The Book of the Honeycomb's Flow

Sēpher Nōpheth Sūphīm

THE BOOK OF THE
Honeycomb's Flow

Sēpher Nōpheth Ṣūphīm

BY Judah Messer Leon

First Published at MANTUA, 1475/76

A CRITICAL EDITION
AND TRANSLATION

BY Isaac Rabinowitz

Cornell University Press

ITHACA AND LONDON

THIS BOOK HAS BEEN PUBLISHED WITH THE AID OF A GRANT FROM
THE HULL MEMORIAL PUBLICATION FUND OF CORNELL UNIVERSITY.

First published 1983 by Cornell University Press.
Published in the United Kingdom by Cornell University Press Ltd.,
Ely House, 37 Dover Street, London W1X 4HQ.

International Standard Book Number 0-8014-0870-9
Library of Congress Catalog Card Number 81-15273
Printed in the United States of America
*Librarians: Library of Congress cataloging information
appears on the last page of the book.*
The paper in this book is acid-free, and meets the guidelines for permanence and durability of the Committee on Production Guidelines for Book Longevity of the Council on Library Resources.

Harry Caplan, *memoriae causa:*

מִי כְּהֶחָכָם
וּמִי יוֹדֵעַ פֵּשֶׁר דָּבָר

Who is as the wise man?
And who knoweth a word's presage?
—Ecclesiastes 8:1

Contents

Preface and Acknowledgments

At the genially persuasive suggestion, many years ago, of a good friend who was a foremost authority on the doctrine and history of classical rhetoric, Professor Harry Caplan of Cornell University—now, alas, "departed unto his world"—I undertook to translate Judah Messer Leon's biblically illustrated treatise on the rhetorical art from Hebrew into English. A very wide circle of non-Hebraist students and scholars, I remember Professor Caplan saying, would welcome access to a work which, while a fully representative product of fifteenth-century Italian intellectual life, is yet sufficiently deviant in provenience and contents to make it of potentially great utility in clarifying and illuminating important aspects of the culture and thought of its time and place. This translation, then, in compliance with Professor Caplan's suggestion, is primarily intended for the non-Hebraist; but the difficulties involved in construing and comprehending Messer Leon's language are such that even a skilled reader of medieval Hebrew texts will doubtless now and again be glad of the opportunity to consult another reader's interpretation of the author's meaning.

My attempt to produce a reasonably accurate translation led me in due course to prepare the present critical edition of the Hebrew text. As I proceeded with the work of translation, I came to realize that Adolf Jellinek's edition (Vienna, 1863) of the Hebrew book, while an improvement over the *editio princeps* (Mantua, 1475/76) in a number of places and respects, is nevertheless far too defective to constitute a properly readable or translatable text. I decided, accordingly, to prepare a carefully revised, critical edition of the text, and to base my translation upon it. Messer Leon's "extraordinary treatise . . . the novel *Rhetoric*," as he himself has characterized it, is thus for the first time really accessible to modern readers, Hebraists and non-Hebraists alike.

Except for a single academic year (1961–1962) when I was able to devote myself exclusively to this undertaking, it has been entirely the product of such leisure moments and intervals as I could spare from more pressing responsibilities and commitments. Indeed, but for the help and encouragement generously accorded the project at various junctures, it is doubtful that the work would even now be completed. I am the happier, therefore, herewith to acknowledge most grateful thanks to the following organizations and persons: the John Simon Guggenheim Memorial Foundation, for the fellowship stipend which, supplemented by grants-in-aid from the National Foundation for Jewish Culture and the Samuel Lemberg Foundation, made possible the aforementioned year of concentrated work on the *Nōpheth Ṣūphīm*; the Faculty Research Grants Committee and the Humanities Faculty Research Grant Committee of Cornell University, for grants of funds needed to defray the costs of typing, of preparing the subject-and-name index to the English portions of the work, and of acquiring facsimiles of manuscripts and other pertinent materials; the authorities of the Biblioteca Ambrosiana (Milan), the Biblioteca Palatina (Parma), the Biblioteca Medicea Laurenziana (Florence), the Bibliothèque Nationale (Paris), the Leyden University Library (Leyden), and the Bayerische Stadtbibliothek (Munich), for access to Hebrew and Arabic manuscript materials required for preparation of the critical edition of Messer Leon's Hebrew text and for the writing of the Introduction; William Roth, of New York City, for making available (through the Cornell University Library) a copy of the incunabulum edition of the *Nōpheth Ṣūphīm* (Mantua, 1475/76); the directors and staff of Cornell University Libraries for the use of a library study, and for valuable assistance in procuring access to needed books and papers; the Hull Memorial Publication Fund, and the Hull Memorial Publication Fund Committee, for the generous subvention that made publication of this work possible; the foundations of Messrs. Samuel Lemberg, Edward Isaacs, Julius and Harry Leventhal, Jeffrey S. Aaron, and the late Reuben Frieman, for supplementary contributions to the defraying of publication costs; and Roger Howley, University Publisher, and the able and devoted staff of Cornell University Press, for undertaking, and so beautifully discharging, the onerous task of publishing this work.

The dedication of the book as a memorial of Professor Caplan will, I hope, be regarded as a token, however slight, of the writer's abiding sense of gratitude to him for his contributions to its accomplishment. Not only was he the instigator and inspirer of the translation, but he carefully went over the English both of the initial draft and of the first main revision. Such felicity as the translation possesses is in many passages owed to Professor Caplan's suggestions as to word choice and sentence structure. Although, regrettably, he did not live to see this work in print, it is a solace of sorts that he read through, and approved, the Introduction, and was informed of the fact that the work was in course of production.

Lastly, there is one who stands in relation to this entire long-term project as its paraclete, if not its guardian angel: my wife, Alice. But for her faith and expectation that I would bring the work to completion, her interest, encouragement, and willingness to help—she twice drew upon her small stock of leisure time to type versions of the translation—I should probably never have been able, as Messer Leon might have expressed it, to **make an end of writing the words of this . . . book** [Deut. 31:24].

תונשלב״ע
יצחק בן בצלאל ז״ל רבינוביץ
י״א טבת, תשמ״א

Isaac Rabinowitz
Cornell University
December 18, 1980

Abbreviations and Signs

The Hebrew Text of *Sēpher Nōpheth Ṣūphīm*

Abbreviations

כ Cod. Ambrosiana 91 (Milan), a manuscript of *Sēpher Nōpheth Ṣūphīm* completed by Menahem de' Rossi of Ferrara on October 12, 1474. Biblioteca Ambrosiana.

ד The *editio princeps* of *Sēpher Nōpheth Ṣūphīm*, printed by Abraham Conat at Mantua, 1475/76.

^{R}ד William Roth's copy of the *editio princeps,* used in the preparation of the present edition.

ט Todros Todrosi's Hebrew translation of Averroes' *Middle Commentary on Aristotle's Rhetoric*: *Bēʾūr Ibn Rushd l*^{e} *sēpher Rēṭōriqē, r*[*ōṣeh*] *l*[*ēmōr*], *sēpher ha-h*^{a}*lāṣāh l*^{e} *ʾArisṭū.*

^{g}ט J. Goldenthal, ed., *Averrois Commentarius in Aristotelis de arte rhetorica libros tres, hebraice versus a Todros Todrosi Arlatensi* (Leipzig, 1842): a transcription of cod. Leipzig (heb.) XLI. C. a.

T^{a}ט Cod. Paris 933 (3): manuscript of Todros' *Bēʾūr*. Bibliothèque Nationale.

T^{b}ט Cod. Paris 932 (4): another manuscript of the *Bēʾūr*. Bibliothèque Nationale.

א The original Arabic text of Averroes' *Middle Commentary on Aristotle's Rhetoric*: *Talkhīṣ Kitāb al-Khiṭāba li-ʾArisṭū* (edited on the basis of cod. Leiden Or. 2073 and cod. Laurentiana CLXXX, 54 [Florence] by 'Abdurraḥmān Badawī [Cairo, 1960]).

תנ"ך-ת The *textus receptus* (Massoretic text) of the Hebrew Bible.

J Adolf Jellinek's edition of *Sēpher Nōpheth Ṣūphīm* (Vienna, 1863).

R. ad H. H. Caplan, ed. and trans., Pseudo-Cicero, *Rhetorica ad Herennium* (Cambridge, Mass., and London, 1954).

Signs

[separates text reading from the ensuing variant reading.

[ ] indicates an omission.

< > indicates an addition.

└┐ indicates erasure, or cancellation, of words.

└< >┐ indicates erasure, or cancellation, of an addition.

A dot above a letter indicates a reading that is not certain.

The Annotated English Translation

Source abbreviations

A Averroes' *Middle Commentary on Aristotle's Rhetoric*: the Arabic text, cited as paged in Badawī's edition.

Boethius Boethius' *De differentiis topicis* (in J.-P. Migne, ed., *Patrologia latina* 64).

De I. H. M. Hubbell, ed. and trans., Cicero, *De inventione* (Cambridge, Mass., and London, 1949).

Halm C. Halm, *Rhetores latini minores* (Leipzig, 1863): Victorinus' commentary on *De I.*

LR. ad A. The thirteenth-century Latin version of the *Rhetorica ad Alexandrum,* edited by M. Grabmann (*Sitzungsberichte der Bayerischen Akademie der Wissenschaften,* phil.-hist. Abteilung, 1931/32, Heft 4 [Munich, 1932]). References to this text, by page and line, are followed by the Stephanus page references to the Greek text (*R. ad A.*).

Q. H. E. Butler, ed. and trans., Quintilian, *Institutio oratoria* (London, 1921–1922).

R. ad A. H. Rackham, ed. and trans., Pseudo-Aristotle, *Rhetorica ad Alexandrum* (Cambridge, Mass., and London, 1965).

R. ad H. H. Caplan, ed. and trans., Pseudo-Cicero, *Rhetorica ad Herennium* (Cambridge, Mass., and London, 1954).

Rhet. J. H. Freese, ed. and trans., Aristotle, *The ''Art'' of Rhetoric* (Cambridge, Mass., and London, 1939).

T Todros Todrosi's Hebrew translation of Averroes' *Middle Commentary on Aristotle's Rhetoric,* cited as paged in Goldenthal's edition (^{g}ט).

T/A Todros/Averroes.

Other abbrevations

B The Hebrew Bible: *T^{e}nakh (T[ōrah]- N[^{e}bhī'īm]- K[^{e}thūbhīm]).*

C, ד/C The *editio princeps* of *Sēpher Nōpheth Ṣūphīm,* printed by Abraham Conat at Mantua, 1475/76.

C^{R} The copy of the Conat incunabulum owned by William Roth of New York City, and used in the preparation of this edition.

DML Rabbi David Messer Leon, son of JML.

JML Rabbi Judah Messer Leon, author of *Sēpher Nōpheth Ṣūphīm.*

JV The Jewish Publication Society's English version of B (a revision of the King James Version) (Philadelphia, 1917).

KJV The King James Version of the Old Testament, published 1611.

M, כ/M The Milan Ambrosian Library MS (cod. Ambrosiana 91) of *Sēpher Nōpheth Ṣūphīm,* dated 1474.

N.S. *Sēpher Nōpheth Ṣūphīm*: The Book of the Honeycomb's Flow. [*Ps. 19:11*].

Books of the Bible

Gen(esis) בר׳
Exod(us) שמ׳
Lev(iticus) וי׳
Num(bers) במ׳
Deut(eronomy) דב׳
Josh(ua) יהו׳
Judg(es) שופ׳
1 Sam(uel) שמ״א
2 Sam(uel) שמ״ב
1 Kings מל״א
2 Kings מל״ב
Isa(iah) יש׳
Jer(emiah) יר׳

Ezek(iel) יח׳
Hos(ea) הו׳
Joel יואל
Amos עמ׳
Obad(iah) עו׳
Jonah יונה
Mic(ah) מי׳
Nah(um) נח׳
Hab(akkuk) חב׳
Zeph(aniah) צפ׳
Hag(gai) חג׳
Zech(ariah) זכ׳
Mal(achi) מל׳

Ps(alms) תה׳
Prov(erbs) מש׳
Job איוב
Song of S(ongs) שה״ש
Ruth רות
Lam(entations) איכה
Eccl(esiastes) קה׳
Esth(er) אס׳
Dan(iel) דנ׳
Ezra עז׳
Neh(emiah) נחמ׳
1 Chr(onicles) דה״א
2 Chr(onicles) דה״ב

Introduction

1. The Nature and Importance of the *Nōpheth Ṣūphīm*

Judah Messer Leon's *Sēpher Nōpheth Ṣūphīm* (The Book of the Honeycomb's Flow [Psalms 19:10]) is a treatise on the art of Rhetoric—an *ars rhetorica*—in which the principles and rules of effective and eloquent utterance, formulated in accordance with the doctrine of some of the most authoritative ancient Greek and Latin writings on the subject, are illustrated from, and in turn used to interpret, passages of the Hebrew Bible. Written and published in northern Italy within the third quarter of the fifteenth century, this book, earlier and more clearly than any other single work of Jewish provenience, reflects that deepened and extended concern with classical rhetoric which is taken to be the hallmark of early Renaissance humanism, the most important intellectual movement in the European culture of its day.[1]

As a handbook of rhetoric, no topic, theme, or issue susceptible of persuasive presentation to an audience by a speaker or writer was in principle outside the purview of the *Nōpheth Ṣūphīm*.[2] The work in fact discusses or alludes to a wide variety of theological, philosophical, political, legal, and psychological subjects. It thus constitutes an excellent conspectus of fifteenth-century ideas, set forth from the point of view of a rabbi and Jewish communal leader who was, in addition, an adherent of and a commentator upon the Aristotelian-Maimonist-Averroist philosophy, an educator, and a physician.

In finding exemplification of classical rhetorical doctrine in passages of the Hebrew Bible, Messer Leon was in effect declaring that, although the sacred texts are perfect as God is perfect, they were composed, and are to be interpreted, according to the same rhetorical and poetical principles as those governing works of a secular or profane character.[3] His treatise must, accordingly, rank as one of

1. On the central importance of rhetoric in early Renaissance humanism, see P. O. Kristeller, *Renaissance Thought: The Classic, Scholastic, and Humanist Strains* (New York, 1961), 11 ff., 100 ff., and J. E. Seigel, *Rhetoric and Philosophy in Renaissance Humanism: The Union of Eloquence and Wisdom, Petrarch to Valla* (Princeton, 1968), 221–223.

2. Cf. the definition of rhetoric, derived from Aristotle/Averroes/Todros and cited by Messer Leon at the outset of i.1: "a faculty which undertakes the effecting of whatever persuasion is possible on any given subject."

3. See, e.g., iv.1.2: "For most of what we shall say [regarding Figures of Speech], we shall draw

the earliest monuments of the modern literary and rhetorical criticism of the Hebrew Scriptures. Indeed, Book Four of the *Nōpheth Ṣūphīm,* which consists of descriptions and scriptural illustrations of no fewer than eighty figures of thought and of speech, is still useful as one of the ablest and fullest treatments of these important features of Biblical Hebrew diction and style.[4]

To its own contemporaries, however, and to successive generations of Italian Jewish writers and scholars throughout the Renaissance period, the *Nōpheth Ṣūphīm* was chiefly important for its restatement of the age-old doctrine that all scientific and scholarly knowledge is essentially scriptural or Israelite in origin, hence licit for Jewish study, and for its utility as a practical guide to effective speech and writing. It is no accident that Azariah de' Rossi, whose *Mᵉ'ōr 'Ēnayim* (first published at Mantua, 1573–75) is the ablest Jewish historical work to appear between the second and the nineteenth centuries, quotes one of the two notable passages of the *Nōpheth Ṣūphīm* in which Messer Leon defends his recourse to Gentile ideas and teachings; nor that the other is quoted in Judah Moscato's *Nᵉphūṣōth Yᵉhūdhāh* (first published at Venice, 1589), the volume through which Moscato is held to have "metamorphosed the form and vitalized the content of the Jewish sermon."[5] An interesting memorandum, dated 1538, attests the fact that the professional scribes (*sōphᵉrīm*) employed by Italian Jewish communities to compose official letters, addresses, petitions, and other public documents were paid according to their competence in rhetoric.[6] The

---

upon Book IV of the [*New*] *Rhetoric* written by Tully [i.e., Ps.-Cicero, *Rhetorica ad Herennium*], and upon the account given by the Philosopher [Aristotle] in Book III of his *Rhetoric*. The examples of the Figures, however, I have taken from **our holy and our beautiful house** [Isa. 64:10], from the words of prophecy and the divinely inspired narratives **that sit first in the kingdom** [Esth. 1:14] of agreeableness and elegance, that are **sweeter . . . than honey** [Ps. 19:11]." At i.7.22 ff., rules of human rhetoric laid down by Aristotle and Quintilian are found to be illustrated in, hence used to interpret, Abraham's colloquy with the Hittites (Gen. 23:3 ff.) and Abigail's speech to David (I Sam. 25:24 ff.); and there are many other such examples. While Messer Leon is careful to state that the excellence of human rhetoric is to be judged in terms of the standards found in and demonstrated by the Holy Scriptures, and that the Scriptures' excellence is not to be judged in terms of human rhetorical or literary artistry, his procedure throughout the *Nōpheth Ṣūphīm* shows that he thought the difference between the Scriptures and other products of rhetorical-literary art to be one of degree, not of kind. Other characteristic expressions of Messer Leon's in this regard occur at i.13.13, iv.55.1, iv.68.1, and iv.82.2.

4. The two best-known discussions of the Biblical Hebrew figures in later Hebrew literature are those of M. H. Luzzatto's *Sēpher Lᵉshōn Limmūdhīm* (Mantua, 1727) and S. Löwisohn's *Mᵉlīṣath Yᵉshūrūn* (Vienna, 1816). Although Luzzatto almost certainly knew of the *N.S.*, and Löwisohn may have known of it, neither, so far as I have been able to ascertain, makes any allusion to Messer Leon's work. Nor, apparently, was Book IV of the *N.S.* consulted by E. König, whose *Stilistik, Rhetorik, Poetik in Bezug auf die biblische Literatur* (Leipzig, 1900) is the fullest modern treatment of the Biblical Hebrew figures.

5. *N.S.* i.13.14 is quoted, in abridged form, in *Mᵉ'ōr 'Ēnayim* i.75 (Vilna, 1863); Moscato, *Nᵉphūṣōth Yᵉ hūdhāh* (Lemberg, 1859) Sermon 5, 19b, quotes *N.S.*, Preface: 14. The remark on Moscato's role in the history of Jewish preaching is from Israel Bettan, *Studies in Jewish Preaching* (Cincinnati, 1939), 194. De' Rossi's and Moscato's quotations of the *N.S.* are also discussed by A. Altmann in his *Essays in Jewish Intellectual History* (Hanover, 1981), 110–113.

6. Alexander Marx, "Glimpses of the Life of an Italian Rabbi of the First Half of the Sixteenth

Nōpheth Ṣūphīm was doubtless as widely used in the training of such official secretaries as in the preparation of young men for the study of medicine and of philosophy at the Italian universities that would admit them.[7] In the seventeenth century (1623), we find Joseph Solomon Delmedigo recommending study of Messer Leon's *Nōpheth Ṣūphīm,* along with Aristotle's *Rhetoric* and *Poetics,* to whoever might wish to dispose of "**the excellence of dignity and the excellence of power** [Gen. 49:3] in language."[8] Our treatise was still in use as late as the eighteenth century: Shimshon Kohen Modon (or, as he signed himself, Sansone Sacerdote Modone), a well-known rabbi and poet who in 1722 was appointed Scholar (*ḥākhām*) and Secretary (*sōphēr*) of the Mantua Community, once owned, and quite certainly studied, the William Roth copy of the Incunabulum used in preparing the present edition.[9]

As the first work in Hebrew literature wholly devoted to the new, rhetoric-centered outlook upon life and letters that characterizes the Italian Renaissance, the *Nōpheth Ṣūphīm* most fittingly and deservedly has the honor of being the first Hebrew book printed and published in its author's lifetime.[10]

2. The Author

Regrettably, we know all too little about the life and career of Rabbi Judah ben Jehiel Rophé, "titled Messer Leon," author of the *N.S.* and certainly fifteenth-century Italian Jewry's nearest equivalent of the archetypal "Renaissance man." Rabbi, educator, physician, exegete, and author, at various times in a life course

Century (David ibn Yahya)," HUCA I (1924), 605–624. R. David's remark, paraphrased above, reads (p.620): . . . כל קהל שׂוכר סופר קבוע . . . וכפי מדרגתו בהלצה ככה שכרו Note, too, his remark (p. 621): במלכות הלז אין חזון נפרץ מההלצה הלשונית ("In this kingdom, **there is no frequent vision** [1 Sam. 3:1] apart from rhetorical language").

7. That training in rhetoric was a requisite of Jewish medical students and physicians was apparently one of the reasons that induced Messer Leon to circulate the *N.S.* See his rather obscure *m*ᵉ*līṣāh* statement of the point in the Preface: 11 and note 12.—The *N.S.* is cited as a standard work in the field of rhetoric by Baruch b. Uzziel Ḥazqīṭō, Rabbi in Ferrara in the sixteenth century; cf. R. Bonfil, *The Rabbinate in Renaissance Italy* [Heb.] (Jerusalem, 1979), 191–192.

8. The quoted words are from the *Epistle ('Iggereth 'Āḥūz)* prepared by Delmedigo on behalf of the Qaraite, Zeraḥ ben Mᵉnaḥem of Troki. The *Epistle,* first published by Abraham Geiger in *M*ᵉ*lō' Ḥophnayim* (Berlin, 1840), was reprinted, in part, by A. Cahana, *Siphrūth Hahisṭōriyyā Hayyis-r*ᵉ*'ēlīth* (Warsaw, 1923), 152–163; the reference to the *N.S.* is found on pp. 155–156. The reference is also included in the excerpt from the *Epistle* given in S. Assaf's *M*ᵉ*qōrōth L*ᵉ*thōl*ᵉ*dhōth Haḥinnūkh B*ᵉ*yisrā'ēl* (Tel Aviv, 1936), III, 99.

9. On Modon, who wrote one of the approbationary poems included in the opening pages of Luzzatto's *L*ᵉ*shōn Limmūdhim,* see S. Simonsohn, *History of the Jews in the Duchy of Mantua* [Heb.] (Jerusalem, 1965), II, 522 (Eng. trans. [Jerusalem, 1977], 703). Several marginal notes in the William Roth Incunabulum show that the writer (Modon?) compared Messer Leon's text with that of the *Rhetorica ad Herennium.* According to C. Bernheimer, *Paleografia Ebraica* (Florence, 1924), 399, Modon was owner of an outstanding collection of Hebrew books and manuscripts.

10. The *N.S.* was printed and published by Abraham Conat, at Mantua, most probably in 1475, and certainly no later than 1476; see my discussion, below, of the date of the *editio princeps,* and L. Goldschmidt, *Hebrew Incunables: A Bibliographical Essay* (Oxford, 1948), 75–76.

that spanned the last three quarters of the *quattrocento* he resided and worked in some of the most important centers of the burgeoning Renaissance Italian culture, including Ancona, Padua, Venice, Bologna, Mantua, and Naples. Judah Messer Leon's biography, if it were known in sufficient depth and detail, would yield rich stores of insight into the inner life and problems of a Jewish community that, for a century or so, was more tolerated and freer than any in the world prior to the nineteenth century. The brief outline of Judah Messer Leon's life presented in the following pages is, I believe, the first completely accurate statement of all the basic chronological and residential facts that have thus far become known.[11]

11. The best assemblage of biographical data on Judah Messer Leon that has thus far appeared is Daniel Carpi's essay, ר' יהודה מיסיר ליאון ופעולתו כרופא, "R. Judah Messer Leon and His Activity as Physician," in *Michael I* (Publications of the Diaspora Research Institute, Tel-Aviv University, Vol. I [1972]), 277–301, reprinted in slightly revised form in *Koroth* (a journal devoted to the history of medicine and science), 6, no. 7–8 (1974), 277–301; a recasting of the Hebrew essay in English, "Notes on the Life of Rabbi Judah Messer Leon," is in E. Toaff, ed., *Studi Sull' Ebraismo italiano in memoria di Cecil Roth* (Barulli [1974]), 36–62. Carpi's paper (hereinafter "Carpi" is the revised Hebrew original, "Carpi^{e}" is the English version) not only brings together and discusses the findings and views of other scholars, but for the first time makes available a group of notarial documents bearing upon Judah Messer Leon which are preserved in the state archive of Padua. These documents constitute a most welcome and valuable accretion to the small body of securely known data on Judah Messer Leon.

Carpi's presentation of the facts of JML's biography, excellent and judicious though it is in many respects, is unfortunately vitiated by a fundamental chronological error that has led to other mistakes in dating various events and stages of JML's career, and has entailed a partially incorrect ordering of the sequence of his residencies. Carpi has denied and rejected the correct date of an event known to have taken place at Venice: the birth there, on December 10, 1471, of JML's son, David. A key statement in the establishment of this date, namely, David's remark (p. 64 of his legal disquisition on rabbinical authority and ordination [*s^{e}mīkhā*], *K^{e}bhōdh Ḥ^{a}khāmīm*, ed. S. Bernfeld [Berlin, 1899]) that his own ordination was received on his eighteenth birthday, which fell on the Sabbath of Hanukkah [November 21, 1489], seems to have been regarded by Carpi as a textual error. This opinion, however, is untenable. The true date of David's birth (though not the place), was worked out by S. Rosanes, *History of the Jews in Turkey* [Heb.], I (Jerusalem, 1930), 85, n. 120, on the basis not merely of the one passage of *K^{e}bhōdh Ḥ^{a}khāmīm,* but on the basis of three other passages as well (pp. 5, 28, and 53). One passage might be suspected of textual error, but hardly four, whose testimony is all to the same effect. The several statements establish the fact as certain that David had reached the age of forty in the year 5272 (1511–1512); the "Sabbath of Hanukkah" on which his eighteenth birthday fell was, therefore, the 27th of Kislev of the year 5250, or November 21, 1489; reckoning back from this, the date of his birth is fixed as Tuesday, the 27th of Kislev, 5232, or December 10, 1471. (The date correspondences are those of the tables in E. Mahler, *Handbuch der jüdischen Chronlogie* [Leipzig, 1916].) This date is further corroborated: among the passages utilized by Rosanes, that on p. 5 of *K^{e}bhōdh Ḥ^{a}khāmīm* exhibits a synchronism between David's attainment of age forty (the year of the dispute treated in his legal opinion) and the year of the accession (not the death, as stated by Rosanes!) of the Ottoman sultan, Selim I, namely the year 1512. Thus, the date of David Messer Leon's birth is certain. The several statements which all indicate December 10, 1471 as the date of David Messer Leon's birth cannot be dismissed as scribal or textual errors; and because he must have known the date of his own birth, no arguments contradictory of his statements, however plausible, can invalidate, or be preferred to, his testimony on this point. The strongest of Carpi's negative arguments rests on his acceptance of a needless emendation, by Cassuto, in the letter of David Messer Leon to David of Tivoli which (in my translation) appears below. By virtue of this "correction" (pointed out in n. 36 below, as well as *ad loc.*), DML is made to claim that he and David of Tivoli were fellow-students and friends in Bologna at a time when the former was still an

The place of JML's birth and early rearing may, with fair plausibility, be inferred from several of the notarial documents which he executed, now preserved in the archives of both Padua and Mantua; in these he is named as "the Jew, Leo, son of a certain Vitalis, of Monticulus."[12] Since he himself executed the documents, he must have so identified himself to the notaries in each case. He thought of himself, that is to say, as "of Monticulus," meaning that "Monticulus" was the place where he was born and raised.[13] Because, however, several northern and central Italian towns bear the name "Monticulus" (the Latin form of the more familiar "Montecchio"), the one of which JML considered himself native is not definitely certain.[14] V. Colorni, followed by Daniel Carpi,

---

infant, and the latter already a grown man. As will be seen, however, David Messer Leon makes no such claim.

In the preface to his *Māghēn Dāwīdh* (S. Schechter, "Notes sur Messer David Léon tirées des manuscrits," *Revue des études juives,* XXIV [1892], 121). David tells us that Venice was the city of his birth. The entailed presence of his father, JML, in Venice in December 1471—doubted by Carpi mainly on the basis of his rejection of the date of David's birth—is thus virtually a certainty, and fits in very well with a datum provided by another source; see below, n. 40.

In addition to Carpi's papers, the following publications are especially valuable for JML's biography: (a) U. Cassuto, s.v. "Jehuda ben Jechiel," *Encyclopaedia Judaica* (Berlin, 1931), VIII, cols. 999-1001, includes a nearly complete bibliography to 1931. (b) H. Rosenberg, "Cenni biografici di alcuni Rabbini e Literati della Comunitá Israelitica di Ancona," *Estratto dal saggio degli scritti in lingua ebraica degli Eccelentissimi Rabbini Vivanti e Tedeschi d.v.m.* (Casale Monferrato, 1932), XXV-XXXVIII, summarizes the biographical data contained in the letters published by D. Frankel, דברי ריבות בשערים (Husyatyn, 1902), and other documents. (c) V. Colorni, "Note per la biografia di alcuni dotti ebrei vissuti a Mantova nel secolo XV," *Annuario di Studi Ebraici diretto da Umberto Cassuto,* Vol. I: 1934 (in memoria S. H. Margulies, Rome, 1935), 169-182, publishes the gist of Mantuan notarial documents dated March 11, 1473, March 13, 1475, and April 26, 1475, the first two of which were executed by Messer Leon, while the third contains a reference to R. Joseph Colon. (d) S. Simonsohn, תולדות היהודים בדוכסותמנטובה, I–II (Jerusalem, 1963, 1965), esp. 456–457, 521; translated as *History of the Jews in the Duchy of Mantua* (Jerusalem 1977), 626–627, 717, shows the baselessness of G. ibn Yaḥya's perniciously influential story of the "quarrel" between Messer Leon and Joseph Colon, and their alleged expulsion from Mantua; contains an admirably full bibliography, and a terse, but quite correct, estimate of Messer Leon's historical importance. (e) J. Buxbaum, תולדות רבינו יוסף קולון ושיטתו ["R. Joseph Colon and his Legal Thought"] in E. D. Pines, שו"ת ופסקי מהרי"ק החדשים [*New Responsa and Decisions of Rabbi Joseph Colon*] (Jerusalem, 1970), י"ט-מ"ח [19–48], the best available account of the relations between Joseph Colon and Messer Leon. (f) I. Rabinowitz, "A Rectification of the Date of Judah Messer Leon's Death," in C. Berlin, ed., *Studies in Jewish Bibliography, History and Literature in Honor of I. Edward Kiev* (New York, 1971), 399-406, refutes the widely accepted speculation that Judah Messer Leon was executed in Moscow on April 22, 1490; shows, on the basis of a hitherto unpublished document and of other evidence that the death of Judah Messer Leon "occurred between some time in the year 1497 and early September of the year 1499."

12. Carpi, 285 and 287 (Carpi^{e}, 56 and 59): ". . . Leonem hebreum qm Vitalis de Monticulo . . . ," ". . . Leoni hebreo filio qm Vitalis de Monticulo . . .". Colorni (p. 173): ". . . Leo filius quondam Magistri Vitalis de Monticulo . . . ," ". . . Leonis hebrei . . . filii quondam Vittalli [*sic*] de Monticulo. . . ."

13. That it is JML, and not merely his father, who is described as "of Monticulus" is shown by Paduan Document 5 (Carpi, 301, Carpi^{e}, 62). Notarial usage, abundantly exemplified in these documents, evidently required that persons named be always further identified by paternity and place of origin, sometimes by present address as well.

14. See, e.g., the several small cities and towns listed under "Montecchio" in *Grande Dizionario Enciclopedico . . . Torinese,* XII (3d ed., Turin, 1970).

thought the Montecchio of the region of Le Marche the likeliest such locale, as this is the Montecchio nearest Ancona, where, having been accepted as Rabbi while still in his early manhood, JML was in residence by 1453.[15] But it is, I think, rather more probable that the small town in Vicenza Province known today as Montecchio Maggiore was the "Monticulus" in question. Both Padua and Mantua are much closer to Montecchio Maggiore than to the Montecchio situated in Le Marche between Pesaro and Urbino. A Paduan or Mantuan notary, hearing JML designate himself as "of Montecchio" would most naturally and immediately understand this to mean the place now known as Montecchio Maggiore; and since, in the documents prepared for JML, the notaries wrote "Monticulus" without other regional qualification, it may most easily be supposed that Montecchio Maggiore was the place they had in mind.

The earliest dated records we have of JML are: (1) the colophon of *Libh^{e}nath Hassappīr*, his Hebrew grammar, finished September 11, 1454;[16] (2) the colophon of *Mikhlal Yōphī,* his minor textbook on logic, begun January 7, 1455, and finished February 6, 1455;[17] (3) a letter of his, dated January 8, 1455, sent from

15. Colorni, 175, esp. n. 4; Carpi, 283, n. 34 (Carpi^{e}, 54–55, n. 63).

16. See G. Margoliouth, *Catalogue of the Hebrew and Samaritan MSS in the British Museum* [rpt., London, 1965], no. 978, III, 305; A. Neubauer, *Catalogue of the Hebrew MSS in the Bodleian Library* (Oxford, 1886), no. 1491, col. 527; I. A. Benjacob, *Ozar Ha-Sepharim* (Vilna, 1880), 256 (no. 61); and H. Loewe, *Catalogue of the MSS in the Hebrew Character . . .* [*at*] *Trinity College* (Cambridge, 1926), no. 88, 84–85. Two facts about *Libh^{e}nath Hassappīr* are pertinent here: (1) JML tells us only the date of his completion of the work, not, as he does in the case of his minor work on logic, both the date when it was begun and the date of completion; and (2) in marked contrast to his customary practice of including his title when referring to himself ("*Messer* Leon"), in the case of this book, as Margoliouth has pointed out, the preface and each successive chapter begins with a reference to himself without title: "saith Leon . . . (*'āmar Lē'ōn*)." The explanation of these facts may be that JML had begun to write *Libh^{e}nath Hassappīr* some time before he received his honorific, that is, before 1452, and that although by the time he finished the book he could already refer to himself as "Messer Leon," he did not take the trouble to change the openings of his preface and of the succeeding chapters. Or it may be that by the 18th of Ellul, 5214 (September 11, 1454), when the book was finished, he had not yet decided always to use his title in referring to himself. The first known instance of his self-designation as "Messer Leon" is his signed, initial round robin letter on female purification (D. Frankel, ed., *Dibh^{e}rē Rībhōth Bashsh^{e}'ārīm* [Husyatyn, 1902], fols. 1–2a); we know this was sent from Ancona in 1454, but as the document itself is undated, we do not know exactly when in 1454 it was sent, whether before or after September 11.

17. These dates are as given by H. Zotenberg, *Catalogues des mss. hébreux et samaritaines de la Bibliothèque Impériale* (Paris, 1866), No. 998 (1°), 179: "Il est dit dans un post-scriptum que l'auteur avait commencé cet ouvrage le 17 tebeth 5215 (1455 de J.C.), et l'avait terminé le 18 schebat de la même année." See M. Steinschneider, *Die hebräischen Uebersetzungen des Mittelalters* (Berlin, 1893), 79–80, for a listing of other MSS of *Mikhlal Yōphī*. Steinschneider, apparently misled by a reported reading of the colophon of the Florence MS, thought the work was produced a year earlier than in fact it was. "Aus dem Epigraph erfahren wir," he writes (p. 80), "dass er [JML] das Werk von Dienstag 17. Tebet bis Donnerstag 18. Schebat 214 (also vom 21. Dec. 1453 bis 20. Jan. 1454, in einem Monat) verfasst habe." Now in 5214, that is 1453/4 C.E., "17. Tebet" was not "21. Dec." but December 12, and "18. Schebat" was not "20. Jan.," but January 17; the Hebrew month dates given by Steinschneider, however, do coincide with those of the Paris MS, and he informs us that the colophon of the Petersburg Firkovitch MS (copied by Abraham Farissol in 1471) gives the composition date as 1455—again as in the Paris MS. Moses ben Shabbethai Levi, the scribe of British Museum MS no. 1117 (Margoliouth, *Catalogue* III, 543–44), reports the work as having

Ancona to the Florentine Jewish community;[18] and (4) the sharply negative response, dated April 6, 1455 of Rabbi Benjamin Montalcino of Florence to the open letters, circulated from Ancona, in which JML urged stricter observance of the rules of female ritual purification, and interdicted the study of Rabbi Levi ben Gershom's commentary on the Pentateuch (as advocating a view of the divine omniscience that was tainted with heresy).[19] Following the indications of date in the letter to the Florentine community and in Rabbi Benjamin's adverse response, we note that the controversial letters circulated by JML, then already settled as a rabbi and *Rōsh Y^{e}shībhāh* (head of academy) in Ancona, were written and sent out by him in the year 1454. Thus, with allowance for the time required to establish himself securely enough to feel able to circulate such letters,[20] the date of his arrival in Ancona can hardly have been later than the year 1453, and may have been as early as 1452.[21]

It is a fair guess, then, that JML was born between 1420 and 1425, for, brilliant and accomplished though he was, he could scarcely have been accepted as a rabbi and *Rōsh Y^{e}shībhāh* in so important a community as Ancona if he were not close to thirty years of age, or older.[22] On the other hand, he could not have been much older than thirty when he took up his duties there, since in another letter to the Jewish community of Florence—this one undated, but also adverting to the interdiction of Rabbi Levi's commentary and to the admonition on female purification of his circular communications—he speaks of himself as *'ūl yāmīm* ("an infant of days" [Isa. 65:20]).[23]

JML received the honorific which he thenceforward used in referring to himself, and which ultimately became part of his name,[24] in the first half of the

---

been begun by JML "on Tuesday, the 16th of Tebet, 215" and finished "on Thursday, the ____ of Shebat, 215"; the date in Shebat was apparently omitted by mistake, and Moses ben S. has also mistakenly made the 16th of Tebet, 215 a Tuesday, instead of the Monday it in fact was. Three MSS, then, report 5215 as the year of composition, and one 5214; the month dates of the Paris MS also fall on a Tuesday and Thursday respectively, and are thus exactly paralleled by those of Steinschneider's report. The dates as given in the Paris MS are, accordingly, those best corroborated, and are most probably correct.

18. As published by Frankel, *Dibh^{e}rē Rībhōth,* fols. 1b–2a, the letter is without date, but the copy included in MS 223 of the Hebrew University Library gives the date as "the 18th of Tebeth, 215" (Wednesday, January 8, 1455, the day following that on which JML began the composition of his *Mikhlal Yōphī*). See S. Assaf, "From the Treasures of the Jerusalem Library," in *Sources and Investigations in Jewish History* [Heb.] (Jerusalem, 1946), 218 ff., 221.

19. Two of JML's three letters on these matters, and R. Benjamin Montalcino's adverse response, are published in Frankel's *Dibh^{e}rē Rībhōth,* Documents 1–3, fols. 1a–4a; the text of the third letter is presented in S. Assaf's "Treasures of the Jerusalem Library," 221–225. These letters and the several other documents pertaining to the controversy are ably summarized by Rosenberg, "Cenni," XXV–XXX, by Carpi (283 ff.; Carpi^e, 46 ff.), and by Simonsohn, *Jews in Mantua* (456 f. [Heb.]; 626 f. [Engl.]).

20. Cf. Rosenberg, "Cenni," XXVIII and n. 1; Carpi, 283 and n. 34 (Carpi^e, 46–47 and n. 30).

21. The *terminus a quo,* 1452, is the year in which JML received his honorific.

22. Cf. Carpi, 283, n. 34.

23. Assaf, 225: "ואם את משפטי תמאסו מצד חלשת המזהיר כי הוא נתעב ונאלח ועול ימים . . ."

24. *Supra,* n. 16.

year 1452, during the first visit to Italy of the emperor Frederick III.[25] The fact is established by a statement in Rabbi Benjamin Montalcino's letter of April 6, 1455, in which we are informed that JML's title was "directly or indirectly" conferred upon him by the pope and the emperor.[26] While Rabbi Benjamin thus professes not to know (he is perhaps unwilling to assert) that the pope and the emperor conferred the title upon JML in their own persons, his statement attests his knowledge that they could have done so, and this means that the title must have been conferred at a time when the emperor was in Italy. The only such period prior to 1454—by which time, as we have seen, JML was already using his honorific—was that of the emperor's first Italian visit, January 1 to June 3, 1452. It is, accordingly, within this period that Rabbi Judah b. Jehiel Rophé, also known as "Leon," was titled "Messer Leon."[27]

Of JML's career before the year 1452 we know very little, and that mainly by inference. Like his father, he was licensed to practise medicine;[28] indeed, if his skill and accomplishments as a physician had not already won him more than local acclaim, he would probably never have been knighted by the emperor and the pope.[29] By this time, moreover, he must have been married,[30] and his daugh-

25. Frederick came to Italy in 1452 in order to receive his imperial crown at the hands of Pope Nicholas V, and to be married to the sixteen-year-old Princess Leonora of Portugal; cf. L. Pastor, *History of the Popes,* II (London, 1899), 138–162. During Frederick's second visit to Italy, in 1468–69, (Pastor, IV, 160 f.), Messer Leon was even more signally honored.

26. The statement (*Dibh^{e}rē Rībhōth,* fol.2b top) reads: "דיו לעבד היות כרבו ואחר שהאפיפיור והקיסר יר"ה אשר מכחם או כח כחם מכונה מסיר ליאון נמנעים מצד מוסרם לצוות ולגזור גזרות על תושבי הארצות האלה אעפ"י שעמם הם כי אינם כפופים תחתם ראוי שימנע מזה ג"כ הבא מכחם:." "'It is enough for the servant to be as his master' [T.B. Ber. 58b]: Since the Pope and His Majesty, the Emperor—by whose authority, directly or indirectly, Leon is titled 'Messer'—scrupulously refrain from enjoining orders and decrees upon the inhabitants of these lands (for although they are their own people, they are not subject to them), so too should refrain one whose authority is derived from theirs." Cf. Carpi^{e}, 43, n. 17. By "these lands" R. Benjamin means Tuscany and other territories not directly ruled by the pope or the emperor.

27. Frederick entered Italy on January 1, 1452 (Pastor, II, 141). He was at Pordenone on January 2 and, in course of his journey back to Vienna, again on June 3, 1452 (A. Benedetti, *Storia de Pordenone* [Pordenone, 1964], 84). It was at Pordenone, seventeen years later, that Frederick conferred an extraordinary privilege, as well as a double doctorate, upon JML.

28. The Mantuan notarial document of March 3, 1475, cited by Colorni ("Note," 173, refers both to JML and to his father as "magister," the title bestowed upon persons licensed to practise medicine; cf. Carpi, 287 (Carpi^{e}, 44–45). According to the colophon of the manuscript of *Libh^{e}nath Hassappīr* quoted by Benjacob (*Ozar Ha-Sepharim,* 256), which was written in 1455, יחיאל הרופא ישר"ו ("Jehiel the physician, m[ay] he l[ive] m[any] g[oodly] y[ears]"), JML's father, was then still alive.

29. How or why JML's precocious knighthood was procured we do not know. It is virtually certain, however, that the circumstances or the achievements were connected with his activity in the field of medicine, because no other of his several competencies could have offered occasion to either the pope or the emperor thus signally to honor him. The argument is supported by the manner in which he is referred to in the several official documents which he caused to be notarized. The Paduan documents refer to him as "artium et medicine doctorem praestantissimum" (Carpi, 295; Carpi^{e}, 56), "tam in cirugia quam in fisica . . . fidedignorum Christicolarum testimonio . . . clarum et expertum" (298; 59), "milite et artium ac medicine doctore celeberrimo" (299; 60), and "spectabilis militis artium et medicine doctoris et fisice" (301; 62). One of the Mantuan documents calls him "Leonis hebrei arcium et medicine doctoris et militis, nec non legis hebraice doctoris", another "eximius arcium et medicine doctor Dominus Magister Leo" (Colorni, "Note," 173).

30. JML apparently was married at least twice; see Paduan Document 6 (Carpi, 301; Carpi^{e}, 62).

ter, Belladonna, may already have been born.[31] He had also already opened, or was about to open, his famous *ye shībhāh*, an academy in which students, while receiving a thorough Jewish education, could be trained in the secular disciplines necessary for higher studies in the humanities, in philosophy, and in medicine.[32] Finally, he had doubtless already embarked on the composition of his grammar, the first of the series of textbooks he designed for the use of students seeking to complete the religio-secular curriculum of his academy.[33]

How long beyond the year 1455 JML maintained his residence in Ancona[34] we do not know, nor does the evidence now at our disposal permit absolute certainty of where he settled after he left Ancona. His residence at Padua by February 27, 1470, is, however, documentarily established;[35] and such other indication as we have of his residence during the fifteen years following his attested presence in Ancona also points rather to Padua than to any other locale.[36] The extraordinary

---

The name of his first wife, the mother of Belladonna, is not on record, nor do we know when or how this marriage was terminated. JML's second wife, named in Paduan Document 6, was Stella, daughter of Benjamin ben Joab of Fano; she was the mother of their son, David.

31. We learn from Paduan Document 3 (Carpi, 299; Carpi^e, 60) that on May 21, 1470, JML paid 135 gold ducats, the dowry of his daughter, Belladonna, to Bonaventura son of Aleuccio, of Padua, in virtue of her marriage to Aleuccio, Bonaventura's son. If we suppose that contemporary Italian Jewish custom was followed in the case of this marriage, Belladonna would have been between about 14 and 20 years old at the time. which would mean that she was born between 1450 and 1456.

32. His *ye shībhāh* is known to have functioned wherever JML established his residence until approximately 1495, when in consequence of the anti-Jewish disturbances that attended the French occupation of Naples, he and David Messer Leon probably left that city. As outlined in the open letter published at Mantua in 1564 and circulated throughout northern Italy, the curriculum of R. David Provenzali's proposed Jewish college was essentially the same as that of JML's *ye shībhāh*. See S. Assaf, *Sources for the History of Education in Israel,* Vol. II [Heb.] (Tel-Aviv, 1931), 115-120, and J. R. Marcus, *The Jew in the Medieval World* (Cincinnati, 1938), 381-388.

33. The indication that JML had begun to compose *Libh^e nath Hassappīr* before he was knighted is given above (n. 16). David Messer Leon's letter of May 4/5, 1484, lists the several main curricular texts in the order in which his father composed them; see below. JML's commentary on Jedaiah Bedersi's *B^e ḥīnath 'Ōlām,* a noncurricular text not mentioned in David's letter, was also composed before 1452: the copyist of the Vienna MS that includes the work, Mordecai b. Solomon of Camerino, states in the colophon that he finished his task on April 25, 1449; see A. Z. Schwarz, *Die hebräischen Handschriften der Nationalbibliothek in Wien* (Leipzig, 1925), 175. Schwarz's doubt of JML's authorship is groundless, as it is based merely on what he considered the rather too early date of this copy. Significantly, this commentary also exhibits the pre-knighthood formula ("saith Leon") found in *Libh^e nath Hassappīr;* see the portion of the text quoted by M. Steinschneider, "Mazkereth Hammazkir," Kobak's *Jeschurun* VIII (Hebrew part, 1875), 68, and the remarks of U. Cassuto, *Gli ebrei a Firenze nell' età del rinascimento* (Florence, 1918), 262-263 (in M. Hartom's Hebrew translation [Jerusalem, 1967], 205).

34. As mentioned above, Rabbi Benjamin Montalcino's critique of the pronouncements issued by JML from Ancona, which refers to JML as currently in residence there, is dated April 6, 1455.

35. Carpi, Document 1, 295 ff. (Carpi^e 56 ff.).

36. Carpi, 285 f. (Carpi^e, 48 f.) holds that during the 1460's, before JML settled in Padua, he was resident in Bologna. This view, however, is untenable. It rests upon the mistaken rejection of David Messer Leon's statement of the date of his birth, and upon the equally mistaken belief that a passage in David Messer Leon's letter to David of Tivoli, dated May 4/5, 1484, (p. 120 of Schechter, "Notes sur Messer David Léon") proved both to have been fellow students under JML at Bologna. The latter error rests upon Cassuto's needless emendation of the passage in question ("La famiglia di David da Tivoli," *Corriere Israelitico* XLV [1906/7], 261, n. 2): by "correcting" the text's actual ". . . in Bologna; and I was then **by him** [*sc.* JML] **as a nursling** [Prov. 8:30]" to ". . . in Bologna; and you were then,"—i.e., by emending *hāyīthī* ("I was") to *hāyīthā* ("you were")—a self-reference of

writ of privilege issued in JML's favor by the emperor Frederick III at Pordenone on February 21, 1469, while it does not specify the city where he was then residing, speaks of the testimony offered by "reliably credible Christians" to the effect that these have known him for a long period of time, and currently know him, to be engaged in the practice and teaching of medicine.[37] As the University of Bologna, the only seat of higher learning other than that of Padua wherein JML might possibly have been so described, is known not to have welcomed Jews as professors and students of medicine at this time,[38] it is probably Padua to which Rabbi Judah transferred his household and his *y^{e}shībhāh* upon leaving Ancona.[39]

At Padua, accordingly, JML remained between the date, after 1455, when he removed from Ancona, and the date in the latter part of 1470 or in 1471, when we find him in Venice.[40] He thus lived longer in Padua than anywhere else in Italy, except for his native town ("Monticulus" or Montecchio Maggiore) and Naples, the last of his major residencies, where he lived upward of fifteen years.[41] Considering how attractive Padua at this time must have seemed to a

---

DML's has been changed into a reference to David of Tivoli. DML is here saying that, during the period of his father's residence in Bologna, he, David, was a mere infant, too young to have begun his studies; see the annotated translation of this important letter, given below.

37. Carpi, Document 2, 298 (Carpi^{e}, 59): "te . . . tam in cirugia quam in fisica ut fidedignorum christicolarum testimonio qui diu longoque tempore . . . experientiam atque doctrinam tuam experti sunt et continuo experiuntur edoti sumus [*sc.* Fredericus] clarum atque expertum evasisse. . . ."

38. Carpi, 287, n. 60, 289 (Carpi^{e} 45, n. 26, 49). In JML's letter to the Jewish community of Bologna, sent from Mantua in 1474, he refers to his days there as having been spent in disputation with Gentile scholars. In his letter to the Florentine community, however, he speaks of "*lecturing* in the great academies, **in the midst of many peoples** [Mic. 5:7] since **ancient years** [Mal. 3:4] on **all learning and wisdom** [Dan. 1:17]," a statement more likely to have been accurate respecting Padua than Bologna. Full English translations of these two important letters are given below.

39. Paduan Document 6 (Carpi, 301 [Carpi^{e}, 62]) attests JML's residency there until at least October 11, 1470; he was at Venice on December 10, 1471, when DML was born, and he is documented as at Mantua by March 11, 1473 (Colorni, "Note," 173). Accordingly, his sojourn at Bologna (attested both by his own 1474 letter from Mantua and by that of DML to David of Tivoli in 1484) could have lasted for only a little more than a year. Did he come to Bologna with some purpose in mind which brought him into conflict with Christian scholars there and caused him to engage in the disputations mentioned in the passage of his letter cited above (n. 38); and did he leave Bologna when the issues at controversy were not decided to his satisfaction?

40. According to M. Steinschneider (*Gesammelte Schriften* [Berlin, 1925] 219, n. 10), MS Paris 621 contains a notice (verified by A. Neubauer in a private letter to Steinschneider) to the effect that "Jehuda ben Moses aus Cologna in der Schule (ישיבה) des Jehuda ben Jechiel he-Rofe am 1. Tebet 232 [so it should read; Steinschneider has '272'] (13. [Steinschneider erroneously writes '3.'; see the table in Mahler, *Chronologie,* 574] Dec. 1471) vor den Schulern in Schlachtregeln geprüft worden." Only three days before this examination, on Tuesday, December 10, 1471, JML's son is recorded as having been born at Venice; it is, therefore, practically certain that, as Colorni has suggested ("Note," 174, n. 3), JML, his household, and his *y^{e}shibhāh,* were then in Venice. The objection that Jews were forbidden to reside in Venice at this time (Carpi, 291; Carpi^{e} 52, n. 51) does not have much force, since the ban was plainly more honored in the breach than strictly maintained (see *Jewish Encyclopedia,* s.v. "Venice"), and besides, physicians such as JML were exempted from the ban. JML may have settled in Venice before the end of the year 1470; the removal of their household (including the *y^{e}shībhāh*) from Padua to Venice may have been the reason that Stella, JML's wife, on October 11, 1470, granted the power of attorney over her Paduan property and interests which is recorded in Document 6 (Carpi, 301; Carpi^{e}, 62).

41. *Ca.* 1480 to *ca.* 1495.

man of JML's professional and scholarly interests—its great university, unusually tolerant of Jews, was renowned alike for its medical school and for its hospitality to Averroist Aristotelianism—the wonder is less that he should have settled and remained there for so long than that he should ever have left.[42] During these years in Padua, he lectured at the university,[43] continued to teach and practise medicine,[44] brought to completion two more of his curricular texts,[45] and probably began to write, but did not finally redact, a third.[46] It was during his Paduan residency, too, that his daughter, Belladonna, grew up and was married,[47] and that he himself married Stella, daughter of Benjamin ben Joab of Fano, the lady who, at Venice on December 10, 1471, was to give birth to their son David.[48] And it was while JML was resident at Padua, finally, that he traveled to Pordenone in order to meet his royal patron, the emperor Frederick III, then ending his second visit to Italy. Here, on February 21, 1469, the emperor bestowed upon him what must surely rank as the most extraordinary writ of privilege ever accorded an individual European Jewish academician: not only a double doctorate, in medicine and in the liberal arts, but also the right to confer such doctorates upon other Jews of proved and demonstrated worthiness.[49]

As the Paduan archival documents attest, JML exercised the right granted him

42. See Carpi, 289f. (Carpi^{e}, 50 f.) on Padua's attractiveness to Jewish scholars. It is interesting to note that JML's residence in Padua must certainly have antedated the establishment there, *ca.* 1463, of the famous *y^{e}shībhāh* of R. Judah Minz. Was he perhaps helpful in its establishment? His respect for this great Ashkenazi center of Talmudic and rabbinic scholarship, and the esteem in which he held its head, are shown by the fact that years later he sent his son David, already then an ordained rabbi, to pursue advanced studies there under R. Judah, and thus to obtain an additional *s^{e}mīkhāh* from this well-known authority on Jewish law (*K^{e}bhōdh Ḥ^{a}khāmīm,* 64).

43. As he says in his 1474 letter to the Florentine community (n. 38, above).

44. As stated in the passage of the writ of privilege quoted above (n. 37). Since teachers and practitioners of medicine were required by university statute to wear a distinctive form of the *cappa,* or academic gown, it was at Padua that the question whether the wearing of this garment was permissible according to Jewish law became actual for JML. The question turned on whether or not the wearing of the *cappa* constituted a violation of Num. 15:37-41, Deut. 22:12, and Lev. 20:23, as rabbinically interpreted. Together with another concerned rabbi, Samuel da Modena, JML wrote a legal opinion holding that the wearing of a *cappa,* so made as not to be liable to the scriptural fringes requirement, was indeed licit; as parties of interest in the matter, however, they appealed to the foremost expert on Jewish law in Italy at that time, R. Joseph Colon. Colon, who in 1455 had upheld JML in his controversial views and admonitions regarding female ritual purification, now (*ca.* 1460?) approved the views of JML and Samuel da Modena on the wearing of the *cappa;* see his *Responsa* (No. 88 in most editions). Some years later, in another *responsum* (No. 149), Colon entered into greater detail on how the *cappa* must be made in order to be free of liability to the fringes requirement. Summaries of the relevant *responsa* are contained in Pines and Buxbaum, *New Responsa and Decisions of Rabbi Joseph Colon,* 317-318. See also Rosenberg, "Cenni," XXXIII, n. 2; on the *cappa,* cf. W. N. Hargreaves-Mawdsley, *A History of Academical Dress in Europe until the End of the Eighteenth Century* (Oxford, 1963), 19, 190-193.

45. The two were the *N.S.* and the *Super-commentary on Isagoge-Categories-De Interpretatione;* see the translation of David Messer Leon's letter to David of Tivoli, and the fuller discussion of the composition date of the *N.S.,* both given below.

46. His *Super-commentary on the Posterior Analytics;* see the remark on its redaction in his 1474 letter from Mantua to the Florentine Jewish community, translated below.

47. N. 31 above.

48. N. 30 above.

49. Carpi, Document 2, 297-299; 289-291 (Carpi^{e}, 59; 46, 51-52).

by Frederick III at least twice: on February 27, 1470, he conferred the degree of doctor of liberal arts and of medicine upon Johanan, son of Isaac Alemanno, of Mantua, and on June 15, 1470, he bestowed the same degree upon Benedict, son of Jacob de Gallis, of Parma.[50] Although we are not further informed about Benedict of Parma, Johanan Alemanno is quite well known as an author, and even more widely known as one of Giovanni Pico della Mirandola's teachers of Hebrew and of Judaic literature.[51] An unpublished work of Alemanno's (his *Liqqūṭīm* [''Miscellanies''],[52] is said to include JML's *N.S.* and one of his works on Aristotelian logic in a listing of the books Alemanno considered the essential core of ''an ideal curriculum of Jewish education.''[53] If the logical work in question was JML's *Super-commentary on Isagoge-Categories-De Interpretatione,* as seems likely, Alemanno has thus indicated his abiding respect for two of the textbooks that must have been made available to him when he was their author's student at Padua.

We unfortunately do not know whether JML conferred doctorates upon others besides Alemanno and Benedict of Parma, nor do we know how long his right so to act continued in effect. For such an educator as he had become and was to remain throughout most of his life, so much prestige and economic advantage obviously attached to the right to confer the doctorate, that he must certainly have exercised it in many more than the aforementioned two instances had he remained in uncontested possession of this authorization; and at least some of these instances, for doctorates (especially in medicine) were economically valuable, would have been recorded in various notarial archives, and thus become known to us. The absence of such records makes it probable that JML never awarded other doctorates than those given to Alemanno and Benedict of Parma.[54] Was he perhaps restrained from exercising his privilege at Padua? Was his move from Padua to Venice not long after he conferred the second of these double doctorates connected with the imposition of such a restraint? And was this extraordinary, imperially given privilege one of the issues at controversy in the disputations with Gentile scholars in which he says he engaged while at Bologna?[55]

Whatever the cause or causes of JML's abandoning Padua, we find him next

50. Carpi, Documents 1 and 4, 295–297, 299–300 (Carpi[e], 56–58, 61). On the degree of ''doctor of liberal arts,'' see F. M. Powicke and A. B. Emden, *The Universities of Europe in the Middle Ages, by the late Hastings Rashdall* (Oxford, 1936), I, 20 and 241, n. 4.

51. U. Cassuto, *Gli ebrei a Firenze nell' età del rinascimento,* 301 ff. (Heb., 235 ff.); G. dell' Acqua-L. Münster, ''I rapporti di Giovanni Pico della Mirandola con alcuni filosofi ebrei'' (in M. Salmi, et al., *L'opera e il pensiero di G. Pico della Mirandola nella storia dell'umanesimo* [Florence, 1965]), 162 f.

52. Cassuto, *Gli ebrei,* 312 (Heb., 243); Neubauer, *Hebrew MSS in the Bodleian*, 2234 (col. 771).

53. D. B. Ruderman, ''An Exemplary Sermon from the Classroom of a Jewish Teacher in Renaissance Italy'' (in *Italia,* I [1978]), 10, n. 7.

54. An outstanding student of JML's at Naples who later himself became a distinguished scholar and teacher, Abraham de Balmes of Lecce is recorded as having received the double doctorate in 1492. Significantly, the bestower of the degrees in this instance was not JML, but Pope Innocent VIII (H. Friedenwald, *The Jews and Medicine* [Baltimore, 1944], II, 573).

55. In the letter translated below from Mantua to the Bolognese Jewish Community in 1474.

successively at Venice and at Bologna, in each of which he remained for about a year (late 1470–1472).[56] Of his stay at Venice we know no more than that his son David was born there on December 10, 1471, and that three days later, in the presence of the students of his *y^eshībhāh,* a young man from Cologna was examined in the rules of ritual meat slaughtering.[57] Concerning JML's Bologna sojourn, our sole clear item of information is the aforementioned fact that he there engaged in disputations with Christian scholars.[58]

We are far better informed about the next stage in JML's career, the two years or so of his residence in Mantua (1473–1475).[59] We not only have several important notices by others about him at this time, but we have, as it were, an autobiographical statement: the two letters that he sent in 1474 to the Jewish communities of Bologna and of Florence, in which he defended himself against the slanders and falsehoods of a treacherous erstwhile protegé.[60]

In Mantua, JML established his *y^eshībhāh* and living quarters in close proximity[61] to the home of Rabbi Joseph Colon, the great legal authority and Talmudist who in 1455 had upheld him in his views on female purification, and who, in the 1460s, had done so again on the issue of the *cappa.*[62] Rabbi Joseph had settled in Mantua in 1470 or 1471;[63] he is documentarily attested as having remained there until at least April 26, 1475.[64]

While both rabbis were thus fellow townsmen and neighbors, JML figured personally in a rather grim legal matter on which Rabbi Joseph had been asked to rule, and of which we have a fairly detailed account in two of his responsa.[65] As

56. N. 39, above.
57. N. 40, above.
58. N. 55. The text of the passage in David Messer Leon's 1484 letter to David of Tivoli, in which JML's stay at Bologna is mentioned, is unfortunately corrupt. Judging by JML's statement in his 1474 letter to the Florentine Jewish community, he either continued writing, or may have completed but left unredacted, his *Super-commentary on the Posterior Analytics* during the brief period of his stay at Bologna.
59. Two notarial documents (adverting to a sum of 170 ducats deposited by JML with the Norsa brothers and subsequently withdrawn) attest him as living in Mantua between at least March 11, 1473, and March 13, 1475. Cf. Colorni, "Note," 173. For the Norsa brothers, Abraham Farissol made the copy of JML's *Super-commentary on Isagoge-Categories-De Interpretatione* now preserved in the Bodleian Library (Neubauer, *Hebrew MSS,* 1392). This manuscript is dated January 15, 1472; the author's fame as a scholar and teacher had thus plainly reached Mantua well in advance of the establishment of his *y^eshībhāh* there. According to A. Freimann, "Jewish Scribes in Medieval Italy" (in S. Lieberman, ed., *Alexander Marx Jubilee Volume* [Eng. Section, New York, 1950]), 313, fourteen-year-old Samuel b. Samuel da Modena finished the MS copy of JML's grammar now in the Library of the Jewish Theological Seminary on Tammuz 24 (June 29), 1475. If, as seems likely, the copying was done in JML's *y^eshībhāh,* this may indicate that JML, as late as the date mentioned, was still living in Mantua.
60. Reference and translation given below.
61. According to Colorni ("Note," 175), they lived on the same street, the "contrada dell'Orso" (p. 171).
62. N. 44 above.
63. Buxbaum and Pines, *New Responsa,* כ"ב.
64. Colorni, "Note," 171.
65. The earlier and shorter of the two, in which R. Joseph explains his assumption of jurisdiction over the case, is Buxbaum and Pines, *New Responsa,* no. 17, p. 88; the later, in which JML is cited,

described by Rabbi Joseph, the case concerned a father and a son, Naphtali Herz Cohen and Asher Cohen, German Jews resident in Verona. They had quarreled, and the father had resorted to various expedients (including having his son severely beaten in the synagogue)[66] in order to force the younger man and his family to abandon their shared dwelling and household goods; the son, however, had managed (mostly by dint of the relief he was able to elicit from Rabbi Joseph) to thwart all his father's attempts to victimize him. Cohen *père,* realizing that he was not likely to succeed in dislodging his son if the case were tried or arbitrated under Jewish auspices, at length resorted to a measure considered little short of sacrilege: pretending that Asher had refused, when requested, to have the case tried before a Jewish tribunal, Naphtali Herz brought charges against his son before the Gentile courts of Verona, had him arrested, and, as he was unable to furnish bail, remanded to prison.[67] It was at this juncture, according to Rabbi Joseph's account, that JML happened to be in Verona.[68] He protested the unjustified bringing of the matter before a Gentile court; his protest, however, went unheeded, nor was he properly requested, as he ought to have been, to adjudicate the matter.[69] Upon arrival in Mantua, accordingly, he made a full report of the incident to Rabbi Joseph.[70] The latter at once dispatched his decree-in-judgment,

---

is no. 149 of שו"ת מהרי"ק [*Responsa of R. Joseph Colon*] (in all editions except that of Warsaw, 1870, where it is no. 194). An account of the case, based only on the second of R. Joseph's two responsa (and otherwise not strictly accurate), is given by M. Güdemann, *Geschichte des Erziehungswesens und der Cultur der abendländischen Juden,* III (Vienna, 1888), 256.

66. He was beaten, says Colon (no. 149), "to the point that his blood was spilled upon the ground; they tore his prayer-shawl and phylacteries, and the blood poured over the prayer-book he was using, as I have been told. Can such blood be of acceptance, or can it **come up for a sweet savour** [Lev. 2:12]?"

67. "One of the supreme duties of the Jew in every age, but more especially after the beginning of the Crusading epoch, was the obligation to keep Jewish affairs from the ordinary law-courts" (I. Abrahams, *Jewish Life in the Middle Ages* [Philadelphia, 1896], 49). As Colon makes plain in this responsum, a matter could be brought before a Gentile court only in the event the summoned party refused to appear before a Jewish tribunal, and then only with the express permission of the Jewish court. In this case, the fact that Asher had not replied immediately to the suddenly voiced, peremptory command of his father that he name judges, but had gone into a room and closed the door behind him, was distorted by Naphtali Herz into a refusal on Asher's part to appear before a Jewish tribunal; but the father of course had no authorization from the Jewish court (R. Joseph's *bēth-dīn,* since he had taken jurisdiction over the case) to lay the matter before the Gentile courts of Verona.

68. He seems to have been merely passing through Verona—possibly after a visit at Montecchio Maggiore?—en route to Mantua.

69. "The father," writes R. Joseph (Responsum 149), "was insisting on having his claims [to the domicile and the household goods] fully satisfied before he would remove his pressure upon his son and not hale him into the Gentile court, according to the statement of the distinguished notable, teacher and scholar, R. Messer Leon, who was there present, but whose voiced protest against the perpetrators of this deed went unheeded by them. There are here several counts of sin and blame. First, they did not properly petition him to render a Jewish legal decision, but merely hastily and arrogantly. . . ."

70. Including his testimony, as a witness, that the son had in fact consented to have the case tried before a Jewish court, but that the father then refused to have his son released from jail and the power of the Gentile court "except on condition that he [the son], his wife and his children leave his house" and abandon all claim to the household goods.

ordering Naphtali Cohen, under penalty of excommunication, to have his son immediately released from jail and restored to their house, to withdraw the case from the jurisdiction of the Gentile courts, and to arrange with his son for a prompt and definitive settlement of their dispute under proper Jewish auspices.[71]

As Rabbi Joseph's account of the foregoing episode clearly shows, he and JML had great respect and regard for each other, and were the friendliest of neighbors. We have no reason to suppose that the excellent relations between the two, thus depicted—as, indeed, in the several other responsa by Colon in which JML is named—ever deteriorated or altered.[72] The sole contrary indication, an otherwise uncorroborated, brief report in Gedaliah ibn Yaḥya's *Shalsheleth ha-Qabbālāh* (Chain of Tradition, first printed in 1587),[73] is not merely later by about a century than the circumstances it purports to describe, but its misstatements of definitely known facts show that it is totally devoid of credibility.[74] Acceptance of this demonstrably false report has nevertheless until quite recently dominated—and vitiated—practically the whole of the scholarly literature on JML.[75]

We learn from David Messer Leon's letter to David of Tivoli that his father's work "on four books of the *Physics*" was composed in Mantua; here too, certainly, JML finished the redaction of the *Super-commentary on the Posterior Analytics* of which he speaks in his own letter to the Florentine Jewish community.[76] And it was also at this time—the slightly more than two years of JML's Mantuan residency—that Rabbi Abraham Conat allowed the copy of the manuscript of the *Nōpheth Ṣūphīm*, which he had some time before made for himself, to

71. I.e., Responsum 149.

72. As pointed out by Buxbaum (Pines, *New Responsa*, כ"ז), there is not the slightest suggestion in any of Colon's responsa of any difference of opinion with JML. The introduction of R. Joseph's lengthy responsum of support for JML on the matter of female purification (*New Responsa*, 229 ff.) consists of a *m*ᵉ*līṣāh*-passage in which JML is described in terms of extravagant praise.

73. *Editio princeps* (Venice), 62b; (Jerusalem, 1962), p. 143. The report reads: "R[abbi] Judah, called Messer Leon, was in Mantua, and he composed *Sēpher Nōpheth Ṣūphīm*. He was the opponent-at-law [*ha-bar p*ᵉ*lugtēh*] of *M*[*ōrēnū*] *h*[*ā*] *-R*[*ābh*] *Y*[*ōsēph*] *Q*[*ōlōn*], and the community became so divided that the Duke [*Dūkās*] drove both of them out of the city."

74. (a) Contrary to the statement in the report, the *N.S.* was not composed in Mantua; (b) the ruler of Mantua at the time (Lodovico), as S. Simonsohn (*Jews in Mantua*, p. 457, n. 111; Eng. trans., 627) has pointed out, was not a "Duke" but a "Marchese." According to M. Steinschneider (*Jewish Literature from the Eighth to the Eighteenth Century* [London, 1857; rpt. N.Y., 1965], 251), Joseph Delmedigo (early seventeenth century) called the *Chain of Tradition* a chain of lies. Oddly enough, Steinschneider himself, though recognizing that the source of the report was both late and unreliable, nevertheless accepted it as factual; see his *Gesammelte Schriften* (Berlin, 1925), 219, and his *Hebr. Uebersetzungen*, 77.

75. Simonsohn is the first scholar to have argued that ibn Yaḥya's report must be rejected; he has been followed in this opinion by virtually all others who have studied the original sources, including Carpi and Buxbaum. Demonstrably false as the report is, someone must have transmitted the gist of it to ibn Yaḥya; he certainly did not invent it. Perhaps there is here an echo of one of the "Sephardi's" slanders against JML, slanders which could have persisted in Sephardi circles long after their perpetrator had been shown by JML (in the letters translated below) to be a forger, a liar, and an informer.

76. See the translations of both letters.

be copied by Menaḥem ben Elijah de' Rossi of Ferrara, and then, on the basis of his own returned copy, printed it[77] in the printing house he had just established in Mantua.[78] Thus, for the very first time in the history of Hebrew literature, a work by a living author was printed and published after the manner of a modern book.

Although the *editio princeps* of the *N.S.* does not indicate the year and place of its printing, we know from those of Conat's imprints which do bear such indications that the place was definitely Mantua, and that the year, which cannot be later than early in 1476, was most probably 1475.[79] Thus the probability is very great that JML must still have been residing in Mantua when Conat first began to print the *N.S.* He undoubtedly knew that Conat had made a manuscript copy of his book, and he may have known of Conat's intention, through the newly available printing process, to issue the work in multiple copies. It is certain, nevertheless, that JML, for all that he was the original author of the *N.S.*, played no part whatever in its production as a printed book: he neither edited it nor corrected it in proof. Comparison of the text of Menaḥem de' Rossi's manuscript copy—based, it will be remembered, on the earlier copy made by Conat—with that of the incunabulum edition, shows clearly that Conat, in course of printing the volume, made many errors both of omission and of

77. In his colophon to the *editio princeps,* Conat tells us how and why he came to print the *N.S.* From the fact that de' Rossi, in his colophon, includes the lines of verse—the "parable"—with which Conat ends the book, we see that de' Rossi's copy was made from Conat's own manuscript copy; the *Vorlage* of the latter had probably reached Mantua at about the same time as that of the *Super-commentary on Isagoge-Categories-De Interpretatione* which Farissol copied for the Norsa brothers. The variants between the text of the de' Rossi manuscript (now in the Ambrosian Library, at Milan) and that of the *editio princeps* establish that de' Rossi made his copy from an unretouched form of the same text Conat used in printing the volume.

78. Pietro Adamo de' Micheli introduced the recently invented art of printing at Mantua in the year 1472; cf. L. Pescasio, *L'arte della stampa a Mantova nei secoli XV-XVI-XVII* (Mantua, 1971), 11. Conat's printing office followed de' Micheli's by no more than three years, as indicated by the facts set forth in the next-following note.

79. See A. M. Habermann, "The Printer Abraham Conat and his Letters" [Heb.], *'Ālīm,* II (1935/6), 81 ff., and L. Goldschmidt, *Hebrew Incunables: A Bibliographical Essay* (Oxford, 1948), 11, 75-76; also the excellent bibliographical description of a copy of the incunabulum edition by M. Marx, "A Catalogue of the Hebrew Books Printed in the Fifteenth Century Now in the Library of the Hebrew Union College," *Studies in Bibliography and Booklore,* I (1953/4), 36f. The colophon of Jacob ben Asher's *Ṭūr 'Ōraḥ Ḥayyīm* states that Conat finished printing his edition of this volume at Mantua on June 6, 1476; the printing of the next volume of Jacob ben Asher's work, the *Ṭūr Yōreh Dēʿāh,* though begun at Mantua by Conat, was not finished by him there, but was completed at Ferrara by Abraham ben Ḥayyim of Pesaro on July 25, 1477. Conat's activity as a printer was thus confined to Mantua, and is unattested beyond the year 1476. The six works issued by him without indication of date or place must therefore all have been printed at Mantua between the date when he established his printing-office—probably late in 1474 or early in 1475—and some time in the summer or fall of 1476. Various typographical details indicate that the *N.S.* was one of the first three of these six Conat imprints. Now Conat could not have begun to print the *N.S.* until after Menaḥem de' Rossi had returned Conat's own manuscript copy of the work, and as we learn from de' Rossi's colophon, Conat's manuscript copy was being used by him in Ferrara until October 12, 1474. Accordingly, Conat could not possibly have commenced printing the *N.S.* until the end of the year 1474, at the very earliest, and probably (since it is virtually certain that the two other first imprints preceded it) did not begin it until the second half of 1475; almost certainly, however, it was off the press before the end of the year 1475.

[Job 18:14]. Moreover, as one that tramples down[92] was he with them, **as a madman who casts firebrands, arrows and death** [Prov. 26:18].[93]

"Therefore I administered no rebuke when they scorned and taunted him on the day of the convocation, **for he deserves to die** [1 Sam. 20:31] and ought properly to be overthrown: **because of the perpetual ruins** [Ps. 74:3], his name and memory ought to be made to perish. **Let** not an enemy **do evil in the sanctuary** [Ps. 74:3], but let him be delivered up to reproaches and insults. **Happy is the man that does this** [Isa. 56:2], because he **fights the battles of the Lord** [1 Sam. 25:28].[94]

"As for his having **opened his mouth wide against me** [Ps. 35:21], **gushing out, speaking arrogantly** [Ps. 94:4] with **tongue that speaks proud things** [Ps. 12:4], **I had** almost quite **held my peace, I had been still and refrained myself** [Isa. 42:14] from answering him at all, for **my** people have **known my name** [Isa. 52:6] from **the months of old** [Job 29:2]. But now **this has come to pass in your days** [cf. Joel 1:2], that a base fellow **should stand up in the assembly and cry out** [Job 30:28] that **I have not learned wisdom** [Prov. 30:3], and that **I am brutish,**[95] **unlike a man** [Prov. 30:2]. For the mad fool, the enemy of the Lord and His holy Torah, **he that is girded with new armor** [2 Sam. 21:16], **comes from afar** with **his tongue full of indignation** [cf. Isa. 30:27], says to me as follows: 'You are **sunk in the mire of** folly [Ps. 69:3]; **with you it dwells, in the midst of you** [Deut. 23:17]; **carry** it **in your bosom**' [Num. 11:12].[96]

"Are they not **in full strength and likewise many** [Nah. 1:12], of the wise men of the Gentiles, today **in the land of** your **sojournings** [Gen. 37:1] **that have seen the mighty hand** [Deut. 11:2] with which the Lord graced me **in the way of discernment** [Isa. 40:14]? Also, **you yourselves are witnesses this day** [Ruth 4:9] that, all the days when **I stood at the threshold of** your **courts** [Ps. 84:11], my **heart was not turned back** [Ps. 44:19] **by reason of the prancings, the prancings of the mighty ones** [Judg. 5:22] of the controversies. Yet who has said, 'Nay, but it is [**out of his mouth**][97] **that come the knowledge and the**

92. Emendation: כרמם for כרסם.

93. Far from hating him, JML would have been happy to sing his praises. Witnesses, however, have testified against him that he sought to seduce the students of JML's *y^eshībhāh* into beliefs and acts that would assuredly send them down to hell, and expose them to its satanic terrors. His demeanor with the students was destructive rather than helpful.

94. JML, apparently assailed by the Sephardi for not having rebuked the students when, at a convocation in the synagogue, he had been scorned and taunted by them, replies that he was in fact deserving of far harsher treatment: because the damage he had done to many was eternal and irreparable, he deserved utter obliteration. JML would not permit an enemy of the Sephardi to do him physical harm in the place of divine worship, but he believes that one subjecting him to scorn and reproach should be praised and blessed as defending the cause of God and true religion.

95. Emendation: ובער (as at Prov. 30:2) for ונער.

96. Though the Sephardi's vicious attack upon JML's good name is too obviously incredible to need refutation, his public denunciation of JML as an ignorant boor, steeped in folly, has made JML decide to reply.

97. Text omits מפיו.

commission, errors that JML would never have overlooked or allowed to stand had he had anything to do with seeing the work through the press.[80]

Closely associated with JML's *y^eshībhāh* in Mantua, whether as student or teaching assistant or both, was a young scribe and scholar from Ferrara named Abraham Farissol.[81] Farissol, who later gained considerable fame as an author in his own right,[82] was throughout much of his life a skilled and indefatigable copyist of manuscripts, many of which are still preserved. Among these is MS Parma 1957, which, besides some materials composed by Farissol himself, contains an assortment of texts by various authors; the codex is a portmanteau volume of school texts and other materials used, or deemed useful, by Farissol in his work as a teacher.[83] One of the texts (number 9 in de' Rossi's list), for example, bears the superscription, "These are the theses of the *y^eshībhāh* of Messer Leon (his Rock and his Redeemer preserve him!)," and consists of a series of propositions headed respectively "in the Torah," "in Logic," and "in Grammar"—apparently propositions listed for discussion by Messer Leon at sessions of the courses in these subjects given in his *y^eshībhāh* during a particular term.[84] An entire group of these texts, again (numbers 11–13 in de' Rossi's list), consists of letters, by various hands, which Farissol used as examples in teaching the scribal and epistolary art (the *ars dictaminis*). Included in this group of texts, and thus luckily preserved to us, are the two letters (number 12, as listed) sent by JML in 1474 to the Jewish communities of Bologna and Florence.[85]

80. Examples of omissions from the text of the incunabulum edition, restored in the present edition mainly on the basis of Menaḥem de' Rossi's manuscript copy, preserved in the Ambrosian Library, occur at ii.10.24, iii.13.1, iii.16.5, iii.18.6, iv.5.2, iv.19.4, and iv.20.1; see the *apparatus criticus* of my Hebrew text. A particularly egregious example of an error of commission occurs in iv.70; Conat has here arbitrarily shifted several lines of text from the end of the chapter, where (as similar usage in chapters 69, 75, 76, and 77 shows) they were originally placed by JML, to the beginning of the chapter. If JML had had anything to do with the printing of his book, as some scholars have imagined, he would never have countenanced such a displacement of what he wrote. Cf. what is said below on the Hebrew text of the present edition.

81. On Farissol, see Simonsohn, *Jews in Mantua,* 537; Eng., 707; to the bibliography cited there now should be added D. B. Ruderman, "An Exemplary Sermon from the Classroom of a Jewish Teacher in Renaissance Italy."

82. Farissol is perhaps best known for his cosmographical treatise, *'Iggereth 'Orḥōth 'Ōlām* (Epistle on the Ways of the World), published at Ferrara (1524), at Venice (1586), and, with a Latin translation by Thomas Hyde, at Oxford (1691). This was the first Hebrew book to give an account of the epoch-making Portuguese and Spanish voyages of discovery of the late fifteenth century, including those of Columbus to the New World.

83. Now in the Biblioteca Palatina di Parma, MS 1957 once belonged to G. B. de' Rossi (I. B. de-Rossi), who numbered it "Cod. 145" and listed its contents in his *MSS Codices Biblioth. I. B. De-Rossi* (Parma, 1803), 95–97.

84. The first three theses, published by P. Perreau in J. Kobak's *Jeschurun VII* (1871), Heb. part, 82, n. 1, read as follows: "In Torah: It was in the essential nature of the Tree of Knowledge of Good and Evil to increase the bodily appetites. In Logic: The First Kind of the First Figure has been the most useful syllogism. In Grammar: The intensive *pu'al*-conjugation does not constitute an individual conjugation in and of itself."

85. The letters, transcribed from Cod. De-Rossi 145 (now MS Parma 1957) by P. Perreau, were published by M. Steinschneider in Kobak's *Jeschurun VII* (1869), Heb. part, 26 ff. (cf. p. 82);

Messer Leon's Letters (1474) to the Jewish Communities of Bologna and of Florence

The occasion of these letters was the fact that a teaching assistant whom JML had found it necessary to dismiss, a Spanish Jew (Sephardi) named David (patronymic unknown), was seeking to avenge himself upon his former employer and teacher by libeling and slandering him however and wherever he could. JML plainly felt constrained to refute these calumnies in the larger and more influential Jewish communities, particularly in Bologna, where he had been in residence just before coming to Mantua, and in Florence, where the Jewish community already then included many Sephardim; his defense in each letter is modulated—as might be expected from the writer of the *N.S.*—according to his anticipated readership and audience, and presumably, also, according to what he had heard of the acceptance accorded his opponent's falsehoods.[86] The care JML has evidently taken with these letters, including his effort to enhance their dignity by writing them in phrases drawn mainly from the Scriptures (*mᵉlīṣāh*),[87] shows that the affair was of more than passing concern to him. The letters are of unusual historical interest because, self-revelatory as they are, they afford a rare and most welcome glimpse into the feelings and personal opinions of this early Renaissance Jewish scholar and communal leader.

His Letter to the Jewish Community of Bologna (MS Parma 1957 [= Codex De-Rossi 145] : 12a)

"[Farissol's superscription]: This is the copy of the letter composed by Messer Leon (may his Rock protect him) and sent by him to Bologna because of a certain Sephardi who was opposed to him in Mantua in the year 234 of the l[esser] s[pecification] [= 1474 C.E.].

"[Messer Leon's text]: I have heard that **the cry is gone round about the borders** [Isa. 15:8] of Bologna, has **broadened and wound about higher and higher** [Ezek. 41:7] **in the full assemblies** [Ps. 68:27]. In your **house of prayer** [Isa. 56:7] **my glory** has been **put to shame** [Ps. 4:3] by **men of blood and deceit** that **shall not live out half their days** [Ps. 55:24]. It is **an enemy that taunts me** [Ps. 55:13], and all the **people perceive the thunderings** [Exod. 20:15].[88]

according to Kobak (n. 1, p. 26), corrections to the text, as transcribed, were contributed by Steinschneider. S. Z. H. Halberstam, and himself. A microfilm of the manuscript, kindly furnished me by the authorities of the Biblioteca Palatina di Parma, has enabled me to check, and here and there to improve, the readings of the published transcription; it is upon the text as thus slightly revised that my translation is based.

86. Cf. *N.S.* i.7 and i.10.

87. *N.S.*, i.14.

88. I.e., an enemy's slanderous vilification of JML has been spread throughout the whole of the Jewish community of Bologna. He has been held up to public obloquy even in the house of divine

"Now, therefore, **hear, O ye priests** [Hos. 5:1], **ye shepherds** [Eze understanding and intelligence, **the people in whose heart is the** Lor [Isa. 51:7].[89] How **the mighty man glories** [Jer. 9:22]—in evil! **What speak? or how shall** he **clear** himself [Gen. 44:16]? For he has **uttered ness against the Lord so as to practise ungodliness** [cf. Isa. 32:6]. **edged sword is in his hand** [Ps. 149:7] to **cast down many wounded** [cf. 7:26], victims of destructiveness and of denial of God. **The sword, it is pened, yea, it is furbished** [Ezek. 21:16], for to **hunt** down **souls** [Ezek. 13: in order to **break down** the **towers** [Ezek. 26:4] of the Torah. **Smoother t cream are the speeches of his mouth** [Ps. 55:22] so as to **cast** men **into t depths** [Mic. 7:19] of heresy and apostasy. His **wine is the venom of serpen** [Deut. 32:33], he is **a root that bears gall and wormwood** [Deut. 29:17].[90]

"And if it be said that thus **to lay wanton charges against** him [Deut. 22:14] is **had of my hand** [Isa. 50:11] because **I hate** him **with utmost hatred** [Ps. 139:22], **was not David hiding himself with** you [1 Sam. 23:19] ere ever he came **to appear before** me [Exod. 34:24]? And **wise men** that **shall be wise** [Prov. 13:20] had heard from him **the voice of adjuration** [Lev. 5:1], **the voice of** one **shouting for mastery** [Exod. 32:18] **in order to rend the enclosure of hearts** [Hos. 13:8], **and** the voice of one **speaking words against the highest** [Dan. 7:25]. And I **knew that for their sake he suffered taunts** [Jer. 15:15], that men had **struck him in the open sight of others** [Job 34:26] in the **land of your sojournings** [Gen. 17:8], whereas **his voice was not heard** [Ps. 19:4] **when he went in unto the holy place** [Exod. 28:29], **though there was enough contempt and wrath** [Esth. 1:18].[91]

"Indeed, **his statutes would have been my songs** [Ps. 119:54] **in the midst of congregation and assembly** [Prov. 5:14]. But witnesses have testified against him that he wished to make those athirst **to hear the words of the Lord** [Amos 8:11] drink of **the beaker, even the cup of staggering** [Isa. 51:17]; that he sought to seduce and **to thrust down** those gleaning before me from their **height** [cf. Ps. 62:5], and covertly placed before them ordinances which, **straying from the way of understanding** [cf. Prov. 21:16], would lead to the **uttermost parts of the nether-world** [cf. Isa. 14:15], would **march them to the king of terrors**

worship by destructive and deceitful persons, who accordingly are under the curse of a shortened life span.

89. JML addresses himself to the intelligent and sincerely religious leaders of the community.

90. This Sephardi, able as he is, delights in evil; the fact cannot be argued away. So plausible is he in the exposition of pernicious and blasphemous doctrine that he is capable of seducing many into heresy and apostasy, to their ultimate damnation and to the subversion of Judaism.

91. JML denies that hatred of David the Sephardi (as presumably alleged) is his reason for preferring the aforementioned serious charges against him. In proof of his denial he cites the fact of his acceptance of David at Mantua despite the latter's unseemly behavior earlier at Bologna, where he tried to induce others to rebel against the community's leadership. JML had nevertheless received David because he had suffered blows and insults for his stated views, yet during public worship he had contained his anger out of respect for the holy place.

discernment' [Prov. 2:6]? **Have I** not **conceived the people** [Num. 11:12] of **knowledge and skill** [Dan. 1:17] since **old time** [Ezek, 38:17]? Or **have I** not **brought them forth** [Num. 11:12]? Or have **all the wise men of the Gentiles and all their kings** [cf. Jer. 10:7], when **they saw my glory** [Isa. 66:17], not said, **'There is none so discreet and wise as he'** [Gen. 41:39]?[98]

"**Bring it to your minds** [cf. Isa. 46:8], **and ask for the old paths** [Jer. 6:16]: **When men rose up against us** [Ps. 124:2], when **the enemy said 'I will pursue, I will overtake, I will divide the spoil'** [Exod. 15:9], **many times** [Ps. 106:43], even **in the days of my youth** [Job 29:4], **was** not **God with me** [Gen. 28:20] to shatter **the horn of** our **adversaries** [Lam. 2:17], to **be for the people** [Exod. 18:19] **a preserver of life** [Gen. 45:5]? Was it not my hand **that pierced the dragons** [Isa. 51:9] of terror, **that made the depths of the sea** of troubles **a way for the redeemed to pass over** [Isa. 51:10]? Yet **because of this my heart is not haughty, nor mine eyes lofty; neither do I exercise myself in things too great, or in things too wonderful for me** [Ps. 131:1]. If I have **done mighty and tremendous things** [cf. Deut. 10:21], it was the **Lord,** blessed be He, He for **Whom they that wait shall not be ashamed** [Isa. 49:23], that **gave power to the faint** [Isa. 40:29] to **do valiantly** [Ps. 108:14], **and to him that had no might He increased strength** [Isa. 40:29]. He made **my heart take courage** [cf. Ps. 27:14] and **gave me the tongue of them that are taught, that I should know how to sustain with words him that is weary** [Isa. 50:4].[99]

"**Though** I **am little in** my **own sight** [1 Sam. 15:17], and know that **I have not the understanding of a man** [Prov. 30:2], for **who am I and what is my life** [1 Sam. 18:18], the fact is, indeed, that **I will say 'Behold me'** [Isa. 65:1] to everyone **that searches** and to everyone **that seeks** [cf. Ezek. 34:6], and that my **hands are spread forth** [1 Kings 8:54] **to strangers and settlers** [Lev. 25:23] and foreigners whom I do not know. **And brought down, I would speak from the ground** [Isa. 29:4] for any man **sore bestead and hungry** [Isa. 8:21], though my **speech should be low out of the dust** [Isa. 29:4]. None crying out for deliverance **is my ear too dull to hear** [Isa. 59:1]. Nor have I been afraid to go **into the land of great drought to proclaim liberty to the captives** [Isa. 61:1] of terror, **release to them that are fettered** [Isa. 61:1] by panic, and to come **from**

98. Many Gentile scholars in Bologna can attest JML's learning, discretion and wisdom, and thus give the lie to the Sephardi's allegations. Many of the Bolognese Jewish community, too, witnessed the courage, intelligence, and learning displayed by JML in his controversies, throughout the period of his stay in their city, with the most formidable of the Gentile scholars. Yet none—here JML mildly rebukes his addressees—has taken the trouble thus factually to contradict the Sephardi's assertions. None has pointed out that, far from being the ignorant and brutish fool depicted by the Sephardi, JML is the man who for years has trained up scholars and has fully justified the honors accorded him by the scholars and rulers of the Gentiles.

99. Consider what has happened in the past: from his youth onward, God being with him, JML has successfully defended his people against their enemies. His achievements have, nevertheless, not made him haughty, nor left him with an exaggerated notion of his own powers. He believes it is the Lord who has given him the strength, courage, and skill needed to succour and sustain his people.

the lions' dens, from the mountains of the leopards [Song of S. 4:8], **in order to bring to pass as it is this day, to save much people alive** [Gen. 50:20].[100]

"To whom **turned I a stubborn shoulder** [Zech. 7:11] **when any man came nigh to prostrate himself before** me [2 Sam. 15:5]? **And what is the case even now** [1 Kings 14:14]? If I were able to do something that would be good for you, either in general or specifically, **upon my belly would I go and dust would I eat** [Gen. 3:14]. I would **not turn back** before anyone [Prov. 30:30] **until I had performed the purposes of** your **heart** [Jer. 23:20]. Why, then, should you **hear the reproof which puts me to shame** [Job 20:3]? **The foreigner who has come from a far land** [Deut. 29:21] **has a harlot's forehead** [Jer. 3:3] **to have given** me **to reviling** [Isa. 43:28] **upon the highest places of the city** [Prov. 9:3]. **Your eyes have seen** it [Deut. 4:3], **but there is none of you that is sorry** [1 Sam. 22:8] over my cause of sorrow.[101]

"Now, then, **judge betwixt me and** [Isa. 5:3] Master **David, that littlest one** [cf. 1 Sam. 17:14]. Consider **all the goodness that** I **showed** [1 Kings 8:66] him before he **multiplied transgression** [Amos 4:4] and turned to sacrilege.[102] **It came to pass upon a day** [1 Sam. 1:4] that he **came nigh to prostrate himself before** me [2 Sam. 15:5]; he **entreated me with** his **mouth** [Job 19:16], and said that because of my name he had come **from the ends of the earth** [Isa. 41:9] that I might **teach him knowledge and make him to know the way of discernment** [Isa. 40:14]. He was garbed in patches, **and spot cleaved to his hands** [Job 31:7], but I was attentive to him, looked upon him, and my **eye pitied** him [Ezek. 16:5], so I **brought him home into** my **house** [Deut. 22:2] for **a long time** [Num. 20:15]. I **made great provision** for him [2 Kings 6:23], and **made** him **joyful in the house of my** renown[103] [cf. Isa. 56:7]. I **spoke kindly** to him [Gen. 50:21], and arranged that he read for my students [al-Ghazali's] *Principal Purposes of the Philosophers*,[104] in order that they might **put** their **money in** his **sack** [Gen. 43:22] and there **not be withholden from** him that **which** he might **pur-**

100. Without self-importance and self-confidence, JML has nevertheless never refused a request for his aid from any needy person, whether acquaintance, stranger, or foreigner; nor, however reduced his own personal circumstances, would he ever turn a deaf ear to a cry of distress. He has not been afraid to jeopardize himself in order to relieve the fears, and to save the lives, of victims of oppression.

101. Can the Jews of Bologna cite a single case in which JML rejected a plea for assistance? Even now, as they are well aware, he would do everything he could to accomplish some good for them. Why then should they have listened to the foreigner who had the effrontery to revile JML for alleged behavior which they know to be completely uncharacteristic of him? None, apparently of those present at the time felt sufficient concern for JML to give the lie to the Sephardi's obloquy.

102. Here follows JML's "Statement of the Facts"; cf. *N.S.* i.8, and the remarks in i.11.4 on the placing of the "Statement" within the sequence of the parts of the discourse.

103. Paronomasia: *tᵉhillāthī* ("my renown") for *tᵉphillāthī* ("my prayer").

104. *Kawwᵉnōth Happīlōsōphīm,* the translation (*ca.* 1352), by Judah Nathan b. Solomon of Provence, of al-Ghazali's *Maqāṣid al-Falāsifa*. Cf. S. Munk, *Mélanges de philosophie juive et arabe* (Paris, 1859), 369 ff.; J. Klatzkin, *Anthology of Jewish Philosophy* [Heb.] (Berlin, 1926), 17, 273–276.

pose to do [cf. Gen. 11:6]. I solemnly warned him, however, not to discuss with the students, outside my presence, any matter that is religiously heterodox.

"Thus I **magnified and exalted** him [cf. Isa. 1:2] and made him a **head of nations** [Ps. 18:22].[105] And I gave him daily instruction in the *Posterior Analytics,* **until David exceeded** [1 Sam. 20:41].[106] But **when he had been** here **a long time** [Gen. 26:8], and I came to know that **he devised to thrust down** [Ps. 62:5], I **drove** him **out so that** he **should not cleave unto the inheritance of** holy ones [1 Sam. 26:19]. **Then his spirit passed over** [Hab. 1:11]: he **has turned into another man** [1 Sam. 10:6], and **in the broad places** he **utters** his **voice** [Prov. 1:20].[107]

"Therefore **consider, I pray you, and see** [2 Kings 5:7] that I **have** not **transgressed and have** not rebelled [Lam. 3:42] **in making a difference between the unclean and the clean** [Lev. 11:47].[108] **Of a truth I know that** [Job 9:2] **the man will not be quiet** [Ruth 3:18], will not fail to return answer to these words of mine, but will **puff out lies** [Prov. 6:12]. But as for me, this **once have I spoken** [Job 40:5], and have **declared you my opinion** [Job 32:6]. **I will not smite him the second time** [1 Sam. 26:8] lest I **turn back from the service** of my **work** [Num. 8:25], stop **the work of holiness** [Exod. 36:4] in order to **walk after things of nought** [Jer. 2:5]. *Finis.*"

His Letter to the Jewish Community of Florence (MS Parma 1957 [= Codex De-Rossi 145]: 12b)

"[Farissol's superscription]: Another letter by our teacher, Rabbi Leon, sent from Mantua to Florence because of the aforementioned Sephardi.

"[Messer Leon's text]: **The captivity of Jerusalem that is in Sepharad** [Obad. 20] is that which **sits first in the kingdom** [Esth. 1:14] of the Torah-observant life, is that which has **built in the heavens the upper chambers** [Amos 9:6] of the faith. They are such as **can order the battle-array** [1 Chr. 12:39]: **every man has his sword upon his thigh** [Song of S. 3:8] so as to smite the God-denying **with an incessant stroke** [Isa. 14:6], **with the stroke of the sword, and with slaughter and destruction** [Esth. 9:5]. **Unto them alone has been given the** entire **land** [Job 15:19] of scientific inquiry. **Him that speaks falsehood** [Ps. 101:7], the destructive sects that **utter wickedness against the Lord** [Isa. 32:6], **they have hurled down to utter** [Ps. 73:18] **and perpetual ruin** [Ps. 74:3]; **them that have set their mouth against Heaven** [Ps. 73:9] they

105. The *y^eshībhāh* students, that is, who were apparently not only of Italian Jewish provenience, but from other European Jewish communities as well.

106. Cf. the more detailed account in Messer Leon's Letter to the Jewish community of Florence.

107. Cf. nn. 93 and 96, above.

108. To have separated the Sephardi from the *y^eshībhāh* was no sin.

hunt with thrust upon thrust [Ps. 140:12]; **their tongue walketh through** [Ps. 73:9] **the land of great drought** [Hos. 13:5]. **They built the palaces** [Hos. 8:14] of knowledge; **of unhewn stones** [Deut. 27:6] did **they set up** its **towers** [Isa. 23:13], made them **as high as the eagle** [Obad. 4]; their **place of defence** [Isa. 33:16] was **the fortresses of their Rock** [cf. Ps. 31:4]. **Above the stars of God** have they **exalted** their **throne** [Isa. 14:13], **and** their **righteousness endures forever** [Ps. 111:3].[109]

"'Now, however, **a rod of pride** [Prov. 14:3] **has come forth out of the stock** [Isa. 11:1] **of righteousness, the planting of the Lord wherein He might glory** [Isa. 61:3]. **It is a root that bears gall and wormwood** [Deut. 29:17], one that is **the cruel poison of asps** [Deut. 32:33], and that **has no compassion** [Jer. 21:7]. His tongue, **like a sharp sword** [Isa. 49:2], is used to **cast down many wounded** [Prov. 7:26], the victims of his destructiveness. A rebel **against his King and his God** [Isa. 8:21], **he speaks words against the highest** [Dan. 7:25] in order **to cast down from** the heights **the beauty of** [Lam. 2:1] the perfect religion. His **fool's mouth is his ruin** [Prov. 18:7] as he **gushes out, speaks arrogancy** [Ps. 94:4].[110]

"Is it that my **anger is kindled against the rivers** of intellect, **or my wrath against the sea** [Hab. 3:8] of understanding? My **mariners and my pilots** [Ezek. 27:27] in **gallant ship** [Isa. 33:21], in **swift ships** [Job 9:26] do not **do business in great waters** [Ps. 107:23], do not thus **firm their mast, not spread sail** [Isa. 33:23] among the wrecks that are **in the deep** [Ps. 107:23] around them. **Shall one man sin** [Num. 16:22], and shall **I be sore displeased** [Zech. 1:2] **with all the** innocent **congregation** [Num. 16:22] **in whose mouth are the high** praises of God [Ps. 149:6]? **Shall** my **wrath burn like fire** [Ps. 89:47], and shall my mouth **speak froward things** [Prov. 2:12]? Is not **all that is with** me **in the house** [Josh. 6:17] of insight and **in the field** [Exod. 9:3] of scientific investigation received **at their mouth** [cf. Prov. 2:6] or from their writings? I have set them **at the head over me as familiar friends** [Jer. 13:21], for it is they—**the mighty men that were of old** [Gen. 6:4], **of whom I said 'In their shadow** I **shall live'** [Lam. 4:20]—who **teach Jacob** the **ordinances** of perfection, **and the Torah** of wisdom and knowledge **to Israel** [Deut. 33:10]. Do they not time and again **put incense before** me **and whole burnt-offering upon** my **altar** [Deut. 33:10]? **And wherefore would I lift** myself **up above the assembly of the Lord** [Num. 16:3]? **Should the axe boast itself against him that hews**

109. The better to mark the contrast with the particular Spanish Jew blamed in this letter to the Florentine Jewish community, JML devotes his introduction (cf. *N.S.* i.6.7) to an encomium upon Spanish Jewry in general—of whom, also, a considerable number were apparently among his addressees. Spanish Jewry is praised for the true piety and extensive scientific knowledge which have constituted them such able defenders of the faith.

110. Spanish Jewry, a noble and virtuous stock, has now produced a vicious and ignoble son, David the Sephardi. Eloquent and persuasive, though pitiless, and an enemy of God and of the Jewish community's leaders, David, through misuse of his abilities, has both destroyed the faith of many Jews and accomplished his own ruin.

therewith [Isa. 10:15]? Now, therefore, God forfend that I should **present a stubborn shoulder** [Neh. 9:29] and **commit trespass against** [Num. 5:6] those **who have made me and fashioned me** [Ps. 119:73], caused the light to shine upon me **in dark places** [Ps. 88:7], and cleared my way of **stone of offense and rock of stumbling** [Isa. 8:14].[111]

"**And who has feeling** for the glory of the sons of Spain, **if not I** [Eccl. 2:25]? Was it not just a few days ago that one of the men of our congregation **opened** his **mouth without measure** [Isa. 5:11] in our prayer house, **in the sight of all the people** [Exod. 19:11], against the Sephardi? **His tongue was as a devouring fire** [Isa. 30:27], and beyond **David he exceeded** [1 Sam. 20:41], his **throat an open sepulchre** [Ps. 5:10]. But **my lips were full of indignation** [Isa. 30:27], and **crying out in the assembly** [Job 30:28], I took care **to contend with him** [Job 9:3] **with tongue speaking proud things** [Ps. 12:4] **of a people revered from their beginning onward** [Isa. 18:7]; **for it has been a people of understanding** [Isa. 27:11] from of old, and **over lands have they called upon their names** [Ps. 49:12].[112]

"Accordingly, if I have now become **very wroth, and** my **anger has burned within** me [Esth. 1:12], it is because of **an adversary and an enemy** [Esth. 7:6] who has rebelled and gone far in wickedness. I know that **better than the fat of rams** [1 Sam. 15:22], **better than a bullock, does it please the Lord** [Ps. 69:32] **that I show zeal against the arrogant** [Ps. 73:3]; for **to hold it in I cannot** [Jer. 20:9] when a man, **upon coming in unto the holy place** [Exod. 28:29], lifts up his voice in heresies and delusions **that hunt souls as birds** [Ezek. 13:20].[113]

"Now in order that no one imagine or consider that **my hand has done this** [Isa. 41:20] because of **the hatred wherewith I hated** him and so **have laid wanton charges against** him [Deut. 22:14], I have said to our dear friend from Bologna:[114] 'Cause judges, such as **you choose and bring near** [Ps. 65:5], to sit,

111. JML denies—as, apparently, this particular Sephardi has alleged—that he is prejudiced against Sephardi scholars and thinkers in general. True, those Sephardim by whom he has been influenced and guided are not such as bring one into religious and intellectual peril. He would certainly not condemn all Sephardim for the derelictions of an individual Sephardi. Indeed, all that JML most esteems in philosophy and in science has been received from Sephardim, whether as translators ("at their mouth") or as original authors. It is such Sephardim who have taught him how to live properly as a religious Jew. It is scarcely reasonable to suppose that so dedicated a servant of the Jewish community as JML would seek to exalt himself above the community, and not at all to be imagined that he would willingly commit arrogant trespass against those who have contributed so much to his own intellectual progress, enlightenment, and moral development.

112. JML yields to none in solicitude for the honor of Spanish Jewry. Not long since, in JML's own Italian Jewish congregation, a member, in the course of denouncing David the Sephardi, went too far and attacked Sephardim in general. Protesting this, JML reminded the congregation that the intelligence and insight of Sephardic Jewry, since earliest times, were justly renowned throughout the world.

113. JML's anger has been aroused not because David is a Sephardi, but because he has proved himself to be a vicious and confirmed enemy of God. To show zeal against the arrogant is known to be more pleasing to God than animal sacrifices. In any case, it is impossible for JML to countenance the Sephardi's promulgation of soul-destroying heresies in his *y^{e}shībhāh* ("the holy place").

114. The person mentioned is almost certainly one of those to whom the Sephardi sent his

and to his face righteous men will testify on oath that he has **devised to thrust down** [Ps. 62:5], **depart from the path** [Isa. 30:11], **turn aside unto crooked ways** [Ps. 125:5], in order **to trust in vanity** [Job 15:31] and falsehood, in order **to break down the towers** [Ezek. 26:4] of the faith. His **guests are** to be **in the depths of hell** [Prov. 9:18].[115]

''And if **the former** counts **should be void** [Num. 6:12], **added besides unto them** [Jer. 36:32] is an iniquitous act of transgression too great to be borne. For having slanderously informed against several of the students, he came into my house at eventide **with great power and with a mighty hand** [Exod. 32:11], with police officers of the (marchese's) court armed with lances and swords, in order to arrest one of the students, **to hurt his foot with fetters** [Ps. 105:18]. The Lord, however, **suffered him not to hurt** us [Gen. 31:7], for he **turned back by reason of** his **shame** [Ps. 70:4].[116]

''Again, he wrote to Bologna and to other places falsehoods **past searching out** [Isa. 40:28], namely that **I surely hired** him [Gen. 30:16] to magnify my name and to **praise my works in the gates** [cf. Prov. 31:31]; also, that he should **make** me **to know the way of discernment** [Isa. 40:14], **he that put his holy spirit in the midst of** me [Isa. 63:11].[117]

''Again, too, he copied the *Super-Commentary on the Posterior Analytics* that I had made, but which had not previously been redacted. Inasmuch as I was in process of redacting the work at the time—or just prior to that time—that I was giving him instruction in it, **he brought up an evil name against** me [Deut. 22:14], namely, that although I had committed gross errors and mistakes, he had taught me how **to make straight the crooked** [cf. Eccl. 1:15], had given **righteous judgments upon** me [Jer. 39:5] so as **to devise a skillful work** [Exod. 31:4] on **knowledge and all understanding** [cf. Exod. 31:3]. Yet more: he excised the page containing the book's preface, and wrote **according to these words** [Gen. 24:28]: 'This is the commentary that Maestro Paulo made and that Messer Leon translated from the Christian tongue into Hebrew.'[118]

---

denunciation of JML. As indicated by the wording, he is a friend both of JML and of the member of the Florentine community who is the primary recipient of the present letter. The latter, according to Cassuto (*Firenze,* 263, n. 2 [Heb. 205, n. 12]), was probably the 'Immanuel Ḥai b. 'Uzziel 'Azriel da Camerino at whose request JML composed his commentary on Bedersi's *B^{e}ḥīnath 'Ōlām* (cf. n. 33 above).

115. JML's action against the Sephardi is neither arbitrary nor based on trumped-up charges. Sworn testimony is available to the effect that the Sephardi has sought to subvert the Jewish faith; those whom he has seduced are certain to find themselves in the depths of hell.

116. One of the Sephardi's evil deeds is particularly heinous and intolerable: he falsely informed against several of the *y^{e}shībhāh* students, and had one of them arrested and taken in shackles from JML's house by armed police of the marchese's court. Shame, however, prevented him from pressing his charges.

117. In communications to Bologna and elsewhere the Sephardi made grossly false statements about his relationship with JML. He claimed to have been hired in order to enhance JML's reputation; also that he, having inspired JML, would make a scholar of him.

118. JML's completed, but as yet unredacted, super-commentary on Averroes' Middle Commentary on Aristotle's *Posterior Analytics,* copied by the Sephardi, was pressed by him into the service

"Let now, therefore, **the wise men make answer with knowledge** [cf. Job 15:2]: **see, yea, see** [1 Sam. 24:12] how **exalted is his stature** [Ezek. 31:5], how he **speaks insolence with a haughty neck** [Ps. 75:6], and his **tongue devises destruction** [Ps. 52:4]. **Have you not known, have you not heard** [Isa. 40:28] **from the ends of the earth** [Isa. 41:9]? The **statutes** of the intellectibles **have been my songs** [Ps. 119:54] from **months of old** [Job 29:2]: **I was set up from the beginning** [Prov. 8:23] **to teach the people knowledge** [Eccl. 12:9], to **pronounce aloud** [Isa. 58:1] **upon the highest places of the city** [Prov. 9:3] lectures on the sciences, natural and divine. **Before the mountains** planned by Him **were brought forth** [Ps. 90:2], **from the beginning, or ever the earth was** [Prov. 8:23], **the crown and the insignia** [2 Kings 11:12] had been placed upon my head, and **the rod of God in** my **hand** [Exod. 4:20]; so the **sheaves** of the true ideas have drawn near, **and bowed down to my sheaf** [Gen. 37:7].[119]

"Alas for the eyes that thus see an ungodly man, flawed in intelligence and in character, **rise up to bear perverted witness against me** [Deut. 19:16], denying what is palpable and self-evident, and, in his initial words, attempting to **profane my name amongst the Gentiles** [cf. Ezek. 36:23]! **Woe unto him that strives with his maker** [Isa. 45:9], that opposes his master; **a potsherd with the potsherds of the earth** [Isa. 45:9] **that says to a father, 'What are you begetting?'** [Isa. 45:10]! Who, then, is he that has been lecturing in the great academies, **in the midst of many peoples** [Mic. 5:7] since **ancient years** [Mal. 3:4], on **all learning and wisdom** [Dan. 1:17] **after its kind** [Gen. 1:12]? Or who is he that fights battles before the **peoples and the princes** [Esth. 1:11], **that rends the mountains and breaks in pieces the rocks** [1 Kings 19:11], **that turns wise men backward** [Isa. 44:25], as have I? This is **because the Lord has been with me** [Gen. 39:23].[120]

"And if I am likened to the fly's wings and **the spider's webs** [Isa. 59:5], **with whom took I counsel, and who instructed me** [Isa. 40:14] when, **these twenty years** ago now [Gen. 31:41], I worked out and composed my rules of grammar, which are **sweeter than honey** [Ps. 19:11] to those who **eat of their venison**

---

of his campaign to blacken JML's reputation. The Sephardi falsely claimed to have shown JML how to correct his many mistakes, and how the work might be made into a valuable treatise on philosophical and scientific method. Moreover, he removed JML's preface from his copy, and in its stead introduced a statement saying that Maestro Paulo—i.e., Paul of Venice (d. 1429)—had written the book, and that JML had merely translated it from Latin into Hebrew.

119. The Sephardi, JML says at the outset of his refutation, is overbearing, insolent, and destructive. JML is known by all to have carried on his philosophical and scientific work for many years. He was born to teach, to lecture on science and philosophy at the greatest centers of learning. He was predestined to eminence as an interpreter of works of philosophic and scientific truth.

120. The Sephardi has borne false witness against JML, denying self-evident facts and trying to denigrate JML's excellent reputation among Gentiles. His opposition to his master, his aspersions against his teacher's creative work, must ultimately bring him to grief. In brief refutation, JML mentions that he has for many years been lecturing to students of many nations (as, e.g., at Padua) on many different philosophical and scientific subjects; and that, God helping him, he has successfully engaged in public controversies with scholars of great reputation.

[Gen. 27:19], and which have been disseminated in **the isles afar off** [Isa. 66:19]?[121] Or who **taught** me **knowledge** [Isa. 40:14] in the case of my *Supercommentary on Isagoge-Categories-De Interpretatione?*[122] Or in the case of that extraordinary treatise, in the case of the novel Rhetoric,[123] **who has given me anything beforehand, that I should repay him** [Job 41:3]? Or in the case of the summary of logic,[124] which **is altogether delight** [Song of S. 5:16]? For **David, when he changed his demeanour** [Ps. 34:1], asserted that it was his **power and the might of** his **hand** that **got me this wealth** [Deut. 8:17]. And why **should his face not now wax pale** [Isa. 29:22] when he calls my compositions 'translations'? Cannot **eye see and ear hear** [cf. Prov. 20:12], in **an instant suddenly** [Isa. 29:5], that **the witness is a false witness** [Deut. 19:18]?

"'One [prayer] have I spoken **with** my **hands spread forth toward heaven** [1 Kings 8:54]: '**Lord, remember unto David all** my **affliction**' [Ps. 132:1]. May God judge between him and me; [**the heavens**] **shall reveal his iniquity, and the earth shall rise up against him** [Job 20:27]. *Finis.*"

No record remains of the effect, if any, produced by the foregoing letters, written and circulated in 1474, nor do we know if the bitter and ugly affair depicted therein was a factor in terminating Messer Leon's residence at Mantua. A notarial document attests him as still in the city on March 13, 1475, when—possibly in anticipation of his imminent departure—he received back from the bank of the Norsa brothers the sum of 170 ducats which he had deposited with them two years earlier (March 11, 1473),[125] and a manuscript copy of his grammar, dated June 29, 1475, if it may be assumed to have been made in his *ye shībhāh,* quite possibly signifies that he did not move his household and school from Mantua until a time subsequent to this date.[126] It is even possible that, while JML did not participate in the production of the first printed edition of the *N.S.*,[127] he was still in Mantua throughout the time that the volume was in press. In such case, since as previously noted the printing is best assigned to the second half of 1475,[128] JML may not have terminated his residence at Mantua until some time in the year 1476.

121. If JML were indeed such a scholarly "lightweight" as the Sephardi has asserted, how, alone and unaided twenty years ago, could he have composed *Libh^e nath Hassappīr*, a work sufficiently prized to have achieved circulation overseas.

122. *Supra,* n. 45.

123. . . . ובחבור הנפלא בהריטוריק' החדשה. That החדשה here means "novel," or "original," rather than "recent" or "new" (in the sense of "newly finished"), follows, I believe, from the fact that the context is JML's refutation of the Sephardi's allegation that he is not an original scholar. Note, too, his belief that the *N.S.* is an "extraordinary" composition. As Conat had not yet begun to print the *N.S.* when this letter was written, החדשה cannot be a reference to the appearance of the *editio princeps.*

124. *Mikhlal Yōphī.* (n. 17, above).

125. Colorni, "Note," 173.

126. *Supra,* n. 59.

127. *Supra,* n. 80.

128. *Supra,* n. 79.

discernment' [Prov. 2:6]? **Have I** not **conceived the people** [Num. 11:12] of **knowledge and skill** [Dan. 1:17] since **old time** [Ezek, 38:17]? Or **have I** not **brought them forth** [Num. 11:12]? Or have **all the wise men of the Gentiles and all their kings** [cf. Jer. 10:7], when **they saw my glory** [Isa. 66:17], not said, **'There is none so discreet and wise as he'** [Gen. 41:39]?[98]

"**Bring it to your minds** [cf. Isa. 46:8], **and ask for the old paths** [Jer. 6:16]: **When men rose up against us** [Ps. 124:2], when **the enemy said 'I will pursue, I will overtake, I will divide the spoil'** [Exod. 15:9], **many times** [Ps. 106:43], even **in the days of my youth** [Job 29:4], **was** not **God with me** [Gen. 28:20] to shatter **the horn of** our **adversaries** [Lam. 2:17], to **be for the people** [Exod. 18:19] **a preserver of life** [Gen. 45:5]? Was it not my hand **that pierced the dragons** [Isa. 51:9] of terror, **that made the depths of the sea** of troubles **a way for the redeemed to pass over** [Isa. 51:10]? Yet **because of this my heart is not haughty, nor mine eyes lofty; neither do I exercise myself in things too great, or in things too wonderful for me** [Ps. 131:1]. If I have **done mighty and tremendous things** [cf. Deut. 10:21], it was the **Lord,** blessed be He, He for **Whom they that wait shall not be ashamed** [Isa. 49:23], that **gave power to the faint** [Isa. 40:29] to **do valiantly** [Ps. 108:14], **and to him that had no might He increased strength** [Isa. 40:29]. He made **my heart take courage** [cf. Ps. 27:14] and **gave me the tongue of them that are taught, that I should know how to sustain with words him that is weary** [Isa. 50:4].[99]

"**Though I am little in** my **own sight** [1 Sam. 15:17], and know that **I have not the understanding of a man** [Prov. 30:2], for **who am I and what is my life** [1 Sam. 18:18], the fact is, indeed, that **I will say 'Behold me'** [Isa. 65:1] to everyone **that searches** and to everyone **that seeks** [cf. Ezek. 34:6], and that my **hands are spread forth** [1 Kings 8:54] **to strangers and settlers** [Lev. 25:23] and foreigners whom I do not know. **And brought down, I would speak from the ground** [Isa. 29:4] for any man **sore bestead and hungry** [Isa. 8:21], though my **speech should be low out of the dust** [Isa. 29:4]. None crying out for deliverance **is my ear too dull to hear** [Isa. 59:1]. Nor have I been afraid to go **into the land of great drought to proclaim liberty to the captives** [Isa. 61:1] of terror, **release to them that are fettered** [Isa. 61:1] by panic, and to come **from**

98. Many Gentile scholars in Bologna can attest JML's learning, discretion and wisdom, and thus give the lie to the Sephardi's allegations. Many of the Bolognese Jewish community, too, witnessed the courage, intelligence, and learning displayed by JML in his controversies, throughout the period of his stay in their city, with the most formidable of the Gentile scholars. Yet none—here JML mildly rebukes his addressees—has taken the trouble thus factually to contradict the Sephardi's assertions. None has pointed out that, far from being the ignorant and brutish fool depicted by the Sephardi, JML is the man who for years has trained up scholars and has fully justified the honors accorded him by the scholars and rulers of the Gentiles.

99. Consider what has happened in the past: from his youth onward, God being with him, JML has successfully defended his people against their enemies. His achievements have, nevertheless, not made him haughty, nor left him with an exaggerated notion of his own powers. He believes it is the Lord who has given him the strength, courage, and skill needed to succour and sustain his people.

the lions' dens, from the mountains of the leopards [Song of S. 4:8], **in order to bring to pass as it is this day, to save much people alive** [Gen. 50:20].[100]

"To whom **turned I a stubborn shoulder** [Zech. 7:11] **when any man came nigh to prostrate himself before** me [2 Sam. 15:5]? **And what is the case even now** [1 Kings 14:14]? If I were able to do something that would be good for you, either in general or specifically, **upon my belly would I go and dust would I eat** [Gen. 3:14]. I would **not turn back** before anyone [Prov. 30:30] **until I had performed the purposes of** your **heart** [Jer. 23:20]. Why, then, should you **hear the reproof which puts me to shame** [Job 20:3]? **The foreigner who has come from a far land** [Deut. 29:21] **has a harlot's forehead** [Jer. 3:3] **to have given** me **to reviling** [Isa. 43:28] **upon the highest places of the city** [Prov. 9:3]. **Your eyes have seen** it [Deut. 4:3], **but there is none of you that is sorry** [1 Sam. 22:8] over my cause of sorrow.[101]

"Now, then, **judge betwixt me and** [Isa. 5:3] Master **David, that littlest one** [cf. 1 Sam. 17:14]. Consider **all the goodness that I showed** [1 Kings 8:66] him before he **multiplied transgression** [Amos 4:4] and turned to sacrilege.[102] **It came to pass upon a day** [1 Sam. 1:4] that he **came nigh to prostrate himself before** me [2 Sam. 15:5]; he **entreated me with** his **mouth** [Job 19:16], and said that because of my name he had come **from the ends of the earth** [Isa. 41:9] that I might **teach him knowledge and make him to know the way of discernment** [Isa. 40:14]. He was garbed in patches, **and spot cleaved to his hands** [Job 31:7], but I was attentive to him, looked upon him, and my **eye pitied** him [Ezek. 16:5], so I **brought him home into** my **house** [Deut. 22:2] for **a long time** [Num. 20:15]. I **made great provision** for him [2 Kings 6:23], and **made** him **joyful in the house of my** renown[103] [cf. Isa. 56:7]. I **spoke kindly** to him [Gen. 50:21], and arranged that he read for my students [al-Ghazali's] *Principal Purposes of the Philosophers,*[104] in order that they might **put** their **money in** his **sack** [Gen. 43:22] and there **not be withholden from** him that **which** he might **pur-**

100. Without self-importance and self-confidence, JML has nevertheless never refused a request for his aid from any needy person, whether acquaintance, stranger, or foreigner; nor, however reduced his own personal circumstances, would he ever turn a deaf ear to a cry of distress. He has not been afraid to jeopardize himself in order to relieve the fears, and to save the lives, of victims of oppression.

101. Can the Jews of Bologna cite a single case in which JML rejected a plea for assistance? Even now, as they are well aware, he would do everything he could to accomplish some good for them. Why then should they have listened to the foreigner who had the effrontery to revile JML for alleged behavior which they know to be completely uncharacteristic of him? None, apparently of those present at the time felt sufficient concern for JML to give the lie to the Sephardi's obloquy.

102. Here follows JML's "Statement of the Facts"; cf. *N.S.* i.8, and the remarks in i.11.4 on the placing of the "Statement" within the sequence of the parts of the discourse.

103. Paronomasia: *tᵉhillāthī* ("my renown") for *tᵉphillāthī* ("my prayer").

104. *Kawwᵉnōth Happīlōsōphīm,* the translation (*ca.* 1352), by Judah Nathan b. Solomon of Provence, of al-Ghazali's *Maqāṣid al-Falāsifa.* Cf. S. Munk, *Mélanges de philosophie juive et arabe* (Paris, 1859), 369 ff.; J. Klatzkin, *Anthology of Jewish Philosophy* [Heb.] (Berlin, 1926), 17, 273–276.

pose to do [cf. Gen. 11:6]. I solemnly warned him, however, not to discuss with the students, outside my presence, any matter that is religiously heterodox.

"Thus I **magnified and exalted** him [cf. Isa. 1:2] and made him a **head of nations** [Ps. 18:22].[105] And I gave him daily instruction in the *Posterior Analytics,* **until David exceeded** [1 Sam. 20:41].[106] But **when he had been** here **a long time** [Gen. 26:8], and I came to know that **he devised to thrust down** [Ps. 62:5], I **drove** him **out so that** he **should not cleave unto the inheritance of** holy ones [1 Sam. 26:19]. **Then his spirit passed over** [Hab. 1:11]: he **has turned into another man** [1 Sam. 10:6], and **in the broad places** he **utters** his **voice** [Prov. 1:20].[107]

"Therefore **consider, I pray you, and see** [2 Kings 5:7] that I **have** not **transgressed and have** not rebelled [Lam. 3:42] **in making a difference between the unclean and the clean** [Lev. 11:47].[108] **Of a truth I know that** [Job 9:2] **the man will not be quiet** [Ruth 3:18], will not fail to return answer to these words of mine, but will **puff out lies** [Prov. 6:12]. But as for me, this **once have I spoken** [Job 40:5], and have **declared you my opinion** [Job 32:6]. **I will not smite him the second time** [1 Sam. 26:8] lest I **turn back from the service** of my **work** [Num. 8:25], stop **the work of holiness** [Exod. 36:4] in order to **walk after things of nought** [Jer. 2:5]. *Finis.*"

His Letter to the Jewish Community of Florence (MS Parma 1957 [= Codex De-Rossi 145]: 12b)

"[Farissol's superscription]: Another letter by our teacher, Rabbi Leon, sent from Mantua to Florence because of the aforementioned Sephardi.

"[Messer Leon's text]: **The captivity of Jerusalem that is in Sepharad** [Obad. 20] is that which **sits first in the kingdom** [Esth. 1:14] of the Torah-observant life, is that which has **built in the heavens the upper chambers** [Amos 9:6] of the faith. They are such as **can order the battle-array** [1 Chr. 12:39]: **every man has his sword upon his thigh** [Song of S. 3:8] so as to smite the God-denying **with an incessant stroke** [Isa. 14:6], **with the stroke of the sword, and with slaughter and destruction** [Esth. 9:5]. **Unto them alone has been given the** entire **land** [Job 15:19] of scientific inquiry. **Him that speaks falsehood** [Ps. 101:7], the destructive sects that **utter wickedness against the Lord** [Isa. 32:6], **they have hurled down to utter** [Ps. 73:18] **and perpetual ruin** [Ps. 74:3]; **them that have set their mouth against Heaven** [Ps. 73:9] they

105. The *y^e^shībhāh* students, that is, who were apparently not only of Italian Jewish provenience, but from other European Jewish communities as well.

106. Cf. the more detailed account in Messer Leon's Letter to the Jewish community of Florence.

107. Cf. nn. 93 and 96, above.

108. To have separated the Sephardi from the *y^e^shībhāh* was no sin.

hunt with thrust upon thrust [Ps. 140:12]; **their tongue walketh through** [Ps. 73:9] **the land of great drought** [Hos. 13:5]. **They built the palaces** [Hos. 8:14] of knowledge; **of unhewn stones** [Deut. 27:6] did **they set up** its **towers** [Isa. 23:13], made them **as high as the eagle** [Obad. 4]; their **place of defence** [Isa. 33:16] was **the fortresses of their Rock** [cf. Ps. 31:4]. **Above the stars of God** have they **exalted** their **throne** [Isa. 14:13], **and** their **righteousness endures forever** [Ps. 111:3].[109]

"'Now, however, **a rod of pride** [Prov. 14:3] **has come forth out of the stock** [Isa. 11:1] **of righteousness, the planting of the Lord wherein He might glory** [Isa. 61:3]. **It is a root that bears gall and wormwood** [Deut. 29:17], one that is **the cruel poison of asps** [Deut. 32:33], and that **has no compassion** [Jer. 21:7]. His tongue, **like a sharp sword** [Isa. 49:2], is used to **cast down many wounded** [Prov. 7:26], the victims of his destructiveness. A rebel **against his King and his God** [Isa. 8:21], **he speaks words against the highest** [Dan. 7:25] in order **to cast down from** the heights **the beauty of** [Lam. 2:1] the perfect religion. His **fool's mouth is his ruin** [Prov. 18:7] as he **gushes out, speaks arrogancy** [Ps. 94:4].[110]

"Is it that my **anger is kindled against the rivers** of intellect, **or my wrath against the sea** [Hab. 3:8] of understanding? My **mariners and my pilots** [Ezek. 27:27] in **gallant ship** [Isa. 33:21], in **swift ships** [Job 9:26] do not **do business in great waters** [Ps. 107:23], do not thus **firm their mast, not spread sail** [Isa. 33:23] among the wrecks that are **in the deep** [Ps. 107:23] around them. **Shall one man sin** [Num. 16:22], and shall **I be sore displeased** [Zech. 1:2] **with all the** innocent **congregation** [Num. 16:22] **in whose mouth are the high** praises of God [Ps. 149:6]? **Shall** my **wrath burn like fire** [Ps. 89:47], and shall my mouth **speak froward things** [Prov. 2:12]? Is not **all that is with** me **in the house** [Josh. 6:17] of insight and **in the field** [Exod. 9:3] of scientific investigation received **at their mouth** [cf. Prov. 2:6] or from their writings? I have set them **at the head over me as familiar friends** [Jer. 13:21], for it is they—**the mighty men that were of old** [Gen. 6:4], **of whom I said 'In their shadow** I **shall live'** [Lam. 4:20]—who **teach Jacob** the **ordinances** of perfection, **and the Torah** of wisdom and knowledge **to Israel** [Deut. 33:10]. Do they not time and again **put incense before** me **and whole burnt-offering upon** my **altar** [Deut. 33:10]? **And wherefore would I lift** myself **up above the assembly of the Lord** [Num. 16:3]? **Should the axe boast itself against him that hews**

109. The better to mark the contrast with the particular Spanish Jew blamed in this letter to the Florentine Jewish community, JML devotes his introduction (cf. *N.S.* i.6.7) to an encomium upon Spanish Jewry in general—of whom, also, a considerable number were apparently among his addressees. Spanish Jewry is praised for the true piety and extensive scientific knowledge which have constituted them such able defenders of the faith.

110. Spanish Jewry, a noble and virtuous stock, has now produced a vicious and ignoble son, David the Sephardi. Eloquent and persuasive, though pitiless, and an enemy of God and of the Jewish community's leaders, David, through misuse of his abilities, has both destroyed the faith of many Jews and accomplished his own ruin.

therewith [Isa. 10:15]? Now, therefore, God forfend that I should **present a stubborn shoulder** [Neh. 9:29] and **commit trespass against** [Num. 5:6] those **who have made me and fashioned me** [Ps. 119:73], caused the light to shine upon me **in dark places** [Ps. 88:7], and cleared my way of **stone of offense and rock of stumbling** [Isa. 8:14].[111]

"**And who has feeling** for the glory of the sons of Spain, **if not I** [Eccl. 2:25]? Was it not just a few days ago that one of the men of our congregation **opened** his **mouth without measure** [Isa. 5:11] in our prayer house, **in the sight of all the people** [Exod. 19:11], against the Sephardi? **His tongue was as a devouring fire** [Isa. 30:27], and beyond **David he exceeded** [1 Sam. 20:41], his **throat an open sepulchre** [Ps. 5:10]. But **my lips were full of indignation** [Isa. 30:27], and **crying out in the assembly** [Job 30:28], I took care **to contend with him** [Job 9:3] **with tongue speaking proud things** [Ps. 12:4] **of a people revered from their beginning onward** [Isa. 18:7]; **for it has been a people of understanding** [Isa. 27:11] from of old, and **over lands have they called upon their names** [Ps. 49:12].[112]

"Accordingly, if I have now become **very wroth, and** my **anger has burned within** me [Esth. 1:12], it is because of **an adversary and an enemy** [Esth. 7:6] who has rebelled and gone far in wickedness. I know that **better than the fat of rams** [1 Sam. 15:22], **better than a bullock, does it please the Lord** [Ps. 69:32] **that I show zeal against the arrogant** [Ps. 73:3]; for **to hold it in I cannot** [Jer. 20:9] when a man, **upon coming in unto the holy place** [Exod. 28:29], lifts up his voice in heresies and delusions **that hunt souls as birds** [Ezek. 13:20].[113]

"Now in order that no one imagine or consider that **my hand has done this** [Isa. 41:20] because of **the hatred wherewith I hated** him and so **have laid wanton charges against** him [Deut. 22:14], I have said to our dear friend from Bologna:[114] 'Cause judges, such as **you choose and bring near** [Ps. 65:5], to sit,

111. JML denies—as, apparently, this particular Sephardi has alleged—that he is prejudiced against Sephardi scholars and thinkers in general. True, those Sephardim by whom he has been influenced and guided are not such as bring one into religious and intellectual peril. He would certainly not condemn all Sephardim for the derelictions of an individual Sephardi. Indeed, all that JML most esteems in philosophy and in science has been received from Sephardim, whether as translators ("at their mouth") or as original authors. It is such Sephardim who have taught him how to live properly as a religious Jew. It is scarcely reasonable to suppose that so dedicated a servant of the Jewish community as JML would seek to exalt himself above the community, and not at all to be imagined that he would willingly commit arrogant trespass against those who have contributed so much to his own intellectual progress, enlightenment, and moral development.

112. JML yields to none in solicitude for the honor of Spanish Jewry. Not long since, in JML's own Italian Jewish congregation, a member, in the course of denouncing David the Sephardi, went too far and attacked Sephardim in general. Protesting this, JML reminded the congregation that the intelligence and insight of Sephardic Jewry, since earliest times, were justly renowned throughout the world.

113. JML's anger has been aroused not because David is a Sephardi, but because he has proved himself to be a vicious and confirmed enemy of God. To show zeal against the arrogant is known to be more pleasing to God than animal sacrifices. In any case, it is impossible for JML to countenance the Sephardi's promulgation of soul-destroying heresies in his *y^eshībhāh* ("the holy place").

114. The person mentioned is almost certainly one of those to whom the Sephardi sent his

and to his face righteous men will testify on oath that he has **devised to thrust down** [Ps. 62:5], **depart from the path** [Isa. 30:11], **turn aside unto crooked ways** [Ps. 125:5], in order **to trust in vanity** [Job 15:31] and falsehood, in order **to break down the towers** [Ezek. 26:4] of the faith. His **guests are** to be **in the depths of hell** [Prov. 9:18].[115]

"And if **the former** counts **should be void** [Num. 6:12], **added besides unto them** [Jer. 36:32] is an iniquitous act of transgression too great to be borne. For having slanderously informed against several of the students, he came into my house at eventide **with great power and with a mighty hand** [Exod. 32:11], with police officers of the (marchese's) court armed with lances and swords, in order to arrest one of the students, **to hurt his foot with fetters** [Ps. 105:18]. The Lord, however, **suffered him not to hurt** us [Gen. 31:7], for he **turned back by reason of** his **shame** [Ps. 70:4].[116]

"Again, he wrote to Bologna and to other places falsehoods **past searching out** [Isa. 40:28], namely that **I surely hired** him [Gen. 30:16] to magnify my name and to **praise my works in the gates** [cf. Prov. 31:31]; also, that he should **make** me **to know the way of discernment** [Isa. 40:14], **he that put his holy spirit in the midst of** me [Isa. 63:11].[117]

"Again, too, he copied the *Super-Commentary on the Posterior Analytics* that I had made, but which had not previously been redacted. Inasmuch as I was in process of redacting the work at the time—or just prior to that time—that I was giving him instruction in it, **he brought up an evil name against** me [Deut. 22:14], namely, that although I had committed gross errors and mistakes, he had taught me how **to make straight the crooked** [cf. Eccl. 1:15], had given **righteous judgments upon** me [Jer. 39:5] so as **to devise a skillful work** [Exod. 31:4] on **knowledge and all understanding** [cf. Exod. 31:3]. Yet more: he excised the page containing the book's preface, and wrote **according to these words** [Gen. 24:28]: 'This is the commentary that Maestro Paulo made and that Messer Leon translated from the Christian tongue into Hebrew.'[118]

---

denunciation of JML. As indicated by the wording, he is a friend both of JML and of the member of the Florentine community who is the primary recipient of the present letter. The latter, according to Cassuto (*Firenze,* 263, n. 2 [Heb. 205, n. 12]), was probably the 'Immanuel Ḥai b. 'Uzziel 'Azriel da Camerino at whose request JML composed his commentary on Bedersi's *B^{e}ḥīnath 'Ōlām* (cf. n. 33 above).

115. JML's action against the Sephardi is neither arbitrary nor based on trumped-up charges. Sworn testimony is available to the effect that the Sephardi has sought to subvert the Jewish faith; those whom he has seduced are certain to find themselves in the depths of hell.

116. One of the Sephardi's evil deeds is particularly heinous and intolerable: he falsely informed against several of the *y^{e}shībhāh* students, and had one of them arrested and taken in shackles from JML's house by armed police of the marchese's court. Shame, however, prevented him from pressing his charges.

117. In communications to Bologna and elsewhere the Sephardi made grossly false statements about his relationship with JML. He claimed to have been hired in order to enhance JML's reputation; also that he, having inspired JML, would make a scholar of him.

118. JML's completed, but as yet unredacted, super-commentary on Averroes' Middle Commentary on Aristotle's *Posterior Analytics,* copied by the Sephardi, was pressed by him into the service

commission, errors that JML would never have overlooked or allowed to stand had he had anything to do with seeing the work through the press.[80]

Closely associated with JML's *y^eshībhāh* in Mantua, whether as student or teaching assistant or both, was a young scribe and scholar from Ferrara named Abraham Farissol.[81] Farissol, who later gained considerable fame as an author in his own right,[82] was throughout much of his life a skilled and indefatigable copyist of manuscripts, many of which are still preserved. Among these is MS Parma 1957, which, besides some materials composed by Farissol himself, contains an assortment of texts by various authors; the codex is a portmanteau volume of school texts and other materials used, or deemed useful, by Farissol in his work as a teacher.[83] One of the texts (number 9 in de' Rossi's list), for example, bears the superscription, "These are the theses of the *y^eshībhāh* of Messer Leon (his Rock and his Redeemer preserve him!)," and consists of a series of propositions headed respectively "in the Torah," "in Logic," and "in Grammar"—apparently propositions listed for discussion by Messer Leon at sessions of the courses in these subjects given in his *y^eshībhāh* during a particular term.[84] An entire group of these texts, again (numbers 11–13 in de' Rossi's list), consists of letters, by various hands, which Farissol used as examples in teaching the scribal and epistolary art (the *ars dictaminis*). Included in this group of texts, and thus luckily preserved to us, are the two letters (number 12, as listed) sent by JML in 1474 to the Jewish communities of Bologna and Florence.[85]

80. Examples of omissions from the text of the incunabulum edition, restored in the present edition mainly on the basis of Menaḥem de' Rossi's manuscript copy, preserved in the Ambrosian Library, occur at ii.10.24, iii.13.1, iii.16.5, iii.18.6, iv.5.2, iv.19.4, and iv.20.1; see the *apparatus criticus* of my Hebrew text. A particularly egregious example of an error of commission occurs in iv.70; Conat has here arbitrarily shifted several lines of text from the end of the chapter, where (as similar usage in chapters 69, 75, 76, and 77 shows) they were originally placed by JML, to the beginning of the chapter. If JML had had anything to do with the printing of his book, as some scholars have imagined, he would never have countenanced such a displacement of what he wrote. Cf. what is said below on the Hebrew text of the present edition.

81. On Farissol, see Simonsohn, *Jews in Mantua,* 537; Eng., 707; to the bibliography cited there now should be added D. B. Ruderman, "An Exemplary Sermon from the Classroom of a Jewish Teacher in Renaissance Italy."

82. Farissol is perhaps best known for his cosmographical treatise, *'Iggereth 'Orḥōth 'Ōlām* (Epistle on the Ways of the World), published at Ferrara (1524), at Venice (1586), and, with a Latin translation by Thomas Hyde, at Oxford (1691). This was the first Hebrew book to give an account of the epoch-making Portuguese and Spanish voyages of discovery of the late fifteenth century, including those of Columbus to the New World.

83. Now in the Biblioteca Palatina di Parma, MS 1957 once belonged to G. B. de' Rossi (I. B. de-Rossi), who numbered it "Cod. 145" and listed its contents in his *MSS Codices Biblioth. I. B. De-Rossi* (Parma, 1803), 95–97.

84. The first three theses, published by P. Perreau in J. Kobak's *Jeschurun VII* (1871), Heb. part, 82, n. 1, read as follows: "In Torah: It was in the essential nature of the Tree of Knowledge of Good and Evil to increase the bodily appetites. In Logic: The First Kind of the First Figure has been the most useful syllogism. In Grammar: The intensive *pu'al*-conjugation does not constitute an individual conjugation in and of itself."

85. The letters, transcribed from Cod. De-Rossi 145 (now MS Parma 1957) by P. Perreau, were published by M. Steinschneider in Kobak's *Jeschurun VII* (1869), Heb. part, 26 ff. (cf. p. 82);

Messer Leon's Letters (1474) to the Jewish Communities of Bologna and of Florence

The occasion of these letters was the fact that a teaching assistant whom JML had found it necessary to dismiss, a Spanish Jew (Sephardi) named David (patronymic unknown), was seeking to avenge himself upon his former employer and teacher by libeling and slandering him however and wherever he could. JML plainly felt constrained to refute these calumnies in the larger and more influential Jewish communities, particularly in Bologna, where he had been in residence just before coming to Mantua, and in Florence, where the Jewish community already then included many Sephardim; his defense in each letter is modulated—as might be expected from the writer of the *N.S.*—according to his anticipated readership and audience, and presumably, also, according to what he had heard of the acceptance accorded his opponent's falsehoods.[86] The care JML has evidently taken with these letters, including his effort to enhance their dignity by writing them in phrases drawn mainly from the Scriptures (*m*ᵉ*līṣāh*),[87] shows that the affair was of more than passing concern to him. The letters are of unusual historical interest because, self-revelatory as they are, they afford a rare and most welcome glimpse into the feelings and personal opinions of this early Renaissance Jewish scholar and communal leader.

His Letter to the Jewish Community of Bologna (MS Parma 1957 [= Codex De-Rossi 145] : 12a)

"[Farissol's superscription]: This is the copy of the letter composed by Messer Leon (may his Rock protect him) and sent by him to Bologna because of a certain Sephardi who was opposed to him in Mantua in the year 234 of the l[esser] s[pecification] [= 1474 C.E.].

"[Messer Leon's text]: I have heard that **the cry is gone round about the borders** [Isa. 15:8] of Bologna, has **broadened and wound about higher and higher** [Ezek. 41:7] **in the full assemblies** [Ps. 68:27]. In your **house of prayer** [Isa. 56:7] **my glory** has been **put to shame** [Ps. 4:3] by **men of blood and deceit** that **shall not live out half their days** [Ps. 55:24]. It is **an enemy that taunts me** [Ps. 55:13], and all the **people perceive the thunderings** [Exod. 20:15].[88]

according to Kobak (n. 1, p. 26), corrections to the text, as transcribed, were contributed by Steinschneider. S. Z. H. Halberstam, and himself. A microfilm of the manuscript, kindly furnished me by the authorities of the Biblioteca Palatina di Parma, has enabled me to check, and here and there to improve, the readings of the published transcription; it is upon the text as thus slightly revised that my translation is based.

86. Cf. *N.S.* i.7 and i.10.

87. *N.S.*, i.14.

88. I.e., an enemy's slanderous vilification of JML has been spread throughout the whole of the Jewish community of Bologna. He has been held up to public obloquy even in the house of divine

"Now, therefore, **hear, O ye priests** [Hos. 5:1], **ye shepherds** [Ezek. 34:7] of understanding and intelligence, **the people in whose heart is the** Lord's **Torah** [Isa. 51:7].[89] How **the mighty man glories** [Jer. 9:22]—in evil! **What shall** he **speak? or how shall** he **clear** himself [Gen. 44:16]? For he has **uttered wickedness against the Lord so as to practise ungodliness** [cf. Isa. 32:6]. **A two-edged sword is in his hand** [Ps. 149:7] to **cast down many wounded** [cf. Prov. 7:26], victims of destructiveness and of denial of God. **The sword, it is sharpened, yea, it is furbished** [Ezek. 21:16], for to **hunt** down **souls** [Ezek. 13:20], in order to **break down** the **towers** [Ezek. 26:4] of the Torah. **Smoother than cream are the speeches of his mouth** [Ps. 55:22] so as to **cast** men **into the depths** [Mic. 7:19] of heresy and apostasy. His **wine is the venom of serpents** [Deut. 32:33], he is **a root that bears gall and wormwood** [Deut. 29:17].[90]

"And if it be said that thus **to lay wanton charges against** him [Deut. 22:14] is **had of my hand** [Isa. 50:11] because **I hate** him **with utmost hatred** [Ps. 139:22], **was not David hiding himself with** you [1 Sam. 23:19] ere ever he came **to appear before** me [Exod. 34:24]? And **wise men** that **shall be wise** [Prov. 13:20] had heard from him **the voice of adjuration** [Lev. 5:1], **the voice of** one **shouting for mastery** [Exod. 32:18] **in order to rend the enclosure of hearts** [Hos. 13:8], **and** the voice of one **speaking words against the highest** [Dan. 7:25]. And I **knew that for their sake he suffered taunts** [Jer. 15:15], that men had **struck him in the open sight of others** [Job 34:26] in the **land of your sojournings** [Gen. 17:8], whereas **his voice was not heard** [Ps. 19:4] **when he went in unto the holy place** [Exod. 28:29], **though there was enough contempt and wrath** [Esth. 1:18].[91]

"Indeed, **his statutes would have been my songs** [Ps. 119:54] **in the midst of congregation and assembly** [Prov. 5:14]. But witnesses have testified against him that he wished to make those athirst **to hear the words of the Lord** [Amos 8:11] drink of **the beaker, even the cup of staggering** [Isa. 51:17]; that he sought to seduce and **to thrust down** those gleaning before me from their **height** [cf. Ps. 62:5], and covertly placed before them ordinances which, **straying from the way of understanding** [cf. Prov. 21:16], would lead to the **uttermost parts of the nether-world** [cf. Isa. 14:15], would **march them to the king of terrors**

---

worship by destructive and deceitful persons, who accordingly are under the curse of a shortened life span.

89. JML addresses himself to the intelligent and sincerely religious leaders of the community.

90. This Sephardi, able as he is, delights in evil; the fact cannot be argued away. So plausible is he in the exposition of pernicious and blasphemous doctrine that he is capable of seducing many into heresy and apostasy, to their ultimate damnation and to the subversion of Judaism.

91. JML denies that hatred of David the Sephardi (as presumably alleged) is his reason for preferring the aforementioned serious charges against him. In proof of his denial he cites the fact of his acceptance of David at Mantua despite the latter's unseemly behavior earlier at Bologna, where he tried to induce others to rebel against the community's leadership. JML had nevertheless received David because he had suffered blows and insults for his stated views, yet during public worship he had contained his anger out of respect for the holy place.

[Job 18:14]. Moreover, as one that tramples down[92] was he with them, **as a madman who casts firebrands, arrows and death** [Prov. 26:18].[93]

"Therefore I administered no rebuke when they scorned and taunted him on the day of the convocation, **for he deserves to die** [1 Sam. 20:31] and ought properly to be overthrown: **because of the perpetual ruins** [Ps. 74:3], his name and memory ought to be made to perish. **Let** not an enemy **do evil in the sanctuary** [Ps. 74:3], but let him be delivered up to reproaches and insults. **Happy is the man that does this** [Isa. 56:2], **because** he **fights the battles of the Lord** [1 Sam. 25:28].[94]

"As for his having **opened his mouth wide against me** [Ps. 35:21], **gushing out, speaking arrogantly** [Ps. 94:4] with **tongue that speaks proud things** [Ps. 12:4], **I had** almost quite **held my peace, I had been still and refrained myself** [Isa. 42:14] from answering him at all, for **my** people have **known my name** [Isa. 52:6] from **the months of old** [Job 29:2]. But now **this has come to pass in your days** [cf. Joel 1:2], that a base fellow **should stand up in the assembly and cry out** [Job 30:28] that **I have not learned wisdom** [Prov. 30:3], and that **I am brutish,**[95] **unlike a man** [Prov. 30:2]. For the mad fool, the enemy of the Lord and His holy Torah, **he that is girded with new armor** [2 Sam. 21:16], **comes from afar** with **his tongue full of indignation** [cf. Isa. 30:27], says to me as follows: 'You are **sunk in the mire of** folly [Ps. 69:3]; **with you it dwells, in the midst of you** [Deut. 23:17]; **carry** it **in your bosom**' [Num. 11:12].[96]

"Are they not **in full strength and likewise many** [Nah. 1:12], of the wise men of the Gentiles, today **in the land of** your **sojournings** [Gen. 37:1] **that have seen the mighty hand** [Deut. 11:2] with which the Lord graced me **in the way of discernment** [Isa. 40:14]? Also, **you yourselves are witnesses this day** [Ruth 4:9] that, all the days when **I stood at the threshold of** your **courts** [Ps. 84:11], my **heart was not turned back** [Ps. 44:19] **by reason of the prancings, the prancings of the mighty ones** [Judg. 5:22] of the controversies. Yet who has said, 'Nay, but it is [**out of his mouth**][97] **that come the knowledge and the**

92. Emendation: כרמס for כרסם.

93. Far from hating him, JML would have been happy to sing his praises. Witnesses, however, have testified against him that he sought to seduce the students of JML's *y^eshībhāh* into beliefs and acts that would assuredly send them down to hell, and expose them to its satanic terrors. His demeanor with the students was destructive rather than helpful.

94. JML, apparently assailed by the Sephardi for not having rebuked the students when, at a convocation in the synagogue, he had been scorned and taunted by them, replies that he was in fact deserving of far harsher treatment: because the damage he had done to many was eternal and irreparable, he deserved utter obliteration. JML would not permit an enemy of the Sephardi to do him physical harm in the place of divine worship, but he believes that one subjecting him to scorn and reproach should be praised and blessed as defending the cause of God and true religion.

95. Emendation: ובער (as at Prov. 30:2) for ונער.

96. Though the Sephardi's vicious attack upon JML's good name is too obviously incredible to need refutation, his public denunciation of JML as an ignorant boor, steeped in folly, has made JML decide to reply.

97. Text omits מפיו.

Except for a single ambiguous reference in a manuscript of the British Museum, a prayer codex copied by Abraham Farissol and dated in the year 1478,[129] we now lose sight of JML for a period of approximately five years. Our next recorded mention of him—the earliest attestation we have of his long residence in Naples—is in a scribal note which is dated the 12th of Ab, 5240, that is, July 19, 1480; this note is found in another British Museum manuscript, a copy of JML's own *Super-commentary on Isagoge-Categories-De Interpretatione*.[130] That he should have chosen to establish his *y^{e}shībhāh* at Naples at about this time is easily understood. Attracted by the inducements and privileges made available as a matter of deliberate policy by the despotic Aragonese ruler, Ferrante I, Jews from all over northern Italy and from countries outside Italy were then settling in considerable numbers in the Kingdom of Naples.[131]

During the fifteen years or more of his residence in Naples, JML continued to produce works in the several fields of his scientific and scholarly competence;[132]

129. Margoliouth, *Catalogue*, no. 621 (II, 213–214): "'Jeshurun, give voice' (*R^{e}shūth to Bār^{e}khū*, by Messer Leon of Ancona, called in Israel [Our] M[aster], the R[abbi], R[abbi] Judah, [his] Rock and [his Redeemer] p[reserve him])." The text of this prayer, often reprinted, may conveniently be consulted in Simonsohn, *Jews in Mantua* (Heb.), II, 439 (Eng. trans. [rather too freely rendered], 605). We are unfortunately not able to determine whether Farissol, in thus referring to JML as "of Ancona," meant (1) that he knew him then (in 1478) to be living there, or (2) that he believed (mistakenly) that Ancona was JML's native place, or (3) that he knew this *R^{e}shūth* to have been written by JML while formerly resident in Ancona.

130. Margoliouth, *Catalogue*, no. 881 (III, 174–175). The note, by an anonymous scribe who was a student in JML's *y^{e}shībhāh*, is found at the end of the section on the *Categories*, and reads as follows: "12th of Ab (be it of acceptance!) of the year 5240, (its sign of the [year's] specification being **Thus says the High** [רָם (*rām*) = 240] **and Lofty One** [Isa. 57:15]), in Naples, in the Synagogue of the Foreigners: finished and completed, with the cooperation and help of God, in the house of Rabbi Messer Leon. May the Name grant him to publish all his privately-kept works [כל תעלומותיו], to be delivered from the traps of forgery and falsification, and to be unto us as **balm** of **Gilead** [cf. Jer. 8:22] in healing all our souls' ills; and may he bring us to our **desired haven** [Ps. 107:30], **joyful and glad of heart** [1 Kings 8:66], as is our **heart's desire** [Ps. 21:3]. Amen everlasting. *Selah.*" The date and place—"the Synagogue of the Foreigners," the area in Naples where Jewish immigrants from foreign countries, including Italian territories outside the Kingdom of Naples, were quartered—of the note itself are given in the first part of the first sentence; the words "finished and completed," however, refer to the preceding sections of the manuscript: the copying of the text was done in the "house" (i.e., the *y^{e}shībhāh*) of JML. We seem to hear in the note's prayer for JML, particularly in the references to "privately kept works" and to deliverance "from the traps of forgery and falsification," reverberations of the affair of David the Sephardi. The scribe, speaking for himself and for other students in JML's *y^{e}shībhāh*, bears interesting witness to the affection and esteem felt for their teacher.

131. C. Roth, *The History of the Jews of Italy* (Philadelphia, 1946), 276–277.

132. David Messer Leon, in his letter from Naples to David of Tivoli, lists those of his father's works composed between the time of his leaving Mantua (1475/6) and the date of the letter (1484); see the apposite passage, commencing "Then **after** a few **days** [Josh. 23:1]," etc., in the annotated translation given below. At Naples too, between 1484 and 1495, JML must have composed his super-commentaries on Averroes/Aristotle's *Prior Analytics* and *Ethics*, and his *Mōrēh Ṣedheq*, a commentary on Maimonides' *Guide to the Perplexed*. These works are not mentioned in David's 1484 letter, as they unquestionably would have been had they then been in existence; see the lists of JML's works in M. Steinschneider, *Gesammelte Schriften* 220–228; I. Husik, *Judah Messer Leon's Commentary on the "Vetus Logica"* (Leyden, 1906), 6; and U. Cassuto's article in the Berlin *Encyclopaedia Judaica*.

and he brought his *y^eshībhāh* to the acme of its fame and influence. An idea of the nature and importance of the *y^eshībhāh,* as it functioned in the year 1489 is conveyed in a short passage of David Messer Leon's legal disquisition on rabbinical ordination (*semīkhāh*). David's ordination—his first, as he tells us[133]—was received "in my youth when I was eighteen years old, in Naples, in the great *y^eshībhāh* of my lord and father (be his memory for blessing), under whom at the time were twenty-two well-known ordained rabbis. While my lord and father (be his memory for blessing) was a great man in his generation and the Light of our Exile, he himself did not wish to ordain me, because I was his son—this despite the fact that we find in Sanhedrin, Chapter I (5a), that Rabba bar Rav Huna obtained his authorization from his father. So it was, then, that all those rabbis who were there, from France, from Germany, and from other 'tongues,' ordained me. . . . This took place on my birthday, the Sabbath of Hanukkah; and many scholarly researches on the matter of the [proper] date of ordination were presented, some among which brought proof that, although I was but eighteen years old, ordination could be granted to such an one who was worthy. . . ."[134]

One of the well-known rabbis associated with JML's *y^eshībhāh* at Naples was Rabbi Jacob Landau. His historically valuable legal code, *Sēpher Hā'āghūr,* is notable in two additional respects: it follows the *N.S.* as the second Hebrew book printed in its author's lifetime; and it is the first work to carry those approbationary writs (*haskāmōth*) by outstanding rabbis and scholars which became so characteristic and fixed a feature of the Hebrew printed book.[135] JML himself was one of those who, at Rabbi Jacob's request, furnished such a testimonial;[136] other *y^eshībhāh* associates who did so were David Messer Leon, Jacob b. David

133. His second ordination was obtained from R. Judah Minz, at whose *y^eshībhāh* in Padua, David tells us in his legal essay (*K^ebhōdh Ḥ^akhāmīm*, 64), he studied for "a time, times," i.e. for three terms, after he had received his first ordination at Naples on November 21, 1489; cf. nn. 11 and 42 above. The three terms in question must have fallen mainly in the year 1491: David was still at Naples in 1490 when he received Jacob Provenzali's dated responsum to his query on the study of philosophy and the sciences; and he was again at Naples in 1492, when he was one of the several rabbis who furnished approbations of the first printed edition of Jacob Landau's legal code, *Sēpher Hā'āghūr*.

134. *K^ebhōdh Ḥ^akhāmīm,* 64–65.

135. J. Bloch, *Hebrew Printing in Naples* (New York Public Library, New York, 1942), 10, 22–23; J. L. Teicher, "Notes on Hebrew Incunables," *Journal of Jewish Bibliography,* 4 (1943), 56–58.

136. The Hebrew text and an English rendering of JML's *haskāmāh* appear in *The Jewish Encyclopaedia* (New York, 1904), II, 27; D. W. Amram, *Makers of Hebrew Books in Italy* (Philadelphia, 1909), 66–67, has also published a translation. The interest and importance of this approbation are sufficiently great, it seems to me, to justify the following attempt at a more strictly accurate rendering: "I have indeed seen the effort of our colleague, [our] h[onored] t[eacher] the R[abbi], R[abbi] Jacob Landau, composer of the goodly work called *'Āghūr:* that he has collected and brought together the laws of daily worship, of the festivals, and of every forbidden or permitted practice as well as all that is therewith entailed. It is a composition which gives **goodly words** [Gen. 49:21] on matters of custom and on decisions by legal authorities, such as are upright in point of severity. I have, therefore, set my signature upon a **honeycomb of pleasant words** [Prov. 16:24]. The insignificant one, Judah, called Messer Leon."

Provenzali, and Moses b. Shem-Ṭob ibn Ḥabib.[137] Jacob Provenzali, in his responsum on the study, by Jews, of philosophy and the sciences (addressed in 1490 to David Messer Leon), refers to JML as "the paragon of the generation, our guide and master, o[ur] h[onored] t[eacher], the R[abbi], R[abbi] Judah, called Messer Leon."[138] Moses ibn Ḥabib, in the year 1484, composed at Naples a Hebrew grammar, *Peraḥ Shōshān* [1 Kings 7:26] (The Lily's Blossom), in which he makes frequent reference to Judah Messer Leon's grammar, *Libh^e nath Hassappīr*.[139] We also know the names of at least two of JML's younger pupils during the years of the *ye shībhāh*'s existence at Naples. One was Moses b. Shabbethai Levi, who in 1483 wrote for himself (as he tells us in the colophon) the very legible copy of JML's *Super-commentary on Isagoge-Categories-De Interpretatione* preserved in the Biblioteca Casanatense at Rome.[140] The other was Abraham de Balmes of Lecce, recipient of a double doctorate at Naples in 1492, who many years later composed a Hebrew grammar in which he often cites both the work of his teacher, and the work of Moses ibn Ḥabib.[141]

Various writings of David Messer Leon, composed at intervals between 1492 and 1497/98, afford us such meager information as we have about JML's last years.[142] From what David tells us, we infer that both he and his father were among the many Jews who fled Naples in 1495 during the pogrom which followed upon the taking of the city by the French under Charles VIII. By 1497/98 David—almost certainly accompanied by his father—was settled somewhere in the Ottoman Empire, probably at Monastir (formerly "Monasterio," now Bitola), in Macedonia.[143] At any rate, it was "from the city of Monasterio" that a copy of an ordination diploma composed by David Messer Leon was brought to one Berechiah b. Judah Russo; according to the document's superscription, Berechiah received it on Thursday, the 8th of Tishri, 5260, that is, on September

137. Teicher, "Hebrew Incunables," lists the approbationers and reproduces the Hebrew text of David Messer Leon's testimonial.

138. Jacob Provenzali, *Sh^e'ēlāh ūth^e shūbhāh bidh^e bhar limmūdh haḥokhmoth* ("Question and Response on the Study of the Sciences"), published in: Eliezer Ashkenazi, *Dibh^e rē Ḥ^a khāmīm* (Metz, 1849); the citation appears on pp. 70–71. In the excerpt from the responsum published by S. Assaf, *Sources*, etc., II, the citation is given on p. 100.

139. Margoliouth, *Catalogue*, III, 307 (MS 980).

140. G. Sacerdote, *Catalogo dei Codici Ebraici della Biblioteca Casanatense* (Firenze, 1897), No. 154 (Ms. 3127). British Museum MS no. 1117, a copy of JML's *Mikhlal Yophi*, was made by the same scribe in 1481.

141. De Balmes' grammar—*Miqnē 'Abhrām* (Abram's Cattle) [Gen. 13:7], published at Venice in 1524 by Daniel Bomberg in double format, one with a Latin translation, the other (reduplicated at Tel-Aviv, 1972) without—cites JML and Ḥabib together at Quire 8:7b; de Balmes refers to Ḥabib very frequently, more often than not to disagree with him. He quotes JML as "my teacher" at Quire 13:8b.

142. That JML was still alive in 1497/98 is shown by the fact that the latest of these writings (*Ma'amar Shebhaḥ Hannāshīm*) employs the *ante-mortem* formula, "his Rock and his Redeemer protect him" (יצ"ו), following mention of his name. For the list of these writings, and for the question of the date of JML's death, see my paper, "A Rectification of the Date of Judah Messer Leon's Death" (n. 11f, above), esp. pp. 401 ff.

143. Ibid., 402–403.

12, 1499. By this date, since the superscription mentions JML with addition of the post-mortem formula, "remembered be he for the life of the world to come" (ז"לה"ה), the author of the *N.S.* was no longer alive.[144] In fine, our sources indicate that Judah Messer Leon died, probably at Monastir, on a date that fell within the two-year interval between 1497 and 1499.

3. David Messer Leon's Letter (1484) on His Father's Works

The earliest listing we have of JML's works is in a letter sent by David Messer Leon from Naples in 1484 to their kinsman, David of Tivoli. For all its youthful naiveté—David was then but thirteen years old—the annotated bibliography contained in this letter is carefully and intelligently wrought. It is comprised, in the first place, of works by JML then being used, or available for use, in conjunction with the study and teaching carried on in the *ye shībhāh* at Naples. Secondly, the works are listed in the order of their composition. If the latter feature, as we have already seen, makes of the letter a prime source of information on the several stages of JML's career, the former constitutes it an admirable starting point for any detailed consideration of the *N.S.* In the context of this listing of JML's works, we are able to see that the *N.S.* was intended by its author to function as part of a planned curriculum of post-primary and higher education, at once "religious" and "secular": a scheme of education designed to equip young Jews with the intellectual skills and knowledge needed not only for the life in harmony with divine revelation that might earn them a portion in the world to come, but for success in the affairs of this world, whether as persons of consequence in the wider society of their time and place, or, more specifically, as leaders of their own Jewish communities. Here, then, is a translation of the Hebrew text of this interesting document, as thus far partially published and available:[145]

"I know, moreover, that you have **longed greatly** [Gen. 31:30] to know of the books composed by the great Rabbi, 'he who gives light to the earth and those dwelling upon it,'[146] 'the leader of his people,'[147] my l[ord and] f[ather] (his R[ock and [Redeemer] p[rotect him]). I have, accordingly, seen to the mention-

144. The text and a translation of the ordination diploma, an important document, are given on pp. 399-400, 404, n. 5.

145. The main bibliographical section of the letter was published by S. Schechter, "Notes sur Messer David Leon tirées de manuscrits," 120, on the basis of a copy made by M. Margolies of Cod. Laur. 88.12 (Biblioteca Laurenziana, Florence), pp. 1-2a. Schechter omitted the *m^e līṣāh-* introduction, while Margolies declared the final part of the letter, including the date, illegible. U. Cassuto nevertheless succeeded in deciphering the final lines, and published them as Document VI of his essay, "La famiglia di David da Tivoli," *Corriere Israelitico,* XLV (1906-7), 301 f.

146. Quoted from the *Yōṣēr* (adapted from Isa. 45:7), the first of the two benedictions that precede the *Sh^e ma'* in the Morning Liturgy.

147. Sanhedrin 14a, Ketubot 17a.

ing of them for your honor, each one **at its place**[148] [Ps. 37:10], and as he **proclaimed their names over lands** [Ps. 49:12].[149]

"The first [Gen. 2:11][150] is *Libhᵉnath Hassappīr* ["The Pavement of Sapphire" (Exod. 24:10)], a treatise on grammar; **and after that came forth** its **brother** [Gen. 25:26], named *Mikhlal Yōphī* ["The Perfection of Beauty" (Ps. 50:2)], which contains many principles of the science of logic, **new and old** [Song of S. 7:14]. **And the name of the third** [Gen. 2:14] is *Nōpheth Ṣūphīm* ["The Honeycomb's Flow" (Ps. 19:11)], in which he set forth the sweetness and pleasingness of the utterance in the Prophets' speeches; it is **to be much praised** [2 Sam. 14:15].[151] He also composed a [super-]commentary on *Isagoge-Categories-De Interpretatione*[152]. . . .[153] established his hands in Bologna;[154] and I was[155] then **by**

148. I.e., the works are listed in the order of composition.

149. With the titles, given them by JML, by which he caused them to be known both in Italy and abroad.

150. Literally, "the one," i.e., "No. 1."

151. These three school texts, while their subjects reflect the continuing vitality of the tradition of the medieval *trivium* (grammar, logic, rhetoric) in early Renaissance pedagogy, in their contents exemplify, and in part carry out, their author's scheme of an integrated "Jewish-religious" and "secular" education. All three books are "Jewish," because written in Hebrew; each, because it is the handbook of a discipline considered an indispensable prerequisite of higher learning, is also "secular." In the case of the grammar, the "Jewishness" is reinforced by virtue of the fact that the principles of the grammatical art are exhibited as these are found to exist in the language of the Hebrew Bible. The "Jewishness" of the rhetoric is even more strikingly evident; here the rules and principles, drawn from the works of Greek and Latin rhetoricians, are applied to—in some instances found laid down in—passages of the Hebrew Scriptures.

That David Messer Leon has listed these three works in the order of their composition, as he indicates, is externally verifiable and certain. We know the composition dates of *Libhᵉnath Hassappīr* (September 1454) and of *Mikhlal Yōphī* (February 1455); both works are quoted in the *Nōpheth Ṣūphīm,* which for its part is cited by neither. Although JML may have begun the composition of the *N.S.* while he was still in Ancona (at least until April 1455), it was only completed during his residence at Padua (*ca.* 1455–*ca.* 1471): see §2 and n. 45, above, and the fuller discussion below. The several temporal phrases in David's letter—e.g., "Then, **after** a few **days** [cf. Josh. 23:1]," etc.—are further indication that the works mentioned are listed in the order of their composition.

152. "Also" here seems to indicate that this super-commentary was completed at about the same date as the *N.S.*: both works were probably used by Johanan Alemanno at Padua before February 1470. (cf. §2 and nn. 50–53 above). The super-commentary is partially published in I. Husik, *Judah Messer Leon's Commentary on the "Vetus Logica"* (Leyden, 1906).

153. The several dots indicate a lacuna in the text at this point.

154. The subject of the verb "established" (כוננה), as the verb ending shows, could only have been a feminine singular noun. To make "his (i.e., JML's) hands" the subject of the verb, and to take the three Hebrew words here (. . . . כוננה ידיו בבולוניא) to mean that JML composed the [super-] commentary on *Isagoge,* etc. in Bologna, is simply to mistranslate the broken text before us; *pace* Husik (p. 6), Rosenberg, "Cenni," XXXII, and Carpi (285; Carpiᵉ, 48), this text does not say that JML composed this work in Bologna. What the text in fact says is that *something*—expressed by some now missing feminine noun—"established his hands in Bologna," i.e., caused JML to continue his career in Bologna. Was there a reference here to some quality by virtue of which, or to some circumstance because of which, JML was induced to settle briefly in that city? See above, §2, and nn. 55, 58, and 98.

155. Cassuto, "La famiglia," 261, n. 2, here emends the actual reading "I was" (הייתי) to "you were" (היית), and thus obtains the widely accepted, erroneous reference to David of Tivoli as a pupil of Judah Messer Leon; see note 36, above. Although David of Tivoli was certainly an admirer of

him as a nursling [Prov. 8:30] as regards knowing **the discipline of wisdom** [Prov. 1:3], in **making offering to the** work[156] **of Heaven** [Jer. 44:17] **for instruction and for testimony** [Isa. 8:20].[157]

"Now **if those are in full strength** [Nah. 1:12], you dispose of '**pleasant words are as a honeycomb.**' [Prov. 16:24].[158] **And likewise many** [Nah. 1:12] are **in his storehouses**[159] [2 Kings 20:13], of **which,** I think, you **have not heard the fame** [Isa. 66:19], **nor have** you **been told** [1 Kings 10:7] **of their abundance or of their wealth** [Ezek. 7:11]. **And one is** [Gen. 42:13] the [super-] commentary on the *Posterior Analytics,*[160] of which **glorious things are spoken** [Ps. 87:3]: this having reached **the exiles of Jerusalem that are in Sepharad** [Obad. 20] and come into the hands of a scholar, a teacher of righteousness, **he set it in the firmament of the heavens** [Gen. 1:17] for **greatness and glory** [cf. 1 Chr. 29:11].[161] In Mantua he (Judah) also composed a wonderfully fine volume on four books of the *Physics.*[162] It explains Averroes' words, reconciles the Long Commentary with the Latin version and the Middle Commentary, and introduces all the problems discussed in each of these several books, so that one does not need to consult any other volume. So great is its glory that **it is become the chief cornerstone** [Ps. 118:22].[163]

"Then, **after** a few **days** [cf. Josh. 23:1], he began his *Exposition of the Torah,* which includes all the problems that occur to the human mind in matters

---

JML, there is no evidence outside this arbitrary emendation to support the assumption that he was ever JML's student.

156. Word play: *m^e lékheth* "work" for the actual *malkath* "queen" of the verse in Jeremiah.

157. DML is here saying that, during JML's residence in Bologna, he was as yet too young to have begun his own studies, both secular and sacred, with his father. As shown above (n. 39), David must have been brought from Venice to Bologna when he was still not yet a year old; he was only fifteen months old when his father is attested as in residence at Mantua (March 11, 1473).

158. A veritable honeycomb of doctrine—an actualization, as it were, of Prov. 16:24—is at David of Tivoli's disposal if he owns all four of the aforementioned texts composed by JML.

159. Unlike the previously cited four volumes, which are widely disseminated and thus well known, the books about to be mentioned have not been released by JML for public circulation. These are "**in his storehouses,**" i.e., kept by him for his own use, and for others' use only as he permitted. They are the "privately-kept works" mentioned in the scribal note cited above (n. 130). It is because these works were only privately circulated, if at all, that manuscript copies of them are now so much rarer than copies of the four publicly circulated curricular texts (including, of course, the printed *N.S.*).

160. This is the work that figured in the affair with David the Sephardi, described in JML's letter of 1474 to the Florentine Jewish community (*supra,* §2 and n. 118); cf. Margoliouth, *Catalogue* no. 883 (III, 178–179). Note that as late as 1484 JML had still not released it for public circulation, though it was obviously being circulated among Sephardi scholars both in Italy and abroad.

161. Who the Sephardi scholar and legist (for such is the sense here of "teacher of righteousness") was we do not know. It is interesting that David Messer Leon, future author of the legal disquisition on *s^e mīkhāh* (*K^e bhōdh Ḥ^a khāmīm*), thus early knew that the title *rābh* was not used among Sephardim in the sense of one authorized to adjudicate cases of sacred law.

162. Our knowledge of this work is confined to this passage.

163. In the judgment of the students and scholars affiliated with JML's *ye shībhāh* at Naples, this book was apparently reputed to be the most fundamentally important of the author's expositions of Averroist-Aristotelian philosophy.

of divinity. **There is none to be compared to** it [Ps. 40:6]; it encompasses the whole of Genesis, and Weekly Portions *Weʾēlle Shemōth* [Exod. 1:1–6:1] and *Wāʾērā* [Exod. 6:2–9:35].[164]

"**Also**[165] **Judah has appointed** him **a harvest** [Hos. 6:11] in the art of medicine: he has composed a single volume, in the Christian tongue, that comprises all the various kinds of diseases;[166] it **is more precious than rubies** [Prov. 3:15]. He has, in addition, prepared many *novellae* on Book I of Avicenna's *Canon,* Fen I, and explained Fen II thereof.[167]

"Also, [he has prepared] a compendium of his legal decisions, to serve as a remembrance of him. . . .[168] And were **his bread given, his waters sure** [Isa. 33:16], he would occupy himself with these divine studies **day and night** [Josh. 1:8], so that he would write marvellous words on matters of Torah. . . .[169]

"Surely[170] **this, we have** heard **it, so it is** [Job 5:27]: that he whom it is **desired to make wise** [Gen. 3:6] and **to cause to be good** [Ps. 36:4], Master Joab, my kinsman, (his R[ock] and [Redeemer] p[rotect him]), your son, is going from good to good in the pleasantness of his ways—**which cheers God and men**

164. The *Exposition* was only begun shortly after Judah left Mantua; as pointed out above (n. 129), we do not know where he was then in residence. As David's language here suggests, theology and metaphysics are the paramount concerns in the *Exposition.* The work was possibly an outgrowth of the author's effort—mentioned many years earlier (1454) in the letters from Ancona in which he temporarily interdicted study of R. Levi b. Gershom's commentary on the Pentateuch—to prove that R. Levi's view of the divine omniscience is heretical. JML apparently never finished the *Exposition.* That it did, however, extend beyond Exod. 9:35 is indicated by I. A. Benjacob's report of the Firkovitch manuscript of several of JML's writings (*Ozar Ha-sepharim* [Vilna, 1880], 256): this manuscript includes the section of the *Exposition* between *Mishpāṭīm* [Exod. 21:1–24:18] and the end of *Shemīnī* [Lev. 9:1–11:47]. A passage of his father's *Exposition* is quoted by David in *Māghēn Dawīdh;* see Schechter, "Notes sur Messer David Leon," 125.

165. The writing of the *Exposition of the Torah,* begun after JML left Mantua, was continuing at Naples at the composition date (May 1484) of this letter. Hence the term "also," employed here and at the beginning of the next paragraph, probably means "also at Naples."

166. This volume, written in Latin, apparently consisted of a classified list of ailments as described in various medical works, and here presented in summary form. The mention here of these medical text compositions of JML's shows that he was engaged in the teaching of medicine at Naples, and that some of the students of his *yeshībhāh* were also medical students. One such was certainly Abraham de Balmes of Lecce.

167. Fen I, Book I of Avicenna's *Canon* deals with the definition of medicine and its cognate subject headings in natural science; Fen II treats of the classification and categorization of diseases, of their causes, and of cases of disease in general. Cf. the Hebrew text of the preface to the *Canon* as given in J. C. Wolf, *Bibliotheca Hebraea,* IV (Hamburg, 1733), 747–748, and, for the Latin version, *Liber Canonis Avicennae* (Venice, 1507; reprod. Hildesheim, 1964), ii–iii. In the Hebrew version, as in the present letter, "fen" (from Arabic *fann,* "kind," "specimen," "variety"; "field [of work]," "speciality," "scientific discipline"; "art") is *ʾōfen,* "manner," "way." The first printed edition of the Hebrew text of the *Canon,* it is perhaps pertinent to point out, appeared at Naples in 1491, some seven years after this letter's attestation of JML's concern with the work in the same city.

168. This work has not survived. At this point, there is a break in the text.

169. But for the economic necessity which compels him to occupy himself with more mundane matters, such as the teaching and practice of medicine, JML would devote himself entirely to the "way of Torah," as described at *Pirqē ʾĀbhōth* 6:4. Here again the text breaks off.

170. The Hebrew text, from this point to the end of the letter, is that published by Cassuto, "La famiglia" (n. 145, above).

[Judg. 9:13]—and **the purpose of the Lord prospers in his hand** [Isa. 53:10].[171] Now this is my counsel, if you are willing to heed: do send him to us, for he **is bone of** our **bones and flesh of** our **flesh** [Gen. 2:23], **will be to us as eyes** [Num. 10:31], and shall **comprehend words of understanding** [Prov. 1:2] **evening and morning and noonday** [Ps. 55:18].[172]

"And should you retreat **from your holy habitation** [Deut. 26:15] when your **soul has loathed worthless bread** [Num. 21:5], let my lord **make me to hear joy and gladness** [Ps. 51:10] **with pen of iron, with point of diamond** [Jer. 17:1], and **I will be glad and rejoice** [Ps. 31:8] exceedingly.[173]

"Now, therefore, my lord, **behold my land is before you** [Gen. 20:15] **and all that you see is** yours [Gen. 31:43]; **all my bones say** [Ps. 35:10] they would **become subject to you and serve you** [Deut. 20:11]. **Examine me and try me** [Ps. 26:2]; my soul **all the day would speak of your righteousness** [Ps. 35:28], **and cry mightily unto the Lord** [Jonah 3:8]: 'May **He who rescues David** [Ps. 144:10] **make His face to shine upon you**' [Num. 6:25].[174]

"That insignificant one, son of the Luminary of the Exile, [our] t[eacher], t[he rabbi], R[abbi] Judah (his R[ock] and [Redeemer] p[rotect him]) called Messer Leon, your kinsman David, who is writing while in need of more sleep: my eyes have 'a sleep which is not sleep.'[175]

"Tuesday-to-Wednesday night, 24th of the Counting [of the *ʿŌmer*],[176] [5] 244 [May 4–5, 1484]."

4. The Date, Purposes, and Distinctive Character of the *N.S.*

As shown by JML's letter of 1474 to the Florentine Jewish community, and by David Messer Leon's letter of 1484 to David of Tivoli, the *N.S.* was written to constitute the rhetorical member of a set of curricular textbooks devoted to the components of the traditional *trivium,* namely, grammar, logic and rhetoric.[177]

171. Master Joab, son of David of Tivoli, whom his father wishes educated in the sciences and trained in virtue, is reported to be growing ever more charming, and to be making progress in his Jewish studies.

172. Young Joab, suggests DML, should be sent to the household and *y^{e}shībhāh* of JML at Naples, where his kinsmen would regard him as "the apple of their eyes," and where he would be hearing learned discourse morning, noon, and night.

173. Should David of Tivoli suspend the sacred studies which he pursues when he has had more than enough of worldly occupations, then it would please DML very much to have a letter from him with assurances of weal and felicity.

174. DML assures his kinsman of his readiness to serve him and of his prayers for his prosperity and felicity.

175. Talmudic phrase (Pes. 120b, Meg. 18b, Ta'an. 12b, etc.); i.e., "I am dozing off."

176. The fifty-day period between Passover (beginning on the second day) and *Shābhūʿōth* (Pentecost); cf. Lev. 23:15–16.

177. The tripartite nature of JML's initial set of curricular texts (cf. n. 151, above) has been somewhat obscured by the fact that he devoted one volume each to grammar and to rhetoric, but prepared two, the elementary *Mikhlal Yōphī* and the *Super-commentary on Isagoge-Categories-De Interpretatione,* on logic. He apparently intended the *Mikhlal Yōphī,* which he composed in the space

Accordingly, JML's intention to compose the *N.S.* was formed some time before September 1454, when the grammar component of this planned set of curricular texts was completed (n. 16). The decision to compose such a series was quite certainly bound up with the author's decision to open his *y^eshībhāh,* an academy in which, as far as possible, an integrated curriculum of Jewish and "secular" studies was to be followed. Grammar, logic, and rhetoric, JML points out in two interesting passages of the *N.S.*, are the arts proper to the dialectical division of philosophy (i.2.11), the *artes sermocinales* (iv.33.4) which are ancillary to the study of political and ethical philosophy, and indeed to all the "speculative sciences." At the same time, *qua* Hebrew grammar, *qua* logic studied in Hebrew, and *qua* biblically illustrated rhetoric, these were the disciplines considered fundamentally prerequisite to all higher Jewish studies.[178]

The impetus to compose the *N.S.* can thus be traced back to the very outset of JML's arrival in Ancona, if not before (*ca.* 1452), but the work was certainly not completed until the latter part of his sojourn in Padua, between approximately 1465 and 1470. As we have seen (nn. 50–53 above), Johanan Alemanno probably had access both to the *N.S.* and to the *Super-commentary on Isagoge-Categories-De Interpretatione* before he received his double doctorate at JML's hands in February 1470. Abraham Conat, in his colophon, tells us that he first came upon the *N.S.* in "**a nut-garden** [Song of S. 6:11] of perfection," that is, in a library containing works conducive to human perfection. A manuscript of the *N.S.* thus seems to have arrived in Mantua well before its author settled there; if it may be supposed that it arrived there along with its fellow, the *Super-commentary,* it was in Mantua not later than 1471, since we know that Farissol's copy of the *Super-commentary* was finished there by January 15, 1472.[179] Conat had certainly made his own manuscript copy of the *N.S.* by 1473, for, as pointed out above, it was from this copy that Menahem de' Rossi, at Ferrara on October 12, 1474, completed the manuscript now in the Ambrosian Library.[180] Thus, such information as we have on the circulation of the *N.S.* before Conat printed it at Mantua in 1475/76, points to Padua, 1465–1470, as the place and period when JML finished the work, begun more than a decade earlier, and released it for copying by others.

It is Padua, too, which best accommodates the specific reference to Jewish students of medicine in JML's account of his purposes in composing the *N.S.* "Certain commentators on medical works," he tells us in the scripturally derived

---

of a single month (n. 17), to be used not only by beginners, but temporarily, pending completion of his more elaborate logical work, also by more advanced students. It was evidently the *Super-commentary* which he intended as the proper logic component of his set of curricular texts. In his 1474 letter, we observe, the reference to the *Mikhlal Yōphī* (n. 124) is appended to—is cited outside and following—the mention of the trilogy of texts.

178. See n. 151, above.

179. See n. 59, above.

180. M: colophon (as translated *infra*).

phraseology (*mᵉlīṣāh*) of his Preface, were harshly critical of physicians and students of medicine whose education did not include training in rhetoric. Anxious to avoid such criticism, some of JML's students were constantly importuning him to supply them with such training. To help meet this demand, JML was moved to complete and release his *ars rhetorica;* by virtue of the scriptural foundations and examples of the *N.S.*, Jewish students who mastered this textbook would find themselves far better prepared than others in rhetoric.[181] This particular statement of one of the book's purposes, we note—possibly because of the fairly restricted readership of the *N.S.* implied by it—was evidently found unsuitable by the book's first publisher and printer, Abraham Conat. In the incunabulum edition, at any rate, the text's original "certain commentators upon medical works" (כ/M) has been altered to "certain commentators upon the books of prophecy" (ד/C), and the phrase "perfect descriptive statements" (namely, of symptoms, regimens, prescriptions, and so forth) has been changed to "perfect atonement." The original statement of purpose was thus transformed by Conat into an assertion of the book's importance in the broader fields of scriptural exegesis and theology.[182]

In composing the *N.S.*, JML did indeed have a broader purpose in mind than the production of a textbook that would help him train his students in the art of rhetoric—help them learn to speak and to write effectively, persuasively, elegantly. He planned and wrote the book so that it would demonstrate a thesis that he had come to hold, namely, that the fundamental principles of the "science of Rhetoric" are included in, and could best be learned from, the Hebrew Bible. This thesis, first set out at magniloquent length in his *mᵉlīṣāh*-couched Preface, he took care to state a second time, more clearly if more prosaically, in a notable passage at the end of his chapter on Memory (i.13.12–13). The gist of this passage is as follows:

> Every science and every rationally apprehended truth that any treatise may contain is present in our Holy Torah and in the Books of those who speak by the Holy Spirit[183]—present, that is, for those who thoroughly understand the subjects involved. . . . In the days of Prophecy, indeed, **in the months of old** [Job 29:2], when **out of Zion, the perfection of beauty, God shined forth** [Ps. 50:2], we used to learn and know from the Holy Torah all the sciences and truths of reason, including all that were humanly attained, for everything is either latent therein, or plainly stated. What other peoples possessed of these sciences and truths was, by comparison with us, very little. . . . But after the indwelling Presence of God departed from our midst because of our many iniquities . . . we were no longer able to derive understanding of all scientific developments and attainments from the Torah's words; this

181. Preface: par. 11: "Since, moreover, some . . . **are as a mote in weight** [Isa. 40:15]."

182. Conat's emendations are given in the apparatus to Preface: par. 11 of the Hebrew text, and in the notes to the English translation *ad loc.*: בספרי הנבואה for the original בספרי הרפואה, and הכפורים השלמים for הספורים השלמים.

183. I.e., the Pentateuch, Prophets, and Writings, the Hebrew (and Aramaic) Scriptures (תנ"ך).

> condition, however, persists due to our own falling short, our failure to know the Torah in full perfection. Thus the matter has come to be in reverse; for if, after we have come to know all the sciences, or some part of them, we study the words of the Torah, then the eyes of our understanding open to the fact that the sciences are included in the Torah's words, and we wonder how we could have failed to realize this from the Torah itself to begin with. Such has frequently been our own experience, especially in the science of Rhetoric. For when I examined the words of the Torah in the way now common amongst most people, I had no idea that the science of Rhetoric or any part of it was included therein. But once I had studied and investigated Rhetoric, **searched for her as for hid treasures** [Prov. 2:4] out of the treatises written by men of nations other than our own, and afterwards came back to see what is said of her in the Torah and the Holy Scriptures, then **the eyes** of my understanding **were opened** [Gen. 3:7], and I saw that it is the Torah which was the giver... and I marvel how previously **the Spirit of the Lord passed** [1 Kings 22:24] me by, so that I did **not know her place, where** it **is** [Nah. 3:17].

JML's effort to combine demonstration of this thesis with a manual of instruction in rhetoric has determined the content of the *N.S.* and given the work its distinctive character. The principles and rules of rhetoric, which he derives from classical (and medieval) Latin sources and from Aristotle (via Averroes in Hebrew translation),[184] are presented by him in textbook form. These same principles and rules, he is additionally at pains to point out, are also contained in the Hebrew Scriptures, whether implicitly as they are exemplified and illustrated in certain passages and verses, or even explicitly as they are allegorically stated in others. In i.5, for instance, JML describes the various divisions of a speech—Introduction, Statement of Facts, Partition, Proof, Refutation, and Conclusion—as these are defined and set forth in a number of classical and medieval sources; the final portion of the chapter is devoted to a discussion of Judah's address to Joseph (Gen. 44:18–34), which, he points out, exhibits and exemplifies—hence implicitly teaches—every one of these "Parts of Invention." In i.4, on the other hand, the five faculties or competencies that one wishing to be a successful speaker must master—declared in accordance with several classical authorities to be Invention, Arrangement, Style, Memory, and Delivery—are found to be explicitly, though allegorically, referred to at the outset of Moses' Song (Deut. 32:1–2).[185] "The main rules of delivery," we are told (i.12.25), "are clearly expounded by the Holy Books," and King Solomon, in two verses of Proverbs (16:23–24), has summed up the principles of style (i.14.16–17).

God Himself, according to JML, created Rhetoric and implanted it within the human spirit (i.4.11); Israel's most eminent rhetoricians were the Prophets, who

184. Listed below.

185. See the list of all expounded scriptural passages, given in the index. The three groups of such passages are therein differentiated as follows: (a) those held by JML to be sources of rhetorical doctrine, (b) those cited as exemplifications of rhetorical principles and rules, and (c) those which exemplify or illustrate figures of diction and of thought.

"are held to be without peer among the orators of the Nations" (iv. 68.).[186] The *ars rhetorica* exhibited in the Hebrew Bible, accordingly, is finer, more nearly perfect, than any other. The deliberative orator or advocate of policy "who is a son of our people" is admonished to adopt premises "from what is found written in these books of Torah; his words will thus be most completely persuasive. If, in order to bring men closer to virtue and to alienate them from vice, he adopts his premises from moral authorities on government , there is of course no trespass or sin in such procedure; but in this, as in all matters, our books of Torah rank first at **laying for a foundation a stone** of perfection, **a costly cornerstone** [Isa. 28:16]" (ii.18.9). That the Hebrew Scriptures are the best of all sources from which to learn the art of rhetoric is the article of faith which underlies the composition of the *N.S.* and is responsible for the distinctive character of much of its contents.

5. The Extrabiblical Sources of the *N.S.*

In addition to the Hebrew Scriptures, the sources drawn upon by JML in composing the *N.S.*, "the treatises by men of nations other than our own" (i.13.13), are the following:[187]

1. "Aristotle's *Rhetoric*." The work referred to in the *N.S.* as the *Rhetoric* of Aristotle ("the Philosopher") is in fact neither the original Greek text of that book, nor a translation from the Greek original into any of the languages known to JML—Hebrew, Aramaic, Latin, and Italian—but rather Todros Todrosi's Hebrew version (from the Arabic) of Averroes' *Middle Commentary on Aristotle's Rhetoric* (abbreviated as T/A).[188] In thus preferring Averroes' *Middle Commentary on the Rhetoric* to the Latin version of the *Rhetoric* itself best known at the time—that by William of Moerbeke,[189] which must certainly have been available to him—JML was merely exemplifying the belief, characteristic

186. Cf. i.2.15 and iv.68 of the translation.

187. The specific *loci* of JML's references to his extrabiblical sources are indicated in the footnotes to my English translation of the *N.S.* The works according to the pagination or sections of which the *loci* are cited are named in the list of abbreviations at the outset of the Introduction.

188. (a) T(odros): J. Goldenthal, ed., *Bē'ūr Ibn Rushd l^{e}sēpher hah^{a}lāṣāh l^{e}'Arisṭū, he'^{e}thīqō mill^{e}shōn haghrī l^{e}'ibhrī heḥākhām Ṭodrōs Ṭodrōsī mizzera' hayy^{e}hūdhīm: Averrois Commentarius in Aristotelis de arte rhetorica libros tres, hebraice versus a Todros Todrosi Arelatensi* (Leipzig, 1842). Todros' own title (p. 5 of Goldenthal's edition) is given in the list of abbreviations, above. (b) A(verroes): A. Badawī, ed., *Talkhīṣ Kitāb al-Khiṭābah li-'Ariṣṭū, li-'abi al-Walīd Muḥammad ibn 'Aḥmad ibn Rushd: Averrois Paraphrases in Librorum Rhetoricorum Aristotelis* (Cairo, 1960). References are to both of these publications by page, as well as to the respectively apposite passages in the Greek text of the *Rhetoric* (cited, in parentheses, according to the edition published by the Loeb Classical Library, with English translation by J. H. Freese [Cambridge, Mass., and London, 1939]). Another edition of Averroes' *Talkhīṣ*, with extensive commentary, was published at Cairo in 1968 by M. Salīm Sālim.

189. On this version, see J. E. Sandys, *A History of Classical Scholarship from the Sixth Century B.C. to the End of the Middle Ages*, 2d ed. (Cambridge, 1906), 585-588, 591; and J. J. Murphy, *Rhetoric in the Middle Ages* (Berkeley, 1974), 92-101.

of many fifteenth- and sixteenth-century Italian Averroists, that the Andalusian Commentator's works on the writings of Aristotle were the truest and most accurate representations of "the Philosopher's" views.[190] JML understood very well that the *Talkhīṣ/Bēʾūr* (*Middle Commentary*) was not the work of Aristotle himself, but of Averroes. At ii.17.8, for example, he distinguishes the two writers by name; at i.11.9, he names Averroes as the commentator on a work by Aristotle ("the *Metaphysics* . . . according to the New Translation"). When, therefore, JML attributes a statement made by Averroes (in Todros' translation) directly to "the Philosopher, in Book I of the *Rhetoric*," as he repeatedly does in the *N.S.*, the attribution, while not literally correct, is manifestly the result of his belief that the words in question are in fact an accurate representation of the sense intended by Aristotle in that passage. This belief, to be sure, is patently untenable. Let alone the question of Averroes' faithfulness to Aristotle's sense, Todros, whose mastery of Arabic (as he himself acknowledged, and as exhibited in many passages of the *N.S.*) was far from perfect, has not always accurately translated Averroes' text.[191]

2. "The Abridgment of the *Rhetoric* which (Aristotle) made for Alexander": such (or the equivalent) is JML's designation of the work known to us as the pseudo-Aristotelian *Rhetorica ad Alexandrum;*[192] he cites it in twelve passages of the *N.S.*[193] Since JML was unable to read the Greek original of this work, if he used it at all in any form now known he must have done so in one or other of the two extant medieval Latin translations.[194] This, however, is not certain. The one apparently direct quotation in the *N.S.* of a sentence from the "Abridgment"—"The Philosopher, in 10 [*sic*] of the Abridgment of the *Rhetoric* which he made

190. Cf. C. E. Butterworth, *Averroes' Three Short Commentaries on Aristotle's "Topics," "Rhetoric," and "Poetics"* (Albany, N.Y., 1977), vii ff., 2–3, 87. Averroes' commentaries are listed (under the title of each several Aristotelian work) in F. Peters, *Aristoteles Arabus: The Oriental Translations and Commentaries on the Aristotelian Corpus* (Leiden, 1968). On the distinctions between "long," "middle," and "short" ("epitomes") Averroist commentaries on Aristotle's works, see H. A. Wolfson, "Plan for a *Corpus Commentariorum Averrois in Aristotelem,*" *Speculum,* 6 (1931), 423.

191. Cf. Steinschneider's remarks on Todros and his translations (*Hebr. Uebersetzungen,* 62 f.); examples of Todros' inaccuracies are pointed out in the notes to the English translation.

192. H. Rackham, ed. and trans., Pseudo-Aristotle, *Rhetorica ad Alexandrum,* Loeb Classical Library (Cambridge, Mass., 1965), 258–262; W. Rhys Roberts, *Greek Rhetoric and Literary Criticism* (New York, 1928), 42–43; J. W. H. Atkins, *Literary Criticism in Antiquity* (Cambridge, 1934), I, 160; G. Kennedy, *The Art of Persuasion in Greece* (Princeton, 1963), 114–124.

193. i.5.1, 4, 5; i.8.9 (*bis*); ii.4.21, 22; ii.11.27; ii.12.1, 10; ii.14.15; ii.15.2; ii.17.14.

194. On these, see M. Fuhrmann, *Untersuchungen zur Textgeschichte der pseudo-aristotelischen Alexander-Rhetorik* (Mainz: *Abhandlungen der Geistes- und Sozialwissenschaftliche Klasse,* Jahrgang 1964, nr. 7 [Wiesbaden, 1965]), 10 f.; and J. J. Murphy, *Rhetoric in Middle Ages,* 101, n. 44. My source footnote references are to the only one of these thus far published: M. Grabmann, "Eine lateinische Übersetzung der pseudo-aristotelischen Rhetorica ad Alexandrum aus dem 13. Jahrhundert," *Sitzungsberichte der Bayerischen Akademie der Wissenschaften, Philosophisch-historische Abteilung,* 4 (Munich, 1932), 26–81. References to this publication (as "Textausgabe," by page and line, with following indication of the locus of the passage in the Greek text) are prefaced by "cf." because it is not certain that JML's citations are drawn from it.

for Alexander, defines it as follows: 'The Introduction is a short statement whereby the mind of the audience is made receptive, attentive, and well-disposed in respect of what is about to be spoken' '' (i.5.4)—occurs as such neither in ''Chapter X'' of the Greek text, nor in the corresponding section of the published Latin translation. It is possible, accordingly, that JML may here have drawn upon a version of the *Rhetorica ad Alexandrum* (Hebrew? Latin?) that is no longer extant. Considering, however, that all other citations of the ''Abridgment'' in the *N.S.* are paraphrases, and not direct quotations, it is also possible (despite the contrary indication of the wording) that JML intended the definition as given to be understood rather as a summary statement of ''the Philosopher's'' view of the matter than as the repetition of his very words.[195]

Like all his contemporaries, JML believed Aristotle to have been the author both of the *Rhetoric* and of the *Rhetorica ad Alexandrum*[196] Where, accordingly, he found contradictory assertions in the *Rhetoric* and the *Rhetorica ad Alexandrum*—as on whether a Statement of Facts could appropriately form part of a Deliberative discourse—he felt constrained to reconcile the contradictions, or to explain them away.[197]

3. ''The New Rhetoric,'' thought by JML and virtually all his contemporaries to have been written by ''Tully,''[198] is the usual fifteenth-century designation of the work now known as the pseudo-Ciceronian *Rhetorica ad Herennium*.[199] No other of JML's extrabiblical sources, not even the *Middle Commentary on Aristotle's Rhetoric,* has influenced the *N.S.* more pervasively than the *Rhetorica ad Herennium*. In its character as a manual of the art of rhetoric, in its division into four books, and in much of its technical doctrine, the *N.S.* is plainly modeled upon the *Rhetorica ad Herennium*. This is not to say, however, that JML hesitates to differ with the author of the *Rhetorica ad Herennium,* or that he does not know how to adapt the material of his model to his own purposes. In the *Rhetorica ad Herennium,* for example, the Judicial Kind of Cause is treated before Epideictic oratory, because, as the writer explains, he believes his reader will find the material easier to understand if set out in an order from the more to

195. The quotation marks around the definition in this passage are, of course, mine, and not JML's. Quotation marks, it must be remembered, are employed neither in M nor in C.

196. That Aristotle could not have been the author of the *R. ad A.* was first asserted by Erasmus in 1531; cf. Fuhrmann, *Textgeschichte,* 143, and Rackham, *R. ad A.,* 258 ff.

197. *N.S.* i.8.9; cf. ii.14.15 and ii.17.14.

198. Except in the case of ''Aristotle''—written in abbreviated form 'ארסטו = *'Aristō*. or *'Arisṭū*. from the Arabic *'Arisṭū,* or, in full transliteration of the Latin form of the name, אריסטוטלס (*aliter* ארסטוטליס [1.1.5]—JML generally uses the Italian forms of Greek and Latin names. Thus ''Cicero'' is written טוליאו from Tullio = Tully, ''Quintilian'' קוינטיליאנו from Quintiliano, ''Victorinus'' ויטורינו from Vittorino, ''Boethius'' בואציו (בואיציו) from Boezio, ''Demosthenes'' דימושטיני from Demostene (i.12.19), etc. JML never refers to Cicero by this *cognomen,* but always by his *nomen* (Tullius, [i.e. Tullio]); Quintilian, however, is always mentioned by *cognomen,* never by *nomen* (Fabius).

199. According to H. Caplan, *R. ad H.,* ix, it was not until 1491 that the work was definitively ''divorced . . . from Cicero's name.'' On the term ''New Rhetoric,'' see below.

the less difficult.[200] JML, however, cleaving to the opposite pedagogical principle—"the learner's progress should be from the easy to the difficult, and not the reverse" (i.13.8)—gives the priority to the Epideictic Kind of Cause. Again, in treating the Figures, JML arranges them in the same order in which they appear in the *Rhetorica ad Herennium,* and, to the extent permitted by his Scriptural illustrations and the Hebrew language, he models their definitions upon those of his source.[201] Yet he never omits, where necessary, to refashion the definitions into tolerably accurate generalized descriptions of the Figures as they occur in his adduced Scriptural citations.[202] He is, of course, fully aware that the difference between Hebrew and Latin, as languages, will naturally occasion difference in the usage of the Figures. At iv. 55.1, in the case of the Figure of Thought "Dwelling on the Point" (*commoratio* = *hāʿᵃkhābhāh* ["lingering, delay; retention"]), he comments that whereas "Tully" apologizes for his inability to adduce an appropriate example, he, JML, can cite "several important and precious examples from the words of the holy prophets, who were the most pre-eminent of orators."[203]

4. "The Old Rhetoric" (*De inventione*). Whatever the solution to the problem of the relations between the genuinely Ciceronian *De inventione* and the pseudo-Ciceronian *Rhetorica ad Herennium,*[204] JML believed both to be the work of "Tully," and distinguished them as the Old Rhetoric (*hahᵃlāṣāh hayyᵉshānāh* = *Rhetorica Vetus*) and the New Rhetoric (*hahᵃlāṣāh haḥᵃdhāshāh* = *Rhetorica Nova*) respectively.[205] Unlike his proceeding in the case of "Aristotle," Quintilian, and the "Tully" of the *Rhetorica ad Herennium,* JML never cites *De inventione* as an independent, primary source of rhetorical doctrine, but always as in some way ancillary or complementary to one or several of his more important authorities.[206] This proceeding permits him to treat *De inventione* as, for the most part, merely an earlier, less well-considered and complete, form of the *Rhetorica ad Herennium.* In the single instance he cites of an outright contradiction between the two works—on the number and

200. Caplan, *R. ad H.,* 2.1.1 (p. 59).

201. Compare the list of the Figures given at the outset of *N.S.* iv with Caplan's listing, *R. ad H.,* pp. lvi ff.

202. See *N.S.* iv.1, n. 3.

203. *R. ad H.,* 4.45.58 (p. 375).

204. The problem and the several main solutions that have been proposed for it are lucidly summarized by Caplan, *R. ad H.,* pp. xxv–xxxii; see too S. Niccoli, "*Rhetorica ad Herennium*" e "*De Inventione*" (Naples, 1969).

205. According to E. R. Curtius, *European Literature and the Latin Middle Ages,* trans. W. R. Trask (New York, 1953), 153, "... it was usual to refer to Cicero's *De inventione* as *Rhetorica vetus* or *prima* or *prior,* to distinguish it from the *Rhetorica ad Herennium,* which was known as *Rhetorica nova* or *secunda* or *posterior.*" Caplan (p. viii) says that *R. ad H.* was called *Rhetorica Secunda* in the twelfth century because of its position in the manuscripts following *De inventione;* later, "perhaps because of a belief that Cicero wrote the treatise to replace his juvenile *De Inventione,*" it came to be called *Rhetorica Nova.*

206. Books I and II exhibit, *inter alia,* examples at i.1.6; i.2.2, 5, 10, 13; i.8.3, 10, 20; ii.11.20, 27, 29.

classification of the Kinds of Cause (i.6.1)—he follows Victorinus in arguing that the contradiction is more apparent than real.

5. Quintilian's *Institutio oratoria* is the third major extrabiblical source of the rhetorical doctrine in the *N.S.* It is in virtue of Quintilian's (and Cato's) definition of the ideal orator—"a good man skilled in speaking" (12.1.1)—that JML declares Israel's prophets "without compare" as orators (*N.S.* i.2.15); the arguments advanced in JML's scripturally couched (*m*ᵉ*līṣāh*) defence of the rhetorical art (i.2.1ff.) are, in the main, drawn from the *Institutio oratoria.*

Although Rabbi Judah had the whole of Quintilian's work before him, the numbering of the materials in his manuscript copy was not identical with that of the text as now established. I have noted the following discrepancies between the book and chapter enumeration in the text of the *Institutio oratorio* that must have been before JML—very likely a descendant of some *mutilus* eked out by a copy of Poggio Bracciolini's transcript of the manuscript he found in 1416 in the monastery of St. Gall[207]—and that of modern editions:[208]

Modern edd. of Q.	**JML's MS of Q.**	**Passage in *N.S.***
2.15.34	2.16	i.1.5
2.15 ff.	2.16	i.1.8
2.16.1 ff.	2.17	i.2.2
2.16.7 ff.	2.17	1.2.5
12.2.10 ff.	12.3	i.2.11
11.3.2	11.4	i.12.19
3.7.12 ff.	3.9	ii.4.24
8.4.3 ff.	8.5	ii.11.22
3.8.6 ff.	3.10	ii.17.11

Apparently, too, JML's manuscript contained the statement about faults incidental to an Introduction (*N.S.* i.7.17) which does not appear in the *Institutio*'s discussion of such faults (4.1.62 ff.)

6. Sixteen passages of C. Marius Victorinus' commentary on Cicero's *De inventione* ("Victorinus . . . in the Commentary on the Old Rhetoric" [i.2.10]) are cited in the *N.S.* While several of these citations merely corroborate or explain a statement of the *De inventione,* for example i.1.6–7 on the purpose of rhetoric, i.5.7 on the definition of the Proof, and i.7.3 on the defence of a dishonorable case, most are introduced quite independently of the *De inventione,*

207. Cf. M. Winterbottom, "Fifteenth-Century Manuscripts of Quintilian," *The Classical Quarterly,* n.s. XVII (1967), 344–345. The nature of JML's MS of Q. as an eked-out "*mutilus*" may explain his variant references to numbered "Books" of the *Institutio Oratoria* now as *ma'*ᵃ*mar* ("essay, treatise," e.g., i.1.5 and 8, now as *ḥēleq* ("part," e.g., i.2.2).

208. The discrepancies, all solely in the chapter enumeration, with that of JML's text of Q. in each case exhibiting a slightly higher number than that of the editions, may have arisen from the fact that the chapters of JML's MS had not yet been further subdivided into sections, as in the modern editions.

as valuable rhetorical teachings in their own right. Thus, in the discussion of what a well-trained deliberative orator should know (i.2.13), the pertinent definitions of "natural philosophy" (that is, theology) and of "political philosophy" are those of Victorinus; so, too, the definitions of "duty" (i.6.8), of the virtues (ii.14.6), and of the State (ii.15.1).[209]

7. On the analogy of the medieval Hebrew title of Aristotle's *Topics,* JML calls Anicius Manlius Severinus Boethius' *De differentiis topicis* "the *Sēpher Hanniṣṣūᵃḥ* (Book of Dialectic) which he (Boethius) made" (i.4.2).[210] Each of the two references in the *N.S.* to *De differentiis topicis* has to do with Invention: the first (i.4.2) corroborates the definition of Invention as given in the *Rhetorica ad Herennium*, while the second (i.5.3) consists of a rationale of the subdivision of this faculty into its six component parts.

8. JML twice (i.1.5 and i.2.10) cites statements said to have been made by "the commentator Alanus." In the first of these, "Alanus" is said to have defined rhetoric as "the guiding concept and true criterion of utterance"; according to the second, he held that the "perfect orator cannot, in the nature of the case, be other than a good and righteous man." Although neither reference includes the title of the work commented upon by "Alanus," or the name of its author, it is virtually certain that this was pseudo-Cicero's *Rhetorica ad Herennium*. It is not merely that the contexts of the *N.S.*'s two references to "Alanus" seem to exclude the possibilities that the commentary was, like Victorinus', on Cicero's *De inventione,* or on the treatises of Aristotle or Quintilian. There is a more positive fact: an unpublished commentary on the *Rhetorica ad Herennium,* extant in at least nine manuscripts of the fourteenth and fifteenth centuries, is attributed (in three of the manuscripts) to "Alanus," as author. Whether, however, this "Alanus" was the well-known Alain de Lille (d. 1203), or whether the commentary was falsely ascribed to his authorship, has not yet been certainly determined.[211]

209. JML probably had Victorinus' commentary before him in a MS that contained both it and the text of *De I.* That such was the case is suggested by the phrasing of most of the references to the commentary in the Hebrew of the *N.S.* Literally rendered, these read "as the commentator Victorinus says in the Old Rhetoric" (i.2.13), "according to Victorinus in the Old Rhetoric" (i.6.8), "as Victorinus says in the Old Rhetoric" (i.7.3 and 10, i.8.3 and 7, ii.15.1), etc. My English translation, of course, is in these instances not literal, but more accurate; i.e., I write "as Victorinus says in his Commentary on the Old Rhetoric," etc.

210. On *Sēpher Hanniṣṣūᵃḥ* being Aristotle's *Topics,* see M. Steinschneider, *Hebr. Uebersetzungen*, 54 and 62, and J. Klatzkin, *'Ōṣar Hammūnāḥīm*, s.v. *niṣṣūᵃḥ*. Cf. the brief discussion in I. Husik, *Judah Messer Leon's Commentary on the "Vetus Logica,"* 69–70, of Steinschneider's mistaken guess (and Husik's own!) as to JML's name for the *De diff. top.* A summary of the rhetorical doctrine of the *Topica Boetii,* as the "enormously popular" *De diff. top.* was known, is included in J. J. Murphy's *Rhetoric in the Middle Ages,* 67–71; for an English version of the complete text, see now *Boethius's "De topicis differentiis,"* translated by Eleonore Stump (Ithaca, N.Y., 1978).

211. See H. Caplan, "A Medieval Commentary on the *Rhetorica ad Herennium,*" in *Of Eloquence: Studies in Ancient and Medieval Rhetoric,* ed. Anne King and Helen North (Ithaca, N.Y., 1970), 247–270; and cf. my note on the first of the *N.S.*'s references to "Alanus" (i.1.5, n. 3).

The distribution of the foregoing sources throughout the *N.S.* may be summarized as follows: all eight authorities are drawn upon for the doctrinal rhetorical materials brought together in Book I; all the sources but one (Alanus) are cited in Book II; in Book III, the sole doctrinal source is Todros'/Averroes' *Middle Commentary on Aristotle's Rhetoric;* and in Book IV, the main extrabiblical source is the *Rhetorica ad Herennium,* with Todros/Averroes cited only in Chapters 75-77 and 82-83.[212]

In addition to the Hebrew Scriptures and to his doctrinal rhetorical sources, JML makes incidental reference or allusion to the following works in the *N.S.:*

(a) Targum Onqelos: on Num. 12:1 (iv. 74.1):
(b) *Mishnah: Aboth* 1:18 (ii.10.8), 1:1 (ii.13.31), 2:9 (iii.16.4), and 1:12 (iv.50.3); *Sh*ᵉ*buoth* 3:7 ff., *Makkoth* 3:1 ff., 3:10 (iii.20.11 [nn.2 and 3]);
(c) *Babylonian Talmud; B*ᵉ*rakoth* 20a and/or 'Erubin 100a (i.7.27);
(d) Eleazar Kalir: Poem (i.14.5);
(e) "Biblical commentators" (Rashi, Ibn Ezra, et al.,) on Ps. 84:3 (ii.13.18);
(f) David Qimḥi, *Book of Roots* (iv. 10.4);
(g) Immanuel of Rome, *Maḥb*ᵉ*rōth* (ii.4.3);
(h) Averroes, *Commentary on the Metaphysics of Aristotle* (i.11.9);
(i) Aristotle, *Physics* (Preface: 16).

Of his own works, finally, JML once cites his minor Logic, *Mikhlal Yōphī* (iii.18.10), and refers four times to his Grammar, *Libh*ᵉ *nath Hassappīr* (i.11.6, iv.40.9, iv.76.2, and iv.77.3).

6. The Rhetoric of the Hebrew Scriptures, According to the *N.S.*

At once an *ars rhetorica* and a rhetorical interpretation of the "plain meaning" (*p*ᵉ*shāṭ*) of the Hebrew Scriptures, as pointed out by Abraham Conat in his colophon to the *editio princeps,* the *N.S.* is indeed the "extraordinary treatise" that its author proclaimed it.[213] "A like work on the art of Rhetoric did not exist among us," says Conat in his Colophon (par. 3). The remark need not have been confined to Jewish scholarship: in the entire history of biblical scholarship, no work that is really comparable to the *N.S.*, no such systematically rhetorical a treatment of the Hebrew Scriptures by a qualified Hebraist, is attested until late in the nineteenth century.[214] Although the fact has hitherto gone unrecognized,

212. See JML's introduction to the contents of the several Books of the *N.S.* at the end of his Preface (Par. 17), ii.1, iii.1, and iv.1. The more heterogeneous character of the rhetorical materials set forth in Books I and II, as compared with those presented in Books III and IV, helps explain the fact that T/A and *R. ad H.* are the sole extrabiblical sources drawn upon in the latter two books.

213. *Supra,* the letter of 1474 to the Florentine Jewish Community (§2 and n. 123).

214. Book IV of Augustine's *De doctrina Christiana,* although in large part an attempt to show that scriptural eloquence embodies the finest norms of classical rhetoric, naturally adverts more to the New Testament than to the Old, especially as Augustine himself was not a Hebrew scholar; cf. H. J. Vogels, *S. Aurelii Augustini De doctrina christiana libros quattuor* (Bonn, 1930), iv.7.15 (pp. 78-79). Like M. H. Luzzatto's *L*ᵉ*shōn Limmūdhīm* (Mantua, 1727) and Solomon Löwisohn's

modern scholarly study of the rhetoric of the Hebrew Bible has in Judah Messer Leon its earliest qualified protagonist.[215]

But if Rabbi Judah was innovative and well ahead of his time in essaying to study the manner of the Hebrew Scriptures, his conception of the substance of those Scriptures—the conception whose assumptions and corollaries constituted the ambit within which his rhetorical study proceeded—was altogether medieval and, while Maimonist, quite orthodoxly Jewish. Since, as he "believed with perfect faith," God had revealed the Scriptures to Israel through Moses, the Prophets, and others actuated by the Holy Spirit,[216] God is for him in effect the "Author" of the Scriptures; and as He is perfect, then these texts must also be perfect both in content and in form. Not only do they contain, whether explicitly or implicitly, the whole of all truth that men can know (i.13.12–13), they are inerrant in language and expression, grammatically and rhetorically perfect.[217] "As for the Prophets," he writes, "by common consent held to be without peer among the orators of the Nations, . . . there is no anomaly at all in their words; a construction that may be called anomalous by the grammarian may, to the orator developing a subject, prove appropriate to his theme and completely convincing to his hearers" (iv.68.1). What might appear to be a rhetorical gaffe, or even a scribal or grammatical error, will invariably be found to have been deliberately introduced, most often as a Figure of Thought or of Diction. "Strange Usage," for example, "is a Figure of Diction whereby one or more grammatically irregular words are introduced in order to call attention to, enhance, and elevate the

---

Mᵉlīṣath Yᵉshūrūn (Vienna, 1816), R. Lowth's *De sacra poesi Hebraeorum praelectiones academicae* (Oxford, 1753) and J. G. von Herder's *Vom Geist der Ebräischen Poesie* (Dessau, 1782–1783) are more concerned with the poetics than with the rhetoric of the Hebrew Scriptures. Thus, the first detailed, rhetorically oriented analyses of passages of the Hebrew Bible (by a qualified Hebraist) to appear since publication of the *N.S.* are those contained in E. König's *Stilistik, Rhetorik, Poetik in Bezug auf die biblische Literatur* (Leipzig, 1900). On Jewish rhetorical works in general, see the still useful survey by Nehemiah Brüll, "Zur Geschichte der rhetorischen Literatur bei den Juden," *Ben Chananja* VI (1863), pp. 486–490, 509–513, 527–532, 568–573; cf. too A. Altmann's "*Ars Rhetorica* as Reflected in Some Jewish Figures of the Italian Rennaissance" (in the volume of essays cited in n. 5 above), 97–118.

215. On modern study of the rhetoric of the Hebrew Bible, see J. Muilenburg, "Form Criticism and Beyond," *Journal of Biblical Literature* 88 (1969), 1–18; cf. J. J. Jackson and M. Kessler, eds., *Rhetorical Criticism: Essays in Honor of James Muilenburg* (Pittsburgh, 1974), esp. B. W. Anderson, "The New Frontier of Rhetorical Criticism," ix–xviii.

216. This, of course, is the conception of the *Tōrāh Shebbikhᵉthābh*—the Written Torah—affirmed and expressed in Talmud and Midrash. See S. Schechter, *Some Aspects of Rabbinic Theology* (New York, 1923), 116–126, and G. F. Moore, *Judaism in the First Centuries of the Christian Era* (Cambridge, 1927), I, 235–250; and cf. Principles VI–IX of Maimonides' "Thirteen Principles of the Faith" (J. H. Hertz, ed., *The Authorised Daily Prayer Book* [New York, 1948], 251–253). Offhanded references to the conception occur in the *N.S.*, e.g., at i.4.10, ii.18.1, and iv.1.2.

217. "The mediaeval Rabbins concentrated their attention on the plain grammatical sense of Scripture . . . although they never altogether shook off the false principle that a good sense must be got out of everything, and that if it cannot be got out of the text by the rules of grammar, these rules must give way" (W. Robertson Smith, *The Old Testament in the Jewish Church* 2d ed. [New York, 1901], 53–54).

strangeness of the subject matter'' (iv.76.1); three anomalous verb forms which occur in passages in Ezekiel (9:8; 8:16) and Isaiah (63:3) are cited as instances of the Figure. ''In general,'' Rabbi Judah argues, ''whatever is found in Scripture of words of Prophecy and of those speaking by means of the Holy Spirit—**there is nothing perverse or crooked in them** [Prov. 8:8], no truly awkward stammering or real irregularity. For how should the Lord of language and its beauty speak in words that are ungraceful or unrefined? Such an incongruity is past imagining, and reason must all the more reject it'' (iv.82.2).

As the products of God's own rhetorical artistry, the Hebrew Scriptures are necessarily, Rabbi Judah maintains, the very acme, the *ne plus ultra,* of rhetorical excellence. No human works of rhetorical art have ever equalled, nor could they ever hope to equal, the rhetorical excellence of the Scriptures. ''Between the Torah's pleasing words and stylistic elegancies,'' he tells us, ''as well as all the statutes and ordinances of Rhetoric which are included within the Holy Scriptures—and all of the like that all the other Nations possess, the difference is so striking that to compare them is like comparing **the hyssop... in the wall** with **the cedar that is in Lebanon** [1 Kings 5:13]'' (i.13.13). This difference, for all its asserted vastness, is nevertheless clearly understood by JML to be a difference of degree, not of kind. Throughout the *N.S.* he takes for granted that the rules and principles of the art of rhetoric are the same for all, whether in the case of practitioners of the art or of works of this art. The same rules and principles, JML thus affirms throughout the *N.S.,* hold both for God's essays in the field of rhetorical art and for those of human beings; only in the Scriptures, the products of God's artistry, the rules and principles of the art are perfectly applied and exhibited, whereas the artistry in a work by any human practitioner will *ipso facto* be seen to fall far short of that which informs any of God's rhetorical masterpieces. Without in the least relinquishing his medieval and orthodox Jewish belief in the inerrancy and superhuman quality of the Holy Scriptures, Judah Messer Leon, in this fifteenth-century ''extraordinary treatise,'' shows himself to be one of the earliest practitioners of that modern biblical criticism whose watchword is: ''Interpret the Scriptures like any other book.''[218]

JML's scriptural illustrations of classical rhetorical doctrine and his rhetorical biblical exegesis, found in every part of the *N.S.,*[219] are perhaps nowhere more notably or characteristically displayed than in his detailed expositions of the following four passages:

1. Abigail's speech to David (1 Sam. 25:24-31: *N.S.* i.7.25-34). This quasi-

218. Quoted from Benjamin Jowett, ''On the Interpretation of Scripture,'' *Essays and Reviews* (Leipzig, 1862), 327.

219. Book IV, in which the Figures of Speech are treated, is richer in biblical exemplification than any other part of the *N.S.* Those chapters of Book III (iii.2-18) which are devoted to affects, emotions, and norms of human behavior are the least well biblically illustrated.

judicial address,[220] Abigail's successful intercession with David on behalf of her villainous husband, Nabal, is presented by JML as an example of the kind of speech which, according to classical rhetorical doctrine, need not include all six of the Parts of Invention (i.5.2), and in which, rather than an overt Introduction, the Subtle Approach (i.6.4, i.7.1-11) must be brought into play. As Rabbi Judah analyzes it, the speech is pervaded by the Subtle Approach (i.7.25, 32), consists formally only of four of the Parts of Invention—Statement of Facts, Proof, Refutation and Conclusion (*ibid.* 25)—and includes instances of the Figures Paronomasia (25), Hyperbaton (26), Duplication (27), and Antithesis (32). Abigail's success is attributed to her use throughout the speech of the Subtle Approach—the means whereby David was rendered attentive, receptive and well disposed (25, 32)—and to her brilliant deployment of two rhetorical techniques: the shifting of the blame from Nabal to herself, and her well-conceived and executed requesting of pardon (27-28, 29-30).

2. Psalm 45 (ii.4.1-19). JML says of this Psalm, his prime biblical example of an Epideictic utterance, that it deals "with the Messiah, his deeds, and the qualities for which one should praise him." "In sum, then," he writes in the précis with which he concludes his long and detailed rhetorical exposition, "we find that in this Psalm the Psalmist is pronouncing an Epideictic discourse of Praise;[221] that herein are included all the faculties required of the orator—Invention, Arrangement, Memory, Delivery, and Style;[222] further, that it contains the several Parts of a Discourse—Introduction,[223] Statement of Facts,[224] Proof,[225] Refutation,[226] and Conclusion[227]—while, as we have said, the phrase **A Song of loves** in part represents the Partition;[228] that the praise of the subject is drawn from all the categories—Qualities of Character, Physical Attributes, and External Circumstances; and finally, that the Psalmist begins in the Grand and ends in the Middle Style."[229] Figures employed by the Psalmist, as pointed out or referred to by JML in his exposition, include Hyperbaton (ii.4.5, 16), Metonymy (ii.4.6, 14), Refining (13), Asyndeton (14), and Duplication (14).

3. The Tekoan Woman's speech (2 Sam. 13:39-14:20: *N.Ṣ.* ii.13). The speech whereby King David is induced to allow his exiled son, Absalom, to return to

220. In terms of JML's rhetorical taxonomy, the speech is essentially a treatment of a subtype of "the Assumptive Juridical Issue," namely, "the Acknowledgment of the Charge" (i.10.13, ii.9.8-17).

221. *N.S.* i.3.2, 5, 8; ii.3; ii.4.2.

222. Based on exposition of terms in vv. 1-2 (ii.4.5).

223. Vv. 1-3 (ii.4.10).

224. Vv. 4-6 (ii.4.11-12).

225. Vv. 7-10 (ii.4.13-15).

226. Vv. 11-15 (ii.4.16).

227. Vv. 15-18 (ii.4.17).

228. V. 1 (ii.4.4).

229. Based on allegorical interpretation of *ye dhīdhōth* ("loves") in verse 1 (cf. pars. 16, 18). Cf., too, 1.14.17, on shifting from one Style to another.

Jerusalem, assertedly based upon "the arousal of pity and the winning of pardon for the sinner, skills demanded in a speech of the Judicial Kind of Cause," is presented as JML's principal biblical illustration of this class of utterance. The passage, he remarks, is one of "such inordinate difficulty that to this day we have seen no satisfactory exposition of it; nor did we ourselves understand it until . . . we studied some of the disciplines special to rational utterance"—principally, of course, grammar, rhetoric, and logic—"which successfully awakened us to the literal sense and intended meaning of the verses" (ii.13.1).

A listing of seven "of the problems that confuse this literal sense" prefaces the rhetorical exegesis of the passage; these difficulties are then disposed of through explanations derived from five rhetorical and psychological Commonplaces (ii.13.2–24). As analyzed by Messer Leon, the speech consists of two main parts: a successful plea—advanced as a probing of the king's willingness and readiness to relieve a parent's distress—that the king remove a supposititious threat against the life of the Woman's remaining son; and a subtle linkage of the king's professed and sworn readiness to take action on the Woman's behalf with the obtaining of his assent to Absalom's return. The fabricated case is shown to consist of an Introduction (v. 14:4 [27]), a Statement of the Facts (vv. 5–7 [27]), a Confirmatory Proof (v. 7 [28]), a Refutation (v. 9 [29]), and a Conclusion (v. 11 [30]). Following a second Introduction (v. 12), Absalom's return is advocated in a Complete Argument (cf. *N.S.* ii.10.2–3), said here to be developed "with all its several parts": the Proposition (v. 13 [33]), the Reason (v. 14 [34]), Proof of the Reason (v. 14b [35]), Amplification (v. 15 [36]), and Résumé (vv. 16–17a [37]). The two cases, the fabricated case of the Woman's son, and that of Absalom, are shown to be linked and dependent upon each other; the Amplification of the Complete Argument on Absalom's behalf, for example, is construed as also constituting virtually a second Refutation for the portion of the speech devoted to the fabricated case (36). The Conclusion of the Woman's advocacy, a laudation and blessing of the king (v. 17b [38]), is similarly applicable to both cases. An instance of Hyperbaton is pointed out in verse 13 (33); the Amplification of the Complete Argument (v. 15 [36]) is, as elsewhere described (ii.11.1), considered an additional embellishment.

4. Rab-Shakeh's speech counseling Judean submission to the Assyrian king (2 Kings 18:17–36: *N.S.* iv.9). This speech, no less than the many "commandments, admonitions, and reproofs" of contrary theological tendency which, as JML remarks, comprise so "much . . . of what one finds in the Bible, [is] in the category of Deliberative oratory" (ii.18.8). In view of its purport, the speech could not be cited in the chapter entitled "the Giving of Counsel According to the Torah" (ii.18), JML's principal collection of biblical illustrations of the Deliberative Kind of Cause. Its excellence as a biblical example of the category was, however, too obvious to allow it to go unnoticed in such a work as the *N.S.*; and in addition to a main discussion—felicitously set in the context of the

discourse's dominant Figure, "Reasoning by Question and Answer" (iv.9)—Rabbi Judah introduces it in two other passages of his work (iii.18.2 and iv.58.5).

As JML interprets it, the speech is entirely in accord with the rules governing Deliberative discourses laid down in *N.S.* ii.14–16. We have here a deliberation of "which of two possible decisions is the better" (ii.14.1); the aspect of the Advantage involved is that of Security in its subdivisions of Might and Craft, and the commonplaces on which these are severally based (2 Kings 18:19–20; cf. ii.14.4–5, 15, ii.15.4–5, ii.16.1 ff.). Rab-Shakeh's discourse, as JML points out in one of the two subsidiary passages in which he cites it, exhibits an instance of one of the two classes of logical proof that speakers employ, namely an Example, this one an Example drawn from previous events (2 Kings 18:33–35, cf. iii.18.2). In the remaining subsidiary passage, a portion of the address (2 Kings 18:21) is explained as Rab-Shakeh's use of still another Figure of Speech—"Comparison . . . developed for . . . vividness . . . in [the form of] Connection or Relationship"—in order to press home one of his refutative arguments (iv.58.5).

Astonishingly innovative and ahead of its time though JML's rhetorical exegesis of the Hebrew Scriptures is thus seen to be—Book IV of the *N.S.* is even today not superseded as a systematic study of Biblical Hebrew figures of diction and of thought—it is culturally fallacious in two fundamental respects. One of these, as scholars now generally recognize, is that the canons and principles of Greek and Latin rhetorical art may not simply be presumed—as Rabbi Judah believed—to have been functional in the ancient Israelite culture in which the Hebrew Scriptures were produced. The other is this: the assumptions and beliefs about the nature and powers of words that were handed down and received in ancient Israel, how words were culturally perceived to behave and to act—hence, too, the guiding presumptions of word articulation and text formation—are demonstrably quite different from the beliefs and assumptions about the nature and powers of words held in Graeco-Roman and later Western societies and cultures. JML's failure to grasp and to deal in his work with this fundamental difference in cultural perception means that all his rhetorical analyses of biblical texts are necessarily suspect of cultural fallibility. The identical suspicion, we hasten to add, for the same reason—though with far less excuse than in the case of our fifteenth-century scholar!—attaches to practically the whole of our modern rhetorical and literary criticism of the Hebrew Bible. A valid rhetorical understanding of the Hebrew Bible is still, as it was in JML's day, a prime desideratum of biblical scholarship.[230]

230. Cf. my papers, "Towards a Valid Theory of Biblical Hebrew Literature," in L. Wallach, ed., *The Classical Tradition: Literary and Historical Studies in Honor of Harry Caplan* (Ithaca, N.Y., 1966), 315–328; and " 'Word' and Literature in Ancient Israel," *New Literary History,* 4 (1972), 119–139.

7. The Hebrew Text of the *N.S.*

Neither Abraham Conat's *editio princeps* of the *N.S.* (ד/C), printed and published at Mantua late in 1475, nor the edition published by Adolf Jellinek at Vienna in 1863 (J)[231] contains a Hebrew text sufficiently complete and error-free to constitute a satisfactory basis for translation, or indeed for any serious study, of Messer Leon's work. Some of the reasons for considering ד/C an unsatisfactory edition of the text have already been indicated;[232] the apparatus criticus of the present edition, described below, exhibits the plenitude of other instances of such grounds. As for J, which is essentially an attempt to reproduce ד/C in an improved and corrected version,[233] suffice it to point out that, besides innumerable less serious errors, portions of the text have been passed over and left out—omissions which either distort or preclude understanding of Messer Leon's meaning in the affected passages—in twenty-two places.[234]

The manuscript of the *N.S.* which Abraham Conat edited and printed as ד/C, is no longer extant. Fortunately, however, even before Conat edited and printed it in 1475/76, it had been copied by Menaḥem de' Rossi of Ferrara, and this copy, finished October 12, 1474, is preserved in the Ambrosian Library at Milan.[235]

231. Adolf Jellinek, *Nofet Zufim: R. Jehuda Messer Leon's Rhetorik, nach Aristoteles, Cicero und Quintilian, mit besonderer Beziehung auf die Heilige Schrift* (Vienna, 1863). Both the German and the Hebrew title pages carry statements to the effect that Jellinek, "Prediger der israelitischen Cultusgemeinde in Wien," published the volume in honor of the seventieth birthday of another well-known Viennese preacher, Rabbi Isaak Noa Mannheimer. This anniversary fell on October 17, 1863; and Jellinek tells us in the note appended to his reproduction of Conat's colophon that his correction of the proofs of J was done in the ten-day period between Rosh Hashanah and Yom Kippur, 5624, i.e., between September 14 and September 23, 1863. Confronted by a "deadline" that allowed less than a month—interrupted, too, by holidays—for completion of the entire project, Jellinek and the printers obviously and necessarily must have worked in great haste. The signs of their haste are abundantly evident in every part of the text of this presentation edition. Long out of print, J, in an unrevised and uncorrected photographic reimpression, was reissued at Jerusalem in 1971–72.

232. Above, sections 2 and 4, and nn. 80 and 182. For a listing of descriptions and discussions of C as an incunabulum, see F. R. Goff, *Incunabula in American Libraries: Third Census* (New York, 1964), 320.

233. We also owe to Jellinek introduction into the body of the text of the chapter-and-verse numbers of the biblical passages cited by JML for purposes of illustration or of exegesis, one of the several editorial improvements needed in order to facilitate modern use of the *N.S.* JML might have, but generally does not, specify the chapter numbers of his scriptural citations; chapter enumeration, while not usual, had begun to be included in some manuscripts of the Hebrew Bible by his day; note his erroneous reference to Ps. 58 at iv. 24.1. Verse enumeration, on the other hand, appears for the first time only in sixteenth-century, printed Hebrew Bibles. See C. D. Ginsburg, *Introduction to the Massoretico-Critical Edition of the Hebrew Bible* (London, 1897), 25 ff., 107–108.

234. These omissions, not otherwise noticed in the present edition, occur at the following points in J: p. 10, line 34; 18, 5; 26, 34; 44, 3; 46, 26; 66, 26; 81, 3; 81, 33; 86, 15; 86, 26; 91, 17; 102, 26; 105, 31; 128, 34; 138, 30; 153, 21; 161, 4; 162, 11; 174, 5; 188, 1; 189, 16; 193, 25. At 35, 4–5, *per contra*, we find not an omission, but a confusing dittography: a repetition of the words between התלונה (line 2) through יקיים (line 4). J. Klatzkin's *Anthology of Jewish Philosophy* [Heb.] (Berlin, 1926), 175–181, includes *N.S.* i.10 and iv.12–16, reedited on the basis both of C and of J. Although Klatzkin has in these pages successfully corrected a round dozen of Jellinek's lapses, he has retained J's mistakes, or committed errors of his own, in some 18 other instances. *Caveat lector!*

235. The de' Rossi manuscript, cod. Ambrosiana 91, is described by C. Bernheimer, *Codices*

Collation with ד/C of the readings of the de' Rossi manuscript (ב/M)—the earlier form of Conat's twofold witness to the text of the *N.S.*—together with some supplementation from other sources, has made it possible to achieve a text that is certainly less blemished and more exactly proximate to that originally composed by JML—in short a more "satisfactory" text—than either ד/C or J. With ב/M at our disposal we are able to note and to eliminate Conat's later editorial revisions, those now found in ד/C (and consequently in J). We can thus restore the text of the *N.S.* to what it must have been in Conat's no-longer-extant manuscript original of ב/M, to what the text must have been before Conat edited it into the form now before us in ד/C. From Conat's statements in the colophon of ד/C, we gather that his no-longer-extant manuscript was copied from one upon which he came in "a nut-garden of perfection," a library, that is to say, of theological and scientific works.[236] That he made such a manuscript copy—did not print ד/C directly from the manuscript he found in the "nut-garden"—is clearly established by the fact that ב/M, while its colophon omits the greater part of the colophon we find in ד/C, includes, and mentions Conat as the author of, the latter's final verses (his "parable").[237] We are not, of course, informed of the provenience of the "nut-garden" manuscript, but based on what we know about the production of other manuscripts in JML's *y*ᵉ*shībhāh,*[238] and about the composition date of the *N.S.*,[239] it is a fair inference that the "nut-garden" copy was made either directly from JML's autograph of the text or from a copy of such a direct copy. The *stemma* of the Hebrew text of the *N.S.* may, then, be diagrammed as follows:

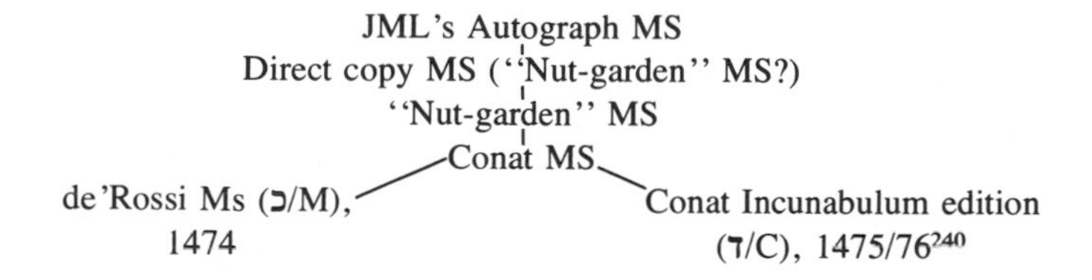

hebraici Bibliothecae Ambrosianae (Florence, 1938), 115. On Menaḥem de' Rossi as a scribe, see A. Freimann, "Jewish Scribes in Medieval Italy," 292–93, and the references there given.

236. The "nut-garden" may well have been the library of the Norsa brothers, for whom Farissol copied JML's *Super-commentary on Isagoge-Categories-De Interpretatione;* cf. n. 59 above.

237. See the two colophons, translated below.

238. *Supra,* §2, and nn.59, 118, and 130.

239. See §4 above.

240. It should be emphasized that M (the de' Rossi MS, cod. Ambrosiana 91) is the only extant manuscript that both antedates C (the printed incunabulum edition) and is not a handwritten copy of C. Two such handwritten copies of C are known: (1) cod. Munich 55² (M. Steinschneider, *Die hebräischen Handschriften der K. Hof- und Staatsbibliothek in Muenchen* [Munich, 1895], p. 37); and (2) cod. Parma 1395¹ [2651¹] (P. Perreau, *Catalogo dei codici ebraici della Biblioteca di Parma non descritti dal de Rossi* [Florence, 1878], no. 18, p. 133). Both these MSS are said to have been copied in the sixteenth century. Mention should also be made of the fact that C itself has been mistakenly thought to be a manuscript; see, e.g., G. Pasini, *Codices Manuscripti Bibliothecae Regii Taurinensis Athenaei,* I, (Turin, 1749), Cod LIX, 21b–22a; and cf. E. Artom, "Gli incunaboli ebraici della Biblioteca Nazionale Universitaria di Torino," *Soncino-Blätter* 1 (1925–1926), 52–53.

In addition to the main witness borne by כ/M and by ד/C to JML's Hebrew text of the *N.S.*, important supplementary witness is afforded by the two Hebrew sources upon which he drew so extensively in composing the work: the *textus receptus* of the Hebrew Bible, and Todros Todrosi's Hebrew translation, from the Arabic, of Averroes' *Middle Commentary on Aristotle's Rhetoric*. Todros' Hebrew version was published in 1842 by J. Goldenthal (ᵍט) on the basis of a single manuscript in the Leipzig Ratsbibliothek.[241] Since, however, the text of Todros' version used by JML was plainly not always identical with that published by Goldenthal, two additional manuscripts (ᵃט and ᵇט) have been consulted for the purposes of the present edition.[242] Where, again, I have had to ascertain the Arabic reading underlying Todros' Hebrew, I have done so in A. Badawī's convenient edition.[243] These several materials—כ/M, ד/C, the Hebrew Bible (ת/B), Todros' translation of Averroes' *Middle Commentary* (ט/T, in its several forms), and Averroes' Arabic text itself (א/A)—are those from which the Hebrew text of the *N.S.* has been constituted. All are cited, as needed or as appropriate, in the first of the two apparatuses that appear at the foot of the main text, the apparatus devoted to the booking of the variant readings.[244]

From what has already been said about כ/M and ד/C, and considering that JML almost certainly had no hand in the editorial operations noted in ד/C, it will be clear that when the texts of כ/M and ד/C vary, and where neither is disqualified by obvious error, the preferred reading will generally be that of כ/M.[245] All rejected variant readings, however, including the rejected errors of either text, are entered in Apparatus I. Even orthographic and abbreviational variants are entered in Apparatus I, especially such as have seemed to me to reveal or illumine fifteenth-century scribal, or early printing, techniques and conventions.

In handling JML's citations (for exegetical or illustrative purposes) of passages of the Hebrew Bible, where both כ/M and ד/C witness to the fact that he has misquoted—he has obviously often cited the biblical text from memory—I have left the misquotation in the body of our text, and given the correct biblical reading in the apparatus. Where the misquotation is present in כ/M, but not in ד/C, and where there is no reason to suspect scribal error in כ/M, I have usually

241. The manuscript of Todros' *Bēʾūr* published by Goldenthal (our ᵍט) is Cod. Leipzig (hebr.) XLI. C. a, as listed in E. W. R. Naumann, *Catalogus librorum manuscriptorum qui in bibliotheca senatoria civitatis Lipsiensis asservantur: Codices orientalium linguarum descripserunt H. O. Fleischer et Fr. Delitzsch* (Grimae, 1838), p. 307.

242. Respectively, cod. Paris 933³ and cod. Paris 932⁴, listed in H. Zotenberg, *Catalogues des mss. hébreux et samaritaines de la Bibliothèque Impériale* (Paris, 1866), p. 164.

243. Badawī's edition (n. 188) is based on the two best-known MSS of the work, cod. Leiden Or. 2073 and cod. Laurentiana Or. CLXXX, 54 (Florence); cf. pp. 12–13 and 15 of his introduction.

244. The abbreviations and signs of this apparatus are included and explained in the list at the beginning of the volume.

245. Where כ/M and ד/C disagree, but are equally correct—e.g. in the manner of indicating the Divine Name, or where the one text abbreviates while the other gives the words in full—I have adopted the form that I thought JML more probably wrote.

treated the matter as an editorial correction on Conat's part, that is, kept the כ/M reading in the main text and booked the correction in the apparatus.[246]

In those passages where JML is quoting, paraphrasing, or abridging Todros/Averroes—he employs all these methods—I have, when the several forms of the text of ט/T vary among themselves, admitted the reading which I think JML most likely had before him, and I have entered the others in the apparatus. There are, of course, places where JML has obviously and deliberately departed from the ט/T reading before him; in each such case, the latter is entered in the apparatus. Occasionally, where a mistaken or more than usually ambiguous rendering of Todros' has affected the text of the *N.S.*, I have thought it necessary to call attention to the underlying Arabic text (א/A).

In Apparatus II are collected the *loci,* by book, chapter, and verse (in Hebrew), of all the scriptural phrases and verbal reminiscences to which JML so often has recourse in order to express—as plainly he thought behooved him in an *ars rhetorica*—what he wishes to say: in a word, his *m^e^līṣāh*. The passage-*loci* are indicated here rather than in the main body of the text—the procedure followed in my English translation—since in their way they too are an external constituent of the Hebrew text of the *N.S.*

Conjectural emendations, where admitted, are indicated in footnotes to the text, following the apparatuses. Emendations of C made by Jellinek, and adopted in the present edition, are credited to him in footnotes (for example, "Correction: J"). "^R^ד" is acknowledged as the source of accepted emendations drawn from among those found written on the margins (or between the lines) of the copy of the incunabulum kindly placed at my disposal by William Roth, of New York City. The marginal annotations of "Roth" are probably the work of Rabbi Shimshon Kohen Modon of Mantua (as he signs himself, "Sansone Sacerdote Modone" [1679-1727]), who once owned the book,[247] but there is no conclusive evidence that such is the case, and the annotations may be those of another reader. All otherwise unattributed emendations are those I have felt constrained to make.

The paragraphing and punctuation of the Hebrew text as here published are the work of the present editor. These details are not separable from the sense of the text, as I construe and perceive it, and therefore, with due allowance for the difference between English and Hebrew sentence structure, are mainly duplicated in the text of the translation. The punctuation marks employed are, with one exception, those that are standard in modern printed Hebrew texts. The

246. ד/C often subsumes an important part of a biblical quotation under the Hebrew equivalent of "etc." ('וכו), where כ/M cites the passage in full. In passages, especially in Book IV, where JML may have cited several biblical passages as examples, ד/C will not infrequently be found to have omitted one. Conat's editorial practice in this regard may have been actuated by a desire to hold down the costs of printing the work.

247. *Supra,* §1 and n. 9.

exception consists of a single point, placed to coincide with the upper point of a colon (·); I use this to mark a separation within the text that is somewhat more extensive than that represented by a comma, but less extensive than that represented by a semicolon. In כ/M and ד/C, separations within the text, if marked at all, are indicated simply by wider than normal spacing between words. To keep the margins even, ד/C makes frequent use of additional letters at the ends of lines, precursive of the opening letters of the word with which the next following line commences (*litterae dilatabiles*); these letters have occasionally caused confusion and error in J.

8. The Annotated English Translation

Intended primarily for non-Hebraist readers, my annotated English translation of the *N.S.* will perhaps not be altogether otiose to Hebraists as well, since the Hebrew original is so often difficult and obscure. The annotation, aside from the full documentation of all the author's biblical and rhetorical sources, is confined to that minimal amount of explanation needed to render this fifteenth-century treatise understood in and of itself. The *loci* of all JML's references and allusions to the Bible (here printed in semibold type) are given, in brackets, within the body of the translation; those of his references to rhetorical works are indicated in the source footnotes to the passages in which they are mentioned. In translating JML's *mᵉ līṣāh* and his biblical quotations, I have in general followed the language of the Jewish Publication Society's *The Holy Scriptures According to the Masoretic Text: A New Translation* (Philadelphia, 1917) (JV); where JML's construction and interpretation of the biblical text differ from those of JV, I have, of course, made my translation reflect his understanding.

In fine, by providing what I hope will be regarded as a clear and readable English version of Judah Messer Leon's *Sēpher Nōpheth Ṣūphīm,* I have sought to make available to all who may be interested what is probably the single most original and important work of Jewish scholarship produced in early Renaissance Italy.

ספר נפת צופים

The Book of the Honeycomb's Flow

ספר נפת צופים

הדור חפץ שפתי דעת, / על מה נרפים אתם נרפים?
הטיבו נגן, הרבו שיר, / כי בא מגיד נפת צופים.
חבר ספר, אמרי שפר, / כשמו כן הוא: נפת צופים.

5 [1] אמר העבד הקטן, האוהב הנאמן, יהודה יצ״ו, הנקרא מסיר ליאון: בימים ההם בהיות אור ישראל כאור החמה, כאור שבעת הימים, בסוד אלוה עלי אהלנו; בשבת עיר על תלה וארמון על משפטו, וככבי השמים וכסיליהם יראים מגשת אלינו לרע; ומטות הממשלה אף ברושים שמחו להם, ארזי לבנון מבין עבותים היתה צמרתם׳ כעב תעופינה בנות המזמה וחכמות שרותיה אל הר־
10 הקדש, וכיונים אל ארבותיהם. אף הלצה מצאה בית, ובת השיר קן לה, בין העומדים, אשר שתה אפרוחיה את מזבחות ה׳ לכבוד ולתפארת. כל ממלכות התבונה בעדן גן אלקים היו, משם יפרדו. שם תרבצנה בנוה טוב, בזאת התורה אשר שם משה; מבין שורותיה יצהירו. בתוך אבני אש התהלכו, אשה רעותה לא פקדו.

1 נפת] נופת[ב] || 5 יצ״ו] יצו[ד] | מסיר] מסי[ב] || 7 אהלנו] אהלינו[ב] || 12 אלקים] אלהים[ד] ||

2 משׁ׳ כ׳ ט״ו | שמ׳ ה׳ י״ז || 3 יש׳ כ״ג ט״ז | תה׳ י״ט י״א || 4 בר׳ מ״ט כ״א | תה׳ י״ט י״א || 5 מל״ב י״ח כ״ד || 6 יש׳ ל׳ כ״ו | איוב כ״ט ד׳ || 7 יר׳ ל׳ י״ח | יש׳ י״ג י׳ | שמ׳ ל״ד ל׳ || 8 יש׳ י״ד ח׳ || 9 יח׳ ל״א ג׳ | יש׳ ס׳ ח׳ | שופ׳ ה׳ כ״ט || 10 יש׳ ס׳ ח׳ | תה׳ פ״ד ד׳ || 11 זכ׳ ג׳ ז׳ | תה׳ פ״ד ד׳ | שמ׳ כ״ח ב׳ || 12 יח׳ כ״ח י״ג | בר׳ ב׳ י׳ | יח׳ ל״ד י״ד || 13 דב׳ ד׳ מ״ד | איוב כ״ד י״א | יח׳ כ״ח י״ד || 14 יש׳ ל״ד ט״ז ||

The Book of the Honeycomb's Flow

O generation desiring **the lips of knowledge** [Prov. 20:15],
Wherefore **are ye idle, are ye idle** [Exod. 5:17]?
Make sweet melody, sing many songs [Isa. 23:16],
For a propounder of **the honeycomb's flow** [Ps. 19:11][1] is come.
He has composed a book, **goodly words** [Gen. 49:21],
Which is even as its name: **The Honeycomb's Flow** [Ps. 19:11].[2]

Messer Leon's Preface

[1] Says that **least . . . servant** [2 Kings 18:24], the faithful friend, JUDAH (may his Rock and Redeemer preserve him!), called MESSER LEON: In those days when the light of Israel was **as the light of the sun . . . as the light of the seven days** [Isa. 30:26], **when the friendship of God was upon** our **tent** [Job 29:4]; when **the city** abode **on its mound and the palace on its wonted place** [Jer. 30:18], and **the stars of heaven and the constellations thereof** [Isa. 13:10] **were afraid to come nigh** [Exod. 34:30] us for ill; while as for the sceptres of rulership,[3] even **the cypresses rejoiced at** [Isa. 14:8] them, **the cedars of Lebanon** [14:8], whose **top was among the thick boughs** [Ezek. 31:3]: then the daughters of Thought and **the wisest of her princesses** [Judg. 5:29][4] **would fly as a cloud** [Isa. 60:8] unto the Holy Hill, **and as the doves to their cotes** [60:8]. Rhetoric, too, **found a house** [Ps. 84:4], and Poesy **a nest for herself** [84:4], **amongst those standing by** [Zech. 3:7], **where she might lay her young at** the **altars of the Lord** [Ps. 84:4] **for splendor and for beauty** [Exod. 28:2]. All realms of understanding were **in Eden the Garden of God** [Ezek. 28:13], **from thence** were they **parted** [Gen. 2:10]. **There were they lying down in a good fold** [Ezek. 34:14], in "**This is the Law which Moses set**" [Deut. 4:44];[5] from **between** her **olive-rows were they making oil** [Job 24:11]. **In the midst of**

1. That is, a teacher of "melifluousness," of discourse composed according to the principles of the art of rhetoric.
2. The verse, as the colophon demonstrates, is by Abraham Conat, the printer of the *N.S.*
3. Israel's rulers; cf. Ezek. 19:11.
4. The arts and the sciences; cf. below, i.13.13.
5. Cf. Par. 10, *infra*.

[2] אז ראינו בנעם השם ונהרנו בחכמה ודעת. במסלה עלינו עד מרומים,
בנינו בשמים מעלותינו. ממעל לכסאות ההנהגה שמנו קננו· בסתר המדרגה
הנשגבה נחבינו, בצלה חמדנו וישבנו.

[3] אז יהפך עלינו המון ים חיל גוים למען דעת צדקות ה׳. שפעת גמלים
5 תכסנו לקחת מפינו תורה; ואניות תרשיש בראשונה, עם נפך ספיר וברקת,
לדעת מוסר השכל. אלה משבה יבאו, ואלה מארץ סינים; זהב ולבונה ישאו
אלו מראש הררי קדם, עם כל אבקת רוכל, להבין אמרי בינה. מה גדלו מעשינו
בימים ההם! מה יקרו רעינו עם אל, ותעלוזנה כליותינו אף גילת ורנן! מה עצמו
ראשי עם קדש, ונפלאו במועצות ודעת, גבהא קומתם! כבוד הלבנון נתן לנו,
10 הדר ההנהגה והתפארת, עד יאמרו בגוים הגדיל ה׳ לעשות עם אלה.

[4] וכאשר חשך עלינו השמש בצאתו, וחפרה הלבנה, כי כבוד ה׳ סר מעלינו,
ויסתר פניו ממנו, ותבקע העיר ההללה, טבעו בארץ שעריה, ובית קדשנו
ותפארתנו היה לשרפה, ממרום משפטים משחיתים באו לנו. קרעו את סגור
לבנו, ולא דמו הסר המלכים איש ממקומו. וספקו עלינו כפים כל עוברי דרך כי
15 ירדנו פלאים; שרקו ויניעו ראשם. אבדה עצה מבנים, ויסכרו מעינות התבונה
ומקוריה; והחכמה באה בחדריה ותסגור דלתיה בעדיה, ותשכון בחגוי סלע
מרום שבתה, ותשב במחשכים, במסתורי התעודה בנתה ביתה; לא תאיר אל
עבר פניה כימי קדם, אין גם אחד תקרא בפתחי שערים כשנים קדמוניות. עתה
תאבל הארץ, קריה נאמנה תפרש כפיה· כי הוכו בניה בסנורים, ירדו במצולות

1 השם] יי[ד] || 5 תכסנו] תכסינו[ר] || 6 משבה] משבא[ת] || 13 משחיתים] משיחתים[ר] || 19 הוכו] הכו[ר] ||

---

1 תה׳ כ״ז ד׳ |במ׳ כ׳ י״ט |תה׳ ס״ח י״ט ||2 עמ׳ ט׳ ו׳ |יר׳ נ״ב ל״ב |עו׳ ד׳ |שה״ש ב׳ י״ד ||3 שה״ש ב׳ ג׳ ||4 יש׳ ס׳ ה׳ |מי׳ ו׳ ה׳ |יש׳ ס׳ ו׳ ||5 איוב כ״ב כ״ב |יש׳ ס׳ ט׳ |שמ׳ כ״ח י״ח |יח׳ כ״ח י״ג || 6 מש׳ א׳ ג׳ |יש׳ ס׳ ו׳ |יש׳ מ״ט י״ב |יש׳ ס׳ ו׳ ||7 דב׳ ל״ג ט״ו |שה״ש ג׳ ו׳ |מש׳ א׳ ב׳ |תה׳ צ״ב ו׳ ||8 תה׳ קל״ט י״ז |מש׳ כ״ג ט״ז |יש׳ ל״ה ב׳ |תה׳ קל״ט י״ז ||9 מש׳ כ״ב כ׳ |יח׳ ל״א ה׳ |יש׳ ל״ה ב׳ ||10 תה׳ קכ״ו ב׳ ||11 יש׳ י״ג י׳ |יש׳ כ״ד כ״ג |שופ׳ ט״ז כ׳ ||12 יש׳ ס״ד ו׳ |יר׳ נ״ב ז׳ |יח׳ כ״ו י״ז |איכה ב׳ ט׳ ||13 הו׳ י״ג ח׳ ||14 תה׳ ל״ה ט״ו |מל״א כ׳ כ״ד |איכה ב׳ ט״ו ||15 איכה א׳ ט׳ |איכה ב׳ ט״ו |יר׳ מ״ט ז׳ |בר׳ ח׳ ב׳ ||16 מל״ב ד׳ ה׳ |עו׳ ג׳ ||17 איכה ג׳ ו׳ |יש׳ ח׳ ט״ז |מש׳ ט׳ א׳ |שמ׳ כ״ה ל״ז ||18 יש׳ נ״א ט׳ |מש׳ א׳ כ״א |מל׳ ג׳ ד׳ ||19 הו׳ ד׳ ג׳ |יש׳ א׳ כ״ו |יר׳ ד׳ ל״א |מל״ב ו׳ י״ח |שמ׳ ט״ו ה׳ ||

stones of fire did they **walk about** [Ezek. 28:14], **none wanting her mate** [Isa. 34:16].

[2] Then did we **behold the graciousness of the Lord** [Ps. 27:4] and were radiant with wisdom and knowledge. **By the highway** [Num. 20:19] we **ascended on high** [Ps. 68:19]; we built our **upper chambers in the heavens** [Amos 9:6]. **Above the thrones of** [Jer. 52:32] civilized mankind did we **set** our **nest** [Obad. 4]: **in the covert of the** highest **cliff** [Song of S. 2:14] were we hidden, **under its shadow did** we **delight to sit** [2:3].

[3] **Then . . . the abundance of the sea . . . the wealth of nations . . . kept turning to** [Isa. 60:5] us **that** they **might know the righteous acts of the Lord** [Mic. 6:5]. **The caravan of camels** would **cover us** [Isa. 60:6] to **receive . . . instruction from** our **mouth** [Job 22:22]; **and the ships of Tarshish first** [Isa. 60:9], with **carbuncle, sapphire** [Exod. 28:18] **and emerald** [Ezek. 28:13], to know **the discipline of wisdom** [Prov. 1:3]. These **would come from Sheba** [Isa. 60:6], **and these from the land of Sinim** [49:12], **bearing gold and frankincense** [60:6] from **the mountain-tops of the East** [Deut. 33:15] **along with all the powders of the merchant** [Song of S. 3:6], **in order to comprehend the words of understanding** [Prov. 1:2]. **How great were** our **works** [Ps. 92:6] in those days! **How precious were** our **thoughts** with **God** [Ps. 139:17], while our **reins rejoiced** [Prov. 23:16] **even with joy and singing** [Isa. 35:2]! **How mighty were the heads** [Ps. 139:17] of the holy nation, how wondrous in **counsels and knowledge** [Prov. 22:20], how their **stature was exalted** [Ezek. 31:5]! **Lebanon's glory was given unto us** [Isa. 35:2], splendor of hegemony and beauty; so that **they would say among the nations "The Lord hath done great things with these"** [Ps. 126:2].

[4] But when **the sun darkened against us in his going forth** [Isa. 13:10], and **the moon was confounded** [24:23], because the glory of **the Lord had departed from** [Judg. 16:20] us and He had **hid** His **face from us** [Isa. 64:6]; when **the renowned city** [Ezek. 26:17] **had been breached** [Jer. 52:7], **her gates had sunk into the ground** [Lam. 2:9], and our glorious holy House had been burnt—from on high ruinous judgements came to us. They **rent the encasement of our heart** [Hos. 13:8] **and ceased not** [Ps. 35:15] to **take the kings away, every man out of his place** [1 Kings 20:24]. **All that passed by clapped** their hands at us [Lam. 2:15], for we were **come down wonderfully** [Lam. 1:9]; **they hissed and wagged their head** [2:15]. **Counsel perished from the prudent** [Jer. 49:7], **the fountains of** understanding and its wellsprings **were stopped** [Gen. 8:2]. Wisdom withdrew into her chambers **and shut** her **doors after her** [2 Kings 4:5]; she **dwelt in the clefts of the rock,** her **habitation on high** [Obad. 3]; she **dwelt in dark places** [Lam. 3:6], **builded her house** [Prov. 9:1] in the coverts of **the Testimony** [Isa. 8:16]. She would not **give light over against** [Exod. 25:37] her presence **as in the days of old** [Isa. 51:9], nor would **she call** anyone **at the entrance of the gates** [Prov. 1:21] **as in ancient years** [Mal. 3:4]. Now **did the land mourn** [Hos. 4:3], **the faithful city** [Isa. 1:26] **spread her hands** [Jer.

ההוללות, כל משברי התלאות וגליהם עליהם עברו. מלכה ושריה בגוים׳ אין תורה כי אם צרה וחשכה, מעוף צוקה. ונביאיה לא מצאו חזון, לא יראו אור ההשגה[1] כי יהל. לא חכמו, ישכילו, ״זאת המנוחה״ כלולת המשכלות, כי טח מראות עיניהם.

[5] עתה רחקו מעלינו כל רועי דעה והשכל; כל עתודי ארץ שמעו אשר נואלנו ואשר חטאנו. ״סורו! טמא!״ קראו לנו׳ היינו ביניהם לנידה׳ כי יאמרו: ״ידנו רמה׳ עלינו במעלות החכמה עד שחקים. הנה עם בני ישראל רם ועצום ממנו — במדרגות הסכלות; בחשכה יתהלכו, עם טמא שפתים, נלעג לשון אין בינה.״

[6] מה אמולה לבתך, הבת השובבה, כי אשר למדת אותם אלופים לראש. והשקיתם מיין הרקח כוס מלא מסך התבונות; מעסיס רמוניך שתו וישכרו וייטיבו לבם עד נפקחו עיניהם בחכמות רמות נעלמות. מראשית עריסותיך עשו להם כוונים לקטר למלאכת[2] השמים. מראשית פרי אדמתך הביאו אל בית האוצר וישנו את טעמם לעיניהם. מגז כבשיך יתחממו. עשו להם במות טלואות אשר שם הרקמה. מהררי קדשך חצבו אבנים גדולות לבנות להם מצודות ומגדלים. ממך פנה, ממך יתד, כללו יפים. ממך יצא כל נוגש יחדיו, ערוך כאיש למלחמה.

[7] ועתה יאמרו לנו: ״השמים עלינו למרום התבונות, שבינו שבינו; בנינו בתים, עליות, והיכלות רבי התפארת בכל מדע והשכל.״ וקראו לך טמאת השם,

3 ההשגה[1]] ההשגו[גד] |המנוחה ‹השלמה›[ד] || 8 נלעג] בלעג[ג] || 12 וייטיבו] וייטבו[ד] |רמות] רבות[ג] || 18 השמים] המים[ד] ||

1 יונה ב׳ ד׳ |איכה ב׳ ט׳ || 2 יש׳ ח׳ כ״ב |איכה ב׳ ט׳ || איוב ל״ז כ״א || 3 איוב ל״א כ״ו |דב׳ ל״ב כ״ט |יש׳ כ״ח י״ב || 4 יש׳ מ״ד י״ח || 5 מש׳ י״ט ז׳ |יר׳ ג׳ ט״ו |יש׳ י״ד ט׳ || 6 במ׳ י״ב י״א |איכה ד׳ ט״ו |איכה א׳ י״ז || 7 דב׳ ל״ב כ״ז |שמ׳ כ׳ כ״ו |תה׳ נ״ז י״א |שמ׳ א׳ ט׳ || 8 תה׳ פ״ב ה׳ |יש׳ ו׳ ה׳ |יש׳ ל״ג י״ט || 10 יח׳ ט״ז ל׳ |יר׳ ל״א כ״ב |יר׳ י״ג כ״א || 11 שה״ש ח׳ ב׳ |תה׳ ע״ה ט׳ |שה״ש ח׳ ב׳ || 12 בר׳ ג׳ ה׳ |במ׳ ט״ו כ״א || 13 יר׳ ז׳ י״ח |דב׳ כ״ו ב׳ |דנ׳ א׳ ב׳ || 14 שמ״א כ״א י״ד |איוב ל״א כ׳ |יח׳ ט״ז ט״ז || 15 תה׳ פ״ז א׳ |דב׳ כ״ז ב׳ || 16 זכ׳ י׳ ד׳ |יח׳ כ״ז ד׳ |זכ׳ י׳ ד׳ |יר׳ ו׳ כ״ג || 18 מש׳ כ״ה ג׳ |תה׳ ס״ח י״ט || 19 יר׳ כ״ב י״ד |הו׳ ח׳ י״ד |דנ׳ א׳ י״ז |יח׳ כ״ב ה׳ ||

[1] J's emendation.

[2] So with many Mss and the *Qᵉrē* of ת: למלכת.

4:31]: for her children had been **smitten with blindness** [2 Kings 6:18]; **they went down into the depths** [Exod. 15:5] of folly; **all** the **waves and billows** of hardship **passed over** them [Jonah 2:4]. **Her king and her princes** were **among the nations; instruction** was **no more** [Lam. 2:9]; but **distress and darkness, the gloom of anguish** [Isa. 8:22]. **Nor did her prophets find vision** [Lam. 2:9]; **they saw not the light** [Job 37:21] of comprehension **when it shined** [Job 31:26]. They were not **wise** enough **to understand** [Deut. 32:29] "**This is the rest**" [Isa. 28:12], the crown of things intelligible, **for their eyes were bedaubed so that they could not see** [44:18].

[5] Now all the **shepherds** of **knowledge and understanding** [Jer. 3:15] **went far from us** [Prov. 19:7]; **all the chief men of the earth** [Isa. 14:9] heard **how we had done foolishly and how we had sinned** [Num. 12:11]. "**Depart ye! unclean!**" they **cried unto us** [Lam. 4:15]; we were **amongst them as a thing impure** [1:17]. For **they would say: "Our hand is exalted** [Deut. 32:27]; we have **gone up by** the **steps** [Exod. 20:23] of wisdom **unto the skies** [Ps. 57:11]. **Behold, the people of the children of Israel are too** exalted **and too mighty for us** [Exod. 1:9]—in the degrees of folly; **they go about in darkness** [Ps. 82:5], **a people of unclean lips** [Isa. 6:5], **of a stammering tongue that thou canst not understand"** [Isa. 33:19].

[6] **How weak was thy heart** [Ezek. 16:30], **O thou backsliding daughter** [Jer. 31:22], **for the friends whom thou thyself didst train were at the head** [13:21]. Yet thou didst **cause** them **to drink of spiced wine** [Song of S. 8:2], **a cup . . . full of the mixed wine** [Ps. 75:9] of understanding; **of the juice of** thy **pomegranates** [Song of S. 8:2] they drank, received benefit,[6] and improved their mind until their **eyes were opened** [Gen. 3:5] in high and obscure sciences. **Of the first of** thy **dough** [Num. 15:21], they **made** them **cakes** in order to sacrifice **to the heavenly creation** [or: **the queen of heaven**] [Jer. 7:18].[7] **Of the first of the fruit of** thy **ground** [Deut. 26:2] they **brought into the treasure-house** [of their gods] [Dan. 1:2], and **changed** their **demeanour before them** [1 Sam. 21:14]. **With the fleece of** thy **sheep were** they **warmed** [Job 31:20]. They **made** them **high places decked with divers colors** [Ezek. 16:16] where there was variegated stuff. Out of thy **holy mountains** [Ps. 87:1] they hewed **great stones** [Deut. 27:2] to build them strongholds and towers. **Out of** thee **came forth the corner-stone, out of** thee **the stake** [Zech. 10:4]; **they perfected** their **beauty** [Ezek. 27:4]. **Out of** thee **came forth every master together** [Zech. 10:4], **set in array as a man for war** [Jer. 6:23].

[7] And now they say to us: "**The heavens for height** [Prov. 25:3] of understanding have we **ascended,** we **have led** our **captivity captive** [Ps. 68:19]; we have **built** the most glorious **manses, roof-chambers** [Jer. 22:14], and **palaces**

6. Play on words: the expected *wayyishk^{e}rū* ("and they became drunk") is here replaced by *wayyissākh^{e}rū* ("and they were benefited"); cf. Gen. 43:34.

7. Here JML follows some 50 Mss. and R. David Qimḥi's commentary in reading למלאכת for למלכת, and understanding the expression in the sense of Ps. 8:4, *q.v.*

סכלה הוללה, גועלת אישה ובניה, מתבוססת בדמי הבטלה, חבקה אשפתות הנבלות לטמאה בם, באין חכמה ותבונה.

[8] ואנכי באש עברתי אמרתי: אסורה נא ואראה, הכצעקתה הבאה אלינו עשו פלילה, וראו, במראות הצובאות פתח ההשגות העיוניות, מראות היצירה התמימה, ושקלו גבעות ההשגה במאזני הבחינה. וחפשתי אמתחותם, וראיתי את כל בית נכאתם. ואלך ביער לכרות לי ארזים, ומראש יונקותם רך קטפתי. ובאתי אל ערוגות הבשם, ואריתי מר ואהלות, לעשות לי גנות ופרדסים.

[9] וכאשר ראיתי אחר כן בחצרי ובטירותי, חדר בחדר, למצוא מקום למגדלות מרקחים אשר חשבתים חדשים, מקרוב באו· וידי נטפו מר ואהלות, קציעות כל בגדותי· אשכול הכפר, נרד וכרכום, עם כל ראשי בשמים נטעו ושורשו בקרן זוית, אשר לא דמיתי ולא עלו על לבי מלפנים, אמרתי: מדושתי ובן גרני לא יחסר כל בו; אך לשקר שמרתי מעט הצאן ההנה במדבר העמים· אף כי זאת אשיב אל לבי, כי לא במחתרת מצאתים ובמקום ארץ חשך, אם לא עמדתי את רוכלים בארצות לרעות בגנים וללקוט שושנים.

[10] לכן קנאתי לה׳ קנאה גדולה, ומלאני לבי להראות העמים והשרים כי עדות ה׳ נאמנה, תמימה, נשגבה, מחכימת פתי. היא חותם תכנית, אשר בה כל מושג ונודע למינהו מציאות מפורסמת או רמוזה, בה ינוחו הלבבות וישקוטו. עמה מקור החיים הנצחיים וההשגחה הפרטית ליראי ה׳ ולחושבי שמו· ידה חלק חלקתה להם בקו. כללה אמתת המציאות בכללו; וכל חכמה, עיונית או מעשית, כללות מסוגל רוחני נתגלה בנבואה ליושבים לפני ה׳, לא שזפתו עין

1 הוללה] והוללה[כ] || 2 לטמאה] לטמא[כ] || 8 אחר כן] א״כ[כ] | ובטירותי] ובטירותם[כ] || 15 <את> העמים[ד] || 16 פתי] פותי[כ] || 19 [חלק][ד] | חכמה] חכמת[כ] ||

---

1 יח׳ ט״ז מ״ה | יח׳ ט״ז כ״ב | איכה ד׳ ה׳ || 2 וי׳ ט״ו ל״ב | שמ׳ ל״ו א׳ || 3 יח׳ ל״ח י״ט | שמ׳ ג׳ ג׳ | בר׳ י״ח כ״א || 4 יש׳ ט״ז ג׳ | שמ׳ ל״ח ח׳ || 5 יש׳ מ׳ י״ב | בר׳ מ״ד י״א–י״ב || 6 מל״ב כ׳ י״ג | יש׳ מ״ד י״ד | יח׳ י״ז ד׳ || 7 שה״ש ו׳ ב׳ | שה״ש ה׳ א׳ | שה״ש ד׳ י״ד | קה׳ ב׳ ה׳ || 8 בר׳ כ״ה ט״ז | מל״ב ט׳ב׳ || 9 שה״ש ה׳ י״ג | דב׳ ל״ב י״ז | שה״ש ה׳ ה׳ || 10 תה׳ מ״ה ט׳ | שה״ש א׳ י״ד | שה״ש ד׳ י״ד || 11 יר׳ י״ב ב׳ || 12 יש׳ כ״א י׳ | שמ״א כ״ה כ״א | שמ״א י״ז כ״ח || 13 איכה ג׳ כ״א | יר׳ ב׳ ל״ד | יש׳ מ״ה י״ט || 14 שה״ש ו׳ ב׳ || 15 מל״א י״ט י׳ | זכ׳ א׳ י״ד | אס׳ ז׳ ה׳ | אס׳ א׳ י״א || 16 תה׳ י״ט ח׳ | יח׳ כ״ח י״ב || 17 בר׳ א׳ י״ב | יש׳ י״ד ז׳ || 18 תה׳ ל״ו י׳ | מל׳ ג׳ ט״ז || 19 יש׳ ל״ד י״ז || 20 יש׳ כ״ג י״ח | איוב כ״ח ז׳ ||

[Hos. 8:14] in every **science and skill**" [Dan. 1:17]. But thee have they called **defiled of name** [Ezek. 22:5], mad fool, **loather of her husband and her children** [16:45], **wallowing in** useless **blood** [16:22], **embracing dunghills** [Lam. 4:5] of shamelessness **to be unclean thereby** [Lev. 15:32], without **wisdom and understanding** [Exod. 36:1].

[8] As for me, **in the fire of my wrath** [Ezek. 38:19] I said: **I will turn aside now and see** [Exod. 3:3] **whether . . . according to the cry of it which is come unto** us [Gen. 18:21] they have **executed justice** [Isa. 16:3], have seen **in the mirrors which serve at the door** [Exod. 38:8] of speculative concepts, visions of the perfect creation, **and** have **weighed** the **mountains** of thought **in the scales** of examination [Isa. 40:12]. So I **searched** through their **sacks** [Gen. 44:11–12] and saw **all** their **treasure-house** [2 Kings 20:13]. I went into the forest to **hew** me **down cedars** [Isa. 44:14] and **cropped off** a tender one from **the topmost** of their **young twigs** [Ezek. 17:4]. I came **to the beds of spices** [Song of S. 6:2] and **gathered myrrh** [5:1] **and aloes** [4:14] to **make me gardens and parks** [Eccl. 2:5].

[9] But when I afterward saw that within the **inner chamber** [2 Kings 9:2] of my own **villages and encampments** [Gen. 25:16] place had been found for the **banks of sweet herbs** [Song of S. 5:13] which I thought **new, come in of late** [Deut. 32:17]; that **my hands dripped with myrrh** [Song of S. 5:5] **and aloes, all my garments with cassia** [Ps. 45:9]; that **a cluster of henna** [Song of S. 1:14], **spikenard and saffron, . . . with all the chief spices** [4:14], which I had never before thought about or noticed, had been **planted** and **taken root** [Jer. 12:2] in a corner, I said: Nothing whatever is lacking in **my threshing and the winnowing of my floor** [Isa. 21:10]. **Surely in vain have I kept** [1 Sam. 25:21] **those few sheep in the wilderness** [17:28] of the nations; although **this I recall to my mind** [Lam. 3:21]: that I **would not have found** them **breaking in** [Jer. 2:34] nor **in a place of the land of darkness** [Isa. 45:19] had I not stood with traffickers amongst [foreign] lands **to feed in the gardens and to gather lilies** [Song of S. 6:2].

[10] Therefore **I was . . . jealous for the Lord** [1 Kings 19:10] **with a great jealousy** [Zech. 1:14], and **presumed in** my **heart** [Esth. 7:5] **to show the peoples and the princes** [1:11] that **the Testimony of the Lord is sure, perfect,** and exalted, **making wise the simple** [Ps. 19:8]. She is a **signet of perfection** [Ezek. 28:12] wherein every conception and object of knowledge **after its kind** [Gen. 1:12] is either a plainly manifest, or else an allegorically stated, reality wherein hearts are **at rest and are quiet** [Isa. 14:7]. **With** her **is the fountain of** eternal **life** [Ps. 36:10], and special providence **for them that fear the Lord and that think upon His name** [Mal. 3:16]; her **hand hath allotted** a portion **unto them by line** [Isa. 34:17]. She comprises the truth of existence in general; and every science, speculative or practical, is a spiritually adapted body of principles[8]

8. Adapted, that is, to the mental and spiritual quality of its knowers and practitioners.

הנשמה מזולת השפעה נבואיית או מקובלת ממנה. לא ידע אנוש ערכה אם לא
יבקשנה ככסף בכל מדינה ומדינה, וכמטמונים יחפשנה.

[11] ויען קצת משרי המלך הפרתמים, בחורי חמד לבושי ההשגה, אוכלי יערי
עם דבשי, יעירוני בבקר בבקר לתת להם לשון למודים, יתנשאו בו לעומתם על
אשר אמרו קצת המפרשים בספרי הרפואה ידברו בצואר עתק בכל חקת
ההלצה ומשפטיה, למען לא נגרע גם אנו מהקריב קרבן הספורים השלמים
למועדו· נתתי את לבי לדרוש ולתור ולגלות את אשר ידעתי בחכמת ההלצה,
עם שהיא נקלה בעניניה. וידעו כל העם אשר אני בקרבו את מעשה ה׳ ופעלו, כי
טוב הוא ונורא הוא על כל סביביו; וכל הגוים מאין ופעלם מאפע· מאפס ותוהו
נחשבו, הן איים כדק יטול.

[12] לכן מצאתי השומרים משמרת הלשון ואסובבה את מזבחותם מזוית אל
זוית, מרחוק ומקרוב. ובאתי בחצריהם ובטירותם, ובידי מנורת זהב טהור, וגולת[3]
הרצון האלהי לשמן ששון על ראשה; יאירו שבעת הנרות אל עבר פני לראות
במו אופל מקום ספיר אבניה. עברתי משך ויון ותובל ותירס, האיים הרחוקים
אלישה ותרשיש, כתים ודודנים ואספתי חיל כל הגוים: זהב ורב פנינים, לשם

5 הרפואה] הנבואה[ד] || 6 הספורים] הכפורים[ד] || 8 בעניניה] בעינינים[כ] |[ה׳][כ] || 9 [מאפע][כ] | <ותוחו>
ותוהו[ד] || 12 וגולת[3]] וגילת[כד] || 13 האלהי] האלקי[כ] || 15 אלישה] אלִשה[כ] |הגוים] גוים[כ] |ורב] ורוב[כ] ||

1 איוב כ״ח י״ג ||2 מש׳ ב׳ ד׳ |אס׳ ד׳ ג׳ |מש׳ ב׳ ד׳ ||3 אס׳ ו׳ ט׳ |יח׳ כ״ג ו׳ |שה״ש ה׳ א׳ ||4 יש׳
נ׳ ד׳ |יח׳ א׳ כ׳ ||5 תה׳ ע״ה ו׳ |במ׳ ט׳ י״ד ||6 במ׳ ט׳ ז׳ ||7 קה׳ א׳ י״ג |8 שמ׳ ל״ד י׳ ||9 תה׳ פ״ט
ח׳ |יש׳ מ׳ י״ז |יש׳ מ״א כ״ד |יש׳ מ׳ י״ז ||10 יש׳ מ׳ ט״ו ||11 יח׳ מ׳ מ״ה |תה׳ כ״ו ו׳ ||12 בר׳ כ״ה
ט״ז |שמ׳ כ״ה ל״א ||13 זכ׳ ד׳ ב׳ |תה׳ מ״ה ח׳ |במ׳ ח׳ ב׳ ||14 תה׳ י״א ב׳ |איוב כ״ח ו׳ |בר׳ י׳
ב׳ | יש׳ ס״ו י״ט ||15 בר׳ י׳ ד׳ |זכ׳ י״ד י״ד |מש׳ כ׳ ט״ו ||

[3] J's correction, based on ת.

which was revealed by prophecy to **them that dwell before the Lord** [23:18], **which no** soul's **eye had seen** [Job 28:7] without prophetic influence, direct or derived. **Man knoweth not the price thereof** [28:13] unless he **seek her as silver** [Prov. 2:4] **in every province** [Esth. 4:3] **and search for her as for hid treasures** [Prov. 2:4].[9]

[11] Since, moreover, some **of the King's most noble princes** [Esth. 6:9], **handsome young men** [Ezek. 23:6] **clothed with** [23:6] attainment, who **have eaten my honeycomb with my honey** [Song of S. 5:1], **rouse** me **morning by morning** [Isa. 50:4] to **give** to them **the tongue of them that are taught** [50:4]; whereby they may **be lifted up beside** [Ezek. 1:20] the statements of certain commentators on medical works,[10] who, using all **the statute of** Rhetoric **and the ordinance thereof** [Num. 9:14], **speak . . . insolence with a haughty neck** [Ps. 75:6], so that we too may not **be kept back from bringing the offering** of perfect descriptive statements[11] at **its appointed season** [Num. 9:7]: **I have,** accordingly, **applied my heart to seek, . . . search out** [Eccl. 1:13], and to disclose what I know about the art of rhetoric, little of the subject though this be.[12] **And all the people among which** I live shall know **the work of the Lord** [Exod. 34:10] and His doing, for He is good **and feared of all them that are round about Him** [Ps. 89:8]; while **all the nations** [Isa. 40:17] **are nothing and** their **work a thing of nought** [41:24]; **they are accounted . . . as things of nought and vanity** [40:17]: **behold, the isles are as a mote in weight** [40:15].[13]

[12] I therefore encountered **the keepers of the charge** [Ezek. 40:45] of language and **compassed** their **altars** [Ps. 26:6] from corner to corner, ancient and modern alike. I entered **their villages** and **their encampments** [Gen. 25:16] holding **a candlestick of pure gold** [Exod. 25:31], **with a bowl** of the divine will **upon the top of it** [Zech. 4:2] for **oil of gladness** [Ps. 45:8]; **the seven lamps gave light** [Num. 8:2] before my face wherewith to behold **in darkness** [Ps. 11:2] the **stones** which **are the place of sapphires** [Job 28:6]. I traversed **Meshech and Javan and Tubal and Tiras** [Gen. 10:2],[14] **the far-off isles** [Isa. 66:19] of **Elishah and Tarshish, Kittim and Dodanim** [Gen. 10:4], and

9. The view expressed in *m^elīṣāh* style here is restated more prosaically at the end of the chapter on Memory (i.13.12–14); cf. Int. §4.

10. The reading of M; C reads: "on the books of prophecy."

11. Thus M; C: "perfect atonement."

12. In this rather obscure paragraph, JML explains an immediately didactic purpose of the *N.S.*: to equip those of his pupils intent upon becoming physicians with the training that certain medical authorities were then holding an essential prerequisite of admission to the practice of medicine. The variant readings mentioned in nn. 10 and 11 above represent Conat's attempt to alter JML's statement here of a relatively narrow pedagogic purpose into the broader one of pertinence to scriptural exegesis and theology. In the fourteenth century, Petrarch condemned the attempt by physicians to subsume rhetoric within medical education and practice; in the following century, on the other hand, Salutati wrote in favor of such study (J. Seigel, *Rhetoric and Philosophy in Renaissance Humanism* [Princeton, 1968], 37–39). JML may well have been aware of this discussion.

13. That is, by virtue of the scripturally based and illustrated *N.S.*, Jewish students will be far better prepared in rhetoric than Gentiles.

14. B: "Javan and Tubal and Meshech and Tiras."

שבו ואחלמה, וסגלת מלכים והמדינות, וכלי יקר, שפתי דעת. ועשיתי עטרות, ומלאתי בהם מלואת אבן יקרה, ושמתים על ראש השרידים אשר ה׳ קורא לצפירת תפארה. אומרים אמור למנאצי: הקבצו יחדיו פליטי הגוים, חזו מפעלות ה׳! צאו וראו בעטרה שעטרה לי אמי, לתורה ולתעודה, ביום חתנתי 5 וביום שמחת לבי· אם תתנו סגור תחתיה? אם יש לכם בכיסכם אבן ואבן, גדולה וקטנה, כאשר יש לנו כל הנמצא לכבודנו? ולמה תרימו קרן, תשמיעו במרום קולכם?

[13] ועם התבונני בכל הנמצא כתוב בספר, בזאת המלאכה עזבתי קצת המאמרים לא יתנו בברותי ראש גיא שמנים; ושלחתים לנפשם, והבאתי 10 תחתיהם אמרות טהורות מדברי הנבואה אשר בהם אתפאר. ואליהם פי קראתי לכונן פשטים נפלאים, חדשים מקרוב באו, לא שערום קצת הקדמונים, והמה גבורי לאפי, עליזי גאותי.

[14] ואתה בן אדם, אם תחשוב האמנתי כי ידברו הנביאים בלשון מדברת גדולות למה שראיתי דבריהם מסכימים עם הנמצא מזה אצל קצת האומות, לב 15 הותל הטך, והמכשלה הזאת תחת ידך, ושכבה בחיקך, עמך ישב בקרבך. בקשתני ולא מצאתני, והייתי נקי מאלתך. ואם העולה על רוחך כי לכן פניתי אל הדברים ההם והאמנתים, להיותם קרובים לדברי הנבואה — יתלכדו ולא יתפרדו — אז רוחי בקרבי אשחרך· וקרא ואנכי אענה, ופי הוא המדבר הנני.

7 קולכם] כולכם[כ] || 10 ואליהם] ואלהם[ד] || 11 לא שערום <לא שערום>[כ] || 15 ידך] ידיך[כ] ||

---

1 שמ׳ כ״ח י״ט | קה׳ ב׳ ח׳ | מש׳ כ׳ ט״ו | זכ׳ ו׳ י״א || 2 שמ׳ כ״ח י״ז | יואל ג׳ ה׳ || 3 יש׳ כ״ח ה׳ | יר׳ כ״ג י״ז | יש׳ מ״ה כ׳ || 4 תה׳ מ״ו ט׳ | שה״ש ג׳ י״א | יש׳ ח׳ כ׳ | שה״ש ג׳ י״א || 5 איוב כ״ח ט״ו | דב׳ כ״ה י״ג || 6 תה׳ ע״ה ה׳ || 7 יש׳ נ״ח ד׳ || 8 דנ׳ י״ב א׳ || 9 תה׳ ס״ט כ״ב | יש׳ כ״ח א׳ | יר׳ ל״ד ט״ז || 10 תה׳ י״ב ז׳ | יש׳ מ״ט ג׳ | תה׳ ס״ו י״ז || 11 דב׳ ל״ב י״ז || 12 יש׳ י״ג ג׳ || 13 יח׳ ב׳ ו׳ | תה׳ י״ב ד׳ || 15 יש׳ מ״ד כ׳ | יש׳ ג׳ ו׳ | מל״א א׳ ב׳ | דב׳ כ״ג י״ז || 16 שה״ש ג׳ א׳ | בר׳ כ״ד מ״א | יח׳ כ׳ ל״ב || 17 איוב מ״א ט׳ || 18 יש׳ כ״ו ט׳ | איוב י״ג כ״ב | בר׳ מ״ה י״ב | יש׳ נ״ב ו׳ ||

gathered **the wealth of all the nations** [Zech. 14:14]: **gold, and a multitude of rubies** [Prov. 20:15]; **jacinth, agate, and amethyst** [Exod. 28:19]; **treasure such as kings and the provinces have as their own** [Eccl. 2:8]; and the **precious jewel, the lips of knowledge** [Prov. 20:15]. I **made crowns** [Zech. 6:11], **set in** them **settings of** precious **stones** [Exod. 28:17], and placed them **for a diadem of beauty** [Isa. 28:5] on the heads of **the remnant, those whom the Lord shall call** [Joel 3:5].[15] **They may surely say unto them that despise me** [Jer. 23:17]: "**Assemble yourselves . . . together, ye that are escaped of the nations** [Isa. 45:20]; **behold the works of the Lord** [Ps. 46:9]! **Go forth . . . and gaze upon . . . the crown wherewith** my **mother hath crowned** me [Song of S. 3:11] **for instruction and for testimony** [Isa. 8:20] **in the day of** my **espousals and in the day of the gladness of** my **heart** [Song. of S. 3:11]. Can ye **get it for gold** [Job 28:15]? Or do ye **have in** your **bag diverse weights, a great and a small** [Deut. 25:13], when we have all true reality for our glory? Wherefore do ye **lift up the horn** [Ps. 75:55–56], **make your voice to be heard on high**" [Isa. 58:4]?

[13] With **all that is found written in the book** [Dan. 12:1], in this work I have omitted some discourses which do not **put into my feast** [Ps. 69:22] **the head of the fat valley** [Isa. 28:1]. I **let them go . . . at their pleasure** [Jer. 34:16], but introduced in their stead **pure words** [Ps. 12:7] of prophetic discourse **by** which **I will be glorified** [Isa. 49:3]. **I cried unto** them **with my mouth** [Ps. 66:17], in order to establish marvellous and new literal interpretations, **which have lately come in** [Deut. 32:17], interpretations which, though not thought of by any of the ancients, are **my mighty ones for mine anger, my proudly exulting ones** [Isa. 13:3].[16]

[14] **And thou, son of man** [Ezek. 2:6], if thou thinkest I believe that the prophets speak with a **tongue that speaketh proud things** [Ps. 12:4] because I consider their words to comport with what, of the same kind, is found amongst some of the nations, **a deceived heart hath turned** thee **aside** [Isa. 44:20], **this ruin is under thy hand** [Isa. 3:6], **lieth in thy bosom** [1 Kings 1:2], **dwelleth with thee in the midst of thee** [Deut. 23:17]. Thou hast **sought** me **but found** me **not** [Song of S. 3:1], and I **shall be clear from** thy **oath** [Gen. 24:41]. But if **that which cometh into** thy **mind** [Ezek. 20:32] is that I have turned to those words and given them credence because they are close to the words of prophecy—**they stick together that they cannot be sundered** [Job 41:9]—then, **with my spirit within me I seek thee earnestly** [Isa. 26:9]; then **call thou, and I will answer** [Job 13:22], **it will be my mouth that speaketh** [Gen. 45:12], **behold, here I am** [Isa. 52:6].[17]

15. We are here informed that, having received the traditional Jewish education and mastered the seven arts of the medieval curriculum, JML studied the works of Gentile scholars and rhetoricians. He thus accumulated rich stores of knowledge which he then sought to restore to Israel as part of Israel's own scriptural heritage; cf. Int. §4.

16. The "recent" interpretations of prophetic passages which JML has, through rhetorical analysis, confirmed have been found by him to be effective in controversy.

17. In other words: it would be wrong and untrue to accuse JML of believing that the excellence of

[15] וקראתי שם זה הספר נפת צופים למה שבו מנעימות הספורים וערבותם, והוא צוף דבש אמרי נעם· הוד והדר יעטרהו, מתוק לנפש ומרפא לעצם.

[16] ויען ידיעת הכללים קודמת לידיעת הפרטים, כאשר התבאר בספר השמע, הלכתי בזה הספר מן הכלל אל הפרט למען ילקטו הדברים אחד אחד· מבלי בלבול והסתבך, רק בסדר אשר ידי הטבע כוננוהו, וימינו היא סמכתהו, למען ירוצו בו חפצי צדקו ולא ייגעו עד ימצא מקום תהלות הספורים לה׳, משכנות שפה ברורה לאביר יעקב· ולשון עלגים תמהר לדבר צחות.

[17] והיה זה הספר בכללו נחלק לארבעה שערים:

השער הראשון, יתבארו בו גדר ההלצה ותכליתה· ואם היא ראויה ליכתב· וגדר המליץ ומשמרתו· וסוגי הדבורים· והדברים הראויים למליץ· וחלקי ההמצאה.

השער השני, ידובר בו איך יושמו בהרגל חלקי המאמר בערך אל שלשה סוגי הדבור, רצוני לומר, מקיים· משפטי· עצתי· ודברים נופלים בעול וחמס· וטענות עצמיות נשגבים בהנהגה.

השער השלישי, יספר בו מן המדות· ומן מיני ההקשה המיוחדים למליץ.

השער הרביעי ידבר מן היפויים ההלציים.

[18] השער הראשון כולל ארבעה עשר פרקים:

הפרק הראשון[4]: פרק גדר ההלצה ותכליתה.

הפרק השני: אם ראויה זאת המלאכה ליכתב· ומי הוא המליץ· ומשמרתו.

1 נפת] נֹפת[כ] || 2 יעטרהו] יעטרידהו[כ] || 6 חפצי] חפיצי[כ] || 7 ברורה] ברוֹרדה[כ] || 11 שלשה] שלש[כ] || 12 רצוני לומר] ר״ל[כ] || 14 השער] שער[כ] || 17 הפרק הראשון] פרק א׳[כ][4] ||

---

1 תה׳ י״ט י״א || 2 מש׳ ט״ז כ״ד | תה׳ ח׳ ו׳ | מש׳ ט״ז כ״ד || 4 יש׳ כ״ז י״ב || 5 שמ׳ ט״ו י״ז | יש׳ נ״ט ט״ז || 6 חב׳ ב׳ ב׳ | תה׳ ל״ה כ״ז | יש׳ מ׳ ל״א | תה׳ קל״ב ה׳ | תה׳ ע״ח ד׳ || 7 תה׳ קל״ב ה׳ | צפ׳ ג׳ ט׳ | תה׳ קל״ב ה׳ | יש׳ ל״ב ד׳ ||

---

[4] Throughout the list כ writes פרק א׳, פרק ב׳, etc., where ד writes הפרק הראשון, הפרק השני, etc.

[15] I have named this book NŌPHETH ṢŪPHĪM [The Honeycomb's Flow (Ps. 19:11)], because of the sweetness and pleasance of its contents, for, indeed, **pleasant words are as a honeycomb** [Prov. 16:24]. It is **crowned with glory and honor** [Ps. 8:6], is **sweet to the soul and health to the bones** [Prov. 16:24].

[16] Now since the knowledge of principles takes precedence over that of particulars, as is explained in the *Physics*,[18] I have proceeded in this work from the general to the particular, in order that the details may **be gathered one by one** [Isa. 27:12]; not with confusion and complication, but in the order which nature's **hands have established** [Exod. 15:17] and which **His own** right hand **has sustained** [Isa. 59:16]; so that all **who delight in** His **righteousness** [Ps. 35:27] **may run . . . in it** [Hab. 2:2] **and not be weary** [Isa. 40:31] **until** there be **found** the **place** [Ps. 132:5] of the **praises of the Lord's tellings** [Ps. 78:4], **dwelling places** [Ps. 132:5] of **a pure language** [Zeph. 3:9] **for the Mighty One of Jacob** [Ps. 132:5], **and the tongue of the stammerers be ready to speak plainly** [Isa. 32:4].

[17] This work has been divided into four books:[19]

Book I, in which are set forth: the definition and aim of Rhetoric; whether the art ought to be presented in written form; the definition and function of the orator; the Kinds of Cause; the competencies of which the speaker should dispose; and the Parts of Invention.

Book II, which discusses how the parts of the discourse are handled in the three Kinds of Cause, to wit, Epideictic, Judicial, Deliberative; cases involving injustice and wrong; and forensic issues of importance in political administration.

Book III describes patterns of human character, and the types of reasoning peculiar to the rhetorician.

Book IV discusses the Figures of Speech.

[18] Book I comprises fourteen chapters:

Chapter 1: The Definition and Aim of Rhetoric

Chapter 2: Whether This Art Ought to Be Presented in Written Form; Who Is the Speaker; and His Function

---

scriptural prophecy consists of its conformity with Gentile discourses of similar character; on the contrary—and this he will gladly admit—he holds such Gentile discourses valuable and credible because they approximate scriptural prophecy. Judah Moscato, *N^e^phūṣōth Y^e^hūdhāh* (Lemberg, 1859), Sermon 5, 19b, quotes this paragraph *verbatim*. Passage i.13.14 below, cited in abridged form by A. de'Rossi, *M^e^'ōr Ēnayim* (Vilna, 1863), i.75, is another, sixteenth-century, articulation of the same idea. Cf. Int. §1.

18. I.e., Aristotle's *Physics* (φυσικὴ ἀκρόασις) [1.1(184a)], in Hebrew called *The Book of the Hearing* (סֵפֶר הַשֵּׁמַע), as here, or *The Book of the Natural Hearing* (סֵפֶר הַשֵּׁמַע הַטִּבְעִי); see J. Klatzkin, *Thesaurus Philosophicus Linguae Hebraicae* (Heb.) (Berlin, 1928–1935), IV, 133. JML read this work in both Latin and Hebrew: subsequently, as mentioned in DML's letter to David of Tivoli (Int. §3, above), he composed a commentary on several of its books. Cf. M. Steinschneider, *Hebräischen Uebersetzungen*, 108ff.; S. D. Wingate, *The Medieval Latin Versions of the Aristotelian Scientific Corpus* (London, 1931), 21–24, 39: F. E. Peters, *Aristoteles Arabus* (Leiden, 1968), 33. To proceed from generalities (κοινά) to particulars ('ἴδια) is to follow the *ordo naturae*, while to proceed from particulars to generalities is the *ordo doctrinae;* cf. G. R. T. Ross, *Aristotle, De Sensu and De Memoria* (Cambridge, 1906), 125.

19. Literally, "gates."

הפרק השלישי: פרק סוגי הרבור.
הפרק הרביעי: הדברים הראויים להיות במליץ.
הפרק החמישי: מחלקי ההמצאה.
הפרק הששי: פרק הפתיחה.
5 הפרק השביעי: פרק הפתיחה הנסתרת.
הפרק השמיני: פרק הספור.
הפרק התשיעי: פרק החלוק.
הפרק העשירי: פרק הקיום וההתרה.
הפרק אחד עשר: פרק הסדור.
10 הפרק שנים עשר: פרק הרמיזה.
הפרק שלשה עשר: פרק הזכירה.
הפרק ארבעה עשר: פרק הצחות ומיניה.
[19] ומהנה נתחיל בעזרת המלמד לאדם דעת:

---

13 תה׳ צ״ד י׳ ||

Chapter 3: The Kinds of Cause
Chapter 4: The Competencies Which the Speaker Should Possess
Chapter 5: Of the Parts of Invention
Chapter 6: Of the Introduction
Chapter 7: The Subtle Approach
Chapter 8: The Statement of Facts
Chapter 9: The Partition
Chapter 10: The Proof and Refutation
Chapter 11: The Arrangement
Chapter 12: The Delivery
Chapter 13: Memory
Chapter 14: On Style and Its Types

[19] And from here we make our beginning with the help of Him **that teacheth man knowledge** [Ps. 94:10].

הפרק הראשון

מה היא ההלצה ומה תכליתה?

[1] אמר אריסטוטילס בראשון מההלצה שענין ההלצה הוא כח עומס על
עצמו ההספקה האפשרית בכל אחד מהענינים הנפרדים. והתבאר שם שהרצון
5 בכח הוא המלאכה אשר תפעל בשני המקבילים, רצוני לומר בדבר והפכו, אלא
שלא יתחיב לה המשך התכלית המבוקש על צד ההכרח. והמשל, שאם היה
המבוקש מהמליץ חזרת האנשים רעי התכונה והמפעלים אל שלמות ההנהגות·
והרבה והפציר במאמרים הלציים בכל היכלת עד שלא הניח דבר ממה
שנתחייב לו לפי תנאי זאת המלאכה ומשפטיה· עם כל זה אפשר שלא ישיג
10 התכלית אשר אליו נשא את נפשו. והנך רואה בעיניך כמה הפליגו הנביאים
ע״ה במאמרות טהורות מזקקות, וקראו אל בני ישראל בחזקה לאמור: שובו
בנים שובבים; ויתנו כתף סוררת, גם מאז לא פתחה אזנם לשוב אל ה׳ אלקיהם.
ונוקשו ונלכדו, עלה הכורת עליהם, ספו תמו מן בלהות.

[2] והמכון ב״עומס על עצמו ההספקה האפשרית״, שיכון במאמר תכלית מה
15 שאפשר בו מן הסדור התקון והיופי לפי חקת המלאכה בענין אשר בו המאמר,
לא יפקד ממנו איש. ומה שאמר, ״בכל הדברים הנפרדים״, הוא ענין לא ימצא
כמהו במלאכות החלקיות, כי הם לא יספיקו בכל הדברים כי אם בענינים שהם

3 הוא] היא[ב] וההלצה היא[ט] || 5 רצוני לומר] ר״ל[כ] || 8 היכלת] היכול[כ] || 9 שנתחייב] שהתחייב[ד] ||

---

10 דב׳ כ״ד ט״ו | מל״ב ז׳ ב׳ || 11 תה׳ י״ב ז׳ | יונה ג׳ ח׳ || 12 יר׳ ג׳ י״ד | נחמ׳ ט׳ כ״ט | יש׳ מ״ח ח׳ | הו׳ ה׳ ד׳ || 13 יש׳ כ״ח י״ג | יש׳ י״ד ח׳ | תה׳ ע״ג י״ט ||

BOOK I

CHAPTER 1

What Is Rhetoric and What Is Its Aim?

[1] In the first Book of the *Rhetoric* Aristotle[a] says that rhetoric is a faculty which undertakes the effecting of whatever persuasion is possible on any given subject. It is there explained that by "faculty" is meant the skill that can accomplish both of two contrary results, that is, both a particular conviction and its opposite, except that achievement of the end sought will not necessarily follow. If, for example, the speaker's object should be the moral reform of men who are evil in disposition and deeds, and if he has often importuned them to such effect in speeches of a rhetoric so able that he has omitted nothing requisite according to the rules and ordinances of this art, it is nevertheless possible that he will not attain the end **upon which he has set his heart** [Deut. 24:15]. **Behold, thou mayest see it with thine own eyes** [2 Kings 7:2] how the prophets (upon whom be peace!) excelled in **pure** and **refined** discourses [Ps. 12:7], and how they **cried mightily unto** [Jonah 3:8] the children of Israel, saying: **Return, O backsliding children** [Jer. 3:14]; but the children of Israel **presented a stubborn shoulder** [Neh. 9:29], **yea, from of old** their **ear was not opened** [Isa. 48:8], **to return unto** the Lord **their God** [Hos. 5:4]. So they were **snared and taken** [Isa. 28:13], the **feller came up against** them [14:8], **they were wholly consumed by terrors** [Ps. 73:19].

[2] By "undertakes the effecting of whatever persuasion is possible" is meant the deliberate endowing of the discourse with the utmost possible order, correctness, and beauty prescribed by the art for such a subject, omitting no individual element.[1] Since he says "on any given subject," he means a faculty whose like does not exist among the several particularized arts, for none of these is capable of effecting persuasion in all cases, but only on such points as are involved in that

1. Literally, ". . . and there lacketh not one man of us" [Num. 31:49].

a. T14/A15; cf. *Rhet.* 1:12 (1355a ff.).

במלאכה ההיא. כאילו תאמר שהרפואה לא יספיק כי אם בדברים הצריכים לחכמת הרפואה· וכן בעל חכמת הגימטריאה אין לו לבאר או להוכיח דבר בלתי מצטרך אל מלאכתו· וכן בכלם, כאשר יתבאר בחפוש.

[3] אמנם ההלצה אפשר לה שתספיק בכל המלאכות ובכל הענינים; כאלו תאמר שהמליץ יספיק למי שמכחיש דבר מה התבאר ענינו בחכמת הטבע שהענין הוא כמו שהתבאר שם· וזה בהפליגו עם האיש ההוא בנעימות הספור וטוב ההלצה, מצורף לאי זו ראיה משובחת או מפורסמת, עד יביאהו לחשוב שהענין ההוא במדרגה מן הפרסום כדברים המורגשים אשר כָל אדם חזו בם. וכן הענין ביתר המלאכות.

[4] והנה הנביאים ע״ה הספיקו לאומה הישראלית בדברים כמעט אין תכלית למספרם, מהם במדות, מהם בדעות. משל הראשון: שמרו משפט ועשו צדקה, וגו׳ [יש׳ נ״ו א׳]; משל השני: שאו מרום עיניכם וראו· מי ברא אלה? המוציא במספר צבאם, וגו׳ [שם מ׳ כ״ו].

[5] ואם נאמר שההלצה היא חכמה אשר בענינים המשתפים והמיוחדים נוהגת דבור מלא ושלם, לפי מה שנמצא בקצת החבורים· או שהיא מלאכה מסדרת להפיק הרצון· או חכמת אמרות מזוקקות, כאשר יגיד קוינטיליאנו בפרק ששה עשר מן המאמר השני· או שהיא השגה מראה דרך ומשפט אמתי מן הדבור, כמו שאמר אלאנו המפרש· הכל שב אל ענין אחד כמעט עם מה שאמר הפילוסוף. כי ענין דבור מלא ושלם במאמר הראשון הוא אשר רמזהו ארסטוטילס בעומס על עצמו כו׳; וענין בכל אחד מן הענינים הנפרדים הוא מה שנאמר הנה היא חכמה אשר בענינים המשתפים והמיוחדים וכו׳. אמנם המאמר השני הוא אומר תכלית ההלצה שהיא הפקת הרצון, וזה לא זכרו ארסטוטילס במאמרו· אבל מאמר השלישי והרביעי הוא מבואר מענינם שהם נכללים במאמר הפילוסוף אשר זכרנוהו.

2 הגימטריאה] הגמאטריאה[כ] || 12 [וגו׳][כ] || 13 [במספר צבאם][כ] || 18 אל ענין] לעניין[כ] || 20 ארסטוטילס] אריסטוטילס[כ] || 23 ארסטוטילס] אריסטוטולו[כ] ||

one field. You might, for instance, say that medicine can persuade only in cases which require medical science; similarly, the geometrician is not qualified to explain or demonstrate a matter in which his skill is not required; and so with all the arts, as is clear by induction.

[3] Rhetoric, however, can effect persuasion in all fields and subjects. For example, a trained speaker can persuade a skeptic that a demonstrated proposition in natural science is indeed as has there been made evident. This the speaker accomplishes with such a person by so skillfully joining pleasing description and excellent presentation with a celebrated or generally accepted proof that he leads his interlocutor to think that this proposition is quite as accepted in common sense as the palpable things which all men perceive. Such too is the case in all other fields.

[4] The prophets (upon whom be peace!) have effected persuasion of the Israelite nation on an almost infinite number of matters, some moral, some intellectual. An example of the first sort is: **Keep ye justice, and do righteousness,** etc. [Isa. 56:1]; an example of the second: **Lift up your eyes on high, and see: who hath created these? He that bringeth out their host by number,** etc. [40:26].

[5] Whether we say that rhetoric is the art of dealing fully and perfectly in speech with both general and specialized subjects, as we find it defined in some treatises; or that it is a skill in arranging to procure assent; or the science of refined words, as Quintilian[b] declares in Chapter 16 of Book II;[2] or is the guiding concept and true criterion of utterance, as the commentator Alanus has said:[3] all these definitions amount substantially to what the Philosopher has stated. For what is said in the first definition's "dealing fully and perfectly in speech" is implied in Aristotle's "undertakes the effecting of whatever persuasion is possible," et cetera; and Aristotle's "on any given subject" is the same as the statement here about "the art of dealing with both general and specialized subjects." It is true that what the second definition says about the aim of rhetoric, namely to procure assent, is not mentioned by Aristotle in his treatise; but it is self-evident from the third and fourth definitions that these are included in that of the Philosopher mentioned above.

2. *Sic,* JML; see source footnote b for the reference in modern editions; cf. Int. §5(5).

3. Literally, "Alano" (אלאנו); this "Alanus" is almost certainly the author of the twelfth-century commentary on the *R. ad H.* described by Harry Caplan in *Of Eloquence: Studies in Ancient and Medieval Rhetoric*, ed. Anne King and Helen North (Ithaca, 1970), 247–270. Like several other scholars, A. Melammed assumes that this "Alanus" was none other than Alain de Lille ("Alanus de Insulis"); see his interesting essay "Rhetoric and Philosophy in the *Nōpheth Ṣuphīm* of R. Judah Messer Leon" (Heb.), *Italia,* I, no. 2 (1978), כ"ז [27]. Professor Caplan, however, noting that the commentary is listed by an authority on Alain (R. de Lage) among works falsely or doubtfully attributed to him, hesitates, pending further study of manuscripts of the commentary, "to assign the work to him" (p. 269). See the Int., §5(8).

b. Q. 2.15.34.

[6] אמנם תכלית ההלצה, כפי מה שהתבאר מדברי טוליאו בראשון מההלצה הישנה ומדברי ויטורינו המפרש, הוא הפקת הרצון במאמר, למה שכל מה שישתדל המליץ ולדבר גבוהה גבוהה, לשון מדברת גדולות, הוא לזה התכלית, רצוני לומר, להמשיך לבב האדם לעשות אשר יחפצהו מן הענינים, 5 לא יסור ממנו ימין ושמאל. ואמתת זה התבאר ממה שאמר שלמה המלך במשלי: שפתי צדיק ידעון רצון ופי רשעים תהפוכות [י׳ ל״ב]. כלומר, שפתי הצדיק, אשר יכוננו דבריהם בתכלית מה שאפשר מנתינת ההספקה, ידעון להשיג התכלית אשר כוונו אליו, והוא רצון האנשים. אמנם פי רשעים, אשר לא ידעו דרכי ההלצה ולא יבינו, בחשיכה יתהלכו, וישיגו דברים רבים הפכיים אל 10 מה שכוונו אליו.

[7] ולקחו בזה הגדר ״במאמר״, למה שהפקת הרצון תעשה בדברים רבים; כאלו תאמר שאדם ישיג מבקשו בתת מנות, כלי כסף וכלי זהב ושמלות· והאשה המנאפת מוכרת עמים בזנוניה וממלכות בכשפיה; ולהבדיל ביניהם אמרו בגדר הנזכר ״במאמר״, שהמליץ מפיק הרצון בסבת מאמריו מיוסדים על 15 אדני[1] פז, מתוקים מדבש ונפת צופים.

[8] אבל מה שיראה מדעות קצת הקדמונים הביאם קוינטיליאנו בפרק הששה עשר ממאמר השני, תכלית המליץ הוא לחבר במאמרו כל מה שאפשר מן הדברים לפי חקת המלאכה ומשפטיה בערך אל השגת ענין וענין. וזה התפרסם מדברי ישעיהו, באמרו: ה׳ אלקים נתן לי לשון למודים לדעת לעות את יעף 20 דבר, כו׳ [יש׳ נ׳ ד׳]. כלומר, שי״י נתן לו לשון האנשים המורגלים המפלגים בהלצה, לדעת לאמר הדברים הנמרצים בעת הראוי את יעף. וכאילו אמר התכלית מזה הלשון למודים הוא לדעת לעות דבר את יעף, רצוני לומר, לדבר דבר בעתו את יעף כפי מה שאפשר. והמכוון ביעף הצמא לשמוע דבר ה׳, כמו

6 [ידעון][כ] ‖ 9 בחשיכה] בחשכה[ד] ‖ 12 מבקשו] מבוקשו[כ] ‖ 15 אדני[1]] אבני[כד] ‖ 16 קוינטיליאנו] קווינטילאנו[כ] ‖ 18 [ומשפטיה][כ] ‖ 19 ישעיהו] ישעייהו[כ] | למודים] לימודים[כ] ‖ 20 [כו׳][ד] ‖ 23 הצמא לשמוע דבר ‹הצמא לשמוע דבר›[כ] ‖

3 שמ״א ב׳ ג׳ | תה׳ י״ב ד׳ ‖ 5 יהו׳ כ״ג ו׳ ‖ 9 תה׳ פ״ב ה׳ ‖ 12 בר׳ כ״ד נ״ג ‖ 13 מש׳ ל׳ כ׳ | נח׳ ג׳ ד׳ ‖ 15 שה״ש ה׳ ט״ו | תה׳ י״ט י״א ‖ 18 במ׳ ט׳ י״ד ‖ 23 מש׳ ט״ו כ״ג ‖

[1] So J, following ת.

[6] The aim of rhetoric, indeed, as is clear from Tully's[c] words in Book I of the Old Rhetoric and from the words of the commentator Victorinus,[c] is the procuring of assent by speech, inasmuch as the orator's entire effort—**exceeding high talk** [1 Sam. 2:3], **the tongue that speaketh proud things** [Ps. 12:4]—is to this end, namely, to attract the human mind to the accomplishing of whatever it is that the orator wishes, **turning not aside therefrom to the right hand or to the left** [Josh. 23:6]. The truth of this is evident from what King Solomon said in Proverbs: **The lips of the righteous know what is acceptable; but the mouth of the wicked is all frowardness** [10:32]. That is, **the lips of the righteous,** who carefully frame their words to be as persuasive as possible, achieve their purpose, which is the assent[4] of men. As for **the mouth of the wicked:** since these **know not** the ways of Rhetoric, **neither do they understand, they go about in darkness** [Ps. 82:5] and frequently obtain results which are the reverse of what they intended.

[7] Tully and Victorinus introduced the words "by speech" into this definition because the procuring of assent may, in fact, be accomplished by many means. For instance, a man may attain what he seeks by the bestowal of gifts, **jewels of silver and jewels of gold, and raiment** [Gen. 24:53]; while the **adulterous woman** [Prov. 30:20] **sells peoples through her harlotries and** kingdoms[5] **through her witchcraft** [Nah. 3:4]. To distinguish among these things, therefore, they say "by speech" in the aforementioned definition, for the orator procures assent because his words are **set upon sockets of fine gold** [Song of S. 5:15], are **sweeter than honey and the honeycomb** [Ps. 19:11].

[8] It would appear, however, from the opinion of some of the ancients which Quintilian[d] has introduced in chapter 16 of Book II[6] that the speaker's object is to include in his discourse all those matters which, **according to the statute of** the art **and . . . the ordinance thereof** [Num. 9:14], may be relevant to the grasping of some proposition. This view is well-known from Isaiah's words, where he says: **The Lord God hath given me the tongue of them that are taught, that I should know how to sustain with words him that is weary,** etc. [Isa. 50:4]. That is to say, the Lord gave him the language of the most expert practitioners of the rhetorical art, so as to know how to address forceful words at the proper time to one who is weary. It is, indeed, quite as if he had said that the object of this "tongue of them that are taught" is to know how to sustain with words one who is weary, that is, to speak, as far as possible, **a word in due season** [Prov. 15:23][7] to the weary. By "the weary" is meant one who thirsts to hear the word

4. In the Hebrew, "what is acceptable" [Prov. 10:32] and "assent" are the same word (רצון).
5. B: "families."
6. *Sic,* JML; cf. Int. §5(5) on the disparity between the numbering of the divisions of Quintilian's work in the text used by JML, and that of modern editions (cited here in source footnote d).
7. There is a play on words here between "to sustain" (לעות) and "in due season" (בעתו).

c. *De I.* 1.5.6; Halm, 173.
d. Q. 2.15.

ומים לשתות את היעף במדבר [שמ״ב ט״ז ב׳], על דרך לא רעב ללחם ולא צמא למים כי אם לשמוע דבר ה׳ [עמוס ח׳ י״א].

[9] ונאמר אנחנו שהגדרים הנזכרים לא יסתרו זה את זה, וגם שניהם כאחד טובים. ולהבנת זה הענין ראוי שתדע שהתכלית, ממנו חיצוני, וממנו פנימי; כאלו תאמר שתכלית השלחן הפנימי הוא שיעשה על השלמות כפי מה שאפשר בערכו· עוד, השלחן נעשה לאכול עליו, ללמוד, או לעשות דבר מה אחר, וזהוא התכלית החיצוני. וכן במה שאמרנו מן הגדרים תכלית ההלצה הוא: עשיית מה שאפשר מן המאמרים לא יפול דבר מתנאי ההלצה נקרא תכלית פנימי· אמנם הפקת הרצון הוא התכלית חיצוני, על מדרגה שהאכילה והלימוד תכלית חיצוני לשלחן.

פרק שני

אם ראויה זאת המלאכה להכתב· ומי הוא המליץ· ומשמרתו.

[1] שלשה המה מטיבי צעד, יביעו ידברו עתק: לא תקום ולא תהיה ההלצה אחת מן המלאכות, ובמספר החכמות לא תבא.

[2] ראשונה, כי בכל דור ודור קמו אנשים, בני בליעל, אשר אמרו: ללשוננו נגביר, ויבקשו לשלוח יד במלך והשרים; שתו בשמים פיהם, שמו תבל לשמה ועריו הרסו. קבר פתוח גרונם להטות מדין דלים, ואת הישרה יעקשו. אמרו לרשע צדיק אתה· לכילי נדיב יהללוהו בקהל עם· נבל נבלה ידבר, במושב זקנים

1 ומים] והיין[ת] | [את][ת] || 2 דבר] את דברי[ת] || 3 הנזכרים] הנז׳[כ] || 7 וזהוא] וזהו[כ] || 11 שני] ב׳[כ] ||

3 קה׳ י״א ו׳ || 14 מש׳ ל׳ כ״ט | תה׳ צ״ד ד׳ | יש׳ ז׳ ז׳ || 15 איוב ג׳ ו׳ || 16 מל״א כ״א י׳ | תה׳ י״ב ה׳ || 17 אס׳ ב׳ כ״א | אס׳ א׳ ט״ז | תה׳ ע״ג ט׳ | יש׳ י״ד י״ז || 18 תה׳ ה׳ י׳ | יש׳ י׳ ב׳ | מי׳ ג׳ ט׳ || 19 מש׳ כ״ד כ״ד | יש׳ ל״ב ה׳–ו׳ | תה׳ ק״ז ל״ב ||

of the Lord, as in . . . **and** water[8] **that such as are weary**[9] **in the wilderness may drink** [2 Sam. 16:2], taken in the sense of **Not a famine of bread, nor a thirst for water, but of hearing the word**[10] **of the Lord** [Amos 8:11].

[9] We ourselves would say that the aforementioned definitions do not contradict each other, even that **both are alike good** [Eccl. 11:6]. In order to understand this matter you must know that an aim may be both extrinsic and intrinsic. For instance, one may say that the intrinsic aim of a table is that it be made as perfect as anything of the sort can be. Again, a table is made to eat on, study at, or do something else, and this is the extrinsic aim. So with the definitions of the end of rhetoric which we have cited: the making of all the statements that can be made, while omitting nothing rhetorically essential, we would call the intrinsic aim; whereas the procuring of assent is the extrinsic aim, just as eating or study is the extrinsic aim of the table.

CHAPTER 2

Whether This Art Ought to Be Presented in Written Form; Who Is the Speaker; and His Function

[1] **There are three things which are stately in their march** [Prov. 30:29], **they gush out, they speak arrogancy** [Ps. 94:4]: Rhetoric **shall not stand, neither shall it come to pass** [Isa. 7:7] as one of the arts, nor shall **it come into the number of** [Job 3:6] the sciences.[1]

[2] First, in every generation, **men, base fellows** [1 Kings 21:10], have arisen **who have said: "Our tongue will we make mighty"** [Ps. 12:5], **and** who have **sought to lay hands on the king** [Esth. 2:21] **and the princes** [1:16]; who **have set their mouth against the heavens** [Ps. 73:9], **made the world a desolation**[2] **and destroyed the cities thereof** [Isa. 14:17]. **Their throat is an open sepulchre** [Ps. 5:10] **to turn aside the needy from judgment** [Isa. 10:2], **and they pervert . . . equity** [Mic. 3:9]. They say **unto the wicked: "Thou art righteous"** [Prov. 24:24], laud the **churl** as **noble** [Isa. 32:5] **in the people's assembly, . . . praise . . . in the seat of the elders** [Ps. 107:32] **the vile person who**

8. B: "and the wine."
9. JV: "faint."
10. B: "words."

1. Objection to Rhetoric and its study has been made on three essentially false grounds; these are presented and refuted in the following paragraphs.
2. B: "as a wilderness"; cf. Isa. 13:9.

יהללוהו. דורש משפט ומהיר צדק — סורו טמא, קראו למו· זקנים משער
ישביתו. ולשונם תהלך בארץ להרוס מגדלים· כל חומה בצורה יפילו. מי יתן
החרש יחרישון! והנה טוליאו בתחלת ההלצה הישנה, וקוינטיליאנו בפרק
שבעה עשר מהחלק השני, ספרו מה שהשחיתו אלה מן הארצות והישובים.
5 משאתם יגורו אלים· רבים חללים הפילו· ואין יתרון לבעל הלשון.

[3] זאת, ועוד אחרת: אשר ידי הטבע עשוהו ויכוננוהו, היצלח למלאכה?
היאמר, כאשר מימי קדם קדמתה, כי חלו בה ידי החכמה להכין אותה ולסעדה,
והיא תבא במשפט הטבעים עם זקני עמה ושריה? תתן לראשה לוית חן, ולא
ידעו גבולה איה· עטרת תפארת תמגנם, ולא הבינו את דרכה. כי יד ה׳ עשתה
10 זאת להגדיל כבוד ולהפליא תושיה עם בני אדם. להם לבדם נתנה למורשה,
ונעלמה מעיני כל חי. ומי הוא זה, ואי זה הוא, אשר לא יספר, ידבר, יגיד, ומלין
יכביר לפי הצורך והשעה? ויכלכל דבריו במשפט, ולא למד חכמה ודעת
קדושים לא ידע.

[4] ועוד: מי יתן לי מתבונות ודעת, ומה יעשה למלאכה לשון רמיה?
15 והחכמה תעוז לחכם באמרות טהורות כסף מזקק בעליל הארץ; וזאת הרשעה
היוצאת למדה לשונה דבר שקר, שוא ודבר כזב לא הרחיקה, שמה עלילות
דברים, לא לאמונה גברה בארץ. תפיח כזבים ורכו דבריה משמן; תפתח פיה,

2 תהלך] תיהלך[ב] || 3 וקוינטיליאנו] וקווינטיליאנו[ב] || 5 משאתם] משאיתם[ב] | רבים] רב׳[ב] | [הפילו][ב] ||
10 נתנה] ניתנה[ב] || 11 ומלין] ומלים[ד] || 15 באמרות] במאמרות[ב] ||

---

1 יש׳ ט״ז ה׳ | איכה ד׳ ט״ו | איכה ה׳ י״ד | 2 תה׳ ע״ג ט׳ | יח׳ כ״ו ד׳ | יש׳ ב׳ ט״ו || 3 איוב י״ג ה׳ ||
5 איוב מ״א י״ז | מש׳ ז׳ כ״ו | קה׳ י׳ י״א || 6 תה׳ קי״ט ע״ג | יח׳ ט״ו ד׳ || 7 יש׳ כ״ג ז׳ | איכה ד׳
ו׳ | יש׳ ט׳ ו׳ || 8 יש׳ ג׳ י״ד | מש׳ ד׳ ט׳ || 9 מש׳ ד׳ ט׳ | איוב כ״ח כ״ג | יש׳ מ״א כ׳ || 10 יש׳ כ״ח
כ״ט | שמ׳ ו׳ ח׳ || 11 איוב כ״ח כ״א | אס׳ ז׳ ה׳ | איוב ל״ה ט״ז || 12 תה׳ קי״ב ה׳ || 13 מש׳ ל׳ ג׳ ||
14 איוב ל״א ל״ה | מש׳ ב׳ ו׳ | יח׳ ט״ו ה׳ | תה׳ ק״כ ג׳ || 15 קה׳ ז׳ י״ט | תה׳ י״ב ז׳ | זכ׳ ה׳ ח׳ ||
16 זכ׳ ה׳ ג׳ | יר׳ ט׳ ד׳ | מש׳ ל׳ ח׳ | דב׳ כ״ב י״ד || 17 יר׳ ט׳ ב׳ | מש׳ י״ד ה׳ | תה׳ נ״ה כ״ב | מש׳ ל״א
כ״ו ||

speaks villainy [Isa. 32:6]. As for **one . . . that seeketh justice and is ready in righteousness** [Isa. 16:5]—**"Depart ye! unclean!" they cry unto them** [Lam. 4:15]; they make **the elders cease from the gate** [Lam. 5:14]. **And their tongue walketh through the earth** [Ps. 73:9] to **break down . . . towers** [Ezek. 26:4]; they cast down **every fortified wall** [Isa. 2:15]. **O that** they **would altogether hold** their **peace** [Job 13:5]! Indeed, both Tully,[a] at the beginning of the Old Rhetoric, and Quintilian,[b] in Chapter 17 of Book II,[3] have told of the countries and domains which such men have ruined. **When** they **raise** themselves **up, the mighty are afraid** [Job 41:17]; they have **cast down many wounded** [Prov. 7:26]; **and the master of language is without profit** [Eccl. 10:11].[4]

[3] This, and yet another: that which **the hands** of nature **have made . . . and fashioned** [Ps. 119:73], **is it profitable for any work** [Ezek. 15:4]?[5] Is it to be said, as **in antiquity, in ancient days** [Isa. 23:7], that the **hands** of science **fell upon her**[6] [Lam. 4:6] **to establish her and to uphold her** [Isa. 9:6], and that she **enters into judgment** of natural things **with the elders of** her **people and the princes thereof** [3:14]? **She will give to** her **head a chaplet of grace** [Prov. 4:9]; though they know not her confine, where she is, **a crown of glory will she bestow on them** [Prov. 4:9], though they **understand** not **her way** [Job 28:23]. **For the hand of the Lord hath done this** [Isa. 41:20] to magnify honor and to **make wisdom wondrous** [Isa. 28:29] amongst the sons of man. To them alone hath He **given her for a heritage** [Exod. 6:8], **seeing it is hid from the eyes of all the living** [Job 28:21]. **Who is he, and where is he** [Esth. 7:5], that will not tell, speak, declare, and **multiply words** [Job 35:16] as necessity and the moment dictate? And he **ordereth his words rightfully** [Ps. 112:5], though he has **not learned wisdom** nor **has the knowledge of holy men** [Prov. 30:3].[7]

[4] And again:[8] **Would that I had** [Job 31:35] some **discernment and knowledge** [Prov. 2:6], **but how will a deceitful tongue** [Ps. 120:3] **be meet for any work** [Ezek. 15:5]? **Wisdom is a stronghold to the wise** [Eccl. 7:19] through **pure words, as silver refined in a crucible on the earth** [Ps. 12:7]. But **this wickedness** [Zech. 5:8] **that goeth forth**[9] [5:3] has **taught** her **tongue to speak lies** [Jer. 9:4], has not **removed far . . . falsehood and lies** [Prov. 30:8], has **laid wanton charges** [Deut. 22:14], has **grown mighty in the land but not for truth** [Jer. 9:2]. She **breatheth forth lies** [Prov. 14:5] and her **words are softer than**

3. *Sic,* JML; modern reference as in source-footnote b.
4. JV: "then the charmer hath no advantage."
5. Is native ability alone sufficient, or must it be improved by training? The belief that native ability is sufficient is the basis of the second objection to Rhetoric.
6. I.e., Rhetoric.
7. JV: ". . . of the Holy One."
8. The third objection: the immorality of Rhetoric.
9. I.e., Rhetoric.

---

a. *De I.* 1.2.3 ff.
b. Q. 2.16.1 ff.

תענה עזות והמה פתיחות, ברחובות תתן קולה.
[5] והנה טוליאו בתחלת ההלצה הישנה, וקוינטיליאנו בשבעה עשר מהשני,
ורוזנים אחרים נוסדו יחד להציב גבולות ההלצה, להכין אותה ולסעדה במשפט
ובצדקה. ויקראו בקול גדול לאמר: מה לכם תדכאו הרכה, הענוגה, בית נתיבות
5 נצבה? עוד תוסיפו סרה להסירה מגבירה, הרים המצנפת והסר העטרה? והיא
בהכלי מלך ולפני כל יודעי דת ודין לבנות ולהרוס בחקת התורות ומשפטם. מות
וחיים ביד לשון לתת לאיש כפעלו. הלא היא בנתה מזבחות ההנהגה אבני גזית,
חצבה עמודיה שבעה? תתן לכל ממלכות את הנזר ואת העדות. איכה תרעה
כל מדינה ומדינה ועם ועם? ליד שערים ומבוא פתחים תרון ותאמר לאדם: הן
10 יראת ה׳ חכמה! עלו זה במעלות התבונה; הסיר מלכי הפחיתיות איש ממקומו,
ומלאי חמת ה׳ המטים עקלקלותם, אלה וכחש רצוח וגנוב ונאוף פרצו. אל
תטמאו בכל אלה, תקריבו הריק והמלא תסיעו. עברו משער לשער במחנה
וראו: מי הוא הצד ציד החשיבות, יביא בפריו אלף כסף הכשרונות, ורבוא רבבן
מגמלי אדון המציאה קדמוהי יקומון, נושאים נכאת וצרי ולוט, להסיר מאיש או
15 אשה כי יעשו אחת התועבות· גם כל חולי וכל מכה, פצע וחבורה ומכה טריה,

וקולה] קולב[ד] ||4 נתיבות] נדיבות[כ] ||9 ומבוא] ומבא[ד] |לאדם] לאדן[כ] ||11 [וגנוב][ד] ||13 ורבוא רבבן] ורבא רבוון[ד] ||15 אשה] מֹאשה[כ] ||

1 מש׳ י״ח כ״ג |תה׳ נ״ה כ״ב |מש׳ א׳ כ׳ ||3 תה׳ ב׳ ב׳ |דב׳ ל״ב ח׳ |יש׳ ט׳ ו׳ ||4 מל״ב י״ח כ״ח |יש׳ ג׳ ט״ו |יש׳ מ״ז א׳ |מש׳ ח׳ ב׳ ||5 יש׳ א׳ ה׳ |דה״ב ט״ו ט״ז |יח׳ כ״א ל״א ||6 מש׳ ל׳ כ״ח |אס׳ א׳ י״ג |יר׳ מ״ה ד׳ |במ׳ י״ט ב׳ |במ׳ ט׳ י״ד ||7 מש׳ י״ח כ״א |מש׳ כ״ד י״ב |מל״א ה׳ ל״א ||8 מש׳ ט׳ א׳ |מל״ב י״א י״ב |שה״ש א׳ ז׳ ||9 אס׳ ג׳ י״ב |מש׳ ח׳ ג׳ ||10 מש׳ ט״ו ל״ג |יח׳ מ׳ כ״ב |מל״א כ׳ כ״ד ||11 יש׳ נ״א כ׳ |תה׳ קכ״ה ה׳ |הו׳ ד׳ ב׳ ||12 וי׳ י״ח כ״ד |מל״ב ד׳ ד׳ |שמ׳ ל״ב כ״ז ||13 בר׳ כ״ז ל״ג |שה״ש ח׳ י״א |דנ׳ ז׳ י׳ ||14 בר׳ כ״ד י׳ |דנ׳ ז׳ י׳ |בר׳ ל״ז כ״ה ||15 במ׳ ה׳ ו׳ |דב׳ כ״ח ס״א |יש׳ א׳ ו׳ ||

oil [Ps. 55:22]; **she openeth her mouth** [Prov. 31:26], **answereth impudently** [18:23] with words that are **keen-edged words** [Ps. 55:22], and **uttereth her voice in the broad places** [Prov. 1:20].

[5] Now Tully,[c] at the beginning of the Old Rhetoric, Quintilian[d] in Chapter 17 of Book II[10] and other **rulers have taken counsel together** [Ps. 2:2] to **set the borders of** [Deut. 32:8] Rhetoric, **to establish it and to uphold it through justice and through righteousness** [Isa. 9:6]. And they have **cried with a loud voice** [2 Kings 18:28], saying: "**What mean ye that ye crush** [Isa. 3:15] the **tender and delicate one** [47:1] that **standeth where the paths meet** [Prov. 8:2]? Will **ye stray away more and more** [Isa. 1:5] to **remove her from being queen** [2 Chr. 15:16], **to take off the mitre and remove the crown** [Ezek. 21:31]?[11] **Yet is she in kings' palaces** [Prov. 30:28] and before **all that know law and judgment** [Esth. 1:13] to **build** and to **break down** [Jer. 45:4] by means of **the statute of the laws** [Num. 19:2] **and . . . the ordinance thereof** [9:14]. **Death and life are in the power of a tongue** [Prov. 18:21], to give **to every man according to his work** [24:12]. Is it not she that built the altars of civilization **with hewn stone** [1 Kings 5:31], that **hath hewn out her seven pillars** [Prov. 9:1]?[12] She gives all realms **the crown and the insignia** (2 Kings 11:12]. **Where does she shepherd** [Song of S. 1:7] **every province and . . . every people** [Esth. 3:12]? **Beside the gates, . . . at the coming in at the doors, she crieth aloud** [Prov. 8:3], and she says to mankind: Verily, **the fear of the Lord is . . . wisdom** [15:33]! **Ascend,** now, **the steps** [Ezek. 40:22] of understanding! **Take the kings** of baseness **away, every man out of his place** [1 Kings 20:24], and those **full of the fury of the Lord** [Isa. 51:20] who **turn aside unto their crooked ways** [Ps. 125:5], who, **swearing and lying, murdering and stealing and committing adultery, break all bounds** [Hos. 4:2]. **Defile not ye yourselves in any of these things** [Lev. 18:24], bringing near the empty and **setting aside that which is full** [2 Kings 4:4]. **Go . . . from gate to gate throughout the camp** [Exod. 32:27], and see: **Who . . . is he that hath taken the venison** [Gen. 27:33] of esteem, whose **fruit brings in a thousand pieces of the silver** [Song of S. 8:11] of advantage, **before whom stand ten thousand times ten thousand** [Dan. 7:10] **of the camels of** the **Master** [Gen. 24:10] of existence, **bearing spicery and balm and laudanum** [37:25], in order to prevent that **a man or woman should commit** [Num. 5:6] some abomination; to remove **also every sickness and every plague** [Deut. 28:61], **wounds, and bruises, and festering**

10. *Sic,* JML, modern reference as in source-footnote d.
11. B: ". . . to remove . . . take off. . . ."
12. A reference to the sevenfold division of the sciences (the *trivium* plus the *quadrivium*); see H. A. Wolfson, "The Classification of the Sciences in Medieval Jewish Philosophy," *Hebrew Union College Jubilee Volume* (Cincinnati, 1925), 236–315.

c. *De I.* 1.1.1. ff.
d. Q. 2.16.7 ff.

גם כל מדוה מצרים יתנו יקר מזולל? אותו תלבישו מלכות, לתת בידו מקל עוז ומטה תפארה, ובלעדו לא ירים איש את ראשו ואת רגלו; הוא ישא הוד וישב על כסא רם ונשא· הוא ישפוט תבל בצדק, יעודד ענוים, ישיב רשעים לשאולה, יכה עמים בעברה, כל גוים שכחי אלקים.

[6] הן אלה קצות דרכיה. והיתה סחרה ואתננה קדש לה׳ מדי יום ביומו· לא יותן סגור תחתיה, נופך ספיר וברקת. ומי יספר כל תהלתה? ואם מימים ימימה באו פריצים וחללו יפעתה, נשאו את רדידה מעליה, ויעדו מלבושיה, שש ומשי ורקמה, להשתחוות ולזבוח לעשתורת אלהי צדונים, או למלכם שקוץ עמונים· העל זאת תאבל הארץ? והכרת תכרת הנפש ההיא התמימה, לרשת משכנות הקצף — וחרון על כל המונה — לבנות את במות התופת וגיא בן הנום· תגלה ערותה, ותעל צחנתה, והיתה דראון לכל בשר?

[7] שוטטו נא בחוצות היצירה, תחת שמי ה׳ מים עד ים, באיים הרחוקים, ומנהר עד אפסי ארץ· ובקשו ברחובותיה אם תמצאו אור כי יהל תמיד, לא יחשה. ולא יבואו ימי הפקדה בארץ עיפתה כמו אפל? ולא יגיעו ימי השילום, להיות ענן לבושו וערפל חתלתו? ומי משלנו ידמה לעליון, בל יסע יתדותיו לנצח, מתנשא לאמר: אני אמלוך לעולם ועד, במשפט ובצדקה יגה שביב אשי, ונגע לא יקרב באהלי· וילעג לשאת לספחת ולבהרת? מי יאמר: זכיתי לבבי· אשכיר חציו מדם העצלה, ממותי חללים תמות, וחרב תאכל בשר התאוה· בצדקתי החזקתי ולא ארפה· לא אמוט לעולם· היעזוב מצור שלג לבנון? כי מי

1 מדוה] מדוי[ד] | לתת <אותן>[כ] || 3 ישיב] ישֹׁוב[כ] || 5 והיתה] והיה[ת] | מדי] מידי[כ] || 8 צדונים] צידוני׳[כ] || 10 וחרון] והחרון[כ] | וגיא] וגי[ר] || 14 כמו] כמ[כ] | השילום] השלום[ר] || 15 יתדותיו] ידותיו[כ] || 16 ועד] וועד[כ] || 17 באהלי] באהלו[כ] | זכיתי] זיכיתי[כ] || 18 ממותי] מימותי[כ] || 19 ארפה] ארפיה[כ] ||

---

1 דב׳ כ״ח ס׳ | יר׳ ט״ו י״ט | אס׳ ה׳ א׳ | יר׳ מ״ח י״ז || 2 בר׳ מ״א מ״ד | זכ׳ ו׳ י״ג || 3 יש׳ ו׳ א׳ | תה׳ צ״ו י״ג | תה׳ קמ״ז ו׳ | תה׳ ט׳ י״ח || 4 יש׳ י״ד ו׳ | תה׳ ט׳ י״ח || 5 איוב כ״ו י״ד | יש׳ כ״ג י״ח || 6 איוב כ״ח ט״ז | יח׳ כ״ח י״ג | תה׳ ט׳ ט״ו | שמ״א א׳ ג׳ || 7 יח׳ ז׳ כ״ב | יח׳ כ״ח ז׳ | שה״ש ה׳ ז׳ | יח׳ ט״ז י״ג || 8 שמ״א א׳ ג׳ | מל״א י״א ה׳ || 9 יר׳ ד׳ כ״ח | במ׳ ט״ו ל״א | חב׳ א׳ ו׳ || 10 יח׳ ז׳ י״ב | יר׳ ז׳ ל״א || 11 יש׳ מ״ז ג׳ | יואל ב׳ כ׳ | יש׳ ס״ו כ״ד || 12 יר׳ ה׳ א׳ | איכה ג׳ ס״ו | תה׳ ע״ב ח׳ | יר׳ ל״א י׳ || 13 תה׳ ע״ב ח׳ | יר׳ ה׳ א׳ | איוב ל״א כ״ו || 14 יש׳ ס״ב ו׳ | הו׳ ט׳ ז׳ | איוב י׳ כ״ב | הו׳ ט׳ ז׳ || 15 איוב ל״ח ט׳ | תה׳ פ״ט ז׳ | יש׳ י״ד י״ד | יש׳ ל״ג כ׳ || 16 מל״א א׳ ה׳ | שמ׳ ט״ו י״ח | יר׳ ד׳ ב׳ | איוב י״ח ה׳ || 17 תה׳ צ״א י׳ | וי׳ י״ד נ״ו | מש׳ כ׳ ט׳ || 18 דב׳ ל״ב מ״ב | יח׳ כ״ח ח׳ | דב׳ ל״ב מ״ב || 19 איוב כ״ז ו׳ | תה׳ ל׳ ז׳ | יר׳ י״ח י״ד ||

sores [Isa. 1:6]; even **all the diseases of Egypt** [Deut. 28:60] do they render **precious out of vile** [Jer. 15:19]. Him should ye garb in **royal apparel** [Esth. 5:1], giving into his hand **the strong staff** and **the beautiful rod** [Jer. 48:17]; **without** him **shall no man lift his head or his foot** [Gen. 41:44]; **he shall bear the glory and shall sit** [Zech. 6:13] **upon a throne high and lifted up** [Isa. 6:1]: **he will judge the world with rightousness** [Ps. 96:13], **uphold the humble** [Ps. 147:6], make **the wicked return to the nether-world** [Ps. 9:18], **smite the peoples in wrath** [Isa. 14:6], **even all the nations that forget God** [Ps. 9:18].

[6] **"Lo, these are but the outskirts of** her **ways** [Job 26:14]. **And her gain and her hire are holiness to the Lord** [Isa. 23:18] each day: **it cannot be gotten for gold** [Job 28:15], the **carbuncle, sapphire,** or **smaragd** [Ezek. 28:13]. Who **may tell of all** her **praise** [Ps. 9:15]? But if, **from year to year** [1 Sam. 1:3], **robbers shall enter** [Ezek. 7:22] **and . . . defile** her **brightness** [28:7], **take away** her **mantle from** her [Song of S. 5:7], and remove her **raiment . . . of fine linen, and silk, and richly woven work** [Ezek. 16:13] in order **to worship and to sacrifice unto** [1 Sam. 1:3] **Ashtoreth the goddess of the Zidonians** or unto **Milcom the detestation of the Ammonites** [1 Kings 11:5]: **for this shall the earth mourn** [Jer. 4:28]? Shall **that** innocent **soul utterly be cut off** [Num 15:31], so as **to possess** the **dwelling places** [Hab. 1:6] of wrath—**for wrath is upon all the multitude thereof** [Ezek. 7:12]—to **build the high places of Topheth** and **the valley of the son of Hinnom** [Jer. 7:31]? **Shall** her **nakedness be uncovered** [Isa. 47:3], her **ill savour come up** [Jocl 2:20], **and** she **be an abhorring to all flesh** [Isa. 66:24]?

[7] "**Run ye to and fro now through the streets of** [Jer. 5:1] creation, **under the heavens of the Lord** [Lam. 3:66] **from sea to sea** [Ps. 72:8], **in the isles afar off** [Jer. 31:10], **and from the River**[13] **unto the ends of the earth** [Ps. 72:8]; **and seek in the broad places thereof if ye can find** [Jer. 5:1] **a light which shall shine** [Job 31:26] **and never cease**[14] [Isa. 62:6]. Do not **the days of visitation come** [Hos. 9:7] upon a **land of darkness thick as darkness itself** [Job 10:22]? And will not **the days of recompense** [Hos. 9:7] arrive, **the garment** whereof is **the cloud and thick darkness the swaddling band for it** [Job 38:9]? **Who** of our kind **can be compared unto** [Ps. 89:7] **the Most High** [Isa. 14:14], **whose stakes shall never be plucked up** [Isa. 33:20]? Who can **exalt himself, saying, 'I will be king** [1 Kings 1:5] **forever and ever** [Exod. 15:19]; **in justice and in righteousness** [Jer. 4:2] **shall the spark of my fire . . . shine** [Job 18:5], **nor shall any plague come nigh my tent,'** [Ps. 91:10]; and scoff at **rising . . . scab and . . . bright spot** [Lev. 14:56]? **Who can say: 'I have made my heart clean** [Prov. 20:9]; **I will make** its **arrows drunk with** the **blood** [Deut. 32:42] of idleness, which **shall die the deaths of them that are slain** [Ezek. 28:8], and the **sword shall devour the flesh** [Deut. 32:42] of lust; **my righteousness I hold fast**

13. The Euphrates.
14. JV: ". . . be silent."

הנהר העצומים והרבים, ושטפו כפעם בפעם עיר ויושביה׃ או כי ארצות
ומדינות תהומות יכסיומו מטעם המלך וגדוליו׃ כי הרבו לפשוע, ויבאו המים
בקרבם.

[8] ואם יצאה אש אלקים ותאכל בקצה המחנה׃ ולהבה תלהט הרים מנפש
5 ועד בשר תכלה׃ העל זה תכחד מן הארץ, לא תבא עוד אלינו, לא תראה ולא
תמצא? גם כי תחוד חידה, ותמשול משל, ובשקר תסתר שרתי במדינות מדי
חודש בחדשו׃ הלכן יסחבוה צעירי הצאן סחוב והשלך, ויז מדמה אל הקיר,
ברגלים תרמס, ועל עפר תשכב? יעלו עליה קהל לאמר: אל תפקדו את
הארורה הזאת׃ שמטוה, וישמטוה? הלא אלה כעדי תלבש לדעת לעות את יעף
10 דבר; ותקשרם ככלה להורות דעה, להבין שמועה. וכי כבדה אזן משמוע אם לא
תברא חדשה, אז תהפוך אל עמים בשפה ברורה, בתודה וקול זמרה תטיב נגן
תרבה שיר, בנתה טורים בחרוזים למען תזכר; גם כי שמעה קול אלה במחנה,
בשנאה תעורר מדנים, תפקד צבא מלחמה, תטיב את דרכה לבקש אהבה,
וישנה את נערותיה לטוב. ומה תכעיסוה גם כעס? מה פשעה ומה חטאתה?
15 ומה שמץ דבר נמצא בה!

[9] והנה זה מה שהשיבו האנשים האלה תשובה נצחת על הראשון והאחרון
מהמאמרים המדברים סרה על זאת המלאכה. והמאמר הנשאר התירו
הפילוסוף בראשון מההלצה, באמרו: וימצאו הרבה שיגיעו למכוונם בזה הפעל.

1 הנהר] נהר[כ] ‖ 6 מדי] מידי[כ] ‖ 7 יסחבוה] יחסבוה[כ] ‖ 8 תרמס] תרמסנה[כת] ‖ 10 דעה] דעת[כ] | להבין] ולהבין[כ] ‖ 13 מלחמה] המ֗לחמה[כ] ‖ 18 וימצאו הרבה] וימצא הרבה מהם[ט] | שיגיעו] יגיע[gט] יגיעו[aט bט] ‖

---

1 יש׳ ח׳ ז׳ | יר׳ מ״ז ב׳ ‖ 2 שמ׳ ט״ו ה׳ | יונה ג׳ ז׳ | עמ׳ ד׳ ד׳ ‖ 4 במ׳ ט״ז ל״ה | במ׳ י״א א׳ | תה׳ פ״ג ט״ו ‖ 5 יש׳ י׳ י״ח | שמ׳ ט׳ ט״ו | שופ׳ י״ג ח׳ ‖ 6 יח׳ י״ז ב׳ | יש׳ כ״ח ט״ו | איכה א׳ א׳ ‖ 7 יש׳ ס״ו כ״ג | יר׳ מ״ט כ׳ | יר׳ כ״ב י״ט | מל״ב ט׳ ל״ג ‖ 8 יש׳ כ״ח ג׳ | איוב כ׳ י״א | יח׳ כ״ג מ״ו | מל״ב ט׳ ל״ד ‖ 9 מל״ב ט׳ ל״ג | יש׳ מ״ט י״ח | יש׳ כ״ח ט׳ | יש׳ נ״ט א׳ ‖ 10 יש׳ מ״ט י״ח | יש׳ כ״ח ט׳ | יש׳ נ״ט א׳ ‖ 11 יש׳ ס״ה י״ז | צפ׳ ג׳ ט׳ | יש׳ נ״א ג׳ ‖ 12 יש׳ כ״ג ט״ז | וי׳ ה׳ א׳ ‖ 13 מש׳ י׳ י״ב | יש׳ י״ג ד׳ | יר׳ ב׳ ל״ג ‖ 14 אס׳ ב׳ ט׳ | שמ״א א׳ ו׳ | בר׳ ל״א ל״ו ‖ 15 איוב כ״ו י״ד ‖ 17 דב׳ י״ג ו׳ ‖

and will not let it go [Job 27:6]; **I shall never be moved** [Ps. 30:7]; **doth the snow of Lebanon fail from the rock'** [Jer. 18:14]? If **the waters of the river** are indeed **mighty and many** [Isa. 8:7], **and they overflow,** now and then, **a city and its inhabitants** [Jer. 47:2], or if **the deeps cover** [Exod. 15:5] lands and provinces **by the decree of the King and His nobles** [Jonah 3:7], it is because they have **multiplied transgression** [Amos 4:4] that the waters have come into their midst.

[8] ''And if the **fire** of God has **come forth** [Num. 17:35] **and devoured in the uttermost part of the camp** [Num. 11:1], **if the flame that setteth the mountains ablaze** [Ps. 83:15] **consumes both soul and body** [Isa. 10:18]: shall Rhetoric on this account **be cut off from the earth** [Exod. 9:15], not **come again unto us** [Judg. 13:8], neither be seen nor found? Moreover, because **the princess**[15] **among the provinces** [Lam. 1:1] **from one new moon to another** [Isa. 66:23] **puts forth a riddle and speaks a parable** [Ezek. 17:2] or **hides** herself **in falsehood** [Isa. 28:15]: shall **the least of the flock** therefore **drag** her **away** [Jer. 49:20], **drawn and cast forth** [Jer. 22:19]? Shall **some of her blood** be **sprinkled on the wall** [2 Kings 9:33], **shall** she **be trodden under foot** [Isa. 28:3], and **shall** she **lie down in the dust** [Job 20:11]? **Shall an assembly be brought up against** her [Ezek. 23:46], saying: '**Look** not **after this cursed woman** [2 Kings 9:34]; **throw her down**'; so shall **they throw her down** [9:33]? Does she not **clothe** herself **with** these things **as with an ornament** [Isa. 49:18], **that** she **should know how to sustain with words him that is weary** [50:4]? She **girds** herself **with them, like a bride** [49:18], in order to **teach knowledge, . . . make the message understood** [28:9]. For when the **ear is heavy, that it cannot hear** [59:1] if she **create** not . . . **a new** [65:17] thing, **then** she **turns to the peoples with a pure language** [Zeph. 3:9]; with **thanksgiving and the voice of song** [Isa. 51:3] she **makes sweet melody, sings many songs** [23:16], constructs lines in verses so that the message be remembered. Moreover, when she **heareth the voice of adjuration** [Lev. 5:1] in the camp, that with **hatred stirreth up strife** [Prov. 10:12], that **mustereth the host of battle** [Isa. 13:4], she **trims her way to seek love** [Jer. 2:33]; and it has **advanced her and her maidens to the best** [Esth. 2:9]. Why, then, **vex her sore** [1 Sam. 1:6]? **What is** her **trespass, what is her sin** [Gen. 31:36]? **And how small a whisper** [Job 26:14] can be found against her!''

[9] What has just been said is the convincing reply made by these men [Tully, Quintilian, and others][e] to the first and last of the statements which **speak perversion against** [Deut. 13:6] this art. As for the remaining charge, the Philosopher[f] refuted it in Book I of the *Rhetoric,* where he says: ''Many succeed

15. I.e., Rhetoric.

e. *De I.* 1.1 ff.; Q. 1.16.1 ff.
f. T6/A4; cf. *Rhet.* 1.1 (1354a).

ומבני אדם מי שיפעל זה בהזדמן, ומהם מי שיפעלהו בהרגל וקנין קיים. וידוע שמי שיפעל זאת המלאכה בקנין קיים הוא יותר חשוב ממי שיפעלנה בהזדמן, כי אשר ידע בסבה אשר בה יפעל פעולתו יותר תמים ויותר מעלה. וזה הענין ידעוהו ההמון, כל שכן היחידים סגלות· לכן היה מחויב שיוחקו חלקי זאת המלאכה בספר, ולא יהיה מספיק הנמצא מזה בטבע לבד ולא בהרגל, כמו הענין בהרבה מהמלאכות ההקשיות.

[10] אמנם מהו המליץ הוא דבר הוקשה אל קצת המחברים, מצד שקצתם שיחשבו, כמו שאמר קוינטיליאנו בפרק השני מן החלק השנים עשר (גם ויטורינו בפירוש ההלצה הישנה, והמפרש אלאנו), שימנע בחק המליץ השלם שלא יהיה אדם טוב וצדיק. והביאו לזה צדדים רבים מצד הפרסום להוכיח דעתם: מהם, שהמליצים הנמרצים שהיו בכל דור ודור היו בריאי ההנהגה וטובים, קראו בשמותם עלי אדמות· ומהם, שהניחו שאי אפשר למליץ שיספיק בדברים תמימי ההספקה אם לא יהיו פיו ולבו שלם. רצוני לומר, כי היאך יעורר על הצדק והיושר באופן הראוי ולבו יקבץ און לו לעות אדם בריבו?

[11] והנה יביא במאמר השלישי מהחלק השנים עשר הדברים הראוים למליץ, וקודם מחלק הפילוסופיא לשלשה חלקים כפי חלוקת קצת המחברים, רצוני לומר, לטבעית מדינית דברית. ואין ספק שהחלק השלישי, רצוני לומר, הדברית, כלה ראויה למליץ: אם הדקדוק, לדעת ענין השם והפעל והמלה ואת מוצאם ואת מובאם, ולהבין כל מה שימשך אליהם מן ההוראות והשמושים באופן שלם; ואם ההלצה, לא יפקד ממנה מאומה כי היא מלאכתו המיוחדת, דדיה ירווה בכל עת; ואם ההגיון, צריך לו מאד להתוכח עם שכנגדו ולהבדיל בין הכזב והצדק, בין הטמא ובין הטהור; אלא שלא יצטרך לרדת עד תכלית דקדוקיו ופלפוליו, כי אין מחק המליץ להוכיח הדבר בדיוקים ועמוקות כאשר יעשה בעל מלאכת ההגיון, אלא שיתחייב בערכו להביא דברים תמימי

1 וקנין] ובקנין[ט] || 2 וידוע שמי שיפעל] וידוע שאשר יפעל[ט] | [הוא][ט] | ממי שיפעלנה] מאשר יפעלנה[ט] || 3 כי אשר ידע בסבה] וכאשר היה זה כן הנה אשר (מי ש'[טa bv]) יפעלנה בקנין קיים וידע בסבה[ט] | הענין] ענין[טg bv] || 4 סגלות] הסגלות[טg] | לכן] ולכן[ט] || 5 בטבע] הטבע[כ] || 8 השני] שני[כ] || 16 קצת המחברים <קצת המחברים>[כ] || 19 ואת מובאם] ומובאם[כ] || 20 [כי][כ] ||

11 תה׳ מ״ה י״ח || 12 תה׳ מ״ט י״ב || 14 תה׳ מ״א ז׳ | איכה ג׳ ל״ו || 18–19 שמ״ב ג׳ כ״ה || 20 שמ״א כ״ה כ״א || 21 מש׳ ה׳ י״ט || 22 וי׳ י״א מ״ז ||

in achieving their purpose through exercise of this faculty. Some men do this by chance, others by virtue of habit and of permanent endowment. Of course, one whose practice of this art is by virtue of permanent endowment is worthier than one whose practice is by chance; for he who knows the cause whereby he achieves his effect is the more complete and more excellent. Now the general public has some knowledge of this matter, to say nothing of the chosen few.[16] Inevitably, therefore, the several divisions of this art have been written down in book form, since neither will any natural aptitude alone, nor what may be acquired through habit, be sufficient, just as is true in many of the dialectic arts."

[10] Objection has, indeed, been raised against certain writers with the question, "What, then, distinguishes and defines the orator?" For there are some who think, as Quintilian[g] says in Chapter 2 of Book XII (Victorinus[h] too, in the commentary on the Old Rhetoric, and the commentator Alanus[17]), that a perfect orator cannot, in the nature of the case, be other than a good and righteous man. In proof of their opinion, they have presented many obviously valid arguments. One of these is that the most effective speakers **in all generations** [Ps. 45:18] have been morally sound and good men: **lands are called after their names** [Ps. 49:12]. In another they affirm that it is impossible for a speaker to succeed in persuading with even the most wholly persuasive of words unless both his mouth and his heart be whole. For how, that is to say, can he fittingly arouse others to righteousness and uprightness while **his heart gathereth iniquity to itself** [Ps. 41:7] **to subvert a man in his cause** [Lam. 3:36]?

[11] Now in Chapter 3 of Book XII,[18] [Quintilian][i] cites the disciplines proper to a speaker, first following several other writers in partitioning philosophy into three divisions: natural, ethical, and dialectical. There can be no doubt that the third division—the dialectical—is entirely proper to the speaker: whether as Grammar, **to know** noun, verb and particle and their **going out and** their **coming in** [2 Sam. 3:25], and to have sound understanding of all their entailed meanings and usages; or as Rhetoric, of which **nothing** may **be missed** [1 Sam. 25:21] because that is the speaker's own special art, whose **breasts satisfy** him **at all times** [Prov. 5:19]; or as Logic, much needed by him in debate with his opponent, and in distinguishing between the false and the true, **between the unclean and the clean** [Lev. 11:47]. The orator need not plumb the depths of logic in all its fine points and subtleties, for it is not absolutely essential to his function that he demonstrate his proposition with as profoundly accurate precision as the professional logician, but it is his obligation in this regard to introduce the most

16. JML and T[ab]: היחידים סגלות (T[g]: היחידים הסגלות) < A: الخواص = "the educated."
17. *Supra*, chap. 1, n. 3.
18. *Sic*, JML; modern reference as in source-footnote i.

g. Q. 12.2.1 ff.; cf. 2.16 ff.
h. Halm, 168.
i. Q. 12.2.10 ff.

ההספקה עם המשלים וראיות מפרסמות יעמדו עליהם השומעים בקלות.

[12] ואם החלק השני, רצוני לומר, הפילוסופיא המדינית, התחייבה אליו בשלמות, כי כל זאת המלאכה תבנה עליה: אם שירצה ליעץ לשבח או לגנות, ולהבין ארחות משפט, שהם אשר יסוב עליהם המליץ, כל זה הוא דבר יתבאר 5 ענינה בפילוסופיא המדינית.

[13] ואם החלק הראשון, הוא מבואר שהוא גם כן מן הדברים הראוים לו, למה שיפול הדבור הרבה בסוג העצתי בעבודת האלקים, כמו שיתבאר: עם שראוי לדעת הנהגת השם יתעלה בעולם למען יוכל האדם להתקרב אל בוראו, ולשמור חקותיו ותורותיו, ולכוון בכל כח אל זאת ההנהגה, ויברח מפני זה 10 מתאוות העולם ותענוגות בני אדם אשר לא יתנוהו השב רוחו אל האלקים אשר נתנה. ואל תפלא באמרנו בחלק הראשון בעבודת האלקים, עם שהיא הפילוסופיא טבעית, למה שהמכוון אצלם בטבעית החכמה האלקית, כמו שאמר ויטורינו המפרש בהלצה הישנה: שהטבעית היא אשר תספר מענינים האלקיים, והפילוסופיא המדינית היא האומרת מענינים המיוחסים לאדם 15 בהנהגת המדינות. סוף דבר, לפי דברי זה החכם, המליץ הוא אדם טוב, בקי[1] בלשון לימודים: ומשמרתו הוא שיוכל לדבר, כפי מה שאפשר, בכל הדברים שהם מיוסדים מצד הדתות והמדות אל ההרגל המדיני עם הפקת רצון השומעים, כמו שאמר טוליאו בהלצה החדשה: או שהוא הדבור כפי הראוי להפקת הרצון, כאשר אמר בישנה.

20 [14] והנה אם תתבונן בדברי שלמה המלך, יתבאר לך כל מה שאמרנו למעלה ממאמר אחד קצר אשר בו מן הפלא מה שלא יעלם, וזה שהוא אמר: כסף נבחר לשון צדיק: לב רשעים כמעט [משלי י׳ כ׳]. והרצון בכסף הנבחר, הכסף אשר הוא נקי מן הסיגים בתכלית מה שאפשר בערכו מן השלימות. ורמז בזה אל הספור הנאות אשר בתכלית; וכאלו אמר שלשון הצדיק הוא הספור 25 הנאות אשר בתכלית, והתנה במליץ הטוב והשלם שיהיה צדיק. והנה זה שב

2 התחייבה] התחייב^ג || 4 יתבאר] התבאר^ד || 8 יתעלה] ית׳^ג || 12 הפילוסופיא] הפילוסופיאה^ג | האלקית] האלהית^ג || 13 הישנה] היישנה^ג || 14 האלקיים] האלהיים^ג || 15 בקי[1]] נקי^כד 11

4 מש׳ ב׳ ח׳ || 9 בר׳ כ״ו ה׳ || 10 איוב ט׳ י״ח || 11 קה׳ י״ב ז׳ || 16 יש׳ נ׳ ד׳ ||

[1] Emended in accordance with the text at p. 38, line 2.

perfectly persuasive of arguments, together with examples and commonsense proofs that his audience can easily understand.

[12] As for the second division—ethical philosophy—the whole of it is needed by the speaker, for the entire art of Rhetoric is built upon it. Whether he intends to give counsel, to praise or to censure, or to offer understanding of **the paths of justice** [Prov. 2:8], these being undertakings to which a speaker must address himself, in every case there is an argument whose point will be demonstrated by means of ethical philosophy.

[13] And as for the first division it is also obvious that it too must be among the disciplines proper to the orator, since in theology much of the speaking is clearly going to be of the Deliberative type. In addition, one must know the order instituted by God (be He exalted!) in the world, so that man can draw near to his Creator, **keep**. . . His **statutes** and His **laws** [Gen. 26:5], and try with all his might to conform to this order; he may thus be able to escape the lusts of the world and the pleasures of mankind which **do not suffer** him **to restore** [Job 9:18] his **spirit . . . unto God who gave it** [Eccl. 12:7]. Be not surprised at our referring to theology as in the first division, or that, additionally, we refer to it as natural philosophy, since what these Gentiles mean by ''natural'' is God's wisdom. As Victorinus,[j] the commentator on the Old Rhetoric, says: ''Natural philosophy is an account of divine matters, ethical philosophy that which treats of matters of human concern in the political order.'' In fine, according to this scholar, the orator is a good man, well versed in **the tongue of them that are taught** [Isa. 50:4]; and, as Tully[k] has said in the New Rhetoric, it is his function as far as possible to be able to discuss all the matters which are ordained by law and custom for the uses of citizenship, and this, moreover, to the satisfaction of his hearers. Or, as he said in the Old,[l] the speaker's function is to speak in the manner best adapted to satisfying his hearers.

[14] Now if you study the words of King Solomon, all that we have said above will be obvious to you from one short statement which is too marvellous to go unremarked, the one in which he says: **The language of the righteous is choice silver; the heart of the wicked is little worth** [Prov. 10:20].[19] By ''choice silver'' he means the silver which is as entirely free of dross as it possibly can be. He has thus alluded to the most appropriate sort of verbal communication; it is as though he had said that the language of the righteous is the most appropriate kind of verbal communication, and had set as the condition *sine qua non* of the good

19. JML uses allegorical (i.e., ''philosophical'') interpretation in the case of those Biblical passages (like this one) in which he believes rhetorical principles are taught and enjoined. Biblical passages which he considers applications, exemplifications, or illustrations of rhetorical doctrine are generally interpreted by him according to his conception of their literal sense.

---

j. Halm, 160.
k. *R. ad H.* 1.2.2.
l. *De I.* 1.5.6.

אל גדר המליץ אשר ספרו קוינטיליאנו, שהוא אדם טוב בקי בלשון למודים. כי
כל אדם טוב, בקי בלשון למודים, יצדק עליו שהוא צדיק לו הספור הנאות
בתכלית, כי זה הוא המכוון בלשון למודים. וכן להפך, שהצדיק, בעל הספור
הנאות אשר בתכלית, הוא האדם הטוב הבקי בלשון למודים. והמכוון בצדיק
5 הנה האדם אשר לו הצדק אשר במדות ובדעות; ולהורות על זה אמר אחר כן
לב רשעים, והיה ראוי שיאמר, להסכים עם ראשית הפסוק, וכסף סיגים לשון
רשע· אלא שרצה בזה המאמר להורות שלא התחייב למליץ השלם השלמות
אשר במדות לבד, אמנם התחייב לו גם כן השלמות בדעות. ולזה אמר שהרשע
אי אפשר שיעשה זה, כי עם היותו בעל הפחיתיות שהוא רשע — כי כן יקרא
10 הרשע סתם — הוא גם כן חסר השכל, אין תבונה בו, אשר זה בחלוף מה
שהתחייב אל המליץ השלם כמו שהתבאר. וזה מה שרצה בלב רשעים כמעט;
ותהיה הכ"ף לאמת, כמו אותו כהיום תמצאון אותו [שמ"א ט׳ י"ג]. ולו אמר
בלבד כסף נבחר לשון צדיק וכסף סיגים לשון רשע, היה המכוון בצדיק שלם
המדות· וכן היה המובן ברשע פחות המדות; ובמה שיצא משטתו ואמר לב
15 רשעים כמעט תחת מה שהיה ראוי לאמר כסף סיגים לשון רשע, גלה דעתו
שהרצון בצדיק בזה המקום שלם המדות והדעות· והמכוון ברשע חסר המדות
והדעות והנה התנה במליץ הטוב שיהיה חכם ושלם במדות, כמו שהתפרסם
למעלה מדברי קוינטיליאנו. ויען הדבר המתואר בו הצדיק אין ספק בטובו
וביפיו, והיה שלמות הלשון אשר היא ההלצה מתואר לצדיק, התחייב מזה
20 שזאת המלאכה ראויה וטובה וגדולת השלמות והתועלת· גם כי היא דבר יתוקן
במלאכה, כאשר הענין כן בכסף.

1–2 [כי כל אדם טוב בקי בלשון למודים]ᶜ || 5 אחר כן] א"כᶜ || 12 ולו] ולאᶜ || 14 המובן] המכוןᶜ ||
19 שלמות] משלימותᶜ ||

---

1 יש׳ נ׳ ד׳ || 10 ער׳ ז׳ ||

and sound speaker that he be a righteous man. Now this, of course, adverts to the definition of the orator as described by Quintilian,[m] that he is a good man, well versed in **the tongue of them that are taught** [Isa. 50:4]. For it will be true of any good man, well versed in **the tongue of them that are taught,** that he is a righteous person whose powers of verbal communication are of the most appropriate kinds, since such is the meaning of **the tongue of them that are taught.** Conversely, too, the righteous man, the master of extremely appropriate communication, is the good man, well versed in **the tongue of them that are taught;** by "righteous" here is meant the man who possesses both ethical and intellectual rectitude. To indicate this Solomon goes on to say **the heart of the wicked is little worth,** though what should have been said, for the sake of consonance with the first half of the verse, is "but silver dross is the language of the wicked." We may infer, therefore, that by saying this, Solomon intended to teach that the sound speaker requires not only soundness in ethics, but soundness in matters of intellect also. This, moreover, is why he says that it is impossible for the wicked man to be made into a sound speaker: because the wicked man, in addition to possessing viciousness—which is wickedness, for wickedness in the abstract will so be called—is also deficient in intelligence; he is one **in whom there is no discernment** [Obad. v. 7]—the very opposite of what is required of the sound speaker, as has been made clear. This, then, is what Solomon meant by **the heart of the wicked is little worth.** The *kaph* of *kim^{e}'at* ["little worth"; literally, "like" or "as a little"] is used to indicate precision,[20] as **At this time** [k^{e}hayyōm] **ye shall find him** [1 Sam. 9:13]. If he had merely said "The language of the righteous is choice silver, but silver dross is the language of the wicked," "righteous" would have meant "one who is ethically sound," and similarly "wicked" would have been taken to mean "one who is ethically defective"; but by departing from his normal course to say "the heart of the wicked is little worth" instead of "silver dross is the language of the wicked," as might have been said, he has made plain his thought that "righteous" in this passage means "one who is ethically and intellectually sound," whereas the intended meaning of "wicked" is "one who is ethically and intellectually deficient." In this way, then, he has made it a condition *sine qua non* that the good speaker must be both wise and ethically sound, the same condition as that pointed out above on the basis of Quintilian's[n] words. Now since there can be no doubt of the goodness and beauty of the term "the righteous" by which the orator is described, and since soundness of language, which is Rhetoric, is attributed to "the righteous," it necessarily follows that this art is worthy, good, and of the greatest soundness and utility; also that it is a matter susceptible of improvement through art, just as is the case with silver.

20. Cf. Qimḥi's commentary *ad loc.*, where *kayyōm* of Gen. 25:33 is cited as a parallel.

m. Q. 12.1.1 ff.
n. Q. ibid.

[15] והנה אם כן עלה בידינו מזה הפסוק שההלצה היא נאותה וראויה ליכתב· ושהמליץ השלם יוכללו בו שלשה דברים: שיהיה חכם, שלם המדות, ומכלכל דבריו במשפט בכל מה שאפשר בערכו. וזה מה שאמר שלמה המלך גם כן: שפתי צדיק ידעון רצון ופי רשעים תהפוכות [משלי י׳ ל״ב]· לב חכם ישכיל פיהו ועל שפתיו יוסיף לקח [שם ט״ז כ״ג]· ופסוקים הרבה זולתם. ולזה מפלגי ההלצה היו בחירי האומה וסגולתה, כמעט נשלמו בהם המעלות כלם, רצוני לומר, הנביאים אשר אין ערוך אליהם.

[16] וכל זה יחזק דברי קוינטיליאנו. אמנם משמרת המליץ, אמרה שלמה המלך אחר הפסוק הנזכר, באמרו: שפתי צדיק ירעו רבים [שם י׳ כ״א]. והנה המשיל בכאן תמימות ההספקה בכל ענין וענין למזון המיוחד לכל איש ואיש; כי כמו שצריך המזון להיות נאות לניזון ודומה לו, כפי מה שאפשר, באופן ישוב הוא הוא, כן גם כן התחייב בחק המאמר להיות נאות ודומה לשומע, באופן יפיק רצון המליץ כאלו היה המליץ בעצמו. ולזה אמר ירעו רבים, כי דרך הלשון לכנות המאכל במרעה, כמו ירעו בשן וגלעד [מיכה ז׳ י״ד]; וכן נרמזה בו גם השגת השכל, כמו ורעו אותם דעה והשכל [ירמי׳ ג׳ ט״ו]. ואמר רבים, כי מהראוי לו שיספיק ויאמר הראוי בכל הענינים; והנה זה שב אל מה שגדרנו למעלה במשמרת המליץ:

פרק שלישי

בסוגי הדבורים אשר תעיין בהם ההלצה.

[1] חשבו קצת הקדמונים, כמו שאמר טוליאו בהלצה הישנה, שהדבורים אשר תעיין בם ההלצה הם בלתי בעלי תכלית, רצוני לומר, שאין ענין וחקירה אשר לא תעיין בה ההלצה· כאלו תאמר, החקירה אם הריקות נמצא או לא,

6 וסגולתה] וזולתה[כ] || 14 וגלעד <כימי עולם>[כ] || 15 אותם] אתכם[ת] | דעה] דעת[כ] || 18 שלישי] ג׳[כ] ||

3 תה׳ קי״ב ה׳ ||

[15] If the foregoing is true, then from this verse we have successfully concluded that the art of Rhetoric is one which it is fitting and proper to preserve in writing; and that the sound orator should possess three general qualifications: he must be wise, ethically sound, and one **that ordereth his words rightfully** [Ps. 112:5] in every possible pertinent respect. This has also been stated by King Solomon in the verses: **The lips of the righteous know what is acceptable, but the mouth of the wicked is all frowardness** [Prov. 10:32], **the heart of the wise teacheth his mouth, and addeth learning to his lips** [16:23]; and many others besides. Thus the eminent in Rhetoric were the elect of the nation and its special treasure, in whom all the virtues were very nearly perfect—I mean the prophets, who are without compare.

[16] All this corroborates the words of Quintilian.[o] With respect to the function of the orator, this is stated by King Solomon just after the aforementioned verse, where he says: **The lips of the righteous feed many** [Prov. 10:21]. He has here likened the effecting of complete persuasion in any one subject to the food which is particularly suited to each individual person. For just as the food must be adapted to the person fed, and be as assimilated to him as possible, so that he will return to his very own self, just so is it characteristic of the discourse that it must necessarily be adapted to the hearer, and so assimilated to him that he will be as satisfied by the speaker as if he were the speaker himself. Solomon says "feed many" because it is colloquial usage in Hebrew to call the act of eating "feeding," as for example, **Let them[21] feed in Bashan and Gilead** [Mic. 7:14]. The word is likewise used allegorically of intellectual perception, as in **who shall feed them[22] with knowledge and understanding** [Jer. 3:15]. And Solomon says "many" because the orator's proper function is to be persuasive, and able to say what ought to be said on all subjects. And this, of course, adverts to the definition we gave above of the orator's function.

CHAPTER 3

The Kinds of Cause with Which Rhetoric Is Concerned

[1] Some of the ancients, as Tully[a] tells us in the Old Rhetoric, thought that the causes with which Rhetoric is concerned are infinite in number, that is, that there is no subject or investigation with which Rhetoric will not be concerned; for

21. "Thy people."
22. B: "you."

---

o. Q. as *supra*.

a. *De I.* 1.5.7 and 1.6.8.

ומהו הזמן והמקום, וזולתם מן החקירות טבעיות אלקיות, איך ומה שתהיינה.
[2] וחלק עליהם הפילוסוף והנמשכים אחריו, רצוני לומר, טוליאו וקוינטיליאנו
וזולתם. וזה לשון הפילוסוף בראשון מההלצה: "וכבר ימצאו סוגי הדבורים
אשר תעיין בם ההלצה מהענינים הרצוניים שלשה, כמו שימצא מספר מיני
5 השומעים למאמר ההלצי שלשה. וזה כי הדבור מורכב משלשה: מאומר, והוא
המליץ· ומנאמר לו, והוא אשר יעשה לו המאמר· ומאשר יתחייב אליהם
המאמר, והם השומעים. והתכלית במאמר, אמנם הוא פונה מול אלו
השומעים. והשומעים בלי ספק אם חולק, ואם שופט, ואם המכוון לתת לו
הספקה. והשופט, אם שיהיה שופט בענינים העתידים, והם המועילים
10 והמזיקים· ואם בענינים שכבר היו. והענינים אשר כבר היו, מהם אשר ימצאו
לאדם בבחירתו, כמו המעלות והפחיתיות· מהם שימצאו לאדם בזולת בחירתו,
אבל מאדם אחר, והוא העול והיושר. והשופט בענינים העתידים הוא הראש·
והשופט בענינים ההווים הוא אשר יפקדהו הראש, כמו הדיין במדינותינו אלה.
ואמנם החולק, הנה אמנם יחלק בכח הקנין ההלצי. אם כן, סוגי המאמר ההלצי
15 שלשה: עצתי, ועצומי, וקיומי." עד כאן דבריו.

[3] אמנם קוינטיליאנו, בפרק רביעי מהחלק השלישי, אומר שלא ימנע אם
שתהיה משמרת המליץ בדבר נוגע במשפט, או חוץ ממנו. אם ינתן הראשון,
יהיה בידנו סוג אחד מסוגי ההלצה, והוא העצומי או המשפטי. והדבר אשר הוא
חוץ מהמשפט, לא ימנע גם כן אם שיהיו בערך אל זמן העתיד, ויולד העצתיי·
20 שהעצה היא בדברים העתידים· ואם שיהיו בערך אל הזמן העבר, ויצמח
המקיים, למה שהשבח והגנות המיוחדים במקיים יביטו הזמן העבר. עוד באופן
אחר, שלא ימנע אם שיהיה הדבר בודאי אצל המליץ, ומזה יצמח המקיים,
שהוא מחייב שבח או גנות בודאי· אם שיהיה זה אצלו בספק. וזה לא ימנע אם
שהוא בבחירתנו, ויתחייב מזה העצתי, ואם שהדבר תלוי בספק זולתנו, וימשך
25 העצומי.

[4] ואחר התישב זה, ראוי שנגדור כל אחד מאלו הסוגים כאשר נוכל להבין
מהפילוסוף, בראשון מההלצה, וטוליאו בראשון מההלצה החדשה והישנה,
וזולתם.

4 שימצא] שימצה[ד] || 5 ההלצי] הלצי[כ] || 10 אשר ימצאו] מה שימצאו[ט] || 11 בבחירתו] בביחרתו[ד] | כמו] ואותם הם[ט] | מהם שימצאו] ומהם מה שימצאו[ט] || 12 אחר] אחד[טgu טav] (اخر[א]) || 13 יפקדהו] יפקידהו[ט] || 14 ואמנם] ואולם[ט] | ‹הנה› אם כן[ט] || 19 אם][כ] || 26 התישב] שהתיישב[כ] | אחד] אחת[כ] ||

example, the investigation into whether or not the vacuum is an existent thing, what time and space are, and other such theologico-scientific investigations, of whatever nature or kind they may be.

[2] The Philosopher and his followers, however—I mean Tully, Quintilian, and others—disagreed with these writers. This is the Philosopher's[b] language in Book I of the *Rhetoric:* ''Now the Kinds of Cause,[1] of matters subject to human volition, with which Rhetoric is concerned are found to be three in number, just as the kinds of hearers of a rhetorical discourse are three. For a speech is a combination of three elements: a sayer, that is, the orator; that in regard to which something is said—that about which the orator makes his discourse; and those to whom the discourse must be addressed, the hearers. The purpose of the discourse indeed, is conformed to these hearers. Hearers doubtless will either be an opposing party, or else a judge, or else the party at whom the persuasion is directed. The judge is either a judge of future things, and these may be advantageous or harmful; or of past things, some of which, such as the virtues and the vices, pertain to a man by his own choice, while others come to him not by his choice but from some other person—effects, namely, of wrongdoing and uprightness. The judge of future things is a chief-of-state, while the judge of present affairs is an appointee of the chief authority, like the magistrate in these cities of ours. And as for the opponent, he will make his dissent by virtue of the rhetorical skill he has acquired. It follows, then, that the kinds of rhetorical discourse are three: Deliberative, Forensic, and Epideictic.''

[3] Thus far Aristotle. Quintilian,[c] however, in Book III, Chapter 4, says that the orator's charge must necessarily be concerned either with a matter connected with law, or with one outside this sphere. Given the first, we obtain one of the kinds of Rhetoric, namely the Forensic or Judicial. The extrajudicial cause must also necessarily refer either to future time, in which case the Deliberative Issue is engendered—for deliberation is concerned with events to come—or to past time, which produces Epideictic; since the praise and censure which are peculiar to Epideictic contemplate time past. Regarded in another way, again, the cause must necessarily be either one which the orator holds to be certain, giving rise to Epideictic, which makes positive assertion of praise or of blame; or the matter must be one of which the orator is in doubt. The latter is necessarily either within our own choice, and so must give rise to the Deliberative, or the matter depends upon the doubt of others, which results in the Forensic.

[4] This determined, we must define each of these Kinds as we are able to understand them from the Philosopher[d] in Book I of the *Rhetoric,* from Tully[e] in the first Books of the New and of the Old Rhetoric, and from others.

1. T/A: ''kinds of things'' (סוגי הדברים < جناس الاشياء).

---

b. T23/A28; *Rhet.* 1.3 (1358b).
c. Q. 3.4.6–8.
d. T24 ff./A29 ff.; cf *Rhet.* 1.3 (1358b).
e. *De I.* 1.7.9, 1.9.12; *R. ad H.* 3.6.10.

[5] ונאמר שהמקיים הוא אשר יכלול שבח או גנות בערך אל אדם מה· והשבח הוא שהדברים הרצוניים אשר ידוברו מאדם מה הם מעלה וחשיבות לנפשו· והגנות הוא כשהדברים האלה ישובו גנות, פחיתות, וחסרון לנפש אשר ידובר אלה בערכו.

[6] אמנם העצתי הוא שכאשר יושם בעצם תמצא בו הרשאה או מניעה· וזה שכל מי שיעץ, בין לאחד מאנשי המדינה בין לכלל המדינה, הנה לא ימנע אם שיעץ בהרשאה או במניעה. וההרשאה הוא המאמר העצתי המספיק על שהדבר ראוי שיעשה· והמניעה הוא מאמר העצתי המספיק על שהדבר אינו ראוי שיעשה. ואין ראוי שיעלם שהצואה, והאזהרה, והגערה, והפיוס, והתחנה, והנוהג מנהגם הם תחת זה הסוג.

[7] ואם העצומי או המשפטי, הוא דבר, שכאשר יושם מחלקת, בו תלונה או התנצלות ממנה. והתלונה היא אשר יכוון בה לבאר שפלוני עשה הפך מן הראוי, רצוני לומר, שהגיע ממנו רע לפלוני· וההתנצלות הוא אשר יכוון בו לבאר שלא עשה הפך מן הראוי, ולא הגיע מפלוני לפלוני רע· והתוכחה תחת התלונה.

[8] וראוי שתדע שהיותר ראוי שבזמנים בערך אל המקיים הוא הזמן העומד, או קרוב אליו, כי מה שישובח או יגונה הוא בדברים הנמצאים בו בעת השבח והגנות. ולפעמים ישבח אדם, או יגנה, לתחבולה מהתחבולות, ואז יכוון בשבח או בגנות זולת מה שספרנוהו.

[9] והתכליות לאלה הסוגים לפי המכוון מהפילוסוף בראשון מההלצה: אם בערך אל העצתי, יהיה המועיל או המזיק, רצוני לומר, שירשה במועיל או ביותר מועיל, וימנע מההזק או מיותר הזק· ותכלית העצומי הוא היושר והעול· ותכלית המקיים הוא השבח והגנות. ואם ישתמש אחד מאלו בתכלית חברו, הנה זה לא יהיה על הכונה הראשונה· והמשל, שאפשר שהיועץ יספיק על שהדבר יושר או עול, ויכוון בזה ליעץ בהרשאה או במניעה, רצוני לומר, שיעץ שהדבר שהוא ישר ראוי שיעשה, אמנם הדבר שהוא עול ראוי האדם להתרחק ממנו. וכן גם כן כשישתמש במעלה או בפחיתות, יכון בזה ליעץ התקרב אל המעלות או התרחק מן הפחיתיות.

9 והגערה ‹והתחינה›[ג] || 12 אשר] כאשר[ג] | יכוון] יכווין[ג] | שפלוני] שפלו׳[ג] || 13 ממנו] ממנ״ה[ג] || 15 התלונה] התלנה[ד] || 16 [ראוי][ג] || 20 והתכליות] והתכלית[ג] ||

[5] We say, then, that Epideictic includes praise or censure of some person: praise, when the matters subject to human volition mentioned in connection with some individual are of advantage and importance to his soul; censure, when these matters bring disgrace, disesteem, and disadvantage to the person in connection with whom they are mentioned.

[6] The Deliberative type of speech is essentially one in which you find the urging of an authorization or of a prohibition; for one who gives counsel, whether to an individual citizen or to the citizenry as a whole, must necessarily advise either the authorization or the prohibition of some proposed course of action. The Speech for Authorization is a Deliberative discourse which establishes the conviction that some proposal ought to be enacted, while the Speech for Prohibition is a Deliberative discourse which establishes the conviction that some proposal ought not to be enacted. Nor should we fail to note that speeches of Injunction, Warning, Rebuke, Mollification, Supplication, and the like are subvarieties of this Kind of Cause.

[7] The Forensic, or the Judicial, is a kind which, when a disputation is in process, contains an accusation or a defence against an accusation: the purport of the Accusation is to show that A has done the contrary of what he ought to have done, something, that is to say, which has brought harm to B, while the purport of the Defence is to show that A has neither done the contrary of what he ought to have done, nor has harm come to B because of A. The Rebuke is a subvariety of the Accusation.

[8] One must also know that the time most appropriate to Epideictic is the present or near-present, for what is to be praised or censured consists of things in existence at the time of the praise or censure. Sometimes, too, a man may be praised or censured as a kind of device, in which case the purport of the praise or censure will be other than as we have described.

[9] The ends of these Kinds of Cause according to the meaning of the Philosopher's[f] words in Book I of the Rhetoric, are as follows: In the Deliberative kind, the end is the advantageous or the harmful, that is, that the advantageous or more advantageous be authorized, the harmful or more harmful be prohibited. The end of the Forensic is justice and injustice, that of the Epideictic honor and dishonor. Should one of these kinds be used for the end of one of the other kinds, this need not be a contradiction of the primary intention. For example, a counsellor may try to prove that some proposal is just or unjust, because he thus intends to counsel authorization or prohibition; his advice, that is, will be that it is the just act which ought to be done, whereas one should shun the act which is unjust. The case is similar, too, when a counsellor employs virtue and vice as means, his intention in so doing being to urge the embracing of the virtues or the avoidance of the vices.

f. T25/A29–30; cf. *Rhet.* 1.3 (1358b).

פרק רביעי

הדברים הראויים להיות במליץ.

[1] אמר קוינטיליאנו בפרק השלישי מהחלק השלישי, כי קצת מן הקדמונים לא הסכימו במספר הדברים הראויים למליץ עם מה שאמר טוליאו בראשון מההלצה החדשה׃ אלא שהאמת הוא מה שכתבו, שהתחייב אל המליץ המצא אצלו אלה החמשה דברים, רצוני לומר: ההמצאה, והסדר, הצחות, והזכירה, והרמיזה.

[2] וההמצאה היא חקירת הדברים האמתיים, או נראים אמתיים, אשר ישימו הענין מפורסם. ומה שאמר ״אמתיים או נראים אמתיים״, למה שקצת הדברים הם אמתיים ואינם נראים, וקצתם נראים ובלתי אמתיים, וקצתם אמתיים ונראים, וקצתם בלתי נראים ובלתי אמתיים, כמו שאמר בואציו בספר הנצוח שעשה. משל הראשון: ״שהשמש גדול מן הארץ כמה פעמים״׃ זה, עם היותו אמתיי ומבואר במופת, הוא בלתי נראה ובלתי מפורסם. משל השני: ״אין שום אם הורגת את הבן״׃ זה המאמר מפורסם עם היותו בלתי צודק, למה שהרבה מהם הרגו בניהם, כמו שנמצא בספרי דברי הימים (וגם בספרי הקדש, במלכים) מהנשים שאכלו בניהם. משל השלישי: ״שהשמים הם כדוריים״׃ בזה יתקבצו שניהם יחד, רצוני לומר, האמתות עם מה שיראה ממנו. משל הרביעי: ״שהכל אינו גדול מן החלק״ ו״אפשר הדבר היות לבן ושחור יחד.״ ואמרנו בזה שישים הדבר מפורסם באמצעות הדברים האמתיים או הנראים, כי זה מספיק למליץ שהוא מוכיח מן המפורסמות ומהדברים שיש להם פנים מן ההראות. והנה אם יאמר: ״האשה הזאת ילדה׃ אם כן, שכב איש אותה״׃ הנה באר והוכיח באמצעות דבר אמתי. אמנם אם יאמר: ״האיש הזה חטא׃ והאות, שנתאדמו פניו אצל זכרון החטא״׃ באר מבקשו באמצעות דבר יש לו פנים מן ההראות.

[3] ואם הסדר, הוא סדור וחלוק הדברים אשר יביא במקום הראוי להם, למה שאם הקדים המאוחר או להפך׃ או שהביא במקום הראיות החזקות החלושות, או להפך׃ או זולת זה מן הפוך הסדר׃ הוא מבואר שיצא בזה מן הדרך האמתי והנאות.

1 רביעי] ד׳[ג] || 3 בפרק השלישי] בפרק שלישי[ג] || 9 מפורסם] מפרסם[ד] || 11 בואציו] בואיציאו[ג] || 13 מפורסם] מפרסם[ד] || 14 אם הורגת] איש הורג[ג] | המאמר ‹הוא›[ג] | [מפורסם עם היותו][ג] || 15 במלכים] במלאכים[ג] || 17 ממנו] ממנָה[ג] || 23 החטא] החט[ד] || 25 [המאוחר][ג] | הראיות] הראוי להם[ג] ||

CHAPTER 4

The Competencies Which the Speaker Should Possess

[1] In Book III, Chapter 3, Quintilian[a] says that some of the ancients did not agree, in regard to the number of competencies the speaker should possess, with what Tully[b] says in Book I of the New Rhetoric; but that what Tully wrote is true, namely, that the orator is required to have the following five faculties at his disposal: Invention, Arrangement, Style, Memory, and Delivery.

[2] Invention is the searching out of the propositions, true or plausible, which will make the case generally accepted as true. Tully says "true or plausible" because, as Boethius[c] declares in his book on the *Topics*[1] (1) some propositions are true but not plausible, (2) some plausible but untrue, (3) some both true and plausible, and (4) some neither plausible nor true. An example of the first: "The sun is several times larger than the earth;" this, while true and demonstrated by proof, is neither plausible nor generally accepted as true. An example of the second: "No mother slays her child." This proposition is generally accepted as true, although it is, in fact, untrue; for many mothers have slain their children, as we find in books of chronicles (even in the Holy Bible, in Kings)[2] cases of women who have eaten their children. An example of the third: "The heavens are spherical"; herein both coincide, that is, truth and plausibility. An example of the fourth: "The whole is not greater than the part"; or "A thing can simultaneously be both white and black." Of Invention, then, we say that it makes the case generally accepted as true by means of propositions either true or plausible; for it suffices the speaker to prove his case from considerations commonly accepted as true, and from propositions that have verisimilitude. Thus, if he should say: "As this woman has borne a child, a man has lain with her," he has demonstrated and proved the case by means of a true proposition. If, however, he should say: "This man has sinned, the sign being that he has blushed at the mention of sin," the speaker has demonstrated his point by means of a proposition that has verisimilitude.

[3] Arrangement is the ordering and distribution of the arguments, which the speaker should introduce where they properly belong. For if he should place first what ought to come last, or vice versa, or should introduce the weaker arguments where the stronger should be, or vice versa, or otherwise get them wrong way to, he would thereby obviously depart from the true and fitting method.

1. Literally, "in *The Book of the Dialectic* which he made." "*The Book of the Dialectic*" (סֵפֶר הַנִּצּוּחַ) was the medieval Hebrew designation of Aristotle's *Topics;* see the Int., §5(7) and n. 210.
2. 2 Kings 6:24–30.

---

a. Q. 3.3.1 ff.
b. *R. ad H.* 1.2.3.
c. Boethius, *De differentiis topicis,* bk. II (Migne, *Pat. Lat.* 1180–1182).

[4] ואם הצחות, הוא הבאת התבות או המאמרים הנאותים בענין ענין.

[5] ואם הזכירה, היא חזקה קיימת מהענינים, המלות, והסדרים; ואמר "חזקה קיימת" כדי שיובן מזה הזכירה המלאכותית, רצוני לומר, הנעשת מצד המלאכה כמו שיתבאר, למה שהזכרון[1] הטבעי הוא דבר ראוי שיתבאר בספרי הטבעים, והוא זולת מהמכון ממנו בזה המקום.

[6] ואם הרמיזה, היא תקון הקול, הפנים, והאברים עם ההאתות לענין· רצוני לומר, שאם יאמר דבר יעורר על העצבון, ראוי שיתקן הקול והפנים במדרגת המקוננים והבוכים; וכן תנועות האברים· כאילו תאמר, שיכה כף אל כף, או תנועה אחרת מסכמת לעצבון, וכן ביתר האברים. ואם יעיר על השמחה, יתקן כל הדברים הנזכרים בהפך· וכן בכל ענין וענין כפי מה שיאות לו מן הרמיזות.

[7] והנה, אם תתבונן היטב, אלו החמשה דברים הושמו לפי הסדר הראוי להם הקדימה והאחור. כי אי אפשר שההמצאה לא תקדם, כי הסדר אינו נופל כי אם בענינים הנמצאים. גם המצא הצחות הוא בערך אל ההמצאה והסדור, והיא מתאחרת להם, וכן הזכרון הוא בערך אל שלשתם ורודף אחריהם; והרמיזה היא האחרונה, שאם לא ימציא, יסדר, ידבר צחות, ויזכר, על אי זה דבר תפול הרמיזה?

[8] וראוי שתדע שאמר קוינטיליאנו, בשלישי מהחלק השלישי, שאפשר היות המאמר במדרגה מן הקצור עד לא יתחייב למליץ בערכו החמשה דברים הנזכרים. ואמר טוליאו בהלצה החדשה שהחמשה הדברים הנזכרים, תקל עלינו עשייתם או הוצאתם אל הפועל אם מצד המלאכה, אם מצד ההדרכה, אם מצד ההשתדלות. המלאכה היא נימוס מה נותן דרך ומשפט הדבור· ההדרכה היא אשר למענה נתעורר עם ציור אמתי להדמות אל קצת האנשים במדרגת הדבור· וההשתדלות הוא מנהג והרגל תמידי מן הדבור. ואמר ויטורינו בהלצה הישנה שההשתדלות הוא תמידות הפעל.

[9] ואם ישאל שואל באי זה מקום מן המאמר ראוי שימצאו אלו החמשה ענינים, נשיב שהראוי להם להיות מפזרים בכל המאמר, עד שבכל חלק ממנו תהיה ההמצאה והסדור הראוי, והצחות והרמיזה כפי הענין, במדרגת הדם שהוא מתפשט בכל הגוף.

4 שהזכרון[1]] שהזכרנו[גד] || 5 מהמכון] מהבין[ג] || 7 על] אל[ג] || 11 היטב] הטיב[ג] | אלו] אלה[ג] || 13 [המצא][ד] || 19 הדברים] דברים[ג] || 20 הוצאתם] הוצאתה[ג] || 22 למענה] למעינה[ג] || 23 וההשתדלות] והשתדלות[ג] || 24 הישנה] הישינה[ד] || 25 אלו] אילו[ד] ||

[1] Corrected text; so too in ד[R].

[4] Style is the introduction of the words or the phrases which suit a given subject matter.

[5] Memory is the firm retention of the various subjects, words, and arrangements. Tully[d] says "firm retention," so that from this we will understand that this is "the artificial memory," the memory, I mean, which is wrought by art, as will be explained; for the "natural memory" is something which ought properly to be explained in treatises on natural phenomena, and is not the same as the memory meant here.

[6] Delivery is the regulation of the voice, countenance, and limbs in the manner appropriate to the subject. If, that is, the speaker should say something to evoke sadness, he should regulate his voice and countenance in the manner of those who keen and weep. So, too, the movements of his limbs: he should, you might say, smite palm against palm, or make some other movement comporting with sadness; and put the other limbs of the body to similar use. Or, if he would arouse joy, he should execute movements to opposite effect; and so in any given case, the details of voice, countenance, and limbs should be arranged according to the Delivery appropriate to that case.

[7] Now plainly, if you consider the matter carefully, these five functions are set in the proper sequential order. For it is impossible that Invention not come first, since Arrangement occurs only with matters that already exist. The existence of Style, too, is incidental to, and subsequent upon, Invention and Arrangement, just as Memory is relative to, and follows after, the three of these; while Delivery must come last, since if one does not invent, or arrange, speak with style, nor remember, what occasion will there be for Delivery?

[8] You must know, too, that Quintilian,[e] in Book III, Chapter 3, says that a discourse may be so short that the orator does not need for it the five abovementioned departments. And Tully[f] in the New Rhetoric, says that the execution or the practical utilization of the aforementioned five faculties may become easier for us whether by dint of art, by guidance, or by effort. "Art" is a certain canon of usage that provides a definite method and system of speaking; by "guidance" we are stimulated to a true and faithful approximation of the manner of speaking of certain individuals; and "effort" is the custom and constant practice of speaking. Victorinus,[g] on the Old Rhetoric, says that "effort" is assiduous performance of the act.

[9] If one asks what is the proper place in the discourse for each of these five departments, our reply is that they should pervade the whole discourse, so that the right Invention and Arrangement, the Style and Delivery that accord with the subject, will come into every part, just as the blood distributes itself throughout the body.

d. *R. ad H.* 1.2.3.
e. Q. 3.3.2 ff.
f. *R. ad H.* 1.2.3.
g. Halm, 160.

[10] והנה התבאר מה שנאמר בזה הפרק מהחמשה דברים הנזכרים ממה
שאמר משה רבינו ע״ה, האזינו השמים ואדברה כו׳ [דברים ל״ב א׳], למה שהוא
מביא אלו הענינים כלם במה שאמר[2]: יערוף כמטר לקחי כו׳ [שם שם ב׳]. וה כי
תבת לקח בלשוננו תאמר על הדבור הערב, שהוא כאלו לקח האדם אשר ידבר
אליו לעשות בו כרצונו, כמו: הטתו ברוב לקחה [משלי ז׳ כ״א]; הלוקחים לשונם
וינאמו נאם [יר׳ כ״ג ל״א], ר״ל, שלוקחים לבב האנשים להטותם אל אשר
ירצו. והנה רמז בזה המאמר, ר״ל יערוף לקחי [דב׳ ל״ב ב׳], שלשה דברים, ר״ל,
ההמצאה, והסדר, והצחות. אם ההמצאה והצחות, במה שאמר, לקחי, כי היא
תורה על הערבות כמו שבארנו· גם כי הוא דבר לקחו לפרסם מה שירצה לספר,
והוא ענין ההמצאה; אם הסדר, יובן ממה שאמר, יערוף כמטר, ר״ל שידבר
בסדור מפלג ובמאמרים מופסקים בהדרגה, באופן יובנו בשלמות אצל
השומעים, במדרגת המטר היורד טפה אחר טפה בסדר נאות כפי ענינו; ואם
הזכירה, יתבאר ממה שאמר, תזל כטל אמרתי [שם שם]· וזה כי משה רבינו ע״ה
למד מה שלמד מפי הגבורה, והיו נגד עיניו ולבו תמיד כמו הטל, שהוא ענין
תמידי בלתי נעצר. והנה אמרותיו היו מסודרות מהזכירה אשר בתכלית; לא
ששכח במקצת ממה שנאמר לו עד יפול בדבריו ספק שיאמר דבר בלתי מסכים
עם מה ששמעו מפי השם. ואמר א״כ: כשעירים עלי דשא וכרביבים עלי עשב
[שם שם]. וראוי שתדע שהרצון בשעירים המטר הדק: אם מצד שיגיד עליו ריעו,
ר״ל שתבת רביבים תורה עליו· אם מצד שהוא מלשון ושער שחור צמח בו [וי׳
י״ג ל״ז], כלומר, שהוא במדרגה מן הדקות כמו השערות. והנה אם כן, יהיה יחס
הדשא בערך אל העשב יחס השעירים בהצטרף אל הרביבים, ר״ל, שהדשא
יהיה העשב הדק בתחלתו אשר יספיקו לו השעירים· והעשב יקרא בהיותו
נשלם ונגמר, ויצטרך אל מטר רב ממה שהיה צריך לזה הדשא. והוא מבואר
שאילו היה הסדר נהפך, ר״ל, שיהיו הרביבים בערך אל הדשא והשעירים בערך
אל העשב, לא היה נשלם מה שנקוה מן העשב והדשא, כי הדשא היה נפסד

3 שאמר[2]] שאמ׳[ג] שאמ[ד] ||7 ר״ל] רל[ד] ||13 רבינו] רבנו[ג] ||17 וכרביבים] וכרבבים[ג] ||19 שתבת]
שמלת[ג] |ושער] ושיער[ב] ||

[2] So J.

[10] Now what has been said in this chapter about the aforementioned five faculties is demonstrable from what our Master, Moses (upon whom be peace!), has said in the Chapter, **Give ear, ye heavens, and I will speak,** etc. [Deut. 32:1 ff.], since all these matters are introduced by him in the words: **My doctrine shall drop as the rain,** etc. [32:2].[3] For in our Hebrew tongue the word for "doctrine" [*leqaḥ:* from the root *lāqaḥ* = "to take"] is used of the pleasing speech which, as it were, "takes" the person addressed, to make him do as the speaker wishes. For example: **With her much fair speech (**leqaḥ**) she causeth him to yield** [Prov. 7:21]; [the false prophets] . . . **that take (**lōqᵉḥīm**) with their tongues**[4] **and say: "He saith"** [Jer. 23:31], that is, that "take" the hearts of men, bending them to their desire. Now Moses, in saying **My doctrine shall drop as the rain** [Deut. 32:2] was alluding to three of the faculties, namely, Invention, Arrangement, and Style. He refers to Invention and Style in "my doctrine," because this, as we have explained, indicates pleasing speech; because, moreover, it is the word he has chosen to make what he wishes to describe seem generally accepted as true, which is a matter of Invention. For its part, Arrangement is to be understood from his words "shall drop as the rain," that is, that he is going to speak in such distinctive order and progressive sequence of sentences as will ensure perfect understanding on the part of the audience, just as the rain comes down drop after drop in its own typically appropriate arrangement. As for Memory, it is clearly indicated by his words **My speech shall distill as the dew** [Deut. 32:2]; for our Master, Moses (upon whom be peace!), learned what he learned from the mouth of the Almighty, and these things were continually before his eyes and heart like the dew, which is a constant and never restrained occurrence. His sayings were, indeed, arranged out of a memory which could not be more accurate; he did not forget part of what was said to him, which would make his words subject to the doubt that he might be saying something out of keeping with what he had heard from the mouth of the Lord. Immediately thereafter Moses says: **As the small rain upon the tender grass, and as the showers upon the herb** [32:2]. You must know that the meaning of *sᵉʿīrīm* here is "small rain," whether because this is indicated by its parallel, the word *rᵉbhībhīm,* which means "showers," or by the sense of *sēʿār* itself, as in the passage ". . . and black hair (*sēʿār*) be grown up therein" [Lev. 13:37]: the rain called *sᵉʿīrīm,* that is to say, is in degree of fineness like hairs. If this is so, the relation of "grass" to "herb" is that of "small rain" to "showers": that is, "the tender grass" is the thin, early grass for which "small rain" is sufficient, whereas it will be called "herb" when, having reached full growth, it needs much more rain than does the "tender grass." Now clearly, if the order were reversed—if "showers" were used in connection with "tender grass" and "small rain" with "herb"—our expectation of "herb" and

3. See note 19 of Chapter 2.
4. JV: "that use their tongues."

מרוב המטר, והעשב ימולל ויבש כי לא ירוה צמאונו בשעירים. ובזה האופן, ר״ל שספר הכתוב באמרו כשעירים עלי כו׳, ימצא לכל אחד מה שיאות לו, לא יחסר דבר. והנה אמר משה רבינו ע״ה שדבריו יהיו באופן מהשלמות עד שיאותו בערך אל כל ענין וענין· כקטן כגדול ישמעון. והראוי שלא יבצר ממנו התכלית אשר כוון אליו עם שרמז בזה אל הרמיזה שתהיה כפי מה שיאות לענין ענין, כי האותות הדבור וערבותו כבר רמזו בתבת לקחי. ושעור המאמר כלו הוא כאלו אמר על דרך משל לשמים וארץ: תהיו לי לעדה כי יבאו דברי עם ישראל באופן מן השלמות עד לא יחסר בהם דבר מתנאי הדבור השלם, ר״ל, מההמצאה, הסדר, הצחות, הזכרון, והרמיזה, אשר ראוי למי אשר אלה לו שיגיע אל מה שכוון אליו. ואם בזה לא יוסרו לי, תהיה תוכחה גמורה על קשי ערפם. ותשאר זאת הבחינה מבוארת הצדק· אם היה חסר במאמר אפילו דבר מועט מאשר התחייב אל דבור השלם, היה אפשר שיאמר שזה קרה מחסרון המאמר, והיה בהם בזה קצת התנצלות.

[11] והנה זאת השירה בכללות היא במדרגה גדולה מהדבור הנשא לא תסלה בכתם אופיר. ואיך לא, וי״י הכין דרכה; עשאה ויכוננה השם רוח אדם בקרבו.

פרק חמישי

מחלקי ההמצאה.

[1] אחר שקדם מה שהתחייב למליץ שימצא אתו, ראוי שנבאר חלקי המאמר לפי מה שבארם ארסטו׳ בשלישי מההלצה ובקצורו ששלח לאלכסנדר, ולפי מה

5 כוון] כון[ד] |עם] עד[כ] ||6 כבר ולקחו[כ] ||7 תהיו] ..יו[כ] ||10 שכוון] שכיון[כ] |גמורה] גדולה[כ] ||
15 לא] לו[כ] |ויכוננה] ויכוננה[ד] ||17 חמישי] ה׳[כ] ||20 ארסטו׳] ארסטו[כ] ||

1 תה׳ צ׳ ו׳ ||2 דב׳ ב׳ ז׳ ||4 דב׳ א׳ י״ז ||7 בר׳ כ״א ל׳ ||8 דב׳ ב׳ ז׳ ||10 וי׳ כ״ו כ״ג ||15 איוב כ״ח ט״ז |מש׳ כ״א כ״ט |דב׳ ל״ב ו׳ |זכ׳ י״ב א׳ ||

of "tender grass" would not be fulfilled, since the "tender grass" would be ruined by too much rain, while the "herb" would **fade and wither** [Ps. 90:6] because the "small rain" could not sate its thirst. But in the manner depicted by Scripture in the words **As the small rain upon the tender grass,** etc., to each kind of grass is vouchsafed what is appropriate to it, **lacking nothing** [Deut. 2:7]. We see, then, that our Master Moses (upon whom be peace!) has here asserted that his words are so finished as to be appropriate to any given subject: **the small and the great alike** would be **heard** [1:17]. He cannot properly be denied the end he sought to achieve; nor can it be denied that he has here allegorically suggested that the Delivery accord with what suits a given subject; for in the word "my doctrine" (*liqḥī*) he has in fact alluded to appropriate and pleasing speech. The import of the whole passage is as if, addressing the heavens and the earth, he had parabolically said: "Ye shall **be witness unto me** [Gen. 21:30] that my words addressed to Israel shall be presented with such finish that **not one** of the conditions of perfect utterance will be **lacking** [Deut. 2:7], to wit, Invention, Arrangement, Style, Memory, and Delivery, the faculties which enable the speaker who possesses them to accomplish his purpose. And if they **will not** thus **be corrected unto me** [Lev. 26:23], there shall be the sternest chastisement for their stubbornness." This criterion remains plainly right: if even a minor aspect of what is essential to perfect utterance had been lacking, it could be said that that was so because the statement was incomplete, and this deficiency could then have been used by Israel as a partial defence.

[11] Truly, then, this entire Song is on so high a level of the Grand Style that **it cannot be valued with the gold of Ophir** [Job 28:16]. How should this not be so, since it was the Lord who **looked well to** her **way**[5] [Prov. 21:29]? **He... made** her, **and He established** her [Deut. 32:6] as **the spirit of man within him** [Zech. 12:1].

CHAPTER 5

Of the Parts of Invention

[1] Having dealt above with the faculties which must be at a speaker's disposal, we now may treat the divisions of a discourse as these are set forth by Aristotle[a] in Book III of the *Rhetoric* and in his Abridgment which he sent to

5. I.e., Rhetoric's "way."

a. T214 ff./A305 ff.; cf. *Rhet.* 3.13 ff. (1414a); *LR. ad A.* 61.15ff. (1436a ff.).

שבארם טוליאו בא׳ מההלצה החדשה והישנה עם ויטורינו המפרש, ולפי
קוינטיליאנו ברביעי מספרו.

[2] ונאמר שההמצאה תחלק אל ששה חלקים: פתיחה, ספור, חלוק, קיום,
התרה, חתימה. ואמרו קצת המפרשים שלא בלבד ההמצאה תחלק אל אלו הו׳
5 חלקים, אבל אפשר היות הענין כן גם בסדר, בצחות, בזכרון, וברמיזה.

[3] וראוי שתדע שאמר בואציאו ברביעי מהנצוח כי למה שמדרך המליץ
להוכיח, לא ימנע אם שיעשה זה בהביא ראיה, ואם שיעשה זה בלתי ראיה.
ואם יעשה בלתי ראיה, לא ימנע אם שיעשה זה בלתי משית השומע מקשיב,
מתלמד, מחבב — וזה על שני פנים: אם דרך ספור לבד, ויולד הספור· אם דרך
10 באור מה שבינינו ושכנגדנו, ויתחייב החלוק — אם שיעשה זה בדברים נאותי
ההספקה בלתי ראיה למה שיעשה השומע מחבב, מקשיב, מתלמד. לא ימנע
אם שיעשה זה בהצטרף אל העתיד להאמר, אם בהצטרף אל הדבר שכבר אמר;
אם ינתן הראשון, תתחייב לנו הפתיחה· ואם השני, תמשך מזה החתימה. ואם
שיעשה זה בהביא ראיה, לא ימנע אם שיביא ראיה להוכיח דעתו, ויולד הקיום·
15 אם שיביא ראיה לבטל דעת החולק, ותצמח ההתרה. ולזה היו החלקים ששה
לבד, לא פחות ולא יתר.

[4] אמנם הפתיחה היא מאמר באשר יוכן לב השומע להאזין ולהבין מה
שיאמר· וזה כאשר נעשה אותו מכח דברינו מקשיב, מחבב, מתלמד. והפילוסוף,
בי׳ מקצור ההלצה אשר עשה לאלכסנדר, גודר אותה ככה: ״הפתיחה היא
20 מאמר קצר באשר נעשה לבב השומעים מתלמד, מקשיב, ומחבב בערך אל מה
שידובר בעתיד.״ אמר קוינטיליאנו בד׳ שאלו הדברים, ר״ל שיהיה לב השומע
מוכן ושנביא אותו אל שיהיה מקשיב, מחבב, מתלמד, הוא דבר ראוי לעשותו

1 והישנה] והישינה[ב] || 4 [הו׳][ב] || 11 מתלמד] מלמד[ב] || 17 יוכן] יובן[ד] || 18 דברינו] דברנו[ד] ||
19 לאלכסנדר] לאלכסנ׳[ד] ||

Alexander; and as expounded by Tully[b] in Book I of the New Rhetoric and Book I of the Old (with the commentator Victorinus),[c] and by Quintilian[d] in Book IV of his work.

[2] We say, then, that Invention subdivides into six parts: Introduction, Statement of the Facts, Partition, Proof, Refutation, Conclusion. Some commentators say that it is not only Invention which is divisible into these six parts, but that the same could hold as well for Arrangement, Style, Memory, and Delivery.

[3] You should know, too, that Boethius,[e] in Book IV of the *Topics,*[1] says that since normally the speaker's function is to establish a case, he unavoidably must accomplish this either by adducing evidence, or without adducing evidence. If without adducing evidence, he unavoidably must establish his case either without making the audience attentive, receptive, and well disposed—and this in one of two ways: either simply, through an account of what took place (hence is born the Statement of the Facts), or through a clarification of the issue between us and our opponent (which entails the Partition)—or he must establish his case with words apt to persuade even without evidence because he makes the audience well disposed, attentive, and receptive. He unavoidably must so render the audience in connection either with what is going to be said, or with something that he has already said: given the first situation, we necessarily have the Introduction; if the second obtain, this will result in the Conclusion. If the speaker is to establish his case by adducing evidence, he unavoidably must either present evidence to support his stand, whence the Proof is born, or evidence to nullify the case of his opponent, whence springs the Refutation. Accordingly, the parts of Invention are six only, no less and no more.

[4] The Introduction, indeed, is the statement by which the mind of the hearer is prepared to heed and to comprehend what is going to be said—when, by virtue of our words, we make him attentive, well disposed, and receptive. The Philosopher,[f] in [Chapter?] 10 of the Abridgment of the *Rhetoric* which he made for Alexander, defines it as follows: "The introduction is a short statement whereby the mind of the audience is made receptive, attentive, and well disposed in respect of what is about to be spoken."[2] Quintilian,[g] in Book IV, says that these ends—that the mind of the hearer be prepared and that we render him

1. Cf. Chapter 4, n. 1.

2. Although the quoted words are a condensed version of the cited passage in the *Rhetorica ad Alexandrum,* they are present as such in no text of the work now available; nor do we know of any "Chapter 10" or "Section 10" of the work in which the quoted words appear. This is the only directly quoted—or seemingly directly quoted—citation of the *R. ad A.* in the *N.S.;* see the discussion in the Int., §5.

---

b. *R. ad H.* 1.3.4 ff.

c. *De I.* 1.4.19 ff.; Halm, 194–195.

d. Q. 4.Pr., ff.

e. Boethius, *De differentiis topicis,* bk. IV (Migne, *Pat. Lat.* 1208).

f. Cf. *LR. ad A.* 61.19 f.

g. Q. 4.1.5.

בכל חלקי המאמר· אלא שזה יותר הכרחי בפתיחה, להמתיק לבב השומע באופן נביאהו לחשוק אל מה שימשך מהמאמר.

[5] הספור הוא הגדת הדברים האמתיים או כאלו הם אמתיים, ר״ל שיש להם פנים מן הראות. אמנם הפילוס׳, בקצור ההלצה שעשה לאלכסנדר, גודר הספור באשר בו נספר הדברים העוברים, או נבאר הענינים ההוים, או שנגיד העתידים.

[6] החלוק הוא באשר יתבאר הדבר אשר יסכים בו עם החולק, ואשר ישאר במחלקת· או שהוא באשר יתבאר מה שרוצה לאמר בעתיד. וקוינטיליאנו ברביעי גודר אותה ככה: החלוק הוא מספר הדברים אשר בינינו לבין החולק במחלקת, ואשר נסכים עליהם יחד.

[7] הקיום הוא מאמר כאשר תתבארנה ראיותינו עם קיום דעתנו· או שהוא אשר בהביא ראיות על עניננו המאמר, מוסיף בו חזוק וקיום, כאשר גדרו טוליאו, גם ויטורינו המפרש, בהלצה הישנה.

[8] ההתרה היא מאמר באשר תתבאר הפלת הראיות והספקות הקורות לענין נחזיק בו, וזה אם בכל אם במקצת.

[9] החתימה היא גבול ותכלית מלאכותי מכל מה שנאמר. אמנם אמרנו בזה הגדר מלאכותי, שראוי שיתוקן באופן יעורר השומע אל הרחמנות, או אל האכזריות והכעס· או שישנה במאמר קצר כל הנאמר למעלה.

[10] והמשל לחלקי המאמר מאמר יהודה עם יוסף, פרשת ויגש· וזה כי אמרו ויגש אליו יהודה ויאמר בי אדני כו׳ [בר׳ מ״ד י״ח], כל הפסוק הראשון, הוא הפתיחה. והנה נמצאו בו שלשה תנאי הפתיחה, ר״ל: לעשות השומע מחבב· וזה מצד ההכנעה והתחנה שעשה לפניו באמרו בי אדני, ואל יחר אפך בעבדך· גם מצד מה שאמר כי כמוך כפרעה, ששבח אותו עד שעשאו בדבריו במדרגה אחת עם המלך; עוד יעשהו מקשיב ומתלמד, במה שאמר ידבר נא עבדך דבר·

5 באשר] אשר[ר] || 9 הדברים] הד׳.רים[כ] | לבין] לבן[כ] || 12 בהביא] הביא[כ] || 16 מכל] בכל[כ] | אמרנו] אומרינו[ר] || 23 שאמר] שאמרת[כ] | שעשאו] עשאו[ר] ||

attentive, well disposed, and receptive—ought properly to be achieved throughout all the parts of the discourse, but that in the Introduction it is especially necessary so sweetly to win the heart of the hearer that we make him long for the next section of the discourse.

[5] The Statement of Facts is the telling of the true, or the quasi-true, facts, those, that is, with an appearance of plausibility. The Philosopher,[h] indeed, in the Abridgment of the *Rhetoric* which he made for Alexander, defines the Statement of Facts as that in which we recount things past, explain events which are occurring at the present, or predict future events.

[6] The Partition is a means of making clear wherein one agrees with one's opponent and what remains in dispute; or is a means of setting out what one intends to say later. Quintilian,[i] in Book IV, defines it as follows: "The Partition states the propositions in dispute between ourselves and our opponent, and those on which we in common agree."

[7] It is the Proof when both our evidence and the fact that it substantiates our hypothesis are simultaneously made clear. Or it is that which, when the discourse presents the evidence for our case, adds to it corroboration and substantiation, as Tully (and the commentator, Victorinus, also)[j] defined it in the Old Rhetoric.

[8] The Refutation is a statement by means of which it will be clear that the evidence contrary, and the doubts incidental, to the view we hold have been overthrown, whether in whole or in part.

[9] The Conclusion is the setting of an artistic limit and end to all that has been said. We use the word "artistic" in defining this Part, because the Conclusion ought to be prepared in such manner as to arouse the hearer to pity, or to heartlessness and anger; or it should recapitulate in a brief statement all that has previously been said.

[10] An example of the several divisions of the discourse is afforded by Judah's address to Joseph (Gen. 44:18–44:34) in the Weekly Lection *Wayyiggash* [**Then Judah came near,** etc.: Gen. 44:18–47:27]. For the whole of the first verse—**Then Judah came near unto him, and said: "Oh my lord, let thy servant, I pray thee, speak a word in my Lord's ears, and let not thine anger burn against thy servant; for thou art even as Pharaoh"** [44:18][3]—constitutes the Introduction. As we see, the three conditions of the Introduction are met in it: first, to render the hearer well disposed—this is achieved partly by Judah's submissiveness before Joseph, and his entreaty: "**Oh my lord," and "let not thine anger burn against thy servant,"** and partly by his words: "**for thou art even as Pharaoh,**" words in which he has so highly praised Joseph as to make him of equal degree with the king. Secondly and thirdly, Judah makes Joseph

3. JML cites the verse through "lord," and subsumes the rest under "etc."

h. Cf. *LR. ad A.* 64.23 f. (1438a f.).
i. Q. 4.5.1.
j. *De I.* 1.24.34; Halm, 213 ff.

כי לזה הספור יתחייב שני הדברים יחד, כמו שיתבאר. ומה שהתחיל, אדני שאל
את עבדיו, וכו׳ [שם שם י״ט], כל זה הוא ספור עד והורדתם את שיבתי ברעה
שאלה [שם שם כ״ט], שהוא מספר הדברים שנפלו בזה הענין. ומה שאמר, והיה
כבואי אל עבדך אבינו והנער איננו אתנו, ונפשו קשורה בנפשו׳ והיה כראותו כי
5 אין הנער ומת [שם שם ל׳—ל״א], הוא חלוק, כי בו יתפרסם הדבר אשר לא
יסכימו עליו, ר״ל, על עזיבתו. וכאלו אמר: ״זה התפרסם לנו, כי ימות אם לא
יראה הנער׳ ולזה הוא הדבר שאין ראוי לנו לעשות״; אלא שלא פרסם, לדברו
בענוה ובמוסר כעבד לפני המלך. גם מזה הפסוק יובן מה שהסכימו עליו עם
יוסף, רצוני לומר, בביאת בנימין שמה׳ וכאלו אמר: ״במקצת מה שרצית
10 הסכמנו, על ביאת בנימין במצרים; ומה שנשאר במחלקת הוא העזיבה, הנה כי
אנחנו לא נסכים בזה.״ זה ענין החלוק, אלא שבא כאן ברמז לסבה שבארנו. א״כ
אמר[1]: והורידו עבדיך את שיבת עבדך אבינו ביגון שאולה [ל״א]׳ וזהו הקיום.
וכאלו אמר: ״הראיה שאין לנו להסכים עמך בזה היא, כי אם נעשה זה ימצאנו
עון גדול, למה שנסבב מיתת אבינו ביגון שאולה, וזה עון פלילי.״ ומה שאמר כן,
15 כי עבדך ערב את הנער [ל״ב], היא ההתרה. כי היה אפשר שיאמר: ״מדוע אתה
לבדך תרבה תדבר גבוהה גבוהה, ואחיך יתאפקו?״ והוא מתיר זה במה שאמר,
כי הוא ערב אותו והיה ראוי שישתדל בהשבתו לו יותר מן האחרים. והנה
מאמר ״כי עבדך ערב״ לא היה נופל עם טוב ההבנה על מה שנאמר קודם, אם
לא שנאמר שנרמז למעלה שהם לא יניחוהו ולא יעזבוהו, כמו שבארנו. אמר
20 א״כ: ועתה ישב נא עבדך תחת הנער כו׳, כי איך אעלה אל אבי והנער איננו
אתי כו׳ [ל״ג—ל״ד]: זאת היא החתימה, כאשר כלל במאמר קצר מה שאמר
למעלה. והנה לנו, בזה המאמר כלו, פתיחה, ספור, חלוק, קיום, התרה, חתימה.

3 והיה] ועתה^ת || 4 אבינו] אבי^ת |והנער] והער^כ || 12 אמר[1] אמרו^כד |אבינו] אביו^ד || 19 [שנרמז]^כ ||
20 [ועתה]^כ || 21 שאמר] שנאמ׳^כ ||

---

13 מל״ב ז׳ ט׳ || 14 איוב ל״א כ״ח || 16 שמ״א ב׳ ג׳ ||

---

[1] Correction, as in ^R ד.

attentive and receptive by saying "**let thy servant, I pray thee, speak a word,**" for the Statement of Facts here requires that the hearer be simultaneously attentive and receptive, as will be clear. Beginning with the words "**My lord asked his servants,**" etc. [44:19], all this, as far as "**ye will bring down my gray hairs with sorrow to the grave**" [44:29], is the Statement which Judah gives of the facts involved in this case. His saying, "**And it shall be, when I come to thy servant our father,**[4] **and the lad is not with us; seeing that his soul is bound up with the lad's soul; it will come to pass, when he seeth that the lad is not with us, that he will die**" [44:30–31], forms a Partition, for in this the point of their disagreement is clearly brought out—the disagreement, that is, on the point of leaving Benjamin behind. It was as though Judah had said: "It is obvious to us that Jacob will die if he should not see the lad; hence to leave him behind is something which we must not do"; but he did not say this openly because he was speaking with humility and tact, like a servant before a king. From these verses, also, may be understood the point wherein the brothers agreed with Joseph—the coming of Benjamin thither; it was as though Judah had said: "We have agreed to part of what you wish, the coming of Benjamin into Egypt; what remains in dispute is the question of leaving him behind, for to this, indeed, we will not agree." This was the actual Partition, but it is only hinted at here for the reason already explained. He next says: "**and thy servants will bring down the grey hairs of thy servant our father with sorrow to the grave**" [44:31]; and this is the Proof. It was as though he had said: "What proves that we ought not agree with you in this is, that if we should so act, great **punishment would overtake us** [2 Kings 7:9], for we would thereby have brought about the death of our father 'in sorrow to the grave'—**a criminal deed**" [Job 31:28].[5] Judah's words "**For thy servant became surety for the lad**" [Gen. 44:32] form the Refutation. For it was possible that Joseph would say, "Why do you alone **multiply exceeding proud talk** [1 Sam. 2:3], while your brothers refrain?" but Judah refuted this by saying that he had become surety for Benjamin and that it was quite proper for him to make a greater effort than his brothers to restore the lad to his father. The statement "**For thy servant became surety**" would not make good sense alongside what had previously been stated unless we say that, as explained, it had previously been hinted that they would neither leave nor abandon Benjamin. Thereafter Judah said: "**let thy servant, I pray thee, abide instead of the lad . . . for how shall I go up to my father if the lad be not with me?**" etc. [44:33–34]. This is the Conclusion, when, in a short statement, Judah summed up what he had previously said. Thus, within the whole of this discourse, we have an Introduction, a Statement of Facts, a Partition, the Proof, the Refutation, and a Conclusion.

4. B: "Now therefore when I come to thy servant my father."
5. JV: "an iniquity to be punished by the judges."

פרק ששי

מהפתיחה.

[1] אמר טוליאו, בהלצה החדשה במאמר הראשון, שסוגי הדבור הם ארבעה, ר״ל, הגון, ומכוער, ספק, ושפל; והקשה עליו ויטורינו, בהלצה הישנה לו, ממה שאמר הוא בעצמו למעלה שסוגי הדבור הם שלשה. ואמר בהתרת זה הספק שלא ימנע שדבר אחד בעצמו יחלק בחלוקות מתחלפות, אחר שהחלוקות הנה אינם במדרגה אחת. והמשל בזה שאנחנו נאמר שהחי, ממנו מדבר, וממנו בלתי מדבר· וזאת היא חלוקה אחת; עוד נאמר החי, ממנו מהלך, ממנו מעופף, ממנו שט על פני המים· זאת היא חלוקה אחרת. ושתי החלוקות אמתיות, אלא שהחלוקה הראשונה היתה בערך אל הדברים העצמיים, והחלוקה השנית היא בהצטרף אל הדברים המקריים. וכן גם כן אם נאמר שהחי, ממנו אדום, ממנו לבן, ממנו שחור, ממנו מרוקם· עוד נאמר שהחי, ממנו גדול, ממנו קטן, ממנו בינוני· הנה אלו החלוקות כלם אמתיות, ואם הם בלתי מסכימות במספר החלקים, אלא שהאחת ביחס אל מקרה הכמות, והאחרת ביחס אל מקרה האיכות. ובכלל אומר שהעצם האחד בעצמו יחלק אל חלוקות רבות בלתי מסכימות האברים ביחס אל מקרים מתחלפים, מבלתי שיקרה מזה בטל. וכן הענין באלה החלוקות שנתן טוליאו: שהראשונה בערך אל הקיום והעצה ועצום, שהם איכות מה· והשנית בערך אל איכיות אחרות, ר״ל הגון, מכוער, ספק, ושפל, שהם איכיות אחרות· וכל אלה הם נשאים על הדבור. עוד השיב באופן אחר: שהחלוקה הראשונה היא בהצטרף אל הדבור, וזאת השניה היא בהצטרף אל מקרה הדבור, ר״ל בהצטרף אל המקיים והעצומי והעצתי, כי כל אחד מהם יחלק אל הגון, מכוער, ספק, ושפל.

[2] ואחר התישב זה, נגדור הדברים הנזכרים כפי אשר גדרם טוליאו בחדשה, ונאמר: ההגון הוא כאשר נכוון התנצלות לדבר שראוי זה בו בערך אל כל אדם· או שנכוון התלונה והתרעומת על דבר ראוי זה לו בערך אל כל אדם. המכוער הוא שנכוון המחלוקת והתלונה על דבר ההגון· או שנכוון ההתנצלות על המכוער. הספק הוא אשר לו צדדי המכוער וההגון, ר״ל, שימצא בו צד הגון אל

1 ששי] ו׳[ג] || 4 הישנה] היישנה[ג] || 6 אחר] אחד[ד] || 10 היתה] היה[ג] || 13 אלו] אלה[ג] || 17 טוליאו] טולאו[ד] || 18 איכות] איכו׳[ד] |איכיות אכויות[ג] || 19 איכיות] אכיות[ג] || 20 בהצטרף] בהצטף[ג] || 26 שנכוון] שנכווין[ג] || 27 אשר ו<לא>] לו[ג] ||

CHAPTER 6

Of the Introduction

[1] In Book I of the New Rhetoric, Tully[a] says that the Kinds of Cause are four: honorable, discreditable, doubtful, and petty; and, in his Commentary on the Old Rhetoric, Victorinus[b] has raised the possible objection that Tully himself had previously said that the Kinds of Cause are three. Victorinus resolves the difficulty by asserting that it is not impossible for one and the same thing to be subject to different classifications, since classifications are not all of a single kind and degree. We may, for example, assert of living things that some use speech and some do not, and this is one kind of classification; or, again, we may assert of living things that some walk, some fly, and some swim: this is another classification. Both classifications are valid; the first, however, has to do with substantive matters, the second with accidental. Likewise, if we assert of living things that some are red, some white, some black, and some variegated; or, again, that some are large, some small, and some intermediate in size, all such classifications are valid though disparate in the number of their several parts. It is only that one group relates to the accident of quantity, and the other to that of quality. In fine, he says that the selfsame substance is subject to many disparately membered classifications, depending as these severally relate to different accidents, and this without resultant invalidity. Such, then, is the case with the classifications offered by Tully: the first relates to Epideictic, Deliberative, and Judicial causes, which are of one particular quality, whereas the second has to do with other qualities—I mean, namely, honorable, discreditable, doubtful, and petty—which, quite different as they are, are nevertheless all potentially definitive of the utterance. Victorinus answers the objection in yet another way: the first division is concerned with the substance of the utterance, whereas the second is concerned with the accident of the utterance, that is, with the utterance as Epideictic, Forensic, or Deliberative, for each of these kinds of cause is divisible into honorable, discreditable, doubtful, and petty.

[2] This difficulty settled, we shall define the aforementioned qualities according to Tully's[c] definitions in the New Rhetoric. We say, then, that the cause is honorable when it is our purpose to defend some course which it would behoove any man to defend, or when it is our purpose to prosecute a complaint and an accusation against some course which it would behoove any man to prosecute. The discreditable cause is one in which it is our purpose to dispute and contend against something creditable, or to defend something discreditable. The doubtful has aspects of both the discreditable and the honorable, that is, an aspect found

a. *R. ad H.* 1.3.5–1.4.6.
b. Halm, 195–196; *De I.* 1.5.7 and 1.9.12.
c. *R. ad H.* 1.3.5.

השומעים, וצד מכוער. השפל הוא כאשר יבא לפני הדיין דין שפל.

[3] אמנם בהלצה הישנה אומר שסוגי אלה הסבות הם חמשה: הגון, נפלא, שפל, ספק, וחשוך. ואמר שההגון הוא אשר לב השומע יכוון בו ההתנצלות אף אם לא נאמר דבר· והנפלא הוא אשר יפרד ממנו לבב השומעים· והשפל הוא 5 הנעזב מן השומעים, ואין להם חפץ להטפל בו· והספק הוא כאשר נטיית לבב השומעים בספק, או שיש בו צד לכאן ולכאן מצד עצמו· והחשוך הוא אשר בו השומעים מתונים, או שהוא דבר מבולבל מהדברים שהם קשי ההבנה. וזאת החלוקה האחרונה מביאה גם קוינטיליאנו בא׳ מהחלק השביעי; ואמר ויטורינו המפרש שאלה הגדרים לא נלקחו מעצמות הדברים כי אם בהצטרף אל לבב 10 השומעים. והנה אלה החמשה דברים — הגון, נפלא, שפל, ספק, חשוך — לא נלקחו במוחלט, אלא כפי מה שיסברו בו השומעים. והנה הגדרים שהביאם בהלצה החדשה — יען אמר בגדרים ההם שיהיו כן בערך אל כל אדם — אין ספק שלקח אותם מהדברים בעצמם, מבלתי הצטרף אל סברת השומעים·כי הדבר שהוא ראוי לכל אדם הוא מצד שכן הוא בטבע. אמנם קצת המפרשים 15 חשבו לחבר את האהל, וכתבו שגם שם המכוון בהגון מכוער וזולתם לפי סברת השומעים, והוא זולת מה שנחשבהו אנחנו בזה המקום.

[4] והנה החלוקות הנזכרות תחייבנה חלוף גדול בפתיחות, לפי הענינים אשר הפתיחות האלה בערכם. ולזה אמר טוליאו שהפתיחה היא על אחת משתי פנים: אם מה שממנה בנגלה, ותקרא פתיחה סתם· אם מה שממנה בהעלם, 20 ותקרא פתיחה נסתרת.

[5] והפתיחה סתם כבר גדרנוה למעלה, שהתחייב אצלה שתעשה השומע מחבב, ומתלמד, ומקשיב. ואם יקרה לנו ענין מסופק, נתחיל מהחבוב, למען לא ינגד לנו צד הכעור אשר בו. ואם מה שיקרה לנו יהיה שפל, נשתדל לעשות מקשיב. ואם יהיה המכוער, נעשה בזה הפתיחה הנסתרת, אשר נבאר ענינה

2 הם] הן[c] || 8 ויטורינו] וטורינו[d] וּויטורינו[c] || 12 בגדרים] בגדרי[d] || 13 השומעים] השומעי[d] || 16 שנחשבהו] שנשבחיהו[c] || 19 מה שממנה] ממה ממנה[d] || 23 ינגד] יגד[c] | לעשות] להיות[c] ||

15 שמ׳ כ״ו י״א ||

creditable by the audience, and an aspect found discreditable. It is the petty cause when what comes before the judge is an unimportant case.

[3] In the Old Rhetoric, to be sure, Tully[d] says that the Kinds of these Causes are five: honorable, extraordinary, petty, doubtful, and obscure. He says that an honorable cause is one in which the purpose to defend will be formed in the hearer's mind even though we say nothing; that the extraordinary is one from which the mind of the hearers will be aloof; that the petty is soon abandoned by the hearers, as being a cause with which they have no desire to deal; that the cause is doubtful when the inclination of the hearers' mind is in doubt, or if the cause in and of itself has two separate aspects; and that the obscure is one about which the hearers have reservations, or is a cause which is confused as a result of matters difficult to grasp. This last division is also introduced by Quintilian[e] in Chapter 1 of Book VII;[1] and the commentator Victorinus[f] says that these definitions are not derived from the substance of the matters, but are relative to the mind of the hearers. These five Kinds of Cause—honorable, extraordinary, petty, doubtful, obscure—are indeed not derived absolutely, but according to the hearers' opinion of the Cause. The definitions given in the New Rhetoric, however—since Tully[g] says of those definitions that they are so for any man—were doubtless derived by him from the Causes themselves, quite apart from the hearers' opinion. For the Cause which is appropriate to any man is such because it is appropriate by nature. Some commentators, indeed, thinking to **couple the tent together** [Exod. 26:11], have written that there[2] too Tully's meaning was "honorable," "discreditable," and the rest, according to the hearers' opinion, but this is contrary to our own interpretation of this passage.

[4] The above-mentioned divisions will result in Introductions which differ considerably, according to the matters they severally deal with. Thus, Tully[h] says that the Introduction appears in either of two aspects: one whose effect is explicit, which is called the Direct Opening, without further qualification, or one whose effect is implicit, and which is called the Subtle[3] Approach.

[5] We previously defined the Direct Opening as one whose function it is to make the hearer well disposed, receptive, and attentive. If we find ourselves dealing with an ambiguous matter, we should begin by attempting to create good will, so that the discreditable side of the case may not be used against us. If our Cause happens to be petty, we must try to make the audience attentive. If it is discreditable, we will use the Subtle Approach (which we shall discuss in the

1. *Sic.*, both M and C; the error here, however (confusion of שביעי/רביעי), is more likely Conat's than JML's.
2. I.e., the passage in *R. ad H.*
3. Literally: "hidden," "concealed," "covert."

d. *De I.* 1.15.20 ff.
e. Q. 4.1.40–41.
f. Halm, 195–196.
g. *R. ad H.* 1.3.5.
h. *R. ad H.* 1.4.6.

אחר זה, זולת אם יקרה דבר מה באשר נוכל להשען לעשות החבוב, כאלו
תאמר, שבתלונה הנעשת ממנו מן אשר כנגדנו נגרום החבוב. והמשל: אם נקבע
אחד מחברו אל השופט, וצוה ליכנס במאסר, ואמר מתלונן: אני נענש שלא
כדין· ואז השיב חברו שקבעו: אתה תכנס במאסר על אפך ועל חמתך, כדין או
5 שלא כדין· ואז יאמר אותו העני אל הדין: ראה, אדני, אם גבה לב האיש הזה
לאמר כדברים האלה· זה יביא אל שהדין יכמרו רחמיו, וימשך מפני זה
שהנקבע ההוא לא יכנס במאסר. והנה בזה האופן קרה שעשינו הפתיחה, וחיבה
החבוב לשומע, במקום לא היתה ראויה בו כי אם הפתיחה הנסתרת.

[6] ואם הדבר אשר לפנינו הגון, אז הרשות בידינו לעשות הפתיחה או לבלתי
10 עשותה. ואם נרצה לעשותה, ראוי לנו שנוכיח שהדבר ההוא הגון· או שנאמר
בקצור מאי זה ענין הכונה ממנו לדבר. ואם לא נרצה לעשות הפתיחה, ראוי
שנתחיל להוכיח המבקש מן הדת או מן הכתב, ר״ל, מאי זה שטר יהיה
בעזרתנו, או מאי זו ראיה חזקה יתבאר בה מה שכוונוהו. ואמרו קצת המפרשים
שהרצון הנה בדת אי זו דת שתהיה, אלהית או אנושית.

15 [7] ואחר התישב זה, ראוי שנאמר היאך יעשה השומע מתלמד, מקשיב, או
מחבב. אמנם נעשהו מתלמד: או נספר כלל מה שנרצה לומר בקצור· או
שנעשהו מקשיב, למה שהמתלמד הוא אשר יכין לבו, תקשיב אזנו, להבין
היטב; וראוי שתדע שמי שהוא מתלמד הוא מקשיב, אבל לא יתהפך. אמנם
האופן באשר יעשה מקשיב: אם נאמר שהכונה ממנו לדבר בענינים הגדולים,
20 חדשים מקרוב באו· או מהדברים שהם הכרחיים לכללות, או אל השומע
בעצמו, או מהדברים נוגעים בעבודת האלקים; או שנבקש ממנו שתהיינה אזניו
קשובות לדברינו, שנאמר לו מספר הענינים אשר יהיה בהם המאמר.

[8] אמנם אפשר שנעשהו מחבב באחד מד׳ פנים: אם מצד עצמנו, אם מצד
המנגדים, אם מצד השומעים, אם מצד הענינים בעצמם. והאופן אשר נעשהו
25 מחבב מצד עצמנו: אם נשבח[1] משמרתנו ומעשנו בלתי ההנשאות (והמשמרת
היא, לפי ויטורינו המפרש בהלצה הישנה, הדבר המוטל עלינו להשלימו אם
מצד הדתות, אם מצד הטבע); או שנספר היאך הועלנו לכללות, והיאך הפלגנו
בכבוד הורים ורחם עליהם, ושהטבנו לאחוזת מרעינו, גם כי גמלנו טובה אל
השומע, אם הדברים האלה כלם נכונים להאמר בהצטרף אל הענין אשר אנחנו

2 ממנו] ממנהֹ[כ] || 3 ליכנס] לכנס[ד] || 6 מפני זה] מזה[כ] || 7 [וחיבה][כ] || 9 בידינו] בידנו[כ] || 12 המבקש] המבוקש[כ] | מאי זה] מאי זו[כ] || 14 שכוונוהו] שכווננוהו[ד] || 22 לדברינו] לדברנו[כ] || 24 בעצמם] בעצמן[ד] || 25 נשבח[1]] נקח[כ] נשכח[ד] || 27 הדתות] הדתו[ד] || 28 לאחזת] לאחוזת[כ] ||

17 תה׳ י׳ י״ז || 20 דב׳ ל״ב י״ז || 21 תה׳ ק״ל ב׳ ||

[1] Correction, as in ד[R]; cf. *R. ad H.* 1.4.8 (“laudabimus”).

next chapter) unless circumstances upon which we may rely to create good will happen to be present; if, for example, we can procure good will through the very accusation made against us by our opponent. To illustrate: A, haled by B before a judge and sentenced to jail, protests and says: "I am being unjustly punished"; the lodger of the charge, B, replies: "You will go to jail, like it or not, justly or unjustly." When the poor wretch then says to the judge: "Consider, my lord, whether this person must not be arrogant to use such language," the judge is thereby induced to feel compassion, with the result that that arraignee does not go to jail. We here have an instance in which we have used the Direct Opening and it has procured the hearer's good will, where properly only the Subtle Approach seemed indicated.

[6] If the matter before us is honorable, then the choice is ours whether or not to use an Introduction. Assuming that we wish to use one, we should demonstrate that the matter is in fact honorable, or else we briefly announce what matters we propose to discuss. But if we do not wish to use a Direct Opening, we should begin to prove our case from a law or text, that is, from some helpful document at our disposal, or from some strong proof through which our case will be demonstrated. Some commentators[4] say that "law" here means any kind of law, whether divine or human.

[7] This settled, we must now state how the hearer will be made receptive, attentive, or well disposed. As for our making him receptive: we either give a brief and summary account of what we propose to say, or we make him attentive, since the receptive person is one who **directs** his **heart, causes** his **ear to attend** [Ps. 10:17], in order to understand aright. You must also know that the receptive hearer is attentive, but not vice versa. Now as to the method of making him attentive: either we will say that we propose to speak of important matters, **new** things **that came up of late** [Deut. 32:17], or of matters that are of vital concern to the public or to the hearer himself, or of things appertaining to the worship of God; or else we will request the hearer to **let** his **ears be attentive** [Ps. 130:2] to our words as we enumerate for him the points to be treated in our discourse.

[8] We can make our hearer well disposed by any of four approaches: from the discussion of ourselves, of our opponents, of our hearers, or of the subject matter itself. It is the method of making the hearer well disposed from the discussion of ourselves, (a) if we praise[5] our duty and deeds without arrogance. (According to Victorinus,[i] the commentator on the Old Rhetoric, "duty" is the task which either law or nature obliges us to fulfill.) Or (b) we may describe how we have promoted the general welfare, the surpassing honor and compassion which we have shown our parents, the improvement we have brought to the lot of our friends, and the benefits, too, that we have conferred upon the hearer; provided,

4. I.e., on *R. ad H.* 1.4.6.
5. Emended text; M: "take"; C: "forget."

i. Halm, 197.

בו; עוד נספר עמלנו ולחצנו, שאנחנו נעזבים ונטושים אין עוזר לנו, וכי צרותינו נגדנו תמיד· או נתחנן לפניו שיהיה לנו לישועה, ושנאמר לו שאין לנו בטחון כי אם עליו. והוסיף טוליאו בהלצה הישנה שכמו כן הענין אם ננהג עמו ההכנעה ובקשות ותחנות, או אם נדחה מה שיצא עלינו קול מהדבות.[2]

[9] והאופן שאפשר שנביא החבה מצד[3] המנגדים הוא, אם נביא המנגדים באיבה או בקנאה או במחלוקת. וענין שנביאהו באיבה הוא, אם נספר איזה דבר נעשה מהם כמיאוס והתנשאות וחסרון אמונה, באכזריות או בעזות, במרמה, במרד בי״י, ברב תאוה. אמנם נביאם בקנאה אם נספר גבורותם, וכחם, והתקשרם, ועשרם, ועזרתם, ויחסם· וסעודתם, והמסובים עמהם תמיד, וקרוביהם· ומנהגם בהתנשאות, ושכל מה שהם עושים הוא בעד תועלתם, לא בעבור האמת. והאופן הביאנו אותם במחלקת הוא, שנספר שהחולקים עלינו הם יושבי קרנות, בעלי עצלנות והתרשלות, ורב תאוה.

[10] אמנם מצד השומעים, נביא החבה אם נאמר שמעשיהם כלם הם נעשים בחכמה, ודעת, וענוה, במשפט וצדקה· או אם נפרסם מה גדלה תפארתם בלב האנשים, ויחלו כמטר להם, ידמו למועצותיו.[4]

[11] ואם מצד הדברים בעצמם נביא החבה, נרמם ענינגו ונשבח אותו· וענין החולקים עלינו, ודברי ריבותם, נשפילם עד ארץ, נגיעם עד עפר.

פרק ז׳

מן הפתיחה הנסתרת.

[1] המנע העשות הפתיחה סתם היא באחד מג׳ פנים: אם שהדבר אשר בידנו מכוער, ר״ל שהענין ההוא גורם אל שירחק ממנו לבב השומעים מצד כעורן· אם

1 עמלנו ולחצנו] עמלינו ולחצינו[ר] || 2 או ‹אם› נתחנן[ד] || 5 שאפשר] שאפאר[ר] | מצד[3]] צד[כד] || 9 וסעודתם] וסועדתם[כ] || 12 עצלנות] עצלנת[כ] || 14 ודעת] ובדעת[כ] | וצדקה] ובצדקה[כ] | מה גדלה] מהגדלת[כ] || 16 ענינגו] עינינו[ר] || 21 לבב] לבב[כ] ||

1 דב׳ כ״ו ז׳ || 15 איוב כ״ט כ״ג | איוב כ״ט כ״א || 17 יש׳ כ״ו ה׳ ||

[2] *Sic,* both כ and ד. Read מדהבות? Cf. Isa. 14:4.

[3] Correction, as in [R]ד.

[4] Points to reading לְמוֹעֲצָתִי instead of לְמוֹ עֲצָתִי at Job 29:21.

of course, that all these references are pertinent to the matter under discussion. Or, again (c) we may describe **our toil and our oppression** [Deut. 26:7]—say that we are abandoned and forsaken with none to help us, and that we face hardships continually; or we may beg our hearer to save us, and say that except for him we have none upon whom to rely. In the Old Rhetoric, Tully[j] adds that the effect will be similar, if, with our hearers, we make use of submissive language, prayers and entreaties, or if we refute any slanderous rumor which may have circulated concerning us.

[9] It is the method of making the hearer well disposed from discussion of our opponents if we proceed by bringing our opponents into hatred, envy, or controversy.[k] We shall bring them into hatred if we tell of some deliberately repulsive, high-handed and treacherous deed that they have committed cruelly, brazenly, in defiance of God, with great delight. We shall bring them into envy by telling of their might and strength, connections, wealth, power to aid, and high birth; of their banqueting, their constant banquet guests, and their intimates; of their arrogant conduct, and how everything they do is done for their own profit, not for the sake of truth. The way to bring our adversaries into controversy is to describe them as idle gossips, lazy, indolent, and excessively self-indulgent.

[10] From the discussion of our hearers we shall procure goodwill if we say that all their deeds are done with wisdom, knowledge, and modesty, with justice and righteousness; or if we acclaim the greatness of their glory in the hearts of men, who **wait for** them **as for the rain** [Job 29:23], **keep silence for** their **counsels** [29:21].[6]

[11] If from the discussion of the facts themselves we would secure the goodwill, we extol and praise our own cause, while **laying . . . low even to the ground, bringing . . . even to the dust** [Isa. 26:5] the cause and contentions of our adversaries.

CHAPTER 7

Of the Subtle Approach[a]

[1] The Direct Opening may not be used in any of these three contexts: (1) if our case is dishonorable, that is, when the matter is sure to alienate the mind of

6. B: יִדְּמוּ לְמוֹ עֲצָתִי; JML: ידמו למועצותיו.

j. *De I.* 1.16.22.
k. *R. ad H.* 1.5.8.

a. *R. ad H.* 1.6.9 ff; *De I.* 1.17.23 ff.

כשלבב השומע הספיקוהו מי שקדמו לדבר לפנינו· או שהוא נלאה משמוע מצד המדברים ההם שקדמונו.

[2] ואם הדבר מכוער, נאמר שראוי לדיינים להביט יותר אל הטוב שאפשר שיגיע מזה החוטא יותר ממה שיביטו אל העון, אם הוא אדם גדול המעלה שאפשר שיאמר זה בערכו; או שראוי שיביטו אל מעלת אבותיו וחשיבותם, ומה שעשו מהטובות; או שראוי שיביטו אל הפלגת חכמת זה החוטא ומלאכתו היקרה יותר ממה שיובטו אליו; או שיאמר שיותר ראוי להביט אל האיש הנכבד הזה, גדול העצה ורב העליליה, יותר משתפקד חטאתו וחרפתו לא תמחה.

[3] והנה אם תתבונן בהתנצלות הראשון, נלקח דבר תמורת דבר· ובשני, אדם תמורת אדם· ובשלישי, הדבר תמורת האדם· וברביעי, האדם תמורת הדבר. ובזה האופן ראוי לבאר דברי טוליאו בזה המקום, כמו שאמר ויטורינו בישנה.

[4] או ראוי לנו שנכביד העון, ונאמר שמה שאמרו המנגדים הוא עון מופלג וחטאת עצומה, אין כמוה ואין ערוך אליה בתעצומה ורומה; ואחר שהפלגנו בזה, נאמר שזה הדבר הרע אשר בתכלית ימנע שיוחס בחק האיש הזה אשר הפליגו התלונה בו. והנה הכבדת החטאת והפלגתה הועילה לנו להוכיח שעון כמהו בחק האיש הזה נמנע, למה שלא נמצא מעולם שעשה כדומה לזה.

[5] או שנביא ראיה ממה שנעשה כבר בדומה לזה או גדול ממנו, כאלו תאמר שאם נרצה להציל המכה את חברו מן העונש, נביא ראיה ממי שעשה בזה או ממי שהרגו, שהוא עון יותר גדול, ונמחל לו· וכן ראוי למחול לזה.

[6] או שנביא ראיה ממה שנעשה לקטן ממנו, ר״ל, שבזמן פלוני קרה זה הענין בערך אל פלוני, שהיה קטן מזה האיש במעלה, ומחלו לו הדיינים· וכל שכן שראוי שתמחלו לזה אתם. ואחר שנרגיש שלבו פונה אל הרחמנות, ראוי שנלך בזה ההתנצלות לאט, עם הבאת הדמיונים.

[7] אם שנספר רעות גדולות מהמנגדים ונפליג בספור רשעתם, עם שנאמר שלא נרצה לדבר בהם איך הם בערך אל ההנהגות, כמי שיאמר: אחריש אתאפק, ולא אספר חטאתיך ומה שעשית כך וכך. וזה אחד מן היפויים, הנקרא

5 [שאפשר][c] || 6 מהטובות] מן הטובות[c] | הפלגת חכמת] הפלגת ‹רוב› החכמה[c] || 8 העליליה] העללייה[c] || 9 תמורת] תמורה[c] || 12 שנכביד ‹הדבר›] העוון[c] || 15 והפלגתה] והפלגת[c] || 18 ממי] מימי[c] || 24 [גדולות][c] ||

8 יר׳ ל״ב י״ט | מש׳ ו׳ ל״ג || 25 יש׳ מ״ב י״ד ||

our hearers because of its ugliness; (2) if the hearer has been fully persuaded by the previous speakers; or (3) when the previous speakers have made the hearer too weary to listen further.

[2] (1) Given a dishonorable case, (a) we shall say that the judges should look more to the good which might come of this sinner than to his act of iniquity, if, indeed, he is a person of such high excellence that this can be said about him. (b) Or we will say that the judges ought to consider the virtue and importance of his forebears and the good they accomplished; (c) or that they should pay more heed to the exceptional wisdom and valuable skill of this sinner than to himself. (d) Or it may be said that it is better to have regard for this distinguished person, so **great in counsel and mighty in work** [Jer. 32:19], than that his sin be punished **and his reproach . . . not be wiped away** [Prov. 6:33].

[3] Now plainly, if you study the first defence mentioned above, one thing has been substituted for another thing; in the second, the substitution is of persons; in the third, a thing has been substituted for a person; and in the fourth, a person for a thing. This is how Tully's words in the present passage should be interpreted, as Victorinus[b] says in his Commentary on the Old Rhetoric.

[4] (e) Or, to continue, it may behoove us to emphasize the seriousness of the offence, and to say that our opponents' accusation concerns a crime of such magnitude, a sin of such enormity, as to be without like or compare in size and scope; having expatiated upon this theme, we may say that this act of utmost evil cannot possibly be ascribed to the character of this man, who has been accused of too great a crime. Here, then, is an instance in which magnification and exaggeration of the criminal act are advantageous, enabling us to prove that such a crime is a constitutional impossibility for this defendant, as he could never possibly have committed anything of the kind.

[5] (f) Or, again, we may introduce as evidence a previous act which equals or transcends in seriousness the present one: if, for instance, we wish to acquit a person who has committed an assault, we may introduce as evidence the case of someone who committed this same act, or even killed the victim—a greater crime—and yet was acquitted; and so our defendant, too, should be set free.

[6] (g) Or we may introduce as a precedent what was done in a case involving a lesser man, as follows: "In A's time, there was a case of this same kind involving B, a man of lower standing than our defendant, and whom the judges acquitted; how much the more, then, does it behoove you to acquit this man." Once we sense that the judge is inclining to clemency, we should proceed slowly along this line of defence, and introduce other examples as well.

[7] (h) Or we may describe major iniquities committed by our opponents, amplifying the tale of their wickedness, and saying, too, that we have no desire to discuss the quality of their morals; as though to say, "**I will be still, I will refrain myself** [Isa. 42:14], and not tell the tale of your sins, nor about this-and-

b. Halm, 198; *De I.* 1.17.24.

העלמה· ובזה ירחק לבב השומע מבעלי התלונות.

[8] ואם נראה שלבב השומע פונה אל המנגדים מצד שהספיקו אליו בדברם· כי זה ידעהו בקלות מי שהרגיל מלאכת התלונה וההתנצלות· נבטיח הדיין לספר מה שחשבוהו החולקים מן הראיות למבצר, ומשגב, ובית מקדש מלך, ושנשברהו. או שנתחיל ממה שספרו המנגדים, וביחוד ממה שדברו באחרונה כי שם חביון עזם· כי כאשר יראה השומע המתנצל מוכן להשיב, יחשוב שהאמת אתו. או שנאמר כמספק שלא נדע מאי זה מקום וראיה נכוון ההתחלה, לרוב הראיות אשר לנו כנגד החולקים.

[9] ואם לבב השומע נלאה מרב דברים ששמע מבעלי התלונות, נתחיל מאי זה דבר מעורר השחוק, כגון חידה, או בדיאה, או[1] הדרכה אשר לה פנים מן ההראות; כגון שידבר בלשון אחרת, ר״ל, שאם היה ספרדי יתחיל לדבר בלשון אשכנזי· או שיעשה אי זה פעל מתדמה לאחר, כגון שעשה עצמו בעל חטוטרת, או שדבר בלעגי שפה· או הקריאה בטעות, כגון שקרא שמן בחולם· או אי זה הפוך במאמר, כגון שאמר, אשמע בעיני ואראה באזני· או אי זה דבור מסופק, כגון שיאמר דבר שאפשר שישוב לשני ענינים, כמו שלף איש נעלו [רות ד׳ ז׳]· או אי זה חסרון אות, כגון שרצה לאמר הצלחה ואמר הצחה· או אי זה חשד, כגון שידבר או יעשה פועל יובן ממנו חשד מה כנגד בעלי התלונות, כגון שנראה עצמנו לבלתי אמר דבר מהם, אלא שנטה עצמנו אל אזן אחד מן האנשים, אשר זה יוליד חשד גדול בלב השומע· או לעג, כגון שנאמר לשומע, ״זה בעל התלונות לא היתה חכמה אשר שגבה ממנו, כל סתום לא עממוהו·״ או אי זה פעל שטות שנספר להסיר הלאות מן השומע, או אי זו הפלגה, כגון שיאמר, ״פלוני עשה לו כנפים לעוף בשמים״· או אי זה דמיון, כגון שיאמר לשומע, ״זה בעל התלונות כאריה יכסוף לטרוף״, כי זה יביא להרחיק לבב השומע מן המנגד· או חלוף אותיות, כגון שיאמר ״בעל התנולות״ במקום ״תלונות״· או שנעמד מלאמר, כי זאת אחת מן הסבות שהשומע יהיה מקשיב· או אי זה משל, כגון

1 העלמה] ההעלמה[ג] || 2 בדברם ‹אתו›[ד] || 3 וההתנצלות] וההתצלות[ד] || 5 ושנשברהו] ונשברהו[ג] || 7 כמספק] במספק[ד] || 9–10 מאי זה דבר] מאי הדבר[ג] | או[1]] תו[גד] || 13 שקרא] שקרה[ד] || 16 לאמר] לומ׳[ג] || 24 התנולות] התלונות[ג] ||

4 עמ׳ ז׳ י״ג || 6 חב׳ ג׳ ד׳ || 20 יח׳ כ״ח ג׳ || 23 תה׳ י״ז י״ב ||

[1] Correction as in J and ד[R].

that which you did." Now this is one of the Figures of Speech, that called Paralipsis;[1] the hearer's sympathy is thereby alienated from the accusers.

[8] (2) If we see that the hearer inclines to favor our opponents,[c] whose speaking has served to convince him—and one experienced in the art of accusation and defence will detect this easily—we may promise the judge that we shall review and demolish the points of evidence regarded by our adversaries as their stronghold, fortress, and **king's sanctuary** [Amos 7:13]. Or we may begin with our opponents' views, and particularly with their final words since **there is the hiding of** their **power** [Hab. 3:4]—for when the hearer observes that the defendant is quite ready to make answer, he will assume that the truth is with him. Or, as if perplexed, we may say that, since we have so much evidence to cite against our adversaries, we do not know where, and with which point, to begin.

[9] (3) If the hearer's mind has been wearied by the overabundant words of the prosecution,[d] we may begin with something humorous, a riddle, say, or a joke; or some plausible bit of homely wisdom. One might, for example, speak in a foreign language, that is, if the orator is a Spaniard he might start speaking in German. Or one might mimic somebody else—pretend one has a hump, or stammer, or commit a ridiculous error in reading, like pronouncing *shemen* [= "oil"] with o's instead of e's; or use some inversion—for example, "I hear with my eyes and see with my ears"; or use some double-entendre—for instance, say something that has two different meanings, like **a man** [or: **each**] **drew off his shoe** [Ruth 4:7]; or omit a letter from a word, like saying "proper" when you mean "prosper." Further, something might be said or done implying a certain suspicion of the prosecution; for instance, while obviously avoiding saying anything about them openly, to bend down and whisper into the ear of somebody present, a maneuver which will arouse great suspicion in the hearer's mind. Or sarcasm might be used: we may, for instance, say to the hearer, "This accuser, now, there was never any wisdom too lofty for him, **no secret that they can hide from** him! [Ezek. 28:3]." Again, to banish the hearer's weariness, we might tell an anecdote involving some foolish or extravagant act—for instance, say, "So-and-so made himself wings to fly through the skies." Or use may be made of some simile: we might, for example, say to the hearer, "This prosecutor is **like a lion that is eager to tear in pieces**" [Ps. 17:12], for this may induce the hearer to feel aversion for our opponent. Or there may be a transposition of letters in a key word—for example, to say *ba'al hithnawwᵉlūth* [= "ugly" or "disgraced"] for *ba'al hattᵉlūnōth* [= "prosecutor"].[2] Or we may stop short of saying something, for this is one of the reasons why a hearer will be attentive; use some fable,

1. See iv.24.1 below.
2. Heb. התנולות/התלונות; the text, however, omits the ה from the second word: בעל התנולות במקום תלונות.

c. *De I.* 1.17.25; *R. ad H.* 1.6.10.
d. *R. ad H.* 1.6.10; cf. *De I.* 1.17.25.

שאומר לבעלי התחבולות שועלים· או שנספר חדשות ודברים לא נודעו· או אי
זה חרוז שנאמר· או שנגיד אי זה מעשה שהיה, או שיהתלו שניהם זה בזה.

[10] וראוי שתדע, כמו שאמר ויטורינו בישנה, שהדברים שזכרנו אין ראוי
לעשותם מבלתי הבטה אל מה שצריך, כי ראוי שהאדם יתבונן מה טוב לעשות
5 ויעשה לפי מה שיראה שהשעה משחקת לו ולפי הצורך. גם אם לא יראה דרך
לדברי ההתול והשחוק, אולי יפותה במה שיעירו אל העצבון והדאגה מן
המעשים, הספורים, והדבורים, או דבר בו מן הפלא והתימ׳, כי גם זה יסירהו מן
הלאות. או שיבטיח השומע לבלתי אמור כמו האחרים המאריכים בדבריהם,
אמנם יכלכל דבריו בתכלית הקצור. זה תכלית מה שנאמר בהסרת הלאות.

10 [11] אמנם ההבדל בין הפתיחה סתם והפתיחה הנסתרת כי בפתיחה סתם,
תכף במאמרים נגלים ומפורסמים נגרום אל שלבב השומע יהיה מתלמד,
מקשיב, מחבב· והפתיחה הנסתרת תחייב כל אלה, אלא שתעשה כל זה
בהעלמה והסתר כמו שבארנו. ואין ראוי שיעלם שזה הענין צריך שיהיה שמור
בכל חלקי המאמר, ר״ל לעשות השומע מחבב, מקשיב, מתלמד, אלא שזה
15 בפתיחה הוא הכרחי יותר.

[12] וראוי לנו שנחלק ההטעאות הנופלות בפתיחה, ונאמר:

[13] ראשונה, ראוי שתהיה הפתיחה טובת ההבנה, בלשון בינוני מבלתי
צחיות, למען לא יחשוב אדם בה תחבולות אם תעבור הרגל הלשונות.

[14] עוד, ראוי להשמר שלא ילקח בה דבר על צד הסבה אפשר שילקח בכל
20 דבר, כגון שנאמר: ״הנה באתי אליך כדורש משפט, כי ידעתי לא יעלם ממך דבר
המשפט, להגיע לכל אחד מבעלי דינים מה שראוי לו״· הוא דבר כולל שאפשר
להביא זאת הסבה בכל ענין, לכן אין ראוי להרגילה בפתיחות.

[15] עוד, שלא יאמר מה שאפשר שיאמרהו המנגד, כגון שיאמר לשומע:
״זכור תזכור שאני הייתי למשמעתך כמה שנים״, עם שהמנגד גם כן היה אתו
25 בזמן ההוא.

3 אין [ראוי]ד || 5 שהשעה] שהשעד || 6 [והדאגה]כ || 18 צחיות] צחויותכ || 23 יאמר] י..רכ | מה] דברכ || 24 [גם כן]כ ||

for example, one in which schemers are termed "foxes"; or describe recent developments and things hitherto unknown; or recite a bit of verse; or tell the story of some actual happening; or about two persons trying to deceive each other.

[10] As Victorinus[e] says in his Commentary on the Old Rhetoric, you should know that the suggestions mentioned above ought not to be carried out without careful consideration of what is needed; for a man ought to take thought of what is best to do, and should act according as he sees that the moment is propitious and as the need requires. Moreover, if the way should not seem clear for using satire and humor, the hearer may perhaps be beguiled by some incident, story, saying, some strange or astonishing matter, which will stir him to sadness and anxiety; for such too can banish his weariness. Or a speaker may promise his audience that he will not discourse, like the others, at inordinate length, but will confine his words to the briefest compass. This is all that we shall say about ways to overcome weariness.

[11] The difference between the Direct Opening and the Subtle Approach is this:[f] in the Direct Opening, through language whose meaning is perspicuous and commonly accepted, we straightway make the mind of the hearer receptive, attentive, and well disposed; whereas the Subtle Approach, while it can produce all these effects, achieves them in a concealed and covert way, as we have explained. Nor should it go unremarked that this same care—to make the audience well disposed, attentive, and receptive—must be taken throughout all the parts of the discourse, save that this aim is even more essential in the Introduction.

[12] Since we should analyze the faults incidental to the Introduction, let us say:

[13] First, that the Introduction should be easy to understand, in language that is dignified[3] without being elegant, so that no one will suspect it of intent to deceive should it pass beyond the locutions of ordinary speech.

[14] Second, in the Introduction, care should be taken not to adopt, as premise, a consideration that might be applicable in any case. If, for example, we say "I come to you as one seeking justice, because I know that you are not heedless of the meaning of justice, namely, to give each of the litigants his due," that is too general a consideration, since it might be adduced as the premise in any matter; it is improper, therefore, to employ it in Introductions.

[15] Third, one should not say what can as well be said by one's opponent; for instance, to say to the hearer, "Kindly remember that I have been in your service for so-and-so many years," when the adversary has also been with him for a like length of time.

3. Literally, "middle-style."

e. Halm, 199–200.
f. *R. ad H.* 1.7.11.

[16] עוד, ראוי להשמר לאמר דבר שהמנגד אפשר שיביאהו לעזרתו עם מעט השתנות, והמשל: אם אני השתדלתי לבקשת השומע בדבר מעטי התועלת והכבוד· ושכנגדי כבר השתדל, והשיג למענו השומע דבר יותר מעלה וגדול ממה שהשיג למעני· ואם כן, אם אומר לשומע שיזכור מה שהועלתי אותו בענין כך, אז המנגד יאמר שיזכור התועלת הגדולה אשר הגיע לו ממנו; והנה יאמר דברי ממש עם שנוי ענין התועלת, ואין ספק שזה ישוב לי להזק גדול.

[17] עוד, ראוי להשמר מהפתיחה שיש לה מן הצחות שעור רב, או שהיא ארוכה ביותר. וזה אפשר שיהיה באחד מג׳ פנים, כמו שיאמר קוינטיליאנו: אם שהפתיחה בעצמה תהיה ארוכה· אם שהיא ארוכה להיותה מעורבת עם יתר החלקים· אם שהיא ארוכה בהצטרף אל סוג הדבור, ר״ל סוג העצומי והעצתי, אשר ראוי בערכם שתהיה הפתיחה קצרה.

[18] עוד, ראוי להשמר שלא יהיה בפתיחה דבר שהוא זר מהענין אשר אנחנו בו, כגון שתרצה לקבוע אדם אל המשפט מפני הרצח,ותעשה הפתיחה בענין הנואף.

[19] עוד, הפתיחה הטעאיית אם במקום שראוי לעשות השומע מחבב, אני עושה אותו מקשיב או מתלמד, או להפך. עוד הפתיחה ההטעאיית: אשר אינה מחייבת אל השומע לא התלמדות, ולא קשב, ולה חבה.

[20] זה מה שאמר טוליאו בחדשה. אמנם בישנה אמר שהמקומות ההטעאיים בהצטרף אל הפתיחה, אשר ראוי להשמר מהם בחזקת היד, הם ז׳ רצוני לומר, הכולל, המשותף, המשתנה, הארוך, הנפרד, המחלף, ואשר הוא כנגד תורת הפתיחה. הכולל הוא אשר הוא אפשר שילקח בערך אל ענינים רבים; המשתף הוא שאפשר שילקח מכל אחד משני החולקים; המשתנה הוא כאשר אפשר שכל אחד יקחהו עם מעט שנוי; הארוך הוא כשהתבות או המאמרים יותר ארוכים ממה שצריך; הנפרד הוא כשלא יולד מהסוג ההוא, ואינו, כמו אבר, דבק עם יתר החלקים; המחלף הוא המחלף הסדר ממה שיבקש סוג הדבור, כאלו תאמר שבמקום שראוי לעשות השומע מחבב או מאזין, הוא עושהו מתלמד, או להפך; ואשר הוא כנגד תורת הפתיחה וכלליה הוא שאינו עושה השומע לא מחבב, לא מאזין, ולא מתלמד.

5 הגדולה] הגדול[כ] || 9 [ארוכה][כ] || 11 אשר ‹נאמר› ראוי[כ] || 16 ההטעאיית] ההטעיית[ד] || 18 ‹בהלצה› בחדשה[כ] ||

[16] Fourth, one should beware of saying anything that one's adversary can, with slight alteration, turn to his own advantage. An example: if, at the hearer's request, I have made some endeavor in a matter of slight utility and honor, while my opponent has also previously made such an effort; and if, because of him, the hearer has obtained something greater and more advantageous than that which he obtained because of me; then if I tell the hearer to remember the advantage I procured for him in this-or-that matter, my adversary may say that he should remember the greater advantage obtained because of him. Here he may indeed use my very words, merely altering the particulars of the advantage; and this would no doubt prove severely damaging to me.

[17] Fifth, one must beware of using an Introduction that has elegance in great measure, or that is too long. As Quintilian[g] says, this can happen in one of three ways:[4] the Introduction may in itself be too long, too long because mixed with the other parts of the discourse, or overlong for its Kind of Cause—for the Forensic or the Deliberative type, that is, in which the Introduction ought to be kept short.

[18] Sixth, care should be taken to keep the Introduction free of any matter extraneous to the issue before us; an example would be to have your Introduction deal with adultery when you wish to bring a man to justice for murder.

[19] Seventh, an Introduction is faulty if, where the hearer ought be rendered well disposed, I make him attentive or receptive, or vice versa. Again, that Introduction is faulty which fails to produce receptiveness, attentiveness, and good will in the hearer.

[20] The foregoing is what Tully says in the New Rhetoric. In the Old,[h] however, he says that there are seven faulty commonplaces in connection with the Introduction, which we should try as hard as we can to avoid: the too-general, the in-common, the interchangeable, the overlong, the unconnected, the out-of-place, and the contradictory of the fundamental principle of the Introduction. The too-general consists of that which could be adopted in many cases; the in-common is that which could be adopted by either of the opponents; it is the interchangeable when it could be adopted by either side with little alteration; it is the overlong when the words or the sentences are longer than necessary; it is the unconnected when not germane to the particular Kind of Cause, and is not, like a limb, joined to the remaining parts of the speech; the out-of-place produces a change in order from that which the Kind of Cause requires—as that where the hearer ought to be made well disposed or attentive, the speaker makes him receptive, or vice versa; and the contradictory of the fundamental law and principles of the Introduction is that which makes the hearer neither well disposed, nor attentive, nor receptive.

4. Q. does not list these as such in his discussion of faulty *exordia* (4.1.62 ff.).

g. Q. 4.1.62 ff. (?).
h. *De I.* 1.18.26.

[21] ויש לדעת שקוינטיליאנו, בראשון מהרביעי, אומר כי לפעמים הפתיחה היא דבר יתר· כשהדיין זולת זה הוא מוכן לשמוע, או שהענין אינו צריך להכנה[2]; ואמר אריסטו שאינו מחוייב שתעשה לפני דיין ישר (למה שהדיין הוא נלאה מעסקי רבים, מצד שהזמן קצר, ועוד שבשאר חלקי המאמר לפעמים אנו 5 עושים מה שנעשה בפתיחה מן ההתלמדות, והחבוב, וההקשבה) ואומר לדיינים שיטו אזניהם לשמוע. ואמר הפילוסוף בשלישי מההלצה כי רוב מה שיצטרכו הפתיחה והחתימה הוא בחלק העצתי, ולפעמים בדבור המדיני, וכשהמאמר קצר לא יצטרך אליה. ואמר א"כ: "וכאשר היה הענין כן באלו החלקים כמו שספרנו, הנה החלקים הכרחיים הם שנים, הכונה והאמות· וכל מה שידחה בו 10 בעל הריב, הנה הוא מהאמותים"· והנה כלל ההתרה בכלל האמותי. וא"כ אמר: "וראוי שיונחו לאלה הענינים, כשהיו מתחלפים לשמות, כמו שיעשוהו אנשי המלאכות." ואמר בראשון: ירצה "שיקרא החלק הראשון פתיחה· והשני הכונה· והשלישי הספור· והרביעי האמות· והחמישי החתימה"; וההתרה כללה באמות.

15 [22] והנה, אם תתבונן בספרי הקודש, תמצא כי מה שאמ' אריסטו וקווינטיליאנו הוא אמת, אין ספק בו· וזה כי אם תבקש המאמרים הנמצאים בספרינו והספורים, המעט מהם אשר ימצא בו כל החלקים. ובכלל, זאת החלוקה אינה הכרחית· אלא אפשר שימצאו במאמרים החלקים כלם, וזה יצא אל הפעל על המעט.

20 [23] והנה אברהם אבינו, עליו השלום, כשבקש המערה מאנשי חת, אמר: גר ותושב אנכי עמכם, כו' [בראשית כ"ג ד']. והנה היה הדבר הגון, ובסוג העצתי, ולזה לא עשה בו פתיחה אחרת, אלא שביאר שהדבר הגון, אשר היא הפתיחה

3 להכנה[2]] להבנה[כד] | אריסטו] ארסטו[כ] | מחוייב] מחויב[ר] || 5 שנעשה] שנעש[ר] || 8 [כן][ט] || 9 הכרחיים] ההכרחיים[ט] | [הם][טa] | הכונה ‹המכוונת›[ט] || 11 לאלה] לאלו[ט] | הענינים ‹החמשה›[ט] || 12 [ואמר בראשון][ט] | שיקרא] שיקרו[טb] || 16 וקווינטיליאנו] וקוינטליאנו[ר] || 17 בספרינו] בספרנו[ר] || 21 [כו'][כ] || 22 שביאר] שבאר[כ] | הגון] ההגון[כ] ||

[2] Corrected in J's list of errata, p. 208; cf. Quintilian 4.1.72.

[21] It should be noted that Quintilian,[i] in Chapter 1 of Book IV, says that there are times when the Introduction is superfluous, as when the judge is ready to hear the case without such preliminaries, or when the case requires no preparatory comment.[5] Aristotle[6] too says the Introduction need not be made before an upright judge (on grounds of the judge being wearied with public business) in case time is short; and moreover, we can sometimes use the remaining parts of the discourse to achieve the receptiveness, goodwill, and attentiveness which we normally produce through the Introduction; so that one can merely bid the judges to incline their ears to hear. In Book III of the *Rhetoric,* the Philosopher[j] says that the Introduction and the Conclusion are mostly necessary in the Deliberative Kind, and sometimes in political discourses, but are unnecessary when the speech is short. Following this, he[k] says: "And since, with respect to these Kinds the case is as we have described, the essential parts are two, namely, the Thesis and the Verification; everything urged by a litigant is part of the Verification"; the Refutation is here included under Verification. And further on he[l] says: "The terminology of these matters, as they have been variously named, should follow the usage of the professional practitioners." Of the first part he says he meant "that the first part should be called Introduction, the second the Thesis, the third the Statement of Facts, the fourth the Verification, and the fifth the Conclusion";[7] the Refutation he includes under the Verification.

[22] Now if you study the Holy Books, you find that what Aristotle and Quintilian say is true beyond doubt. For if you investigate the speeches and narratives in our Books, it is only a small minority of the cases in which the Parts of Invention are all present. A division into parts of such scope is generally not essential—although it is possible to find all the parts among the speeches—and such partitioning was seldom put into practice.

[23] We see that our forefather, Abraham (upon whom be peace!), seeking to purchase the Cave of Machpelah from the Hittites, said: "**I am a stranger and a sojourner with you; give me a possession of a burying-place with you, that I may bury my dead out of my sight**" [Gen. 23:4].[8] Since the Cause was honorable, and Deliberative in type, he made no other Introduction than to make it clear that the matter was honorable; just this, in fact, is the Introduction in an

5. J's emendation, corroborated by the reading at Quintilian 4.1.72. Both M and C read "understanding" (הבנה) rather than "preparation" (הכנה).

6. Citation according to the passage in Q.

7. JML's insertion of the words "of the first part he says" has resulted in the awkwardness here. The original sentence read: "in use with professional practitioners, meaning that the first part should be called," etc.

8. Not cited in full by JML.

---

i. Q. 4.1.72.

j. T214/A306; cf. *Rhet.* 3.13 (1444b).

k. T215/A306.

l. T215/A307.

בדבר הגון, כאשר התבאר באמרו גר ותושב· כי מזה הצד היה ראוי שיתנו לו
אחוזת קבר לפחות במכירה. ומה שאמר, תנו לי אחזת קבר, הוא הספור; והנה
אין בכאן חלק אחר מהמאמר. וכאשר גם כן השיבו בני חת, אמרו, נשיא אלקים
אתה בתוכנו [שם ו׳]· וזאת היא הפתיחה, ועשו החבוב בשבח השומע; ואחר[3]
כן אמר׳[4] הספור, רצוני לומר, במבחר קברינו קבור את מתך· וחתמו באמרם,
איש ממנו את קברו לא יכלה ממך. ותשובת עפרון [שם י״א] לא כללה כי אם
פתיחה, ספור, וחתימה: הפתיחה היא אמרו, לא אדוני שמעני, בקשו ממנו
שישמעהו; ושאר מה שנמשך, עד לך נתתיה, הוא הספור· ומה ששנה אחר כן,
לעיני בני עמי נתתיה לך, היא החתימה.

[24] גם אליעזר עבד אברהם התחיל מהספור, זולת אם נאמר שמה שאמר
קודם, לא אוכל עד אם דברתי דברי [שם כ״ד ל״ג], היא הפתיחה, שהוא כאלו
יבקש שישמעוהו. ויחסרו הנה הרבה מהחלקים· והנה אלה כלם בסוג העצתי.

[25] והנה אביגיל עזבה הפתיחה, והתחיל׳[4] מן הספור ואמרה שחטאה במה
שכתוב: בי אדני העון [שמ״א כ״ה כ״ד]. ואחר כן עשתה דוד מחבב ומתלמד
ומקשי׳: אם שעשאהו מחבב, בדבריה עם תכלית ההכנעה· אם שעשאהו
מתלמד ומקשיב, באמרה שתדבר דבר וישמע את דברי אמתו· לפי שזה הענין
ראוי לעשותו עד סוף המאמר, כמו שהתבאר למעלה. אח׳ כן אמרה: אל נא
ישי׳ אדני, כו׳ [שם כ״ה]· כלומר, שלא ישית לבו אליו, לחשוב שהוא בחטא
כלל. ואחר כן אמרה: כי כשמו כן הוא· נבל שמו ונבלה עמו; זה הקיום, אשר בו
הוכיח׳[4] שראוי לו לבלתי השים אל לבו, כי בטבעו הוא לשלם רעה תחת טובה;
והנה בכאן אחד מן היפויים ההלציים, ר״ל, ההעתקה. ומפני שהיה לדוד צד
תרעומת על אביגיל, אם היה שידעה הדבר הרע הזה ולא בקשה למחות כפי

2–3 והנה אין] ואין[כ] | גם כן השיבו] השיבו גם כן[כ] || 4 ואחר[3]] ואם[כד] || 5 אמר׳[4]] אמר[כד] | מתך] מתיך[כ] || 8 אחר] אחרי[כ] || 9 [בני עמי][ד] || 11 [עד][ד] | הפתיחה] פתיחה[כ] || 12 שישמעוהו] שישמעהו[ד] || 13 והתחיל׳[4]] והתחיל[כד] || 14 כן] כך[כ] || 15 ומקשי׳] ומקש׳[ד] || 17 שהתבאר] שהתבא[ד] | אח׳ כן] א״כ[כ] || 18 ישי׳] ישי[ד] | בחטא] בחט[ד] || 19 אמרה] אמר[ד] || 20 הוכיח׳[4]] הוכיח[כד] || ומפני] ומנה[כ] || 22 [הרע][כ] ||

[3] Correction: ד[R].

[4] Abbreviation not indicated in כ or ד.

honorable Cause. This became clear when he said **a stranger and a sojourner,** for on this account it behooved them to grant him **a possession of a burying-place,** if only by purchase. His saying **"give me a possession of a burying-place,"** etc. is the Statement; this particular speech by Abraham contains, then, no other of the parts of a discourse. When, similarly, the Hittites replied, they said, "**Thou art a mighty prince among us**" [23:6], that was the Introduction, and they thus effected goodwill through praise of the hearer; following this they provided the Statement, namely, "**in the choice of our sepulchres bury thy dead,**" and finally, the Conclusion, saying "**none of us shall withhold from thee his sepulchre.**" Ephron's response to Abraham [23:11] also included only an Introduction, a Statement, and a Conclusion. The Introduction was his saying "**Nay, my lord, hear me**"—his request that Abraham listen to him. In the rest of what he said—**"the field give I thee, and the cave that is therein, I give it thee; in the presence of the sons of my people give I it thee"**[9]—the continuation as far as the words "**I give it thee**" is the Statement, while the immediately succeeding repetition, "**in the presence of the sons of my people give I it thee,**" is the Conclusion.

[24] Eliezer, Abraham's servant, also began his speech [Gen. 24:34 ff.] with the Statement, unless we are to regard what he had said just before—"**I will not eat until I have told my errand**" [24:33]—as the Introduction, since he is, as it were, asking to be heard. The speeches of this passage—all of the Deliberative type—lack many of the parts of a discourse.

[25] Abigail, we note, omitted the Introduction, began her speech to David [1 Sam. 25:24 ff.] with the Statement and, in these words of Scripture, argued that it was she who had sinned: "**Upon me, my lord, upon me be the iniquity**" [25:24].[10] Immediately thereafter, however, she made David well disposed, receptive, and attentive: well disposed, by the extreme submissiveness of her words; receptive and attentive, by saying that she had something to express, and he should hear his handmaid's words. As has been explained above, these are effects that should be achieved throughout a discourse, to its very end. She next said: "**Let not my lord, I pray thee, regard this base fellow, even Nabal**" [25:25]; that is, David should disregard Nabal, holding him to be generally sinful. Following this she said: "**For as his name is, so is he; Nabal** [vile person] **is his name, and vileness is with him**" [25:25]. This is the Proof, wherein she established that David ought not to pay attention to Nabal, on the ground that it is Nabal's nature to repay good with evil;[11] here we see one of the Figures of Speech, namely, Paronomasia.[12] Now because David might have had ground for complaint against Abigail, if she had in fact known of this specific act

9. Not cited in full by JML.
10. JML thus regards the speech as a treatment of "the Acknowledgment of the Charge," or subtype of the "Assumptive Juridical Issue"; cf. i.10.13–14, ii.9.8, 10 below.
11. Cf. 25:21.
12. See iv.18 below.

יכלתה, אמרה אחרי כן: ואני אמתך לא ראיתי את נערי אדני אשר שלחת· וזה
החלק הוא ההתרה. וא״כ עשתה החתימה נפלאה, באשר כללה כל הנאמר עם
התועלת אשר ימשך אליו מזה. והנה כללה בזה מה שאמרה, נבל שמו ונבלה
עמו, במה שאמרה: יהיו כנבל אויביך [שם כ״ו], ר״ל שיהיו משלמי רעה תחת
5 טובה כמוהו, כי אז בודאי יפלו ולא יוכלו קום, יאבד זכרם המה; כי אשר הם
בזאת התכונה· — אף מריעיו ירחקו ממנו· וינטשו על פני השדה, ויהיו דראון
לכל בשר.

[26] ובמה שאמרה, חי ה׳ אשר מנעך מבוא בדמים וכו׳, [שם כ״ו], עם רמזה
בזה המאמר שלא ישית אל לבו, כללה בכאן גם מה שימשך לדוד מזה, שלא
10 ישפוך דם נקי. כי הוא לא היה חייב מיתה על דרך האמת, וזה יהיה סבה אל
שיושיע ידו לו, וידבר עמים תחתיו, עם שתחי נפשו לעד בעולם האמתי הרוחני·
כמו שנשנה זה המאמר א״כ באמרה: והיתה[5] נפש אדוני צרורה כו׳ [שם כ״ט].
והנה התמצע חי נפשך בין חי ה׳ והושע ידך[5] לך [שם כ״ו]· והוא מן היפויים
ההלציים, הנקרא הבלבול. ושעור הפסוק הוא כן: ועתה אדני, חי ה׳ אשר מנעך
15 מבא בדמים, והושע ידך לך, וחי נפשך, כו׳; כלומר, מזאת המניעה יתחייב
שתושע לך ימינך, גם שתחי נפשך לעולם הבא.

[27] ויש בזה מן הפלא. למה לא אמר׳[6] תכף שישא[7] לפשע אמתו אחרי
נכנסה במקום החוטא, קודם שתספר מה שימשך מן הגמול? והנה אמרה הגמול
קודם בקשת המחילה, והוא בחלוף מה שראוי, למה שהגמול נמשך למחילה.
20 ועתה שא נא עיני שכלך וראה מה שבזה הספור מן החכמה היקרה עד יקשה

1 אחרי] ·זה[ד] | ואני] ואנכי[כ] || 2 וא״כ] ואכ[ד] | ‹עשתה› עשתה[כ] || 4 כנבל] כנבלה́[כ] | ר״ל] רל[ד] | רעה] ה́רעה[כ] || 8 שאמרה] שאמ׳[ד] | מבוא בדמים][ד] | עם] עד[כ] | 12 א״כ] אח׳ כן[ד] | והיתה[5]] והיה[כד] || 13 ידך[5]] נפשך[כד] || 14 כן] כך[כ] || 17 אמר׳[6]] אמר[כד] | שישא[7]] שתשא[כד] || 20 הספור][כ] ||

5 תה׳ י״ח ל״ט | תה׳ ט׳ ז׳ || 6 מש׳ י״ט ז׳ | יר׳ ט׳ כ״א | יש׳ ס״ו כ״ד || 11 תה׳ י״ח מ״ח || 20 בר׳ ל״א י״ב ||

[5] Restored in accordance with ת.

[6] Abbreviation not indicated in כ or ד.

[7] Correction required by context.

of villainy, and not sought to protest against it as best she could, she next said "**but I thy handmaid saw not the young men of my lord, whom thou didst send**" [25:25]; and this part is the Refutation. She next developed a remarkable Conclusion,[13] in which she included, besides all that had thus far been said, the resultant benefit to David. Her previous statement, "Nabal is his name, and vileness is with him," is here included in her words: "**Now therefore let thine enemies, and them that seek evil to my lord, be as Nabal**" [25:26]; the enemies, that is, would become like Nabal, repayers of good with evil, in which case they would be certain to fall **so that they** would **be not able to rise** [Ps. 18:39], **their very memorial** would **perish** [Ps. 9:7]; for with somebody of this sort—**even his friends go far from him** [Prov. 19:7]: they will be abandoned **upon the open field** [Jer. 9:21] and **shall be an abhorring unto all flesh** [Isa. 66:24].

[26] In her words, "**As the Lord liveth and as thy soul shall live,**[14] **seeing the Lord hath withholden thee from blood-guiltiness,**" and the rest [1 Sam. 25:26], she has included not merely the suggestion that David should disregard Nabal, but also the consequences entailed, that David would not shed innocent blood. For Nabal, in strict truth, was not so guilty as to deserve death, and this sparing of Nabal would be a reason why David's own hand would **find salvation for** [25:26] him **and subdue peoples under** him [Ps. 18:48]; in addition, his soul would live forever in the true, spiritual world. This point is later repeated when she says: "**yet the soul of my lord shall be bound in the bundle of life with the Lord thy God**" [1 Sam. 25:29]. Now the words **as thy soul shall live** [25:26] come between **as the Lord liveth** and **thine own hand**[15] **shall find salvation for thee**; this is a Figure of Speech, the one called Hyperbaton.[16] The true sense of the verse is grasped in the following arrangement: **Now, therefore, my lord, as the Lord liveth, seeing that He hath withholden thee from blood-guiltiness, thine own hand shall find salvation for thee, and thy soul shall live,** etc.[17] In other words: "The certain result of this restraint will be that thy right hand shall procure thee salvation as well as that thy soul shall live on in the world to come."

[27] There is, moreover, something remarkable here. Why did not Abigail urge David to "forgive . . . the trespass of [his] handmaid" [25:28] immediately after she had herself taken the place of the real miscreant, and before she described what the resultant recompense would be? As we see, she stated the reward [25:26] before making her request for pardon[18] [25:28]—the reverse of the proper order, since the reward was to be the consequence of the forgiveness. But, reader, lift **up now** the **eyes** of your understanding, **and see** [Gen. 31:12]

13. For Conclusions in other parts of the discourse, cf. ii.11.8.
14. JV: "liveth."
15. M and C: "soul"; cf. citation, *infra*.
16. *Bilbūl* = "confusion"; see iv. 42, below.
17. JML here takes וְחֵי־נַפְשְׁךָ as identical with וְחַי־נַפְשְׁךָ; there is one such case in B [Lev. 25:36].
18. Cf. "the Acknowledgment of the Charge" and the requesting of pardon i.10.14, below.

למצא ספור כמוהו בשלמות בספרי הקדש. וזה כי לא ראתה אביגיל למצא
התנצלות לנבל כי אם בהעתקה העון, למה שהתקבצו שם בדברים מונעים
המחילה, ר״ל, האיש הבליעל והפעל המגונה. והנה רק רע כל היום מצד האיש
ומצד המעשה, ולא נשאר לה דרך אחר מצדו· ולזה ראתה שתעתיק העון ממנו
5 אל מי שימצא חן בעיני דוד מצד עצמו. וחשבה שהיא תהיה בזה התואר עם מה
שבטחה, אחר בטחון בבורא ית׳, בנעימות מדותיה וערבות דבריה, ונכנסה בזה
במקום בעלה. והיה עתה בדבר צד טוב וצד רע: הצד הטוב בערך אל נושא
העון, והצד הרע בהצטרף אל העון בעצמו· והנה בא הדבר מן הרע משני צדדים
אל רע מצד אחד לבד. ובזה האופן היה אפשרות בקשת המחילה מצד הטוב, כי
10 קודם זאת ההעתקה לא היה בו אפשרות בקשת המחילה מצד נבל, כאשר
יתבאר בזאת המלאכה. ולזה, תכף הגיעה אל דוד, אמרה בי אני אדני העון [שם
כ״ד], כי זה היה היסוד אשר עליו בנתה כל ההצלה הזאת· והיסוד הוא קודם
לבנין בהכרח. ואמרה בי אני אדני, בהכפל כנוי המדבר בעדו, להורות בזה
המאמ׳ שלא נשא׳ ממנו, כלומ׳, אצל נבל· כאלו אמרה: ״בי העון, ואני, העון
15 בעצמ׳״· עם שזה אחד מן היפויים ההלציים, כאשר התפרסם בזה הספר. והנה
בקבל דוד זאת ההעתקה, לא תשאר תרעומת לדוד על נבל זולת אם יאמר
שהוא במדרג׳ מי שהיכולת בידו למחות ואינו מוחה· כי הוא שב בזה הענין,
שהעון נהפך לאיש אחר, והשתדל להסיר ממנה התרעומת. ואמרה אל ישים
אדני כו׳ [שם כ״ה], כלומר, לבו אל נבל אפי׳ להחזיקו בתורת מי שבידו[8] למחות
20 ואינו מוחה, כי נבל שמו ונבלה עמו, ר״ל, שהוא מוטבע על הנבלה, גם כי היא
אתו בקנין ובהרגל. ואחר שמטבעו הוא מוטבע על שישלם רעה תחת טובה,
שהיא ענין הנבלה, היאך יחשב לו לעון העדר הנתינה בשב ואל תעשה? והבן
חכמת זה המאמר, שלא אמר שישא עונו (כמו שאמרה שא נא לפשע אמתך

6 וערבות] ועריבות[כ] || 7 והיה] והיא[כ] || 8 צדדים] צדדין[כ] || 12 היה] היתה[כ] || 13 ואמרה] ואמ׳[ד] | אדוני ‹העוון›[כ] || 14 נשא׳] נשאר[כ] | כלומ׳] כלו׳[ד] | אמרה] אמ׳[ד] || 15 בעצמ׳] בעצמה[כ] | התפרסם] התפרס׳[ד] || 17 במדרג׳ מי] במדרגה מן[כ] | שהיכולת] שהיכ׳[ד] || 18 אחר] אח׳[ד] | ואמרה] ואמר׳[ד] | ישים] ישי׳[ד] || 19 שבידו[8]] שידו[כד] | למחות] למחו[ד] || 23 כמו שאמרה] כאשר אמר[ד] ||

3 בר׳ ו׳ ה׳

[8] Correction required by context.

that the store of precious wisdom in this account is such that its peer in perfection is scarce to be found in the Holy Books. Abigail saw no other way to defend Nabal than through a shifting of the blame,[19] since they were there at issue over matters that precluded pardon, namely, the base fellow himself and the discreditable act. To make either the man or the act the starting point of the defense **was only evil continually** [Gen. 6:5]; so, as there was no other way, she saw that she must shift the blame from Nabal to someone who might personally find favor in David's eyes. Relying upon the charm of her manners and the pleasant aptness of her words, which were second only to her trust in God (blessed be He), she thought that she herself might fit this description, and thus introduced herself in her husband's stead. The case now had both a favorable aspect and an unfavorable, favorable so far as concerned the bearer of the blame, but unfavorable so far as concerned the offense itself. At this point the case, from being unfavorable on both scores, had come to be unfavorable merely on one. In this way a favorable approach to the possibility of asking forgiveness had emerged, for, prior to this shifting of the onus, the approach from the person of Nabal included no possibility of asking forgiveness, as the art of rhetoric clearly establishes.[20] So, at once upon meeting David, she said "**Upon me, my lord, upon me be the iniquity**" [1 Sam. 25:24], for this was the foundation upon which she built the whole of her successful defense, the foundation that necessarily precedes the building. She used the first-person pronoun twice in saying *bī ʾᵃnī ʾᵃdhōnī*[21] in order to show that she did not bear the onus because of him, that is to say, as an accessory of Nabal; it was as if she had said: "Upon me be the iniquity, for as for me, the iniquity is upon myself alone"; in addition, this is one of the Figures of Speech, as demonstrated in the present book.[22] David, by his acceptance of this shifting of the onus, obviously had no remaining ground for complaint against Nabal except to maintain that Nabal was in the position of one who can protest but fails to do so; for with such the case, with the guilt transferred to another person, he quite reversed his role and endeavored to acquit her of the charge. She further said, "**Let not my lord . . . regard,**" and so on [25:25]—that David should, in effect, not regard Nabal even to the point of holding him as one able to protest yet failing to do so—because "Nabal is his name and vileness is with him," meaning that vileness was his by nature as well as by acquired habit and practice. Since it was his inborn nature to repay good with evil—the essence of vileness—how could mere non-giving, a case of "sit-and-do-nothing,"[23] be ascribed to him as iniquity? Understand the wisdom of this statement: it did not

19. On this technique, cf. i.10.11, ii.8.7, and ii.9.9, 17.
20. Cf. e.g., ii.9.15.
21. Literally: "upon me, I, my lord." In classical Hebrew, a subject pronoun may be introduced to emphasize a preceding object pronoun or possessive pronoun.
22. "Duplication" (iv.80) is presumably the figure meant.
23. Cf. Bab. Talm. Bᵉrākhōth 20a, ʿĒrūbhīn 100a. On JML's conception of vileness, see iv. 21.3–8, below.

[שם כ״ח]), רק אמר שלא ישיב אפילו אל לבו לחשוב בו צד קטון מעון.

[28] והנה התנצלה מצד שלא ראתה הנערי׳, ואמרה: ואני אמתך לא ראיתי וכו׳ [שם כ״ה]. כי אם היתה במעמד, היו לה שני עונות: האחד, העון מנבל אשר העתיקה אליה׳ והאחר, העון שלא מחתה בזה העון המגונה כפי יכלתה. והנה אפשר שלא ימחול לה דוד בהקבץ שני הדברים יחד.

[29] ומה שעלה בידו עד הנה הוא הנקות נבל מכל עון, והיות אביגיל במקום נבל על החט ההוא לבד; והנה ספרה מה שימשך לדוד מן הגמול מקבול זו ההעתקה, כמו שבארנו למעלה. וחטא אביגיל במקומו לא נמחל עדיין׳ ולא בקשה עליו מחילה, כי יראה ולא בטחה בנפשה שישלם לה זה מבלי פעל אחר. ולזה נתנה הדורון קודם, עם דברים בהם מן הערבות וההכנעה מה שלא יעלם,[9] עד ישלם לה מה שקותה משכוך כעס דוד וחרון אפו. כי ראתה כי כלתה לנבל הרעה׳ ואתה יודע מה שאמר הפילוסוף בא׳ מההלצה מענין הדורון, שהוא דבר נכסף מאד מאד. ואחר כל זה בקשה המחילה מהעון אשר קבלה על נפשה, ואמרה: שא נא לפשע אמתך [שם כ״ח]. ויעדה לו מן הטוב שימשך לו בעבור זה נוסף על מה שאמר׳[10] למעלה, ואמרה כי יעשה ה׳ לו בית נאמן, ר״ל, שיהיה ביתו נכון עם אל, ותמשך ותתקיים המלוכה בידו לדורי דורים.

[30] ואחר כן שבה לשבחו, כי תמיד יראה מפני האף והחימה, ואמרה: כי מלחמות ה׳ אדני נלחם ורעה לא תמצא בך מימיך [שם]. והנה שבחתו במה שהיה נוגע בהנהגת המלכות, באמרה כי מלחמות ה׳ אדני נלחם, עם שבחה אותו מצד המדות; וכאלו אמרה שהוא ראוי ללחום מלחמת ה׳, שהוא ענין נפלא התועלת, לא שילחם עם איש הבליעל הזה, עם נבל. ומכל זה היה

1 אמר] אמרה[ב] || 2 ואני] ואנכי[ב] || 3 האחד] אחד[ד] || 7 נבל] הנבל[ב] || 10 [יעלם[9]][כד] || 14 אמתך] אמתיך[ב] || 15 שאמר׳[10]] שאמר[ד] שאמרה[ב] || 17 ואחר כן] וא״כ[ב] |[יראה][ב] |ואמרה] ואמ׳[ד] || 19 [ה׳][ב] || 20 מלחמת] מלחמ׳[ד] || 21 שילחם] שישלחם[ב] ||

16 יש׳ נ״א ח׳

[9] Restored omission: ד[R].

[10] Abbreviation not indicated in ב or ד.

say that David should forgive Nabal's iniquity (as when she said "**Forgive, I pray thee, the trespass of thy handmaid**" [25:28]), but only that it should not even enter David's mind to consider Nabal responsible for the least iniquity.

[28] Abigail now based her own defense on the fact that she had not seen the young men, and said: "**but I thy handmaid saw not the young men of my lord whom thou didst send**" [25:25]. For had she been in a position to see them, she would have had to account for two acts of iniquity: the one, the crime of Nabal, the responsibility for which she had transferred from Nabal to herself; the other, the iniquity of not having protested this shameful crime as best she could. It was therefore possible that David might not forgive her if the two charges were combined and taken together.

[29] What the speech had thus far succeeded in accomplishing was Nabal's acquittal of any crime, and the substitution of Abigail for Nabal as liable for that one sin alone; and, as we have explained above, she had recounted the benefit that would come to David as a result of his acceptance of this transfer of the responsibility. But the sin of Abigail as Nabal's replacement had not yet been forgiven; nor had she asked forgiveness for it, for she was apprehensive and lacked confidence that this could wholly be won for her without some further action on her part. That is why she first presented the gift [25:27], which she accompanied with strikingly[24] agreeable and submissive words, so that she might gain that complete abatement of David's anger and wrath for which she had hoped. For she saw that evil was definitely in store for Nabal [cf. 25:17]; and you know what the Philosopher[m] in Book I of the *Rhetoric* says of the gift, namely, that it is something most highly prized. It was subsequent to all this, then, that Abigail requested pardon for the iniquity which she had taken upon herself: "**Forgive I pray thee, the trespass of thy handmaid**" [25:28]. And, promising David that he would derive from such forgiveness a benefit over and beyond that which she had previously mentioned, she said that the Lord would make him "a sure house," that is, that his house would be firmly established with God, and that the kingdom would remain in their possession **unto all generations** [Isa. 51:8].

[30] Thereafter she turned again to praise of David, for she was in constant dread of his anger and wrath, and said: "**because my lord fighteth the battles of the Lord, and evil is not found in thee all thy days**" [I Sam. 25:28]. Thus, in saying "because my lord fights the battles of the Lord," she at the same time praised him for that which pertains to royal leadership and for his own good traits of character. It was as if she had said that he was worthy to fight the battles of the Lord, an enterprise of marvellous benefit, and not merely to fight against this base

24. The deficient Hebrew text has here been restored according to a suggestion (made by S. H. Modone?) in the margin of C[R].

m. T35/A44f.; cf. *Rhet.* 1.5.9 (1361b).

מתחייב שימחול לה, שלא היה בטבעו לעשות רע, עד שלא עשה רע כל ימי
חייו; וכאלו אמרה: "והיאך תעשה הרעה הזאת?"

[31] וא"כ[11] ספרה רשעת שונאיו ורוע מעלליהם, ואמרה: ויקם אדם לרדפך
ולבקש את נפשך [שם כ"ט]· רצוני לומר, שהיו מבקשים את נפשו חנם, לשפוך
5 דם נקי. וזה המאמר בכאן היתה הערמה הגדולה, כי רמזה לו בזה שהוא היה
בענין ההוא במדרגת נבל, רצוני לומר, שכמו שהאנשים היו רודפים אחריו
לשפוך דם נקי, כן היה ענינו עם נבל, שהיה דוד רודף אחריו לשפוך דם נקי גם
כן. והיאך היה מקוה התשועה מהשם משונאיו, אם היה נופל בזה העון בעצמו?
אדרבה, זה פעל היה סבה שימדוד לו ה' מדה כנגד מדה· ולכן היה ראוי
10 להתרחק ממנו הרחוק אשר בתכלית.

[32] והנה חייבה בכל המאמר החבוב לדוד או מצד מה שבדוד מן המדות, או
מצד רוע תכונות שונאיו, ואם כן, אמרה: והיתה נפש אדני, כו' [שם]· ספרה מה
שימשך מן הגמול לו, ומן העונש לאויביו. ועשתה יפוי אחד מן היפויים
ההלציים, הנקרא החלוף, ואמרה שתהיה נפשו צרורה בצרור החיים עם ה'
15 יתברך — רצוני לומר, שתשוב אל מקורה אשר ממנה חוצבה, תמיד מתענגת
מזיו הבורא יתברך — ונפש האויבים תקולע בתוך כף הקלע. והנה צרורה
בצרור החיים הפך תקולע, כי הדבר אשר יקולע מטלטל בהכרח, והדבר הצרור
בצרור הוא נח במקומו הטבעי ולא ילך אנה ואנה; ורמז בזה אל שהכרת תכרת
הנפש ההיא [במ' ט"ו ל"א].

20 [33] ואחר כן[11] חתמה דבריה באופן מלאכותי מפואר, כאשר כללה כל
האמור למעלה: והיה, כי יעשה ה' לאדני ככל אשר דבר [שמ"א כ"ה ל'] מן
הטוב וההצלחה, לא יהיה בו דבר לאבן נגף ולצור מכשול, ולמזכרת עון.
ורצתה, באמרה בזאת, המחילה המיוחדת שאם לא ימחול, תהיה לו למכשול

2 והיאך] ואיךᶜ || 3 וא"כ[11]] ואם כןᶜᵈ || 5 דם] דכᵀ | בכאן] כאןᶜ || 9 ה'] השםᶜ || 10 הרחוק] הריחוקᶜ || 12 תכונות] תכונתᶜ | ואם כן] וא"כᶜ | כו'] כלᵀ || 13 אחד] אחרᵀ || 14–15 ה' יתברך] השם ית'ᶜ || 16 יתברך] ית'ᶜ || 16–17 בתוך... תקולע]ᶜ || 20 ואחר כן[11]] ואם כןᶜᵈ ||

---

22 יש' ח' י"ד | במ' ה' ט"ו ||

---

[11] Emendation: דᴿ.

fellow, Nabal. It followed from all this that David must forgive her, that to do evil was not in his nature; indeed, that he had refrained from doing evil all the days of his life. "How, then," she as much as asked, "will you commit this particular evil?"

[31] Then, setting forth the wickedness of David's enemies and the evil of their deeds, she said: "**And though man be risen up to pursue thee, and to seek thy soul**" [25:29]; that is, there were those who were seeking David's life without just cause, seeking to shed innocent blood. Such a statement at this juncture was most subtly prudent, for she thus suggested that David's own position in that matter was of a kind with Nabal's in this; just as men were pursuing David in order to shed innocent blood, so too was he acting with Nabal: David was pursuing him in order to shed innocent blood. How, then, could David hope that God would save him from his own enemies, if he should himself fall into the same iniquity? On the contrary, such a deed would be reason enough for the Lord to mete out to him measure for measure; it therefore behooved David to keep himself at the farthest possible remove from this sinful act.

[32] Throughout the entire discourse, indeed, Abigail rendered David necessarily well disposed, either as possessing some fine trait of character, or on the score of the base characteristics of his enemies. It is for this reason that she said: "**yet the soul of my lord**[25] **shall be bound in the bundle of life with the Lord thy God; and the souls of thine enemies, them shall He sling out as from the hollow of a sling**" [25:29]—her description of the reward that would accrue to him and the punishment in store for his enemies. She developed a certain Figure of Speech, that called Antithesis,[26] and said that David's soul would be bound up in the bundle of life with the Lord, blessed be He—his soul, that is, would return to the Source whence it was hewn to rejoice constantly in the splendor of the Creator, blessed be He,—whereas the souls of his enemies would be slung out as from the hollow of a sling. "Bound up in the bundle of life" is the antithesis of "be slung out," for something slung is necessarily in motion, while what is bound up in a bundle is at rest in the place natural to it, and does not proceed to this place or to that. Allusion was thus made to the Scriptural **that soul shall utterly be cut off** [Num. 15:31].

[33] Summing up next, and including all that was previously said, Abigail brought her words to a splendidly artistic conclusion: "'**And it shall come to pass, when the Lord shall do to my lord according to all that He hath spoken**' [1 Sam. 25:30] of weal and success, there will be nothing against him to constitute **a stone of stumbling and a rock of offence** [Isa. 8:14], **bringing iniquity to remembrance**" [Num. 5:15].[27] By these words she meant the specific act of

25. At this point the text reads "etc.," and omits the rest of the citation.
26. Cf. iv.57, below.
27. JML apparently found the quotations from Isaiah and Numbers more apt to his purpose at this point than the actual conclusion of Abigail's speech in 1 Sam. 25:30–31. He has the Samuel passage in mind, however, in what he says about the shedding of innocent blood, and the rest of the conclusion paraphrases 25:31.

ולפוקה· גם לא תהיה שישפוך השופך דם נקי. וזהו שב אל דוד· כי אם לא היה מוחל, והיה שופך דם נקי, יהיה נשפך דמו גם כן, שהיה נקי בהצטרף למי שהיו רודפים אותו. ולא ישאר בו דבר רע יבטל הישועה ומה שירצה השם להטיב לו· ואחר זה יזכור את אמתו, ותברכנה נפשו, למה שסבבה אליו מן הטובות.

[35] והנה כלל זה הספור רבים מחלקי המאמר, עם יפויים רבים, ערבות, והכנעה. לא יערכנו זהב וזכוכית.

פרק שמיני

ענין הספור.

[1] אמר טוליאו בהלצה החדשה: ״מיני הספור הם שלשה״. האחד כשנספר דבר מה נעשה לתועלתנו, לכוון בו הנצחון· ויבוקש ענינו בדברים אשר ננתן בהם הפסק דין בעתיד. והסוג השני מן הספור הוא אשר יקרה באחד מחמשה פנים: אם לכוון בו ההאמתה, כמו שאמר: כה עשו אבותיכם בשלחי אותם מקדש ברנע, וכו׳ [במ׳ ל״ב ח׳], שזה הספור הוא בא למען יתאמת העונש אם יעמדו במרדם; אם שנכון בו התלונה והתרעומת כמו: לך רד כי שחת עמך אשר הוצאת מארץ מצרים [שמ׳ ל״ב ז׳], שזה הספור בא על צד התלונה והתרעומת על אשר חטאו ישראל והרבו לפשוע; אם על צד ההעתקה מענין לענין, כמו: ונסע מחורב ונלך את כל המדבר הגדול והנורא ההוא אשר ראיתם דרך הר האמורי כאשר צוה ה׳ אלקינו אותנו ונבא עד קדש ברנע [דב׳ א׳ י״ט], והוא מבואר שזה הספור הוא בא לפרסם בו אופן העתקתם ועברם ממקום למקום; אם שיכוון בו יפוי הענינים ותקונם, כמו הספור ממשתה אחשורוש, כמו שנאמר: חור כרפס ותכלת אחוז בחבלי בוץ וארגמן על גלילי כסף ועמודי שש

1 שישפוך השופך] השופך שישפוך[כ] || 3 שירצה] שירצ[ד] || 4 זה] זת[ד] |יזכור] יזכיר[כ] || 7 שמיני] ח׳[כ] || 13 יתאמת ‹להם›[ד] || 14 התלונה והתרעומת] התרעומ׳ והתלנה[ד] || 15 הוצאת] העלית[ת] || 17 אשר] אש[ד] || 19 הספור] הספו[ד] || 21 ותכלת אחוז ‹ותכלת אחוז›[ד] |ועמודי] ועמו[ד] ||

---

6 איוב כ״ח י״ז ||

pardoning—the act which, if one fails to perform it, constitutes an offence and a stumbling block for him; she also meant that there must be none to shed innocent blood. This last was a reference to David; if he himself should fail to forgive, and should shed innocent blood, his own blood—innocent blood, previously, for those in pursuit of him—might also be shed. Let, however, no evil remain against him which would nullify his salvation and God's will to deal well with him [cf. 1 Sam. 25:31]: then subsequently he would remember his handmaid, and his soul bless her, for the meed of good she had caused him to obtain.

[34] This narrative thus includes several of the Parts of a Discourse, along with a number of Figures, agreeableness, and submissiveness. **Gold and glass cannot equal it** [Job 28:17].

CHAPTER 8

The Statement of Facts

[1] In the New Rhetoric, Tully[a] has said: "There are three types of Statement of Facts." It is one type when we present the account of some action that is to our advantage, the aim in which is victory; this kind is called for in Causes on which a decision is yet to be rendered. The second type of Statement occurs in one of five modes: (1) when our aim in using it is to verify, as in the passage: "**Thus did your fathers, when I sent them from Kadesh-barnea to see the land,**" etc. [Num. 32:8], a Statement introduced in order to verify the punishment in store for the Reubenites and Gadites if they should persist in their rebellion; (2) for purposes of incrimination and indictment, as: "**Go, get thee down, for thy people, that thou broughtest forth**[1] **out of the land of Egypt, have dealt corruptly**" [Exod. 32:7], a Statement made as an incrimination and indictment of Israel for having sinned and frequently transgressed; (3) to effect a transition from one point to the next, as: **And we journeyed from Horeb, and went through all that great and dreadful wilderness which ye saw, by the way to the hill-country of the Amorites, as the Lord our God commanded us; and we came to Kadesh-barnea** [Deut. 1:19], where it is obviously the purpose of the Statement to make plain how they moved and passed from one place to another; (4) when the intention is to embellish and properly set out the details, as in the account of Ahasuerus' feast, where it is said: **there were hangings of white, fine**

1. B and JV: "... broughtest up."

a. *R. ad H.* 1.8.12.

מטות זהב וכסף על רצפת בהט ושש ודר וסוחרת, כו׳ [אס׳ א׳ ו׳]· כל זה הספור בא על צד היפוי והתקון, יתבאר בהם הפלגת הענינים במשתה ההוא; אם שיכוון בו שבח או גנות לדבר, כמו הספור הגדול שעשה יחזקאל הנביא מצור ומלכה, עם שבאו בו דברים רבים על צד היפוי והתקון. ובהלצה הישנה, במקום
5 השבח והגנות, אומר:״אם שיבא מצד ההרחבה במאמר.״ הסוג השלישי הוא כאשר יתבאר באי זה אופן יותר מעלה ויותר מתוקן נוכל להגיד הב׳ סוגים הראשונים· וזה לא ימנע אם שיהיה בענינים בעצמם, אם עם הבאת אנשים מדברים במאמר.

[2] עוד, אשר הוא בענינים הוא נחלק לג׳ חלקים, ר״ל, הגדה, חידה, בדיאה.
10 ההגדה הוא סיפור הדברים הנעשים הרחוקים מזמננו. והחידה היא מאמר יבאו בו דברים בלתי אמתיים, גם אין בהם פנים מההראות, כמו שנאמר ביחזקאל: חוד חידה ומשול משל, וכו׳· הנשר הגדול גדל הכנפים ארך האבר מלא הנוצה אשר לו הרקמה בא הלבנון ויקח את צמרת הארז, וכו׳ [יח׳ י״ז ב׳—ג׳]; וכן מה שאמר יותם: הלוך הלכו העצים למשוח עליהם מלך ויאמרו לזית מלכה עלינו
15 [שופ׳ ט׳ ח׳]. אלה הדברים והנוהג מנהגם מבואר מענינם שהם נמנעו הצדק, כל שכן שאינם אמתיים, אלא שיורו על מה שירצו לומר באופן יותר צח ומתוקן. הבדיאה היא מאמר יבאו בו דברים בלתי אמתיים, אמנם הם אפשרי הצדק; והמשל ממאמר נתן אל דוד, באמרו: שני אנשים היו בעיר אחד עשיר ואחד רש· לעשיר היה צאן ובקר הרבה מאוד· ולרש אין כל, וכו׳ [שמ״ב י״ב א׳—ג׳]; וכן
20 מאמר התקועית אל דוד גם כן: אבל אשה אלמנה אני וימת אישי· ולשפחתך שני בנים וינצו שניהם בשדה, וכו׳ [שם י״ד ה׳—ו׳]. אלה הדברים וזולתם, ואם היו ענינים בדו מלבם, מ״מ מבואר מענינם שהם אפשריים· ואלה מתחבולות תקון הענינים ויפוים.

1 כו׳] כו[ד] || 3 שיכוון] שייכוון[כ] |[הנביא][ד] || 4 רבים] רבי[ד] || 6 הב׳] הב[ד] || 8 מדברים] מדברי[ד] || 9 בענינים] בענייניּם[כ] |לג׳] לג[ד] |ר״ל] רוצה לומ[ד] || 10 מזמננו] מזמנינו[כ] || 12 וכו׳] וכוליה[ד] |ארך] אורך[כ] || 13 בא ‹אל›[ת] |הארז ‹אשר›[כ] |וכו׳] וכולי[ד] || 15 מענינם] מהעניינים[כ] || 16–17 יותר... בו ‹יותר... בו›[ד] || 17 יבאו |‹בו יותר צח ומתוקן›[כ] || 18 בעיר ‹אחת›[ת] || 20 [אבל][ד] ||

cotton, and blue, bordered with cords of fine linen and purple, upon silver rods and pillars of marble; the couches were of gold and silver, upon a pavement of green, and white, and shell, and onyx marble, etc. [Esth. 1:6]: this whole Statement is cited for its embellishment and descriptive detail, as a means of making it clear that the circumstances of that banquet were extraordinary; and (5) when the aim is to praise or censure, like the prophet Ezekiel's great Statement on Tyre and its king [Ezek. 26:1-28:20], which also includes many features of embellishment and of descriptive detail. In the Old Rhetoric, instead of mentioning the Statement aimed at praise or censure, Tully[b] says: "Or it may be introduced for the purpose of amplification." It is the third type when it is clear that the first two types can be handled by us in some way that is more advantageous and accurate; this kind of narrative must be based either on the facts alone, or must include citation of what persons speaking have said.

[2] Tripartite, again, is the narrative based on the facts, namely, historical, fabulous,[2] fictitious. The historical is a narrative of things done long before our time. The fabulous includes matters which are neither true nor plausible, for example, the passage in Ezekiel: **Put forth a fable,[3] and speak a parable. . . . A great eagle with great wings and long pinions, full of feathers which had divers colours, came** [unto][4] **Lebanon and took the top of the cedar,** etc. [Ezek. 17:2-3 f.]. So, too, Jotham's words: **The trees went forth on a time to anoint a king over them, and they said unto the olive-tree, "Reign thou over us,"** etc. [Judg. 9:8 f.]. These and similar narratives, while of themselves unbelievable, not to say also untrue, bring home in clearer and better style what they have to say. The fictitious narrative contains things which, though not true, are nevertheless credible. An example is Nathan's speech to David: "**There were two men in a[5] city: the one rich, and the other poor. The rich man had exceeding many flocks and herds; but the poor man had nothing, save one little ewe lamb,**" etc. [2 Sam. 12:1-3 f.]. Another, again, is the speech of the woman of Tekoa to David: "**Of a truth I am a widow, my husband being dead. And thy handmaid had two sons, and they two strove together in the field, and there was none to part them, but the one smote the other, and killed him,**" etc. [14:5-6 f.].[6] Although these and other stories are the fabrications of their authors' fancy, yet, as is clear from their contents, they could have been fact; they are among the devices used in better formulating and embellishing the facts.

2. Literally: "riddle"; but cf. Ezek. 17:2 where the word is used of an allegory, and Prov. 1:6, in which allegorical and figurative sayings are meant.
3. JV: "riddle."
4. Omitted by JML.
5. JV: "one."
6. Cf. ii.13.6, 21, 27 below.

b. *De I.* 1.19.27.

[3] ומה שנעשה מזה הסוג, עם הבאת האנשים מדברים, ושואלים זה לזה ומשיבים, כמו שאמר ויטורינו בישנה. ויען מקצת האנשים הם חכמים ונבונים, מקצתם סכלים, מקצתם רכי הלבב, מקצתם גבורים, או זולת זה, ראוי לספר באופן אחר ענין החכמים ממה שנספר ענין הסכלים· כי ההגדה ראיה שתהיה מתדמה לאנשים אשר נביא אותם בהגדה ההיא. א״כ ראוי שיהיה לך, מן ההאותו׳ והצחות לפי הענין: כבדות, קלות, תקוה, יראה, חלוף הדעות, חשד, חשק, בדיאה, רחמנות, חלוף הענינים, השתנות המזל, תלאה נעדרת התקוה, שמחה פתאומית, תכלית נאה לענינים· כל אחד לפי מה שידרשהו טבע האנשים הובאו במאמר.

[4] עוד, התחייב בערך אל הספור ג׳ דברים: האחד, שיהיה קצר· השני, שיהיה מפרסם· השלישי, שיהיה לו פנים מן ההראות. הקצר, כשלא נתחיל לספר מתחלת הענין, כמו: והיה כי ישאלך בנך מחר לאמר מה זאת ואמרת אליו בחוזק יד הוציאנו י״י ממצרים מבית עבדים, כו׳ [שמ׳ י״ג י״ד]· הנה הוא מספר מה שצריך ואינו מתחיל לספר השתלשלות ביאת מצרים והמשך הענינים זה אחר זה; ושנאמר הדבר כולל, כמו: ששת ימים עשה י״י את השמים ואת הארץ [שם כ׳ י״א], ואינו מגיד מה שנעשה דבר יום ביומו; ושלא נבא אל תכלית הענין, אלא עד מקום הצריך לנו, כמו: ויהי כי הקשה פרעה לשלחנו ויהרוג י״י כל בכור בארץ מצרים מבכור אדם ועד בכור בהמה על כן אני זובח לה׳, כו׳ [שם י״ג ט״ו]· הנה עזב מה שנעשה על הים להיות זה השעור מן הספור, בערך אל מה שצריך לנו ממנו בזה המקום, מספיק; ושלא נצא מענין אל ענין אחר בלתי צריך במקום ההוא, ושלא נטעה מאשר התחלנו לספר· ושנספר היציאה מן המדינה ותשאר הביאה מובנת בעצמה, כמו: הנה עם יצא ממצרים הנה כסה את עין הארץ, כו׳ [במ׳ כ״ב ה׳]. ושנעזוב הדבר שלא יועיל ולא יזיק, וכ״ש המזיק לבד; ושלא נאמר דבר אחד בעצמו ב׳ פעמים או יותר, זולת אם יהיה לצחות, כמו הענין בקצת היפויים.

[5] אמנם נעשהו מפרסם כשנביא הענינים ראשון ראשון, ואחרון אחרון, בשמרנו סדר הענינים והזמנים; ושלא נבלבל הסדר המיוחד בלשון מקדימת התיבות ואחורם; ושלא נדבר בזרות לפי הלשון, ושנשמור מהדבר שמשמעו לב׳ פנים; ושלא נצא מהמבוקש, ולא נספר מראשית הענין, גם לא נבא עד

2 בישנה] בישינה[כ] || 5 [מתדמה][כ] || 6 ההאותו׳] האותות[כ] || 10 השני] ב׳[ד] || 11 השלישי] ג׳[ד] || 12 לספר... כי ‹לספר...כי›[ד] || 13 [יד][כ] |ממצרים] מצרים[כ] || 18 על כן] לכן[ד] |כו׳] וכו׳[כ] || 20 אל ענין] לעניין[כ] || 23 וכ״ש] וכשם[כ] || 27 המיוחד] המיוחדת[כ] || 28 ושנשמור] ושנשמ׳[ד] || 29 לב׳] לשני[כ] ||

[3] The use to be made of this type, when also persons who speak, or question and answer one another are introduced, is as stated by Victorinus'[c] Commentary on the Old Rhetoric. Now since some people are wise and intelligent and some are fools, some timorous and some courageous, or the like otherwise, a narrative dealing with intelligent persons should be told in quite a different manner from one dealing with fools, for the telling should comport with the character of the persons introduced in the particular narrative. Hence, you should have appositeness and style, according as the subject may warrant: dignity, lightness, hope, fear, change-of-opinions, suspicion, desire, hypocrisy, compassion, reversal in life's circumstances, change of luck, hopeless disaster, sudden joy, a happy outcome—each as the nature of the characters introduced requires.

[4] Three requisites, furthermore, are needed in a Statement of Facts: (1) that it be brief; (2) that it be clear; (3) that it be plausible. It is brief when we do not start our narration from the very outset of the matter. For example: "**And it shall be when thy son asketh thee in time to come, saying: What is this? that thou shalt say unto him: By strength of hand the Lord brought us out from Egypt, from the house of bondage,**" etc. [Exod. 13:14 f.]; here Moses, while recounting all that is needful, does not begin the narrative with the development of the descent into Egypt and the succession of events that followed. It is brief too, when summarily stated, as in the following: **for in six days the Lord made heaven and earth,** etc. [20:11], without saying what was made on each and every day. Again, it is brief when we do not advance clear to the end, but only as far as we need to go, as in the following: "**and it came to pass, when Pharaoh would hardly let us go, that the Lord slew all the first-born in the land of Egypt, both the first-born of men, and the first-born of beast; therefore I sacrifice to the Lord,**" etc. [13:15]; here Scripture has omitted the action at the Red Sea, because this much of the narrative is all that at this point we need to have. The narrative will likewise be brief if we make no contextually unnecessary digression and do not wander from the account we have begun to set forth; so, for example, we tell about the exodus from the country while leaving the entry into it to be understood of itself, as in this verse of Scripture: "**Behold, there is a people come out of Egypt; behold they cover the face of the earth,**" and so on [Num. 22:5]. Finally, brevity will be achieved if we omit whatever neither helps nor harms our case, especially, of course, if we omit only that which is harmful, and if we do not say the same thing twice or more, save, as in the case of certain Figures of Speech, for stylistic effect.

[5] We make our narrative clear, indeed, when, as we introduce the facts from first to last, we preserve the sequence and chronological order of their occurrence; if we do not confuse the word order proper to the language; if we do not use far-fetched verbiage, and are wary of ambiguous language; if we neither digress from the main point, nor tell the story from its remotest origin, nor carry

c. Halm, 202–3.

סופו; ושלא נעזוב הצריך בדבר; ושנשמור מה שנאמר מן הקצור, לפי שהמאמר הקצר באופן ראוי הוא יותר מפורסם ותקל הבנתו.

[6] אמנם היאך יהיה לספור פנים מההראות הוא בזה האופן: אם יסכים לדעת אנשי המדינה ולפי הרגלם וטבעם; אם יהיה בו שעורי הזמן כפי מה שיאותו לענינים, והעצות הראויות, והמקום הנאות, ואופן הדבור כפי מנהג המובאים בספור; ושאי אפשר שנסתור אותו מצד שהזמן היה קצר ממה שצריך· או מצד שלא היה לו סבה תבוא[1] לזה· או מצד שהמקום לא היה ראוי לכך· או שהיה נמנע בחק האנשים ההם, אם מצד שלא יוכלו עשוהו, אם שאפילו היה היכולת בידם, לא היו עושים מצד מדותיהם.

[7] ויש לדעת שהדברים ההכרחיים בכל פעל הם שבעה, כמו שאמר ויטורינו בישנה: ראשונה, מי הוא העושה· ב׳, מה עשה· ג׳, באי זה מקום· ד׳, עם מַי[2] עשה· ה׳ בסבת מה· ו׳, באי זה אופן ·ז׳, מתי נעשה. והמשל: יואב הרג את עמשא· הנה לנו שנים, ר״ל, מי הוא, שהיה יואב, ומה נעשה, נהרג עמשא; באי זה מקום: עם אבן הגדולה אשר בגבעון; עם מַי[2]: עם החרב, כמו שכתוב: ויואב חגור מדו לבושו ועליו חגור חרב מצומדת על מתניו בתערה, וכו׳ [שמ״ב כ׳ ח׳]; בסבת מה: מפני שהיה ירא פן דוד ימנהו שר צבא תחתיו; באי זה אופן: כמו שאמר הכתוב: ויאמר יואב אל עמשא, השלום אתה אחי· ותאחז יד ימין יואב בזקן עמשא לנשק לו, ועמשא לא נשמר מהחרב אשר ביד יואב, ויכהו בה אל החומש, וישפך מעיו ארצה, וכו׳ [שם שם ט׳—י׳]; מתי: ביום כשרדפו יואב ואבישי אחר שבע בן בכרי.

[8] ואפילו אם הדבר הוא אמת, מ״מ צריך לחקור כל אלה החקירות כדי שיהיו לענין פנים מן ההראות, למה שדברים הרבה הם אמתיים עם שאינם נראים. ואם אין הדבר כן, כ״ש שראוי לחקור אותו באמתות. והנה אלה הדברים צריך שנחקור אותם בתחבולה רבה· ונוכל להעזר בהם מכח אי זה נימוס או עדות מהאנשים הגדולים.

[9] וראוי שתדע שקוינטיליאנו, בפ׳ ב׳ מחלק ד׳, מביא מחלקות רבות מהספור מדעות הקדמונים, ושרבים חשבו שהספור הוא בערך סוג העצומי לבד, ובהצטרף אל זמן העבר· ולזה יראה שיסכימו קצת דברי טוליאו. אמנם, לפי מה

1 שהמאמר] שהמקצר[כ] || 2 יותר מפרסם] יותרמ פרסם[ד] | ותקל הבנתו] ותקלה בנתו[ד] || 7 שצריך] שצר[ד] | [מצד שלא... או][כ] | תבוא[1]] תבוא׳[ד] || 8 אם מצד] או מצד[כ] || 8–9 [אם שאפילו... עושים][כ] || 11 ב׳] שנית[כ] | מַי[2]] מי[כד] || 13 עמשא] עמשה[כ] | עמשא] עמשה[כ] | 14 אבן] האבן[ת] | בגבעון] בגבע[ד] | מַי[2]] מי[כד] || 15 מדו] מידו[ד] || ירא] מתירא[כ] || 18 מהחרב] בחרב[ת] || 19 ארצה] ארצם[כ] | וכו׳] וכ׳[ד] || 21 אם <את> הדבר[כ] || 22 שיהיו] שיהי׳[ד] || 23 כ״ש] כש[ד] || 28 טוליאו] טולאו[ד] | אמנם] אמנ[ד] ||

[1] Abbreviation mark removed.

[2] Vocalization not indicated in כ or ד.

it to its utter end; and if we omit nothing that is essential. And the narrative will be clear if we observe what was said of brevity, since the properly brief discourse is clearer and will be easier to follow.

[6] The Statement of Facts will have plausibility[d] as follows: if it conforms to the mind, habits, and nature of the citizenry; and if it contains the timing that is consistent with the facts, the due deliberation, the appropriate scene, and the characteristic manner of speech of the persons involved in the narrative; and if it is impossible to contradict on the ground that the time was too short, or that there was no motive, or that the place was unsuitable, or that it was by nature impossible for those particular persons so to have acted—either because this was physically impossible, or because, though possessing the physical ability, it was morally impossible for them to commit the deed.

[7] It should be borne in mind that the essential factors in any deed are seven, as Victorinus[e] says in his Commentary on the Old Rhetoric: (1) who the doer is; (2) what he did; (3) in what place; (4) with what[7] as aid he did it; (5) for what cause; (6) in what way; (7) when the deed was done. An example: Joab slew Amasa [2 Sam. 20:4–10]; here are two of the essential elements, namely, the doer, Joab, and what was done, the slaying of Amasa; in what place: **at the great stone which is in Gibeon**] [20:8]; with what as aid: with the sword, as Scripture says: **And Joab was girded with his apparel of war that he had put on, and thereon was a girdle with a sword fastened upon his loins in the sheath thereof,** etc. [20:8]; for what cause: his fear that David would appoint Amasa captain of the host in his stead [cf. 2 Sam. 19:14]; in what way: in the words of Scripture, **And Joab said to Amasa, "Is it well with thee, my brother?" And Joab took Amasa by the beard with his right hand to kiss him. But Amasa took no heed to the sword that was in Joab's hand; so he smote him therewith in the groin, and shed out his bowels to the ground,** etc. [20:9–10]; when: the day when Joab and Abishai pursued Sheba the son of Bichri [20:7,11].

[8] Even if our contention is true, all these investigations must nevertheless be made in order that the case have plausibility; for many things are true though they may seem not to be. And if the contention is not really true, it ought all the more thoroughly be investigated. These, then, are the several particulars that we will proceed to investigate with great circumspection; we will be able, through them, to avail ourselves of some legal principle, or invoke the witness of important personages.

[9] Know also that Quintilian,[f] in Book IV, Chapter 2, cites a number of the different theories held by the ancients concerning the Statement of the Facts. Several authorities thought it relevant only to the Judicial Kind of Cause, and connected with past time—a view with which, apparently, some of Tully's

7. Text: "... whom" (מי; or vocalize מַי?).

---

d. *R. ad H.* 1.9.16; *De I.* 1.21.29–30.
e. Halm, 206–7 ff.
f. Q. 4.2.2.

שיראה מדברי הפליוסוף בקצור ההלצה אשר עשה לאלכסנדר, הספור אפשר
שילקח בערך אל כל הזמנים ובערך אל כל סוגי הדבור, ר״ל, בעצתי ובמקיים
ובעצומי, אלא שבג׳ מההלצה אמר דבר זה ענינו: ״ואולם, הדבור העצתי הנה
אין בו ספור כלל, לפי שלא יתכן ספור במה שיהיה בעתיד; אמנם הספור הוא
5 במה שכבר היה, או שהוא הוה עתה.״ והנה בין שני אלה המאמרים סתירה.
ואפשר שנאמ׳ שהפילוסוף לקח בקצורו תבת ״ספור״ באופן רחב, ר״ל בעד כל
הגדה, הווה תהיה, עוברת, או עתידה· ובג׳ מההלצה לקחה ביחוד בערך אל
העבר וההווה לבד; או שלפעמים יפול הספור גם בסוג העצתי, כשההלצי נעתק
אל השבח מהעצה, כמו שאמ׳ הוא אחר כן.

10 [10] עוד, אמר קוינטיליאנו בפרק הנז׳ שנפלה מחלוקת בין הקדמונים, אם
התשובה בשלילה, בסוג המריבי, תקרא ספור או לא. כאלו תאמר: המתרעם
אומר, ״ראובן הרג את הנפש״: והמתנצל משיב ״לא הרגתי״· אם זאת התשובה,
ר״ל אמרו ״לא הרגתי״, היא ספור? והשיב כי התשובה היא ספור, לא מצד מה
שהיא שוללת, אלא מצד שיתחייב אצלו לסתור ראיות בעלי התלונות, או
15 להביא אי זו ראיה או סברה לדבריו. גם מדברי הפילוסוף בשלישי מההלצה
יראה שתשובת המתנצל בשלילה תהיה ספור.

פרק ט׳

ענין החלוק.

[1] אמר טוליאו בהלצה הישנה שהחלוק יחלק לב׳ חלקים: האחד, המודיע
20 באי זה דבר נסכים עם המתנגדים ומהו הענין הנשאר במחלוקת· אשר מזה

3 העצתי] העצתיי[ט][a] || 4 אמנם] ואמנם[ט] | [הוא][ט] || 12 משיב] אומר[כ] | [אם זאת][כ] || 15 הפילוסוף] הפלוסו׳[ד] ||

remarks agree. As may be seen from the words of the Philosopher[g] in the Abridgment of the *Rhetoric* which he composed for Alexander, the Statement of Facts can, indeed, be employed in connection with all temporal contexts and in connection with all the types of discourse, Deliberative, Epideictic, and Forensic. But in Book III of the Rhetoric, he[h] has put the matter, in effect, as follows:[8] "Deliberative discourse, on the other hand, contains no Statement of Facts at all, inasmuch as there can be no such Statement about what is yet to be; the Statement deals only with what has already taken place, or with what presently is the case." These two assertions thus contradict each other. Perhaps we may say that in his Abridgment the Philosopher took the word "Statement" in a broad sense—to represent any kind of narrative, present, past or future—whereas in Book III of the *Rhetoric* he has taken the word as having particular relevance to the past or present only; or we may say that the Statement may at times occur even in the Deliberative Kind, when the orator has moved from the giving of counsel to praise, as the Philosopher[i] subsequently says.

[10] Moreover, in the chapter cited above, Quintilian[j] says that the ancients were divided as to whether or not the simple Denial, in the Judicial Kind of Cause, may be called a Statement of Facts. When, for instance, the prosecution says that "Reuben killed so-and-so," and the defendant answers "I did not kill him," is this response ("I did not kill him") a Statement of Facts? Quintilian's answer is that such a response is indeed a Statement of Facts, not as a Denial, but because the defendant is under the necessity of refuting the evidence of the prosecution, or of introducing some evidence or authority for the defendant's own words. It may be seen also from the words of the Philosopher[k] in Book III of the *Rhetoric* that the defendant's Denial constitutes a Statement.

CHAPTER 9

The Partition

[1] In the Old Rhetoric Tully[a] says that the Partition is itself partitioned into two parts. One tells what we and our opponents agree upon, and what is left in

8. Literally: "... he said a word whose matter is this."

g. Cf. *LR. ad A.* 64.23 f. (1438a f.).
h. T224/A323; cf. *Rhet.* 3.16 (1417b).
i. Ibid.
j. Q. 4.2.9 ff.
k. T223/A319; cf. *Rhet.* 3.13 (1442a).

a. *De I.* 1.22.31; cf. *R. ad H.* 1.10.17.

יעשה רושם חזק בלב השומע כאשר צריך שיתבונן היטב; והחלק האחר, כשנבאר בקצור הדברים שנרצה לדבר בהם בחלקנו אותם לחלקים מה. ושניהם מגלים הדבר ומולידים המחלוקת. וראוי לנו שנבאר בקצור היאך ראוי שיפול כל אחד מהם בהרגל.

[2] אמנם החלק הראשון, ראוי שיטהו המתרעם לתועלתו באופן זה: ״בזה דעת המנגד מסכמת עמנו, ר״ל שיואב הרג אבנר, כי הם יודו בזה; אמנם אם הרגו בדין או לא, זה נשאר במחלקת״. והנה הביא זה הענין לתועלתו באמרו שאפילו המנגדים מודים אליו במקצת.

[3] והחלק האחרון, הנקרא באור, הוא כולל ג׳ דברים, ר״ל, קצור, התכה, מעוט. הקצור כאשר לא ילקח בו כי אם המאמר ההכרחי׳ וזהו תועלתיי מצד שאין ראוי שנחזיק בלב השומע בתבות נכריות או ביפויים רחוקים, כי אם בענינים בעצמם ובחלקי סבותיהם. ההתכה היא כאשר נכלול בחלוק כל הדברים אשר תחת הענין אשר בו המחלקת, כאשר ראוי להתבונן היטב שלא נעזב דבר מה תועלתיי; כאלו תאמר שנחלק ״החי״ אל ״מדבר״ ואל ״בלתי מדבר״, או שנחלק אותו אל ״שח, מעופף, והולך״, ולא עזבנו אחד מן החלקים ההכרחיים. המעוט כשנלקח הסוגים בלתי מעורבים עם חלקיהם, כגון שנקח העצם, הכמות, והאיכות וזולתם, מזולת חלקיהם. והנה מי שיאמר: ״מפני הפחיתות, והכילאות, והעזות, באו לכלל צרות רבות ורעות״, הוא חוטא לפי המעוט, למה שהפחיתות הוא סוג לכילות ולעזות; והוא מעורב א״כ הסוג עם חלקיו, וראוי שאדם ישמר מזה, ר״ל, כשהסוג בחלוקה לבלתי יערב עמו אחד מחלקיו.

[4] ואמר בהלצה החדשה, שאחר ראותנו הדבר אשר בו נסכים עם המנגדים והנשאר במחלקת, כמו שהתבאר, ראוי שיושם בהרגל הבתור. והוא נחלק לב׳ חלקים, אשר אחד מהם הספירה, ר״ל, שהוא מונה החלקים; והמשל, שיאמר: ״אני רוצה להוכיח המבקש בג׳ פנים.״ ואמר שאין מן ההכרח שילקח מספר יותר גדול מג׳, פן ישכח אחד מן החלקים, ויכנס השומע בחשד באופן המליץ לא יאמן עוד. והחלק האחר נקרא הבאור, והוא כשנבאר ענינו בקצור מבלי מספר, באמר׳:״מצד שמו הרע, מצד מדותיו, מצד אותות רבות אוכיח המבוקש.״

1 יעשה ‹מזה›[כ] || 2 בחלקנו] בחל...ו[כ] || 5 הראשון] הא׳[ד] || 14 נעזב] נעזוב[כ] || 16 החלקים] החלקים׳[ד] || 20 שאדם] שהאדם[כ] || 24 מהם ‹הֹםׄ›[כ] || 26 ישכח] נשכח[ד] ||

---

18 תה׳ ע״א כ׳ ||

dispute: this makes a strong impression upon the hearer, as it requires his careful attention. In the second part we briefly set forth the matters we intend to discuss, and divide them into several separate points. Both reveal the Issue and engender the conflict. We must, therefore, briefly explain the proper occasion for the use of each of these parts.

[2] As for the first part, the plaintiff should turn it to his own advantage in this way: ''Our opponents agree with us in this, namely, that Joab killed Abner, for they admit the fact; but whether or not Joab had the right to slay Abner remains in dispute.'' Here, by saying that even his opponents make partial admission, the plaintiff has turned the matter to his own advantage.

[3] The second part, called the Exposition, comprises three qualities: Brevity, Inclusiveness,[1] Conciseness. It is Brevity when the Partition includes nothing save what is essential; this is of advantage, as we must not cause our hearers' minds to fasten upon foreign words or extraneous embellishments of style, but upon the facts of the case themselves and their several causes. It is Inclusivenesss when we embrace in the Partition all that appertains to the issue in dispute, when great care must be taken lest we omit some useful argument. If, for instance, one says we divide the category ''living'' into ''speaking and nonspeaking,'' or divide it into ''swimming, flying, and walking,'' we have omitted none of the essential divisions. There is Conciseness when we use classes without confusing them with their members, as when we bring in the categories of substance, quantity, quality, and the like without mention of their subdivisions. Thus, one sins against Conciseness if he says, ''Defective character, avarice, and insolence have caused them **many and sore troubles**'' [Ps. 17:20], for ''defective character'' is the class embracing ''avarice'' and ''insolence''; here, then, the class is confused with its members, whereas this is precisely what one should be careful to avoid—in the Partition, that is, not to confuse the class with any of its members.

[4] In the New Rhetoric, Tully[b] says that after we have seen what we and our opponents agree upon and what is left in dispute, as previously explained, we should draw upon the Distribution. This has two parts. Of these, one is the Enumeration—the numbering, by the speaker, of the points to be covered; he may, for example, say, ''I intend to prove my proposition by establishing three main points.'' Tully says that we should not bring in a larger number than three, lest one of the points be forgotten and the hearer be rendered so suspicious that the speaker will no longer be believed. The second part, called the Exposition, consists in briefly setting forth the matter at hand without specifying the number of points; as when a speaker says, ''I shall proceed to prove my proposition on the basis of his bad name, his moral character, and many telling signs.''

1. Literally, ''fusion'' (הַתָּכָה), JML's rendering of *absolutio* (''completeness'' [*De I.*]).

b. *R. ad H.* 1.10.17.

[5] ואמר קוינטיליאנו בה׳ מן החלק הד׳, כי פעמים רבות החלוק הוא יתר
במאמר, אבל הצורך אליו, הוא מאיר אותו מאד ומפרסמו, וישא המליץ חן
מהשומעים למענו; וידומה כמו שהוצאו הענינים מהכלל ההמוני ויושמו לעיני
הדין. וראוי שיהיה מפורסם וגלוי, כי איך יהיה המאמר המאיר כלו חשוך, כל
5 חשך טמון לצפוניו. הנה נשלם זה הפרק.

פרק עשירי

פרק הקיום וההתרה.

[1] אחר שבארנו ענין הפתיחה והספור והחלוק, ראוי לנו שנבאר ענין הקיום
וההתרה אשר עליהם תשען כל תקות הנצחון והפקת הרצון, למה שתכלית׳
10 הנצחון. ואם הפתיחה המכוון בה הקנאת החבוב וההתלמדות וההקשבה·
והרצון בספור להגיד ענייננו בסתם· ובחלוק תתברר הכונה ממנה· אלה שניהם
הושמו לתקות השגת הנצחון. כי כאשר נוכיח כונתנו, אשר זה יעשה בקיום·
ונתיר ראיות המנגדים, אשר זה פעל ההתרה· השגנו פרי ההלצה ותכליתה.
[2] אבל זה לא יעשה אם לא נדע קודם ענין הטענה וחלקיה. ואמר טוליאו
15 בחדשה, שכבר חשבו קצת מהקדמונים שהיא תחלק אל ד׳ חלקים; אמנם הוא
קבל מרבו שאינם כי אם שלשה, למה שאחד מאלה החלקים חשבו האנשים
ההם שהם שנים, וזה בחלוף מה שהתברר אצלו.
[3] אמנם הטענה היא המניעה הראשונה מהמתנצל מחוברת אל תרעומת
בעל התלונות. והמשל, בעל התלונות אומר: ״הרגת את הנפש״ והמתנצל
20 אומר: ״לא הרגתי״, זו היא המניעה הראשונה; אבל מה שימשך א״כ מהדברים,
אם זה עשאו כדין או לא, וזולתם מן התרעומת, המניעה בערכם לא תקרא

2 חן] הן[כ] || 3 ויושמו] וישמר[כ] || 4 שיהיה] שיה[כ] || 5 הנה] והנה[כ] || 6 עשירי] י׳[כ] || 9 תקות] תקוות[כ] | שתכלית׳] שתכלית[כ] || 12 לתקות] לתקוות[כ] || 13 המנגדים] המתנגדים[כ] || 14 יעשה] נעשה[כ] || 15 מהקדמונים] מהקודמים[ד] || 20 מה] מי[ד] ||

4–5 איוב כ׳ כ״ו

[5] Quintilian,[c] in Book IV, Chapter 5, says that while the Partition is often superfluous, there is need for it if the discourse is to be made quite lucid and plain, and that because of it the speaker will find favor with his hearers. It will seem as if the points have been made to stand out from the general run and to be present before the eyes of the judge. The Partition should be obvious and plain, for how may that which makes the entire discourse lucid be itself obscure, **all darkness . . . laid up for its treasures** [Job 20:26]? Here ends the present chapter.

CHAPTER 10

The Proof and the Refutation

[1] Having explained the Introduction, the Statement of Facts, and the Partition, we must now consider the Proof and the Refutation. On these depends all hope of victory and persuasion, since victory is their end and goal. If the Introduction is a means of obtaining goodwill, receptiveness, and attention; if with the Statement of Facts we intend simply to give an account of our case; and if, through the Partition, the purpose of this account is clarified: then these two parts, Proof and Refutation, are devoted to the hope of achieving victory. For when we prove what we are intent upon showing (and this is accomplished by means of the Proof) and invalidate the proofs of our opponents (the function of the Refutation), we have gained the fruit of Rhetoric and its goal.

[2] This, however, cannot be accomplished without some prior knowledge of the Issue and Types of Issue. In the New Rhetoric, Tully[a] says that some of the ancients regarded the Issue as divisible into four types; he had it on the authority of his own teacher,[1] however, that there were but three, since one of these types was considered by those ancients—contrary to his own clearly stated view—to be two.

[3] Now the Issue is determined by the joining of the primary plea of the defense with the charge of the prosecution. If, for example, the prosecutor says "You killed that person," and the defendant says "I did not," this latter is the primary plea of the defense; the pleas, however, that are based upon implications of these words—whether or not the defendant acted lawfully—and that are made

c. Q. 4.5.1 ff., 22, 26.

1. Cf. Caplan, *R. ad H.*, xxiii, and 32–33.

a. *R. ad H.* 1.11.18.

ראשונה. ואמר ״מחוברת אל תרעומת בעל התלונות״, כי זולת זה לא תקרא
טענה; כגון שיאמר המתרעם ״הרגת״, והוא אינו משיב כלום.
[4] והטענה תחלק אל ג׳ חלקים, ר״ל, סבריית, ראויה, ומשפטית. ויש לדעת
שהאנשים שהזכרנו היו מוסיפים אל אלו הג׳ הטענה הגדריית; אמנם היא תחת
5 הראוים, על צד האמת.
[5] הטענה הסבריית היא כאשר תפול המחלקת על הענין בעצמו, והמשל:
נהרג אדם מה וראינו אחד יוצא עם חרב בידו מלאה דם׃ הסברה נותנת כי הוא
הרגו אחר שהוא לבדו נראה בזה התואר. והנה אם נקבע אותו אל השופט,
ונאמר שהוא אשר מצאנו החרב בידו הרגו, וישיב ״לא הרגתי״, זאת היא הטענה
10 הסבריית.
[6] וטענה הראויה כאשר יולד המחלוקת מחמת המכתבים, ותחלק לו׳
חלקים, ר״ל, הטענה מן הנכתב והמשמעות, מן הדתות ההפכיות[1], מן המסופק,
מן הגדר, מן ההעתקה, מהדומה.
[7] מהמכתב והמשמעות, כאשר האחד מביא ראיה מאי זה שטר, ושכנגדו
15 אומר שמשמעותו אינו כן.
[8] מן הדתות ההפכיות, כגון שנמצאו שתי דתות מדברות בענין, ואחת מהם
אוסרת או שאינה לא מתרת ולא אוסרת; אם המתרעם ישען על אחת מהם,
ישיבהו המתנצל שהדת האחרת המספרת גם כן מן הענין אינה מסכמת בזה׃
״ומה ראית לסמוך על האחת יותר מן האחרת״.
20 [9] מן המסופק, כגון שמאמר המצוה, על דרך משל, יובן בשני פנים עד לא
נדע באי זה מהם רצה; ואם לפי משמעות אחד היה ראוי שיקבל ראובן מזאת
הירושה ק׳ דוקא׳; ולפי המשמעות השני אינו ראוי שיקבל דבר׃ אם יטעון ראובן
על אלה הק׳ דוקא׳ מכח אחד מאלה המשמעיות, ושכנגדו[2] מתנצל מכח
המשמעות האח׳, היתה זאת הטענה טענה ראויה מן המסופק.
25 [10] מן הגדר, כגון שהיה שם מה בדתות או במכתבים שיסבול שני פירושים;
אם המתרעם יקבוע לשכנגדו[2] אל השופט להענש כפי מה שיורה אחד מן
הפירושים, והמתנצל פוטר עצמו מן העונש לפי הפי׳ האחר שאפשר שיעשה בו,
היתה זאת הטענה טענה ראויה מן הגדר, ר״ל שתולד מכח פירושים מתחלפים
שתסבול התבה ההיא.
[11] מן ההעתקה, כגון שהתנצלו הוא מכח ההעתקה מענין לענין; כגון

9 לא] לו[ג] || 11 המחלוקת] המחלק׳[ר] ההכרחיות[ג] || 12 ההפכיות[1]] ההכריות[ר] | מן] ומן[ג] || 14 ושכנגדו] וכשכנגדו[ג] || 16 שתי] שני[ג] | ואחת] ואחד[ג] || 17 אם המתרעם <אם המתרעם>[ג] || 19 מן האחרת] מהאחרת[ג] || 20 שמאמר המצוה] שאמ׳ המצווה[ג] || 23 ושכנגדו[2]] וכשכנגדו[ם] | מתנצל] מתנצ׳[ר] מתנצח[ג] || 24 האח׳] האחר[ג] || 25 שיסבול] שיסבולו[ג] | פירושים] פרושים[ר] || 26 לשכנגדו[2]] לכשכנגדו[ג] לכשנגדו[ר] || 28 שתולד] שתוולד[ג] | פירושים] פרושים[ר] || 29 שתסבול] שתסבור[ג] ||

[1] Correction: ד[R].

[2] Correction indicated by context.

in connection with the rest of the indictment will not be called primary. Tully says "the joining of the primary plea . . . with the charge of the prosecution," for without this joining there is, properly speaking, no Issue; as when, for instance, the prosecutor says "You killed . . ." and the defendant makes no response at all.

[4] The Types of Issue[b] are three: Conjectural, Legal, and Juridical. It should be noted, too, that the aforementioned ancients added to these three the Issue of Definition, although it really is a subtype of the Legal.

[5] The Issue is Conjectural when the dispute concerns a question of fact. Example: A certain man was killed, and we saw somebody coming away from the scene with a bloody sword in his hand; conjecture yields the inference that this person slew the other, since he alone was observed as thus described. If, now, we hale him before the judge and say that the person in whose hand we found the sword slew the other man, and he responds "I did not kill him," this is an instance of the Conjectural Issue.

[6] The Issue is Legal when the conflict is engendered by written texts. It is divided into six subtypes: Letter and Spirit, Conflicting Laws, Ambiguity, Definition, Transference, and Reasoning from Analogy.

[7] It is an Issue of Letter and Spirit when one of the parties introduces evidence from some document, and his opponent asserts that the meaning of the text is not as thus construed.

[8] The Issue arises from Conflicting Laws when, for instance, two laws are found to apply to a particular deed, and one of them forbids, or else neither expressly permits nor expressly forbids. Should the prosecutor base his case upon the one law, the defendant may respond that the other law, which also deals with the matter, is not in accord with the prosecutor's argument. "And what justification have you," the defendant may ask, "for finding support in the one law any more than in the other?"

[9] The Issue is one of Ambiguity when, for example, a testator's statement may be understood in two ways, so that we do not know which is the meaning he intended. Reuben, according to one possible sense of a will ought to receive one hundred ducats from the estate, but according to the other possible sense ought to receive nothing; if, then, Reuben should claim the hundred ducats on the basis of the one interpretation, and his opponent should defend his claim on the basis of the other, this would constitute a Legal Issue created by Ambiguity.

[10] The Issue arises from Definition when some term in the pertinent laws or documents can sustain two interpretations. If the prosecutor recommends his opponent's penalization by the judge, as indicated by the one possible interpretation of the term, while the defendant seeks acquittal in accordance with the other possible interpretation, this is a Legal Issue arising from Definition; that is, the Issue is born of the differing interpretations which that term can sustain.

[11] The Issue is one of Transference when the defendant bases his case upon a

b. *R. ad H.* 1.11.18 ff.

שיאמר שאלה הדיינים אין בידם לשפוט זה הדין וראוי שיעתק הענין אל דיינים אחרים· או שיאמר שאין זה אשר התלונה עליו ראוי להענש, והנה ראוי שיעתק העונש מאיש לאיש· או שיאמר שזה אינו זמן ראוי לזאת הטענה, והנה תעתק מזמן לזמן.

5 [12] מן הדומה, כגון שלא ימצא לענין אשר אנחנו בו מאמר מיוחד בדתות או בנימוסים או בדברים אחרים, וירצה המתרעם לדמותו אל אי זה מאמר אחר אשר מכחו היה ראוי המתנצל להענש· והמתנצל אומר שאינו דומה, זו טענה ראויה מכח הדומה. הנה נשלמו חלקי הטענ׳ הראויה.

[13] אמנם הטענה המשפטית היא כאשר יודה המתנצל על עשית הדבר,
10 אבל אם נעשה בדין או לא זה ישאר במחלקת; ותחלק אל שלמה וגרועה. הטענה המשפטית השלמה היא כאשר המתנצל מודה ואומר שעשה כראוי· ונקראת זאת הטענה טענה שלמה למה שלא תצטרך לדבר מחוץ יקוה בו המתנצל ההלצה. הטענה המשפטית הגרועה היא כאשר הטענה מצד עצמה חלושה אם לא תשען על דבר מבחוץ; וזאת תחלק אל ד׳ חלקים, ר״ל, הודאה,
15 הרחקת העון, העברת העון, ההערכה.

[14] וההודאה היא כשהוא מודה[3] על החטא ומבקש מחילה עליו; ותחלק אל הוכחה ותחנה. וההוכחה כאשר יתנצל שלא עשה זה בכונה, ותחלק אל סכלות, מקרה, והכרח: סכלות, כגון שהוא מתנצל מצד שלא היה יודע שזה חטא· שאם היה יודע לא היה עושה; מקרה, כגון שמתנצל על שלא עשה הדבר
20 שהיה מחוייב לעשותו מצד מקרה שקרה· כגון שהגשמים מנעוהו, או כל הדומה לה; הכרח, כגון שמתנצל שהוא הוכרח לעשות הדבר או לבלתי עשותו. והתחנה היא שהוא מודה שחטא, ושעשה זה בכונה, אבל הוא מבקש מחילה עליו; וזה בלתי אפשר שיעשוהו הדיינים, כי הם אינם רשאים לעבור על מה שיגזרהו הדת או הנימוס מן העונשים· אמנם זה ראוי אל המלכים ואל הראשים
25 אשר אין למעלה מהם.

[15] הרחקת העון כשיודה שחטא ושעשה בכונה, אלא שחטא אחרים הביאתהו לזה. והמשל מאחד שהרג אמו, והתנצל שאמו גרמה זה מפני שהרגה

2–3 [שאין... שיאמר][כ] || 8 נשלמו] נשלמת[כ] || 11 המשפטית השלמה] המשפטית· השלמה[כ] || 13 כאשר ‹הגרועה›[כ] || 15 הרחקת העון] הרחקה· העון·[כ] | העברת העון, ההערכה] העברת העון. ההערכה[כ] || 16 מודה[3] מורה[כם] | החטא] החט[ד] || 17 הוכחה] הוכׄחׄה[כ] | וההוכחה] והתוכחה[כ] | יתנצל] ינצל[כ] || 19 עשה] עשא[ד] || 22 שהוא מודה שחטא] שמודה ‹שעשה› שחטא[כ] || 23 רשאים] רשאין[כ] || 24 אל המלכים] למלכים[כ] ||

[3] Correction: J.

shift from one feature of the case to another; for example, he asserts that the judges are incompetent to pass judgment on such a case and that the matter should be transferred to other judges; or it is maintained that the accused is not properly liable to penalty, hence that the liability must be shifted from one individual to another; or it is contended that the present is not the right time for trying the case, and hence that there should be a shift in the time set for the trial.

[12] The Issue is one of Analogy in case no citation specifically applicable to the matter at hand can be found amongst the laws, ordinances, or other regulations. If, then, the plaintiff tries to establish a similarity between the present matter and some other legal utterance by virtue of which the defendant should be punished, whereas the defendant denies the similarity, this constitutes a Legal Issue based on Analogy. We have now finished the several subtypes of the Legal Issue.

[13] The Issue is Juridical[c] when the defendant admits the act, but whether or not he had a right to commit it is in question. This Issue subdivides into the Absolute and the Assumptive. It is the Absolute Juridical Issue when the defendant admits the act and contends that he acted rightly; this Issue is called Absolute because it requires no extraneous consideration on which the defendant must prepare to speak. It is the Assumptive Juridical Issue when the case by itself is too weak without the support of extraneous considerations. This Issue, in its turn, divides into four subtypes: Acknowledgment of the Charge, Removal of the Responsibility, Shifting of the Responsibility, Comparison with the Alternative Course.

[14] It is the Acknowledgment of the Charge when the defendant admits the crime and requests pardon for it. The Acknowledgment subdivides into the Exculpation and the Plea for Mercy. The Exculpation is the defendant's denial that he acted with intent. For its part, the Exculpation subdivides into pleas of Ignorance, Accident, and Necessity: Ignorance, as when a defendant pleads that he did not know the act was criminal—that, had he known, he would not have committed it; Accident, as when the defendant pleads that, because of some chance occurrence, he failed to do that which he was required to do—that the rains or the like prevented him; Necessity, as when a defendant pleads that he was forced to do or to refrain from doing something. It is the Plea for Mercy when the defendant confesses both the crime and its premeditation, yet begs for pardon. Now it is impossible for magistrates to grant this Plea, for they do not have authority to bypass such penalties as the law or the ordinance decrees; the Plea for Mercy is, however, in keeping before kings and supreme heads [of state].

[15] It is Removal of the Responsibility when the defendant admits both his misdeed and its premeditation, yet contends that it was the wrongdoing of others which induced his own. As an example we may cite the case of a man who killed

c. *R. ad H.* 1.14.24; cf. *De I.* 1.11.15.

אביו· ובזה האופן העתיק החטא ממנו ושמו על אמו.

[16] העברת העון הוא על שני פנים: אם שיעבירהו על אדם אחר, או על ענין מן הענינים. משל הראשון, אם הדיינים לא יכלו להמית בדין אדם מה מצד גדלו ורוממותו, וצוו לאחד מן הפריצים שיהרגהו כי לא יבואהו עונש מזה, והלך 5 הפריץ והרגו; אחר כן נקבע הפריץ ההוא אל המשפט, והתנצל שעשה זה במצות הדיינים· והנה בטל ממנו העונש למה שהעביר העון אל הדיינים. משל השני, שאחד צוה לבניו בעת מותו שיעשו באר למקום מן המקומות אשר נימוס העיר יזהיר מזה; כאשר נעשתה התלונה על הבנים שלא עשו מה שצוה אביהם, התנצלו מצד הנימוס, ר״ל, שהנימוס יזהיר שלא יעשה· והנה העבירו 10 החטאת מעליהם ושמוה על הנימוס.

[17] אמנם ההערכה היא: כשימנע מבלתי עשות אחת משתים, ראוי שהאדם יעשה היותר בטוח מן המכשולים, כאשר נעריך אחד אל חברו. ואם קרה זה הדבר אל שר הצבא על דרך משל, שהיה באופן שלא היה יכול להנצל מן האויבים כי אם באחד מב׳ פנים, ועשה אחד מהם שהיה נראה לו יותר מעט 15 הנזק· הנה, אם נקבע אל המלך או אל מנהיגי המדינה, יתנצל שאחר שההצלה היתה נמנעת בזולת נזק, ברר מה שהיה בו פחות מן הנזיקים.

[18] והנה בארנו הטענה ומיניה· והנה ראוי שנספר היאך תושם בהרגל, אחר שנבאר מה שצריך לעשות למתרעם ולמתנצל בסבה העצומיית.

[19] וזה כי בהמצא הטענה, תכף ישאל ההתנצלות מן המתנצל אשר הוא 20 סבת המחלוקת· למה שאם לא יהיה כאן התנצלות, יעדר המחלקת, כי הדיין יתן הפסק דין לפי התרעומת. וזה כי אם אדם יודה שהרג את הנפש, אם לא יתנצל ויתן סבה למה עשה זה, יענש מיד. אחר כן, צריך שיביא הסבה, כי בזולת זה אין מקום למחלקת. ואחר התבאר זה מן המתנצל, צריך שהמתרעם יקיים התלונה ויחזקה שהוא כנגד מה שהביא המתנצל; שאם אמר המתנצל שהרג

3 יכלו] יוכלו[ד] || 4 כי] סי[כ] || 7 בעת] בשעה[ד] || 8 [העיר][כ] || 11 אחת] אחד[כ] || 13 הדבר אל] הדבר על[כ] || 16 הנזיקים] הנזיקין[כ] || 18 העצומיית] העצמותית[כ] || 20 המחלוקת] המחלק[י׳ד] ||

his mother, and argued, in defense, that his mother had herself induced the committing of this crime, because she had murdered his father;[2] in this way he has moved the wrongdoing away from himself, and lodged it against his mother.

[16] Shifting of the Responsibility may occur in two forms: the defendant may either transfer the responsibility to another person, or attribute it to some circumstance. An example of the first[3] is a case in which magistrates, unable to have a man legally executed because of his eminence and high station, enjoined a certain nobleman to kill him, since the nobleman would not be liable to punishment therefore. The nobleman accordingly proceeded to kill the other man; and when, subsequently, he was haled into court, his defense was that he had acted on the orders of the magistrates; thus, by transferring the responsibility to the magistrates, he escaped scot-free from punishment. An instance of the second,[4] attribution to a circumstance: A certain man, as he was dying, commanded his sons to dig a well at a spot where such was prohibited by a city ordinance. When an accusation was lodged against the sons for having failed to obey their father's orders, they based their defense on the ordinance, that is, the ordinance's prohibiting of the act; thus they transferred the responsibility away from themselves, and lodged it against the ordinance.

[17] It is Comparison with the Alternative Course when to refrain from doing one or the other of two things is impossible and a man properly prefers the safer of the dangerous alternatives, as these are normally appraised. Suppose, for example, that a general happened to find himself in a position where he could extricate himself from the enemy only by one of two maneuvers, and that he executed that one which seemed to him the less dangerous; if he is then haled before the king or the ruling authorities of the State, his defense will be that, since there was no possibility of safety without risk, he had chosen the less dangerous course.[5]

[18] Having thus explained the Issues and their subtypes, we must now tell how they may be applied. But first we shall set forth what plaintiff and defendant are constrained to do in a Forensic Cause.

[19] As soon as the Issue has been determined, the Line of the Defence is demanded of the defendant, and this forms the crux of the dispute. In the absence of a Line of Defence there would be no controversy, and the judge would render a decision conforming with the Accusation. For if a man admits that he killed some other person, unless he offers a Defence and gives a Justifying Motive for his act, he is liable to immediate punishment. He must, consequently, present the Justifying Motive, for without this there is no actionable conflict. Once this motive has been placed in evidence by the defendant, the prosecutor must establish and confirm the Central Point of the Accusation in opposition to the Justify-

2. The original personae of this example are, of course, Orestes, Clytemnestra, and Agamemnon; cf. *R. ad H.* 1.15.25 ff.

3. Taken from *R. ad H.* 1.15.25.

4. Apparently JML's own example.

5. The example is adapted from the story about Gaius Popilius given at *R. ad H.* 1.15.25.

את הנפש מפני שהרג בנו, אז המתרעם יקיים התרעומת כשיאמר: ״היה לך להביאו בדין, לא להרגו אתה׃ עם שאפי׳ הדיין לא היה יכול להענישו טרם שיודה החוטא.״

[20] והנה יולד מזה ההתעצמות, ר״ל, ממה שהתנצל בו המתנצל, ומאחר שקיים התרעומת המתרעם, המשפט מהדיין אם היה מן הראוי שיהרוג את הנפש מפני שהרג את בנו או לא. והנה בזה האופן יצמח המשפט; וכאשר שפט הדיין מה תיראה לו, צריך לקבץ כל מה שהביא המתרעם וכל מה שהתנצל בו המתנצל ולהביאם אל מקום המשפט.

[21] בכל הטענות וחלקי הטענות ראוי לדרו׳ זה הדרך, זולת בטענה הסבריית׃ כי אין צריך לשאול בה למה עשה, כי הוא מבקש זה ואומר שלא חטא. אלא אחר שהמתרעם נתן התרעומת מכח הסברה, כמו שאמרנו למעלה, מפני שיצא מן המקום עם חרב מלא׳ דם׃ והמתנצל אמר שלא הרג׃ נשאר זה בדעת הדין להתבונן מה ראוי לדון, אם שהרג אם שלא הרג, ואם הסברה דבר ראוי להשען בה או לא. ואם היו טענות רבות במחלקת אח׳, והיו המשפטים גם כן רבים.

[22] וזה היה מנהג הרומיים במשפטים בימים הם. והנה באלה המאמרים באו קיומים והתרות, והתבארו מיני ההמצאה; אלא שלא התחייב אצלנו לאמר בחתימה יותר ממה שנאמר בתחלה, לקלות העמידה על עניניה:

פרק י״א

פרק ענין הסדור.

[1] אמר קוינטיליאנו בראשון מהז׳: במדרגת מה שהתחייב לבונים מבנין הבית כי לא יספיק אליהם לבד המצא[1] להם הדברים הצריכים לבנין, ר״ל,

6 את] בנו[ג] || 9 לדרו׳] לדרוש[ג] || 10 למה עשה][ג] || 11 שאמרנו] שאמ׳[ד] || 12 מלא׳] מלא[ג] | אמר] אומר[ג] || 14 אח׳] אחר[ג] || 18 עניניה] עינינה[ג] || 22 המצא[1]] היוצא[גד] ||

[1] Emendation required by context.

ing Motive advanced by the defendant. If the defendant has said that he killed the deceased because this person had slain the defendant's son, the prosecutor must then establish the Central Point of the Accusation by saying: "You should have brought him to law, not killed him yourself; moreover, even one who is a qualified judge is not empowered to impose punishment upon a criminal before he confesses."

[20] Thence arises the Point to Adjudicate, that is to say, after the defendant's statement of his Line of Defence, and after the prosecutor's establishment of the Central Point of the Accusation, comes the Point of Adjudication by the judge—whether or not the defendant was right in killing the deceased because this person had slain the defendant's son. This, then, is how the Point to Adjudicate is developed; and when the judge has decided what he regards as the Point to Adjudicate, all that the prosecutor has charged, and all the defensive arguments presented by the defendant must be gathered together and introduced at the trial in court.

[21] It is proper to proceed in this way in all the Types of Issue and their subdivisions, except the Conjectural. Here there is no need to ask the accused why he committed the act, for he himself raises this question in arguing that he did not commit the crime. But when the prosecutor has made his conjectural Accusation, as we said above, on the ground that the accused had left the scene with a bloody sword, and when the defendant has denied the murder, what is left for the judge to consider is the judgment that should be rendered: whether the accused did or did not commit the murder, and, indeed, whether or not conjecture is something that should be relied upon. If there are several Types of Issue in a single controversy, there will likewise be several Points to Adjudicate.

[22] Such was Roman practice in judicial matters in those days. Proofs and refutations obviously belong in speeches of this character, and the presence of certain kinds of Invention has been explained. Since, however, the data on Invention are so easy to understand, we need say no more about it in concluding this chapter than was said at the beginning.

CHAPTER 11

The Arrangement

[1] In Book VII, Chapter 1, Quintilian[a] says that just as it does not necessarily suffice the masons engaged upon building a house merely to have the essential

a. Q. 7.Pr.1.

הסיד, והאבנים, ועצי ארזים או ברושים, וזולתם, אבל הצורך הגדול הוא לחבר
הענינים האלה, ולתקנם על סדר, ולכונן הבנין חלק אחר חלק, לא יאחר
המוקדם ולא יקדים המאוחר· כן גם כן צריך לעשות במאמרים. כי עם היות לנו
ספורים, אמרים, וראיות, ותשובות והתרות כהנה וכהנה, לא יועילו ולא יצילו
5 אם לא ישמר הסדור המיוחד בהם. ולזה היה הסדור דבר גדול והכרחי׳ במאמר,
ובלעדו המליץ להבל וריק שמו· יכלה ולא תעשינה ידיו תושיה: לא יענה עזות,
ולא יקרא לשבוים דרור, ולאסורים פקח קוח. לכן ראוי שנדבר בענינו.

[2] וזה שמו אשר יקראו טוליאו בג׳ מההלצה, וזה גדרו אשר גדרו: הסדור
הוא מאמר באשר המאמרים שהמצינו יסודרו, כל אחד מהם במקומו המיוחד
10 לו. והוא על ב׳ פנים: אם שיהיה כפי חקת המלאכה ומשפטיה· אם שיהיה כפי
הראוי לזמן אשר בו המאמר.

[3] אמנם כפי המלאכה יהיה הסדור האמתי כשנתחיל מן הפתיחה, ואחריה
הספור, וימשך א״כ החלוק, ואחריו הקיום· עוד נכוון ההתרה, ולבסוף נסיים
בחתימה, כאשר התבאר למעלה. ולא בלבד חלקי המאמר העקריים צריך
15 שיבאו על סדר, אבל זה הענין בעצמו התחייב בחלקי כל חלק מהם; כאלו
תאמר שנביא כל חלקי הראיה (אשר יתבארו במה שיבא) איש על דגלו באותות,
בסדר מסגל כפי מה שיאות, לא ידח ממנו נדח.

[4] וזה מה שממנו לפי המלאכה. והסדור לפי הזמן הוא שנסדר כל אחד מן
החלקים אשר במאמר לפי הצורך והשעה. והוא כי נצטרך לפעמים להתחיל מן
20 הספור, או מאי זו ראיה חזקה, או מראיית המכתבים, או מן הקיום, או מן
הדומה לאלו מהפוך הסדרים אשר אין לעשותם אלא כשהשעה צריכה לכך.
וזה כי אם נראה השומע במדרגה מן הלאות עד תכבדנה אזניו משמוע, או כי
רבוי הדברים המנגדים ושועתם עלו באזניו, או ענין אחר זולת זה, אז ראוי

6 המליץ] המלי״ |שמו] כמו״ ||

6 יש׳ ל׳ ז׳ |איוב ה׳ י״ב |מש׳ י״ח כ״ג ||7 יש׳ ס״א א׳ ||16 במ׳ ב׳ ב׳ ||17 שמ״ב י״ד י״ד ||22 יש׳ נ״ט א׳ ||23 שמ״ב כ״ב ז׳ ||

building materials available—the lime, stone, timber of cedar or cypress, and the like—but the most important requirement is to put these materials together, to arrange them in order, and to build the structure part after part—neither postponing what has priority, nor assigning priority to what should be postponed—just so is it necessary to do in the case of discourses. For even though we have thus-and-thus many statements of fact, arguments, and proofs, and as many replies and refutations, they will neither profit us nor save us unless the arrangement specifically proper to them is carefully retained. The Arrangement, therefore, is a matter of great and compelling importance in the speech. Without it, the speaker has made the speech **in vain and to no purpose** [Isa. 30:7]; he finishes, but his **hands can perform nothing substantial** [Job 5:12]: he will neither **answer strongly** [Prov. 18:23][1] nor **proclaim liberty to the captives and the opening of the eyes to them that are bound** [Isa. 61:1]. It behooves us, therefore, to discuss the matter.

[2] Tully[b] calls it by this name, Arrangement, in Book III of the [New] Rhetoric, and defines it as follows: Through the Arrangement the several statements which we have invented are set in order, each in its own special place. The kinds of Arrangement are two: it is either developed on essentially the same lines as the rhetorical art itself and its principles, or else it is appropriately accommodated to the occasion of the speech.

[3] The Arrangement modeled upon the rhetorical art is truly such when we begin with the Introduction, follow it with the Statement of Facts, continue with the Partition and after it the Proof; give next place to the Refutation, and end with the Conclusion, as was explained above. It is not merely the fundamental parts of the discourse which must be arranged in order, but the identical operation is required for the subdivisions of each several part; we must, for instance, introduce all the Parts of Evidence (which will be explained later) **each at its post according to the signs** [Num. 2:2],[2] in the appropriately apposite order, taking care **that no banished one be outcast from** it [2 Sam. 14:14].[3]

[4] So much, then, for the Arrangement modeled upon the rhetorical art. In the Arrangement accommodated to the occasion we set each of the several parts of the speech in an order determined by the need and the moment. That is, we may sometimes need to begin with the Statement of Facts, or with some strong argument, or with the evidence of documents, or with the Proof, or make some like change in the order which, but for the need of the moment, would be ill-advised. For if we see that the hearer is weary to the point that **his ears are heavy, that they cannot hear** [Isa. 59:1] or that the multiplicity of our opponents' arguments and their **cry** have gone up **into his ears** [2 Sam. 22:7], or that

1. JV: "imprudently."
2. JV: "... every man with his own standard according to the ensigns."
3. JV: "... that he that is banished be not an outcast from him."

b. *R. ad H.* 3.8.16.

להניח הפתיחה ונתחיל מהספור או מאי זו ראיה חזקה· וא״כ, אם יאות לנו,
נחזור אל הפתיחה. ואם הספור בלתי מפרסם למה שאין לו פנים מן ההראות,
נתחיל מראיה מה חזקה. ובכן, ראוי לנו לנהוג ההפוכים האלה וחלופי הסדרים
אם יבואנו ההכרח לשנות הסדר שהוא לפי המלאכה.

[5] והסדר הראוי בקיומים והתרות הוא שהראיות החזקות תהיינה בראשונה
ובאחרונה, והחלשות והבינוניות — אשר הם לבדם מעטות ההאמתה, אמנם
יקנו האמתה עם האחרות אם תמצאנה יחד — ראוי שיושמו באמצע. וזה כי
תכף השלם הספור יצפה לב השומע אמות המבוקש· לכן ראוי שיהיה האמות
בראשונה מן החזקות שבראיות. ויען הנאמר באחרו׳ ישמרהו השומע בקלות
ותקל עליו זכירתו, אין ספק שראוי לסיים באי זו ראיה קיימת וחזקה. והנה
הסדור בזה האופן יצליח המליץ במדרגה סדור המערכות באופן הראוי
במלחמה, אשר בו מן התוחלת והתקוה על הנצחון דבר לא יעלם.

[6] ואנחנו הביאנו למעלה הרבה מן הפסוקים המעידים על הפוך הסדר.
והנה משה רבינו, עליו השלום, בהתפללו בעד כל ישראל בענין המרגלים,
התחיל מהראיה החזקה שבראיות, על שהיה ראוי לה׳ ית׳ למחול להם, ואמר:
ושמעו מצרים כי העלית בכחך את העם הזה מקרבו: ואמרו אל יושב הארץ,
כו׳ [במ׳ י״ד י״ג—י״ד]. כלומר, ״אם תעשה את הדבר הזה, ושמעו מצרים —
אשר נראה בהם כחך הגדול לכל האותות והמופתים, והעלית את העם הזה
מקרבו — ואמרו שאמנם היה זה, ר״ל, שהרגת אותם עתה, בעבור יושבי הארץ
הזאת, שהם במדרג׳ מן היכולת והרוממות שלא יכלת אליהם להוריש בני
ישראל את ארצם.״ וזאת היא ראיה גדולה על שאין מן הראוי להשמיד את
ישראל, כי מה יעשה לשמו הגדול? ויהיה אל בזה המקום [במ׳ י״ד י״ד] במקום
בעבור, כמו ויאמר אברהם אל שרה אשתו [בר׳ כ׳ ב׳] שהוא כמו בעבור, כאשר
התבאר בלבנת הספיר. והנה ימשכו מזה למצרים ב׳ דברים: אחד, שישמחו

3 וחלופי] וחלופ׳[ר] || 9 באחרו׳ (=באחרונה)] באחרות[כ] || 15 למחול] ימחול[כ] || 18 והעלית] והעליתי[כ] || 20 במדרג׳] במדרגת[כ] || 23 אברהם] אברם[כ] | שרה] שרי[כ] ||

some other such condition obtains, then we should leave out the Introduction and begin with the Statement of Facts or with some strong argument. Later, if it suits our purpose, we can revert to the Introduction. If the Statement of Facts containing some implausible feature is not credited by all, we should begin with some strong argument. Such, accordingly, are the transpositions and changes that we should effect if we are obliged to alter the Arrangement that is modeled upon the rhetorical art.

[5] In the Proof and Refutation the proper Arrangement is to place the strong arguments at the beginning and at the end, while the weak and the indifferent—which in themselves are not very convincing, but which gain the power to convince if present conjointly with the other arguments—should be placed in the middle. For as soon as all the facts have been stated, the hearer is set to anticipate the proving of the case; the very beginning of the validation should therefore consist of the strongest of the proofs. And since what has been said last is most easily retained and remembered by the audience, there can be no doubt that one ought to end with some unassailably strong proof. Thus fashioned, the Arrangement will assure success to the speaker in quite the same way as, during a battle, the proper method of deploying the troops is the device which affords no small expectation and hope of victory.

[6] We have already cited several of the Biblical verses which attest a transposition in the order. Our Teacher, Moses (upon whom be peace), praying for all Israel during the episode of the spies, began with the strongest possible proof of the thesis that the Lord (blessed be He) ought to forgive the Israelites, and said: "**When the Egyptians shall hear—for Thou broughtest up this people in Thy might from among them—they will say: (it is) on account of the inhabitants of this land,**" and the rest [Num. 14:13 f.].[4] In other words, "If Thou shouldst do this thing, the Egyptians—amongst whom Thy great power was made manifest in all the signs and wonders, and out of whose midst Thou broughtest up this people—will hear and will say that Thy destruction now of Israel has come to pass on account of the inhabitants of this land, because they are so powerful and exalted that Thou couldst not prevail over them and give the Children of Israel possession of their land." This was a strong proof: Israel ought not to be destroyed because of what their destruction would do to His great Name. The preposition *'el* [= "to, unto"] in this passage [Num. 14:14] stands for *ba'ᵃbhūr* [= "on account of, for the sake of"], as in **And Abraham said on account of** ('el) **Sarah his wife: "She is my sister"** [Gen. 20:2],[5] where *'el* means much the same as *ba'ᵃbhūr*, as explained in *Libhᵉnath Hassappīr* [The Pavement of Sapphire].[6] For the Egyptians there would be two consequences of such destruc-

4. JV: ". . . they will say to the inhabitants of this land," etc.

5. JV: "And Abraham said of Sarah," etc.

6. JML's Hebrew grammar (1454), still unpublished. The title is taken from Exod. 24:10. See the Int. §2 and n.16, §3 and n.151, and §5 (end), where the three additional citations of this work are listed.

וישישו אף גילת ורנן, כי ראו נקמתם מהרעות הגדולות וצרות רבות ורעות סבלו למענם; ועוד, שיחשבו שזה היה מבלי יכלת, כו׳ [במ׳ י״ד ט״ז]. ומפני שהיה אפשר שיאמר שזה לא יתחיב, כי מה שהושיע׳ הש׳ יתב׳ במצרים היה מפני שהיו ישראל במדרגה ראויה אל שיעשו אליהם הנסים והנפלאות ההנה· אמנם עתה על רוב פשעיהם הדיחם, הסתיר פניו מהם והיו לאכול, ובא להם העונש הגדול מצד רב העונות והמרדים, ולזה לא יתחייב ממנו חסרון מה ביכלת הש׳. אמר א״כ: שמעו כי אתה י״י בקרב העם הזה אשר עין בעין נראה אתה י״י ועננך עומד עליהם, כו׳ [שם י״ד]. כלומר, זה אינו, למה שימצא׳ בישראל דברי[2] ההשגחה הפרטית, שהיא הפך הסתר הפנים, והם כל אלה שזכר, באשר נפלאו ישראל מכל העם אשר על פני האדמה. וזאת היא ההתרה. ואמר אחר כן: אם תמית את העם הזה כאיש אחד, לא מצרים לבד יאמרו זה, אבל כל הגוים אשר שמעו את שמעך יאמרו מבלתי יכולת [שם ט״ו — ט״ז]. וזאת היא ראיה אחרת, אלא שבמצרים יתקבצו ב׳ דברים: השמחה הגדולה שהתחייבה אליהם מצד הנקמה· ושיאמרו מבלתי יכולת. לכן היה מחק השם ית׳ שלא לשמח נפש אויביו, גם שלא יוכלו לאמר הדבר הרע הזה.

[7] ואחר הראיות שב אל הפתיחה ואמר שיגדל כחו וגבורתו כאשר דבר, ושיזכור מדותיו המזקקות אשר בהם מנהיג ישראל, ר״ל, שהוא ארך אפים ורב חסד, כו׳ [שם י״ח], כמדרג׳ מה שנעשה האדם מחבב בזכרו שבחיו מצד המדות המפלגות ההנה. ואחר כן אומ׳: סלח נא לעון העם הזה כגודל חסדך [שם י״ט], וזהו הספור.

[8] וכל זה הבלבול התחייב מפני האף והחמה, כי כאשר היה הענין כן צריך שהמליץ יתחיל מהראיות לשכך מיד חמת השומע, כלומ׳: אם תעשה זה,

1 הגדולות] הגדול[ד] |רבות ורעות] רעׄות ורׄבות[כ] || 2 מבלי] מבלתי[ת] || 3 הש׳ יתב׳] המ׳ ית׳[כ] || 4 ישראל] ישרל[כ] || 6 הש׳] הׄ ית׳[כ] || 8 עליהם <יומם>[כ] || 9 שימצא׳] שימצאם[כ] |[דברי[2]] דברי׳[ד] דברים[כ] || 12 [את][כ] || 15 יוכלו] יכלו[כ] || 16 וגבורתו] וגבורת[ד] || 17 המזקקות] המזיקיקות[כ] || 17–18 ורב [חסד][ד] |כמדרג׳] כמדרגה[כ] || 19 [אומ׳][כ] |חסדך] חסדיך[כ] ||

[2] Correction: J.

tion. First, they would be glad, would rejoice **even with joy and singing** [Isa. 35:2], since they would have seen their vengeance for the great disasters and many sore afflictions they had suffered on Israel's account: and secondly, they would think that this had come about **because the Lord was not able,** and the rest [Num. 14:16]. Now it might be said that the result would not necessarily ensue, since Israel's deliverance by the Name (blessed be He) in Egypt came because Israel quite deserved that those signs and wonders should be performed for their sake, whereas now, for **the multitude of their transgressions** He had **cast them down** [Ps. 5:11], had **hidden** His **face from them and they should be devoured** [Deut. 31:17], and severe punishment for their multiple iniquities and rebellions had overtaken them; thus, it would not necessarily follow that there be any incapability on the part of the Name. Following this, accordingly, Moses said: "**who have heard that Thou Lord art in the midst of this people; inasmuch as Thou Lord art seen face to face, and Thy cloud standeth over them,**" and so on [Num. 14:14]. In other words: This argument is untenable, because the manifestations of special providence—the opposite of the hiding of the divine Countenance—are found in Israel; the manifestations are all those things which he has mentioned, those by virtue of which Israel is more miraculous than any people on the face of the earth. This, then, is the Refutation.[7] Next Moses said: "**Now if Thou shalt kill this people as one man**" [14:15], not only the Egyptians, but all "**the nations which have heard the fame of Thee**" will say: "**Because the Lord was not able**" [14:16]. This is still another proof; in the case of the Egyptians, however, two points are combined: (1) the great joy that would come to them in consequence of their revenge, and (2) that they could say "**Because the Lord was not able.**" Moses argued, accordingly, that it was in the nature of the Name (blessed be He) neither to rejoice the soul of His enemies[8] nor to enable them to say this wicked thing.

[7] After presenting these proofs, Moses returned to the Introduction, and urged that the Lord's power and might be great according as He had spoken, and that He remember the purely ethical character of His guidance of Israel, namely, that He "**is slow to anger, and plenteous in loving kindness,**" and the rest [14:18], quite as a human being might be rendered well disposed at having the praise he has received for those outstanding virtues recalled to his mind. Following this Moses says: "**Pardon, I pray Thee, the iniquity of this people according unto the greatness of Thy** loving kindness" [14:19]; and this is the Statement of Facts.

[8] All this disordering of the Arrangement was made necessary by the divine wrath and anger, for in such circumstances the speaker must begin with proofs in order at once to abate the hearer's anger. He must, in effect, say: "If you do this,

7. I.e., of the argument that Israel's destruction would be attributed to her own unworthiness and not to the Lord's inability to save.

8. Cf. Pss. 30:2, 89:43.

יתחייב כך וכך; וילך בהדרגה אל הפתיחה ואל הספור כפי צורך הענין.
[9] אמנם אפשר שיסופק כי אם ההתחלה מן הראיות תתחייב על הכעס והחרון, למה לא עשה זה משה רבינו עליו השלו׳ בהתפלל עליהם על ענין העגל? והוא מבואר שחטאו ישראל בפעם ההיא חטאז גדולה, מרו ועצבו את
5 רוח קדשו. והנה אז התחיל מן הספור, ואמר: למה י״י יחרה אפך בעמך, כו׳ [שמ׳ ל״ב י״א]; והלך ממנו אל הראיה, ואמר: למה יאמרו מצרים לאמר ברעה הוציאם, כו׳ [שם י״ב]. כלומר, שהיה ראוי שימחול להם כי מה יאמרו מצרים, כו׳ [שם], ר״ל, שנצדקו בדבריהם כאשר אמרו: ראו כי רעה נגד פניכם [שמ׳ י׳ י׳]· ושהשם ית׳ היה אלקי הרעות לבד, כאשו׳ חשבו קצת מהקודמים, כמו
10 שאמר בן רש״ד בבאורו בספר מה שאחר לפי ההעתקה החדשה. עוד, למה לא שב אל הפתיחה, כמו שעשה בכאן באמרו י״י ארך אפים, וכו׳ [במ׳ י״ד י״ח]? ואדרבה, בפעם ההיא היה ראוי לעשות במדרגה מה שיגרום החבוב לבני אדם, כי גדלה חמת י״י עליהם עד לאין מרפא. אמנם התשובה על אלה הספקות היא ממה שיקל: כי במעשה העגל אמר השם ית׳, ועתה הניחה לי [שמ׳ ל״ב י׳]·
15 והנה רמז לו בזה שאם יתפלל עליהם ינחם על הרעה ולא יעשה כלה. והנה לא היה צריך לגרום החבוב ולשכך החמה תכף, ולזה גם כן לא הצרך לפתיחה.

פרק י״ב

פרק ענין הרמיזה.

20 [1] אמר הפילוסוף בנ׳ מההלצה דבר זה ענינו: קדם שנדבר במלות, הנה ראוי שנדבר בענינים הנעשים עם המלות על צד העזר בטוב נתינה ההבנה, והפלת

3 רבינו עליו השלו׳] רבי׳ ע״ה[c] || 10 בבאורו] בבאו״[r] || 13 אלה] אלו[c] || 14 השם ית׳] ה׳ י״י[c] || 20 נתינה] נתינת[t] ||

4 שמ׳ ל״ב ל״א | יש׳ ס״ג י׳ || 13 דה״ב ל״ו ט״ז || 15 שמ׳ ל״ב י״ד | יר׳ ה׳ י״ח

then thus-and-thus must necessarily ensue;'' and he must proceed gradually to the Introduction and to the Statement of Facts, according as the matter at hand requires.

[9] Now it is possible to raise the question. Why, if anger and wrath make it necessary to begin with proofs, did not our Master Moses (upon whom be peace) do this when he prayed for the people in the episode of the golden calf?[9] At that time, it is clear, Israel had **sinned a great sin** [Exod. 32:31], had **rebelled and grieved His holy spirit** [Isa. 63:10]. On that occasion, however, Moses began with the Statement of Facts, and said, ''**Lord, why doth Thy wrath wax hot against Thy people,**'' etc. [Exod. 32:11]; advancing from this to the Proof, he said, ''**Wherefore should the Egyptians speak, saying: For evil did He bring them forth?**'' etc. [32:12]. That is, it was fitting that He should pardon them, for ''Wherefore should the Egyptians speak,'' etc.—namely, be justified in having said, ''**See ye that evil is before your face**'' [Exod. 10:10], and that the Name, blessed be He, was a God of evil only. This last is what some of the ancients believed, as Averroes says in his *Commentary on the Metaphysics* (according to the New Translation).[10] Again, why did Moses [in Exodus 32] not revert to the Introduction as he did in the passage in Numbers cited just above, when he said, ''The Lord is slow to anger,'' etc. [Num. 14:18]? It was rather on the occasion of that passage that he ought to have proceeded gradually to render the Lord well disposed toward men, for His wrath had waxed against them **till there was no remedy** [2 Chr. 36:16]. The answer to these questions is easy to provide, for in the episode of the golden calf, the Name (blessed be He) said, **"Now therefore let me alone**'' [Exod. 32:10]; this was in fact His suggestion: that if Moses should pray for the Israelites He would **repent of the evil** [32:14] and **not make a full end** [Jer. 5:18]. Thus there was no need to make Him well disposed and at once to abate His wrath; and so no Introduction was necessary.

CHAPTER 12

The Delivery

[1] The Philosopher,[a] in Book III of the *Rhetoric*, makes a statement to the following effect: We ought, before discussing diction, to discuss the operations

9. Exod. 32:11-14.

10. On this translation, included in the Latin version of Averroes' commentary, see G. Lacombe et al., *Aristoteles Latinus I* (Rome, 1939), 64-65, and F. E. Peters, *Aristoteles Arabus* (Leiden, 1968), 50-51.

---

a. T179/A250; cf. *Rhet*. 3.1.3 f. (1403b-1404a).

ההצדקה, והגעת הכונה המכוונת· והם אשר היה כבר מנהג הקדמונים שיקראום רמיזת הפנים. וזה שהדברים האלו, למה שהיה מדרכם שיטו השומעים אל ההאזנה וההשמעות והסברת הפנים למדבר, והרחבת הנפש למה שיניחהו, הושאל להם זה השם.

5 [2] ואלו הדברים ב׳ מינים: אם תמונות, אם קולות ונעימות. והתמונות, מהם מה שהם תמונות לגוף בכללו, ומהם מה שהם תמונות לחלקי הגוף, כידים והפנים והראש· ואלו הם יותר רבי העשות אצל ההלצה.

[3] והתמונות בכלל יכוון בהם אחד משני ענינים: אם נתינה הבנת הדבר ודמותו המפיל האמות· ואם דמיון להפעלות מה או מדה מה. וזה, אם במדבר· 10 רצוני, שידומה בו שהוא כאותו ההפעלות או המדה, כמו שידבר אדמוני הפנים, מתפעל בהפעלות הפחד, כאשר רצה להגיד שהוא מפחד, או במתון ואבירות לב מביא לחשוב שהוא משכיל; ואם באשר[1] אליו הדבור, כאשר רצה שיציירהו בצורת מפחד או משכיל; ואם שיפול אותו ההפעלות בנפש השומע, או אותה המדה, עד שיהיה מוכן אם מול האמת הנופל מאותו ההפעלות או המדה, ואם 15 מול הפעל המגיע ממנו.

[4] ואולם הנעימות, הנה הם תעשינה במאמר ההלצי לפנים· מהם לדמות ההפעליות או המדות, וזה גם כן לג׳ פנים. אחד מהם אצל מה שרצה המדבר שיביא לדמות את השומעים שהוא באותו ההפעלות או המדה; כמו שהוא, כאשר רצה שידומה בו הרחמנות, יחנן קולו· וכאשר רצה שידומה בו הכעס, 20 תבער חמתו· וככה במדות; ואמנם היה זה כן שאלו הקולות נמצאות בטבע מגיעות מאשר יתפעלו כמו אלו ההפעליות. והאופן השני: שתהיה כונתו הנעת השומעים מול הפעלות מה, או מדה מה, אם כדי שיגיע להם האמות המגיע מאותו ההפעלות או המדה, או הפעל המגיע ממנו. והג׳ אצל מה שיספר ספור מאנשים יתארם באותו ההפעלות או המדה. ומהם עוד, שהם תעשינה במין מן 25 המשקל בדבור ההלצי, כפי מה שנאמרהו אחר זה. ומהם עוד, שתעשינה שירים בפתיחת המאמר וחתימתו, ומקומות העמידה, וכו׳.

1 היה כבר] כבר היה[כ] || 4 הושאל] הושואל[כ] || 8 נתינה] נתינת[ט] || 11 במתון ואבירות] במתון או [באבו͗רות] ואבירות[כ] || 12 באשר[1]] כאשר[כד] || 13 שיפול] שיפיל[טbg] || 14 מוכן] מובן[ד טa] || 17 אצל] אבל[כ] || 23 והג׳] והשלישי[כ] || 24 באותו] מאותו[טg] |שהם] שהן[ט] || 26 וכו׳] וכ׳[ד] ||

19 מש׳ כ״ו כ״ה || 20 תה׳ פ״ט מ״ז ||

[1] So ט.

which accompany diction as an aid to effective communication, to winning a victorious verdict, and to achieving the end in view: the operations which the ancients were accustomed to call "suggestion-of-countenance."[1] This term was adopted for these procedures because they normally inclined the hearers to be attentive and compliant, moved them favorably to "countenance" the speaker, and rendered them more hospitable to his proposals.

[2] Such procedures are of two sorts: either of physical representations, or of sounds and tones. Of physical representations, some are of the whole body, some of parts of the body, such as the hands, face, and head, these being the most often used in oratory.

[3] Physical representations generally have one of two purposes: either to provide a convincing imitation of some matter which is in course of being explained, or to simulate some emotion or trait of character. The means of accomplishing the latter may be the speaker himself; that is to say, he may seem to manifest that emotion or trait of character. For example, he might speak with face flushed, manifestly affected by fear, when desiring to convey that he is afraid, or he might speak with composure and courage and so make the audience think him intelligent. Or this may be done by the person being discussed, when the speaker wishes to depict him as either frightened or intelligent. Or, finally, that emotion or trait of character may so be projected into the hearer's soul that he will be ready either for the conviction produced by that emotion or trait, or for the action which is its outcome.

[4] For their part, the tones used in a rhetorically able speech are of several different kinds, one being the kind used in order to simulate emotions or traits of character. Such simulation is likewise of three sorts. One of these is in place when the speaker wishes to make his hearers imagine him to be feeling, or to be governed by, a particular emotion or moral trait. If, for example, he wishes it to be imagined that he feels pity, he **will make his voice gracious** [Prov. 26:25],[2] when he wishes it to be imagined that he feels anger, his **wrath will burn** [Ps. 89:47]; and so, too, in the case of moral traits. This kind of simulation is thus effective because such are the sounds which naturally and actually emanate from persons experiencing those emotions. The second sort is called for when it is the speaker's purpose to move his audience to feel, or be governed by, some emotion or moral trait, in order that they should either come to hold the conviction resulting from such emotion or trait, or take the action which is its outcome. And the context of the third sort is a speaker's narrative about people described as feeling, or governed by, such an emotion or trait. Another kind consists of the tones used in conjunction with a sort of meter when the speaking style is hortatory, as comports with what we say below. Still another consists of their use as verse at the beginning and end of the discourse, at pauses, and so on.

1. JML and T: רמיזת הפנים; A: الاخذ بالوجوه "facial imitation." This is the rendering of ὑπόκρισις found in the Old Arabic version of the *Rhet.*; see Badawī's ed. of A, 184.

2. JV: "speaketh tenderly."

[5] עוד אמר: ״וראוי שתדע שהרמיזה בפנים אין לה צורך בהלצות הכתובות, אמנם צריכה בנאמרות פנים בפנים״, כו׳. עוד אמר: ״והרמיזה בפנים אמנם היא מועילה ברוב בהלצות[2] המסדרות על צד המחלקת, לפי שהאדם אמנם יצטרך אל ההעזר בכל הדברים הנותנים הספקה במקום המחלקת כדי שיפול הנצחון״. עד כאן.

[6] ואמר טוליאו בשלישי מההלצה החדשה: הרמיזה תחלק אל ב׳ חלקים, ר״ל, בתאר הקול ותנועות הגוף. ותאר הקול יחלק אל שלשה חלקים: אל חזק, וקיים, ורך. וחוזק הקול יתוסף מן הטבע והולך ומתגדל כפי גדול האדם, וההנהגה הרפואית שומרת אותו. וקיום הקול יתוסף מן הטבע גם כן, אלא שהרגל הקריאה והצעקה שומר אותו. ורכות הקול הוא אשר נוכל לכוף אותו כשנדבר באופן יאות לנו וכרצוננו· וביחוד עושה זה האותות הצעקה. מחוזק הקול וחלק מהקיום, אשר אחד מהם עושה אותו הטבע והאחר הטבע שומר אותו, אין לנו שנדבר בו בזה המקום; אמנם מן חלק מהקיום אשר ישמרהו הרגל הצעקה, ומרכות הקול ההכרחי אל המליץ והוא נקנה מהאותות הצעקה, ראוי שיסופר.

[7] הנה היאך נוכל לשמור הקול, שיהיה במדרגה אחת מן הקיום, הוא בזה האופן: אם בתחלה יהיה נמוך, שפל, שח; למה שאם היה זולת זה בתחלה, ר״ל, אם היה חזק, יזיק אל הלחיים קודם שנרגילהו בקול שפל עם מנוחות ארוכות· למה שבזה ינפשו הקו׳, והנשימה, והלחיים. והנה צריך שנעזוב הצעקה התמידית; נלך בהדרגה אל המאמר, ונכוון ההשתנות עד שלפעמים נגביה הקול, לפעמי׳ נשפיל· ובזה האופן יתקיים ויתמיד הקול, ולא יעשה צרוד; והחדות והצעקה יכו בלחיים ויזיקו להם, ותכף יפסידו ערבות הקו׳. אמנם באחרי׳ המאמ׳, בצעקה מתמדת ובנשימה אחת ראוי שיאמרו דברים רבים, כי כבר נתחממו הלחיים בהדרגה ולא יוזקו מן הקול. והנה עלה לנו מזה שבתחל׳ הקול יהיה נמוך· ובאמצע עם ההשתנות, פעם נמוך פעם חזק· ובאחרונה על מדרגה אחת מן הצעקה, לא זולת זה.

[8] והנה בזה האופן יחס הקול אל השומע מתדמה יחס הקול אל המדבר. כי כמו שיוזק המדבר מהקול החזק והקול החד, ויהיה נאות לו בתחלה הקול החלש, זה הענין בעצמו יקרה לשומע· כי הוא יתפעל מן החד ויוזק, ויערב לו החלש. וכן, כמו שבאמצע בהשתנות[3] הקול עם מנוחות ארוכות ישבות וינפש

3 בהלצות[2]] כהלצות[כד] || על צד] אל צד[טagv] || 7 הגוף] הקול[כ] || 8 האדם] האדה[ד] || 9 וההנהגה] והנהגה[כ] || 12 [אותו][כ] || 17 [שח][כ] | בתחלה] בתחלת[ד] || 19 ינפשו] ימשפו[כ] | הקו׳] הקולות[כ] || 21 יעשה צרוד] יעשה <כל> צרור[כ] || 22 והחדות והצעקה] וחדות · והצעקה[כ] || 23 באחרי׳] באחרים[כ] || 24 שבתחל׳] שבתחלת[כ] || 30 בהשתנות[3]] השתנות[כד] ||

[2] So ט.

[3] Correction required by context.

The Philosopher also says: "And you should realize that while suggestion-of-countenance is not needed in written rhetorical pieces, it is certainly a necessity in discourses pronounced face-to-face," etc. He further says: "Suggestion-of-countenance is of greatest advantage in controversial speeches, since where there is debate the speaker really needs the help of all the devices which yield persuasion in order to bring off the victory." Thus far the Philosopher.

[6] Tully,[b] in Book III of the New Rhetoric, says that Delivery is divided into two parts, Voice Quality and Physical Movement. Voice Quality is tripartite: strong, stable, and flexible. Strength of Voice is subject to natural increase, becomes progressively greater as the human being grows, and is conserved by medical procedures. Stability of Voice is also subject to natural increase, but practice in pronouncing and declaiming conserves it. Flexibility of Voice is our ability, as we speak, to inflect the voice in the manner we deem appropriate and as we like; it is this capacity, particularly, that declamatory modulation makes possible. Vocal Strength and, in part, Vocal Stability—the one of which is produced, the other conserved, by nature—need not be discussed by us here. Some account, however, ought to be given of the category of Vocal Stability that is conserved by declamatory exercise, and of the Vocal Flexibility—essential to the orator—that is acquired by declamatory modulation.

[7] Now we will be able to conserve the voice so that it will retain its stability if, at the outset, it is soft, subdued, and low. For if it is otherwise at the beginning—that is, if it is strong—it will injure the vocal chords[3] sooner than we can habituate it to subdued tones as well as to long rests; for it is in this way that voice, breath, and chords will be refreshed. We must, accordingly, refrain from declaiming at full voice; we will proceed by scaling the voice to what is said, and deliberately effect change, so that sometimes we will raise our voice, sometimes lower it; in this way the voice will be stable, will last, and will not become cramped. Shrill and declamatory tones assail and damage the chords, and soon make the voice become less pleasing. At the end of the speech, however, long periods may safely be delivered in a tone of unbroken declamation and in a single breath, for by then the chords will gradually have become warm, and will not suffer damage from the voice. Our net result, then, comes to this: at the outset the voice should be soft, in the middle it should be varied, now soft and now strong, and at the end it should be sustained on no more than a single tonal level.

[8] It thus appears that the relation between the voice and the hearer is like that between the voice and the speaker. For just as the speaker will be injured by the strong and shrill voice, and the mild tone is more appropriate for him at the outset, so will the hearer have the same experience, since he too will be adversely affected by the shrill voice and find the mild tone pleasant. Similarly, as in the

3. Literally, "jaws."

b. *R. ad H.* 3.11.19–20.

המדבר, כן זה ישוב אל השומע לנחת רוח ולערבות גדול, והמנוחות תעזורנה
לו להבנת הענין והשגתו. וכמו שבאחרונה תאות התמדת הקול עם צעקה מה
למדבר, ולא תזיק לו לסבה שזכרנו, כן השומע, מצד הצעקה המתמדת, יחוקה
הדבר בלבו, ויעשה רושם גדול לשמירת הדבר, ויעירהו כאיש אשר יעור
5 משנתו. והנה יתחייב מזה שדבר אחד בעצמו יתמיד הקול על מדרגה אחת
מהקיום ויחייב ערבות, וטעם, ומתיקות בנפש השומע· כמו שהענין כן בהרבה
מהדברים הטבעיים שימצאו תועלות רבות לדבר אחד, כי רוב העשבי׳ הם
במלאכת הרפואה מועילים לדברים רבים.

[9] ואחר שכבר התבאר ענין קיום הקול, ראוי שנאמר מרכותו[4], שהוא דבר
10 ראוי למליץ, ונאמר שהוא יחלק לג׳ חלקים, ר״ל: הדבור, שהוא כולל הפתיחה,
הספור, והחלוק; והמחלקת, שהוא כולל הקיום וההתרה; וההרחבה, שהיא
כוללת החתימה. הדבור הוא מאמר שפל קרוב אל הדבור תמידי. המחלקת הוא
מאמר חזק נעשה לקיים ולהתיר. ההרחבה הוא מאמר יעורר האדם אל הכעס
או אל הרחמנות.

15 [10] הדבור יחלק אל ד׳ חלקים: אל ההאותות, אל הרומז, אל הספור, אל
השחוק. ההאותות הוא מאמר עם כבדות מה עם שפלות הקול. הרומז הוא
מאמר המורה עם קול שפל אם אפשר שיעשה הדבר או לא יעשה. הספור הוא
באור הדברים הנעשים או נראים. השחוק הוא מאמר מאי זה דבר אשר לו פנים
מן ההראות, ואפשר שיקנה שחוק עם בשת וותרנות.

20 [11] המחלקת[5] יחלק אל התמדה וחלוק. ההתמדה היא צעקה נחוצה
מהמאמר המסופר. החלוק הוא מאמר במחלקת מתמיד עם מנוחות קצרות,
לפעמים עם צעקה חזקה.

[12] ההרחבה תחלק אל המקציף והמחונן. המקציף הוא מאמר מרחיב העון,
מעורר השומע אל החמה והכעס; והמחונן הוא מאמ׳ מרחיב הצרות והתלאות,
25 ויעורר לבב השומע אל הרחמנות.

[13] יען רכות הקול הוא נחלק לג׳ חלקים, ואלה החלקים יחלקו לח׳ חלקים
אחרים, ראוי שיתבאר היאך תיאות הרמיזה בערך אל כל אחד מהם.

2 תאות] תאוות^ב || 3 המתמדת] התמדת^ב || 9 מרכותו[4]] מדבורו^ב מדבותו^ד || 11 וההרחבה] והרחבה^ב || 15 אל ד׳ חלקים] אל חלקי׳^ב | ההאותות] האותות^ב || 20 המחלקת[5]] המחלק^בד || 22 צעקה] הצעקה^ב || 23 ההרחבה] ההתחלה^ב || 26 רכות] רבות^ד ||

4 זכ׳ ד׳ א׳ ||

[4] So J; cf. *R. ad H.* 3.12.23.

[5] Emendation required by context.

middle of the speech variation of voice and long pauses enable the speaker to rest and be refreshed, so will the hearer find this enjoyable and most pleasing, while in addition the pauses will help him to understand and grasp the matter at hand. And as, at the end, the sustaining of a particular tonal level is appropriate for the speaker, and will not injure him for the reason we have mentioned, so, by virtue of the sustained tone, the words will engrave themselves upon the hearer's mind, will make an impression deep enough to be retained, and will arouse the hearer **as a man that is wakened out of his sleep** [Zech. 4:1]. Necessarily, then, the self-same means avails both to sustain the voice at a particular degree of stability and to produce an effect of agreeableness, good sense, and pleasantness in the hearer's soul. The like is true of many other things in nature: many uses can be found for some one thing, as in the medical art most herbs are useful for numerous purposes.

[9] Having explained stability of the voice, we must now discuss its flexibility,[4] an asset which a speaker should command. We may say that it has three aspects: the Tone of Conversation, which is in common appropriate to the Introduction, the Statement of Facts, and the Division; the Tone of Debate, which is in common appropriate to the Proof and the Refutation; and the Tone of Amplification, which is generally appropriate to the Conclusion. The Conversational Tone is a relaxed manner of speaking which is close to that of daily speech. The Tone of Debate is an energetic manner of speaking employed both in affirming and refuting. The Tone of Amplification is a manner of speaking used in order to move others to indignation or to pity.

[10] Conversational Tone comprises four kinds: Dignified, Explicative, Narrative, and Facetious. The Dignified is a manner of speaking with a certain impressiveness, yet keeping the voice down. The Explicative points out in a calm tone whether something can or cannot be done. The Narrative is an exposition of things done or seen. The Facetious is an account of some event that plausibly might have occurred, which, told with modesty and indulgence, will provoke laughter.

[11] The Tone of Debate divides into the Sustained and the Broken. The Sustained is an urgent, full-voiced delivery in the propounding of the facts. The Broken combines a sustained tone in debate with brief pauses, sometimes with sharp vociferation.

[12] The Tone of Amplification divides into the Incensing and the Supplicating. The Incensing, by enlarging upon a crime, incites the hearer to wrath and indignation. The Supplicating, by enlarging upon sufferings and hardships, arouses the heart of the hearer to feel pity.

[13] Since Flexibility of Voice has three parts, and these in turn subdivide into eight others, how each of these will be appropriately delivered must now be explained.

4. Emended reading [*rakkūthō*]; M: "its speaking" [*dibbūrō*]; C: "its causing to speak"? [*dabbōthō?*]; cf. *R. ad H.* 3.13.23.

[14] הדבור באשר הוא עם ההאותות ראוי שיסופר בפה מלא עם קול שפל, אבל לא שנבא אל הדמעות והבכי. ואם הוא עם הרומז, צריך שיעשה בקול מדוקדק מעט, עם מנוחות תכופות ועם חלוקים, למען יתבארו הדברים היטב ויכנסו בלב השומעים. ואם הוא עם הספור, צריך לשנות הקול כפי מדרגת 5 הספור: שאם הוא בעניני המלחמות, נגיד הדבר במהירות ובענין מיוחס אל המלחמה; ואם בענינים אחרים, נדבר באחור יותר· ולפעמים בשמחה לפעמים בעצבון, לפעמי׳ בחוזק ולפעמי׳ בחלשה, לפעמי׳ במדרגת שואל או משיב או זולת זה: בכל דבר וענין שיבא בספור כפי הראוי לו. ואם עם השחוק, צריך שיאמר בקול חרד מעט עם דבר מה מן השחוק, לא שימשך אליו עד יראה סכל. 10 ואם המחל׳, אם הוא בהתמדה, צריך שיתוסף באופן בינוני עם דברים מחוברים אחד אל אחד, ולאמר הדברים עם צעקה מהירה; ואם בחלוק, תתחייב אליו צעקה ברורה עם מלאוי הפה, ויכוון שיהיה שעור משך הקולות בשעור משך המנוחות אשר ביניהם. ואם ההרחבה, אם תהיה במקציף, צריך שיהיה הקול נמוך עם צעקה חלקה, והברה[6] שוה, והשתנות תכוף עם מהירות גדול; ואם 15 תהיה במחונן, צריך שיעשה עם קול שפל והברה[7] נוטה, עם מנוחות תכופות, והמשכיות ארוכים, והשתניות גדולות. והנה נשלם ענין הקול.

[15] אמנם תנועות הגוף הוא תקון תמונת הגוף והפנים באופן יאות אל המדבר. וזה שצריך שיהיה בשת בפנים ומעט כעס, והתמונות לא תכוון בהם הלבשה המפוארה בתכלית, גם לא הנבזת, למען לא נראה או מכת הלוצצים 20 או מעובדי האדמה.

[16] וצריך שיהיו התמונות והפנים מיוחסים אל הקולות: שאם היה הדבור עם ההאותות, ראוי להניע מעט היד הימנית עם עמידת הגו׳·[8] והעצבון, והשמחה, והדבר הממוצע בין שניהם יהיו כפי שיאות לדבור. ואם הוא ברומז, צריך שיעשה זה עם הטיית הראש מעט, לפי שזה הדבר הוא בטבע· כי כל אשר 25 נקרב הראש אל השומעים, יבינו יותר הדבר אשר נלמדם וישיגוהו. ואם הוא בספור, תהיה התנועה מתדמה למה שאמרנו בהאותות; ואם הוא בשחוק, צריך שנראה השמחה בפנים מזולת תנועת התמונות.

6 ולפעמים] לפעמים^ג || 9 המחל׳] המחלה^ג || 10 שיתוסף] שיותסף^ד || 11 מלאוי] מלוי^ג || 14 והברה[6]] והכרח^כד || 15 והברה[7]] והכרה^כד || 17 יאות] יאותו^ד || 19 המפוארה] המפוא׳^ד || 22 [הגו׳[8]]^ג | והעצבון] והעצבו׳^ד ||

[6] So J; cf. *R. ad H.* 3.14.25.

[7] So J.

[8] Abbreviation mark omitted in ד.

[14] A statement in the Dignified Conversational Tone should be delivered with full mouth and subdued tone, yet without coming to the point of tears and weeping. If the statement is in the Explicative Conversational Tone, a rather thin-toned voice is required, as well as frequent pauses and intermissions, so that the points will be very clear and penetrate the minds of the hearers. And if in the Narrative Conversational Tone, one must vary the voice to suit the nature of the account. Thus, if our narrative deals with warfare, we should tell it rapidly and in a warlike manner; while if it deals with other matters, we should speak more slowly—sometimes gaily and sometimes sadly, sometimes strongly and sometimes softly, and sometimes as one would in asking a question, or making a reply, or the like: the manner should correspond to the content of the narrative in every detail. If the statement is in the Facetious Conversational Tone, it must be enunciated with a gentle quaver and with some slight suggestion of a smile, —but not so that the speaker risks seeming a buffoon. In the Sustained Tone of Debate, there must be a moderate increase of the vocal volume as well as an uninterrupted flow of words rapidly declaimed; while in the Broken Tone of Debate, clear exclamation is required, as well as use of the full mouth, and one should contrive that the duration of hearing sounds equal the duration of the intervening pauses. For the Tone of Amplification, if the Incensing, a thin-toned voice is necessary, as well as smooth enunciation,[5] an even flow of sound, and both frequent variation and great speed; and if the Supplicating, it must be executed with subdued voice and a declining flow of sound, as well as frequent pauses, long intermissions and marked changes. And here ends our treatment of Voice.

[15] Physical movement is the control of the body and mien in the manner most appropriate to the speaker. Thus, the countenance must bear an expression of modesty, and of some excitement, while there should be no attempt to have the physical representations take on either extreme elegance or extreme vulgarity, lest we appear to be either buffoons or peasants.

[16] Physical and facial representations must also correspond to the several Tones of Voice. Thus, if the speaker is using the Dignified Conversational Tone, he should make slight motions with his right hand, while his body stays in position—and with such sadness, happiness, or an emotion intermediate as would be appropriate to the Conversational Tone. If the Explicative Conversational Tone is used, it should be accompanied by a slight inclination forward of the head—a natural gesture, for the closer our head to our hearers the more clearly will they grasp the thought we are trying to impart. With the Narrative Conversational Tone the movement should be virtually the same as that which we have prescribed for the Dignified; with the Facetious Conversational Tone, we should show gaiety in our countenance, but omit any other expressive movement.

5. So JML understands *clamore leni* (*R. ad H.* 3.14.25).

[17] ואם המחלקת, אם הוא בהתמדה, צריך שנניע הזרוע במהירות· והפנים, ותהיה בהם מהוראת הכעס. ואם הוא בחלוק, ראוי שיעשה עם הושטת הזרוע במהירות ותנועת הרגל הימין, עם פנים קיימים בכעס.

[18] ואם ההרחבה, אם היא במקציף, נכוון התמונות והפנים כאשר במחלקת בהתמדה, עם אחור יותר; ואם במחונ׳, זה יעשה עם פנים מלאי עצבון, ובכי במדרגת הנשים, והכות בראש ובחזה עם עמידת הגוף.

[19] ואמ׳ קוינטיליא׳, בד׳[9] מחלק הי״א, שהרמיזה היא דבר גדול, ויש לה כח מפלג במאמרים ההלציים עד לא יאמנו הדברים והראיות אשר יביאם המליץ אם לא תעשה בערכם הרמיזה כפי מה שיאות. עוד אמר שכבר שאלו לדימושטיני מה הוא היותר מעולה בכל מלאכת ההלצה, ונתן מקל עוז ומטה תפארת לרמיזה; וכן שאלו פעם שניה ושלישית, וישיבם כדברים הראשונים. ואמר שהקול במלחמה ראוי שיהיה נש׳ בכל היכולת; ובכעס, אכזריי, עז, וקשה, עם נשימות תכופות; ובקנאה, יותר קל; בחנפיות, בהודאות, בפורענות, ובפיוסי׳,[10] קל ושפל; במספיקים, ומניעים, ונודרים, ויועצים, כבד; בפחד ובשת, שפל; ברחמנות, רך; בבאורים, אמצעי בין חד וכבד.

[20] אמנם, שהתמונות ורמיזות הפנים יועילו להראות לאדם מה שיחו הוא דבר מבואר בנפשו, למה שנותנות ההספקה וההבנה אף בלא דבור, כאשר יעשו החרשים. גם בתנועות העפעפים והעינים תובן הכונה; וההשתחואה הגד תגיד לנו כי תכנע הנפש העושה· וכן נכיר הכעס, השמחה, והדאגה והחנפות אף בבעלי חיים בלתי מדברים. גם הצורות המחוקות בקיר תורנה על הכעס, הדאגה, והשמחה וזולתם, ואין אומר ואין דברים.

[21] העורף ראוי להיות זקוף, והצואר מתקבץ ומתפשט. הכתפים מורים על העברה ועל העבדו׳,[7] בהתקבצם וכאשר יקצרו העורף, ולפעמי׳ על הערמה: כאשר יראו על החניפות, והתימה, והיראה עם קצת הושטה מהזרוע עם עוצר הכתפים או התפשט׳.[10]

[22] אמנם הידים, כמעט תמצאנה להם תנועות עד לאין תכלית; עד יאמר

1 שנניע] שנענע[כ] || 5 במחונ׳] כמחונ׳[ד] | עצבון] העצבון[ד] || 10 לדימושטיני] לדימוסטיני[כ] || 10–11 מקל עוז ומטה תפארת] מטה עוז ומקל תפארה[ת] | ושלישית] ושלישי[ד] || 12 נש׳] נשמעת[כ] || 14 ובפיוסי׳[10]] ובפיוסי[כד] | ומניעים] ובמניעים[כ] | ונודרים] ונודדים[ד] || 23 העבדו׳[7]] העבדו[כד] || 24 החניפות] החנפות[ד] || 25 או] עם[כ] | התפשט׳[10]] התפשט[כד] ||

10–11 יר׳ מ״ח י״ז || 16 עמ׳ ד׳ י״ג || 18 שמ״א י׳ ט״ז || 20 יח׳ ח׳ י׳ || 21 תה׳ י״ט ד׳ ||

[9] *Sic.*

[10] Abbreviation not indicated in כ and ד.

[17] With the Tone of Debate, if the Sustained, we must make quick movements of the arm, while as for the countenance, it should bear some indication of excitement. If the Broken Tone, it should be accompanied by a rapid extension of the arm and a movement of the right foot, and also by keeping a look of excitement on the face.

[18] If our Tone of Amplification is the Incensing, we will contrive our physical and facial representations as in the Sustained Tone of Debate, though with more deliberateness. Employment of the Supplicating Tone of Amplification should be accompanied by a mien that is altogether sad, by weeping like a woman, and by beating one's head and breast while the body stays in position.

[19] In Book XI, Chapter 4,[6] Quintilian[c] says that the delivery is an important faculty and has such extraordinary power in oratory that the words and proofs presented by the speaker are not credited unless the delivery appropriate to them is employed. He says, moreover, that Demosthenes, once asked what is the most useful skill in the whole art of rhetoric, awarded to delivery **the strong rod** and **the beautiful staff**[7] [Jer. 48:17]; and asked the same question a second and a third time, he replied to the same effect as he did the first. Quintilian further says that in [depicting] battle the voice should be lifted up as much as possible; in anger, it should be fierce, intense, and harsh, and accompanied by frequent drawings of breath; in expressing zeal, lighter; in flattery, admission, retribution, and conciliation, light and subdued; in persuading, swaying, vowing, and counseling, grave; in expressing fear and shame, humble; in appeals for pity, tender; in expositions, pitched half-way between sharp and grave.

[20] That gestures and facial expressions do indeed avail to show **unto man what is his thought** [Amos 4:13] is self-evident, for they can induce conviction and understanding even without the spoken word, as the dumb manage to do. Meaning may be conveyed even by movements of the eyelids and the eyes. Prostration **tells us plainly** [1 Sam. 10:16] that the recumbent person is submissive; and we may similarly recognize anger, joy, anxiety, and fawning even in animals incapable of speech. Also forms **portrayed upon the wall** [Ezek. 8:10] may connote anger, anxiety, joy, and other emotions, although **there is no speech, there are no words** [Ps. 19:4].

[21] The back of the neck should be erect and straight, the throat taut and extended. When the shoulders are hunched up and thus shorten the neck they are indicative of transgression and servility, and sometimes of guile—as when, held back or straight and accompanied by a slight extension of the arm, they suggest flattery, wonder, and fear.

[22] As for the hands, the gestures invented for them are almost without limit.

6. *Sic*, JML; in modern editions Book XI has three chapters only; cf. Int., §5(5) and nn. 207-208.
7. B: "... **staff** ... **rod**."

---

c. Q. 11.3.2.

להם שהם מדברות, נודרות, מבטיחות, קוראות, מניחות, מתחננות, יראות, מבקשות, מואסות· שמחה, עצבון, ספק, הודאה, תשובה, רבוי מספר, זמן מפרסמות· מצוות, מזהירות, מבארות, מתמיהות, מתבישות; עד כמעט הם בלשון אחד משותף לכל בני העולם. וכן האצבעות: מה ייטיבו דרכן לבאר, ולחלק, ולהראות, ולספור! מה יגידו, ירבו ידברו! ולפעמי׳, עם קצת תנועת הכתפים, עצמו מספר. גם החזה והבטן, עם קצת תנועת, עוזרים אל פרסום הענינים, ולפעמי׳ הבאת היד עליהם, וזה על המעט; אמנם, כאשר יעשה, אין להסיר הבגדים מעליהם. וכן בתנועת הרגלים לפעמים נעזור להספיק בערך אל קצת הספורים.

[23] ואין ספק שבתנועות האלה בעצמם יפלו דברים הטעאיים אשר ראוי להשמר פן יפלו בהרגל. אמנם הדבר הראוי שהמליץ יתבונן עליו הרבה הוא לראות מי הוא המדבר, ומול מי ישוב הדבור, ולפני מי; למה שהוא מבואר שאין ראוי לעשות מרמיזות הפנים, התנועות, והתמונות לפני המלך, או שר הצבא, או נשיאי העדה, ולפני דלת עם הארץ באופן מתדמה.

[24] ובכלל, קוינטילאנו האריך בזה המקום אריכות לא מעט, ואנכי דלגתי דבריו וקצרתי, למה שרובם נכללים בדברי טוליאו, אחד באחד יגשו.

[25] והרמיזה בכללה, אין ספק שהיא מפרסמת מספרי הקודש. אם מתארי הקולות, אמר ישעיה הנביא ע״ה: קרא בגרון אל תחשוך כשופר הרם קולך והגד לעמי פשעם, כו׳ [יש׳ נ״ח א׳]; והנה הורה בזה שהקול בתוכחה ראוי להיות גדול. וכן להפך, קול האמללים ובעלי התחנה ראוי שישפל, כמו שנאמר: ושפלת מארץ תדברי ומעפר תשח אמרתך והיה כאוב מארץ קולך, כו׳ [שם כ״ט ד׳]. וכן: אין קול ענות חלושה ואין קול ענות גבורה קול ענות אנכי שומע [שמ׳ ל״ב י״ח]; קול מלחמה במחנה [שם י״ז]; קול ששון וקול שמחה קול חתן וקול

4 ייטיבו דרכן] יטיבו דרכם[ד] || 5 תנועת] תנועה[ד] || 7 אמנם] אומנם[כ] || 15 האריך ‹הרבה›[כ] | אריכות] אריכו[ד] | דלגתי] דגלתי[ד] || 18 [ע״ה][כ] || 22 ענות חלושה... גבורה] ענות גבורה... חלושה[ת] | ואין] אין[כ] ||

4 יר׳ ב׳ ל״ג || 5 שמ״א ב׳ ג׳ || 6 תה׳ מ׳ ו׳ || 14 במ׳ ל״ב ב׳ | מל״ב כ״ד י״ד || 16 איוב מ״א ח׳ ||

It may thus be said of the hands that they speak, vow, promise, summon, abandon, supplicate, express fear, seek, and reject; express joy, sorrow, doubt, confession, penitence, multiple number, and time; command, warn, explain, and express wonder and shame: so that they almost constitute a single common language for all mankind. And the fingers, too, how they **trim** their **way** [Jer. 2:33] to explain, apportion, point out, and enumerate! How they declare, and **multiply . . . talk** [1 Sam. 2:3]! Sometimes, indeed, accompanied by certain movements of the shoulders, **they are more compelling than a spoken statement** [Ps. 40:6].[8] The chest and abdomen, too, accompanied by certain gestures, promote general understanding of the matters under discussion, and sometimes, though seldom, full mastery of them; when, however, a speaker uses these bodily parts, the clothing over them should not be pulled back. So, too, by movements of our feet we sometimes contribute to the persuasiveness of certain kinds of narratives.

[23] There can be no doubt that these same gestures are subject to errors against which one must be vigilant, lest they become a matter of habit. But what merits a great deal of study on the part of an orator is to consider who is to be the opposing speaker, to whom the discussion is to advert, and in whose presence the speech is to be made. For it is clear that it is inappropriate to enact facial expressions, movements of the body, and gestures in the presence of the king, or of the commander-in-chief of the army, or of the **princes of the congregation** [Num. 32:2] in the same way as before **the poorest sort of the people of the land** [2 Kings 24:14].

[24] In sum, Quintilian[d] dwells at considerable length upon this topic, but I have made omissions and have condensed his words, since most of them are implicit in Tully's, **one is so near to another** . . . [Job 41:8].

[25] There can be no doubt that the main rules of delivery are clearly expounded by the Holy Books. As for qualities of voice, the prophet Isaiah, upon whom be peace, says: **Cry aloud,**[9] **spare not, lift up thy voice like a horn, and declare unto my people their transgression,**" etc. [Isa. 58:1]. He here points out that the voice, when expressing reproof, should be loud. By the same token, on the other hand, the voice of the unfortunate and of suppliants ought to be subdued, as was said: **And brought down thou shalt speak out of the ground, and thy speech shall be low out of the dust; and thy voice shall be as of a ghost out of the ground,** etc. [Isa. 29:4]. Likewise: "**It is not the voice of them that cry for being overcome, neither is it the voice of them that shout for mastery, but the voice of them that sing do I hear**" [Exod. 32:18];[10] "**there is**

8. So, apparently, JML here intends עָצְמוּ מִסַּפֵּר to be understood. JV: ". . . more than can be told."

9. Literally, "with throat."

10. *Sic*, JML; B: ". . . mastery . . . for being overcome."

d. Q. 11.3.1 ff.

כלה [יר׳ ז׳ ל״ד, ט״ז ט׳]. כל זה יורה על השתנות הקול כפי הנאות לדבר דבר.
ואמר בתנועת הראש: בזה לך לעגה[11] לך בתולת בת ציון· אחריך ראש הניעה
בת ירושלם [מל״ב י״ט כ״א; יש׳ ל״ז כ״ב]. עוד, בתנועת הידים עם הראש: ספקו
עליך כפים כל עוברי דרך שרקו ויניעו ראשם [איכה ב׳ ט״ו]. ואמר עוד בתנועת
5 הידים: כי קול כחולה שמעתי צרה כמבכירה קול בת ציון תתיפח תפרש כפיה,
כו׳ [יר׳ ד׳ ל״א]; וביחזקאל: וגם אני אכה כפי אל כפי והניחותי חמתי, כו׳ [יח׳
כ״א כ״ב]· והנה הכיתי כפי אל בצעך אשר עשית, כו׳ [שם כ״ב י״ג];וכן: גם מאת
זה תצאי וידיך על ראשך [יר׳ ב׳ ל״ז]. וכן, בתנועות הרגלים והידים יחד,
ביחזקאל: כה אמר ה׳ אלקי׳ הכה בכפיך ורקע ברגלך ואמור אח [יח׳ ו׳ י״א].
10 וכן, על תמונות הגוף: למה תהיה כאיש נדהם כגבור לא יוכל להושיע [יר׳ י״ד
ט׳]; וכן: רום עינים ורחב לב [מש׳ כ״א ד׳]· לב שמח ייטיב פנים [מש׳ ט״ו י״ג].
ואמר עוד: עוצה עיניו לחשוב תהפוכות קורץ שפתי׳ כלה רעה [שם ט״ז ל׳];
אדם בליעל איש און הולך עקשות פה; קורץ בעיניו מולל ברגליו מורה
באצבעותיו [שם ו׳ י״ב — י״ג].
15 [26] וזה תכלית מה שנאמר בזה הפרק מהרמיזה.

פרק י״ג

פרק ענין הזכירה.

[1] אמר טוליאו בחדשה: הזכירה, ממנה טבעית, ממנה מלאכותית. הטבעית
הוא כח תקוע בנפשנו עם מחשבה· וכאלו אמר שהוא כח מה בנפש אשר בו
20 נזכור הדברים הדמיוניים והשכליים. והמלאכותית היא אשר תקוים מצד
המלאכה וההרגל; במדרגת מה שנמצא מהדברים הטבעיים שהמלאכה תקיים

2 לעגה[11]] לעגת^ם || 7 הכיתי] הכתי^ד |אל] על^כ || 8 בתנועות] בתנועת^ד || 12 עוצה עיניו] עוצם עינו^ר |שפתי׳] שפתים^כ || 20 הדמיוניים] הדמיונים^ד ||

[11] So ת, followed by J.

a noise of war in the camp'' [32:17]; **the voice of mirth and the voice of gladness, the voice of the bridegroom and the voice of the bride''** [Jer. 7:34; 16:9]; all statements of this kind teach that the voice should be varied in the way suited to the specific circumstances. On movement of the head, Scripture says: **The virgin daughter of Zion hath despised thee and laughed thee to scorn; the daughter of Jerusalem hath shaken her head at thee** [Isa. 37:22; 2 Kings 19:21]. Again, movement of both hands and head: **All that pass by clap their hands at thee; they hiss and wag their head** [Lam. 2:15]. Also on gesticulation of the hands: **For I have heard a voice as of a woman in travail, the anguish as of her that bringeth forth her first child, the voice of the daughter of Zion, that gaspeth for breath, that spreadeth her hands,** etc. [Jer. 4:31]; and in Ezekiel: ''**I will also smite My hands together, and I will satisfy My fury,''** etc. [21:22]; ''**Behold, therefore, I have smitten My hand at thy dishonest gain which thou hast made,''** etc. [22:13]. Likewise: **From him also shalt thou go forth, with thy hands upon thy head** [Jer. 2:37]. So too, on movements of both hands and feet in unison, in Ezekiel: **Thus saith the Lord God: "Smite with thy hand, and stamp with thy foot, and say, alas!''** [6:11]. Again, on physical representations: **Why shouldest Thou be as a man overcome, as a mighty man that cannot save?** [Jer. 14:9]. So too: **A haughty look, and a proud heart** [Prov. 21:4], **A merry heart maketh a cheerful countenance** [15:13]. Scripture further says: **He that shutteth his eyes, it is to devise froward things; he that biteth his lips bringeth evil to pass** [16:30]; **A base person, a man of iniquity, is he that walketh with a froward mouth; that winketh with his eyes, that scrapeth with his feet, that pointeth with his fingers** [6:12–13].

[26] Our discussion of delivery in the present chapter has here reached its limit.

CHAPTER 13

Memory

[1] Tully[a] says in the New Rhetoric: Memory is in part natural, in part artificial. The Natural Memory is a faculty implanted in our souls along with thought; he says, in effect, that it is a certain power in the soul by means of which we can recollect both imaginary things and matters of mind. The Artificial Memory is that memory which is confirmed by training and practice; just as there are natural

a. *R. ad H.* 3.16.28.

אותם ויוסיף בהם ואם הם שלמים, כן הענין בכאן, שעם היות לאדם הזכירה
רבת המעלה והשלמות, מכל מקום המלאכה תקיים אותה ותוסיף בשלמות
ההוא. ואם כן, הזכירה הטבעית ראוי לחזקה ולקיימה במלאכה למען תהיה
יותר שלמה· ולזה התחייב לנו לדבר בזאת המלאכה הנה, ולתת לה חקים
5 ומשפטים טובים.

[2] ונאמר שזאת הזכירה המלאכותית תעשה באמצעות המקומות והצורות.
והמכון במקומו׳[1] שיהיו קטנים, ושלמים, ומסומנים, נעשים מצד הטבע או מצד
המלאכה, כדי שנוכל להחזיקם בזכירה בקלות: כמו הבתים, והמרחב אשר בין
שני העמודים, והזוית, וקשת הפתחים, והנוהג מנהגם. והצורות הם חקויים,
10 סימנים, והמשלים לדבר שנרצה לזכרו, כמו הסוסים, והאריות, והנשרים· וצריך
שנשים הצורות במקום מן המקומות אם נרצה לזכרם.

[3] וראוי לנו לבאר היאך נמצא המקומות והיאך נתקן בהם הצורות. כמו
שיודעי האותיות יוכלו לכתוב אותם, ואחר כן לספר אותם מבחוץ· כן גם כן
יודעי החכמה יוכלו להושיב במקומות הדבר אשר ידעו, ואחר כן לפרסם מבחוץ
15 מצד הזכירה. והמקומות דומים לשעוה או לנייר, והצורות לאותיות, והושבת
הצורות במקומות מתדמה לכתיבת האותיות בנייר. ואם נרצה לזכור דברים
הרבה, התחייב לנו למצוא מקומות רבים באשר נושיב צורות הרבה. וממה
שהתחייב אצלנו הוא שיהיו המקומות ההם מסודרים בסדר מיוחד, עד לא
נתבלבל אם נתחיל מהראשון או מהאחרון או מהאמצעי; כמו שהשמות אשר
20 נזכור אותם, אם הם עם סדור מוגבל מאי זה צד שנתחיל לספרם, על הסדר. כן
הענין במקומות בשוה, למה שהמקומות הם בדמיון השעוה או הנייר: שאם לא
נצטרך אל הצורות החתומות בשעוה, או אל האותיות הכתובי׳ בנייר, מ״מ
השעוה והנייר ישארו קיימים אחר מחיקת הצורות והאותיות; וכן, בהעבירנו
הצורות מהמקומות בהעדר הצורך אליהם, ראוי שהמקומות בעמדם יעמודו·
25 מרוב ימים יפקדו. עוד ראוי שנסמן כל חמשי במספר: כאלו תאמר שבמקום
החמישי נשים היד מזהבת, כדי שיובן לנו מה׳ אצבעות היד שהמקום ההוא הוא
החמשי; וכן בחמשי השני התחייב אצלנו לשום בו דבר יורה על מספר העשירי;
וכן בחמישי השלישי דבר יורה הט״ו; וכן בכלם על הסדר. אמנם, לקחנו המספר
החמישי למה שאיננו לא קרוב ולא מופלג.

2 רבת] רבה^כ |אותה] אותם^כ || 14 להושיב] להשיב^כ |לפרסם] לספרם^ד || 16 בנייר] בעיר^ד ||
28 הט״ו] הטור^כ ||

4–5 דב׳ ד׳ ח׳ || 24 יח׳ א׳ כ״א || 25 יש׳ כ״ד כ״ב ||

[1] Abbreviation not indicated in כ and ד; stroke inserted: ^Rד.

qualities which art will confirm and enhance, even though they are in themselves perfectly sound, so here, while a man may have an exceptionally fine and sound Natural Memory, art can nevertheless confirm it and add to that soundness. Such being the case, the Natural Memory must be strengthened and confirmed by art in order to become sounder; and this is why we must here discuss this art and provide it with goodly **statutes and ordinances** [Deut. 4:8].

[2] We say, then, that this Artificial Memory operates through the mediacy of backgrounds and images. By backgrounds we mean scenes of small compass, complete, and identifiably marked, the products either of nature or of art, so that we can easily hold them in the memory: for example, houses, the space between two columns, the corner, the doorway arch, and the like. Images are portraits, marks, and likenesses of the thing we wish to remember—as, for example, horses, lions, and eagles—and we must set the images in one or another background if we wish to remember them.

[3] We should also explain how to invent the backgrounds and to arrange the figures therein. Just as those who know the letters of the alphabet can write them down and later read them out again, so, too, those who know the science [of mnemonics] can set something they know into backgrounds and afterwards set [it] forth again by memory. Backgrounds are like a wax tablet or paper, images like the letters of the alphabet, and the setting of the images in the backgrounds is like inscribing the letters on paper. If, therefore, we wish to memorize a large number of items we must necessarily invent many backgrounds in which to set a large number of images. It is also obligatory that these backgrounds be ordered in a particular sequence, so that we will not become confused if we begin with the first, with the last, or one in between; in the case of names, for example, if they stand in a definite order we will remember them in order no matter from what point we begin to cite them. The same is equally true of backgrounds, since the backgrounds are like the wax tablet or the paper. Though we may not have further need of the images impressed upon the wax or the letters written on the paper, the wax and the paper nevertheless remain in existence after the figures and letters have been effaced; so, too, when we remove the images from the backgrounds because we no longer need them, the backgrounds should continue to **stand where they stood** [Ezek. 1:21]:[1] **after many days shall they be visited**[2] [Isa. 24:22]. We should, moreover, provide each fifth background in the numbered series with an identifying mark. Say, for example, that in the fifth background we set a gilded hand, so that that background will be understood by us to be the fifth from the five fingers of the hand; then in the second fifth, likewise, we need to set something that will indicate the number "ten"; in the third fifth, again, something that will indicate "fifteen," and so with all of them in order. Our reason for adopting the fifth in number is, of course, that it is neither too near nor too distant.

1. JV: "... when these stood, these stood."
2. JV: "... punished."

[4] עוד, אין ראוי שיוקחו מקומות יעברו בהם האנשים תדיר, כי זה הוא מה
שיבלבל הזכירה מאד. וזה מבואר בנסיון, שהדבר הנעשה במסתורים לא יעבור
מנפשותינו, ועושה בנו רושם חזק, ויתקיים, מה שלא יתחייב בערך אל הדבר
הנעשה בפרהסיא, ובתשואות ובהמון קריה, כי לא נחזיק בו: ויעבור והנה איננו.
5 ובכלל, המקומות ההם יהיו כאשר אין העברת האנשים תכופה ותדירה בהם, כי
זה יקיים ויחזק ויעמיד הדבר, ולא נשכחהו. עוד, לא יהיו המקומות דומים זה
לזה ויוכר הבדלם והתחלפם, בין שיהיו המקומות מעשה ידי אמן, כבתי׳ ועליו׳
וזולת· בין יהיו טבעיים, כמו הרים וגבעות, בקעות, והנוהג מנהגם; כי זולת זה
יהיה הטעות בהם קרוב, וזה דבר לא יעלם. עוד, המקומות יתחייב בערכם שיהיו
10 מתדמים לצורות בגודל, ר״ל, שהמקום[2] יהיה בגודל ראוי ביחס אל המקום, לא
שנושיב דבר קטן במקום גדול או להפך, כי זה יחייב הבלבול; אמנם, ראוי
שיושב דבר דבר במקום נאות לו לפי הקטנות והגודל. גם לא יהיו המקומות
חשוכים מאד או להפך, כי אם בתואר אמצעי ביניהם· כי החשוך לא יראה מצד
חשכותו, גם המזהיר הרבה יעלם מצד רב זהרו לעין בערך אל השמש. עוד,
15 המרחק בין מקום למקום יהיה קרוב לשלשים רגלים, לא יוסיף או ימעט ממנו
הרבה, כדי שיקל אל הדמיון לעצור אותו במדרגת השיג חוש העין אשר לו
ברוחק ראות לא יותר רחוק או יותר קרוב ממנו.

[5] ואם לא ייטב בעיני האדם לקחת המקומות הנמצאים, יוכל לציירם
בדמיונות ולהמציאם בטוב בעיניו. כי ביכלתו לצייר מדינות, עירות, ארמונות;
20 ומי שיאמר לו, ״מה תעשה?״ אמנם, ישמור הכללים הנזכרים לבלתי יפקד מהם
איש. וזה תכלית מה שיאמר טוליאו מהמקומות.

[6] אמנם הצורות הם על ב׳ פנים: אם שתהיינה צורות הדברים בעצמם· אם
שתהיינה צורות המאמרים. ואם צורות הדברים, התחייב בערכם שיהיה להם
צד דמיון עם הדבר׳[3] אשר להם צורות; והמשל, אם המתרעם יאמר שפלוני הרג
25 את הנפש בסם המות בסבת הירושה, ושהוא יוכיח ויבאר על פי עדים, אז
המתנצל ראוי לו שיזכור כל הפרטי׳ האלה כדי שיוכל להציל את נפשו מיד
להבה. כי אם יפקד אחד מהם, לא יוכל לקחת התנצלות על הדבר ההוא

1 זה הוא] זהו[ב] || 10 שהמקום[2]] שהמקומ׳[ד] שהמקומות[ב] || 12 נאות] נאו׳[ד] | והגודל] והגדלו[ב] ||
16 במדרגת] במדרג׳[ד] || 17 ראות] ראו׳[ד] || 19 עירות] עיירות[ב] | ארמונות] ארמונו[ד] || 24 הדבר׳[3]]
הדבר[בד] || 25 עדים] עדם[ד] ||

---

4 איוב ל״ט ז׳ | תה׳ ל״ז ל״ו || 20 איוב ט׳ י״ב | במ׳ ל״א מ״ט || 26 יש׳ מ״ז י״ד ||

---

2 Correction required by context.

3 Abbreviation not indicated in ב and ד.

[4] Furthermore, scenes that are constantly traversed by people ought not to be adopted, for such tends to confuse the memory excessively. Experience demonstrates that the action carried on in places concealed from view will not pass from our souls, but makes a strong and enduring impression upon us; which is not necessarily true of the action carried on in public, in the **shoutings** and **tumult of the city** [Job 39:7], for this we will not hold fast: it will have **passed by and, lo, it is not** [Ps. 37:36].[3] In general, the scenes to be adopted should be of the kind in which there is no frequent and constant passing to and fro of people, for a quiet scene of this kind will afford stability, force, and durability to the thing to be remembered, and we shall not forget it. Again, backgrounds should not resemble one another, but be recognizably different and distinguishable, whether, like houses and upper stories and other structures, they are the work of the artisan's hands, or, as in the case of mountains, hills, valleys, and the like, natural phenomena; for otherwise mistakes by means of them can easily be made, a matter of no small importance. It is necessary, furthermore, that the backgrounds and images be congruous in size; that is, the background[4] must be of the right spatial proportions, lest we set a small thing in too large a background, or vice versa, for this is bound to result in confusion. Indeed, any given thing ought to be set in the proportionately small or large background that is appropriate for it. Backgrounds should also be neither too dark nor the opposite, but of intermediate quality, for what is dark will not be seen because of its dimness, while what shines too brightly will also fail to be looked at, because, like the sun, it is too glaring for the eye. Moreover, the interval between backgrounds should be about thirty feet, not much more nor less, so that the imagination can as easily retain it as the sensory eye can grasp anything in its purview that is neither too far away from it, nor too near.

[5] If the speaker is not content with actual backgrounds, he can conceive backgrounds in his imagination, inventing them as seems to him best. For he is quite able to picture provinces, cities, and palaces; and who is there to **say** to him: "**What doest thou**" [Job 9:12]? He should, however, observe all the aforementioned rules, so that **there lacketh not one** [Num. 31:49] of them. With this Tully[b] ends his treatment of backgrounds.

[6] As to images, they are of two kinds: images of subject matter, or images of words. Images of subject matter must bear some resemblance to the objects of which they are images. If, for example, the prosecutor says that so-and-so has killed somebody by poison, that an inheritance was the motive, and that he will prove and demonstrate the case by witnesses, the defendant must remember all these details in order to be able to **deliver** himself **from the power of the flame**

3. JV: "But one passed by, and, lo, he was not."
4. Emended text.

b. *R. ad H.* 3.19.32.

הנפקד, ויפול ולא יוסיף קום. לכן, למען לא ישכח דבר מן הדברים, ראוי לו לקחת צורה מתדמה יתבארו בה כל מה שאמר המתרעם. וזה כשנציר מטה אחת בו חולה אחד נוטה למות, והחשוד לפני המטה מחזיק בימינו כוס התרעלה ובשמאלו שטר צואה, ובאצבע קמיצה ביצי הטלה. ובזאת הצורה יהיה כל הענין חקוק לפנינו, למה שהחולה שהוא במטה ידמה המת מהסם· ואשר לפניו עם כוס התרעלה ידמה ההורג בהסם[4]· והשטר יורה לנו שהוא בסבת ירושה· וביצי הטלה יביאנו להזכיר ענין העדים.[5] ודומה לזה ראוי לעשות בנוהג מנהגם: לקחת, תמורת הדבר שנרצה להזכירו, ענין ידמהו ויביאהו למזכרת. וזה ענין צורת הדברים.

[7] ואם צורות המאמרים, הם מהדברים הקשי׳, וצריכות השתדלות והסתכלות ורגילות יותר, והוא: שבאמצעות צורות מה נבא אל זכרון מאמרים נאמרים. כאילו תאמר שבעשיית המצות נבא אל מזכרת זה המאמר שצוה הש׳ ית׳, באמרו: שבעת ימים מצות תאכלו [וי׳ כ״ג ו׳]; וכן, בראתנו תאר הסכה נזכור תכף מה שכתוב בתורה: בסכות תשבו שבעת ימים [שם שם מ״ב]. ולזה יצטרך זכרון טבעיי הגון ונאות, כי זולת זה יהיה הענין ממה שיקשה מאד. אמנם, אם הטבע יסכים, תעזרהו המלאכה העזר לא יעלם, ויהיה אז מה שתעשה המלאכה בזה דבר יותר גדול ממה שיעשהו הטבע.

[8] ולמה שהתבאר בנסיון שהדברים המרגלים והשפלים, שהם נגד עינינו תמיד, לא יחדשו רושם חזק בזכרון, והדברי׳ החדשים אשר אינם כמנהג הם אשר יבנו בדמיוננו בית זבול להם· כמסרגת הנערים, שהם כל מה שראו ולמדו בקטנותם, להיות להם בזמן ההוא כל הדברים חדשים, מקרוב באו, יפלא[4] מהם המדמה· אם כן, הצורות המביאות אל מזכרת המאמרים ראוי שתהיינה בזה התאר, ר״ל, דבר שיש בו מן החדוש והפלא; כי אז יתעורר הזוכר להחזיקו, יאחזהו ולא ירפהו. כי לא יתעורר האדם מזריחת השמש והערבו, שהוא דבר תמידי ומורגל, כאשר יתעורר מלקיות השמש והלבנה הבאים לעתים רחוקות. ולזה הזקנים, שאי׳ בערכם כמעט דבר חדש או פלא, הם בעלי השכחה

6 בהסם[4]] בהס[ר] בהם[כ] || 12 מזכרת] המזכרת[כ] || 13 בראתנו] בראותינו[ר] || 14 [שבעת ימים][כ] || 19 כמנהג] במנהג[כ] || 20 שראו ולמדו] שלמדו וראו[ר] || 21 יפלא[4]] ויפלא[כד] || 25 מלקיות] מלקיו[ר] || 26 שאי׳] שאינם ||

1 יש׳ כ״ד כ׳ || 3–4 יש׳ נ״א י״ז || 20 מל״א ח׳ י״ג || 21 דב׳ ל״ב י״ז || 24 שה״ש ג׳ ד׳ ||

[4] Correction required by context.

[5] The following note is in the margin of ד[R]: באור זה כי בלשון לאטינו Testes רוצה לומ׳ העדי׳ ור״ל ג״כ הבצים וא״כ כשיהיה בזכרונו הבצים יהיו בזכרונו העדי׳.

[Isa. 47:14]. For should one of these details be lacking, he will be unable to adopt a defence against that missing item, **and** he **shall fall, and not rise again** [24:20]. In order, therefore, not to forget any one point, he should adopt a resembling image whereby all that the prosecutor has said will be kept clear. We shall obtain such an image if we picture a bed in which lies a sick man on the point of death, with the suspect at the bedside holding **the cup of poison**[5] [51:17] in his right hand, in his left a documentary will, and on the fourth finger a ram's testes. By means of this image the entire matter will present itself to us in sharp relief: the sick man in the bed will represent the person who died of poison; the man before him with the cup of poison will represent the murderous poisoner; the document will indicate that the motive was an inheritance; and the ram's testes will bring us to recollect the fact that there are witnesses.[6] The like should be done whenever the subject matter is similarly complex—substitute, in place of the detail which we wish to remember, something that will resemble it and bring it into recollection. So much, then, for images of subject matter.

[7] Images of words are difficult to form, and require more effort, insight, and training: through the mediacy of certain images we are led to recollect the words said. It is as if you should say that through the making of the unleavened bread we come to remember these words of the commandment pronounced by the Name, blessed be He: **Seven days ye shall eat unleavened bread** [Lev. 23:6]; or, again, that by seeing the booth's lineaments we straightway remember the Torah's prescription: **Ye shall dwell in booths seven days** [23:42]. For such recollection an adequate and appropriate natural memory is required, since without it the task will prove to be very difficult. But if nature assent, it will be aided not inconsiderably by art; and what art can then accomplish with this technique will be greater than what nature alone could effect.

[8] Since experience has demonstrated that the ordinary petty things which are constantly present to our sight will not create a strong impression upon the memory, while novel things, being unusual, will **build . . . a house of habitation** [1 Kings 8:13] for themselves in our imagination—like boys, whose ability to image all that they have seen and learned as small children is extraordinary, because all things were then **new** to them, things **that came up of late** [Deut. 32:17]—it follows, accordingly, that the images that bring words to memory must be of this quality, must, that is, consist of something that contains some novelty or wonder; because then the person who is to remember will be stimulated to grasp it, **hold** it, and **not let** it **go** [Song of S. 3:4]. For nobody will be as stimulated by the rising and setting of the sun, an ever-recurring and routine phenomenon, as by solar or lunar eclipses, which occur at infrequent intervals. It is for this reason, too, that the aged, for whom scarcely anything is novel or

5. JV: "staggering."
6. Cf. *R. ad H.* 3.20.33; note that JML assumes his Hebrew reader will know that Latin *testes* means both "witnesses" and "testicles."

העצומה, ויקשה להם לזכור הדברים קשי נפלא. ולזה ראוי שהמלאכה תדמה לטבע, למה שהיא תקון הטבע, ולא זולת זה, כמו שאמ׳ קוינטיליאנו. ונקח, אם כן, לגרום זכירת המאמרים, הדברים החדשים והנפלאים, כגון הענינים שיש להם הפלגה מה בחשיבות או ביופי, נעדרי הרבוי וקלות התנועה; וכן הענינים המכוערים אשר בתכלית יגרמו הזכרון, להיותם גם כן בלתי מרגלים, אלא שלא יעשו זה במדרגת החשובים[6] והנשאים והיפים. או שנלביש הצורה בגדי מלכות, שש ורקמה, ואבן יקרה או עטרת מלכות בראשה; או שנעשה בהפך זה, ר״ל, שנכו׳ בה׳ הפלגה מה מהכיעור, כאלו תאמר שהם מלכלכות בדם, או בוכו׳, או עם אי זה מראה מכוער, או עם קרנים בראשם, ובכלל אי זה דבר מביא לשחוק. ותהיה הפלגה מן יופי או כעור, למען אלה החדושים[6] וההפלגות יגרמו הזכי׳. וכל זה ראוי לעשות בהשתדלות ורגילות מופלג, עד שבזכרנו המקומות עם הצורות תכף נבא לזכור המאמרים אשר יחקום.

[9] וטוליאו, בזה המקום, סותר דעת קצת היונים שהיו לומדים לתלמידי׳ כמעט צורות לבלתי תכלית, ואמר שאין ראוי למלמד לתת לתלמיד זולת ההתחלות, ולצאת מן הענינים במשל אחד· ומזה יבא המתלמד לעשות כן בנוהג מנהגם. וקצרתי, להיותם בלתי מועילים למה שנרצהו; אמנם, מה שאמר בזה המקום ובמקומות אחרים — שהסדר הטוב בלמוד להתחיל מן הכבד, כי כאשר ידעהו יבי׳ ממנו תכף הקל — זהו זולת מה שנחשבהו ומה שנמצא מזה בספרים, כי העתקת המתלמד ראויה שתהיה מן הקל אל הכבד, לא להפך.

[10] וכאשר תתבונן בתורתינו הקדושה, זולת התועלות האחרות הנמצאות בעשיית המצוות, רבות מהם רצו׳ זה המרו׳[7] להזכיר. אמר בענין השבת, בדברות הראשונות: זכור את יום השבת לקדשו· ששת ימים תעבדו, וכו׳ [שמ׳ כ׳ ח׳–ט׳]; ואחר כן אמר: כי ששת ימים עשה י״י את השמים ואת הארץ את הים ואת כל אשר בם, וכו׳ [שם י״א]; ואמר בדברות האחרונות: וזכרת כי עבד היית בארץ מצרים ויוציאך י״י אלקיך משם... על כן צוך י״י אלקיך... [דב׳ ה׳ ט״ו]. והנה זמן עשיית זאת המצוה, עם חקותיה ומשפטיה, ידמו המקומות

2 ולא] לא[ד] || 6 החשובים] ההשובי׳[ד6] | והיפים] והייפויים[כ] || 8 שנכו׳] שנזכור[כ] | בה׳] בהם[כ] || 10 החדושים[6]] ההדושי׳[כד] | הזכי׳] הזכים[כ] || 12 יחקום] יחקו׳[ד] || 13 <שהם לומ׳> שהיו לומדים[כ] | לתלמידי׳] לתלמידים[כ] || 18 יבי׳ [יביא[כ] || 19 הכבד] הכ׳[ד] || 22 תעבדו] תעבד[ת] || 23 [י״י][ד] || 25 אלקיך] אלקי׳[כ] ||

7 יח׳ ט״ז י״ג ||

[6] Corrected: J and [R]ד.

[7] I.e., המרומם.

marvellous, are the most forgetful and find it extraordinarily difficult to remember things. Art, then, should imitate nature, since art is nothing but a re-formation of nature, as Quintilian[c] says. To bring about the recollection of words, therefore, we should choose things novel and extraordinary, matters, say, that have some exceptional importance or beauty, yet lack complexity and speed of motion. Matters that are extremely ugly will likewise bring about recollection, since they too are not usual; but they are not as effective as important, sublime, or beautiful things. We may either dress the image in royal garments, **fine linen . . . and richly woven work** [Ezek. 16:13], with a precious stone or royal crown on its head; or we may do the opposite, I mean see that the images contain some distinctive ugliness: make them bloodstained, you might say, or weeping, or somehow hideous in appearance; or endow them with horns on their heads—with something, in sum, that will arouse a laugh. Exceptional beauty or ugliness should be present so that these novelties and exaggerations may induce recollection. We should practise this entire technique so energetically and so regularly that at once upon remembering the backgrounds and the images we come immediately to recollect the words of which they are the semblances.

[9] At this juncture Tully[d] contradicts the opinion of certain Greeks, who, for their pupils' sake, would study out a virtually infinite number of images. He says that an instructor ought to give a student first principles only, and that he should acquit himself of specific instances by means of a single example; from this the learner will come to act likewise in similar circumstances. I have here been brief, because such instances are of no advantage to our purpose; his statement, however, both in this and other passages—that the best order in learning is to commence with the difficult, because when this is known the easy is at once understandable from it—differs from our own belief and from pronouncements on the subject in literature, namely, that the learner's progress should be from the easy to the difficult, and not the reverse.[7]

[10] Study of our holy Torah shows that, apart from the other advantages brought about by the performance of the commandments, the purport of many a commandment is to facilitate recollection of its particular sublime idea. In the earlier listing of the Ten Commandments, Scripture says concerning the Sabbath: **Remember the Sabbath day to keep it holy. Six days shall ye[8] labor,** etc. [Exod. 20:8–9]; and immediately thereafter: **For in six days the Lord made heaven and earth, the sea, and all that in them is,** etc. [20:11]. In the later listing of the Ten Commandments, it says: **And thou shalt remember that thou wast a servant in the land of Egypt, and the Lord thy God brought thee out thence . . .; therefore the Lord thy God commanded thee . . .** [Deut. 5:15].

7. Cf. ii.1.1, and Int. §5(3).
8. B: ". . . shalt thou. . . ."

c. Q. 2.17.9.
d. *R. ad H.* 3.24.39.

והצורות אשר למענם יגרמו זכרון הדברים. והעדר אכילת החמץ תביאנו לזכור
שנשאו בצקם טרם יחמץ בצאתם ממצרים, כמו שאמר: והגדת לבנך ביום
ההוא... בעבור זה עשה י״י לי בצאתי ממצרים [שמ׳ י״ג ח׳]. ואמר בענין
התפילין: והיה לך לאות על ידך ולזכרון בין עיניך למען תהיה תורת י״י בפיך כי
5 ביד חזק׳ הוציאך י״י ממצרים [שם ט׳]. ואמר בקדשת הבכורות: והיה כי ישאלך
בנך מחר לאמר, כו׳... ויהי כי הקשה פרעה לשלחנו ויהרוג י״י כל בכור בארץ
מצרים מבכור אדם ועד בכור בהמה· על כן אני זובח לי״י כל פטר רחם הזכרים,
וכל בכור בני אפדה [שם י״ד — ט״ו]. הנה אלה המצות יגרמו זכרון קצת הנסים
נעשו ביציאת מצרים. וענין המשכן, והארון, והמנורה, והמזבחות, והשלחנות,
10 וכל הכלים, ובית העולמים, והעבודות: מי לא ידע בכל אלה שהם יחקו
מהעולם העליון הרוחני דברים גדולים, וגורמים לזכור מהאלקיות דבר׳ גדול׳
זולת מה שידמו מענין שכל האדם, ועניניים אחרים נפלאים? ואלה הם המשלים
ודמיונים באופן נפלא עד לאין תכלית יותר ממה שידמו המקומות והצורות
הדברים אשר הם להם דמיונים. ואמר בפרשת אמור, בר״ה: זכרון תרועה מקרא
15 קדש [וי׳ כ״ג כ״ד], ר״ל, שהוא ידמה ההכנעה ושברון הלב הראוי בימים ההם,
וגורם לזכור אותו; מלשון תרועם בשבט ברזל [תה׳ ב׳ ט׳]· רוע התרועעה הארץ
[יש׳ כ״ז י״ט]. וכן גם תרועת השופר תחקה היללה והקינה, כי מה יתאונן אדם
חי, גבר על חטאיו [איכה ג׳ ל״ט]. ואמר בחג הסוכות: בסוכת תשבו שבעת ימים,
וכו׳ [וי׳ כ״ג מ״ב]· ואמר אחר כן: למען ידעו דורותיכם כי בסכות הושבתי את
20 בני ישראל [שם מ״ג]. וכן, בענין הציצית גם כן אמר: והיה לכם לציצית וראיתם
אותו וזכרתם את כל מצות י״י ועשיתם אותם, וכו׳ [במ׳ ט״ו ל״ט]· ואמ׳ אחרי
כן: למען תזכרו ועשיתם את כל מצותי [שם מ׳]. והנה זאת המצוה תביאנו

2 בצקם] בציקם[כ] |בצאתם] בצאתים[כ] |והגדת] והגדתם[ד] |לבנך <לבנך>[כ] ||3 [י״י][כ] |ואמר] וכן[כ] ||
4 עיניך] עניך[ד] |י״י] אל[ד] ||5 ביד חזק׳] בחוזק יד[כ] ||6 [והיה][כ] ||6 [לאמר][ד] ||10 העולמים] עולמים[ד] ||
11 וגורמים] וגומרים[כ] ||14 להם] לה׳[י] ||16 רוע] רעה[ת] ||18 [שבעת ימים][כ] ||20 הציצית]
הצצית[ד] |לציצית] לצצית[ד] ||

Now the time specified for the enactment of this commandment, and, in addition, its several other statutes and ordinances, are like the backgrounds and images by virtue of which words are caused to be remembered. Abstention from eating leaven brings us to remember that, when the children of Israel left Egypt, they **took their dough before it was leavened** [Exod. 12:34], as Scripture says: **And thou shalt tell thy son in that day . . .: It is because of that which the Lord did for me when I came forth out of Egypt** [Exod. 13:8]. Concerning phylacteries, Scripture says: **And it shall be for a sign unto thee upon thy hand, and for a memorial between thine eyes, that the law of the Lord may be in thy mouth; for with a strong hand hath the Lord brought thee out of Egypt** [13:9]. Regarding the sanctification of firstlings, Scripture says: **And it shall be when thy son asketh thee in time to come, etc.; . . . and it came to pass, when Pharaoh would hardly let us go, that the Lord slew all the first-born in the land of Egypt, both the first-born of man, and the first-born of beast; therefore I sacrifice to the Lord all that openeth the womb, being males; but all the first born of my sons I redeem** [13:14–15]. These commandments, then, cause remembrance of some few of the wonders wrought at the time of the Exodus from Egypt. The prescription, too, of the tabernacle, ark, candlestick, altars, tables, all the vessels, the temple, and the services: who does not know of all these that they are great symbols of the spiritual world on high? They cause remembrance of great truths of divine revelation, although they may also symbolize products of human reason and other wonders. These marvelously constituted examples and likenesses are infinitely more effective than are backgrounds and images for the matters of which they serve as likenesses. In the Torah-portion *ʾEmōr* [Lev. 21:1–24:23], speaking of Rosh Hashanah, Scripture says: **. . . a memorial proclaimed with the blast of horns, a holy convocation** [23:24]. The horn-blast here depicts the humbling and breaking of the heart that is appropriate during those days, and causes this to be remembered; the terminology here (*teruʿāh*) is derived from "to break"[9] as in **Thou shalt break them** (terōʿem) **with a rod of iron** [Ps. 2:9]; **the earth is broken, broken down** (rōʿāh hithrōʿaʿāh) [Isa. 24:19]. The blast of the ram's horn, moreover, is an imitation of wailing and lamentation, for **How[10] doth a living man complain, a strong man because of his sins!** [Lam. 3:39]. Concerning the Feast of Booths, Scripture says: **Ye shall dwell in booths seven days,** etc. [Lev. 23:42], and thereafter **. . . that your generations may know that I made the children of Israel to dwell in booths** [23:43]. So, too, on the subject of fringes, it says: **And it shall be unto you for a fringe, that ye may look upon it, and remember all the commandments of the Lord, and do them,** etc. [Num. 15:39]; and thereafter: **. . . that ye may remember and do all My commandments** [15:40]. This,

9. JML has here confused two roots: *rūaʿ* (רוּעַ) and *rāʿaʿ* (רָעַע), the former meaning (*hiphʿīl* form) "to raise a shout" or "to give a blast on a horn," the latter "to break."

10. JV: "Wherefore. . . ."

לזכור מה שצוה לנו י״י מן המצוות באופן רבותי׳, והיה בדמיון צורות המאמרים.

[11] והנה התפרסם כי מקצת תועלות המצות הוא שהם חקוים, דמויים, והמשלים לענינים יקרים ונכבדים, לא יערכם זהב וזכוכית; ובהם יחקו הדברים ההם באופן יותר שלם עד לאין תכלית מאשר יעשו המקומות הנזכרים, עם צורותיהם, מהדברים שגורמים לזכרם· כי הם מעשי ידי השם ית׳, הוא עשאם ויכוננם, ואלה מעשי ידי אדם, ומה יצדק אנוש עם אל?

[12] ולא זו בלבד, אבל כל חכמה, וכל תבונה אשר תמצא בחבור מן החבורים, היא בתורתנו הקדושה ובספרי המדברים ברוח הקדש — למבינים עניניהם, ולאשר האיר י״י עיני שכלו בתכלית מה שאפשר מן השלמות. וזהו מה שאמ׳ המשורר ע״ה: תורת י״י תמימה משיבת נפש [תה׳ י״ט ח׳]. כלל בזה הפסוק ב׳ ענינים: אחד מהם שהתורה היא תמימה, ר״ל, שלא יחסר בה דבר כי כן ענין התמים, עד היא נימוס שלם לכל השלמיות, לא יחסר ממנו איש· ומזה יתחיב שתכלול האמתיות בכללם, ברמז אם בפרסום; והאחר שהיא תשיב הנפש אל מקום חוצבה, ולא יצטרך לה בזה דבר אחר כי היא מספקת בעצמה· כי כמו שכללה כל השלמיות, כן תכלול כל מה שצריך אל השארות הנפש והדבקה באלקים, שהוא השלמות האחרון. והנה סוף הפסוק ואחריתו יתחייב מראשיתו, כי למה שהי׳ תמימה יתחייב בהכרח שיהיה ספק בידה להושיב הנפש אל המלוא העליון: ושבה אל בית אביה כנעוריה· י״י בדד ינחנה ואין עמו אל נכר.

[13] והנה בימי הנבואה, בירחי קדם, כאשר מציון מכלל יופי אלקים הופיע, היינו לומדים ויודעים מן התורה הקדושה כל החכמות והתבונות, וכל ההשגות האנושיות בכללם, כי הכל בה בהסתר או במפורסם. והיה מה שנמצא מה׳ אצל האומות מעט מצער בערכנו, עד היו אומרי׳ הגוים אשר שמעו את שמענו: רק עם חכם ונבון הגוי הגדול הזה. אמנם, אחרי הסתלק׳ השכינה מבינינו בעונותינו הרבים, ופסק׳ הנבואה והדעה, וחכמ׳ נבוננו נסתרה, לא נוכל להבין מדברי

1 [י״י][כ] | רבותי׳] רבו[ד] | בדמיון] בדמיו[ד] || 3 תועלות] תועלו[ד] || 6 מעשי] מעשה[כ] | השם] ה׳[כ] || 7 מעשי] מעשה[כ] || 9 המדברים] ובלשון[כ] || 12 הפסוק] הפסו[ד] || 13 התמים] התמי[ד] || 18 שהי׳] שהיה[כ] || 19 ינחנה] ינחינה[כ] | עמו] עמה[כ] || 23 מה׳] מהם[כ] || 25 הסתלק׳] הסתלקת[כ] || 26 ופסק׳] ופסקה[כ] | והדעה] והדעת[כ] | וחכמ׳] והחכמה[כ] ||

4 איוב כ״ח י״ז || 7 איוב ט׳ ב׳ || 10 תה׳ י״ט ט׳ || 15 יש׳ נ״א א׳ || 19 וי׳ כ״ב י״ג | דב׳ ל״ב י״ב || 21 איוב כ״ט ב׳ | תה׳ נ׳ ב׳ | 24 במ׳ י״ד ט״ו || 25 דב׳ ד׳ ו׳ || 26 יש׳ כ״ט י״ד ||

indeed, is the particular injunction that leads us to remember any other of the Lord's commandments in the manner explained by our Rabbis; in function, therefore, it is like the images of words.

[11] Evidently, then, the value of the commandments consists in part of the fact that they are imitations, likenesses, and illustrations of matters so precious and important that **gold and glass cannot equal** them [Job 28:17]. Through them an infinitely more perfect resemblance is achieved for these matters than that which the aforementioned backgrounds and images can achieve for the matters they recall, since the commandments are the handiwork of the Name Himself, blessed be He, Who made and established them, while backgrounds and images are the handiwork of man—**and how can man be just with God?** [Job 9:2].

[12] Not only is this the case here, but every science, every rationally apprehended truth that any treatise may contain, is present in our holy Torah and in the books of those who speak by the Holy Spirit—present, that is, for those who thoroughly understand the subjects involved, and for whom the Lord has **enlightened the eyes** [Ps. 19:9] of understanding as perfectly as possible. This is what the Psalmist, upon whom be peace, means when he says: **The law of the Lord is perfect, restoring the soul** [Ps. 19:8]. In this verse he has included two ideas. The first is that the Torah is so complete—meaning that nothing is lacking therein, for such is completeness—that it is a Law entirely perfect, deficient in no single respect; from this it necessarily follows that the Torah must include the entirety of all truths, either implicitly or explicitly. The other idea is that the Torah is able to restore the soul to the place **whence** she **was hewn** [Isa. 51:1]; for this the soul needs nothing else, since the Torah is in itself alone sufficient. For as the Torah includes all perfection, so it includes all that is necessary for the ultimate perfection, the survival of the soul and her cleaving to God. The latter and concluding portion of the verse is thus the necessary consequence of its beginning, for since the Torah is complete it must necessarily be equal to the task of restoring the soul to the citadel on high: **if she returned unto her father's house as in her youth** [Lev. 23:13], **the Lord alone shall lead** her, **and . . . no strange god with Him** [Deut. 32:12].

[13] In the days of Prophecy, indeed, **in the months of old** [Job 29:2], when **out of Zion, the perfection of beauty, God shined forth** [Ps. 50:2], we used to learn and know from the holy Torah all the sciences and truths of reason, including all that were humanly attained, for everything is either latent therein or plainly stated. What other peoples possessed of these sciences and truths was, by comparison with us, very little, so that **the nations which heard the fame of** us [Num. 14:15] were wont to say: "**Surely this great nation is a wise and understanding people**" [Deut. 4:6]. But after the indwelling Presence of God departed from our midst because of our many iniquities, when Prophecy and insight ceased, and the science of our men of understanding was hid,[11] we were

11. Cf. Isa. 29:14.

התורה כל השלמיות וההשגות· והוא מצד חסרוננו, לבלתי יודענו התורה על השלמות. לכן היה הענין בהפך; כי אחרי ידענו כל החכמות או חלק מהם, א״כ נתבונן בדברי התורה, אז תפקחנה עיני שכלנו שהם נכללות בדברי התורה, ונתמה איך לא הבננו זה ממנה מתחל׳ הענין· כאשר קרה לנו פעמי׳ רבות, וביחוד בחכמת ההלצה. כי בהתבונני בדברי התורה ההתבוננות הנופל עתה אצל רב האנשים, לא שערתי תהיה בה זאת החכמה או חלק ממנה; אמנם, אחרי למדתיה וחקרתיה, וכמטמונים חפשתיה מחבורי זולתינו מהאומות, אחר כן שבתי לראות מה ידובר בה בתורה ובספרי הקדש, אז נפקחו עיני שכלי וראיתי כי היא הנותנת. ובין ערבות אמריה וצחיותיה — וכל חקת ההלצה ומשפטיה אשר יוכללו בספרי הקדש — ובין כל מה שנמצא מזה אצל כל יתר האומות, הבדל מופלג, עד ידמו כאזוב אשר בקיר בערך אל הארז אשר בלבנון; ונפלאתי איך עבר רוח י״י אותי מלפני׳, ולא ידעתי מקומה איו. וכן תוכל להקיש ביתר החכמות.

[14] ומזה התבאר הטעות והשגיאה הרמה תנוח בחיק קצת החכמים בעיניהם מאנשי אומתנו עתה, האומ׳: ״לא תחזו לנו נכוחות מאשור וממצרים; לא תשתו מים קרים נוזלים מאמנה ופרפר וכל נהרות דמשק. ולנו המים, מקור מים חיים מצור שלג לבנון. ומה לנו אל ארץ מצרים לשתות מי שיחור? כי מי ידלה לנו עתה מים עמוקים להשקות את הצמא במדבר; מי יראה לנו עיינות ותהומות יוצאים בבקעה ובהר, או יוציא מים מצור החלמיש?״ והנה, עם כונתם לרומם התורה ולנשאה, הם משפילים אותה בדבריהם, כי יניאו לבב האנשים לבלתי יראו מסתוריה ויחקרו מה שבה מן השלמות והתבוננות, לבלתי יבואו

3 נכללות בדברי [התורה][ר] || 4 ממנה מתחל׳ הענין] מתחלה ממנה העניין[ר] || 7–8 אחר כן] א״כ[ר] || 17 שיחור] השיחור[ר] || 18 עיינות] מעינו[ד] || 19 ובהר] בהר[ד] ||

---

7 מש׳ ב׳ ד׳ || 8 בר׳ ג׳ ז׳ || 11 מל״א ה׳ י״ג || 12 נח׳ ג׳ י״ז || 14 קה׳ ז׳ ט׳ | יש׳ ה׳ כ״א || 15 יש׳ ל׳ י׳ | יש׳ י״א י״א || 16 יר׳ י״ח י״ד | מל״ב ה׳ י״ב | בר׳ כ״ו כ׳ || 17 יר׳ ב׳ י״ג | יר׳ י״ח י״ד | יר׳ ב׳ י״ח || 18 שמ׳ ב׳ י״ט | מש׳ י״ח ד׳ | שמ״ב י״ז כ״ט || 19 דב׳ ח׳ ז׳ | דב׳ ח׳ ט״ו || 20 במ׳ ל״ב ט׳ ||

no longer able to derive understanding of all scientific developments and attainments from the Torah's words; this condition, however, persists due to our own falling short, our failure to know the Torah in full perfection. Thus the matter has come to be in reverse;[12] for if, after we have come to know all the sciences, or some part of them, we study the words of the Torah, then the eyes of our understanding open to the fact that the sciences are included in the Torah's words, and we wonder how we could have failed to realize this from the Torah itself to begin with. Such has frequently been our own experience, especially in the science of Rhetoric. For when I studied the words of the Torah in the way now common amongst most people, I had no idea that the science of Rhetoric or any part of it was included therein. But once I had studied and investigated Rhetoric, **searched for her as for hid treasures** [Prov. 2:4] out of the treatises written by men of nations other than our own, and afterwards came back to see what is said of her in the Torah and the Holy Scriptures, then **the eyes** of my understanding **were opened** [Gen. 3:7], and I saw that it is the Torah which was the giver. Between the Torah's pleasing words and stylistic elegancies—and, indeed, all the statutes and ordinances of Rhetoric which are included within the Holy Scriptures—and all of the like that all other nations possess, the difference is so striking that to compare them is like comparing **the hyssop . . . in the wall** with **the cedar that is in Lebanon** [1 Kings 5:13]; and I marvel how previously the spirit of the Lord passed me by aforetime, so that I did not know her place, **where** it **is** [Nah. 3:17].[13] You could apply the same comparison to all other sciences.

[14] This clearly is the source of the error and great mistake that **rest in the bosom of** [Eccl. 7:9] some **that are wise in their own eyes** [Isa. 5:21] amongst the men of our nation nowadays, who say: "**Prophesy not into us right things** [30:10] **from Assyria and from Egypt** [11:11]; drink not **cold, flowing waters** [Jer. 18:14] from **Amanah and Pharphar** and all **the rivers of Damascus** [2 Kings 5:12]. **The water is ours** [Gen. 26:20], **a fountain of living waters** [Jer. 2:13] **from the rock** of **Lebanon's snow** [18:14]. What have we **to do** with the land of Egypt, **to drink the waters of Shihor** [2:18]? For who now will **draw for us** [Exod. 2:19] **deep waters** [Prov. 18:4] and give to drink the **thirsty in the wilderness** [2 Sam. 17:29]? Who will show us **fountains and depths, springing forth in valleys and hills** [Deut. 8:7], or will bring forth **water out of the rock of flint** [8:15]?" Although the intention of these people is to elevate and exalt the Torah, they in fact abase her by such talk, since **they turn away the heart** [Num. 32:9], so that men neither see her implications nor search out the perfection and

12. I.e., knowledge of the Torah, ultimately—as in ancient Israel—essential to complete and perfect understanding of the secular sciences, can now itself not be fully attained without the aid of the secular sciences. For JML's *m*^{e}*līṣāh* expression of this idea, see Preface: 1 ff., 10–11, and n. 12; cf. Int., §1 (nn. 5 and 7), and the fuller discussion in §4.

13. It was a main purpose of the *N.S.* to demonstrate the thesis adumbrated in the preceding passage (from ". . . every science [par. 12] . . ."): that the fundamental principles of the "science of Rhetoric" are laid down in, and can best be learned from, the Hebrew Scriptures. Cf. Int., §4 (following n. 182).

בחדריה ותעלומה יוציאו אור. וישארו עם הנראה מקצת פשטיה ומקצת סודותיה המקבלים אצלנו, ורב טוב הצפון בה אין דורש ואין מבקש. וחטאתם לפני י״י על שגגתם; על אלה והדומי׳ לאלה אמר הנביא ע״ה: הוי האומרי׳ לרע טוב ולטוב רע שמים חשך לאור ואור לחשך... מר למתוק ומתוק למר [יש׳ ה׳ כ׳].

פרק י״ד

פרק הצחות ומיניה.

[1] אופני הדבור, הנקראים אצל קצת החכמים צורות, יחלקו אל ג׳, ר״ל, אל דבור הנשא, הבינוני, והשפל. ולא ימלט מאמ׳ שלא יהיה באחד מאלה הפנים, זולת אם היה הטעאיי. הנשא הוא אשר יורכב ממאמרי׳ נשאים עם הרכבה צחה ונקלה; הבינוני הוא אשר יורכב ממאמרים אשר הם במדרגה בינוני בין הנשא והשפל; והשפל הוא אשר יורכב ממאמרי׳ שפלים עד לא יעבור הדבור המורגל בין האנשים.

[2] והרגל הדבור הנשא הוא בזה האופן: אם נקח בו תיבות שהם בתכלית הצחות, מיוחדות או משאלות; ואם נביא בו מאמרים נשאים, אשר בהרחבה והרחמנות; ואם יורכב מיפויי המאמרים או התבות אשר להם התנשאות. והמשל לזה האופן רוב מאמרי ישעיהו וקצת מספורי יחזקאל, כמו: שמעו שמים והאזיני ארץ כי י״י דבר בנים גדלתי ורוממתי והם פשעו בי׳ ידע שור קונהו, וכו׳... הוי גוי חוטא עם כבד עון זרע מרעים בנים משחיתים עזבו את י״י נאצו את קדוש ישראל נזורו אחור׳ על מה תכו עוד תוסיפו סרה, וכל הענין [יש׳ א׳ ב׳—ה׳, וגו׳]. וזה, כי הם תיבות שהם בתכלית הצחות; עוד, נמצאו בזה

1 ומקצת] וקצת[ר] || 2 וחטאתם] וחטא׳[ר] || 3 והדומי׳ לאלה] והדו׳ [לאלה][ר] || 4 לאור <לאור>[כ] || 10 זולת] וזולת[כ] ||

---

1 איוב כ״ח י״א || 2 תה׳ ל״א כ׳ | יח׳ ל״ד ו׳ || 3 במ׳ ט״ו כ״ה ||

understanding that are in her, neither enter her chambers nor bring forth **the thing that is hid . . . to light** [Job 28:11]. They are left with what can be discerned from the letter of some verses of the Torah and from some of the verses whose latent sense is received amongst us by tradition; there is, however, **none to search and seek** [Ezek. 34:6] the **abundant goodness** that is **laid up** [Ps. 31:20] in her. But **their sin-offering is to come before the Lord for their error** [Num. 15:25]; concerning these men and their ilk the Prophet, upon whom be peace, has said: **Woe unto them that call evil good, and good evil; that change darkness into light, and light into darkness . . . bitter into sweet, and sweet into bitter** [Isa. 5:20]![14]

CHAPTER 14

On Style and Its Types

[1] The styles of utterance, called by some scholars forms of utterance, are divided into three: the Grand, the Middle, and the Simple.[a] A discourse, unless faulty, cannot escape being in one or another of these styles. The Grand is composed of elevated statements which are elegantly and smoothly combined, the Middle of statements which are of a quality intermediate between the Grand and the Simple, and the Simple of statements so commonplace that it does not transcend the level of common, everyday speech.

[2] The Grand Style is practised as follows: if we adopt for it words that are the most elegant possible, whether literal or figurative; if we introduce elevated statements in any Amplification and in any Appeal to Pity; and if it is composed of Figures of Thought or of Diction which have grandeur. Most of Isaiah's discourses and certain of Ezekiel's descriptions illustrate this Style; for example: **Hear, O heavens, and give ear, O earth, for the Lord hath spoken: Children I have reared, and brought up, and they have rebelled against Me. The ox knoweth his owner,** etc. . . . **Ah sinful nation, a people laden with iniquity, a seed of evil-doers, children that deal corruptly; they have forsaken the Lord, they have condemned the Holy One of Israel, they are turned away backward. On what part will ye be yet stricken, seeing ye stray away more and more?** and indeed the entire passage [Isa. 1:2–5 ff.]. This is the Grand Style

14. The foregoing paragraph is quoted (in abridged form) by Azariah de'Rossi, *Mᵉ'ōr 'Ēnayim*, ed. Benjacob (Vilna, 1863), i.75; the idea is also expressed at Preface: 14 above, a passage quoted by R. Judah Moscato, *Nᵉphūṣōth Yᵉhūdhāh* (Lemberg, 1859), Sermon 5, 19b. Cf. Int., § 1 and n. 5.

a. *R. ad H.* 4.8.11 ff.

המאמר מן היפויים ההלציים אשר יבוקש ענינם בדבור הנשא, כמו הקריאה, והצחות, וזולתם; ויש בו עניני׳ נשאים הלקוחים ממקום ההרחבה, כי ימצא בו מן ההרחבה במאמר מה שלא יעלם. וכן: מי זה בא מאדום חמוץ בגדים מבצרה זה הדור בלבושו צועה ברוב כחו אני מדבר בצדקה רב להושיע· מדוע אדום ללבושך ובגדיך כדור׳ בגת, וכל הענין [שם ס״ג א׳—ב׳, וגו׳]. וכן: נדרשתי ללא שאלו נמצאתי ללא בקשוני אמרתי הנני הנני אל גוי לא קורא בשמי· פרשתי ידי כל היום אל עם סורר, וכל הענין [שם ס״ה א׳—ב׳, וגו׳], כי בזה המאמר מן ההרחבה, וההתנשאות, והיפויים אשר יבוקש ענינם בדבור הנשא, מה שלא יעלם. וכן ביחזקאל: נבואת צור ומלכה [יח׳ כ״ו ב׳, וגו׳]· ופרשת הודע את ירושלם את תועבותיה [שם ט״ז ב׳, וגו׳]· וזולתם רבים.

[3] אמנם ההרגל מהדבור הבינוני הוא אם נמעט דבר מה מהצחות וההתנשאות ממה שהוא בדבור הנשא, אבל לא שנבא אל המורגל והשפל, כמו: כה אמר י״י ולקחתי אני מצמרת הארז הרמה ונתתי מראש יונקותיו רך אקטוף ושתלתי אני על הר גבוה ותלול· בהר מרום ישראל אשתלנו, וכן כל הענין [יח׳ י״ז כ״ב—כ״ג, וגו׳]; וכן: ואתה בן אדם התשפוט התשפוט את עיר הדמים והודעת את כל תועבותיה· ואמרת כה אמר י״י עיר שופכת דם בתוכה, וכו׳ [שם כ״ב ב׳—ג׳, וגו׳]; וכן: בן אדם שתים נשים בנות אם אחת היו· ותזננה במצרים בנעוריהם זנו שמה מעכו שדיהם ושם עשו דדי בתוליהן· ושמותם אהלה, וכו׳ [שם כ״ג ב׳—ד׳, וגו׳].

[4] אמנם ההרגל מהדבור השפל הוא לדבר במנהג כללות העם, בלשון מורגל אליהם, כמו ספור ירמיהו מעני׳ גדליהו בן אחיקם, ומחרבן הבית· וספ׳ יהושע, שמואל, ומלכים, כמעט רובם, אשר לא יעברו ההרגל והספור הנהוג בכללות האנשים.

[5] וראוי שנשמר פן נפול באופנים ההטעאיים אשר יראו קרובים אל אלה

2–3 הלקוחים... ההרחבה ‹הלקוחים הרחבה›[ר] || 7 [עם][כ] | המאמר] העניין[כ] || 10 ירושלם] ירושלים[כ] || 13 י״י] אדני ה׳[ת] || 14 אשתלנו] אשתולנו[ר] || 16 י״י] אדני ה׳[ת] || 17 שתים] שתי[ר] || 18 במצרים] במצרי[ר] | בנעוריהם] כנעוריה׳[ר] בנעוריהן[ת] | שדיהם] שדיה[ר] שדיהן[ת] | ושם] ושמה[כ] | בתוליהן] בתוליה׳[ר] | ושמותם] ושמותן[ת] || 21 מעני׳] מענייני[כ] | גדליהו] גדליה[כ] || 24 ההטעאיים] ההטעיים[ר] ||

because these are words of the utmost elegance; moreover, in this passage are found some Figures of the sort called for in the Grand Style, such as Apostrophe,[1] Refining,[2] and others; and it contains sublime ideas derived from the topic of Amplification,[3] for Amplification is notably in evidence here. So too in the Grand Style: "**Who is this that cometh from Edom, with crimsoned garments from Bozrah? This that is glorious in his apparel, stately in the greatness of his strength?"—"I that speak in victory, mighty to save."—"Wherefore is Thine apparel red, and Thy garments like his that treadeth in the winevat?"** and the entire passage [63:1-2 ff.]. And again, the following: **I gave access to them that asked not for Me, I was at hand to them that sought Me not; I said: "Behold Me, behold Me," unto a nation that was not called by My name. I have spread out My hands all the day unto a rebellious people,** and the rest [65:1-2 ff.], for in this speech amplification, sublimity, and the Figures of Speech demanded by the Grand Style are present in marked amount. In Ezekiel, similarly, the prophecy against Tyre and her king [26:2-28:19], the section beginning "**. . . cause Jerusalem to know her abominations**" [16:2]; and many others are also in Grand Style.

[3] We practise the Middle Style if we abate somewhat the elegance and sublimity of the Grand Style, yet do not approximate the familiarity of the Simple Style. For example: **Thus saith the Lord**[4]**: "Moreover I will take, even I, of the lofty top of the cedar, and will set it; I will crop off from the topmost of its young twigs a tender one, and I will plant it upon a high mountain and eminent; in the mountain of the height of Israel will I plant it,"** and so throughout the passage [Ezek. 17:22-23 ff.]. Again: "**Now, thou, son of man, wilt thou judge, wilt thou judge the bloody city? Then cause her to know all her abominations. And thou shalt say: Thus saith the Lord**[4]**: O city that sheddest blood in the midst** of her,"[5] etc. [22:2-3]. Also: "**Son of man, there were two women, the daughters of one mother; and they committed harlotries in Egypt; they committed harlotries in their youth; there were their bosoms pressed, and there their virgin breasts were bruised. And the names of them were Oholah,**" etc. [23:2-4].

[4] To practise the Simple Style is to speak in the fashion of the generality of the populace, in language familiar to them, as in the Book of Jeremiah's account of the episode of Gedaliah the son of Ahikam [40:6-41:18], and the account of the destruction of the Temple [52:12-23]; and as in the Books of Joshua, Samuel, and Kings, which for the most part do not transcend the ordinary usage and narrative manner customary with the generality of men.

[5] We must be careful not to fall into the defective types of Style which

1. iv.7.
2. iv.54.
3. ii.11. 22-23 (esp. 23) below.
4. B and JV: ". . . Lord God."
5. JV: ". . . in the midst of thee."

האופנים. אם בערך אל הדבור הנשא, צד אחד הטעאיי כרוך בעקבו ודבק בו, שהוא במדרגת הנפח אל עבי הגוף וגסותו הטבעי, שהאדם לא ירגיש בהבדלם כי אם בהתבוננות, ויחשבוהו הסכלים לדבור הנשא; כגון שיכון ההתנשאות לדבר אין הצורך אליו, או ידבר בלשונות כבדות או תבות נכריות, או יביא במאמר השאלות בלתי נאותות· כמו שיאמר "נציי" במקום "נצים", מפני שמצא זה בדב׳ הקליר, כי זה הלשון עתה אינו כמנהג· או שעשה בנין הפעיל מן "שמר" ואמר "השמיר", ורצה לחדש גזרה לא נמצאה· או שיאמר: "עיני כשלה מני עני וברכי ימררו בבכי"· כי אלה אינם השאלות נאותות, כי לא יפול הכשלון על העין והבכיה על הברכים. ואף על פי שחבר מאלה וכיוצא בהם מאמרים יראה בהם ההתנשאות וההרחבה במאמר, אלה הם מאמרים הטעאיי׳, מיוחסי׳ לגסי הרוח אשר אמרו ללשוננו נגביר, ויחשבו לרומם הדבור בזריות וחדשים מקרוב באו. אמנם הם נראים קרובים אל זה הסוג מפני חדושם ונכריותם, עד יראו רחוקי׳ מאד מהדבור השפל, שהוא הדבור המורגל.

[6] ואם בערך אל הדבור הבינוני: כשלא יסודרו התיבות והמאמרים בסדור הראוי, עד יקשה אל השומע להבינו; במדרגת מי שיאמ׳, תמורת מה נאנחה בהמה, נבכו עדרי בקר, כי אין מרעה להם, גם עדרי הצאן נאשמו [יואל א׳ י״ח]· "מה בהמה נאנחה, בקר נבוכו עדרי, כי להם מרעה אין, עדרי גם נאשמו הצאן"·

2 אל] על[ר] ‖ 4 הצורך] צורך[ר] ‖ 5 נאותות] נאותו[ר] | נציי] נצניים[ר] ‖ 6 בדב׳] בדבר[ר] | עתה אינו כמנהג] אינו כמנהג עתה[ר] ‖ 8 אלה] אילו[ר] ‖ 10 ההתנשאות] התנשאות[ד] | וההרחבה] והחרבה[ר] | מיוחסי׳] מיוח׳[ד] ‖ 12 [באו][ר] ‖ 13 מהדבור] מן הדבור[ר] ‖ 15 אל השומע] לשומע[ר] ‖

7 תה׳ פ״ח י׳ ‖ 8 יש׳ כ״ב ד׳ ‖ 11 תה׳ י״ב ה׳ | דב׳ ל״ב י״ז ‖

appear closely akin to these. In the case of the Grand Style, one such defective kind is hitched on behind it and adheres to it so closely, that, quite like a swelling relative to the body's natural stoutness and robustness, a man can perceive the difference between them only through close observation. The inexperienced, however, will think it the Grand Style, when, for instance, a speaker aims at sublimity for a theme that does not require it; or uses difficult locutions or foreign words; or introduces inept metaphors—saying "blossomings," for instance, instead of "blossoms" (because he found this among Kalir's words),[6] for this locution is now obsolete; or if he should use the *hiph'īl* form of the root *shāmar* ["to guard, keep"] and say *hishmīr* ["he caused to keep"], wishing to innovate a conjugation that does not exist; or if he should say "**Mine eye** tottereth **by reason of affliction** [Ps. 88:10] and my knees **will weep bitterly**" [Isa. 22:4]—inappropriate metaphors, since an eye may not totter nor may knees weep. Although a lover of these and similar verbal mannerisms may see sublimity and amplification in them, they are fallacious diction, characteristic of the gross in spirit, **who have said: "Our tongue will we make mighty"** [Ps. 12:5] and who think to elevate their utterance by irregularities and novelties **that came up of late** [Deut. 32:17]. Indeed, such discourses do appear to approximate the Grand Style because they are novel and bizarre, so that they seem far removed from the Simple Style, the kind of speech that is in common use.

[6] The Middle Style is faulty when the words and sentences are improperly arranged, so that the audience has difficulty in understanding. Thus, if instead of saying:

> **How do the beasts groan!**
> **The herds of cattle are perplexed,**
> **Because they have no pasture;**
> **Yea, the flocks of sheep are made desolate** [Joel 1:18],

one should say:

> "How groan the beasts!
> Of cattle are perplexed the herds,
> Because pasture have they not,
> The flocks, yea, are made desolate, of sheep,"

6. On Eleazar Kalir (also: Kallir, Qallir, Killir, Qillir) see I. Elbogen, *Der jüdische Gottesdienst in seiner geschichtlichen Entwicklung* (Frankfurt-am-Main, 1931 [rep. 1962]), 310–319; A. Z. Idelsohn, *Jewish Liturgy and Its Development* (New York, 1932), 36–37 and 356–357; and S. Spiegel, "On Medieval Hebrew Poetry" (in L. Finkelstein, ed., *The Jews* [Philadelphia, 1949], II, 548 and 560–561). Regarding Kalir's liberties with the Hebrew language, see, in particular, the strictures expressed by Abraham ibn Ezra in his commentary on Eccl. 5:1 (cf. Idelsohn, p. 356). Ibn Ezra does not, however, include the example given here by JML, nor have I been able to locate the *piyyūṭ* by Kalir in which it occurs.

זהו מאמר הטעאיי בערך אל הבינוני; ויקראוהו מותך בלתי שקט, שהוא כמו
הדבר המותך המפסיד תמונתו, ושאין אדם יכול לעמוד על ענינו להיותו בלתי
שקט; ולא יחייב לשומע ההקשבה בשום פנים.

[7] ואם בערך אל הדבור השפל: אם יחטא בדקדוק המלות וסדרם בתבות
5 ובמאמרים המורגלים, וראוי להקרא חסר, כמי שיאמר: ״הלך שפחתך בשוק״·
וא״כ יאמר: ״עבדך תקע באזני״· וא״כ: ״זאת אשיב אל לבי.״ זהו חסר, ומאמר
הטעאיי, ואינו שומר מדרגת הדבור השפל, שהוא נגלה, מפורסם, וברור, בלשון
נאות ואם הוא מורגל; גם כי אינו משלים הדברים, ואומר אותם לפרקים, ולא
יתנו הבנה שלימה אל השומע.

10 [8] ויש לדעת כי בכל אופני הדבור ימצאו יפויים נאותים להם; ואם יושמו
באופן הראוי, ישימו המאמר צח, וההפך להפך. עוד, במאמ׳ אחד בעצמו, ראוי
שנבא לפעמי׳ מן הדבור הנשא אל הבינוני, ומן הבינוני אל השפל, והרגל אלה
ההתחלפיות פעמים יצליחו.

[9] וכאשר התבארו אופני הדבור בערך אל הצחות—ר״ל שהם ג׳: נשא,
15 כשידובר מהענינים הנשאים· ובינוני, כשיסופר מהדברים אשר הם במדרגה
האמצעית· ושפל, כשידובר מהעניני׳ ההמוניים—נספר הדברי׳ אשר יותאר
בהם הצחות הראוי והשל׳. ונאמ׳ שהם ג׳, ר״ל, היופי, ההרכבה, וההאותו׳.

[10] היופי, כשידובר בנקיות ובאופן נגלה מבואר; ויחלק אל ב׳ חלקים, אל
היושר והפרסום.

20 [11] והיושר, כאשר המאמר נקי מטעיות הדקדוק; וזה הטעות באחד מב׳
פנים: אם שיהיה באופן הקריאה, אם זולת זה. ואם הוא באופן הקריאה, כגון
שיקרא התיבה שהיא מלעיל מלרע, או להפך; ואם שיהיה זולת זה, כגון שלא
יבדיל בין מה שראוי להבדיל לפי הדקדוק, ר״ל, בין זכר לנקבה, יחיד ורבים, עבר
ועתיד, וזולתם· וזה יתבאר במלאכת הדקדוק.

25 [12] והפרסום הוא הנותן המאמ׳ נגלה ומבואר; וזה, כשידובר בתיבות
ומאמרים המיוחדים לדברים, ואשר הם בהרגל.

[13] וההרכבה היא שיהיה חבור התיבות צח מכל צד; וזה, כשנשמר מתכיפת
אותיות הנוח, או יתר האותיות העושות המאמ׳ כבד[1] ונשחת. משל הראשון

1 הטעאיי] ההטעאיי[ד] || 3 יחייב] יתחייב[כ] || 4 הדבור] הדבו[ד] || 8 אותם] אות׳[ד] || 12 אל הבינוני <הבינוני>[ד] || 14 התבארו] יתבארו[כ] || 15 מהענינים] מעניינים[כ] || 16 מהעניני׳] מהענים[כ] || 17 והשל׳] והשל[כ] | ונאמ׳] ונא׳[ד] | וההאותו׳] והאותות[כ] || 20 והיושר] והיוש[ד] | באחד מב׳] בא׳ מב׳[כ] || 22 שיהיה] יהיה[כ] || 25 המאמ׳] מאמר[כ] || 28 העושות] העוש׳[ד] | כבד[1]] כבד׳[כד] ||

[1] Abbreviation mark removed.

this is expressed in faulty Middle Style. They call this Drifting Incoherence,[7] because it is like a melted thing that has lost its shape, and which, since it is not at rest, nobody can properly grasp it. Such incoherence cannot possibly compel the hearer's attention.

[7] The Simple Style is faulty if there are mistakes in the accidence and syntax of ordinary words and sentences, and when the expression may fittingly be called defective, as in the case of one who first says: "Your maid-servant, he was walking in the marketplace"; next: "Your man-servant blasted in my ear"; and then: "I'll bear this in mind." This is defective, faulty in expression, and out of keeping with the quality of the Simple Style, which should be perspicuous, readily intelligible and clear, couched in apt, if ordinary, language. The speaker's words, moreover, are incomplete, are disjointed, and convey no complete understanding to the hearer.

[8] One should be aware that there are embellishments appropriate to each of the several Styles.[8] These, if rightly employed, will confer elegance upon the discourse, but if incorrectly used, will have the opposite effect. Also, during the self-same discourse, there are times when we should pass from the Grand Style to the Middle, and from the Middle to the Simple; such alternations in Style will on occasion bring success to the speaker.

[9] Having now made clear the Types of Style—that these are three: the Grand when the discourse turns upon grand themes, the Middle, when the account deals with matters of an intermediate quality, and the Simple, when ordinary affairs are discussed—we may proceed with an account of the attributes of an appropriate and finished Style. These, we say, are three: Beauty, Artistic Composition, and Appropriateness.

[10] Beauty is present when the Style is formed with purity and perspicuity. It has two subdivisions, Correctness and Clarity.

[11] The language is correct when it is free of grammatical errors. Such an error may be one of two sorts: in pronunciation, or in any other grammatical category. It is an error in pronunciation, for instance, when a word that should not be accented on the final syllable is thus accented, or vice versa. The other sort of incorrectness appears when, for example, one fails to observe the proper grammatical distinctions—namely, between masculine and feminine, singular and plural, past and future, and the like—as shown in the art of grammar.

[12] Clarity renders the discourse plain and perspicuous. A discourse is clear when couched in words and sentences which are both specially proper to the subject and are in current use.

[13] Artistic Composition consists of a uniformly elegant combining of the words. We achieve this when we take care to avoid the recurrence of the vowels in too close succession, or of consonants that make the sentence too heavy. An

7. Literally, ". . . melted without being at rest. . . ."
8. See Book IV, *passim*.

אם אמר: "חבה או איבה אחזתך"; משל השני: "חקרת חקקת חשבת חשבונות". במאמר הראשון נכפל נחות הה׳, שהיא מאותיות הנוח, ובשני נשנת הח׳ פעמי׳ רבות. עוד ראוי להשמר מתכיפת תיבה אחת בעצמה, כמו שיאמר: "מהסבה הראשונה היתה הסבה האחרונה לסבה לעלולים רבים". עוד, ראוי שנשמר מהרגל נפילת התיבה באופן מתדמה, כגון: "חברים מקשיבים מלעיבים מכאיבים". עוד, נשמר מחלק התבה לחלקים, כגון שיאמר: "חכם אתה מדני — כל סתום לא עממוהו — אל" [יח׳ כ״ח ג׳]· חלק "דניאל" לשני חלקים. עוד, נברח חבור ארוך מהתבות או מהמאמרים עד שיקוצו האומר והשומעים.

[14] ההאותות הוא הנותן המאמר כלול מהיופי, מצד החלוף הנמצא בו; ותחלק אל יופי המאמרים, ויופי הענייני׳. יופי המאמרי׳, כאשר נמצא במאמר מן הקשוט והעדי דבר לא יעלם· ויופי הענינים הוא, כאשר יופי זה הדבר בענינים בעצמם. ואמר "מצד החלוף הנמצא בו", כי כאשר המאמר הולך באופן אחד, הוא נעדר היופי וההאותות· במדרגת מה שהיה מראה אחד, לבן, או שחור, או זולת זה. והנה הצייר יפאר מלאכתו במראים מתחלפים, כי כאלה יחפצו האנשים· וכן הענינים במאמרים.

[15] גם אין ראוי שיעלם כי מה שנאמר הנה מהכפל, וההשנות, וזולת זה ממה שספרנו, אינו הותר מה שנאמר מהם ביפויים ההלציים; כי המכוון מהם הנה, כשיפסידו צחות הלשון וערבותו, וינהגהו בכבדות· ואם מה שיאמר ביפויים הוא זולת זה.

[16] והנה שלמה המלך כלל כל הנאמר בכאן בב׳ פסוקים, והוא מה שאמר במשלי: לב חכם ישכיל פיהו, ועל שפתיו יוסיף לקח· צוף דבש אמרי נועם, מתוק לנפש ומרפא לעצם [מש׳ ט״ז כ״ג — כ״ד]. וזה, כי במה שאמר "לב חכם

1 השני] הב׳[ד] ‖ 3 תיבה] תבת[ד] ‖ 5 מקשיבים מלעיבים] מלעיבים מקשיבי׳[כ] ‖ 8 האומר] האומרים[כ] | והשומעים] והשומעי[ד] ‖ 14 יפאר] יתפאר[ב] ‖ כי מה] כימה[ד] ‖ וערבותו] ועריבותו[כ] ‖ 22 ומרפא] ומרפה[ד] ‖

example of the first: if one should say *ḥibbāh 'ō 'ēbhāh 'ªḥāzathᵉkhā.*[9] An example of the second: *ḥāqartā ḥāqaqtā ḥāshabhtā ḥeshbōnōth.*[10] In the first sentence there is a double occurrence of the vowel indicated by *hē,* one of the *matres lectionis,* while in the second there are too many repetitions of the consonant *ḥeth.* We must also be on our guard against too immediate repetition of the same word, like saying: "Because of the former cause, the latter cause became a cause of many caused effects." Further, we should carefully avoid overemployment of the same word ending, as: *ḥª bhērīm maqshībhīm mal'ībhīm makh'ībhīm.*[11] Again, we should beware of sundering a word into parts, as to say: "**Thou art wiser than Dan—there is no secret they can hide from** him—**iel!**" [Ezek. 28:3], with the name "Daniel" divided into two parts. And we should also avoid combinations of words or sentences of such length as to disgust both speaker and hearers.

[14] Appropriateness confers upon the discourse a finished beauty derived from the variety present in it. It divides into Figures of Diction and Figures of Thought. It is a Figure of Diction when the wording includes no small amount of embellishment and adornment, a Figure of Thought when such beauty is that of the thought itself. Tully[b] says[12] "beauty derived from the variety present in it" because when the discourse proceeds monotonously, it is as lacking in beauty and appropriateness as anything which is all of one color, white, black, or any other. The painter, indeed, adorns his work by using different colors because people find such variety pleasing; the content of speeches should likewise be varied.

[15] It should not go unnoticed, also, that what has here been said about recurrence, repetition, and the like, is no mere superfluous addition to what we say about these matters in our discussion of the Figures of Speech.[13] Our point in discussing them here is to show that they are capable of marring the elegance and agreeableness of the language, and make it ponderous; our discussion of them as Figures, however, is of a quite different character.

[16] Now all that has been set forth in the present chapter was summed up by King Solomon in two verses,[14] his statement in Proverbs, which reads:

> **The heart of the wise teacheth his mouth,**
> **And addeth learning to his lips.**
> **Pleasant words are as a honeycomb,**
> **Sweet to the soul, and health to the bones**
>
> [16:23–24].

9. "Love or enmity hath seized thee"—illustrating hiatus.
10. "Thou hast searched, thou hast prescribed, thou hast reckoned reckonings"—alliteration.
11. "Attending, scoffing, pain-inflicting companions."
12. Literally, ". . . and he said. . . ."
13. In Book IV.
14. Here allegorically interpreted; cf. i.2, note 19 above.

---

b. *R. ad H.* 4.13.18.

ישכיל פיהו״, רצה הדבור השפל, אשר אין המכוון ממנו כי אם ההשכלה, ר״ל, שישכילו האנשים. ואמר ״חכם״, כי זה אחד מתנאי המליץ, כאשר התבאר למעלה; והרצון ב״לב״, שכל, כמו: לבי ובשרי ירננו אל אל חי [תה׳ פ״ד ג׳]. ושעורו הוא, ששכל החכם ישכיל השומעים מאמרו; ויהיה ״ישכיל״ יוצא לשלישי. והנה אין ספק שזה המאמר הוא על דבור השפל, אשר יבוקש ממנו לבד שיעמדו האנשים על אמתת הספור בנקלה. ואחר כן אמר: ״ועל שפתיו יוסיף לקח״: רצה בזה המאמר הדבור הבינוני, לכן אמר ״יוסיף לקח,״ ר״ל, שיוסיף בו ערבות ומתיקות מה שלא היה בדבור השפל; ואשר זה ענינו הוא הדבור הבינוני. ולזה אמר בלשון הוספה לבד, כי יספיק לו מעט מהתוספת עד שיעבור השפל. והנה בא בזה המאמר בהדרגה מן הפחות אל הנכבד; וכבר התפרסם למעלה הנרצה בתיבת ״לקח״. ואחר כן אמר: ״צוף דבש אמרי נועם״: הגיע עתה לתכלית מה שאפשר מן הצחות והנעימות אשר בדבור. ורצה בזה שיבא אל אשר הוא נעים וצח מכל הצדדים, שהוא הדבור הנשא; ולזה אמר: ״אמרי נועם״ — המאמרי׳ אשר בהם מן הנעימות כפי מה שאפשר — ראויים שיהיו כמו ״צוף״, אשר בו מן המתיקות מה שלא יעלם. ואמר אחר כן: ״מתוק לנפש ומרפא לעצם״, ר״ל, שיהיה זה הנעימות אמתי, לא הטעאיי, עד שראוי שיושג בו המבוקש מצד ערבותו אל נפש השומעים, ויקבל בזה השומע תועלת, אל מה שהוא נוגע בהצלחת הנפשות והצלחת הגוף גם כן, כפי הענין במאמ׳; וזה לא יעשה במאמרים ההטעאיים.

[17] גם רמז אל ההעתקת המאמר מן השפל אל האמצעי, ומן הבינוני אל הנשא, במאמר אחד. ושעור הכתוב, שהחכם הוא מתחיל לפעמי׳ מן הדבור השפל, והולך ממנו בהדרגה אל הבינוני, עולה מן הבינוני אל הנשא. אמנם, שיבא מן השפל אל הנשא בזולת אמצעי, זה אינו, כי העתקת הענין מן ההפך אל ההפך בזולת אמצעי הוא ממה שימנע.

[18] ועד הנה הגיע הנרצה ממנו לאמרו בזה החלק:

4 ישכיל] יסכיל[ד] | ישכיל] יסכיל[כ] || 10 וכבר] וכבד[ר] || 16 הנעימות] הניעמות[ר] || 21 לפעמי׳] לפעמ׳[ר] || 22 עולה] עו׳[ר] ||

Solomon's words, **the heart of the wise teacheth his mouth,** are a reference to the Simple Style, the sole purpose of which is enlightenment, that is, so that people may achieve understanding. He said **the wise,** because wisdom is one of the requirements indispensable to the speaker, as was explained above;[15] and **heart** means intellect, as in the verse **My heart and my flesh sing for joy unto the living God** [Ps. 84:3]. Solomon is saying, in effect, that the wise man's intellect will enlighten all who hear his discourse; the verb **teacheth** is transitive and requires an object [''mouth'' = discourse]. There can be no doubt, then, that this statement refers to the Simple Style, of which it is required only that people readily understand the facts as described. By the immediately following statement, **And addeth learning to his lips,** Solomon meant the Middle Style; he therefore said **addeth learning:** the speaker, that is, should add to it the pleasing quality and sweetness which the Simple Style lacks; the Style thus endowed is the Middle Style. His particular reason for using the term **addeth** was this, that a little supplementation is enough to enable the Middle Style to transcend the Simple. In this statement, then, he has gone gradually from the less to the more highly esteemed; what was meant by the word **learning** has already been made plain. Next he said: **Pleasant words are as a honeycomb;** now he has come to the acme of elegance and pleasantness in Style. By this he meant that the wise man should achieve what is pleasant and elegant in all possible respects, to wit, the Grand Style; and that is why he said: **Pleasant words**—discourses of the utmost pleasantness—should be **as a honeycomb**, that in which sweetness is so eminently present. And next: **Sweet to the soul and health to the bones,** that is, that this pleasantness should be genuine, not faulty, so that by virtue of its pleasingness to the soul of the hearers, the speaker's purpose is deservedly achieved, and so that the hearers, too, receive a benefit, alike psychological and physical, corresponding to the content of the discourse; such will not be the effect of faulty speeches.

[17]Solomon also made allusion to the shifting of the style from Simple to Middle, and from Middle to Grand, within a single discourse. The import of the passage is that the wise speaker, sometimes beginning with the Simple Style and passing gradually from it to the Middle, ascends from the Middle to the Grand. He does not, of course, proceed from the Simple directly to the Grand with nothing between, since an unmediated shift from one opposite to another is scarcely possible.

[18] What we meant to say in this Book has here reached its limit.

15. Cf. i.2. 14–16 above.

השער השני

כולל י״ח פרקים.

4–20 פרק ב׳, פרק ג׳, וכו׳] [פרק] ב׳, [פרק] ג׳, וכו׳[ד] || 6 וקווינטיליאנו] וקינטיליאנו[ד] || 8 החמוסים] ההחמוסים[כ]

BOOK II[1]

Comprising Eighteen Chapters:

1. Literally, "The Second Gate."

פרק א׳

פרק ההצעה לזה המאמר.

[1] אחרי התבארו סוגי הדבורים, והה׳ הדברים הצריכים למליץ, וחלקי
ההמצאה — ר״ל פתיחה, ספור, חלוק, קיום, התרה, חתימה — ראוי לנו
5 שנלמוד איך יושמו בהרגל אלה החלקים בהצטר׳ אל ג׳ סוגי הדבור, ר״ל,
המקיים, והמשפטי, והעצתי. ויען המקיים הוא בשבח וגנות, כאשר התבאר, וזה
אפשר בערכו שיהיה בהצטרף אל פרטי מה· ותקון הפרט הוא קודם לתקון
הכלל, כי לא ישוער תקון הכלל או קלקולו כי אם מצד הפרטים המרכיבים
אותו· ראינו להתחיל בזה בסוג המקיים, ולהקדימו גם אל המשפטי מצדדים:
10 אם מצד שהמשפטי הוא יותר כבד, והעתקת המתלמד היא מן הקל אל הכבד,
אבל לא להפך; אם מצד שקודם יפול באדם השבח או הגנות ממה שישיגהו
היותו מתעצם במרירות לפני כל יודעי דת וד׳· והוא מבואר שאפי׳ קטן בעריסה
אפשר שנכון בו השבח או הגנות בתארי גופו, ובדברים זולת אלה. וא״כ נתחיל
מן סוג המקיים· עוד נלך בהדרגה אל המשפטי, שהוא דבר אפשרי שיפול
15 ביחידים· ונסיים בעצתי, שהוא ענין נופל בכללות ובהנהגת המדינות:

פרק ב׳

מהדברים המדותיים אשר ישובח בהם האדם.

[1] ויען קצת מהשבח והגנות נופל במדות, ראינו להביא בזה המקום קצת מן
הדברים המדותיים אשר ישובח בהם האדם, כפי מה שיאמר הפילוסוף בא׳
20 מההלצה, אחרי אשר נגדור הנאה והמעלה.

5 בהצטר׳] בהטרכם[c] || 12 [וד׳][c] | בעריסה] בערסה[c] || 14 מן סוג] מסוג[c] ||

---

12 אס׳ א׳ י״ג ||

CHAPTER 1

The Introduction to This Book

[1] Now that we have explained the Kinds of Cause, the five Faculties needed by the orator, and the Parts of Invention—namely, Introduction, Statement of Facts, Division, Proof, Refutation, and Conclusion—we must learn how these parts should be handled in the three Kinds of Cause—Epideictic, Judicial, and Deliberative. Since Epideictic includes Praise and Censure, as has been explained,[1] since praise or blame is possible only as attaching to something specific, and since the amendment of the specific must precede amendment of the general—for amendment or vitiation of the general is inconceivable except in terms of the specific instances which compose it—we have thought it best to begin here with the Epideictic Kind of Cause. The following considerations, moreover, have decided us to give priority to the Epideictic even over the Judicial: in the first place, the Judicial Kind is the more difficult, and the learner should be made to advance from the easy to the difficult, rather than the reverse. Second, a man will encounter praise or censure long prior to any involvement in bitter judicial controversy before **all that know law and judgment** [Esth. 1:13]; obviously, we may praise or find fault with even an infant in the cradle for its physical attributes and other characteristics. This being so, we shall begin with the Epideictic Kind, then proceed gradually to the Judicial—the potential experience of some individuals—and end with the Deliberative, which affects the generality of men and the government of States.

CHAPTER 2

The Ethical Qualities for Which a Man Is Praised

[1] Since praise and blame are in part incidental to character, we think it well to introduce at this juncture some of the ethical qualities for which a man will be praised, according to what the Philosopher[a] says in Book I of the *Rhetoric*.[1] First, however, let us define what is excellent, and virtue.

1. i.3.5, above.

1. While JML generally follows T in this section, he alters, abridges, omits, and adds comments of his own.

a. T56 ff./A72 ff.; cf. *Rhet.* 1.9 (1366a ff.).

[2] אמנם הנאה הוא הדבר המשובח, וטוב, וערב, מצד מה שהוא טוב הנבחר בגלל עצמו. והמעלה היא קנין משער לכל פעל הוא טוב מצד אותה ההשערה, או יחשב בו שהוא טוב. ואולם חלקי המעלה הם: החסידות, ר״ל, היושר הכולל· הגבורה· הותרנות· יראת חטא· גודל המחשבה· ענוה· נדיבות· לבוב· 5 חכמה. ואלה המעלות, מהם בהצטרף אל האנשים, ומהם לא. אולם אשר הם בהצטרף אל האנשים, הם כמו הגבורה, והנדיבות, והותרנות, וזולתם; וייוחדו אלה מאשר אינם בהצטרף, למה שאלה יקבלו הפחות והיתר בערך אל העתים ובערך אל האנשים. כי הגבורה יותר טובה בעת המלחמה ממה שתהיה בעת השלום, ומעלת הנדיבות והותרנות יותר תשובח אצל הצריכים מאשר תשובח 10 אצל הבלתי צריכים. אמנם אשר אינם בהצטרף אל האנשים, כגון היראת חטא והלבוב, הם טובים בכל עת בשוה.

[3] ואחר התישב זה, נספר גדרי המעלות הנזכרות, ונאמר: החסידות היא מעלה יתרה, אשר למענה ינתן לכל איש מבני אדם חקו הראוי לו, כשעור מה שתצוה הדת; והעול הוא הפך זה. הגבורה היא מעלה יפעל האדם בה 15 הפעולות המועילות בעריצות וחוזק, כפי מה שתצוה הדת; ומורך לבב הפך זה. היראת חטא היא מעלה המונע מרדוף אחר תאות הגוף על זולת מה שתצוהו הדת; והבלתי ירא חטא הפך זה. הנדיבות היא מעלה פועלת הנאה המפרסם בממון; והנבלה הפך זה. אמנם, מעלת הותרנות תבדל מהנדיבות בפחות ויתר, שהותרנות יותר רב מהנדיבות; ולכן יותר ראוי שנאמ׳ שהותרנות הפכו הנבלה, 20 והנדיבות הפכו הכילות. וגדל המחשבה היא מעלה יהיה בה נעימות הפעולות הנשגבות; וקטן הנפש הפכה. והענוה היא מעלה יפעל בה מן הרוממות וההתנשאות כפי הראוי; והגאות הפך זה. והלבוב היא מעלת השכל אשר בה יהיה נעימות ההסתכלות והעצה, עם מציאות המעלות המדותיות לו, אשר המה מכשרון התבונה. אמנם גדר החכמה, ומיניה וחלקיה, החקירה בה בזולת 25 זה המקום.

[4] ובכלל, פעלות המעלות יהיו משובחות כאשר היו משוערות ביושר. ומה

4 חטא] חט^ד || 9 אצל] אל^כ || 10 צריכים] הצריכים^כ || 13 יתרה] ישרה^ט | כשעור] בשעור^ט || 15 בעריצות וחוזק] בעריצות^gט בחריצות^aט העריצות^bט في الجهاد ^א | שתצוה] שתצוה׳^ד || 24 התבונה] התכונה^ט || 26 היו] יהיו^כ ||

[2] The excellent is the praiseworthy thing, good and somehow justly pleasing, that is chosen for its own sake. Virtue is a bent for determining that some act either is, on grounds of the very appraisal, good, or will be thought to be good. Now the components of virtue are: scrupulous righteousness, that is, complete uprightness; courage; liberality; fear of sin; high-mindedness; humility; generosity; intelligence; wisdom. Of these virtues, some are relative to other persons, some are not. Those which are relative to other persons are, for example, courage, generosity, liberality, and the like; and these are set apart from the virtues which are not relative to others, inasmuch as they may take on less or more importance, depending on the times and the persons involved. For courage is a greater excellence in a time of war than in a time of peace, while the virtue of generosity or of liberality will receive more praise among the needy than among those who are not in want. As for the virtues which are not relative to other persons, like fear of sin and intelligence, they are goods that at all times are equally great.

[3] So much established, we may proceed to define the aforementioned virtues. Scrupulous righteousness, we may say, is the preeminent[2] virtue whereby every individual human being will be given his proper due in accordance with the measure enjoined by law; the contrary of this is injustice. Courage is the virtue whereby a man will perform beneficial actions with force[3] and power as enjoined by the law; and the contrary is timidity of heart. Fear of sin is the virtue which restrains the pursuit of illicit bodily pleasures; to lack fear of sin is the contrary of this. Generosity is the virtue that effects what is patently excellent by means of money; and meanness is its contrary. (The virtue of liberality is, of course, distinguished from generosity in degree of magnitude, liberality far exceeding generosity; it would be more proper, therefore, to say that the contrary of liberality is meanness, while the contrary of generosity is niggardliness).[4] High-mindedness is the virtue that produces the fairest of noble deeds, while smallness of soul is its contrary. (Humility is the virtue that effects the right sort of elevation and exaltation, pride being the contrary of this).[5] Intelligence is that virtue of the intellect which makes possible the grace of insight and counsel, and the existence, as well, of those moral virtues which derive from soundness of understanding.[6] As for the definition of wisdom, its kinds and divisions, this is the subject of inquiry elsewhere.

[4] In general, the acts effected by the virtues will be praised when they are

2. JML: יְתֵרָה; T/A: יְשָׁרָה < عادلة = "upright, straightforward, impartial.

3. JML: עֲרִיצוּת = "tyranny, causing dread, force"; *sic* T^{g}, but T^{a} reads חֲרִיצוּת = "diligence, industry," and this goes back to a misreading of Averroes' في الجهاد "in war" as اجتهاد = "diligence." The other Paris MS (T^{b}) reads: "forceful, beneficial actions" (הָעֲרִיצוֹת).

4. This sentence is a comment by JML; it is unrepresented in T.

5. Sentence unrepresented in T.

6. *Sic*, JML; T/A: ". . . from fittingness-of-disposition." The reading in JML's text (תְּבוּנָה) differs from that of Todros (תְּכוּנָה) by a single letter (כ/ב), each easily mistaken for the other.

שישובח בהם האדם הפעולות העצומות המצערות, אשר יהיה תגמולם הכבוד
לבד, כי הפעולות אשר תגמולם הכבוד טובות מהפעולות אשר תגמולם הממון;
והפעולות אשר אין המכוון בהם תועלת עצמו — אדרבה, אפשר שישיגהו
מהם נזק — ראוי שישובח בו האדם. עוד אמר הפילוסוף, שאשר לא יטמאו
בפעולות אשר יתנולו בהם אנשי הזמה, אבל יוכיחם בפעל ומעשה, הם בעלי
מעלה ראוי שישובחו בה. וכן לבישת הבושת אצל זכרון הגנויות תורה על
המעלה, לפי שכבר יחשב באדם שהבושת ימנעהו מאותו הפחיתות. ויהיה
לפעמים ג״כ העדר הבשת אצל זכרון הנוולים אות ישובח האדם בו, וזה שכבר
יחשב שהאדם יעטה בשת וכלימה אצל זכרון הגנויות כאשר פעלם, או הגיעו[1]
לידו, או הוא תאב שיפעלם. ואמר עוד, שאהבת הנצוח ואהבת הכבוד ממה
שישובח האדם בם, לפי ששניהם אותות יורו על בחירת המעלות, לא להשגת
ממון: אם אהבת הנצוח, הנה תורה על בחירת הגבורה· ואם אהבת הכבוד,
תורה על בחירת כל המעלות. ולכן, היו המעלות הנכספות הנבחרות אשר לא
יכוין בהם בעליהם השגת הממון וקנייתו, לפי שזה יורה על רוממות המעלה. גם
הפעולות אשר ישובח בהם האדם הם שישאר זכרם שמור לנצח אצל בני אדם.
והראוי שישובח בו ג״כ האדם, שיהיה נותן לאוהביו וזולת אוהביו, לנכרים
אצלו או בלתי נכרים, שכבר יחשב שרוממות מעלת הנדיבות היא נתינת הממון
לכל.

[5] אמנם ההמון יטעו בקצת מה שנאמ׳, וישבחו מי שאין ראוי זה לו לחשבו
מעלה· כגון שיחשבו המוסר עצמו לסכנות גבור, והמפזר ותרן, וכן בנוהג
מנהגם. עוד אמר, שראוי שישובח האדם בפני האוהבים, ויגנה בפני השונאים;
גם ישבח בדברים אשר הם שבח אצל בעלי המקום, ויגנה בהפכם, כי אין כל מה
שישובח ויגונה שוה בערך אל המקומות:

1 [המצערות][ט g] המשערות[ט a] الشاقة [א] || 3 אדרבה] אדרבא[כ] || 9 הגיעו[1]] הגיע[כד] || 12 אם] או[כ] ||
14 יכוין] יכווין[כ] || 15 בהם] בה׳[ד] || 19 וישבחו] ויחשבו[כ] || 21 בפני... בפני <בפני...בפני>[ד] ||
23 שישובח [ויגונה][כ] ||

6 תה׳ ל״ה כ״ו || 9 תה׳ ק״ט כ״ט ||

[1] So ט.

deemed just. Those for which a man will be praised are the mighty, burdensome acts whose sole recompense is honor, for acts whose meed is honor are better than those whose reward is money; and acts that are not motivated by selfish advantage—such as may, on the contrary, result in injury to one's self—are those for which a man should be praised. The Philosopher[b] also says that those who do not defile themselves with the acts by which men of evil purpose disgrace themselves, but who rebuke the latter for such act or deed, possess a virtue for which they deserve praise. Similarly, to feel shame[7] when disgraceful acts are mentioned is indicative of virtue, since a feeling of shame may be confidently expected to deter one from the particular shortcoming involved. Sometimes, however, the absence of shame when disgraceful acts are mentioned may also be an indication that a man is on this account praiseworthy, since it may be assumed that he will **put on . . . shame** [Ps. 109:29] and humiliation at the mention of disgraceful acts only when he has actually committed them, or if they have come to hand for him to commit, or if he has felt an overwhelming desire to commit them. Again, the Philosopher[c] says that love of victory and love of honor are among the qualities for which a man is to be praised, for both are signs that the virtues are preferred, not the gaining of wealth: love of victory since it indicates a preference for courage, love of honor since it indicates preference for the virtues *en bloc*. The virtues which are most favored and preferred, therefore, are those not intended by their possessors to be the means of obtaining and holding wealth, for such disinterestedness is indicative of the loftiness of the virtue. The acts, moreover, for which a man will be praised are such as are likely to be forever preserved in human remembrance. And it is praiseworthy in a man to be one who gives both to those who love him and to those who do not, both to those known to him and to those whom he does not know, for the giving of financial aid to all alike may be regarded as the virtue of generosity at its height.

[5] The mass of mankind, to be sure, will err in regard to some of the instances that have been discussed, and will praise one who properly ought not to be thought virtuous. They may, for instance, think, that one who deliberately puts himself into jeopardy is courageous, that a spendthrift is liberal, and so in all like instances. The Philosopher[d] also says that a man should be praised in the presence of his friends and censured in the presence of his enemies; further, that he should be praised for things which are held worthy of praise by the people of that particular place, and should be blamed in respect of the contrary, for not everything worthy of praise or of blame is equally so everywhere.

7. Literally, "... being clothed with shame," a reminiscence of Ps. 35:26; Todros thus renders A's "being embarrassed" (خجل).

b. T58/A74; cf. *Rhet.* 1.9 (1367a).
c. T59/A76; cf. *Rhet.* 1.9 (1367a).
d. T63/A82; cf. *Rhet.* 1.9 (1367b).

פרק ג׳

היאך יושמו בהרגל חלקי המאמר בערך אל סוג המקיים.

[1] אמר טוליאו בג׳ מההלצה החדשה, שהקדמות השבח או הגנות ילקחו מאחד מג׳ ענינים: אם מן הדברי׳ אשר מחוץ· אם מעניני הגוף· אם מעניני הנפש.

[2] אם מן הדברים אשר מחוץ, כגון הדברים הבאים בקרי והזדמן אם טוב ואם רע, כגון: היחס, ההתלמדות, הממונות, מיני היכלת, התפארת, המדינה, האהבי׳, וזולתם· והדברים ההפכי׳ לאלו. אם מעניני הגוף, הם אשר לגוף בטבע מן התועלת והעדרו, כמו: הזריזות, העריצות, היופי, והבריאות· או ההפכי׳ לאלו. אם מעניני הנפש, הם הדברים הבאים מצד העצה והמחשבה, כגון: התבונה, אשר קראנוה למעלה הלבוב· והצדק, הנקרא למעלה היושר הכולל, או חסידות· הגבורה, או גדלת הנפש· ההגונות, אשר קראנוה למעלה ירא חטא, וגדרו טוליאו בשהוא אשר בלבו הגונות התאוות, ר״ל, לקיחת התאוו׳ באופן הגון וראוי; וכן גם כן ההפכיים לאלו.

[3] ואחר התישב זה, נאמר שהפתיחה בזה הסוג ראוי שתלקח אם מצד עצמנו, אם מצד האיש אשר בערכו המאמר, אם מצד השומעים, אם מצד הדבר בעצמו.

[4] אם מצד עצמנו, כגון שנאמר לשומעים: ״רבותי, אני משבח פלו׳, מצד שהכרח הוא שישובחו האנשים מאשר בהם מין מהמעלות״[1]. או שנאמר: ״אני משבח אותו בכונה, לתכלית יודעו צדקותיו וטובותיו, שזאת ההודעה לא תהיה ערומה מהתועלת.״ או שנאמר: ״אני משבח אותו כדי שתדעו בזה טוב לבבי, שאינו יכול להתאפק לבלתי שבח הראוי לו.״ ואם נכוון הגנות, נאמר ההפך, כגון שנאמר: ״אני מגנה פלני על צד ההכרח, כי ראוי הוא לכל אדם לגנות האנשים הראויים לו.״ או: ״שבכונה ראוי לעשות זה, לתכלית תודענה חטאתיו ומדותיו המגונות, למען ישמר האדם ממנו ולא יחשבהו לירא אלקי׳ וסור מרע״. או: ״שאני מגנה אותו כדי שתראו צדקתי, כי לא ידעתי אכנה, ולחמול או לכסות על בעלי הפחיתיות״.

8 ההפכי׳] ההפכים[כ] || 13 הגונות התאוות] הגונות וד התאוות[ד] |[ר״ל לקיחת התאוו׳][כ] || 19 מהמעלות[1]] מה עלות[כד] || 25 אלקי׳] אלוקים[כ] ||

25 מש׳ ג׳ ז׳ || 26 איוב ל״ב כ״ב ||

[1] Correction indicated by context.

CHAPTER 3

The Handling of the Parts of the Discourse in the Epideictic Kind of Cause

[1] In Book III of the New Rhetoric, Tully[a] says that premises of praise or blame are taken from one of three categories: External Circumstances, Physical Attributes, and Qualities of Character.

[2] If from External Circumstances, the premises will be such as come about by accident or chance, whether for good or for ill: descent, education, wealth, kinds of power, glory, country, friendships, and others, and the contraries of these. If from Physical Attributes, the premises will derive from such advantage or lack of advantage as the body may have by nature: agility, strength, beauty, health, or the contraries of these. If from Qualities of Character, the premises will be manifestations of counsel and thought: the understanding which above we called intelligence, the justice which is above called all-inclusive uprightness or scrupulous righteousness,[1] courage or greatness of soul, the seemliness which above we called fear of sin—and which Tully defines as the state of one in whose heart is a seemliness of the appetites, that is, a seemly and proper manner of indulging the appetites—and so, too, the contraries of these.

[3] This established, we may say that the Introduction in this type of cause should be drawn from our own person, or from the person under discussion, or from the hearers, or from the subject matter itself.

[4] If the Introduction is drawn from our own person, we may, for example, say to our hearers: "Gentlemen, I am praising so-and-so because, when people have any kind of virtue in them, it is our duty to praise them." Or we may say: "I praise him purposely so that his righteous deeds and the good he has done may become known to others, for to make this known will not be devoid of utility." Or: "I praise him in order that you may come thus to know the goodness of my own heart, which is unable to refrain from giving praise to one deserving of praise." If our intention is to censure, we speak to the contrary effect; for example, we may say: "I am constrained by duty to censure so-and-so, for it behooves everyone to censure those who deserve censure". Or: "It is proper to do this to the end that his sins and shameful traits of character may become known, so that one will be on guard against him and not regard him as one who **fears God and departs from evil**" [Prov. 3:7]. Or: "I censure him in order that you may see that I am myself just, **for I know not to give flattering titles** [Job 32:22], nor to spare or give protective concealment to the vicious."

1. I.e., "saintliness" (חֲסִידוּת).

a. *R. ad H.* 3.6.10 ff.

[5] אם מצד האיש אשר בערכו המאמר, אם נכוון השבח, נאמר: ״שהוא נמנע בערכי לספר כל תהלותיו״; או: ״שראוי לשבחו בראש הומיות, ועל גבי מרומי קרת;״ או: ״שנאמר שטובותיו רבו כמו רבו, עד תלאה לשון בני אדם לבא עד תכליתם.״ ואם נכוון הגנות, נאמר באופן הפכי למה שנאמר בשבח.

[6] אם מצד השומעי׳, כגון שנאמר, אם נכוון השבח: ״שאין דברי בפני גמולי מחלב, עתיקי משדים, שהם חכמים, ונבונים, וידועים בדרכי פלו׳ ומעלליו, יותר ממני.״ ואם הם אינם מכירים בו, נאמר:״שישר בעינינו לספר בשבחיו לפני השומעים האלה, כי הם, למעלתם, ידמו פעולות החסידים ובעלי הכשרונות; יהיה זה השבח שב גם כן אליהם, שהם במדרגתו מן השלמות, או יותר גבוהה.״ ואם נכוון הגנות, נאמר ההפך, כגון שנאמר: ״שיש לי לספר דברים מעטים בזה, למה שהם מצד חכמתם ותבונתם מכירים בו יותר ממנו.״ ואם אינם יודעים בו, נאמר: ״שראיתי לדבר בפניהם מפעולותיו הנשחתות, כדי שיוכלו להשמר ממנו· גם כי ידעתים באופן מן השלמות יגנו אותו יותר ממני.״

[7] מצד הדבר בעצמו, כגון שנאמר: ״שהענין בעצמו במדרגה מן השלמות עד יראתי פן אחטא בלשוני, וישמטו ממני רוב תועלותיו ושבחיו״; ואם נכוון הגנות, נאמר בהפך.

[8] אמנם הספור בזה הסוג, אם נרצה לעשותו, נספר דבר מה ממעשיו מכוערים או הגונים, עם שמירת מה שנאמ׳ למעלה מענין הספור, שיהיה בלשון נגלה, ולו[2] פנים מן ההראות, וזולתם ממה שהתבאר.

[9] ואם החלוק, ראוי שנגיד הדברים שנרצה לשבחם או לגנותם, כגון שנא׳: ״אני משבח פלני (או: מגנהו) מצד שלשה דברים״; אחר כך ראוי לנו שנאמר סדרם לפי הזמן, ר״ל, ״זה עשה בזמן פלוני, וזה בזמן פלוני״, וכן בהדרגה.

[10] ואם הקיום, נתחיל בו מעניני הנפש, שהם היותר חשובים ועקריים, ואחר כך מעניני הגוף, הגונים או בלתי הגונים, או מהענינים אשד מחוץ. ואם

2 גבי] גפי[ת] || 6 וידועים] ויודעים[ד] || 8 האלה] האלו[ג] || 10 נכוון [<אל>][ג] || 19 ולו[2]] ולא[כד] || 24 [ואם][כ] ||

2 תה׳ ט׳ ט״ו | מש׳ א׳ כ״א || 2–3 מש׳ ט׳ ג׳ | זכ׳ י׳ ח׳ || 5–6 יש׳ כ״ח ט׳ | דב׳ א׳ י״ג || 15 תה׳ ל״ט ב׳ ||

[2] Corrected in accordance with i.8.4, above.

[5] When the Introduction is drawn from the person under discussion, if praise is our purpose, we may say: "It is a thing impossible for me to **tell of all** his **praises**" [Ps. 9:15]; or: "It were fitting to praise him **at the head of the noisy streets** [Prov. 1:21] and **atop the heights[2] of the city**" [9:3]; or we may say: "His acts of goodness so **increase as they have increased** [Zech. 10:8] that it would wear out the human tongue to reach their end." If censure is our purpose, we shall express the contrary of what we say in praise.

[6] When the Introduction is drawn from the person of the hearers, if our purpose is to praise, we may, for example, say: "My words are not addressed to **them that are weaned from the milk, them that are drawn from the breasts** [Isa. 28:9], since these are **wise men, and understanding and knowledgeful** [Deut. 1:13], more than am I, of the ways and doings of our subject." If the listeners are unacquainted with the man, we may say: "We deem it right to recount his praises before those in this audience, for they, in their virtuous deeds, are comparable to saints and men of high principle;[3] let this praise of him apply to them as well, since the degree of their perfection is equal to or above his." If our purpose is censure, we shall say the contrary; for example: "I have but little to tell my hearers about this man, since they, by virtue of their wisdom and insight, know more about him than I do." In the event that they do not know him, we may say: "I think I should speak of his immoral acts in the presence of those in this audience so that they may be on their guard against him; for I know, too, that the state of their perfection is such that their censure of him will exceed mine."

[7] When the Introduction is drawn from the subject matter itself, we may, for example, say: "The matter is in itself so perfect that I fear lest **I sin . . . with my tongue** [Ps. 39:2] and leave unmentioned most of its advantages and praises." And if our purpose is to censure, we shall say the contrary.

[8] As to the Statement of Facts in this Kind of Cause, if we should wish to make one, we may give some account of the man's deeds, abominable or worthy as the case may be; and we should observe, as well, what has been said above about the Statement of Facts[4]—that it must be clear and plausible and possess the other qualities that have been set forth.

[9] In the Partition, we should announce the several things we desire to praise or to blame. We may, for example, say: "I am going to praise (or: censure) so-and-so on three counts"; we should then state these in their chronological order, to wit, "Such-and-such he did in so-and-so's time, and thus-and-thus in the time of so-and-so," and so on, step by step.

[10] In the Proof, we should begin with Qualities of Character, since these are the most important and fundamental, and then go on with either Physical Attributes, adequate or inadequate, or with External Circumstances. When dealing

2. *Sic*, JML; B: ". . . upon the highest places . . ." (גַּבֵּי for גַּפֵּי [B]).
3. Literally, "possessors of fittingness."
4. See i.8.4, above.

מהענינים אשר מחוץ, אם מהיחס אם הוא גדול, נאמר (אם נכוון השבח נאמר[3])
שהוא הולך בעקבות אבותיו, או שהוא גדול המעלה מכל מה שלפניו מבני
משפחתו; ואם הוא שפל היחס, נאמר שעם היותו נעדר המסייעים מצד בני
היחס והמשפחה, מכל מקום הוא בא מעצמו אל זה השלמות הגדול, וידיו רב
5 לו. ואם נכוון הגנות, אם יחסו טוב, נאמר שהוא כלימת המשפחה וחרפת
אבותיו· ואם אין יחסו הגון[4], נאמר שהוא מוסיף עון על עונם וחרפה על
חרפתם. ואם מההתלמדות, אם נכוון השבח, נאמר שהוא כבר התלמד במעלות
ובכשרונות ובטוב הפעלות בכל ימי הנערות· ואם נכוון הגנות, נאמר ההפך.

[11] ואחר כך נבא אל עניני הגוף, הגונים או בלתי הגונים. אם נכוון השבח,
10 אם מהיופי, נאמר שיפיו לא הזיק לו כמו שהזיק לרבים אחרים, כאלו תאמר
לאבשלום וזולתם, ולא היה אליו לחרפה; ואם הזריזות והעריצות, נאמר שהוא
לא נהנה כי אם בדברים החשובים וההגונים; ואם הבריאות, נאמר שזה הוא לו
מצד חכמתו ותבונתו, להיותו בלתי נשמע אל התאוה, ועושה עניניו במשקל
ובמשורה. ואם נכוון הגנות, אם עניני גופו הגונים, נאמר שהוא מרגילם בעברה·
15 היופי בזנות, העריצות להרוג האנשים מבלי פשע, ולהכות באגרוף רשע; גם
בריאותו מרגילו בכל תועבות.

[12] ואחר כך נחזור אל הדברים אשר מחוץ משותפים עם עניני הנפש,
ונראה: אם לו מן הממונות וגנזי זהב וכסף, או אוצרות חשך, העניות והדלות?
מה לו ממיני היכלת והתפארת? מן האהבים ומן השונאים? ומה היה ענינו עם
20 השונאים, ומי גרם לו השנאות? ובאי זו אמונה, או חבה, או משמרה, הרגיל
האהבות? והיאך היה ענינו עם הממונות או עם החסרונות? היאך הרגיל כחו
ויכלתו? כאלו נאמר אם היה גדול הנפש וגבור כנגד השונאים, או אם מדותיו
גרמו לו השנאות; ואם היה ותרן נדיב בממונו, או להפך; ואם הרגיל היכלת
במשפט וביושר, או עות אדם בריבו· או הרגיל בגאוה ורוממות, או בענוה. ואם
25 מת, ראוי שנאמר מה היתה סבת מיתתו; ונשוב אל ד׳ מדות העקריות
והראשיות, ר״ל, התבונה, הגבורה, הצדק, והיראת חטא, ונראה אם התנהג[5]

1 [מהענינים אשר מחוץ][כ] | [מהיחס] מהיחש[כ] || 3 ואם הוא שפל היחס <ואם הוא שפל היחס>[ד] |
המסייעים] המייעים[כ] || 6 הגון[4]] הגוף[כד] || 8 הפעלות] המעלות[כ] || 10 לא] לו[כ] || 19 ממיני] מימיני[כ] ||
20 השנאות] הנשאות[כ] || 21 הרגיל] הרגילם[כ] || 25 היתה] היה[ד] || 26 חטא] חט[ד] | התנהג[5]] תתנהג[כד] ||

5–4 דב׳ ל״ג ז׳ || 15 איוב ל״ג ט׳ | יש׳ נ״ח ד׳ || 18 יש׳ מ״ה ג׳ || 24 איכה ג׳ ל״ו ||

[3] *Sic*, both כ and ד.

[4] Correction based on context.

[5] Correction indicated by context.

with the External Circumstance of descent, if this should in his case be illustrious and our purpose is to praise, we may say that he walks in the footsteps of his forefathers, or that he is more virtuous than any previous member of his family; if he should be of humble descent we may say that, though he lacked the support of kinsmen and family, he yet managed alone to achieve this great degree of perfection: **his hands . . . contend for him** [Deut. 33:7]. If blame is our purpose, and his descent should be noble, we may say that he is the shame of his family and a disgrace to his forebears; but if his ancestry is ignoble, we may say that he has added his own crime to theirs, and his disgrace to theirs. On the score of education: if praise is our purpose, we shall say that he has been schooled in virtue, sobriety of character, and good deeds throughout his entire childhood and youth; and the contrary, if we would censure.

[11] Coming next to Physical Advantages or Disadvantages, if our purpose is to praise the subject on the score of beauty, we may say that his beauty never harmed him as it harmed many others—Absalom,[5] for example, and others; nor did it ever become a cause of reproach to him. On the point of agility and strength, we may say that he used these gifts to advantage only in causes which were important and honorable. As to health, we may say that it is his by virtue of his wisdom and understanding, in that he does not give way to lust, but in matters affecting health acts with due proportion and moderation. If our purpose is to censure, and this in respect of our subject's Physical Advantages, we may say that he habitually uses these for vicious ends: his beauty for prostitution, his strength to slay men who are **without transgression** [Job 33:9], **and to smite with the fist of wickedness** [Isa. 58:4], and even his health for the practice of every kind of abomination.

[12] Then we shall revert to External Circumstances and Qualities of Character in combination, and consider: Does the subject possess wealth, stores of gold and silver, or are his **the treasures of darkness** [Isa. 45:3]—poverty and penury? What kinds of ability and what titles to fame are his? What kinds of friends or enemies does he have? What was his quarrel with his enemies? Who has procured him enmity? With what faithfulness, devotion, or sense of responsibility has he practised friendship? How has he dealt with wealth or with want? How has he habitually used his power and abilities? We shall, for example, say whether he has been magnanimous and courageous toward his enemies, or, on the other hand, whether his character has brought him enmity; whether he has been liberal and generous with his wealth, or the contrary; whether he has always used his abilities with justice and uprightness, or, on the contrary, so as **to subvert a man in his cause** [Lam. 3:36]; whether it has been his habit to act proudly and arrogantly, or, on the contrary, with gentle humility. If he is dead, we should tell what was the cause of his death. We should, moreover, have recourse to the four essential and cardinal traits of character—intelligence, courage, justice, and fear

5. Cf. 2 Sam. 14:25-26, 18:9-15.

בצדק, בתבונה, בגבורה, וביראת חטא, או בהפכם.

[13] והנה בארנו כל הצדדים אשר יפול בהם השבח והגנות· אלא שלא יתחייבו כלם לכל מאמר שישובח או יגונה, אבל ראוי שילקחו הצדדים הנופלים באמת, וההכרחיים לפי ענין וענין.

[14] אמנם החתימות ראוי שתהיינה קצרות, ותתמצענה ביניהם הרחבות תכופות וקצרות, כאילו נאמר: ״הנה בארנו שבח פלוני מעניני הנפש והגוף, והדברים אשר מחוץ; ומפני שהצדק הוא שרש כל המעלות, וזה נמצא בו על השלימות, ראוי א״כ שישובח במקהלות, ויהללוהו בשערים.״ ומה שהבאנו כאן, ״שהצדק הוא שרש כל המעלות״ כו׳, היא הרחבה· ושאר מה שנמשך לזה מבואר.

פרק ד׳

הפסוקים המעידים על מה שנאמר· עם דברים מה מהפילוסוף וקווינטיליאנו.

[1] כאשר תתבונן בספרי הקדש בשבח וגנות, שהוא רוב מה שדברו בו הנביאים לרומם המעלות ולהשפיל הפחיתיות עד עפר, תמצא כל הצדדים הנאמרי׳ למעלה אשר בערכם ילקחו השבח והגנות; והמשל במזמור מדוד האומר: למנצח על שושנים לבני קרח [תה׳ מ״ה א׳].

[2] ויש לדעת, קודם שנבא אל באור הפסוקים, שזה המזמור נעשה ברוח הקדש על המשיח, ופעולותיו, והדברים שראוי לשבחו, בין מעניני הגוף, בין מעניני הנפש, בין מהדברים אשר מחוץ, כאשר יתבאר; והוא מחקה את המשיח כאלו היה נמצא אז בזמן ההוא ומדבר אתו פנים בפנים; הנה זה המאמר בדבור המקיים, ובשער השבח ממנו. עוד ראוי שתדע שהשושן, לפי מה שנחשוב, הוא

1 וביראת] או ביראת[כ] || 13 וקווינטיליאנו] וקינטיליאנו[ד] || 14 בספרי הקדש] בספרי׳ הקדשי׳[ד] || 16 והמשל] והמשו׳[ד] | מדוד] מד׳[כד] ||

8 תה׳ ס״ח כ״ז | מש׳ ל״א ל״א || 15 יש׳ כ״ו ה׳ ||

of sin, and consider whether he has conducted himself with justice, intelligence, courage, and fear of sin, or with the opposite of these.

[13] We have now explained all the categories into which praise and censure fall, although not all are required in every discourse of praise or censure. Choice should be made, however, of those categories which are in fact pertinent and essential in each case.

[14] Concluding remarks should be brief; frequently, however, brief amplifications may be inserted. We may, for example, say: ''We have now shown the qualities of character, the physical advantages, and the external circumstances for which our subject is praised; and since justice, the root of all the virtues, is found in him to perfection, it is fitting that he be praised **in full assemblies** [Ps. 68:27], that **they praise** him **in the gates**'' [Prov. 31:31]. Our introducing here of the words ''justice, the root of all the virtues,'' and so forth, is an amplification; the rest, the consequence of this premise,[6] is thus demonstrated.

CHAPTER 4

Verses of the Bible Which Attest What Has Been Said Above; and Some Remarks by the Philosopher and by Quintilian

[1] When you study praise and censure in the Holy Books—the main content of the speeches made by the prophets for the purpose of extolling the virtues and of **laying** the vices **low . . . even to the dust** [Isa. 26:5]—you find all the considerations mentioned above with regard to which praise and blame are formulated. This is exemplified in the Davidic Psalm entitled: **To the Leader. In the mode of Shoshannim, for the sons of Korah** [Ps. 45:1][1]

[2] Before proceeding with the exposition of the verses, it should be understood that this Psalm, composed through the instrumentality of the Holy Spirit, deals with the Messiah, with his deeds, and with the qualities for which one should praise him—Physical Attributes, Qualities of Character, and External Circumstances, as will be shown. The Psalmist[2] depicts the Messiah as if the Messiah were alive at that time, and the Psalmist were speaking with him face to face. This discourse, then, belongs in the class of Epideictic and, within this

6. The consequence: ''it is fitting that he be praised. . . .''

1. Translation in accordance with JML's conception of the Psalm.
2. Hebrew ''he.''

הפרח שקורי׳ יילאו׳ יש לו ו׳ עלין, והו׳ מגזרת שש; ושפתותיו שושני׳ [שה״ש ה׳ י״ג], ר״ל, דמיו׳ בריח, כמו שסוף הפסוק מעיד עליו באמרו, נוטפות מור עובר, שמבואר בעצמו כי הרצון בו דמיון מצד הריח. והנה מהדברים ריחניים נבא אל השגת בעל הריח׳ וכן מתכונות המשיח ופעולותיו, שהיו לו בלבו ברוח הקדש, הוא בא אל השגת המשיח וענינו. ועם שאפשר לומר כי ״שושנים״ היה אולי אחד מכלי הנגון, או מין ממיני יחסי השיר נסכלים אצלנו, מכל מקום רמז בזה גם שידבר בעניני משיח מאמר שלם, עם כל חלקיו — שהם ששה, ר״ל, פתיחה, ספור, חלוק, קיום, התרה, חתימה, כמו שיתפרסם — במדרגה נעימה וערבה, כאשר יערבו לנפש ויחזיקו הלבבות, במדרגת הדברי׳ הריחניים.

[3] עוד, אין ראוי שיעלם שתבת ״שיר״ בלשון הקדש לפעמים תורה על דבר סתום, כוזב לפי הנגלה — על דרך ״מיטב השיר כזבו״׳ ולפעמי׳ על דבר נאמר על צד נעימות המוסיקא, אף על פי שפשטו אמתי ונגלה. משל הראשון, שיר השירים אשר לשלמה [שה״ש א׳ א׳]׳ משל השני, ותען להם מרים, כו׳ [שמ׳ ט״ו כ״א]; ובזה האופן האחרון נלקחה תיבת ״שיר״ בזה המקום.

[4] ומה שאמר ״ידידות״, מן מה ידידות [תה׳ פ״ד ב׳], והיא תיבה נאמרת בלשון הקדש על הפלגת החבה; ובאה בזה המקום בחסרון המתואר, ומשפטו ״דברות ידידות״, כמו כעדר הקצובות [שה״ש ד׳ ב׳]; ועשיר יענה עזות [מש׳ י״ח כ״ג]. ורצה ב״דברות ידידות״ שני אופני הדבור, ר״ל, הנשא והבינוני, שהם נכספים מאד לבני אדם. וכאלו עשה החלוק, ואמר שהוא ידבר בזה המזמור באחד מב׳ פנים, ר״ל, פעם בדבור הנשא, ופעם בדבור הבינוני, ולא ירד אל השפל כלל.

2 דמיו׳] דמיון[ג] || 6 אחד] א׳[ד] | ממיני] מימיני[ג] || 8 יתפרסם] יתפרס[ד] || 12 שפשטו] שפשוטו[ג] || 15 מן] מין[ג] | נאמרת] נאמר׳[ד] || אדם] האדם[ג] ||

---

9 מש׳ י״ג י״ט ||

class, in the division[3] of "praise." You should, moreover, note that the *shūshan* (*shōshān*) is, as we think, the flower called "lily" (*giglio*);[4] it has six sepals, being etymologically derived from *shēsh* [= "six"]. **His lips are as lilies** [Song of S. 5:13] means comparable in fragrance, as is attested by the end of the verse, **dropping with flowing myrrh,** where, as is obvious, the intended meaning is a comparison in point of fragrance. Plainly, then, from things that are fragrant we come to understand a possessor of fragrance; and so too, from the qualities and deeds of the Messiah which, through the Holy Spirit, the Psalmist had in mind, he came to understand the Messiah and his function. While it is possible to say that *shōshannīm* was perhaps a musical instrument, or one of the metres of poetry which we no longer know, the Psalmist's use of this term at any rate also suggested that he would pronounce, on the attributes and qualities of the Messiah, a complete discourse with all its parts—which are six, namely, Introduction, Statement of Facts, Partition, Proof, Refutation, and Conclusion, as is well known—parts altogether as sweet and pleasing when they are **sweet to the soul** [Prov. 13:19] and captivate hearts, as fragrant things.

[3] It should, furthermore, not go unnoticed that the term *shīr* ["song"] in the holy tongue sometimes refers to a composition which is unclear in meaning and, on the surface, false—in the sense of "The best of the song is its falsity"[5]—while at times it denotes an utterance set to music, even though its literal sense is factual and plain. An example of the first is **The Song of Songs, which is Solomon's** [Song of S. 1:1], of the second, **And Miriam sang unto them,** etc. [Exod. 15:21]. It is in this latter sense that the term "song" is to be taken in the passage under consideration.

[4] The Psalmist's usage here of *ye dhīdhōth* ["loves"][6] may be understood from *may-ye dhīdhōth,* **How lovely . . .** [Ps. 84:2]; in the holy tongue it is a term employed hyperbolically to express esteem. It appears here with omission of the noun it modifies, the full expression being "lovely [utterances]"; comparable uses are **like a flock of shorn** [ewes] [Song of S. 4:2] and **the rich** [person] **answereth impudent** [answers] [Prov. 18:23]. By "lovely utterances" the Psalmist meant the two Styles of Utterance, namely, the Grand and the Middle, which men so highly prize. He was here forming a Partition, as it were, saying that he would speak in this Psalm in one of two styles, now in the Grand Style and now in the Middle, but would not descend to the Simple at all.

3. Literally, "gate."

4. Hebrew transliteration, reflecting JML's pronunciation of Italian: ייליאו. Commonly translated "lily," the *shūshan* still constitutes a problem to students of biblical botany. See *Encyclopaedia Biblica* [Heb.], VII (Jerusalem, 1976), s.v.

5. Attributed to Aristotle, this saying (no. 2861 in I. Davidson's *ʾŌṣar happithgāmīn w^e hamm^e shālīm* [Jerusalem, 1964]) is twice cited in the thirteenth-century *Maḥb^e rōth ʿImmānūʾēl hāRōmī* [The Cantos of Immanuel of Rome], VIII, 227, and XXI, 161–62; see D. Jarden's edition (Jerusalem, 1957), 149, and 390. L. Dukes, *Naḥal Q^e dhūmīn* (Hanover, 1853), 54–59, points out that Immanuel also cited the *bon mot* in his commentary on the Song of Songs. JML's knowledge of the saying may well have derived from either of these works by Immanuel.

6. Here taken by JML as an adjective meaning "lovely [ones]," i.e., an adjective used substantively.

[5] ואחר התישב זה, נחזור אל הפסוקים. ונאמר ששעור הפסוק הראשון הוא כן: ״משכיל שיר ידידות״, ר״ל, הנותן ההשכלה התמימה כפי מה שראוי נתן למנצח, ועל ידו נתן לבני קרח, לשורר אותו ״על שושנים״: אם יהיה הרצון ב״שושנים״ אחד ממיני הנגון, או מנעימות המוסיקא. אמנם, אם רצה לרמוז ב״שושנים״ ששה חלקי המאמר כמו שבארנו, יהיה שעורו ככה: ״זה שיר ידידות על שושנים״ — ר״ל שנעשה על דרך המאמרים השלמים — ״נתן למנצח, ועל ידו לבני קרח״; ועשה בזה אחד מהיפויים ההלציים, הנק׳ הבלבול. ותבת ״מנצח״ הוא לשון חוזק ונצחון, כמו וגם[1] נצח ישראל לא ישקר [ש״א ט״ו כ״ט]· ויז נצחם על בגדי [יש׳ ס״ג ג׳], שהדם הוא חוזק הגוף ותקפו; והוא החזק שבמשוררים, הפקיד עליהם, כמו לנצח על מלאכת בית י״י [דה״א כ״ג ד׳].

[6] אחר כן אמר: רחש לבי דבר טוב, כו׳ [תה׳ מ״ה ב׳]. תבת ״רחש״ בלשון הקדש מורה על התנועה, ולזה יקרא הכלי שתורגש בו תנועה אצל החוש, בשעת אפיית הדברים בו או בשולם, ״מרחשת״ [וי׳ ב׳ ז׳]; וכאלו אמר: ״לבי הניע דבר טוב״. ולקח הנה העלה תמורת העלול, כי זאת התנועה והרחישה שבא אל השפתים שהם עלולות מהלב. וזה הענין יוחס אל תחלת המאמר, שראוי להתחיל בקול נמוך וכאלו לא יורגש כי אם התנועה, כמו שהתבאר בפרק הרמיזה.

[7] וא״כ אמר: אומר אני מעשי למלך [שם שם]. ויהיה ״מעשי״ בזה המקום מלשון קנין או תקון; משל הראשון, את הנפש אשר עשו בחרן, כו׳ [בר׳ י״ב ה׳]· משל השני, וימהר לעשות אותו [שם י״ח ז׳], ועשתה את צפרניה [דב׳ כ״א י״ב]. ואם הוא מלשון קנין, המכון מזה שאלה הדברים אשר הם בשכלו בקנין — ר״ל, במדרגת קשי ההתרה, שהוא ענין הקנין כאשר התבאר — במאמרות הוא אומר בעבור המלך. ואם הוא לשון תקון, יהיה שעורו שהדברים האלה, המיוסדים בתכלית התקון, נאמרים בעבור מלך המשיח. ואפשר שבא זה הלשון כדי

4 ממיני] מימיני[ר] || 7 הנק׳] הנקראים[ב] || 8 וגם[1]] את[ד] וגם נצח את[ב] | לא ישקר <ולא ינחם>[ב] || 12 החוש] החיש[ר] || 15 שהם] שה״[ד] | יוחס] ייוחס[ב] ||

---

[1] Corrected in accordance with ת.

[5] This established, we may now return to the verses of the Psalm. The import of the first verse, we may say, is as follows: *Maschil. A Song of loves:* that is, the Giver of appropriately perfect understanding[7] gave to the *Leader* and, through him, to *the sons of Korah* this song to be sung in the mode of *shōshannīm*—if, indeed, *shōshannīm* means some type of melody or some musical key. If, however, the Psalmist meant to suggest by *shōshannīm* the six Parts of a Discourse, as we have explained, the import of the verse would then be the following: "This song in lovely Styles of Utterance, in the mode of *shōshannīm*"—a song composed after the manner of perfect discourses—"has been given to the *Leader* and, through him, to *the sons of Korah*"; the Psalmist has here formed one of the Figures of Speech, the one called Hyperbaton.[8] The term *Leader (m^e naṣṣē ^a ḥ)* connotes strength and triumph, as in the passages **And also the Glory** (neṣaḥ) **of Israel will not lie** [1 Sam. 15:29]; **And their lifeblood** (niṣḥām) **is dashed against My garments** [Isa. 63:3]—the blood being the body's strength and might. Thus the "Leader" is the most powerful of the singers, the officer appointed over them, as in the verse **to oversee** (l^e naṣṣē ^a ḥ) **the work of the house** [1 Chron. 23:4].

[6] The Psalmist next says: **My heart is astir** (rāḥash) **with a goodly matter** [Ps. 45:2a]. The term "to be astir" in the holy tongue indicates motion; therefore the vessel in which, during baking or boiling, motion is perceptible, is called *marḥesheth* ["stewing pan] [Lev. 2:7]. It is as though he had said: "My heart has set in motion a goodly matter." Here he has taken the cause for the effect,[9] for this motion, and the stirring that comes to the lips, which are effects, come from the heart. And this effect is closely connected with the beginning of the discourse, for, as has been explained in the chapter on Delivery,[10] one ought to begin in a low voice and almost as if the motion of the lips alone should be perceptible.

[7] The Psalmist continues: **I say, 'My work is for a king'** [2b]. **My work** (ma'^a sai) here denotes either an acquiring or a setting in order. An example of the first meaning: **the souls that they had gotten** ('āsū) **in Haran** [Gen. 12:5]; of the second: **and he hastened to dress** (la'^a sōth) **it** [18:7], **and she shall pare** (w^e 'ās^e thā) **her nails** [Deut. 21:12]. If it denotes an acquiring, the intent is that these ideas, which are in his intelligence through having been acquired[11]—that is, are the kind that are hard to dislodge, for this is the meaning of such acquisition—he is going to put into words on behalf of the king. If, however, the word denotes a setting in order, the import is that these words, arranged with the utmost orderliness, are going to be pronounced on behalf of a king, the Messiah.

7. A noun, *haskālāh,* formed on the same root and stem as "Maschil." The latter is a participle meaning "one who causes to understand."

8. iv.42.

9. Metonymy; cf. iv.40.6.

10. Cf. i.12.7 above.

11. He means ideas learned and remembered, as shown by the next following paragraph (8).

שיובנו ממנו ב׳ הענינים יחד, ר״ל, התקון והקנין. ואמ׳ לשון אמירה באמצע, שהאמירה בסתם לא תאמר נמיכות הקול או רוממותו לבד, כי לשון אמירה נופל בשניהם; וזה הוא ענין הקול הראוי באמצע כאשר התבאר. ואמר א״כ: לשוני עט סופר מהיר [שם], כי זה הקול הנאות באחרונה, כמו שהתפרסם מפרק הרמיזה.

[8] והנה כלל זה הפסוק דברים רבים: תכונת הקול הראוי בכל חלקי המאמר, וזאת היא הרמיזה; והסדור והזכירה, מתבת ״מעשי״, שהוא לשון כולל שניהם כמו שהתבאר; ותתחיל מהם ההמצאה, כי היא הקודמת אליה׳, עם שתיבת ״מעשי״ ר״ל הענינים שהיו נמצאים ועומדים בלבו. וכבר עשה אחד מהיפויים ההלציים בפסוק הראשון· הנה לנו, אם כן, עד הנה כל הדברים הצריכים למליץ, ר״ל, המצאה, סדור, רמיזה, זכירה, צחות. גם רמז בזה הפסוק שהוא ידבר בדבור הנשא באמרו ״למלך״, למה שהוא דבר יותר ראוי בעניני המלכים.

[9] ואל יחשב לנו לזרות מה שאמרנו, שתיבת ״מעשי״ כוללת תקון וקנין, כי אדרבה, אם לא נאמר כן, היה הענין זר בחק המליץ השלם, ר״ל, לדבר בתבות המשותפות, כאשר התבאר בג׳ מההלצה; למה שראוי שידבר בתבות קלות ההבנה, נותנות ההשכלה התמימה. ולזה, אם נאמר שעשה זה בכונה, כי שני הענינים נופלים בענין ולא יפול בו הטעות, נצא מזאת המבוכה; זולת אם יאמר שהיא[2] תורה ג״כ ״מעשה״, מלשון ועשית ארון, כו׳ [דב׳ י׳ א׳]; והנה היא תבה משותפת מורה על אחד מג׳ דברים, ר״ל, על העשיה סתם, ועל התקון, ועל הקנין. וענין העשיה בכאן שקר, אלא שהתר זה הספק למה שיקל שאין יסופק עליו, וזה שאין בכאן עשיה סתם; והנה לא תפסד מפני זה ההכנה השלמה הראויה במאמרים הצחיים.

[10] ונשוב אל באור הפסוקי׳. אחר שספר המשורר דרך כלל מה שרצה לאמר, ובאי זה אופן, שהם דברים ראוים בפתיחה, כאשר התפרסם ממה

1 [ב׳]ג || 3 וזה הוא] וזהוג || 8 אליה׳] אליהםג || 18 שהיא[2]] שהואגד || 21 עשיה] <כלל>ג ||

[2] Correction: J.

Possibly this expression was introduced so that both meanings together might be understood, that is, both setting in order and acquiring. The Psalmist put his "I say" in the middle of the verse because use of a form of the verb "to say," unless otherwise qualified, does not indicate that the tone of voice should be either exclusively soft or exclusively loud, but "to say" is found in usage with both tones; this is an instance of the rule about the tone of voice that is appropriate to the middle part of a statement, as previously explained.[12] He then says: **My tongue is the pen of a ready writer** [2e], for this tone of voice is appropriate to the end of a statement, as is plain from the chapter on Delivery.[13]

[8] This verse, therefore, includes a number of principles: the Quality of Voice appropriate for each of the Parts of the Discourse, this being the Delivery; the Arrangement and Memory implied by the words "my work," a phrase which, as was explained, includes both these functions; while Invention is presupposed by Arrangement and Memory, both because it is their premise and because "my work" refers to matters previously invented and now present in the Psalmist's mind. As he had already formed a Figure of Speech in the first verse, we at this point have all the faculties needed by the orator: Invention, Arrangement, Delivery, Memory, and Style. In this same verse, moreover, the Psalmist, in the words "for a king," has intimated that he will speak in the Grand Style, which is best adapted to dealing with the affairs of kings.

[9] Our assertion that the words "my work" imply both setting in order and acquiring should not be thought anomalous, for on the contrary, if we do not so hold, this would be alien to the fundamental principle of the ideal orator, namely, to use words of ordinary language, as is set forth in Book III of the *Rhetoric;*[a] for it is fitting to speak in words that are easy to understand and afford complete comprehension. If, therefore, we say that the Psalmist purposely contrived to have both senses simultaneously applicable so that there should be no chance of error, we emerge from this perplexity. We emerge, that is, unless it be held that the phrase "my work" also denotes a "making" in the sense of ". . . **and make thee an ark,**" etc. [Deut. 10:1]. In such case, "work" would be a common word that might have any of three denotations: a "making" in the literal sense, an ordering, and an acquiring. Now the literal "making" is not the true sense here; the possible doubt is resolved to the point of nearly complete insignificance because there is no literal "making" in the context. Thus, the notion of the complete preparation that elegant discourses require will not on this account be vitiated.

[10] Let us now return to our exposition of the verses of the Psalm. After the Psalmist has told us in a general way what he wishes to say and how he proposes to say it [Ps. 45:1-2]—these being fitting words in an Introduction, as is plain

12. At i.12.7 above.
13. i.12.7-8.

a. T181/A252 f.; cf. *Rhet.* 3.2 (1404b).

שקדם, אמר: יפיפית, כו׳ [שם שם ג׳]. התחיל לשבח המשיח מעניני הגו׳, שהם קודמים לעניני הנפש, ואמר שיש בו מן היופי אשר בתכלית עד אין כמהו באדם; ולזה אמר "יפיפית", בהכפל הפ׳ והע׳, כי זה ענין הכפל בס׳ הקדש, ר"ל, להורות על חוזק הענין, כמו "ירקרק", "אדמדם", וזולתם. עוד שבחו בעניני הנפש, ואמר שיש לשון למודים ידע לדבר בכל ענין על השלמות· וזה ראוי למלכים, למען יהיו דבריו מקובלים אצל השומעים קבול יערב להם, כי זה ענין מתמיד יותר ממה שיקבלו דבריו על צד היראה והפחד; ולזה אמר: הוצק חן בשפתותיך [שם]. וכן אמר ישעיהו ג"כ ע"ה, לא יצעק, ולא ישא, ולא ישמיע בחוץ קולו [יש׳ מ"ב ב׳], ר"ל, שיקובלו דבריו בזולת צעקה, מצד ערבותם, "ומתק שפתים יוסיף לקח". ובכלל, הדבור השלם הוא הכרחי לבעלי ההנהגה; אלא שהוא מן הפלא למה יחס אלה התארים — הברכה מאת האלקי׳, והגמול הגדול (במה שאמר, על כן ברכך אלהי׳ לעולם [שם]) — טרם אומרו הדברים הגדולים, ר"ל הצדק, והאמת, והגבורה, וזולתם מראשוני ההנהגות. ונאמר אנחנו שאמנם היה הענין כן, כי המדות וההנהגות הם מתחייבות באדם לפי מזגו; עד שמי שמזגו שלם כפי מה שאפשר, כן תהיינה פעלות השכל בו שלמות לפי מה שאפשר. ולזה, כאשר תאר המשיח ביופי הגו׳ ותארו המורה על שלמו׳ המזג, הוא מבואר שתהיינה מדות תכונותיו והנהגותיו בזה האופן מן השלמות ג"כ; והנה תתחייב אליו הברכה, חיים עד העולם. והנה נשלמה הפתיחה.

[11] וא"כ אמר: חגור חרבך, כו׳ [שם שם ד׳—ו׳], והוא הספור, שהוא מספר דברים שעשה. ותהיינה אלה התיבות, "חגור", "צלח", "רכב", מן המקור, ר"ל, שאלה הענינים הם בו לעולם: הגבורה, הנצוח כנגד האויבים, והענוה והצדק

2 מן היופי] מהיפוי[ג] || 3 ענין] העניין[ג] | בס׳] בסבה[ג] || 8 ישעיהו <הנביא>[ג] || 12 אלהי׳] אלקים[ד] || 14 [שמי][ג] || 16 הגו׳] הגוף[ג] || 19 שהוא] והוא[ג] || 21 הגבורה <הנוח>[ג] ||

5 יש׳ נ׳ ד׳ || 9–10 מש׳ ט"ז כ"א ||

from the preceding Book[14]—he says: **Thou art fairer than the children of men,** etc. [45:3]. Beginning his praise of the Messiah with Physical Attributes, since these precede Qualities of Character, he asserts that the extreme beauty found in the Messiah is without compare among men. This is why he says *yophyāphīthā* ["thou art fairer"], with doubling of the first and second radicals, for just this is the function of doubling in the Holy Books, namely, to indicate intensification, as *y^eraqraq* ["very green," e.g., Lev. 13:49], *'^adhamdām* ["very red," 13:49], and the like.[15] Again, he praises the Messiah in respect of Qualities of Character, asserting that here is a **tongue of them that are taught** [Isa. 50:4] which knows how to speak correctly and well on any subject; and a king should possess such a tongue, in order that his words find pleasurable acceptance with his hearers, for acceptance of this kind is more lasting than if the hearers accept his words in fear and trembling; this, then, is why the Psalmist says: **Grace is poured on thy lips** [Ps. 45:3]. In like vein, too, Isaiah, upon whom be peace, says, **He shall not cry, nor lift up, nor cause his voice to be heard in the street** [Isa. 42:2], meaning that his words should find acceptance without vehement outcry, because of their pleasantness and because the **sweetness of the lips increaseth learning** [Prov. 16:21]. The ability to speak correctly and well is, in general, essential to political leaders; but one wonders why the Psalmist has connected these forensic attributes with God's blessing and the supreme reward (in the words **Therefore God hath blessed thee forever** [Ps. 45:3]) before he has made mention of the great qualities—righteousness, truth, courage, and the other first principles of civilized conduct. We, for our part, would say that this is the case[16] because a man's character and conduct are necessarily relative to his disposition; so that if someone's disposition is as sound as it can possibly be, acts of intelligence performed by him will correspondingly be as sound as possible. When, therefore, the Messiah is endowed with the attribute of physical beauty and with that quality which indicates soundness of disposition, it is obvious that his ethical character and conduct must also be equally as sound; and thus the divine blessing—eternal life—is necessarily ascribed to the Messiah. Here the Introduction ends.

[11] Next, the Psalmist says: **The girding of thy sword,** and the rest [Ps. 45:4–6].[17] This is the Statement of Facts, since it recounts acts which the Messiah will have performed. The words, **gird, prosper, ride,** are in the infinitive,[18] meaning that the following characteristics are to be his forever: courage, victori-

14. E.g., i.6.7.
15. Translated in accordance with JML's interpretation. JV and modern lexica: "greenish," "reddish."
16. I.e., the Psalmist's introduction of "forensic attributes" ahead of great qualities of character.
17. JV: **Gird thy Sword upon thy thigh, O might one, thy glory and thy majesty. And in thy majesty prosper, ride on, in behalf of truth and meekness and righteousness; and let thy right hand teach thee tremendous things. Thine arrows are sharp—the peoples fall under thee—[they sink] into the heart of the king's enemies.**
18. So JML, but they are commonly regarded as imperatives; cf. JV.

בהצטרף אל האוהבים· עם שהוא "רוכב על דבר אמת", ר"ל, שהוא מושל
בעיוניות ומנהיג אותם כרצונו, כמדרגת הרוכב בהנהגת הבהמה. ומזה ימשך לו
"הוד והדר"· והם שתי מלות נרדפות, נאמרות על השבח והכבוד אשר בתכלית,
ואלה תכונות רמות במלכים. ותהיה "וענוה צדק" כמו "וענוה וצדק", בחסרון
5 וי"ו, כמו שמש ירח [חב׳ ג׳ י"א]. אמנם גדר הגבורה, והענוה, והצדק התבארו
למעלה, ושעור הפסוק הוא כן: "אתה, הגבור" — לשון קריאה — "מעשיך
העוברים הם אלה: חגור חרבך על ירך לנצח האויבים" — ר"ל, במלחמת גוג
ומגוג — "אשר מזה נמשך לך הוד והדר, וגם צלח, רכב על דבר אמת, וענוה
צדק· תמיד ימינך תורך נוראות ונפלאות מהפלגת הנצחון." וחציך שנונים· עמים
10 תחתיך יפלו, כו׳ [שם ו׳]: אמר "בלב אויבי המלך," שהוא לנוכח ושלא לנוכח
בפסוק אחד, כי כן מנהג הלשון, על דרך: שמעו עמים כלם [מל"א כ"ב כ"ח];
ואל משה אמר, עלה אל ה׳ [שמ׳ כ"ד א׳]. ושעור הפסוק הוא כן: "חציך שנונים
בלב אויבי המלך, עד שעמים תחתיך יפלו"· והנה התמצעו, בין "חציך שנונים"
ו"בלב אויבי המלך", "עמים תחתיך יפלו"· וזהו ההתמצעות, שהוא אחד מן
15 היפויים. ואלה שבחים משתפים מצד הנפש והענינים אשר מחוץ, למה
שהגבורה, והצדק, והענוה הם דברים בנפש, והנצחון, ופעולות הגבורה, הם
מהענינים החצוניים. ועד הנה הגיע הספור.

[12] ואל תפלא באמרנו הדברים העוברים בהצטרף אל המשיח, כי המדבר
ברוח הקדש מדבר בעתיד בתכונת עבר· וספר הנצחון מגוג ומגוג, שיעשה על יד
20 המשיח, כאלו עבר; ובערכו שב "חגור חרבך על ירך", "עמים תחתיך יפלו",
ו"חציך שנונים", וכו׳, כי אחרי זה יהיה שלום בארץ, ולא ילמדו עוד מלחמה. גם

9 וחציך] חציך[ת] || 11 מנהג] דרך[כ] || 14 ובלב] ולב[כד] || 16 הגבורה] מהגבורה[כ] ||

---

21 וי׳ כ"ו ו׳ | יש׳ ב׳ ד׳ ||

ous mastery in confronting enemies, meekness and righteousness in relations with friends; he is a ''rider,'' as well, **on the word of truth,** by which is meant that he controls the speculative sciences and directs them at will, like a rider directing a beast. Consequently, **glory** and **majesty** are to be his, these two words being synonyms, used to express extremely great praise and honor, since they are high qualities in kings. **And meekness** [. . .] **righteousness** is the equivalent of **and meekness** [and] **righteousness,** the particle ''and'' being omitted as in **sun** [and] **moon** [Hab. 3:11]. Clear definitions of ''courage,'' ''meekness,''[19] and ''righteousness'' having been supplied above,[20] the import of the verse is as follows: ''As for thee, O mighty one''—a vocative—''thy past deeds are these: the girding of thy sword upon thy thigh in order to gain victory over the enemy''—that is, in the war against Gog and Magog—''the consequence of this being that glory and majesty are thine, prospering, also, riding on the word of truth, and meekness [and] righteousness; thy right hand always teaches thee tremendous acts and prodigies of extraordinary victory.'' **Thine arrows are sharp—peoples fall under thee—**[they sink] **into the heart of the king's enemies**'' [Ps. 45:6]: the Psalmist says **into the heart of the king's enemies,**[21] thus using both second and third person forms in the course of a single verse, for such is the usage of the language. Parallels are: **Hear, ye peoples, all of them** [1 Kings 22:28];[22] **And unto Moses He said: "Come up unto the Lord**'' [Exod. 24:1]. Now the import of our verse is as follows: ''Thine arrows are sharp—[they sink] into the heart of the king's enemies—so that peoples fall under thee.'' Thus the words **peoples fall under thee** have been interposed between **thine arrows are sharp** and **into the heart of the king's enemies;** this is the Interposition, one of the Figures of Speech.[23] These verses,[24] then, consist of praises common both to Qualities of Character and to External Circumstances, since courage, righteousness, and meekness are qualities within the soul, while victory and deeds of valor belong to External Circumstances.

[12] Thus far the Statement of Facts. Do not wonder at our mention of past events in connection with the Messiah, for one who speaks by the instrumentality of the Holy Spirit can speak of the future as past; and the Psalmist has given an account of the victory over Gog and Magog, which is yet to be achieved through the Messiah, as though this event were already past. It is to this event that the words **the girding of thy sword upon thy thigh . . . peoples fall under thee . . . thine arrows are sharp,** etc. refer, for subsequent to this event there will be **peace in the land** [Lev. 26:6], and **neither shall they learn war any**

19. Or: ''humility.''
20. At ii.2.3.
21. Not ''. . . **thine** enemies,'' as might be expected.
22. JV: ''. . . all of you.''
23. Not listed among the figures discussed by JML in Book IV; presumably this is one of those to which he alludes in iv.68.1.
24. Ps. 45:4–6.

המקור בא במקום העבר, כמו ילדה ועזב [יר׳ י״ד ה׳].

[13] ואמר אחר זה: כסאך אלקים עולם ועד, וכו׳ [שם שם ז׳ — ח׳]; זה החלק מיוחס אל הקיום. והוא מתחיל בו מעניני הנפש, כאשר התבאר למעלה, ואמר שכסאו תמיד, הוא השופט צדק לעולם; ולקח הנה המקום תמורת המקומות, 5 והנה תאר אותו בתארים הנפשיים כאלה לעולם, ואמר שהוא ״אלקים עולם ועד״, לא יהיה פעם בזה התאר, פעם בהפכו. ובא ״אלקים״ בזה המקום על דרך אלהי׳ לא תקלל [שמ׳ כ״ב כ״ז], שהרצון בו השופטים האמתיים והמנהיגים החשובים. גם שבט מלכותו הוא שבט מישור [שם ז׳], כלומ׳, שכל מה שיצוה מצד השלטונות והממשלה הוא דבר ישר, לא זולת זה· וכפל הענין על צד 10 ההרחבה במאמר. ועשה אחד מהיפויים ההלציים, הנקר׳ צחות, ואמר: אהבת צדק ותשנא רשע [שם ח׳], והוא מדמה מה שאמר, כסאך אלהים [שם ז׳]. והנה התחייב מכל זה, ר״ל, מצד הצדק והיושר המפלג, שיהיה לו ״הוד מלכות״, ״נגיד ומצוה לאומים״, ״כי בצדקה יכון כסא״· וזאת היא אחת מן המדות הראשיות, ואולי הגדולה שבכולם, וביחוד אצל המלכים. וזהו המכוון ב״על כן משחך 15 אלקי׳ אלקיך שמן ששון מחבריך״ [שם ח׳]; כלומר, שכמו שהוא מופלג בתכונת הצדק יותר משאר האנשים, כן התחייב על צד הגמול הראוי שיהיה לו שלטונות וממשלה על כלם. וכנה המלכות ״במשיחה״, כי היו מושחים אותו כמין נזר ביום חנכת מלכותו, כאשר התבאר מדוד ושלמה; ואין ספק, התחייב מן זאת המשיחה שמחה, ששון, ויקר לבעליה.

20 [14] וא״כ שב לשבחו מענינים אשר מחוץ, ואמר: מר אהלות קציעות כל בגדותי׳ [שם שם ט׳]· ר״ל, שבגדיו בתכלית הפאר והיופי, מקוטרים מכל אבקת

1 [בא][כ] | ועזב] ועזוב[ת] || 3 מעניני] בענייני[כ] || 6 ועד] וועד[כ] | יהיה] שיהיה[ר] || 7 אלהי׳] אלוקי׳[כ] || 9 השלטונות] השולטנות[כ] || 12 מלכות] המלכות[כ] || 17 כי היו] שהיו[ר] | כמין] כמן[ר] || 20 אהלות] ואהלות[ת] ||

4 תה׳ ט׳ ה׳ || 12 דנ׳ י״א כ״א || 12–13 יש׳ נ״ה ד׳ | מש׳ ט״ז י״ב || 19 אס׳ ח׳ ט״ז || 21 שה״ש ג׳ ו׳ ||

more [Isa. 2:4]. The infinitive, too appears in place of a finite past tense, as in **the hind . . . has calved and forsaken** [(infinitive)'āzōbh] **her young** [Jer. 14:5].

[13] The Psalmist next says: **Thy throne, O Judge, is eternal and everlasting;**[25] **a sceptre of equity is the sceptre of thy kingdom. Thou hast loved righteousness and hated wickedness; therefore God, thy God, hath anointed thee with the oil of gladness above thy fellows** [Ps. 45:7–8]. This section is devoted to the Proof.[26] The Psalmist begins it with the Qualities of Character set forth above, and says that the Messiah's throne is everlasting, since he is **the righteous Judge** [Ps. 9:5] forever. He has here adopted a single topic as surrogate for many, thus endowing the Messiah with attributes of soul that are similarly eternal, and says of him that he is **a Judge, eternal and everlasting,** not of one description at one time, and of its opposite at another. In this passage, the use of *'Elōhīm* [''God''] is after the manner of **Thou shalt not revile** 'Elōhīm [Exod. 22:27], where the meaning intended is ''true judges and important leaders.'' The sceptre of the Messiah's kingdom, moreover, is **a sceptre of equity** [Ps. 45:7]: that is, his every order as head of State and ruler is an act of uprightness, and only this; the repetition of the term **sceptre** is of the kind which amplifies a statement. Employing a Figure of Speech, the one termed Refining,[27] the Psalmist says **Thou hast loved righteousness and hated wickedness** [45:8], which resembles his previous statement, **Thy throne, O Judge,** etc. [45:7]. Now the necessary consequence of all this—the result of such extraordinary justice and equity—is that the Messiah is to have **the majesty of the kingdom** [Dan. 11:21], is to be **a prince and commander to the peoples** [Isa. 55:4]; **for the throne is established by righteousness** [Prov. 16:12]—which is one of the cardinal virtues, perhaps even the highest of all, especially in kings. This too is what is meant by **Therefore God, thy God, hath anointed thee with the oil of gladness above thy fellows** [Ps. 45:8]: in other words, just as the Messiah is far superior to the rest of mankind in the quality of righteousness, so necessarily, as equitably he ought, must he come to have political authority and rulership above them all. The Psalmist uses ''anointing'' as a term for kingship, for they used to anoint the king, as a kind of consecration, on the day of his royal inauguration; this is clear from the instances of David and Solomon.[28] The necessary consequence of such anointing to those possessed of it was doubtless **gladness and joy and honor** [Esth. 8:16].

[14] Next the Psalmist again derives his praise of the Messiah from External Circumstances, saying: **Myrrh, and aloes,** [and] **cassia are all thy garments;**

25. The translation of the verse is here made to accord with JML's exposition. Also, here as often elsewhere, I have given the full citation from the Bible. JML frequently gives the opening words of a citation, and subsumes the rest under an ''etc.''

26. I.e., vv. 7–10.

27. Cf. iv.54, and note what is there said about the relation of Refining to Synonymy.

28. David: 2 Sam. 2:4, 4:3; Solomon: 1 Kings 1:39.

רוכל, עם שהם בהיכלים היקרים והנכבדים, ר״ל, בהיכלי שן [שם]. ומר, וקציעות, ואהלות הם מיני בשמים ריחני׳; ובאה תיבת ״קציעות״ בחסרון ו׳, וכאלו אמר, ״מר ואהלות וקציע׳.״ ותיבת ״מני״ [שם] בתוספ׳ יוד, כמו: מני אפרים שרשם בעמלק [שופ׳ ה׳ י״ד]; ״והיכלי שן״ נמשכת אל ״מני״ על דרך כעל גמולות, כו׳ [יש׳ נ״ט י״ח], שהוא כאלו אמר: ״כעל גמולות, כעל גמולות ישלם״; וכן בכאן, כאלו אמר: ״מן הכלי שן, מן הכלי שן״ ב׳ פעמים; והוא אחד מן היפויים החלציים מורה תוקף העניין והפלגתו. ושעור הפסוק הוא כן: ״כל בגדותיך מן הכלי שן, מן הכלי שן שמחוך בהם, שהוא ענין נפלא הפאר שימצאו ההיכלים משן; הם עם זה מר, אהלות, קציעות, כלומר, ריח להם כלבנון וכערוגת הבשם.״ ובאה העלה תמורת העלול, שזה אחד מן היפויים ההלציים, וזה כי הריח עלול לבעל הריח.

[15] אחר כן אמר: בנות מלכים ביקרותיך [שם שם י׳]. שב לשבחו גם מהענינים אשר מחוץ, ואמר שבין הבנות היקרות אשר תהיינה לו כפלגשים תמצאנה בנות מלכים· על דרך והיו מלכים אומניך ושרותיהם מניקותיך [יש׳ מ״ט כ״ג]; וכאלו אמר ״בנות מלכים ביקירותיך״, ותנועת היוד נבלעה בדגש. והשגל [שם], שהיא המלכה, תהא נצבת לימינו בכתם אופיר [שם], כלומר, מלובשת בגדי זהב אשר להם הרקמה עם אבן יקרה. ועד הנה הגיע הקיום, וגם זה מה שבזה המזמור מהדבור הנשא.

[16] ואמר אחר כן: שמעי בת, כו׳ [שם י״א — ט״ו]; התחיל לדבר בבינוני. ויען

2 ריחני׳] ריחנים[ג] ‖ 3 מני] מיני[ג] | בתוספ׳ יוד] בתוספת י׳[ג] | מני] מיני[ג] ‖ 6 ב׳] שני[ג] ‖ 7 העניין] העני׳[ד] ‖ 9 [הם][ג] ‖ 12 ביקרותיך] ביקירותיך[ד] ‖ 13 מהענינים] מעניינים[ג] ‖ 14 מלכים] מלכם[ג] | על דרך [<בנות מלכים ביקרותיך>][ג] ‖ 15 ביקירותיך] ביקרותיך[ג] ‖ 16 בכתם] בכתר[ד] ‖ 17 בגדי] מבגדי[ד] ‖

9–10 הו׳ י״ד ז׳ | שה״ש ה׳ י״ג ‖

out of ivory palaces, out of [ivory palaces] **they have made thee glad** [Ps. 45:9].[29] That is, the Messiah's garments are of the utmost magnificence and beauty, **perfumed . . . with all powders of the merchant** [Song of S. 3:6], and, moreover, are such as are worn in the most precious and dignified places, namely, **in ivory palaces.** Myrrh, cassia, and aloes are species of fragrant spices; "and," though lacking before the word "cassia," is understood, as though the Psalmist had said "Myrrh, and aloes, and cassia."[30] The word *minnī* ["out of"] has an added *yōdh,* like the same word in **Out of** (minnī) **Ephraim came they whose root is in Amalek** [Judg. 5:14]. "Ivory palaces" is the attracted complement of the preposition *minnī* here [Ps. 45:9], just as "deeds" is the attracted complement of *kᵉ'al* ["according to"] in **According to their deeds, accordingly, He will repay** [Isa. 59:18], which verse is to be understood as if it read "According to their deeds, according to their deeds, He will repay." Similarly, in the verse here being considered, it is as though the Psalmist had twice said **Out of ivory palaces:** "Out of ivory palaces, out of ivory palaces, they have made thee glad"; the device is a rhetorical Figure indicating the force and extraordinary quality of the circumstance.[31] The import of the verse, then, is this: "All thy garments are from ivory palaces, from ivory palaces in which they have made thee glad, for it is a circumstance of wondrous magnificence that the palaces are actually of ivory. In addition, the garments are 'myrrh, aloes, cassia'; that is to say, they have a **fragrance as Lebanon** [Hos. 14:7] and **as a bed of spices** [Song of S. 5:13]." Here the cause is substituted for the effect, this being one of the Figures of Speech,[32] for fragrance is an effect of the possessor of the fragrance.

[15] Next the Psalmist says: **Kings' daughters are among thy glorious women; at thy right hand doth stand the consort in gold of Ophir** [Ps. 45:10]. He is again praising the Messiah, and here too on the score of External Circumstances. He says that daughters of kings will be found amongst the glorious young women who are to be his as concubines; this is after the manner of **And kings shall be thy foster-fathers, and their queens thy nursing mothers** [Isa. 49:23]. It is as though the Psalmist had said "Kings' daughters are among thy beloved women," the vowel represented by the second *yōdh* having been absorbed into the preceding doubled letter.[33] The consort, who is the queen, is to stand at the Messiah's right hand in gold of Ophir, that is, dressed in garments of gold-stuff worked with embroidery and precious stones. The Proof extends to this point; here too is the terminal point of the material in Grand Style in this Psalm.

[16] Following this, the Psalmist says: **Hearken, O daughter, and consider**

29. Translated in accordance with JML's interpretation.
30. Comma (iv.13.1); on the distinction between Comma and Asyndeton, cf. iv.34.2.
31. Duplication (iv.80).
32. Metonymy; cf. iv.40.5.
33. According to JML's interpretation, B's *bᵉyiqqᵉrōthekhā* ("among thy glorious women") is here merely a by-form of *bᵉyaqqīrōthekhā* ("among thy beloved women").

אפשר שיסופק היאך המשיח, בחיר י״י וקדושו, יתערב עם זרים ויחבק היק
נכריה, הוא מתיר זה הספק בשאלה יעזבו דתם וישכחו עמם ובית אביהם [שם
י״א]; וזה החלק הוא ההתרה מחלקי המאמר. ואמר לכל אחת מבנות המלכים
שתעזוב דתה ובית אביה ותשוב לבית ישראל, ובזה האופן יתאו המלך יפיה
5 [שם י״ב], עם שראוי שתכנע אליו ותשתחוה כאחת השפחות לפני אדניה. ואמר
שלא תתאונן לעזבה עמה, אלקיה, ומולדתה, כי באה אל מעלה גדולה ורמה
להיות פילגש המשיח, עד שבת צור — ר״ל, עדת צור, שהיא העיר
המעטירה — תבא אליה במנחה [שם י״ג], שתליץ[3] בעדה אל מלך המשיח, ופניה
יחלו עשירי עם [שם]; ותהיה לה כל כבודה, מסגלת מלכים והמדינו׳, נפך, ספיר,
10 וברקת פנימה [שם י״ד], באוצרותיה· וממשבצות זהב לבושה [שם]. וכאלו אמר:
״כל כבודה לבת מלך פנימה״, ר״ל, כל דבר נכבד ויקר יהיה בגנזיה; ונחסרה
הלמד, כמו: שני שרי גדודים היו בן שאול [שמ״ב ד׳ ב׳], שהרצון בו לבן שאול.
ובכן, תובל למלך [שם ט״ו] מעלפת ספירים, בבגדי זהב ורקמה, ובתולות
ריעותיה אחריה; ובאה ״אחריה״ קדם ״ריעותיה״, והוא אחד מן היפויים
15 החלציים.

[17] ואחר כל זה שב להשלים שבחו׳ המשיח והצלחתו, ואמר, מובאות לך
[שם ט״ו]: אלה בנות המלכים, עם הפלגת התפארת וההוד שספרנו, ״מובאות
לך״, וסרות אל משמעתך לעשות בהם כרצונך, ותובלנה בשמחות וגיל, ותבאנה

1 היאך] איך^ג || 2 [הוא]^ג || 4 יתאו] יתאב^ג || 5 כאחת] באחת^ד || אלקיה] אלוהיה^ג || 8 שתליץ[3]] שהליץ^גד ||

1 משׁ׳ ה׳ כ׳ || 7–8 ישׁ׳ כ״ג ח׳ || 9 קה׳ ב׳ ח׳ | יח׳ כ״ח י״ג || שה״ש ה׳ י״ד || 18 שמ״א כ״ב י״ד | נחמ׳ ט׳ כ״ד ||

[3] Correction: J.

and incline thine ear: Forget also thine own people, and thy father's house; so shall the king desire thy beauty; for he is thy Lord; and do homage unto him. And the daughter of Tyre, the richest of the people, shall entreat thy favour with a gift. All riches [has] **the king's daughter within the palace; her raiment is of chequer work in-wrought with gold. She shall be led unto the king on richly woven stuff, the virgins, her companions, in her train** [Ps. 45:11-15]. The Psalmist has here begun to use the Middle Style. Now since the cause might be brought into doubt over how the Messiah, the Lord's Elect and Holy One, could be on intimate terms with strangers, **and embrace the bosom of an alien** [Prov. 5:20], the Psalmist refutes such doubt by asserting that these women would forsake their religions and forget their own peoples and fathers' houses; so this section constitutes, of the several Parts of the Discourse, the Refutation. The Psalmist, bidding each king's daughter to forsake her religion and her father's house and turn to the household of Israel, since in this way the king would come to desire her beauty, adds that she ought humbly do him homage, like a maid-servant before her lord. Nor, says the Psalmist, should she feel sad at abandoning her people, gods, and native land, for, in becoming the Messiah's concubine, she is entering upon a rank so great and exalted that the **daughter of Tyre** [Ps. 45:13]—meaning the community of Tyre, **the crowning city** [Isa. 23:8]—will come to her with a gift, begging her to intercede with the Messianic King on the city's behalf; **the richest of the people** will **entreat** her **favor.** She is to have **all riches** [Ps. 45:13-14], **treasures such as kings and provinces have as their own** [Eccl. 2:8], **carbuncle, sapphire and the smaragd** [Ezek. 28:13],[34] **within the palace** [Ps. 45:14], in her storehouses; and **her raiment** is to be **of chequer work inwrought with gold** [45:14]. It is as though the Psalmist had said: "The king's daughter has all riches within the palace," that is, every sort of magnificent and precious object is to be among her stores. The *lāmedh* of possession is omitted here in the Hebrew, as in **Saul's son two men that were captains of bands** [2 Sam. 4:2], where the meaning intended is "Saul's son had," etc. And so **she shall be led unto the king** [Ps. 45:15], **overlaid with sapphires** [Song of S. 5:14], in garments of goldstuff and embroidery, with **the virgins, her companions, in her train** [Ps. 45:15]. In the Hebrew, "in her train" precedes "her companions," this constituting a Figure of Speech.[35]

[17] After all this the Psalmist resumes, and completes, the Messiah's praises and the description of his future prosperity, saying, **Brought unto thee** [45:15]: these daughters of kings, as well as the extraordinary glory and majesty which we have described, are to be **brought unto thee,** will **give heed unto thy bidding** [1 Sam. 22:14] for thee **to do with them as thou wilt** [Neh. 9:24]; **they shall be led**

34. "The sapphire, carbuncle, and the smaragd." Cf. Pref.: 3 and i.2.6; the changed order indicates that JML, in this *m^{e}līṣāh*-passage as frequently, is citing Scripture from memory.
35. Hyperbaton (iv.42.).

בהיכל מלך [שם ט״ז]. ושב לשבחו מצד יחס האבות, ואמר: תחת אבותיך יהיו
בניך [שם י״ז], ר״ל, שהוא מזרע המלוכה, מגזע ישי המפואר שהיו בו מלכים
נוראים; ומברך אותו במדרגת הנפטר מהמלך — כמו, ויברך יעקב את פרעה
[בר׳ מ״ז י׳] — ואמ׳ שבניו ג״כ יהיו בזה האופן מן ההצלחה, וימליכו תחת
5 אבותיו, ושהוא יזכיר שמו לעולם במקהלות, עד שכל העמים יודו אותו [שם
י״ח], כל גוים יאשרוהו. וזאת היא החתימה.

[18] ומ״שמעי בת״ [שם י״א] עד סוף המזמור דבר במדרגת הדבור הבינוני,
כמו שיעד במה שאמר, ״שיר ידידות״ [שם א׳], כאשר התפרסם ממה שקדם,
ולא שתף בזה המזמור מהדבור השפל קטנה או גדולה.

10 [19] והנה עלה בידינו שבזה המזמור מדבר בסוג המקיים, בשער השבח; ובו
כל הדברים הצריכים למליץ, ר״ל, המצאה, סדור, זכירה, רמיזה, צחות; עוד
חלקי המאמר, ר״ל, פתיחה, ספור, קיום, התרה, חתימה· ומאמר ״שיר ידידות״
מדמה החלוק בקצת, כמו שאמרנו; והוא משבח מכל הצדדים, ר״ל, מעניני
הנפש, ועניני הגוף, ומהדברים אשר מחוץ; גם כי הוא מתחיל מהדבור הנשא,
15 ומשלים בבינוני.

[20] וביחזקאל, ובירמיה, ובקצת מדברי ישעיה, תמצא מאמרים רבים בסוג
המקיים, משער הגנות.

[21] ואמר הפילוסוף, בקצורו מן ההלצה אשר עשה לאלכסנדר, שאם נשבח
איש מה מצד יחס האבות ומעלותיהם, אם היו כלם חשובים, ראוי שנספר
20 אותם אחד לאחד עד שנגיע אל האיש ההוא אשר נכון בו השבח. ואם
הראשונים היו בעלי המעלה, עם שאשר הם קרובים אל האיש היו אנשי דמים
ומרמה, ראוי שנשבח הראשונים אחד לאחד, ונדלג אלה האמצעיים עם
התנצלות וערמה, באמרנו כי לא רצינו להאריך ולהרבות דברים· עם שמעלות
אבותיו של פלני נודעה בשערים, והוא מן המפרסמות. ואם היה הדבר בהפך,

8 שיעד] שייעד[כ] || 12 ספור <חלוק>[כ] || 18 אשר עשה] שעשה[כ] || 20 שנגיע] נגיע[ד] || 23 לא] לו[כ] ||

---

24 מש׳ ל״א כ״ג ||

with gladness and rejoicing, and **shall enter into the king's palace** [Ps. 45:16]. Again praising the Messiah, this time on the score of distinguished ancestry, the Psalmist says: **In the stead of thy fathers shall be thy sons whom thou shalt make princes in all the land** [45:17]; he means to say that the Messiah is of the royal seed, of the illustrious **stock of Jesse** [Isa. 11:1], which produced revered kings. And blessing the Messiah quite as one blesses a king on taking leave of him—for example, **And Jacob blessed Pharaoh** [Gen. 47:10]—the Psalmist declares that the Messiah's sons too would enjoy prosperity of this kind and hold the kingship **in the stead of** his (and their) forefathers [Ps. 45:17], and that he (the Psalmist) would make the Messiah's **name to be remembered** [45:18] forever **in full assemblies** [Ps. 68:27], so that all **the peoples would praise** [Ps. 45:18] him, **all nations call him happy** [Ps. 72:17]. This is the Conclusion.

[18] From the words **Hearken, O daughter** [Ps. 45:11] to the end of the Psalm, the Psalmist's utterance is on the level of the Middle Style; this is as he had promised in saying **A song of loves** [45:1], as was made plain above, nor did he include in this Psalm any admixture, slight or extensive, of the Simple Style.

[19] In sum, then, we find that in this Psalm the Psalmist is pronouncing an Epideictic discourse of Praise; that herein are all the faculties required of the orator, Invention, Arrangement, Memory, Delivery, and Style; further, that it contains the several Parts of a Discourse—the Introduction, Statement of Facts, Proof, Refutation, and Conclusion—while, as we have said,[36] the phrase "A song of loves" in part represents the Partition; also, that the praise of the subject is drawn from all the categories—Qualities of Character, Physical Attributes and External Circumstances; and finally, that the Psalmist begins in the Grand and ends in the Middle Style.

[20] You will find many Epideictic Discourses of Censure in Ezekiel, Jeremiah, and in some parts of Isaiah.

[21] In the Abridgment of the *Rhetoric* which the Philosopher[b] made for Alexander, he says that if our praise of a man is to turn in some way upon his well-born ancestors and their virtues, where all the ancestors are men of esteem, we should describe them one by one individually until we come to the particular person whom we intend to praise. If the more ancient ancestors were men of virtue, while those closer in time to our subject were bloodthirsty and deceitful, we should praise the earlier forebears individually but pass over the intermediate ones with a prudent apology, saying both that we do not wish to speak at excessive length and that the high virtue of our subject's ancestors is **known in the gates** [Prov. 31:23], is a matter of public renown. If, however, the reverse is

36. *Supra,* par. 4.

b. Cf. *LR. ad A.* 69.24 ff. (1440b ff.).

ר״ל, שהראשונים היו אנשי רשע, והאמצעיים טובים, נתחיל מן האמצעיים ונספר אותם אחד לאחד, ונתנצל שלא התחלנו לספר מראשית היחס לבחרנו הקצור, עם שהוא מפורסם שאלה האנשים, שהם גדולי המעלה, אי אפשר שיבאו מפחותי עמים ואנשי בלי שם. ואם לא נמצא לו יחס אבות כלל, אז נאמר
5 שכחו ועוצם ידו עשה לו את החיל הזה, ובו הגיע כל השלמו׳ שהיה ראוי לכל המשפחה, לא יחסר כל בו. ובשער הגנות נעשה מה שנאמר בהפך.

[22] ואמר עוד, שאם נשבח אותו מצד מעשיו ותכונותיו, נתחיל מהצדק, ואחריו התבונה, ואחריה הגבורה, ואחריה היראת חטא, ואחריה יתר המדות. עוד אמר, שראוי לישמר, בשער הגנות, פן נאמר עניני הנוולים והנבלות כי אם
10 ברמז וחידה, ושראוי לנהוג בגנות הגזומים על צד ההתול למנגדים.

[23] ואמר בא׳ מספר ההלצה שהשגבת הענין ועלויו הוא על פנים רבים: אם שיאמר שהוא היה הראשון באותו הפעל, כמו שנאמר בקין שהוא היה ראש לרוצחים, ובאברהם שהיה תחלה לגרים; אם שהוא פעל בזמן מועט מה שדרכו ליפעל בזמן מרובה, או שפעל בזמן מה תקשה פעלתו. אלה הדברים יפליגו
15 הענין, אם טוב ואם רע.

[24] ואמר קוינטיליאנו, בתשיעי מן השלישי, שהשבחים הלקוחים מעניני הנפש הם השבחים האמתיים, והם לעולם שבחים; אמנם הלקוחים מעניני׳ אשר מחוץ, ומעניני הגוף, הם שבחים אם נרגילם בטוב ההנהגות. כאלו תאמ׳ שהעושר ורבוי הקנינים אינו שבח מצד עצמו, כי אם בהרגילנו אותו בנדיבות,
20 וותרנות, ומתנות לאביונים; וכן היכלת הוא שבח אם ירדוף דרכי הצדק והיושר; והיופי, ותאר האברים, הוא שבח אם לא תמשך מזה הרדיפה אל התאוה. ובכלל, אלה מצד עצמם אין בהם שבח או גנות, כי אם בהצטרף אל הנהגתם והרגלם· ואם הנדיבות, והיושר, וזולתם מן ההנהגות, הם לעולם אמתיים בשבח. והנה נשלם מה שרצינו זכרו בסוג המקיים:

5 לכל] אל כל[כ] || 7 מעשיו] פעולותיו[כ] || 8 חטא] חט[ד] || 10 וחידה] וחיד[ד] || 12 בקין] מקין[כ] || 13 פעל] פועל[כ] || 14 או] אם[כ] ||

---

1 איוב ל״ד ח׳ || 4 איוב ל׳ ח׳ || 5 דב׳ ח׳ י״ז ||

the case, if, that is to say, the earlier ancestors were **wicked men** [Job 34:8] while the intermediate ones were virtuous, we should start with the intermediate ancestors, describe them one by one, and apologize for not beginning the account at the outset of the genealogy, saying that we have not only chosen to be brief, but it is well-known, too, that these persons were so high in rank that they could not possibly have come of the baser sort of people, or could not possibly have been **ignoble men** [Job 30:8]. And if in fact he has no illustrious ancestors, then we say that his **own power and the might of** his **own hand have gotten** him **this wealth** [Deut. 8:17], that the perfection which the whole family ought to have attained has been achieved in him, since he is without shortcoming. In a discourse of Censure, we formulate what has been said to opposite effect.

[22] The Philosopher[c] also says that if we are going to praise the subject for his deeds and qualities we should begin with righteousness, next take up intelligence, then courage, fear of sin, and following this, the other virtues. He says, further, that in a discourse of Censure we should take care not to mention the details of shameful and immoral matters, except allusively or enigmatically, but that in Censure it is proper to use exaggeration in ridiculing our opponents.

[23] In Book I of the *Rhetoric*[37] the Philosopher[d] says that there are a number of ways in which to magnify and enhance the subject. It may be said of a man that he was the first to perform a particular deed; in the case of Cain we may say that he was the first of murderers, of Abraham, that proselytes began with him. Or it may be said that the subject did something in far less time than such an act ordinarily requires, or at a time when such an accomplishment is usually hard to achieve. Such statements make the matter, whether good or bad, outstanding.

[24] In Book III, Chapter 9,[38] Quintilian[e] says that praises derived from Qualities of Soul are the truest and most lasting kind of praises; those derived from External Circumstances and Physical Attributes are only praiseworthy if we put them to honorable use. For example, you may say that wealth and abundance of possessions are not in themselves grounds for praise except as we put them to use in generosity, liberality, and gifts to the poor; likewise, ability is ground for praise when one pursues the path of righteousness and uprightness; and beauty and fine physique are grounds for praise if they do not result in the pursuit of lust. In general, such qualities are intrinsically neither praiseworthy nor blameworthy except as connected with the way they are used and put into practice; whereas generosity, uprightness, and the other virtues are everlastingly true grounds for praise. Here ends our intended treatment of the Epideictic kind of discourse.

37. Here JML paraphrases T/A.
38. *Sic,* JML; modern reference as in source-footnote **e.** Cf. Int., §5(5).

c. Cf. *LR. ad A.* 70.32 ff. (1444b ff.).
d. T62/A80; cf. *Rhet.* 1.9 (1368a).
e. Q. 3.7.12 ff.

פרק ה׳

מסוג העצומי· וקודם מענין העול.

[1] אמר הפילוסוף בא׳ מההלצה, שהעול הוא הזק יהי ברצון על דרך העברה בדת הנימוס. והנימוס, ממנו מיוחד, ממנו כולל. והנימוס המיוחד הוא הכתוב, למען לא ישכח המיוחד בעם ועם, אומה ואומה; ואמנם הנימוסים הכוללם הם הבלתי כתובים שהכל מודים בם, כמו כבוד ההורים ותת תודה למטיב. והפעולות אשר היו ברצון, מהם בהסתכלות ובחירה קודמת להם, ומהם מה שיהיה לא מהשתכלות קודם, אבל מחלשת השתכלות למקום מדה רעה או הרגל. וכל פועל דבר על דרך העול, ולא ימנע אם שיפעלהו מצד עצמו לבד, מרצונו ובחירתו, ואם שלא יפעלהו מצד עצמו ובחירתו· וזה אם שיפעלהו בהזדמן, ונקרא קרי, ואם שיפעלהו בהכרח. ואשר יפעלהו בהכרח, מהם מי שיפעלהו מצד טבעו, להיותו רע בטבע, ואם שיפעלהו מפני מכריח מחוץ. ואשר יפעלהו מצד עצמו, הוא לבדו עלת הויתו, לא דבר אחר מחובר בו מחוץ. ולא ימנע אם שיפעלהו מפני הרגל רע או מדה רעה, אם מפני תאוה ותשוקה; ואם מפני התשוקה, לא ימנע אם שיהיה מפני תשוקת דברית, ואם מפני תשוקה דמיונית· וזה לא ימנע כי ממנו מפני תשוקת כעסנית, וממנו מפני התאוה. והנה א״כ העולנים יעולו לאחד מז׳ סבות: א׳) מפני ההזדמן· ב׳) מפני הטבע· ג׳) מפני האונס· ד׳) בגלל ההרגל והמדה· ה׳) מפני הדבריות· ו׳) מפני הכעס· ז׳) מפני התאוה; וכל אלה חלקי חלשת הסברה, זולת הדבריות.

[2] ואשר יפעלו בהזדמן אין להם תכלית מוגבל, גם לא יהיה העול שבהם מתמיד, כי ההזדמן הוא אשר על המעט, כאשר התבאר במקומותיו. ואשר הוא מטבע המעול הוא מתכונה קיימת, שקועה, ותכליתו הוא תכלית ההפעליות הרעות אשר ידובר בהם אחר זה; ואולם אם יהיה מצד השגעון והשטות, לא יוחס אל הטבע כי אם אל אשר הוא בקרי ובהזדמן. ואשר הם מצד האונס, תכליתם תכלית הפעולות הנעשות בבחירה, אחר שהאונס יקרא לכל הפעלות[1] אשר יפעלו בבחירה. ואשר הם מצד הדבריות, תכליתם הדברים אשר יחשב בהם שהם מועילים, ואם הדברים הערבים. אמנם העול שהוא מהכעס, תכליתו בקשת הנקמה, ואולם העול אשר יהיה במדה או בהרגל, או שהוא מצד התאוה,

3 יהי] יהיה[ט] || 4 ממנו כולל] וממנו כולל[כט] || 5 ואומה] באומה[כ] || 6 כמו] כגון[כ] || 12 מכריח] הכרח[כ] || 14 אם מפני] או מפני[כ] || 15 תשוקת דברית] תשוקת דברנית[כ] תשוקה נחשבת דבריית[ט] || 16 תשוקת] תשוקה[ט] || 18 האונס] האנסות[ט] || 21 במקומותיו] בספר המופת[ט] || 22 מתכונה] מתכונת[כ] || 23 לא] לו[כ] || 25–26 [אחר שהאונס...בבחירה][כ] | הפעלות[1]] ההפעלו[ד] || 27 הערבים] המועילים[כ] ||

[1] So ט.

CHAPTER 5

The Judicial Kind of Cause; but First, on Wrongdoing

[1] In Book I of the *Rhetoric,* the Philosopher[a] says that wrongdoing is the voluntary inflicting of harm in contravention of the law. Law is partly special, partly universal. Special law is the sort recorded in writing, so that the law special to each people or nation may not be forgotten; universal laws, however, are the unwritten kind which all acknowledge, like respect for parents and gratitude to a benefactor. Of voluntary acts, some are premeditated and deliberate, while others are the result not of premeditation but of recklessness due to some bad trait of character or habit. Everyone who does any kind of wrongdoing will necessarily either do it of himself alone, of his own will and choice, or not of himself and of his own choice. In the latter case, he will either do it by chance, and the wrongdoing is then called an accident, or he will do it of necessity. Of those doing it of necessity, some will do it because such is their nature, because they are naturally evil, or will do it because of external compulsion. As for one who does the act of his own accord, he alone, independently of any other external factor, is the cause of its eventuation. This act he will necessarily perform either from a bad habit or a bad trait of character, or from desire and impulse. If from impulse, it will necessarily follow either from a rational impulse, or from an irrational impulse; of acts prompted by irrational impulse, some will necessarily follow from angry impulse, some from desire. Hence wrongdoers commit wrongful acts for one of seven causes: (1) chance, (2) nature, (3) compulsion, (4) habit and character trait, (5) rationality, (6) anger, (7) desire; and all of these, except rationality, come under the heading of weakness in the rational faculty.

[2] Chance acts of wrongdoing have no definite purpose, nor will a particular act of this class occur frequently, for the chance occurrence is a rarity, as shown by its topics.[1] An act that arises from the nature of the wrongdoer is of an enduring, permanently fixed character, and its aim is the same as that of the evil effects to be discussed later; if, however, it arises from madness or lunacy, it is not ascribed to nature but to accident and chance. The aim of acts done by compulsion is the same as that of acts done by choice, since compulsion can cause the occurrence of all acts done by choice.[2] Those based on rationality have, for their aim, things thought to be advantageous, or else pleasant things. Revenge, of course, is the aim of the wrongdoing which arises from anger, while

1. Literally, ". . . as was made clear by means of its topics." T, *ad loc.*: ". . . as was stated in the *Book of the Posterior Analytics* (בספר המופת)"; the phrase is not found in the underlying Arabic of Averroes.

2. Text emended according to T.

a. T64 f./A83 f.; cf. *Rhet.* 1.10 (1368b).

תכליתו התענוג. ולכן, כל הדברים אשר יחשב בהם שהם ערבים יעשו בגלל אחת מאלה הסבות הד׳ אשר יפעלם האדם מצד עצמו, ר״ל, ההשתכלות, והכעס, המדה, וההרגל. ובכלל, כל אשר יפעלו העול מצד עצמם יפעלו בגלל דברים שהם באמת טובות או ערבים, או שיחשבו כן מזולת יהי הענין כן. ולזה, כשנחשוב הגע׳ לעתי׳[2] לאי זה טוב עצום וגדול, נסבול מפני זה מן התלאה והצרה העצומה מה שלא יעלם להגיע אליו· או שנחשוב לפעמים שהרעות טובו׳ מצד שיצילו מענשים גדולים, נקמות, ומארות.

[3] התענוג הוא שנוי אל תכונ׳ מתחדשת פתאום מהרגשת הטבעי לו, והיגון והצער הוא שנוי אל תכונה מתחדשת פתאום מהרגשת דבר בלתי טבעי לו. הערב הוא מורגש אשר יפעל זאת התכונה בנפש, והמצטערים הם המפסידים אשר יפעלו הפך זאת התכונה. והנה כל אשר היה בדבר יותר בטבע, היה יותר חזק התענוג. ולזאת הסבה בעינה היה הדבר אשר במדה והרגל ערב, למה שמה שנרגילהו פעמים רבות ידמה הדבר הטבעי אשר הוא תמידי.

[4] וראוי שתדע שהתאוות, מהם דבריות, מהם בלתי דבריות. והבלתי דבריות הם אשר נשתתף בהם בבעלי חיים, כמו מאכל, משתה, משגל, וזולתם. אמנם תאות השמע והראות — כאילו תאמר: לעשות שרים ושרות· או שנלבש בגדי זהב אם אבן יקרה — אינם ערומות מהדברי׳, כי באלה לא יתענגו הבעלי חיים, ולא נשתתף בהם עמהם; גם כי שני אלה החושים ידמו לדבריות מצד מה: אם השמע, שותף עמו מצד המלות· ואם הראות, מצד הקוים והרמיזות הנעשות אצל המשא ומתן.

[5] גם לא ימנע אם שאשר בו התענוג הוא הווה, ויהיה התענוג בפגישתו· אם שהוא עובר, ויהיה התענוג בזכרונו· ואם שהוא עתיד, ויהיה התענוג בתוחלת. ולזה היה הכעס ערב מצד מה, למה שימצא בו מן התוחלת על נפילת הרע על מי שיכעס עליו; והנה, אחר כך, בקשת הנקמה תערב מצד התקוה, אשר תשיגנו לתת לאיש כפעלו. אמנם הנצוח לא בלבד יערב לאוהבי הנצוח לבד, אמנם יערב לכל בני אדם בכלל· וזה כי הנצוח הוא תשוקה אל ההתנשאות, אשר הוא הנכסף מכל בני אדם ואם יתחלפו בזה בפחות, ביתר. וכן הכבוד, ההגדלה, והרוממות, מבואר מענינם שהם נכספים מכלל המין.

[6] והכפלת הדבר האחד בעינו ערבה מצד הכנסו בהרגל, והמורגל יערב. וכן ההעתקה וההמרה מענין לענין ערב בטבע, מפני הרגשת דבר מתחדש. וכן

4 שיחשבו] שייחייבו[כ] || 5 הגע׳ לעתי׳[2]] הגעת לעתים[כ] || 7 [טובו׳][כ] | מצד] מיד[כ] || 8 תכונ׳] תכונת[כ] | 8–9 [הטבעי...מהרגשת][כ] || 10 והמצטערים] והמצערים[ט] || 12 [שמה][כ] || 15 כמו] כגון[כ] || 19 הקוים] הקיום[כ] || 27 ביתר] ויתר[ט] ||

16 קה׳ ב׳ ח׳ || 17 מל״א י׳ ב׳ ||

[2] I.e., הגענו לעתיד.

that which comes about through character or habit, or is based on desire, has pleasure for its aim. All acts considered pleasing, therefore, as the doer does them for his own sake, are done for one of the following four causes: ratiocination, anger, trait of character, and habit. As a rule, all who commit acts of wrongdoing for their own sakes do so for reasons which really are good or pleasant, or which they so consider even when such is not the case. This is why, if we think we shall in future have gained some great and important good, we will on this account suffer notable hardship and great distress in order to achieve it; or we will sometimes consider evils as goods on the ground that they will deliver us from severe punishment, acts of vengeance, and execration.

[3] Pleasure is an alteration to a suddenly renewed disposition in the soul to feel what is natural to it; pain is an alteration to a sudden disposition to feel something unnatural. The pleasant is a sense experience which effects the former disposition in the soul, and the painful are those injurious experiences that effect the opposite of this disposition. Thus, the more natural the experience, the stronger the pleasure. It is for this very reason that any natively characteristic and habitual action is pleasant: since the act that we are in the habit of doing over and over again is like a constantly recurring phenomenon of nature.

[4] You should know, too, that some desires are rational, some irrational. Now the irrational desires are those which we share with animals, such as those for food, drink, sexual intercourse, and the like. Indeed, even auditory and visual desires—for example, to **get . . . men-singers and women-singers** [Eccl. 2:8], or to be dressed in garments resplendent with **gold . . . and precious stones** [1 Kings 10:2]—are not altogether devoid of rationality, because the animals do not take pleasure in such things, and because we do not share the desire for them with the animals. Both these senses, moreover, resemble rationality in a certain respect: hearing has a side in common with rationality by dint of words, and sight in respect of the delineations and gestures carried out in the course of conversation.

[5] Further, what affords pleasure must necessarily be either now present, in which case the pleasure consists in encountering it; or past, in which case the pleasure consists in remembering it; or future, in which case the pleasure lies in expectation. Hence there is a respect in which anger is pleasant, since it includes some expectation of the falling of evil upon the object of one's anger; it follows, then, that the seeking of revenge is pleasant as a hope, namely, that it will be vouchsafed us to requite the villain according to his deed. Victory, indeed, is pleasant not to those only who love conquest, but to all human beings generally; for winning is a craving for superiority, something yearned for by all men, although in varying intensity, less or more. And it is likewise self-evident that fame, self-magnification, and high station are cravings shared by the general run of mankind.

[6] Repetition of the self-same event is pleasant because it thus enters the category of the habitual, and the familiar is pleasant. Similarly, movement and

הלמוד והחקויים והדמויים ערבים, למה שבאלה יודע הדבקות אשר בין הנמצאות· והתענוג אמנם הוא בהשגת הדבקות אשר בין שני דברים מהדברים הנמצאים בעולם. וענין המציאות, מבואר בעינו שהוא נכסף אצל כל אדם. ולהועיל לקרובים, והשעשוע העיוני, ואהבת הבנים, ואהבת כל אדם פעולותיו ומדותיו שהם טבעיות לו או בהרגל — אין ספק בם שהוא מן הדברים הערבים.

[7] ואחר התישב זה, נאמר שהעול יעוול בחשבו אפשרות עשייתו בערכו, ושיהיה ממה שיעלם ולא יודע, או שיהיה ממה שישכח בזמן מועט אם לא יהיה ממה שיעלם. אמנם בעלי הכח והיכלת והתחבולה הרמה, הם יעשו העו׳ אם לא יעלם, לחשב׳ הנצ׳ מהרע מהפלגת יכלת׳, אם מעשר, אם מקרוב׳, אם מאוהב׳, אם בתחבולות; גם כי יועיל לבעלי התחבולות הוציאם העול באופן לא יחשב עול. גם יקל העו׳ בהצטר׳ אל האוהבים, למה שיקוו מן הרצוי קדם בואם אל מקום הדין. ואוהבי השופטים יעוולו בנקלה, כי לא יפחדו יגיע אליהם העונש מצדם. ודברים רבים זולת אלו יקל העו׳ בערכם, אשר לא זכרתים לבחרי הקצור.

פרק ו׳

מהאנשים החמוסים· והחמס.

[1] הנה בעלי הממון יעשה להם העו׳ לפעמי׳ אם היתה כונת המעוול על הממון, אם לרוב הצרך אליו להיותו עני, אם שהוא יכו׳[1] לשים על עפר בצר ולכנוס סגולת מלכי׳ והמדינות, ומפני זה ירבה מעשה העול. ולזה העשירים יהיו חמוסי׳ מזה הצד, כי אם עוולו העניי׳ לא ישיגו מה שכונו אליו מקבוצת הממון.

[2] והבוטחים בכל אדם עד לא יחושו לרוע תכונות האנשים, יפול בהם העול בנקלה. וכן השומרים מהתבזות במריבות ומחלק׳, גם אלה יחמסו, כי לא יחקרו

4 העיוני] השעשוני[ט] || 5 אין] או[כ] |[בם][כ] || 9 יכלת׳] יכולת[כ] || 11 בהצטר׳] בהצטרך[כ] || 18 יכו׳[1]] יכול[כ] || 19 מלכי׳] המלכים[כ] || 20 חמוסי׳] עשירים[כ] | העניי׳] העניינים׳[כ] || 23 ומחלק׳] ומחלוקת[כ] | יחקרו] יחמסו[כ] ||

18 איוב כ״ב כ״ד || 19 קה׳ ב׳ ח׳ ||

[1] I.e., יכוון.

change from one circumstance to another are pleasant in the case of nature, because a renewal is perceived. Learning and acts of artistic mimesis are also pleasant, since by their means the connectedness of existent things becomes known; the pleasure, indeed, consists of grasping the connection which holds between any two things that exist in the world. It is self-evident that existence is a desideratum with every human being. Also the conferring of benefits upon intimates, intellectual entertainment, the love of children, and the love of every man for the acts and the traits of character which are naturally or habitually his—there is no doubt that each of these belongs among things pleasant.

[7] This determined, we may say that the wrongdoer will commit a wrong when he considers the doing of it possible, and that it will either escape notice and remain unknown, or else, in the event that detection is inevitable, that it will soon be forgotten. Indeed, the strong, able, and exceptionally cunning will even commit a detectable wrong, for they will consider that their extraordinary ability, or their wealth, relatives, or friends, or their cunning will procure them safety from ill; it also avails the cunning to bring off the crime in such manner that it will not be considered a crime. Moreover, the wronging of friends is the more easily perpetrated because they may be expected sooner to be appeased than to come into court. Friends of judges will more easily commit wrong, because they do not fear that punishment will reach them from this quarter. Besides these, there are many other considerations that facilitate wrongdoing, but because I have chosen to be brief, I have not mentioned them.

CHAPTER 6

On the Victims of Unjust Action; and on Unjust Action[a]

[1] The wealthy are those to whom wrong is done if, as may happen, the wrongdoer is intent upon money, whether because the latter is poor and has great need of it, or whether, intending to place **treasure in the dust** [Job 22:24] and to **gather . . . treasure such as kings and provinces have as their own** [Eccl. 2:8], he on this account commits the act of wrong many times. And the reason why the victims of this kind of unjust action are the rich is that to wrong the poor would not achieve the intended garnering of wealth.

[2] Those who are so trusting of every man that they fail to sense the evil in men's dispositions will also easily fall victim to wrongdoing. Likewise, those whose care it is not be abused in quarrels and disputes—they too will be

a. T79 ff./A103 ff.; cf. *Rhet* 1.12 (1372b).

על העול לברחם מהמחלקת. ובעלי העצלה וההתרשלות, ואשר לא ידעו ענין
העול והיושר, ובעלי הבשת, יפול העו׳ עליהם מדי יום ביומו, כי לא יחפשו עליו
ויסכלוהו. גם אשר נבטח בהם שישבחוהו, כגון הקרובים והאחים, או שלא
ירגישו בו, נעוול אותם מבלי פחד למה שאלה לא יחשבו שהאחים יעולו אותו;
5 ואף אם ידע שקבל העול מהם, ישכח׳ קד׳ שיבקר להוציאו מידם במריבה
ומחלק׳. והאנשים אשר נחמסו פעמים רבות, גם אשר הפסידו ריבותם לפני
השופטים, שבו למרמס רגל· וכל אדם יעוולם אחרי היותם בזה האופן מן
החלשה והעדר היכלת, ואין מושיע להם.

[3] והנכרים במדינה, או ביחס, או במדות, או בלשון, או בדת מוכנים שיעשה
10 להם עול למקום התענגות, והעול הנופל בם הוא הבזיון· כי העול יהיה בממון,
והכבוד, והשלום. ופחותי הנפש והפחדנים, אלה יביאו עליהם העול כי לא יירא
האדם מהם כלל· והסבלנים הנשקעים באמת יחמסו ויעולו כי לא יחשב שהם
ינקמו ממנו.

[4] אמנם הדברים הנלקחים בעולנות, הם אם הדברים אשר ראוי שתפול
15 בהם המחילה, ואם שהם יסתרו ויעלמו. אמנם הדברים אשר תפול בהם
המחילה הם הנבזים והמעטים, כי לא יחושו האנשים בהפקדם. אמנם סבות
ההסתר וההעלם הם רבות: אם שיקל שנוי תמונותיהם או גווניהם· או שימצאו
דומים להם אצל העולן עד יחשבו שהם שלו, ולזה יקדימו לקנות ממין הדבר
שירצו לחמום· אם שהם דברים שהם משתנים עם הזמן מבלי שישנה אותם
20 האדם.

[5] אמנם מיני החמס יהיו מול ב׳ דברים, ר״ל אם שיהיה ערב, או מועיל· והם
ימצאו על שני צדדים, אם לדחיית נזק, אם להשארות תועלת; והחמס הוא
שיקח האדם דבר מהעול ברצונו ובבחירתו. ולא יצטרך המתרעם לבד אל שידע
מיני החמסים והפעולות אשר הם עול, והתנאים אשר בהם יהיה חמס ועול,
25 אבל זה ג״כ התחייב בחק המתנצל, למה שהוא יודה[2] לפעמי׳ במציאות הדבר
אשר טען כנגדו, עם שיכחיש שהוא עול; וזה, שיודה בשהוא לקח, לא בשהוא
גנב· בשהוא קלל, לא בשהוא חרף· שהוא בעל בעילת[2] מצוה, לא בשהוא נאף;

5 ישכח׳ קד׳] ישכחם קודם[כ] || 6 ריבותם] ריבות[כ] || 11 יירא] ירא[ד] || 12 והסבלנים] והסכלים[טg] || 18 דומים] דומין[ד] |ממין] מימין[כ] || 22 להשארות] להשארת[ט] || 25 יודה[2]] יורה[כד] || 27 בעילת[2]] בעולת[כד] ||

8 דב׳ כ״ח כ״ט ||

[2] So ט.

victimized because, for the sake of avoiding controversy, they will not prosecute the crime. The indolent, the easygoing, those unacquainted with wrongdoing and uprightness, and the retiring daily fall victim to wrongdoing, because they will not lay it bare, but ignore it. Those too, such as kinsmen and brethren, who may be relied upon to find our act praiseworthy, or not to notice it, we can wrong without fear because they will not deem their brethren capable of such crime; and even when such a victim knows that he has received injustice from them, he will sooner forget it than to seek, in contention and controversy, to bring them to account for it. Men who have been victims many times, and those, too, who have lost their suits-at-law before the magistrates, have repeatedly been trodden under foot; and anybody is liable to wrong them in consequence of the fact that they are so obviously weak and powerless, and have **none to save** [Deut. 28:29] them.

[3] Aliens, whether in citizenship, race, manners, language or religion, are ready targets of a wrong inflicted because it is found pleasurable, the wrong which they incur being disdain;[1] for wrong can involve money, honor, or well-being. The pusillanimous and cowardly bring wrongdoing upon themselves, for the perpetrator will have no fear of them at all; while men of truly profound patience[2] will be victimized and wronged because the perpetrator will not think that they will take vengeance upon him.

[4] Wrongfully taken objects are either thefts which are properly pardonable, or such as may be concealed and go unnoticed. Pardonable thefts are trifles of little value, for people will be unaware that they are missing. Concealment and evasion of notice are attempted for many reasons: either that it will be easy to alter the objects' shapes or colors; or that the criminal already has in his possession things so similar that these will be thought to be his own—and so criminals will even first purchase an object of the kind they intend wrongfully to take;—or that they are things which will change in the course of time without being altered by the criminal.

[5] The various kinds of unjust action have two objectives, namely, either the pleasant or the advantageous; and they are planned along two lines, either for the warding off of injury or for the preserving of advantage. Unjust action is a person's taking, deliberately and of his own choice, to some form of crime. It is not only the prosecutor who needs to know the several varieties of unjust actions, the acts which constitute wrongdoing, and the conditions under which unjust action and wrongdoing take place, but this knowledge is naturally also required of the defendant, since he may have occasion to admit[3] the truth of his opponent's charge while denying that it constitutes wrongdoing. Thus, he may admit that he took but not that he stole, that he cursed but not that he reviled, that he had

1. הבזיון < التهاون
2. A: والصابرون . . . المغضون بالحقيقة "the truly forbearing patient" (105).
3. Text emended according to T (84).

ולזה ראוי לשניהם שידעו מה היא הגנבה, מה הוא החרוף, ומה הוא הנאוף, וזה
כפי התורה הכוללת או המיוחדת באומה.

[6] והחמס אשר לא יקבל התנצלות הוא הנעשה בקדימת ההשתכלות
ובבחירה. ויש חמסים שיורה[3] עליהם שמותם שהם[4] מן החמס אשר בתכלית,
5 ושנעשו בהשתכלות ובבחירה, כמו הגנבה והנאוף, כי אלה אי אפשר מבלי
בחירה; ולזה, כשהודה באלה השמות, לא נשאר לו התנצלות. ויחויב על
המתנצל לבלתי ידה בשמות אלו, ואם הודה, לא יודה אלא בסוג· כמו שיודה
בשהוא קללו, לא בשהוא חרף; וזה, שהחסרונות יתחלפו בגנות לפי הפחות
והיתר· למה שהכילות לא יחשב לחרפה, ואם הנאוף, הנה אין ספק שהוא
10 חרפה נפלאה.

[7] ולפי שהמתרעם יגדיל החמס והמתנצל ימעיטהו, ראוי אחר כן שידובר
מהחמס הגדול ומהמועט. ומה שימצא בדברים המועטים חמס גדול, זה יהיה
אם מגודל הרע בעצמו הנמצא בזה הדבר המועט, אם מעצם הנזק. אולם מעצם
הנזק בדבר המועט הוא כמי שישלול מן העני מכולת ביתו, כאשר היה מועט
15 ואין לאל ידו שיקנה זולתו אכל. וגדל הרע בעצמו בדבר המועט כמי שיגנוב
שקל כסף מן ההקדש, למה ששקל כסף הוא דבר אין ראוי שיחשב למעוטו;
אמנם הוא רע גדול, למה שנשאו לבו למעול באלקים ולקחת ממונו, ולזה הגיע
אל התכלית מה שאפשר מן הרוע; וכאלה אינה ראויה המחילה והסבל כלל.

[8] ומהחמס העצום, שיהיו בעלי הצדק והחסידות מדוכאים על פעולותיהם;
20 אמנם כי זה תפארת לאנשים ההם, כמו שקרה זה להרוגי מלכות, שהגיע להם
מזה תפארת לא ישוער אחר המות· וכן מה שסבל ירמיהו מן המכות ויתר
הדברים שבו לו לתפארת בחייו ובמו׳. ובכלל, כל מי שינזק על הדבר ראוי
שיכובד בו ישיג באותו הנזק כבוד מופלג.

[9] ומן החמס העצום, שיהיה החמס ההוא דבר חדש, לא עשהו אדם לפניו

4 שיורה[3]] שיודה^כד | שהם[4]] שם^כד || 13 מגודל] הגודל^כ || 15 אכל] אבל^ד || 21 [מזה]^כ | לא] ולא^כ ||
22 ובמו׳] ובמות^כ ||

---

17 שמ׳ ל״ו ב׳ ||

---

[3] Corrected on the basis of ט.

[4] So J; cf. ט.

licit sexual relations[4] but not that he committed adultery. Both sides, therefore, must know what theft is, what reviling, and what adultery—and these, moreover, according to universal law or to the special law of the nation.

[6] An indefensible unjust action is one committed with premeditation and by choice. There are unjust actions whose very names indicate[4] that they[5] are extremely unjust and have been committed with premeditation and by choice—for example, theft and adultery, for without a freely made choice these are impossible. When, therefore, an accused person confesses acts so named, no defense for him is left. It is incumbent upon the defendant not to admit the commission of acts called by these names; and if he does confess, he should do so only in generic terms. He may, for example, admit that he cursed the plaintiff, but not that he reviled him. This is because faults will be differently censured, some less, some more; thus, niggardliness is not considered a disgrace, whereas adultery is without doubt shameful in extraordinary degree.

[7] Now since the plaintiff will magnify the unjust action, while the defendant will minify it, we must, in what follows, discuss both the major unjust action and the minor.[b] When, in petty cases, there is a major act of injustice, this will be either because of the intensity of the evil itself involved in this minor affair, or because of the substantial damage inflicted. An example of substantial damage in a minor affair is afforded by one who pilfers the food of a poor man's household when there is little enough of it and the poor fellow lacks the wherewithal to buy other food. And an example of intensity of evil itself in a minor affair is the case of one who steals a silver *shekel* from the treasury of the Temple, for a silver *shekel* is a matter so petty as to merit no consideration; this act is, nevertheless, intensely evil in that the perpetrator's **heart stirred him up** [Exod. 36:2] to commit trespass against God and take money that belongs to Him, and he has thus reached the outermost limit of evil. Such acts as these cannot with propriety be pardoned or tolerated at all.

[8] The action is grossly unjust in kind when righteous and saintly men are oppressed for their deeds. Such oppression, in fact, glorifies such men, as happened in the case of the martyrs slain by the Roman Government,[6] for whom the posthumous result was the attainment of immeasurable glory; and so, too, the blows[7] and other indignities suffered by Jeremiah redounded to his glory both while he yet lived and after his death. It is, indeed, generally true that anyone who suffers injury for the sake of an act for which one should be honored will receive even greater honor because of that injury.

[9] That action is of the grossly unjust type, also, whose originality is such that

4. Text emended according to T (84).
5. Emendation: J.
6. The famous Ten Martyrs, slain during the Hadrianic persecution (*ca.* 135 C.E.).
7. Jer. 37:15.

b. T87/A115.

או לאחריו; עוד, שיהיה הוא ראשון שעשהו, ונמשך אחריו כל מי שעשה זה
הפעל, כענין קין עם הבל; עוד מן החמס העצום המגיע ההפסד והאבדון
למנהיגי העם, יראו להם הדרך ישכון אור, כמו מניחי הנימוסים ואשר יבואו
ממנו טובות אל הכלל; עוד, אשר יפול ממנו בקרובי' והאוהבים, למה שיהיה
5 מחק האדם להטיב לקרוביו ואחזת מרעיו, לא לעול אותם ולחמסם; עוד,
הבגידות, ושבועת שוא, והפרת הברית, ואשר יבושו קויהם, הם מן החמסים
העצומים, וכל שכן אם קבלו מהם טובות· לכן ראוי לתת לאלה הענשים
הגדולים במקום רואים, ובמושב זקנים, במקהלות, על גפי מרומי קרת.

[10] עוד, החמס בנימוסים בלתי כתובים יותר עצום מהחמס בנימוסים
10 הכתובים, כי הבלתי כתובי' הם כמו הענין הטבעי, וכל העולם יסכימו להיות
השכל מורה עליהם, כמו כבוד הורים ותת תודה למטיב. אמנם הנימוס הכתוב
הוא אשר התיחדה בו האומה, ואינם במדרגת הדברים הטבעיים והמסכמים.

[11] ואחרי בארנו הדברים אשר מהם ילקחו הקדמות בערך אל המתרעם
והמתנצל, נחזור אל מה שאמר טוליאו בזה בב' מההלצה החדשה. ונשלם
15 הפרק הששי:

פרק שביעי

מהטענה הסבריית.

[1] ראוי שנאמר מה שראוי בזאת הטענה לעשות למתרעם אחר שהמתנצל
הכחיש הפעל, גם מה שראוי שישיבהו המתנצל.

20 [2] וצד המתר' בספורו שיהיו החשדים מפוזרים בו· כגון שיאמר שכל פעולות

1 שעשהו] שעשאהו[כ] || 11 הנימוס הכתוב] הנימו' הכתו'[ר] || 12 הדברים ‹הדברים›[כ] || 14 ונשלם] נשלם[ר] || 16 שביעי] ז'[כ] ||

---

3 איוב ל"ח י"ט || 5 בר' כ"ו כ"ו || 6 יש' מ"ט כ"ג || 8 איוב ל"ד כ"ו | תה' ק"ז ל"ב | תה' ס"ח כ"ז | מש' ט' ג' ||

no man ever committed it before, nor has since. The act is grossly unjust, moreover, when its perpetrator is the first to commit it and is the prototype for every subsequent committer of this deed, as in the episode of Cain and Abel. Again, a grossly unjust kind of action is that which brings damage and destruction upon those leaders of the people who show them **the way to the dwelling of light** [Job 38:19]—establishers of constitutions, for instance, or any public benefactor. The action is further of this kind that is directed by its perpetrator against relatives and friends, for it is human nature to benefit one's relatives and **the party of his friends** [Gen. 26:26],[8] not to wrong and victimize them. Betrayals, swearing falsely, violation of covenant, and making those **ashamed who wait for** them [Isa. 49:23] are still other acts of the grossly unjust sort, especially so if the perpetrators receive benefits as a result of them; these ought therefore be given the severest of punishments **in the open sight of others** [Job 34:26], **in the seat of the elders** [Ps. 107:32], **in full assemblies** [Ps. 68:27] **upon the highest places of the city** [Prov. 9:3].

[10] An unjust action in violation of unwritten norms, moreover, is more grossly unjust than one that violates the written; for those that are unwritten are the equivalent of a phenomenon of nature, and all the world approves them, since they are indicated by reason—for example, honoring parents, and thanking a benefactor. The written law, however, is the respect in which a particular nation is set apart, and its provisions are not of a kind with things natural and universally approved.

[11] Having clarified the propositions from which premises both for the prosecution and for the defense will be drawn, we may now return to what Tully says on this subject in Book II of the New Rhetoric. Chapter 6 is ended.

CHAPTER 7

The Conjectural Issue

[1] We must set forth how the prosecutor should proceed in a Conjectural cause after the defendant has denied that he committed the deed, and how, also, the defendant should answer.[a]

[2] For the prosecution, the Statement of Facts should contain suspicious particulars interspersed throughout. The prosecutor should, for example, maintain

8. So, following the Targum and Rashi, JML interprets; JV: "... and Ahuzzath his friend."

a. Cf. *R. ad H.* 2.2.3 ff.

החשוד, ודבריו, ועניניו, ומעשיו, ותנועותיו מורות שפעל אותו הפעל. אמנם ספור המתנצל ראוי להיות פשוט וצח, עם נתינת הבנה והחלשת החשדים שהביא המתרעם.

[3] וזאת הטענה נחלקת לו׳ חלקים: מפרסם, יחס, אות, ראיה, המשכות, 5 באור.

[4] המפורסם הוא כאשר תבאר שהחשוד הוכרח לחטוא, ושכל ימיו היה שטוף בזה החטא והכעור. וזה יחלק אל הסבה וההנהגה.

[5] והסבה היא שהניעהו אל החטא, כאלו תאמר תקות התועלת, או בריחת הנזקין. תקות התועלת כאשר ישאל: האם לא עשה זה הענין לתוחלת שישיג 10 ממנו תועלת, או תפארת, או עושר גדול, או שררה, או אהבת הנשים, או תאוה אחרת? ומשל בריחת הנזקין: האם לא עשה זה הענין לברוח מן הנזק, מהשנאות, מהשם רע, מהיגון, מהצער? ובכלל, המתרעם יבנה ענינו על תוחלת השגת התועלת ובריחת הנזקין. אמנם צד ההתנצלות הוא שיכחיש המתנצל כל מה שאמר המתרעם, אם יוכל· ואם לאו, יחליש דבריו, ויאמר שהיא רעה גדולה 15 לחשוד כל אדם שהגיעהו תועלת מצד אי זה דבר, ולאמר שהוא עשהו.

[6] ואם ההנהגה, היא כאשר נחייב הענין ממעשיו הקודמים. ובזה ישתדל המתרעם למצא אם הסכן הסכין לעשות כזה[1]· ואם לא ימצא זה, יתבונן אם נפל בחשד דומה לו, ויראה אם יוכל למצא הסכמה מה מהנהגתו הקודמת אל זה הפעל בזה האופן: שאם החשד הוא שכוון בזה השגת ממון וריוח, נאמר 20 שהנהגתו הקודמת מסכמת בזה שהיה כילי וקובץ על יד כל ימי חייו, ולזה נפל בזה החטא· ואם החשד הוא שעשה לתכלית שררה ושלטונות, נאמר שזה הוא דבר אמתי מבלי ספק, למה שנראה שלעולם רדף אחר הכבודות, מתנשא לאמר, אני אמלוך; ובזה האופן נוכל לקיים החטא והעון מצד ההנהגה. ואם לא תמצא ההנהגה מסכמת עם החטא, נחפש אם נמצא׳ מסכמת מצד מה. והמשל: 25 החשד הוא שחטא לתוחלת ממון, ואין לנו מהנהגותיו הקודמות שהיה כילי, נמצא מה שדמהו במקצת ונאמר שהיה נותן שוחד, בעל אמונה רעה; ובכלל, נחפש עונותיו, פשעיו, להראות שהוא בעל עברות ומדות רעות· לכן, אין מן

2 והחלשת] וחלשת^ב || 7 החטא] החט^ד || 8 או בריחת] ובריחת^ב || 12 מהשם רע מהיגון] מהיגון מהשם רע^ב || 15 ולאמר] ולומר^ב | עשהו] עשאהו^ב || 17 כזה[1]] בזה^בד | [זה]^ב || 21 ושלטונות] ושולטנו׳^ב || 22 מבלי] בלי^ב | שלעולם] לעולם || 24 נמצא׳] נמצא^ב || 25 לנו] לנו׳^ב ||

20 מש׳ י״ג י״א || 22–23 מל״א א׳ ה׳ ||

[1] Emendation required by context; cf. *R. ad H.* 2.3.5.

that all the acts, words, affairs, works, and movements of the suspect indicate that he did the deed in question. The Statement of Facts of the defendant, on the other hand, should be simple and clear, and should, in addition, afford explanations of, and weaken, the suspicions introduced by the prosecutor.

[3] This issue has six divisions: Notoriety, Attribution, Sign, Proof, Consequent Behavior, Confirmatory Proof.

[4] The issue is one of Notoriety when it is shown that the suspect had a compulsion to crime, and that he has been immersed in this kind of crime and foul practice all his life. Notoriety subdivides into Motive and Manner of Life.

[5] The Motive is what has induced the suspect to commit the crime: the hope of advantage, one might say, or the avoidance of injury. It is hope of advantage when the question is, Did he not commit this act in the expectation of procuring some advantage from it—glory, great riches, political power, the love of women, or some other gratification? And to examplify avoidance of injury: Did he not commit this act in order to avoid some disadvantage—enmities, ill-repute, grief, or pain? In general, then, the prosecutor will construct his case on the hope the defendant had of gaining advantage and of avoiding disadvantage. In his defense, on the other hand, the defendant will deny, if possible, everything that the prosecutor has said; if that is not possible, then he will weaken the prosecutor's allegations, saying that it is a gross evil to bring under suspicion every person who has procured some profit from an act, and to charge that he committed it.

[6] As for Manner of Life, this is involved when we draw our proofs of the charge from the defendant's previous deeds. Here the prosecutor will try to discover whether the defendant has definitely been in the habit of committing this kind of misdeed; if he does not so find, he will consider whether the defendant has ever fallen under the suspicion of similar guilt, and will see if some correspondence is discoverable between the previous conduct of the accused and the present crime. The procedure is as follows: if we suspect the motive of the present crime was pecuniary gain and profit, we shall allege that this act corresponds with the previous conduct of the defendant, since he has been avaricious, one **that gathereth little by little** [Prov. 13:11], all the days of his life, and that this is why he fell into this particular crime. If we suspect that the accused committed the crime for the purpose of gaining political power and authority, we shall say that the accusation is true beyond doubt because we see that he has always pursued honors, **exalted himself, saying, "I will be king"** [1 Kings 1:5]; and proceeding in this way we shall be able to establish the present crime or felony on grounds of the defendant's manner of life. But if his manner of life is not found to be entirely consistent with the present crime, we investigate to see if it can be found consistent in part. Example: Suspecting that the defendant committed the crime in the expectation of pecuniary gain, but with no previous record of avarice on his part available to us, we may find what resembles this in part, and can allege that he has been a giver of bribes, a person of bad faith. In general, we analyze his iniquities and transgressions, in order to show that he is a trespas-

התימה אם נפל עתה בזה החטא, ואם עצום הוא.

[7] ואם המתרעם לא יוכל למצא פשע וחטאת מצד הנהגותיו הקודמות, למה שהיה פרוש מאד לפי מה שהתפרסם, ויש לו שם על פני חוץ כאחד הגדולים אשר בארץ, אז יאמר המתרעם שאין להביט אל השם הטוב ופרסום מעשיו אצל האנשים· אמנם ראוי להתבונן היטב כי הוא עשה זה החטא מבלי ספק; ושהוא במדרגת הערומים ובעלי התחבולות מלאו כרסם מכל טומאה כטמאת הנדה בתעלומות והסתר, ומקדישים ומטהרי׳ אל הגנות· גם כי ירבו תפלה וילכו שחוח עד המה בחזקת קדושים ופרושים אצל בני אדם, ושבע תועבות בלבם, ובגלוליהם נפשם חפצה.

[8] וצד התנצלות הוא שיציע המתנצל ההנהגה הקודמת תמימה כפי מה שאפשר, אם יוכל. ואם ימנע, למה שרבו פשעיו מלפנים, יאמר שאז, בימים ההם, היה צעיר השנים, או שהיה שובב, או סכל, או מוכרח, או מפותה· וא״כ הלך בדרך טובים, והתנהג בחסידות, והיה צדק אזור מתניו, עד אין ראוי שיוטל חטא זה עליו מפני זה. ואם היה כל כך מוחזק לרשע בכל הזמן הקודם עד ימנע בערכו לאמר כדברים האלה, יאמר המתנצל שאין ראוי להאמין לקולות ולשמור הרעות, כי הוא נקי מכל פשע וחטאת, וביחוד מזה העון שהוטל עליו; ומי יוכל לעצור באנשים הרעים, השונאים, והאויבים, ומוציאי הדבה, שלא יביעו ידברו עתק· והוא מאמר כולל ומוסכם מכל האנשים שאין להאמין בקולות. ואם התפרסמו עניני רשעו כל כך שאין לו התנצלות כלל מזה הצד, יאמר שאין עתה הכונה להתוכח מהמדות וההנהגות הרעות לפני בעלי ההנהגות, כי אם לברר הפשע לפני הדיינים, אם הוא אמת או לא.

[9] היחס הוא כשהמתרעם אומר שזה הענין לא היה שב לתועלת כי אם לזה שהמתרעם עליו; גם כי לא היה אדם יכול לעשותו כמוהו· או שלא היה אפשר העשותו כי אם בדברים אשר עשהו· או שלא היה אפשר שיעשהו אדם מה אחר באופן כל כך נאות· או מצד רב התאוה לא רצה המתן לעשותו באופנים יותר נאותים. ואז צד ההתנצלות הוא שיבאר ההפך, ר״ל שהיה יכלת באחרי׳ לעשותו כמהו, ובאופן נאות· ואפשר שישוב לתועלת יותר גדול לאחרים ממה

4 אצל] אל[כ] ||7 ומקדישים] המתקדשים[ת] ||14 כל כך מוחזק] כ״כ מחוזק[כ] ||26 באחרי׳] באחר[כ] ||

---

3 איוב י״ח י״ז ||3–4 שמ״ב ז׳ ט׳ ||6 יח׳ ל״ו י״ז ||ד יש׳ ס״ו י״ז ||8 מש׳ כ״ו כ״ה ||9 יש׳ ס״ו ג׳ ||
13 מש׳ ב׳ כ׳ |יש׳ י״א ה׳ ||18 תה׳ צ״ד ד׳ ||

ser and man of bad character, and that it is therefore not really surprising if he has now fallen into this particular sin, heinous as it is.

[7] If the prosecutor should be unable to discover transgression and sin in the defendant's previous manner of life because, as all agree, the defendant has been most self-restrained, and has a **name abroad** [Job 18:17] as one **of the great ones that are in the earth** [2 Sam. 7:9], the prosecutor will then say: "Not ours to consider the good name of the accused and the fame that his deeds have won among men, but we must mark well the fact that he has unquestionably committed this particular crime. He is of the ilk of those cunning ones, those masters of trickery, who secretly and covertly fill their belly with every kind of vileness, as unclean **as the uncleanness of a woman in her impurity** [Ezek. 36:17], yet sanctimoniously[1] **purify themselves to go unto the gardens** [Isa. 66:17]; who, moreover, pray so much, and go about so submissively, that they are held by men to be saints and ascetics, though **there are seven abominations in** their **heart** [Prov. 26:25], **and their soul delighteth in their** idols" [Isa. 66:3].

[8] As his defense, the defendant will, if possible, submit that his previous conduct has been as nearly faultless as possible. But if this line of defense is precluded by reason of his many previous transgressions, he will say that in those bygone days he was immature, unruly, ignorant, or that he was coerced or seduced; later, however, he so much **walked in the way of good men** [Prov. 2:20], his behavior was so saintly, and **righteousness** was so truly **the girdle of his loins** [Isa. 11:5] that in view of such a record this crime ought not be lodged at his door. If, however, he has been so notorious a villain at all times in the past that such pleas are precluded in his case, then the defendant will say that it is not proper to credit rumors and preserve the memory of wrongs, for he is innocent of any transgression or sin, and especially of this act of iniquity with which he has been charged. "Who can restrain evil men—haters, enemies, slanderers—that they do not **gush out . . . speak arrogancy** [Ps. 94:4]? It is the approved consensus of all men that rumors may not be believed." And if the facts of the defendant's villainy are so notorious that he has no defense of this kind at all, he will say that the purpose of the present proceeding is not to hold a disputation on immoral character and conduct before Professors of Ethics, but to determine, before the judges, whether the charge of transgression is or is not true.

[9] The issue is one of Attribution when the prosecutor avers that the act in question could yield advantage to none but his adversary; also, that nobody else had equal ability to do it; or that it could have been carried out by any save the means which the defendant used; or that it would have been impossible for any other man to carry it out so conveniently; or that, from excess of passion, the defendant could not brook waiting to do it by more convenient means. The case for the defense will then consist of showing the opposite, namely, that others were as capable of doing the deed as was the defendant himself, and of doing it as

1. B: ". . . that sanctify themselves. . . ."

שישוב אליו· ושהיה בזה הפעם לאחרים כל מה שצריך.

[10] האות הוא נחלק לו״[2] חלקים: המקום, הזמן, ההמשכות, הסבה, תוחלת ההשלמה, ותקות[2] ההעלמה.

[11] ושאלות המקום הם: אם המקום בדד או מעבר· אם הוא בדד לעולם או
5 זה היה בעת המעשה לבד· ואם הוא מקום הקדש או חול· כולל או מיוחד? ונחפש תארי המקום, אם הוא נגלה או מכוסה, ואם היה אפשר שיראה או שישמע הדבר; ונכתוב כל הדברים שהם שבים להצדיק המתרעם או המתנצל.

[12] שאלות הזמן: באי זה חלק מחלקי השנה· באי זו שעה בלילה או בין השמשות· באי זה יום ובאי זו שעה, בכמה שעות, נעשה? וכן כל הדומה לזה.

10 [13] שאלות ההמשך: אם היה ארוך בערך אל הענין· ואם היה בו המשך מספיק להשלמת הענין· ואם היה יודע קודם שהיה לו המשך יוכל להשלים הענין?

[14] הסבה: אם היתה מספקת לענין, או היתה אחרת טובה הימנה?

[15] תוחלת ההשלמה: שנמצאו בו הדברים הנזכרים, ואם מהצד האחד
15 ימצא כח על הדבר, מעות, עצה, חכמה, פנים מן ההראות· ומצד האחר העדר היכלת, עניות, הוללות, סכלות, בלתי פנים מההראות· אשר מאלה הצדדים היה יכול לדעת אם אפשר שהדבר יבא לתכלית או לא.

[16] תקות[3] ההעלמה תשאל מן החברים, מן המסייעים, מן המשתפי׳, מן הבנים או עבדים, או שניהם· כאלו אמר שזה עשה הפעל הרע, למה שעשאהו
20 עם בניו או עם אנשים שלא יגלו זה על זה.

[17] הראיה היא כשיתבאר הדבר באופן יותר קיים וראיות חזקות, ונחלקו לג׳ חלקי׳: עבר, הווה, עתיד. השאלות מהזמן העבר: אנה היה, אנה נראה, ואם ראוהו א״כ· ואם בא בתנאי עם אנשים מה· ואם אמר לעשות זה הפעל· ואם היה עמו אדם שעשה בחבורתו כדומה לזה· ואם היו לו מן המסייעים ומן
25 העוזרים· ואם עשה זה במקום לא היה רגיל בו, או בזמן אחר? בזמן ההוה: אם

2 לו״[2]] לז״כד || 3 ותקות[2]] ותקווה·כ ותקוה־ד || 9 ובאי זו] ובאי זהכ || 18 תקות[3]] תקוןכד || 22 הווה עתיד] עתיד הווהכ | מהזמן] <מה> מהזמןכ || 24 עמו אדם] אדם עמוכ ||

[2] So J, as required by the context ; cf. *R. ad H.* 2.4.6.

[3] So J; cf. *R. ad H.* 2.4.7.

conveniently; that the act could yield even greater advantage to others than to himself; and that, at the time of the deed, others had all the means needed to commit it.

[10] Sign has six[2] divisions: the Place, the Point of Time, the Duration of Time, the Reason, the Expectation of Fulfillment, and the Hope of Escaping Detection.

[11] Questions on the Place are: Was the place a lonely one or a throughfare? Is it always lonely, or was this the case only at the time of the act? Is it a sacred place or a profane? Public or private? We examine the features of the place, whether it was out in the open or concealed, and whether the deed could have been seen or heard. And we list all the points which are relevant to the justification of the defendant or the plaintiff.

[12] Questions on the Point of Time: In which season of the year, at what time of the night or late afternoon, on what day and at what hour of the day, at what o'clock, was the deed done? And every analogous case is similarly investigated.

[13] Questions on the Duration of Time: Was the time long enough for the proceeding? Was it long enough to carry the deed through, and did the defendant know in advance that there would be time enough for him to accomplish the act?

[14] The Reason: Was it sufficient for the undertaking, or was there another, better one?

[15] There is Expectation of Fulfillment when the factors mentioned above are present, and if there are, on one side, the power to commit, funds, deliberation, wisdom, *a priori* probability, or, on the other side, incapability, poverty, heedlessness, ignorance, *a priori* improbability; for from these considerations the defendant might have ascertained whether his plan could or could not be successfully consummated.

[16] Hope[3] of Escaping Detection will be investigated in terms of the defendant's friends, accomplices, confederates, and his sons or servants, or both; as when the prosecutor has asserted that the defendant did indeed commit the evil deed, since he perpetrated it in association with his own sons or other persons not likely to give each other away.

[17] The issue is one of Proof when the charge will be demonstrated in a manner that is of superior validity and by means of strong evidence which has been divided into three parts: past, present, and future. Questions of time past: Where was the defendant, where was he seen, and did they see him subsequently? Did he enter into a stipulation with any other persons, did he say he would do this deed, was he accompanied by a man who had been his associate in some like deed? Did he have any accomplices or assistants? Did he commit the act in a place which he was not in the habit of frequenting, or at a time for him

2. Both M and C read ''seven'' here by dividing ''Hope'' from ''Escaping Detection.'' This is one of several indications that JML did not correct the text of C as it was being printed.

3. Emended text (תִּקְוַת); M and C: ''Arrangement'' (תִּקּוּן).

נראה בזמן העשיה· ואם נשמע קול פסיעותיו, כשהיה רודף אחריו· ואם שמענוהו צועק עליו, או ששמענו קול כלי זינו, או אם הושג זה באחד החושים, ר״ל ראות, שמע, ריח, טעם, משוש? השאלות מזמן העתיד: אם ישאר דבר אשר למענו אכיר איך היה הענין, או מי עשהו? אם גוף המת נפוח עם שחרות, יורה על שנתן לו סם המות; ומי עשהו נכיר אם הניח החרב, או הבגד, או סמן הרגל· או שנרא׳ בגדיו מלכלכים בדם· אם נראה שב במקום ההוא תכף נעשה המעשה.

[18] ההמשכות הוא כשנשאל מן הסמנים הנמשכים לעושה העברה, או לנקי ממנה. צד המתרעם שיאמר, אם יוכל, שאשר עליו התלונה התאדם או השתחר, או שהיה מגמגם, מתבלבל בדבורו, נדר דבר מה· ואלה כלם סמנים נמשכים לעוברים. ואם לא נראו אלה הסמנים אחר עשית החטא, יאמר המתרעם שזה בערמתו ותחבולתו כבר חשב קודם כל מה שימשך, וגמר בלבו להתחזק ולהתאפק עד לא ימשך לו אחד מהם. וכן עושים המרגילי׳ ברשע ומופלגים בו, שישמרו מההתפעליות יהיו סבה אל הגלות ענינם; וזה יורה על ההרגל העצום, וכחם אשר להם על עשיית התועבות, כי לא יגיעם התפעלות מהם כלל. וצד ההתנצלות, אם קרו ההתפעליות, שהדברים האלה נמשכו לגדל הסכנה אשר ישער התחייב מזה, לא על עשיית החטאת. ואם לא קרו לו הסמנים ההם, יאמר שזה אמנם היה כי נכון לבו, בטוח על היותו נקי שלא תבאהו רגל גאוה, ויד רשע לא תנידהו.

[19] אמנם הביאור הוא אשר נרגילהו באחרונה, אחר קיום החשד; וימצאהו לו מקומות מיוחדים וכוללים. והמיוחדים הם: שאי אפשר שינהג אותם זולת המתרעם· שאי אפשר שינהג אותם זולת המתנצל. הכוללי׳ הם שאפשר שיורגל׳[4] בין מן[4] המתרעם, בין מן המתנצל, מצדדים מתחלפים. אמנם בטענה הסבריית, המקום המיוחד למתרעם כאשר יאמר שאין ראוי הרחמנות על הרעים, וכאשר יפליג אכזריות העון; והמקום המיוחד למתנצל כאשר יבקש על העון המחילה, וכאשר יאמר שהמתרעם התרעם על צד החמס והעדר המשפט. והמקומות הכוללים לשניהם הם: מהעדים וכנגד העדים, מהנגישות וכנגד הנגישות, מהראיות וכנגד הראיות, מהקולות וכנגד הקולות.

[20] מהעדים נאמר לפי מעלתם, והנהגתם, ונאמנותם. וכנגד העדים נאמר

2 זינו] זיינו[ג] || 5 עשהו] עשאהו[ג] || 6 שנרא׳] שנראה[ג] || 8 ההמשכות] ההמחשכות[ד] | לעושה] לעושי[ד] || 10 [שהיה][ג] || 11 החטא] החט[ד] || 16 האלה] האלו[ג] || 17 החטאת] החטא׳[ד] || 19 תבאהו] תבואהו[ג] || 21–22 אותם זולת המתרעם] אדם זולת המתרעם[ג] || 23 שיורגל׳[4]] שיורגל[כד] | בין מן[4] המתרעם] בין המתרעם[כד] | [מן] המתנצל[ג] || 26 וכאשר יאמר] ואמר[ג] ||

18 תה׳ קי״ב ז׳ || 19 תה׳ ל״ו י״ב ||

[4] Emendation required by context; cf. *R. ad H.* 2.6.9.

unusual? In the category of time present: Whether he was seen at the time of the act; whether, if he was pursued, the sound of his footsteps was heard; and whether we heard the victim cry out against him, or heard the sound of his weapons, or the fellow was perceived by any of the senses—sight, hearing, smell, taste, touch? Questions of time future: Whether anything is left which will afford me a clue to the nature of the crime, or to who did it. If the body of the deceased is both swollen and discolored, it signifies that he was poisoned. We will have a clue to the person who committed the deed if he left a sword behind, or a garment, or a footprint; or if his clothes were seen to be bloodstained; or if he was observed again in that place soon after the deed was done.

[18] The issue is one of Consequent Behavior when our questions deal with the signs which the transgressor, or the person innocent of transgression, often manifests. For the prosecution it will be argued, if possible, that the accused blushed, changed color, became hesitant or confused in speech, or made some vow—all signs often manifested by transgressors. If such signs have not been observed after the crime was committed, the prosecutor will say that the defendant, with his shrewdness and cunning, thought out beforehand all that would follow, and resolved to conduct himself with such boldness and self-assurance that not one of these signs would be manifested by him. "Such is the practice of clever and hardened criminals: they are on their guard against the feelings that might effect disclosure of what they have done. And it indicates how hardened they are, and the power at their disposal to commit abominable deeds, that they remain totally unaffected by these acts." The argument of the defense, if these feelings have appeared, is that such manifestations are due to the magnitude of the perilous consequences to himself imagined by the defendant as a result of the accusation, not signs that he committed the crime. And if those signs have not appeared in the defendant, he will say that such is indeed so because **his heart** is **steadfast, trusting** [Ps. 112:7] in the fact of his innocence **not** to **let the foot of pride overtake** him, **and . . . the hand of the wicked drive** him **away** [Ps. 36:12].

[19] Confirmatory Proof is what we employ finally, after suspicion has been established; found belonging to it are both special and common topics. The special topics are: (a) those which only the prosecutor can use; (b) those which only the defendant can use. The common topics are those which, in differing ways, can be employed by either the prosecutor or the defendant. In a conjectural cause, it is the special topic of the prosecutor when he says that the wicked ought not to be pitied, and when he exaggerates the brutality of the crime. The defendant's special topic is when he seeks pardon for the crime, and when he says that the prosecutor has lodged a wrongful and unjust charge. The topics common to both sides are the following: for and against the witnesses, for and against the testimony given under torture, for and against the proofs, for and against the rumors.

[20] In favor of witnesses, our statement will refer to their virtue, fine be-

לפי רוע הנהגתם והעדר נאמנותם, ושאי אפשר שיהיה כמו שאמ׳· או שלא היה
הענין כן כמו שאמרו· או שימנע שהעדים ידעו אותו· או שאמר׳[4] מה שאמ׳
מצד איבה, אהבה, יראה, או בגלל שחד· או שהם מביאים ראיות, ואין בחק
העדים כי אם להשיב כפי מה שישאלו.

5 [21] מצד הנגישות, כשנאמר שדרך הקדמונים היה לחקור האמת במכות
ונגישות גדולות, כדי שיאמרו מה שידעו. וצד המתרעם הוא שיאמר ראוי
לעשות כן לנחשדים, כפי מה שנהגו מימי קדם, כדי שיודו על האמת. ואחר
הגדת או הודאת הנגושים ראוי למתרעם שיקיים דבריו ויאמ׳: ״הלא אמרתי
אליכם, רבותי, כי זה פעל ועשה?״ וכנגד הנגישות, שיאמר המתנצל
10 שהקדמונים בחרו הנגישות כדי שיודו בדברים הודאים, לא במסופקים וחשדים
כאשר אמר המתרעם· שהוא מבואר שאין להביא האנשי׳ לידי נסיון מחמת
תרעומת מה, קול, או חשד היוצא, כי אם בדברים שהם מבוארי[5] ההראות. עוד,
שאין להאמן למה שיאמר בסבת הצע׳, כי אין כל האנשים סובלים בשוה
המכות והנגישות, אבל זה יתחלף לפי החזק והאבירות, והחלש׳ ופחיתו׳ הלב;
15 עד שהחלש, שאין יכול לסבול, חרף נפשו למות, ויודה מה שיחשו׳ שירצה
הדיין, כדי שלא יתייסר תמיד· עוד, יתבונן מה שיחפוץ בו הדיין, ואם הוא שקר.
ולפעמי׳, בהודאתם, ישימו חטא מות על איש צדיק תמי׳· וכל זה להנצל
מהיסורים. והנה ישפך דם נקי הרבה, וירבה העול, אם נלך אחר הנגישות.
אמנם, זה ההתנצלות יועיל כאשר השיבונו לכל מה שהושם במחלקת מן
20 המתרעם, וסתרנו דעותיו בראיות מספיקות.

[22] מהראיות, והאותות, ויתר המקומות המגדילים החשד, ראוי לעשות בזה
האופן: כאשר יסכימו ראיות ואותות רבות על הדבר, ואמר שענין ברור
ומפרסם, לא חשד לבד, הוא אשר התחייב מהם; עוד, שראוי להאמין יותר
בראיות ובאותות ממה שיאמן בעדים, למה שהעדים מפני היראה, או שחד, או
25 אהבה, או איבה העידו מה שהעידו, וזה נמנע בחק הראיות והאותות. וכנגד
הראיות, והאותות, והחשדים אחרים, נאמר בזה האופן, והוא: שיאמ׳ המתנצל
שאי אפשר המצא במדרגה מן התמימות, והיושר, והנקיות שלא יפול בו החשד
מצד מה· לכן, אין לקחת ראיה על האנשים הטובים להחזיקם מכחה במדרגת
הרשעים. עוד, ראוי שנחליש החשדי׳, ושנאמ׳ שאפשר שהחשדים ההם בעצמם
ילקחו בערך זולתנו· ונאמ׳ שהוא עון גדול ללכת אחרי הסברה והחשד, להחזיק

1 שאמ׳] שאמר[c] || 2 שאמר׳[4]] שאמר[cd] || 12 מה֗ [קול][c] | מבוארי[5]] מבואר[cd] || 13 הצע׳] הצעקה[c] ||
14 והחלש׳ ופחיתו׳] והחלשה והפחיתות[c] || 17 חטא] חט[d] || 26 שיאמ׳] <והוא שיאמר>[c] ||
30 [ללכת][c] ||

---

9 יש׳ מ״א ד׳ || 15 שופ׳ ה׳ י״ח || 17 דב׳ כ״ב כ״ו | בר׳ ו׳ ט׳ ||

---

[5] Correction: J.

havior, and reliability. Against witnesses, it will refer to their evil manner of life and their unreliability, and we shall say that the matter could not possibly be as they assert; or that it did not happen as they allege; or that the witnesses could not have known it; or that their statements are actuated by enmity, friendship, fear, or bribery; or that, while it is absolutely improper for witnesses to do anything save answer the questions asked, these witnesses have been trying to introduce proofs of the charge.

[21] We speak in favor of the testimony given under torture when we say that the method of the ancients was to search out the truth by means of painful beatings and tortures so that people should tell what they knew. The prosecutor's argument will be that suspects should be treated as was customary in ancient days in order to make them confess to the truth. Following the statement or confession of those tortured, the prosecutor should declare that it confirms his charges, and say, "Did I not say to you, gentlemen, that he is the one who **wrought and did it** [Isa. 41:4]?" Against the testimony given under torture the defendant will say that the ancients selected the method of torture in order to make people confess things that are demonstrably certain, not things ambiguous and suspect as alleged by the prosecutor; for clearly men should not be brought into such testing because of some complaint, rumor, or suspicion that is abroad, but only in the case of matters which are clearly plausible. "Moreover, what is said because of pain is not to be believed, for not all men suffer beatings and tortures equally, but this will vary according to strength and valor, or weakness and disheartenment. Thus the weakling, unable to endure, will have **jeoparded** his **life unto the death** [Judg. 5:18], and make whatever confession he thinks will satisfy the judge in order to avoid incessant torment; will, furthermore, try to divine what will please the judge even though it be false. Sometimes, through such confessions, a **sin worthy of death** [Deut. 22:26] is fastened upon **a man righteous and whole-hearted** [Gen. 6:9]—all to escape the agonies of torment. Much innocent blood will thus be shed, and injustice increase, if we follow extorted testimony." Such a defense is most truly effective when we have replied to everything disputed by the prosecutor, and rebutted his views by means of adequate proofs.

[22] In favor of proofs, signs, and the other topics used to heighten suspicion, it is proper to proceed as follows: When many proofs and signs concur on the issue, then say that the necessary result is a clear and self-evident fact, not merely a suspicion. "Moreover, it is proper to give greater credence to proofs and signs than to witnesses, since witnesses can have offered their testimony out of fear, bribery, friendship, or enmity, while this is intrinsically impossible with proofs and signs." Against proofs, signs, and other such means of casting suspicion we will argue as follows: "It is impossible," the defendant will say, "to find anyone so perfect, upright and innocent that he will not fall under some sort of suspicion; a proof, therefore, which forces us to hold that good men are of the same quality as the wicked is unacceptable." Further, we should weaken the grounds for suspicion, asserting that the self-same means of casting suspicion could possibly be used in connection with others than ourselves; and then we shall say that it is

בהם האנשים כרשעים, בזולת העדים.

[23] מן הקולות, צד המתרעם הוא: שיאמר שלא יתפרסם לעולם אי זה קול או חשד שלא יהיה אמת בכל או במקצת· עוד, שיאמ׳ שזה הקול לא יצא בסבת איבה, אהבה, שחד, או יראה, להיות כל אלה הסבות נעדרות בענין· עוד, שיאמ׳ שאפי׳ היו כל הקולות האחרים כוזבים, זהו אמתי, כאשר נבאר בראיות. כנגד הקולות: כשיביא המתנצל משלים מקולות וחשדים[6] יצאו על האנשים והיו כוזבים; גם כי הקולות מוצאים לפעמים מחמת שנאה, אם גם כן מהאנשים הרעים אשר למדו לשונם דבר שקר, והולכי רכיל אשר אין להאמין בהם; עוד, שיאמר המתנצל למתרעם: ״אין להאמין בקולות, כי גם אני שמעתי עליך היום קול וחשד מדבר פלוני, ולא האמנתי· וכן ראוי שלא תאמין בו אתה· גם כל אדם יוכל לעשות בדיאה ולהוציא שם רע על האנשים, מזולת שיהיה הענין כן.״ ואם הקול חזק מאד וקשה ההעתקה, צריך שנבאר מכח הסברה ונוכיח, עד שישאר האמת במקומו.

[24] ואמר הפילוסוף בא׳ מההלצה אצל הנגישה, שראוי לשופטים שלא ישתמשו בזה המין בלקיחת ההודאה, אבל ירגילו ויעשו בהודאות האחרות; כי הרבה מן האנשים, בבריאות גופותיהם ונסיון נפשותיהם, יסבלו הצער סבל חזק ולא יודו בצודק· ואולם רכי הלב ואנשי החלשה, הנה כבר יודו על עצמם בכוזב קודם שיראו הצרות; ולכן אין בנגישות דבר ראוי לבטוח בו:

פרק שמיני

מהטענה הראויה.

[1] כבר בארנו במאמר הראשון לזאת הטענה ששה חלקים· ועתה נשים בהרגל בערך אל[1] המתרעם והמתנצל חלקיה, אחד לאחד.

6 וחשדים[6]] וההשדים^כ וחשדי^ר || 7 [גם] כי^כ || 19 שמיני] ח׳^כ || 22 אל[1]] לא^כד ||

8 יר׳ ט׳ ד׳ | יר׳ ו׳ כ״ח ||

[6] So J.
[1] So J.

grossly unjust to follow conjecture and suspicion and, using these in the absence of witnesses, to hold men for villains.

[23] In favor of rumors, it is for the prosecution to hold that no rumor or suspicion which is not either entirely or partially true would ever be generally accepted; moreover, that this particular rumor was not issued because of enmity, friendship, bribery, or fear, since all these motives are absent in the present instance; and again, that even though all the other rumors may be false this particular one is true, "as we shall demonstrate by proofs." Against rumors: when the defendant brings examples of the issuance against men of rumors and suspicions that turned out to be false; and points out, too, that rumors are sometimes circulated because of hatred, or, as also happens, are spread by evil men who **have taught their tongue to speak lies** [Jer. 9:4], and by those who, **going about with slanders** [6:28], are not to be believed. The defendant will, moreover, say to the prosecutor: "Rumors are not to be credited. Why only today I heard a rumor and suspicion unfavorable to you mentioned by so-and-so, but I did not believe it, and so you yourself ought likewise to discredit rumor; moreover, anybody can produce an ugly fiction and give people a bad name without justification in fact." If, however, the rumor is very strong and difficult to dislodge, we shall need to use logically valid demonstration and proof so as to replace the rumor with the truth.

[24] With reference to torture, the Philosopher[b] says in Book I of the *Rhetoric* that judges ought not to use means of this sort to obtain a confession, but should accustom themselves to proceed by means of confessions that are otherwise obtained; for many men, thanks to their physical vigor and their psychological stamina, will bear up most staunchly under pain without confessing to a just charge, while, on the other hand, timid and weak men are likely to confess to a false charge against themselves sooner than to see themselves suffer. Nothing said under torture, therefore, should be relied upon.

CHAPTER 8

The Legal Issue

[1] Already in Book I[1] we distinguished six subtypes of this Issue; now, keeping both prosecutor and defendant in mind, we set forth, one by one, how these six subtypes should be brought into play.[a]

b. T95/A127; cf. *Rhet.* 1.15 (1377a).

1. At i.10.6ff.

a. Cf. *R. ad H.* 2.9.13 ff.

[2] ונניח קודם שרצון הכותב הדת יראה מתחלף למה שנכתב בה· אם נרצה
להרגיל הכתב, נרגיל המקומות האלה על צד הספור: קודם, שנשבח הכותב
הדת, ונאמ׳ שהיה חכם גדול· גם הדת הגונה מאד, מעלפת ספירים. עוד, נספר
לפני הדיינים: ״הדת אומרת כך וכך״. עוד נאמר: ״לא ימנע, רבותי, או המנגדים
ידעו זאת הדת, או לא ידעו אותה; אם ידעו אותה, חטאו בכך· ואם לאו, ג״כ
חטאו״. אחר כך ראוי להעריך מהו יותר טוב: ללכת אחר הדת ולשמור הדת· או
ללכת אחר המחשבה העמוקה, להתבונן ברצון הכותב, למה שיראה שראוי
ללכת אחר הדת; עוד א״כ ראוי שנסתור מה שהעמיקו שחתו המנגדים שהיה
רצון מניח הדת. א״כ נאמר: ״למה לא נכתב בדת זאת המחשבה שאמרתם· מה
הזק היה בדת· או אם לא היה ספק ביד המניח הדת לכתוב״? א״כ נמצא פסק
כפי מה שנראה לנו בהבנת דברי הדת, ונבאר שזה הוא הדת בעצמה· ושלא
רצה דבר אחר המניח כי אם מה שנכתב בה בפרסום· ושאותו המאמר הוא צח
ומפורסם, מתוקן בשלמות עם ראיה ברורה. עוד, נביא המשלים שכאשר נפלה
זאת הטענה בין האנשים, יצא הפסק שנעשה כפי הכתוב בדת; עוד, ראוי
שנספר שיש מן הסכנה הגדולה למי שאינו הולך אחר כתב הדת, ולחשוב בו
מחשבות; עוד, שהמודה שעשה כנגד מה שכתוב בדת, אלא שרוצה להתנצל
מרצון המניח הדת, המקום הכולל הוא שיענש אחר שעבר על דברי הדת.

[3] ואם נרצה להשען על מה שיראה שיהיה רצון המניח הדת, קודם, ראוי
שנשבח המניח הדת, וחכמתו, ותבונתו· ושכלכל דבריו במשפט ובקצור ראוי,
ולא רצה שיכתב בדת כי אם ההכרחי, ר״ל, אשר ימנע להבין מבלתי שיכתב,
אבל הדבר המובן בעצמו לא רצה שיכתב בה. עוד, נאמר שכן דרך המטעים
והמזייפים, להשען על הכתב לבד, מזולת שיתבוננו ברצון המניח הדת ההיא,
או הנימוס, התבוננות שלם. עוד, שנאמר כי לפי מה שיראה הפשט אי אפשר
שיעשה· גם כי אינו טוב להעשות, לא[2] לפי הדת, ולא לפי ההנהגה, ולא לפי
הטבע, ולא לפי היושר; ולא יחשוב אדם חכם שזו תהיה כונת מניח הדת בשום
פנים. עוד, מה שנאמר אנחנו הוא דבר נפלא הצדק; אמנם פסק המנגד׳ הוא
הבל וריק· או שטות· או נעדר הצד׳· או דבר לא יתכן· או נמנע שיעשה· או

1 שרצון] שהרצון[ג] |מתחלף] מחלף[ג] ||3 נספר] נאמ׳[ג] ||8 שנסתור] שנסתו[ר] |שחתו] שיחתו[ג] ||
10 המניח] מניח[ג] ||12 [בה][ג] ||16 [בדת][ג] ||18 המניח] הֹמניח[ג] ||20 להבין] להבי׳[ר] ||21 המטעים]
המטים[ג] ||24 לא[2]] לו[כד] ||27 הצד׳ (=הצדק) הצד[ג] ||

3 שה״ש ה׳ י״ד ||8 הו׳ ט׳ ט׳ ||19 תה׳ קי״ב ה׳ ||27 יש׳ ל׳ ז׳ ||

[2] Emendation required by context.

[2] Assuming the intention of the framer of the law appears to be at variance with the letter of the written text, if we wish to employ the letter, we shall employ the following topics in our Statement of the Facts: We shall first praise the framer, saying that he was a man of great wisdom, and that the law, too, is of surpassing worth, **overlaid with sapphires** [Song of S. 5:14]. Next, we shall state the law before the judges: "The law says thus and thus." Continuing, we shall then say: "Gentlemen, our opponents either knew, or did not know, this law; if they knew it, they are *ipso facto* guilty, and if they did not know it, they are nevertheless also guilty." After this we should assess which is better: to follow the text in keeping the law, or, following the thought behind it, to consider the framer's intention, as it is only apparently proper to follow the letter of the law. At this point, furthermore, we should refute our opponents' **deeply corrupted** [Hos. 9:9] presentation of what the original framer of the law intended, and thereafter say: "Why was this interpretation of yours not expressly written into the text of this law? What harm would there have been in the law so written? Or was the original framer unable adequately to write it down?" We shall next find a previous judgment that conforms to our idea of how the words of the law should be understood, and show that this substantially is the law, that the framer intended nothing else than what is plainly in the written text, and that the statement is clear and self-evident, completely correct and clearly proved so to be. We shall, moreover, cite examples of cases in which, when the issue between the contending parties happened to be of this kind, the judgment rendered was in conformity with the letter of the text. We must also affirm the fact that it is a gravely dangerous proceeding for one who does not follow the written text of the law to read notions into it. And against one who confesses that he has acted contrary to what is written in the law, yet means to base his defence upon what the original framer intended, the commonplace is that he should be punished because he has transgressed the prescriptions of the law.

[3] If, however, we wish to base our case upon what was apparently the intention of the original framer, we ought first to praise the framer of the law, his wisdom, his insight, and the fact that he **ordered his words rightfully** [Ps. 112:5] and with proper conciseness: he intended that only what was necessary should be written in the law, that is, what could not be understood unless it were written; but he did not intend to include anything self-evident in the written text. Next we shall say that it is the method of cheats and forgers thus to base their case upon the written text alone, without complete and thorough study of the intention of the framer of such a law or ordinance. We shall say, moreover, that the law, in its apparent literal meaning, cannot be carried out, and that to carry it out would not be a good thing, not according to Statute Law, Legal Custom, the Law of Nature, or Equity; nor will any wise man suppose that this literal construction in any way constitutes the intention of the framer. Further, our own construction is eminently just, whereas the interpretation advanced by our adversaries is **vanity and emptiness** [Isa. 30:7], an absurdity, unjust, impossible, impracticable, not

שאינו מסכים עם מה שנאמר בדת בראשונה ובאחרונה· או שאינו מסכים עם הדת הכוללת, או עם דתות אחרות כוללות· או שהוא חלוק מן הפסקים שנתנו כבר בזה הענין בזמן העובר. עוד, שנגיד המשלים מפסקי׳ נתנו בעד רצון מניח הדת, ולא בעד מה שנכתב; עוד, נביא דתות ונמוסים רבים שאנחנו הולכים בערכם אחר רצון מניח הדתות והנימוסים ההם. עוד, שהמקום הכולל הוא, שיענשו הנשענים על המכתב, ומניחים רצון הנכתב.

[4] ראוי שנראה בתחלה, כאשר שתי דתות תהיינה הפכיות אחת לאחת, אם אחת שוללת האחרת בכל או במקצת· או שהם הפכיות באופן שאחת מצוה, ואחת מזהרת· או שאחת עוצרת, ואחת מנחת. ומי שהתנצל שלא עשה מה שהאחת עוצרת מפני הדת האח׳ המנחת, כוון להתנצלות שהוא בתכלית החלשה, למה שהעצור הוא יתר גדול מההנחה, והיה לו לשמור הדת העוצרת. וכן, מי שהתנצל שעשה כפי הדת הראשונה, מבלי שישים לב אל הדת האחרונה השוללת הראשונה בכל או במקצת, התנצל באופן חסר מאד, כי כאשר הענין כן, ראוי ללכת אחר הדת האחרו׳. וכאשר יפול הענין במחלקת, ר״ל, שהדתות תהיינה הפכיות, ראוי שבתחלה נקח הדת שהיא בעזרתנו ונשבח אותה, ונספר אותה, ונבארה, ואא״כ נפרסם מה הרצון בדת האחר׳, ונמשוך אותה לתועלותינו· עוד, נביא מהמשפטית בסתם[3], ונחקור ממנה חלקי הדין[4] אשר יתבארו במה שיבא, ונראה אם מסכימים עמה או לא.

[5] ואם הדת אפשר שתובן בפנים רבים, קודם, ראוי שנחפש אם הוא כן שהוא מסופקת; ועוד, נחפש היאך היא כתובה, ובאי זה אופן, ואם פתרון המנגדים אפשר שייושב על הכתב או לא; ואח׳ כן נוכיח שפתרוננו ייושב בה· ושהוא אפשר, והגון, וישר· ושהוא אפשר שיעשה, באופן טוב ושוה, כפי הדת, ההנהגה, והטבע, וזה הדבר בחק פתרון המנגדים הוא בהפך· ולא תהיה הדת מסופקת אם יצדקו בערכה כל אחד מהפתרונים.

[6] וכאשר נרגיל הגדר, ראוי שנגדור ראשונה התבה בקצור, באופן נאות אלינו; ואא״כ נבאר שענינו מסכים עם הנרצה בתבה והמכוון בה; ואא״כ נסתור גדר המנגד, באמרנו שהוא כוזב, או בלתי תועלתיי, או מכוער, או מנוול.

[7] ובהעברת העון, ראוי שישאל אם ראויה הטענה שתעשה באופן אחר, או בזמן אחר, או במקום אחר, או לפי דת אחר, או שיהיה אדם אחר[4] השואל או

10 האח׳ (=האחרת)] האחת[ד] | בתכלית] בתחלית[כ] || 14 האחרו׳ (=האחרונה)] האחרון[כ] || [שהיא][כ] || 16 האחר׳ (=האחרת)] האחרון[כ] || 17 לתועלותינו] לתועלתינו[כ] | בסתם[3]] בסתר[כד] | הדין[4]] הדיין[כד] || 21 שייושב] שיושב[כ] | ואח׳ כן] ואא״כ[כ] || 29 [או במקום... אדם אחר][כ] | אדם אחר[4]] אדם אחד[ד] ||

[3] Correction: J.

[4] Required emendation.

in accord with ancient and modern legal interpretations, in disagreement with the common law or other generally binding rules of law, or at variance with previous decisions in cases of this kind. Next, we shall offer instances of decisions rendered in favor of the intention of the original framer, but not in favor of the letter of the text, furthermore citing many laws and ordinances in which we follow the intention of the framer. Here again, the commonplace is that those who rely upon the letter and ignore the intention underlying the written words should be punished.

[4] When two laws conflict, we must first see whether the one negates the other wholly or in part, or whether their disagreement is such that one commands while the other prohibits, or that one restrains while the other permits. The defendant who pleads that he did not comply with the restraint of the one law because of the permission granted by the other has conceived a defence that is extremely weak, for restraint is greater than permission, and it was his obligation to keep the law which restrains. The line of defence taken by the defendant who pleads that he acted in conformity with a former law without heeding a later law which negates the earlier in whole or in part is similarly very defective, for when such is the case one ought to follow the later law. When the case happens to be controversial, that is, when the laws conflict, we should first take up and praise the law favorable to us, state the facts about it and expound it. Then we shall elucidate the intention of the other law, and appropriate it for the advantage of our cause; we shall, moreover, introduce the Absolute Juridical Issue, and examine its several departments of Law[2]—to be explained in the next chapter—and see whether or not the conflicting laws are consistent with this Issue.

[5] If a law can be understood in more than one way, we ought first to investigate whether it is indeed ambiguous. Then we shall investigate the manner and style in which it is written, and whether or not our opponent's interpretation can be borne by the text. Next we shall show that our own interpretation can be borne by the law—that it is practicable, suitable, and ethical; that it can be carried out well and equitably in conformity with Statute Law, Legal Custom, and the Law of Nature, whereas the opposite is true essentially of our opponents' interpretation; and that the law will no longer be ambiguous if the judges will affirm the correctness of either one of its possible interpretations.

[6] When we employ the Issue of Definition, we must first briefly define the term in question in a way that suits our purpose; next we shall show that our conduct is consistent with the intended meaning of the term; and then we shall refute the definition of our opponents, asserting it to be false, disadvantageous, immoral, or disgraceful.

[7] In cases involving Transference of the Guilt, the question should be raised whether the charge ought properly to be made in another manner, or at another time, or in another place, or according to another law, or that the examiner or the

2. Emended text: "... Law" (דין) for "... judge" (דיין).

הפועל; וכל זה יתבאר בדתות והנהגות לפי הטוב והיושר, כאשר יתבאר בטענה המשפטית בסתם.

[8] וכאשר נוכיח מן הדומה, ראוי שישאל בראשונה אם בדברים הדומים, גדולים או קטנים ממנו, או בדברים בלתי דומים, נמצא כתוב בזה האופן· או שנפסק כמוהו; וא״כ לראות אם הענין דומה ממש למה שאנחנו בו, או בלתי דומה· ואם נכתב בכונה, ר״ל, שכן היה כמו שנכתב, או שעל צד התחבולה והשמירה כוון שהיה דומה לדבר אחר נעשה בזה האופן, כדי שלא יבטל.

[9] וזה מה שרצינו אמרו מהטענה הראויה:

פרק ט׳

מהטענה המשפטית בסתם· ומהגרועה.

[1] אמנם הטענה המשפטית היא כשנודה בפעל, ונאמר שהדבר נעשה במשפט, מבלתי לקיחת התנצלות נכרי. וראוי שנשאל בה אם הדבר נעשה כמשפט, או לא· וזה יודע כשנכיר המשפט, מאי זה חלקים יורכב. לכן, נאמר שהמשפט יורכב מאלה החלקים, ר״ל, מהטבע· מהדת· מהמנהג· מהנפסק[1]· מהשוה מהטוב· מהתנאי.

[2] מהטבע, כשנעשה הדבר מצד החמלה והרחמנות· אשר על זה הצד האבות יאהבו הבנים, והבנים האבות.

[3] מהדת, הענין הנעשה מהסכמת העם שהוא דת באומה ההיא.

[4] מהמנהג הוא כשהדבר הורגל, מזולת דת, כמו דבר ראוי והגון.

[5] מהנפסק הוא כשהדבר כבר נתן בו הפסק דין, או כוונת הדיין בו נודעת; וזה הענין נופל באופנים מתחלפים, למה שמה שיפסק האחד לא יפסוק האחר· גם יראה לאחד מן הדיינים זולת ממה שיראה אל האחר.

[6] מהשוה והטוב הוא כשהדבר יבוקש אל האמת ותועלת הכללי.

1 כאשר] וכאשר^c || 5 שנפסק] שנספק^c || 14 מהנפסק[1]] מהנספק^{cr} || 16 החמלה] החמחלה^c || 20 הפסק] הסֹפֹק^c || 23f. הכללי. והמשפט מהתנאי] הכללי והמשפט. מהתנאי^c ||

[1] Correction: J.

bringer of the action ought to be some other person. The means of demonstrating any such argument will be Statute Laws and Legal Customs that are fair and equitable, as will be explained in connection with the Absolute Juridical Issue.

[8] When we derive our proof from Analogy, we must first inquire whether, on similar matters of greater or less importance than the present case, or on matters that are not similar, there exists a text written in this style, or a like decision. Next, we must see whether the matter is or is not in fact similar to ours, and whether it was intentionally so written, that is, as worded in the text; or whether the similarity to another, similarly styled enactment was intended as a contrivance and a safeguard to prevent complete annulment.

[9] This, then, is what we wished to say about the Legal Issue.

CHAPTER 9

The Absolute Juridical Issue; and the Assumptive

[1] It is the Juridical Issue when we admit the deed but, without adopting any extraneous defence, contend that the act was lawfully committed. Herein it is proper to inquire whether the act was or was not in accord with the Law; and this will be ascertained when we know the departments of which the Law is constituted. We may say, then, that the Law is constituted of the following departments: Nature, Statute, Custom, Previous Judgments, Equity, and Agreement.[a]

[2] It is Natural Law when some act is done out of compassion and mercy; in accordance with this kind of Law, parents love their children, and children their parents.

[3] Statute Law is that kind of Law which is enacted by consent of the people to be Law in that nation.

[4] It is Legal Custom when, in the absence of a statute, a practice has come to be habitually done as the thing that is fitting and proper.

[5] It is a Previous Judgment when the case is one on which a legal decision has previously been rendered, or on which the intention of the previous judge in the case is known. There will be instances of contradictory kinds of Previous Judgment, since what one judge decides another will not, and also, what will seem reasonable to one judge may be altogether different from what will seem reasonable to another.

[6] It is a matter of Equity when the question turns upon the truth and the general welfare.

a. Cf. *R. ad H.* 1.14.24; 2.13.19 ff.

[7] והמשפט מהתנאי הוא כשהתנו זה עם זה, ובאו בפשרה, שראוי לקיים כל אחד מה שהתנה.

[8] אבל בטענה המשפטית הגרועה, אם עשה הערכה ואמר שעשה הטוב מב׳ ענינים הנופלים בענין, ראוי לראות בראשונה אם אמת הוא שמה שעשה המתנצל היה רב התועלת יותר ממה שהיה ראוי לעשות, לפי המתרעם· אם הוא יותר הגון, יותר נקל להעשות. אחר כן, ראוי לשאול אם היה נוגע לו לתת זה הפסק דין, ר״ל, שזה הוא יותר תועלת, או שזה הפסק הוא מוטל על הכלל. אחר כן, יתמצע אי זה חשד מן המתרעם, מצד הטענה הסבריית, שלא עשה כהוגן להקדים הרע אל הטוב, אלא שעשה זה בסבת שקר או דבר אחר, ויביא לזה אי זו סברה; עוד, שהיה יכול קודם לראות דרך ולמצוא אופן, עד לא היה צריך לעשות מה שעשה. וצד ההתנצלות הוא שיתנצל, מצד הטענה הסבריית אשר קדם זכרם, כנגד כל מה שאמר המתרעם· ולהוכיח, קודם, שהיה יותר מועיל, ושלא עשה זה בשביל שחד או דבר אחר, ושלא היה יכול למנוע לבלתי יפול בזה הענין. עוד, ירגיל המקום הכולל שמי שיקדים הרע אל הטוב, ויעשה הדבר אשר אין ברשותו ויכלתו לעשות, ראוי לענש גדול; והמתנצל ירגיל המקום הכולל מצד המחלקת, ושישאל למתרעם או לדיין שישימו לנגד עיניהם בחירתו, והמקום, והזמן, והענין, ומה היו עושים אם יהיו כמוהו בתוך לבאים, גדר מזה וגדר מזה, בין הצרות הגדולות והמהומות העצומות· ושאם יתבוננו בו היטב, יראו כי טוב עשה בתוך עמיו, יבאו ויגידו צדקתו.

[9] אבל היאך תפול בהרגל העתקת העון או העברתו? ראוי לשאול קודם, אם זאת ההעברה נעשת באמתות; ועוד, יש להתבונן אם העון במדרגה שוה בהצטרף אל המתנצל ובערך אל אשר הועבר עליו; עוד, אם הוכרח אחד לחטוא מפני שחטאו אחרים; עוד, היה ראוי לעשות הוא בעצמו זה המשפט; עוד, אם לא נעשה משפט מאותו עון אשר הועבר באחר, אם היה מן החיוב לעשות משפט בדבר שלא בא עדין לפני השופטים. והמקום הכולל בערך אל המתרעם הוא שראוי לענש גדול מי שיחשוב שהכח היה יותר גדול מהמשפט. אמנם המתנצל, ראוי שיספר האכזריות הגדול שהיה בפעל הראשון, אשר גרם לו לחטא, ולשים הענין, והזמן, והמקום נגד העיני׳, כדי שישערו השו׳ שלא היה ראוי לעשות באופן אחר· ״כי אולי היה בורח, אם היינו ממתינים ביאת הענין לפני הדייני׳״.

14 ירגיל] נרגיל[כ] || 16 שישימו] שישי׳[ד] || 17 [יהיו][כ] || 19 יבאו] יבאו׳[ד] || 22 עליו] אליו[כ] || 24 מן החיוב] ראוי[כ] || 28 העיני׳] העניין[כ] || 30 הדייני׳] הדיין[כ] ||

17 תה׳ נ״ז ה׳ || 18 במ׳ כ״ב כ״ד || 19 יח׳ י״ח | תה׳ כ״ב ל״ב ||

[7] The Law is founded on Agreement when the parties have made a contract with one another and settled that each must fulfill what he had contracted to do.

[8] In the Assumptive Juridical Issue, on the other hand, if the defendant has made a comparison and says that he carried out the better of the two available courses of action, we must first consider whether it is in fact true that what the defendant did was more advantageous than that which, according to the prosecutor, he ought to have done, or more worthy, or more practicable. Next, we should ask whether it was the defendant's right to make this judgment, that is, to decide that his was the more advantageous act, or whether this decision was the responsibility of the general public. Then one or another suspicion will be interposed by the prosecutor, as in a Conjectural cause, to the effect that the defendant has not only acted improperly in preferring the worse to the better, but was led to do this by fraud, or by some other motive as to which the prosecutor can introduce a plausible opinion; that, moreover, the defendant could previously have seen a way and found the means which would have obviated the need to do what he did. Using, in defence, the conjectural arguments previously outlined, the defendant will refute all that the prosecutor has said, and show, first, that his act was more advantageous, next, that he did not commit it for sake of a bribe or any other consideration, and finally, that he could not avoid his having fallen into this affair. The prosecutor, again, will employ the commonplace that one who prefers the worse to the better, and does something which one is neither authorized or empowered to do, ought to be severely punished. The defendant, employing the same commonplace to contradictory effect, will ask the prosecution or the judge to envisage the alternatives he confronted, and the place, time, and circumstances, and ask what they would have done had they been, as he was, **among lions** [Ps. 57:5], **a fence being on this side and a fence on that side** [Num. 22:24], caught between great afflictions and serious troubles; and he will suggest that, if they consider the matter diligently, they will see that he **did that which is . . . good among his people** [Ezek. 18:18], and **they shall come and shall declare his righteousness** [Ps. 22:32].

[9] But how may use be made of the Shifting or the Transfer of the Question of Guilt? It should first be asked whether this Transfer can truthfully be made; we have further to consider whether the question of guilt is as serious for the defendant as for the person to whom it has been transferred; again, whether one can be compelled to sin because others have sinned; also, whether the defendant ought to have made this judgment by himself; yet again, if there has been no adjudgment of the particular crime transferred to another, whether it is our obligation to adjudicate a matter that has not yet come before the judges. The commonplace of the prosecutor: "Anyone who considers that might is greater than justice ought to be severely punished." The defendant, on his part, should describe the vicious brutality of the original act which brought about his own misdeed, and he should cause the judges so to envisage the circumstances, time, and place that they will deem it improper to have acted otherwise: "For he might perhaps have fled had we waited until the matter could come before the judges."

[10] ההודאה היא אשר למענה נשאל המחילה; והיא נחלקת אל הוכחה ותחנה, כאשר כתבנו למעלה, ואלה מקומו׳:

[11] בקשת המחילה מצד ההוכחה כשנכחש שהדבר נעשה בשאט בנפש; ותחלק אל הכרח, מקרה, סכלות· ונבקש תחלה מאלה הג׳ הענינים, וא״כ נשוב אל התחנה. ונתבונן, קודם, אם היה הפשע סבה להכרח מצד מה, או כי היה שתו׳ עמו, או אם ההכרח היה סבה לפשע. עוד, יש לשאול אם היה יכול לבטל, או למנוע, או למעט ההכרח ההוא; עוד, אם חשב מחשבות, או נסה, לעמוד כנגד ההכרח ולדחותו. עוד, ילקחו החשדים מן הטענה הסבריית, כי הוא עשה זה בכונה, ושהכרח קרה בענין. עוד, עם ההודאה שקרה לו הכרח גדול שלא היה בידו לדחותו, אם ראוי שיהיה סבה מספקת למחילה.

[12] מצד שסכל בדבר, אם יאמר החוטא שחטא, יש לשאול ולהתבונן: אם היה יכול לדעת או לא; עוד, אם השתדל לדעת אותו; עוד, אם העדר הידיעה היה במקרה או בפשע· למה שאם קרה זה מצד שכרות, או חשק, או כעס, או כדומה לאלו, זה יקרא פשע, לא סכל, ולא יוכל להתנצל מצד הסכלות. עוד, נחקור מהטענה הסבריית אם זה ידע או סכל בדבר, ונתבונן אם ראוי שהעדר הידיעה יהיה לעזר מספיק אחר שנדע שהחטא נעשה.

[13] עוד, אם יבקש המחילה מצד שקרה זה הדבר במקרה, יש לחקור בו כל מה שחקרנו בהכרח, למה שכל ג׳ חלקי ההוכחה הם קרובים בענין עד שנוכל ליחס להם דברים משותפים.

[14] והמקומות הכוללים לאלו: שיאמ׳ המתרעם שאחר שהודה הוא עצמו בדבר, והוא מחזיק בדיי׳ בדבריו עד יאחר המשפט, ראוי לענוש אותו; וצד ההתנצלות שיאמר המתנצל שהרחמנות, והחמלה, וטוב הרצון הם ראוים בכל הדברים, והוא מבואר שהדבר שלא נעשה בכונה אין ראוי לחשבו מרמה.

[15] אמנם נרגיל התחנה כשנודה על החטא ולא נתנצל מצד מהצדדים הנז׳, ר״ל, מצד ההכרח, מקרה, או סכלות, ומ״מ נבקש מחילה עליו. ואלו המקומות

2 מקומו׳ (=מקומותיה)] מקומות[כ] || 6 שתו׳ (=שתוף)] שתו[כ] || 16 שהחטא] שהחט[ד] || 21 בדיי׳] בדיין[כ] || 22 שהרחמנות] שהרחמ׳[ד] ||

---

3 יח׳ כ״ה ט״ו ||

[10] The Acknowledgment is that for the sake of which we plead for pardon. Its divisions are the Exculpation[1] and the Plea for Mercy, as we have written above,[2] and its topics are the following:

[11] The asking of pardon is exculpatory when we deny that the act was done **with disdain of soul** [Ezek. 25:15]. The Exculpation divides into Necessity, Accident, Ignorance; we will base our request, at the outset, on these three factors, and thereafter return to the Plea for Mercy. First, then, we consider whether the transgression was somehow a cause of, or a contributory factor to, the stated necessity, or whether the necessity was a cause of the transgression. There is next to inquire whether the defendant could have nullified, avoided, or lightened such necessity; whether, also, he devised means against, or tried to withstand and to banish, the necessity. Also to be included are grounds, drawn from the Conjectural Issue, for suspecting that his act was done intentionally, while this necessity was in the affair by accident. Again, upon the defendant's Acknowledgment that he had encountered a necessity too great for him to banish, whether this must be accounted sufficient cause for granting him pardon.

[12] If, in a Plea of Exculpation based on ignorance, the sinner owns that he has sinned, there is to inquire and consider: whether or not he could have informed himself; next, whether he tried to acquire knowledge of the matter; then, whether the lack of awareness was accidental or criminal. For if such ignorance came about through drunkenness, lust, anger, or the like, he will be termed criminal, not ignorant, and he will be unable to defend himself on the ground of ignorance. Furthermore, proceeding as in a Conjectural cause, we shall seek to discover whether he was informed or ignorant of the matter, and consider whether lack of awareness properly constitutes a sufficient recourse once we know that the crime was committed.

[13] If, moreover, the defendant asks pardon on the ground that the act happened accidentally, there will be investigation of all the points that we investigate in the case of Necessity, since all three divisions of the Exculpation are so much akin in content that we can ascribe to them features in common.

[14] Commonplaces which belong to these causes are the following: the prosecutor will say that since the defendant, who has himself confessed to the act, is holding the judges up with speeches to the point of delaying justice, it is proper to punish him; for his part, the defendant will say that mercy, compassion, and goodwill are fitting in all cases, and that an unintentional act clearly ought not to be reckoned one of criminal guile.

[15] We shall use the Plea for Mercy when, confessing the crime, we shall not, in defence, resort to any of the aforementioned kinds of exculpation—Necessity, Accident, or Ignorance—and yet ask for pardon. The topics special to the Plea

1. Hebrew הוֹכָחָה = "proof," "evidence" (from *hiph'il* of יָכַח, which can mean, in addition to other things, "show to be right").

2. i.10.14. JML considers Abigail's speech to David (1 Sam. 25:24–31) as essentially a treatment of this subtype of the Assumptive Juridical Issue; cf. 1.7.25 ff., and Int. §6.

המיוחדים לה: קודם, שנאמר שמספר הטובות שעשינו היה יותר גדול הרבה
ממספר הרעות, ולכן אין להביט אל הרע הנעשה. עוד, נבקש מצד המעלות
והחשיבות שהם לאיש אשר נבקש בעדו המחילה· עוד, מצד יחס האבות
וחשיבותם. עוד, מצד שיש בו תוחלת ותקוה אל שיתחייבו ממנו טובות לכלל,
5 אם יונח מבלתי עונש. עוד, נאמר שרוב הענוה, והשפלות, והרחמנות, והחמלה
שהרגיל בה בין בני אדם בפקידותו תחייב ג״כ לנו שנמחול לו זה העון· וכאשר
עשה, כן נעשה לו. עוד, אם נאמר שלא חטא מצד האיבה, או האכזריות, או
שהעמיק להרע, אלא לכונה טובה נתכוון, וחשב לנהוג פקידות ישר וראוי·
ונעלם ממנו מה שהיה אפשר להגיע אלינו מן הנזקין וסכנות מצד זה הפעל,
10 ובא לכלל טעות. עוד, אם נביא המשלים שכבר נמחל לאחרים זה העון בעצמו.
עוד, אם נאמר שמזאת המחילה לא תתחייב סכנה או נזק לכללות. עוד, שלא
נקבל מפני זה, מתושבי ארצנו או ארץ אחרת, בשת וחרפה. והמקומות
הכוללים בזה הענין: שנביא דברים רבים מהבנת האדם אל החוטאים,
מהמקרים הקורים, מהרחמנות, ומהשתנות עניני העולם, ולהוכיח מהם שראוי
15 למחול לו; והמתרעם יאמר אלה הדברים כלם בהפך, עם הרחבה ומספר
החטאים. וענין המחילה אין דבר מתיחס אל הדיין, כמו שאמר למעלה, כי אם
אל המלכים, והשרים, ובעלי המדינה היושבים ראשונה.

[16] והפילוסוף, בא׳ מההלצה, מביא קצת מינים מבקשת המחילה אשר לא
נזכרו הנה. מהם, שיאמרו שלא יביט אל הנימוס עצמו, המחייב העונש· אמנם,
20 יביט אל מה שהיה במניחו מן הרחמנות והחמלה. ומהם, שלא יחוייב שיעויין
אל נגלה זאת התורה או הנימוס, כי אם אל מה שכוון בו· וזה במקום שיהיה
המובן מן הלשון הפך מה שיחייב נגלהו מן העונש. ומהם, שאין ראוי שיענש על
מה שהיה על המעט, אבל על מה שיהיה נכפל מהפושע· וזה כאשר לא קדם
ממנו אותו הפעל. ומהם, שיזכירהו בטובות אשר הגיעו מאשר הפשע אליו אל
25 הפושע, כי זה יניעהו שתהא המחילה מכלל אותן הטובות. ומהם, שיזרזהו על
המתינות אצל החמס, כשיאמ׳ לו שאין ראוי שימהר האדם, כאשר הגיעו עול
מאדם אחר, להשיב גמולו בראשו תכף, אבל יעמוד, כי אולי יהיה באחרית זה

6 שהרגיל] שהרגילה[c] || 9 הנזקין] הנזקים[c] || 20 שיעויין] שייעויין[c] || 22 שיחייב] שייחייב[c] ||

17 אס׳ א׳ י״ד || 27 יואל ד׳ ד׳ ||

for Mercy are as follows: First, we may say that our good deeds far outnumber our bad, and that, therefore, it is not alone the evil done that should be noticed. Again: our plea is set forth in terms of the virtues and the standing of the man for whom we are asking pardon, and of the nobility and distinction of his forebears. Next: if he is left unpunished, it may be hoped and expected that he will prove to be a source of benefit to the public. Further: the great gentleness, humility, mercy, and compassion which he was wont to show to men while he was in power also places us under the obligation to forgive him for this act of iniquity: as he has done in the past, so should we do unto him. Again: he did not sin out of hatred or cruelty, or because he had plunged deep into evildoing, but to noble purpose, thinking he was discharging his responsibility uprightly and properly; he was unaware of the injuries and dangers that could overtake us in consequence of this particular act, and so he fell into error. Further: we cite examples of others who have received forgiveness for this very iniquity. Again: we assert that pardoning this fault entails no danger or injury to the public. And again: we shall not because of thus pardoning him incur the reproach of shame and disgrace either from the citizens of our own country or from those of any other. Commonplaces of the Plea for Mercy: we cite many instances of the understanding shown by our man toward sinners; introduce instances of the accidents of fortune, pity, and the mutability of worldly things, and try to show from these that the defendant ought to be pardoned. All these commonplaces, reversed, will be used by the prosecutor, along with an Amplification and an Enumeration of the defendant's sins. Pardoning is not a function that properly belongs to a judge, as he [Tully][b] has stated above, but to kings, princes, and political authorities **who sit first** [Esth. 1:14] in the State.

[16] The Philosopher,[c] in Book I of the *Rhetoric,* cites several kinds of plea for pardon which have gone unmentioned here.[3] Of these, one is that the defendants say that the judge should look not just to the law itself, which makes punishment mandatory, but to the mercy and compassion characteristic of the law's original framer. Another: that it is our duty to study, not the letter of this law or the ordinance, but its intention—where the language may be understood as contrary to what the letter requires in the way of punishment. Another: that a transgressor ought not to be punished for an offense that seldom occurs, but for one that might be repeated—this when the misdeed in question has never previously been committed by him. Another: to remind the victim of the transgression of his benefactions to the transgressor, for this may induce him to include pardon amongst those kindnesses. Another: to urge patience with an unjust action, saying to the plaintiff that a man who has suffered wrong at the hands of another ought to be in no haste straightway to **return . . . retribution upon** the

3. I.e., where JML has been following *R. ad H.*

b. *R. ad H.* 1.14.24.
c. T86/A113; cf. *Rhet.* 1.13 (1374b).

טוב יגיענו. ומהם, שנאמר שראוי לאדם להיות מקל עם האנשים, יספיקהו מהם המאמ׳ הנאה מבלעדי הפעל· ושלא היה חזק החקירה. ומהם, שראוי האדם שיהא נקי מהמדוים והענשים.

[17] אמנם, ההתנצלות מצד העברת העון הוא כשנעביר הפשע אל דבר מה, או אל אדם מה. ואם נעבירהו אל האדם, כגון שנאמ׳ שהיה סבה אשר הביאתהו לפשוע, נחקור אם האיש ההוא היה במדרגת מן היכלת כאשר יאמר החשוד· ואיך ואם היה יכול זה, מבלי סכנה או באופן הגון, לעמוד כנגדו· ואם ראוי לנו להאמין לחשוד שאחרים הביאוהו לזה הפעל. א״כ נמשך העני׳ אל המחלקת הסבריי, ונתוכח אם הוא נעשה בכונה. ואם נעביר העון אל דבר מה, כגון שנאמ׳ שדבר מה הטענו, נחקור בזה האופן בעצמו, ובאופן כתבנו למעלה בהכרח:

פרק י׳

משלימות ההקשות ותקונם· וקצת ההטעאות אשר בערכם.

[1] אמר טוליאו בב׳ מהחדשה שמציאות הראיות הצריכו׳ בענין ענין אינו ממה שיקשה· אמנם, לתקנם באופן הראוי ובמקום הראוי, ושלא ירבו על מה שצריך גם לא ימעטו ממנו, ושלא לכפול דבר אחד בעצמו גם שלא להניח הענין שהתחלנו, ולהביא כל דבר בתכלית הסדור והשלמות לא יחסר דבר, זה אינו ממה שיקל.

[2] לכן נאמ׳ שההקשה השלמה ותמימה מכל צד תחלק אל ה׳ חלקים, ר״ל, אל הצעה· אמות· קיום האמות· יפוי· וכלל. ההצעה היא כאשר נציע בקצור מה שנרצה להוכיח. האמות הוא המוכיח אמתת מבוקשנו בקצור. קיום האמות הוא אשר יוכיח בהקשות רבות האמות הנאמ׳ בקצור. היפוי מה שננהג מן

3 מהמדוים] מהמדנים[ט] (= الخصومات [א]) || 4 הוא] אוא[ד] || 6 הביאתהו] הביאת׳[ד] || 7 מבלי] בלתי[כ] | כנגדו] בנגדו[ד] || 8 העני׳] העניינים[כ] || 13 ההטעאות] הטעאות[ד] || 14 הצריכו׳] הצריכו[כ] || 16 להניח] הניח[ד] ||

other's **head** [Joel 4:4], but should tarry, for this could perhaps end in his gaining of some good. Another: that we say that a man ought to be lenient with people, contenting himself with courtesy of speech on their part, if not of deed; and that the defendant was not harsh in cross-examination. Another: that our man deserves to be free of afflictions[4] and of punishments.

[17] Our defense is based upon Transfer of the Guilt when we transfer the blame for the transgression to some circumstance or person. If we transfer it to a person, as when it is alleged that he was responsible for causing the suspect to transgress, we shall investigate whether that man was as able to do this as the suspect asserts; how and if the suspect could safely or honorably have resisted him; and whether it is proper for us to believe a suspect's allegation that others brought him to commit such a deed. Then the case is developed into a controversy of the conjectural kind, and we debate whether the deed was done with premeditation. If we transfer the Guilt to some circumstance, as when we assert that some circumstance led us astray, we investigate in the same manner as has just been set forth, and as we wrote above in dealing with Necessity.

CHAPTER 10

On Complete Arguments, Their Improvement, and Some Defects in Connection Therewith

[1] In Book II of the New Rhetoric, Tully[a] says that to find the proofs needed in each case is not difficult; to set them out in the proper manner and in the proper place, however, neither in greater nor in lesser number than necessary, and neither to dwell overlong on any one topic nor to abandon the line of argument that we have begun, but to bring every topic into the finest possible arrangement and completeness, lacking nothing—this is not at all easy.

[2] We may say, then, that the most complete and altogether perfect argument is comprised of five parts, to wit: the Proposition, the Reason, the Proof of the Reason, the Embellishment, and the Résumé. The Proposition is our setting forth summarily of what we intend to prove. The Reason briefly demonstrates the truth of our basic proposition. The Proof of the Reason demonstrates, by means of several additional arguments, the validity of the briefly-stated Reason. The Embel-

4. JML: מֵהַמַּדְוִים = "of afflictions, diseases"; T: מֵהַמְּדָנִים = "of contentions," and so A: *al-khuṣūmāt* = "quarrels, controversies, feuds, lawsuits"; the text should possibly be corrected accordingly. I am assuming that JML read מהמדוים for מהמדנים.

a. *R. ad H.* 2.18.27 ff.

התיקונים והיפויים על צַד ההגונות וההשמנה להקשה המקויימת. הכלל הוא
מאמ׳ קצר מקיף בכל חלקי ההקשות.
[3] ואלה הה׳ חלקי׳ הם כוללים ההקשה והראיה התמימה, אלא שאין כלם
הכרחיים, למה שאם הדבר קצר שהזכרון מחזיקו בקלות, אנחנו נחסר הכלל;
5 ואם הענין הוא שפל ואינו סובל מן ההשמנה וההרחבה, נחסר היפוי; ואם
יתקבצו ב׳ הדברים יחד, ר״ל, שהענין קצר והוא ג״כ שפל, אז נחסר הכלל
והיפוי. וא״כ, ההקשה התמימה והרחבה היא כוללת כל הה׳ דברים שזכרנו·
והיותר קצרה היא הכוללת ג׳ חלקים· והבינוני׳ היא בעלת ד׳ חלקים, עם חסרון
היפוי או הכלל.
10 [4] ראוי שתדע שאופני ההקשות ההטעאיות הם שנים: אחד מהם הראוי
להוכיח מן המנגד· ואחד מהם שאינו ראוי להוכיח, מצד שהוא מלא דבר, והוא
מפורסם הכזב, ואין לו פנים מההראות. ובידיעת אלה הדרכים ההטעאים
נשמור מההטעאות שהם בהקשות· עוד נלמד להוכיח מי שאינו נשמר מהם.
ויען אמ׳ שחלקי ההקשה השלמה הם ה׳, נאמ׳ מההטעאות המיוחדת לכל אחד
15 למען נוכל להשמר ממה שבכל אחד מההטעאות, או להוכיח בהם המנגד.
[5] ההצעה ההטעאיית, כשנלך מחלקים מה, או מרובם, אל הכלל, כמי
שיאמ׳: ״שכל העניים חפצים יותר בקניית הממון ברשע מהעמידה בעניות עם
הצדק.״ אם יאמ׳ בזה האופן מבלתי שיספר מה הראיה על זה, נוכיח כנגדו
בקלות כשנאמ׳ לו: ״שזה יצדק בקצת העניים, אבל שיצדק כן בערך כלם הוא
20 שקר.״
[6] עוד, ההצעה הטעאיית, כשהדבר שהוא אפשרי על המעט יוכחש בסתם
ובמוחלט, כמי שיאמ׳: ״אין שום אדם אפשר שיבא אל אהבת דבר מה בהבטה
אחת״; כי זה הענין הוא אפשרי לפעמי׳, ואם על המעט, והוא מכחישו בכלל.
[7] עוד, ההצעה היא הטעאיית, כשנאמר שלקטנו כל הדברים, ונניח מהם אי
25 זה ענין הגון וראוי, כמו שנאמ׳: ״זה הנהרג, לא ימנע אם שנהרג מן הלסטים, או
מן האויבים, או ממך, שעשאך יורש מקצת נכסיו; והוא מבואר שאין לו אויבים,
גם לא נראו במקום ההוא לסטים מעולם· וישאר, אחר כן, שזה נהרג ממך.״
והנה התבארה זאת הטעאה, כשנאמר שהריגתו היתה אפשרית גם על יד
אחרים, רוצה לומר, על יד אחד מעבדיו או מאשתו, שאינם אחד מן הנזכרים.
30 [8] עוד, ההצעה היא הטעאיית כשניעד אי זה דבר במספר, ואניח מהמספר
אשר יעדתי· והמשל, אם אומ׳ שזה הענין כולל שלשה דברים, ולא אביא כי אם

1 להקשה] להקשת[כ] || 3 ואלה] ואילו[כ] | התמימה] תמימ׳[ד] || 7 [כל][ד] || 9 או הכלל] והכלל[ד] || 10–11 הראוי להוכיח] ראוי להוכחה[כ] | שאינו] שאין[כ] | להוכיח] להוכחה || 12 ההטעאים] הטעיי׳[ד] || 13 מההטעאות] מההטאות[כ] || 14 [השלמה][כ] || 15 מההטעאות] מההטעות[כ] || 19 בערך] ‹אל›[כ] || 21 ההצעה] הצעה[כ] | [על][כ] | בסתם] בסת׳[ד] || 24 ההצעה] הצעה[כ] | היא] והיא[כ] | שלקטנו] שלקיטת[כ] || 27 אחר כן] א״כ[כ] || 28 הטעאה] ההטעאה[כ] || 30 ההצעה] הצעה[כ] || שלשה] ג׳[כ] ||

11 עמ׳ ו׳ י״ג ||

lishment consists of the arrangements and adornments we use to dignify and enrich the confirmed argument. The Résumé is a brief statement drawing together all the parts of the argument.

[3] These five parts together constitute the perfectly developed argument and demonstration, but not all five are always essential. For if the matter is brief enough to be readily grasped by the memory, we may omit the Résumé; if the subject is too ordinary to tolerate enrichment and amplification, we may omit the Embellishment; and if both conditions coincide, that is, if the matter is both brief and ordinary, we may then leave out both the Résumé and the Embellishment. Thus the fullest and most perfect argument includes all five of the parts we have mentioned, the briefest three, and the mean four, omitting either the Embellishment or the Résumé.

[4] You must know that there are two sorts of defective arguments: one that must be refuted by the opposing speaker, and the other that need not be refuted, as being **a thing of nought** [Amos 6:13], plainly false, and implausible. Knowledge of these defective modes will enable us to be on our guard against faults in arguments; and we shall, in addition, learn how to refute anyone not on his guard against them. And since Tully says that the perfect argument consists of five parts, we shall treat the faults special to each single part, so that we may ourselves be able to guard against the faults in each, or, again, to refute our opponent by their means.

[5] The Proposition is defective when we proceed from a few parts, or from a majority of the parts, to the whole class, as if one should say: "All the poor would rather do wrong and acquire wealth than remain poor and do right." If one makes this sort of assertion without presenting the evidence for it, we shall easily refute him when we say to him: "This may be true of *some* poor men, but that it is equally true of *all* is false."

[6] Again, the Proposition is defective when something that is rarely possible is denied categorically and absolutely, as, for example, one who says: "No man can fall in love at a single glance." For this is sometimes, even though rarely, possible, and yet the speaker denies the possibility altogether.

[7] Again, the Proposition is defective when we assert that we have assembled all the relevant possibilities, but leave out some one possibility which is pertinent and worthy of consideration, as that we say: "This victim must either have been slain by robbers, by enemies, or by you, whom he made part-heir of his estate. Now it is clear that he had no enemies, and also that robbers have never been seen in that place; it remains, then, that this man was slain by you." But the fallacy here will be exposed as soon as we have pointed out that his murder could have been committed by others, say by one of his servants, or by his wife, neither of which possibilities was among those mentioned.

[8] Again, the Proposition is defective when, having assigned a given number of points to some topic, I then leave out part of the assigned number; for example, if I should say that the case in question is comprised of three elements,

ב׳ מהם. וכן הצעה היא הטעאיית, אם אומר יותר מהדבר אשר יעדתי במספר, כאמרי: ״על ג׳ דברים העולם עומד: על הדין, ועל האמת, ועל השלום, ועל היראת חטא״. וכן ההצעה הטעאיית, אם יסופר בה דבר מזמן יותר רחוק ממה שצריך, כמו שנתחיל בספור יציאת מצרים מבראשית ברא אלקי׳. וכן, בנוהג מנהגם.

[9] והאמות הטעאיי הוא שאינו מיוחס אל ההצעה, או מפני חלשתו, או מפני שהוא הבל. אמנם הוא חלוש כשלא יחייב מה שהוצע בהכרח, והמשל: אם ההצעה היתה שהרבית הוא דבר רע, ורציתי לאמתו מצד שהגזל הוא רע, זה לא יחייב ההצעה, כי יש לאומ׳ שיאמ׳ שהגזל הוא נטל על כרחו של אדם, והריבית ברצונו. וההבל הוא הבא מסבה כוזבת, במדרגת מי שיאמ׳ שהפילוסופיה היא רעה, שהיא תוליד ההפרדה׃ והוא מבואר שאף אם לא תהיה הסבה כוזבת, מכל מקום, ההצעה האומרת שהפילו׳ היא רעה, היא שקר.

[10] עוד, האמות הוא הטעאיי כשנקחהו במדרגת האמות, ואינו מוסיף על ההצעה דבר׃ במדרגת מי שיאמ׳ שהכילות הוא רע מפני שעצירת היד היא רעה. אלה המאמרים מסכימים, ואין לאחד מהם תוספת על חברו, ואם הם במלות שונות.

[11] עוד, האמות הוא הטעאיי כשנביא לענין סבה למטה ממדרגתו, כמי שיאמ׳[1]: ״טוב שיהיו לאדם אהבים רבים, כדי שיהיו לו עם מי ישחק״; וכן: ״החכמה היא תועלתיית, מפני שהחכמים הם אוהבי הרחמנות.״ הוא מבואר שאלה הסבות הם חסרות בערך הדבר׳[2] אשר הם אליהם סבה.

[12] עוד, האמות הוא הטעאיי שאפשר בערכו להלקח בערך אל הצעות רבות, והמשל, כמי שיאמ׳ שהחכמה היא טובה מפני שהיא מעלה; עם זה האמות בעצמו אוכיח שהחשיבות[3] הוא טוב, וכן הצדק, וכן הגבורה, וזולתם.

[13] בקיום האמות צריך שנשמור מדברים רבים, גם התחייב בערכנו לשמור עניני׳ אחרים רבים, למה שקיום האמות באופן הראוי הוא מוכיח כל ההקשה ההוכחה אשר בתכלית.

3 חטא] חט[ד] |הצעה] הצעה היא[ג] |יסופר] סופר[ג] || 6 הטעאיי] ההטעאיי[ג] || 8 שהרבית] שרבית[ג] || 11 שהפילוסופיה] שהפילוסופיאה[ג] || 18 שיאמ׳[1]] שנאמ׳[כד] |שיהיו] שיהא[ד] || 20 הדבר׳[2]] הדבר[כד] || 23 וכן הגבורה] והגבורה[ג] |וזולתם] וזולתן[ג] ||

4 בר׳ א׳ א׳ ||

[1] Correction as required by grammar; cf. usage below (l. 22).

[2] Corrected according to context.

[3] Read חסידות, as at ii.2.2–3 above?

but then introduce only two of them. The Proposition is likewise defective if I mention a greater number of items than I have enumerated, as that I should say: "By three things is the world sustained: by justice, truth, peace, and the fear of sin."[1] And the Proposition is also defective if its narrative proceeds from a time more remote than is needful, as that we should begin the story of the Exodus from Egypt with **In the beginning God created** [Gen. 1:1]. So too, with other instances of this kind.

[9] The Reason is defective when it is unrelated to the Proposition, either because it is weak, or because it is nonsense. It is weak, indeed, when it does not require us to conclude that what was proposed is necessarily true. For example,[2] if the Proposition is that usury is an evil, and if I intend to prove the truth of the Proposition on the ground that robbery is an evil, this will not necessarily validate the Proposition, for it can be said that robbery is a taking of something from a person against his will, whereas usury is a taking with his consent. The Reason is nonsense when it comes from a false cause, as when somebody says that philosophy is an evil because it engenders divisiveness; whereas it is clear that even if the cause is not false, at any rate the Proposition, which states that philosophy is an evil, is untrue.

[10] Again, the Reason is defective when we take it as the Reason, though it adds nothing to the Proposition, as when somebody says that niggardliness is an evil because tight-fistedness is an evil. These terms are synonymous; neither constitutes an addition to the other, although different words are used.

[11] Again, the Reason is defective when we introduce, respecting a subject, a cause not adequate to it, as when one says: "It is good for a man to have many friends, in order that he may thus have persons with whom he can jest"; or similarly: "Wisdom is useful, because the wise are lovers of mercy." Such causes are clearly deficient in relation to the matters of which they are so adduced.

[12] Again, the Reason is defective if it can be applied to many Propositions: as when, for example, someone says that wisdom is good because it is a virtue. With this same Reason, I might "prove" that excellence[3] is good, and so, too, that justice, bravery, and other qualities are good.

[13] In the Proof of the Reason, we need to ward off many allegations, and also in regard to what we ourselves say, we must be observant of many other details, for a proper Proof of the Reason affords the most cogent support of the whole argument.

1. Inexact quotation of *Mishnah Ābhōth* 1:18.

2. This example rebuts an important point in the contemporary Christian polemic against the Jewish loan bank, the economic mainstay of Italian Jewish life in the quattrocento.

3. The Hebrew here reads חשיבות "importance," "estimableness," etc., but I suspect that the original reading was rather חסידות, as above, ii.2.2–3, where I have rendered it "scrupulous righteousness."

[14] ואנחנו נרגיל, עם השתדלות בקיום האמות, הקשה נכפלת בזה האופן כמו שהביא טוליאו המשל מאחת מהבנות, שהיתה מוכיחה אביה למה שהיה רוצה להפרידה מבעלה, והיתה אומרת: ״אבי, לא טוב הדבר אשר אתה עושה״ — וזאת היא ההצעה; ואמ׳ אחר כן: ״למה שאתה עושה לי חרפה ובושה גדולה להפרידני מבעלי״ — ועד הנה האמות; ואחר כן, מביאה קיום האמות: ״שלא ימנע, אם שהיית יודע מתכונות האיש קודם, או לא· ואם היית יודע זה קודם, למה נתתני לו לאשה· ואם לא היית יודע, שהיית מחזיק אותו בתורת אדם טוב, למה תבחר עתה להפרידני ממנו?״ וזה האופן, אפשר שנוכיח זיופו באחד מב׳ פנים: אם שנקח הפך ב׳ החלקים· ואם ההפך מאחד מהם. משל הראשון, שישיב האב לבת: ״לא עשיתי לך חרפה או כלמה, למה שאם הוא חשוב, יפה עשיתי שנתתיך לו לאשה· ואם אינו חשוב, אני אושיעך מההזקין ומהרעו׳ כשאפרידך ממנו.״ משל השני, שישיב האב: ״למה שאמרת, שאם אינו חשוב למה נתתיך לו לאשה, אשיב שאז, בשעת החופה, היה נראה לי חשוב· וטעיתי, ואחר כן הכרתי בו, לכן הסכמתי להפרידך.״ וא״כ, הוכחת זה ההמשכות הוא על שני פנים, הראשון יותר חד, והאחרון יותר נקל.

[15] עוד, קיום האמות הטעאיי הוא כאשר הדבר המורה על דברים רבים אקח אותו כאלו לא יורה כי אם על אחד; והמשל: אם אומ׳ שהכרח הוא, אחד שהתלבן, שיהיה חולה· או אחת שמחזקת בילד, הכרח שילדה· למה שאלה אינם סמנים מובהקים אם לא ישתתפו עמהם סמנים אחרים, ואם ישתתפו, אין ספק שיגדילו החשד.

[16] עוד, קיום האמות הוא הטעאיי כשהדבר שאומ׳ אפשר שישוב גם כן אלי, כגון שאומר, ״אוי להם לנושאי הנשים״· מפני שיאמר, ״גם אתה נשאת אחת מהם.״

[17] עוד, קיום האמות הוא הטעאיי אם אתנצל בדבר כולל, כמו שאומ׳ ״שחטאתי מחמת הבחרות, או מחמת הכעס, או מחמת החשק״· שזה התנצלות הוא כולל לכל דבר, ויאמ׳ המתרעם: ״אם זה הוא התנצלות אמתי, לכל עון יהיה לו התנצלות.״

[18] עוד, הקיום הטעאיי כשילקח דבר מה בודאי שעתה הוא בספק, וגם

2 שהביא] שמביא[כ] || 5 להפרידני] להפרידי[ד] || 6 שהיית] שהיה[כ] || 7 בתורת] בתור׳[ד] || 8 להפרידני] להפריד׳[ד] || 11 מההזקין] מהזקי׳[כ] || 14 וא״כ] ואח׳ כן[ד] | ההמשכות] המשכות[ד] || 15 והאחרון] ואחרון[ד] || 18 שהתלבן שיהיה] שנתלבן שהיה[ד] | אחת] אחד[כ] || 21 כשהדבר] הדבר[ד] || 23 מהם] מה[ו]ן[ם][כ] ||

[14] In attempting to Prove the Reason, we shall employ a Dilemma like that in the example presented by Tully[b]—of the young woman who rebuked her father for wishing to separate her from her husband. "Father," said she, "what you are doing is not a good thing"—and this is the Proposition. "For," she continued, "you are bringing disgrace and humiliation upon me in separating me from my husband"—thus far the Reason. Then, introducing the Proof of the Reason, "Necessarily," she said, "either you had prior knowledge of the man's character, or you did not. If you had such prior knowledge, why did you give me to him for wife? And if you had no such knowledge, since then you held him for a good man, why do you now choose to separate me from him?" We can demonstrate the fallacy in this type of argument in either of two ways: by reversing the two parts, or by adopting the opposite of merely one of them. In illustration of the first, the father might reply to his daughter: "I have not brought disgrace or shame upon you, for if he is an estimable man I did well in giving you to him for wife; but if he is not worthy of esteem, I shall, by separating you from him, save you from injuries and ills." In illustration of the second, the father might reply: "To your question why, if he is not worthy of esteem, I gave you to him for wife, I may rejoin that then, at the time of the marriage ceremony, he appeared to me to be thus worthy; I was, however, mistaken, and having later come to know him for what he is, I have accordingly decided to separate you." Thus, the rebuttal of such a conclusion is twofold, the first sharper,[4] the second easier.

[15] Again, the Proof of the Reason is defective when I take that which points to several things as though it were to point to one thing only. To illustrate: if I say of a person gone pale that he must be sick, or of a woman holding a child that it must be her child. For these are not indubitably clear signs unless they are associated with still other signs, but if there is concurrence of such signs, they undoubtedly increase suspicion.

[16] Again, the Proof of the Reason is defective when my own allegation can be brought home to myself as well; for example, if I should say "Woe unto them that marry wives!" this would be defective, because it might be said, "Yet you too have married one!"

[17] Again, the Proof of the Reason is defective if my defence consists of a banal generalization, like "I sinned because of youth—or anger—or lust"; for such a defense is all-inclusive, and the prosecutor can say: "If this is a valid defence, the defendant will have an excuse for any crime whatsoever."

[18] Again, the Proof is defective when something is taken as a certainty

4. JML may have read "acutior" for "auctior" ("fuller") in his Latin text.

b. *R. ad H.* 2.24.38.

מקדם, כמו שיקח מרבע העגול כאלו הוא בודאי.

[19] עוד, הקיום הוא הטעאיי, אם תכף השלמת דבר מה אומ׳: ״אם הייתי זוכר, או היה עולה על לבבי, לא הייתי מניח בא הענין עד המקום הזה· כי הייתי עושה כך וכך, אבל לא עלה זה במחשבה.״

[20] עוד, הקיום הוא הטעאיי כאשר החטא הוא מפורסם, ורוצה להתנצל עם התנצלות קטן בענין· כענין התנצלו׳ שאול עם שמואל, שחמל העם על מיטב הצאן [שמ״א ט״ו ט״ו].

[21] עוד, הקיום הוא הטעאיי אם יאמ׳ בו דבר יוכל אדם לחשבו לרעה· כמי שהוא גדול המעלה וחזק יאמר בעצה שהוא יותר טוב להרגיל המלכים, ר״ל, להיות תחת המלכים, מהיות תחת הדתות; זהו מאמר מסוכן שיביא האדם לחשוב שאמ׳ אלה הדברים בעד עצמו, שיחפוץ למלוך ולהשתרר.

[22] עוד, להרגיל הגדרי׳ הכוללי׳ או הכוזבים הוא הטעאיי; משל הכוזבים, כמי שיאמר במוסר עצמו לסכנות, שהוא גבור· ובנעדר הרגשת החרפה, שהוא ענו; משל הכוללים, כמי שיאמר בגדר הצדק, שהיא תכונה טובה בנפש· כי זה הגדר הוא כולל המדות הטובות כולם.

[23] עוד, הוא הטעאיי ליקח דבר בראיה שהוא המסופק אשר נחקור עליו; כמי שהוא רוצה להוכיח הגנב, ויוכיחנו מצד שזה האדם הוא איש בליעל, כילי, ומטעה· והעד על זה, שגנב. ו״ך הוא לקח בראיה אשר ראוי שיחקר עליו· שאפשר היותו בליעל, ומטעה, וכילי מזולת שיהיה גנב.

[24] עוד, הוא הטעאיי להתיר מחלקת ממחלקת אחר, כאלו יהיה במחלקת ובספק אם ראובן גנב או לא, לא נוכל להתיר זה הספק מצד שזה המחלקת בעצמו הוא בשמעון· למה שלא התיר הספק מדבר כבר בספק ונתר, כי אם מדבר שהוא במחלקת במדרגת אשר נחפוץ להתירו.

[25] עוד, הוא הטעאיי להוכיח הדבר שהוא חזק המחלקת בדבר בלתי מספיק לבארו הטב; והמשל, אם ימות ראובן בלא יורשים, ויאמ׳ ראובן שכל נכסיו יהיו לאיש דומה לו, ויבא שמעון ויאמ׳ כי לו משפט הירושה, למה שהוא דומה לראובן ביחס, ובתארי הגוף, ובחכמה· אין ספק במה שאמ׳ להוכיח שתנתן לו הירושה, למה שאינו דומה לו מכל הצדדין.

[26] עוד, קיום האמות הוא הטעיי, אם יאמ׳ בו אדם דברי׳ סותרי׳ זה את זה

1 מרבע] מרובע[כ] || 6 התנצלו׳] ההתנצלות[ד] || 9 להרגיל] להדגול[כ] || 10 להיות] להיו[ד] | זהו] זה הוא[כ] || 15 הטובות] טובות[ד] || ו״ך] לך[כ] || 22 [מדבר כבר בספק ונתר][ד] || 26 לאיש דומה] לדומה[ד] ||

which is in doubt now, even as it was in ancient times; for instance, to take the squaring of the circle as a certainty.

[19] Again, the Proof is defective if, immediately after finishing some line of argument, I say: "Had I remembered, or had it entered my mind, I should not have permitted the case to come to this point; for I should have done this or that, but it did not come to mind."

[20] Again, the Proof is defective when the transgression is plainly evident, yet the sinner contents himself with a defence based upon an insignificant detail, like the point in Saul's defence before Samuel, namely, that **the people spared the best of the sheep** [1 Sam. 15:15].

[21] Again, the Proof is defective if one can reckon something said therein for ill; as that a personage of high rank and power should say, in offering counsel, that it is better to get used to kings—meaning to be under kings—than to be under laws. This is a dangerous statement which might lead one to suppose that the speaker has uttered these words on his own behalf, because he wishes to be king and ruler.

[22] Again, it is a fault to use general or false definitions. An example of false definition: Somebody says of a man who delivers himself to dangers that he is valiant, or of a man insensitive to shame that he is meek. An example of general definition: Defining righteousness, someone says that it is a good quality of the soul; this definition is faulty because it applies to all good traits of character.

[23] Again, it is faulty to take as proof the very thing in question which we are investigating; as that, wishing to prove a man a thief, a speaker should prove it on the ground that the man is a base, avaricious, and deceitful fellow—and the evidence for this is that he has committed theft. The speaker has thus taken as proof that which properly is to be investigated, since it is quite possible for the man to be base, deceitful, and avaricious without being a thief.

[24] Again, it is a fault to refute one disputed point by another disputed point. If, for example, the question in doubt and dispute is whether or not Reuben committed theft, we cannot resolve this question on the ground that the self-same point is in dispute in the case of Simeon, since our question has not been resolved on the ground of a previously entertained and resolved question, but on the ground of a case which is just as much under dispute as that which we wish to resolve.

[25] Again, it is a fault to attempt to prove a strongly disputed matter by something that is inadequate to explain it thoroughly. If, for example, Reuben dies without heirs, and has said that all his property should go to a man like himself, and thereupon Simeon comes and says that the inheritance should be adjudged his because he resembles Reuben in ancestry, physical characteristics, and wisdom, what he has said is inadequate to prove that the inheritance should be turned over to him, since he does not resemble Reuben in all respects.

[26] Again, the Proof of the Reason is faulty if in it a speaker makes inconsis-

בערך אל דבר אחד בעצמו; כמי שיאמ׳ ״שאין לענות לכסיל, כדי שלא נחשב היותנו דומים לו״, ובסוף יאמ׳ ״שהוא ראוי לענות לאותו כסיל בעצמו, פן יהיה חכם בעיניו״; הנה אלה הדברים סותרים זה את זה.

[27] עוד, הוא הטעאיי אם נאמ׳ דבר שירע בעיני הדיינים ובעיני השומעים, כגון שנשבח שונאיהם, או נגנה קרוביהם ואוהביהם· כי זהו כנגד כללי זאת המלאכה, לקנות החבוב מהשומעים.

[28] עוד, הוא הטעאיי אם לא נוכיח כל החלקים הנופלים בהצעה.

[29] עוד, הוא הטעאיי ההעתק מענין לענין במאמ׳, כאילו תאמר: שההתחלה היתה בגנב, ואחר כן אלך ממנו אל הורג נפש; כמי שמתחיל המאמ׳ בחכמה אחת, וילך אל חכמה אחרת. וכן, ראוי לשמור בכל היכלת שלא יתוסף דבר במאמ׳ שאינו מענין שהתחלנו· גם לא נחסר בו דבר צריך אליו.

[30] עוד, הוא הטעאיי לחרף ולבזות שום חכמה וידיעה מפני מה שנראה בעלי החכמה ההיא מרוע התכונות והמעללים· כמי שמבזה הפילוסופיא מפני שראה קצת מבעליה הולכים הדרך לא טוב.

[31] עוד, הוא הטעאיי כאשר יתבאר ענין החטא, אלא שלא נדע מי היה, ויכוון האדם המאמ׳ כלו בענין החטא ההוא· כמי שיאמר: ״הוא מת נפוח מבלתי מראה; א״כ, הוא נהרג מסם המות.״ והוא הטעאיי, כי הצרי׳ לנו לדעת הוא מי הרגו, לא באי זה אופן נהרג; כי זה התפרסם לנו, והנה לא יוכיח זה המאמ׳ לנו דבר ממה שצריך אלינו.

[32] עוד, הוא הטעאיי כאשר נעריך דבר אל דבר, ונאריך במה שיתחייב מאחד מהם, והשני נעזב ולא נאמ׳ ממנו דבר· כמי שיאמ׳: שרוב החטים דבר יותר מועיל למדנה מרוב השעורים, למה שהחטים הם כך וכך; וירבה בספר התועלת הנמשך מהם, ולא יאמר מהשעורים דבר.

[33] עוד, הוא הטעאיי, בהעריכנו דבר אל דבר, שנשבח אחד מהם ונגנה האחר· כמי שיאמ׳ שהיראת חטא מדה יותר מעולה מהנדיבות, ויספר בשבח היראת חטא ובגנות הנדיבות; וזה הוא הטעאיי, כי עם היות דבר מעולה מדבר, לא יתחייב שאחד מהם יהיה רע ויהיה ראוי בו הגנות· אדרבה, יתחייב ששניהם טובים, אלא שהאחד יתואר במדרגה יותר מעולה.

5 זהו] זה הוא[ב] || 8 [במאמ׳][ב] || 9 שההתחלה] שהתחלה[ב] |נפש] הנפש[ב] || 14 הדרך] בדרך[ר] || 17 הצרי׳] צריך[ב] || 22 [למדנה][ר] || 24 בהעריכנו] בהעריכות[ר] |אחד] דבר[ב] ||

3–2 מש׳ כ״ו ה׳ || 14 יש׳ ס״ה ב׳ ||

tent statements about one and the same matter; as when one says, "A fool should not be answered, lest we be thought to resemble him,"[5] but ends by saying, "It is proper to answer that same fool, **lest he be wise in his own eyes**" [Prov. 26:5]. These statements obviously contradict each other.

[27] Again, it is faulty if we say something which the judges and hearers may take amiss, as that we should praise their enemies or censure their kinsmen and friends; for to do that would be to violate the rules of this art on gaining the goodwill of the audience.[6]

[28] Again, it is faulty if we do not prove all the subdivisions found in the Proposition.

[29] Again, it is a fault to shift the discussion from one subject to another, as if you should say: "Having begun with a thief, I now go from that to a murderer." This is like one who, beginning a discourse on one science, proceeds with a treatment of a different science. Similarly, we should take all possible care to allow nothing that is not part of the theme upon which we embarked at the outset to be added to the discourse; also to omit nothing necessary to the subject.

[30] Again, it is faulty to disparage and depreciate a science or body of knowledge because of the evil qualities and deeds discernible in practitioners of that science; like the person who disparages philosophy because he has observed that some philosophers **walk in a way that is not good** [Isa. 65:2].

[31] Again, it is a fault when the fact that a crime was committed is evident, but we do not know who committed it, and the speaker devotes his entire argument to the fact of that crime; as one who says: "That corpse was swollen, disfigured; therefore the man was killed by poison." This is faulty because what we need to know is who killed the man, not the manner in which he was killed; for the method is sufficiently plain to us, and such a statement, therefore, will not establish for us any useful point.

[32] Again, it is a fault when, in comparing one thing with another, we treat at length what the one entails, but abandon the other and say nothing about it; as one who, saying, "Abundance of wheat is more advantageous to a State than abundance of barley, since wheat is thus and-thus," then gives a copious account of the advantages accruing from wheat, but says not a word about barley.

[33] Again, it is a fault, when we are comparing two things, to praise one and disparage the other; for example, one who, averring that fear of sin is a higher virtue than liberality, argues in praise of fear of sin and in censure of liberality. This is faulty, because while one thing may be more excellent than another, it does not necessarily follow that either of them is bad and blameworthy; on the contrary, it must be affirmed that both are good, but that the one may be described as the higher virtue.

5. A paraphrase of Prov. 26:4; this verse and the next are in fact inconsistent, and might in themselves have been used by JML as his example, but, perhaps because he was unwilling to show Scripture as inconsistent, he has paraphrased here.

6. See i.6.9–10.

[34] עוד, הוא הטעאיי לחלוק על דבר מה מפני השתנות השמות; והמשל, שהדת אומרת שהגנב יתלוהו על העץ, ואחר כן נקרא הגנב בשם "לסטס"· אין לאומ׳ שיאמ׳ שמי שגנב לא יתלוהו על העץ מפני שעתה אין שמו "גנב", כי אין להשתנות השמות ענין אחר, שהפעל הוא בעינו:

פרק י"א

מהטעאות קצת חלקי ההקשה התמימה; מהספירה, ומהההרחבה, והרחמנות.

[1] יען היפוי הוא מורכב מדברים דומים, והמשלים, וענינים אשר נתן בהם הפסק· ומהרחבות וענינים אחרים המגדילים ומשמינים ההקשה· ראוי שנדבר גם מההטעאות האפשריות בערכם.

[2] ונאמ׳ שהדומה הטעאיי הוא שמצד אחר הוא בלתי דומה, ויערך מהצד הבלתי דומה; או שהמכוון ממנו לדמותו דמיון כולל, או שהוא כנגד האומ׳.

[3] וההמשל הוא הטעאיי אם הוא שקר, או בלתי ראוי, או יותר גדול או יותר קטן ממה שהוצרך אליו.

[4] הדבר אשר נפסק ממנו הדין הוא מסופר באופן הטעאיי כאשר לא ידמה למה שאנחנו בו· או שהוא כענין בלתי נוגע המחלקת· או שהוא בלתי ראוי· או שהמנגדים יוכלו להביא אותו בעזרתם, והוא יותר מיוחד בעניינם.

[5] עוד, הוא הטעאיי להוכיח מה שכבר הודה בו המנגד, למה שהוא ראוי אז להגדילו, לא להוכיח מציאותו.

[6] עוד, הוא הטעאיי להגדיל ולהרחיב הדבר שלא הוכיחו עדיין· כאלו תאמ׳: "שנגדיל ענין הריגת הנפש טרם הוכיחנו שפלו׳ הרגו."

[7] אמנם הטעאות הכלל, מהם, כשלא יכלל מה שנאמ׳ בסדר· עוד, אם לא יכללם בקצור· ואשר לא ישאיר אי זה דבר ודאי וקיים על צד הספירה, ר"ל, מה שהתבאר בהצעה, ובאמות, ובקיום האמות, ובכל ההקשה.

4 ענין] במין[כ] || 5 פרק] פ׳[כ] || 9 ומהרחבות] ומהההרחבות[כ] || 10 מהההטעאות] מהטעאות[כ] || 11 שמצד] שמצ׳[ד] || 12 האומ׳] האחת[כ] || 14 שהוצרך] שהצורך[ד] || 15 מסופר] מסופק[ד] | הטעאיי] הטעאי[ד] || 17 יוכלו] יכולים[ד] | מיוחד בעניינם] מיוחס בענינים[ד] || 18 ראוי אז] אז ראוי[ד] || 22 יכלל] נכלל[ד] | בסדר] בסתר[כ] || 23 [לא][ד] || 24 ובכל] וכל[כ] ||

[34] Again, it is a fault to build a dispute upon a change in names. For example, the law states that a thief shall be hanged on the gallows, but the thief is subsequently termed "brigand": it cannot be contended that he who committed the theft should not be hanged on the gallows on the ground that he is not now termed "thief," for the change in names has no different significance, since the act involved is precisely the same.

CHAPTER 11

Of Faults in Some of the Parts of the Complete Argument; of Enumeration, Amplification, and the Appeal to Pity

[1] Since Embellishment is made up of similes, examples, and previous decisions, as well as of amplifications and other means of enlarging and enriching the argument, we must also discuss the faults to which these are liable.[a]

[2] We may say that a Simile is faulty if it has another dissimilar side, and the comparison is based on the dissimilar side; or if the similarity meant to be indicated is too general, or is prejudicial to him who presents it.

[3] An Example is defective if it is false, or unseemly, or greater or smaller in scope than it needs to be.

[4] The recounting of a previously decided case is at fault when that one is unlike our present case, or when the resemblance is to a matter that does not bear on the disputed issue, or if it is discreditable, or if our opponents can introduce it in their own support and it is more apposite to their case.

[5] Again, it is a fault to prove what has already been admitted by our opponent; for then it is appropriate to enlarge upon this admission, not to prove that it is the case.

[6] Again, it is a fault to enlarge and amplify an as yet unproved proposition; as if you should say: "Before proving that so-and-so was the murderer, we shall enlarge upon homicide."

[7] Among defects of the Résumé are the following: when what has been said is not summed up in exact order; also, if the summary is not brief; and if it does not leave some certain and valid conclusion through recapitulation, that is, what has been made clear through Proposition, Reason, Proof of the Reason, and the entire argument.

a. *R. ad H.* 2.29.46 ff.

[8] יש לדעת שהחתימות, אשר יקראום היונים ״כלל העולה״, נחלקות אל ג׳ חלקי׳, ר״ל, ספירה· הרחבה· חנינה. ואפשר בערכנו להרגיל החתימות באחד מד׳ מקומות, ר״ל, בפתיחה· בספור· באי זו הקשה קיימת· ובחתימה. ואין ראוי שיעלם שהרצון ב״חתימה״ הנה אינה החתימה אשר היא אחת מחלקי המאמ׳,
5 אשר כבר התבאר ענינה, כי אז לא היה צודק המצאה כי אם בחתימה· אמנם, המכוון בה בזה המקום תכלית וחותם מאמ׳ מה, או חלק מאמ׳. וזה אפשר המצאו בפתיחה, כמו שנקח בסוף הפתיחה אי זה משל יחתמה; וכן ביתר החלקים, ר״ל, שימצא בסוף הפתיחה, ובסוף הספור, ובסוף אי זו הקשה קיימת, ובסוף החתימה.

10 [9] ונחזור לדברינו, ונאמ׳ שהספירה היא כאשר נכלול ונזכור בקצור מה שבארנו. וראוי שנספרם על צד מחודש, לא שנשנה הדברי׳ בעצמ׳, כי זה יקרא השנות. וראוי שהספירה תהיה על סדר הדברים, כדי שיביא השומע לזכור הדברים אשר סדרם בזכרון. גם אין ראוי שתתחיל הספירה לא מההתחלה ולא מהספור, שלא יראה אי זה דבר מתוקן ומסודר במלאכה· או אי זו תחבולה או
15 בדיאה להראות העמים והשרים כי זוכר כל הנשכחות אשר מעולם. ולזה, ראוי שתתחיל מהחלוק, וממנה, על הסדר ובקצור, בקיום ובהתרה.

[10] ההרחבה היא מאמ׳ נלקח לעורר השומעים על החמה והכעס מצד המקומות הכוללים; והמקומות הכוללים ילקחו מעשרה כללים באופן הגון להגדיל העון.

20 [11] המקום הראשון הוא מספרי הקודמים, כשנספר במה היה גודל זה החטא אצל השם יתברך, ואצל השופטים, ומנהיגי המדינות, והחכמים בכל דור ודור, ובעלי העצה· ונביא מה שנכתב מזה בדתות ובנמוסים.

[12] המקום השני, שנתבונן בערך מי העון הנעשה: אם הוא דבר שב אל האלקים· או בערך כל בני האדם· או בהצטרף אל היותר גדולים· או אל אשר
25 הם במדרגה שוה עם החוטא בעניני הנפש, והגוף, וההצלחות אשר מחוץ· או בערך אל אשר הם למטה ממנו במדרגה. ובאלה הבחינות יתבאר גודל העון או קטנו.

1 נחלקות] נחלקי[כ] || 5 התבאר] הת׳[ד] || 8 שימצא] שתמצא[כ] || 11 שבארנו] שאמרנו[כ] | הדברי׳] הד׳[ד] | בעצמ׳] בעצמה[כ] || 12 שיביא <שיביא>[כ] || 13 הספירה] מהספירה[ד] || 15 <הוא> אשר[ד] || 20 המקום] והמקום[ד] | מספרי] מספורי[כ] | החטא] החט[ד] || 22 מזה] ומה[ד] || 24 האדם] אדם[ד] | בהצטרף] בהצטרך[כ] || 26 ובאלה] וכאלה[ד] ||

---

15 אס׳ א׳ י״א | בר׳ ו׳ ד׳ ||

[8] It should be noted that Conclusions, what the Greeks call "summary,"[1] are divided into three parts: the Recapitulation, the Amplification, and the Appeal to Pity. It is possible for us to employ Conclusions in any of four places: in the Direct Opening, in the Statement of Facts, in case of some unshakable argument, and in the Conclusion. It should not go unnoticed that by "Conclusion" here is not meant the previously explained conclusion which is one of the Parts of the Discourse, for in that case it would be incorrect to find it in any place other than at the end of the speech; but "Conclusion" in the present context means the final close of some argument or part of an argument. Such a Conclusion can appear in the Direct Opening, as when we adopt some example to bring the Opening to an end. And so too, in the remaining Parts of the Discourse: that is, a Conclusion may occur at the end of the Direct Opening, of the Statement of Facts, of some unshakable argument, and of the main Conclusion.

[9] Returning now to our subject, we may say that it is the Recapitulation when we gather together and briefly recall the points we have made. Our Recapitulation should be made in a fresh way; we should not reiterate the very words, for this will be termed repetitious. The Recapitulation should also preserve the order of the several points so as to bring the hearer to recall the points which he has set in a definite order in his memory. Moreover, the Recapitulation should begin neither with the Introduction nor the Statement of Facts, lest it seem artificially contrived and arranged, or seem a kind of trick or fabrication **to show the peoples and the princes** [Esth. 1:11] that the speaker remembers all things forgotten **that were of old** [Gen. 6:4]. The Recapitulation should therefore begin with the Partition, and thence, in order and briefly, proceed with the Proof and the Refutation.

[10] Amplification is a speech device adopted in order, through commonplaces, to stir the hearers to wrath and indignation. Commonplaces will be drawn from ten formulae in the way best suited to magnifying the iniquity.

[11] The first commonplace is taken from the books of the ancients: we describe why this particular sin has been regarded as so heinous by the Name, blessed be He, and by judges, heads of State, sages in every generation, and counselors; and we introduce what is written about this sin in laws and ordinances.

[12] The second commonplace is that we consider whom the iniquitous deed affects: whether it is something that adverts to God; or affects all mankind; or involves our superiors; or those who are the sinner's peers in qualities of soul and body, and in favorable external circumstances; or concerns our inferiors. Through application of these criteria, either the seriousness or the insignificance of the crime will become clear.

1. The term used here, כלל העולה, is the medieval Hebrew equivalent of *summa, summarium:* see Klatzkin, *'Ōṣar hammūnāḥīm happilosophīyīm,* [Thesaurus Philosophicus Linguae Hebraicae] (Berlin, 1928), II, 92, s.v.

[13] המקום השלישי, שנספר מה שאפשר שיתחייב, אם יותר זה העון לכל וילך החוטא נקי מכל עונש, מן הנזקין, והסכנות, ורעות רבות וצרות.

[14] המקום הרביעי, שאם נשא זה העון ולא נעניש החוטא, אנשים אחרים גם כן לא ייראו מעשות תועבות גדולות מאלה, למה שיקוו המחילה מהם, ושיצאו מבלי עונש. ויבדל זה המקום מאשר למעלה ממנו, שהמקום השלישי הוא בבחינת הרע שאפשר שיתחייב בסתם ובמוחלט, וזה המקום הוא לקוח ביחוד מצד יצר האדם רע, ועושה עולה.

[15] המקום החמישי, שאם יצא הפסק דין זולת מה שראוי בחק האיש הזה, יהיה מעוות לא יוכל לתקון לעולם, וחסרון במשפט לא יוכל להמנות; ואף על פי שדברים רבים מתרפאים בטוב העצה ובמשך הזמן, זה יהיה במדרגת שחין מצרים אשר לא יוכל להרפא· צרעת ממארת הוא.

[16] המקום הששי, שנבאר שזה נעשה בכונה ורצון, בידיעה ובהכרח· ולא יוכל להתנצל בשום צד· ולא תצדק בכאן התחנה והבקשה באחד מן הפנים.

[17] המקום השביעי, כגון שנאמ׳: ״שזה העון, אין למעלה ממנו אכזריות נפלא ולקיחת השררה שלא כדין, כמו חרפת הנשים, או דבר אחר המביא חרב איש ביד רעהו להשמיד, להרוג, ולאבד.״

[18] המקום השמיני, שנאמר: ״שזה אינו מעונות המורגלים· אמנם כי הוא מיוחד ברוע ובהפלגת הפשעים, אשר ראוי לקחת למענו הנקמה מבעליו באכזריות, חמה, ושטף אף· ולהב אש אוכלה.״

[19] המקום התשיעי, כגון שנגדיל העון דרך ההצטרפות, כגון שנאמר: ״שהריגת האנשים הוא עון יותר גדול מאונס הבתולה, למה שההריגה אינה מקבלת תקון, אמנם ענין האונס יתוקן.״

[10] המקום העשירי, שנספר מה שהיה קודם המעשה, ובשעת המעשה, ואחריו, לעשות הדבר כאילו הוא נגד העינים· ולספר כל דבר ודבר עם תלונה גדולה ותרעומת, והפלגת העון והגדילו בכל פרטי המעשה.

[21] ובהלצה הישנה, מוסיף ה׳ מקומות אחרים: אשר האחד מהם, שנאמר שזה העון נעשה מאדם שלא היה לו לעשות· אדרבה, היה לו למחות אם יעשוהו אחרים. השני, שנאמר שזה הוא דבר חדש בערכנו, ושלא שמענו כמוהו

1 השלישי] הג׳[ד] || 2 [נקי][כ] | הנזקין] הנזקים[כ] || 6 ובמוחלט] ומוחלט[ד] || 7 [רע][כ] || 8 בחק] בחק׳[ד] || 9 במשפט] המשפט[כ] || 11 הוא] היא[כ] || 14 השביעי] הז׳[ד] || 15 ולקיחת] ולקחת[כ] || 16 להרוג] ולהרוג[כ] || 17 השמיני] הח׳[ד] || 20 התשיעי] הט׳[ד] || 26 האחד] אחד[כ] || 27 למחות] למחו׳[ד] ||

---

2 דב׳ ל״א י״ז || 7 בר׳ ח׳ כ״א | תה׳ ל״ז א׳ || 9 קה׳ א׳ ט״ו || 10–11 דב׳ כ״ח כ״ז | וי׳ י״ג נ״ב || 15–16 שופ׳ ז׳ כ״ב | אס׳ ג׳ י״ג || 19 מש׳ כ״ז ד׳ | יואל ב׳ ה׳ ||

[13] The third commonplace is that we relate the injuries, dangers, **and many evils and troubles** [Deut. 31:17] which could ensue if this iniquity were permitted to all, and whoever sinned were to get off scot-free.

[14] The fourth commonplace: if we tolerate this iniquity and fail to punish the sinner, others too will not be afraid to commit even greater abominations, since they will expect to be pardoned and go unpunished. This commonplace is distinguished from that immediately above in that the third commonplace is about evil consequences that, speaking abstractly and in general. may possibly ensue, whereas the present commonplace is a specially adopted form of the idea that **the inclination of man . . . is evil** [Gen. 8:21], and he is an **evil-doer** [Ps. 37:1].

[15] The fifth commonplace: if the judgment rendered should be other than this man justly deserves, it will be **a crooked thing which can** never **be made straight, and a loss** in justice **which cannot be numbered** [Eccl. 1:15];[2] and although many ills can be remedied through excellent counsel and in the course of time, this ill will be of a kind with **the boil of Egypt . . . which cannot be healed** [Deut. 28:27], which **is a malignant leprosy** [Lev. 13:52].

[16] The sixth commonplace: we show that the act was done intentionally and willfully, consciously, and under compulsion; that it is altogether indefensible; and that any kind of plea or request for mercy is here quite unjustified.

[17] The seventh commonplace: as that we say, "No extraordinary cruelty or illegal seizure of power, the shaming of women, for example, or any other matter that brings a **man's sword against his fellow** [Judg. 7:22] **to destroy, to slay and to cause to perish** [Esth. 3:13], is higher in infamy than this crime."

[18] The eighth commonplace: that we say, "This is no ordinary crime, but one so evilly and viciously unique that it should be avenged upon its perpetrators with **cruelty, wrath, and anger overwhelming** [Prov. 27:4],[3] with **a flame of fire that devoureth** [Joel 2:5]."

[19] The ninth commonplace is to make the iniquity greater through association; we may, for example, say: "Homicide is a greater crime than the rape of a virgin, since murder is irreparable whereas rape can be amended."

[20) The tenth commonplace: we describe what happened before, during, and after the act, making the affair seem to be taking place before our very eyes, accompanying the narration of each detail with sharp incrimination and denunciation, and heightening and enlarging upon the crime by means of all the particulars of the act.

[21] In the Old Rhetoric, Tully[b] gives five additional commonplaces. The first of these: we say that this crime was committed by one who not only should not have committed it himself, but on the contrary had a duty to protest if others were going to do it. The second: we say that this is a novel crime to us, and that we

2. Slightly altered from JV.
3. Slightly altered from JV.

b. *De I.* 1.54.104–105.

מעולם. השלישי, שנאמ׳ אלה הדברים עם כלמות חרפות מהחוטא, לעורר הכעס והחמה והאיבה לשומעים עליו. הרביעי, שנבקש מהשומעים שיחשבו שזה החטא נעשה בערכם· כאלו תאמר, שאם היה החטא בבנים או בנשים, יחשבו שזה נעשה בבניהם ונשותיהם. החמישי, שאפי׳ בעיני אויבינו ומבקשי נפשינו היה רע עליהם המעשה הזה.

[22] ואמר קוינטיליאנו, בחמישי מהמאמר השמיני, שההרחבה היא נחלקת אל ארבעה חלקים, רוצה לומר, הוספה· הערכה· הבדל· ואחדות.

[23] אמנם ההוספה, הוא מאמר מתחיל מן השפל והולך במדרגה עד מרומים; והמשל בזה בישעיה: הוי גוי חוטא, עם כבד עון· זרע מריעים, בנים משחיתים· עזבו את י״י, נאצו את קדוש ישראל, נזורו אחור [יש׳ א׳ ד׳]. המכוון ב״נזורו אחור״ שנזורו אחור, בסתם ובמוחלט, מכל מצוה ומכל מדה טובה· וזה גדול מכל מה שנאמר. ואין ספק ש״עם כבד עון״ מוסיף על גוי חוטא, אלא שאפשר שעם היותו ״כבד עון״ לא הגיע עדין למדרגה שיריע לאחרים· והנה אם כן, ״זרע מרעים״ מוסיף על ״כבד עון״. והנה יתכן שהמכון ב״מרעים״ יהיה שירעו מעט לאנשים, אבל לא יעשו כלה· ולזה, ״בנים משחיתים״ מוסיף על ״זרע מרעים״, שהמכוון בזה המאמר שהם משחיתים את הארץ ברוע מעלליהם. ועם כל זה, אפשר שיהיו עם י״י בקצת המצות· והנה הוא מבואר ש״עזבו את ה׳״ מוסיף על ״בנים משחיתים״, אלא שעם כל זה אפשר שלא יעשו ביד רמה, בשאט בנפש, להכעיס; והתחייב מזה שמה שאמר, ״נאצו את קדוש ישראל״, שהמכוון בו שהיו עוברים להכעיס, יוסיף על ״עזבו את י״י״. ועם כל

1 השלישי] הג׳[ד] || 2 הרביעי] הד׳[ד] || 3 החטא] החט[ד] | החטא] החוטא[ד] || 4 שאפי׳ <אל>[כ] || 6 בחמישי] בה׳[כ] | השמיני] הח׳[כ] || 7 ארבעה] ד׳[כ] || 10 [את][כ] || 12 שנאמר] שאמ׳[כ] | שעם] טעם[כ] || 13–14 אם כן] אחר כן[ד] ||

16–17 יש׳ א׳ ט״ז | במ׳ י״א כ״ט || 19 במ׳ ט״ו ל׳ | יח׳ כ״ה ט״ו | מל״א כ״א ו׳ ||

have never heard of anything like it. The third: that we are presenting these facts together with the sinner's scornful insults, so as to arouse against him the anger, wrath, and hostility of the hearers. The fourth: we ask our hearers to imagine this crime as affecting themselves; for example, if the crime was perpetrated upon children or women, we ask them to imagine that this crime was perpetrated on their own children or wives. The fifth commonplace: that even to our enemies and those who seek our lives this deed would seem repugnant.

[22] In Book VIII, Chapter 5,[4] Quintilian[c] says that the Amplification is divisible into four parts: Augmentation, Comparison, Differentiation, and Amalgamation.

[23] Augmentation is a speech device which begins with the comparatively insignificant and proceeds gradually to the highest degree. We have an example of this in Isaiah:

> **Ah sinful nation,**
> **A people laden with iniquity,**
> **A seed of evil-doers,**
> **Children that deal destruction,**[5]
> **They have forsaken the Lord,**
> **They have contemned the Holy One of Israel,**
> **They are turned away backward** [Isa. 1:4].[6]

The purport of **they are turned away backward** is that they turned away, categorically and absolutely, from every commandment and from every kind of virtue; and this is the climax of the entire passage. Now **a people laden with iniquity** undoubtedly constitutes an increase over **sinful nation,** but leaves the possibility that, though **laden with iniquity,** the people might not have reached that degree of sin wherein they would do evil to others; so, then, **a seed of evil-doers** augments **laden with iniquity.** At this point, **evil-doers** could conceivably mean those who, while they may do some harm to other people, yet do not wreak complete destruction: **children that deal destruction,** therefore, augments **a seed of evil-doers,** the purport of this phrase being that they are destroying the land with **the evil of their doings** [Isa. 1:16]. Despite all this, they might yet be **the Lord's people** [Num. 11:29] with regard to some of the commandments; clearly, therefore, **they have forsaken the Lord** augments **children that deal destruction.** Even so there remains the possibility that their acts were not committed **with a high hand** [Num. 15:30], **with disdain of soul** [Ezek. 25:15], **to provoke Him** [1 Kings 21:6]; consequently, the statement, **they have contemned the Holy One of Israel,** the purport of which is that they were transgress-

4. *Sic,* JML; modern reference as in source-footnote c.
5. JV: "... deal corruptly."
6. Cf. i.14.2.

c. Q. 8.4.3 ff.

זה, אפשר שתהיה בהם אי זו מדה טובה· לכן אמר אחרי כן, ״נזורו אחור״.
[24] וההערכה הוא מאמר שהולך וגדל, אבל על צד ההערכה, שהוא מעריך דבר לדבר· והמשל בזה בהושע: לא אפקוד על בנותיכם כי תזנינה, ועל כלותיכם כי תנאפנה· כי הם עם הזונות יפרדו, כו׳ [הו׳ ד׳ י״ד]. התחיל בזה הפסוק מזנות ״הבנות״, ר״ל, שלא היו לאיש עדין· והלך מזה אל נאוף ״הכלות״, שהוא דבר יותר גדול, שהם נשואות בעל· ולזה אמר ״תנאפנה״, שהוא דבר יותר מיוחד באשת איש. עוד נעתק מזה אל דבר יותר גדול, ואמר: ״כי הם עם הזונות יפרדו״, ר״ל, כי הם בעצמם, ר״ל, האבות, שהיו להם להזהר מן הפשעים יותר מן הכלות, מצדדים: אם מצד שהם מלאי ימים יותר, ובישישי׳ חכמה· אם מצד שלא תבער בם כל כך שלהבת הבחרות; אם גם כן מצד שהזכרים דעתם יותר קיימת מהנקבות· גם כי מחוק גדולי הבית להוכיח אשר תחתיהם. עם כל זה, הגיע מרוע תכונתם, שבהיותם תמיד עם הזונות, מכל אשר בחרו ואפילו הנשואות, ירגישו בזה בעליהם, כי לא יוכלו לחשוב סבה אחרת לזה ההתקרבות הגדול, ויקנאו את נשותיהם עד יפרדו מהם· והנה הם סבה להפריד האנשים משוכבת חיקם. ותהיה תיבת ״יפרדו״ יוצאת לשלישי, על דרך ומכתבים עמל כתבו [יש׳ י׳ א׳]; או ירצה ב״יפרדו״ שהם, בהיותם עם הזונות תמיד, יפרדו נשותיהם מהם לזנות באנשי הארץ גם הם, כי יקנאו בבעלים· וזה להם שכר חלף עבודתם, והנה מלאה הארץ זמה; או ירצה בזה, כי מרוב תאותם להיות עם הזונות, כל אחד מפרד אשתו ממנו בכונה, ומשכיבה עם חברו, ומתחלפים נשותיהם זה בזה, כי ינעם להם לחם סתרים, ותערב לנפשם

1 אחרי] אחר[ד] || 2 הוא] היא[כ] || 12 תמיד] תמי[ד] || 13 יוכלו] יכלו[כ] ||

9 יר׳ ו׳ י״א | איוב י״ב י״ב || 12 בר׳ ו׳ ב׳ || 15 מי׳ ז׳ ה׳ || 18 במ׳ י״ח ל״א | וי׳ י״ט כ״ט || 20 מש׳ ט׳ י״ז | מש׳ י״ג י״ט ||

ing in order to provoke Him, augments **they have forsaken the Lord.** With all this, there might still possibly be some sort of virtue in them, and that is why the prophet says the next following words, **they are turned away backwards**.

[24] Comparison is also a speech-device of progressive magnitude, but of a kind that evaluates one instance of some act in terms of another. Hosea provides an example:

> **I will not punish your daughters when they commit harlotry,**
> **Nor your daughters-in-law when they commit adultery;**
> **For they themselves cause separation in consort**[7] **with lewd women,** etc. [Hosea 4:14].

In this verse the prophet's point of departure was the harlotry of the **daughters,** that is, those who as yet had no husband. From this he went on to the adultery of the daughters-in-law, a greater matter, since they were married; he therefore says **they commit adultery,** this being the more specific term used in the case of a man's wife. Passing on thence to something still more serious, he says **for they themselves cause separation with lewd women: they themselves,** that is, the fathers, whose duty it was to be even more heedful of transgressions than the daughters-in-law. Such was their duty for several reasons: whether because the fathers are more **full of days** [Jer. 6:11], and **wisdom is with aged men** [Job 12:12]; or because the flame of youth does not burn in them so ardently; or even because males are more stable in mind than are females; and also because it is natural for the senior members of the family to correct those who are subject to their authority. All this notwithstanding, it resulted from their evil character that, consorting always with harlots, **whomsoever they chose** [Gen. 6:2], and even with married women, the husbands of these women, unable to imagine any other reason for such great intimacy, would remark the fact and be so suspicious of their wives' unfaithfulness that they would separate from them; and so it was the fathers who caused the separating of husbands from those **that lie in** their **bosoms** [Mi. 7:5]. The verb form *y^{e}phārēdhū* thus is transitive and causative, in the same way as *kittēbhū* in **Woe . . . to the writers that cause the writing of iniquity** [Isa. 10:1].[8] Or, by *y^{e}phārēdhū,* Hosea may have meant that the fathers, through their constant association with harlots, would cause their own wives to separate from them and to commit harlotry with the men of the land, because they would suspect the infidelity of their husbands. This being the fathers' **reward in return for** their **service** [Num. 18:31], **the land** was indeed **full of lewdness** [Lev. 19:29]. Or the meaning of the term may be that, because of their passionate desire to consort with harlots, each father deliberately would cause his own wife to separate from himself and sleep with his friend; and that they would exchange wives with each other because to them **bread eaten in**

7. JV: "For they themselves consort with . . ."; KJV: "For they themselves are separated with whores. . . ."

8. JV: ". . . that write iniquity."

זאת הזמה הגדולה אשר אין למעלה ממנה.

[25] ההבדל, כשיתואר שבח או גנות האחד בנבדל ממנו: כמו שהאריך הפסוק בתארי גלית, כמו שכתוב: גלית שמו, מגת, גבהו שש אמות וזרת· וכובע נחשת על ראשו, ושריון קשקשים הוא לבוש, ומשקל השריון חמשת אלפים שקלים נחשת, וכו׳ [שמ״א י״ז ד׳—ה׳] — מאריך ומספר מתעצומות׳[1], ורומו, ולבו כלב הארי; והיה זה האריכות כלו על צד ההרחבה לשבח דוד שנצח אותו. וכן מה שאמ׳ בישבי בנוב — אשר בילידי הרפה, ומשקל קנו שלש מאות משקל נחשת [שמ״ב כ״א ט״ז] — הוא על צד ההרחבה לשבח אבישי שהרגו. והדומים לזה הרבה בלשוננו.

[26] והאחדות הוא, כשתעשה ההרחבה בתבות מתחלפות אחדות בטעם, או במאמרים מתחלפים אחדים בטעם, ר״ל, שאין שם תוספת או חסרון; והמשל בישעיה: שבעתי עולות אילים וחלב מריאים· ודם פרים וכבשים ועתודים לא חפצתי [יש׳ א׳ י״א]. הרצון בכל אלה שי״י מאס בקרבניה׳, עולותיהם, וזבחיהם על רוב פשעיהם, ולבלתי הטהרם מהם ושובם בתשובה גמורה.

[27] עוד אמר קוינטיליאנו שגם ימצאו מיני ההמעטה, כמו שימצאו מיני ההגדלה וההרחבה. והנה טוליאו לקח ההרחבה, בהלצה הישנה והחדשה, בהגדיל העון לבד, כמו שנראה מגדרה אשר גדרה. אמנם, קוינטיליאנו לקח ההרחבה על צד שתובן ממנה הגדלה ותוספת בכל ענין, בשבח או גנות או זולת זה· כמו שהתבאר ג״כ בהרחבות והגדלות הנמצאות בספרי הקדש, וביחוד ביחזקאל בנבואת צור [יח׳ כ״ו], ובנבואת חירם [שם כ״ח], ובנבואת פרעה מלך מצרים [שם כ״ט], וזולתם. ואמ׳ הפילוסוף בקצור ההלצה שמיני ההרחבה

4–5 אלפים שקלים] שקלים אלפים^ד |וכו׳] ובר^כ |מתעצומות׳[1]] מתעצומו^כ || 7 קנו] קינו^ת || 9 לזה] בזה^ד || 12 אילים...מריאים] אלים...מראים^ד || 13 שי״י] שהשם^ד |בקרבניה׳] בכל קרבניהם^ד || 18 שתובן] שתוב׳^ד || 21 ואמ׳] ואמו^ד ||

14 איכה א׳ ה׳ ||

[1] Abbreviation not indicated in ד.

secret is pleasant [Prov. 9:17], and because such unsurpassably great lewdness was **sweet to** their **soul** [13:19].

[25] It is Differentiation when someone's praise or blame is depicted through the description of one distinguished from him. An example is the passage which dilates upon the qualities of Goliath, as follows: **And there went out a champion from the camp of the Philistines, named Goliath, of Gath, whose height was six cubits and a span. And he had a helmet of brass upon his head, and he was clad with a coat of mail; and the weight of the coat was five thousand shekels of brass,** etc. [1 Sam. 17:4–5]—a long description of Goliath's abundant might, height, and lion-heartedness. The whole of this lengthy description is a way of amplifying the praise of David, who vanquished Goliath. Likewise, the statement about Ishbi-benob, **who was of the sons of the giant, the weight of whose spear was three hundred shekels of brass** [2 Sam. 21:16], is a way of amplifying the praise of Abishai, who killed him. Usages similar to this kind of Amplification abound in our language.

[26] It is Amalgamation when the Amplification is accomplished by means of words or sentences which, while varying, are one in meaning, that is, where there is neither increase nor decrease in the meaning. Our example is found in Isaiah:

I am full of the burnt-offerings of rams,
And the fat of fed beasts;
And I delight not in the blood
Of bullocks, or of lambs, or of he-goats [Isa. 1:11].

The intent of all these expressions was that the Lord had rejected the people's oblations, burnt-offerings, and sacrifices **for the multitude of** their **transgressions** [Lam. 1:5], and for their failure to be cleansed of these and to return to Him in complete repentance.

[27] Quintilian[d] says, further, that there are various kinds of Attenuation, just as there are various kinds of Enlargement and Amplification. Now Tully,[e] in both the Old Rhetoric and the New, conceived of Amplification only in connection with the enlarging of the crime, as we see from his definition of the term. Quintilian, however, took Amplification as connoting enlargement and supplementation of any subject, whether in praise, blame, or any other connection; as is clear, also, in the case of the amplifications and enlargements found in the Holy Books, particularly in Ezekiel's prophecies on Tyre [26–27], Hiram [28:2 f.],[9] Pharaoh King of Egypt [29:2 f.], and others. And the Philosopher,[f] in

9. Ezekiel's "prince of Tyre" is, apparently, identified by JML as the "Hiram" of 1 Kings 5:15 ff. and many other passages.

d. Q. 8.4.28
e. *De I.* 1.53.100; *R. ad H.* 2.30.47.
f. Cf. *LR. ad A.* 38.33 f. (1426b f.).

ראויים בסוג המקיים יותר מיתר הסוגים.

[28] ונשוב לדברי טוליאו. בב׳ מההלצה החדשה, בענין החנינה, אמר שאנחנו נעורר השומעים אל החנינה מצדדים רבים. מהם, שנספר שנוי עתותינו והעתקתם מטוב אל רע. ומהם, שנעריך ימי המהומה והצער אל ימי ההצלחה הגדולה, כלומר: ״ראו במכאוב הגדול אשר עולל לי, עם שכבר הייתי ממעל לכוכבי אל.״ ומהם, שנספר מה יתחייב לנו מן הרע הגדול אם לא נמצא חן בעיניהם. ומהם, שנאמר שהננו להם לעבדים, ובידיהם אנחנו לעשות לנו כטוב בעיניהם. ומהם, שנאמר מה שימשך מן הצרות לאבותינו, לבנינו ולבנותינו, ולנשותינו אם לא יפנו אלינו· ושעל זה היה דוה לבנו, לא ממה שאפשר שיגיע לנו בעצמנו. ומהם, שנספר מה רבו מעשינו, וחסדינו אשר מעולם, לכל דורש ולכל מבקש. ומהם, שנספר רוע מזלנו, ועניינו ולחצנו, מימים רבים. ומהם, שנספר היאך סבלנו אותם בסבר פנים יפות וביראת השם.

[29] זה מה שאמר בחדשה; אמנם בישנה, אמר טוליאו, ווטורינו המפרש, שהחנינה היא מאמר מעורר האנשים אל החנינה· ומוסיף במקומות החנינה, כגון שנאמר: ״שמרוב קשי זמננו, כאשר נצפה שיעבור זמן התלאות והיגונות, וישן מפני חדש נוציא, יתחדש כנשר נעורינו, אז נפלנו בענין יותר רע ממה שהיינו בתחלה.״ ומהם, שנעביר המאמ׳ אל בעלי חיים בלתי מדברים, או אל הדוממים, כאלו נשים הבתים והשדות מדברים, לעורר יותר לבב השומעים. ומהם, שנביא פרטי הצער והיגון, ונספרם בבכי· כגון, אם נתאונן על הבנים, נספר שעשועם, ולמודם, ומזונותיהם בבכי ויללה; וכן ביתר הענינים. ומהם, שנספר שאין לנו מנחם· וקרובינו ואחינו עזבונו, נטשונו, אף כי מריעינו רחקו ממנו· ואשר גמלנו אותם טובות, ועשינו עמם חסד ואמת, שכחונו ולא זכרו ברית אחים:

6 ומהם] ומה[ר] || 7 ובידיהם] ובידיכם[כ] || 10 רבו] שרבו[כ] | מעשינו וחסדינו] מעשנו וחסדנו[ר] || 12 [יפות][כ] | השם] ה׳[כ] || 13 בישנה] בישינה[כ] | אמר] אמ׳[כ] | ווטורינו] וויטורינו[כ] || 21 מריעינו] מריענו[כ] ||

6–5 יש׳ י״ד י״ג || 10 תה׳ ק״ד כ״ד | תה׳ כ״ה ו׳ | יח׳ ל״ד ו׳ || 11 תה׳ מ״ד כ״ה | יהו׳ כ״ג א׳ || 16 וי׳ כ״ו י׳ | תה׳ ק״ג ה׳ || 21 איכה א׳ כ״א | מש׳ י״ט ז׳ || 22 בר׳ מ״ז כ״ט || 23–22 עמ׳ א׳ ט׳ ||

the Abridgment of the *Rhetoric,* says that the several varieties of Amplification are more fittingly employed in Epideictic than in the other Kinds of Cause.

[28] Let us now return to Tully's[g] words. In the New Rhetoric, Book II, discussing the Appeal to Pity, he says that there are numerous ways of stirring pity in our hearers. One is to recount the alteration in our fortunes, how they have gone from good to bad. Another is to compare our present days of trouble and distress with the days of our great prosperity, as follows: "Consider the great pain inflicted upon me, and consider, besides, the fact that I was once **above the stars of God**" [Isa. 14:13]. Another way is to describe to our hearers the great ill that must necessarily follow for us if we fail to find favor in their eyes. Another: to say that we are as slaves to our hearers, and are in their hands to do with as they may deem best. Another: to point out the resultant distress of our parents, sons and daughters, and wives, if our hearers should not decide in our favor; it is because of this that our heart would be sore, not because of what threatens to overtake ourselves. Another: to recount **how manifold** were our **works** [Ps. 104:24], and our **mercies** which **have been from of old** [Ps. 25:6], for any **that did search or seek** [Ezek. 34:6]. Another: to describe our ill fortune, **our affliction and our oppression** [Ps. 44:25], of **many days** [Josh. 23:1]. And another: to describe how we have borne these sorrows with good countenance and with reverence for the Name.

[29] This is what Tully says in the New Rhetoric. In the Old, however, Tully[h]—as also the commentator Victorinus[i]—defines the Appeal to Pity as a speech device for arousing pity in men; and he makes several additions to the commonplaces of the Appeal to Pity. One such is that we say: "Among the worst of the many disasters dealt us by fortune was that, just as we were hoping that the time of hardships and troubles was over, and we should **bring forth the old from before the new** [Lev. 26:10], our **youth be renewed like the eagle** [Ps. 103:5], at that very moment we fell into a worse plight than we were in to begin with." Another such commonplace: to transfer the discourse to dumb animals or inanimate objects, for instance to endow houses and fields with the power of speech, in order more deeply to stir the minds of our hearers. Another: to introduce the details of our sorrow and trouble and to weep while describing them; for example, if showing grief over children, to weep and wail while telling how they played, studied, and took their meals; and thus too, with all other such details. Another: to tell how **there is none to comfort** [Lam. 1:21] us; our kinfolk and brethren having abandoned and forsaken us, **how much more do** our **friends go far from** [Prov. 19:7] us; and how those to whom we have rendered good and with whom we have **dealt kindly and truly** [Gen. 47:29] have forgotten us **and remembered not the brotherly covenant** [Amos 1:9].

g. *R. ad H.* 2.31.50.
h. *De I.* 1.55.106 ff.
i. Halm, p. 257.

פרק י״ב

היאך יושמו בהרגל חלקי המאמר, ר״ל פתיחה, ספור, חלוק, קיום, התרה, חתימה, בערך אל סוג העצומי.

[1] אמר הפילוסוף, בקצור ההלצה אשר עשה לאלכסנדר, שאם נכוון המאמ׳ בסוג העצומי, נתחיל הפתיחה באופן התבאר במה שקדם; ואם הוא המתרעם, יציע הענין אשר עליו התלונה לגרום ההקשבה לשומע. עוד, נגרום החבוב באופן התבאר למעלה — אמנם כי הוא יותר ראוי לכונן שבח השומעים מהדברים יותר נפלאים ויותר מיוחדים בשומעים — עם שנעורר אותם אל הכעס והאיבה כנגד המנגדים באמרנו שהם רעים וחטאים. עוד, אם התרעם בעבור אנשים אחרים בדבר איננו נוגע לו, ראוי שיאמר שאינו עושה זה לתקות שכר, רק לאהבת האנשים או לשנאת המנגדים· או שהוא היה במעמד וראה הענין על השלמות· או שהוא עושה זה לתועלת הכללות· או מפני שנכמרו רחמיו בראותו שזה הסובל הנזק והחרפה, הוא נעזב מכל האנשים ואין דורש משפטו, מוכה אלקים ומעונה.

[2] ואחר הפתיחה נבא אל הספור· אם שנספר התלונה בחלקים מפוזרים, אם שנכלל הכל ביחד.

[3] ואחר הספור נבא אל החלוק, להודיע הדבר אשר הוא בהסכמה עם המנגד, ואשר ישאר במחלקת.

[4] ואחר החלוק נבא אל הקיום, לקיים התלונה באחד מאופני הקיומים. ונתחיל בהם מן העדים, גם מאשר בידינו מן ההודאות על התלונה· מהראיות· מהדתות· מהמנהגים· מהחשדים· מהאותות וההקשות· או זולתם, לפי מה שיבקש ענינו, ולפי ענין הטענה הסבריית תהיה ראויה או משפטית.

[5] אחר כן, נחשוב מה שאפשר שישיב המתנצל ויטעון, ונתיר אותם· וזאת תהיה ההתרה. ואם השיבו המתנצלים וטענו על הקיומים שעשינו, ראוי שנרחיב אותם, ושנתיר כל מה שאמ׳ ושנופל במחשבתנו שיוכלו לאמר; ואופן

1 פרק] פ׳ג || 2 [חלקי]ג || 8 עם] עדד |שנעורר] שכעוררג || 10 איננו] אינוג |[זה]ג || 11 לאהבת] לאהבתוג |[היה]ג || 21 מהמנהגים] מהמנהיגיםג || 22 ענינו] ענינינוג |הסבריית] סברייתג || 24 שעשינו] שעניינוג || 25 ושנופל] ושנפלד ||

14 יש׳ נ״ג ד׳ ||

CHAPTER 12

The Handling of the Parts of the Discourse, i.e., Introduction, Statement of Facts, Division, Proof, Refutation, and Conclusion, in the Judicial Kind of Cause[1]

[1] The Philosopher,[a] in the Abridgment of the *Rhetoric* which he made for Alexander, says that if our purpose is to speak in a judicial Kind of Cause, we begin the Introduction in the manner previously explained; and if the speaker is the plaintiff, his setting forth of the grievance is intended to make the hearer attentive. Next, we procure goodwill in the manner explained above—although it is better to base praise of the hearers on their more extraordinary and specially characteristic qualities—and in addition, we arouse them to indignation and hostility against our opponents by asserting that these are evil and sinful men. Further, if the speaker is acting for others in prosecuting a case of no direct personal concern, he should say that he is doing so not from hope of reward, but only from friendship for these men, or from hatred of their opponents; or because he happened to be so situated that he saw the entire affair; or that he is acting in the public interest, or because his compassion was stirred when he saw this sufferer of injury and insult forsaken by all, with none to seek justice for him, a man **smitten of God and afflicted** [Isa. 53:4].

[2] After the Introduction we come to the Statement of Facts: we either state the facts of the grievance under several separate counts, or bring them together into a unified whole.

[3] After the Statement of Facts, we come to the Partition, making known wherein we agree with our opponents and what remains in dispute.

[4] After the Partition, we come to the Proof, establishing the accusation through one of the several methods of substantiation. Herein we begin with the witnesses and with such admissions of the charge as are in our hands; with evidence derived from laws, customs, grounds for suspicion, signs, reasoned arguments, or still other proofs, as the case may require, and depending as the Issue is Conjectural, Legal, or Juridical.

[5] Next we consider the possible replies and arguments of the defense and rebut them, this constituting the Refutation. Should the defendants reply to and argue against the proofs we have offered, we must amplify these proofs and refute all that they have said and whatever occurs to us that they may be able to

1. Cf. i.3, 5–10; ii.5, 7–9, 11.

a. Cf. *LR. ad A.* 71.20 ff. (1441b–1442a ff.).

הטענות והתשובות שיוכלו להשיב האחד על האחר כבר בארנו למעלה.
[6] ואחר כל זה, ראוי שנספר באופן מחודש ובקצור מה שנאמר על צד הספירה; ושנעורר הדיינים בקצור על המנגד אל הכעס, או האיבה, או הקנאה, אם נוכל· ונעורר אותם עלינו אל האהבה, והחן, והחנינה, כפי מה שאפשר.
[7] אמנם המתנצל, גם הוא יעשה הפתיחה באופן התבאר· ונספר בו שדעתנו להתיר כל ראיות המתרעם, ולהשיב אל כל מה שאמר.
[8] ואחר הפתיחה, נשיב אל כל דברי התרעומת, ונתיר הראיות וההקשות באופן התבאר למעלה, כפי מה שתבקש הטענה; ויאמר: "שזה המתרעם עשה כאיש בליעל ורשע, לכונן התרעומת הכוזב כאשר יעשו אנשי דמים ומרמה· ובזה הודיע חכמתו ומעלליו". וזה, אם יוכל להתנצל באופן שלם· ואם לאו, ירגיל מקומות ההוכחה, והתחנה, ובקשת המחילה אשר זכרונם; גם נתיר כל מה שעלה במחשבתנו שיוכל לאמת המתרעם.
[9] ואחר כן, על צד הספירה, בקצור נספר מה שנאמר, ונחתום המאמר.
[10] ואמר הפילוסוף, בקצורו הנזכר, שזה הענין, ר"ל, ספור מה שנאמ' למעלה, הוא דבר נפלא בכל מיני הדבור ובכל אחד מהחלקים, וביחוד בתרעומת ובהתנצלות. ואין המכוון בזה לבד ספור מה שנאמ', כאשר בשבח ובגנות, לא דבר אחר; אמנם ראוי, בתרעומת והתנצלות, שנעורר השומע אל החנינה וההטבה בערכנו, ואל האיבה, והכעס, והקנאה בהצטרף אל המנגדים, בספרנו הנאמ' למעלה; למה שמביא זאת החזרה, ר"ל, ספור הנאמ', לזכור פעולתינו הנשכחות וכשרון מעשנו, ורשעת המנגדים ורוע מעלליהם· כי זרע מרעים המה, בנים משחיתים. וזה יעשה בלב השומע רושם נפלא, וכל שכן אם נאמר שהם בעצמם, הדיינים, לא ימלטו לבלתי יקבלו מן האנשים האלה מן הכלימות ההזקים והחרפות, אם לא יענשו באופן הראוי· ושאנחנו באופן מן ההכנעה אליהם עד כלנו להם לעבדים, ונדרש לעולם אל אשר ישאלו, ושלא נסור מכל אשר יצוונו ימין ושמאל:

9 [ומרמה]ג || 12 לאמת] לאמר ד || 15 ובכל] וכל ד || 16 ובהתנצלות] והתנצלות ד || 19 בספרנו] בספורנו ג || 23 [לזכור]ג || 23 ושאנחנו] ושאחנו ד || 25 יצוונו] תצונו ד ||

9 תה' נ"ה כ"ד || 19–20 יש' א' ד' || 24–25 דב' י"ז כ' ||

say. We have explained above the sort of arguments and replies which each side can make against the other.

[6] After all this we should present what was said afresh and briefly in the form of an Enumeration; and we should be brief in arousing, if we can, the indignation, hatred, or zeal of the judges against our opponent, and to stir them as far as possible to friendship, favor, and compassion toward ourselves.

[7] For his part, the defendant will also form the Introduction in the manner explained. In it we set forth our intention to refute all the prosecutor's proofs and to reply to everything he has said.

[8] After the Introduction, we reply to all the counts of the complaint and refute the proofs and arguments in the manner explained above, as the Issue may require. "This plaintiff," it may be said, "has acted like a worthless and wicked fellow in concocting the kind of false accusation which is the expedient of **men of blood and deceit** [Ps. 55:24]; in so doing, he has made known his wisdom and his deeds." This will be said if the defendant can defend himself completely; but if he cannot, he will employ the commonplaces of the Exculpation, the Plea for Mercy, and the Plea for Pardon which we have mentioned. We shall also refute everything that we suppose the plaintiff might be able to affirm.

[9] Finally, in the form of an Enumeration, we shall briefly restate what has been said, and so bring the speech to an end.

[10] In his aforementioned Abridgment, the Philosopher[b] says that this feature, namely, the restatement of what was previously said, is of great importance in all the Kinds of Cause and in all their subspecies, but especially in the case of speeches of accusation and defence. This does not mean that the restatement should be confined solely to what has been said, and include nothing else, as in speeches of praise and blame. Indeed, in accusation and defence, we should arouse the hearer to pity and favorable action with respect to us, and to hatred, indignation, and zeal as regards our opponents, through our manner of retelling what was previously said. For such repetition, that is, the restatement of what has been said, can bring to recollection our forgotten achievements and the worthiness of our action, and also the wickedness of our opponents and the evil of their deeds: that they are **a seed of evil-doers, children that deal corruptly** [Isa. 1:4]. This will make a profound impression upon the hearers, the more so if we say that they, the judges themselves, will not escape the most insolent abuse and insults from these fellows unless they are properly punished; whereas our submissiveness to the judges is such that we are entirely their servants, and are forever applying ourselves to whatever they require; we **turn not aside from** whatever they **command** us, **to the right hand or to the left** [Deut. 17:20].

b. Cf. *LR. ad A.* 76.28 ff. (1444b ff.).

פרק י״ג

ענין האשה התקועית.

[1] יען ענין התקועית נבנה על התעוררות החנינה והמחילה לחוטא, שהוא
דבר יבוקש ענינו בדבור המשפטי, כאשר התבאר ממה שקדם, הסכמנו לדבר בו
5 הנראה בעינינו ממנו בזה המקום; למה שבו מהקשי העצום עד שלא ראינו
פירוש תתישב בו דעתנו עד היום הזה; גם אנחנו לא הבינונו אותו מלפנים עד
פקח י״י עיני שכלנו, והתבוננו בקצת החכמות המיוחדות לדבור· אשר העירונו
לפשט הפסוקי׳ הבאי׳ בזה הענין, ולמכוון בהם, הערה נחשוב בה באנו עד מרום
קצו, יער כרמלו.

10 [2] וקודם שנתחיל בבאור הפסוקים, נעיר על קצת הספקות יבלבלו זה הפשט
וישימוהו במטמוני מסתורים, ובארץ חשך וצלמות, וישב שם עד היום הזה.

[3] ראשונה, כי אחר שראה יואב, וידע כי לב המלך על אבשלום, כמו שמעיד
הכתוב [שמ״ב י״ד א׳], למה לא שאל הוא בעצמו המחילה עליו, עד שהוצרך
ללכת בתחבולות כאלה?

15 [4] ועוד, למה עשה זה על יד אשה, ולא מצא איש חכם ישים הדברים בפיו,
אחר שהיה הדבר נעשה על פי עצתו? ומה מצא יתרון באשה מבאיש בענין
הזה?

[5] עוד, למה לא ביאר הכתוב ביאת האשה אל המלך? שאמר הכל בלשון
אמירה, כמו שכתוב: ותאמר האשה התקועית, ״אל המלך!״ ותפול על אפיה
20 ארצה, ותשתחו, ותאמ׳, ״הושיעה המלך!״ [שם שם ד׳]. והנה חסרה בכאן
ביאת האשה מתקועה[1] ירושלם לפני המלך; והראוי שיאמ׳: ״ותבא האשה
התקועית אל המלך, ותפול על אפיה ארצה״, וכו׳.

[6] ועוד, מה ענין המשל שהביאה משני בנים [שם ה׳–ז׳]· ושהיה נמשך מזה
הכרת השם לבעלה, אם יהרג גם האחר? וזה לא היה דומה לענין אבשלום
25 כלל· כי מה היה מפסיד דוד אם אבשלום לא היה חוזר לירושלם? ולמה לא

1 פרק] פ׳[ɔ] || 2 ענין] מעניין[ɔ] || 3 על <ענין>[ɔ] || 4 המשפטי] משפטי[ר] || 5 שלא] לא[ר] || 7 והתבוננו] והתבוננו[ר] || 9 באנו] באט[ר] || 21 ביאת] בזאת[ר] || 23 שהביאה] שהביא[ɔ] || 25 לירושלם] לירושלים[ר] ||

7 מל״ב ו׳ י״ז || 9 יש׳ ל״ז כ״ד || 11 יש׳ מ״ה ג׳ | איוב י׳ כ״א | מל״ב ט״ז ו׳ ||

[1] *Sic;* ת (non-locative): תְּקוֹעַ.

CHAPTER 13

The Episode of the Woman of Tekoa

[1] Since the episode of the Woman of Tekoa[1] is based upon the arousal of pity and the winning of pardon for the sinner, skills demanded in a speech of the Judicial Kind of Cause as is clear from what has gone before, we have agreed to present our views on the passage here. For in the passage there is such inordinate difficulty that to this day we have seen no satisfactory exposition of it;[2] nor did we ourselves understand it until the **Lord opened the eyes of** [2 Kings 6:17] our intellect and we studied some of the disciplines special to rational utterance. These have so successfully awakened us to the literal sense and intended meaning of the verses contained in this passage that we think we **have entered into its farthest height, the forest of its fruitful field** [Isa. 37:24].

[2] Before beginning our explanation of the verses, let us note some of the problems that confuse this literal sense and set it amongst **hidden riches of secret places** [Isa. 45:3], in **the land of darkness and of the shadow of death** [Job 10:21], where it has **dwelt . . . unto this day** [2 Kings 16:6].

[3] In the first place, since, as Scripture testifies, Joab saw and **perceived that the king's heart was toward Absalom** [2 Sam. 14:1], why did not Joab himself ask pardon for Absalom before finding it necessary to resort to such cunning?

[4] Second, why did Joab act through a woman? Why, since the plan was to be carried out according to his counsel, did he not find a wise man into whose mouth to put the words [14:3, 19]? What advantage did he find in employing a woman rather than a man in this proceeding?

[5] Third, why is the text unclear on the coming of the woman to the king? For as written, the text expresses all this in the term "said": **And the woman of Tekoa said, "Unto the king!" She then fell on her face to the ground, and prostrated herself and said: "Help, O king"** [14:4].[3] Thus, the woman's coming from Tekoa to Jerusalem into the king's presence has here been left unsaid. Properly, the text should say: "And the Tekoan woman came unto the king, and she fell on her face to the ground," and so on.

[6] Fourth, what was the point of the fable which she introduced of the two sons [14:5–7], according to which the consequence would have been the cutting off of her husband's name if the second son also were to be slain? The case of this fable bore no resemblance at all to that of Absalom; for what loss would David

1. 2 Sam. 13:39–14:21

2. Cf., in addition to the commentaries on the passage included in rabbinic Bibles (*Miqrā'ōth Gᵉdhōlōth*), Profiat Duran's expository epistle (late fourteenth century), appended to his *Ma'ᵃsē 'Ēphōdh* in the edition of J. Friedlander and J. Kohn (Vienna, 1865), 198–205.

3. JV: "And *when* the woman of Tekoa *spoke* to the king, she fell on her face to the ground," etc. "*When*" is not in the Hebrew at all; "*spoke*" represents the word usually rendered "said." I have translated above in accordance with JML's understanding of the passage.

עשתה משל דומה בענין?

[7] ועוד, אחר שאמר לה המלך: "לכי לביתך, ואני אצוה עליך" [שם ח'], מה הוצרכה לאמר: "עלי, אדני המלך, העון", וכו' [שם ט'].

[8] ועוד, למה חזרה לאמר, "יזכר נא אדני המלך את י"י אלקיך" [שם י"א], והנה עשה מה ששאלה באמרו: "המדבר אליך, והבאתו אלי", כו' [שם י']?

[9] ועוד, מה ענין למים הנגרים ארצה אשר לא יאספו [שם י"ד] להשיב המלך את נדחו [שם י"ג]?

[10] ועוד בלבולים אחרים מאלה; ובכלל, כל המאמר במדרגה מן הבלבול עד יראה מן התמה הגדול איך קרא הכתוב זאת האשה "חכמה", ואמר שיואב שם דבריו בפיה· כי לפי העולה על הדעת בתחלה, היה בזה הענין מן הסכלות מה שלא יעלם.

[11] וקודם שנבוא אל התרת[2] הספקות, ראוי שתדע ענינים מה:

[12] הראשון, שטבע האדם יתעורר מן החדשות, ויקוץ בדברים המרגלים· במדרגת היפויים ההלציים, שהכונה הכוללת בהם היא להוציא האנשים מן הלשון המורגל אשר לא יתעורר ממנו האדם, לא מעט ולא הרבה. והנה התבאר בנסיון שאפי' הגדול שבתענוגים והשעשועים, נקוץ בו מצד הרגילות והתדירות, והדבר שיש בו קצת מן הצער הבא לפעמי' נשתוקק אליו· כמו שיבחר האדם לפעמי' התעמלות על המנוחה, להיותו קץ במנוחה, ואף אם לא תהיה בזה סבה אחרת.

[13] הב', שהבודה בדיאה צריך שיתקנה באופן לא יוכר בה שהיא בדיאה, כמו שהתבאר בזה הספר; כאלו תאמ' שמי שירצה להראות שהוא שוטה ומשוגע צריך שיביא האנשי' לחשוב שכן הוא באמת, וזה בעשותו כל מפעלו' השוטה ותנועותיו· כמו שעשה דוד עם אכיש מלך גת [שמ"א כ"א י"ד].

[14] הג', שהוא מבואר כי מי שיש בו מן המרירות הגד', ומן החרדה העצומה פן תבואהו שואה לא ידע שחרה, ויהיה דבר אפשר בו שימנע מצד המלוכה, לא ינום האיש ולא יישן, ולא יאחרו פעמיו, אך ימהר ויחיש מלאכתו, הולך וזועק

2 לביתך] לביתיך[ד] || 3 לאמר] לומ'[כ] || 4 [אדני][ת] | [המלך][כ] || 6 ארצה] ארצם[כ] || 12 התרת[2]] היתר[כ] | התר[ד] || 15 האדם ‹כלל›[כ] || 20 הב'] השנית[כ] | שהבודה] שהבודא[ד] || 22 [באמת][ד] | [מפעלו'] פעולות[כ] || 24 הג'] השלישית[כ] | הגד'] הגדול[כ] || 26 ולא יאחרו] גם לא יאחרו[כ] ||

---

25 יש' מ"ז י"א || 26 תה' קכ"א ד' | שופ' ה' כ"ח | יש' ה' י"ט | חב' א' ב' ||

---

[2] Correction: J; cf. par. 17, below.

suffer if Absalom should not return to Jerusalem? Why, then, did she not construct a fable which would resemble the case at hand?

[7] Fifth, after the king had said to her, **"Go to thy house, and I will give charge concerning thee"** [14:8], why did she find it necessary to say, **"My lord, O king, the iniquity be upon me,"** and so forth [14:9]?

[8] Sixth, why did she repeat [her request], saying, **"I pray thee, let my lord the king**[4]**remember the Lord, thy God, [that the avenger of blood destroy not any more"**—14:11], when, in fact, the king had already done as she had asked by saying, **"Whosoever saith aught unto thee, bring him to me, and he shall not touch thee any more"** [14:10]?

[9] Seventh, what relation is there between the **water spilt on the ground which cannot be gathered up again** [14:14] and the king's fetching **home again his banished one** [14:13]?

[10] In addition, there are still other perplexities. The whole discourse, in fine, is so confusing that it would seem a matter of great astonishment how Scripture can call this woman **wise** [14:2] and say that Joab put his words in her mouth [14:3]; for the thought that at first comes to mind is that the folly in this proceeding was plain and unconcealed.

[11] Before we come to the resolution of these difficulties, there are certain facts which you should know:

[12] First, it is human nature to be stimulated by the new but to feel the loathing of surfeit for the hackneyed; hence, for example, rhetorical embellishments, whose general purpose it is to free us from language grown over-familiar, by which one can be neither slightly nor greatly stirred. Indeed, experience has shown that over-familiarity and too frequent indulgence will make us come to loathe even the greatest of pleasures and delights, and we may even find occasion to long for something in which there is a little pain; just as a person will sometimes prefer strenuous physical exertion to rest for no reason other than that he is surfeited with inaction.

[13] Second, one who practices a deception must arrange it in such a manner that the fact that it is a deception will go unrecognized, as was made clear in this very Scriptural Book. One who wishes to seem a fool and madman, say, must cause people to think that he is really such by committing all the acts and performing all the movements of the fool, as David did when he was with Achish, king of Gath [1 Sam. 21:14].

[14] Third, it is clear that a person who is suffering great sorrow and is, at the same time, in a state of the utmost anxiety lest a **ruin come upon** him . . . which he **will not know how to charm away** [Isa. 47:11]—some possible action by the government against him which he would prevent—such a person will **neither slumber nor sleep** [Ps. 121:4], his footsteps will not tarry, but **he will make speed and will hasten his work** [Isa. 5:19], **crying out . . . of violence** [Hab. 1:2] as

4. B omits "my lord"; M omits "the king."

חמס· גם כי יבואו דבריו במדרגה מן הבלבול יכירו בו האנשים כי נפשו מרה לו.

[15] הד׳, כי כאשר ימנע בערכנו להביא משל ודומה לענין ידמיהו באמתות, נקח אשר נחשוב בעיניינו שיספיק לנו לבחון בו מה שנרציהו· והוא כשנראה בענין יתרון, או חסרון מצד אחר יעמוד במקום מה שחסר המשל; וכאשר יהיה הענין כן לא יחשב זה הדמיון הטעאיי, כי הוא נלקח על צד הבחינה, לא על צד הביאור.

[16] הה׳, שיתחייב בחק האדם המדבר עם המלכים או השופטים שישים לבו אל דבריהם וידקדק בהם דקדוק רב ועצום, עד אם יבין מכח דבריו אי זה רמז על ענין באופן נסתר, אז ידבר דבר יגלה לו הענין הנעלם ההוא· פן יחשוב השיגו מהם דבר שאינו כן, ויפטר מלפניו בדבר מועט התועלת, או שאין בו תועלת כלל, ובכפיו דבק מאום.

[17] ואחר התישב זה נשוב אל התרת הספקות:

[18] ונאמ׳ אל הספק הראשון, כי אמת שנכספה גם כלתה נפש דוד לצאת אל אבשלום, ר״ל, לראותו מבלתי שיבא אבשלום לירושלם, כמו שאמ׳ הכתוב: לצאת אל אבשלום [שמ״ב י״ג ל״ט]. ותהי׳ תבת ״ותכל״ מלשון ״נכספה, גם כָּלְתָה נפשי״ [תה׳ פ״ד ג׳]· משרש כָּלָה, מן הדגוש· ולשון נקבה שב אל מחשבת דוד, תאותו, או נפשו, כמו שאמ׳ קצת המפרשים. והנה, עם זה שהתאוה לראותו, היה אפשר שתהיה דעת דוד שיעמוד אבשלום לעולם בגשור, כי לא יעשה אדם כל שיתאוהו· ואתה רואה כי עם היות בו זאת התשוקה אמ׳: ״יסוב אל ביתו ופני לא יראה״ [שמ״ב י״ד כ״ד]. והנה בא לב דוד אל מדרגה מה ממדרגות התשוקה, כי קודם זה לא היה לבו אליו כלל; והרגיש יואב זאת ההטיה מלבב דוד אל אבשלום· אם שרמז זה באי זה דבור, אם בזולת דבור, הרגיש שלא היה עומד במדרגה הראשונה· כי אולי היה מספר דוד רעות מאבשלום כפעם בפעם על דבר אמנון, או שהיה מתמלא חימה אצל זכירת[3] שמו, מה שלא היה עושה עתה, או כדומה לזה. לכן אמר: וידע יואב כי לב המלך אל אבשלום [שם שם א׳], ר״ל, שכבר נטה לבו אל צד האהבה דבר מה,

1 יבואו דבריו] דבריו יבא[כ] || 2 הד׳] הרביעית[כ] | ידמיהו] ידמה[ד] || 3 בעיניינו] בעינינו[ד] | שנרציהו] שנרצ׳[ד] || 7 הה׳] החמשית[כ] | או השופטים] והשופטים[כ] || 15 ותהי׳] ויהיה[כ] || 16 מחשבת] מחשב[ד] || 20 בא] בה[ד] || 21 ממדרגות] ממדרגתו[ד] || 24 דבר] דבר׳[ד] | זכירת[3]] זכירי[כ] זכירה[ד] || 25 מה שלא] מהשל׳[ד] || 26 אל] על[ת] ||

---

1 מל״ב ד׳ כ״ז || 11 איוב ל״א ז׳ || 13 תה׳ פ״ד ג׳ ||

---

[3] Correction: J.

he goes; moreover, his words will become so incoherent that people will recognize that his **soul is bitter within** him [2 Kings 4:27].

[15] Fourth, when it is not possible for us to introduce a true analogue to the case at hand, we take up a case whose substance we think will serve us adequately as a probation for the one we are intent upon establishing. It is an analogue of this kind when we see that the case at hand contains an additional element not in the parallel, or a deficiency that makes it actually rather different from the parallel. When such is the case, an analogy of this sort is not considered faulty, for it has been adopted as a probation, not as part of the exposition.

[16] Fifth, a person conversing with kings or judges will naturally be so attentive to their words and will subject these to such minute and intense scrutiny that, if he notes in his interlocutor's words some suggestion of a hidden concern, he will then say something to bring that hidden concern into the open. He will do this lest, thinking that he has obtained from these authorities something which in fact he has not obtained, he leave his interlocutor's presence with something of only little advantage, or of no advantage at all **if any spot has cleaved to** his **hands** [Job 31:7].[5]

[17] This established, we come back now to the resolution of the difficulties:

[18] As to the first of these, we say that truly David's **soul yearned, yea, pined** [Ps. 84:3] **to go forth unto Absalom** [2 Sam. 13:39],[6] that is, to see him, without Absalom's coming to Jerusalem, as the text says: **And the soul of King David pined to go forth unto Absalom; for he was comforted concerning Amnon, seeing he was dead** [13:39]. *Watt*^{e}*khal* ("and . . . pined") may be understood from its use in **My soul yearneth, yea, even pineth for the courts of the Lord** [Ps. 84:3]. It is a form of the active intensive stem, from the root *kālāh,* a *feminine* form because it refers to a feminine noun as subject, David's **thought,** his **desire,** or his **soul,** as some of the commentators state.[7] Now although David wished to see Absalom, he quite possibly might have made up his mind that Absalom should remain permanently in Geshur. For nobody does everything that he wishes to do; and you see that even though David felt this longing he nevertheless said, **"Let him turn to his own house, but let him not see my face"** [2 Sam. 14:24]. Plainly, too, David's heart had just reached a certain intensity of longing, for previously his heart had not at all been **toward Absalom** [14:1]. It was this inclining of David's heart toward Absalom that Joab perceived; whether the king gave hint of this by some utterance, or without utterance, Joab perceived that David's heart was no longer disposed as formerly. For perhaps David formerly would from time to time speak harshly of Absalom on account of Amnon, or become furious at the mention of Absalom's name, but was now doing neither; or might give some similar indication. The text therefore says: **Now Joab . . . perceived that the king's heart was toward Absalom** [14:1], that is to say,

5. JV: "And if any spot hath cleaved to my hands."
6. Thus B literally; JV: ". . . failed with longing for Absalom."
7. E.g., Rashi, Ibn Ezra, et al.; cf. *Miqrā'ōth G*^{e}*dhōlōth, ad loc.*

וזה לא היה עד היום הזה; ולזה אמר: ״אולי יש תקווה, עם התחכמות
ותחבולה, שיחזור גם בירושלים, ועל עמדו יעמוד.״ והיה זה הדבר, עם כל זה,
מסופק מאד וקשה ההשגה בעיני יואב, לגודל החטא· ואם שהיה זה נמנע,
כאשר היה בתחלה, לא חשב, אמנם היה רואה כי היה הדבר ראוי להתחכמות
5 גדולה, ובתחבולות יעשה מלחמה. והנה שב הענין מן הנמנע, לפי שהיה חושב
יואב, אל קצת אפשרות, ואם היה רחוק. ובכן הותר הספק הראשון.

[19] ואמנם, היה טוב בעיניו לעשות הדבר על יד אשה לסבות. מהם, שלא
יכיר דוד בתחבולה, כי חשד התחבולות הוא בנשים מעט, לחלשת שכלם ושעור
סברתם המעטית והפחותה מטבע. ומהם, שתקון המאמר וסדרו באופן שלם
10 הוא מעטי בנשים ובבריאה חדשה· וזה היה סבה אל שיתעורר דוד יותר על ידה.
ומהם, שהאדם בטבע נמשך יותר אל הרחמנות והחמלה בנקבות ממה שימשך
ממנו בזכרים, להיותם יותר רחוקות מן ההצלחה ומן ההשתדלות להשיג
מבוקשם, וכל אשר היה הדבר ברחוק יותר מן הטוב כן טבע הרחמנות נמשך
אליו יותר· עם גם כן שהאדם אוהב את הנקבות בטבע. ולזה ראה יואב לעשות
15 זה הדבר על יד אשה; וזה מה שנשיב אל הספק השני.

[20] ואל השלישי נאמ׳ שהאשה, ליתרון התחכמותה, אחרי עשותה מה
שאמ׳ לה יואב מן האבלות והעדר הסיכה, עשתה עצמה ממש כדמיון אשה
מצרה, וחרדה לכליון חרוץ, נחפזת ללכת הלוך וזועקה: ״אל המלך!״ [שמ״ב י״ד
ד׳]. והנה נראה כאילו הגיעה אל המלך בזולת תנועה· לכן, בפסוק לא התבאר
20 רק מה שהיתה צועקת ״אל המלך!״ תמיד וכאשר ישאלוה; וזהו מה שאמ׳
״ותאמ׳ האשה התקועית ׳אל המלך!׳״ וכו׳ [שם], כי זה היה דבורה תמיד· כי
תקנה הבדיאה הזאת באופן מופלג כמו שראוי, כאשר התבאר. וזאת היא
תשובת הג׳.

[21] ונשיב אל הרביעי כי זה הדמיון לוקח הנה לבחינה, כמו שהתפרסם· וזה,
25 כי אם היתה מביאה משל דומה ממש לענין, היה דוד תכף מרגיש בזאת

3 [זה][ד] || 4 כאשר [היה][כ] || 5 גדולה] גדול[ד] || 10 ובבריאה] בריאה[כ] || 11 הרחמנות] רחמנות[כ] | שימשך] שימש[ד] || 15 אשה; ‹גם כי כבר נסה קצת מחכמת הנשי׳, ר״ל, מהאשה החכמה אשר באבל, מענין שבע בן בכרי (שמ״ב כ׳ ט״ז, וכו׳)›[כ] || 16 השלישי] הג׳[ד] | עשותה] עשות[ד] || 19 הגיעה] תגיע[ד] || 20 וזהו] וזה הוא[כ] || 23 תשובת] תשובה[ד] | הג׳] השלישית[כ] || 24 הרביעי] הרביעית[כ] || 25 בזאת] לזאת[ד] ||

1 איכה ג׳ כ״ט || 2 דה״ב ל״ד ל״א || 5 מש׳ כ׳ י״ח || 17–18 יר׳ מ״ח מ״א | יש׳ י׳ כ״ב ||

that the king's heart had now turned to some extent in the direction of love, which had not been the case before that day. Joab therefore thought: **"Perhaps there may be hope** [Lam. 3:29] that, with skillful handling and wise contrivance, Absalom may also return to Jerusalem and **stand . . . in his place"** [2 Chr. 34:31]. Withal, however, this seemed to Joab exceedingly dubious and difficult to achieve because of the magnitude of Absalom's sin; and if he did not consider that it was altogether impossible, as it had been at the outset, he yet saw that the matter must be managed with great skill, and that **with wise counsel** he should **carry on war** [Prov. 20:18]. The affair thus turned from being one impossible of accomplishment, as Joab had previously considered it, to being partly, if remotely, feasible. In this way, then, our first difficulty is resolved.

[19] For several reasons, indeed, it seemed best to Joab to act in the matter through a woman. One was that David would not detect the stratagem, for women, because of their native weakness of intellect and naturally slight and deficient reasoning power, are little suspect of cunning stratagems. Another reason was that the ability to arrange and perfectly to order a discourse is seldom found in women and the newly fledged; and this was ground for supposing that David would be more deeply stirred through her agency. Another: that a man is naturally more easily induced by women than by men to show mercy and compassion, because women are farther removed from prosperity and from endeavoring to obtain what they seek, and the more removed from the good a thing is, the more is mercy naturally attracted to it; it may be added, too, that a man is by nature fond of women. Joab therefore decided to act in this matter through a woman;[8] and this is our answer to the second difficulty.

[20] As to the third problem, we say that when the woman, with her more than ample skill in managing affairs, had carried out Joab's suggestions regarding mourning and omitting to anoint herself [14:2], she made herself a veritable replica of **a woman in her pangs** [Jer. 48:41], one a-tremble because **an extermination is determined** [Isa. 10:22], moving in agitated haste and crying out as she went, **"Unto the king!"** [2 Sam. 14:4]. It thus seemed as if she got to the king without purposive motion; in the verse [14:4], accordingly, only the fact that she kept crying out **"Unto the king!"** constantly, and whenever she was questioned, is expressly stated. The text reads **And the woman of Tekoa said, "Unto the king,"** and so on, because this was her constant utterance; for she had arranged this fabrication in properly exaggerated style, as has been explained. This, then, is the answer to the third problem.

[21] Our answer to the fourth problem is that the analogy was plainly adopted to serve as a probation. For if the woman of Tekoa had introduced an example genuinely analogous to the case at hand, David would at once have perceived the

8. Here M adds: ". . . because, moreover, he had already experienced some womanly wisdom, namely, that of the wise woman in Abel, of the episode of Sheba the son of Bichri" [2 Sam. 20:16 ff.]. Since this episode took place *after* that of the Tekoan woman, the reference here is anachronistic, and realization of this may have induced Conat to omit these words from C.

התחבולה, ולא היתה מגעת אל מבוקשה. והערימה לקחת משל תשלם בו הבחינה, ואם הוא בלתי דומה· כי כונתה לעשות באופן יבחן רצון לב דוד משיבת אבשלום, לא זולת זה. ושקלה, שאם יתרצה לה המלך במה שבדאה מלבה מענין הבן, מצד הרע שימשך לה מזה, ר״ל, מהכרת שם הבעל, כל שכן
5 — או לפחות לא מעט — יתרצה לעשות מה שתשאל גם מענין אבשלום; כי יתרון אהבת האדם את בנו לעשות בעדו יותר ממה שהיה עושה בעד אחרים· והתשוקה בו תעמוד במקום הנזק המגיע לאשה, עד שאם היה מסכים בהסרת הנזק ההוא היה גם כן מסכים בהשלים תשוקתו אל אבשלום; כי אולי היה חפץ יותר בהגיע אל תכלית התשוקה הזאת ממה שהיה חפץ בהסרת הנזק
10 מהאחרים, או לפחות לא מעט. וזה היה התבוננות גדול מצד האשה ויואב, ושקול הדעת אין כמוהו; ובכן התבאר הספק הרביעי.

[22] ואל הספק החמשי נשיב כי מה שאמר דוד לאשה, ״אני אצוה עליך״ [שם ח׳], היה אפשר שיהיה ענינו על זולת שיתרצה לאשה במה ששאלה; כי אמר ״אני אצוה עליך״ סתם· המובן ממנו: מה שהיה ברצון דוד. לכן האשה,
15 העומדת תמיד עם התבוננות לראות מה ידובר בה, אמ׳ בלבה: ״אולי יחשוב המלך כי אין הדבר כן כמו שאמ׳ לו מענין הרצח, שלא היה באופן יהיה הבן חייב מיתה או גלות· ויחרד ויפחד פן ישיגנו מזה עון.״ לכן אמרה: ״עלי, אדני המלך, העוון, ועל בית אבי· והמלך וכסאו נקי״ [שם ט׳]; כלומר, שהיו הדברים ממש כמו שספרה· וכי יפטור המלך את הבן השני מן המיתה ומן הגלות, אין
20 בזה פשע כלל מצד המלוכה; כי מן ההכרח שנאמ׳ שלא היה זה הרוצח חייב מיתה או גלות, לפי משפטי התורה. ובזה הותר הספק הה׳.

[23] ואל הששי נאמר שרמזה במאמ׳ ההוא, ש״יזכור י״י״ [שם י״א], דרך שבועה, להיותה בטוחה יותר, ושתהיה בחינתה שלמה. וזהו מה שאמר אחרי כן: ״חי י״י, אם יפול משערת ראשו ארצה״ [שם]; והנה הותר זה הספק.
25 [24] ואל השביעי נאמ׳ שהתקועית בארה מבוקשה, ר״ל, שישיב המלך את

10 האשה] האשׁ ‖ 14 האשה] האישהׄ ‖ 15 אמ׳] אמרׄ ‖ 16 הרצח] הרוצחׄ | הבן חייב] הנתחייבׄ ‖ 18 העוון] העו׳ׄ ‖ 21 ובזה] ובכןׄ | הה׳] חמשיׄ ‖ 23 אחרי] אחרׄ ‖ 24 ראשו] בנךׄ | 25 נאמ׳] נמׄארׄ ‖

stratagem, and she would not have attained her object. She therefore cunningly adopted an example by means of which the testing of him might be accomplished, though the example itself was not truly analogous; for her purpose was to act in such manner as would probe the wish of David's heart to have Absalom return, this and this alone. She reasoned that if the king, in the case she had fabricated about her son, should consent to help her because of the evil that would be its result for her, namely, the cutting-off of her husband's name, he would all the more—or, at least, no less—consent to do as she would ask in the matter of Absalom as well. For it is the superiority of the love a man feels for his son that he will do more on behalf of his son than he would on behalf of others; and David's longing for Absalom would so far parallel the harm that might overtake the woman, that if he should agree to the removal of such threatened harm, he would also agree to fulfill his own longing for Absalom; for the chances were that his wish to attain the aim of this longing would be stronger than his wish to remove harm from others, or, at least, would be no less strong. This was a brilliant flash of insight on the part of the woman and Joab, a matchless feat of reasoning; and thus the fourth difficulty is explained.

[22] Our answer to the fifth problem is that David's statement to the woman, **"I will give charge concerning thee"** [14:8], could have meant that he would not consent to do what the woman asked; for he had merely said "I will give charge concerning thee," meaning whatever charge David might will. Therefore the woman, persistently and constantly on the alert to consider what was to be spoken through her, thought to herself: "Perhaps the king is thinking that the facts about the slaying may not be as I have set forth to him—that the slaying was not of the sort which would make my son liable to death or banishment; and he may be uneasy and fearful lest some resultant guilt of iniquity overtake him." She therefore said: **"My lord, O king, the iniquity be on me, and on my father's house; and the king and his throne be guiltless"** [14:9]; the facts, that is, were really as she had described them to be, and if the king should acquit her second son of the penalty of death or banishment, there would be in this no transgression at all on the sovereign's part; for we are obliged to say that, according to the laws of the Torah, this slayer was not liable to death or banishment. This, then, is the solution of the fifth problem.

[23] In answer to the sixth problem, we say that with the statement **"Let the king remember the Lord"** [14:11], the woman was suggesting that the king do this in the course of an oath, so that she might be surer, and her probation be completely carried through. This accounts for David's immediately following statement: **"As the Lord liveth, there shall not one hair of his head [9]fall to the earth"** [14:11]; and herewith this problem is solved.

[24] In answer to the seventh problem, we say that the woman of Tekoa proved what she was advocating—**that the king . . . fetch home again his banished**

9. B: ". . . of thy son. . . ."

נדחו [שם י״ג], מן ההפך. וזה, שהיתה רואה בשכלה, שאין לדחות הדבר דחוי
עולמי כי אם דבר נעדר ממנו האפשרות על הגעת הטוב והשלמות, כי בזה אין
ספק שאין ראוי להשתדל בו כלל· אבל ענין אבשלום לא היה בזה האופן, כי היו
בהשבת הנדח ההוא צדדים אפשרי התועלת; לכן היה ההשתדלות בו ראוי.
5 וכאילו אמרה: ״הדבר הנעדר אפשרות הגעת התועלת ראוי שידחה דחוי עולמי,
כי לא יכשר בו ההשתדלות אל ההקרבה; ויתחייב מזה, שהדבר שהוא אפשרי
על הגעת התועלת לא יהיה נדחה דחוי עולמי, מצד הטוב האפשרי להיות בו·
וא״כ, מצוה ההשתדלות בערכו לקרבו, כדי שיצא לפעל מה שבו מן האפשרות
על הטוב.״ והנה בארה זה הענין מצד המיתה, כי לא ישאר בגוף יותר אפשרות
10 אל הגעת הטוב והשלמות בטבע; לכן היא בדמיון המים הנשפכים במקום
מדרון, במקום נמנע התקבצם, כי אז לא ישאר במים אפשרות על הגעת שלמות
מה מהם· גם כי אין ראוי לעשות בזה ההשתדלות. ולזה אמרה[4]: ״אשר לא
יאספו״ [שם י״ד], ר״ל, שאין מי שישתדל בזה; והנה נשאר שראוי ש״ישיב
המלך נדחו״ [שם י״ג]. והנה הותר הספק השביעי בכללו.

15 [25] ונשוב אל הפסוקים. ספר הכתוב מה שאמר לה יואב מענין האבלות
והעדר הסיכה [שם ב׳], ואין ספק שהאשה עשתה כל מה שצוה אותה יואב,
ואם דלג הפסוק העשיה· כי בדברים המבוארים לפעמים ידלג הפסוק לפעמי׳
המצוה, לפעמי׳ העשיה, כאשר התפרסם מהרבה מקומות.

[26] וספר שיואב שם הדברים בפיה [שם ג׳], ואמר אחר כן: ותדבר האשה
20 התקועית, ״אל המלך!״ [שם ד׳], ר״ל, שהיתה הולכת הלוך וזועקה, אומרת
הדברים האלה, ומשיבה לכל שואליה. ודלג התנועה לרמוז שלרוב מהירותה
וחפזה כמעט לא נרגשה בה תנועתה.

[27] והשתחוה על אפיה ואמרה: ״הושיעה המלך!״ [שמ״ב י״ד ד׳]; וזה
המאמר יגרום החבוב, כאשר התפרסם ממה שקדם· וזאת היא הפתיחה מחלקי
25 המאמ׳. ואחר כן ספרה, כאשר שאלה המלך, שהיא אשה אלמנה, וימת אישה
[שם ה׳], להורות שבעלה היה מן האנשים החשובים הראוי להקרא ״איש״·
ולזה, היה בו דבר ראוי שלא יכרת שמו על פני חוץ, אשר היא השאלה אשר

בהגעת] הגיע[ד] || 8 וא״כ] ואחר כך[ד] || 11 התקבצם] להתקבצם[ד] || 12 אמרה[4]] אמר[כד] || 16 שצוה] שצוותה[כ] || 18 [המצוה לפעמי׳][ד] || 19 ותדבר] ותאמר[ת] || 21 הדברים] כדברי׳[כ] || 24 כאשר] כאש[ד] || 25 וימת] וימות[ד] | אישה] אשה[כ] || 27 היא] הוא[כ] ||

---

27 איוב י״ח י״ז ||

---

[4] Correction: J.

one [14:13]—from the contrary. Her intelligence enabled her to see that only what is incapable of gaining in goodness and soundness should be eternally banished, for in such case, doubtless, it deserves no effort at all. Absalom's case, however, was not of this kind, for there were aspects of possible benefit in the restoring of that particular banished one; the effort in his instance was, therefore, worth making. It was as though she had said: "What is incapable of improvement ought to be banished forever, for in such case no effort to make it come closer to good can succeed. From this, however, it follows logically that what is capable of improvement should not be forever banished because of the good which it may possibly come to contain; and if this be so, the effort involved in making it approximate good, so that its potential good become actual, is an act of religious merit." She here used the fact of death to demonstrate this proposition, for with death no further possibility of obtaining natural good and perfection is left in the body [14:14]. Death is therefore analogous to waters spilt on a slope; a place where it is impossible for them again to collect, for in such circumstances there is no possibility of their achieving any wholeness; also, to make any such attempt is not worthwhile. That is why she said "... **which cannot be gathered up again**" [14:14]—in other words, no one will make the effort in such case. Hence it remained worthwhile that the king ought to "... **fetch home again his banished one**" [14:13]. The seventh problem has thus received its complete solution.

[25] Let us now return to the verses. The text narrates what Joab said to the woman about mourning and omitting to anoint herself; and the woman doubtless did all that Joab had commanded her to do, although the verse omits to mention the doing [14:2]. For, as is evident from many passages, where matters are clear, it may happen that the verse sometimes omits the command, sometimes the actual doing.

[26] Having told how **Joab put the words in her mouth** [14:3], the text goes on to say: **And the woman of Tekoa spoke,**[10] **"Unto the king!"** [14:4], meaning that she kept crying out as she went, saying these words in response to all who questioned her. The text omits mention of her purposive motion in order to intimate that, because her haste and agitation were so great, her purposive motion went practically unnoticed.

[27] She then **prostrated herself and said: "Help, O king!"** [14:4]. Such a statement will engender goodwill, as has previously been made plain; of the several Parts of the Discourse this is the Introduction.[11] Next, as the king asked her to do, she presented a Statement of the Facts: she was a **widow**, her **husband being dead** [14:5]. Her choice of the word *'īsh* ["man"] for *husband* was to indicate that her spouse was one of those persons of importance worthy of this designation; in his case, therefore, it was fitting that his **name abroad** [Job

10. *Sic.* = וַתְּדַבֵּר, although in the two earlier citations of this verse, וַתֹּאמֶר ("and she said") is used; B: "... said ..." (וַתֹּאמֶר). This is another of JML's numerous slight errors in citing B—the result, no doubt, of his habit of citing from memory.

11. Cf. i.6.8.

שאלה. וספרה מחלקת הבנים, ושדרך המקרה הגיעה המיתה לאחד מהם אל
האחר באופן שלא היה חייב מיתה או גלות, לפי משפטי התורה; ועם כל זה,
יצר בעלי המשפחה גדל מאד, והיו רוצים להמית גם את השני. ובתבת "ויכו"
(האחד, וכו'), בא הכנוי טרם הידיעה, כמו: ותפתח ותראהו, את הילד [שמ' ב'
5 ו']· אשר לא יעבדו אותו, את נבוכדנאצר [יר' כ"ז ח'].

[28] אחר כן אמרה מה שימשך מן הרעה הגדולה, אם בני המשפחה ימיתו
את הבן האחר, והוא הכרת שם "האיש" ההוא החשוב [שם ז']; וזה אחד
מאופני ההתעוררות על החנינה, כאשר התבאר ממה שקדם· ובזה אמתה
שראוי הוא שינצל מזה הצד.

10 [29] ומפני שדוד לא ידע הדברים האלה כי אם מפיה, ואפשר שהיה הענין
באופן יצטרך לקחת ממנו נקמה, אמ': "לכי לביתך, ואני אצוה עליך" [שם ח']·
כלומ', "אצוה מה שיראה לי אחר החקירה והדרישה, איך היה הדבר." כי אם
היה חייב באי זה דבר מצד התורה לא יחייבהו המלך, היה זה עון וחטאת בחק
המלוכה. ולזה, בהתבונן האשה הענין הזה, אמרה: "עלי, אדני המלך, העון,
15 ועל בית אבי" [שם ט']· כלומ', שאמת יהגה חכה, ואין בזה עון כלל. והאמין
המלך לקול האות האחרון, ואמר: "המדבר אליך, והבאתו אלי, ולא יוסיף עוד
לגעת בך" [שם י']; ואמ' "והבאתו אלי", שהוא לשון זכר, למה שצוה על האשה
אחד מנעריו, להביא המדבר אליה, או מי שיגע בה אפי' באצבע קטן, באופ' לא
יוסיף עוד לגעת בה.

20 [30] ואחרי כן האשה רמזה לו שישבע שבועה, ואמ': "יזכור נא המלך את י"י
אלהיך" [שם י"א]. וכל זה עשתה לבחון לבב המלך — אם עושה זה בכל נפשו
ובכל מאודו, או בלב ולב — כדי שתשלם לה הבחינה מענין אבשלום. והנה
נשבע: "חי י"י, אם יפול משערת ראשו ארצה" [שם]· והנה נשלמה הבחינה,
ובטחה שכן יעשה בענין אבשלום על כל פנים.

25 [31] ואפשר שיסופק עוד: כי אחר שלא היה לבן משפט מות, למה תלתה

1 המקרה הגיעה] מקרה הגיע[ד] || 2 שלא] לא[ד] || 3 גדל] גדול[ד] | ובתבת] וכתבת[ד] || 4 וכו'] כו'[כ] ||
5 [אותו][ד] | נבוכדנאצר] נבוכ'[ד] || 6 אחר כן] א"כ[כ] || 8 מאופני] מאופן[ד] || 11 לביתך] לבתך[ד] ||
16 והבאתו] והבאתי[ד] || 17 והבאתו] והבאתי[ד] || 18 [באופ'][כ] || 20 ואחרי כן] וא"כ[כ] || 21 אלהיך]
אלקיך[כ] || 24 על כל פנים] עכ"פ[כ] ||

15 מש' ח' ז' || 16 שמ' ד' ח' || 21–22 דב' ו' ה' | תה' י"ב ג' ||

18:17] should not be cut off; and this was the boon she asked. She described the dispute between her sons, and how, accidentally, one of them had brought about the death of the other—in such manner that, by the laws of the Torah, he was not liable to a penalty either of death or of banishment. All this notwithstanding, the impulse to evil of the men of the clan had become very great, and they were in favor of killing the second son too [2 Sam. 14:6–7]. In the word *wayyakkō* (**but . . . smote**), the object pronoun anticipates the defined noun to which it refers,[12] just as in **And she opened it, and saw** it, **even the child** [Exod. 2:6], and in **which will not serve the same Nebuchadnezzar** [Jer. 27:8].[13]

[28] Next she stated the great ill that would result if the members of the clan should kill her other son—the cutting-off of the name of that important "man" [2 Sam. 14:7]. As has previously been explained, this is one of the methods of arousing pity;[14] she thereby presented a Confirmatory Proof[15] that her son was on this score worthy of deliverance.

[29] But because David knew of these things only from her mouth, and it was possible that the case was such that vengeance would have to be taken upon her son, the king said to the woman: **"Go to thy house, and I will give charge concerning thee"** [14:8], that is, "I will give such charge as I deem proper after investigation and inquiry into the precise circumstances of the case." For if the surviving son were liable, by the Torah, to some punishment which the king should not make him suffer, that would be an iniquity and a sin against the law of the realm. Understanding this, the woman therefore said: **"My lord, O king, the iniquity be on me, and on my father's house; and the king and his throne be guiltless"** [14:9]; that is, her **mouth uttereth truth** [Prov. 8:7], and in proceeding accordingly there is no iniquity at all. So the king **believed the voice of the latter sign** [Exod. 4:8] and said: **"Whosoever saith aught unto thee, bring him to me, and he shall not touch thee any more"** [2 Sam. 14:10]. The gender of the word **bring** in the king's statement is masculine because he gave charge concerning the woman to one of his young men, namely, to bring before him whoever might say anything to her or so much as lay a little finger upon her, so that he could not again touch her.

[30] The woman, intimating that the king should swear an oath, next said: **"I pray thee, let the king remember the Lord thy God"** [14:11]. She did all this to assay the king's heart—to determine whether he was making this promise **with all his soul and all his might** [Deut. 6:5], or **with a double heart** [Ps. 12:3]—so that she might have a thorough probation of Absalom's case. And the king did swear: **"As the Lord liveth, there shall not one hair of his head**[16] **fall to the earth"** [2 Sam. 14:11]; the probation was thus complete, and she was confident that the king would in every respect act similarly in Absalom's case.

[31] There is perhaps this further difficulty: since the woman's son could not

12. Literally, ". . . but smote-him the one the other," where "him" refers to "the other."
13. Literally, ". . . which will not serve him, Nebuchadnezzar."
14. Cf. ii.11.28–29.
15. Cf. ii.7.19.
16. B: ". . . of thy son. . . ."

האשה ענין ההצלה בהכרת השם? היה ראוי שתאמר כי בני המשפחה עושים
אתה חמס להמית הבן, אשר אינו בדין שימות, והמלך מחייב לעשות הדין· מה
היה בזה המקום מן החסד והחנינה עד שיבחן בזה שכן יעשה בענין אבשלום.
ונשיב לזה: שעם שהדין הוא כך, הרשות ביד המלך והשופטים לעשות זולתו
5 על צד הסיג והגדר, לפי הצרך והשעה. לכן ספרה הנזק הגדול אשר יתחייב
ממנו, לעורר הרחמנות· והיה בחינה: שאם יתרצה המלך בזה, יכמרו רחמיו על
אבשלום כמו שאמרנו.

[32] והנה עשתה פתיחה אחרת, ועשאתו מקשיב ומתלמד באמרה: "תדבר
נא שפחתך אל אדני המלך דבר" [שם י"ב].

10 [33] וא"כ עשתה[5] ההקשה השלימה עם חלקיה, ואמ': "למה חשבת כזאת
על עם אלקי'· ומעשות המלך הדבר הזה כאשם, לבלתי השיב המלך את נדחו"
[שם י"ג]: ומאז דבר המלך את הדבר הזה היה כאשם וחוטא. ואמ' זה בכ"ף
הדמיון מפני הכבוד, שלא ליחס למלך עון וחטאת, אלא שהוא ידמהו בזה
הפעל; או תהיה הכ"ף לאמת, כמו: אותו כהיום תמצאון אותו [שמ"א ט' י"ג];
15 ויהיה המכוון בזה שמאז אמרו שהנדח לא ישוב, היה בעון ואשמה. ויהיה
שמוש המ"ם כמ"ם "מאז הבקר ועד עתה" [רות ב' ז']· "מדי עברו יקח אתכם"
[יש' כ"ח י"ט]. והנה בזה המאמ' בלבול החלקי', והוא אחד מן היפויים
ההלציים; וזה המאמ' הוא ההצעה מחלקי ההקשה התמימה, שהציע'[6] בקצור
אשר רצתה להוכיח.

20 [34] וא"כ אמרה: "כי מות נמות, וכמים הנגרים ארצה אשר לא יאספו"

1 עושים] עושין[ד] || 2 מה] ומה[כ] || 4 שעם] טעם ‹היות›[כ] || 7 [כמו שאמרנו][ד] || 10 עשתה[5]] עשאה[כד] || 11 אלקי'] י"י[ד] | ומעשות] ומעשת[כ] ומדבר[ת] | [את][ד] || 12 ‹למה חשבת כזאת על עם י"י לבלתי השיב המלך את נדחו› ומאז[ד] | בכ"ף] בכף[ד] עם כ"ף[כ] || 13 הדמיון] הד'[ד] || 14 תמצאון] תמצאו[כ] || 15–16 ויהיה שמוש] ותהיה שמוש[כ] | המ"ם כמ"ם] המ' כמ'[ד] | הבקר] הפקד[ד] | מדי] מידי[כ] || 18 ההצעה] הצעה[ד] | שהציע'[6]] שהציע[כד] ||

[5] Correction: J.
[6] So J.

lawfully be sentenced to death, why did she link the deliverance she was seeking with the cutting off of the name? She should have stated that the members of the clan were about to commit a wrong against her in killing her son, since he would die illegally, whereas it was the king's duty to carry out the law. There would have been enough of an appeal to kindness and pity in this commonplace to have probed the king's willingness to act similarly in Absalom's case. Our answer to this problem is as follows: while such might be the letter of the law, the king and the judges had authority to act otherwise as a hedge and a fence [to its principle],[17] as the need and the moment required. Therefore, in order to arouse compassion, she described the great harm to which her son's death would necessarily lead; and this constituted a probation: if the king should consent to help her in this, he would, as we have said, be moved to compassion for Absalom.

[32] At this point she made another Introduction, rendering the king attentive and receptive by saying: **"Let thy handmaid, I pray thee, speak a word unto my lord the king"** [14:12].

[33] She next developed a Complete Argument, with all its several parts,[18] and said: **"Wherefore[19] hast thou devised such a thing against the people of God? for from the effecting of[20] this word the king is as one that is guilty, in that the king doth not fetch home again his banished one"** [14:13]: from the time that the king spoke this word, he had become as one that is guilty and a sinner. In saying this she used the particle of resemblance, k^{e}- ["as"], out of respect, so as not directly to attribute guilt and sin to the king, but to liken him to one thus derelict. Or the particle here may be used to express confirmation, as in **for at this** *very* **time ye shall find him** [1 Sam. 9:13]; in our passage the force of the particle would be that from the moment David said that "the banished one should not return", he was *indeed* in a state of sin and guilt.[21] The use of the particle *mē*- to express "from" here is paralleled in **from the morning until now** [Ruth 2:7], **as often as it passeth through** [literally: "from the enough-times-of its passing through"] **it shall take you** [Isa. 28:19]. Now this statement by the woman contains a "confusion of the parts," one of the rhetorical Figures.[22] And of the several parts of the Complete Argument, this is the Proposition, her brief setting forth of what she wished to prove.[23]

[34] Next she said: **"For we must needs die, and are as water spilt on the ground, which cannot be gathered up again"** [2 Sam. 14:14]. As we have

17. Cf. *Mishnah Abhōth* 1:1, "Make a fence around the Law." JML is arguing that while the son might not be liable to death according to the letter of the law against homicide, the king and the judges could extend the applicability of the law to include his case when the times warranted additional strictness in order to prevent the law from being disregarded completely.

18. Cf. ii.10.2.

19. B: "Wherefore, then . . . ."

20. B: ". . . from speaking this. . . ."

21. I.e., as the particle k^{e}- of k^{e}*hayyōm* at 1 Sam. 9:13 means "at this *very* time," so the same particle k^{e}- of k^{e}'*āshēm* at 2 Sam. 14:13 means "is *indeed* a guilty one."

22. Hyperbaton: iv.42.

23. Cf. ii.10.2,5–8.

[שמ״ב י״ד י״ד]· בארה שהמלך היה באשמה מצד ההפך, על צד שבארנו; וזה המאמ׳ הוא האמות, מחלקי ההקשה התמימה.

[35] אחר כך אמרה: ״ולא ישא אלקים נפש, וחשב מחשבות״, כו׳ [שם]· וזה המאמר הוא קיום האמות, מחלקי ההקשה. ואמ׳ שהראיה על זה עוד, שאשר בו אפשרות תועלת אין ראוי לדחותו דחייה עולמית, הוא ש״לא ישא אלקי׳ נפש״, ר״ל, שלא יטול אותה לדחותה דחייה עולמית, כמו שעשה מן הגוף· אדרבה, הוא ״חושב מחשבות״ ש״לא ידח ממנו נדח״ [שם], בדברים שהם עם אפשרות התועלת. ותהיה תבת ״ישא״ על דרך: וינשאם וינטלם [יש׳ ס״ג ט׳]· או שהיא לשון ״שרפה״, כמו: וישאם דוד ואנשיו [שמ״ב ה׳ כ״א]. והוא מבוא׳ שאינו לשון ״נשיאות פנים״, כמו: לא תשא פני דל [וי׳ י״ט ט״ו], להעדר תיבת ״פני״; ואינה סברה שיהיה העקר חסר בספר, כי הדבר הזה יעמד במדרגת ההבדל להבדילו מיתר ההוראות.

[36] ״ועתה אשר באתי לדבר אל המלך את הדבר הזה״, כו׳ [שמ״ב י״ד ט״ו]: הכונה ממנה שעדיין לא יאמן[7] דוד, שמה שאמ׳ לה הוא אמת. והוא כדמות התרה, כי היה אפשר שיאמ׳ דוד, ״מה לך לדבר אלי על אבשלום?״ לכן אמרה שאם המלך יעשה דבר אבשלום, ג״כ יאמינו האנשים יותר ברצות המלך הצלת בן האשה· כי זולת זה, יתמהו העם שיעשה המלך לה מה שלא עשה לעצמו. כי באה לדבר אל המלך את הדבר הזה, למה שיש בו מן העזר בערך אל מה שבקשה, שזה תהיה סבה שייראוה העם ויאמינו בה שהוא כן· לפיכך, חשבה

1 היה] היתה[כ] || 7 אדרבה הוא] אדרבא שהוא[כ] || 8 וינשאם וינטלם] וינטלם וינשאם[ת] || 13 <את> אשר[כ] || 14 יאמן[7]] יאמין[כד] || 16 ברצות] ברצון[כ] | הצלת] הצלה[ד] || 19 שהוא כן] שכן הוא[כ] ||

[7] Emendation required by context.

already explained, she thus showed from the contrary that the king was in a state of guilt. This, then, of the several parts of the Complete Argument, is the Reason.[24]

[35] Thereafter she continued: **"Neither doth God take away any soul, but He deviseth means that one that is banished be not an outcast from Him"** [14:14].[25] This declaration represents, of the several parts of the Argument, the Proof of the Reason.[26] She argued that there was this further proof of her contention that what had possibility of advantage ought not to be banished forever, namely, that **neither doth God take away any soul:** that is, He does not take the soul to banish it forever, as He does in the case of the body; on the contrary, **He deviseth means** whereby, in the case of things potentially advantageous, **one that is banished** may **not be outcast from Him** [14:14]. The word *yissā* [''take away''] is here used after the manner of **And He carried them and bore them** [Isa. 63:9],[27] or it denotes ''burn,'' as in **And David and his men burned them** [2 Sam. 5:21].[28] It clearly does not denote ''lift up the face,'' ''show favor (for a person in judgment)'' as in **Thou shalt not respect the person** [literally: lift up the face] **of the poor** [Lev. 19:15], because the word ''face'' is lacking here; nor is it reasonable to suppose that the main point should be left unexpressed in the Book, for the presence of this word ''face'' is precisely what enables this meaning of the verb to be distinguished from the other meanings it may bear.

[36] **"Now therefore, as to why I am come to speak this word unto my lord the king, it is so that the people may respect me; and thy handmaid said: I will now speak unto the king; it may be that the king will perform the request of his servant"** [2 Sam. 14:15].[29] By this she meant that David would not[30] yet be believed actually to have said to her what he had said. These words virtually comprise a Refutation,[31] for it was possible that David might say to her: ''Of what concern is it to thee to speak to me about Absalom?'' She therefore said that if the king should act favorably in the case of Absalom, people would also be more inclined to believe that the king wished to save the woman's son; for otherwise the people would think it strange that the king should be doing for her what he had not done for himself. Her reason for coming to speak this word to the king was that herein lay some hope of aid in connection with what she sought, since this act on the part of the king would cause the people to respect her and to

24. Cf. ii.10.2,9-12.
25. JV: ''Neither doth God respect any person; but let him devise means,'' etc. I have translated here in accordance with JML's interpretation.
26. ii.10.2,13 ff.
27. JV: ''And he bore them, and carried them''; ''carried'' is from the same Heb. root as ''take away.''
28. JV: ''And David and his men took them away.'' JML here follows the Targum and Qimḥi, q.v.
29. This translation differs from JV in conformity with JML's interpretation.
30. ''Not'' is not in the Hebrew text, but the correction is required by the context.
31. i.10.1 ff.

לאמר למלך גם זה הדבר. והרחיבה בזה המאמ׳ ליפותו· גם שתראה, שמכח שנדר לה לקיים הבן, יתחייב ג״כ שיעשה דבר אבשלום, כי זה תלוי בזה.

[37] והנה כללה אחר כן כל מה שנאמ׳ מהצלת הבן וענין אבשלום· ואמ׳ כי הכלל העולה הוא, ״כי ישמע המלך להציל אמתו מיד האיש״ [שם ט״ז] כוון להשמיד אותה ואת בניה. וזו היא הצלת הבן· ואחר כן אמרה: ״ותאמר שפחתך, יהיה נא דבר אדני המלך למנוחה״ [שם י״ז]; בזה רמזה שיבת אבשלום, כי על ידה ינוחו לבבות האנשים להאמין מה שצוה מענין הבן, כמו שבארנו.

[38] וחתמה בשבח המלך, שהוא חכם ״כמלאך האלקים לשמוע בטוב וברע״ [שם], ר״ל, הטוב על צד ההקרבה, והרע על צד ההסרה· והוא ג״כ טוב, כי הסרת הנזקי׳ טוב מה. וברכה את המלך כדרך הנפטרי׳ מלפני המלכים, ואמרה: ״וה׳ אלקיך יהיה עמך״ [שם].

[39] והנה, בכל זה המאמ׳, כוונה להעלים הענין אל המלך· ולא עלה לידה, כי הרגיש המלך לבסוף והבין הבדיאה, ושאלה: ״היד יואב אתך?״ [שם י״ט], שהרגיש בו שהיה אוהב אבשלום. והנה האשה אמרה לו האמת, ושבחה אותו לבסוף שהוא ״חכם כמלאך האלקים, לדעת את כל אשר בארץ״ [שם כ׳]· ר״ל, שהוא במדרגה מן ההתבוננות והשלמות עד ידע הכל, ולא יוכל האדם להטעותו בדבר.

[40] וישאר מה שנמשך לזה מבואר:

פרק י״ד

היאך יושמו בהרגל חלקי המאמר בסוג העצתי.

[1] אמר טוליאו, בג׳ מההלצה החדשה, כי לפעמי׳ יפול בדברים העצתיים לראות מה הוא יותר טוב משני ענינים· ולפעמי׳ מה הוא נפלא התועלת

4 להציל ‹המלך›[כ] | מיד] מכף[ת] || 5 אמרה] אמר[ר] || 6 יהיה] יהי[ר] || 8 בטוב וברע] בטוב והרע[ר] הטוב והרע[ת] || 10 הנזקי׳] הנזקין[ר] | ‹הוא› טוב[כ] | כדרך ‹כל›[ר] | הנפטרי׳] הנפטרין[ר] || 10–11 וה׳ אלקיך] וי״י אלהיך[ר] | יהיה] יהי[ת] || 13 והבין] והכין[ר] | ושאלה] ושאל[ד] || 16 במדרגה] במדרגת[ר] || 17 להטעותו] להטעאותו[כ] || 19 פרק] פ׳[כ] || 22 הוא יותר טוב] טוב הוא יותר[כ] ||

believe that the king's action would be the same in her own case; she had, accordingly, thought to say this word, too, to the king. She thus used Amplification[32] to embellish her speech; she would thereby also show that, by virtue of the fact that the king had given her his oath to preserve her son, he would necessarily act similarly in the case of Absalom, for each case was dependent upon the other.

[37] As we see, she next made a Résumé[33] of all that had been said about the saving of her son and about Absalom. The sum of the matter, she declared, was that **"the king hear to deliver his servant out of the hand of the man"** who desired to destroy her and her progeny [14:16]. After this reference to the saving of the son, she went on to say: **"And thy handmaid said: Let, I pray thee, the word of my lord the king be for rest"** [14:17]; she thus made subtle reference to the restoration of Absalom, because, as we have explained, such a reinstatement would be the means of setting people's minds at rest—so that they would believe what the king had commanded in the case of her son.

[38] She closed with a laudation of the king: he was wise **as an angel of God . . . to discern good and bad** [14:17], that is to say, the good which should be brought nigh, and the bad which should be averted—also a good, because the averting of injuries is a kind of good. Then she blessed the king after the manner of those who depart the presence of royalty, saying: **"And the Lord thy God be with thee"** [14:17].

[39] Now her intention throughout this entire discourse was to keep the king unaware of the real issue. But in this she did not succeed, for the king finally sensed and understood the fabrication, and asked her, **"Is the hand of Joab with thee in all this?"** [14:19], for he had noticed that Joab was Absalom's friend. The woman hereupon told him the truth, praising him, finally, for being **wise as . . . an angel of God, to know all things that are in the earth** [14:20]; he was, in other words, of such high and perfect understanding that he knew everything, and no mere mortal could mislead him in any respect.

[40] The ensuing remainder is sufficiently clear.

CHAPTER 14

The Handling of the Divisions of the Discourse in the Deliberative Kind of Cause

[1] In the New Rhetoric, Book III, Tully[a] says that in Deliberative causes there is frequent occasion to consider which of two possible decisions is the better; and

32. ii.11.1,22 ff.; cf. ii.10.2.
33. ii.11.7,9.

a. *R. ad H.* 3.2.2.

מדברים רבים. משל הראשון ממה שבא בעצת בני שכם וחמור, אם ראוי שימולו או לא [בר׳ ל״ד כ׳–כ״ד]; משַל השני, אם ישאל בעצה, ״מה הוא נפלא התועלת מאלה השלשה: עשות משפט, ואהבת חסד, והצנע לכת עם י״י?״ [מי׳ ו׳ ח׳].

[2] עוד, הדברים העצתיים, מהם ראוי שיועצו בעבור עצמם· מהם ראוי שיועצו בעבור אי זה דבר מחוץ לבד· מהם ראוי שיועצו בעבור שניהם יחד. משל הראשון, מה שהיה אומ׳ הנביא אל בית דוד: ״דינו לבקר משפט, והצילו עשוק מיד עושק״ [יר׳ כ״א י״ב]; וכן: ״אמת ומשפט שלום שפטו בשעריכם״ [זכ׳ ח׳ ט״ז]. אלה נופלים בעצה מצד עצמם· כי אין צורך בהם לדבר מחוץ, כי הם טובים מצד עצמם; ומזה המין כמעט כל עצות הנביאים בישראל. משל השני, העצה שנתן יוסף לפרעה, באמרו: ״ויפקד המלך פקידים בכל מדינות מלכותו״, וכו׳· ״ויקבצו את כל אוכל השנים הטובות״, כו׳ [בר׳ מ״א ל״ד–ל״ה]; כי העצות אשר בזה האופן הם לדבר מחוץ, ר״ל, לתועלת המגיע שהוא מהדברים אשר מחוץ. ומזה המין היתה העצה שנתן ירמיהו. לשרי החיילים, שלא ילכו למצרים [יר׳ מ״ב ז׳ — כ״ב]· ולצדקיהו, שיכנע למלך בבל [שם ל״ח י״ז, וגו׳]. משל השלשי, מהעצה שנתיעץ אברהם אבינו להציל את לוט מיד המלכים [בר׳ י״ד ח׳, וגו׳]· כי זה כלל התועלת מהממון, שהוא דבר מחוץ, ומהו ראוי מצד עצמו, ר״ל, הצלת הקרובים.

[3] ולעולם ראוי שיתבוננו בעלי העצה הדבר הנופל בעצה מהו, כדי שיוכלו לסדר כל המאמרים בערכו.

[4] התועלת בדברי׳ העצתיים יחלק אל ב׳ חלקי׳, ר״ל, אל הבטוח ואל ההגון.

[5] הבטוח הוא אשר יכונן השמירה מהסכנות האפשריות, בקרוב או לזמן רחוק, באי זה אופן שיוכל· ויחלק אל הכח והתחבולה. אמנם הכח הוא בהרגל החיילות וערכי המלחמה, בכלי זיין, בדוגיות שבייה, באסיפת האנשים וקבוצם, והנוהג מנהגם; התחבולה תורגל במעות, נדרים, ונדבות· בבדיאות, זיופים, ומסירות, וזולתם מן הדומים לאלה.

[6] ההגון יחלק אל ישר ומשובח. הישר הוא ענין נעשה במעלה מן המעלות· ויחלק אל התבונה, והצדק, והגבור׳, והיראת חטא, שהם המדות הראשיות.

3 עם י״י] וכו׳[ד] עם אלהיך[ת] || 7 [הנביא אל בית][ד] || 8 עשוק] גזול[ת] |[שלום][ד] || 10 כמעט כל] רב[ד] | בישראל] לישראל[כ] || 11 [המלך][ת] | בכל מדינות מלכותו] על הארץ[ת] || 12 וכו׳] כו׳[ד] || 13 לדבר] דבר[ד] | לתועלת] לתולעת[כ] |[שהוא][ד] || 16 השלשי] הג׳[ד] || 17 מהממון] מהממ׳[ד] | ומהו] מה שהיה[ד] || 18 הצלת [הקרובים][ד] || 23 והתחבולה] והתבולה[ד] || 24 שבייה] שביים[כ] || 28 והגבור׳] גבורה[כ] ||

often occasion to consider which of a number of courses of action is the most advantageous. An example of the first is the question that the men of Shechem and Hamor had to deliberate upon: should they, or should they not, undergo circumcision [Gen. 34:20–24]? It would exemplify the second kind if the question under deliberation should be, "Which of these three is the most advantageous: **to do justly,** or **to love mercy,** or **to walk humbly with the Lord"**[1] [Mic. 6:8]?

[2] Again, some Deliberative causes ought to be advocated on their own account, others on account of some extraneous consideration only, and some on account of both together. An example of the first group is what the prophet said to the house of David: **"Execute justice in the morning, and deliver the oppressed**[2] **out of the hand of the oppressor"** [Jer. 21:12]; so too: **"Execute the judgment of truth and peace in your gates"** [Zech. 8:16]. These are courses which should be advocated on their own account: they need no extraneous motive, for they are good in themselves. Nearly all the courses counseled by Israel's prophets are of this kind. An example of the second group is Joseph's counsel to Pharaoh: "And **let** the king[3] **appoint overseers over** all the provinces of his realm . . . **and let them gather all the food of these good years,**" etc. [Gen. 41:34–35]. Counsels of this kind have an extraneous motive, that is to say, some advantage derived from external circumstances. Of this sort was the counsel that Jeremiah gave to the captains of the forces, that they should refrain from going to Egypt [Jer. 42:7–22], and the advice given to Zedekiah, that he should submit to the king of Babylon [38:17 ff.]. An example of the third group: the deliberation in which Abraham, our forefather, determined to save Lot out of the hand of the kings [Gen. 14:8 ff.], for this course of action included both the pecuniary advantage, an external circumstance, and a matter proper on its own account, namely, the saving of kinsmen.

[3] Counsellors must always study the nature of the matter under deliberation so that they may be able to arrange all their statements in relation thereto.

[4] Advantage, in Deliberative causes, has two aspects: Security and Honor.

[5] Security sets up guard against potential dangers, whether imminent or farther off in time, by whatever method possible. Security subdivides into Might and Craft. Might is obtained by using armies and battle-arrays, by means of weapons, slave-galleys, the recruiting and mustering of men, and the like. Craft is exercised by means of money, vows, and gifts, by fabrications, frauds, delations, and other like means.

[6] The Honorable is divided into the Right and the Praiseworthy. The Right is an action performed with one or another of the virtues; it subdivides into Understanding, Justice, Courage, and Fear of Sin, which are the cardinal virtues. We

1. B here has ". . . thy God"; "the Lord" is the reading of M; C has "**to walk humbly**, etc." JML doubtless wrote what M reads.
2. B: "spoiled." JML's text is "corrected" by Jellinek in his list of errata to conform with B.
3. "The king" is not in B, but in JML's citation, here partly exact, partly paraphrase.

וכבר כתבנו גדרם בשם הפילוסוף, ולהם יסכימו גדרי טוליאו אלא שיקראם בשמות מתחלפים. וגדר אותם ויטורינו בהלצה הישנה בזה האופן: התבונה היא ידיעת הדברים הטובים והרעים בכל הזמנים; הצדק הוא קנין בנפש קיים, הנותן מה שיאות לכל התגמולים; הגבורה היא לקיחה משוערת מהסכנות וסבל ההתעמלות; ההגונות היא שררת הנפש ונצחונה בערך אל הדברים בלתי הגונים ובלתי תועלתיים.

[7] אמנם חלקי התבונה יושמו בהרגל בעצתיי, אם נעריך התועלות אל הנזקים, וניעץ ההתקרבות אל התועלות והבריחה מן הנזקים; או שניעץ בדבר מה אשר לנו בו ידיעה היאך אפשר שיעשה, ובאי זה אופן; או שניעץ דבר מן הדברים מצד מה שראינו וששמענו, ונוכיח מה שראוי לעשות בהבאת המשלים מהדברי׳ העוברים.

[8] אמנם נרגיל חלקי הצדק בעצתי, כגון: — שניעץ שראוי לחמול לעניים ולמבקשי המחילה. — עוד, שניעץ לתת תודה למי שגמלנו טובה. — עוד, לקחת הנקמה ממי שהרעו לנו. — עוד, לשמור האמונה בכל היכלת. — עוד, לשמור הדתות, והנימוסים, וההרגלים· שראוי לאהוב חבירינו ואחוזת מריענו עם טוב ההשתדלות. — עוד, נראה שראוי לאהוב האלוה ית׳, והאבות, וארץ מולדתינו. — עוד, אם נאמ׳ שראוי לאהוב, במשפט ובפרישות מן החטא, האנשים אשר הם תחת משמעתנו, ואשר התארחנו עמם, והקרובים, בין מצד האב בין מצד האם. — עוד, שנאמ׳ שאין ראוי לצאת מהדרך הישר, לא לתקות שכר, או חן, או סכנה, או על צד הבדיאה. — עוד, שנאמר שהמשפט ראוי שיהיה שוה לכל.

[9] אלו הדברים והדומים להם אם יפלו בעצה, נאמר שהם מדרכי הצדק וראוי ללכת אחריהם· ונוכיח שהפכיהם ראוי למאוס, ושהם דרכים על זולת

1 שיקראם] שיקראום[כ] || 2 התבונה] התכונה[ר] || 3 הדברים] האברים[ר] || 5 שררת] שרדף[כ] || 7 התבונה] התכונה[ר] | בעצתיי] העצתי[ר] | התועלות] התועלת התועלת[ר] || 9–10 מן הדברים] מהדברי[כ] || 12 הצדק] הצד[ר] | בעצתי] בעצתיי[כ] || 13 תודה] טובה[כ] | 14 ממי] למי[כ] || 15 לאהוב] לאהו[ר] | חבירינו] החברות[ר] || 17 במשפט] המשפט[ר] || 18 [הם][ר] | תחת] קצת[כ] ||

---

15 בר׳ כ״ו כ״ו ||

have already written their definitions, in the Philosopher's name,[4] and Tully's definitions agree, save that he calls them by different names.[5] Victorinus,[b] commenting on the Old Rhetoric, defines them as follows: Understanding is the knowledge at all times of things good and bad; Justice is an abiding disposition in the soul that bestows fairness upon all requitals; Courage is a calculated taking of risks and the patient endurance of suffering; Seemliness is self-mastery and control exercised with respect to things unseemly and unprofitable.

[7] Topics under the head of Understanding are brought into play in the Deliberative discourse,[c] when, comparing advantages with disadvantages, we counsel proximation to the one and flight from the other; or if we advocate some course of action in connection with which we possess the knowledge of how and in what manner it can be carried out; or if we urge one or another course of action based on what we have seen and heard, and show what ought to be done by adducing examples from history.

[8] Under Justice, in a Deliberative discourse, we may draw upon such topics as the following:

We may urge that it is proper to pity the poor and those who ask for pardon.

Again, we may urge that thanks should be given those who have dealt kindly with us.

Again, that vengeance should be taken upon those who have harmed us.

Again, that we should do everything possible to keep faith.

Again, that we should observe our laws, manners, and customs; that we ought, with the best of endeavor, to show love for our friends[6] and **the company of our companions** [Gen. 26:26].[7]

Again, we may show that we should love the Deity, blessed be He, our parents, and our native land.

Again, if we say that it is proper to show love, with justice and with abstention from sin, for those subject to our discipline, for those with whom we have exchanged hospitality, and for our relatives, whether on the paternal or maternal side.

Again, we may say that there should be no departure from the right path whether for hope of reward, favor, or avoidance of peril, or because of any kind of falsehood.

Again, we may say that justice should be evenhanded for all.

[9] Whenever these and the like topics find place in a deliberation, we shall maintain that they are of a kind with those paths of Justice which we ought to

4. ii.2.2–3.
5. *R. ad H.* 3. 2. 3.
6. C reads "fellowship" or "societies."
7. Cf. Rashi, *ad loc.*

---

b. Halm, p. 156; *De I.* 2.53.159 ff.
c. *R. ad H.* 3.3.4.

הצדק והמשפט.

[10] אמנם חלקי הגבורה נרגיל בעצות באמרנו: — שראוי שנחשוק בדברים הגדולים והרמים ונרדוף אותם, כי כן דרך הגבורים, ושנמאס בדברים הפחותים והשפלים. — עוד, שאין ראוי להפטר משום דבר הגון מפני סכנה מה גדולה, או התעמלו׳. — עוד, שניעץ סבל המות קודם ממה שנבא לידי בזיון וחרפה. — עוד, שלא נפטר מפקידותינו ומשמרתנו בעד כל צער שבעולם. — עוד, שלא נירא משנאת אדם מה מחמת האמת. — עוד, שראוי ליכנס בסכנה בעד האבות, והאהובים, והקרובים, ואשר ראוי שנאהב אותם לפי המשפט.

[11] ונרגיל חלקי ההגונות, ר״ל, יראת חטא, כשנאמ׳ שראוי לבזות רבוי התאוות והתענוגים, הכבודות והמעות· ואם נגביל כל דבר בגבול מה טבעי אשר אין לצאת מהגבול ההוא.

[12] אלה הם החלקי׳ אשר ראוי להרחיבם בעצה, אם הכונה ממנו ליעץ על ההקרבה אליהם. ואם נרצה ליעץ על ההרחקה, נעשה בזה האופן: שמה שאחרי׳ קורי׳ אותה תבונה, נוכיח שהיא סכלות והוללות ושראוי שנרחק מהם· ומה שקראוהו צדק, הוא חמס ושוד ישמע בו על ענינו· ומה שקראוהו גבורה, הוא עזות לא גבורה· וכן מה שקראוהו הגונות ויראת חטא, הוא דבר רע נשחת, נתעב ונאלח. ובכלל, כאשר הכונה להמעיט ולהרחיק, נכחיש, במה שחשבוהו מעלה, שיהיה הענין כן· אדרבה, נפציר עצמנו להוכיח שהוא פחיתות.

[13] המשובח הוא אשר ממנו יתחייב דבר הגון הוה ועתיד. ולא הבדלנו המשובח מהיושר להורות שחלקי היושר לא יהיו גם תחת המשובח· אמנם, אף שהמשובח יולד מהיושר, מ״מ הם חלוקים במאמ׳; למה שאם ניעץ אחת מהמעלות והנזכרו׳ מבלי זכירת שבח כלל, אז יקראו חלקי היושר· אבל אם נשבח אותם במאמרנו, שנאמ׳ שהם דברים משבחים, אז יהיו חלקי המשובח. וזה כי אין לרדוף אחר הדברים הישרים והמעלות לתכלית השבח לבד, אבל אם יתחייב השבח לישר, ייטב בעינינו הרצון המתאוה הישר ונשמח בו. וכאשר נראה שהדבר הוא ישר, אין ספק שנראה אותו שהוא משובח ג״כ מבעלי

5 התעמלו׳] התעלמות[כ] || 6 מפקידותינו] מפקדוננו[כ] || 7 משנאת] שנאת[ד] | עוד] עו׳[ד] || 8 ואשר] אשר[ד] || 10 בגבול מה] מה בגבול[כ] || 14 אותה] אותו[כ] || 17 שחשבוהו] שחשבו[ד] || 20 אף] אע״פ[כ] || 21 למה שאם] למה ש׳[ד] || 22 והנזכרו׳] הנז׳[כ] | כלל] כללי[ד] || 23 נשבח] נשכח[ד] ||

15 יר׳ ו׳ ז׳ || 17 איוב ט״ו ט״ז ||

follow; and we shall demonstrate that we ought to reject their contraries, which are paths leading to unrighteousness and injustice.

[10] In Deliberative causes we draw upon topics under Courage, when we say:

That we should desire and pursue courses noble and lofty, for such is the way of the brave, but ought to reject courses mean and base.

Again, that it is unworthy to shirk any honorable course on account of some great peril or toil.

Again, that we would sooner counsel the suffering of death than fall into shame and disgrace.

Again, that we would not abandon our office and our duty by dint of any grief in this world.

Again, that we will not fear being hated by any person whatsoever because of the truth.

Again, that it is proper to face danger on behalf of parents, friends and relatives, and those whom it is just for us to love.

[11] Finally, we draw upon topics of Seemliness, that is, Fear of Sin, when we say that we should despise overindulgence in lust and pleasure, in the piling up of wealth and money; and if we set, for every matter, some natural limit beyond which we must not go.

[12] Such are the divisions of the virtues which should be amplified in a deliberation if we intend to counsel adherence to them. But if we wish to urge a policy of avoidance, we shall perform as follows: what others call Understanding, we shall demonstrate to be a folly and madness from which we ought to stay removed; what they have called Justice is really a matter over which **"Violence and spoil!" is heard** [Jer. 6:7]; what they have called Courage is not this, but rashness; and likewise, what they have called Seemliness and Fear of Sin is an act evil and corrupt, **abominable and impure** [Job 15:16]. In general, when the intention is to minimize and urge aloofness from the policy of others, we shall deny that what they consider a virtue is really such; on the contrary, we shall tax ourselves to demonstrate that it is a defect.

[13] The Praiseworthy is that of which an honorable circumstance, present and future, is necessarily affirmed. We have distinguished the Praiseworthy from the Right, not in order to teach that the subdivisions of the Right may not also be listed under the Praiseworthy, but because, although the Praiseworthy is engendered by the Right, the two are nevertheless to be differentiated in making a speech. For if we urge one of the virtues and counsels noted above without mention of praise at all, then they are called topics under the Right; but if, in our speech, we praise those virtues and counsels, declare, that is, that they are laudable courses of action, then they are topics under the Praiseworthy. This is because right actions and the virtues are not to be pursued only for the sake of praise; but in case praise is required for right action, we shall approve, and rejoice over, the yearning for the right. In showing that the act is right, we shall doubtless show that it is also held worthy of praise by those who possess the

המעלות, אם יהיה דבר משובח אצל בני המעלה ומגונה אצל האנשי׳ הפחותי׳·
או שהוא משובח מחבירינו, ומכל בני המדינה, ומעמי׳ אחרים, ומבנינו אשר
יהיו אחרינו.

[14] והפתיחה בזה הסוג תהיה באופן כתבנו במשפטי[1]; גם כי נוכל להתחיל
מהפתיחה נסתרת, בהזדמן הסבה תמנע הפתיחה סתם, ואם יקרה בזה ספור
מענין מה בעתיד.

[15] יען התכלית באלה הענינים הוא התועלת, והוא נחלק אל בטוח והגון,
אם אפשר בערכנו להוכיח שניהם, נדר להראות במאמרנו שתכלית הדבר אשר
ניעץ עליו יהיו אלה שניהם יחד· ואם ימנע בערכנו להוכיח כי אם אחד מהם,
נאמר בספור מה הדבר אשר נוכיח אותו. והנה לקח "הספור" הנה באופן רחב,
ר"ל, בערך אל הגדת העתיד· והוא זולת מה שאמ׳ בגדר הספור, שהוא בערך
אל זמן העובר; ונמשך בזה אל דברי הפילוסוף בקצור ההלצה אשר הביאונוהו
למעלה.

[16] אמנם נרגיל החלוק בזה האופן: שאם נאמר מה בטוח, נחלק אותו אל
הכח והתחבולה; ואם נאמ׳ מה[2] ישר על דרך משל, ויפלו בו כל חלקי הישר,
נאמר שהוא נחלק לארבעה חלקים· ואם לא יפלו בו כח החלקים, נחלקהו
לחלקי׳ אשר הנפילה בהם אפשרית לפי מאמרנו.

[17] ונרגיל הקיום וההתרה מהמקומות אשר יקויים בהם הבטוח וההגון.
כגון, שנוכיח שראוי לעשות מלחמה ולנצח האויבים, אם נרצה לשבת לבטח·
ויביא ראיות על המלחמה יותר מהשלום. ואם ירצה להוכיח הבטוח מצד
השלום, יאמר שאין דבר למעלה ממנו, ושהוא המציל מהנזקי׳ ומהסכנות· כי מי
יודע תכלית המלחמה? ויביא המשלים מהטובות שגרם השלום בזמנים
העוברי׳, מהרעות שבאו מצד המלחמה, וזולתם מן הראיות.

[18] ואם ירצה להוכיח ההגון, כגון הגבורה, יאמר שראוי לאדם לסבול המות
טרם יצא ממנו· וכי טוב הוא למות בכבוד ממה שיחיה בחרפה ובבזיון;
ושאבותינו לא פחדו מהמות להשיג הכבוד והתפארת, כמו שעשו מלכי בית
חשמונאי; ושהאבירים, שהם הגבורים אשר מעולם, לא פחדו מהסכנות והיתה

2 מחבירינו] מחברנו[ד] || 4 במשפטי[1]] המשפטיו[כ] המשפט[ד] || 5 בזה] מזה[כ] || 7 התועלת] תועלת[ד] ||
8 נדר] נרד[ד] || 10 אשר] שאר[ד] || 11 בגדר] שבגדר[כ] || 12 דברי] דבר[ד] || 14 מה בטוח] מהבטוח[ד] |
[אותו][ד] | 14–15 אל הכח] לכח[ד] | מה[2] ישר] מהישר[כד] || 17 אפשרית] אפשרי׳[ד] || 18 הבטוח]
הבטחון[כ] || 19 לשבת לבטח] לשכון בטח[כ] || 21 [דבר][ד] | מהנזקי׳] מהנזקין[כ] | ומהסכנות] מהסכנות[ד] ||
24 [המות][כ] || 25 ממה] למה[כ] | שיחיה] שיהיה[ד] || 26 מהמות] מהמוה[ד] || 27 <אשר> שהם[כ] ||

2–3 דב׳ כ״ט כ״א || 19 וי׳ כ״ה י״ט ||

[1] Corrected text; cf. par. 19, below.

[2] Corrected, as in מה בטוח, immediately above.

virtues, if the act is indeed held in honor by the virtuous but held to be blameworthy by the vicious; or we shall show that it is worthy of praise by our friends, by all our fellow citizens, by other peoples, and by our children **that shall** be **after** us [Deut. 29:21].

[14] The Introduction in this Kind of Cause will be of the sort we described for the Judicial.[8] We can also start with the Subtle Approach if there is reason not to use the Direct Opening, and if the speech happens to include a Statement of Facts on some future matter.

[15] Since the end in these causes is Advantage, and Advantage breaks down into Security and Honor, if it is possible for us to demonstrate both kinds of Advantage, we shall promise to show in our speech that the end of the course of action we are counselling will consist of both conjointly; but if it should be possible for us to prove only one of these kinds of Advantage, we shall mention, in our Statement, the specific consideration that we are going to prove. "Statement" here is, to be sure, rather broadly conceived, that is, it relates to a telling of the future; and this differs from Tully's definition—that the Statement of Facts relates to past time. Here he agrees with the Philosopher's remarks in the Abridgment of the *Rhetoric,* which we cited above.[9]

[16] We shall treat the Partition as follows: if Security is our theme, we will divide it into Might and Craft; and if we would proceed by way of example in speaking of the Right, and there is occasion to use all the subdivisions of the Right, we shall say that it can here be divided into four categories; but if not all the divisions are applicable, we shall divide it into those of its categories that are admissible, depending on our speech.

[17] Our handling of the Proof and the Refutation will be in terms of the topics by which the considerations of Security and of Honor can be established. To demonstrate, for example, that if we wish to **dwell . . . in safety** [Lev. 25:19] we must wage war and defeat the enemy, a speaker will introduce arguments showing that war is more advantageous than peace. But if a speaker wishes to base his demonstration of Security on peace, he will say that no value is higher than peace: it is peace which preserves us from injuries and perils, for who can be certain how the war will end? And he will introduce examples of the blessings conferred by peace in times past, of the evils that have come through war, and other such arguments.

[18] If the speaker wishes to demonstrate the advantage of a course of Honor—of bravery, for example—he will say that a man ought to suffer death sooner than depart from Honor, and that it is better to die gloriously than to live in shame and disgrace; that our forefathers, in order to achieve glory and honor, did not shrink from death, as witness the kings of the Hasmonean house; that the gallant knights, the heroes of long ago, feared no perils, but had their minds ever

8. ii.12.1.
9. i.8.9.

מחשבתם דבקה לעולם בענינים רבי ההדר והתפארת; וכן בנוהג מנהגם: כפי מה שירצה ליעץ, ראוי לקחת ההקדמות המיוחדות בדבר דבר.

[19] והחתימות ראוי שנקחם כמעט כמו שנלקחו בסוג המשפטי.

[20] והנה נשלם מה שאמ׳ טוליאו בזה בהלצה החדשה· וזה ראינוהו מספיק בזה הפרק: 5

פרק[1] ט״ו

מה היא המדינה· והדברים אשר ייעץ בהם ההלציי.

[1] אמר וטורינו בישנה: המדינה היא רבוי מקובץ מהאנשים לחיות כפי המשפט.

10 [2] אמנם הענינים אשר ייעץ בהם ההלציי, הביאם הפילוסוף בא׳ מההלצה· ואמר שלא ימנע, אם שהמליץ ייעץ לאחד מבני המדינה, אם שייעץ על אנשי המדינה בכללם. והדברים שתהיה בהם העצה, בעניינים הגדולים מעניני המדינות, יעלו אל מספר חמשה: הא׳, בקבוץ הממונות הנאצרות למדינה· הב׳, במלחמה או שלום· הג׳, בשמירת הארץ ממה שירד עליה מחוץ· הד׳, במה 15 שיכנס בארץ או שיצא ממנה· הה׳, בשמירת התורות והנימוסים. ואמר, בקצור ההלצה אשר עשה לאלכסנדר, שמה שראוי ליעץ בראשונה אצל בעלי העצה וההמון הוא בעניני האלקי׳: מהעבודות, מהקרבנות והזבחים, וזולתם, וכו׳. ורוב מה שייעצו בו הנביאים הוא מזה הסוג, ר״ל, מענין השם, ית׳ ויתעלה, לשמור מצותיו חקותיו ומשפטיו, כאשר התפרסם זה מדבריהם.

20 [3] ומי שייעץ בקבוץ הממונות צריך שידע ג׳ דברים: א׳, שידע תבואות המדינה, וסחרה ואתננה, מה הם· שאם יחסר מהמעולה, ייעץ להוסיף עליו; הב׳ שידע הוצאת אנשי המדינה כלם; הג׳, שידע מיני האנשים אשר במדינה·

1 דבקה] דבוקהב || 4 החדשה] בחדשהד || 6 פרק1 ט״ו] פקר ט״רד פ׳ ט״רב || 7 ייעץ] יעץב || 8 וטורינו] ויטורינוב | בישנה] בישינהב | לחיות] להיותד || 10 ייעץ] יעץב || 11 ימנע] מנעב | המדינה] תמדינהד | שייעץ] ייעץב || 12 בעניינים] בדבריםד || 13 הא׳] האחתב | הב׳] השניתב || 14 הג׳] השלישיתב | הד׳] הרביעיתב || 15 או שיצא] ויצאד | הה׳] החמישיתב || 18 השם] ה׳ב | [ויתעלה]ב || 20 ומי] ומהד | הממונות] ההמונותב | ג׳] שלשהב | א׳] אחתב || 22 הב׳] השניתב | הג׳] השלישיתב ||

[1] Corrected text.

fixed upon concerns of the greatest dignity and honor; and so on in like vein. Depending upon what the speaker wishes to urge, he should adopt the premises special to each course of action.

[19] The Conclusions that we should adopt are virtually the same as in the Judicial Kind of Cause.

[20] Here ends Tully's treatment of the Deliberative Kind of Cause in the New Rhetoric; and we think that what we have said is sufficient for the present chapter.

CHAPTER 15

What the State Is; and the Matters on Which the Trained Orator Gives Counsel

[1] Victorinus,[a] in his Commentary on the Old Rhetoric, says: The State is a multiplicity of persons brought together to live in accord with law.

[2] In Book I of the *Rhetoric,* the Philosopher[b] introduces the matters on which the public speaker gives counsel. He says that the speaker necessarily will give counsel either to some individual member of the State, or to the citizens of the State as a whole. The subjects dealt with in deliberating the most important affairs of State amount in number to five: (1) the collection of the monies laid by for the State; (2) war or peace; (3) the defence of the country against any descent upon it from without; (4) what may enter or leave the country; (5) the keeping of laws and ordinances. In the Abridgment of the *Rhetoric* which he made for Alexander[c] he says that what may fittingly be deliberated upon by counsellors and the mass of citizenry is, in the first place, divine matters, such as cults, offerings, sacrifices, and the like.[1] Most of what the Prophets urge is in this category; as is plain from their words, that is, their counsel, dealing with the Name, be He blessed and exalted, favors the keeping of His commandments, statutes, and laws.

[3] One who offers counsel on the gathering of monies must know three things: (1) what the State's products, trade, and income are, so that if the yield is less than first rate he will urge its increase; (2) the State's public expenditure; (3) the

1. Religious matters are first in the list of seven such subjects mentioned *ad loc.* in *LR. ad A.* (1423a).

a. Halm, p. 158; cf. *De I.* 1.1.1.
b. T28/A34 f.; cf. *Rhet.* 1.3 (1358b).
c. Cf. *LR. ad A.* 31.37 (1423a).

שאם יהיה שם ריק בטל, נעדר המלאכה, ייעץ לגרשו מן הארץ.

[4] ואולם היועץ במלחמה או שלום צריך שידע כח מי שילחם, וכח אשר ילחם עמו· ושעור הענין שאפשר שיגיע במלחמה, האם הוא קטן או עצום· וענין המדינה, הבמחנים או במבצרים, ואם הם באופן שיוכלו להלחם. וצריך שידע 5 אל מה הביאו המלחמות הקודמות: שאם הביאו אל האבדון והמות, ייעץ בשלום· ואם הביאו אל הנצחון, ייעץ במלחמה. וצריך שלא יעלם ממנו ענין החיילות וכל חלק מחלקי המלחמה.

[5] ומי שייעץ בשמירה, ראוי שידע אופני שמירת הארץ ההיא, ומה שיצטרך לשמירה לפי מה שיתחדש, וכמה מיני השמירה· וידע המקומות אשר ראוי 10 שישמרם שמירה מעולה, ואשר ראוי שישימרם שמירה פחותה, כדי שיוכלו לכוון השמירה באופן הנאות למקום מקום, ולהוסיף ולחסר כפי מה שיצטרך.

[6] ומי שייעץ בענינים היוצאים מן הארץ והנכנסים בה, צריך שידע שעור מה שיצטרך שיצא מן הארץ מן הענינים היוצאים, ושעור מה שצריך שיכנס מן הדברים הנכנסים, באופן יספיק לאנשי המדינה· כדי שיוכל ליעץ על התוספת 15 והחסרון, כפי הצורך והשעה. ולא יעלם ממנו גם כן מה העניינים הנמצאים במדינה, ומה הענינים הבלתי נמצאים בה וצריך שיבאו אליה מבחוץ, כדי שייעץ על הבאת מה שצריך והוצאת מה שצריך.

[7] ומי שייעץ בהנחת הנמוסים והדתות, צריך שידע ויתבונן לכוון הדת והנימוס כפי מה שיאות לכל מדינה ומדינה, לפי טבע האנשים ותכונותיהם; כי 20 אין כל המדינות שוות בזה, והנימוס שהוא טוב במקום מן המקומות לעמידת אנשי המקום ההוא, אפשר שיהיה סבת השחתת מקום אחר, והפסד הכלל· כי אין כל האנשים צריכים לאזהרה שוה ולנימוס שוה, כי זה יתחלף לפי המקומות והטבעים. וצריך שידע כל מיני ההנהגות, ר״ל, מה שצריך להנהגת המלכים, ולהנהגת החרות, וזולתם, כדי שיוכל ליעץ בהם הראוי; ושידע הדתות 25 וההנהגות אשר הועילו לאנשי מדינה ומדינה בזמנים הקודמים, ואשר מצאו בהם אנשי המדינות הזק, כדי שיוכל ליעץ הקרבה אל המועילים והבריחה מן המזיקין, ולהעמיד המדינה במה שישמרה מן ההנהגות.

[8] ואמ׳ הפילוסוף, בא׳ מההלצה, כי לכל אדם תשוקה טבעית לטוב אשר יכספהו, וזה הטוב בכלל הוא כשרון התכונה; וכשרון התכונה הוא האותות הפעל עם מעלה· ואורך ימים· וחיים נעימים וערבים עם הבריאות· והרחבת

1 בטל] בטלן[ב] || 10 שיוכלו] שיוכל[ד] || 15 מה העניינים] מהענינים[ר] || 21 סבת] סבה[ר] | והפסד] והפסר[ב] || 27 המזיקין] הנזקין[ר] || 28 בא׳] באחת[ב] || 29 התכונה...התכונה] התבונה...התבונה[ר] ||

classes of the State's citizenry, so that if there is any unskilled, idle ne'er-do-well in the country, the counsellor will urge that he be ejected.

[4] In regard to war or peace, the counsellor needs to know the strength both of the attacking belligerent and that of the attacked; the measure of what might be achieved by war, whether this be small or great; the State's situation, whether in respect of armies or of fortifications, and if these are ready and able for war. He needs to know, too, the results of previous wars: if these have led to ruin and death, he will counsel peace, if to victory, war. And he must have some understanding of strategy and of every other of the elements involved in war.

[5] A speaker giving counsel on defence ought to know the methods of defending that particular country, what is needed for defence in the light of what might happen, and the several kinds of defence; and he should know the positions which must be most stoutly defended and those which may be less well defended, so as to be able to fix upon the kind of defence best suited to each position, and so as to propose increase or decrease in strength as needful.

[6] A speaker giving counsel on a country's exports and imports needs to know in what amounts exports must leave the country, and imports enter, so as to suffice the people of the State. This he must know in order to be able to counsel increase and decrease, as need and the hour require. He must not be ignorant of the material resources found in the State, nor of those not found therein that must come in from the outside, so that he can offer counsel on what needs to be imported and what exported.

[7] He who would give advice on the framing of ordinances and laws needs to know and understand how to adapt the law and ordinance appropriate to any one State to the nature and characteristics of its citizens. For not all States are alike in this respect; and the ordinance that, in some one locality, is helpful to the survival of the people there may possibly cause the destruction of another locality, and bring loss to all; for all men do not need the same warning and the same statutory enactment, since this varies according to the locality and the nature of the people. He needs to know, too, all the various types of government, that is to say, what is necessary to a monarchy, to a free republic, and to the other kinds, in order to be able to offer the appropriate counsel about them. And he must also know the laws and forms of government that in earlier times were of advantage to the citizens of each State, as well as those which the citizens of States have found injurious, so that he may be able to advocate approximation of the advantageous and escape from the injurious, and maintenance of the State in the form of government that will preserve it.

[8] In the *Rhetoric,* Book I, the Philosopher[d] says that every man has a natural desire for a good after which he yearns, and this good generally is rightness-of-state.[2] Rightness-of-state is seemliness of action combined with virtue, longev-

2. כשרון התכונה < صلاح الحال < εὐδαιμονία, i.e., "happiness."

d. T32/A40; cf. *Rhet.* 1.5 (1360b).

הממון· ונעימות התכונה אצל בני אדם· עם הגעת הדברים השומרים לאלו הדברים, והפועלים להם. וכבר יראה שזה הוא רושם כשרון התכונה, כי כל בני אדם יראו שזה כשרון התכונה, או קרוב מזה. וחלקי כשרון התכונה הם: היחס· רבוי האחים והבנים· והעושר· והאותות הפעל והכבוד· והישישות המשובח· ומעלות הגוף, כמו הבריאות, והיופי, והאמיצות, והעריצות, והחריצות, והגסות· והשבח· וההגדלה· וההצלחה· והמעלה וחלקיה, כמו השכל, והענוה, והגבורה, והיושר, והחסידות.

[9] היחס: האנשים המיוחסים הם אשר אבותיהם[2] היו הראשונים אשר יסדו המדינה, או הראשונים אשר חנו בה· ויהיו עם זה ראשיה שופטיה ושוטריה, בעלי שם טוב ורבי מספר· ושיהיו עם זה בני חורין לא עבר עליהם רע. או המיוחסים הם שהרגילו העניינים היפים המקובלים אצל בני אדם, ואם לא יהיו שופטים ושוטרים, ולא ראשים. וטוב שיהיה זה היחס מצד האב והאם; ואם נפסק הנשיאות והקצינות בסוג ההוא אשר הוא מהם בשכבר הימים, לא יהיה מיוחס; וייעץ ההלצי בזה כפי המפרסם באומה אומה.

[10] ונעימות התכונה בילדים היא רבוי הנערים וכשרונם במעלות הגוף ובמעלות הנפש. מעלת הגוף בד׳: העריצות, והיופי, והחוזק, והחריצות; מעלות הנפש ענוה וגבורה. וכשרון התכונה בנקבות ג״כ יהיה במעלות הגוף והנפש; מעלות הגוף הם ב׳, והם יחס האברים כפי מה שראוי והמראה, כמו שנ׳ ברחל: יפת תאר ויפת מראה [בר׳ כ״ט י״ז]; אמנם אריסטו׳ אמ׳: ״...ורבוי הבשר הטבעי, לא המראה והיופי״. ומעלות הנפש הם ג׳: יראת חטא, ואהבת המוסר, ואהבת העמל.

[11] העושר הוא רבוי הדנרים, והארצות, וההיכלות, ומקנה, ועבודה רבה, וזולתם מן הקנינים. וההנעמה בממון הוא ההשתמשות על דרך ההתעדנות ממנו, לפי שההקנאה היא פועלת העושר, וההשתמשות הוא העושר בעינו· ולזה אמ׳ בגדר הנז׳ ״ההשתמשות״.

[12] והכבוד הוא למשגיח באנשים עם נעימות הפעולה· והוא תגמול להם על דרך היושר והאמת, אחר שהיו אלה הפעולות לא יהיה תגמולם זהב, ולא

1 התכונה] התבונה[ד] || 2 התכונה] התבונה[ד] | כל ‹זה›[ד] || 4 והבנים] והאחים[כ] || 8 אבותיהם[2]] אבותיו[כד] || 11 המיוחסים] מיוחסים[כ] | העניינים] מענייני[ד] || 14 וייעץ] ויען[ד] || 16 מעלת] מעלות[כ] || 17 במעלות ‹במעלות›[כ] || 18 ב׳] שנים[כ] || 19 ויפת מראה] וכו׳[ד] | אריסטו׳] ארסטו[כ] | הבשר] הכשר[כ] || 20 ג׳] שלשה[כ] | ואהבת המוסר] ואהבה המוסר[ד] || 22 והארצות] ומארצת[ד] || 23 ההתעדנות] ההתערבו׳[ד] ההתעדנות[ט] || 25 ההשתמשות] המשתמשות[ד] ||

9 יהו׳ כ״ג ב׳ ||

[2] Corrected text.

ity, a delightful and pleasant life combined with health, ample funds, and pleasantness-of-state[3] in the opinion of mankind, as well as availability of the things that conserve and effect these goods. That such is indeed the design of rightness-of-state is shown by the fact that all men consider this, or the close approximation of this, to be rightness-of-state. The constituent parts of rightness-of-state are the following: good birth, numerous brethren and children, wealth, seemliness of action and honor, and a fine old age; also bodily advantages, like health, beauty, sturdiness, great strength, athletic prowess, and robustness; and glory, high station, and success; and virtue with its component parts—intelligence, modesty, courage, uprightness, and scrupulous righteousness.

[9] Good birth: men of good lineage are those whose forefathers were the first to found the State, or were the first to settle there; were, in addition, its **heads . . . judges . . . and . . . officers** [Josh. 23:2], of whom many possessed excellent reputation; and who were, besides, free men upon whom evil had not come.[4] Or distinguished ancestors are those who instituted the good manners in common human acceptance, even though they were neither judges and officers nor heads. It is well that this distinction of lineage should derive from both the father's and the mother's side. If, however, leadership and rulership were already before his day extinct in the family from which a man comes, he is not of distinguished birth. A speaker's Deliberative discussion of this subject will conform with accepted public opinion in each several nation.

[10] Pleasantness-of-state in respect of male children consists of having numerous boys endowed with excellences of both body and soul. Bodily excellence is fourfold: great strength, beauty, energy, and athletic prowess; excellences of soul are modesty and courage. Rightness-of-state in respect of female children is also determined by their excellences of body and soul. Feminine excellences of body are two: proper proportion of the limbs and fair appearance, as was said of Rachel: . . . **of beautiful form and fair to look upon** [Gen. 29:17]; though Aristotle says ". . . and abundance of natural flesh, not fair appearance and beauty."[5] Feminine excellences of soul are three: fear of sin, love of moral discipline,[6] and love of labor.

[11] Wealth is abundance of *dinars,* lands, palaces, livestock, many servants, and other such perquisites. Enjoyment of money consists in using it in such manner as to derive pleasure from it, for while acquisition is the efficient cause of wealth, the using of wealth is in and of itself wealth; and this is why Aristotle brings "use" into the aforementioned definition.

[12] Honor belongs to one who shows consideration for people by his fair treatment of them; it is the just and true recompense for such deeds, since gold

3. נעימות התכונה < حسن الحال.
4. A: ". . . upon whom enslavement had not come." T misread سباء for a form of the root ساء = "to be evil, wicked," etc.
5. *Sic,* T34/A42.
6. A mistranslation (?) of T: A says "love of affection" (الأُلْفَة / מוסר).

יתן סגור תחתיהם; ואלה, יחוייב להם כבוד אפי׳ שלא בשעת הפעולה. וההשגחה בבני אדם אשר תחייב הכבוד היא ההשגחה בהצלתם מהרעות אשר אין ההצלה מהם נקלה, או הקנאתם הטובות אשר אין הקנאתם נקלה. והדברים הכוללים אשר יהיה בהם הכבוד הם: המדרגות במושבות, והאזנה לדברי האדם ועזיבת מחלקתו, והתשורות אשר יחייבו האהבה והקרבה; כי התשורה תקבץ ב׳ ענינים, הוצאת הממון והכבוד, וזה כי בבני אדם ג׳ מינים: מין אוהב כבוד, ומין אוהב ממון, ומין אוהב שניהם יחד· והתשורה תקבץ אלה המינים הג׳.

[13] ואמנם מעלת הגוף הנה היא הבריאות, שיהיו מופשטים מן החלאים לגמרי· כי זולת זה לא יהיה נעים התכונה בערכו.

[14] ואולם יופי הנערים הוא שיהיו מוכנים אל חמשה דברים, ר״ל: מרוצה, רכיבה, האבקות, פזוז, כרכור. ויופי הבחורים שיהיו ערבי המבט אצל מעשה המלחמה. ויופי הישישים הוא התענגות פעלותיהם בענינים אשר הם הצלחה, ושיהיו נראים בלתי תוגה או דאגה· כי הישישות המשובח הוא התמדת הגדולה בהעדר התוגה.

[15] אולם החריצות הוא כח יניע בו האדם זולתו כפי רצונו, בדחיה או הגבהה, או בלחיצה או במה שדומה לזה.

[16] והגסות הוא גדול האדם באורך, ברוחב, ובעומק· ותהיינה תנועותיו עם זה בלתי נטרחות· ויהיה גסותו אין סבתו שומן.

[17] והעריצות היא תכונה מורכבת מהגסות[3], האמיצות, והקלות· כי אשר קבץ הגסות, והכח, והקלות, הוא עריץ.

[18] ורבוי החברה, וכשרון התכונה באחים, הוא שיהיה כל אחד פועל הטוב אשר יועיל בו האחר, לא הטוב אשר יקבל בו תועלת בעצמו לבד; וזהו ענין הידיד והחבר.

[19] ואולם כשרון מזל ההצלחה הוא שיהיה ההזדמן לאדם עלה למציאות הטובות לו, אם מהטובות הנמצאות לו בעצמותו, ואם מהטובות הנמצאות לו מחוץ.

[20] ואולם, הודעת המעלות הם משער השבח, למה שהמשבח יעיין בם מצד מה שהם הוות, והיועץ מצד מה שהם עתידות. והוא מבואר, שמה שבפעל יותר נכבד ממה שבכח: והשבח והגדולה הם דברים נמשכים למעלות· והנה המיעץ ייעץ לתכלית השגת הדברים הנזכרים, ויזהיר מהפכיהם.

3 הקנאתם] הנחתם[ג] |אשר] השר[ד] |[אין][ג] ||4 והאזנה] וההזנה[ג] ||6 ב׳] שני[ג] |ג׳] שלשה[ג] ||8 הג׳] השלשה[ג] ||9 ואמנם] ואולם[ד] |מעלת] מעלות[ד] ||10 יהיה] תהיה[ד] ||11 [הוא][ד] |חמשה דברים] הדברים[ג] ||12 ערבי המבט] ערכי המכני[ג] ||13 [הוא][ד] ||14 [נראים][ד] ||16 אולם] אמנם[ג] |האדם] אדם[ד] ||17 הגבהה] בהגבריה[ג] |בלחיצה] הלחיצה[ג] |במה שדומה] כמד שידמה[ג] ||20 מהגסות[3]] מהעריצות[גד] ||22 התכונה] התבונ[ד] ||23 האחר] האחד[ג] ||30 ממה שבכח] משבכח[ד] |והגדולה] הגדלה[ד] |הם דברים] דבר[ד] ||

1 איוב כ״ח ט״ו ||

[3] Corrected from ט.

will not recompense them, they **cannot be gotten for gold** [Job 28:15]. Such deeds make mandatory the bestowal of honor, although not while the action is being performed. The consideration for mankind that necessarily elicits honor is one that delivers men from evils from which deliverance is not easy, or is one that procures men benefits not easy to acquire. Common means of showing honor are the following: rank in assemblies, respectful attention to a man's words, avoidance of controversy with him, and the gifts which love and intimacy enjoin. For a gift fuses two components: an expenditure of funds, and honor; this is because there are three sorts among men, a sort that loves honor, a sort that loves wealth, and a sort that loves both honor and wealth, and the gift includes all three.

[13] Bodily excellence means good health, of course, complete freedom from ailments; for otherwise one is not pleasant-of-state in respect of the body.

[14] The beauty of boys consists of their adeptness at five things: running, riding, wrestling, leaping, and circling.[7] The beauty of young men resides in their pleasingness to look upon as they execute the maneuvers of war. The beauty of old men is the pleasure they take in their accomplishments in matters that turn out well, and that apparently are free of grief or anxiety; for the most praiseworthy old age consists in the continuance of dignity in the absence of grief.

[15] Athletic prowess is the physical strength whereby one man moves another as he wills by pushing, lifting, pressing him down, or the like.

[16] Robustness is a man's well-developed height, breadth, and depth, despite which his movements are unimpeded, and in the case of whom the robustness is not caused by fat.

[17] Great strength is a quality compounded of robustness,[8] sturdiness, and swiftness; for whoever combines robustness, strength, and swiftness is endowed with great strength.

[18] We are blessed with numerous friends, and enjoy rightness-of-state in respect of brethren, when each does the kind of good that will benefit the other, not the kind from which only the former himself receives benefit. This, in fact, is the essential meaning of "friend" and "comrade."

[19] It is prosperous good fortune of the right kind when what happens to a man is a cause of his coming to have goods, whether of goods that he comes by within himself, or of those that he comes by from outside.

[20] To afford knowledge of the virtues, to be sure, is part of any consideration of praise in oratory, since the Epideictic orator will treat the virtues as actual and present, the Deliberative orator as future. Clearly, what is actual is more honored than what is potential: glory and high station are consequences of the virtues; obviously, too, the Deliberative orator gives his counsel for the purpose of attaining the perquisites just mentioned, and warns against their opposites.

7. The list in T as here; A: "running, riding, fencing, wrestling, boxing." I am not sure T did not mean fencing by "leaping" and boxing by "circling."

8. JML here: "force"; I have emended on the basis of T/A.

[21] והנה אלה כלל הדברים הערבים והמועילים. אמנם, מן ההטבות המועילות אשר יגדל שעורם אל המקבלים הוא, כשיהיה אדם מה נשגב השעור, ולו[4] ג״כ שונא נשגב השעור, ואחד מן האנשים יפעל הטוב באחד מהם והרע בשונאו· זה יחשב לפעל נשגב ולהטבה גדולה אין כמוה. כמו שקרה לאומירוש עם היונים ושונאיהם: כי הוא הגדיל בשבח אחד מגדולי היונים, והגדיל בבזיון שונא מופלג היה לו· וגדלוהו היונים הגדלה גדולה עד שחשבוהו לאיש אלקי׳.

[22] והתגמול אשר לא תשובח נפילתו הוא, אם שיהיה חסר מן ההטבה אשר הגיעה אליו, אם בכמות ואם בתועלת· ואם שיהיה זה מותר אצל הגומל, ולא יצטרך אליו. והתגמול הישר הוא ההטבה השוה אשר הגיעה אליו.

והנה נשלם זה הפרק:

פרק י״ו

המקומות אשר מהם יוכיח המליץ שהדבר יותר מועיל.

[1] יען יצטרך ההלצי לפעמי׳ לבאר שדבר יותר מועיל מדבר, יתחייב המצא אצלו המקומות והמשקולות אשר בהם ישקל היות הדבר יותר מועיל ויותר משובח.

[2] מהם, שהדבר שהוא מועיל בכל הדברים יותר מועיל ממה שהוא מועיל בקצתם.

[3] ומהם, שהיותר מתמיד הוא יותר מועיל ממה שהוא על המעט מתמיד.

[4] ומהם, שאשר יותר גדול התועלת הוא יותר מועיל מהקטן.

[5] ומהם, שהיותר רב הוא יותר מועיל מהיותר מעט.

[6] ומהם, שאשר קבץ מתארי הטוב יותר הוא יותר מועיל. ותארי הטוב אשר בתכלית הוא: שיהיה הדבר נבחר בגלל עצמו, לא בִגלל זולתו· ושיהיה נכסף

3 ולו[4]] ולא[כד] || 6 שחשבוהו] חשבו[ד] || 7 אלקי׳] האלקים[ד] || 9 הגיעה] הגיע[ד] || 12 פרק] פ׳[כ] || 14 ההלצי] להלצי[כ] | שדבר] דבר[ד] || 19 [על][כ] || 20 שאשר <הם>[ד] || 22 שאשר] אשר[כ] || 23 נבחר] נכחד[ד] ||

[4] Corrected according to ט[ab].

[21] These, then, comprise the class of things agreeable and advantageous. Now the following is a beneficial act of goodness of the kind highly prized by the recipients: when one man of high rank has an enemy of equally high rank, and some third party does good to the one but ill to his enemy, this will be considered by the former as a noble deed and act of incomparably high favor. Just this happened to Homer in relation to the Greeks and their enemies: he had highly praised one of the great men of the Hellenes and brought a distinguished enemy of his into profound dishonor; the Greeks then magnified Homer to the point of considering him a man of God.[9]

[22] The recompense which, though actually made, will not be praised, is either one that falls short of the good obtained by the original beneficiary whether in quantity or degree of advantage; or is something that the requiter regards as superfluous and not needed. A just recompense is the equivalent of the good which the original beneficiary obtained.[10]

Here ends this chapter.

CHAPTER 16

The Topics from Which the Speaker Demonstrates the Policy of Greater Advantage

[1] Since the speaker must at times show that one policy is more advantageous than another, it follows that he should have at his disposal the topics and the considerations by means of which to weigh the course of greater advantage and excellence.[a]

[2] One of these topics: that what is of advantage in all things is superior in advantage to what is advantageous merely in some.

[3] Another, that the more lasting is more advantageous than that which rarely is lasting.

[4] Another, that the larger in benefit is more advantageous than the smaller.

[5] Another, that the quantitatively greater is superior in advantage to the quantitatively smaller.

[6] Another, that that which brings together more attributes of the good is of superior advantage. The attributes of consummate good: that the object is pre-

9. For the final phrase, cf. T42/A54; I am unable to locate Averroes' source.
10. T43/A55. JML has here abbreviated T's not very felicitous translation of A.

a. Cf. T44 ff./A 56 ff.; cf. *Rhet.* 1.7 (1363b ff.).

אצל הכל· ושיהיו בעלי החכמה והחשיבות כוספים אותו. והקרוב אצל זה הטוב הוא יותר מועיל ממה שהוא יותר רחוק ממנו. גם אם היה בסוג מה מן הסוגים דבר הוא יותר מעולה מדבר שהוא בסווג אחר, יתחייב היות זה הסוג אשר תחתיו המעולה ההוא יותר נכבד מהסוג האחר; והמשל בזה, אם האיש מעלה מהאשה, יתחייב היות הזכרים מעולים מן הנקבות· וזה כי יחס הנכבד אל סוגו כיחס הנכבד האחר אל סוגו, והיה יחס הסוג אל הסוג כיחס הנכבד אל הנכבד.

[7] ומהם, שהדבר אשר יתחייב ממנו דבר אחר, ולא יתהפך, הוא יותר נכבד מאשר התחייב ממנו; והמשל, שמהממשלה יתחייב העושר ומהעושר לא תתחייב הממשלה· ואם כן, הממשלה היא יותר נכבדת ויותר מעולה מהעושר.

[8] ומהם, שאשר יפעל הטוב היותר מועיל הוא יותר מועיל; והמשל מן העריצות והיופי, כי שניהם מועיל[1], ויען העריצות יפעל בו טוב יותר גדול ממה שיפעל ביופי, והוא א״כ יותר רב תועלת. וככה הבריאות והתענוג, ששניהם מועילים, והבריאות יפעל בו טוב יותר נכבד, וא״כ, הבריאות הוא יותר מועיל.

[9] ומהם, שהנבחר בסתם הוא יותר מועיל מהנבחר עם תנאי מה; והמשל, שהבריאות הוא נבחר בסתם, אמנם היופי הוא נבחר בתנאי, ר״ל, עם הבריאות· והנה א״כ, הבריאות יותר מועיל.

[10] ומהם, ששני דברים מועילים, אחד שלמות ואחר דרך אליו, השלמות הוא יותר מועיל; כאלו תאמר, החכמה והלמוד, שהחכמה היא שלמות, והלמוד דרך אליה· ואם כן, החכמה היא יותר מועילה.

[11] ומהם, שהדבר הנבחר בעבור עצמו יותר מועיל מהנבחר בעבור זולתו; כמו החכמה והעושר, שהחכמה נבחרת בעבור עצמה, והעושר בעבור זולתו· ואם כן, החכמה יותר מועילה.

[12] ומהם, שהדבר אשר ישים בעליו יותר מעט צורך אל האוהבים הוא יותר מועיל מאשר ישימהו יותר רב צורך.

[13] ומהם, ששני דברים מועילים, שהאחד צריך לשני, ולא יתהפך, הדבר שאינו צריך לאחר הוא יותר מועיל; כמו הבנים והעושר, שהבנים צריכים אל העושר, ולא יתהפך, כי העושר אינו צריך אל הבנים· והתחייב א״כ, שהעושר הוא יותר מועיל.

7 אחר] אחד[ד] || 12 תועלת] התועלת[כ] || 16 הבריאות ‹הוא›[ד] || 19 והלמוד] והתלמוד[כ] | מועילה] מעולה[כ] ||

---

[1] *Sic,* ט < א: فإنّ كليهما نافع.

ferred for its own sake, and not for the sake of something else; that it is an object craved by all; and that the wise and the estimable long[1] for it. What is proximate to such consummate good is superior to what is farther from it. If, also, some one class contains a member of greater distinction than that which is in another class, it will necessarily follow that the first class, under which that distinguished member is subsumed, is more distinguished than the other. For example, if the best man is superior to the best woman in some regard, it will follow that human males are superior in that regard to females; for the relation of the one distinguished member to its class is as the relation of the other distinguished member to its class, and the relation of the one class to the other class is as the relation of the distinguished member of the one to the distinguished member of the other.

[7] Another: that thing of which some other thing is a consequence, but of which the reverse is not true, is more distinguished than that which is its consequence. For example, wealth is the consequence of dominion, but dominion is not the consequence of wealth; such being the case, dominion is more distinguished than wealth and superior to it.

[8] Another: that which brings about the more useful good is of superior advantage. For example, great strength and beauty: both are advantageous, but because greater good is brought about by great strength than by beauty, the former is accordingly of greater value. So also with health and pleasure: both are advantageous, but it is by health that the good of greater importance is brought about, and health is therefore the more advantageous.

[9] Another: what is preferred absolutely is more advantageous than what is preferred on some condition. Health, for example, is preferred absolutely, while beauty is only conditionally preferred, that is to say, preferred only if combined with health; health, then, is the greater advantage.

[10] Another: of two advantageous things, the one a consummation, the other a way to it, the consummation is the more advantageous. Of wisdom and learning, one might say, since wisdom is a consummation, and learning a way to it, wisdom is therefore the greater advantage.[2]

[11] Another: a thing preferred for its own sake is more advantageous than one preferred for the sake of something else. As with wisdom and wealth: wisdom is preferred for its own sake, wealth for the sake of something else; wisdom, then, is the more advantageous.

[12] Another: what renders its possessor less in need of friends is more advantageous than that which places him in greater need.

[13] Another: of two advantageous things, one of which needs the other, while the reverse is not true, the one which does not need the other is more advantageous. As with children and wealth: children need wealth, but the reverse is not true, for wealth does not require children; it therefore follows that wealth is the more advantageous.

1. *Sic,* JML: T and A: "prefer."
2. This example differs from the one given by T/A: "health and pleasure."

[14] ומהם, כאשר היו שני דברים התחלות לשני דברים אחרים, ההוה מההתחלה היותר עצומה הוא יותר מועיל.

[15] ומהם, שאשר מציאותו יותר מועט יותר מעולה מאשר מציאותו רב, כמו הזהב בערך אל הבדיל; וג״כ יש צד הפך זה, שמי שיגדל מציאותו הוא יותר מעולה ממה שימעט מציאותו, לרבוי תועלותיו· כמו שנאמ׳ שהמים טובים לרבוי מציאותם וכללות תועלתם.

[16] ומהם, שמה שהוא קשה המציאות הוא יותר מעולה, לפי שמה שימעט מציאותו הוא נכרי, ויתפארו בו האנשים; וגם כן יש צד הפך זה, שמה שיקל מציאותו הוא יותר מעולה, לפי שהוא ימצא בכל עת שישתוקק אליו.

[17] ומהם, שהדבר אשר הפכו יותר עצום הנזק הוא יותר מעולה.

[18] ומהם, שהדבר אשר העדרו יותר חזק הרוע הוא יותר מעולה.

[19] ומהם, שהתכליות שהם יותר מועילות, המביאים אל אלה התכליות הם יותר מועילים.

[20] ומהם, שאהבת האדם, בעל הממון, יותר מעולה מאהבת הממון.

[21] ומהם, שהדברים אשר תאותם מעולה יותר מעולים מאשר תאותם בלתי מעולה; והמשל, שתאות החכמה מעולה, ותאות המאכל והמשתה בלתי מעולה· א״כ החכמו׳ הם מעולות מהמאכל והמשתה. וכן גם כן הפך זה, שמי שהוא יותר מעולה, הנה תאותו יותר מעולה· למה שהחכמה מעולה יותר מהמשגל, ואם כן, מי שיתאוה לו החכמה יותר מעולה ממי שיתאוה המשגל.

[22] ומהם, שהחכמות שהם יותר מעולות, פעולותיהם יותר טובות; משל זה, שלמה שהיו החכמות המדעיות יותר מעולות מהמעשיות, היתה פעולתם, אשר היא הצדק, יותר מעולה מאשר פעולתם המעשה. והפך זה גם כן, שהפעולה היותר מעולה היא מהחכמה היותר מעולה· שהעמידה על האמת, שהיא יותר מעולה מהמעשה, היו המלאכות המדעיות יותר מעולות מהמעשיות; וכח זה ההתחיבות הוא שיחס פעולה לפעולה כיחס מלאכה אל מלאכה.

[23] ומהם, שאשר ישפוט בו הכל, או הרוב, או המלובבים והטובים והישרים בלבותם, שהוא טוב ויותר מעולה, הנה הוא יותר מעולה במוחלט ובעצמו כאשר שפטו זה כפי יצירתם, והיו חכמי לב לא לפי מה שקנוהו מהדעות מחוץ.

3 מועט] מעט[ד] || 5 שהמים] שמים[ל] || 11 [הוא][ל] || 17 א״כ החכמו׳] והחכמות[ל] | שמי] שמה[טא] || 19 [לו][ל] || 23 [היא][ל] | שהיא] שהיה[ל] || 25 שיחס] שייחס[ל] | לפעולה] אל פעולה[ל] ||

28 שמ׳ כ״ח ג׳ ||

[14] Another: when two things are first principles of two other things, that which results from the greater principle is the greater in advantage.

[15] Another: that which exists in lesser amount is more prized than that of which plenty exists, as is gold in comparison with tin.[3] But there is also a contrary of this, namely, that the good which exists in larger quantity is more valuable than that which exists in smaller amount, because it has more uses; we may say, for example, that water is excellent because it exists in abundance and because it is universally useful.

[16] Another: what is hard to find is more prized, since what is more rarely found is not well known, so that people will boast of it. But there is also a contrary of this: what is easy to find is the greater good inasmuch as it is there whenever desired.

[17] Another: that of which the contrary has the greater power to harm is the greater good.

[18] Another: that thing the absence of which constitutes the more serious evil is the superior in excellence.

[19] Another: things that lead to ends of greater advantage are themselves of superior advantage.

[20] Another: the love of the friend who possesses money is nobler than the love of money.

[21] Another: those things, the desire for which is noble, are better than those for which the desire is not noble. An example: the desire for wisdom is noble, but the desire for food and drink is not noble; hence, the sciences are nobler than food and drink. Similarly, too, the reverse of this: whichever is nobler, the nobler the desire for it; since wisdom is nobler than sexual intercourse, then one who craves wisdom is nobler than one who lusts after sexual gratification.

[22] Another: the nobler the sciences, the better their effects. An example: since the speculative sciences are nobler than the practical, their effect, which is truth,[4] is better than the effect of the others, praxis. And the reverse of this too: since the nobler effect is that of the nobler science, since the understanding of truth is nobler than praxis, the speculative arts are nobler than the practical. In virtue of this consecution, effect is related to effect as art to art.[5]

[23] Another: that which all, or the majority, or the intelligent and the good and upright in heart, judge to be good and more excellent is absolutely and in itself of greater excellence, when such judgment is in accord with their innate

3. T/A: "iron." "Tin" is either a misreading (בדיל for ברזל), or else JML deliberately altered the example.

4. T, followed by JML, has here merely transliterated the Arabic *ṣidq* ("truth") into the Hebrew *ṣedeq* ("righteousness, justness, correctness").

5. Literally: "The strength of this necessary consecution is that the relation of effect to effect is as the relation of art to art." T: "And indeed these two *topoi* are necessitated inasmuch as the relation of art to art is the relation of effect to effect." A: "And indeed these two *topoi* are inseparable because the relation of art to art is the relation of effect to effect."

כי המלובבים מבני אדם כבר יאמרו ביצירתם המעלות והטובות מה הם, וכמה הם, ואצל אי זה דבר הם, ואם היה מה שיעמדו עליו ביצירתם זולת מה שתהיה העמידה עליו מזה בחכמות. והרצון ב״אשר יכספוהו הכל״, הנאמר בגדר הטוב, ר״ל, כפי יצירתם הטבעית· כי מה שתכספהו היצירה הלבביית הוא טוב מוחלט, 5 או הוא יותר מעולה מטוב, כמו ידיעתם שהגבורה, והמוסר, והעריצות טובות, ותשוקתם אליהם.

[24] ומהם, שמה שהיה מן הטובות עמו תענוג, הנה הוא יותר נבחר ממה שאין עמו תענוג· ומה שהיה יותר רב תענוג, הנה הוא יותר נבחר.

[25] ומהם, שמה שיבחרוהו הכל הוא יותר מעולה ממה שלא יבחרוהו כל 10 ההמון.

[26] ומהם שמה שיבחרוהו רוב בני אדם הוא יותר נבחר ממה שיבחרוהו המעט מהם.

[27] ומהם, שמה שיבחרוהו השופטים הראשונים, אשר לא לקחו המשפטים מזולתם והם מניחי התורות, יותר מעולה ממה שלא יבחרוהו.

15 [28] ומהם, שהמקובל אצל בני אדם, שאשר כבודותיהם יותר גדולות הם יותר נבחרות· שהכבוד, למה שהיה תגמול המעלה, כל מה שגדל כבוד האיש יחשב בו שגדלה מעלתו. והמין מבני אדם אשר הגיעם ההזק העצום והצער הנפלא למקום המעלות, הם גם כן מקובלי המאמרים מאד, כמו סקראט וזולתו· ואשר התקבצו בו שני הדברים יחד, ר״ל, הכבודות וההזק הרב מפני המעלות, 20 יהיו יותר מעולים ויותר נבחרים.

[29] ומהם, שהדברים אשר יעשו בזמן אשר אין מדרכם שימצאו בו, או שיעשום מי שאין מדרכם שיעשום, יחשבו יותר נשגבים ויותר מעולים אצל בני אדם· כמו להיות מליץ בימי הנערות, או שיפעל החלש פעל החזק, והחולה פעל הבריא.

25 [30] ומהם, שהחלק הנשגב מדבר אחד בעצמו הוא מהדברים שהם יותר מעולים· כמו הלב מהב״ח, או האביב מהשנה, והבחור מהמדינה.

[31] ומהם, שהמועיל במה שהצורך אליו יותר מועיל, והפכו הוא יותר מזיק· כמו הבריאות בישישות, שהוא יותר נבחר מהבריאות בנער.

[32] ומהם, מה שהיה מן הדברי׳ יותר קרוב אל התכלית הוא יותר מעולה.

30 [33] ומהם, שמה שדרכו להיות באחרית החיים הוא יותר מעולה· כמו החכמה, והידיעה, וזולתן מן המעלות, אשר ישלמו עם אורך החיים.

2 היה] היתה[ר] || 3 הנאמר] נאמ׳[כ] || 18 המעלות] התועלות[ר] |סקראט] סקרט[ר] || 19 הדברים] דברים[כ] || 22 מעולים] מועילי׳[ר] || 25 מדבר] בדבר[ר] || 26 מעולים] מועילים[ר] |מהב״ח] מב״ח[כ] || 27 שהצורך] שהוצרך[כ] || 28 הבריאות] תהבריאות[ר] || 30 ומהם] מהם[ר] || 31 וזולתן] וזולתו[ר] ||

character and they are **wise-hearted** [Exod. 28:3], and when the judgment does not depend upon opinions acquired from without. For the intelligent of mankind may be expected to consult their own innate character in declaring what virtues and goods are, how many they are, and in what particular connection they are, and whether that which they understand by virtue of their own character is other than what the sciences enable them to understand. By "object that all crave," mentioned above[6] in the definition of the good, is meant what all crave in conformity with their natural character; for what the innate character of intelligent men craves is absolute good, or the good that is of superior excellence; as, for example, knowing that courage, morality, and great strength are goods, their longing for these.

[24] Another: a good accompanied by pleasure is preferred to one not thus accompanied; and the more pleasurable the good, the more preferred.

[25] Another: that which all choose is better than what is not chosen by all.

[26] Another: that which is chosen by the majority of mankind is preferable to that which is chosen by the minority.

[27] Another: that which is preferred by the first judges—those who, not adopting statutes from others, themselves are the framers of the laws—is better than that which they do not prefer.

[28] Another: the well-received among men, because those whose honors are greater are those more preferred; for, since honor is the recompense of virtue, the greater a man's honor, the greater will his virtue be thought to be. But the words of the class of men who have sustained great injury and extraordinary misfortune by reason of the virtues are also very well-received, those of Socrates, for example, and others; and the class in whom both attributes are joined, that is to say, both honors and great injury because of the virtues, are superior and more to be preferred.

[29] Another: things accomplished at a time when they are not wont to be encountered, or accomplished by those not wont to accomplish them, are thought by men to be grander and more excellent, like becoming a spokesman while young, or like the weak performing the feat of the strong, or the sick that of the healthy.

[30] Another: the most important part of some one phenomenon is itself classed among the things that are of higher value, like the heart in the living creature, or the spring of the year, and the young people of the State.

[31] Another: what is serviceable when needed is more beneficial, and the opposite is more noxious; health in old age, for example, is more favorable than health in childhood.

[32] Another: whichever of two things is closer to the end in view is the better.

[33] Another: what is wont to come at the end of life is of superior excellence, like wisdom, knowledge, and the other virtues, which grow sounder with length of life.

6. Par. 6.

[34] ומהם, שמה שפעולתו מועלת לעצמו, אף אם לא ידענו שום אדם, הוא יותר נבחר מהדבר שהיותו נבחר תלוי בשידע· כמו הבריאות והיופי, שהבריאות נבחר בעצמותו, והיופי לזולתו.

[35] ומהם, שהמועילים בדברים רבים הם יותר מועילים; ולזה יחשב שהבריאות והעושר נשגבים, שהם מועילים בדברים רבים, ר״ל, שהם יקבצו העזיבה מהתוגה והפעל בתענוג· ר״ל, שהבריאות הוא סבת הפעל בתענוג, והעושר סבת עזיבת התוגות· וכל אחד משני אלה, ר״ל עזיבת התוגות והפעל בתענוג, מעולה ונבחר בנפשו, וכאשר קובצו באדם, שמוהו רב ועצום מכל דבר.

[36] אלה מה שראינו להביא בזה המקום ממקומות אשר מהם יתבאר היות הדבר יותר מועיל; אלא שיתחייב להלצי, שכאשר הביא אלה ההקדמות, לחזקם בהמשלים הלקוחים מן האנשי׳ אשר פעלו אותם הפעולות והשיגם התועלת או הנזק; ולזה, מה שיחוייב להלצי, שיהיה שומר הספורים וההגדות:

פרק י״ז

מנתינת העצה בנימוסים.

[1] אמר הפילוסוף בא׳ מההלצה, שהחפץ לתת עצה בנימוסים המועילים, וההספקה בם אשר בתכלית, צריך שידע מיני ההנהגה, והמדות והנימוסים אשר ייחדו הנהגה הנהגה· למה שבכל אחת מההנהגות, נימוסים מועילים בה, אשר בהם תהיה הצלת אותה המדינה וקיומה. והנימוסים מופלגי הפאר והתועלת הם הנימוסים הישרים אשר ירשמם הראש הראשון במדינה ההיא, או הנפקד עליה ממנו; והנימוסים ההם הישרים יתחלפו בהנהגות בהתחלף תכליתם, ומספרם לפי מספר ההנהגות.

[2] וההנהגות בכלל הם ד׳: ההנהגה הקבוצית· וההנהגה הפחותית· והנהגת הממשלה· והנהגת האחדות, והוא הכבוד. ואלה ההנהגות כלם, המכוון

1 שום] טוב[כ] || 7 אלה] אילו[כ] אלו[ט] || 10 להלצי] ההלצה[כ] || 12 הנזק] נזק[ד] || 13 פרק] פ׳[כ] || מההלצה] מן ההלצה[כ] || 17 מההנהגות] מהנהגות[ד] || 22 והנהגת] וההנהגת[ד] || 23 והנהגת] וההנהגת[ד] ||

[34] Another: that which by itself works benefit, even though no one is aware of it, is preferable to the thing which must depend upon awareness in order to be preferred; of health and beauty, for example, health is preferred of and for itself, beauty for something other than itself.

[35] Another: things beneficial in numerous respects are more advantageous. Thus health and wealth are highly valued, since they are beneficial in many respects; that is to say, they combine freedom from sadness with active pleasure, meaning that health is the cause of active pleasure, wealth the cause of freedom from sadness. Each of these two—freedom from sadness and active pleasure—is in itself excellent and *per se* preferred, and when an individual disposes of both in combination, they make him greater and stronger than can any other thing.

[36] These, then, are the several topics from which to demonstrate that something is of greater advantage that we have thought it desirable to introduce here. The speaker, however, when he has introduced such premises as these, will be obliged to support them with examples of persons who followed those courses of action, and so gained advantage or suffered injury. And that is why the speaker of necessity becomes the preserver of stories and tales.

CHAPTER 17

The Giving of Counsel on Laws

[1] In the *Rhetoric*, Book I, the Philosopher[a] says that he who wishes to give counsel on the legal enactments of greatest advantage, and to deal with them as convincingly as possible, needs to know the several types of government and the principles and norms peculiar to each type; for in the case of each of the several types there are legal measures of advantage to that type, the means of saving and preserving that particular kind of State. By far the finest and most beneficial measures are the sets of just laws drawn up by the sovereign authority in that kind of state, or by the appointee of the sovereign authority; these just sets of laws vary in the several types of government as the aims of these governments vary, and their number accords with that of the several governments.[1]

[2] In general, there are four types of government: democracy, oligarchy, aristocracy, and monarchy, or timocracy.[2] The laws laid down in all these sys-

1. In this section, as in the previous chapter, JML follows T/A. Whole phrases and sentences are cited *verbatim*, others with slight changes. JML also will often abridge T.

2. Literally, "collective government, scanty government, government-of-rulership, government-

a. T53 ff./A68 ff.; cf. *Rhet.* 1.8 (1365b) ff.

בנימוסים המונחים בהם הוא המדינה והכל, לא האיש.

[3] אם המדינה הקבוצית, הנה היא אשר תהיה הראשות בה בהזדמן והמַזל, לא בחק ראוי, אחר שאין בזאת המדינה יתרון לאחד על האחר.

[4] ואם פחיתות הראשות, הוא אשר יתמנו בו הממונים על המדיניים בהנחת
5 המסים והעלות על צד שיגיע קבוץ הממון לראש הראשון, לא לעשות אוצרות ומטמוניות למדינה, או ההוצאה למשמרת וחזוק. ואם חנם חלק מקבוץ הממון, היה ראשיות קבוץ הממון· ואם לאו, היה ראשיות הנצחון; והיו במדרגת העבד לראש הראשון, ותהיה שמירתו מהם כמדרגת שמירת האדם מעבדו.

[5] ואם טוב הממשלה, היא אשר תהיה על דרך המוסר וההמשך במה
10 שיחייבהו הדת או הנימוס; כי אשר ייעצו במה שיחייבהו הנימוס, הם מושלים בטוב הממשלה. וזאת היא הממשלה אשר יגיע בה כשרון אנשי המדינה וההצלחה האנושית; ולזה היו אנשי מעלות ובעלי יכלת על הפעולות אשר יתנו הצלחה למדינה, ובעלי זריזות ושמירה במה שדרכו שיפסיד המדינה מבית או מחוץ· ולכן נקראת זאת המדינה בזה השם. וזאת הממשלה, הם שני מינים:
15 ראשות המלך, והיא המדינה אשר יהיו דיעותיה ופעולותיה כפי מה שיחייבוהו החכמות העיוניות· והשנית ראשות הטובים, והיא אשר יהיו פעולותיה ודעותיה מעולות לבד; וזאת תקרא הכהניית, ויאמ׳ שהיא היתה נמצאת בפרסיים הראשונים, לפי מה שספרו אבונצר.

[6] ואם אחדות הממשלה, הנה היא הראשות אשר יאהב המלך שיתיחד בו
20 בכבוד הראשיי, ולא יבצר ממנו דבר ישותף לו בו זולתו; וזה בהפך מדינת

1 הוא] והוא[כ] || 4 הראשות] הראשון[כ] | המדיניים] המדינה[ד] || 5 <לא> על צד[כ] || 6 ההוצאה] ההוצאת[כ] | למשמרת] לשמרת[כ] | וחזוק] וחוזק[ד] || 7 [היה][כ] | ראשיות] ראשתות[כ] || 10 שיחייבהו] שיחייבה[ד] | במה] כמה[כ] || 11 כשרון <תכונת>[ט] || 15 יהיו] היו[ד] ||

tems of government are aimed at the State and the whole society, not at any particular person.

[3] A democratic State is one in which headship is achieved through chance or luck, not through being really deserved, since in this sort of state no one individual has superiority over any other.

[4] Oligarchic rule[3] is that in which those set over the citizens to levy taxes and imposts are appointed to assure accrual of the collected funds to the prime authority, not so as to create stores of funds and reserves for the State or for outlay on defense and fortification. If the first authority favors the oligarchs with a share in the collected wealth, it is a plutocracy; if not, it is rule-by-domination.[4] Their status is that of servant to the first authority; and his protection of them is as the protection which a man accords to his servant.[5]

[5] Aristocracy[6] is government by way of disciplined morality and of faithful adherence to the obligations imposed by the law or the constitution; for those who urge as policy what the constitution requires exercise the best kind of rulership. This is the type of government through which the citizens of the state come to have rightness [-of-state][7] and human felicity; the rulers, therefore, are men endowed with the virtues and with the ability to perform the acts that will bring prosperity to the State, and who are zealous to guard against whatever tends to injure it from within or from without; and that is why such a State is called by this name.[8] There are two varieties of such rulership: royal supremacy, this being the State whose opinions and actions conform to the logical requirements of the speculative sciences; and secondly, supremacy of the best, a State whose actions and opinions are virtuous only. The latter is called a priestly State, and, according to Abū Naṣr's account, is said to have been in existence among the ancient Persians.[9]

[6] Monarchy is the form of supremacy in which the king desires to be the sole person to have the honor of being head of state, without any exception in which

---

of-oneness, which is honor.'' T/A has ''government of becoming-less'' instead of ''scanty government'' (הנהגת הפחותות < سياسة الخسة instead of ההנהגה הפחותית).

3. ML and T: ''lessening-of-headship'' (פחיתות הראשות) < A: ''becoming-less-of-headship'' (خسة الرئاسة).

4. I.e., what Aristotle, in the *Politics* (1272b, 1292b, 1293a), calls δυναστεία.

5. The language here is ambiguous because T has translated A too literally. My translation represents the sense of A.

6. Literally, ''goodness-of-rulership'' (טוב הממשלה < جودة التسلط).

7. The bracketed words translate a term omitted by JML, but found in T.

8. I.e., aristocracy (''goodness-of-rulership'').

9. The statement here attributed by JML and T/A to al-Fārābī (Abū Naṣr Muḥammad ibn Muḥammad ibn Ṭarkhān al-Fārābī [870–950 C.E.]) does not appear in any work of this philosopher that has come down to us. Averroes refers to this statement not only at the parallel in T/A (54/69)—whence JML introduced it here—but also in his *Epitome of Plato's Republic* (R. Lerner, *Averroes on Plato's Republic* [Ithaca, N.Y., 1974], 102). E. I. J. Rosenthal has conjectured that the source may be a passage in al-Fārābī's lost commentary on the *Nichomachean Ethics;* cf. his *Political Thought in Medieval Islam* (Cambridge, 1958), 201, and the discussion, including allusion to the present passage in JML's *N.S.*, in his *Studia Semitica* II, 56, n. 72.

הטובים. ואלה המדינות, לפעמים היו הנימוסים המונחים בם[1] מוגבלים, בלתי מומרים, אחדים[1] לנצח, כפי מה שעליו הענין בנמוסי הישמעאלים; ולפעמים היו בלתי בעלי נימוסים מוגבלים, אבל יונח הענין בם אל המושלים עליהם כפי היותר מועיל בעת עת, כפי מה שעליו הענין בהרבה מהנימוסים הרומיים היום.

[7] ותכליות אלה ההנהגות הם אלה: תכלית ההנהגה הקבוצית החרות· ותכלית פחיתות הראשות קבוץ הממון· ותכלית טוב הממשלה המעלה והחזקת הנימוס· ותכלית האחדות הכבוד. וההנהגות אשר לא יונחו בם נימוסים בלתי מומרים, הנה תכלית מניחם הוא השמירה והנצירה מהטעות הנופל בנימוסים בהמרת הזמנים והמקומות.

[8] ואמר בן רשד שאלה ההנהגות אשר ספרם אריסטו׳ לא ימצאו פשוטות, ואמנם ימצאו ברוב מרכבות, כגון הענין בהנהגה הנמצאת עתה; כי היא, כשנסתכל בה, נמצאה מורכבת ממעלה, כבוד, חרות, ונצחון.

[9] והנה כאשר נדע מיני ההנהגות, נוכל לדעת המדות והנימוסים אשר יביאו אל תכלית כל אחת מאלה, ונוכל ליעץ הדברים המועילים בערכם. האמנם כי ראוי שנתלבש באותן המדות אשר נשתדל ההספקה בהן, כי בזה האופן יהיו דברינו נותנים ההספקה; כי כשתמצא בנו המדה אשר ניעץ עליה היה מאמרנו בזרזנו עליה יותר חזק הספקה. ולכן, ראוי שלא ניעץ אלא במה שהוא נמצא לנו ואנחנו תאבים על שימצא לנו.

[10] והנה התבאר מאין נספיק המועיל בנימוסים בהנהגה הנהגה, וכמה צדי ההנהגות והנימוסים אשר נפנה למולם, כפי מה שיספיק לזאת המלאכה.

[11] ואמר קוינטיליאנו, בעשירי מן החלק השלישי, שהמיעצים בזה הסוג ראוי שידברו באופן מתחלף כפי התחלף תכונות השומעים ומעלותיהם· עד שידבר בפני בעלי העצה היושבים ראשונה באופן ראוי אליהם ובערכם. תאות

1 בם[1]] בה[כד] || 2 באחדים[1]] אחרים[כד] || 3 בעלי] מעלות[כ] בעלות[טag] | בם] בה[כ] || 6 הראשות] ה׳[כ] || 9 בהמרת] כהמרת[כ] || 10 ההנהגות] ההנג׳[ד] | אריסטו׳] ארסטו[כ] || 12 נמצאה] נמצאת[ד] | ממעלה] ממעלת[ד] || 14 אחת] אחד[ד] || 15 בהן] בהם[כ] || 16 ההספקה ‹לשומעים›[כ] || 17 הספקה] ההספקה[ד] || 19 נספיק] נפסיק[כ] || 20 למולם] למולה[ד] || 21 קוינטיליאנו] קִנטיליאנו[כ] | השלישי] הג׳[ד] || 22 [כפי התחלף][כ] || 23 תאות] תאיות[כ] ||

23 אס׳ א׳ י״ד ||

[1] Corrected from ט.

anybody else shares his honor. This is the opposite of the aristocratic state. Sometimes the constitutions laid down in monarchical states are strictly delimited, unalterable, everlastingly the same, as is the case with the constitutions of Muslim[10] powers. Sometimes, however, monarchical states are without defined constitutions, the policy of greatest advantage at any particular time being left, instead, to their rulers, as is the case with many of the Christian[11] state constitutions today.[12]

[7] The aims of these several forms of government are the following: of democratic government, freedom; of oligarchy, the accumulation of wealth; of aristocracy, virtue and adherence to the laws; and of monarchy, honor. As for governments in the case of which the constitutions laid down are not unalterable, the aim of the framers of such constitutions is precaution and watchfulness against the defectiveness to which constitutions are subject as times and situations change.

[8] Averroes[b] says that the several kinds of government described by Aristotle are not found in pure and unalloyed form, but are for the most part composite, as is true of the type of government that now[13] exists. For this type, when we study it, we find to be a composite of virtue, honor, freedom, and mastery.

[9] Now knowledge of the several species of government will make it possible for us to know the ethics and legal norms that will lead to the end of each form, and we will be able to counsel the courses of greatest advantage in each respectively. We should, in fact, ourselves assume those ethical attitudes of which we attempt to persuade others, because in this way our words will be found convincing. For when the ethical trait whose adoption we are counselling is found in ourselves, the speech in which we urge its adoption will be the more strongly persuasive. It is therefore fitting that we should advocate only that which is true of ourselves and that which we wish to be true of ourselves.

[10] From what premises we may persuade others of the kind of laws that would be most advantageous in each several form of government, has now been explained, and also—sufficiently for this present treatise—some of the aspects of the several forms of government and of legal institutions to which we may advert.

[11] In Book III, Chapter 10,[14] Quintilian[c] says that in this Kind of Cause[15] counsellors should speak in a manner varied to conform with the varying dispositions and ranks of their hearers. Accordingly, one will speak in the presence of

10. "Ishmaelite" (T) < "Islamic" (A).
11. "Roman" (T/A).
12. "Today": Averroes' day (twelfth century C.E.).
13. "Now": Averroes' day.
14. *Sic*, JML; modern reference as in source-footnote c.
15. I.e., the Deliberative.

b. T55/A70.
c. Q. 3.8.6 ff.

הפתיחה בזה הסוג מתדמה לפתיחה הנעשת בסוג המשפטי, כי נשיאי העדה קריאי מועד ידמו הדיינים אשר אליהם המשפט. ובכלל, בכל המאמר, ישמור מה שראוי לשמור המדבר לפני הגדולים. ואם היה הדבור העצתי לפני המון העם, ראוי לכונן ההספקה בענינים יאותו להמון, ולדבר דברים אשר מדרכם 5 שיקובלו כפי מדרגתם; כי דבר אחד בעצמו לא יקובל מבעלי הדעת השלמה ומההמוניים בשוה· לכן, צריך המליץ בזה להערמה גדולה, לתת לכל אחד דבר יערב לו ויטעמהו ויקבלהו.

[12] וכן, ג״כ, אין ראוי שכל האנשים ידברו באופן מתדמה, כי המאמ׳ יקבל ג״כ התחלפות מצד התחלפות מדרגת האנשים המדברים. והוא מבואר שאין ראוי 10 לזקן, מלא חכמה וחותם תכנית, לדבר באופן ידבר אחד מהבחורים, חדשים מקרוב באו לדבר ליד שערים· גם כי המלך והשרים לא ידברו באופן מתדמה לדלת עם הארץ· רק איש ואיש ידבר כפי מה שיאות למדרגתו, לא יטה ממנה ימין ושמאל.

[13] ובכלל, צריך שיתבונן המליץ לעולם בג׳ ענינים: א׳, הדבר אשר בערכו 15 תנתן העצה· הב׳, מדרגת היועץ· הג׳, מדרגת האנשים אשר להם הכח להסכים אל מה שיוועץ, או למנוע ממנו.

[14] עוד אמ׳ כי הספור אין בזה הסוג מצד עצמו, כי אם במקרה, שאין מי שיסכל הדבר אשר ייעץ עליו עד יתחייב לספרו. האמנם, כי המשלי׳ בזה הסוג יצליחו יותר ממה שיועילו ביתר הסוגים, להיות הדברים העתידים מתדמים 20 לעוברים עד נקח ראיה מהם על מה שאפשר שימצא בעתיד· והנה יהיה במאמ׳ העצתי ספור מהדברים העוברים במקרה. גם מצד שידמה לפעמי׳ לסוג המשפטי· כי הרבה מה שנעורר האנשים אל הכעס, והאבה, היראה, והחנינה, ואהבת הדבר והתרחק ממנו בסוג העצתי, כאשר הענין כן בסוג המשפטי. אמנם, אם נקח הספור באופן רחב מצד שיכלול כל הגדה, אם מהעבר אם 25 מהעתיד, כמו שהתבאר למעלה מדברי טוליאו בג׳ מהחדשה ומדברי הפילוסוף

5 הדעת] הדיעה[ב] || 6 דבר] דברי[ד] || 17 המשלי׳] ההמשלים[ב] || 20 במאמ׳] באמ׳[ב] || 21 העוברים] העתידים[ב] | [מצד][ד] || 25 מהעתיד] העתיד[ב] | בג׳] בלישי[ב] | מהחדשה] מהההחדשה[ד] ||

1–2 במ׳ ט״ז ב׳ || 10 יח׳ כ״ח י״ב || 10–11 דב׳ ל״ב י״ז | מש׳ ח׳ ג׳ || 12 מל״ב כ״ד י״ד || 12–13 מש׳ ד׳ כ״ז ||

counsellors **who sit first** [Esth. 1:14] in a manner appropriate and relevant to them. The Introduction, in this Kind of Cause, should resemble that made in the Judicial Kind of Cause, because **princes of the congregation, the elect men of the assembly** [Num. 16:2] are like the judges to whom a judicial cause is brought. In general, throughout his entire discourse, the orator should exercise all the care that one speaking in the presence of the great must exercise. But if it is a Deliberative speech before the multitude of the people, it is fitting to establish conviction by means adapted to the multitude, and to use words which, depending on their quality, will normally be accepted. For one and the same word is not equally acceptable both to the completely educated and the ordinary run of the multitude; here, therefore, the speaker needs great astuteness in providing each group with the word that will please it, that it will find agreeable to its taste, and will accept.

[12] So, too, all men should not speak alike, for a speech can also sustain variation in terms of the difference in the quality of the individual speakers. It clearly does not behoove an elder, **full of wisdom** and **seal most accurate** [Ezek. 28:12], to speak as would any of the younger men, **new ones that came up of late** [Deut. 32:17] to speak **beside the gates** [Prov. 8:3]; nor should king and princes speak in the same fashion as the **poorest sort of the people of the land** [2 Kings 24:14]; but each individual should express himself in a way comporting with his station in life, **turning** from it **not to the right hand nor to the left** [Prov. 4:27].

[13] In general, too, there are three considerations that the orator must ever bear in mind: (1) the subject on which his counsel is to be given; (2) the personal quality of the speaker giving counsel; (3) the rank of the persons who have the power either of assenting to the counsel given or of dissenting from it.

[14] Quintilian[d] further says that the Statement of Facts is not present in this Kind of Cause because it is substantially germane, but by chance, for no hearer will be so ignorant of the matter on which the speaker is offering counsel that the speaker will be obliged to give a complete account of it. The fact remains, however, that in this Kind of Cause examples are more productive of success and advantage than they are in the other Kinds, since future instances will be enough like those of the past that the latter may be used as our proof of what possibly could eventuate in the future; hence a Deliberative speech may by chance include a historical account of past events. It may also include a Statement of the Facts because a Deliberative discourse will sometimes resemble one of the Judicial Kind; for much of the arousing of people to indignation, hatred, fear, and pity, to love of something or alienation from it, that we shall do in the Deliberative Kind of Cause is precisely what is done in the Judicial Kind of Cause. Of course, if we conceive the Statement of Facts broadly, holding it to include any narrative, whether of the past or of the future, as was made clear above from Tully's words

d. Q. 3.8.10 f.

בקצור הנז׳, היה בזה הסוג מן הדבור הספור בעצם:

פרק י״ח

מנתינת העצה לפי התורה.

[1] אתה בן אדם, אם תשכיל כל הנאמ׳ למעלה מהנהגת טוב הממשלה,
5 אשר אמר בה הפילוסוף שהיא תגיע ההצלחה האנושית עד שהיא תהיה על
דרך המוסר, וכפי מה שיחיבהו הדת והנימוס, אשר ידי השכל יסדוהו, ואדם ירה
אבן פנתו· אז תדע מה גדלה מעלת האומה הישראלית על כל בני אדם, מה
טובו אוהליה ומשכנותיה, ומה יפו פעמי הנהגותיה; אשר לה משפטים צדיקים
ותורות אמת לא הלו בם ידים· נתונים נתונים המה לנו מאדון המציאה, בורא
10 השמים ונוטיהם, אשר גבהו דרכיו מדרכינו, ומחשבותיו ממחשבותינו, כאשר
גבהו שמים מארץ.

[2] ויען יחס פעלה אל פעולה כיחס הפועל אל הפועל· והיה הפועל בדתנו
ונימוסנו הש׳ ית׳, שאין לו יחס ודמיון עם אחד מברואיו· התחייב מזה שאין יחס
וערך לגמול הנפלא אשר נצפה אם נשמור לעשות ככל התורה והמצוה אשר
15 צונו ה׳ אלקינו, לאשר יקוו הם השג באמצעות הנימוסים השכליים; כי המצוה
הזאת יש לה תועלות רבות זולת אשר ישיגם השכל, לא יוכל האדם לעמוד
עליהם כי אם בנבואה או בקבלה. והנה אמר הנביא: אל מי תדמיוני ואשוה
יאמ׳ קדוש [יש׳ מ׳ כ״ה]· למי תדמיוני ותשוו ותמשילוני ונדמה [שם מ״ו ה׳];

2 פרק] פ׳[כ] || 3 מנתינת] מנתנת[כ] || 4 [כל][כ] || 5 [שהיא] תגיע[ד] | [עד] אם[ד] | שהיא תהיה] שהיא עד שתהיה[כ] || 6 שיחיבהו] שייחייבידהו[כ] || 7 פנתו] פינתה[כת] | הישראלית] הישאלית[ד] || 8 ומה יפו] ומה ייפו[כ] || 10 השמים] שמים[כ] || || 13 הש׳] ה׳[כ] || 14 [והמצוה][כ] ||

---

3 יח׳ ב׳ ו׳ || 6 זכ׳ ד׳ ט׳ || 6–7 איוב ל״ח ו׳ || 7–8 במ׳ כ״ד ה׳ | שה״ש ז׳ ב׳ || 8–9 נחמ׳ ט׳ י״ג | איכה ד׳ ו׳ | במ׳ ג׳ ט׳ || 9–10 יש׳ מ״ב ה׳ | יש׳ נ״ה ט׳ || 10–11 יש׳ נ״ה ט׳ || 14 דב׳ ו׳ כ״ה | שמ׳ כ״ד י״ב || 14–15 דב׳ א׳ מ״א || 15–16 דב׳ ו׳ כ״ה ||

in the New Rhetoric, Book III, and from the Philosopher's words in the aforementioned Abridgment,[16] what is substantially a Statement of Facts has a place in this Kind of Cause.

CHAPTER 18

The Giving of Counsel According to the Torah

[1] **Thou, son of man** [Ezek. 2:6], if you comprehend all the aforementioned observations about aristocratic government,[1] of which the Philosopher says that it results in human felicity so long as it keeps to the way of moral discipline and functions as law and constitution require—that moral discipline of which **the hands** of the intelligence **have laid the foundation** [Zech. 4:9] and mankind has **laid the corner-stone** [Job 38:6]; then you will know how great is the advantage of the Israelite people above all the sons of men, **how goodly are** its **tents** . . . and **dwellings** [Num. 24:5], and **how beautiful are** the **steps** [Song of S. 7:2] of its social ethics. For it possesses righteous **ordinances and laws of truth** [Neh. 9:13] upon which **no hands fell** [Lam. 4:6]: **they are wholly given unto us from** [Num. 3:9] the Lord of existence **That created the heavens and stretched them forth** [Isa. 42:5], Whose **ways are higher than** our **ways, and** Whose **thoughts than** our **thoughts** [55:9], **as the heavens are higher than the earth** [55:9].

[2] Now since effect is to effect as efficient cause is to efficient cause, and since the efficient cause in the instance of our law and constitution is the Name, blessed be He, between Whom and any of His creatures there exists neither proportion nor comparability, it perforce follows that there is neither proportion nor commensurability between the wondrous recompense that we may expect **if we observe to do** [Deut. 6:25] according to all **the law and the commandment** [Exod. 24:12] **that the Lord our God has commanded us** [Deut. 1:41] and that recompense which others may hope to obtain by means of laws produced by human intelligence. For **this commandment** [6:25] has many advantages not attainable by intelligence, advantages which man could come to know only through prophecy or through tradition. Indeed, the Prophet says: **To whom then will ye liken Me that I should be equal? saith the Holy One** [Isa. 40:25]; **to whom will ye liken Me, and make Me equal, and compare Me, that we may**

16. i.8.9 and ii.14.15; the reference to *R. ad H.* III is unverifiable, and may be erroneous.

1. ii.17.5, above; cf. T54/A69 and *Rhet.* 1.8 (1365b).

לאמר שאין לו יחס ודמיון כלל עם אחד מברואיו, וכן אין יחס בין פעולותיו ופעולות ברואיו. ולזה מנהיגי האומה, שופטיה ושוטריה, יוכיחונו על עברנו על המצות והתורות ההנה, ומיעד לעוברים עונש גדול; וכן יצוונו לשמור את כל החקים והמשפטים עם יעוד הגמול ליראי ה׳ ולחושבי שמו.

[3] אמר במצות השכליות, ר״ל, התלויות באמונה: שמע אלי יעקב וישראל מקוראי· אני הוא אני ראשון אף אני אחרון; אף ידי יסדה ארץ וימיני טפחה שמים [יש׳ מ״ח י״ב—י״ג]. עוד אמר: שאו מרום עיניכם וראו מי ברא אלה· המוציא במספר צבאם לכלם בשם יקרא [שם מ׳ כ״ו]. עוד אמ׳: מי מדד בשעלו מים ושמים בזרת תכן וכל בשליש עפר הארץ, וכו׳ [שם שם י״ב].

[4] ואמר, להזהיר מן העברות: הוי מגיעי בית בבית שדה בשדה יקריבו· עד אפס מקום, וכו׳ [שם ה׳ ח׳]. ואמ׳ בהטיות הדין והמשפט: הוי החוקקים חקקי און ומכתבים עמל כתבו [שם י׳ א׳]. ואמר מיכה: שמעו נא זאת ראשי בית יעקב וקציני בית ישראל המתעבים משפט, כו׳ [מי׳ ג׳ ט׳]; ואמר: על הרע כפים להטיב השר שואל והשופט בשלום והגדול דובר הות נפשו, כו׳ [שם ז׳ ג׳]. ואמ׳ יחזקאל: וימרו בי הבנים בחקותי לא הלכו ואת משפטי לא שמרו לעשות אותם אשר יעשה אותם האדם וחי בהם ואת שבתותי חללו, וכו׳ [יח׳ כ׳ כ״א]; כאלו באר הפסוק שאין נימוס בעולם תתחייב אליו הצלחת הנפש, אשר רמז וחי בהם, כי אם התורה לבדה.

[5] ואמר יחזקאל בעבודה זרה: מה אמולה לבתך נאם ה׳ אלקים בעשותך את כל אלה, כו׳ [שם ט״ז ל׳]; ואמר אחר כן: בבנותיך גבך בראש כל דרך ורמתך עשית בכל רחוב, כו׳ [שם שם ל״א]. ואמ׳ עוד: ואבא ואראה והנה כל תבנית רמש ובהמה שקץ וכל גלולי ישראל מחוקה על הקיר, כו׳ [שם ח׳ י׳]; ואמ׳ עוד: והמה משתחויתם קדמה לשמש [שם שם ט״ז].

[6] ואמ׳ ירמיהו בשמירת השבת: השמרו בנפשותיכם ולא תוציאו משא ביום

2 ושוטריה <ונביאי׳>[ד] |יוכיחונו] יוכיחוני[כ] || 3 עונש] עון[ד] || 4 ומהמשפטים] ועמשפטי׳[ד] || 6 הוא אני][ד] |אף אני] ואני <הוא>[ד] || 8 צבאם <וכו׳>[כ] |לכלם בשם יקרא][כ] || 11 וכו׳] כו׳[כ] || 12 ומכתבים] ומכתבי[כ] || 13 המתעבים] המענים[ד] |להטיב] להיטיב[ת] || 15 משפטי] משפטיי[כ] || 16 ואת] את[ת] || חללו וכו׳] וכו׳ חללו[כ] || 17 אשר] אפר[ד] |רמז <בהם>[כ] || 19 בעבודה זרה] בע״ז[כ] || 21 ורמתך] וראיתך[כ] || 22 <בית> ישראל[ת] |מחוקה] מחזקה[כ] || 23 משתחויתם] משחיתים[כ] || 24 ולא תוציאו] ואל תשאו[ת] ||

2 דב׳ ט״ז י״ח || 4 מל׳ ג׳ ט״ז ||

be like? [46:5]. There is, that is to say, neither proportion nor comparability at all between Him and any of His creatures, and so there is no proportion between what He effects and what His creatures effect. It is for this reason that the people's leaders, its **judges and officers** [Deut. 16:18] and prophets, admonish us against transgressing those commandments and laws, while severe punishment is promised for transgressors. Similarly, their charging us to keep all the statutes and ordinances is accompanied by a promise of reward **for them that fear the Lord and that think upon His Name** [Mal. 3:16].

[3] On the commandments involving the intellect—that is, those dependent upon faith—Isaiah says: **Hearken unto Me, O Jacob, and Israel My called: I am He; I am the first, I also am the last; yea, My hand hath laid the foundation of the earth, and My right hand hath spread out the heavens** [Isa. 48:12–13].[2] Again, he says: **Lift up your eyes on high, and see: who hath created these? He that bringeth out their host by number, He calleth them all by name** [40:26]. Again: **Who hath measured the waters in the hollow of his hand, and meted out heaven with the span, and comprehended the dust of the earth in a measure?** etc. [40:12].

[4] To warn us against transgressions Isaiah says: **Woe unto them that join house to house, that lay field to field, till there be no room!** etc. [5:8]. On perversions of law and of justice he declares: **Woe unto them that decree unrighteous decrees, and to the writers that write iniquity!** [10:1]. Micah says: **Hear this, I pray you, ye heads of the house of Jacob, and rulers of the house of Israel, that abhor justice, and pervert all equity,** etc. [Mic. 3:9]; and: **Their hands are upon that which is evil to do it diligently; the prince asketh, and the judge is ready for a reward; and the great man, he uttereth the evil desire of his soul** [7:3]. Ezekiel says: **But the children rebelled against Me; they walked not in My statutes, neither kept Mine ordinances to do them, which if a man do, he shall live by them; and[3] they profaned My Sabbaths,** etc. [Ezek. 20:21]; this verse virtually proves that no other constitution in the world necessarily leads to the soul's felicity—alluded to in the words **he shall live by them**—save the Torah alone.

[5] On idolatry Ezekiel says: **How weak is thy heart, saith the Lord God, seeing thou doest all these things,** etc. [16:30]; and he continues: . . . **in that thou buildest thine eminent place in the head of every way, and makest thy lofty place in every street,** etc. [16:31]. Again: **So I went in and saw; and behold every detestable form of creeping things and beasts, and all the idols of Israel,[4] portrayed upon the wall,** etc. [8:10]; and again: . . . **and they worshipped the sun toward the east** [8:16].

[6] On keeping the Sabbath Jeremiah says: **Take heed for the sake of your**

2. Here M is perfectly accurate in citing B, while C does not cite accurately.
3. "and": not in B.
4. B: "of the house of Israel."

השבת [יר׳ י״ז כ״א]; ואמ׳ עוד: לא תוציאו משא מבתיכם ביום השבת וכל מלאכה לא תעשו׳ וקדשתם את יום השבת, כו׳ [שם שם כ״ב].

[7] ואמ׳ בצווי על שמירת קצת המצות: שמרו משפט, כו׳ [יש׳ נ״ו א׳]. ואמ׳ בהושע: זרעו לכם לצדקה קצרו לפי חסד [הו׳ י׳ י״ב]; ואתה באלהיך תשוב [שם י״ב ז׳]. ואמ׳ בצפניה: בקשו את י״י כל ענוי הארץ, וכו׳ (צפ׳ ב׳ ג׳). ואמ׳ בזכריה: משפט אמת שפטו וחסד ורחמים עשו איש את אחיו [זכ׳ ז׳ ט׳]; אמת ומשפט שלום שפטו בשעריכם [שם ח׳ ט״ז]. ונחתמה הנבואה בפסוק המצוה בכלל על כל הכתוב בספר התורה הזאת, ואמ׳ בסוף מלאכי: זכרו תורת משה עבדי אשר צויתי אותו בחורב... חקים ומשפטים [מל׳ ג׳ כ״ב]. והנה אמר הש׳ ית׳ ליהושע: רק חזק ואמץ מאד לשמור ולעשות ככל התורה אשר צוך משה עבדי, כו׳ [יהו׳ א׳ ז׳]; ואדננו דוד צוה לשלמה בנו: ״ושמרת את משמרת י״י אלקיך״, וכו׳ [מל״א ב׳ ג׳].

[8] והנה רוב מה שתמצא בספרי׳, וכמעט כל מה שנאמ׳ לנו מן המצוו׳ האזהרות והתוכחות — שהם בסוג העצתי, כאשר התבאר בתחלת הספר — הוא בעניני התורה התמימה. וכל זה להיותה נימוס שלם, לא יחסר כל בה, מביאה אל הצלחת הגוף והנפש, כמו שנאמ׳: אורך ימים בימינה ובשמאלה עושר וכבוד [מש׳ ג׳ ט״ז]; כלומ׳, שעל הכוונה הראשונה היא תתן לנו אורך ימים וחיים נצחיים· ועל הכוונה השנית, אשר כנה בשמאלה, תביא אל הצלחת העולם הזה, אשר מן הנפלאים הנמצאים בו הם עשר וכבוד, כאשר התפרסם במה שקדם.

[9] והנה עלה בידינו מכל מה שאמרנו, שההלציי מבני אומתנו ראוי שיקח הקדמותיו ממה שנמצא כתוב בספרים האלה התוריים, ובזה יהיו דבריו תמימי ההספקה. אמנם, אם יקח הקדמותיו מבעלי ההנהגה המדותיים להביא האנשים אל המעלות ולהסירם מן הפחיתיות, אין כאן פשע וחטאת· אלא שבזה, ובכל הענינים, ספרינו התוריים הם היושבים ראשונה ליסד אבן השלמות, פנת יקרת,

1 [עוד][כ] |לא] ולא[ת] || 3 משפט ‹ועשו צדקה כי קרובה ישועתי לבא וכו׳›[כ] || 4 זרעו] זכרו[כ] |תשוב ‹קצרו לפי חסד›[כ] || 5 וכו׳] אשר משפטו פעלו בקשו צדק בקשו ענוה[כ] || 6 וחסד] חסד[ד] || 7 שלום שפטו בשעריכם] וכו׳[ד] || 9 הש׳] ה׳[כ] || 10 מאד לשמור] לשמור מאד[ד] |ולעשות] לעשות[ת] || 11 [כו׳][כ] |בנו] בנ[ד] |את] א[ד] || 12 וכו׳] ללכת בדרכיו לשמור מצוותיו חוקותיו ומשפטיו ועדותיו ככתו׳ בתורת משה[כ] || 13 המצוו׳] הצִיוּוים[כ] || 14 כאשר] כאשת[כ] || 16 כמו] כמה[כ] | ובשמאלה] בשמאולה[ת] || 16–17 ובשמאלה עושר וכבוד] וכו׳[ד] || 19 [הנמצאים][ד] |עשר] העושר[כ] || 21 שההלציי] שההליציי[כ] |מבני אומתנו] מבני אומתינו ‹מבני אומתינו›[כ] || 23 הקדמותיו] הקדמות[כ] |המדותיים] המדיית[כ] ||

8 דב׳ כ״ח ס״א || 15 תה׳ י״ט ח׳ || 25 אס׳ א׳ י״ד |יש׳ כ״ח ט״ז ||

souls, and bear no burden on the Sabbath day [Jer. 17:21]; and he further says: . . . **neither carry forth a burden out of your houses on the Sabbath day, neither do ye any work, but hallow ye the Sabbath day,** etc. [17:22].

[7] Scripture speaks in the imperative mood on the keeping of certain commandments: **Keep ye justice,** etc. [Isa. 56:1]. In Hosea it says: **Sow to yourselves according to righteousness, reap according to mercy** [Hos. 10:12]; . . . **therefore turn thou to thy God** [12:7]. In Zephaniah: **Seek ye the Lord, all ye humble of the earth,** etc. [Zeph. 2:3]. In Zechariah: **Execute true judgment; show**[5] **mercy and compassion every man to his brother,** etc. [Zech. 7:9]; . . . **execute the judgment of truth and peace in your gates,** [8:16]. The prophetic canon of Scripture draws to a close with a verse of general commandment embracing everything **written in the book of this law** [Deut. 28:61], and reads at the end of Malachi: **Remember ye the law of Moses My servant, which I commanded unto him in Horeb . . . even statutes and ordinances** [Mal. 3:22]. Note, too, that the Name, blessed be He, uses the imperative in saying to Joshua: **Only be strong and very courageous, to observe and to do according to all the law which Moses My servant commanded thee,** etc. [Josh. 1:7];[6] and our ruler, King David, commands Solomon his son: "**. . . and keep the charge of the Lord thy God,**" etc. [1 Kings 2:3].

[8] Much, indeed, of what one finds in the Bible, and nearly all that is said to us in the form of commandments, admonitions, and reproofs—which, as was made clear in the initial part of our book,[7] are in the category of Deliberative oratory—concerns matters of **the Torah . . . that is perfect** [Ps. 19:8]. All of this is there because the Torah, being a perfect constitution in which nothing is lacking, leads to felicity of body and of soul, as it is said: **Length of days is in her right hand; and**[8] **in her left hand are riches and honour** [Prov. 3:16]. In other words, the Torah is primarily intended to give us length of days and eternal life, and secondarily—expressed here as **in her left hand**—she is intended to lead to felicity in this world, in which, as has previously been made plain,[9] wealth and honor are among the most preeminent of existent goods.

[9] The sum and substance of all that we have said is that the speaker who is a son of our people should adopt his premises from what is found written in these books of Torah; his words will thus be most completely persuasive. Of course, if he adopts his premises from moral authorities on government in order to bring men to the virtues and to keep them away from the vices, there is no trespass or sin in such procedure; but in this, as in all matters, our books of Torah rank first[10]

5. B: "and show."
6. So JML, according to M. B: "Only be strong and very courageous, to observe to do according to all the law," etc. C: "Only be strong and courageous, to be very observant and to do," etc.
7. i.3.6.
8. B omits "and."
9. ii.15.11-12, above.
10. Literally, "are those sitting first," a phrase taken from Esth. 1:14.

וידיהם תבצענה בתי הנשמה, להכין אותה ולסעדה; כעל גמולות בעל תשלם.
ובזה נשלם זה החלק הב׳:

1 בעל] כעל[ת] | תשלם] ישלם[תד] || 2 [הב׳][כ] ||

---

1 זכ׳ ד׳ ט׳ | יש׳ ט׳ ו׳ | יש׳ נ״ט י״ח ||

at **laying . . . for a foundation a stone** of perfection . . . **a costly corner-stone** [Isa. 28:16], and their **hands**[11] **shall also finish** [Zech. 4:9] the temples of the soul, **to establish it and to uphold it** [Isa. 9:6]; **according to deeds** [59:18] will it repay the possessor.[12]

Here ends this second Book.

11. I.e., the constructive powers of the books of the Torah.

12. JML here alters the citation slightly to produce a play on words. For *kᵉʿal gᵉmūlōth kᵉʿal yᵉshallēm,* he substitutes *kᵉʿal gᵉmūlōth baʿal tᵉshallēm* (C ''corrects'' to *yᵉshallēm*). JV: ''According to their deeds, accordingly He will repay.''

השער השלישי

כולל כ״ב פרקים.

הפרק הראשון: פרק ההצעה לזה המאמר.
פ׳ שני: מהכעס.
5 פ׳ שלישי: מהשקט הכעס.
פ׳ רביעי: מהאהבה והחבה.
פ׳ חמישי: מהשנאה והאיבה.
פ׳ שישי: מהפחד.
פ׳ שביעי: מהגבורה והבטחון.
10 פ׳ שמיני: מהבשת והחרפה.
פ׳ תשיעי: מקיום החסד ותת תודה לו.
פ׳ עשירי: מהעצבון.
פ׳ אחד עשר: מהגאוה.
פ׳ שנים עשר: מהקנאה.
15 פ׳ שלשה עשר: מהשמחה.
פ׳ ארבעה עשר: מהיגון ואנחה.
פ׳ חמשה עשר: ממדות הבחורים.
פ׳ ששה עשר: ממדות הישישים.
פ׳ שבעה עשר: ממדות הגבירים.
פ׳ שמנה עשר: מהסמן וההמשל.
פ׳ תשעה עשר: מהסברה.
פ׳ עשרים: מהמקומות המקיימים.
פ׳ אחד ועשרים: ממקומות התוכחת.
20 פ׳ שנים ועשרים: מהמקומות המטעים.

3 הפרק הראשון] א׳[ד] || 4 פ׳ שני מהכעס] ב׳ פרק הכעס[ד] || 5 פ׳ שלישי] ג׳ פרק[ד] || 6 פ׳ רביעי] ד׳ פרק[ד] || 7 פ׳ חמישי] ה׳ פרק[ד] || 8 פ׳ שישי] ו׳ פרק[ד] || 9 פ׳ שביעי] ז׳ פרק[ד] || 10 פ׳ שמיני] ח׳ פרק[ד] || 11 פ׳ תשיעי] ט׳ פרק[ד] | ותת] ולתת[כ] || 12 פ׳ עשירי] י׳ פרק[ד] || 13 פ׳ אחד עשר] י״א פרק[ד] || 14 פ׳ שנים עשר] י״ב פרק[ד] || 15 פ׳ שלושה עשר] י״ג פרק[ד] || 16 פ׳ ארבעה עשר] י״ד פרק[ד] || 17 פ׳ חמשה עשר] ט״ו פרק[ד] || 18 פ׳ ששה עשר] י״ו פרק[ד] || 19 פ׳ שבעה עשר] י״ז פרק[ד] || 20 פ׳ שמנה עשר] י״ח פרק[ד] || 21 פ׳ תשעה עשר] י״ט פרק[ד] || 22 פ׳ עשרים] כ׳ פרק[ד] || 23 פ׳ אחד ועשרים] כ״א פרק[ד] | ממקומות] מהמקומות[ד] || 24 פ׳ שנים ועשרים] כ״ב פרק[ד] | מהמקומות] ממקומות[כ] | המטעים] המניעים[ד] ||

BOOK III[1]

Comprising Twenty-Two Chapters:

1. Literally, "The Third Gate."

פרק א׳

ההצעה לזה המאמר.

[1] אחרי בארנו בחלקים הראשונים מה שחשבנוהו מספיק בידיעת סוגי הדבור, וחלקי המאמר, והדברים הראויים למליץ· ולמדנו האדם להרגיל עצמו בכל סוג מהם כפי מה שיאות, ולכונן חלקי המאמר באופן ראוי והגון לענין ענין· והראנו המקומות אשר ילקחו מהם הקדמות לדבר מה שצריך בסוג העצתי, עצומי, או מקיים, עם השמירה מן ההטעאות· ראינו לדבר בשני חלקים האחרונים בדברים המשותפים לכל המלאכות.

[2] ויען מיני ההפעליות, כגון הקנאה, והאיבה, והכעס, וזולתם, מצד מה ששבו קנין באדם במדרגת המדות — ר״ל שהיו אלה תכונות נפשיות בטבע או בהרגל — יפול בהם השבח והגנות, והיו מסוג המקיים· ומצד מה שהם הפעליות, יבקש ענינם לפעמים בסוג המשפטי והעצתי, בהצטרכנו לעורר הלבבות אל אחד מהם, כאשר התפרסם מהדברים הקודמים· היו אלה א״כ משותפים לכל המלאכות.

[3] והוא מבואר בנפשו ג״כ שמיני ההקשה אשר ינהגם המליץ אינם דברים מיוחדי׳ בסוג מה מהם· כי הסמן וההמשל, שהם כלי ההלצי כאשר יבקש המבוקש, ילקחו בכל אחד מהסוגים.

[4] לכן, הסכמנו על עצמנו לדבר מאלה השנים בזה החלק, ר״ל, ממיני ההפעליות וממיני[1] ההקשה. עוד, נדבר בחלק האחרון מהיפויים ההלציים, שהם דברים משותפים ג״כ. ואין ספק, לפי מה שנחשוב, שזה הסדור הוא נפלא מאד, מבואר היופי והתקון, לא יערכנו זהב וזכוכית:

1 פרק] פ׳[כ] || 4 עצמו] נפשו[ר] || 6 לדבר] לבאר[כ] || 16 ההלצי] ההלציי[כ] || 18 על] את[ר] || 19 וממיני[1]] ומימני[ר] ומימיני[כ] ||

---

21 איוב כ״ח י״ז ||

---

[1] So J.

CHAPTER 1

Introduction to the Present Book

[1] In the first parts of our work, we set forth what we considered sufficient to know about the Kinds of Cause, the Parts of a Discourse, and the Faculties proper to a speaker; we taught the student to familiarize himself with what is suitable in each Kind of Cause, and to arrange the Parts of his Discourse in the manner fitting and proper to each subject; and we presented the topics from which the premises for speaking as required in a Deliberative, a Judicial, or an Epideictic cause should be drawn, and showed, too, how to guard against faults. Now, then, in the two final sections, we have chosen to discuss matters that all aspects of the art have in common.

[2] Since the various affects, like envy, hatred, anger, and the rest, in the degree in which they become permanently fixed in a person as traits of character—as qualities of the soul, either natural or acquired by habit—are subject to praise and blame, and thus appertain to the Epideictic Kind of Cause; and, on the other hand since, being affects, they are sometimes demanded by the Judicial and Deliberative Kinds of Cause (when we need to stir hearts to feel one or another of them, as our previous discussion has made plain)[1] the several affects, then, are common to all the several forms of the art.

[3] It is also self-evident that the different kinds of reasoning practised by the orator are not special to some particular Kind of Cause; for the Enthymeme and the Example, the speaker's instruments in seeking what he is after, are applicable in every one of the several Kinds.

[4] We have, therefore, taken it upon ourselves to discuss both these subjects in this part of our work, namely, the various affects and the several varieties of reasoning. In the last part, moreover, we shall discuss the Figures of Speech, as these too are common to all the Kinds of Cause. There is no doubt, to our way of thinking, that this order is most excellent, patently beautiful, and correct, such that **gold and glass cannot equal it** [Job 28:17].

1. See especially ii.5, 11, 12, 14 and 17.

פרק ב׳

מהכעס.

[1] אמר הפילוסוף בב׳ מההלצה: הכעס הוא תוגה או רושם נפשיי, תהיה ממנו תשוקה מן הנפש אל עונש יהיה מחוייב במי שהכעס עליו, מפני בזיון ממנו באיש הכועס, או במי שהוא לרגלו ודבק אליו. והבזיון הוא אשר יקרא הקטנת הנפש, לפי שהיא תקטן כאשר ידמו בה הדברים הקטנים ויבזוה.

[2] ומיני הבזיון הם ג׳: הקלאה· התול· ולעג.

[3] וההקלאה היא הזכרת הקלונות אשר יעשה האדם במי שיחשבהו חרפת אדם ובזוי עם, כשכוון בה הגעת צער או בזיון בערך אל הנקלה בהזכירו מומיו מבלתי שיכוון לתועלתו כלל; אמנם, כשכוון בה הגעת התועלת אל מי שיקלהו ויחרפהו, כמו שיוכיח אדם חברו לטובתו עם חרפות וגדופים, זה לא יקרא בזיון.

[4] וההתול הוא הסכמה נראה עם המהותל בדבר מה, מזולת שיהיה הענין כן על דרך האמת· כמו: ויהי בצהרים, ויהתל בהם אליהו, ויאמר: ״קראו בקול גדול· כי אלקים הוא· כי שיח, וכי שיג לו, וכי דרך לו· אולי ישן הוא ויקץ״ [מל״א י״ח כ״ז]. והוא מבואר שהיה נראה שאליהו יסכים עמהם עד שהאמינו בו כמו שנא׳: ויקראו בקול גדול, ויתגודדו כמשפטם, וכו׳ [שם שם כ״ח].

[5] והלעג הוא בזיון מה בדברים או ברמיזות באופן ירגיש בו הנלעג, בלי הזכרת מומין; ועל הרוב יעשה עם רמיזה מה, כמו: בחנפי לעגי מעוג חרוק עלי[1] שנימו [תה׳ ל״ה ט״ז]. אמנם, נקרא לעג בשלא יכוון בו דבר אחר כי אם הקנטת הנלעג והבזיון בו; אמנם, אם כוון בזה תועלת לעצמו, כמו שיעשו העומדים לפני המלכים לתת להם תענוג ושעשוע, יקרא ״לוצץ״, כמו: משך ידו את לוצצים [הו׳ ז׳ ה׳].

[6] ואין ספק שהכעס והבזיון הוא עם תענוג מה לבעליהם: אם הכעס, למה

3 נפשיי] נפשי׳[ר] || 4 במי] כמי[כ] || 5 והבזיון] ובבזיון[כ] | הקטנת] הקטות[כ] || 6 תקטן] תקטין[כ] | בה] בו[ר] | ויבזוה] ויבזוהו[ר] || 8 יעשה] יעשיהו[כ] || 9 [ובזוי עם][ר] | <וזה> כשכוון[ר] || 10 הגעת] בהגעת[כ] || 12 [מה][ר] || 14 שיג] [לו][כ] | [הוא][ר] || 18 [מה][ר] | עלי[1]] עלי׳[ר] עליו[כ] || 19 שנימו] שינמו[כ] || 20 [בו][כ] | אמנם] אם[כ] || 21 משך] ומשך[כ] ||

8–9 תה׳ כ״ב ז׳ ||

[1] Corrected according to ת.

CHAPTER 2

Of Anger

[1] In Book II of the *Rhetoric,*[1] the Philosopher[a] says that anger is a sadness of soul, or a psychic impression, resulting in a craving of the soul for the imposition of punishment upon the person against whom the anger is directed because of some disdain shown by the latter for the man thus angered, or for some follower or adherent of his. Disdain is what the Philosopher calls a diminishment of soul, for the soul is diminished when it is thought of in paltry terms and held in contempt.

[2] There are three kinds of disdain: insult, sarcasm, and mockery.

[3] Insult is the pejorative reference that a person makes in the case of one whom he considers **a reproach of men and despised of the people** [Ps. 22:7], when his purpose is to bring pain or contempt upon the insulted party by reminding him of his faults without the least intention of benefiting him. When, however, his purpose is to benefit the one whom he is insulting and taunting—as when a man rebukes his friend for his own good with taunts and abuse—this is not called disdain.

[4] Sarcasm is a seeming to be in agreement about something with the person against whom the sarcasm is directed, when in strict truth this is not the case. Example: **And it came to pass at noon, that Elijah used sarcasm with**[2] **them, and said: "Cry aloud; for he is a god; either he is musing, or he is gone aside, or he is in a journey, or peradventure he sleepeth, and must be awakened"** [1 Kings 18:27]. Elijah, it is clear, seemed to be in such patent agreement with the prophets of Baal that they believed him, as is thus stated: **And they cried aloud, and cut themselves after their manner,** etc. [18:28].

[5] Mockery is a kind of disdain with words or gestures such that the mocked person perceives it, though no mention is made of faults. For the most part, mocking is accompanied by some gesture, as: **With the profanest mockeries of backbiting they gnash at me with their teeth** [Ps. 35:16]. Now we call mockery that which has no other purpose than to irritate and show disdain of the victim; but if the mocker's aim herein is to serve his own advantage, like the aim of courtiers in affording kings pleasure and amusement, he is called a "jester," as, for example: **Our king . . . stretcheth out his hand with jesters**[3] [Hos. 7:5].

[6] There is no doubt that anger and disdain are attended by a certain pleasure

1. In this section, JML rather paraphrases than excerpts T.
2. JV: "mocked," B: וַיְהַתֵּל, from which הִתּוּל "sarcasm," is derived; "them" refers to the priests of Baal.
3. JV: "scorners."

---

a. T100 ff./A134 ff.; cf. *Rhet.* 2.2 (1378a ff.).

שיתגדל בנפשו האדם לחשבו שינקם ממנו· ולזה לא יכעס האדם על מי שהוא
גדול ממנו מאד, כי לא תפול בזה מחשבה על הנקמה· גם לא יכעס על מי
שהוא קטון ממנו מאד, למה שלא יחשוב לנפשו התגדלות בהנקם ממנו. ואם
המבזה, ימצא תענוג בנפשו בחשבו יש לו מעלה על הנבזה· כי לא יבזה האדם
5 למי שיחשבהו גדול ממנו.

[7] אמנם אשר יכעסו על זולתם, הם אשר יחשבו ימצא להם יתרון עליהם
בצד מן הצדדים, כמו שיכעס העשיר על העני· והשקט על שמריו לנכון למועדי
רגל· ואשר יחשוב בנפשו שהיא מוכנת למעלה מן המעלות על נעדרי ההכנה
אל השלמות· והמלכים והשרים על אשר תחתיהם. עוד, יכעסו ויהיו חזקי
10 הקפדנות מבקשי הנקמה אשר לא יתפייסו מהפושע עליהם בדבר מועט. עוד,
יכעסו אשר היה להם חק הטבה מה מזולתם, וימנעו ממנה בכונה מעושה
הטבה· כי אלה יכעסו בחשבם עזיבת ההטבה ההיא אליהם לבזיון.

[8] גם התכונות המחייבות הכעס הם: ההשתוקקות אל דבר עם דאגה וצער,
שאלה לקוצר רוחם יחשבו העשות דבר כנגדם ואם לא נעשה. ומהם, אשר להם
15 דברים יצערום כמו עני או חלי וזולתו, וישתוקקו אל הסרת אותו הצער· כי אלה
יכעסו על כל דבר. ומהם, האדם אשר נכזבה תוחלתו, כי ימהר אליו הכעס
בראותו מחשבותיו בטלות, לא יועילו ולא יצילו; ועל הדומה לזה אמר ישעיהו
הנביא: ועבר בה נקשה ורעב· והיה כי ירעב, והתקצף, וקלל במלכו ובאלהיו,
ופנה למעלה [יש׳ ח׳ כ״א].

20 [9] אבל האנשים אשר נכעס עליהם הם אשר יחשב בהם העדר התועלת
לזולתם בפעל או במאמר· ועל זה הצד תפול ההקלאה בחכמים והמעולים
מההמון, למה שתכונותיהם ועניניהם ומעלותיהם הם אצלם נעדרי התועלת
לגמרי; ולזה, כאשר ירגישו בפעולותיהם מן התועלת, יתחרטו מן ההכלמה
ויבקשו מהם מחילה ויתנצלו במה שעבר, וזה בעת הצרך אליהם.

25 [10] גם נכעס על האנשים אשר יפסקו טובותיהם הנהוגות· או שלא יגמלו
האדם על פעלו כפי מה שראוי לו· או שיגמלו רעה תחת טובה· שזה יחשבוהו
האנשים לבזיון.

[11] גם האוהבים יפול הכעס עליהם כאשר לא ידברו טובות באוהביהם

3 שהוא קטון] שקטן[כ] || 4 מעלה] טענה[כ] || 7 הצדדים] הצדדין[ד] | על] אל[ת] || 9 [על][כ] || 10 לא] ל[ד] || 11 להם] עליהם[ד] || 14 העשות] לעשות[ד] | <אי זה> דבר[ד] || 15 יצערום] יצערו[ד] || 16 נכזבה] נתבזה[כ] || 18 בה] בם[כ] | ובאלהיו] ובאלקיו[כ] || 20 העדר] עלילת[כ] || 24 במה] ממה[כ] || 25 נכעס] נכנס[כ] || 26 האדם <האדם>[כ] | [לו][כ] ||

---

7 יר׳ מ״ח י״א | 7–8 איוב י״ב ה׳ || 17 שמ״א י״ב כ״א ||

for those experiencing them. Anger is pleasurable, in that a man's thought of his vengeance raises his self-esteem; hence a man will not be angry with one who is far greater than himself, for here there can be no thought of vengenace. Nor will he be angry with one who is far inferior to himself since he will not esteem himself enhanced in prestige by avenging himself of such a person. As for the disdainful person, he finds inward pleasure in thinking that he outranks the disdained; for one will not disdain a person whom he considers greater than himself.

[7] Those who display anger toward others are such as consider themselves in some way superior to these. For example, the rich will display anger toward the poor; he that **hath settled on his lees** [Jer. 48:11] toward one **ready for them whose foot slippeth** [Job 12:5]; he that thinks his soul inclined to any of the virtues toward those not inclined to perfection; and kings and princes toward those who are beneath them. Seekers of vengeance, again, who will not be appeased by a light punishment of the one who wrongs them, will display anger and be violently hot-tempered. Again, they display anger, who, having a right to some benefit from others, are then deliberately denied it by the doer of the favor; such persons will be angry because they will regard the omission to do that favor as a slight.

[8] There are also dispositions of mind that lead to anger. These include the state of mind in which one's longing for something is accompanied by anxiety and a sense of grievance; persons in such a state will, because of their impatience, fancy themselves the victims of an act of hostility even if nothing of the kind has been committed. Another is the disposition of those beset by such troubles as poverty, sickness, and the like, who long for the removal of the affliction; for these persons will display anger over everything. Another is the state of the man whose hope has been disappointed, for anger is quick to seize him when he realizes that his fancies are vain things **which cannot profit nor deliver** [1 Sam. 12:21]. Of one who is in such case the prophet Isaiah says: **And he shall pass this way that is sore bestead and hungry; and it shall come to pass that, when he shall be hungry, he shall fret himself, and curse by his king and by his God, and turn to look upward** [Isa. 8:21].

[9] But the persons against whom we will display anger are those thought to be of no benefit to others, in deed or in word. Into this category falls the insulting of the wise and the virtuous by the mob, for, to the mob, the qualities, functions, and virtues of the wise and the virtuous are totally devoid of utility. And that is why, when the masses do sense some benefit in the accomplishments of such men, they regret having affronted them, crave their pardon, and apologize for their past behavior—but this at a time when the mob has need of them!

[10] We also display anger against people who stop their customary favors, or who refuse a man the deserved recompense of his deed, or who return evil for good, since this sort of thing will be regarded by people as a slight.

[11] Even friends incur anger if they do not speak well of their friends when

כאשר יצטרך· או שלא יגערו במי שמזכיר אותם לרעה· או שלא ישתתפו בצרתם, ויהיו להם מעיר לעזור, כמשפט האוהבים· או שיחשבו רעה מאוהביהם ויחשדום בדבר· למה שכל אלה הדברים הם פעולות השונאים.

[12] גם יפול הכעס על אשר יבזו האדם בדברים שהם חוץ ממנו; ואלה ה׳ 5 מינים: א׳, כאשר יקל באשר תכבדהו· ב׳, אשר יבזה מי שהוא מופלא אצלך, ואם אינו מופלא· ג׳, שלא יהיה מופלא אצלו מה שתחפוץ היותו מופלא אצל בני אדם, אף על פי שאין הענין כן· והד׳, שיבזה באנשים אשר תתפלא מהם, או יתפלאו ממך· ה׳, שלא יתבייש מהדברים שתתבייש מהם. ואמנם יכעס האדם על הענינים האלה, לפי שיראה לו שלא יעזרו לו אוהביו על הדבר הראוי· ככעס 10 האבות על הבנים כאשר הוא נעדר העזר מהם על הדברים הנאותים, או יחשבו בם שהם נאותים.

[13] גם נכעס על האוהב אם ישכח מה שראוי שיזכרהו· כמו שישכח שם האוהב, או מה שצוה עליו, והוא נקל השמירה, למה שהוא יחשבהו לבזיון. גם יכעס האדם על מי שיכירהו כאוהב לו, וייטיב לזולתו ולא ייטיב אליו.

15 [14] והנה התבארו מי הם האנשים המוכנים שיכעסו· ואשר יפול הכעס עליהם· והדברים הפועלים לכעס:

פרק ג׳

מהשקט הכעס.

[1] השקט הכעס הוא העדר הכעס או רפיונו; וזה נעשה בהפכי הענינים 20 השלשה הנזכרים, ר״ל, שאנשים שוקטי הכעס הם בהפך הכועסים· גם אשר לא יפול עליהם הכעס ראוי שיהיו בהפך אשר הכעס יפול עליהם· והדברים הפועלים להשקט הם בהפך הדברים הפועלים לכעס.

[2] ולזה, כשנשער שהמבזה אינו עושה מה שעושה בכונה, אם שתהיה שגיאה או אונס, יהיה סבה להשקט כעסנו· כי הכעס הוא בערך אל הבזיון 25 הנעשה ברצון. עוד, הצער והאונס בכועס ישקיטוהו מכעסו, וישכיחוהו הבזיון.

5 א׳] אחד[כ] |באשר] כאשר[ר] |ב׳] שנים[כ] |מופלא] מופלה[ר] |אצלך] אצלר[כ] ||6 ג׳] שלישי[כ] ||7 <כל> בני אדם[ר] |והד׳] והרביעי[כ] |שיבזה] שבזה[ר] ||8 ה׳] החמישי[כ] ||9 ככעס] בכעס[כ] ||17 פרק] פ׳ || 19 בהפכי] בהפך[ר] ||20 השלשה] הג׳[ר] ||21 שיהיו] שיהיה[ר] ||

---

2 שמ״ב י״ח ג׳ ||

they should; or if they fail to rebuke one who makes unfavorable mention of their friends; or if they fail to share their friends' distress and **be ready to succour** them **out of the city** [2 Sam. 18:3], as friends should; or if they think ill of their friends and suspect them of some baseness; for all these are the acts of enemies.

[12] Anger will also be incurred by those who slight a man over matters external to himself. Such matters are of five kinds: (1) when what you hold in honor is lightly esteemed; (2) disdain of one whom you regard as admirable, even though he is not so; (3) refusal to regard as admirable what you wish all men to regard as such, even when it is not really so; (4) disdain of persons whom you admire or who admire you; (5) not being ashamed of things that you are ashamed of. A man will indeed become angry over matters such as these, because it will seem to him that his friends are not supporting him when such support is appropriate; as fathers will be angry with their sons when there is no support from them in matters that are, or that they consider to be, worthy.

[13] We will also direct our anger against a friend if he forgets what he ought properly to remember, for example, his friend's name, or some easily observable injunction that his friend has laid upon him, for his friend will consider this to be a slight. And a man will be angry, too, with one whom he knows to be his friend, who yet does favors for another but not for him.

[14] Who the persons are that readily display anger, those upon whom anger is likely to fall, and the things that provoke anger have now been made clear.

CHAPTER 3

Of the Calming of Anger

[1] The calming of anger[a] consists in its removal or mollification, and is accomplished when the opposites of the three aforementioned factors obtain. Persons, that is, whose anger has been allayed are the opposite of the angry; those, moreover, upon whom anger does not fall are properly the opposite of those who incur anger; and the things that have calming effect are the opposite of those that excite anger.

[2] So, then, when we suppose that the committer of a disdainful act is not doing it on purpose, or that it is an inadvertence or done under duress, here are grounds for the calming of our anger; for anger occurs in connection with an intentional act of disdain. Pain, again, and mishap, will cause the anger of an angry person to subside, and make him forget the slight. Again, we calm anger

a. T106 ff./A142 ff.; cf. *Rhet.* 2.3 (1380a).

עוד, נשקיט הכעס כשנעשה בעצמנו מה שחשב הכועס לבזיון עליו· כי אז יחשב שלא נעשה זה על צד הבזיון כי לא יחשב שאדם יבזה עצמו.

[3] עוד, ההודאה בעון והתשובה ממנו — שידור שלא ישוב אליו לעולם — ישקיטו הכעס· כי הוא כמי שקבל עליו העונש ממה שעשה. והוא מבואר 5 שההודאה תקל העונש, כי כשאמר דוד אל נתן "חטאתי לי״י", אז אמר נתן: "גם י״י העביר חטאתך· לא תמות" [שמ"ב י"ב י"ג]. וכן אמר משה רבינו, בענין העגל מתודה: "אנא, חטא העם הזה חטאה גדולה!" [שמ' ל"ב ל"א]; וכן בענין הקרבנות: והתודה אשר חטא עליה [וי' ה' ה']. והנה התבאר בנסיון שאנחנו נכביד העונש על האנשים הכופרים הטוענים על עצמן, ויחדל הכעס מאשר יודו 10 בעונש הבא עליהם שהוא יושר; ועוד התחייב, כי הכפירה היא עזות פנים ויוהרא, ואין לעג ובזיון כזה; אמנם, כאשר אין העון גלוי, לא תחשב אז הכפירה לבזיון.

[4] עוד ישקיט הכעס, כשישים האדם עצמו דכא ושפל רוח, במדרגת מה שנראה מהכלבים· כי הם לא יחרצו לשונם על היושבים והשקטים· אמנם ינשכו 15 האנשים הנמהרים. והעניות והצער באדם ישקיט הכעס, כי זה יחשבהו האדם בעונש הראוי והיורד עליו. ואשר לא יחזיקו במריבה ישקיטו הכעס, כי זה עומד מקום ההכנעה ושפלות הרוח.

[5] ואשר אין דרכם לזכור מומי האנשים להתל או להלעיג, או אשר יעשו על המעט· או לא יכעס האדם עליהם, או, אם נפל בהם הכעס, ישקוט במהרה. עוד, 20 האנשים שהם טובי הנפשות, נעימי המדות, וסבלנים· או לא יכעוס האדם עליהם, או ישקוט מהם הכעס במהרה, כי לא יחשב באלה שיעשו מה שיעשו על צד הבזיון. גם האנשים הנוראים, אשר מוראם וחתתם על הבריות, לא יפול עליהם הכעס, כי אי איפשר שיכעס עליו ויירא ממנו יחד. ואשר יתביש ממה שפעל, ישקוט ממנו הכעס.

25 [6] והדברים אשר אין ראוי שיכעוס עליהם, הנה הם אם שלא יכעס האדם עליהם, אם שישקוט הכעס במהרה; כמו בזיון המלמד על צד התוכחת· ופעולת

1 יחשב] יתברר[ב] || 3 ‹וה֗הודאה› והתשובה[ב] || 5 כי כשאמ׳ דוד ‹כי כשאמ׳ דוד›[ב] || 8 עליה] עליו[ב] || 10 היא] הוא[ד] || 15 ישקיט] ישקי״[ד] || 19 [או] לא[ד] || 22 וחתתם] וחתיתם[ב] || 23 אי] אי״[ד] || 26 שישקוט] שישקו[ד] | התוכחת] התוכחה[ד] ||

---

13 יש׳ נ״ז ט״ו || 14 שמ׳ י״א ז׳ || 22 בר׳ ט׳ ב׳ ||

when we commit upon ourselves what the angry person considered an act showing disdain of him, for he will then think that this was not done in disdain, because he will not imagine that a person would slight himself.

[3] Again, confession of wrongdoing and repentance of it—the vow of the perpetrator never again to repeat the wrong—will calm anger; for one thus repentant is like one who has paid the penalty for his deed. Confession clearly mitigates punishment, for upon David's saying to Nathan, **"I have sinned against the Lord,"** Nathan said: **"The Lord also hath put away thy sin; thou shalt not die"** [2 Sam. 12:13]. So, too, Moses our Teacher, making confession in the incident of the golden calf, said: **"Oh, this people have sinned a great sin!"** [Exod. 32:31];[1] and dealing with the sacrifices, Scripture likewise says, **he shall confess that wherein he hath sinned** [Lev. 5:5].[2] Indeed experience demonstrates that we inflict heavier punishment upon persons who deny guilt and advance arguments in their own defense, but that anger desists from those who admit the justice of the punishment to be meted out to them. This, moreover, is reasonable, for denial of the obvious is insolence and effrontery, and there is no mockery or disdain like it. When, however, the wrongdoing is not obvious, the denial is then not considered a slight.

[4] It further calms anger if the person who is its object makes himself **of a contrite and humble spirit** [Isa. 57:15]. Just this is manifest in the behavior of dogs, for they do not **whet . . . tongue** [Exod. 11:7] against those who are seated and relaxed, whereas they may bite quickly moving persons. Poverty and pain in a man will calm anger, for this will be regarded by the angered person as the fitting punishment which should come down upon the former. Again, those who do not persist in contention calm anger, as such abstention is a surrogate for capitulation and humbleness of spirit.

[5] Nor will a man be angry with those who are not wont to make sarcastic or mocking reference to the faults of others, or who do this only seldom; or if anger does fall upon them, it is quickly calmed. Again, one will either not be angry with people who are noble souled, pleasant mannered, and tolerant, or else the anger provoked by them is quickly calmed, for it will not be thought that what such people do is done with disdain. Awe-inspiring persons, too, **the fear . . . and the dread** [Gen. 9:2] of whom is upon their fellow men, do not incur anger, for it is impossible to be at the same time both angry with a person and in awe of him. And if a person is ashamed of what he has done, the anger he has provoked will be calmed.

[6] As for things over which it is improper to grow angry, a person either does not in fact grow angry over them, or else his anger speedily subsides; like the disdain displayed by a teacher in reproval, and the acts of disdain of which

1. The "mitigation" is stated in v. 33.
2. The "mitigation," i.e., forgiveness, is stated in v. 10.

הבזיון אשר יכוון בה הגעגוע בעת אשר יכוו׳ בהם הגעגוע· או אשר יכוון בהם השעשוע בעת היה המכוון בהם השעשוע. והגעגוע, לפי מה שאמר אריס׳, הוא אשר יכוון בו להטיב נפש אשר אליו הגעגוע, מזולת שיגיע מאותו הגעגוע תענוג· והשעשוע יכוון בו שיתענג המתענג עם אשר אליו השעשוע; ולכן יגעגעו הטובים, ולא ישתעשעו. וכן הבזיון, אשר המכוון ממנו היסור על צד העונש אצל הפשעים, ישקוט ממנו הכעס. וכן, כשיספיק האדם הצורך בדבר מועט ונבזה, הוא דבר אשר לא יכעס האדם עליו, או ישקוט ממנו הכעס, אחר שבאותו הנבזה קצת מהספקת צרכו.

[7] ובכלל, כל פעל מפעולות הבזיון או המבזה, כאשר לא יכוון בו הזק למבוזה ולא תענוג מגונה, או תחובר בו תקוה ותוחלת, לא יכעס ממנו; משל הראשון, הבזיון על צד התוכחת· משל השני, הגעגוע אשר לא יבא אל הזמה· משל השלישי, שיחובר בו טוב הספקת הצורך.

[8] גם ארך הזמן ישקיט הכעס, אם לא יכפל בו הפעל המחייב לכעס.

[9] גם גאולת הדם, אם בעצם הפושע ואם במי שדבק בו, תשקיט הכעס העצום. עוד, נפילת הרעות העצומות בפושעים תשקיט הכעס, לפי שהיא עומדת במקום גאולת הדם. עוד, החמוסים לא יפול הכעס עליהם ממה שיעשו כנגד החומסים, לפי שהחומסים יחשבו שהפעולות ההם הם יושר· ואין לאחד שיכעס על היושר; ובזה הענין, ראוי שהחמוסים יראו לחומסים שזה על צד העונש עליהם, על מה שקבלו מן החמס· אלא שהרעים והתקיפים לפעמים יכעסו אף על היושר, לרוע תכונתם.

[10] ואשר לא ישערו בבזיון והקלאה לא יכעסו, וזה לסכלותם. וגדולי הנפש לא יכעסו, כי לא יחשבו שפעלות הבזיון יחייבו להם בזיון; אדרבה, יחפצו בזה שהאנשים ישללו מהם הרבה מפעלות המעלות, כדי שיראו גודל נפשם: שאף על הדברים הגדולים לא יכעסו. ובכלל, כל מי שלא יצטער בבזיון, אם מפני קוטן שעור המבזה ואם מפני גודל שעור המבוזה, הנה הוא לא יכעס.

[11] עוד, הגוססים לא יפול הכעס עליהם, כי נפלו ברע יותר עצום מן הרע שקוה האדם בהם· כי אשר נפל בו פגע המות ירוחם, אחר שהוא היותר עצום שבפגעים.

1 אשר יכוו׳] שיכווין[ב] || 2 אריס׳] ארסטו[ב] || 5 היסור] הויכור[ב] הויסור[ט] || 11 יבא] יביא[ד] || 12 השלישי] הג׳[ד] || 17 שהחומסים] שהחמוסים[ד] || 19 מן החמס] מהחמס[ד] || 26 נפלו] נפל[ד] || 27 ירוחם] ידוחם[ב] | אחר] אחד[ב] | היותר] יותר[ד] ||

teasing (?)[3] is the purpose when teasing is deliberately intended, or those of which the purpose is amusement when the amusement is deliberately intended. Teasing, according to Aristotle,[4] may be intended to improve the soul of the teased, not to obtain pleasure from the teasing. Amusement aims at the pleasure both of the merrymaker and of the person amused. The good, therefore, may tease, but they will not indulge in amusement. Similarly, the anger aroused by disdain which is aimed at the disciplining and castigation of moral lapses will be calmed. So, too, when a man satisfies a need with something petty that has evoked disdain, this is something over which the man will not become angry, or the anger provoked will be calmed, since in that disdained object there is some satisfaction of his need.

[7] All in all, then, any disdainful act, or any disdainful person, so long as the intention is neither harm to the person disdained nor some discreditable pleasure, or so long as some hope or expectation is combined with it, will not provoke anger. An example of the first is the disdain of reproof; of the second, the teasing that does not come to wantonness; of the third, that with which is combined the good of satisfying a need.

[8] A long lapse of time will also calm anger if meanwhile the act that caused it is not repeated.

[9] Blood vengeance, too, whether upon the offender himself or upon an adherent of his, will calm violent anger. Again, the falling of grievous ills upon the offenders calms anger, since this is a surrogate for blood vengeance. Further, victims of unjust action will not incur anger over what they do against their oppressors, for those who commit injustice will regard those acts as justice, and one does not become angry over justice. Here it behooves the wronged to demonstrate to the oppressors that the present action is a way of punishing them for the injustice suffered; yet wicked and powerful men, owing to their evil character, will sometimes grow angry even over justice.

[10] Those who fail to discern disdain or insult will not become angry, this because of their stupidity. And highminded men will not become angry because they will not consider that acts of disdain must necessarily lead to disdain of them; on the contrary, they may wish people to deny them the credit of their many acts of virtue, so that their highmindedness—the fact that even the most flagrant instances of such disdain will not provoke them to anger—may be evident. In general, one who does not feel offended by disdain, whether because of the insignificance of the disdainful person or the great worth of the disdained, will not grow angry.

[11] The dying, moreover, will not incur anger, for they have fallen into an ill more grievous than that which the angry person hoped for them; one upon whom death's blow has fallen is pitied, for death is the most grievous affliction of all.

3. All three manuscripts of T, like JML, have the reading גַּעְגּוּעַ which normally means "longing," or "yearning." Averroes here has *mazḥ* = "joking."
4. T/A: "And the difference between teasing [or: joking] and amusement, in the view of Aristotle," etc.

[12] הנה כבר התבאר מאי זה מקומות ילקחו הקדמות לעורר הכעס או להשקיטו. והכעס בכלל ישקוט וינוח מששה מינים מבני אדם: אחד מהם, מן הנוראים· הב׳, אשר יתביישו מהם בני אדם· הג׳, נעימי המדות וטובי הנפשות· הד׳, פועלי הבזיון לא בבחירה· הה׳, מי שכבר ירד עליהם[1] רע יותר גדול מאשר ישתוקקהו הכועס עליהם· הו׳, שיהיו כבר נאבדו ונפסדו.

וזה תכלית מה שנאמ׳ בכעס הנה:

פרק ד׳

מהאהבה והחבה.

[1] האהבה היא שיהיה האדם כוסף הטוב לאדם אחר בגלל עצמות אותו האדם, לא בגלל עצמות נפשו· ושיהיה לו כח יפעל בו הטוב לו. וההתאהבות הוא שיהיה כל אחד משניהם בזאת התכונה; והתחייב מזה שהאוהב האמתי יחבב ויחובב יחד. ויחשב שיהיה באהבה התמימה תנאי שלישי: שכל אחד משניהם, עם שהוא אוהב הטוב לחברו מפני עצמות חברו, ידע כל אחד משניהם אהבת חברו לו.

[2] וכאשר היה זה מונח לנו בגדר האהבה, התבאר שהאוהב הוא אשר יתענג בטוב אשר יהיה לחברו, וישתתף עמו בנזקין ובעצבונות אשר ירדו בו, לא מפני עצמותו אבל מפני עצמות אוהבו. וכאשר היה האוהב בזה התואר, כל אחד מאוהביו ישיש וישמח בו· ולכן יהיו האנשים המשתתפי׳ בטבע ברעות ונזקין מחובבים.

[3] והשונאים הם בהפך אלו: שהטובות הנופלות בשונאיהם יהיו להם לצער גדול, ויתענגו ברעות הנופלות בהם.

[4] ואם כן, מאותות האהבה התמימה הוא שיתאונן אל הרע הנופל באוהב, וישמח בטוב המגיע אליו. גם מאותותיה, שיהיה פעל האוהב הפכי לפעל השונא בדבר האחד בעינו, כאשר הוקש אחד מהם באחר; והמשל, שאדם יחשוב להנצל על יד שני אנשים, וימצא שאחד מהם עזרו, והאחר מסרו· והנה

2 ישקוט] ישקיט[ד] || 3 הב׳] השני[ב] | הג׳] השלישי[ב] || 4 הד׳] הרביעי[ב] | הה׳] החמישי[ב] | עליהם[1]] עליו[בד] במ[ט] || 5 ישתוקקהו] ישתוקק[ד] | הו׳] הששי[ב] || 6 שנאמ׳] שנא׳[ד] | הנה <נשלם הפרק>[ד] || 7 פרק] פ׳ || 8 מהאהבה] פרק האהבה[ד] || 12 יחבב] ידובב[ב] || 15 זה] זא[ד] || 16 ובעצבונות] ועצבונות[ד] || 18 המשתתפי׳] המשותפים[ד] || 19 מחובבים] מחובבין[ד] || 21 הנופלות] הנופלים[ב] || 22 באוהב] באהבתו[ב] באוהבו[ט] || 24 באחר] באחד[ב] || 25 [מהם][ב] ||

18 תה׳ מ׳ י״ז ||

[1] Emendation suggested by ט.

[12] The kind of topics from which lines of argument useful for arousing or calming anger may be drawn have now been made clear. In general, anger will subside and abate from six kinds of persons: (1) the awe-inspiring; (2) those before whom men feel abashed; (3) the pleasant mannered and the noble souled; (4) those whose act of disdain is involuntary; (5) those upon whom there has already come down an evil greater than that ardently desired for them by the person whom they have angered; (6) those who will soon have perished and passed away.

This concludes our treatment here of anger.

CHAPTER 4

Of Friendship and Love

[1] Friendship[a] is the desiring by one person of another's good for the other's own sake, not for his own, and his wishing to be capable of doing the other good. It is mutual friendship when each of the two is of this disposition; it follows, then, that in mutual friendship a true friend both loves and is loved at the same time. It is thought, too, that there is a third condition of perfect friendship, namely, that each of the two, in addition to desiring good for his friend for his friend's own sake, be conscious of his friend's love for him.

[2] This being laid down for us in the definition of friendship, it clearly follows that a friend is a person who rejoices in the good that his friend may come to have, and who shares with him the hurts and sorrows that may descend upon him, not for his own sake but for his friend's. When a friend is of this description, each of his friends will **rejoice and be glad** [Ps. 40:17] in him; and so persons who naturally share the ills and hurts[1] of others come to be loved.

[3] Enemies are the opposite of these: the strokes of good fortune that befall their enemies pain them greatly, whereas they rejoice in the evils that beset these enemies.

[4] Such being the case, indications of perfect friendship include sorrow over the evil that falls upon a friend and gladness over the good that comes to him. Another such indication is that a friend's act will be the opposite of an enemy's in the same matter, when the one is compared with the other. For example, a man counting upon two persons to be his means of deliverance, then finds that one of

1. So T and JML; A: "... who naturally share with others both for better and for worse...."

---

a. T110 ff./A148 ff.; cf. *Rhet.* 2.4 (1380b ff.).

אין ספק שאשר עזרו הוא האוהב, ואשר מסרו הוא השונא.

[5] ואחר שכבר התבאר שהאוהב הוא אשר יכסוף הטוב לאוהבו מפני עצמות אוהבו, הנה התבאר שההטבה אחד מפועלי החבה.

[6] ואוהב האוהב אהוב· ואשר יאהבו הנאהבים אהובים; וכן, אשר יאהבום האהובים· ואשר ישנאו מי שישנא האדם· ואשר ישנאום שונאי האדם: כל אלה אהובים. ובכלל, האוהב יחשב הטוב שהוא לאוהבו הוא לו בעצמו, וכן הרע· ולזה, ישתתפו באוהבים ובשונאים, ובכל הדברים.

[7] והטובי[1] הנפשות אשר תערב חברתם, ולא יקוצו בהם האנשים להיותם מתענגים בם, הם אהובים לנעימות מדותיהם· כי לא יתעוררו אלה לרעה מן הרעות, או לשלח מדנים ותגרה עד תחוייב בהם השנאה.

[8] גם המשבחים והמשובחים הם אוהבים זה את זה; ואשר ירגילו נקיות במלבושיהם ובעניניהם, הם נופלים בחן האנשים מצד אותו הנקיות, והם אוהבים; גם אשר ישקטו מהכעס מהרה, ואינם נוטרים איבה, ובכלל לא יחפצו במדון וברע שיגיע מהם לשום אדם, הם אוהבים. ואשר יתפלאו מזולתם בדבר עצמו אשר יתפלאו מעצמם אהובים· כי לא תחשב זאת להערמה, כי אין מי שיתפלא מעצמו כי אם בדבר יחשוב היותו אמת.

[9] והשמחים באדם, במה שיש לו מן הטובות, אהובים· והמכבדים והמכובדים אהובים זה לזה. והאנשים אשר יחפוץ האדם יקנאו לו קנאה מצד מעלותיו — באופן לא תגיע מזאת הקנאה הלשנה או דבר רע, אלא שיכסוף שיעמדו על מעלותיו — הם אהובים· למה שיעמדו על הטובות והמעלות אשר באדם מצד קנאתם; וזה אשר יכספו, אם לא תגיע הקנאה למדרגה תתחייב ממנה נזק או חרפה במקונא.

[10] ואשר ייטיבו לאנשים אהובים לאשר ייטיבו, אם לא תחובר בזאת ההטבה עבודה גדולה, או דבר יותר רע ועצום מן ההענקה ההיא.

[11] ואשר יאהבו הקרובים והרחוקים, החיים והמתים, יאהבו מבני אדם, לשערם נעימות מדותיהם· כי כבר יחשב שהאוהב את הנכרי או המת, כל שכן שיאהב הקרוב או החי.

[12] ואשר לא יעזבו האנשים לעת צרכם אהובים, למה שבהם מטוב ההנהגה· כי האדם יאהב הטובים, איך ומה שיהיה.

2 [התבאר[ד] || 6 לאוהבו] לאהובו[ד] || 7 באוהבים] באהובים[כ] || 8 והטובי[1]] והטוב[כד] והטובות[טb] || 10 ותגרה] ותגרא[ד] || 12 הנקיות] נקיות[כ] || 13 אוהבים] אהובים[ט] محبوبون [א] || 14 אוהבים] אהובים[טא] | ואשר ‹לא›[ד] || 15 עצמו] בעצמו[כ] || 19 מעלותיו] מעלות[ד] | [אלא][כ] || 20 שיעמדו ‹אלה›[כ] || 21 יכספו ‹האנשים›[כ] || 23 אהובים] אוהבים[ד] || 27 הקרוב] בקרוב ||

10 מש׳ ו׳ י״ט ||

[1] Corrected according to [ag]ט < א: والطّيبو النفوس.

them helped him while the other betrayed him: there is no doubt that the helper is a friend, the betrayer an enemy.

[5] Since it has been clearly established that a friend is one eager for his friend's good for the latter's own sake, it is now clear that the conferring of benefit is among the acts that create affection.

[6] A friend's friend is liked; and they who like those that are liked are themselves liked. So, too, those whom the liked like, those that hate whom a person hates, and those whom a person's enemies hate—all these are liked. In general, a friend will consider his friend's good his own, and similarly the evil; and because of this they will share friends and enemies, and in all matters.

[7] The noble souled whose companionship is agreeable, and of whom others never grow tired because they delight in them, are liked for the loveliness of their characters; for these cannot be incited to any kind of wickedness, nor to the **sowing** of such **discord** [Prov. 6:19] and contention as would perforce bring them into hatred.

[8] Those who praise, and those praised by them, are also friends, each of the other. And those that practise cleanliness in their dress and in their habits incur men's favor for this quality, and are friends.[2] Those, too, are friends[3] whose anger quickly subsides, who do not nurse a grudge, and who, in general, have no wish to be the cause of bringing discord and evil to anybody. And they who admire others for the very quality that they consider admirable in themselves are liked; since nobody admires himself save for something that he believes to be true, such admiration will not be thought hypocrisy.

[9] Those who rejoice in a person, in the blessings that are his, are liked; and givers and recipients of honor are each other's friends. Persons whom a man would have envy him his virtues—not so that this envy should result in slander or vilification, but rather out of desire to have his virtues understood—are liked, because out of their rivalry with him, they understand the man's excellence and virtue; and this will be their desire if the envy does not reach the point where it must necessarily result in harm to, or abuse of, the person envied.

[10] Benefactors are liked by their beneficiaries unless the benefaction entails enormous labor, or some worse and greater ill ensues from that favor.

[11] Those friendly both to near kindred and to persons remote from them, to the living and to the dead, will be loved by men, since their characters will be supposed lovely; for it will certainly be thought that one who befriends the alien or the dead must all the more be friendly to his near kinsman or to the living.

[12] They too are liked who, because of the nobility of their conduct, do not abandon people in the hour of their need; for a person, whatsoever his quality and nature, likes those who are of noble character.

2. So JML; T: "liked."
3. T: "liked."

[13] ופעלת האהבה הם: החברה· וההתקרבות עם הבריות· וחזקת יד האוהב וההטבה לו· ושלא יספר בטוב שעשה· וכן יתר הדברים שיפעלום האוהבים קצתם לקצתם:

פרק ה׳

מהשנאה והאיבה.

[1] השנאה היא בהפכי האנשים אשר תחוייב אליהם האהבה; ופעולותיה הפכיות לפעולת האהבה, כגון עשיית מה שיכעיס את בני אדם· ונתינת המום בם· וההרעה אליהם באחד ממין הרעות. ואשר לא יתביישו מהעברות ולא יוכחו מהפשעים, ובכלל כל בעלי החסרנות, אנחנו נשנא אותם.

[2] ותבדל השנאה מהכעס, למה שהכעס הוא בערך אל אדם עשה לנו מה שיחויב ממנו הכעס· אמנם נשנא האנשים, ואם לא פעלו כנגדנו דבר, מצד רוע מעלליהם ופחיתות מדותיהם. עוד, שהכעס הוא בערך אל הפרטי, כאלו תאמר ראובן, או שמעון, או זולתם· אמנם השנאה תפול בין שני גוים כלם, כאלו תאמר בין הישמעאלים והנוצרים. ועוד, שהכעס ישקוט באורך הזמן, אף אם לא נעשה דבר מאשר כעסנו עליו להשקיט הכעס ממנו· אמנם השנאה לא תעבור לעולם, כי אם בהבטל הענין אשר יחייב השנאה. ועוד, שהכועס ישתוקק יגיע אל אשר יכעס עליו רע מה מוגבל, תשוער בו לקיחת הנקמה· אמנם השונא ישתוקק הרע לשונאו אי זה רע שיהיה, מוגבל או בלתי מוגבל. ועוד, כי בכעס ישותף קצת תענוג, כמו שהתבאר, ובשנאה לא ימצא תענוג. ועוד, כי הכועס ישתוקק שירד באשר הכעס עליו רע לא יעבירהו מן העולם· אמנם השונא יחפוץ המות למי שישנא, ויכסוף הפקדו מארץ החיים.

[3] הנה, ממה שאמרנו בזה הפרק ובפרק האהבה, יבקש המליץ הקדמות

2 שיפעלום] שיפעלו[ד] || 3 קצתם] קצת[ד] || 4 פרק] פ׳[כ] || 7 שיכעיס] שנכעיס[כ] |ונתינת] ונקיבת[כ] || 8 וההרעה] וההרע[ד] |ממין] מימין[כ] || 9 יוכחו] יווכחו[כ] || 16 לעולם] לעול[ד] |אשר][כ] || 19 לא <לא>[ד] ||

11–12 יר׳ כ״ג כ״ב || 21 איוב כ״ח י״ג ||

[13] Acts of friendship are: comradeship, intimacy, assisting and benefiting the friend, omitting reference to a favor one has oneself done, and the remaining actions of this sort that certain friends do for certain others.

CHAPTER 5

Of Hatred and Enmity

[1] Hatred[a] is incurred by the opposite of those persons whom we inevitably like. Acts of hatred are the opposites of acts of friendship; for example, doing what makes men angry, finding fault with them, and harming them through an act of evil of some kind. Shameless transgressors and incorrigible offenders, and, in general, all the vicious, we hate.

[2] Hatred is distinguished from anger in that anger is associated with the person who has done that to us of which our anger is perforce the consequence, whereas we may hate certain people even though they have done nothing against us personally, on the score of **the evil of their doings** [Jer. 23:22] and the viciousness of their character. Anger, moreover, is connected with a specific individual, with Reuben, say, or Simeon, or someone else, whereas there can be hatred between two entire peoples, as for instance, between the Muslims and the Christians.[1] Again, anger subsides with the lapse of time, even if the person with whom we are angry has done nothing to calm our anger; whereas hatred will never pass away except through removal of the circumstances which perforce result in the hatred. Again, the angry man longs to have the object of his wrath overtaken by some definite evil which can be construed as the exacting of vengeance, whereas the hater longs to have his enemy harmed by any kind of ill, definite or indefinite. Again, some pleasure is associated with anger, as has been explained,[2] whereas no pleasure is found in hatred. Again, the angry man craves that an evil may befall the object of his wrath, yet not such an evil as will remove the victim from the world, whereas the hater wishes the death of him whom he hates, and is eager to have him disappear from **the land of the living** [Job 28:13].

[3] From what we have said in the present chapter and above in the chapter on friendship,[3] it is evident that the speaker will seek lines of argument by which to

1. The example is not in T/A, which here refers to "ourselves" (i.e., the Arabs of Spain) and "the Berbers."
2. iii.2.6.
3. iii.4, passim.

a. T114 f./A154 f.; cf. *Rhet.* 2.4 (1382a).

יבאר בהם ענין השנאה והאהבה, ומי הם האוהבים ומי הם השונאים; גם היאך נעורר אל אהבת ענין או שנאתו; עם שיקובל תועלת בידיעת ענין השנאה והכעס בקיום העול, שהם מן הסבות אשר בגללם יעול המעול· כמו שנקיים שראובן מעול עלינו מצד השנאה אשר בינינו:

5

פרק ו׳

מהפחד.

[1] הפחד הוא עצבון או ערבוב מדמוי רע יירא האדם שיפסידהו או יצערהו. והנרצה בעצבון, הדאגה והצער אשר תשיג הנפש· ובערבוב, השתבשות ההשתכלות· ובהפסד, האבדון והמות· ובצער, מה שלמטה ממנו. אמנם, אין 10 הפחד מהדברים הנופלים בזמן הרחוק, כי זה דבר לא יפול הפחד עליו· כאשר לא נפחד מהמות עם ידיעתנו שנמות בלי ספק, למה שלא נדעהו היותו קרוב; אבל הפחד הוא בערך אל דבר יפול חדושו בזמן העתיד הקרוב, ויהיה עם זה גדול ועצום הרע· כי מהרע המועט לא יפחד האדם.

[2] ויתחייב מזה שהדברים המפחידים הם אשר להם כח גדול על ההפסדים 15 הגדולים, אם המות ואם שיהיה מן המצערים אשר בתכלית, ויהיה אפשרות חדוש פעולתו בזמן קרוב. וכאשר החמסן יחייב החמס כאשר יתקבצו בו שני דברים, הרצון על החמס והכח על עשיתו — כי הרצון זולת הכח, או הכח זולת הרצון, לא יתחייב ממנו דבר — כן ג״כ המפחיד יביא הפחד כאשר ספק בידו לעשות, ורצונו עליו. ולזה לא נפחד מהחלשי׳, ואף אם ירצו בעשיית הפחד, ולא 20 מן הגבורים והחזקים, כאשר נדע מענינם שלא ירצוהו. והרע אשר ראינוהו נופל באדם אחר, נירא יותר ממנו.

[3] ואשר הם מועדים לעשות הרעות הגדולות, בני אדם יראים מהם בטבע. וכן, אשר להם יכלת על הענשים הגדולים מפחידים, אם לא שתהיה בהם מדת

4 שראובן] שרואבן[כ] || 5 פרק] פ׳[כ] || 8 השתבשות] הסתביות[כ] || 9 ההשתכלות] ההסתקלות[כ] ההסתכלות[ט] || 10 דבר] הדבר[ד] || 11 קרוב] בקרוב[כ] || 13 המועט] המועיל[ד] || 14 ויתחייב] והתחייב[ד] | המפחידים] המפחדים[כ] || 16 שני] ב׳[ד] || 21 אחר] אחד[כ] ||

demonstrate hatred and friendship, and to show who are friends and who enemies. It will also be evident how we may arouse others to the love or hatred of something, and that there is advantage, as well, in knowing about hatred and anger in establishing the proof of a crime, since both are among the reasons on account of which a miscreant will commit crime. We will establish, for example, that Reuben's crimes against us are committed because of the hatred that obtains between us.

CHAPTER 6

Of Fear

Fear[a] is an affliction or confusion arising from the imagining of an evil by a person who is afraid that it will destroy or hurt him. By "affliction" is meant the anxiety and suffering that overtake the soul; by "confusion," the disordering of reflection; by "destruction," ruin and death; and by "hurt," a lesser degree of destruction. There is, to be sure, no fear of things expected to happen in the remote future, for such an event will not occasion fear; as that we will not fear death, despite our awareness that we are indubitably going to die, because we may not know that death is imminent. Rather, fear has to do with something which will very soon start to take place, and which, in addition, is grossly and powerfully injurious; for a man will not fear a minor ill.[1]

[2] It follows from this that the things which induce fear are such as possess great power to inflict the worst disasters, whether death or some extremely painful form of suffering, and the onset of which is an imminent possibility. Just as the wrongdoer will inevitably perpetrate his unjust act when two factors are simultaneously present in him, the will to commit the unjust act and the power to execute it—for the will without the power, or the power without the will, must come to nothing—so too the inspirer of fear induces fear when power enough to carry out the act is at his disposal, and he has the will to commit it. We do not, therefore, fear the weak even though they may have the will to make us afraid, nor the great and powerful, when we know of them that they lack this will. And we are more apprehensive of that evil which we have seen befall another person.

[3] People naturally fear attested doers of acts of great evil. So, too, those who possess the power to inflict severe punishment inspire fear, unless it is charac-

1. The reading of M and of T/A; the reading of C: ". . . an evil that is productive of advantage."

a. T115 f./A156 f.; cf. *Rhet.* 2.5 (1382a ff.).

המחילה. ואשר להם יכלת על הנזק מפחידים אשר בהם הנזק ההוא אפשרי· כגון שהגנבים מפחידים בעלי הממון, לא מי שאין להם ממון. ואשר יפול בהם החמס לפעמי׳, ויחשבו שיחמסו בעתיד, הם יראים לעולם, כמו אנשי המס· וכן אשר ימצאום חלוף מה שיקוו, הם לעולם פחדנים. ובעלי השררה והממשלה
5 הם מפחידים, וכל שכן כאשר יתאוו להזיק. ואשר יפחדו מהם בעלי השלמיות והמעולים שבבני אדם, הם מפחידים; ואוהבי החמוסים מפחידים החומסים אותם· וכן אוהבי השנואים מפחידים השונאים אותם.

[4] ואין בעלי החמה הגדולה והרגזנות מפחידים אצל הכעס והחמה, כי אלו יסור כעסם במהרה; ואמנם, המפחידים הם בעלי הישוב והמעצור אשר לא
10 יפרסמו ענינם, ואין מי שיכיר מה שבלבם· כי בתחבולות יעשו מלחמה, והם נוטרי איבה בסתר. וכל הדברים המפחידים, כאשר לא תשוער ההצלה מאשר יגרמו בצד מן הצדדים, אז יהיה מהם הפחד אשר בתכלית.

[5] ובכלל, הדברים המפחידים, הם מפחידים למקום ההדמות· כי הישיש יפחד כאשר קרה המות לישיש כמוהו, לא כאשר קרה לבחור. והנה הפחד
15 בהכרח יהיה לאנשים יחשבו שיגיעום רעות· ומהרעות אשר יחשבו שהם יגיעום אצל האנשים אשר יחשבו שהם יחייבו הגעת זה להם· ובעת אשר יחשבו הגעת הרע אליהם.

[6] ואחר התבאר שהפחדנים הם אלו, התחייב מזה שאשר יחשבו שלא תאונה אליהם רעה, הם בריאי הגופות, נעימי התכונות מפני הדברים אשר
20 מחוץ; ואשר יחשבו בעצמם כי הם בשתי אלה התכונות, ואם לא יהיו כן — ר״ל, בריאות הגוף והאותות הדברים אשר מחוץ — אלה ג״כ לא יפחדו. ולזה, מי שיחשוב בעצמו בריאות הגוף וחזקו, כמו הבחור, לא יפחד· אדרבה, יעול ויחמוס וימסור עצמו לסכנות; וכן, מי שהוא רב הממון ורב העזר מהאחים הקרובי׳ והאוהבים, יחשוב עצמו נעים התכונה מהדברים אשר מחוץ. והפכי
25 אלו שכבר שערו עצמם מטרה לכל צרה, והם חלושים אצל הרעות כמי שנפל בו אלה הרעות בפעל· אלא שלאילו תקוה על ההצלה, והם משתדלים בהגעתה; והאות על זה, שהם מבקשים העצה על ההצלה· והוא מבואר ששאלת העצה היא בדבר אשר יפחד ממנו, ויקווה בו ההצלה. ולכן, גדר הפחד

5 ואשר] וכאשר[ב] || 6 ואוהבי] ואוהב[ד] | מפחידים] מפחדים[כ] || 15 ורעות] הרעות[כ] | יחשבו שהם יגיעום] יחשבום שהם יגיעו[ד] || 18 ואחר] ואשר[כ] || 20 ואם] אם[כ] || 26 שלאילו] של אלו[ד] | תקוה] תקו׳[ד] || 28 היא] הוא[כ] | ויקווה] ויהיה[ד] | בו] בה[כ] | ולכן] לכן[ד] ||

10 מש׳ כ׳ י״ח ||

teristic of them to mete out pardon. And those capable of inflicting injury inspire fear in persons susceptible to such injury; thieves, for example, inspire fear in those who possess wealth, not in those who do not. Those occasionally subject to unjust action, and who think that they will again be victims in the future, are always apprehensive—men liable to special taxation,[2] for instance; so, too, those who keep meeting the contrary of their hopes are forever in fear. Those who hold political authority and ruling power inspire fear, especially when they enjoy doing harm. Again, those who are feared by the finest and best among mankind inspire fear. And the friends of the victims of unjust action inspire fear in those who victimized them; so, too, the friends of the hated inspire fear in the haters.

[4] The hot-tempered and choleric do not inspire fear with their anger and rage, for the anger of such persons vanishes quickly. But those who do inspire fear are the composed and the restrained who do not divulge what they are intent upon, with the result that nobody can discern what is in their hearts; for **with wise strategies they carry on war** [Prov. 20:18] and nurse the grudge of enmity in secret. All fear-inspiring things will arouse the utmost fear when it is supposed that there is no way at all of escaping what they threaten to bring about.

[5] In general, things that inspire fear do so because some comparison is relevant; for an old man will be in fear when death has come accidentally to another old man like himself, but not when it has come to a young man. Fear, then, necessarily comes to people who anticipate that evils will overtake them; is inspired by the evils that they think they may receive from those considered likely to make these overtake them; and occurs at a time when they think evil may overtake them.

[6] Such, then, are the fearful. This clear, it necessarily follows that those who think that no evil is likely to come to them are the physically healthy, the pleasant-of-state by dint of external circumstances; and those who believe themselves to be in these two states even if they really are not—that is, in physical health and in agreeable external circumstances—these too will not be in fear. Thus, one who regards himself as physically healthy and strong, a young man, for example, will not entertain fear; on the contrary, he may commit crimes and unjust acts and expose himself to dangers; and so, too, will one who, amply provided with wealth and the support of brethren, kinsmen, and friends, regards himself as in pleasant case in respect to external circumstances. The opposites of these are they who, already supposing themselves a target for every woe, are as defeated by evils as one upon whom these evils have actually fallen; such as these, however, have hope of deliverance and make efforts to achieve it. It is the sign of such hope that they seek counsel on how to be delivered; it is obvious that the asking of advice will concern something feared in the case of which there is

2. The Hebrew expression thus translated is T's rendering of A's *'ahl aḍ-ḍimma:* tolerated non-Muslim subjects of Muslim states who, in return for paying a poll tax, were permitted to dwell in safety in those states.

הוא אשר יחדל למענו הפחדן מענין מה כוון אליו. והוא הפחד המכוון בזה
המקום, אשר יעוררהו ההלצי אצל הדיין, או אצל בעלי העצה, באמרו שאם
יעשה כך וכך, תבואינה רעות רבות וצרות· עד ייעץ שיחדלו ממנו, פן מרה
תהיה באחרונה, כמו שקרה בזמן העובר לאנשים קשי עורף: עמדו במרדם עד
5 הגיעום רעות רבות לא שערום, ומהאנשים לא עלתה על לבם הגעת הרע
אליהם מצדם:

פרק ז׳

מהגבורה והבטחון.

[1] הגבורה והבטחון הם הפך הפחד; והם יהיו דמיון או מחשבה לתקות
10 ההצלה אשר כאלו היא קרובה; וידמו העדר המפחידים או רחוקי האפשרות,
ומה שיחייבו הגבורה לנגד עיניהם תמיד· כגון הממון, ועזר האחים ואנשים
גדולים ימנעו הגעת הרע אליו.

[2] והבטחון הוא באנשים אשר אין ביניהם הקנטה· כי יבטח האדם במי שלא
גמלהו רע, וכל שכן במי שהטיב לו או שרחם עליו. גם יבטח האדם באשר
15 יאהבו שיזכרו פעולותיהם לטובה, וירוממום בקהל עם והם הולכים בדרכי
המעלה והנשיאות· כי לא יחשב שהאנשים האלה יעשו עולה, או יהיו לאנשים
לסלון ממאיר ולקוץ מכאיב.

[3] והאנשים אשר יחשבו יסירו מעליהם גם כל חלי וכל מחלה, וכל בהלה
ומהומה, אצל ההתגברות על הרע הנופל, עד שלא ישיגו ממנו אבדון ומות, או
20 מה שיכאיבם, הם רבי הבטחון והתקוה. וכן אשר כבר נסו פעמים רבות מהרע
העצום, ויצילם י״י.

[4] גם האנשים בלתי יראים מהרעות הנופלות, אם שלא ניסו הדבר המפחיד

3 [ממנו]ד || 6 מצדם <נשלם הפרק>ד || 7 פרק] פ׳כ || 9 לתקות] לתקוןכ || 10 [אשר]ד | כאלו] באלהכ ||
13 יבטח] יבחרד || 14 וכל שכן במי] כל שכן במהכ || 17 לסלון] לסילוןכ || 19 שלא] לאד ||

3–4 שמ״ב ב׳ כ״ו || 15 תה׳ ק״ז ל״ב || 17 יח׳ כ״ח כ״ד || 18 דב׳ כ״ח ס״א || 19 איוב כ״ח כ״ב ||
21 שמ׳ י״ח ח׳ ||

hope of deliverance. Fear may therefore be defined as that on account of which a fearful person will desist from carrying out some intended course of action. This is the kind of fear meant here, the kind that the speaker arouses in the judge, or in those who deliberate, when he says that if this-or-that is done, many evils and troubles will ensue; so that he urges them to desist from it, lest there **be bitterness in the end** [2 Sam. 2:26], as happened in time past to certain stiff-necked men: they persisted in their rebellion until overtaken by many evils, evils such as they had never imagined, and emanating from men through whom it never occurred to them that harm could come to them.[3]

CHAPTER 7

Of Courage and Confidence

[1] Courage and confidence[a] are the opposite of fear; they consist in an imagining or thinking of the hope of deliverance as if it were near; the imagining, too, of fear-inspiring things as absent or only remotely possible, but of sources of encouragement as always in view—wealth, for instance, and the aid of brethren and of important persons able to prevent one from being overtaken by evil.

[2] Confidence is present in men between whom there is nothing to provoke anger; for a person will feel confidence in one who has done him no ill, and all the more in one who has done him good or has shown him compassion. A person will also feel confidence in those eager that others should speak well of their deeds, should **exalt** them **in the assembly of the people** [Ps. 107:32] for walking in the ways of virtue and nobility; for it will not be thought that such men will do wrong, or be to other men **a pricking brier and a piercing thorn** [Ezek. 28:24].

[3] Men who think that, with a bold attack upon the impending evil, they will avert from themselves **also every sickness and every disease** [Deut. 28:61],[1] every dismay and discomfiture, so that the evil would bring them neither **destruction and death** [Job 28:22], nor anything that might cause them pain—these are the abundantly confident and hopeful. So, too, are those who have already on many occasions had experience of gravely dangerous evil, **and the Lord delivered them** [Exod. 18:8].

[4] Confident, also, are the men who are unafraid of impending evils, whether such as have not experienced, and do not know, the fear-inspiring agent, or who

3. C adds: "The chapter is ended."

1. B: ". . . and every plague"; JML substitutes מַחֲלָה for the מַכָּה found in this verse.

a. T119 f./A161 f.; cf. *Rhet.* 2.5 (1383a f.).

ולא ידעוהו, ואם שנסוהו ויודעים בו, והמשל מיורדי הים באניות· כי אשר לא
ראו הטביעות הגדולות במצולות, בלב ימים, לא יראו כי יהמו יחמרו מימיו, כי
לא שערו הסכנה הנופלת; ואשר עשו מלאכה במים רבים תמיד, וראו גבורות
י״י, ונפלאותיו במצולה, וכי טבעו אנשים בתהומות פעמים רבות — גם הם
5 יבטחו ולא יפחדו, אצל שערם ההצלה באש׳ מלפנים עברה עליהם בים צרה,
ואור נגה עליהם.

[5] ואשר יחשבו שהם יותר מעולים מהמושלים עליהם, או שכן הם באמת
יותר מעולים, או שוים אליהם, לא יראו מהם. ומה שיתן הבטחון גם כן, שלא
ימצא אדם חומס לאחר זולת שונאו, כי אז לא יפחד האדם מאשר אינו שונא לו
10 גם מתמול גם משלשום.

[6] וכן עבודת האלוה, ושמירת חוקיו ומשפטיו, יתנו הבטחון אשר בתכלית·
כי יבטח האדם על עושהו, ולא יירא מרבבות עם.

[7] ונעימי ההנהגה אצל בני האדם, וביחוד אצל החכמים, רבי הדעה,
והמליצים הנמרצים אשר להם לשון מדברת גדולות, יבטחו בהם· וכל שכן
15 שלא ייראו יגיעם רע מזולתם.

[8] והכעס הוא מהדברים הנותנים לאדם בטחון. גם החמוסים יבטחו בה׳,
בהאמינם כי הוא מושיע החמוסים וחוסי בו. וכאשר יחשוב האדם שלא יבואהו
רע· או שאם יפול, יבטלהו ויצודהו למדחפות, לא יירא ולא יחת:

פרק ח׳

20 ## מהבשת והחרפה.

[1] הכלימה, או הבישנות, הוא עצבון או ערבוב יקרה אצל עשיית הפעולות
בלתי נאותות ישימו האדם בלתי משובח, אם בהווה, אם בעבר, אם בעתיד.

3 גבורות] גבורת[ד] || 5 באש׳] כאשר[כ] || 9 אינו] אינינר[ד] || 15 ייראו] יראו[ד] || 17 וחוסי] וחוסיי[ד] | וכאשר] ואשר[ד] || 18 ויצודהו] ויצורהו[כ] || 19 פרק] פ׳[כ] || 22 בהווה...בעבר] בעבר...בהווה[ד] ||

---

1 תה׳ ק״ז כ״ג || 2 יונה ב׳ ד׳ | תה׳ מ״ו ד׳ || 3 תה׳ ק״ז כ״ג || 3–4 תה׳ ק״ו ב׳ | תה׳ ק״ז כ״ד || 5 זכ׳ י׳ י״א || 6 יש׳ ט׳ א׳ || 9 דב׳ י״ט ד׳ || 10 שמ׳ ד׳ י׳ || 12 תה׳ ג׳ ז׳ || 14 תה׳ י״ב ד׳ || 17 תה׳ ב׳ י״ב || 18 תה׳ ק״מ י״ב | דב׳ א׳ כ״א ||

have experience and knowledge of it. **They that go down to the sea in ships** [Ps. 107:23] furnish an example: for those who have not seen great founderings **in the depths, in the heart of the seas** [Jonah 2:4],[2] are not afraid when **the waters thereof roar and foam** [Ps. 46:4], because they cannot appraise the impending danger; but those who have constantly done **business in great waters** [Ps. 107:23], who have observed **the mighty acts of the Lord** [Ps. 106:2] **and His wonders in the deep** [Ps. 107:24] and frequently seen men drowned in the sea's depths—these, too, will feel confidence and not be afraid, since their assumption of rescue will be based on the fact that aforetime there had **passed over** them at **sea affliction** [Zech. 10:11], yet **upon them . . . the light shined** [Isa. 9:1].

[5] They who think themselves better than their rulers, or who truly are better, or are their equals in excellence, will not stand in fear of them. It also inspires confidence when a man is found to commit outrage against none but his enemy, for then one will be unafraid of him who has **hated him not** [Deut. 19:4] **heretofore** [Exod. 4:10].

[6] So, too, the worship of God and the keeping of His statutes and laws inspire the highest confidence; if a man relies on his Maker, he will not be **afraid of ten thousands of people** [Ps. 3:7].

[7] They whose deportment is held pleasing by mankind, particularly by the wise, the very learned, and the skilled orators who have **the tongue that speaketh proud things** [Ps. 12:4], inspire confidence, and especially in those who do not fear being overtaken by evil at the hands of others.

[8] Anger is one of the circumstances that give a man confidence. Even victims of unjust acts feel confidence in the Lord, believing that He delivers the oppressed **that take refuge in Him** [Ps. 2:12]. And when a person thinks that no evil will come to him, or, if this should indeed happen, thinks that he will be able to nullify it, to **hunt it down with thrust upon thrust** [Ps. 140:12], he **fears not, neither is he dismayed** [Deut. 1:21].

CHAPTER 8

Of Shame and Disgrace

[1] Ignominy, or shame,[a] is a pain or disturbance which attends the committing of the unseemly acts that render a man unpraiseworthy, whether with refer-

2. Inexactly cited by JML.

a. T121 f./A164 f.; cf. *Rhet.* 2.6 (1383b f.).

ואולם עזות הפנים הוא בזיון, ומעוט כאב והצטערות, בחדוש הדברים אשר יהיה מהם הבשת. והנה התחייב מזה שהאדם יבוש ויכלם בהראות בו אחת מפעולות הרעים, או מפעולות הפחותים; משל הראשון: גזל וגנבה, כפירת הפקדון, רדיפת החמס, וזולתם מהדברים שיתחייב מהם נזק אל זולתו· משל השני: כמו המורך לבב, והפחד, ונעדר הרגשת הבושה, והנוהג מנהגם מהחסרונות אשר לא יתחייב מהם נזק אל בני אדם. ומהרעות המגונות אשר יתבייש האדם: התחתן, או התקרב, או היות בחברה עם בעלי הנבלה והפחיתות.

[2] ומהדבר׳[1] שראוי להתבייש האדם הוא: שיהיה עשיר ולא יקובל ממנו תועלת, או מה שיקובל הוא מועט; או שישאל העניים ויצטרך מהם; או שייעד האדם בדבר מה, וכאשר יבקש ממנו אותו הדבר, ישאלנו הוא גם כן דבר מה, כדי שידחהו בזה, לבלתי עשות מה שייעדו; או בהפך זה, שכאשר נשאל דבר מה, יבקש הוא לשואל מה שהיה כבר יעדו בו, כדי שידחה מנפשו השאלה.

[3] וממה שיתבייש האדם ממנו: שישבח האדם בעת צרכו אליו, ולא ישבחהו בזולת העת ההוא; וכאשר נכזבה תוחלתו ממה שהיה מקוה הגעתו אליו מן התועלת בחק האיש ההוא, אולי יתהפך לגנות.

[4] וממה שיתבייש האדם, שישבח האדם ביותר ממה שבו כאשר יעשו החנפים· או יוציא הנבלות והפחתיות בצורת המעלות· או שיראה התלאות והיגונות הקורות לבני האדם יותר חזקות הכאב והצער ממה שהם· וכן הנוהג מנהגם ממיני החניפות.

[5] וממה שיתבייש ממנו האדם הוא: שתהיה בעיניו התלאה המעטה הקורה אליו תלאה עצומה, כמו שיקרה לישישים ולמעונגים, שהם כואבים ללא דבר, ולאשר לא ראו בצרה שיתעלפו כמעט ממנה; כי אלה תכונות מגונות מעידות על ההכנעה והשפלות.

[6] ומה שראוי להתבייש ממנו: להכלים פעולות החשיבות, כגון שיגנה הנדיבות והותרנות, החמלה והרחמנות· או שישבח נפשו, ויספר ממנה פעולות נאות· או שייחס לנפשו פעולות זולתו.

[7] ומהמגונה לאדם, שתהיינה פעולותיו בצורת מה שהוא מגונה, ואם לא היו מגונות על דרך האמת· כמו שהיה ממשפחה או אנשי מדינה שהם אנשי גנויות.

[8] וממה שיכלם בו האדם, שיהיו דומיו ובני גילו מבני אדם יפעלו פעלות נאות, ולא ישתתף הוא להם בם. והרצון בדומיו: השוים בסוג, ואשר הם

9 ומהדבר׳[1]] ומהדבר[כד] | ומהמדות[ט] || 10 העניים] העניינים[כ] || 12 שייעדו] שיידעהו[ד] | שכאשר] כאשר[כ] || 14 שישבח] שישכח[כ] || 15 ישבחהו] ישכחידהו[כ] | וכאשר] ואשר[ד] || 18 בצורת] בצוות[כ] || 19 האדם] אדם[ד] || 20 ממיני] מימיני[כ] || 21 בעיניו] בעניו[ד] || 22 כמו שיקרה] כשיקרה[ד] || 26 והותרנות] והתורנות[כ] ||

[1] Corrected.

ence to the present, past, or future. Impudence, on the other hand, is disdain of, and little pain and distress at, instances which should engender shame. Hence it follows that a man will feel shame and ignominy when an act characteristic of the wicked, or of the morally inferior, comes to be known of him. Examples of wicked acts are robbery and theft, withholding a trust, following unjust pursuits, and other practices that perforce result in harm to others. Examples of moral faults are cowardice, fear, insensitivity to shame, and such similar defects of this kind as do not necessarily result in harm to mankind. And among the unfavorable circumstances that reflect discredit and of which a man will be ashamed: to have ties of marriage, kinship, or association with the wanton and the morally inferior.

[2] Among things of which a man ought properly to be ashamed are the following: to be rich without accrual of advantage, or when such accrual is small; or to ask of the poor and be in need of them; or to promise another man something and then, when this other requests him to fulfill this promise, himself to ask the other for something too, in order thus to put the latter off and to avoid doing what he had promised him; or, conversely, when asked for some favor, to demand of him who asks it the fulfillment of what the latter had previously promised him in order thus to turn the request away from himself.

[3] Among the acts of which a person is ashamed are the following: to praise another at a time when he has need of the other, and to praise him at no other but such time; and, when the hope of obtaining some naturally expected benefit from the other person has been disappointed, perhaps to reverse himself and censure the other.

[4] A man will also be ashamed to praise another more than he deserves, as flatterers do; or to present villainies and vices in the guise of virtues; or to consider the hardships and sorrows that ordinarily befall mankind as more deeply painful and grievous than in fact they are; and so, too, with every like kind of flattery.

[5] A man will further be ashamed to fancy the trifling hardship which befalls him to be one that is very burdensome, as happens with old men and with the self-indulgent, who agonize over what is nothing at all, and with those who have not seen distress because they are virtually veiled off from it; for such blameworthy characteristics are testimony of humiliation and degradation.

[6] An act one ought to be ashamed of is to cast reproach upon worthy deeds, as, for instance, to asperse generosity and liberality, pity and compassion; or to praise oneself and credit oneself with numerous fair accomplishments; or to attribute to oneself the accomplishments of another.

[7] It brings a man into disgrace if his deeds can be represented as disgraceful even though they are not truly so; if, for example, he belongs to a family or citizenry comprised of men of vile habits.

[8] It is a cause of reproach to a man not to participate in the honorable deeds done by other men who resemble him and are his contemporaries. By those who

ממדינה אחת; והרצון בבני גילו: בעלי השנים המתקרבים· ואשר הם בענין אחד, ר״ל, באהבה, או בחברה, או שהם מול תכלית אחת· ובכלל, כל אשר ישתוו בדבר אחד, כמו שיהיו אנשי מלאכה אחת, או עסק אחד. והנה הענין כן למה שהוא מגונה שלא ישתתף האדם עם אוהביו, בני משפחתו, או מדינתו, אם בטוב ואם ברע.

[9] והכלימות אשר ישיגו האדם מפאת זולתו, ר״ל, על צד הדבוק בו או כדומה לזה, כמו הזמות בנשים ובנערים, יתחייב מהם הבזיון אשר בתכלית, הנבלה וההקלאה. והרצון ב״נבלה״: הפרסום אצל בני אדם בענין מגונה; ״וההקלאה״: כגון שיבוזה ויחמס, ולא ימצא מושיע לו· ומזה המין, הגזל, והגנבה, וזולתם· וממה שיתבייש ממנו האדם כאשר לא יבקש גאולת דמו.

[10] ויען הכלימה הנה אמנם תהיה מפני דמוי העדר השבח· ויצטער ממנו האדם מזה כאשר היה מפאת הנכבדים מבני אדם, ר״ל, שיעדר שבחו מפיהם· הנה יתבייש האדם בכלל מאשר יחשבוהו גדול ויכבדוהו או מאשר בעיניו בזה התואר מן הכבוד והמעלה. ואשר יאהב האדם שיהיה מכובד אצלם הם דומיו, ובני גילו, והאנשים אשר יחשב בם שאמונותיהם אמונות צודקות, כמו הישישים ובני המעלה.

[11] והדברים המפרסמים, הנראים לעין, ונעשים בפרהסיא, יכלם האיש מהם יותר מזולתם; ולזה, יתבייש האדם מהקרובים אליו ומביטים אל עניניו יותר. ואשר לא יתבישו מאלו הם המגונים והרעים מבני אדם אשר הכלם לא ידעו· הכרת פניהם ענתה בם.

[12] והמין מהאנשים אשר ישמר האדם מהם, ולא יאמין בם, יתבייש מהם· כי אלה יגנוהו, אם יראו בו פעל מה מגונה, וינבלוהו; ולזה, לא יתבייש התלמיד מרבו, ומהאוהבים אשר יתנהג האדם עמהם בנחת· כי אלה יראו לו אי זה הדרך ישכון אור, שלא ישיג מהם כלמה יהיה נבזה אצל בני אדם.

[13] והאנשים אשר ישמרו גנויות בני אדם, והמבזים והמלעיגים, יתבישו בני אדם מהם. ובכלל, יתביש האדם מכל מי שיחזיקהו במדרגה מעולה ויהלל אותו.

9 וההקלאה] ובהקלאה[כ] | ולא] או לא[כ] || 11 [השבח][כ] || 12 [שיעדר][כ] || 13 יחשבוהו] חשבוהו[כ] | גדול <ונשא>[כ] || 18 [האדם][ד] | [אליו][כ] | ומביטים] ומכינים[כ] || 19 המגונים] המגינים[כ] || 22 יגנוהו] יגינוהו[כ] || 24 ישכון] ישכן-[ת] | שלא] ולא[כ] || 26 [האדם][ד] ||

---

9 דב׳ כ״ב כ״ז || 19 –20 יר׳ ח׳ י״ב | יש׳ ג׳ ט׳ || 23–24 איוב ל״ח י״ט ||

resemble him I mean such as are of equal rank and are fellow citizens. By contemporaries I mean persons of approximately the same age; those who are in some particular relationship to him, friendship, say, or colleagueship, or who have the same ends in view; and, in general, all who are equal in some one respect, like practitioners of the same art or profession. The reason for such reproach is that it is disgraceful for a man to fail to join with his friends, the members of his family, or his fellow-citizens, whether for good or for ill.

[9] The disgraceful habits that come upon a man because of another, that is, through attachment or the like to that other, for example, abominable acts with women and with boys, will necessarily result in the extremest contempt, infamy, and disrespect. By "infamy" I mean making a disgraceful matter notorious amongst men; by "disrespect" I mean, for example, that the person will be considered contemptible and fall victim to unjust acts—of the kind that includes robbery, theft, and the rest—and find **none to save** [Deut. 22:27] him. And it is one of the circumstances of which a man will be ashamed if blood-redemption on his behalf is not sought.

[10] Now since the feeling of disgrace can certainly be aroused by an imagined lack of praise, and since a man will be distressed by such lack of praise on the part of those held in honor by mankind—when, that is, praise of him out of their mouths is lacking—then he will in general feel shame before one whom men consider great and hold in honor, or before one whom he deems of this honorable and virtuous description. A man likes to be held in honor by those who resemble himself, by his contemporaries, and by those whose beliefs he thinks to be true, like the venerable and the virtuous.

[11] A person will be more ashamed of events that are commonly known, open to view, and publicly done than of such as are not; and that is why a man may feel shame before his intimates, who are close observers of his affairs. Such as do not feel shame before these are the blameworthy and wicked among men that **know not how to blush** [Jer. 8:12]; **the show of their countenance doth witness against them** [Isa. 3:9].

[12] A man will feel shame before the class of persons against whom he is on his guard and whom he does not trust, for these may censure him if they think some act of his to be blameworthy, and may bring him into infamy. This is why a pupil does not feel shame before his master and before friends with whom he can be at ease, for these show him **where is the way to the dwelling of light** [Job 38:19], how not to obtain for his acts the ignominy of being held in contempt by mankind.

[13] Men will feel shame before persons who remember their moral lapses, before the contemptuous, and before mockers. In general, too, a man will feel shame before anyone who holds him to be of high excellence and who speaks in praise of him.

[14] ולא יתביש האדם לבד מהגנויות· אמנם, יתביש גם מהאותות המורות עליהם; כאלו תאמר, שלא יתביש האדם מהזנות לבד, אבל מהראיות אשר יורו על הזנות, כגון דבור הנבלות וזולתם. ואפשר המצא מינים אחרים יתביש מהם האדם, זולת אשר זכרנום. אמנם, לא יתביש האדם מאחיו, קרוביו, עוזריו, אשר ישקיפו על עניניו ויוכל להאמין בם; גם לא יתביש האדם מהנבזים הפחותים, כי אלו לא יביטו למה שהוא גנות או שבח, במדרגת הבהמות והנערים.

[15] ואין בישנות האדם ממכיריו ומהרחוקים בשוה, למה שהבושת אשר יהיה לעיני מי שיכירך יהיה ממה שהוא באמת מגונה· וממי[2] שלא יכירך יהיה ממה שהוא במחשבה והמפורסם מגונה.

[16] ומיני האנשים המתפעלים מהבשת הפעלות רב הם: מאמינים בעצמם שהם גדולי המעלה· כי אלה תמהר אליהם החרפה, פן יגונו בעיני האנשים אשר במושב זקנים יהללוהו; וכן, האנשים אשר יכספו יהיו נוראים וחשובים אצל בני אדם; ואשר הם רבי הצרך אל העוזרים תמהר אליהם החרפה. גם האנשים אשר אינם בתכלית השבח או בתכלית הגנות יתביישו, כי ייראו פן ימהר אליהם הגנות. גם האדם החרפה תקדימהו כשיביטו אליו האנשים אשר יתבייש מהם· לכן, מי שירצה לחזק הכלימה ולהגדילה יחקה שהפעל המגונה נעשה במקום רואים.

[17] ולא ישיג האדם כלימה בלבד מעניניו, כי גם יתבייש מפעולות הנטפלים אליו· כאלו תאמ׳ בניו, ואשתו, ואחיו, ואבותיו, וזולתם. גם תגדל הכלימה אם יתרשל האדם משמירת מה שראוי שישמרהו, כמו המלכים, והשרים, והמדינות· ותכפל עם הבטת שונאיהם.

[18] ובמה שאמרנו בענין הבשת, יובנו עניני העזות בדבר שהוא נודע בהפכו· וזה, כשנדע הפך האנשים המתביישים, ומאשר יתבייש, ומאי זה דבר יתבייש.

[19] ומזה, ההלציי יוכל לעמוד על התעוררות הבשת, או להליץ ממנו מה שראוי:

3 מינים] מונים[ב] || 6 אלו] אלה[ב] || 8–9 [באמת... שהוא][ד] || 8 וממי[2]] וממה[ב] || 10 הפעלות] הפעליות[ד] || 14 השבח] בשבח | ייראו] יראו[ד] || 15 תקדימהו] תקראהו[ב] || 16 מהם <לחזק>[ב] || 18 מעניניו] בעניניו[ב] || 20 יתרשל] ישתדל[ב] | משמירת <האדם>[ב] || 24 ההלציי] ההלצי[ד] ||

12 תה׳ ק״ז ל״ב ||

[2] Corrected according to ט.

[14] A man will be ashamed not merely of acts that are disgraceful, but also of the signs indicative of disgraceful acts; he will, you might say, be ashamed not only of whoring, but also of the signs that point to whoring, like obscene speech and the like. There may be classes of persons other than those we have mentioned before whom a man will feel ashamed. A man will not, however, feel ashamed before his brethren, kindred, helpers, those who are privy to his affairs and whom he can trust. Nor will he be ashamed before persons disdained as inferior, for these, quite like animals and young children, are unconcerned with censure or praise.

[15] The shame a person feels before his friends is not the same as that which he feels before those remote from him, since the shame felt in the presence of one who knows you will be that aroused by what is in truth disgraceful, while that before one who does not know you will be that aroused by what is considered and generally held to be disgraceful.[1]

[16] The kinds of men who are greatly affected by shame are the following: those who believe themselves to be of high virtue, for to such as them the feeling of disgrace will be quick to come, from fear that they may appear blameworthy in the eyes of the men who **praise Him in the seat of the elders** [Ps. 107:32]; so, too, men who long to enjoy the admiration and esteem of mankind, and men who are in great need of others' assistance, are quick to feel disgrace. Even men who are susceptible neither to extreme praise nor to extreme censure may feel shame, as they may fear lest their censure come swiftly. The feeling of disgrace also comes sooner to a person when men before whom he will feel shame are observing him; one, therefore, who wishes to intensify and enhance the shame will picture the blameworthy act as done in a place where such men see it.

[17] A person may suffer ignominy not merely from his own circumstances; he will also be ashamed of acts committed by those who are attached to him—for example, his children, wife, brethren, ancestors, and others. Great ignominy also results if a man is negligent in defending that which it behooves him to defend, such as kings, princes, and States; doubly so when, in addition, their enemies are looking on.

[18] Through what we have said about shame, the several aspects of shamelessness may severally be understood as, in each case, the known opposite—this, if we know the opposite of the persons who feel shame, the opposite of those before whom shame is felt, and the opposite of whatever circumstance of which one will be ashamed.

[19] From this exposition, the trained speaker will understand how to arouse, or how properly to treat, the feeling of shame.

1. Through scribal error (homoioteleuton) C here omits "... in truth disgraceful, while that before one who does not know you will be that aroused by what is...." M also errs in reading "before that which" for "before one who"; I have here corrected according to T.

פרק ט׳

מקיום החסד ותת תודה לו.

[1] החסד הוא אשר למענו יאמר לבעל החסד שהוא חסיד. והענינים שיקראו ״חסדים״ הם אחד משני ענינים: אם העזר בגוף, ואם בממון וכבוד· וכבר יהיה העזר בגוף או ממון מפני הכבוד.

[2] ואמנם, תקרא ההטבה ״חסד״ כאשר לא ימצאה מקבל ההטבה מאדם אחר, זולת המטיב· וגם שלא יגיע לפעלו ממנו דבר, אבל יהיה כלו בגלל המקבל.

[3] ולפעמים תהיה ההטבה המעטה נשגבה בהצטרף אל אחד מחמשה פנים: אחד מהם, כשהיה רוב הצרך אליה; הב׳, בעת שאין דרך בני אדם להשגיח על יד אח׳, כמו בסכנות העצומות; הג׳ שהיה הוא לבדו המטיב; הד׳, שהיה הוא הראשון; הה׳, שהיתה הטבתו עודפת על הטבת זולתו.

[4] והדברים אשר אצלם חוזק הצורך שלשה מינים: הא׳, הנכספים ההכרחיים בחיים; הב׳, אשר ישתוקק האדם אליהם, ואם לא יהיו הכרחיים, כמו המגדים; והג׳, מה שהיה מן הדברים מכאיב הפקדו, או מצער. ואשר הם בזה התואר שנים מינים: מין[1] מורגל ונכסף, והם החשוקים; ומין ישתוקק האדם ויתאוה למקום הסכנה הגדולה והתלאה העצומה· כי מי שהוא בצרה נפלאה יתאוה היציאה ממנה. ולכן יגדל החסד אצל אשר הם בתכלית ההכנעה או בריחה משונאיהם, כאשר שמרום והסתירום ממבקשי נפשם; ואם היתה ההטבה בעצמה מעטה, הנה היא גדולה בהצטרף אל חוזק הצורך וקשי הזמן.

[5] והנה התבאר מאין ילקחו ההקדמות אשר יקויים בהם החסד. אמנם מאין ילקחו ההקדמות אשר יסולק בהם החסד, הם על שמנה פנים: א׳, שתהיה ההטבה חוזרת אל המטיב; הב׳, שתהיה מעוטה ממה שתחוייב; הג׳, שתהיה בעת אשר לא יצטרך אליה; הד׳, כשנפלה ההטבה בהזדמן; הה׳, כשתהיה ההטבה באונס; הו׳, כשכוון בהטבה התגמול על הטבה אחרת ממקבל ההטבה אל המטיב; הז׳, שיכוון בהטבה לפרסמה, ולקבל עליה תשואות חן; הח׳, שהמטיב הטריח מקבל ההטבה בענין מה או צורך בעבורו:

1 פרק] פ׳[כ] || 4 אחד משני] א׳ מב׳[ד] || 6 ימצאה מקבל] ימצא המקבל[כ] || 7 אחר] אחד[כ] | לפעלו] לפעלת[כ] || 9 אל אחד מחמשה] על אחת מה׳[ד] || 10 כשהיה] כשיהיה[ד] | הב׳] השני <שהיה>[כ] || 11 אח׳] אחר[כ] | הג׳] השלישי[כ] | הד׳] הרביעי[כ] || 12 הה׳] החמישי[כ] | הטבתו] הטבת[כ] | עודפת] עורפת[כ] || 13 אצלם] אצלה[ד] | שלשה] ג׳[ד] | הא׳] האחד[כ] || 14 הב׳] השני[כ] | לא] לו[כ] || 15 והג׳] והשלישי[כ] | הפקדו] הפרדו[ד] || 16 שנים] ב׳[ד] | מין[1]] מן[כד] || 17 ויתאוה] ויאוה[ד] || 18 החסד] חסד[ד] || 19 היתה <היתה>[כ] || 21 התבאר] יתבאר[כ] || 22 שמנה] ח׳[ד] | א׳] אחת[כ] || 23 הב׳] השנית[כ] | הג׳] השלישית[כ] || 24 הד׳] הרביעית[כ] | הה׳] החמשית[כ] || 25 הו׳] השישית[כ] | התגמול] והתגמול[כ] || 26 הז׳] השביעית[כ] | בהטבה] בכוונה[כ] | הח׳] השמינית[כ] || 27 בעבורו <והנה נשלם זה הפרק>[ד] ||

19 יר׳ י״ט ט׳ || 26 זכ׳ ד׳ ז׳ ||

[1] Corrected according to ט.

CHAPTER 9

Of Kindness and Gratitude[1]

[1] Kindness[a] is that quality by virtue of which the possessor of kindness is said to be kind. Acts termed "kindnesses" are of two sorts, either physical aid, or aid in wealth and honor; and physical or monetary aid is sometimes rendered because of honor.

[2] Now a favor is called an act of kindness only when it can be obtained from no one but the benefactor; and also when the doer gains nothing from his favor, but does it entirely for the recipient's sake.

[3] A small favor becomes relatively great when conferred in one of five situations: (1) when it is most urgently needed; (2) if done at a time when men are not wont to look after others, as in situations of very great danger; (3) when the benefactor was the only one to do it; (4) when he was the first to confer it; (5) when the favor done by him surpasses that conferred by anyone else.

[4] Urgent needs are of three kinds: (1) the eagerly desired essentials of life; (2) things that a man craves though they are nonessential, like choice fruits; (3) things of which it is harmful or painful to be bereft. Wants of this last-mentioned description are of two kinds: a kind familiar and desired—beloved things and persons; and a kind that a man yearns for and desires in a situation of great danger and inordinate hardship; for one who is in extraordinary distress craves release from it. The kindness is magnified, therefore, from the point of view of those who are in utterly abject state or in flight from their enemies, when they are protected and concealed from those **that seek their life** [Jer. 19:9]. Even if the favor in itself is small, it is great indeed relative to the urgency of the need and the difficulty of the time.

[5] Whence to take premises in demonstration of kindness has now been made clear. As for sources of premises in refutation of kindness, there are eight such topics: (1) that the favor is one which redounds to the advantage of the benefactor; (2) that it falls short of what it should have been; (3) that it was conferred at a time when not needed; (4) when its being a favor is accidental; (5) when it is a favor done under compulsion; (6) when the favor is intended by the recipient of another favor as recompense of his benefactor; (7) that the purpose of the favor is to publicize it, to receive for it **shoutings of grace** [Zech. 4:7]; (8) that the benefactor has charged the recipient of the favor to undertake some business or fill some need on the benefactor's behalf.

1. Literally: "Of the Affirmation of Kindness and the Giving of Thanks for It." T: "The Statement on the Affirmation of Kindness and the Giving of Thanks for It." A: "The Statement on the Affirmation of Kindness and Being Grateful for It, and on the Denial of It and Being Ungrateful for It."

a. T127 f./A163 f.; cf. *Rhet.* 2.7 (1385ab).

פרק י׳

מהעצבון.

[1] העצבון הִיא דאגה מה משגת מפני רע מפסיד או מצער יקרה לאדם לבלי חק· וזה כאשר יהיה ירא שיחודש הרע עליו, או על אחד מן נטפליו, והיה קרוב הנפילה. והרצון ב״מפסידים״, אשר ישנו הגוף· וב״מצערים״, אשר יפעלו הכאב הנפשי.

[2] והתבאר מזה שהבלתי עצב יחשוב שלא תאונה רעה, לא אליו ולא לאחר הנטפל בו. ולכן, לא יעצבו אשר כבר ירדו עליהם הרעות העצומות, כמו אשר מתו בניו; ולא אשר יחשבו שהם מצליחים· וזה, שאשר יחשבו זה יחשבו שהם לא יגיעם דבר מהרע. גם כן לא יעצבו אשר יחשבו שהם לא יכאבו, לא מפני גופותיהם ולא מפני נפשותיהם; וזה, אם מפני שכבר קדמום רעות ונצולו מהם· ואם מפני שהם ישישים, כבר ארך הרגלם לרעות· ואם מפני רבוי הנסיון· ואם למקום מנהג נהגו בו להנעים נפשותיהם כהנעמת[1] נפשות המקובלים המצליחים· ואם מחמת פרסומם לבני אדם, שיראו, מפני זה, שהרעות רחוקות מהם מצד שעוריהם אצל בני אדם עד כלם ישתדלו בהצלתם. ומכלל אלו האנשים אשר מחשבותיהם נאות למקום מציאות האבות להם, והבנים, והנשים· אשר לא יכאיבום, ולא יצערו׳, ולא יעציבום הימים באחד מהם. ומכלל אלו ג״כ בעלי ההפעליות המיוחסות לגבורה, כמו הכעס, וחוזק הלב· כי אלו לא יעצבו, ולא ייראו ממה שייראו ממנו הכל. והאנשי׳ הרעים, נותני המומים המבזים זולתם לחסרון יצירתם, לא יעצבו, לפי שלא יעלה במחשבתם שיפול בהם רע.

[3] אבל האנשים אשר יעצבו הם אמצעיים בין מי שיבטח בזמן כל הבטחון, ובין מי שיתיאש כל היאוש, לפי שהמינים אשר בקצוות לא יעצבו. והאנשים אשר יפחדו מאד מאד לא יעצבו לזולתם, לפי שהנבהלים מהפחד לא ידאגו באחרים להיותם טרודים בכאב הנופל בהם. ואשר יחשבו באחד שהוא עני ופחות, הנה לא יעצבו לו, לפי שהם יראוהו ראוי לנפילת הרע בו· או לא יראו שנפילת הרע בו רעה.

1 פרק] פ׳[כ] || 5 אשר יפעלו] שיפעלו[ד] || 9 מתו] מיתו[כ] || 10 גם כן] ג״כ[ד] || 11 ונצולו] ונצלו[כ] || 12 כבר] כפי[ד] || 13 כהנעמת] בהנעמת[1][כד] || 15 <כי> מצד[כ] | כלם] כלים[כ] | אלו] אילו[כ] || 17 יצערו׳] יתערום[כ] | הימים באחד] הימי׳ באח׳[ד] || 18 אלו] אילו[כ] | וחוזק] וחזק[ד] || 20 המומים המבזים] המומין המבזין[ד] || 22 יעצבו] יעציבו[כ] | כל הבטחון] בלי בטחון[כ] || 24 שהנבהלים] הנבהלים[כ] ||

[1] Corrected according to ט.

CHAPTER 10

Of Anxiety[1]

[1] Anxiety[a] is a certain concern occasioned by a destructive or painful evil that may befall a person who does not deserve it; it is felt when he fears that the evil will befall himself, or some connection of his, and that this evil is imminent. By "destructive evils" I mean those that disfigure the body, by "painful evils" those that inflict psychic hurt.

[2] From this it is clear that one who is not anxious thinks that evil will betide neither himself nor another who is connected with him. Those, therefore, are not anxious upon whom the worst evils have already descended—for example, one whose children are already dead; nor are those anxious who think that they are fortunate, since those who think this also think that nothing evil will overtake them. Nor are they anxious who think that they will suffer no pain whether of body or of soul: whether because they have previously been confronted by evils and been delivered from them; or because they are old men, already long accustomed to evils;[2] or because of much experience; or because they are in the habit of making themselves agreeable in the manner of persons who are well-liked and successful; or, because of the fame they enjoy with men, they think it due to this that evils are remote from them, as the esteem in which men hold them is such that all would endeavor to preserve them. With men like these, furthermore, are classed those persons whose thoughts are serene regarding the continuing existence of their parents, children, and wives, persons who think that the days will bring them no hurt, pain, or sorrow because of any one of these. In the same class, too, are those given to feeling the affects traceable to courage, such as anger and boldness of heart, for such persons are not anxious, nor do they fear what people generally fear. Nor are evil men anxious—those who, from want of character, are the disdainful vilifiers of others—since it does not enter their minds that evil may befall them.

[3] But those persons are anxious who are midway between him who is supremely confident of good luck and him who is in utter despair, as the kinds at the extremes will not be anxious. Nor will persons in excessive fear be anxious concerning others, for the terrified are too deeply preoccupied with their own present agony to worry over others. And those who consider that a particular poor individual is also morally inferior will not be anxious for him, since they

1. The Arabic word (اهتمام.) to which the term thus translated goes back means "concern," "anxiety," "solicitude." The Hebrew word used (עִצָּבוֹן) is more usually rendered "toil," "pain," "sorrow," or "grief."
2. So M and T/A; C: ". . . old men according to the length of their habituation to evils."

a. T129 f./A176 f.; cf. *Rhet*. 2.8 (1385b ff.).

[4] ופועלי העצבון הם כל הדברים המפסידים לגוף ומצערים לנפש, וביחוד
אם היה מן המפסידים המביאי׳ אל המות. ומהמפסידי׳ המביאים אל המות הם
כאבי הגוף והמהומה, התמהון והחלי, והצרך אל מכלת הבית. וכן העדר
האחים או מעוטם, למה שהיה מרוע המזל, יהיה מהרעות המעציבות
5 המפסידות. והעמידה מהתנועה וההתעסקות, וקצת מהחלאים, הם ממה
שיפעלו העצבון. וממה שיפעל העצבון הוא: אם ילך האדם בדרך אשר בו
ימצאו האנשים טוב, והוא לא ימצא ממנו כלום· או אם הוא הולך ומכון אל
הטוב, וכל אשר יקוה[2], וימצאוהו[2] רעות רבות וצרות· או שהוא הולך אל הטוב
בזמן לא יוכל ליהנות ממנו, כמו העשר בימי הזקנה.

10 [5] אמנם הקרובים אשר הם בתכלית הקרבה ממנו, כמו האב והבן, יעצב
עליהם האדם כאשר יירא ירידת הרע בהם· או שיחמול עליהם כאשר כבר ירד
עליהם; וזה ההבדל בין העצבון והרחמנות· כי העצבון בערך אל העתיד,
והרחמנות בערך אל הדבר שכבר בא. אמנם, כאשר נפל הרע באדם, הנה לא
יאמר שהוא ירחם עצמו· וכאשר יירא נפילתו, לא יאמר שהוא עצב, אבל
15 מפחד; אמנם יעצב האדם על הדומים לו במדות, והמחשבות, והמדרגות,
והיחסים, כאשר היו התלאות קרובות הנפילה בהם.

[6] ובכלל, יעצב האדם מהרעות והכאבים קרובי הנפילה, לא מנמנעי
המציאות או אשר תדומה נפילתם במה שעבר פעמים רבות. והזכרון גם כן לא
יפעל הפחד או העצבון.

20 [7] והאותות והראיות אשר יורו על הרע, כמו אשר ידמו בקולותיהם
ותכונותיהם כאילו נפל הרע, או שהוא קרוב הנפילה, הם מפועלי העצבון;
ובפרט, כאשר יחשב שאלו אשר נראה אות הרע נופל עליהם יהיו נשחתים· וכל
שכן אם היו נכבדים· ויותר מזה אם היה השחתתם בעת אשר הצורך אליהם
יותר, או התקוה בהם יותר אפשרית· כמו שיהרגו או ימותו בחורים. כי אילו
25 כלם יפעלו העצבון יותר מזולתם, ר״ל, השחתת המעולים אשר לא יהיו ראוים
לזה בעת אשר הצורך אליהם בו חזק.

2 המביאי׳] המביא[ג] || 8 יקוה[2] וימצאוה[2]] יקוהו ימצאוהו[גד] || 9 ליהנות] להנות[ג] | כמו העשר] כעושר[ד] || 13 הדבר] דבר[ג] || 15 מפחד] יפחד[ד] | הדומים] הדומין[ד] || 18 המציאות] המציאת[ג] | במה] כמה[ג] || 21 כאילו] כאלו[ד] || 22 שאלו] שאילו[ג] || 24 התקוה] התקנה[ג] ||

3 מל״א ה׳ כ״ה ||

[2] Corrected text.

will think that he deserves the evil which has come down upon him; or they will not consider the falling of evil upon him a bad thing.

[4] The efficient causes of anxiety are all things injurious to the body and hurtful to the soul, particularly if the cause is one of the injurious things that lead to death. Injurious things that lead to death include bodily aches and trouble,[3] bewilderment,[4] and disease, and want of **food for** the **household** [1 Kings 5:25]. Similarly, the lack or paucity of brethren, when good luck has gone bad, is among the destructive evils that cause anxiety. Paralysis of the ability to move and be active, and certain other ailments, are among the efficient causes of anxiety. And it causes anxiety if a man walks in the way in which other men find good, yet he finds none there; or if he sets out toward the good and all that he hopes for, yet[5] many evils and troubles light upon him; or if he sets out toward the good at a time when he can no longer enjoy its full benefit, like seeking riches in old age.

[5] A man will be anxious on behalf of his closest kinsmen—like father and son—when he fears the descent of evil upon them, or will pity them when evil has already descended upon them. And this is the difference between anxiety and compassion, for anxiety has reference to the future, but compassion to what has already come. To be sure, when the evil has fallen upon the man himself, he will not say that he feels compassion for himself, and when he fears its coming he will not say that he is anxious, but rather that he is in fear; it is rather on behalf of those who resemble him in character, outlook, station, and birth that a man feels anxious when calamities are about to descend upon them.

[6] In general, a man will be anxious over evils and hurts that are imminent, not over those that cannot possibly be encountered, nor over those imagined to have happened many times in the past. And memory, too, is an efficient cause neither of fear nor of anxiety.

[7] Physical signs and manifestations that point to evil, as in the instance of persons who by their tones and bearing give the impression that the evil has occurred, or is on the point of occurring, are among the efficient causes of anxiety; particularly when it may be thought that the persons who exhibit the signs of suffering an evil will be ruined. This is especially true if they are distinguished men, and even truer if their ruin comes at a time when the need of them is greater, or when what is hoped concerning them seems likely to be realized: for example, if young men should be slain or die. For all such considerations are more effective of anxiety than others; such considerations, I mean, as the ruin of the excellent, who do not deserve such a fate, at a time when the need of them is urgent.

3. So JML and T; A: جهد = "strain," "overwork," "exhaustion." The Hebrew word here (מהומה) more usually means "confusion," "tumult," "discomfiture."

4. A: "old age" (كبر); JML and T: "bewilderment" (תמהון). Possibly *senility*, the bewilderment of old age, was intended. Cf. γῆρας (*Rhet*. 1386a).

5. Corrected Hebrew text.

[8] גם תהיה הדאגה על אשר יגיעם טוב לבלי חק· והוא אשר יקרא ״גאוה״, לפי שהעצבון הוא הדאגה — שהיא הפכית לעצבון — על הרע אשר יגיע למי שאינו ראוי לו, וזה ההפעלות האחר הוא מדת נשיאות, ר״ל, הדאגה על מי שהגיעו טוב לבלי חק. כי אשר ילכו אל זולת מה שיהיו ראויים מטוב או רע, הנה ראוי לדאג עליהם מאד מאד. ואשר ילכו אל הרע מהסבות הראויות שיבא מהם רע, יראו בני אדם שהם ראוים לזה; ואולם, אשר ילכו אל אלה הדברים מדרכים בלתי ידועים, הנה ראוי שיהיו באמצע בין אלו: שלא נאמין בם שהרע שמצאם הוא ראוי או בלתי ראוי, אבל ראוי שיונח ענינם אל האל; לפי שמה שיגיע אל האדם מהעול והרע מדרכיו הידועים, הנה סבתו העול והרוע אשר באדם ההוא· ואולם, מה שהגיעו מזה מזולת דרכיו הידועים, הנה אנו נעזוב ידיעת זה אל האל ית׳.

[9] והקנאה יותר הפכית לעצבון מהדאגה על הטוב אשר הגיע למי שאינו ראוי לו, אשר קראנוה ״גאוה״; וכאלו זה ההפעלות קרוב שיהיה באמצע בין העצבון והקנאה· וזה, שהדאגה בטוב כמו שהקנאה בטוב; ואמנם, ההבדל ביניהם, שהקנאה דאגה בטוב השיג מי שיהיה ראוי לו· וזה דאגה בטוב השיג מי שאינו ראוי לו.

[10] ואשר ידאג להגעת הטוב למי שהוא ראוי לו ולמי שאינו ראוי לו, ירפא מזה הכאב בנפילת הרע בהם, ר״ל, ביותר רעים שיהיו אשר לא יהיו ראוים לטוב. ולכן, המין מן האנשים אשר יכו אבותיהם, או ישקצו נפשותיהם ברציחה, כל אדם ישמח בנפול עליהם העונש, לפי שהיא במדרגת השמחה אשר תהיה כשהגיע הטוב לנאותים· כי שני הענינים יחד הם יושר. והטובים והחכמים ישמחו בירידת הטוב במי שראוי לו, וירידת הרע גם כן במי שראוי לו, שכל אחד מאלו נאה; והסכלים והרעים ישמחו וידאגו בהפך מה שישמחו מהם החכמים או ידאגו מהם.

[11] הנה התבאר מאין ילקחו הקדמות לקיים העצבון או לעוררו:

3 האחר] האחד[כ] || 4 ראויים ‹לו›[כ] || 5 עליהם] עליו[ד] | מאד [מאד][ד] || 7 אלו] אילו[כ] || 8 שמה] מה[כ] || 10 מה] המ׳[ד] || 11 ית׳] יתברך[ד] יתעלה[bgv] || 14 ואמנם] ואולם[ד] || 18 שיהיו ‹ר״ל›[כ] || 19 ישקצו] ישקיטו[כ] || 20 העונש] העוני[כ] || 23 נאה] בזה[כ] | מה] מזה[ד] || 25 התבאר] יתבאר[כ] ||

[8] Concern will also be felt on account of those who have come by a good undeservedly. This is what should be termed "resentment,"[6] since anxiety is the concern—concern is not the same thing as anxiety—over an evil that may overtake one who does not deserve it, while this other affect—resentment—is a characteristic of high station, the concern, I mean, over one who has come by an undeserved good. For when people attain some good or evil that they do not deserve, they are properly the object of very great concern. As for those who attain evil for reasons which properly should result in evil, men will think that they deserve this fate. Those, however, who come to such things in consequence of ways unknown will properly be in the middle ground between these two extremes: in their case we shall not believe that the evil that has befallen them is either deserved or undeserved, but that their case must be left to God. For the injustice and evil that overtake a man in consequence of his known ways are caused by the injustice and evil in that particular individual; but as for the injustice and evil that overtake him which are not in consequence of his known ways—the understanding of this problem we leave to God, blessed be He.

[9] Envy is even more a contrary to anxiety than is the concern over a good which comes to one who does not deserve it, the emotion we have called "resentment"; and this latter affect is quite near to being in the middle ground between anxiety and envy, since the concern in resentment is over a good, just as envy is concerned with good; the difference between them, however, is that envy is concern over a good that has overtaken one deserving of it, while resentment is a concern over a good that has overtaken one undeserving of it.

[10] He who feels concern both when good comes to the deserving and when it comes to the undeserving will be cured of this pain when evil falls upon them—[will be more easily cured], that is, the more wicked are they who are undeserving of good.[7] Everyone, therefore, will rejoice when punishment falls upon the sort of men who beat their parents or make themselves abominable by murder, since this is tantamount to the rejoicing felt when good overtakes those worthy of it; for these two events together constitute justice. Further, the good and the wise will rejoice at the descent of good upon one who deserves good, and also at the descent of evil upon whoever deserves evil, since each of these events is fair. But fools and the wicked will rejoice and feel concern over the contraries of the things over which the wise rejoice and feel concern.

[11] Whence to derive premises to prove or stimulate anxiety has now been made clear.

6. The Hebrew word here (גַּאֲוָה), normally translated "pride," is T's rendering of Arabic *nafāsa*, which he apparently took as verbal noun from *nafusa*, "to be of high account" or "excellent." *Nafāsa*, however, can also be a verbal noun from *nafisa* = "to think (a person) not worthy (of something)," and this was apparently the meaning intended by A here.

7. The awkwardness here is due to JML's abridgment and alteration of T. The latter says that a person who is both "envious" and "resentful" will cease to have these feelings when the persons against whom they are directed are afflicted by misfortune; and that such a "cure" is worthy in proportion as the afflicted are both more wicked and less deserving of good.

פרק י״א

המאמר בגאוה.

[1] אמר הפילוסוף בב׳ מההלצה, שאם היה המתגאה הוא אשר ידאג לטוב ונעימות ענין יהיו לאיש לבלי חק, הנה התחייב מזה הגדר בנפשו שלא תהיה הגאוה בכל הטובות; לפי שהאדם לא יתגאה על אח׳ בגבורה, ולא בחסידות, ובכלל בכל המעלות אשר תהיינה לאדם מן הרצון· כמו לא ידאג במציאות הפכי המעלות לו; ואמנם תהיה הגאוה בממון, והכח, ובכלל בטובות המוצאות האדם מחוץ ממה שכבר יראה שהטובים יהיו ראוים להם, והרעים אינם ראוים להם, כמו הרשות והממון.

[2] ואמנם, יתגאה האדם באלו כשהיו חדשים· כי הקודמים מזה, יחשב בם שהם קרוב מהענין המחויב אשר בטבע. ולכן, לא יתגאו בני אדם בממונות הבאות בירושה, ולא בראשיות הקודמות ברוב; ואולם יתגאו, בלי ספק, בטובות המתחדשות, כמו הממשלה המתחדשת, והמון הממון והאחים, וזולת זה מן הטובות; וסבת זה, שהאנשים הם יותר חזקי חימה על אשר יתעשרו מחדש מאשר להם העושר בירושה· וכמו כן הענין בשאר הטובות אשר מחוץ. והסבה בזה שני דברים: אחד מהם, שהם יראו שאותו הטוב המתחדש הם היו ראוים לו יותר ממנו; והשני, שהם יראו שהמחויב בו היה התחבר ענין הקדום לו, ר״ל, שאשר היה לו מקדם הוא ראוי לו· והוא העני, דרך משל, או ההכנעה. ולכן, לא יתגאו בני אדם בטובות הקודמות, לפי שהם ממה שכבר הורגלו, וכאילו הם מחוייבות להם.

[3] והטוב אשר האדם אינו ראוי לו, אצל המתגאה עליו, מתחלף· וזה, שהטוב אשר יהיה ראוי לו אחד אחד מבני אדם מתחלף בהאותות והשעור; וזה, שאין כל טוב נאות לכל אדם, ולא השעור מזה אחד, אבל לכל אדם טוב נאות ושעור מתיחס. כי משא כלי המלחמות והתכונות המלחמיות הם טובות, אבל הם בלתי נאותות בנזירים, ואמנם הם נאותות באנשי הגבורה. וככה, ההפלגה

1 פרק] פ׳[ג] ‖ 5 אח׳] אחד[ג] | בחסידות] בחסידו[ר] ‖ 6 ידאג] ידא׳[ר] ‖ 8 מחוץ] בחוץ[ר] ‖ 10 כשהיו] בשהיו[ר] ‖ 11 שהם] שהוא[ר] ‖ 12 בירושה] מירושה[ר] ‖ 16 שני] ב׳[ר] | [היו][ר] ‖ 19 יתגאו] יתקנאו[ג] ‖ 22 [יהיה][ר] ‖ 24 מתיחס] התיחס[ר] | והתכונות] והתבונות[ג] ‖

CHAPTER 11

On Resentment

[1] In Book II of the *Rhetoric,* the Philosopher[a] says that if the resentful person is one who feels concern when an undeserving man has good fortune and is in easy circumstances, it necessarily follows from this same definition that resentment is not felt with respect to all goods; since no one will be resentful of another's courage, nor of his piety, nor, in general, of any of the virtues that man can acquire by exercise of will; just as it would not be a concern to anyone that the other be found to have the contraries of the virtues. But there will be resentment of wealth, power, and, in general, of all the advantages that may fall to a man's lot except those which good men will be thought to deserve and the wicked not to deserve, like political primacy and wealth.

[2] Now a man will resent the possession of these goods only insofar as they have been recently acquired, for older acquisitions will be looked upon as almost the effect of natural necessity. Men, therefore, do not resent inherited wealth, nor political honors won long in the past. Undoubtedly, however, they do resent newly acquired goods, like recently won ruling power, abundant wealth and brethren, and other such advantages; this is because men's anger burns more fiercely against the self-made newly rich than against the possessors of inherited wealth, and likewise in the case of all the other external goods. The reason is twofold: first, they consider that they are more deserving of the particular good which has been recently acquired than is its possessor; and second, they think that what is needed in his case is continued adherence to him of his former condition—that, in other words, he deserves what he previously had, poverty, for example, or humbleness. Men therefore do not resent[1] the possession of older goods, since these are among the things to which they have grown accustomed, and which, as it were, those possessing them ought properly to have.

[3] The good which, in the opinion of the resentful person, its possessor does not deserve, varies, for the good that any one man deserves will vary in appropriateness and measure. This is because not every good is appropriate to each and every man, nor is the measure of this good one and the same, but for every man there is a good that is appropriate and of relatively proper measure. For the bearing of arms and the making of military dispositions are goods, but they are inappropriate to the devout[2] and appropriate only to the powerful. Thus, too, extravagance

1. M: "... feel jealousy over ...," "... are not envious of. ..."
2. Literally: "Nazirites"; so T translates A's النُّساك = "hermits," "recluses," "pious men," "devotees."

---

a. T134 f./A184 f.; cf. *Rhet.* 2.9 (1386b ff.).

במשגל לא תאות באשר עשרם חדש, ואמנם תאות לאשר להם עושר קדום· לפי שהחדש בעושר יצטרך אל שמירת העושר, ואולם קדום העושר הנה כאלו עשרו דבר קיים, לא יפחד עליו.

[4] וכאשר היה האדם יאות בו טוב מה, ולא יגיעהו, בשרו עליו יכאב, ונפשו עליו תאבל. וכאשר הגיע לאדם מהטובות מה שהוא נשגב ממנו באיכות או השעור, הנה הוא מתת אלקים, והחנינה, והחק והגזרה אשר יאמ׳ בו שהוא מאצל[1] הש׳ ית׳. וזה כמו שיתגבר הקטן בגדול כאשר יהיה שונא, או הנקלה בנכבד, והעבריין בנזיר אלקים· ואם לא, הנה אין לעבריין שיתגבר בנזיר, כי הנזיר מעולה יותר מהעבריין. ומכאן יתבארו הטובות אשר יאמר בם שהאנשים יגיעו אליהם בגזירה אלהית, וזה: שאלה הטובות, ודמיוני אלו האנשים, הם אשר ייוחסו[1] הטובות היורדות בם אל הגזירה האלקית.

[5] ומאשר יתגאו עליהם בני אדם אשר יהיו אליהם הטובות העצומות אשר יהיו ראויים להם הטובים מבני אדם, לא הרעים מהם; ולכן, יאנח האדם ויתגאה כאשר המעולים לא יוכלו להתגבר במה שיהיו ראוים, ויתגבר בם מי שלמטה מהם.

[6] ואולם אשר יתגאו, הנה הם האנשים האוהבים הכבוד ושאר הענינים אשר יתגבר בם מי שאינו ראוי להם· כי זה המין מבני אדם, בכלל יאנח ויתגאה בכל הענינים אשר יראו נפשותיהם ראויות להם, ולא יראו זולתם ראוים להם, בהבצרם מהם והגיעם לזולתם. אמנם המסתפקים מבני אדם, ואשר יראו שאצלם תחבולה בהבאת הטובות, לא יתגאו, לפי שלא יראו שבכאן דברים הם יותר ראוים בהם מזולתם· ואם ראו זה בעלי התחבולה, לא יראו שהם יבצרו מהם.

[7] ומהדברי׳ הנזכרים יתכן שנטה השופט אל הגאוה על בעל[1] הריב, או הרחמנות לו, או העצבון בו; וזה, שאשר היו בכאן אנשים ראוים, והם כבר התגברו והצליחו· אם יהיו בכאן אנשים בלתי ראוים, ולא יתגברו ולא יצליחו· הנה אין ראוי שידאג עליהם, אבל ישמח בזה; ובהפך, אם היו בכאן רק אנשים

1 באשר <כאשר>[ד] |לאשר] באשר[ב] || 2 [הנה][ב] || 4 [בשרו][ד] || 7 מאצל[1]] אצל[כד] |הש׳] י׳׳[ב] |ית׳] יתעלה[ט] |כאשר יהיה] כשיהי׳[ד] || 9 מעולה יותר] יותר מעולה[ב] || 10 בגזירה אלהית] בגזרת אלקית[ד] |אלו] אלה[ד] || 11 ייוחסו[1]] יוחסו[כד] |הגזירה] הגזרת[ד] || 12 יתגאו] יתקנאו[ב] || 13 הטובים] הטהורים[ב] || 14 בם] בהן[ב] || 16 הענינים] ענינים[ב] || 18 ולא [יראו][ב] || 21 יבצרו] יכבדו[ב] || 23 על] אל[ב] |בעל[1]] בעלי[כד] |או] א[ב] || 24 [בו][ד] || 26 הנה] הני[ב] |רק] הק[ד] ||

4–5 איוב י״ד כ״ב ||

[1] Corrected according to ט.

in getting married[3] is not suitable for the newly rich, and is appropriate only to those whose wealth is of long standing; since the newly rich needs to conserve wealth, whereas the wealth of the long wealthy is, as it were, a permanent condition concerning which he has no fear.

[4] When the man is one for whom some good would be appropriate, and it does not come to him, **his flesh grieveth for** it **and his soul mourneth over** it [Job 14:22][4] And when a man obtains some particular good that is too grand for him in quality or measure, then this is a divine gift, a boon, an enactment and decree of which it will be said that it comes from[5] the Name, exalted be He. This is like the victory of the small over the great when the latter is the enemy, or of the dishonored over the honored, and of the transgressor over the devout—or else no transgressor could prevail over the devout because the devout is of higher excellence than the transgressor. The goods of which it will be said that men attain them by divine decree may be explained in this way: these goods and the likes of these men are such that the goods which descend upon them must be attributed to the divine decree.

[5] Among persons resented[6] by others are those to whom come the important goods which the best of men, not the wicked, deserve. A man is aggrieved[7] and resentful, therefore, when the virtuous are unable to win the things that they deserve, and one inferior to themselves succeeds in winning them.

[6] Resentful, indeed, are those who covet the honor and all the other emoluments which one who is undeserving of them may win; for persons of this sort generally feel chagrin and resentment at all the emoluments which they think they themselves deserve and others do not, when such emoluments are withheld from themselves but come to the others. The contented among men, however, and those who think they have a means of attracting advantages, will not be resentful, since the contented will not think that there are things which they deserve more than others do; and if those who have the means of gaining advantages thought they deserved them, they would not think that these advantages would be withheld from them.

[7] From the considerations that have been mentioned it will be possible to incline a judge to feel resentment against a litigant, or compassion for him, or anxiety concerning him; that is, if those involved are deserving men who have now prevailed and succeeded, or are undeserving men who do not prevail or succeed, it is not proper to feel concern on their account, but to rejoice at the

3. T and JML: "sexual intercourse"; but the Arabic word thus rendered means both that and the contracting of marriage (نِكَاح).

4. T's citation.

5. Reading corrected on the basis of T and A.

6. M: "envied."

7. Literally: "sighs"; the underlying Arabic word (يأسف) means "feel grief, regret, sorrow, chagrin."

ראוים לטוב, ולא יתגברו, הנה כבר ראוי שיחמול עליהם ושידאג לענינם. ובכלל, מכאן יקח המליץ הקדמות לקיים הגאוה[2] או לעוררה:

פרק י״ב

מהקנאה.

[1] הקנאה היא דאגה תקרה לאדם מפני הצלחת הזולת וטוב מזלו· וזה, כאשר נמצאו לו מהטובות, כמו הטובות המתוארות בשער הגאוה, ומציאותם לבני אדם שהם ראוים להם ויאותו בם. והיתה אותה הדאגה מהמקנא אינה לפי שהוא תאב שיהיה לו אותו הטוב לבד, או יסור מהמקונא ויהיה לו, אבל לשיסור לבד מהמקונא.

[2] והתחייב מזה שהמקנא אמנם יקנא המין מבני אדם שהם דומים לו ובני גילו· או יחשב בם שהם דומיו ובני גילו. וארצה ב״דומים״, המתדמים לאיש בסוג, ביחס, בשנים, בקנין, בשבח, ובממון· כי אלו הם המקונאים. והרצון ב״סוג״, כפי מה שאמר הפילוסוף בג׳ מההלצה, נערות או זקנה, אשה או איש, ערבי או[1] רומי.

[3] ואולם הקנאים הם אשר ירוממו השלמות בטובות אשר יקנאו עליהם· אלא שהם לא ישלמו בזה, ולא הגיעום כל הטובות, ולא נפקדו מהם כלם יחד, אבל מעט מהם. ולכן מה שלא ימצאו פועלי הפעולות הנשגבות — רצוני, בעלי השעורים הנשגבים, ובעלי המזל המצליחים בדברים הצלחה תמימה — מקנאים: לפי שהם יראו שכבר לא יבצר מהם דבר, ושכל דבר להם; וככה, המין מהאנשים אשר ינושאו בדבר מן הדברים, ויכובדו בסבתו, וכ״ש בחכמה וכשרון

2 הגאוה[2]] הקנאהד הקאנהג || 3 פרק] פ׳ג || 7 הדאגה] הגאוהג || 8 [אבל]ג || 10 [אדם]ג | דומים] דומיןד || 11 בדומים] בדומיןד || 12 בקנין...המקונאים <בקנין...המקונאים>ד | ובממון] וממוןד || 13 בג׳] בשלישיג || 14 [או[1]]גד || 17 פועלי] פעוליג || 18 השעורים] השעורד || 19 [מקנאים]ד ||

[2] Corrected text.

[1] Corrected text.

event; and contrariwise, if the persons involved deserve only good, and yet do not prevail, it is indeed proper for him to pity them and to be concerned over their plight. In general, then, the speaker will take from here the premises from which to prove or to arouse resentment.[8]

CHAPTER 12

Of Envy

[1] Envy[a] is a concern that may beset a person on account of another's prosperity and good fortune—this, when the other has gained possession of goods, like those described in the chapter on resentment,[1] which really belong and are appropriate to men who deserve them. This concern of the envious person is no passionate desire to be possessed of the good in question, or that, eluding the envied person, it should become his, but only that it should elude the envied person.

[2] From this it necessarily follows that one who is envious will envy only the sort of persons who resemble and are of one kind with himself, or are thought to resemble and be of one kind with himself. By "persons who resemble" I mean those similar to the man in class, lineage, age, acquirement, distinction, and wealth, for these are the things that excite envy. By "class" is meant—according to the Philosopher[b] in Book III of the *Rhetoric*—youth or old age, woman or man, Arab or Roman.[2]

[3] The envious, indeed, place high value upon possessing *all* the goods that excite envy; they feel incomplete only in this respect: neither have all goods come to them, nor have they ever lacked in all of them at the same time, but only a small part of them. This is why the doers of sublime deeds—the noble men of high worth, and the fortunate who are completely successful in affairs—do not find enviers; for those capable of envy will think that surely nothing should be withheld from the noble, but that everything is properly theirs; this is likewise true of the sort of men who are distinguished in some respect and who are for that reason held in honor, especially for wisdom and soundness-of-state.[3] And those

8. Corrected text; C: "envy" (הקנאה); M: הקאנה (a misreading of הגאוה?).

1. iii.11.1.
2. *Sic*, A and T.
3. *Sic*, T; JML: "soundness-of-understanding" (תבונה instead of תכונה).

a. T136 f./A187 f.; cf. *Rhet*. 2.10 (1387b f.).
b. T199/A280; *Rhet*. 3.7 (1408a).

התכונה[2]. ואוהבי הכבוד יותר חזקי קנאה מאשר אינם אוהבי כבוד; והחכמים
יחפצו שיכובדו בכבודות הראויות לחכמים, ולכן יקנאו באשר יכובדו באילו
הכבודות; ובכלל, כל מי שיאהב שישובח על דבר מהדברים, הנה הוא יקנא
זולתו בדבר ההוא בעינו· ולכן אשר יכספו שיכובדו על דבר מה יקנאו על אותו
5 הדבר בעינו. והאנשים הקטני נפשות, הם גם כן קנאים, לפי שכל דבר יגדל
אצלם יקנאו עליו, ואם היה בעצמו קטן. ואולם במה יקנאו, הם יקנאו
בהשתוקקם לכתר השבח וכתר שם טוב, ולמעלות הממון והעבדים; ובכלל,
בכל אופני ההצלחות והמזל, ובכל דבר נעים· וכל שכן, בענינים אשר יתאוום,
או יחשבו שכבר יחוייב שיהיו להם.

10 [4] והקנאה תהיה במין מן האנשים אשר להם אצל האדם דמיון או התקרב:
כאשר היו בזמן אחד או קרוב, ובמקום אחד או קרוב. ולכן לא יקנא הישיש
בנער, ולא יקנא אשר יבאו אחריו בזמן, או אשר עברו ונפסדו, וביחוד משנים
רבות; וכן לא יקנאו זה את זה מי שהם רחוקים במקום, כאלו תאמר, יושבי רומי
ליושבי מצרים; ולא יקנא האדם האנשים אשר הם יותר חסרים ממנו הרבה או
15 שהם יותר שלמים ממנו מאד.

[5] ואמנם יקנאו מי שבינו ובינם שתוף· וזה, בחולקים בדבר אחד, ואוהבים
לדבר אחד. ובכלל, כל שני אנשים מתאוים לדבר אחד, וכל אחד מהם יאהב
שלא יהיה לחברו דרך שיתאחד בו ויתפרד· ולזה, היתה הקנאה יותר ראויה
שתהיה לאלו. וזה כמו המפואר והמתפאר: כי אלו יתאוו דבר אחד, וכל אחד
20 מהם יכסוף שיפרד בו· ואמנם יקנא המפואר למתפאר בדברים אשר כשקנה
אותם היה בם דומה לו.

[6] והדאגה באלה הדברים תחלה, והאנחה עליהם כאשר השתרשה מהנפש,
תחודש ממנה הקנאה לאשר ימצאו להם הטובות האלו, או הם תאבים שימצאו
להם בעתיד, או כבר נמצאו במה שעבר. ולכן, כבר יכנסו אשר נאמרו בשער
25 האנחה, והגאוה בשער הקנאה, לפי שהאנחה, כאשר התחזקה מהנפש, שבה
קנאה.

1 התכונה[2]] התבונה[כד] || 2 באשר] כאשר[כ] | באילו] באלה[ד] || 3 ובכלל] והכלל[ד] | [שיאהב][ד] | על דבר
מהדברים] בדבר מן הדברים[ד] || 5 [לפי][ד] || 6 במה] כמה[כ] || 7 שם] שום[כ] || 10 והקנאה] והקנא[ד] ||
14 ליושבי מצרים] למצריים[ד] || 16 ובינם] לבינם[כ] || 16–17 ואוהבים לדבר אחד] ואוהבים לדבר
אחר[ד] || 20 כשקנה] תוקנה || 21 [לו][כ] || 22 השתרשה] השתבשה[gט] השתרשה[abט] || 23 ממנה] ממנו[ד] |
לאשר] לאמר[ד] | או הם] אז הם[ד] || 25 והגאוה] הגאוה[ד] ||

[2] Corrected according to ט.

who are covetous of honor are more strongly envious than those who do not covet honor. The wise wish to be accorded the honors befitting wise men, and so envy those who receive such honors. In general, anyone who desires praise for something will envy someone else on account of that very thing; therefore those who yearn to be honored for some reason will feel envy over that very reason. And the pusillanimous, too, will be envious, for they feel envy over everything that seems great to them, even though it is really slight. As for the circumstances in which envy is felt, people become envious when they covet the crown of praise and the crown of a good name,[4] and the advantages of wealth and servants. In general, envy is excited by every manner and kind of prosperity and good fortune, by everything pleasant, and especially by things that people crave for themselves or think it obligatory for them to have.

[4] Subject to envy are the class of men to whom the envious person bears some resemblance or form of nearness: when they are his contemporaries or nearly so, and of the same or a nearby place. For this reason an old man will not envy a boy, nor will he envy his successors in time, or those who have passed away and are no more, especially if this happened many years ago. Similarly, those who are distant in place will not envy each other, for example, inhabitants of Rome and inhabitants of Egypt.[5] Nor will a man envy those who are either far less, or far more, perfect than he.

[5] Those may be envied, indeed, between whom and the envious person there is a sharing: those at odds over one and the same thing and those who love one and the same thing. In general, should any two persons covet some one particular thing, then each desires the other to have no way of getting it for himself alone; and for this reason, the envy that these will experience is more patent. This is like the case of the possessor of glory and the glory seeker: for these covet the same one thing, and each is eager alone to have it. The already glorious will envy the glory seeker only the things which, when acquired by the seeker, will enable the latter to resemble himself.

[6] Initial concern over these matters, and chagrin over them when concern has become rooted in the soul,[6] result in envy of those who actually possess these goods, or those who long to acquire them in the future, or those who have already possessed them in the past. What has been said, therefore, might be included in the chapter on chagrin, and resentment in the chapter on envy,[7] since chagrin, when it has taken possession of the soul, turns into envy.[8]

4. *Mishnah Ābhōth* 4:13.

5. In T/A, the example is "Greeks . . . and those at the Images [*sic*] of Hercules of the Andalusian peninsula, our country."

6. T and JML: ". . . of the soul." T has here taken over, and incorrectly used, the Hebrew cognate (מן) of a correctly used preposition (مِن) in A.

7. iii.14 (chagrin); and the present chapter (envy).

8. The Hebrew here is very awkward: T's translation is of words rather than of sense. My English follows A's sense.

[7] ומי שהיה מהנערים גדול בשנים, הוא יקנא הקטן ממנו בשנים כאשר הגיע הקטן לטוב לא השיגהו היותר גדול, או שהשיג טוב כמהו. וכן, יקנא מי שהשיג הדבר בהנהגה גדולה למי שישיגהו בהנהגה יותר מעוטה; וכמו כן, אשר השיגו דרושם בהשתדלות, ואיחור, ויגיעה, יקנאו לאשר השיגוהו קל מהרה.
5 [8] ומאלה הדברים, יקח המליץ ההקדמות לעורר הקנאה או לקימה:

פרק י״ג

מהשמחה.

[1] והוא ידוע גם כן במה ישמחו השמחים, ולמי ישמחו, ובאי זה תכונות יהיו השמחים. אחר שהיו הדברי׳ אשר בהם ישמח האדם הם בהפך הדברים אשר
10 בהם ידאג ועליהם יקנא, כאשר התבאר במה שקדם, ככה אשר ישמח הוא הפך אשר יקנא, ואשר ישמחו בני אדם בו הוא הפך אשר יקנאו בו. ולזה התחייב, שאם היתה הקנאה דאגה בטוב ישיגהו מי שראוי לו, שהשמחה תהיה משוש בטוב ישיגיהו מי שראוי לו.
[2] ומאלה הדברים, התבאר לנו דרך אשר בו נעורר השופטים על החמלה או
15 על הקנאה על אחד מבעלי דינים· והיאך יקויים היות האדם חומל ומקנא:

6 פרק] פ׳כ || 8 במה]כ | השמחים] האנשי׳ד | ישמחו] ישמחד || 9 הדברי׳] כדבריםכ || 10 ידאג] ידעgט ידאגabט | במה] ממהכ || 12–13 שהשמחה...לו]ד || 15 דינים] דיניןכ ||

[7] Of boys, the older will envy his junior when the junior has obtained a good not obtained by him, or has obtained one that equals his. Likewise, one who has achieved some object by means of more skillful management will envy whoever achieves it with less skillful management. And similarly, too, those who have obtained what they sought at the expense of strenuous effort, long delay, and fatigue, will envy those who have obtained the same end easily and swiftly.

[8] From such considerations as these the speaker may derive the premises from which to arouse or to prove envy.

CHAPTER 13

Of Gladness[1]

[1] Familiar enough, too, are the things over which the glad[2] will be glad, the persons for whom they will be glad, and what conditions will dispose them to be glad.[a] For since the things over which a man will be glad are the contrary of those which, as shown above, cause him concern and excite him to envy, then one who feels glad is the contrary, accordingly, of one who feels anxious, and the person for whom men are glad is the contrary of one whom they envy. It necessarily follows, therefore, that, if envy is concern over a good reached by one who deserves it, gladness is rejoicing over a good obtained by one who is deserving of it.[3]

[2] These considerations have now made clear to us the method by which we will arouse in the judges pity for, or envy of, a particular litigant, and how it can be proved that a person is compassionate and envious.

1. The word so translated is שִׂמְחָה, T's rendering of غِبْطَة = "state of happiness, delight, rapture, felicity."
2. So M and T; C has altered this to "men."
3. The words "gladness . . . it" are omitted in C, but are present in M and, in slightly different form, in T.

---

a. Cf. T138 f./A190 f.

פרק י״ד

המאמר ביגון ואנחה.

[1] האנחה היא דאגה מה תראה בפנים להפקד טובות נכבדות יכספם האדם לנפשו, או למי שהוא לרגלו; וזה בערך אל הטובות האפשריות, והיה אותו האדם, כפי טבעו או סוגו או הוריו הקדומים, ממי שראוי לטוב ההוא· מזולת שיכסוף שלא יהיו אותם הטובות לזולתו, ואמנם יכסו׳ שיהיו לו, וידאג מפני שלא היו לו. והנה התחייב מזה שהאנחה והיגון טוב, ושהם לא יהיו אלא לטובים· ושהקנאה רע וחסרון, ושהיא לא תהיה אלא לרעים. למה שהיגון ישים האדם בצד שיהיה מוכן להשיג הטובות ויהיה ראוי להם — כי זה ההפעלות לא יקרא אלא למי שיראה נפשו מוכנת אל הטובות וראויה להם — ויהיה זה סבה להקנאת המעלות· ואולם הקנאה תשים האיש בצד שיהיה מוכן לא לשישיג טוב אחר.

[2] ואין ספק שלא יצטער האדם בהפקד ממנו הענינים שהם מועטי הטוב, או שהם בלתי טובים, גם לא יכסוף אשר לא יראה נפשו ראויה להם; ולזה, אשר יאנחו הם אשר יראו נפשותם ראויות לטובות אינם להם; ואשר הם בזאת התכונה הם הבחורים וגדולי הנפשות. גם אשר לא תהיינה להם הטובות אשר יהיו ראוים להם נכבדי האנשים וטוביהם, כמו העושר ורבוי האחים, יאנחו על מה שיבצר להם מהטובות האלה; כי מי שיש לו עושר יאנח על מה שיבצר ממנו מהרשות· ואשר לו רשות מבלעדי עושר יאנח על מה שיבצר ממנו מן העושר· וכבר יאנחו אלה על מה שיבצר מהם מהתוספת והרבוי בטובות האילו יותר ממה שימצא לזולתם. אמנם קרה לאלה זה ההפעלות כי הם יחשבו בנפשותם שיהיו טובים, או קרוב שיהיו טובים, אחר שימצא להם הדבר הראוי לטובים. משל זה, שכאשר אחז אחד הראשות והעושר, חשב שהוא טוב אחר שהיו שני אלו מן הדברים הראוים לטובים· ולזה, מצא האנחה על מה שיבצר לו מזה.

[3] ואשר אבותיהם הראשונים וקרוביהם מכובדים, יקרה בם זה ההפעלות הרבה ביחס אלה הטובות, לפי שהם יחשבו שהם נאותות להם בירושה ושהם ראויים להם.

[4] וכאשר יהיו הענינים אשר בם האנחה ענינים נשגבים ומפוארים, יחוייב שיהיו אם מעלות נפשיות· או ענינים משובחים, ר״ל, טובות גופניות או מחוץ·

1 פרק] פ׳[ב] || 2 ואנחה] ובאנחה[ד] || 4 האפשריות] באפשריות[ב] || 6 יכסו׳] בסוף[ב] || 9 הטובות] טובות[ד] || 10 יקרא] יהיה[ד] יקרה[ט] | שיראה] שידאה[ב] || 11 לשישיג] להשיג[ב] || 12 אחר] אחד[ט] || 14 יראה] ידאה[ב] || 15 יראו] ידאו[ב] || 16 הטובות] טובות[ד] || 18 להם] מהם[ט] || 19 מהרשות] מן הרשות[ד] מהראשות[ט] || 20 מהתוספת] מהתופסת[ד] | בטובות האילו] לטובות כאלו <הוא>[ד] || 21 יחשבו] חשבו[ב] || 24 הדברים] הדברי[ד] || 27 בירושה] כירושה[ד] || 29 יחוייב] יחוייבו[ב] ||

CHAPTER 14

Of Distress and Chagrin

[1] Chagrin[a] is a certain facially manifested concern at failure to obtain highly valued advantages that a person eagerly desires for himself, or for some associate of his. It occurs with reference to possible advantages, and when that person is by nature, class, or previous ancestry deserving of that advantage; while not anxious that those goods belong to nobody else, he is eager that they be his, and is concerned because they are not. It follows, then, that to feel chagrin and distress is a good, and that only good men will experience these emotions, whereas envy is an evil and a defect that only the wicked will possess. Since distress disposes a man to become prepared to acquire goods, and disposes him to be deserving of them—for this emotion is experienced only by one who considers himself prepared to come by, and to be worthy of, good things—distress is a motive for acquiring the virtues; envy, however, disposes a man to be prepared to prevent the acquiring of good by another.

[2] A man will doubtless not be troubled when he fails to obtain things that are of little or no value, nor will he long for those which he does not think he deserves. The chagrined, therefore, are those who consider themselves deserving of advantages they do not have. Those also susceptible to this mental state are the young and the high-minded; those, too, who do not have the goods that the honored and best of men deserve, such as riches and abundance of brethren, will feel chagrin over the withholding of such goods in their case. For one who has riches will be chagrined over the leadership that is withheld from him, and the person who has leadership without riches will be chagrined over the riches withheld from him; and these may be expected to be chagrined over the withholding from themselves of more increase and multiplication in such goods than others are to obtain. This emotion is experienced by such persons because they may think of themselves as excellent, or near to being excellent, only in consequence of possessing the thing that excellent men deserve. An example is the person who, holding leadership and riches, has thought himself excellent inasmuch as these two advantages are among the things that the excellent deserve, and, so thinking, comes to have chagrin over whatever good of this sort is withheld in his case.

[3] Those whose early ancestors and kinsmen are held in honor are frequently susceptible to this emotion in relation to such goods, since they consider them suitably theirs by inheritance, and themselves as deserving of them.

[4] Since the matters over which chagrin is felt are noble and exalted, they will necessarily be either psychical excellences, or else excellent circumstances, by

a. Cf. T139 ff./A191 ff.; cf. *Rhet.* 2.11 (1388b ff.).

ואלה כל הדברים אשר בם תועלת, נעימות ושלמות, ואם ערבות. ולכן, כבר יכבדו האנשים בעלי אלו המינים השלשה, ר״ל, המטיבים אליהם, והם אנשי התועלת; והטובים, והם האנשים נעימי הפעלות; ואשר בם התעדנות, והם הערבי׳׳ ושוה היתה ההטבה וההתעדנות בם לנפשותם או למי שידבק בם.

[5] והנה היגון יהיה על תכונת האנשים אשר ימצאו להם הענינים הנכבדים אשר זכרנום, כמו הנוי, והעושר, והגבורה, והחכמה, והראשות. אמנם, היה הראשות מהענינים אשר יאנח האדם על הפקדם[1], לפי שאנשי הראשיות יוכלו להטיב אל רוב בני אדם; ומהיותר עצומה שבפעולותיהם היא הנהגת הצבאות· והדרשות, וזולת זה מקניני הראשיות ותכונותיהם, אשר יפעלו בהם ההטבה לבני אדם.

[6] ואשר ישתוקקו הרבה מהאנשים שיהיו כמותם, או אשר יתפלאו מהם הרבה מן האדם, יכספו האנשים להדמות להם. ומזה המין, אשר ידברו בפרסום שמם המשוררים, והמליצים, ומשאירי הספרים לנצח· כי הם אשר ידברו בתושבחות האדם ופרסום שמו.

[7] ואשר להם כל הטובות, או גדולי השעור מהם, לא יאנחו ולא יצטערו.

[8] והנה, מאלה יוכל ההלצי לקיים היגון והאנחה, או לעורר האדם אליהם:

פרק ט״ו

ממדות הבחורים.

[1] יען תמצאנה מדות מיוחדות לפי השנים, הסכמנו להביאם בזה המקום, כפי מה שהביאם הפילוסוף בב׳ מההלצה, למען לא יבצר מהמליץ אשר יזם לעשות לדבר במדות המתחלפות לפי השנים, לקיים ולעורר כפי הצורך והשעה.

1 כבר] כבד[ג] || 2 המינים] המינין[ג] | השלשה] הג׳[ד] || 3–4 [והטובים... הערבי׳][ג] | וההתעדנות] ובהתעדנות[ד] || 7 הפקדם[1]] הפקרה[ג] הפקדה[ד] הפרדם[טa] | הראשיות] הראשות[ד] || 8 היא] הי׳[ד] || 13 הספרים] ספרים[ד] || 16 ההלצי] ההלציי[ג] || 17 פרק] פ׳[ג] || 19 להביאם] למביאם[ד] || 20 שהביאם הפילוסוף בב׳ מההלצה] שאמ׳ הפילוסו׳ בג׳ מהלצ׳[ד] ||

20–21 בר׳ י״א ו׳ ||

[1] Corrected according to ט[g].

which I mean physical or external advantages; and these are all the things in which there are benefit, loveliness, and perfection or delight. Men may, therefore, be expected to honor those who dispose of these three species of good: those, namely, who do them good, the beneficent; those who are good, the men whose acts are fine; and those through whom there is delight, the pleasing, whether the good done and the delight afforded be for their own benefit or for that of someone connected with them.

[5] Now distress is felt on account of the state of the persons whose actual circumstances are the respected ones we have mentioned, like beauty, riches, courage, wisdom, and leadership. Leadership, however, is among the circumstances over whose absence[1] a man will feel chagrin, because men in authority are able to benefit a great many others. Among the most significant of their acts is generalship; and oratorical ability, as well as other such aptitudes and qualities of leadership, are the means employed by them to procure benefit for mankind.

[6] And those whom many men yearn to be like, or whom many of humankind admire: it is these whom men are eager to resemble. To this class belong those whose names are celebrated by poets, orators, and such as leave lasting books behind them,[2] for these tell a man's praises and the renown of his name.

[7] Those who possess all the advantages, or those of greatest significance, will neither be chagrined nor troubled.

[8] From these considerations, then, the speaker will be able either to prove distress and chagrin, or to arouse these emotions in another person.

CHAPTER 15

The Character of Young Men

[1] Since there are traits of character specific to the several periods of life, we have decided to introduce them at this juncture, as the Philosopher[a] did in Book II[1] of the *Rhetoric,* so that **nothing will be withholden from** the speaker **which** he may **purpose to do** [Gen. 11:6] in dealing with traits of character that vary according to age, and so that he can prove and arouse as need and the moment require.

1. Corrected text.
2. A adds: "I mean the historians."

1. The reading of M; C: ". . . in III of *Rhetoric*" (*sic*).

a. T141 ff./A194 ff.; cf. *Rhet.* 2.12 (1388b ff.).

[2] ונתחיל ממדות הבחורים, ונאמר: הבחורים הם אשר עברו שני שבועות משנותיהם אל צד ג׳ שבועות. הנה ממדותיהם שהם יבחרו כל דבר, והם נמהרים אל מה שיתאווהו· והתאוות הגופניות הגוברות עליהם יותר מיוחסות אל הנוגה. והם מהירים ומתהפכים, יתאוו הדבר במהרה ויתעבוהו במהרה. והסבה בהשתוקקם כל דבר שדעותיהם מבולבלות, לא נתיישבו עדין על מה שראוי לבחור מהענינים העולמיים, ואין סברותיהם קיימות.

[3] והם עם זה מהירי הכעס עד יאנסו ממנו, למה שהם מרוב אהבתם את הכבוד לא יסבלו אם יקלם מקלה, אבל יצטערו כאשר יחשבו שהם יבזום. והם אוהבים הכבוד, ועל הכל הנצחון· וזה, שהבחרות ישתוקק ההתפארות, והנצחון דבר מן ההתפארות. ויכספו הכבוד והנצחון יותר מהממון, כי הם לא נסו ההוצאה.

[4] ומחשבתם נעימה ותוחלתם רחבה לחמימות טבעם; לא יחלשו ולא ילאו· יסבלו הצער ויבזוהו, וזה לכח חמימותם. והם ברוב יחיו[1] בתוחלת, לפי שהתוחלת הוא בהצטרף אל העתיד, והזכרון לעובר; והעתיד לנערים נמצא יותר מן העובר, לפי שהם בראשית מציאותם, ולזה ייחלו יותר מאשר יזכרו.

[5] והם מאמינים לכל דבר, וזה שמדרכם שיאמינו מבלתי ראיה, או בראיה חלושה; לכן יצדיקו בכל דבר· וכאשר יכוון להטעותם בהוראה, תקל הטעאתם.

[6] גם הם גבורים, עם שהם מנעימי התוחלת, כי הגבורים כעסנים נעימי התוחלת. ואולם, נעימות התוחלת יחדש להם שלא יחרדו· וזה, שכח[2] התקוה בהתגברות יתן להם גבורה, ותוחלת הטוב הוא אחד ממה שיתן הגבורה. ואולם הכעס הנה יחדש להם חוזק הלב, לפי שאין אחד שיפחד מהאדם ויכעס עליו.

[7] וממדתם שהבשת יגבר עליהם, לפי שהם אינם מכירים עדיין בין הדברים אשר יחוייב להתבייש מהם, ובין הדברים אשר אין להתבייש מהם; והם, לחשדם נפשותיהם בכל, יתביישו מכל דבר מיראתם שכבר טעו.

2 ג׳] שלש[ג] || 3 <הם> מיוחסות[ג] | 6 [לבחור][ד] || 7 [את][ד] || 8 יקלם] יקלה[ג] | יבזום] יבוזום[ג] || 10 [הם][ד] || 12 יחלשו] יחלישו[ג] || 13 יחיו[1]] יהיו[כד] || 14 והזכרון] הזכרו׳[ד] || 16 לכל] בכל[ד] || 18 כעסנים) כעסני[ג] || 19 התוחלת] תוחלת[ד] | שכח[2]] שבח[כד] || 21 יחדש] יחזק[ד] || 22 שהם אינם] שאינם[ג] || 24 בכל] מכל[ד] | טעו] תעו[ד] ||

[1] Corrected according to ט and א.

[2] Corrected according to ט.

[2] Beginning, then, with the character traits of young men, we say: young men are they who have moved past two heptads[2] of their years on the way to three heptads. It is characteristic of them that they will make a choice of some kind, and be off in a rush toward whatever it is they desire; and the bodily lusts that chiefly govern them are those ascribed to the influence of the planet Venus. The young are given to sudden change, are quick to desire a thing, and as speedily find it abominable. What prompts their random cravings is that their ideas are confused, unsettled as yet with respect to what worldly things ought be preferred, and their opinions are unstable.

[3] They are, in addition, quick to anger and even dominated by it, for owing to their great love of honor they cannot tolerate it if anyone slights them, but are aggrieved when they imagine that they are disdained. They love honor, and above all victory: youth longs to appear magnificent, and victory is magnificence of a sort. They are more eager for honor and victory than for money, for they have not experienced [the drain of] expenditure.[3]

[4] Their thoughts are pleasant and their hopes expansive, owing to the warmth of their nature; they neither weaken nor grow weary,[4] but will endure and be disdainful of pain—this also owing to the force of their warmth. For the most part they live[5] in hope, for hope is of the future and memory of the past. To the young the future is more actual than the past, since they are at the beginning of their own existence, and so they indulge more in hope than in memory.

[5] They believe anything, for they are wont to give credence without proof or with weak proof; therefore they will declare any proposition true, and when it suits someone's purpose to mislead them about evidence they are easily deceived.

[6] Further, they are at the same time brave and optimistic, for the courageous are angry optimists. It is their optimism, indeed, that is responsible for the fact that they do not fear: the force[6] of their hope of prevailing gives them courage, and the expectation of some advantage is a factor of encouragement. As for anger, it is responsible for their resoluteness of heart, for no one is afraid of a man while in anger at him.

[7] And it is characteristic of the young to be overcome by shame, inasmuch as they are as yet unable to discriminate between the things of which one properly should be ashamed and those of which one need not be ashamed. Because they doubt themselves in all respects, they are likely to be ashamed of anything out of fear of having made a mistake.

2. Literally: "weeks," the reading, too, of A; cf. Dan. 9:24–27.
3. A: "poverty." T seems to have read the Arabic here as *nafaqa* (نفقة) = "expense," instead of as *fāqa* (فاقة), the reading of both the Leiden and Florence MSS, which means "poverty."
4. A: "flinch."
5. JML: "are," but A and T give the true reading; cf. *Rhet*. 2.12.8 (1389a).
6. Corrected according to T; M and C: "praise" (שֶׁבַח/שֶׁכֹּחַ).

[8] והם מחזיקים בנימוסי׳ מאד, ואוחזים בהם· והסבה בזה, שהם לא יפנו אל[3] העיון בהם עד שיובדל להם מה מהם יושר ממה שאינו יושר.

[9] והם גדולי הנפשות, ויחשבו שלא יהיו עניים לעולם, כי לא נסו הגלגולים וההפסדות. וישתוקקו לעולם מפעלות גדולי הנפשות, הנשגבות מהם· וזה 5 מדרך התרחבות תוחלתם.

[10] וממדותיהם שהם יבחרו הנאה יותר מבחירתם המועיל, למעוט התבוננותם בתמורות הזמן; ובחירתם לנאה מפני בחירתם למעלות· ובחירתם למעלות מפני השבח והגנות.

[11] והם מחבבים חבריהם יותר משאר בני אדם, לפי שמתמימו׳ התענוג 10 והשמחה המצא החברה והשתתפות האחים. והם לא ידרשו המועיל בדבר מהדברים ולא באוהבי׳; וטעותם בדברים רב מה שיהיה בדברים המועילים אשר יבחרום הזקנים. ופעולותיהם בלתי מוגבלות ובלתי משוערות, כי הם יחבבו מאד וישנאו מאד· ובכלל, הנה יפליגו בכל דבר, וזה לרוע הכרתם תמורות הזמן.

15 [12] והם יחשבו שהם יודעים כל דבר, וזה בסבת השתוקקם לכל דבר. והם ירכבו החמס באנסות, והדברים אשר מהם המום והקלון, וזה גם כן להתפארותם והפלגתם בדברים. והם רחמנים, לפי שהם יחשבו בבני אדם יחד שהם טובים צדיקים; והם למיעוט רעתם ישנאו אנשי הרוע, לפי שהם יחשבו כי אנשי הרוע יפעלו מה שאיננו ראוי.

20 [13] והם אוהבים הלצנות והשעשוע; ונטותם מהדבר הוא קל מהרה, לפי שמהירות הנטיה מחלשת הסברה:

1 בנימוסי׳] מנימוסים^ד || 2 אל^2] על^כד || 5 התרחבות] התחרבות^כ || 7 התבוננותם] התבוננו׳^ד | מפני] מבנ^כ | למעלות] המעלו׳^ד || 9 חבריהם] חביריהם^כ | שמתמימו׳] שמתמיאות^כ || 10 המועיל] במועיל^ד || 11 מהדברים] מן הדברים^ד | באוהבי׳] האוהבי׳^ד || 12 יבחרום] יכירום^כ || 13 הכרתם] הבנתם^כ || 16 באנסות] באניסות^כ | והקלון] וקלון^ד || 17 [יחד] יחד^ד || 18 צדיקים] וצדיקים ||

[3] Corrected according to ט.

[8] They set great store by traditional usages and hold fast to them, the reason being that they do not devote enough study to such usages to discriminate what is right about them from what is wrong.

[9] They are nobly highminded, and think that they will never be poor, for they have not experienced reversals and losses. They are forever yearning after the deeds of souls nobler and loftier than their own—a byproduct, this, of the expansiveness of their hopes.

[10] It is further characteristic of them to prefer what is ethically fine to what is expedient, because they give such little thought to the vicissitudes[7] of fortune. They prefer what is fine because they prefer the virtues, and the virtues because of praise and blame.

[11] And they are fond of their friends, more so than are the rest of mankind, since the actuality of comradeship and fraternal communion is a most perfect pleasure and joy. They do not look for that which is advantageous in the case of some particular thing or in the case of their friends; regarding things, they make more mistakes than old men do respecting the useful things which they prefer. The actions of the young are unrestrained and immoderate, for they love and hate to excess, and, in general, will carry everything too far because they are so little acquainted with vicissitudes in fortune.

[12] They think they know everything just because they long[8] for everything. They will commit[9] outrage with violence and acts that result in taint and dishonor—this, too, because of their tendency to boastfulness and to exaggeration in words. But they are compassionate, since they assume that human beings as a whole[10] are good and righteous; but because their own wickedness is inconsiderable, they hate vicious persons, since they assume that the vicious will do what ought not be done.

[13] They love jesting and merriment; and they turn aside easily and quickly from the matter at hand, for the haste to shift attention is a product of weakness in reasoning power.

7. T thus renders an Arabic word (عَوَاقِبُ) that means "ends, outcomes, upshots; issues, effects, results, consequences."

8. So JML; T: "are immersed in" (השתקעם); he prefers this meaning of the Arabic (إغرَاقِهم) to the alternative "carry everything to excess," which is what A meant. Such examples of mechanical translation abound in T.

9. Literally: "ride": an Arabic idiom transposed into Hebrew.

10. The Heb. word translated "as a whole" (יחד) is T's rendering of an Arabic word (جَمِيعًا) in A; it is present in M, but omitted in C—one of the indications that Conat revised the text before, or while, printing it. See the Int., §2 and n. 80, and cf. n. 246.

פרק י״ו

ממדות הישישים.

[1] והישישים אשר עברו שנות הזקנה, הנה הם הפכי למדות הבחורים, ר״ל, לאהבת הלצנות והשעשוע· ותשוקת התאוות הגופניות· והרחמנות לאנשים· והפתוי· ומהירות הכעס· וחזק הלב· ואהבת הכבוד והנצוח· והמשכת התוחלת· וגודל הנפש· ורכיבת החמס· ושאר זה המין. והיה זה כן לפי שהם חיו[1] זמן ארוך, וקצרה תוחלתם· ונבגדו הרבה וחטאו הרבה. והיתה מחשבתם בבני אדם רעה, לנפילתם על סבות הבגידה וחטאת הכונה בנסיון· ורוב הפעלות הנפלות בם היו כלם רעות, או מביאות אל הרעות.

[2] וממדותיהם שהם לא יספקו בדבר במה שבינם לבין עצמם; ולא יתפלאו מדבר ירד עליהם, לפי שהוא כבר הוכפל עליהם; ולמה שהם נסו כל דבר, כאלו הם לא יקוו דבר. ולא יצטערו בשבח וגנות, לפי שכוונתם האמתיות; גם לא יגזרו אומר על דבר לעולם בזולת ״שמא״ ו״אולי״, לרוב הכזבת תוחלתם. והם רעים, בקצת מדותיהם, לרוע מחשבתם בכל דבר· וזה למעוט אמנתם, והאמנתם מעט היא לרבוי נסיונם. ולא יאהבו ולא ישנאו בהפלגה, ולא יגלו אהבתם ושנאתם כי אם באונס והכרח; והידיד והאויב אצלם הם להם על דמיון אחד· וזה, לרוב הבגידה והטעות שנפל בהם לארך ימיהם.

[3] והם קטני נפשות: יבזו בדברים הנשגבים, ולא ישתוקקו אל דבר זולת מה שבו המחיה; והם בלתי בעלי חן וכבוד לרוב צורך העולם בענינים ההכרחיים לחיות· ואמנם היה להם זה לרוב הנסיון; ולזה הם בעלי כילאות, לעמידתם שהשגת הקנינים קשה· וביחוד בשנות הישישות, שההפסד מוכן לחלשת גופותם.

[4] והם ״רואים את הנולד״, למה שנסו מענין הזמן; ויש להם מורך ופחד לקרירות מזגם — בהפך הבחורים, שהם בעלי חמימות ותבערה. והם אוהבים

1 פרק] פ׳[כ] || 2 הישישים] הבחורים[כ] || 3 הפכי] הפכים[כ] || 6 ורכיבת] ורבינת[כ] | חיו[1] היו[כד] || 14 מחשבתם] תוחלתם[ד] || 15 בהפלגה] ההפלגה[ד] || 16 באונס והכרח] בהכרח ואונס[כ] || 17 שנפל] שנפלו[ד] || 19 צורך] צור׳[ד] | העולם] העמלם[כ] || 20 לחיות] לחיוית[כ] || 24 והם] הם[ד] ||

---

13 איוב כ״ב כ״ח || 17 דב׳ ל׳ כ׳ ||

---

[1] Corrected according to ט.

CHAPTER 16

The Character of Old Men

[1] Old men,[a] those who have passed into the senior years of life, are of a tendency opposite to the character traits of the young—in respect, that is, of their love of jesting and merriment, sharpness of physical appetites, compassion for others, gullibility, swiftness to anger, boldness, love of honor and victory, extensiveness of hope, high-mindedness, the committing of unjust acts, and the rest. Such is the case because the old have lived[1] for a long time and their expectation of life is short; they have often been treacherously deceived and have often sinned themselves. They have a poor opinion of mankind, because they have in experience encountered the motives of treacherous deception and devious purpose, and because most acts affecting them turned out to be wholly evil or such as lead to evils.

[2] It is characteristic of the old not to be in any doubt about themselves; nor are they surprised by anything that comes upon them, inasmuch as it has repeatedly happened to them before; and since they have experienced everything, it is as if they hope for nothing. They do not worry about praise and blame, for they are intent upon the facts; moreover, they never **decree a thing** [Job 22:28] about any course, without a "perhaps" or a "maybe," because their expectation has so often proved false. That they are evil in some few of their characteristics is due to their pessimistic view[2] of everything—this because they have little faith—while that their trust is slight is due to their frequent experience. They neither love nor hate in excess[3] and will disclose their love and hatred only if coerced and constrained by necessity. Friend and foe, they maintain, look to them exactly alike—this owing to the numerous instances of treacherous deception and error that have befallen them in consequence of **the length of** their **days** [Deut. 30:20].

[3] They are mean of soul: disdainful of lofty things, they crave nothing save the means of sustaining life; and they are neither kindly, nor respectful of the world's great need in matters necessary for survival, an attitude which has become theirs solely in consequence of long experience. Thus, they are avaricious because they well understand that the gaining of possessions is difficult, and that, particularly during the years of old age, physical infirmity facilitates ruin.

[4] They "see what will be,"[4] in virtue of their experience of fortune; but they are cowardly and apprehensive owing to the coldness of their temperament—in contrast with young men, who are warm and fiery. They love life even when

1. Text: "been"; T, A, and Aristotle read "lived"; cf. iii.15.4 and n. 5, above.
2. So T, A, and M; C: "because they expect evil."
3. So T and M; C: ". . . hate excess."
4. A quotation of *Mishnah Ābhōth* 2:9—not in Todros.

a. Cf. T144 ff./A198 ff.; cf. *Rhet.* 2.13 (1389b ff.).

לחיות אף אצל סוף חייהם, לא להתעדן מהתאוות — לפי שסבות התאוות כבר
נעדרו זולת תאוות המאכל מבין שאר החושים· כי היא תמצא בהם הרבה, לפי
שהמאכל הכרחי להם, ויהיה שם ההכרח עם ההתעדנות — אמנם, יאהבו
החיים מצד עצמם לבד.

5 [5] וחבתם ואהבתם לבני אדם היא מפני המועיל, לא מפני הנאה, לפי שהם
אוהבים נפשותיהם· והמועיל הוא בהצטרף אל נפשו, והנאה הוא בערך אל
זולתו. ובייּשנותם הוא מועט, למה שיבחרו המועיל יותר מן הנאה, והבשת הוא
יראת הבצר הנאה· ולמה שהדברים שהם טוב גמור או שהוא על הרוב, הם
מעטי המציאה ויצטרך זמן ארוך אל הקנאתו, כאשר התבאר אליהם בנסיון.

10 [6] ואשר נשאר מחיי הישישים מעט, תמעט תוחלתם. ורוב מחיתם ועדונם
אמנם הוא בזכרונות, לא בתוחלת, בהפך מה שעליו הענין בבחורים· כי הזכרון
הוא בערך אל העובר, והישישים כבר עברו רוב חייהם; ולזה, הם טובי הראיה
והאומד במה שיהיה.

[7] וכעסם, מצד מעוט סבלנותם[2], הוא מהיר חד· אמנם הוא חלוש, מצד
15 חלשת חמימותם; והם יראי חטא להפסק תאוותיהם; וינזרו מדרישת היותר
משובח אל מה שהוא הכרחי ומועיל. וממדתם החמס, אבל במרמה ואונאה, לא
בקלונות כמו העניין בבחורים.

[8] והם סובלים הכאבים בנחת, לפי שהמתינות והנחת הם הפך הלצנות
אשר הם ממדות הנערים. והם רחמנים, אבל זה הוא מפני חלשתם ודמותם
20 קלות הפלת הרע במי שיחמלו עליו, לא מפני אהבתם לבני אדם, כרחמנות
הבחורים:

פרק י״ז

ממדות הגבירים, ר״ל, אשר הם בין הישישות והבחרות.

[1] ואולם אשר הם בתוקף החיים, שהם הגבירים אשר יקראם ארסטו׳ זקנים,
25 מדותיהם אמצעיות בין אלו המדות, והם מתרחקים מהקצוות. לכן הם יותר

2 [הרבה][ג] || 3 ההכרח] הכרח[ג] || 7 ובייּשנותם] ובייּשבותם[ג] |הוא] הו׳[ד] || 8–9 [או שהוא... זמן][ד] ||
11 בזכרונות] בזכרוננו[ג] || 13 במה] כמה[ג] || 14 סבלנותם[2] סבלותם[ג ד] || 15 חטא] חט׳[ד] |להפסק]
להפסיק[ד] |מדרישת] מדרושת[ג] || 17 העניין] ענין[ד] || 20 שיחמלו] שימחלו[ג] |כרחמנות] ברחמנות[ג] ||
22 פרק] פ׳[ג] || 24 ארסטו׳] ארסטו[ג] ||

---

[2] Corrected according to ט.

their own is nearly at an end, not in order to indulge the appetities—since the causes of the appetities have now vanished save, of remaining sensations, the appetite for food (which often persists because they must eat, and necessity here coincides with indulgence)—but simply because they love life as life.

[5] Their love and friendship for others is based on expediency, not honor, because they love themselves, and the expedient concerns oneself, the honorable another than oneself. Their sense of shame is exiguous, because they prefer the expedient to the honorable, while shame is a dread of being dishonorable; and because things that are altogether, or for the most part, good, are rare and take a long time to acquire, as experience has made clear to them.

[6] As the remaining portion of old men's lives is brief, their hope is slight. What most sustains and delights them consists of memories rather than of anticipation, in contrast to what is true of young men; for memory is of the past, and the greater part of old men's lives is already past. But it is for this reason that they excel in foreseeing and surmising what is to be.

[7] Since their tolerance is small, their anger is sudden and sharp, although it is feeble because their warmth is weak; they are fearers of sin, owing to the curtailment of their lusts; but they refrain from seeking the more praiseworthy course in favor of the necessary and the useful. It is within their character to commit wrong, but by cunning and deception rather than by openly disgraceful acts, as in the case of the young.

[8] They suffer injuries quietly, as composure and quiet are the contrary of the jesting[5] characteristic of the young. They feel pity, but this is because they are weak and are thinking of the ease with which evil has fallen upon the person whom they are pitying, not because they love mankind, as when young men feel pity.

CHAPTER 17

The Character of Men in Their Prime, That Is, Those between Old Age and Youth

[1] Now as for those who are in the prime of life, the vigorous men[1] whom Aristotle[a] calls middle-aged,[2] their traits of character are intermediate between

5. T's rendering of A's *hazl* (هزل). May the originally intended Arabic reading have been *haul* (هول) = "terror, alarm, dismay"?

1. JML's term (גְּבִירִים), not found in T.
2. T renders A's "middle-aged" (كهول) by the Hebrew זְקֵנִים = "elders"; JML while taking over זְקֵנִים from T, is careful to point out that the word here has the sense of גְּבִירִים.

a. T146 f./A201 f.; cf. *Rhet*. 2.14 (1390a).

ישרים· והם גוברים על מה שראוי, בעת הראוי ובשעור הראוי, מזולת שיסתכנו. והם לא יצדיקו בכל דבר, ולא יכזיבו בכל דבר, אבל יציירו הענינים כפי ישותם הנמשכת לטבע׳. והם מכוונים אל הנאה והמועיל יחד; ואינם אנשי הצדק׳ גמורה, ולא התלוצצות גמור· וכן בתאוה והגבור׳, רצוני, שהם יראי חטא עם גבורה; והבחורים גבורים תאוניים, והישישים רכי לבב יראי חטא. ובכלל, יש להם הממוצע בין התוספת והגרעון הנמצְאים בבחורים ובזקנים. ושנות הזקנה הם מל״ה שנים עד נ׳ שנה.

[2] וזה מה שרצינו אמרו ממדות הזמני׳ בזה המקום:

פרק י״ח

מהסימן וההמשל.

[1] הנה הגיע המקום, לפי מה שיעדנו, לדבר במיני ההקשה אשר יקח ההלצי; כי אלה גם כן אין ספק בם שהם משתפים לכל הסוגים הג׳, ר״ל, עצתיי קיומיי משפטי. ונאמ׳, כי לפי מה שיאמ׳ הפילוסוף בב׳ מההלצה, הם ב׳ סוגים: המשל וסמן· והסברה היא חלק מהסמן. וההמשל דומה לחפוש במלאכת הנצוח· והסמן דומה להקש.

[2] וההמשל, בזאת המלאכה הם ב׳ מינים. אחד, שיהיה לקוח מדברים כבר היו ונמצאו, כמו שעשה רב שקה; למה שכאשר רצה לבאר נצחון מלך אשור על יהודה וירושלם, הביא ראייה מהדברים שכבר היו, ר״ל, ממה שקרה לאומות האחרות, שלא יוכלו לעמוד לפני מלך אשור, ואמר: ״ההצל הצילו אלקי

1 ובשעור] וביעוד[ב] || 3 לטבע׳] לטבעיהם[ב] | הצדק׳] צדקה[ב] || 4 התלוצצות] ההתלוצצות[ד] | והגבור׳] וגבורה[ב] || 5 חטא] החטא[ב] || 6 בבחורים ובזקנים] בזקנים ובחורים[ב] || 7 נ׳] נ״[ב] || 9 פרק] פ״[ב] || 12 משתפים] משתתפים[ד] || 13 ונאמ׳] ובאמ׳[ב] | בב׳] בבי׳[ב] | ב׳] בי׳[ב] || 15 דומה להקש] דומה לך לבקש[ב] || 16 שיהיה] שיהיו[ב] || 17 רב שקה] רב שקא[ד] רבשקה[ת] || 18 לאומות] לאמת[ד] || 19 יוכלו] יכלו[ב] ||

those of the young and the old just considered, and they avoid the extremes of either. Therefore the middle-aged are more upright, and they venture forth courageously upon whatever they must, when and in the measure that they must, but without rashly exposing themselves to danger. They neither believe nor disbelieve everything, but depict things as they are in consequence of their nature. They are intent upon what is simultaneously honorable and expedient. They are neither exclusively earnest nor exclusively frivolous, and the same is true with respect to lust and courage; I mean that they are both sin-fearing and brave, while young men are brave but lustful, and the old are cowardly but sin-fearing. In general, theirs is the mean position between the excess and the deficiency found in young men and in the aged.[3] The years of maturity[4] are from thirty-five to fifty.

[2] This concludes what we intended to say in this place about the traits characteristic of the several stages of life.

CHAPTER 18

Enthymeme and Example

[1] We have now reached the proper place to discuss, in accordance with our promise, the kinds of logical proof which the speaker uses; for there is no doubt that these too are common to all three kinds of discourse, Deliberative, Epideictic, and Judicial. We say, then, following the statement of the Philosopher[a] in Book II of the *Rhetoric,* that there are two classes of these proofs, Example and Enthymeme, the Maxim being part of an Enthymeme. Example resembles induction in the art of Dialectic, while the Enthymeme resembles the syllogism.

[2] Example, in the art of Rhetoric, is of two kinds. One is drawn from previous events, like the one presented by Rab-shakeh.[1] Wishing to demonstrate that the king of Assyria would be victorious over Judah and Jerusalem, he brought evidence from previous events, that is, from what had befallen other nations, to the effect that the Judeans would be unable to withstand the king of Assyria. He said: **"Hath any of the gods of the nations ever delivered his land**

3. Here זְקֵנִים instead of יְשִׁישִׁים, as above.
4. Literally: "old age," "elderhood" (זִקְנָה).

1. Misspelled in C and treated as two words, not as in our edd. of B (2 Kings 18:17 ff.). M here spells correctly, but also treats the term as two words; so both M and C below, par. 8.

a. T153 ff./A211 ff.; cf. *Rhet.* 2.20 (1393ab).

הגוים״, וכו׳ ״איה אלקי חמת וארפד״, וכו׳ ״מי בכל אלקי הארצות״, וכו׳
[מל״ב י״ח ל״ג—ל״ה]. והנה באר מזה, לפי מחשבתו, המנע הצלת ירושלם גם
כן.

[3] והמין השני מן ההמשלים, שהמליץ ימציא המעשה ויבדאהו בדיאה; וזה
5 לפעמים היה הקדמה, ולפעמים מאמ׳ ארוך. והארוך, לפעמי׳ היה ידוע הכזב
אצל המדבר והשומע· כמו הבדיאה שעשה יותם על בעלי שכם ועל בית מלוא,
שהמליכו עליהם אבימלך, באמרו: ״הלוך הלכו העצים למשוח עליהם מלך,
ויאמרו לזית מלכה עלינו״, וכו׳ [שופ׳ ט׳ ח׳]· שרצה להוכיח באותה הבדיאה
שתצא אש מאבימלך ותאכל את בעלי שכם ואת בית מלוא [שם כ׳], כמו שאמ׳
10 בהמשל הבדוי ש״תצא אש מן האטד, ותאכל את ארזי הלבנון״ [שם ט״ו].
ולפעמים לא יהיה ידוע הכזב, כהרבה[1] מן החידות אשר יעשום בעלי ההנהגות.

[4] ושם ״הדמוי״ יותר מיוחד בהקדמה הבדויה אצל ארסטו· ואשר הוא
בדברים הנמצאים יקרא ״המשל״ סתם. ותועלת הדבור הבדוי שהוא יותר נקל
מהנמצא, לפי שיקשה להביא דמיון במאמ׳ מהדברים כבר עברו; ואמנם הדבור
15 הבדוי כבר יקל· וזה אמנם יהיה, כשהיה לאדם כח על לקיחת הדומה והמתיחס,
ומתחייבי הדברים והענינים ההווים מהם. ותועלת ההמשל הנמצא שהוא יותר
מספיק בסוג העצתי, שהקורות הנופלות בעתיד הם ברוב דומות אל העוברות.
והדמויים יותר מועילי׳ בשהם יותר נקלים, ובאשר האדם אפשר שישימם חזקי
הדמיון אל הענינים אשר בם הדבור. והענינים העוברים אשר יביאם בהמשל
20 לפעמי׳ לא יהיו חזקי הדמיון, אלא שהם כמו שנ׳ יותר חזקי ההספקה.

[5] ואמר בא׳ מההלצה, שהמאמרים אשר יהיה בם הקיום והבטול כמו שהם
במלאכת הנצוח ב׳ מיני׳: אחד מהם החפוש, ומה שיחשב בו שהוא חפוש·
והמין השני ההקש, ומה שיחשב בו שהוא הקש. ככה, המאמרים המקיימים
והמבטלי׳ לזאת המלאכה, אחד מהם דומה לחפוש, והוא ההמשל· והאחר[2]
25 דומה להקש, והוא הסימן. והסימן, אם כן, הוא ההקש ההלצי· וההמשל הוא
החפוש ההלצי. וההלציים, כאשר יבחן ענינם, יגלה שהם אמנם יפעלו כלל
האמותים אשר יהיו במאמ׳ בשני אלו המינים, ר״ל, אם בהמשל, ואם בסמן,

1 איה] איה[כ] || 2 מזה לפי מחשבתו] לפי זה מחשבתו[כ] || 4 ההמשלים] המשלים[ד] || 8 [ויאמרו לזית מלכה עלינו][ד] || 10 בהמשל] במשל[ד] || 11 כהרבה[1]] בהרבה[כד] || 12 ארסטו] ארסטו׳[ד] || 15 כשהיה] כשיהיה[ד] || 18 והדמויים] והדומיים[כ] |מועילי׳] מועלים[כ] || 19 בם ‹הדמיון›[כ] || 20 כמו שנ׳] כמה שנאמ׳[כ] || 21 והבטול] ויבטול[כ] || 22 מיני׳] מינין[כ] |אחד] א׳[ד] |ומה שיחשב] ושיחשב[ד] || 24 אחד] א׳[ד] |והאחר[2]] והאחד[כ] וא׳[ד] || 27 ואם] אם[ד] ||

[1] Corrected according to ט[g] (and א).

[2] Corrected according to ט.

out of the hand of the king of Assyria? Where are the gods of Hamath, and of Arpad? . . . Who are they among all the gods of the countries, that have delivered their country . . . ?" [2 Kings 18:33-35]. Thus, it was from these events that he believed he had shown that the deliverance of Jerusalem was impossible.[2]

[3] The second kind of Example consists in the invention and fabrication of a fictitious tale by the speaker. This may either constitute a premise or be a long statement. As for the long statement, both speaker and audience may be aware of its untruth, as in the case of the fiction Jotham devised against the men of Shechem and Beth-millo who had made Abimelech king over them: **"The trees went forth on a time to anoint a king over them; and they said to the olive tree: 'Reign thou over us,'"** etc. [Judg. 9:8].[3] By means of this fiction, Jotham wished to show that fire would **come out from Abimelech, and devour the men of Shechem, and Beth-millo** [9:20], just as, in the fictitious example, he had said that fire would **come out of the bramble and devour the cedars of Lebanon** [9:15]. Sometimes it will not be known that the statement is a fabricated untruth, as in the case of many of the ambiguous pronouncements made by politicians.

[4] "Comparison" is the more specialized term used by Aristotle for a fictitious premise, while one based on actual facts is simply called "Example." The advantage of a fiction is that it is easier to produce than fact, since it is difficult, in a particular discourse, to bring in an exact analogy from actual events of the past. A fiction, on the other hand, is quite easy to invent, though only when a man is capable of grasping the analogy and the relationship, and the logically necessary corollaries and inferences deriving from these. The advantage of the Example based on actual facts is that it is more persuasive in the Deliberative kind of discourse, for future events will in large part resemble those of the past. Comparisons are more useful in that they are easier to invent and in that it is possible for the speaker to make them resemble more closely the matters under discussion. Past circumstances introduced by the speaker as his Example may not be so closely analogous, but, as was said, they are more strongly persuasive.

[5] In Book I of the *Rhetoric,* the Philosopher[b] says that the arguments used in proof and disproof, as found in the art of Dialectic, are of two kinds; one is induction and apparent induction, and the second is the syllogism and the apparent syllogism. Likewise, of arguments that effect proof and disproof in the art of Rhetoric, one kind resembles induction and is the Example, and the other resembles the syllogism, and is the Enthymeme. The Enthymeme, then, is the rhetorical syllogism, while the Example is rhetorical induction. Careful examination of the practice of speakers reveals that all the proofs in a discourse are accomplished by means of these two forms of statement only, that is, either by means of an

2. Rab-shakeh's speech is discussed in greater detail in iv.9, and further cited in iv.58.5.
3. Cf. i.8.2.

b. T16 f./A18 f.; cf. *Rhet.* 1.2 (1356ab).

וזה, שהם יכונו ההדמות להקש ולחפוש. ואשר יפעלו מזה, אמנם יפעלוהו במה שהוא המשל באמת וסמן באמת, או במה שיחשב בו שהוא כן.

[6] וההקש בנצוח יותר בטוח מן החפוש, וההמשל בהלצה יותר מספיק מהסימן. משל הסימן מה שנא' בירמיהו: נבער כל אדם מדעת, הוביש כל צורף מפסל· כי שקר נסכו ולא רוח בם [י' י"ד]. ואלו עשינו הקש שלם, היה זה ענינו: "מכל אשר שקר נסכו, ראוי שיהיה נבער כל אדם מדעת· והפסל שקר נסכו· א"כ, מהפסל, ראוי שיהיה נבער כל אדם מדעת"; והנה השמיט הכתו' ההקדמה הגדולה, ולכן נקרא סמן, ר"ל, הקש בלתי שלם.

[7] וכן בישעיהו: שרשם כמק יהיה, ופרחם כאבק יעלה· כי מאסו את תורת י"י צבאות, כו' [ה' כ"ד]. הוא סמן גם כן; ולו היה הקש שלם, היה בתואר ככה: "כל המואס תורת ה' צבאות, שרשם כמק יהיה, ופרחם כאבק יעלה· וישראל מאסו את תורת י"י צבאות· א"כ, שרשם כמק יהיה", כו'. והנה בכאן ג"כ נשמטה הגדולה.

[8] ומשל ההמשל התבאר למעלה, מדברי רב שקה.

[9] גם ראוי שתדע שההבדל בין החפוש וההמשל הוא, שהחפוש הוא הקשה מכל הפרטים אל הכלל; כמי שיאמ' שאין אדם אחד שלא ידבר, למה שראובן מדבר, שמעון מדבר, לוי מדבר, וכן כל פרטי האדם מדברים· ויתחייב מזה שכל אדם ידבר; ולו[3] חסר פרטי אחד, ההקדמה הכוללת היתה שקרית. אמנם ההמשל, אפשר שתהיה הקשה מפרטי אחד לבד אל פרטי אחר; כאלו תאמ': "ראובן, מפני שעשה כך, קרה לו כך· וכן ג"כ שמעון, אם יעשה כמוהו, יקרה מה שקרה לו".

[10] ושאר מה שצריך לזה בארתי בקצורי לחכמת הדבר; וזה מספיק הנה בידיעת הסימן וההמשל:

1 וזה] מה[ד] || 3 בנצוח ‹הוא›[ד] | ‹וההמש'› וההמשל[ד] || 4 שנא'] שנאמ'[כ] | מדעת ‹וכו'›[ד] | 5–4 [הוביש... בם][ד] || 7 השמיט הכתו'] השמינו דכתו'[כ] || 8 נקרא] נקרא'[כ] || 10 בתואר] כתאר[כ] || 12–13 ג"כ נשמטה הגדולה] נשמטה הגדולה ג"כ[כ] || 14 מדברי] מדב'[ד] || 18 ולו[3]] ולא[כד] || 20 לו [כך][כ] ||

[3] Corrected text.

Example or by means of an Enthymeme, since it is the purpose of these to resemble syllogism and induction. Such proving as speakers do they accomplish only by means of genuine Example and genuine Enthymeme, or of what may be considered such.

[6] In Dialectic, the syllogism is more reliable than induction, but in Rhetoric Example is more persuasive than Enthymeme. The use of an Enthymeme is illustrated in a passage in Jeremiah: **Every man is brutish, without knowledge: every goldsmith is confounded by the idol: for the molten image thereof is falsehood, and there is no breath in them** [10:14].[4] Were we to give the complete syllogism, it would run as follows: ''As a result of anything whereof the molten image is falsehood, every man must be brutish, without knowledge; an idol is a thing whereof the molten image is falsehood; therefore, as a result of the idol, every man must be brutish, without knowledge.'' Scripture has here left out the major premise, and this is therefore called an Enthymeme, that is to say, an incomplete syllogism.

[7] Again, in Isaiah: **Their root shall be as rottenness, and their blossom shall go up as dust; because they have rejected the law of the Lord of hosts,** etc. [5:24]. This too is an Enthymeme; if it were a complete syllogism, it would take the following form: ''The root of all who reject the law of the Lord of hosts shall be as rottenness, and their blossom shall go up as the dust; the people of Israel have rejected the law of the Lord of hosts; therefore, their root shall be as rottenness, etc.'' Here, too, the major premise has been omitted.

[8] An instance of Example, drawn from the words of Rab-shakeh, was set forth above.[5]

[9] You must know also that the difference between induction and Example is that induction is an inference from all the individual particulars to the general principle. One may say, for instance, that there is no man who does not speak, since Reuben speaks, Simeon speaks, Levi speaks, and so, too, do all individual members of the class, Man, speak; hence it necessarily follows that every man will speak. But if even one particular is wanting, the general principle is fallacious. In the case of Example, on the other hand, there can be an inference from merely one particular to another particular; you might, for instance, say: This or that has happened to Reuben because he did such-and-such; and so too with Simeon—if he does the same as Reuben, what has happened to Reuben will happen to him.

[10] I have explained the remaining essentials of this subject in my Compendium of Logic;[6] but the foregoing constitutes, for present purposes, sufficient knowledge of the enthymeme and the example.

4. Translation based on KJV.
5. Par. 2 (and note 2).
6. A reference to JML's *Mikhlal Yōphī* (''Perfection of Beauty,'' [Ps. 50:27]), extant in manuscript in various libraries. See the Int., §2 and n. 17, §3 and n. 151.

פרק י״ט

מהסברה.

[1] הסברה היא גזרה נושאה ענינים כלליים, לא חלקיים· וזה, בענינים הנבחרים והמרוחקים, לא בענינים העיוניים· כאשר היתה הגזרה תולדת סמן והתחלה לסמן אחר, מזולת שיפורש ההקש המוליד אותה, ולא ההקדמה השנית אשר תעשה עמה חלק סמן, ולא התולדה המחוייבת ממנה. וזה שהגזר׳ הכללי׳ לא תמלט שתהיה אם התחלת סמן ואם תולדת סמן, או מה שיקבץ שני העניינים.

[2] וזאת היא אשר קראנוה ״סברה״ הנה; והמשל מאשר ירצה לדבר על לב חברו, לנחמו על עניו, ויאמר: ״לא ראיתי צדיק נעזב, וזרעו מבקש לחם״; כי זה כאלו אמר לו: ״אתה לא תעזב באופן תהיה נודד ללחם, כי לא ראיתי צדיק נעזב, וזרעו מבקש לחם״; והנה, היא התחלה לסמן. ואם היה הקש שלם, היה נעשה על זה התאר; ״אין שום צדיק, לפי מה שאחשב, נעזב וזרעו מבקש לחם· ואתה צדיק· א״כ, כו׳; והנה, השמיט בזה המקום הקטנה. אמנם, היא תולדה לסמן בזה האופן: ״לא ראיתי צדיק נעזב, וזרעו מבקש לחם, כי יודע י״י דרך צדיקים״.

[3] ואמר הפילוסוף שהסברה נחלקת אל ארבעה חלקים: החלק הראשון, הסברה אשר יקבלה השומע בזולת זרות, ר״ל, שתהיה מן הדברים המפרסמים אל רוב בני אדם; החלק השני[1], שתהיה מפורסמת אל המשכילים והחכמים שבהם; החלק השלשי, הסברה הזרה מצד מה; החלק הרביעי[2], אשר זרה ומסופקת הרבה. משל הראשון: אם יאמ׳ אומר, ״לפי מה שאחשוב, ולפי מה שאסבור, ראוי שיהיה האדם בריא״; משל השני: אם יאמ׳, ״יראה לי שאינו אהוב מי שלא יאהב תמיד״; משל השלישי: ״שאין ראוי שיקובל מאמ׳ מי

1 פרק] פ׳[ב] || 3 הסברה] והסברה[ב] || 5 והתחלה] והתחלת[ב] | מזולת] מ׳[ד] | שיפורש] שיפורט[ב] || השנית] השני׳[ד] | המחוייבת] מחוייב׳[ד] || 6–7 שהגזר׳ הכללי׳] שהגזירה הכללייתּ[ב] || 9 והמשל] ומשל[ד] | מאשר ירצה] במי שירצ׳[ד] || 11 אמר] אומ׳[ד] | [לו][ב] || 14 היא] הא׳[ב] || 15 נעזב וזרעו] וזרעו נעזב[ב] | י״י] ה׳[ב] || 17 שהסברה] שהסברא[ב] | ארבעה] ד׳[ד] | הראשון] הא׳[ד] || 19 החלק השני[1]] החלק השנית[ב] והב׳[ד] | מפורסמת] מפורסמ׳[ד] | והחכמים] וחכמי׳[ד] || 20 החלק השלשי] הג׳[ד] | החלק הרביעי[2]] החלק הרביעית[ב] הד׳[ד] || 21 ומסופקת] מסופ׳[ד] | הראשון] הא׳[ד] || 22 השני] הב׳[ד] | שאינו] שאינינו[ב] || 23 השלישי] הג׳[ד] | [מי] מה[ב] ||

9–10 רות ב׳ י״ג || 10 תה׳ ל״ז כ״ה || 11 איוב ט״ו כ״ג || 15–16 תה׳ א׳ ו׳ ||

[1] Corrected according to ט.

[2] Corrected text.

CHAPTER 19

Of the Maxim

[1] The Maxim[a] is a judgment the subject matter of which consists of generalizations, not of particular details—of generalizations on what practical courses should be preferred and which avoided, not generalizations of a theoretical sort. It is a Maxim when the judgment is the conclusion of an Enthymeme or the beginning of another Enthymeme, without explicit statement of the syllogism that generates it, or of the second premise conjoined with which it would function as part of an Enthymeme, or of the conclusion that necessarily follows from it. The generalized judgment, that is, cannot escape being either the beginning or the conclusion of an Ethymeme, or a combination of both.

[2] Such, then, is what we here term "Maxim."[1] Example: a man who, wishing to **speak to the heart** [Ruth 2:13] of his friend in order to comfort him for his poverty, says, **"I have not seen the righteous forsaken, nor his seed begging bread"** [Ps. 37:25]. Now this is as if he had said to his friend: "You will not be so forsaken as to become one that **wandereth abroad for bread** [Job 15:23], for **I have not seen the righteous forsaken, nor his seed begging bread**"; this judgment, then, is the beginning of an Enthymeme. If it were a complete syllogism, it would take the following form: "No righteous man, I believe, is forsaken, nor does his seed beg bread. You are a righteous man. Therefore," etc.; here, as we see, the minor premise has been omitted. The same judgment, however, might form the conclusion of an Enthymeme, as follows: **"I have not seen the righteous forsaken, nor his seed begging bread** [Ps. 37:25], **for the Lord regardeth the way of the righteous"** [Ps. 1:6].

[3] The Philosopher[b] says that the Maxim is divisible into four classes: (1) the Maxim which the hearer will accept as not paradoxical, I mean one of those sentiments which are self-evident to the majority of mankind; (2) the Maxim which is self-evident to the intelligent and the wise amongst men; (3) the Maxim which is in some respect a paradox; (4) the Maxim which is greatly paradoxical and open to doubt. An instance of the first: if one says, "As I think and believe, it behooves a man to be healthy." An instance of the second: if one says, "It seems to me that he is not beloved[2] who does not everlastingly love." An

1. The Hebrew word *s^e bhārā* (סְבָרָה: T's rendering of رأى), here = γνώμη, has many other meanings, the commonest of which is the approximate equivalent of Latin *opinio*—Cf. iv. 10.1 ff., where *māshāl* (מָשָׁל) is the term for the Figure, "Maxim."

2. So JML, following T, although the underlying Arabic word (محبا) might equally well have been read as the active, instead of as the passive, participle, and thus been translated "lover."

---

a. T154 ff./A215 ff.; cf. *Rhet*. 2.21 (1394a–1395b).

b. T155 f./A216 f.

שיהיה בתאר מה במה שיחשוב בו ויסבר״; משל הרביעי, אם יאמר: ״שסברתו
היא מהאדם, שלא ישים כעסו בלתי מת, אחר שהיה הוא מת״. וזה המין, ראוי
שתחוזק בסימן, בזה האופן, שיאמ׳: ״כי הכעס מן הדברים אשר הוא סבתם״.
[4] וכאשר היו הסברות מגונות נכריות, ראוי שיקדים לפניהם דבר המסיר
5 גנותם, כמי שיאמר: ״אני איני מקנא לאחד מבני אדם, ולא מזכיר עונות וסברות
בטלות, כי איני ראוי להוכיח ולתת מוסר השכל״.
[5] והמנהג בסברות, שתאמר בה תבה תורה עליה, כמו: ״לפי מה שיראה
לי״ או: ״לפי מה שאחשוב״· והנוהג מנהגם. גם כי היא תאות בישישים יותר,
למה שסברתם תשען על מה שבחנו ונסו מן הדברים. ואפשר שתעשנה הסברות
10 דרך דמיון וחקוי, כמי שיאמ׳: ״אני חושב שאבות יאכלו בוסר, ושני הבנים
תקהינה״. ולפעמים הסברה תענג הנפש ויכאיבה, למה שתסבול שני הדברים
יחד· כמי שיאמר: ״אל ירע בעיניך כי כבר הכרתי מדותיך״· כי זה המאמ׳ יסבול
הוכחה והגדלה.
[6] והדבור המדותיי, כשיעשה על צד הסברה, הוא יותר מועיל· כמי שיאמר:
15 ״אין לנו שנאהב בשעור מה שנשנא״· ר״ל, שהאהבה ראויה שתהיה יותר. וראוי
שיהיה מה שיליץ האדם בו בדברים המדותיים כפי מחשבת השומע, וכפי מה
שיכשר בעיניו מן המדה, ויהיה כמוס בו בכח· כי בזה יהיה המאמר לו יותר
מועיל, לפי שהוא ישים מה שבכח בנפשו מהרה אל הפעל. כמו שיראה האדם
ישיש פועל פעל נער, ויאמ׳ לו: ״זה בלתי נאה לישישים, אבל הנאות בם כך
20 וכך״· כי כשירד זה המאמר על מי שבנפשו מחשבת אותה המדה, התנועע
אליה.
[7] ותועלות הסברה: הא׳, ששכל ההמון לא יקיף בענינים הכלליים כי אם
בחלקיים· וכאשר נליץ להם הכללי באותן החלקיות אשר השיגו׳, שמחו
מהכללות אשר הקנינו להם· כי האנשים יאהבו בטבע ההקנאות.
25 [8] והב׳, כי לכל אדם ימצאו לו דברים יכספם, ודברים לא יכספם; וכאשר
נליץ אותו במה שלא יכספהו בכללי המשותף בינו ובין מה שיכספהו, ימהר
לקבול הכללי מפני צרכו אליו· ואלו לא הביאו קרוב, לא יקבלהו ולא תפול לו

1 במה] כמה[ב] | ויסבר] ויספריהו[ב] ויסברהו[ט] | הרביעי] הד׳[ד] | שסברתו] סברתו[ב] || 5 מקנא] מקצה[ב] |
מזכיר] מכביר[ד] || 6 בטלות] כלילות[ב] || 10 [יאכלו][ב] || 10–11 הבנים תקהינה] בנים תקהנה[ד] | שני]
ב׳[ב] || 13 והגדלה] הגדלה[ד] || 14 הסברה] הסברא[ב] || 19 [בם][ב] || 22 ותועלות] ותועלת[ב] | הא׳] האחד |
הכלליים] הכוללים[ד] || 23 השיגו׳] השיגום[ב] || 24 מהכללות] מהכלל[ד] || 25 והב׳] והשנית[ב] ||
26 המשותף] המשו׳[ד] | [ימהר][ב] ||

---

6 מש׳ א׳ ג׳ || 10–11 יח׳ י״ח ב׳ || 12 בר׳ כ״א י״ב ||

instance of the third: "It is not proper to accept the statement of anyone of the sort that he esteems and approves." An instance of the fourth: one says "that his opinion is based upon Man, who, since he is mortal, cannot render his anger immortal." This last variety should be strengthened by an Enthymeme, by some such remark as "that anger is among the things of which Man is the cause."

[4] When Maxims are discreditable or bizarre, it is proper to preface them with a word that obviates their discreditableness; for instance, one may say: "As for me, I neither envy any man, nor do I bring crimes and absurd opinions into recollection, for I am not one to admonish others and to administer **the discipline of wisdom**" [Prov. 1:3].

[5] It is customary, when using Maxims, to say some word to indicate that you are doing so—"as it seems to me" or "as I think," and the like. The Maxim, moreover, is best suited to older men, for one used by them will have the support of what they themselves have tested and tried. And Maxims can be used as a way to exemplify and to illustrate; for instance, one may say: "I think that **the fathers have eaten sour grapes and the children's teeth are set on edge**" [Ezek. 18:2]. Again, the Maxim may sometimes afford the soul both pleasure and pain, for the soul can sustain both sensations at the same time; one may, for instance, say: "**Let it not be grievous in your sight** [Gen. 21:12] that I have come to know your ways," for such a statement can imply both rebuke and high esteem.

[6] A moral utterance, if couched in the form of a Maxim, is more useful; for instance, one may say: "We ought not to love in the same measure as we hate"; that is to say, love should be greater than hate. The subject matter of a speaker's moral pronouncements should be adapted to the ideals of the hearer, and to the ethical principles which he approves and which are potential within him; the discourse will thus be more useful to him, since it will quickly make actual that which is potential in his soul. For instance, one may see an old man acting the part of a youth, and say to him: "This is unseemly for aged men, but what is seemly in their case is thus-and-thus"; for when a statement of this sort is directed at one in whose soul there is the idea of such moral conduct, he is set in motion toward it.

[7] Of the Maxim's several advantages, the first is this: that the mind of the masses cannot encompass universals except by means of particulars, and so, when we speak of the general in terms of the particulars of which they have a grasp, they rejoice in the generalization we have enabled them to acquire; for men naturally love to make such acquisitions.

[8] Second, there are certain things that every man feels he needs, and certain things that he does not; so when we speak to a hearer of what he does not feel he needs in terms of the universal shared both by this and by what he does feel he needs, he will quickly accept the universal because of his need; whereas if the speaker does not make it seem pertinent,[3] the hearer will not accept it, and will

3. Literally: "... does not bring it close." T's rendering of قريبا —undoubtedly the reading of the Arabic text before him—by its Hebrew root-congener קרוב ("close") has here misled JML,

בו הספקה. והמשל: מי שיש לו בנים כחשים עבריינים, או שכנים רעים, יקבל[3]
מאמ׳ האומ׳ ש״אין בעולם רע מהשכנים או מהבנים״.

[9] הג׳, מה שירוץ המנהג בו מהשמטת ההקש המקיים אותה להראותה,
ושהוא ממה שיוכל להביאו כל אחד מאצל עצמו· וישים השומע בצד שיצייר
5 בנפשו שהוא מבעלי ההכרה והידיעה בהקשו, ויהיה סבה אל שיצדיקהו וימשך
לו.

[10] והד׳, שהאדם, כשהולץ בדבר מה, פעמי׳ ידחה המאמ׳ בזה בתשובתו,
לראותו שהוא מגונה עליו שיכנע למאמ׳ זולתו, למה שהוטבעו עליו הנפשות
מהעצום והמרי· וכאשר הולץ בכללי בערך אל הענין ההוא החלקיי, היה אפשר
10 שלא יסתור המאמ׳ ויקבלהו, אחר שנעלם ממנו אותו הדבר שהיה מכוון
המליץ.

[11] והה׳, היותר עקרי[4] ויותר מעולה, שהסברה תשים הדבור המדותיי; והיה
זה כן, שהסברה היא גזירה כללית בעניינים יובחרו או ירוחקו· והגזירה הכללית
בעניינים אשר יכספם האדם תניעהו אל שיתלבש במדת מי שבחר אותם
15 העניני׳ עצמם, או ירחיקם.

ולכן, היתה הסברה ערבה אצל השומע ואצל המליץ:

20

פרק כ׳

מהמקומות· וקודם, מהמקימים.

[1] ויען המקומות הם יסודות הסימנים — כי אמנם אפשר לנו שנמצא
25 הקדמות הסימנים בדרך מלאכותי בידיעת המקומות, כאשר התבאר בב׳
מההלצה — ראוי שנאמ׳ מהם בזה המקום. ולמה שהיה המקום אם מקיים,

1 יקבל[3]] יקבלו^כד^ יקובל^טg^ || 3 הג׳] השלישי^כ^ || 4 להביאו] להבאיו^ד^ || בנפשו] נפשו^ד^ | סבה] סבת^ד^ || 7 והד׳] והרביעית^כ^ | שהאדם]^ד^ | מה]^ד^ | פעמי׳] פעמי^ד^ | בתשובתו] בתשובות^כ^ || 8 שהוא] שהו^ד^ | שיכנע] שיכני^ד^ | למאמ׳] לאמר^כ^ || 12 והה׳] והחמשית^כ^ | עקרי[4]] עקר^כד^ | המדותיי] מדותיי^ט^ || 13 כללית] כללי^ד^ || 14 שיתלבש] שילבש^כ^ || 17 פרק] פ׳^כ^ || 21 שהיה] שיהיה^כ^ | אם מקיים]^כ^ ||

1 ישׁ׳ ל׳ ט׳ ||

[3] Corrected according to ^ab^ט.
[4] Corrected according to ט.

not be convinced by it. For instance, one that has **lying children** [Isa. 30:9]—transgressors—or wicked neighbors, will accept the statement of a speaker who says: "Nothing in the world is worse than neighbors or children."

[9] Third, since it is normal to suppress the syllogism which, were it to appear, would prove the Maxim, and since the Maxim is thus something that anyone on his own part would be able to adduce, it disposes the hearer to imagine himself as one of the discerning who know the syllogism involved, and it constitutes a reason for him to accept it as true and to follow it.

[10] Fourth, a man, when addressed on some subject, will in reply sometimes reject what has been said, because, owing to the native tendency of souls to be contentious and perverse, he may consider it discreditable submissively to accept the statement of somebody else; but when addressed on that specific subject in generalizations, he will possibly not contradict the statement, but accept it, since he may have failed to discern the import of the speaker's remarks.

[11] Fifth, the most important and best advantage is that the Maxim gives the speech moral character. This is because the Maxim is a generalized judgment about circumstances to be preferred or avoided; and such a generalized judgment about the circumstances which a man would find desirable will move the hearer to assume the moral attitude of one who has preferred or avoided these same circumstances.

Hearer and speaker alike, therefore, find the Maxim pleasing.

CHAPTER 20

Of Topics; and First, of the Demonstrative

[1] Because topics are fundamental to Enthymemes—for only through knowledge of topics is it possible for us artistically to invent the artificial premises of Enthymemes as has been explained in Book II of [Aristotle's][a] *Rhetoric*—we must discuss them here. And since a topic is either demonstrative—one which

---

who added the negative in an attempt to make sense of T. In A, however, the word not only means "nearby, close at hand," but also "simple, easily understood": ". . . and if he [the speaker] introduces it [what the hearer is not in need of] *simply* [i.e., as a "particular," not as a "universal"] he [the hearer] will not accept it. . . ." T's Hebrew, as noted, presupposes an Arabic reading اتا به قريبًا , which differs slightly from that of both the Florence and the Leiden MSS. The former reads اتا به جزئيا (". . . introduced it as a particular"), the latter اوتى به جزئيا (". . . if it is introduced as a particular").

---

a. T162 ff./A225 ff.; cf. *Rhet*. 2.22 ff. (1395b ff.).

והוא אשר יוליד מציאות הענין מההקדמות המודות· ואם מוכיח, והוא אשר יולידהו מההקדמות הנכחשות· גם כי יפול בהם הטעות לפעמים· הנה ראוי לנו שנזכור מין מין מאלה בפני עצמו.

[2] ונתחיל מהמקימים, ונאמר שאחד מהמקומות המקימים הוא הלקוח מההפכים. והמשל, שאם היתה היראת חטא מועילה, התחייב מזה שהתאוה, שהיא הפכה, תהיה מזיק· ואם היתה המלחמה עלת הרעות הקורות, הנה השלום ראוי שיתקן זה ויסלקיהו; וזה, שהוא מבואר שמה שיתחייב אל אחד מההפכים הוא הפך מה שהתחייב אל האחר.

[3] הב׳, שהדברים הנגזרים, חיובם אחד; כמו שנאמר היראת חטא טובה· א״כ, הירא חטא טוב.

[4] הג׳, מהמצטרפי׳: שאם היה הפעל נעים, הנה ההפעלות ג״כ נעים; והמשל, אם המכר נעימות, הנה ההקנאה נעימות.

[5] הד׳, מן הפחות והיתר; כמי שיאמ׳: ״הכה אביו· ואם כן, יכה קרוביו״. כי כשהיה פחות המציאות נמצא, הנה רב המציאות נמצא בהכרח. ואולם בבטול, הוא הפך זה, כי מי שלא יכה הקרובים, יותר ראוי שלא יכה האב.

[6] והה׳, שיסתיר דברי המליץ ממה שפעלו כבר, או פועלהו· או ממה שלא יפעלהו, גם אינו פועלו. — ומהם, שתטריח מי ששאל אותך דברים קשים עליך, או דבר מה, שיפעל הוא מה שיקשה עליו, או לא יוכל לעשותו. — ומהם, שתשאל לזולתך שיפעל מה שתדע שהוא לא יוכל לעשותו, ומה שאיננו לו, כדי שיחשב בך שאתה ממי שאצלו אותו הדבר. — ומהם, שתתן למום על זולתך דבר תדעהו לעצמך, כדי שיחשב שאשר תתנהו מום לזולתך איננו לך; וכמו כן, שתחייב לזולתך זכות אינו בך, כדי שיחשב שהוא בך. — ומהם, הרדפת תוספת התנאים במאמר, עד שישוב טענה· או חסרון התנאים במאמר, עד שישוב טענה. — וממה שיעשה בו תוכחת אל המתרעם: שיבאר מי שעליו התערומת[1] שהוא השתוה לו ברע, ושאינו יותר מעולה ממנו.

[7] והמקום הו׳ לקוח מהגדר או מהרושם, או מה שיחשב בו שהוא גדר או רושם· או המרת שם מקום שם, או הודעת הדבר בסוגו.

[8] והז׳ הוא מקום מהחלוקה, כמו שיאמר אומ׳ ש״מי שיחמוס, יחמוס לאחד

1 יוליד] יוליך[כ] |מההקדמות] מהקדמות[ד] |[והוא][ד] ||2 מההקדמות] מהקדמות[ד] ||3 מאלה] מאילו[כ] || 5 היתה] היה[כ] ||6 שהיא] היא[כ] ||7 ויסלקיהו] ויסקלהו[ד] ||8 הוא] היא[ד] ||9 הב׳] השנית[כ] ||10 חטא] חט[ד] ||11 ההפעלות] ההתפעלות[ד] ||13 הד׳] הרביעית[כ] |ואם כן] א״כ[כ] ||14 כשהיה] כשיהיה[ד] || 16 והה׳] והחמשית[כ] ||17 דברים] בדברים[ד] ||19 כדי] כדיי[כ] ||21 איננו] אינינו[ד] ||22 שיחשב] שתחשב[כ] ||26 הו׳] הששי[כ] ||28 והז׳] והשביעית[כ] |כמו] כגון[ד] |לאחד] לא[ד] |

[1] *Sic*, for תרעומת.

gives rise to an inference from affirmed premises that a proposition is so; or is refutative—one which gives rise to the inference from premises that have been denied—and because both may be subject to error, we must treat each of these kinds of topics separately.

[2] Beginning, then, with the demonstrative kind, we say that one such topic is drawn from opposites. If, for instance, fear of sin is beneficial, it necessarily follows that lust, which is its opposite, is harmful; and if war is the cause of our present evils, peace should correct and relieve this condition. For clearly, the necessary consequence of one of a pair of opposites is the contrary of the necessary consequence of the other.

[3] The second demonstrative topic: that etymologically related terms take the same predicate; if, for example, it is said that fear of sin is good, then the fearer of sin is good.

[4] The third topic is derived from correlative terms: if a certain act is delightful, the corresponding act is also delightful. For example, if the selling is a delight, then the buying is a delight.

[5] The fourth is derived from the less *vis-à-vis* the more; for example, one may say: "He has struck his father; therefore, he will strike his kinsmen." For if the less frequent is found to be true, then the more common is necessarily also true. But in disproving, this is reversed, for one who does not strike his kinsmen is even more apt to refrain from striking his father.

[6] The fifth: to show that the words of the speaker are contradicted by what he has previously done or is doing, or by what he would not do and is not now doing.

(1) An instance of this topic: If someone has asked you difficult questions, or made some oppressive demand, challenge him himself to do something which is difficult for him, or which he will be unable to do.

(2) Another: to demand that somebody else do what you know he cannot do, or ask him for something which he does not have, so that you may be regarded as one to whom such a thing is available.

(3) Another: project upon somebody else a fault that you know you yourself possess, so that it may be thought that you are free of the fault you have ascribed to him; and similarly, attribute to somebody else a merit that you do not possess, so that it may be thought to be yours.

(4) Another: to attach so many—or so few—conditions to a statement that it becomes a mere pretext.

(5) And a topic wherewith to rebuke a plaintiff: when the defendant shows that the plaintiff is his peer in evil and no more virtuous than himself.

[7] The sixth topic is derived from a definition or impression, or what is thought to be a definition or impression; or consists of substituting one term for another, or of characterizing something by its class.

[8] The seventh is a topic derived from logical division, as when one says: "A

משלשה"· ויבאר שאי אפשר שיהיה אחד מהם.

[9] והח' מהחפוש, ר"ל, בלתי שלם, כמי שיאמ': "פלו' החזיק בדת אלקיו, והתמידה ממשלתו, ותכון מלכותו".

[10] הט', שנשפוט בדבר מה מפני שכבר שפט בו מי שכבר קדם באותו הדבר בעינו או בדומהו· וכל שכן, אם היה נעשה על יד כל ההמון, והחכמים עמם או רובם, והיה אותו המשפט תמידי. וככה כאשר שפטו בו מי[2] שיחשב בהם שהם לא ישפטו בתהפוכות בהפך האמת· או בהפך הטוב· או בהפך המועיל· או בהפך היושר· כמו הבנים עם האבות והמלמד.

[11] הי' בחלוקת הנשוא, בבטול המצא הנשוא לנושא· כמו שיאמר: "איך יהיה פלו' חייב מלקות? אי זו שבועה נשבע, או אי זה חק חלף, מהדברים שהעונש בהם מלקות?"

[12] המקום הי"א, שנעיין בכל מה שיתחייב לענין, מטוב ועד רע, כדי שיבחן אם הוא טוב או לא כפי המתחייבים, וכל שכן המתחייבים המתהפכים; כאלו נאמר: "אם טוב למתלמד לקחת מוסר השכל, והנה המתחייב אליו מן הטוב שיהיה חכם, ושיהיה נושא חן ושכל טוב בעיני ה' ואדם· והמתחייב אליו מן הרע שיהיה מקונא· והנה נבחר, כשראוי, שיקח מוסר השכל, כי הטוב גובר עליו".

[13] המקום הי"ב, שנעשה המקום הנז' בהפכים לבד, כמי שיאמ': "אם אדברה, הנני מדבר אם אמת ואם כזב; אם אדבר כזב, ישנאני האל· ואם אדבר אמת, ישנאוני בני אדם".

[14] המקום הי"ג כשיהיה ענין מה יודו בו כל בני אדם בנגלה ובלשון, ובהפכו יודו בו כל בני אדם במשכיות הסתר· כי ההלצי אפשר שיתן הספקה, בדברים כאלה, בדבר והפכו, והוא תחבולה ופלא. המשל, שמי שיכוון להזהיר על הרחקת היין, יאמר שהיין אסור, כי שקץ הוא ומפתח הפשעים· כי זה, בנגלה

1 משלשה] מג"[ד] | אחד] א'[ד] || 2 והח'] והשמינית[כ] | בדת] בידו[כ] || 3 והתמידה] והתמיד'[ד] || 4 הט'] התשיעית[כ] || 5 וכל שכן] וכ"ש[כ] || 6 תמידי] תמידיי[כ] | מי[2]] ממי[כד] || 7 בתהפוכות <או>[ד] || 9 הי'] העשירי[כ] | כמו] כגון[ד] || 12 הי"א] האחד עשר[כ] || 13 לא] לאו[כ] | וכל שכן] וכ"ש[כ] || 14 המתחייב] התחייב[ד] || 18 הי"ב] השנים עשר[כ] | בהפכים] ההפכיים[כ] || 19 אדברה] אדרבה[כ] || 21 המקום הי"ג] המקם שלשה עשר[כ] || 22 כל בני אדם] בני כל אדם[כ] | הסתר] בסתר[כ] | ההלצי] ההלציי[כ] || 23 כאלה] האלה[כ] || 24 [היין][כ] ||

3 מל"א ב' י"ב || 14 מש' א' ג' || 15 מש' ג' ד' || 16 מש' א' ג' ||

[2] Corrected according to ט.

malefactor does wrong from one of three motives,'' and then goes on to show that none of these could here be the case.

[9] The eighth is derived from induction, that is, from an incomplete induction,[1] as in the statement: ''King So-and-so held fast to his religion, and so his dominion persisted **and his kingdom was established** [1 Kings 2:12].''

[10] The ninth: we may make a certain judgment because this was made by a previous body in regard to the same or a like matter; and especially if that judgment was made by the entire body politic, including all, or most of, the wise, and if that judgment proved lasting. The same applies when the judgment is that of persons thought unlikely to make warped judgments, judgments contrary to the truth, to the good, the useful, or the just; like judgments of children made by their parents or their teacher.

[11] The tenth consists in partitioning the predicate when denying the pertinence to the subject of what has been predicated; for example, to say: ''How can so-and-so be held liable to lashes? What sort of 'vain oath' did he swear,[2] which statute did he pass by, of the matters punishable by scourging?''[3]

[12] The eleventh topic: we study all the inevitable consequences, both good and bad, of a proposal, in order to examine whether, by the criterion of the consequences entailed, and especially of those that are contradictory, the proposal is or is not good. For example, we may say: ''Assuming it to be good for a student **to receive the discipline of wisdom** [Prov. 1:3], then the good that will inevitably ensue for him is that he will become wise and obtain **grace and good favor in the sight of the Lord and of man** [3:4];[4] the evil that must inevitably ensue for him is that he will be envied; therefore, as we should, we prefer that the student **receive the discipline of wisdom** [1:3], because the good preponderates.''

[13] The twelfth topic: to use only contrary alternatives in forming the topic just mentioned, like saying: ''Were I to speak, I must speak either truth or falsehood. Should I speak falsehood, God would hate me; and if I speak truth, men will hate me.''

[14] It is the thirteenth topic when the proposition is one that all men[5] outwardly, with lip service, profess, but whose opposite they all acknowledge in their secret thoughts; because a speaker can, in such cases, argue persuasively either in favor of a given course or of its opposite—a debater's trick and a clever paradox. For instance, one whose purpose is to urge abstention from wine may

1. Hence, according to iii.18.9 above, from ''Example.''

2. Cf. *Mishnah Sh^ebhū'ōth* 3:7 ff.; Deut. 25:1 ff.; these examples differ from those of T/A, except for ''. . . which statute did he pass by. . . .''

3. For a list of these, see *Mishnah Makkōth* 3:1 ff.; for the ''forty stripes save one'' = ''lashes,'' ''scourging,'' see *Mak.* 3:10, and Deut. 25:2–3.

4. Inexact citation by JML; the word ''obtain'' that precedes the citation is a reminiscence of Esth. 3:15.

5. *Sic* JML; T: ''all''; A: ''that is professed outwardly and with lip service (literally: with the tongue).''

ובנאה, יודו בני אדם, ר״ל, הישמעאלים; ויאמר אחר שהוא יועיל לאיש בבריאותו, וייטיב תכונתו ושכלו· כי זה יודו בו בני אדם בסתר, ובמשכיות לבב.

[15] המקום הי״ד מורכב משני מקומות ממקומות ההקבלה· אחד משניהם, הרכבת ההפכים· והאחר, הפוך הקדמות ההפכים. וזה כמי שהוכח בעבודת בנו, גדול, שהוא אמר למוכיחים: ״אם אתם תשימו הגדולים מהנערים בכלל אנשים, הנה כבר תחייבו שהקטנים מהאנשים נערים״; כי אמרנו ״הנער הגדול איש״ הפך אמרנו ״האיש הקטן נער״· והאיש והנער מקבילים, וכמו כן הגדול והקטן. ומשל אחר ממי שיאמר: ״אם אתם לא תשימו המבקרים אתכם מתועבי׳ ומרוחקים כאשר עשו נבלות, הנה לא תקרבו ליראי החטא ולא תבקרום.״

[16] ומקום הט״ו: שני המקבילים, יחוייב להם דבר אחד בעינו. כמו שנאמ׳ ש״הנפש היא עצם שכלי, ותמות· או שאינה עצם שכלי, ולא תמות״; שאשר יחוייב מאלו השנים מקבילים הוא ענין אחד, ר״ל, שהנפש אינה נפש.

[17] והי״ו מועיל בלקיחת ההקדמות המתהפכות, והוא: שבכאן, תכונות לדברים, ישיגו אותם התכונות דברים מתהפכים· וכאשר לוקחו אותם התכונות גבולים אמצעיים, היה אפשר לתת בם הספקה בדבר והפכו. וזה המקום מתחלף לשאר המתהפכים, בשאלו[3] התכונות אינם מתהפכות. משל זה, שיאמ׳ אומר: ״אם אני אפחד, לא אהרוג, אבל אברח, שבבריחה אנצל· וכאשר אהיה בטוח, אהרוג״; או יאמ׳: ״כאשר אפחד, אהרוג, כי אני בהריגה אנצל· וכאשר אהיה בטוח, לא אצטרך אל ההריגה״. והמשל בזה, נעשה בו הדברים אשר יחוייבו מהם תכליות שונות· והוא, שנעיין בדברי׳ אשר כשהיו יסבלו ב׳ תכליות מתחלפות, או תכליות רבות· כי אנו, כשלקחנו אותם הדברים גבולים אמצעיים, היה אפשר לנו שנספיק בם בדבר וחלופו. כמו שיאמ׳ אומ׳, בדבר

2 וייטיב] ייטיב || 3 הי״ד] הארבעה עשר | משני] מב׳[ד] | ממקומות] וממקומות[ד] || 5 אמר] אומר[ד] ||
7 [נער][כ] || 11 הט״ו] החמשה עשר[כ] | כמו שנאמ׳] כשנומ׳[ד] || 12 [שכלי] ותמות[ד] || 13 השנים] הב׳[ד] ||
14 והי״ו] והששה עשר[כ] | ההקדמות] המקדמות[ד] | המתהפכות] ומתהפכות[כ] || 15 ישיגו] ישיבו[ד] ||
16 מתחלף] המתחלף[כ] || 17 בשאלו[3]] כשאלו[כד] | <אם> שיאמ׳[כ] || 18 שבבריחה] שבברחה[כ] ||
21 כשהיו] כשיהיו[ד] | ב׳] שני[כ] שתי[ט] || 22 גבולים] גדולים[כ] || 23 [לנו][כ] ||

2 תה׳ ע״ג ז׳ ||

[3] Corrected according to ט.

say that wine is forbidden as being an abomination, a key to sinful deeds; for this is something that men—specifically Muslims[6]—will openly and nobly profess. But another may say that wine is beneficial to a man's health, improving his disposition and his mind; for this is acknowledged by men secretly, and in **the imaginations of their heart** [Ps. 73:7].

[15] The fourteenth is a composite of two of the topics of parallelism, one of which is made up of contraries, while the other is the reverse of the premises of the contraries. An instance is the statement made to his critics by one who was under censure over the liability to service of his son, a tall boy: "If you count the tall boys as men, then you must certainly affirm that the short men are boys"; for to say "a tall boy is a man" is the reverse of saying "a short man is a boy," while "man" and "boy," and so too "tall" and "short," are parallel contraries. Another instance is furnished by one who says: "If you do not consider your visitors abominable and to be avoided when they have committed disgraceful deeds, then you should not consort with those who fear sin nor should you visit them."

[16] The fifteenth: the two parallel contraries have one and the same logically inevitable consequence. An example is the statement: "The soul is either an intelligent substance that is mortal, or else it is an unintelligent substance that is immortal"; for the logical consequence of these two parallel contraries is the same, to wit, that soul is not soul.[7]

[17] The sixteenth is useful in the adoption of contrasting premises. Here, circumstances which are themselves contraries may impinge upon identical mental and emotional states; and when these same states are adopted as middle terms, it is possible by their means to argue persuasively in favor either of a given course or of its contrary. This topic differs from the others that involve contraries in that these states are themselves not contraries. For example, one might say either this: "If I felt afraid, I would not fight,[8] but would flee, since by fleeing I would save myself; but since I feel safe, I will fight"; or he might say this: "Being afraid, I would fight, for by fighting I might save myself; but since I feel safe, I do not need to fight." This topic is exemplified when the circumstances are such as have disparate aims as their consequences. We should, that is, notice circumstances which, having come to pass, tolerate two contrary aims, or many contrary aims; for should we adopt those circumstances as middle terms, we could, by their means, argue persuasively in favor either of a given course or of its contrary. For instance, one person may say of something that a man has

6. JML's note, not in T: A is, of course, the author of the example. "Muslims" is literally "Ishmaelites" in the Hebrew.

7. JML has here deliberately altered the example given in T/A (167/232): " 'God is a created being and immortal, or not a created being and mortal'; for the logical consequence of these parallel contraries is the same, namely, that God is not God." The alteration may have been actuated by fear lest T/A's example be deemed religiously offensive.

8. T, followed by JML: "slay"; A: "fight." T has translated the Arabic verb in the sense it bears in the base stem, but in the stem Averroes uses here (III) it means "fight."

נתנו האדם לזולתו: ״אמנם נתת אותו אליו להכלימו ולהבאישו, כי גחלים אתה חותה על ראשו״; ויאמר אחר שהמתנה מתנת אוהב נאמנה. והוא מקום יעשה בכל הסוגים השלשה.

[18] והי״ז כולל על המריבים והמיעצים, והוא, שנעיין בדברים אשר יכסוף בם האדם או לא· והענינים אשר מפניהם יעשו הדברים כאשר נמצאו, או לא יעשו כשנעדרו. ומזה, שאם היה הענין אפשר, והיה נקל ומועיל לו ולאוהבים, ומזיק לשונאים· או בלתי מזיק, או היה הנזק פחות מהתועלת· הנה ראוי שיעשו אלה ודומיהן. אמנם, אשר יחשוך מהם האדם, או יחדל, הם הפכי אלה. ומאלה יתרעמו המתרעמים וישיבו המשיבים: אם התרעומת, הנה מאשר יכספם האדם· ואם ההתנצלות, מאשר יחשוך מהם.

[19] וראוי שתהיינה ההקדמות אשר יעשו בכאן מהדברים המקובלים בתחלת הדעת, ותפול בם ההספקה בקרוב ובקלות. ומשל מה שתפול בו ההספקה בקרוב ובקלות, מה שאמרו קצת הקדמונים: ״כי הנימוסים יצטרכו אל נימוס יחזקם, כמו שיצטרך הדג אשר בים אל המלח, עם היות הים מלוח· וכמו שיצטרכו הזתים אל שמן הזית, ואם בם שמן הזית.״ כי זה, ואם היה בלתי מספיק, הנה כבר תפול ההספקה בו בקרוב כאשר נוסף אל המלח, כשנרצה השארותו ושמירתו ושיושם בו טעם אחד· וכן יתוסף בזתים כאשר ירצה השארתום ושנוי טעמם, ר״ל, שיושם שמן הזית בם:

1 נתת] נתן[ד] || 3 השלשה] הג׳[ד] || 4 והי״ז] והשבעה עשר[כ] | המריבים] המדינים[ד] || 10 ואם] וא׳[ד] | מאשר] אשר[כ] || 12 בתחלת] בתחלה[ד] | [בם][ד] || אחד] אחר[ט] ||

1–2 מש׳ כ״ה כ״ב ||

presented to another: "You gave it to him only in order to humiliate him and bring him into bad odor, **for thou wilt heap coals of fire upon his head**" [Prov. 25:21];[9] but another person may say that it was the sincere gift of a friend.[10] This topic may be used in all three Kinds of Cause.

[18] The seventeenth topic, common both to litigants and to deliberative orators, consists in examining what a man holds to be desirable or undesirable; and the circumstances because of which, if they obtain, acts will be committed, or, if wanting, not committed. Hence, if the act is possible, easy, and advantageous, to the man and his friends, while hurtful to his enemies—or if the act is not injurious to him, or its harm is outweighed by its advantage—then it must be that these and the like acts will be carried out. On the other hand, the conditions and circumstances which deter a man from acting, or because of which he would forbear to act, are the contraries of these incentives. Plaintiffs' charges and respondents' replies are based on such incentives and deterrents: in the case of the prosecution, upon what the accused holds to be desirable, in the case of the defense, upon the considerations which would deter him.

[19] The premises to be employed in this connection should derive from things that are *a priori* acceptable and that can readily and easily be made to satisfy. An example of what can readily and easily be made satisfying is found in the statement of certain ancients: "Customary norms need a law to strengthen them, just as a fish that was in the sea needs salt, notwithstanding the fact that the sea is salty, and just as olives need olive oil, although they contain olive oil."[11] For the fish, if unsatisfying, can quite readily be made satisfying as soon as more salt is added, should we wish to leave it over and preserve it, and fix its original flavor; and the olives may likewise be supplemented—have olive oil put into them—should it be wished to leave them over and to renew their flavor.

9. The biblical context deals with gifts to an enemy. This illustration is also used (including the quotation from Proverbs) in the corresponding passage in T, but is, of course, not in A.

10. Syllogistically: *Favoring a given course* (A)
"If I give him a gift, I will humiliate him;
I will give him a gift (middle term);
∴ I will humiliate him" (consequence or aim).
Favoring a contrary course (B)
"If I give him a gift, I will be his friend;
I will give him a gift (same middle term as in A);
∴ I will be his friend" (consequence or aim).

11. The ultimate source of the quotation is Androcles of Pitthus, according to *Rhet.* 2.23.22 (1400a).

פרק כ״א

ממקומות התוכחת.

[1] אמנם מקומות התוכחת, מהם, שיעיינו בני האדם בטובות ורעות אשר בהם יזכור הבעל ריב בשבח או הגנות ממה שהוא חוץ מאותו הענין אשר בו המאמ׳· וזה, מה שהיה מהם הגדת חדשות אצל בני אדם ומרגלא בפומהו, או היו מוכנים להרגילו בפיהם ואם לא הגידו בו עדיין· ר״ל, מפעולות בעלי הריב ומאמריהם ההווים והעוברים. ויעשו תוכחת בעלי הריב בזה, אצל מה שיחייבו אותם ענין מה; כמו שיאמר אדם: ״אתם, הנה לא יתן אחד מכם דבר כלל· ואולם אני, הנני כבר נתתי להרבה מכם.״ ובכלל, הנה יהיה העיון בכאן בכל מה שיזכרוהו המריבים יחד, ממה שהוא חוץ מההקדמות אשר יעשו בבאור הדבר.

[2] ומקום אחר לקוח מדומי הפעולות אשר יוכיח האדם בם, ומדמיוניהם, ודומי בעלי הריב מבני אדם. וזה, כשלא יוכל מי שעליו התרעומת שיסור גנות מה שנזכר בו, יתנצל בשדומ׳ אותו הפועל כבר עשאו המתרעם· או כבר היה אותו הפעל בעינו מדומהו מבני אדם; וזהו ההשתנות· ואמנם יפנה ההלצי אליו כשלא יוכל להסיר החשד ממנו באופן אחר.

[3] ומקום אחר: במדרגת מי שיביא ראיה, על מי שגורש מארצו, שהוא מיוחס ממה שכתוב בספר היחסים אצל בני המדינה ההיא.

[4] ומקום אחר: כאשר פעל פעל, ועזב מה שהוא יותר מעולה ממנו.

[5] ומקום אחר: שנעיין אם יעשה היועץ מה שמיעץ לאחרים לעשות, או שיתרחק ממה שייעץ להתרחק ממנו· כי אם לא יסכים דבורו עם מעשיו, והוא לו אפשרי, היה זה מקום תוכחה לו. וזה המקום כוזב· כי כבר ייעץ האדם בדבר, והוא יחשבהו בעת היותו מיעץ בו טוב, וא״כ יתבאר לו שאינו טוב· ולא יפעלהו, והוא כבר יעץ בו.

[6] ומקום אחר: שנעיין אל ב׳ פעולות אשר יפעלם האדם· האם האחת

1 פרק] פ׳[כ] || 2 <המאמר> ממקומות[כ] || 3 שיעיינו] שיעיונו[כ] || 4 שהוא] ששהוא[ד] || 5 בפומהו] בפומיהו[ד] || 6 מפעולות] מפעלות[כ] || 10 המריבים] המדינים[ד] || 12 בעלי] בעל[ד] || 13 בשדומ׳] כשדומה[כ] || 14 ההשתנות] ההשתנות[כ] |ההלצי] ההלציי[כ] || 15 אחר] אחד[כ] || 16 אחר] אחר׳[ד] | ראיה] ראייה[כ] |[על][כ] || 17 בספר] בספרי[ד] || 18 פעל [פעל][ד] פועל[agv] פעל[btv] || 20 שייעץ] שיועץ[ד] || 21 אפשרי] אפשריי[ד] || 22 בו <כי>[ד] ||

CHAPTER 21

Refutative Topics[1]

[1] As for refutative topics,[a] one is that men should examine the goods and evils mentioned by the contesting party in the praise or blame of something outside the subject under discussion, some new development that people have been talking about and is now current in their mouths, or which they will likely make current though it has not yet been reported—some point, that is, having to do with the past and present deeds and words of the contestants. This topic may be used to effect the refutation of the contending parties, inasmuch as their deeds and words impose a certain obligation upon them. A man, for instance, might say: "As for you, indeed, not one of you will give anything at all, but I, on the other hand, have in the past given freely to many of you." In general, the examination called for here should be of anything mentioned by the contending parties that is outside the premises on which the proof of their case will be based.

[2] Another topic is taken from deeds similar to those by which a speaker could effect refutation, from imaginary deeds of this kind, and from persons similar to the contestants. When, that is, the accused cannot elude some discreditable reference to himself, his defence will be that the plaintiff has, in the past, committed a like deed, or that the identical deed was previously committed by a person of his sort. This is the counter-check, but the speaker resorts to it only when he is unable to remove the suspicion from himself in another way.

[3] Another topic is of the kind used when some advocate, on behalf of a person deported from his country, proves from what is recorded in the genealogical registry of the citizens of that State that the deported person is native to the place.

[4] Another topic: when someone has done a deed, but left a better deed undone.

[5] Another: we examine whether a counsellor himself does or avoids what he counsels others to do or to avoid; for if what he says does not comport with what he in fact does when such action is possible for him, then this offers occasion to rebuke him. This topic, however, may be fallacious; for a man may advise a course of action which, at the moment of giving such counsel, he regards as sound, but which subsequently appears to him to be clearly unsound; and so, although he has previously counselled that this should be done, he does not do it himself.

[6] Another: we examine whether, of two acts which a man might do, the

1. Literally: "Topics of Rebuke," or "Censure," "Reprimand," "Reproach," "Reproof," etc.

a. T169 ff./A234 ff.; cf. *Rhet.* 2.23 (1397a ff.).

משתיהם יחויב ממנה, כשפעלה, שלא יפעל א״כ האחרת, ויהיה בזה מקום הוכחה; כמו מי שיגנה האדם, ויתקרב אליו· כי הגנות מורה על הרחוק, והנה הוא מתקרב.

[7] ומקום אחר: שנעיין בדבר אשר הושם ראיה על התרעומת, ונקיים ממנו
5 כשהוא אפשר שיהיה ראיה על ההתנצלות· או אם יהיה הדבר אשר בו יתנצל, יתכן בו שיהיה ראיה על התרעומת. וזה יהיה על שני פנים. אם שיהיה בטבע הראיה: כמו שימצא אדם עומד באמצע הבית ויאמר לו שהוא לסטיס, לפי שהוא נמצא בזה המקום· ויאמר הוא: ״הלא אילו הייתי לסטיס, לא הייתי עומד באמצע הבית״. והאופן השני, שימצא באותו המאמר אשר יתנצל בו המתנצל,
10 או יתרעם ממנו המתרעם, מקום יורה לו הפך הוראתו: ואם היה בהתנצלות, הורה בו על התרעומת· ואם היה בתרעומת, הורה ממנו על ההתנצלות; וזה כמו טעות יקרה במאמר מתוספת, או חסרון, או העלם תנאי מתנאיו. כמו שיחשד אדם שהוא גנב דבר מבית הזדמן שנרצח בעליו בו, ויאמר: ״למה אגנוב ממנו דבר, ואני לא רצחתי בעליו?״ כי בכמו זה המקום, יתחזק
15 החשד עליו, אחר שהיה כבר טעה, ופנה להשיב ממה שלא נשאל ממנו.

[8] מקום אחר הלקוח משם הדבר. משל זה, שאם יזדמן איש ששמו ״נואף״, או ״רוצח״, ויאמר: ״אתה נואף, אתה נואף״· ״אתה, רוצח, אתה רוצח״. ולפעמים היה בהעתק השם ובשנוי מעט· כמו שהיה שמו ״אונן״, ויאמר שהוא עשה ״אונאות״.

20 [9] והתוכחות בכלל יותר מצליחות ויותר מועילות מן הקיומים, לפי שהם יביאו לדמות אל השומע, עם הדבר, הפכו· ויהיה ציורו יותר תמים ויותר ערב; וגם כן כי התוכחות, לקרבת באורם, יחוברו ממלות מעטות, ותהיינה יותר נקלות שמירה ויותר מהירות הכרה לדבר. ושניהם אלה הדברים, הם סבה אל שתהיינה התוכחות יותר מבוארות וגלויות אצל השומע. ושניהם יפעלו
25 ההספקה המניעה הנפש, כל שכן מה שהיה מהם, כאשר התחיל ההלצי במעשהו, הרגיש הוא והשומעים בתכלית המכוון ממנו· ובכלל, שיעמדו ממנו על הדבר המתחייב הנמשך לפתיחת המאמר. כי הסימנים אשר בזה התואר

4 ראיה] ראייה[כ] || 6 שני] ב׳[ד] || 7 לסטיס] לסטס[כ] || 8 אילו] אם[ד] || 10 לו] לנו[ד] || 11 על <צד>[כ] || 15 נשאל] ישאל[כ] || 22 וגם כן] וג״כ[כ] | ממלות <ממלות>[כ] | מעטות] מעוטות[כ] || 23 מהירות] נקלות[ד] || 25 כל שכן] כ״ש[כ] ||

consequence of the one, should he do it, would necessarily be that he then would not do the other; in which case, there will then be occasion for rebuke. Example: one who denounces a man, yet tries to become his close friend; for denunciation implies distance, yet here he is attempting to be on terms of close friendship.

[7] Another: we examine a fact represented as evidence for the accusation, and establish that it can constitute evidence of the defence; or, if the fact should be the means of a successful defence, we establish the possibility that it constitutes evidence for the accusation. This topic is found in either of two forms. (1) It may be in terms of the nature of the evidence, as follows: A man found standing in the interior of the house is accused of being a robber because he was come upon in this place; but he may argue, ''Isn't it true that if I were a robber, I would not be standing here in the interior of the house?'' (2) It is in the second form when, in the very defence offered by the accused, or in the charge presented by the prosecution, a point is found which indicates the contrary of what the statement implies: if found in the defence, the point is indicative of the charge, and if in the accusation, of the defence; and this is like the occurrence, in a statement, of a fault of excessiveness, or of inadequacy, or of failure to notice some necessary precondition. Suppose, for example, a person is suspected of having stolen something from a house in which the owner, as it happened, was murdered, and argues: ''Why would I steal anything from that house, when it was not I who murdered its owner?'' If he advances such a point as this, the suspicion against him will be strengthened, since he has now committed a fault, in having gone out of his way to reply on a matter concerning which no inquiry was made of him.

[8] Another topic is the one taken from the name of the act. This would be examplified if, assuming there could be a man named Adulterer or Murderer, it should be said: ''You, Adulterer, are indeed an adulterer''; ''You, Murderer, are indeed a murderer.'' This topic has sometimes had actual use through the carrying over of a name in slightly altered form; as when, for example, a man's name is Wiley and it is said that he has practised wiles.[2]

[9] The refutative topics are, in general, more successful and useful than the demonstrative, since they present the proposition to the hearer's mind side by side with its contrary, and the depiction of it is more complete and gratifying; also because refutative topics, being virtually self-evident, are composed of few words, and so are more easily retained and make the case more quickly understandable. These two considerations explain why refutative topics may be held by the hearer to be clearer and plainer. But both kinds of topics can effect the persuasion that sways the soul, especially if, at the very outset of the speaker's task, both he and the audience perceive them as part of his purpose, and if, in general, the audience is brought by him to understand the matter that is the logically necessary consequence of what was said at the outset. For speakers, let

2. This is an attempt to reproduce JML's Hebrew *jeu de mots:* אוֹנָאוֹת/אוֹנָן (''deceits, frauds'').

כבר ישמחו בם המדברים כאשר הרגישו מהם זה הענין, כ״ש השומעים.

[10] ואילו המקומות בכלל, כשהגיעו לאדם, היה אפשר לו שישיג בם מהמלאכה הזאת, בזמן קצר ויגיעה מעטה, מה שדרכו שיושג בזמן ארוך ויגיעה רבה:

פרק כ״ב

מהמקומות המטעים.

[1] המקומות המטעים ב׳ מינים, מלות וענינים.

[2] ואולם הסימנים המטעים מפני המלות, הנה אחד ממיניהם הוא שתהיינה תמונות המלות אחדות, ומה שיורו עליו מאותם התמונות מתחלף. והמקום הזה התחלה להקשים רבים׃ כי אלו, כשיחוברו כפי זה האופן, יחודש מהם סימן נחשב, מזולת שיהיה באמת סימן. ומהם, אשר יהיה בהסכמת השם ושתופו׃ כמו אמרנו, במי שיחסו כלבי, שהוא ״כלב״; ואמנם, הטעות בזה ששם הכלב יאמר על משפחת כלב ועל החי הנובח.

[3] ומקום אחר מהדבור הנפרד שיאמר מחובר, ומהמחובר, שיאמ׳ נפרד, לפי שיחשב שהוא דבר אחד. משל מה שיצדק נפרד ויכזב מחובר: שיאמר שאשר ידע אותיות האלפא ביתא, כל אחת בפני עצמה, ידע השיר, לפי שהשיר מחובר מאותיות אלפא ביתא. והמשל ממה שיכזב נפרד, ויצדק מחובר, כמו: ״ב׳ וג׳ הם ה׳ ״.

[4] ומקום מיוחד בהלצה, והוא שישים האומר השומעים בצד שיתדמה להם הענין עד שיפול בנפשותיהם שמי שעליו הטענה עשה אותו העניין אשר טען הוא נגדו, מפני[1] שיקיים הטוען שהוא עשה זה׃ או יפול בנפשותיהם שהטוען

2 ואילו] ואלה[ד] || 5 פרק] פ׳[כ] || 7 המטעים] המעטים[כ] || 8 אחד] א׳[ד] | ממיניהם] מימיניהם[כ] || 11 ומהם אשר יהיה בהסכמת] ומה אשר היה בהם בהסכמת[ד] || 16 אחת] אח׳[ד] || 18 ה׳] ב׳[ד] || 19 שיתדמה] שידמה[כ] || 20 [העניין][ד] ||

[1] *Sic* ט<א: من قبل.

alone the audience, are certain to delight in Enthymemes of this quality once they have noticed that such is their character.

[10] In general, once these topics are at a man's disposal, he can through them gain from this art, in a short time and with little labor, what is ordinarily achieved after a long time and with much labor.

CHAPTER 22

Fallacious Topics

[1] Fallacious topics[a] are classed under two headings, words and meanings.

[2] Of the verbally fallacious Enthymemes, it is one type when the external form of the word is one and the same, while what is denoted by these identical forms differs in each case. This topic is the starting point for many sophisms, for such words, set in syllogistic order, form an Enthymeme that is apparent rather than real. One such Enthymeme is constituted by a convergence and sharing of the same name, as when we should say, of a man of Kelbite extraction, that he is a *kelb*;[1] the fallacy here, however, is that the noun *kelb* [''dog''] designates both the clan Kelb and the barking animal.

[3] Another such topic consists of treating something that is separate as if it were in combination, and something in combination as if, because seeming to be one thing, it were separate. As example of what is true in the case of the separate but false in the case of the combined: to say that whoever knows the letters of the alphabet, severally and separately, knows poetry, since poetry consists of the letters of the alphabet in combination. And an example of what is false of the separate, and true of the combined, is: ''Two and three are five.''[2]

[4] Now a fallacious topic, used only in Rhetoric, is that whereby a speaker can bring the hearers so to conceive of[3] the action at issue as to gain the impression that the defendant committed the act charged against him, even before[4] the prosecutor proves that it was the defendant who perpetrated the act; or make the

1. The illustration, based on the name of a well-known Beduin tribe, is A's; cf. the Biblical name ''Caleb.''

2. Two (separately) are not five; and three (separately) are not five; but two *and* three (combined) are five.

3. *Sic* T, followed by JML; more probably the Arabic of A here means ''to harbor such doubts of.''

4. T and JML: ''on account of the fact that'' (من قبل > מפני, an error due to excessive literalness).

a. T171 ff./A239 ff.; cf. *Rhet.* 2.24 (1401a ff.).

כוזב בטענותיו, מפני[2] שיתנצל מי שעליו הטענה. והראשון יהיה ממה שיאמרהו הטוען, או יפעלהו; כמו שיגדיל מה שטען בו נגדו· או ימצאהו רתת ממנו, ויראה ממנו בעצמו הצטערות. והשני ממה שיפעלהו מי שעליו הטענה, או יאמרהו; כמו שיבכה· או יעמוד ויכה לחייו· ויעלה עפר על ראשו· או יאמר מאמרים יבהיל בהם השומע והשופט· עד שיתנודד, וישגה במה שישגיח בו, ולא יוכל לשערו.

[5] ומקום אחר שהוא הולך בו מן הכולל אל המיוחד· כמי שיאמ׳: ״פלו׳ גנב, מפני שהוא רע״; כי כבר יצדק שהגנב רע, אלא שלא יתהפך, ר״ל, שכל רע יהיה גנב.

[6] ומקום אחר ממה שבמקרה, כמי שיאמ׳: ״שהעכברים עזרונו על שונאינו, לפי שהם כתתו מתרי קשותותם.״

[7] ומקום אחר, שישים מה שאינו עלה לדבר עלה לו· וזה כשיקח ההווה עם הדבר, או אחריו, סבה למציאות הדבר מזולת שיהיה סבה; כאלו יאמר שהנהגת בן אבי עאמר[3] היתה מפני רע כוונו, לפי שהקטטה באנדלוס היתה אחריה.

[8] ומקום אחר, והוא שיהיה הדבר שדרכו שילקח בתאר מה, וילקח בתאר אחר· וזה, אם מזמן, אם מקום, אם תכונה[4], או צד. משל הראשון מהבינוני, שמדרכו שילקח בתאר זמן העומד, ולקחו בתאר עבר, כמו: ופרעה חולם [בר׳ מ״א א׳]. משל השני, שלקח ״שמה״ תמורת ״הנה״. משל השלישי, כגון שהוציא העבר בתכונת ההווה, ואמ׳ ״שומר״, ״שומרת״, וכו׳. משל הרביעי, שמה שראוי להוציא בצד האפשר, ר״ל, ״ראובן אפשר שילך״, הוציאו בצד המחויי׳, ואמר: ״ראובן מחוייב שילך.״ או: יהיה ממה שדרכו שילקח בתואר מה, וילקח מוחלט· כמו שנאמ׳ במי שישר בממונות, שהוא ישר במוחלט.

וזה מה שרצינו לזכרו בזה השער:

2 יפעלהו] יפעילהו[כ] |כמו] או[כ] |רתת] רהת[ד] ||3 בעצמו] בעצמות[ד] |יאמרהו] יאמר[ד] ||4 כמו] במי[ד] ||7 פלו׳] פלני[ד] ||10 שונאינו] שנאיננו[כ] ||12 שישים] שישי[ד] ||14 עאמר[3] עמ̇אד[כ] עמד[ד] עמאר[aט] עמ̇אר[bט] ||17 מקום] ממקום[כ] |אם] או[כ] |תכונה[4] תבונה[כד] ||18 ולקחו] נלקחו[כ] |[כמו][ד] ||19 השלשי] הג׳[ד] ||20 וכו׳] כו׳[כ] |הרביעי] הד׳[ד] ||21 המחויי׳] המחוטב[כ] |[ואמר][ד] ||22 מחוייב] מחטיב[כ] ||23 במי שישר] כי מי שיישר[כ] ||24 לזכרו] זכרו[ד] ||

[2] *Sic* ט<א: من قبل.

[3] Corrected according to [g]ט.

[4] Corrected according to ט.

hearers gain the impression that the prosecutor's allegations are false even before[4] the accused establishes his defence. The first will derive from something the plaintiff says or does; for example, he may enlarge upon the charge made against the defendant, or be seized by agitation because of him, and make his distress over the defendant visible. The second will derive from what the respondent does or says; he may, for example, weep, or stand still and slap his cheeks and put dust on his head, or make shocking statements to audience and judge, or even move about distractedly, fumble for his point and not be able to think what it was.

[5] Another topic is that in which the general is extended to the specific; for example: "So-and-so is a thief, because he is an evil person." While it is certainly true that the thief is evil, the reverse—that every evil person is a thief—is not true.

[6] Another such topic consists of some improbable happening, as that one should say: "The mice aided us against our enemies, for it was they who reduced our enemies' bowstrings to shreds."

[7] Another fallacious topic: to assign as cause of a thing that which is not its cause, as when what happens simultaneously with a thing, or after it, is taken as the cause of the thing's being in existence, although it is no cause; for example, if it should be said that Ibn Abī 'Āmir's administration was actuated by the evil of his aims since civil strife in Andalusia followed.[5]

[8] Another topic: Something normally assumed to have one quality is taken to have a different quality—some quality, that is, of time, place, manner, or mode. (1) An example of the first is a participle which, normally assumed to have the quality of the present tense, is taken to have the quality of the past, as in the verse **And . . . Pharaoh dreamed**[6] [Gen. 41:1]. (2) Example of the second: to take "thither" for "hither." (3) Example of the third: as when the past is expressed in the manner of the present, and one says "he keeps," "she keeps," etc.[7] (4) An example of the fourth: when what should be presented as possible—"Reuben may go"—is presented as obligatory—"Reuben must go." Or: something normally taken in a qualified way is taken absolutely; as when it is said of one who is upright in regard to money matters, that he is altogether upright.

This concludes what we planned to mention in this Book.

5. Abū 'Āmir Muḥammad ibn Abī 'Āmir al-Ma'āfirī (940–1002 C.E.), the great Almanzor, was perhaps the ablest leader Muslim Spain ever had. He was *de facto* ruler of the Peninsula for some 20 years.

6. A participle in the Hebrew.

7. I.e., the "historical present."

השער הרביעי

כולל פ״ג פרקים

פ׳ א׳: ההצעה לזה המאמר.
פ׳ ב׳: ההשנות הקודם.
5 פ׳ ג׳: ההשנות המאוחר.
פ׳ ד׳: המורכב משניהם.
פ׳ ה׳: החזרה.
פ׳ ו׳: ההפוך.
פ׳ ז׳: הקריאה.
10 פ׳ ח׳: השאלה.
פ׳ ט׳: הויכוח.
פ׳ י׳: המשל.
פ׳ י״א: החלוף.
פ׳ י״ב: המדובק.
15 פ׳ י״ג: המחולק.
פ׳ י״ד: המשולש.
פ׳ ט״ו: השוה.
פ׳ י״ו: המתדמה.
פ׳ י״ז: המסכים.
20 פ׳ י״ח: ההעתקה.
פ׳ י״ט: הוכחת השאלה.
פ׳ כ׳: ההדרגה.
פ׳ כ״א: הרושם.
פ׳ כ״ב: ההערה.
25 פ׳ כ״ג: ההגהה.
פ׳ כ״ד: ההעלמה.
פ׳ כ״ה: המיוחד.
פ׳ כ״ו: הנמשך.
פ׳ כ״ז: ההשבה.
30 פ׳ כ״ח: ההכפל.
פ׳ כ״ט: הפתרון.
פ׳ ל׳: הסבובי.
פ׳ ל״א: ההתנדבות.

3 פ׳ א׳] א׳ פרק[ד] |ההצעה] הצעה[כ] ||4 פ׳ ב׳] ב׳ פר״[ר] |ההשנות] השנות[כ] ||5 פ׳ ג׳] ג׳ פרק[ד] ||6 פ׳ ד׳] הד׳ פר״[ר] ||7 פ׳ ה׳] ה׳ פרק[ד] ||8 פ׳ ו׳] ו׳ פר״[ר] ||9 פ׳ ז׳] ז׳ פרק[ד] ||10 פ׳ ח׳] ח׳ פרק[ד] ||11 פ׳ ט׳] ט׳ פרק[ד] ||12 פ׳ י׳] י׳ פרק[ד] ||13 פ׳ י״א] י״א פרק[ד] ||14 פ׳ י״ב] י״ב פרק[ד] ||15 פ׳ י״ג] י״ג פרק[ד] ||16 פ׳ י״ד] י״ד פרק[ד] ||17 פ׳ ט״ו] ט״ו פרק[ד] ||18 פ׳ י״ו] י״ו פרק[ד] ||19 פ׳ י״ז] י״ז פרק[ד] ||20 פ׳ י״ח] י״ח פרק[ד] ||21 פ׳ י״ט] י״ט פרק[ד] ||22 פ׳ כ׳] כ׳ פרק[ד] ||23 פ׳ כ״א] כ״א פרק[ד] ||24 פ׳ כ״ב] כ״ב פרק[ד] |ההערה] ההעדרה[ד] ||25 פ׳ כ״ג] כ״ג פרק[ד] ||26 פ׳ כ״ד] כ״ד פרק[ד] ||27 פ׳ כ״ה] כ״ה פרק[ד] ||28 פ׳ כ״ו] כ״ו פרק[ד] ||29 פ׳ כ״ז] כ״ז פרק[ד] ||30 פ׳ כ״ח] כ״ח פרק[ד] ||31 פ׳ כ״ט] כ״ט פרק[ד] ||32 פ׳ ל׳] ל׳ פרק[ד] ||33 פ׳ ל״א] ל״א פרק[ד] ||

BOOK IV[1]

1. In this Book, I have kept, as the English translations of the Hebrew terms for the Figures, Professor Harry Caplan's widely accepted English renderings of the Latin terms found in the *Rhetorica ad Herennium*. Messer Leon's carefully considered Hebrew translations of the same terms are given, and in most instances glossed, in footnotes at the beginning of each respective chapter.

פ׳ ל״ב: המסופק.
פ׳ ל״ג: ההמשכות.
פ׳ ל״ד: הנבדל.
פ׳ ל״ה: הנפסק.
פ׳ ל״ו: הכלל.
פ׳ ל״ז: ההצעה.
פ׳ ל״ח: התמורה.
פ׳ ל״ט: הכנוי.
פ׳ מ׳: המכנה.
פ׳ מ״א: האריכות.
פ׳ מ״ב: הבלבול.
פ׳ מ״ג: הגוזמא.
פ׳ מ״ד: ההמרה.
פ׳ מ״ה: הבלתי מורגל.
פ׳ מ״ו: ההתיחסות.
פ׳ מ״ז: ההשאלה.
פ׳ מ״ח: המפקד[1].
פ׳ מ״ט: התוכחה.
פ׳ נ׳: ההכנעה.
פ׳ נ״א: ההתבוננות.
פ׳ נ״ב: החלוק.
פ׳ נ״ג: המאסף.
פ׳ נ״ד: הצחות.
פ׳ נ״ה: העכבה.
פ׳ נ״ו: ההגדה.
פ׳ נ״ז: ההתנגדות.
פ׳ נ״ח: הערך.
פ׳ נ״ט: הדמיון.
פ׳ ס׳: הדמות או הצורה.
פ׳ ס״א: הסמן.
פ׳ ס״ב: התואר.
פ׳ ס״ג: הספור.
פ׳ ס״ד: ההעברה.
פ׳ ס״ה: הנותר.
פ׳ ס״ו: המספיק.
פ׳ ס״ז: נגד העין.
פ׳ ס״ח: ההצעה.
פ׳ ס״ט: הנוסף.
פ׳ ע׳: החסר[1].
פ׳ ע״א: המקיף.
פ׳ ע״ב: המוקדם.
פ׳ ע״ג: המגזם.
פ׳ ע״ד: המקביל.
פ׳ ע״ה: המסתיר.
פ׳ ע״ו: הזרות.
פ׳ ע״ז: ההרכבה.
פ׳ ע״ח: הקודם.
פ׳ ע״ט: ההגדלה.

1 פ׳ ל״ב] ל״ב פרק[ד] || 2 פ׳ ל״ג] ל״ג פרק[ד] || 3 פ׳ ל״ד] ל״ד פרק[ד] || 4 פ׳ ל״ה] ל״ה פרק[ד] | הנפסק] הנספק[ד] || 5 פ׳ ל״ו] ל״ו פרק[ד] || 6 פ׳ ל״ז] ל״ז פרק[ד] || 7 פ׳ ל״ח] ל״ח פרק[ד] || 8 פ׳ ל״ט] ל״ט פרק[ד] || 9 פ׳ מ׳] מ׳ פרק[ד] || 10 פ׳ מ״א] מ״א פרק[ד] || 11 פ׳ מ״ב] מ״ב פר׳[ד] || 12 פ׳ מ״ג] מ״ג פרק[ד] || 13 פ׳ מ״ד] מ״ד פרק[ד] || 14 פ׳ מ״ה] מ״ה פרק[ד] | הבלתי] מבלתי[ד] || 15 פ׳ מ״ו] מ״ו פרק[ד] || 16 פ׳ מ״ז] מ״ז פרק[ד] || 17 פ׳ מ״ח] מ״ח פרק[ד] | המפקד[1]] המפקר[כד] || 18 פ׳ מ״ט] מ״ט פרק[ד] || 19 פ׳ נ׳] נ׳ פרק[ד] || 20 פ׳ נ״א] נ״א פרק || 21 פ׳ נ״ב] נ״ב פרק ד׳ || 22 פ׳ נ״ג] נ״ג פרק[ד] || 23 פ׳ נ״ד] נ״ד פרק || 24 פ׳ נ״ה] נ״ה פרק[ד] | העכבה] הערכה[כ] || 25 פ׳ נ״ו] נ״ו פרק[ד] || 26 פ׳ נ״ז] נ״ז פרק[ד] || 27 פ׳ נ״ח] נ״ח פרק[ד] || 28 פ׳ נ״ט] נ״ט פרק[ד] || 29 פ׳ ס׳] ס׳ פרק[ד] | הדמות [או הצורה][כ] || 30 פ׳ ס״א] ס״א פרק[ד] || 31 פ׳ ס״ב] ס״ב פרק[ד] || 32 פ׳ ס״ג] ס״ג פרק[ד] || 33 פ׳ ס״ד] ס״ד פרק[ד] || 34 פ׳ ס״ה] ס״ה פרק[ד] || 35 פ׳ ס״ו] ס״ו פרק[ד] || 36 פ׳ ס״ז] ס״ז פרק[ד] || 37 פ׳ ס״ח] ס״ח פרק[ד] || 38 פ׳ ס״ט] ס״ט פרק[ד] || 39 פ׳ ע׳] ע׳ פרק[ד] | החסר[1]] החסד[כד] || 40 פ׳ ע״א] ע״א פרק[ד] || 41 פ׳ ע״ב] ע״ב פרק[ד] | המוקדם] המקדם[ד] || 42 פ׳ ע״ג] ע״ג פרק[ד] || 43 פ׳ ע״ד] ע״ד פרק[ד] || 44 פ׳ ע״ה] ע״ה פרק[ד] || 45 פ׳ ע״ו] ע״ו פרק[ד] || 46 פ׳ ע״ז] ע״ז פרק[ד] || 47 פ׳ ע״ח] ע״ח פרק[ד] || 48 פ׳ ע״ט] ע״ט פרק[ד] ||

[1] Corrected text.

פ׳ פ׳: הנשנה.
פ׳ פ״א: ההתעוררות.
פ׳ פ״ב: הנסמך.
פ׳ פ״ג: הדברים שצריך להתרחק מהם
5 או להתקרב אליהם.

פרק א׳

ההצעה לזה המאמר.

[1] אחרי שקדם לנו מה שקדם מענייני זה הספר, ונכנסנו בחצריהם ובטירותם, וחפשנו חדר בחדר בדברי המליצים הקדומים והחדשים למצוא דברי 10 חפץ, נשאר לנו שנביא היפויים ההלציים למשפחותם לבית אבותם, כפי מה שיעדנו׳ שהם ג״כ עניני׳ משותפים לסוגי׳ רבים.

[2] ורוב מה שנאמר בזה, נקחהו מד׳ מההלצה שחבר טוליאו, וממה שספר הפילוסוף בג׳ מההלצה. אמנם המשלים להם, הביאותים מבית קדשנו ותפארתנו, מדברי הנבואה והספורים התוריים, היושבים ראשונה במלכות 15 הערבות והצחות, המתוקים מדבש, לא יותן סגור תחתיהם, ותמורתם כלי פז:

פרק ב׳

פ׳ ההשנות הקודם.

[1] ההשנות הקודם הוא השנות תיבה אחת בעצמה בראשונה, בדברים הדומים או בלתי דומים. והמשל בדברי׳ הדומים: אל תרא ביום אחיך ביום

1 פ׳ פ׳] פ׳ פרק[ד] |[הנשנה][כ] ‖ 2 פ׳ פ״א] פ״א פרק[ד] ‖ 3 פ׳ פ״ב] פ״ב פרק[ד] ‖ 4 פ׳ פ״ג] פ״ג [פרק][ד] ‖ 6 <הנה נתחיל סדור הפרקים>[ד] |פרק] פ׳[כ] ‖ 8 מענייני] מענין[ד] ‖ 10 היפויים] היפיים[כ] ‖ 11 עניני׳] עניינים <ענינים>[כ] |לסוגי׳] בסוגים[כ] ‖ 12 מד׳] מרביעי[כ] ‖ 13 בג׳] בשלישי[כ] ‖ 16 פרק] פ׳[כ] ‖ 17 [פ׳][ד] |[הקודם][ד] ‖ 18 השנות] שנוי[ד] ‖ 19 אל] ואל[ת] |תרא [ביום][ד] ‖

8–9 בר׳ כ״ה ט״ז |מל״ב ט׳ ב׳ ‖ 9–10 קה׳ י״ב י׳ |במ׳ א׳ ב׳ ‖ 13–14 יש׳ ס״ד י׳ |אס׳ א׳ י״ד ‖ 15 תה׳ י״ט י״א |איוב כ״ח ט״ו |איוב כ״ח י״ז ‖

CHAPTER 1[1]

The Advance Outline of This Book

[1] In the course of the preceding treatment of the subjects with which the present work is concerned, we entered **their villages . . . and their encampments** [Gen. 25:16] and searched out the **inner chamber** [2 Kings 9:2] of the pronouncements made by both ancient and more recent rhetoricians in order **to find out words of delight** [Eccl. 12:10]. It now remains for us to introduce the Figures of Speech **by their families, by their fathers' houses** [Num. 1:2], as we promised,[2] for these also are matters that more than one of the Kinds of Cause have in common.

[2] For most of what we shall say herein, we shall draw upon Book IV of the [New] Rhetoric written by Tully,[3] and upon the account given by the Philosopher in Book III of his *Rhetoric*. The examples of the Figures, however, I have taken from **our holy and our beautiful house** [Isa. 64:10], from the words of prophecy and the divinely inspired narratives **that sit first in the kingdom** [Esth. 1:14] of agreeableness and elegance, that are **sweeter . . . than honey** [Ps. 19:11], that **cannot be gotten for gold . . . neither shall the exchange thereof be vessels of fine gold** [Job 28:15,17].

CHAPTER 2

Epanaphora[1]

[1] Epanaphora[a] is repetition of an identical initial word in expressions either of like or unlike content. Examples in expressions of like content: **Not have**

1. Added in C, just before "Chapter One": "Here we begin the ordering of the Chapters."
2. See the introduction to Book III.
3. *Supra*, note 1 to the chapter-listing of Book IV.

1. Literally: "Initial Repetition": הַהִשָּׁנוּת הַקּוֹדֵם (*sic*).

a. *R. ad H.* 4.13.19.

נכרו· אל תשמח לבני יהודה ביום אבדם· ואל תגדל פיך ביום צרה [עו׳ י״ב]. הנה תיב׳ ״אל״ נשנת פעמים רבות, בתחלת כל מאמ׳· והם דברים דומים, כי כלם שבים אל מה שהיה עשו שמח בצרת ישראל. עוד בזכריה, בדברים הדומים, ובסוג המקיים לשבח: ממנו פנה, ממנו יתד, ממנו קשת מלחמה· ממנו יצא כל נוגש יחדו [זכ׳ י׳ ד׳]. עוד בצפניה: יום עברה היום ההוא· יום צרה וצוקה, יום שואה ומשואה, יום חשך ואפלה, יום ענן וערפל [צפ׳ א׳ ט״ו].

[2] והמשל בדברים הבלתי דומים, מה שנאמ׳ ביחזקאל: שם אשור וכל קהלה, וכו׳· שם עילם וכל המונה סביבות קברתה, וכו׳· שם משך ותובל, כו׳ [יח׳ ל״ב כ״ב—כ״ו]. עוד בהושע: וארשתיך לי לעולם· וארשתיך לי בצדק ובמשפט...· וארשתיך לי באמונה [הו׳ ב׳ כ״א—כ״ב].

[3] והוא מבואר שאלה המשלים האחרונים הם בדברים הבלתי דומים· כי במשל הראשון, האמות מתחלפות· ובשני, ההמשך הנצחי הוא זולת צדק, ומשפט, והאמונה.

[4] וזה היפוי, יתכן העשותו בסוג המקיים העצתי והמשפטי, ובדבור הנשא והבינוני. ויש לזה היפוי מהצחות וההתנשאות מה שלא יעלם.

פרק ג׳

פ׳ ההשנות המאוחר.

[1] ההשנות המאוחר הוא השנות התבה האחת בעצמה באחרונה. והמשל בישעיהו, בנבואת מצרים: ערות על יאור, על פי יאור· וכל מזרע יאור, יבש נדף

1 אל] ואל[ת] || 2 [הנה...מאמ׳][כ] || 3 בזכריה] בזכריהו[ד] || 4–5 [ממנו] יצא[כ] || 6 וצוקה] ומצוקה[ת] || 8 וכו׳] כו׳[ד] | [סביבות קברתה][ד] | וכו׳] כו׳[ד] | משך ותובל] משך תבל[ת] || 12 הראשון] הא׳[ד] | האמות <הם>[כ] | ובשני] ובב׳[ד] || 14 וזה <נשא בינוני>[כ] || 16 פרק] פ׳[כ] || 17 [פ׳][ד] | ההשנות] השנות[ד] || 18 [התבה][כ] ||

gazed [2]shouldest thou on the day of thy brother in the day of his disaster, not have rejoiced shouldest thou over the children of Judah in the day of their destruction, not have spoken proudly shouldest thou in the day of distress [Obad. v. 12]. Here the word "not," several times repeated, appears at the beginning of every clause;[3] and the expressions are of similar content because they all refer to the fact that Esau took pleasure in Israel's misfortune. Again, in Zechariah, in expressions of like content, and in an Epideictic discourse of praise: **Out of them shall come forth the corner-stone, out of them the stake, out of them the battle bow, out of them every master together** [Zech. 10:4]. Another, in Zephaniah: **A day of wrath is that day,[4] a day of trouble and distress, a day of wasteness and desolation, a day of darkness and gloominess, a day of clouds and thick darkness** [Zeph. 1:15].

[2] Examples in expressions of unlike content: the passage in Ezekiel, **There is Asshur and all her company**, etc.... **There is Elam and all her multitude round about her grave**, etc.... **There is Meshech and[5] Tubal**, etc. [Ezek. 32:22–26]. Again, in Hosea: **And I will betroth thee unto Me forever; and I will betroth thee unto Me in righteousness, and in justice... ; and I will betroth thee unto Me in faithfulness** [Hos. 2:21–22].

[3] In these last examples the expressions are clearly of unlike content, for in the first the several nations are different, while in the second, eternal duration is not the same as righteousness, justice, and faithfulness.

[4] This figure can be used in the Epideictic, Deliberative, and Judicial Kinds of Cause, and in the Grand and Middle Styles. It possesses an elegance and a nobility that will not fail to be noticed.

CHAPTER 3

Antistrophe[1]

[1] Antistrophe[a] is repetition of an identical final word.[2] Examples: in Isaiah, in the prophecy against Egypt: **The mosses by the Nile, by the brink of the**

2. *Sic*, JML and B; JV: "But thou shouldest not have gazed." The Hebrew begins each phrase with the negative particle אַל, and I have tried to represent this.
3. "Here... clause" is in C, but not in M.
4. JV: "That day is a day of wrath," but the Hebrew order is as above.
5. B omits "... and."

1. Literally: "Delayed Repetition," "Final Repetition," "Postpositive Repetition": הַהִשָּׁנוּת הַמְּאוּחָר (*sic*).
2. I.e., of a series of several phrases or other periods.

a. *R. ad H.* 4.13.19.

ואיננו [יש׳ י״ט ז׳]; רוע התרועעה הארץ׃ פור התפוררה ארץ׃ מוט התמוטטה
הארץ [שם כ״ד י״ט]. עוד, ביחזקאל: ונתכה בתוכה טמאתה, תתום חלאתה׃
תאונים הלאת, ולא תצא ממנה רבת חלאתה׃ באש חלאתה [יח׳ כ״ד
י״א — י״ב].
5 וזה היפוי, אפשר העשותו בדברים אשר אפשר ההשנות הקודם בערכם:

פרק ד׳

פ׳ המורכב משניהם.

[1] המורכב משניהם הוא הרכבת שתי הצחיות הנזכ׳ יחד, עד תהיה התיבה
הראשונה נשנת בראשונה, והאחרונה באחרונה. והמשל בצפניה, בסוג העצתי:
10 בטרם לא יבא עליכם חרון אף י״י׃ בטרם לא יבא עליכם יום אף י״י [צפ׳ ב׳ ב׳].
עוד, בירמיה: הנני מביא עליכם גוי ממרחק בית ישראל, וכו׳׃ גוי איתן הוא, גוי
מעולם הוא [יר׳ ה׳ ט״ו]. עוד, בירמיה: כי מי יחמול עליך ירושלם׃ ומי ינוד לך׃
ומי יסור לשאול לשלום לך [שם ט״ו ה׳]. עוד, בירמיה: כי מנאפים מלאה הארץ׃
כי מפני אלה אבלה[1] הארץ [שם כ״ג י׳].
15 [2] וזה, אפשר העשותו בכל הסוגים, ויבוקש ענינו בדבור הנשא והבינוני:

1 ואיננו] ואינינו[ב] | רוע] רעה[ת] | התרועעה] התרועע[ב] | הארץ] ארץ[ד] || 2 הארץ] ארץ[ת] | עוד] והמשל[ד] || 3 הלאת] חלאת[ב] | חלאתה׃] חלאת[ד] || 6 פרק] פ׳[ב] || 7 [פ׳][ד] || 8 הוא] היא[ד] | שתי] שני[ד] | הנזכ׳] הנזכרי[ד] || 9 והאחרונה] האחונה[ד] || 10 עליכם] עליהם[ד] || 11 [וכו׳][ב] | 1,1–12 [גוי איתן... הוא][ד] || 13 יסור] ינוד[ד] || 14 אבלה[1]] אכלה[בד] ||

[1] Corrected according to ת.

Nile, and all that is sown by the Nile, shall become dry, be driven away, and be no more [Isa. 19:7]; **Broken, broken down is the earth; crumbled in pieces is the earth; trembleth, tottereth the earth** [24:19].[3] Again, in Ezekiel: . . . **that the impurity of it may be molten within it, consumed the filth of it; it hath wearied itself with toil, yet from it goeth not forth the great filth of it: in fire shall be the filth of it** [Ezek. 24:11–12].[3]

[2] This Figure may be used in the same Kinds of Cause and Styles as those in which Epanaphora can appropriately appear.

CHAPTER 4

Interlacement[1]

[1] Interlacement[a] is the combining of both the aforementioned elegancies of Style in such a manner that the first word is reiterated at the beginning of the periods, and the last word at the end. Zephaniah contains an example, in a Deliberative context: . . . **before the fierce anger of the Lord come upon you, before the day of the Lord's anger come upon you** (Zeph. 2:2]. Again, in Jeremiah: **Lo, I will bring a nation upon you from far, O house of Israel, etc.; it is an enduring nation, it is an ancient nation . . .** [Jer. 5:15].[2] Another in Jeremiah: **For who shall have pity upon thee, O Jerusalem? Or who shall bemoan thee? Or who shall turn aside to ask about welfare in respect of thee?** [15:5].[3] Further in Jeremiah: **For full of adulterers is the land; for because of swearing mourneth the land** [23:10].[4]

[2] Use of this Figure is possible in all the Kinds of Cause, and its effect is demanded by the Grand and Middle Styles.

3. Translated in the order of the Hebrew.

1. Literally: "the combined of the two of them" (הַמּוּרְכָּב מִשְּׁנֵיהֶם), or "Composite Repetition."
2. It is obviously the last two phrases that JML has in mind here.
3. The last two questions constitute the illustration.
4. Translated in the order of the Hebrew.

a. *R. ad H.* 4.14.20.

פרק ה׳

פ׳ החזרה.

[1] החזרה היא חזרת התיבה ההיא בעצמה מבלתי הסדר השמור בראשונות.

[2] והמשל בשירת דבורה: בין רגליה כרע נפל שכב· בין רגליה כרע נפל· באשר כרע שם נפל שדוד [שופ׳ ה׳ כ״ז]; השנות התיבות ״כרע״ ו״נפל״, הוא מבוא׳, שלא ישמור הסדר כמו הקודמי׳. וכן בנחום: אל קנוא ונוקם י״י· נוקם י״י ובעל חימה· נוקם הוא לצריו, כו׳ [נח׳ א׳ ב׳]; תיבת ״נוקם״ נשנה בהעדר הסדר. וכן בצפניה: לא שמעה בקול· לא לקחה מוסר· בי״י לא בטחה· אל אלהיה לא קרבה [צפ׳ ג׳ ב׳]; וכן: שארית ישראל לא יעשו עולה ולא ידברו כזב ולא ימצא בפיהם לשון תרמית [שם י״ג]; בשניהם תיבת ״לא״ תעתק מבלי סדר. עוד, ביחזקאל: קץ· בא הקץ על ארבע[1] כנפות הארץ· עתה הקץ עליך [יח׳ ז׳ ב׳—ג׳].

[3] ויקרה לזה היפוי שהתיבה הנשנת לפעמים מורה דבר אחר ממה שהורה בתחלה. והמשל בשמשון: ויאמ׳ שמשון: ״בלחי החמור חמור חמורתים· בלחי החמור הכתי אלף איש״ [שופ׳ ט״ו ט״ז]; ״חמור חמורותים״ הוא מגזרת ויצברו אותם חמרים חמרים [שמ׳ ח׳ י׳], שהוא זולת מה שיורה ביתר המקומות.

[4] והשנות דבר אחד בעצמו ג׳ או ב׳ פעמים זה אחר זה מבלתי אמצעי, הוא מזה המין. והמשל: עוה, עוה, עוה אשימנה [יח׳ כ״א ל״ב]; ארץ, ארץ, ארץ, שמעי דבר י״י [יר׳ כ״ב כ״ט]; אנכי, אנכי הוא מנחמכם [יש׳ נ״א י״ב]; עורי, עורי, לבשי עוז, זרוע י״י [שם נ״א ט׳]; התעוררי, התעוררי, קומי, ירושלם [שם שם י״ז]. והוא נפלא לעורר על ענינים מתחלפים.

[5] ואין ראוי שיחשב שההשנות באלה היפויים יהיה מצד חסרון תיבות הצריכות בלשון· אבל הכונה בזה הערבות והצחות לאוזן השומע, עד שהוא

1 פרק] פ׳[כ] || 2 [פ׳][ר] || 5 התיבות] תיבות[כ] || 6 הקודמי׳] הקודמים[כ] || 7 [ובעל...תיבת][ר] | הוא] י״י[ת] || 8 בקול ‹כו׳›[ר] | 8—9 [לא...קרבה][ר] || 9 עולה ‹וכו׳›[ר] | 9—10 [ולא...תרמית][ר] || 11 על] עד[כ] | עתה][כ] | עליך] עליה[ר] || 12 ויקרה לזה] ויקרא זה[ר] | שהורה] שהודה[ר] || 13 [החמור][ר] | חמורתים ‹כו׳›[ר] || 13—14 [בלחי...איש][ר] | מגזרת] מגזרה[ר] || 15 [שיורה][כ] || 17 מזה] בזה[ר] | ארץ ארץ [ארץ][כ] || 22 בזה] בהם[ר] | לאוזן] לחזק[ר] ||

---

[1] *Qᵉrē* for *kᵉthībh* ארבעת.

CHAPTER 5

Transplacement[1]

[1] Transplacement[a] is the recurrence[2] of the identical word without retention of the original word order.

[2] An example occurs in the Song of Deborah: **At her feet he sunk, he fell, he lay; at her feet he sunk, he fell; where he sunk, there he fell down dead** [Judg. 5:27]; the repetition of the words "he sunk" and "he fell," it is clear, does not retain the order of the words as previously given. Similarly, in Nahum: **God is jealous, and the Lord avengeth; the Lord avengeth and is full of wrath; He[3] avengeth Him of His adversaries,** etc. [Nah. 1:2];[4] the word "avengeth" is repeated, but not the word order. So, too, in Zephaniah: **She hearkened not to the voice, she received not correction; in the Lord she did not trust, to her God she drew not near** [Zeph. 3:2];[5] also: **The remnant of Israel shall not do iniquity, and not speak lies, and a deceitful tongue shall not be found in their mouth** [3:13];[5] in both these verses the word "not" is carried over, but not the word order. Again, in Ezekiel: **An end! the end is come upon the four corners of the land; now is the end upon thee** [Ezek. 7:2–3].

[3] It occasionally happens, in the case of this Figure, that the repeated word signifies something other than its initial meaning. Our example is in the Samson narrative: **And Samson said: "With the jawbone of an ass** (ḥªmōr) **heaps upon heaps** (ḥªmōr ḥªmōrāthāyim), **with the jawbone of an ass have I smitten a thousand men"** [Judg. 15:16]; *ḥªmōr ḥªmōrāthāyim* is patterned upon **And they gathered them together into heaps** (ḥºmārīm ḥºmārīm) [Exod. 8:10], which is different from the meaning of *ḥª mōr* ["ass"] elsewhere.

[4] Belonging to this type of Figure is a triple or double use of the same word in uninterrupted succession. Examples: **A ruin, ruin, ruin will I make it** [Ezek. 21:32]; **O land, land, land, hear the word of the Lord** [Jer. 22:29]; **I, I am He that comforteth you** [Isa. 51:12]; **Awake, awake, put on strength, O arm of the Lord** [51:9]; **Awake, awake, stand up, O Jerusalem** [51:17]. The Figure is extraordinarily effective in arousing feeling over impending changes.

[5] It should not be thought that the repetition which appears in these Figures is due to the language's lack of the necessary words; rather, the aim herein is a

1. Literally: "Returning," "Recurrence": הַחֲזָרָה.
2. חֲזָרָה, the word also used for "transplacement."
3. B: "the Lord."
4. The citation in M, which differs slightly from B, is much fuller than in C, where it extends only through the second "avengeth." My translation here differs from JV.
5. Fuller citation in M than in C.

a. *R. ad H.* 4.14.20.

במדרגה מן הפרסום שאין צריך להביא עליו ראיה.

[6] וזה היפוי נופל על הנשא ועל שפל, ועל הבינוני על הרוב:

פרק ו׳

פ׳ ההפוך.

[1] ההפוך הוא מאמר מורכב מהפכים, ועל הרוב מתחיל בטוב ומסיים ברע. והמשל: מעודד ענוים י״י· משפיל רשעים עדי ארץ [תה׳ קמ״ז ו׳]; והוא מבואר ש״מעודד״ הוא הפך ״משפיל״ ו״ענוים״ הפך ״רשעים״· והמאמר הראשון גמול, והשני פורענות. וכן: כל גיא ינשא· וכל הר וגבעה ישפלו [יש׳ מ׳ ד׳]. וכן: כי אתה עם עני תושיע· ועינים רמות תשפיל [תה׳ י״ח כ״ח]; שבעים בלחם נשכרו, ורעבים חדלו· עד עקרה ילדה שבעה, ורבת בנים אוּמללה [שמ״א ב׳ ה׳]; וזה הרבה משיסופר.

[2] וזה היפוי, אם יעשה בתכלית התקון, יבוקש ענינו על הרוב בדבור הנשא· והוא מיוחד בסוג המקיים והמשפטי, ובכל חלקי המאמ׳ זולת החלוק:

2 ועל שפל ועל הבינוני] ועל הבנוני שפל[ב] || 3 פרק] פ׳[ב] || 4 פ׳ ההפוך] מההפוך[ד] || 7 הראשון] הא׳[ד] || 8 והשני] והב׳[ד] | ישפלו] ישפל[ד] || 10 שבעה] ז׳[ד] ||

certain agreeableness and elegance for the hearer's ear,[6] such that what is said is so plainly true as to require no proof.

[6] There is occasion for the use of this Figure in both the Grand and Simple Styles, but it is employed mostly in the Middle Style.

CHAPTER 6

Antithesis[1]

[1] Antithesis[a] is a Figure of Diction compounded of contraries which, for the most part, begins with a good and ends with an evil. Example: **The Lord upholdeth the humble; He bringeth the wicked down to the ground** [Ps. 147:6]; ''upholdeth,'' obviously, is the contrary of ''bringeth down,'' ''humble,'' the contrary of ''wicked''; and the first statement is a reward, the second a punishment. Similarly: **Every valley shall be lifted up, and every mountain and hill shall be made low** [Isa. 40:4]. So too: **For Thou dost save the afflicted people; but the haughty eyes Thou dost humble** [Ps. 18:28]; **They that were full have hired out themselves for bread, and they that were hungry have ceased; while the barren hath borne seven, she that had many children hath languished** [1 Sam. 2:5]. Instances of Antithesis are too many to count.[2]

[2] This Figure, if wrought with the utmost perfection, is an effect called for mostly in the Grand Style; while especially appropriate in the Epideictic and Judicial Kinds of Cause, it is applicable in all the Parts of the Discourse except the Partition.

6. This is the reading of M; C: ''. . . agreeableness and elegance to strengthen the hearer. . . .''

---

1. הַהִפּוּךְ.

2. Cf. the numerous examples of the Figure in the article by Leah Fraenkel, ''Antithesis as a Scriptural Literary Device,'' in *Bible and Jewish History: Studies . . . dedicated to the Memory of Jacob Liver* [Heb.] (Tel-Aviv, 1971), 129–146.

---

a. *R. ad H.* 4.15.20.

פרק ז׳

פ׳ הקריאה.

[1] הקריאה היא המורה צער או כעס או דאגה בסבת אדם מה, מדינה, עם, או מקום, כמו: הוי אריאל אריאל, קרית חנה דוד· ספו שנה על שנה, חגים ינקופו [יש׳ כ״ט א׳]; כי למה שהנביא היה רואה חרבן הבית, היה לו מן הצער הדאגה והכעס מה שלא יעלם. וכן: הוי מראה ונגאלה, העיר היונה [צפ׳ ג׳ א׳]. וכן: הוי שודד, ואתה לא שדוד, ובוגד, ולא בגדו בך· כהתימך שודד, תושד· כנלותך לבגוד, יבגדו בך [יש׳ ל״ג א׳]; היה מלא כעס וחימה על מלך אשור שהרבה לפשוע כנגד כל ישראל. וכן: הוי רב את יוצרו, חרש את חרשי אדמה· היאמר חמר ליוצרו, ״מה תעשה״, ו״פעלך אין ידים לו״· הוי אומר לאב, ״מה תוליד״ [שם מ״ה ט׳—י׳]; רדי, שבי על עפר, בתולת בת בבל, שבי לארץ אין כסא, בת כשדים! [שם מ״ז א׳]; הוי גוי חוטא, עם כבד עון! [שם א׳ ד׳]. הם והנוהג מנהגם מורים מן הצער, הכעס, והדאגה, מה שלא יעלם, עם שמביאים השומעים להתפעל ההתפעליות ההנה בעצמם.

[2] וזה היפוי ראוי שיעשה על המעט, ולפי מה שיבוקש בענין, כי אז ימצא בו מן הצחות שעור רב. והוא כלי נפלא להמשיך הלבבות אל הדברי׳ הנזכרים, ועל הרוב יהיה הרגלו בדבור הנשא. ובא בלשון הקדש לפעמים על התוכחה, כמו: הדור אתם, שמעו דבר ה׳ [יר׳ ב׳ ל״א]; לפעמי׳ זולת על אלה, כמו: שמעו דבר ה׳ [יש׳ ס״ו ה׳]· הקהל, חקה אחת... [במ׳ ט״ו ט״ו]· וזולתם רבים; אלא שעם מלת ״הוי״ תורה על הרוב על מה שנאמ׳ למעלה:

1 פרק] פ׳[כ] || 2 [פ׳][ד] || 4 מקום] קרוב[כ] || 6 מראה] מוראה[ת] | העיר היונה] וכו׳[ד] || 7 [בך][ד] | כהתימך] בהתימך[ד] || 9 [כל][כ] || 10 [לו][כ] || 11 שבי] ושבי[ת] || 14 להתפעל ‹אלה›[כ] || 15 ולפי] לפי[ד] || 17 הנשא ‹נשא›[כ] || 18 שמעו] ראו[ת] | [על][ד] | ‹הדור אתם› שמעו[1כד] ||

9 עמ׳ ד׳ ד׳ ||

[1] Corrected text.

CHAPTER 7

Apostrophe[1]

[1] Apostrophe[a] is the displaying of grief, anger, or anxiety over some person, State, people, or place, as follows: **Ah, Ariel, Ariel, the city where David encamped! Add ye year to year, let them strike away the feasts!** [Isa. 29:1].[2] Since the Prophet's vision was of the destruction of the Temple, the intensity of his grief, anxiety and anger is patent. Similarly: **Woe to her that is filthy and polluted, to the oppressing city!** [Zeph. 3:1]. So too: **Woe to thee that spoilest, and thou wast not spoiled; and dealest treacherously, and they dealt not treacherously with thee! When thou hast ceased to spoil, thou shalt be spoiled; and when thou art weary with dealing treacherously, they shall deal treacherously with thee** [Isa. 33:1]. The prophet was filled with anger and wrath against the king of Assyria, who **multiplied transgression** [Amos 4:4] against all Israel. Thus also: **Woe unto him that striveth with his Maker, as a potsherd with the potsherds of the earth! Shall the clay say to him that fashioneth it, "What makest thou?" or, "Thy work, it hath no hands"? Woe unto him that saith unto his father, "Wherefore begettest thou?"** [Isa. 45:9–10]; **Come down, and[3] sit in the dust, O virgin daughter of Babylon, sit on the ground without a throne, O daughter of the Chaldeans!** [47:1]; **Ah, sinful nation, a people laden with iniquity!** [1:4]. These and like examples of Apostrophe display notably intense grief, anger, and anxiety, and simultaneously lead the hearers themselves to feel these emotions.

[2] This figure should be used sparingly, and as the effect is demanded, for then it will be found to contain a large measure of elegance. It is a marvellous instrument for drawing hearts to the aforementioned objects, and will for the most part be employed in the Grand Style. In the holy tongue it sometimes expresses rebuke: **O generation, hear[4] ye the word of the Lord!** [Jer. 2:31]. Sometimes it serves other purposes: **Hear the word of the Lord** [Isa. 66:5]; **O congregation, there shall be one statute . . .** [Num. 15:15];[5] and there are many other examples. When, however, the word "Ah!" "Woe!" is used, the sense is generally that stated above.

1. "Calling out," "Exclamation": הַקְּרִיאָה.
2. The translation here is in accordance with Rashi, whose interpretation of this verse JML appears to follow.
3. Omitted in JML's text.
4. B: "see."
5. Messer Leon here follows Saadiah, Qimḥi, et al.—who are followed also by Luzzatto, Mendelssohn, and Leeser—in rendering "O congregation." JV follows Ibn Ezra, who denies vocative force to the Hebrew article, and renders "As for the congregation"; KJV and other versions also fail to construe the article as vocative here.

---

a. *R. ad H.* 4.15.22.

פרק ח׳

פ׳ השאלה.

[1] השאלה היא מאמר אשר כשסופרו מן הנשאל דברים אשר בערכם תאות
השאלה, אז ימשך לה הצחות אשר בתכלית, עם לשון מדברת גדולות. והנה
5 ירמיהו, אחר התרעמו מישראל תלונה גדולה על רוב פשעיהם לכל חטאתם,
שאל ואמר: למה תריבו אלי׳ כלכם פשעתם בי, נאם י״י; לשוא הכתי את
בניכם, מוסר לא לקחו, וכו׳ [יר׳ ב׳ כ״ט—ל׳]. וכן: הדור אתם שמעו דבר י״י, וכו׳
[שם שם ל״א]. וא״כ אמר: מה תטיבי דרכך לבקש אהבה׳ גם את הרעות למדת[1]
את דרכך [שם ל״ג]; וחזר ואמ׳: מה תזלי מאד לשנות את דרכיך׳ גם ממצרים
10 תבושי כאשר בשת מאשור [שם ל״ו]. והיתה זאת השאלה בסוג העצתי.

[2] וכן ישעיהו, במפלת מלך בבל אחר הדברים ההם — ר״ל, שבר י״י מטה
רשעים, שבט מושלים, מכה עמים בעברה, כו׳ [יש׳ י״ד ה׳—ו׳] — אמר: איך
נפלת משמים הלל בן שחר׳ נגדעת לארץ חולש על גוים [יש׳ שם י״ב]. וכן
בהוכיחו את ישראל בתחלת הספר, ואמ׳ הוי גוי חוטא, וכו׳ [שם א׳ ד׳], אמר
15 אחרי כן: על מה תכו עוד, תוסיפו סרה, וכו׳ [שם ה׳]; ושב א״כ, כאשר קרא
אותם קציני סדום ועם עמורה, ואמ׳: למה לי רוב זבחיכם יאמ׳ ה׳׳ שבעתי
עולות אילים, וכו׳ [שם י׳—י״א].

[3] והנה בהעשותה כמשפט, יעלה לשמים שיאה; ורוב מה שתבא, כמנהג
הוא בדבור הנשא:

1 פרק] פ׳[כ] || 2 פ׳ השאלה] מהשאלה[ד] || 3 תאות] תאוות[כ] || 4 [לה][ד] || 6 הכתי] הכיתי[ת] || 7 וכו׳] כו׳[ד] | שמעו] ראו[ת] || 8 תטיבי] תיטיבי[ת] | <לכן> גם[ת] || 9 דרכך] דרכיך[ת] | דרכיך] דרכך[ת] חרבך[כ] || 10 תבושי] תבוש[כ] | והיתה] ותיה[כ] || 13 הלל] היילל[ת] | גוים] הגויי[ד] || 14 [וכו׳][ד] | אמר] ואמ׳[ד] || 15 אחרי] אח׳[ד] | [עוד תוסיפו סרה][ד] | וכו׳] כו׳[כ] || 16–17 [יאמ׳ ה׳׳ שבעתי עולות אילים][ד] | וכו׳] כו׳[כ] || 19 בדבור] ברבוי[כ] ||

4 תה׳ י״ב ד׳ || 5 תה׳ ה׳ י״א | וי׳ ט״ז כ״א || 18 איוב כ׳ ו׳ ||

[1] *Q^e rē* for *k^e thībh* למדתי.

CHAPTER 8

Interrogation[1]

[1] Interrogation[a] is a Figure of Diction which results in the utmost elegance, as well as the **tongue that speaketh proud things** [Ps. 12:4], when rightly questionable actions are in this way stated to be those of the party being interrogated. Jeremiah, having bitterly denounced Israel for the multitude of **their transgressions** [Ps. 5:11], **even all their sins** [Lev. 16:21], used Interrogation when he said: **Wherefore will ye contend with Me? Ye all have transgressed against Me, saith the Lord. In vain have I smitten your children, they received no correction,** etc. [Jer. 2:29–30]. Similarly: **O generation, hear[2] ye the word of the Lord: Have I been a wilderness unto Israel?** etc. [2:31]. Following this, Jeremiah said: **How trimmest thou thy way to seek love? . . . Even the wicked ones hast thou taught thy way![3]** [2:33]; and again he said: **Why gaddest thou about so much to change thy ways?[4] Thou also shalt be ashamed of Egypt, as thou wast ashamed of Assyria** [2:36].[5] The context of this Interrogation was a Deliberative Cause.

[2] So, too, Isaiah, when the king of Babylon was overthrown following those prophetic words—**The Lord hath broken the staff of the wicked, the sceptre of the rulers, that smote the peoples in wrath,** etc. [Isa. 14:5–6]—said: **How art thou fallen from heaven, O Lucifer, son of the morning? How art thou cut down to the ground, which didst weaken the nations?** [14:12].[6] Similarly, after Isaiah's rebuke of Israel at the beginning of the Book, where he says **Ah, sinful nation,** etc., he continues: **On what part will ye be yet stricken, seeing ye stray away more and more?,** etc. [1:4–5]; and then when he has called the Israelites **rulers of Sodom** and **people of Gomorrah,** again he says: **To what purpose is the multitude of your sacrifices unto Me? saith the Lord; I am full of the burnt-offerings of rams,** etc. [1:10–11].

[3] Indeed, when this Figure is carried out according to rule, its **excellency mounts up to the heavens** [Job 20:6]. It mostly appears, as customarily used, in the Grand Style.

1. הַשְּׁאֵלָה.
2. Both here and in Chapter 7 where the same quotation is used, M and C have "hear ye" instead of the "see ye" of B. This is probably because JML is citing from memory, though a genuinely variant reading is not impossible. "Have I . . . Israel?" is not in our text, which contents itself with the introductory words only.
3. B: "ways."
4. B: "way."
5. KJV.
6. KJV.

---

a. *R. ad H.* 4.15.22.

פרק ט׳

פ׳ הוכוח.

[1] הוכוח הוא כאשר האדם נושא ונותן בענין מה, וישאל לעצמו, ויתיר הספקות הנופלות בדרוש בפני השומעים. והמשל מרב שקה: כאשר הלך להמשיך הלבבות להכנע תחת מלך אשור, נשא ונתן לעיני אליקים בן חלקיהו ושבנא הסופר ויואח בן אסף המזכיר להוכיח כי הנה מה טוב ומה נעים לעבוד את מלך אשור; והוא היה השואל והמתיר הספקות הקורות בענין, כי הם לא השיבו אליו דבר כמו שבא בכתו׳.

[2] ואמר בתחלה בתכונת שאלה: ״מה הבטחון הזה אשר בטחת?״ [מל״ב י״ח י״ט]; והוא בעצמו השיב לזאת השאלה, ואמ׳: ״אמרת אך דבר שפתים?״ [שם כ׳]. כלומ׳: ״אולי תשיבני כי ׳דבר שפתים׳ — ר״ל, שיפתה אנשיו והעם, בכונו במאמריו הערבות והצחות, עד יהיו לאחדים בידו, ולא תבקע העיר לא במרד ולא במעל; כי הרבה מי שינצלו, עם חלשתם, מצד האחדות וההסכמה אשר ביניהם· ותחשוב ש׳דבר שפתים׳ בזה האופן יצילך מיד צר, והיית מוצק ולא תירא· זה אי אפשר שיעמוד״. והביא לזה ראיה מן המפרסם מן הנהגת המדינות, שהנצחון אמנם ישלם באמצעות שני דברים אשר הם תנאים הכרחיים במלחמה, ואמר: ״עצה וגבורה למלחמה״ [שם כ׳]. כלומ׳: ״אינו כמו שתחשוב. כי מי שרוצה להלחם עם אויביו באופן יקוה הנצחון הגמור, יתחייב לו שיתיעץ ויתבונן היטב אם המלחמה ראויה שתעשה או לא· ואם היא ראויה שתעשה, באי זה מקום, ובאי זה זמן, והיאך; ולא יעלם ממנו ענינו וענין שונאו,

1 פרק] פ׳[כ] ‖ 2 פ׳ הוכוח] מהוכוח[ר] ‖ 3 [לעצמו][ר] ‖ 4 [בדרוש][ר] ‖ 7 והמתיר] ומתיר[ר] ‖ 7–8 לא השיבו אליו דבר <לא השיבו אליו דבר>[ר] ‖ 9 בתכונת] בתכונה[ר] | שאלה] השאלה[כ] ‖ 15–16 הנהגת המדינות] הנהגה המדינית[ר] ‖ 17 הכרחיים] הכרחי[ר] | כמו] כמה[כ] ‖ 19 שיתיעץ] שתיעץ[כ] ‖ 20 ולא] לא[ר] ‖

6 תה׳ קל״ג א׳ ‖ 12 יח׳ ל״ז י״ז | מל״ב כ״ה ד׳ | 12–13 יהו׳ כ״ב כ״ב ‖ 14 תה׳ ק״ז ב׳ | 14–15 איוב י״א ט׳ ‖

CHAPTER 9

Reasonıng by Question and Answer[1]

[1] It is Reasoning by Question and Answer[a] when the person discussing some subject puts questions about it to himself and resolves its difficulties in the presence of the hearers. Our example is furnished by Rab-shakeh:[2] When he went to induce the Judeans to make up their minds to submit to the king of Assyria, he dealt with the matter in the presence of **Eliakim the son of Hilkiah, . . . and Shebnah the scribe, and Joah the son of Asaph the recorder** [2 Kings 18:18] in order to prove **how good and how pleasant it is** [Ps. 133:1] to serve the Assyrian king. And it was he himself who kept raising questions about the matter, and resolving the difficulties involved in it, for, as stated in the text, the Judeans made no reply to his questions.

[2] His first statement in question form was: **"What confidence is this wherein thou[3] trustest?"** [2 Kings 18:19]. Replying himself to this query, he said: **"Sayest thou that it is a mere word of the lips?"** [18:20].[4] In other words: "Perhaps you will in answer say to me that confidence is **a mere word of the lips**—that by carefully contriving to make one's words agreeable and elegant one can so artfully deceive one's soldiers and the people that they will **become one in** his **hand** [Ezek. 37:17], and that no **breach will be made in the city** [2 Kings 25:4] either **by rebellion** or **by treachery** [Josh. 22:22]; for there are many instances of those who, though weak, were able to save themselves by means of the unity and harmony that prevailed among them. You think, then, that **a mere word of the lips** in this style will save you **from the hand of the adversary** [Ps. 107:2], **yea, thou shalt be stedfast and shalt not fear** [Job 11:15].[5] This argument, however, cannot possibly stand up." In proof of this he then cited the well-known political axiom that military victory is accomplished by two means only, the indispensable conditions for making war, and he said: **". . . counsel and strength for war"** [2 Kings 18:20].[6] In other words: "It is not as you think. For he who wants to wage against his enemies the kind of war in which he can expect complete victory must necessarily deliberate and consider well whether or not the war ought to be waged; and, if it ought to be waged, where, when, and how; and the facts of his own condition and that of his enemy should not be

1. "Disputation," "Debate," "Discussion," "Dialectic": הַוִּכּוּחַ.
2. 2 Kings 18:17 ff.; see iii.18.2,8, and iv.58.5.
3. I.e., Hezekiah.
4. Translation slightly different from JV.
5. Note that JML does not hesitate to use scripturally derived phrases (*m^e līṣāh*) in paraphrasing the Assyrian envoy's speech.
6. On the conditions for making war, cf. ii.14.5 (". . . Might and Craft") and ii.15.4.

a. *R. ad H.* 4.16.23.

כדי שיקח הבחינה השלמה אם אפשר שילחם עמו ויכהו, או יכבד, וישב בביתו,
ויהיה לו למס ויעבדהו. ותשועה ברב יועץ; וכל זה איננו שוה לו, אם לא תהיה
לו גבורה: שיוכל להתגבר, אם מצד גבורת אנשיו וחזקם, עם מעוטם· או מצד
רבוים, ואם אינם במדרגה גדולה מן החוזק· או מצד שניהם יחד, ר״ל, החזק
5 והרבוי.״

[3] והנה בחזקיהו לא היה אחד מאלה באופן שיקוה הנצחון עם מלך אשור,
כאשר יבאר אחר כך. ויען למי שנמנעת התשועה בערכו אפשר לו להתגבר על
אויביו מצד העזר אשר לו מאחרים, והיה אפשר שישיב כי בזה העזר יעשה חיל,
ובו יבוס קמיו, אמר א״כ: ״הנה בטחת לך על משענת הקנה הרצוץ הזה על
10 מצרים״, וכו׳ [שם כ״א]. כלומ׳: ״לא תשלם לך התשועה בזה, אם מצד שפרעה
אולי יטעה אותך, ומוצא שפתיו לא ישמר· אם ג״כ מצד שפרעה מלך מצרים
אינו במדרגה מן היכולת שיוכל להושיע את ישראל מיד אויביו, אפי׳ עם שתוף
ישראל עמהם.״ וכאשר היה זה כן, הוא מבואר שהבטחון בפרעה ישוב לו לנזק,
כי לולי זה הבטחון, אולי היה משלים ומציל את נפשו מיד להבה; ולזה,
15 המשילו אל משענת קנה רצוץ, שישוב לנזק אל הסומך עליה, בחלוף מה שקוה
ממנה מן העזר והתועלת.

[4] ואחרי כן הקשה קשיא אחרת גדולה, ואמ׳: ״אולי תאמרו אלי: ׳באלקים
נעשה חיל, כי ליי׳ התשועה, ובו בטחנו לעזרה אשר לא יבושו קויו· גם הוא
היכול האמתי, וספק בידו לעשות חכם לבב ואמיץ כח.׳ והנה דברי׳ כחרש
20 הנשבר, הבל המה, מעשה תעתועים. גם בזה לא תוכלו הועיל, והן נכזבה
תוחלתכם, כי אתם מריתם את פיהו והכעסתם לפניו. והנה אפי׳ אם נודה
שהיכלת בידו לעשות, לא יעשה.״ ולזה, אמר: ״וכי תאמרו״, כו׳... ״הלא הוא

2 ויהיה] ויהי[ד] | איננו] אינינו[כ] || 3 אם מצד] עם מצד[ד] || 6 שיקוה] יקוה[ד] || 7 התשועה] התשובה[ד] ||
8 מאחרים] מאמרי[ד] || 9 [לך][ד] || 9–10 [הזה על מצרים][ד] | וכו׳] כו׳[ד] || 11 מלך] הלך[ד] || 15 רצוץ]
הרצוץ[ד] || 16 [ממנה][כ] || 17 קשיא] קשיה[כ] | אלי <כי>[כ] || 18 גם <כי>[כ] || 19 [בידו][ד] | דברי׳] דבריי[כ] ||
21 והנה אפי׳] הנה אפי[ד] || 22 תאמרו] תאמרון[ת] | הלא] היא[ד] ||

2 דב׳ כ׳ י״א | מש׳ כ״ד ו׳ || 8 תה׳ ק״ח י״ד || 9 תה׳ מ״ד ו׳ || 11 דב׳ כ״ג כ״ד || 14 יש׳ מ״ז י״ד ||
17–18 תה׳ ק״ח י״ד | מש׳ כ״א ל״א | יש׳ מ״ט כ״ג || 19 איוב ט׳ ד׳ || 20 יר׳ י׳ ט״ו | יש׳ מ״ז י״ב ||
20–21 איוב מ״א א׳ | במ׳ כ׳ כ״ד ||

concealed from him, so that he may most thoroughly assay whether it will be possible to fight and defeat the enemy, or whether this will be too difficult, and he should stay at home, **become tributary unto** the enemy **and serve** him [Deut. 20:11]. Now **in the multitude of counsellors there is victory** [Prov. 24:6]. But all this counselling is worthless to him who wants to wage war unless he has the strength and the ability to prevail, whether because of the valor and might of his men, though these be few; or because of their large number, though they be possessed of no considerable degree of might; or of both factors at once, that is, both might and number."

[3] In Hezekiah's case, indeed, neither of these factors was such that he might expect victory over the king of Assyria, as Rab-shakeh goes on to explain. But since one for whom self-deliverance is excluded can yet prevail over his foes with aid obtained from others, and it was therefore possible for Hezekiah to reply that through such aid he would **do valiantly** [Ps. 108:14], would use it to **tread them under that rise up against** [Ps. 44:6] him, Rab-shakeh thereupon said: **"Behold, thou trustest upon the staff of this bruised reed, even upon Egypt,"** etc. [2 Kings 18:21]. In other words, "Deliverance will not be successfully achieved for you in this way, first, because Pharaoh is perhaps deceiving you, and will not keep **that which is gone out of** his **lips** [Deut. 23:24]; and again, because Pharaoh king of Egypt is not powerful enough to deliver Israel out of the hand of their enemies, even with Israel participating alongside the Egyptians." This being so, it was clear that reliance upon Pharaoh must result in harm to Hezekiah, because if he had no such reliance he would perhaps accept the terms of peace and **deliver** himself **from the power of the flame** [Isa. 47:14]. Accordingly, Rab-shakeh likened Pharaoh to the staff of a bruised reed, which will return harm to the person leaning upon it, the very contrary of the aid and advantage expected of it.[7]

[4] Next, Rab-shakeh raised another great difficulty, saying: "Perhaps you will say to me, **'Through God we shall do valiantly** [Ps. 108:14], for **victory is of the Lord** [Prov. 21:31], and it is upon Him that we rely for aid, since **they shall not be ashamed that wait for** [Isa. 49:23] Him; moreover, He it is Who is truly capable and in Whose hand is ample power to make one **wise in heart and mighty in strength** [Job 9:4].' If so, your words are as a broken potsherd, **they are vanity, a work of delusion** [Jer. 10:15]. Not even by this means shall you **be able to profit** [Isa. 47:12], and **behold,** your **hope of Him is in vain** [Job 41:1], for **ye have rebelled against His word** [Num. 20:24] and have made Him angry.[8] Thus, even if we should admit that He has the power to act, He will not act." On this point Rab-shakeh said: "**But if ye say unto me: 'We trust in the Lord our God';[9] is not that He, whose high places and whose altars Hezekiah**

7. Cf. ii.14.17.

8. Literally: "have made angry before Him," as in the Targum (e.g., Jer. 25:6) to avoid anthropopathism.

9. Our text reads "etc." for "We trust in the Lord our God."

אשר הסיר חזקיהו את בבמותיו״? כו׳ [שם כ״ב]. ״והנה לא נשאר לכם הבטחון כי
אם על מצרים.״ ושב לבאר מַה שהניח, שלא תשלם להם התשועה על ידו׳ כי
אנשי המלחמה בירושלם ספו תמו מן בלהות, עד לא יוכלו לתת רוכבים על
אלפים סוסים [שם כ״ג]. והנה כמעט נשאר פרעה לבדו׳ והיה מפורסם שהוא לא
5 יוכל להלחם עם המלך הגדול, מלך אשור, אשר אין ערוך אליו בימים ההם,
וכבש ממלכות ולחם מלחמות, הסיר גבולות עמים ולא התיצב איש לפניו.

[5] והנה עם ההודאה ביכלת י״י ית׳, היה אפשר שישיב רב שקה אחת
משתיים: אם שהסתיר פניו מהם, והיה לאכול מרוב עונם, ורבה משטמה, אבל
לא שיצוה להחרים׳, אלא שלא יושיענו אם תקראנה אותו צרות רבות ורעות׳
10 אם שחרה אפו עליהם עד לכלה, וישלח עליהם שרי החילות להשמיד, להרוג,
ולאבד. והנה שב עתה להשיב זאת התשובה האחרונה׳ אמר שי״י אמר אליו:
״עלה על הארץ הזאת והשחיתה״ [שם כ״ה].

[6] והיה גם כן אפשר שישיב רב שקא לזאת הטענה בהכחשת יכלת הבורא
ית׳, אלא שלא ראה לאמר זה בהיותו מדבר עם אליקים, ושבנא, ויואח, שהיו
15 חכמים וידועים׳ שהיה אליהם זה הדבר מפרסם הכזב, היה מהליש בזה יותר
תְשובותיו. אמנם א״כ, תחשב שההמון יאמין בזה, עם הצלחת מלך אשור
וחלשת שכלם׳ שקרא בקול גדול יהודית [שם כ״ח] להשמיע דבריו אל ההמון,
אז השיב בהכחשת היכלת, ואמר שאין דבר תלוי ביכלת אלוה להציל העם מיד
מלך אשור [שם ל׳]; וזה מה שאמ׳: ״ההצל הצילו״, כו׳... ״איה אלהי חמת

2 להם] לה[ד] || 4–5 שהוא לא יוכל] שלא היה יכול[ד] || 7 [י״י][ד] | אחת] א׳[ד] || 8–9 [אבל לא שיצוה להחרים׳][כ] | יושיענו] ירשיענו[כ] || 10 וישלח] וישליח[כ] | להרוג | ולהרוג[כ] || 11 [זאת][ד] | [שי״י] שהש׳[ד] || 15 היה] והיה[כ] || 16–17 תחשב שההמון...אל ההמון] שקרא בקול גדול יהודית להשמיע דבריו אל ההמון וחשב שההמון יאמין בזה עם הצלחת מלך אשור וחלשת שכלם[ד] || 19 אלהי] מלך[כ] ||

3 תה׳ ע״ג י״ט || 5 מל״ב י״ח י״ט | תה׳ מ׳ ו׳ || 6 יש׳ י׳ י״ג | יהו׳ א׳ ה׳ || 8 דב׳ ל״א י״ז | הו׳ ט׳ ז׳ || 9 דב׳ ל״א י״ז || 10 מל״א ט״ו כ׳ | 10–11 אס׳ ג׳ י״ג ||

hath taken away, etc. [2 Kings 18:22]? Hence, your only remaining ground for confidence is Egypt.'' And he made a further demonstration of his thesis that their deliverance would not be consummated by His hand: that the warriors in Jerusalem were so **wholly consumed by terrors** [Ps. 73:19] that they could not even set riders upon two thousand horses [2 Kings 18:23]. Thus, practically the only ground of confidence left was Pharaoh, and it was obvious that he would not be able successfully to wage war against **the great king, the king of Assyria** [18:19], unto whom in those days **there was none to be compared** [Ps. 40:6], who had subdued kingdoms and waged wars, who had **removed the bounds of the peoples** [Isa. 10:13] with no **man able to stand before** [Josh. 1:5] him.

[5] Now with his aforementioned acknowledgment of the power of the Lord, blessed be He, it was possible for Rab-shakeh to make one of two additional replies: either, that while the Lord had **hid His face from them and they** were to **be devoured** [Deut. 31:17] **for the multitude of** their **iniquity, the enmity being great** [Hos. 9:7], He would not command their utter destruction but would merely refrain from delivering them if **many troubles and evils should come upon them** [Deut. 31:17];[10] or else he could say that the Lord's anger burned against them to the point of destroying them completely, and so He had **sent the captains of... armies against** [1 Kings 15:20] them **to destroy, to slay, and to cause to perish** [Esth. 3:13]. Here, then, he resorted to this latter reply; he averred that it was the **Lord** Himself who had **said unto** him: **"Go up against this land, and destroy it"** [2 Kings 18:25].

[6] It would also have been possible for Rab-shakeh to counter such a Judean contention by denying the power of the Creator, blessed be He, but he did not think it well to make this assertion, seeing that he was speaking with Eliakim, Shebnah, and Joah, who were **wise... and full of knowledge** [Deut. 1:15]; since such an assertion would have been taken by them to be patently and notoriously false, he would thereby have made too weak a rebuttal. Later, however, it could be thought that the crowd would believe such an argument in view of the success of the king of Assyria and of their own weakness of intellect; inasmuch as Rab-shakeh had **cried with a loud voice in the Jews' language** [2 Kings 18:28] in order to make the crowd hear his words, he then used the answer of the denial of the divine power, saying that to save the people out of **the hand of the king of Assyria** [18:30] was a matter independent of the power of God.[11] This was the purport of his words: **"Hath any of the gods of the nations ever**

10. B: ''many evils and troubles....''

11. In C, this sentence has been rearranged as follows: ''Later, however, when he **cried with a loud voice in the Jews' language** [2 Kings 18:28] in order to make the crowd hear his words, and when he thought the crowd would believe such an argument in view of the success of the king of Assyria and of their own weakness of intellect, he then used the answer of the denial of the divine power, saying that to save the people out of **the hand of the King of Assyria** [18:30] was a matter independent of the power of God.''

וארפד״? כו׳ [שם ל״ג — ל״ה].

[7] אמנם, הבטיחם קודם זה בטוב הגדול ובנעימו׳ החיים שיהיה להם אם ישמעו אל מלך אשור, אשר הוא בחלוף התלאה העצומה אשר להם בהיותם תחת ממשלת חזקיהו; כי בזה ימשך לבב העם· ירוצו ולא ייעפו בשמעם היעוד על אשר יקוו מן ההצלחות. וזהו מה שאמ׳ אליהם: ״עשו אתי ברכה וצאו אלי, ואכלו איש גפנו״, כו׳ [שם ל״א].

[8] והנה בכל זה הספור הוא היה השואל והעונה והמתיר הספקות, ואם היה בפני האנשים הנזכרים. וזה היפוי, אפשר לעשותו בכל סוגי הדבורים, ובכל חלקי המאמר זולת החלוק:

פרק י׳

פ׳ המשל.

[1] המשל הוא מאמר קצר בערך אל הנהגת העולם, יתפרסם בו אשר ימשך ממנה בזמן ההוה או בעתיד. ובזה האופן לקחנו המשל הנה כמו שאמר דוד: ״כאשר יאמר משל הקדמוני: מרשעים יצא רשע· וידי לא תהיה בך״ [שמ״א כ״ד י״ד].

[2] ומזה היפוי מלא כל ספר משלי. והוא יחלק לשני חלקים, למה שממנו פשוט, וממנו מורכב. והפשוט גם הוא נחלק לשני חלקים, למה שממנו עם נתינת הסבה, וממנו זולת זה.

[3] משל הראשון: קסם על שפתי מלך· במשפט לא ימעל פיו [מש׳ ט״ז י׳]; לב חכם ישכיל פיהו ועל שפתיו יוסיף לקח [שם ט״ז כ״ג]; אבן חן השחד בעיני

2 ובנעימו׳] ובעימות[כ] || 6 ואכלו איש גפנו][ד] | כו׳] וכו׳[ד] || 10 פרק] פ׳[כ] || 11 פ׳ המשל] מהמשל[ד] || 12 יתפרסם] פרסם[ד] || 13 או][ד] || 14 כאשר יאמר][ד] | וידי לא תהיה בך] וכו׳[ד] || 19 משל] המשל[כ] | קסם] קדם[כ] || 20 השחד] השוח׳[ד] | ישכיל] ישכל[כ] | עשה] עושה[ד] ||

---

4 יש׳ מ׳ ל״א ||

delivered his land out of the hand of the king of Assyria? Where are the gods of Hamath, and of Arpad?" etc. [18:33-35].

[7] Previously, however, he had assured the crowd that great good and a pleasant life would be theirs if they hearkened to the king of Assyria—the very contrary, indeed, of the inordinate hardship which was their lot under Hezekiah's rule. For by such assurance he might win the heart of the people: **they would run . . . and not faint** [Isa. 40:31] upon hearing the promise of the prosperity which they might expect. This is what he said to them: **"Make your peace with me, and come out to me; and eat ye every one of his vine, and every one of his fig-tree, and drink ye every one the waters of his own cistern,"** etc. [2 Kings 18:31 ff.].

[8] Thus, in this entire narrative, it was Rab-shakeh himself who kept asking the questions, supplying the answers, and solving the difficulties, though he was in the presence of the men mentioned above. This figure is applicable in all the Kinds of Cause and in all the Parts of the Discourse except the Partition.

CHAPTER 10

The Maxim[1]

[1] A Maxim[a] is a short saying about the way of the world by means of which a conclusion, presently or in future applicable, is held to be self-evidently true. Thus, we have here taken "maxim" as in David's statement: **"As saith the proverb of the ancients: Out of the wicked cometh forth wickedness; but my hand shall not be upon thee"** [2 Sam. 24:14].

[2] The whole of the Book of Proverbs is made up of this Figure. It is divisible into two classes, as there is a simple form of it, and a complex. The simple Maxim is also found in two sorts, as there is a form without reason given, and one with.[2]

[3] Examples of the first:[3] **A divine sentence is in the lips of the king: his mouth trespasseth not in judgment** [Prov. 16:10]; **The heart of the wise teacheth his mouth, and addeth learning to his lips** [16:23]; **A gift is as a precious stone in the eyes of him that hath it: whithersoever it turneth, it**

1. הַמָּשָׁל: also "proverb," "example," "allegory," "fable," etc.; cf. iii.19.1-2.
2. Text: ". . . a form with . . . and one without."
3. I.e., the simple Maxim, unaccompanied by the reason.

a. *R. ad H.* 4.17.24 ff.

בעליו· אל כל אשר יפנה ישכיל [שם י״ז ח׳]; עשה צדקה ומשפט נבחר לי״י מזבח [שם כ״א ג׳]; אוטם אזנו מצעקת דל· גם הוא יקרא ולא יענה [שם כ״א י״ג]. כל אלה המשלים הם פשוטים, ומבלי סבה מבוארת בכתוב.

[4] משל השני, שהוא עם נתינת הסבה: גדל[1] חמה נושא עונש· כי אם תציל, ועוד תוסיף [שם י״ט י״ט]. המכוון בו כי מי שהוא גדל חמה ימשך לו העונש בהכרח, וזהו המשל; ונותן בו הסבה: כי אם זאת החמה אפשר שתציל בעליה לפעמים — מצד התגברות על אשר יכעס עליו, כי יחם לבבו וינצחהו — ועוד תוסיף בכל פעם זאת החמה להתגבר, עד יבואהו העונש הגדול מהאנשים; כי זה דבר בלתי סובלו הטבע, והנה בהכרח בעל החמה ישא קללות, ומארות, ומכת בלתי סרה באחרונה. עוד משל אחר: סוד רשעים יגורם — זהו המשל — כי מאנו לעשות משפט — זאת היא הסבה [שם כ״א ז׳]. וכן: טוב כעס משחוק· כי ברוע פנים ייטב לב [קה׳ ז׳ ג׳]; טוב עין הוא יבורך· כי נתן מלחמו לדל [מש׳ כ״ב ט׳]. וכן: נפש עמל עמלה לו· כי אכף עליו פיהו [מש׳ ט״ז כ״ו]; כלומר, נפש עמל עמל לצרכו· והסבה בזה כי לא יוכל לעשות מבלי שיעמול לצרכו,״ כי אכף עליו פיהו״, ר״ל, ״פיהו״ כופף אותו על זה העמל, מפני הכרח האכילה והשתיה אשר אי אפשר בלעדם. ויהיה ״אכף״ ו״כפף״ שני שרשים בענין אחד, כמו שאמר ר׳ דוד· ויבא על דרך כל עמל האדם לפיהו [קה׳ ו׳ ז׳].

[5] אמנם, המשל המורכב הוא המחבר ממשלים רבים; וגם הוא יחלק לשני מינים, כי ממנו מבלתי סבה, ממנו עם נתינת סבה. משל הראשון: פורע מוסר מואס נפשו· ושומע תוכחת קונה לב [מש׳ ט״ו ל״ב]; בברכת ישרים תרום קרת· ובפי רשעים תהרס [שם י״א י״א]; ברב דברים לא יחדל פשע· וחושך שפתיו משכיל [שם י׳ י״ט]; עוכר ביתו בוצע בצע· ושונא מתנות יחיה [שם ט״ו כ״ז]; כל אחד מאלה מורכב משני משלים.

[6] והמשל ממה שממנו בסבה: נואף אשה חסר לב· משחית נפשו הוא

2 מצעקת] מזעקת[ת] || 3 הם פשוטים] הפשוטים[ר] || 4 גדל[1]] גרל[תר] || 5 חמה] חימה[ר] || 6 זאת] בזאת[ר] || 7 התגברות] התגברותו[ר] || 9 סובלו] סובלת[ב] | החמה] החמות[ב] || 10 ומכת] ומכה[ר] | סוד] שד[ת] || 14 שיעמול] שיעמו[ר] || 16 כמו שאמר] כדע׳[ר] || 18 המחבר] במחובר[ר] || 19 נתינת סבה] נתינת הס׳[ב] | הראשון] הא׳[ר] || 20 תוכחת] תוכחה[ר] | בברכת ישרים תרום] ברכת תסוב[ב] || 23 משני] מב׳[ר] ||

---

7 דב׳ י״ט ו׳ || 10 יש׳ י״ד ו׳ ||

---

[1] *Q^e rē* for *k^e thībh* גרל.

prospereth [17:8];[4] **To do righteousness and justice is more acceptable to the Lord than sacrifice** [21:3]; **Whoso stoppeth his ears at the cry of the poor, he also shall cry himself, but shall not be answered** [21:13]. All these maxims belong to the simple class, and are without reason explicitly stated in the text.

[4] An example of the second form of simple Maxim, that with the reason given: **A man of great wrath shall suffer punishment; for if it deliver him, yet will it wax again** [19:19].[5] The intended meaning is that punishment inevitably overtakes a person of great wrath, and this forms the Maxim. The reason given is that if such wrath can sometimes deliver its possessor—by waxing great against the object of his anger: because **his heart** will be **hot** [Deut. 19:6] and make him victorious—then such wrath will each time again wax great until stern punishment comes to him at men's hands; for since wrath of this kind is a trait of which nature is intolerant, its possessor must, in the end, inevitably sustain curses, maledictions, and the **incessant stroke** [Isa. 14:6]. Another example: **A cabal**[6] **of the wicked shall drag them away**—the Maxim proper—**because they refuse to do justly**—the reason [Prov. 21:7]. Thus again: **Vexation is better than laughter, for by the sadness of the countenance the heart may be gladdened** [Eccl. 7:3]; **He that hath a bountiful eye shall be blessed, for he giveth of his bread to the poor** [Prov. 22:9]. And again: **The hunger of the labouring man laboureth for him, for his mouth compelleth him** [16:26]. In other words, a laborer's hunger labors for his need, the reason being that he could not function without laboring for his need, "for his mouth compelleth him"—that is, "his mouth" forces him to such labor because food and drink are indispensable necessities. "Compel" (*'ākhaph*) and "force" (*kāphaph*) are two separate roots that have the same meaning, as Rabbi David has said.[7] The verse parallels **All the labour of man is for his mouth** [Eccl. 6:7].

[5] The complex Maxim, in its turn, is a composite of several maxims. It likewise subdivides into varieties, for there is a form without reason given, and another with reason given. Examples of the first: **He that refuseth correction despiseth his own soul, but he that hearkeneth to reproof getteth understanding** [Prov. 15:32]; **By the blessing of the upright a city is exalted, but it is overthrown by the mouth of the wicked** [11:11]; **In the multitude of words there wanteth not transgression, but he that refraineth his lips is wise** [10:19]; **He that is greedy of gain troubleth his own house, but he that hateth gifts shall live** [15:27]. Each of the foregoing examples is compounded of two maxims.

[6] An example of the form with reason given: **He that committeth adultery with a woman lacketh understanding: He doeth it that would destroy his own**

4. KJV.
5. Translation in accordance with Messer Leon's interpretation.
6. B and JV: "The violence. . . ." JML here has written סוד for שׁוד.
7. Rabbi David Qimḥī's *Book of Roots;* see J. H. R. Biesenthal and F. Lebrecht, *Rabbi Davidis Kimchi Radicum Liber* (Berlin, 1847; rep. Jerusalem, 1967), s.v. אכף, col. 30, p. 15.

יעשנה; נגע וקלון ימצא· וחרפתו לא תמחה [שם ו׳ ל״ב—ל״ג]; ואחר אלה המשלים נותן הסבה, והוא אמרו: כי קנאה חמת גבר· ולא יחמול ביום נקם [שם שם ל״ד].

[7] וזה היפוי אפשר העשותו בכל סוגי הדבור, ובכל חלקי המאמ׳ זולת החלוק; ועל הרוב יבוקש ענינו בדבור הבינוני:

פרק י״א

פ׳ החלוף.

[1] החלוף הוא מאמ׳ מורכב מהפכים, אשר מאחד המאמרים יתחייב האחר; ובזה יבדל מההפוך אשר בארנוהו למעלה.

[2] והמשל: גומל נפשו איש חסד· ועוכר שארו אכזרי [מש׳ י״א י״ז]; ״עוכר שארו״ ו״גומל נפשו״, וכן ״איש חסד״ ו״אכזרי״, הם הפכיים, ומזה הצד אין חלוק בין ההפוך ובין החלוף; אלא שבהפוך לא יבקש מאחד מן המאמרים יתחייב חברו, כאשר הענין בחלוף; כי מכח המאמ׳ הראשון, האומר שהעושה טובות לנפשו יקרא איש חסד, יתחייב שהעושה הפך זה, ר״ל, שהוא ״עוכר שארו״, ימשך לו הפך החסידות, והוא האכזריות.

[3] וכן: רשע עושה פעולת שקר· וזורע צדקה שכר אמת [שם י״א י״ח]; כי אם ״פעלת שקר״ תתחייב אל הרשע, הוא מבואר שימשך אל ״זורע צדקה״, שהוא הצדיק, ״שכר אמת״. וכן: אשת חיל עטרת בעלה· וכרק׳ בעצמותיו מבישה; מחשבות צדיקים משפט· ותחבולות רשעים מרמה [שם י״ב ד׳—ה׳]; אוגר בקיץ בן משכיל· נרדם בקציר בן מביש [שם י׳ ה׳]; מבואר מענינם, שמאחד מאלה

2 כי קנאה] כן קנאת[כ] | ולא] לא[כ] || 6 פרק] פ׳[כ] || 7 פ׳ החלוף] מהחלוף[ד] || 8 מאחד] מא׳[ד] | האחר] האחד[כ] || 11 הפכיים] הפכין[ד] || 12 החלוף] ההפוך[כ] || 13 הראשון] הא׳[ד] | <ר״ל> האומר[כ] || 16 פעולת] פעולה[ד] || 17 פעלת] פעל[כ] || 18 וכרק׳] וכרקב[ת] וכרקיו[כ] || 19 ותחבולות] תחבלות[ת] | מרמה] וכ׳[ד] ||

soul; wounds and dishonour shall he get, and his reproach shall not be wiped away. After these maxims, the text gives the reason in these words: **For jealousy is the rage of a man, and he will not spare in the day of vengeance** [6:32–34].

[7] This Figure can be used in all the Kinds of Cause and in all the Parts of the Discourse except the Partition. It is usually in demand in the Middle Style.

CHAPTER 11

Reasoning by Contraries[1]

[1] Reasoning by Contraries[a] is a Figure of Diction composed of paired opposite statements, such that from one of these the other necessarily follows; it is thus distinguishable from Antithesis, which we explained above.[2]

[2] For example: **One that doeth good to his own soul is a merciful man, and one that troubleth his own flesh is a cruel** [Prov. 11:17].[3] "Troubleth his own flesh" and "doeth good to his own soul," like "a merciful man" and "a cruel" are paired contraries, and on this score there is no difference between Antithesis and Reasoning by Contraries. In Antithesis, however, it is not required that one of the contrasting statements must necessarily follow from the other, as in the case of Reasoning by Contraries; for from the force of the first statement, which says that the doer of good to his own soul will be called a merciful man, it necessarily follows that one who does the contrary of this—one who "troubleth his own flesh"—must possess a quality that is contrary to mercy, namely, cruelty.

[3] So too: **The wicked earneth deceitful wages, but he that soweth righteousness hath a true[4] reward** [11:18]; for if "deceitful wages" are what the wicked must eventually receive, then clearly, to one "that soweth righteousness," that is, the righteous, there must necessarily come "a true reward." And so again: **A virtuous woman is a crown to her husband, but she that doeth shamefully is as rottenness in his bones** [12:4]; **The thoughts of the righteous are right, but the counsels of the wicked are deceit** [12:5]; **A wise son gathereth in summer, but a son that doeth shamefully sleepeth in harvest**

1. Literally: "the exchange," "the contrary," "the reverse," "the substitution": הַחִלּוּף.
2. iv.6.
3. Translation here in accordance with JML's interpretation.
4. JV and KJV: "sure."

a. *R. ad H.* 4.18.25 ff.

המאמרים יתחייב האחר בהכרח.

[4] וכאשר יחוברו בקצור ובתכלית התקון, אחד באחד יגשו מבלי הפרדה, אז חיבו מן הערבות לשומעים מה שלא יעלם. וזה היפוי טוב בערך אל כל סוגי הדבור ובכל חלקי המאמ׳, וביחוד בקיום ובהתרה; ויבוקש ענינו על הרוב בדבור הבינוני:

פרק י״ב

פ׳ המדובק.

[1] המדובק הוא מאמר כולל חלקים קצרים ומדובקים זה בזה, שבים אל ענין אחד קודם השלמת המאמר. והמשל: שריך סוררים, וחברי גנבים· כלו אוהב שחד, ורודף שלמונים [יש׳ א׳ כ״ג]. וכן: שבעתי עולות אילים, וחלב מריאים· ודם פרים, וכבשים, ועתודים לא חפצתי [שם שם י״א]. וכן: ותשורי למלך בשמן, ותרבי רקוחיך· ותשלחי ציריך עד מרחוק, ותשפילי עד שאול [שם נ״ז ט׳]. וכן: ותבטחי ביפיך, ותזני על שמך· ותשפכי את תזנותיך [יח׳ ט״ז ט״ו]. וכן: ואלבישך רקמה, ואנעלך תחש· ואחבשך בשש, ואכסך משי [שם שם י׳].

[2] וזה היפוי, אם נעשה כהוגן, הוא בתכלית מה שאפשר לעורר החמה והכעס לרעים, והרצון וטוב הלבב לטובים. ואפשר העשותו בכל סוגי הדבורים, ויבוקש ענינו על הרוב בדבור הבינוני:

1 יתחייב] תתחייב[כ] || 2 ובתכלית] בתכלית[ד] || 3 חיבו] חיבת[ד] || 4 הדבור] הדבורי׳[כ] | [בקיום][ד] | ובהתרה] בהתרה[ד] || 6 פרק] פ׳[כ] || 7 פ׳] פרק[ד] || 13 ותשפכי] ותשפתי[כ] ||

2 איוב מ״א ח׳ ||

[10:5]. It is clear from the content that the second in each of these pairs of statements must necessarily follow from the first.

[4] When such pairs are composed in terse form and with full correctness, with **one so near to another** [Job 41:8] and not separated, then they must afford the hearers no small delight. This Figure will be found excellent for all the Kinds of Cause and in all the Parts of the Discourse, but especially in the Proof and the Refutation; and it is an effect demanded mostly in the Middle Style.

CHAPTER 12

Colon or Clause[1]

[1] Colon or Clause[a] is a sentence structure in which, before the sentence is terminated, several short, interconnected sentence parts that advert to a single thought are brought together. For example: **Thy princes are rebellious, and companions of thieves: every one loveth bribes, and followeth after rewards** [Isa. 1:23]. Thus again: **I am full of the burnt-offerings of rams, and the fat of fed beasts; and in the blood of bullocks, or of lambs, or of he-goats I delight not** [1:11].[2] Again: **And thou wentest to the king with ointment, and didst increase thy perfumes, and didst send thine ambassadors far off, even down to the nether-world** [57:9]. Or again: **But thou didst trust in thy beauty, and play the harlot because of thy renown, and didst pour out thy harlotries . . .** [Ezek. 16:15]. And again: **I clothed thee also with richly woven work, and shod thee with sealskin, and wound fine linen about thy head, and covered thee with silk** [16:10].

[2] This Figure, appropriately used, is most capable of arousing wrath and anger toward the evil, and favor and kindness of heart toward the good. It can be employed in all the Kinds of Cause, and is mostly in demand in the Middle Style.

1. Literally: "the joined together," "the attached": הַמְּדוּבָּק.
2. Translated in the Hebrew order the better to illustrate the Figure.

a. *R. ad H.* 4.19.26.

פרק י״ג

פ׳ המחולק.

[1] המחולק הוא מאמ׳ נופלות בו תיבות רבות מבלי אות קושר. והמשל: אמר אויב, ״ארדוף, אשיג, אחלק שלל״ [שמ׳ ט״ו ט׳]; בין רגליה כרע, נפל, שכב [שופ׳ ה׳ כ״ז]; וביחזקאל: התאחדי, הימיני, השימי, השמאלי· אנה פניך מועדות [יח׳ כ״א כ״א].

[2] וזה היפוי, ואשר למעלה ממנו, כמעט הם מכונים תכלית אחת, אלא שיתחלפו בהמתנה ומהירות· שהקודם הוא יותר מתון, וזהו יותר מהיר. ודמיון הקודם במי שמרים זרועו להכות חברו הכאות רבות; ודמיון זה היפוי במדרגת מי שתוקע חרבו במהרה בבטן אויבו הלוך ותקוע, לא יחדל עד ידקרהו, ויעברהו ממותי חללים ימות.

[3] ואלה שניהם מפלגים בהערת הלבבות לטובה או לרעה· וטובים בערך אל כל סוגי הדבור, ויבוקש ענינם על הרוב בדבור הנשא והבינוני:

פרק י״ד

פ׳ המשלש.

[1] המשלש הוא מאמר כולל ג׳ יפויים יחדו מבלי אמצעי, עם התמדת התבות והוכחת הדרוש. ואלה השלשה יפויים: המשל, והחלוף, וההמשכות.

1 פרק] פ׳[c] || 2 פ׳] פרק[d] || 5 השמאלי] השמאילי[d] השמילי[t][1] || 8 מתון] מתין[c] || 9 במי] כמי[c] || 11 חללים] תחלאים[t] || 13 ענינם] ענינים[c] || 14 פרק] פ׳[c] || 15 פ׳] פרק[d] || 17 השלשה] הג׳[d] ||

11 יר׳ ט״ז ד׳ ||

[1] Massoretic note: חסר א׳.

CHAPTER 13

Comma or Phrase[1]

[1] Comma or Phrase[a] is a sentence structure in which there occurs a succession of several words without conjunctive particle. For example: **The enemy said, "I will pursue, I will overtake, I will divide the spoil"** [Exod. 15:9]; **At her feet he sunk, he fell, he lay** [Judg. 5:27]. And in Ezekiel: **Go thee some one way, go right, direct thyself, go left: whithersoever thy face is set** [Ezek. 21:21].[2]

[2] This Figure and the Figure treated immediately above serve virtually the same purpose. They differ, however, in point of deliberateness and speed, the pace of Colon being more leisurely, that of Comma quicker. The former Figure is analogous to one who lifts his arm in readiness to deal his adversary many blows; while in the latter Figure it is as if one keeps quickly and repeatedly thrusting his sword into his enemy's belly, not ceasing until he pierces him through, so that he comes to experience **shall die of grievous deaths** [Jer. 16:4].[3]

[3] Both these Figures are extremely effective in stirring hearts to good or to ill; they will be found excellent for all the Kinds of Cause, and are mostly in demand in the Grand and Middle Styles.

CHAPTER 14

The Triple Figure[1]

[1] The Triple Figure[2a] is a statement which includes three Figures joined directly together, and in which, as well, we find an uninterrupted succession of the words and a proof of the matter under investigation. These three figures are Maxim, Reasoning by Contraries, and Elimination.

1. Literally: "the divided, apportioned, differentiated, disjointed, separated": הַמְחוּלָּק.
2. Translated in the Hebrew order the better to illustrate the Figure.
3. Text: ". . . the deaths of the slain" (חֲלָלִים instead of תַּחֲלֻאִים).

a. *R. ad H.* 4.19.26.

1. Literally: "the threefold": הַמְשֻׁלָּשׁ.
2. In *R. ad H.*, "Period."

a. *R. ad H.* 4.19.27.

[2] והמשל מספר קהלת, כאשר שלמה המלך רצה להוכיח שהוא טוב
לשמוע גערת חכם משמוע שיר כסילים [קה׳ ז׳ ה׳], ואמר להוכיח זה, בתחלה:
שטוב כעס משחוק [שם שם ג׳]. ואין המכון ב״כעס״ הנה תכונת הכעס ומדתו,
אבל לקח הנה ״כעס״ במקום סותר ההתול והצחוק· רצוני לומר, שראוי לאדם
5 לעמוד בדמות כעוס, טרם שימשך אל ההתול והשחוק. ונתן הסבה בזה ואמר:
כי ברע פנים ייטב לב [שם]; רצה לומר, כי מדרגת השגת החכמות והידיעות —
אשר רמז הנה ב״ייטב לב״, כי הרצון ב״לב״ הנה החלק השכלי, כמו: צור לבבי,
וחלקי עם אלקים לעולם [תה׳ ע״ג כ״ו] — הוא כפי מדרגת ״רוע הפנים״,
שהרצון בו ההתפשט מן התאוות החמריות.

10 [3] והנה זה המאמר הוא משל פשוט עם נתינת הסבה; ויתמיד לזה המשל
החלוף תכף, ואמר: לב חכמים בבית אבל, ולב כסילים בבית שמחה [קה׳ ז׳ ד׳].
כלומ׳ אחר שלב האדם, שהוא הכח השכלי, ״ייטב״ עם ״רוע הפנים״ — ר״ל,
ששלמותו הוא נתלה בהפשטה מן החמריות — אין ספק שהחכמים, המבקשים
השלמות האחרון ושהרוח תשוב אל האלקי׳ אשר נתנה, יכוננו לבם בבית אבל,
15 אשר שם מן ההערה אשר בתכלית אל עזיבת התענוגים ועניני העולם. אמנם
הכסילים, אשר כל כספם ותאותם ישימו בדומם הגוף ותענוגיו, ולשומו לראש
פנה יבזו[1] הידיעות והשגות השכל, יכוונו אל הפך מה שכוונו בו החכמים, רצה
לומר, שלבם בבית שמחה.

[4] והנה מן המשל הנז׳ והחלוף, התחייבה התולדה ש״טוב לשמוע גערת
20 חכם״ — שהוא מעיר אל הטוב שבמדות ובדעות, שהם תכלית מה שכוון מן
יצירת האדם — ״משמוע אל שיר כסילים״ [שם ה׳], אשר יעירו אל התאוות
המדומות, לא יועילו ולא יצילו כי תהו המה. והאריך אחר כן בהפסד ענינם על
צד ההמשל, ואמר: כי כקול הסירים תחת הסיר, כו׳ [שם ו׳].

2 משמוע] מאיש שמע[ת] || 4 רצוני לומר] ר״ל[כ] || 5 בדמות] כדמות[ד] || 6 [כי][ד] | ייטב] יטב[ד] | רצה לומר] ר״ל[כ] || 7 בייטב] ביטב[ד] || 8 [עם][ת] || 9 ההתפשט] התפשט[ד] | החמריות] והחמריות[כ] || 15 אל] על[כ] || 16 [כל][ד] | בדומם] כדומם[ד] | הגוף] לגוף[ד] || 17 יבזו[1]] ויבזו[כד] | בו] אליו[ד] | 17–18 רצה לומר] ר״ל[כ] || 20 שבמדות] שמדות[כ] | ובדעות] וברעות[כ] || 22 אחר כן] א״כ[כ] ||

14 קה׳ י״ב ז׳ || 16–17 תה׳ קי״ח כ״ב || 22 שמ״א י״ב כ״א ||

[1] Emended text.

[2] Our example is taken from the Book of Ecclesiastes: King Solomon, wishing to prove that **it is better to hear the rebuke of the wise than . . . to hear the song of fools** [Eccl. 7:5], in order to accomplish this first said: **Vexation is better than laughter** [7:3]. *Ka'as* [''anger, vexation''] does not here mean the state and moral quality of anger; rather, Solomon used *ka'as* here to represent a position contradictory of sarcasm and derision. That is to say, a man ought sooner to stop short as one vexed than be drawn into sarcasm and derision. Giving the reason for this, he said: **For by the sadness of the countenance the heart may be gladdened** [7:3]. In other words, the degree of attainment in the sciences and disciplines—to which he had alluded in the words **the heart may be gladdened,** for ''heart'' here means the intellectual portion of man, as it does in ''. . . **the rock of my heart, and my portion is** (with) **God forever** [Ps. 73:26][3]—is proportionate to the degree of **the sadness of the countenance,** meaning the abnegation of the materialistic desires.

[3] This statement, then, is a simple Maxim, with the reason given.[4] Continuing with a Reasoning by Contraries[5] directly after presenting this Maxim, Solomon said: **The heart of the wise is in the house of mourning, but the heart of fools is in the house of mirth** [Eccl. 7:4]. Since, that is, man's heart (the intellectual faculty) is ''gladdened'' when there is ''sadness of countenance'' (meaning that his perfection is dependent upon a stripping off of materialism), there is no doubt that the wise—those who seek ultimate perfection, and that **the spirit return unto God who gave it** [12:7]—fix their heart **in the house of mourning** where there is the utmost stimulation to the abandonment of the pleasures and affairs of the world. Fools, on the other hand, who tacitly make the body and its pleasures all that they crave and desire, and who, in order to make the body **the chief cornerstone** [Ps. 118:22], despise[6] the disciplines and intellectual attainments, are directed toward the contrary of the aim of the wise: their **heart is in the house of mirth** [Eccl. 7:4].

[4] Thus, the necessary consequence that follows from the aforementioned Maxim and Reasoning by Contraries is this:[7] **It is better to hear the rebuke of the wise** [7:5]—which stimulates a man to those finest ethical principles and attitudes that are the ultimate purpose of his creation—**than . . . to hear the song of fools**—that arouses him to imaginary delights **which cannot profit nor deliver, for they are vain** [1 Sam. 12:21]. Then elaborating in a simile upon the profitlessness of this characteristic of fools, Solomon said: **For as the crackling of thorns under a pot, so is the laughter of the fool** [Eccl. 7:6].

3. The word ''with'' (עִם) is not in B, but has been read into the verse by JML. Cf. Ibn Ezra and Rashi, *ad loc.*
4. Cf. iv.10.
5. Cf. iv.11.
6. Slightly amended text.
7. I.e., the third member of the Triple Figure, an Elimination, as defined and illustrated in iv.33.1, below.

[5] וההכרחי בזה היפוי הקשר המאמרים הנזכרים וחבורם מבלי אמצעי, לא מצד הזמן ולא מצד המאמרים. וזה היפוי מועיל מאד בקיום ובהתרה, ובכל סוגי הדבורי׳ ויבוקש ענינו בבינוני, ובשפל יותר:

פרק ט״ו

פ׳ השוה.

[1] השוה הוא מאמר כולל חלקים מה שוי התנועות במספר, או נראים שוי התנועות. והמשל: אז תבין צדק ומשפט· ומשרים כל מעגל טוב [מש׳ ב׳ ט׳]; משיב רעה תחת טובה· לא תמיש[1] רעה מביתו [שם י״ז י״ג]; טוב פריי מחרוץ ומפז ותבואתי מכסף נבחר [שם ח׳ י״ט]; אוגר בקיץ בן משכיל· נרדם בקציר בן מביש [שם י׳ ה׳]. כל מאמר מהנזכרי׳ כולל שני מאמרים שוי התנועות במספר· וכאלה רבים במשלי.

[2] וזה הענין יעשהו ההרגל וההתמדה כמעט בלי כונה. ואפשר העשותו בכל סוגי הדבורים· ויבוקש ענינו בבינוני, ובשפל יותר:

פרק י״ו

פ׳ המתדמה.

[1] המתדמה הוא יפוי כולל חלקים מה, אשר בכל אחד מהם תפול תיבה

3 ענינו ‹שפל›ᶜ || 4 פרק] פ׳ || 5 פ׳] פרקᵀ || 7 ומשרים] ומישריםᴺ || 8 תמיש[1]] תמושᴺ | פריי] פריוᶜ | מחרוץ] מחרווץᵀ || 9 ומפז] מפוזᵀ | ותבואתי] ותבואתᶜ || 12 וההתמדה] וההמתדמהᵀ || 14 פרק] פ׳ᶜ || 15 פ׳] פרקᵀ ||

[1] *Kᵉthībh* for *qᵉrē* תמוש.

[5] The essential point of this Figure is the combining and joining of the Figures mentioned without interruption of any kind, whether temporal or verbal. This Figure is very useful in the Proof and the Refutation and in all the Kinds of Cause; its effect is called for in both the Simple and Middle Styles, but more so in the Simple.

CHAPTER 15

Isocolon[1]

[1] Isocolon[a] is a statement in which the several constituent parts consist of an equal, or virtually equal, number of syllables. For example: **Then shalt thou understand righteousness and justice: and the equitable,**[2] **yea, every good path** [Prov. 2:9]; **Whoso rewardeth evil for good: evil shall not depart from his house** [17:13]; **Better my fruit than gold, fine gold: and my produce than choice silver** [8:19];[3] **A son that is wise gathereth in summer: but a shame-bringing son sleepeth in harvest** [10:5].[4] Each of the foregoing statements is composed of two cola, in each of which there is an equal number of syllables; and there are many such in Proverbs.

[2] Experience and constant practice will make the forming of an Isocolon almost instinctive. It can be introduced in all the Kinds of Cause, is called for in the Middle Style, and even more in the Simple.

CHAPTER 16

Homoeoptoton[1]

[1] Homoeoptoton[a] is a figure that brings together several sentence divisions, each of which contains a word whose grammatical form is the same as that of one

1. Literally: "the equal," "equivalent": הַשָּׁוֶה.
2. JV and KJV: ". . . and equity"—changed here in order to make the number of syllables equal in each half-verse. In the Hebrew the number of syllables is eight.
3. Translation slightly altered to keep the number of syllables equal. The number of Hebrew syllables is nine.
4. Translation altered to exhibit the Figure. The number of Hebrew syllables is eight.

---

a. *R. ad H.* 4.20.27 ff.

1. Literally: "the similar," "the homogeneous": הַמִּתְדַּמֶּה.

---

a. *R. ad H.* 4.20.28.

באופן מתדמה לאשר היא בחלק האחר. והמשל: תמת ישרים תנחם· וסלף בוגדים ישדם[1] [מש׳ י״א ג׳]; תיבת ״תמת״ נופלת באופן מתדמה ל״סלף״, שהוא במאמ׳ האחר, וכן מלת ״ישרים״ לתיבת ״בוגדים״. וכן: ושמתי כדכד שמשותיך, ושעריך לאבני אקדח [יש׳ נ״ד י״ב]. וכן: תאות צדיקים אך טוב· ותקות רשעים עברה [מש׳ י״א כ״ג]; ״תאות״ ו״תקות״ נופלות באופן מתדמה, וכן ״צדיקים״ ו״רשעים״. וכן: מחשבות צדיקים משפט· ותחבולות רשעים מרמה [שם י״ב ה׳]. וזה הרבה.

[2] וראוי שתדע שלא ימנע, במאמר אחד, היות יפויים רבים בבחינות מתחלפות. כמו במשל שהבאנו באחרונה, ר״ל, מחשבות צדיקים[2], כו׳, אשר ימצא בו יפוי החלוף גם כן, כמו שהתבאר למעלה; אלא שזה יביט אל נפילת התבות באופן מתדמה, והחלוף אל הרכבת המאמר מההפכים, ושהאחד יתחייב אל חברו.

[3] וזה היפוי נלקח בערך אל השמות, ויבוקש ענינו בבינוני יותר, ואפשר העשותו בכל סוגי הספורים:

פרק י״ז

פ׳ המסכים.

[1] המסכים הוא יפוי כולל חלקים מה, אשר בכל חלק יפול פעל מה באופן

1 האחר] האחד[ד] | תנחם] ינחם[כ] || 2 ישדם[1]] ושדם[ת] || 3 לתיבת] לסלף[ד] || 4 ותקות] תקות[ת] || 5 תאות ותקות] תאוה ותקוה[ד] || 6 ותחבולות] תחבלות[ת] || 9 צדיקים[2]] רשעים[כד] || 10 כמו] כמה[כ] || 13 בבינוני יותר] יותר בבינוני[ד] || 15 פרק] פ׳[כ] || 16 פ׳] פרק[ד] ||

[1] *Qerē* for *kethībh* ושדם.

[2] Corrected according to ת.

in the next division. For example: *Tummath y^{e}shārīm tanḥēm, w^{e}seleph bōgh^{e}dhīm y^{e}shoddēm:* **The integrity of the upright shall guide them, but the perverseness of the faithless shall destroy them** [Prov. 11:3]. The grammatical accidence of the word *tummath* [''the integrity of''] is the same as that of *seleph* [''the perverseness of''] in the next clause;[2] so too, the accidence of the word *y^{e}shārīm* [''the upright''] is the same as that of the word *bōgh^{e}dhīm* [''the faithless''].[3] Thus also: *W^{e}samtī kadhkōdh shimshōthayikh, ūsh^{e}'ārayikh l^{e}'abhnē 'eqdāḥ:* **And I will make thy pinnacles of rubies, and thy gates of carbuncles** [Isa. 54:12].[4] Again: *Ta'^{a}wath ṣaddīqīm 'akh ṭōbh, tiqwath r^{e}shā'īm 'ebhrāh:* **The desire of the righteous is only good, but the expectation of the wicked is wrath** [Prov. 11:23]; *ta'awath* [''desire''] and *tiqwath* [''expectation''] are of the same grammatical accidence, and so are *ṣaddīqīm* [''righteous''] and *r^{e}shā'īm* [''wicked'']. And again: *Maḥsh^{e}bhōth ṣaddīqīm mishpāṭ, w^{e}thaḥbūlōth*[5] *r^{e}shā'īm mirmāh:* **The thoughts of the righteous are right, but the counsels of the wicked are deceit** [12:5]. Homoeoptoton abounds.

[2] You should know, too, that it is not impossible for several different kinds of rhetorical Figures to occur in the same statement. In the last cited example, for instance, **The thoughts of the righteous,**[6] etc. [12:5], we find also the Figure Reasoning by Contraries, as was made clear above.[7] Homoeoptoton, however, looks to words of the same grammatical accidence, while Reasoning by Contraries looks to the opposite expressions of which the sentence is composed, and of which the one necessarily leads to the other.

[3] The present Figure is to be used in connection with nouns, is an effect called for mainly in the Middle Style, and can be applied in all kinds of Statement of Facts.

CHAPTER 17

Homoeoteleuton[1]

[1] Homoeoteleuton[a] is a Figure that brings together several sentence divisions, in each of which there is a verb of like grammatical accidence. For

2. I.e., both are nouns in the construct state.
3. I.e., both are considered by JML to be nouns, masculine plural, in the absolute state.
4. Refers to ''thy pinnacles . . . thy gates.''
5. B: *taḥbūlōth*.
6. Both M and C read ''wicked.''
7. iv.11.3.

1. Literally: ''the agreeing [in ending],'' ''the corresponding [in ending]'': הַמַּסְכִּים.

a. *R. ad H.* 4.20.28.

מתדמה לחברו. והמשל: קחי רחים, וטחני קמח· גלי צמתך, חשפי שובל, גלי שוק, עברי נהרות [יש׳ מ״ז ב׳]; בכל חלק יפול פעל צווי לנקבה. וכן: למי תדמיוני, ותשווּ ותמשילוני ונדמה [שם מ״ו ה׳]; ״תדמיוני״ ו״תמשילוני״ נופלים באופן מתדמה. וכן: הנה צרפתיך ולא ככסף· בחרתיך בכור עוני [שם מ״ח י׳]; וזולתם רבים.

[2] ואפשר העשותו בכל סוגי הדבורים, ויבוקש ענינו בבינוני יותר:

פרק י״ח

פ׳ ההעתקה.

[1] ההעתקה היא כאשר יעתקו התבות במאמר עם חלוף או תוספת אות או אותיות, גזר או גזרים· או עם התחלפות ההוראה. אשר אפשר שתעשה על פנים רבים מתחלפים:

[2] אם שתחזור אותה התיבה בעצמה, עם הוראתה, עם תוספת אותיות השמוש לבד. והמשל בירמיהו: על כן על מואב איליל[1] ולמואב כלה אזעק [יר׳ מ״ח ל״א]; ״מואב״ במאמ׳ הראשון מבלי אות השמוש, ובשני עם תוספת וי״ו ולמד לשמוש.

[3] אם שתחזור אותה התיבה בעצמה עם חסרון אות השמוש והתחלפות ההוראה, והמשל: הבוגד בוגד והשודד שודד [יש׳ כ״א ב׳]; הוא מבואר

1–2 גלי שוק] בלי שוק[ד] | [בכל][כ] || 4 [הנה][ד] | ככסף] בכסף[ת] ככסף <בכו>[כ] | בכור עוני] בבור עיני[ד] || 7 פרק] פ׳[כ] || 8 פ׳] פרק[ד] || 9 [אות][כ] || 13 בירמיהו] בירמיה[כ] | איליל[1]] ייליל[כד] || 16 עם חסרון] בחסרו׳[ד] || 17 ההוראה] הוראת׳[ד] ||

[1] Corrected according to ת.

example: **Take the millstones, and grind meal; remove thy veil, strip off the train, uncover the leg, pass through the rivers** [Isa. 47:2]; each member contains a verb in the feminine singular imperative. Similarly: **To whom will ye liken Me, and make Me equal; and compare Me, that we may be like?** [46:5]; "will ye liken Me" and "will ye compare Me" are similar in accidence.[2] Again: . . . **I have refined thee but not as silver;**[3] **I have tried thee in the furnace of affliction** [48:10]. And there are many other examples.

[2] This Figure can be used in all the Kinds of Cause, and its effect may be called for in the Middle Style.

CHAPTER 18

Paronomasia[1]

[1] Paronomasia[a] is the Figure when the words in a sentence are repeated[2] with a changed or added letter or letters, syllable or syllables, or are repeated in a different meaning of the words. The Figure can be developed in a number of different ways:

[2] (1) The identical word recurs in the same sense, and with addition of preformative and afformative letters[3] only. In Jeremiah, for example, *'al kēn 'al Mō'ābh 'ayēlīl ūl Mō'ābh kullōh 'ez'aq:* **Therefore will I wail for Moab; yea for Moab, all of it, I will cry out** [Jer. 48:31]. "Moab" in the first clause has no preformative letter, but in the second appears with addition of preformative *wāw* ["and" = "yea"] and *lāmedh* ["for"].

[3] (2) The identical word recurs with lack of preformative or afformative letter, but in a different sense, as in the following example: *habbōghēdh bōghēdh whashshōdhēdh shōdhēdh:* **The treacherous dealer dealeth treacherously, and the spoiler spoileth** [Isa. 21:2]. Here, clearly, the first words in each half,

2. I.e., in every respect except that of the *binyān* (derived conjugation) of each: *pi'el* in the case of the first, *hiph'īl* in that of the second.

3. So JV; B has בְּכָסֶף = "as though silver"; Messer Leon has ככסף = "as silver." He had the sense right, but the wording wrong (ב-*essentiae*).

1. Literally: "transfer," "removal"; "copy," "translation"; "change of place," "transposition"; "mutation," "modification": הַהַעְתָּקָה.

2. Literally: "are copied" (יעתקו [*hoph'al*]).

3. Literally: "letters of attendance," a technical term for the letters אית"ן, מש"ה, וכל"ב, the constituent phonemes of the several morphemes and particles (pronominal elements, prepositions, conjunctions, etc.) that may be pre- or post-fixed to word stems.

a. *R. ad H.* 4.21.29.

שהתיבות הראשונות הם עם אות השמוש והם שמות, ר״ל, ״הבוגד״ ו״השודד״· והאחרונות הם פעלים בלי אות השמוש.

[4] אם שתחזור התיבה עם התחלפות מפועל לפעול, ומשם לפעל, כמו: הוי שודד ואתה לא שדוד, ובוגד ולא בגדו בך [שם ל״ג א׳]. במאמר הראשון, נחלף הפועל לפעול; ובשני, נחלף השם לפעל עבר המורה על רבים· ובכן יקרהו גם כן החלוף מן יחיד לרבים. וכן: כהתימך שודד תושד [שם]; התחלף השם לפעל בזאת החזרה. וכן: גם מדמן תדומי [יר׳ מ״ח ב׳]; שב השם לפעל בנפילת המ״ם והנו״ן, ובא תחתיהם התי״ו והיו״ד. וכן: בגת אל תגידו [מי׳ א׳ י׳]; התחלף השם לפעל עם השתנות אותיות, ותוספת, וחסרון, ושנוי הנקוד.

[5] אם שתחזור התבה עם התחלפות חלק אחד מהבנין אל חלק אחר, כמו: כנלתך לבגוד יבגדו בך [יש׳ ל״ג א׳]; התחלף מהמקור לפעל עתיד מורה על רבים· והתחייב גם כן בערכ׳ חלף קצת האותיות, וחסרונם, והשתנות הנקודים.

[6] אם שתחזור התיבה משם לשם, עם השתנות נקוד והוראה, כמו: בבית לעפרה עפר התפלשי[2] [מי׳ א׳ י׳]; וכמו: בתי אכזיב לאכזב [שם י״ד].

[7] אם שתחזור התבה עם תוספת גזר, עם הוראה מסכמת, כמו שנאמר ביחזקאל: לא מהם.... ולא מהמהם [יח׳ ז׳ י״א]· כי הנרצה ב״המהם״ כמו המכוון ב״מהם״, וגזר ״מי־״ נוסף.

[8] ולפעמים תשוב עם תוספת גזר עם הוראה מתחלפת, ושנוי קצת האותיות עם הנקודים, ותוספת ״הא׳״, כמו שנאמר במיכה עוד: היורש אביא לך, יושבת מרשה [מי׳ א׳ ט״ו].

1 שהתיבות] שהתובות[ד] | [ר״ל][ד] || 4 בך] בו[כ] | הראשון] הא׳[ד] || 5 ובשני] והב׳[ד] || 6 [וכן][כ] | כהתימך] בהתימך[ד] || 8 והנו״ן] והנון[ד] | התי״ו והיו״ד] תי״ו ויו״ד[ד] | וכן] וגם[ד] || 12 והתחייב] ויתחייב[ד] | בערכ׳] בערכם[כ] | חלף] הלוך[כ] || 16 לא מהם <ולא מהם> ולא מהמהם[ד] | בהמהם] במהמהם[כ] || 19 [עוד][ד] | אביא] אבי[ת] ||

[2] *Qᵉrē* for *kᵉthībh* התפלשתי.

namely, "the treacherous dealer" and "the spoiler," are accompanied by the preformative letter and are nouns, whereas the last words are verbs and lack the preformative letter.

[4] (3) The word recurs with change from active to passive, or from noun to verb, as follows: *hōi shōdhēdh w^{e}'attāh lō shādhūdh ūbhōghēdh w^{e}lō bhāgh^{e}dhū bhākh:* **Woe to thee, spoiler, and thou not spoiled; and treacherous dealer, and they dealt not treacherously with thee.** [Isa. 33:1][4] In the first clause, the active participle has been changed to a passive. In the second, the noun has been changed to the third person, masculine plural, perfect tense, of the cognate verb; the word has thus also undergone a change from singular to plural. Similarly, *kah^{a}thīm^{e}khā shōdhēdh tushshadh:* **When thou hast ceased to be a spoiler, thou shalt be spoiled** [33:1]: in this repetition, noun has changed to verb. Again in *gam madhmēn tiddōmī:* **"Thou also, O Madmen,[5] shalt be silent"** [Jer. 48:2], the noun has become a verb through the falling away of the *mēm* and the *nūn,* and their replacement by the *tāw* and the *yōdh.* So, too, in *b^{e}ghath 'al taggīdhū:* **Tell it not in Gath** [Mic. 1:10], the noun has changed to a verb with a different ordering of the letters, the addition of some letters, the omission of one letter, and a change in the vocalization.

[5] (4) The word recurs with a change from one part of the conjugation to another, as in *kann^{e}lōth^{e}khā libhgōdh yibhg^{e}dhū bhākh:* **When thou shalt make an end to do treacherously, they shall deal treacherously with thee** [Isa. 33:1],[6] where there has been a change from the infinitive to the finite verb, imperfect tense, third person, masculine plural; correspondingly, also, certain letters have necessarily been changed, omitted, or differently vocalized.

[6] (5) The word recurs as a noun, but with altered vocalization and sense, as in *b^{e}bhēth l^{e}'aphrāh 'āphār hithpallāshī:* **At Beth-le-aphrah[7] roll thyself in the dust** [Mic. 1:10]; or in *bāttē 'akhzībh l^{e}'akhzābh:* **The houses of Achzib shall be a deceitful thing** [1:14].

[7] (6) The word recurs with addition of a syllable, but in much the same sense, as in Ezekiel's words, *lō mēhem . . . w^{e}lō mēh^{e}mēhem:*[8] **None of them . . . nor of any of theirs** [Ezek. 7:11];[9] for the purport of *h^{e}mēhem* is about the same as what is meant by *mēhem,* and the syllable *mē-* has been added.

[8] (7) Sometimes the word reappears with addition of a syllable and with a different meaning, with alteration of some letters and vowel points, and with a supplementary *hē,* as is said, again in Micah: *hayyōrēsh 'ābhī' lākh yōshebheth*

4. JV slightly altered to bring out JML's meaning.
5. Moabite town; cf. Rashi, *ad loc.*
6. KJV.
7. G. W. Wade, *The Books of the Prophets Micah, Obadiah, Joel and Jonah,* (London, 1925), p. 8, suggests "Duston" to show the paronomasia.
8. The form is a *hapax legomenon.*
9. KJV.

[9] ולפעמי׳ תשוב התבה עם הוראתה, עם תוספת נו״ן, עם התחלפות מעתיד לנמצאים לעתיד לנסתרים, כמו: ״אל תטיפו״, יטיפון [שם ב׳ ו׳].

[10] ולפעמים תשוב התבה בהדרגה עם תוספת גזר פעמים, וכמעט עם הוראה מסכמת, וזה מבלתי אמצעי, כמו שכתוב בנחום: בוקה ומבוקה ומבולקה [נח׳ ב׳ י״א]. והנה ״מבוקה״ בתוספת גזר בערך אל ״בוקה״, וכן הענין ב״מבולקה״ בערך אל ״מבוקה״.

[11] ולפעמים תחבור התבה פעמים, גם כן מבלי אמצעי באופן אחר, כמו: ונהה נהי נהיה [מי׳ ב׳ ד׳]. והוא מבואר ש״נהה״ הוא פעל· ויתר ההתחלפות אשר ביניהם מפורסם.

[12] וזה היפוי יותר בינינו במנהג ממה שהוא אצל הנוצרי׳, ובאופן מתחלף במקצת; וביחוד מיכה המורשתי מלא כרסו מעדניו. וקצרה ידי מהביא כל פרטי זה היפוי, כי נשארו מהם הרבה בפסוקים, כמו: כי עזה עזובה תהיה, וכו׳ [צפ׳ ב׳ ד׳]· לא יצאה יושבת צאנן מספד בית האצל [מי׳ א׳ י״א]; כי עד סירים סבוכים, ובסבאם סבואים [נח׳ א׳ י׳]; רתום המרכבה לרכש, יושבת לכיש [מי׳ א׳ י״ג]; וזולתם רבים, והקש מאלה על השאר.

[13] ואלה השלשה יפויים, ר״ל המתדמה והמסכים והחזרה, ראוי לעשותם על המעט, למה שיש בהעשותם מן הקשי מה שלא יעלם. והתדירות בהם יביא האנשים לחשוב שהדבר יש בו מן ההראות מצד המלאכה ההלציית, לא מצד האמת· ויביא אל שהאנשים לא יאמינו במליץ, אשר הוא מן הדברים ההכרחיים בערכו, וישוב במדרגת הנערים; עוד, שבאלה היפויים מן הערבות והנעימות שעור רב, ואין בהם קנין חזקת החשיבות והמעלה במליץ.

1 נו״ן] נון[ד] || 4 מבלתי] שבלתי[כ] | ומבוקה] ובוקה[כ] | ומבולקה] ומבולק[ד] || 9 ההתחלפות] התחלפות[ד] || 10 <הוא> יות[י] | [שהוא][כ] | מתחלף] מתחלק[כ] || 12 [וכו׳][כ] || 13 [לא...האצל][ד] || 14 ובסבאם] וכסבאם[ת] | יושבת] יושבי[ד] | לכיש] לכישה[כ] || 16 לעשותם] לעשותה[ד] || 17 [בהם][ד] || 19 מן הדברים] מהדברים[ד] ||

11 מי׳ א׳ א׳ | יר׳ נ״א ל״ד ||

mārēshah: **An heir will I bring to thee, O inhabitant of Mareshah** [Mic. 1:15].[10]

[9] (8) Sometimes the word reappears in the same sense, but with supplementary *nūn,* and with a change from the second person plural masculine of the imperfect tense to the third person plural masculine of that tense, as in *'al taṭṭīphū yaṭṭīphūn:* **"Preach ye not," they preach** [Mic. 2:6].

[10] (9) Sometimes the word reappears several times with gradual syllabic addition, with retention virtually of the same sense, and without other intervening matter, as in the following text from Nahum: *būqāh ūm^{e}bhūqāh ūm^{e}bhullāqāh:* **She is empty, and void, and waste** [Nah. 2:11]. As compared with *būqāh, m^{e}bhūqāh* has an additional syllable, and the same is true of *m^{e}bhullāqāh* as compared with *m^{e}bhūqāh.*

[11] (10) Sometimes the word recurs several times, again without other intervening matter, but in another grammatical function, as in *w^{e}nāhāh n^{e}hī nihyāh:* . . . **and lament with a doleful lamentation** [Mic. 2:4]. *Nāhāh* is clearly a verb, while *n^{e}hī nihyāh* are nouns; the other differences between them are obvious.

[12] This Figure is more usual with us than with the Christians,[11] and our mode of using it is rather distinctive; **Micah the Morashtite** [Mic. 1:1] has especially **filled his maw with** its **delicacies** [Jer. 51:34]. I am unable here to cite all the particulars of this Figure, for there are too many of them left in the Biblical verses, as for example, in the following: *kī 'azzāh '^{a}zūbhāh thihyeh . . . :* **For Gaza shall be forsaken . . .** [Zeph. 2:4]; *lo yāṣ^{e}'āh yōshebheth ṣa'^{a}nān mispadh bēth hā'ēṣel:* **The inhabitant of Zaanan went not forth to the wailing of Beth-ezel** [Mic. 1:11],[12] *kī 'adh sīrīm s^{e}bhūkhīm ūbh^{e}sobh'ām*[13] *s^{e}bhū'īm:* **For while they be yet folden together as thorns, and while they be yet drinking though drunk . . .** [Nah. 1:10];[14] *r^{e}thōm hammerkābhāh lārekhesh yōshebheth lākhīsh:* **Bind the chariots to the swift steeds, O inhabitant of Lachish** [Mic. 1:13]. There are many other verses besides, identifiable by analogy from these.

[13] These three figures—Homoeoptoton, Homoeoteleuton, and Paronomasia—should be sparingly used since the difficulty of contriving them is not inconsiderable. Too frequent use, moreover, will lead people to think that the cause owes its plausibility to rhetorical artifice rather than to truth; this will make them lose that confidence in the speaker which is a requisite of his success, and he will come to seem childish. Again, while in these Figures there is an abundance of pleasure and delight, the presumption of worth and virtue in the speaker

10. Translation adapted from KJV.

11. JML means orators and writers in the languages of Christian Europe, particularly, of course, Latin.

12. This passage is in M but not in C. The translation follows Ibn Ezra and Qimḥi; the modern versions interpret differently. Qimḥi mentions the fact of paronomasia here.

13. *Sic* both M and C; B: *ūkh^{e}sobh'ām.*

14. KJV (adapted).

ובהתמדתם יקוצו האנשים, במדרגת מה שיביאו הדברים המתוקים, כמו הדבש
והנוהגים מנהגו, אל שהאוכלי׳ מהם הרבה יקוצו בהם בתכלית מה שאפשר.
כמו שנאמר: דבש מצאת אכול דייך· פן תשבענו והקאתו [מש׳ כ״ה ט״ז].
[14] ואפשר העשותו בכל סוגי הדבור· ויבוקש ענינו לפעמי׳ בנשא, ויותר
5 בבינוני:

פרק י״ט

פ׳ הוכחת השאלה.

[1] הוכחת השאלה הוא מאמ׳ אשר, כשיבואו בו שאלות, תכף אחר השאלה
נשא המבוקש ממנו להוכיח מכח השאלה. וזה על שני פנים: אם שהשאלה
10 תשוב אל המנגד· אם שישאל אליו בעצמו השואל.
[2] משל הראשון מיפתח· כשרצה להוכיח שמלך בני עמון לא היה ראוי
שילחם אתו, אחר אותו הספור הארוך היאך התגלגל כבוש ישראל הארצות
ההנה, שאל ואמר: ״הטוב טוב אתה מבלק בן צפור מלך מואב· הרוב רב עם
ישראל אם נלחום נלחם בם?״ ואח׳ כן אמר: ״בשבת ישראל בחשבון ובבנותיה
15 ובערוער ובבנותיה וכל הערים אשר על יד ארנון שלש מאות שנה· ומדוע לא
הצלתם בעת ההיא?״ [שו׳ י״א כ״ה—כ״ו]. ואחר הב׳ שאלות ההנה, נשא
המבקש והוכיחו מכח השאלות, ואמר: ״ואנכי לא חטאתי לך״, כו׳ [שם כ״ז].
כלומ׳, ״ממה שכבשו ישראל הארצות ההנה, אין ראוי שתלחם עמי· כי אם היה
האמת והמשפט אתכם, היתה ראויה זאת המלחמה זה שלש מאות שנה. גם
20 אין ראוי לך להלחם מצד שאני פשעתי כנגדך בדבר מן הדברים· ואם כן, אתה
עושה אתי רעה להלחם בי״ [שם]. וכאלו אמר: ״אם היתה זאת המלחמה
ראויה, לא ימנע אם שתהיה ראויה מצד כבוש הארצות שלא כדין״ — ואם היה

1 במדרגת] במדרגה[ד] || 2 מנהגו] מנהגת[כ] |שהאוכלי׳] האוכלים[כ] || 3 תשבענו] תשביענו[כ] ||
4 [סוגי][ד] || 6 פרק] פ׳[כ] || 7 [פ׳][ד] || 9 ממנו] מהם[ד] |שני] ב׳[ד] || 11 הראשון] הא׳[ד] || 14 נלחום] לחום[כ] ||
15 ובערוער] ובערעור[ת] |וכל] ובכל[ת] |יד] ידי[ת] || 16 הב׳] השני[כ] || 17 ואנכי] ואני[ד] || 19 והמשפט]
המשפט[ד] || 20 כנגדך] נגדך[ד] |ואם כן] וא״כ[כ] || 21 היתה] היה[כ] ||

is not obtainable through them. And when they are used constantly, people become surfeited with them, quite as sweet things such as honey and the like will bring those who overindulge in them to loathe them utterly. As has been said: **Hast thou found honey? eat so much as is sufficient for thee, lest thou be filled therewith, and vomit it** [Prov. 25:16].

[14] Paronomasia can be used in all the Kinds of Cause; it is occasionally called for in the Grand Style, but more often in the Middle.

CHAPTER 19

Hypophora[1]

[1] Hypophora[a] is diction in which, immediately following the introduction of several questions, the point we are called upon to prove is raised on the strength of what has been asked. There are two types: the questioning is either addressed to the adversary, or the poser of the questions asks them of himself.

[2] The first type is exemplified by Jephtha who, when he wished to prove that the king of the Ammonites ought not to wage war against him, posed several questions after delivering that long account of how Israel's conquest of those territories had been brought about [Judg. 11:15–24], and said: **"Art thou any thing better than Balak the son of Zippor, king of Moab? did he ever strive against Israel, or did he ever fight against them?"** And immediately thereafter: **"While Israel dwelt in Heshbon and its towns, and in Aroer and its towns, and in all the cities that are along by the side of the Arnon, three hundred years; wherefore did ye not recover them within that time?"** [11:25–26]. Then, directly following these two queries, he raised the point he was seeking to make, and proved it on the strength of the questions, saying: **"I therefore have not sinned against thee, but thou doest me wrong to war against me,"** etc. [25:27]. In other words: "Since Israel took those territories by conquest, it is not proper for you to war against me now; for if truth and justice were on your side, such a war should have been fought three hundred years ago. Moreover, you cannot properly make war on the ground that I have been in any respect remiss towards you. Therefore, **thou doest me wrong to war against me."** It was as if he had said: "If this war were one that should be fought, it must necessarily either be one that should be fought on the ground that the territories were

1. Literally: "the proof of the question"; "the reproving of the question"; "the deciding, determining, showing-to-be-right, convincing, admonishing etc., of the ~uestion": הוֹכָחַת הַשְּׁאֵלָה.

a. *R. ad H.* 4.23.33–4.24.34.

זה, היתה נעשת בימי בלק בן צפור, כמו שפירש — "אם שתהיה ראויה על אי
זה פשע וחטאת עשיתי כנגדך· וזה אינו, כי אנכי לא חטאתי לך; נשאר, אם כן,
שאתה עושה עמי רעה להלחם בי."

[3] המשל השני מירמיהו, בהנבאותו על בבל, באמרו: על הארץ מרתים, כו'
5 [יר' נ' כ"א—כ"ד]. רצה להוכיח שסבת המפלה העצומה הבאה עליהם היתה
על אשר הפליגו להרע לישראל, ושאל בינו לבין עצמו: "איך נגדע ונשבר פטיש
כל הארץ· איך היתה לשמה בכל הגוים?" [שם כ"ג]. ותכף השיב ואמר: "כי בי"י
התגרית" [שם כ"ד]; ר"ל, שהתגרו בישראל, הנקראים בשם י"י, ועשו עמהם את
הרעה אשר בתכלית. וכאלו אמר: "מפלת בבל לא ימנע אם שתהיה מצד
10 חלשתם ומעוט כחם· אם מצד אי זה פשע וחטאת נפלא, יתחייב אליהם ההכרת
וההשמד על צד העונש מאשר לו הגבורה לאין תכלית. ובטל שיהיה מצד
חלשתם, למה שכבשו כל הממלכות עד יקראו 'פטיש הארץ'; ונשאר, א"כ,
שנלכדו, ונוקשו, ונתפשו על צד העונ' מהבורא ית', בורא השמים ונוטיהם".
וזהו מה שאמר: "יקשתי לך וגם נלכדת, בבל, ואת לא ידעת· נמצאת וגם
15 נתפשת, כי בי"י התגרית" [שם כ"ד].

[4] וכן, כשרצה ישעיהו להוכיח שהשם ית' הוא אוהב את ישראל, ואם
לפעמי' יכהו בשבט התלאות והצרות ויחר אפו בהם, הוא על צד התוכח' כאשר
ייסר איש את בנו, שאל בינו לבין עצמו ואמר: "הכמכת מכהו הכהו· אם כהרג
הרוגיו הורג?" [יש' כ"ז ז']; ותכף השיב: "בסאסאה, בשלחה, תריבנה" [שם ח'].
20 כלומ': אם היה עושה זה על צד השנאה, היה עושה עמהם כלה, כאשר עשה
למלך אשור, שהיה מכהו, וליתר האמות, שהוא מכה אותם בעברה עד
השמדם; וזה אינו, כי הוא אינו מכלה אותם כליון גמור, כאשר משלם לשונאיו,
בלי מדה ושעור על פניו להשמידם; וישאר שיביא עליהם הענש במדה על צד

2 פשע וחטאת] פשע או חטאת[ד] | כנגדך] נגדך[ד] | נשאר] וישאר[כ] | אם כן] א"כ[כ] || 4 [השני][ד] | מרתים] מדתים[כ] || 6 ונשבר] וישבר[ת] || בכל הגוים] ככל הגוים[ד] בבל בגוים[ת] || 8 ר"ל] רוצה לומר[ד] | בישראל] בישראל[ד] | י"י] השם[ד] || 12 א"כ] אחר כך[ד] || 13 ונתפשו] ונתפסו[ד] | [העונ'][כ] || 14 נמצאת וגם] נמצאת גם[ד] || 16 שהשם] שה'[ד] || 17 התוכח'] התוכחת[כ] || 18–19 אם כהרג הרוגיו הורג] וכו'[ד] | בסאסאה] בססאה[כ] || 20 [עושה] זה[כ] | צד] יד[ד] || 23 [וישאר... צד][ד] ||

13 יש' מ"ב ה' || 17 שמ' ל"ב י' || 17–18 דב' ח' ה' || 20 יר' ה' י"ח || 21 יש' י"ד ו' || 21–22 דב' ז' כ"ג || 22 דב' ז' י' ||

conquered illegally''—in which case it should have been fought in the days of Balak the son of Zippor, as he had specifically stated—''or else the war must be one that ought to be fought on account of some sinful wrong I have done to you—and such is not the case, for **I . . . have not sinned against thee.** It remains, therefore, that **thou doest me wrong to war against me.**''

[3] The second type is exemplified by Jeremiah, when, prophesying against Babylon, he said: **Go up against the land of Merathaim,** etc. [Jer. 50:21-24]. Wishing to prove that the reason for the overwhelming ruin which was to engulf the Babylonians was that they had gone too far in inflicting evil upon Israel, he asked himself these questions: **"How is the hammer of the whole earth cut asunder and broken? How is she become a desolation among all the nations?"** [50:23][2] And forthwith he gave the reply and said: **"Because thou hast striven against the Lord"** [50:24]; that is to say, the Babylonians had striven against Israel, those called by the name of the Lord, and had done them the utmost evil. It was as if he had said: ''Babylon's ruin must necessarily be caused either by the weakness of the Babylonians and the dwindling of their power, or by some extraordinary transgression and sin requiring, as punishment, that they be cut off and destroyed by Him to Whom belongs power without end. Now it is absurd to suppose that their ruin will come to pass through their own weakness, for they have made such conquest of all kingdoms that they are called **the hammer . . . of the earth** [50:23]. It remains, therefore, that they will have been **taken, snared,** and **caught** [50:24] as a punishment by the Creator, blessed be He, **He that created the heavens and stretched them forth**'' [Isa. 42:5]. Such is the purport of Jeremiah's words: **"I have laid a snare for thee, and thou art also taken, O Babylon, and thou wast not aware; thou art found, and also caught, because thou hast striven against the Lord"** [Jer. 50:24].

[4] In the same way Isaiah, wishing to demonstrate that the Lord, blessed be He, loves Israel, that if, occasionally, He smites them with the rod of troubles and tribulations and His **wrath waxes hot against them** [Exod. 32:10], He does so by way of correction, **as a man chasteneth his son** [Deut. 8:5], put questions to himself, and said: **"Hath He smitten him as He smote his smiter? Or is he slain according to the slaughter of them that were slain by Him?"** [Isa. 27:7]. To these questions he immediately replied: **"In full measure, when Thou sendest her away, Thou dost contend with her"** [27:8]. In other words: If His acts against Israel were done out of hatred, He would **make a full end** [Jer. 5:18] of him as He had of the king of Assyria, who had been **his smiter** [Isa. 27:7], and of the rest of the nations, whom He **smote . . . in wrath** [14:6] **until . . . destroyed** [Deut. 7:23]. This is not the case, for He is not annihilating Israel utterly in the same way as He **repayeth them that hate Him,** whom He destroys without measure or limit **to their face** [7:10]. It remains, then, that He is bringing punishment upon Israel in measure, by way of correction; and it is this that is the

2. Citation as in M; C: ''. . . as all the nations''; B: ''How is Babylon become a desolation among the nations?''

התוכחת׳ וזהו שאמ׳: ״בסאסאה, בשלחה, תריבנה״.

[5] וזה היפוי הוא גדול המעלה, והרגיל בו יחשב אדם חכם ונבון. ואפשר העשותו בכל סוגי הדבור, ובקיום יותר מכל חלקי המאמר׳ ויבוקש ענינו על הרוב בדבור הבינו׳ והנשא:

פרק כ׳

פ׳ ההדרגה.

[1] ההדרגה הוא מאמר הולך בהדרגה מן הקודם אל המתאחר עם השנות המתאחר, כמו: וארפכשד ילד את שלח׳ ושלח ילד את עבר; ולעבר יולד שני בנים [בר׳ י׳ כ״ד—כ״ה]. וכן: ואלה המלכים אשר מלכו בארץ אדום׳... וימלוך באדום בלע בן בעור, ושם עירו דנהבה; וימת בלע, וימלוך תחתיו יובב בן זרח מבצרה; וימת יובב, וימלוך תחתיו חושם מארץ התימני; וימת חושם, וימלוך תחתיו הדד בן בדד, כו׳ [שם ל״ו ל״א—ל״ה]. וכן: ויסעו בני ישראל מרעמסס, ויחנו בסכת; ויסעו מסכת, ויחנו באיתם אשר בקצה המדבר; ויסעו מאתם וישב על פי החירות, כו׳ [במד׳ ל״ג ה׳—ז׳].

[2] וזה יבוקש ענינו בדבור השפל:

פרק כ״א

פ׳ הרושם.

[1] הרושם הוא מאמר מורכב מדברים המיוחדים לענין בקצור, כמו: הצור

1 [התוכחת][ד] |וזהו] וזה[ד] || 2 הדבור] הדובר[ד] || 4 הבינו׳ והנשא] בינוני נשא[כ] || 5 פרק] פ׳[כ] || 6 פ׳] פרק[ד] || 7 הוא ‹הולך›[כ] | 7–8 [עם השנות המתאחר][ד] || 9 ואלה] אלה[כ] | אדום ‹כו׳›[כ] | 9–10 [וימלוך באדום][ד] || 11 התימני] התמני[כ] || 12 [תחתיו][כ] || 13 באיתם] באיתן[כ] | וישב] ויחנו[ד] || 16 פרק] פ׳[כ] || 17 פ׳] פרק[ד] ||

---

2 בר׳ מ״א ל״ג ||

purport of Isaiah's statement: **"In full measure, when Thou sendest her away, Thou dost contend with her"** [Isa. 27:8].

[5] Hypophora is of great worth, and one skilled in its use will be deemed **a man discreet and wise** [Gen. 41:33]. It can be used in all the Kinds of Cause, in the Proof more than in all other Parts of the Discourse, and its effect is one called for mostly in the Middle Style and the Grand.

CHAPTER 20

Climax[1]

[1] Climax[a] is diction that proceeds in gradation, from the prior to the next following item, with recurrence of the latter, For instance: **And Arpachshad begot Shelah, and Shelah begot Eber, and unto Eber were born two sons** [Gen. 10:24–25]. Similarly: **And these are the kings that reigned in the land of Edom. . . . And Bela the son of Beor reigned in Edom; and the name of his city was Dinhabah. And Bela died, and Jobab the son of Zerah of Bozrah reigned in his stead. And Jobab died, and Husham of the land of the Temanites reigned in his stead. And Husham died, and Hadad the son of Bedad,** etc. [36:31–35], Again: **And the children of Israel journeyed from Rameses, and pitched in Succoth. And they journeyed from Succoth, and pitched in Etham, which is in the edge of the wilderness. And they journeyed from Etham, and turned back unto Pi-hahiroth,** etc. [Num. 33:5–7].

[2] Climax is an effect called for in the Simple Style.

CHAPTER 21

Definition[1]

[1] Definition[a] is a statement that comprises, in summary form, the properties special to some entity. For instance: **The Rock, His work is perfect; for all His**

1. Literally: "gradation," "degree," "ratio"; "doing by degrees, gradually": הַהַדְרָגָה.

a. *R. ad H.* 4.25.34 ff.

1. Literally: "mark," "trace," "sign," "impression": הָרוֹשֶׁם.

a. *R. ad H.* 4.25.35.

תמים פעלו, כי כל דרכיו משפט, כו׳ [דב׳ ל״ב ד׳]; אלה הדברים, בתכלית
השלמות, הם מיוחדים בבורא ית׳. וכן בישעיהו: שאו מרום עיניכם, וראו מי
ברא אלה׳ המוציא במספר צבאם; לכלם בשם יקרא מרב אונים ואמיץ כח [יש׳
מ׳ כ״ו]. כאלו אמר: ״שהשם ית׳ הוא מי שברא והוציא במספר צבא השמים,
5 וקרא לכלם בשם המיוחד לו — ר״ל, שנתן לכל אחד מהם מן השולטנות והכח
כפי מה שאפשר לו; ואמנם, היה זה מרב אונים ואמיץ כח, שהשם ית׳ וכחו לא
יגבלו, והוא בלתי בעל תכלית.״ ואלה הם דברים מיוחדים בו ית׳, אשר לא
יצדקו על זולתו; וקראהו במקום אחר ״קורא הדורות מראש״ [יש׳ מ״א ד׳]׳
ושהוא ״ראשון...ואחרון״ [שם מ״ד ו׳]׳ וכל אלה מה שיוחד בהם האלוק׳
10 מזולתו.

[2] וכן שלמה המלך, בגדרו ״הפתי״, אמר שהוא ״המאמי׳ לכל דבר״,
ו״החכם״ הוא ״המבין לאשורו״ [מש׳ י״ד ט״ו]׳ ואלה הם תארים מיוחדים בפתי
ובחכם; ואמר שתורת החכם היא ״מקור חיים לסור ממוקשי מות״ [שם י״ג י״ד].

[3] והנה ישעיהו הנביא אומר גדר הנבל, והכילי, והנדיב. ואמר בגדר ״הנבל״,
15 כי הוא אשר ״נבלה ידבר, ולבו יעשה און׳ לעשות חנף, ולדבר אל י״י תועה׳
להריק נפש רעב, ומשקה צמא יחסיר״; וגדר ״הכילי״ בש״כליו רעים׳ הוא זמות
יעץ לחבל עניים[1] באמרי שקר, ובדבר אביון משפט״; אמנם, גדר ״הנדיב״ אשר
״נדיבות יעץ׳ והוא על נדיבות יקום״ [יש׳ ל״ב ו׳—ח׳].

[4] ולהבנת זה המאמר, ראוי שתדע ש״הנדיבות״ היא התכונה האמצעית בין
20 הכילאות והפזור׳ והקצה הראשון הוא הפזור, והקצה האחרון הוא הכילאות.
ולזה, הוא מן התימה למה הביא הנבלה אצל הנדיבו׳ למה שהאמצעי בערך
אל הנבלה הוא טוב הלבב, וענין ״הנבלה״ הוא להיות כפוי טובה על אשר
גמלוהו מן הטובות; כמו שנאמר: הלי״י תגמלו זאת, עם נבל ולא חכם [דב׳ ל״ב
ו׳]׳ ר״ל, שהיו כפויי טובה על כל אשר גמלם י״י, ושכחו אל מושיעם; ולזה, אמר
25 אחר כן: הלא הוא אביך קנך [שם]. וכן בענין אביגיל: נבל שמו, ונבלה עמו

2 בישעיהו] בישעהו[כ] || 4 ית׳] יתעלה[ר] || 5 [לו][כ] |ר״ל] רצוני לומר[ר] |[מהם][ר] |מן השולטנות] מהשלטנות[ר] || 6 כפי] לפי[כ] |ית׳] יתעלה[ר] || 9 [בהם][ר] || 11 אמר] אומ׳[ר] |המאמי׳] מאמין[כ] |[לכל][כ] || 12 ואלה] ואלו[ר] || 14 [הנביא][ר] || 17 עניים[1] ענוים[כת] |ובדבר] וכדבר[כ] || 19 ולהבנת] ולהכנת[כ] | האמצעית] אמצעית[ר] || 20 הכילאות] הכלות[כ] |הראשון] האחרון[כ] |הכילאות] הכילות[כ] || 21 הנדיבו׳] הנתיבות[ר] || 23 גמלוהו] גמלהו[ר] |הלי״י] הלה׳[כ] |עם נבל ולא חכם] וכו׳[ר] || 25 אחר] אחרי[כ] ||

24 תה׳ ק״ו כ״א ||

[1] *Qᵉrē* for *kᵉthībh* ענוים.

ways are justice; a God of faithfulness and without iniquity, just and right is He[2] [Deut. 32:4]. These properties, in absolute perfection, exist only in the Creator, blessed be He. So too in Isaiah: **Lift up your eyes on high, and see: who hath created these? He that bringeth out their host by number; He calleth them all by name by the greatness of His might, and for that He is strong in power** [Isa. 40:26]. It is as though Isaiah had said: "The Name, blessed be He, is the One who created the host of the heavens, brought them out by number,[3] and called them all by the name special to each—that is, gave to each the authority and power that it is capable of possessing. And this has indeed been brought about by **the greatness of His might, and for that He is strong in power,** since the Name, blessed be He, and His power are unlimited, and He is infinite." Now these are characteristics that are special in Him, blessed be He, special in a way not true of anyone except Him. God is elsewhere termed by Isaiah **He that called the generations from the beginning** [41:4], and **the first and... the last** [44:6]. All these terms are means of uniquely distinguishing God from what is not God.

[2] King Solomon, similarly, defining **the thoughtless,** said that he is one that **believeth every word,** the wise,[4] one that **looketh well to his going** [Prov. 14:15], these being qualities uniquely characteristic of the thoughtless man and the wise man respectively. He said, too, that the wise man's teaching **is a fountain of life, to depart from the snares of death** [13:14].

[3] Now the prophet Isaiah offers definitions of the vile person, the churl, and the liberal man. Defining the vile person, he said that he is one who **will speak villany, and his heart will work iniquity, to practise ungodliness, and to utter wickedness against the Lord, to make empty the soul of the hungry, and to cause the drink of the thirsty to fail** [Isa. 32:6]. He defined the churl as one whose **instruments... are evil; he deviseth wicked devices to destroy the poor with lying words, and the needy when he speaketh right** [32:7]. His definition of the liberal, however, is one who **deviseth liberal things, and by liberal things shall he stand** [32:8].

[4] In order to understand this passage you must know that liberality is the quality which is the mean between churlishness and prodigality, prodigality being at one extreme and churlishness at the other. The juxtaposition of vileness and liberality is thus a matter of some astonishment, for the mean in relation to vileness is goodness of heart, and vileness connotes ingratitude for favors received. As has been said: **Do ye thus requite the Lord, O vile**[5] **people and unwise?** [Deut. 32:6]; that is, they were ungrateful for all the kindness shown them by the Lord, and **they forgot God their saviour** [Ps. 106:21]; referring to this Moses went on to say: **Is not He thy father that hath gotten thee? Hath He**

2. Text: "etc." for "a God... is he."
3. Cf. Qimḥi, *ad loc.*
4. B: "prudent."
5. JV and KJV: "foolish."

[שמ״א כ״ה כ״ה]; כלומ׳, שהיה כפוי טובה על כל הטוב שעשה עמו דוד, כמו שאמ׳: ״אך לשקר שמרתי את כל אשר לזה במדבר, ולא נפקד מכל אשר לו מאומה״, כו׳ [שם כ״א]. ו״טוב הלבב״ הוא העושה טובה לאשר גמלוהו, ומשלם להם כפעלם.

[5] וכל זה מוסיף ספק וקושי בענין ״הנבלה״ אשר הביאה הנביא הנה. ונאמר אנחנו שאחר שהתכונות האלה שתיהן, ר״ל, טוב הלבב והנדיבות, הם בממון, לא חשש הנביא לכלול בנדיבות גם טוב הלבב· ומזה הצד, היה הקצה האחרון הנבלה, כאשר לקחו גם כן הפילוסוף בא׳ מההלצה.

[6] והנה הנבל והכילי יתחלפו, למה שהכילי, עם שהוא קובץ על יד והוא צר עין, מכל מקום אפשר שישלם לאשר גמלהו כפעלו· אשר הוא זולת ממה שהוא בנב׳, שהגיע מהפלגת התכונה על חמדת הממון ואהבתו עד ישלם רעה תחת טובה, ולזה הוא פחות מן הכילי ויותר רע ממנו. לכן, לא אמר הכתוב, ״לא יאמר עוד לנבל שוע״, כמו שאמר, ״לא יאמר עוד לנבל נדיב, ולכילי לא יאמר שוע״ [יש׳ ל״ב ה׳]· כי אינו נופל בדמיון שיקרא הנבל ״שוע״, להפלגת המרחק אשר ביניהם. אמנם מה שהוא אפשר, וגם הוא זה בזרות, שההמון יחשבו על הנבל שהוא ״נדיב״, ועל הכילי שהוא ״שוע״.

[7] והנה לקח בגדר הנבל, שהוא ״נבלה ידבר, ולבו יעשה און״ [שם שם ו׳], ר״ל, כי להפלגת רשעתו וחמדתו על הממון, מדבר עניין הנבלה בפרהסיא. ואם תאמ׳ כי אולי יאמר, ולא יעשה—למה שאינו מן ההכרח שכל מה שיאמר יוציאהו האדם לפעל, כאשר יפורסם מן החוש — אמר א״כ, ״ולבו יעשה און״ [שם]· ר״ל, שאפי׳ מה שחושב אותו בלבו לבד מפעלות הנבלה, לעולם יביאהו אל הפעל והמעשה· כל שכן שיעשה זה כאשר ימצאו שניהם יחד, הדבור והמחשבה. אחר כן אמר, ״לעשות חונף״, וכו׳ [שם]; אמר שהוא חושב ומדבר לזה התכלית, ר״ל, שיעשה הרשע בפרהסיא, לגזול ולעשוק האנשים, ולהיות כפוי טובה, אפי׳ כנגד הבורא ית׳, עד שיאמ׳ ״עזב י״י את הארץ״, ו״אין אלקי״״

1 שהיה] שהו[ר] | על כל הטוב שעשה עמו] עמ[ר] || 2 אשר לזה במדבר] וכו[ר] || 6 [ר״ל][ר] || 8 הנבלה] והנבלה[ר] || 9 והנה] הנה[ר] || 11 בנב׳] כנבל[כ] || 12 [פחות][ר] | [רע][ר] | אמר] יאמר[ר] || 13 שאמר] שיאמר[ר] || 15 [הוא][ר] || 16 הנבל] נבל[כ] || 18 רשעתו וחמדתו על הממון מדבר עניין הנבלה] רשעו וחמודו לממ׳ ינבל[ד] || 18–19 ואם תאמ׳ כי] וא״ת[ר] | שאינו] שאי[ר] || 20 א״כ] אחרי כן[ב] || 23 אחר כן אמר] א״כ [אמר][ב] || 24 בפרהסיא] בפרהיא || 25 שיאמ׳] יאמר[ב] | ואין] ואן[ר] ||

9 מש׳ י״ג י״א || 25 יח׳ ח׳ י״ב | תה׳ י׳ ד׳ ||

not made thee and established thee? [Deut. 32:6]. Likewise in the incident involving Abigail: **Nabal is his name, and vileness**[6] **is with him** [1 Sam. 25:25]; in other words, Nabal was ungrateful for all the good David had done him, just as David had said: **Surely in vain have I kept all that this fellow hath in the wilderness, so that nothing was missed of all that pertained unto him: and he hath returned me evil for good** [25:21]. The goodhearted person, then, is one who does good to those who have dealt kindly with him, requiting them as their acts deserve.

[5] All that has just been said increases our doubt and difficulty over the "vileness" introduced here by the prophet. Our own opinion is this: since both these qualities—goodness of heart and liberality—are expressible in terms of wealth the prophet did not hesitate to make liberality include goodness of heart as well; from this point of view, vileness was the other extreme, just as the Philosopher[b] also takes it in Book I of the *Rhetoric*.

[6] Now the vile person differs from the churl in that the churl, while he is one **that gathereth little by little** [Prov. 13:11] and is narrowly self-centered, is nevertheless capable of compensating the person who has dealt kindly with him as his acts deserve; which is not the case with the vile person, in whom the disposition to covet and love money has gone so far that he will repay good with evil, and who thus is inferior to, and worse than, the churl. The text, therefore, did not say **The vile person shall be no more called** noble as it did say **The vile person shall be no more called liberal, nor the churl said to be noble** [Isa. 32:5], because the distance between the vile person and the noble is so great that to call the vile person noble is unimaginable. What is possible, however, though the possibility is far-fetched, is that the multitude might think the vile person liberal and the churl noble.

[7] In defining the vile person Isaiah used the words **will speak villany and his heart will work iniquity** [32:6], meaning that the vile person's wickedness and money-lust are carried to such lengths that he speaks vileness openly. And if you say that perhaps the vile person will merely say, but not do, vile things—for a person need not necessarily carry out in action everything he may say, as is obvious from common sense—then Isaiah's next words are, **and his heart will work iniquity.** The vile person, that is, will always carry out in action and perform even those acts of vileness of which the thought alone is in his heart: all the more will he do this when both are simultaneously the case—when both speech and thought of iniquity are present. Isaiah next said **to practise ungodliness,** etc. [32:6]; the vile person, he said, thinks and speaks to that purpose; he will, that is, commit wickedness openly, will rob and oppress people, and prove himself ingrate enough, even toward the Creator, blessed be He, to assert **"The**

6. JV: "churlishness"; KJV: "folly."

b. T57/A73; cf. *Rhet.* 1.9.12 (1366b).

כל מזמותיו. והגיע מהפלגת תכונתו הרעה שיגזול גם את העניים, ואם מה
שאפשר שישיג מהם הוא מעטי; וזה מה שאמר, "להריק נפש רעב, ומשקה צמא
יחסיר" [שם]· כי מעט קט שיקח ממנו, יקח חיותו, לחמו ומימיו, וימות תחתיו
ברעב.

5 [8] זה מה שאמר בגדר "הנבל". אמנם, כל מה שאמר בגדר "הכילי" מוכיח על
היותו במדרגת הרוע למטה מהנבל הרבה; וזה מאחד משני פנים: אם שלא יגיע
מתכונתו לעשות הרעות המפלגות שיעשהו הנבל· אם גם כן שמה שיעשהו
יעשה בערמה, ותעלומות, והסתר. ואמר שה"כילי כליו רעים" [שם שם ז']· ר"ל,
שהוא לא יגזול בפרהסיא, כמו שעושה הנבל, אלא שיכון להונות האנשים
10 במדה, במשקל, ובמשורה, באופן יחשבהו לא יוודע הדבר ולא ישמע בחוץ
קולו; וזהו מה שאמ' "כליו רעים"· ר"ל, שיש לו אבן ואבן, אפה ואפה. עוד
עושה תחבולה אחרת, כי "הוא זמות יעץ" [שם]; ר"ל, שהוא חושב תחבולות
רעות להטות מדין דלים בעדות שקר, או להסיר משפטו באופן אחר, בדבר
שיגיע לו הנאה ממנו· וכל זה בלאט, ובתעלומות, ומביא האנשים לחשוב שהוא
15 רודף אחר צדקה ומשפט. והנה הנבל והכילי שניהם שוים כשירעו לעניים ויקחו
אותו המעט אשר להם· אלא שהנבל עושה זה מהפלגת תכונתו הרעה, שעם
גזלו העשירי' יגזול גם אותו המעט אשר לעניים. אמנם הכילי עושה זה להסתיר
ענייניו· גם כי יקל בעיניו להטות דין העניים יותר מהעשירים; ואם הטיית דין
העשירים היתה לו במדרגה שוה מן ההסתר והקלות להטיית דין העניים, היה
20 מניח העניים על ענינם.

[9] ואמר אחרי כן הנביא בגדר "הנדיב" — "ונדיב נדיבות יעץ" [שם שם ח']
— הפך הכילי, ש"הוא זמות יעץ". ואם תאמ' שהוא מיעץ על הנדיבות, ולא
שיעשהו, לזה אמר: "והוא על נדיבות יקום" [שם]· ר"ל, שהוא יתקיים ויעמוד
בסבת רוב הנדיבות שהוא עושה.

25 [10] וזה היפוי, כאשר יעשה כהוגן, הוא אומר כל כך הדבר בקצור ובלשון
מבואר עד יאות הרבה אל השומעים. ואפשר העשותו בכל סוגי הדבור· ויבוקש
ענינו בבינוני יותר:

1 [את][ג] || 2 שאפשר] אפשר[ג] || 5 זה] וזה[ר] || 7 <מתוכת> מתכונתו[ג] || 8 יעשה] יעשהו[ר] | ר"ל] רצה לומ'[ר] || 9 בפרהסיא] בפרהיא[ג] | שעושה] שיעשה[ר] || 12 [הוא][ר] || 14 בלאט] בלט[ג] || 15 ויקחו] ויקחו[ר] || 20 מניח העניים] מניחם[ר] || 21 אחרי כן] אחר כך[ר] || 23 יתקיים] מתקיים[ר] || 24 רוב] רב[ר] || 25 הדבר] הדבור[ר] ||

---

3 יש' ל"ג ט"ז | יר' ל"ח ט' || 10 וי' י"ט ל"ה | 10–11 יש' מ"ב ב' || 11 מש' כ' י' || 13 יש' י' ב' ||

Lord hath forsaken the land" [Ezek. 8:12], while **all his thoughts are: "There is no God"** [Ps. 10:4]. His disposition to evil is carried to such excess that he will rob even the poor, though what he can obtain from them is quite meagre. This is the import of Isaiah's words, **to make empty the soul of the hungry, and to cause the drink of the thirsty** to fail [Isa. 32:6]; for the very little that the poor man earns the vile person takes from him, his living, **his bread and... his waters** [33:16], **and he is like to die in the place where he is** [Jer. 38:9] of hunger.

[8] These were Isaiah's words in his definition of the vile person. On the other hand, all that he said in defining the churl shows that the churl is far less evil than the vile person. This emerges from one of two points of difference: either the churl's disposition is not such that he will carry evildoing to the lengths that the vile person will; or else, again, what he does he accomplishes by cunning, and in secrecy and concealment. So Isaiah said that **the instruments... of the churl are evil** [Isa. 32:7], meaning that the churl will not openly rob, as does the vile person, but that his purpose is rather to wrong people **in meteyard, in weight, or in measure** [Lev. 19:35] in such a way that, as he thinks, the matter will neither become known nor its **voice... be heard in the street** [Isa. 42:2]. The prophet expressed this in the words, **the instruments... are evil;** the churl, that is, has **diverse weights, and diverse measures** [Prov. 20:10]. Yet another act of cunning which the churl performs is that **he deviseth wicked devices,** etc. [Isa. 32:7]; that is, he contrives wicked schemes **to turn aside the needy from judgment** [10:2] through false testimony, or otherwise schemes to deprive a poor man of his due in some matter from which he himself is obtaining benefit; and all this secretly, covertly, the while making people think that he is pursuing righteousness and justice. Now both the vile person and the churl will alike victimize the poor and take away the little that these have, only the vile person does this because he is so excessively disposed to evil that, together with robbing the rich, he will also rob the poor of what little they have. The churl, however, does this in order to conceal his designs, and because it seems to him that the just claim of the poor is easier to turn aside than that of the rich; but if it were possible for him to turn aside the just claim of the rich with quite as much secrecy and ease as that of the poor, he would leave the poor and their case alone.

[9] The prophet next defined the liberal person—**But the liberal deviseth[7] liberal things** [Isa. 32:8]—as the contrary of the churl, who **deviseth wicked devices** [32:7]. And should you argue that the reference may be to one who counsels liberal things, not to one who does liberal things, as to this the prophet has said, **and by liberal things shall he stand;** that is, he will be preserved and will endure by reason of the many acts of liberality that he performs.

[10] This Figure, properly developed, sets the subject forth so concisely and lucidly that the hearers find it most becoming. It can be used in all the Kinds of Cause, and its effect is very often called for in the Middle Style.

7. Literally: "has counseled" (יָעָץ).

פרק כ״ב

פ׳ ההערה.

[1] ההערה היא מאמ׳ כאשר יסופר בקצור מה שכבר נאמ׳, ומעיר על מה שראוי להאמר. והמשל מה שאמר אליהו לאיוב: ״הנה זאת חקרנוה, כן היא״ [איוב ה׳ כ״ז]· וזהו ספור קצר ממה שנאמ׳; ״שמענה, ואתה דע לך״ [שם]· זאת היא הערה על מה שראוי להאמר; כלומ׳, שיבין מה שנ׳, וידע מה יש לו להשיב.

[2] וכן, מה שאמ׳ דניאל: ״דנא חלמא· ופשריה נאמ׳ קדם מלכא״ [דנ׳ ב׳ ל״ו]· המאמר הראשון הוא קצור מה שנא׳, והאחרון הערה על מה שיאמ׳. וכן, מה שאמ׳ נבוכדנצר אחר ספור החלום: ״דנא חלמא חזית אנא, מלכא נבוכדנצר· ואנת, בלטשצר, פישריה אמר״, כו׳ [שם ד׳ ט״ו]; וכן, מה שאמ׳ דניאל לבלטשצר[1], ״דנא כתבא דרשי׳: מנה מנה, תקל ופרסין· דנא פשר מלתא, וכו׳ [שם ה׳ כ״ה—כ״ו]. בכל אלה, הראשון ספור מה שנא׳, והשני הערה על מה שיאמר; ולכן נקראת הערה, שבה יעיר האדם על מה שראוי להאמר.

[3] ואפשר שיעשה זה היפוי בכל סוגי הדבור· ובחלקי המאמ׳, על הרוב בהתרה ובקיום; ויבוקש ענינו בבינוני יותר:

פרק כ״ג

פ׳ ההגהה.

[1] ההגהה היא מאמ׳ כאשר יעזב בו דבר, ויקח היותר נאות בענין· כאלו הוא

1 פרק] פ׳[כ] || 2 פ׳] פרק[ד] || 3 היא] הוא[כ] |ומעיר] ומעיד[ד] || 4 אליהו] אליפז[ת] || 6 להאמר] להאמן[ד] || 7 דנא] דנה[ת] |ופשריה] ופשרה[ת] || 8 שנא׳] שנ׳[כ] || 9 דנא] דנה[ת] || 10 פישריה] פשרא[ת] || 11 דרשי׳] דראשים[כ] די רשים[ת] |מנה מנה] מנא מנא[ד] |מלתא] מלכא[כ] || 12 הראשון] הא׳[ד] |שנא׳] שנאמ׳[כ] | והשני] והב׳[ד] || 13 נקראת] נקרא[כ] |להאמר] שיאמר[ד] || 14 היפוי] הספור[ד] || 16 פרק] פ׳ || 17 פ׳] פרק[ד] ||

[1] *Sic;* ת: בלשאצר.

CHAPTER 22

Transition[1]

[1] Transition[a] is diction which, presenting a concise account of what has been said, calls attention to what must yet be said. An example is Elihu's[2] statement to Job: **"Lo this, we have searched it, so it is"** [Job 5:27], which is a brief account of what has been said; **"Hear it, and know thou it for thy good"** [5:27]: this notes what must yet be said; Job, in other words, understands what has been said and knows to what he must make reply.

[2] Similarly, Daniel's statement: **"This is the dream; and we will tell the interpretation thereof before the king"** [Dan. 2:36]; the first clause is a concise description of what was previously said, while the second takes note of what is going to be said. So, too, Nebuchadnezzar's remark after the narration of his dream: **"This dream I, king Nebuchadnezzar, have seen; and thou, O Belteshazzar, declare the interpretation,"** etc. [4:15]; and again, Daniel's remark to Belteshazzar:[3] **"This is the writing that was inscribed: MENE MENE TEKEL UPHARSIN; this is the interpretation of the thing,"** etc. [5:25–26]. In each of these examples, the first clause is an account of what was previously said, and the second takes note of what is going to be said. Hence, it is called Transition, since by it a speaker calls attention to what must yet be said.

[3] This Figure can be used in all the Kinds of Cause, and, of the Parts of the Discourse, mostly in the Refutation and Proof. Its effect is very often called for in the Middle Style.

CHAPTER 23

Correction[1]

[1] Correction[a] is a statement employed by a speaker when he discards something he has said, and adopts what is more suitable for his purpose; in effect, he

1. Literally: "rousing," "stirring up"; "remark," "note," "suggestion": הַהֶעָרָה.
2. *Sic,* JML; B: "Eliphaz."
3. *Sic,* JML; B: "Belshazzar."

---

a. *R. ad H.* 4.26.35.

1. Also: "revision," "editing," "proofreading": הַהַגָּהָה.

---

a. *R. ad H.* 4.26.36.

מגיה מה שכבר אמר. והמשל: מפלטי מאויבי· אף מן קמי תרוממני [תה׳ י״ח מ״ט]; כאלו הגיה מה שכבר אמר, ״מפלטי מאויבי״, ואמר שלא ההצלה בלבד עשה מן האויבים, אבל עשה עמו דבר מעולה יותר: שעשה אותו נשא ומרומם יותר משנאיו, שהוא גדול יותר מן ההצלה מהם.

[2] וכן בישעיהו: ולא אותי קראת יעקב· כי יגעת בי ישראל [יש׳ מ״ג כ״ב]. יאמר הנביא כי ה׳ ית׳ יצר ישראל שירוממוהו ויהללוהו בקהל עם· וזהו שאמ׳: ״עם זו יצרתי לי, תהלתי יספרו״ [שם כ״א]. והנה הגיע מרוע תכונת ישראל שלא די שלא יהללוהו, כי גם בעת צרתם לא יקראוהו· והוא המכוון ב״לא אותי קראת יעקב״ [כ״ב]. ועוד עושים רעה גדולה מזו, שהם אומרים כי תשיג להם יגיעה רבה ותלאה עצומה בסבת עבודתו· והוא הנרצה ב״כי יגעת בי ישראל״ [שם]. כאלו הגיה מה שאמ׳, ״לא אותי קראת״; כלומ׳, זהו עון קטן בערך אל מה שהם מתרעמים ומתלוננים, כי הייתי עליהם למשא ולא יוכלו לסבול העמל הגדול אשר ישיג אותם למעני· על דרך: ״הנה מתלאה, והפחתם אותו״ [מל׳ א׳ י״ג].

[3] ועל זה הדרך, מה שנאמ׳ גם כן בישעיהו: והיה לאדם לבער, ויקח מהם ויחם· אף ישיק, ואפה לחם· אף יפעל אל, וישתחו, כו׳ [יש׳ מ״ד ט״ו]; שבמאמ׳ המתאחר, דבר יותר גדול בערך אל חברו.

[4] זה היפוי מעיר לבב השומעים, אשר זה לא יעשה בדבור הכולל והמורגל בפי האנשים. ולזה לא נבא בתחלה אל היותר גדול, כדי שיחודש ממציאות הקטן והגדול יחדיו, באופן הנז׳, ערבות מה אל השומעים· ויצא המאמ׳ ממדרגת הדברים המורגלים אשר לא יעוררו השומעים הערה גדולה או קטנה. ואפשר העשותו בכל סוגי הדבור, ויבוקש ענינו בבינוני יותר:

2 ואמר] אמ׳[ד] || 6 הנביא] הנבי׳[ד] | ה׳] הש׳[ד] || 8 די] דיי[כ] || 12 עליהם] להם[כ] | יוכלו] יכלו[כ] || 15 שנאמ׳] שנ׳[כ] | גם כן][כ] || 16 וישתחו] וישתחוו[כ] || 19 בפי] כפי[כ] ||

6 תה׳ ק״ז ל״ב ||

revises what he has previously said. For example: **He delivereth me from mine enemies; yea, Thou liftest me up above them that rise up against me** [Ps. 18:49]; the Psalmist revised, as it were, his previous words, **delivereth me from mine enemies,** and said that not only had the Lord effected his deliverance from his enemies, but that He had done for him something of greater excellence: He had brought him to a higher and loftier dignity than that of his foes—a greater thing than deliverance from them.

[2] Likewise in Isaiah: **Yet thou hast not called upon Me, O Jacob, neither hast thou wearied thyself about Me, O Israel** [43:22]. The prophet was saying that the Name, blessed be He, had formed Israel **that they might exalt . . .** and . . . **praise . . . Him in the assembly of the people** [Ps. 107:32]; this he said in the words: **This people which I formed for Myself that they might tell of My praise** [Isa. 43:21]. Now, however, because of Israel's evil character, matters have reached such a pass that not only do they fail to praise Him, they do not even call upon Him in their time of trouble—this being the purport of **thou hast not called upon Me, O Jacob** [43:22]. Moreover, they commit an even worse evil: they complain of the great weariness and inordinate hardship that come to them by reason of His service, which is the meaning of **neither hast thou wearied thyself about Me, O Israel** [43:22]. It is as though the prophet revised his prior statement, **thou hast not called upon Me;** in other words, this is a minor iniquity by comparison with the people's murmuring and complaining that I have been a burden unto them, and that they cannot bear the great toil which comes to them for My sake—a thought parallel to that in **Ye say also: "Behold, what a weariness is it!" and ye have snuffed at it, saith the Lord of Hosts** [Mal. 1:13].

[3] Of similar character is the statement, also in Isaiah: **Then a man useth it for fuel, and he taketh thereof and warmeth himself: yea, he kindleth it, and baketh bread; yea, he maketh a god, and worshippeth it, etc.,** [Isa. 44:15]. Each subsequent clause contains a graver dereliction than the one before it.

[4] This Figure stirs the minds of the hearers, something that cannot be effected by means of the common utterance habitually in men's mouths. As to this, we should not come in the beginning to the more important part of our discourse, so that there may be created for our hearers a certain agreeableness from the presence together of the less and the more important in the manner mentioned; and the diction may then transcend the level of commonly used words such as can stir hearers neither in great nor in small degree. Correction can be used in all the Kinds of Cause, and its effect is very often called for in the Middle Style.

פרק כ״ד

פ׳ ההעלמה.

[1] ההעלמה היא מאמ׳ באשר יראה שהכונה היא להסתיר הדבר, או שלא
לאמרו, ומכל מקו׳ יובן מכח המאמ׳. והמשל במזמור נ״ז[1]: האמנם — אלם —
5 צדק תדברון· משרים תשפטו בני אדם? [תה׳ נ״ח ב׳]. ויהיה הרצון ב״אלם״
שתיקה ואלמות, כמו: מי ישום אלם? [שמ׳ ד׳ י״א]; כלומ׳, ״אני רוצה לשתוק
מזה הענין, ולהיות כמו אלם: אם צדק תדברון, ומשרים תשפטו בני אדם״. והנה
יובן מזה המאמ׳ שלא היו עושי׳ כן, כמו שאמ׳ א״כ במפורסם: אף בלב עולות
תפעלון [תה׳ נ״ח ג׳].

10 [2] וכן: לפלגות ראובן, גדולים חקקי לב [שופ׳ ה׳ ט״ו]; כלומר: למה שנחלק
ראובן, ועמד תחתיו מעבר לירדן ולא יצא למלחמה, יש לחשוב עליו מחשבות
רבות, שהיא שותקת מהם. וחזרה זה הדבר פעם אחרת, ואמרה: ״לפלגות
ראובן, גדולים חקרי לב״ [שם ט״ז], להגדיל הענין.

[3] והנה מזה היפוי נולד בלב השומעים חשד יותר גדול ממה שהיה זה
15 מפרסם במאמר. ואפשר העשותו בכל סוגי הדבור, ויבוקש ענינו בבינוני יותר:

פרק כ״ה

פ׳ המיוחד.

[1] המיוחד הוא מאמר באשר יהיה לכל ענין הנאמ׳ בו פועל מיוחד. והמשל
בשירת דבורה: ארץ רעשה· גם שמים נטפו· גם עבים נטפו מים [שופ׳ ה׳ ד׳].

1 פרק] פ׳[כ] || 2 פ׳] פרק[ד] || 3 שהכונה] הכוונה[כ] || 4 ומכל מקו׳] ומ״מ[כ] || 5 משרים] מישרים[ת] ||
8 עושי׳] עושין[כ] | כמו] כמה[כ] || 10 לפלגות] להפלגות[כ] בפלגות[ת] || 11 מעבר] לעבר[כ] || 12 ואמרה]
ואמ׳[ד] || 13 חקרי לב] וכ׳[ד] || 16 פרק] פ׳[כ] || 17 פ׳] פרק[ד] || 18 באשר] כאשר[כ] | [בו][ד] ||

[1] *Sic;* ת: נ״ח.

CHAPTER 24

Paralipsis[1]

[1] Paralipsis[a] is a Figure of Diction in which, while the apparent purpose is to conceal some thought or to abstain from saying it, the thought is nevertheless understood from the force of the statement. For example, in Psalm 57:[2] **Indeed—silence!—do ye speak righteousness, do ye judge with equity the sons of men?** [58:2].[3] The meaning of *'ēlem* here is "silence," "dumbness,"[4] as **Who maketh a man dumb** [Exod. 4:11]. In other words: "I intend to maintain silence and be as one who is dumb on this point, namely, whether you speak righteousness and judge with equity the sons of men." Yet from this very statement it is understood that they were not so speaking and judging; as the Psalmist next openly said: **Yea, in heart ye work wickedness,** etc. [Ps. 58:3].

[2] Similarly: **Touching the divisions of Reuben, great are the heart's thoughts** [Judg. 5:15].[5] In other words: since the tribe of Reuben was of divided mind and remained where it was, across the Jordan, without coming out to battle, this was a matter to which much thought had to be given, a matter about which Deborah was maintaining silence. She repeated this dictum once again, and said, **As to the divisions of Reuben, great are the searchings of heart** [5:16], in order to emphasize the importance of the matter.

[3] Paralipsis can engender a greater suspicion in the minds of the hearers than if the suspicion were openly stated. It can be used in all the Kinds of Cause, and its effect is very often called for in the Middle Style.

CHAPTER 25

Disjunction[1]

[1] Disjunction[a] is diction wherein every statement of fact has a verb of its own. In the Song of Deborah, for example: **The earth trembled, the heavens**

1. Literally: "concealment," "disregard," "neglect," "inattentiveness": הַהַעְלָמָה
2. *Sic;* B: 58.
3. So far as I can see, this interpretation is original with JML.
4. Following Qimḥi, JV and KJV take this word (אֵלֶם) to mean "company." Hence, "Do ye indeed speak as a righteous company?" (JV); "Do ye indeed speak righteousness, O congregation?" (KJV).
5. Translated in accordance with JML's interpretation.

a. *R. ad H.* 4.27.37.

1. Literally: "the special," "specific," "particular": הַמְּיוּחָד.

a. *R. ad H.* 4.27.37-38.

וכן: מן שמים נלחמו· הככבים ממסלותם נלחמו עם סיסרא [שם כ׳]. וכן: מים שאל חלב נתנה· בספל אדירים הקריבה חמאה [שם כ״ה].

[2] ואפשר העשותו בכל סוגי הדבור, ויבוקש ענינו בבינוני יותר:

פרק כ״ו

פ׳ הנמשך.

[1] הנמשך הוא מאמר כאשר יתמצע הפעל והוא נמשך אל הקודם ואל המתאחר יחד. והמשל: מגן אם יראה ורומח [שופ׳ ה׳ ח׳]; ״אם יראה״ הוא באמצע ושב לשניהם. וכן: הרים נזלו מפני י״י· זה סיני, וכו׳ [שם ה׳]; תיבת ״נזלו״ שבה לשניהם. וכן: ידיה ליתד תשלחנה וימינה להלמות עמלים [שם כ״ו]; כאלו תאמ׳, ״ידיה ליתד תשלחנה, וימינה תשלח להלמות עמלים״. וכן: בעד החלון נשקפה ותיבב· אם סיסרא בעד האשנב [שם כ״ח]:

פרק כ״ז

פ׳ ההשבה.

[1] ההשבה היא מאמ׳ כאשר דבר אחד שב לענינים רבים, בין יקדם אותו הדבר או יתאחר. משל הראשון: ימצאהו בארץ מדבר· ובתוהו ילל ישימון [דב׳

1 הככבים] הכוכבי׳[כ] |סיסרא] ססרא[כ] ||2 בספל אדירים הקריבה חמאה] וכו׳[ד] ||4 פרק] פ׳[כ] ||5 פ׳] פרק[ד] ||6 הפעל] בפעל[כ] ||8 וכו׳] כו׳[כ] ||9 ידיה] ידה[ת] ||10 תאמ׳] אמ׳[ד] ||11 האשנב <כו׳>[כ] ||12 פרק] פ׳[כ] ||13 פ׳] פרק[ד] ||15 ילל] יילל[כ] ||

also dropped, yea, the clouds dropped water [Judg. 5:4]. Again: **They fought from heaven, the stars in their courses fought against Sisera** [5:20]. And again: **Water he asked, milk she gave him; in a lordly bowl she brought him curd** [5:25].

[2] Disjunction may be used in all the Kinds of Cause and its effect is very often called for in the Middle Style.

CHAPTER 26

Conjunction[1]

[1] Conjunction[a] is diction in which the verb is placed in the middle and extends both to what precedes it and what follows it. For example: **A shield was there seen, or spear?** [Judg. 5:8];[2] ''was . . . seen'' comes in the middle and applies to both ''shield'' and ''spear.'' Similarly: **The mountains quaked at the presence of the Lord, even yon Sinai,** etc. [5:5]; the word ''quaked'' applies to both ''mountains'' and ''Sinai.'' Again: **Her hands[3] extend for the tent-pin, and her right hand for the workmen's hammer** [5:26]; as if to say, ''Her hands extend for the tent-pin, and her right hand extends for the workmen's hammer.'' And again: **Through the window she looked forth and peered, the mother of Sisera through the lattice** [5:28].

CHAPTER 27

Adjunction[1]

[1] Adjunction[a] is diction in which a single word applies to several phrases, whether that word precedes or follows them. With preceding word, for example:

1. Literally: ''the prolonged,'' ''the drawn after,'' ''the attracted,'' ''the pulled''; also: ''following,'' ''consequent,'' ''continuous,'' ''lasting,'' ''cleaving,'' ''connected'': הַנִּמְשָׁךְ.
2. JV and KJV: ''Was there a shield or spear seen. . . .''
3. JML: ''hands''; B: ''hand.'' JV: ''Her hand she put to the tent-pin, and her right hand to the workmen's hammer.'' The verb in B is third person, feminine plural, as though the subject were ''hands.''

a. *R. ad H.* 4.27.37.

1. הֲשָׁבָה, This word ordinarily means ''a causing to go back,'' ''a restoring,'' ''a returning.'' It is

a. *R. ad H.* 4.27.38.

ל״ב י׳]; תיבת ״ימצאהו״ תשוב לשניהם, והיא קודמת. וכן: אמר אויב, ״ארדוף, אשיג, אחלק שלל· תמלאימו נפשי... תורישימו ידי״ [שמ׳ ט״ו ט׳]; תיבת ״אמר״ הקודמת שבה לכלם.

[2] משל השני: רוכבי אתונות צחורות· יושבי על מדין· והולכי על דרך, שיחו [שופ׳ ה׳ י׳]; תיבת ״שיחו״ תשוב לכלם, והיא באחרונה. וכן: כל יושבי תבל· ושוכני ארץ· כנשוא נס הרים, תראו [יש׳ י״ח ג׳]; תבת ״תראו״ המתאחרת תשוב לשניהם.

[3] והמיוחד, מאלה השלושה יפויים, הוא יותר צח· לכן ראוי לעשותו על המעט, כדי שלא יקוץ בו האדם. אמנם הנמשך וההשבה, שהמכוון בהם הקצור, ראוי לעשותם בתדירות. ואלה השלושה יפויים יבוקש ענינם בבינוני יותר:

פרק כ״ח

פ׳ ההכפל.

[1] ההכפל הוא חזרת הדבר פעם אחרת על צד הכעס או על צד הרחמנות.

[2] משל הראשון: כי הרבה אפרים מזבחות לחטא· היו לו מזבחות לחטוא [הו׳ ח׳ י״א]. וכן: תן להם, י״י, מה תתן· תן להם רחם משכיל, כו׳ [שם ט׳ י״ד]. וכן: אהי דברך, מות, כו׳ [שם י״ג י״ד]. וכן במיכה: אתה תזרע ולא תקצור· אתה תדרוך זית ולא תסוך שמן [מי׳ ו׳ ט״ו]. וכן בנחום: גם את תשכרי, תהי נעלמה·

1 תשוב] תצא[ד] || 2 אחלק...ידי] וכו׳...תמלאמו...‹אריק חרבי›...תורישמו...[ת] || 4 השני] הב׳[ד] || 8 השלשה] הג׳[ד] | לעשותו] לעשות[ד] || 9 האדם] אדם[ד] || 10 בתדירות] בתרידות[כ] | השלשה] הג׳[ד] | ענינם] ענינו[ד] || 11 פרק] פ׳[כ] || 12 פ׳] פרק[ד] || 14 הראשון] הא׳[ד] || 15 תתן ‹להם›[ד] || 16 דברך] דבריך[ת] | כו׳] קטבך שאול[כ] || 16–17 אתה תדרוך...שמן] כו׳[ד] | גם את תשכרי] את תשכרי[כ] ||

He found him in a desert land, and in the waste, a howling wilderness [Deut. 32:10]; the word "he-found-him" applies to both prepositional phrases, and precedes them. Similarly: **Said the enemy "I will pursue, I will overtake, I will divide the spoil; my lust shall be satisfied upon them... my hand shall destroy them"** [Exod. 15:9];[2] the first word, "said," applies to all the following statements.

[2] With following word: **Ye that ride on white asses, ye that sit on rich cloths, and ye that walk by the way, tell of it** [Judg. 5:10]; the word "tell-of-it," placed at the end, applies to all the vocative phrases. Similarly: **All ye inhabitants of the world, and ye dwellers on the earth, when an ensign is lifted up on the mountains, see ye** [Isa. 18:3]; the word "see-ye," which comes last, applies to both vocative phrases.

[3] Of these three last Figures, Disjunction is the most elegant; it should therefore be used only rarely, lest the hearers find it cloying. Conjunction and Adjunction, however, which serve the purpose of conciseness, should be frequently used. The effect achieved by each of these three Figures is called for mainly in the Middle Style.

CHAPTER 28

Reduplication[1]

[1] Reduplication[a] is the repeating one further time of some particular word, whether because of anger or of pity.

[2] Because of anger, for example: **For Ephraim hath multiplied altars to sin, yea, altars have been unto him to sin** [Hos. 8:11]. Similarly: **Give them, O Lord, whatsoever Thou wilt give; give them a miscarrying womb**, etc. [9:14]. Again: **Ho, thy plagues, O death! Ho, thy destruction, O netherworld!** [13:14][2] So also in Micah: **Thou shalt sow, but shalt not reap; thou shalt tread the olives, but shalt not anoint thee with oil** [Mic. 6:15]. And in Nahum: **Thou**

---

a causative noun formation of the root שׁוּב = "to go back," "to return." But one meaning of שׁוּב לְ = "to apply to," "to advert to," "to go back to," and a causative noun of the root in this meaning is intended here, apparently, as an equivalent of *"adiunctio."*

2. JV slightly rearranged to exhibit JML's point.

1. Literally: "the doubling": הַהַכְפֵּל.

2. C here replaces "Ho, thy destruction, O netherworld" with "etc."; M, reading "thy destruction, O netherworld," omits "Ho," the repeated word.

---

a. *R. ad H.* 4.28.38.

גם את תבקשי מעוז מאויב [נח׳ ג׳ י״א]. וכן ביחזקאל: ומפניהם אל תחת, כי בית מרי המה· ודברת את דברי אליהם, אם ישמעו ואם יחדלו· כי בית מרי המה [יח׳ ב׳ ו׳—ז׳]. וכן בישעיהו: כעל גמולות, כעל ישלם, חמה לצריו, גמול לאויביו· לאיים גמול ישלם [יש׳ נ״ט י״ח].

[3] משל השני, כשהוא על צד הרחמנות, בהושע: אפרים, כאשר ראיתי לצור, שתולה בנוה· ואפרים להוציא אל הורג בניו [הו׳ ט׳ י״ג]. וכן בהושע: איך אתנך, אפרים, אמגנך, ישראל· איך אתנך כאדמה, אשימך כצבואים[1]· נהפך עלי לבי, כו׳ [שם י״א ח׳]. וכן במיכה: כי אנושה מכותיה· כי באה עד יהודה, כו׳ [מי׳ א׳ ט׳]. וכן בירמיהו: על כן לבי למואב כחללים יהמה, ולבי אל אנשי קיר חרש כחלילים יהמה [יר׳ מ״ח ל״ו]; על כן על מואב ייליל, ולמואב כלו אזעק [שם שם ל״א].

[4] אמנם, יתחלף זה מכל מיני ההשנות וההשבה שזכרנו למעלה, כי זה היפוי אינו חוזר כי אם פעם אחד, והוא על צד הכעס או על צד הרחמנות, כמו שהתפרסם ממה שקדם· והוא זולת מה שיחוייב ביפויים הנזכ׳. וזה היפוי גדול מאד לעורר הכעס או הרחמנות· והוא כמי שיכה פעמים במקום אחד בעצמו אשר בו מן הכאב והצער דבר לא יעלם. ואפשר העשותו בכל סוגי הדבור, ויבוקש ענינו בנשא ובבינוני:

פרק כ״ט

פ׳ הפתרון.

[1] הפתרון הוא השבת ענין אחד בתיבות מתחלפות· והוא כאלו המתאחרת תפתור הקודמת ויבארה. והמשל: שבעתי עולות אלים, וחלב מריאים· ודם

2 המה] הם[כ] | ודברת <אלי>[כ] | [בית][ת] || 5 השני] הב׳[ר] || 6 להוציא] הוציא[כ] || 7 ישראל] ישרל[כ] | כצבואים[1]] כצבויים[כ] || 9 [בירמיהו][ר] | כחללים] כחלילים[כ] || 10 כחלילים] כחללים[ר] | ייליל] איליל[ת] | כלו] כולו[כ] כלה[ת] || 12 אמנם] ואמנם[כ] | שזכרנו] שהזכרנו[ר] || 13 פעם] בעם[ר] | [על צד] הרחמנות[כ] || 14 הנזכ׳] הנז׳[כ] || 15 כמי] כמו[כ] || 16 הדבור] הספור[כ] || 17 בנשא] נושא[כ] || 18 פרק] פ׳[כ] || 19 פ׳] פרק[ר] || 21 אלים] אילים[ת] ||

[1] *Sic, k^e^thībh; q^e^rē as* כ.

also shalt be drunken, thou shalt swoon; thou also shalt seek a refuge because of the enemy [Nah. 3:11]. Again, in Ezekiel: . . . **nor be dismayed at their looks, for they are a rebellious house; and thou shalt speak My words unto them, whether they will hear or whether they will forbear; for they are most rebellious** [Ezek. 2:6–7]. And again, in Isaiah: **According to their deeds, accordingly**[3] **He will repay, fury to his adversaries, recompense to His enemies; to the islands He will repay recompense** [Isa. 59:18].

[3] An example of the second kind of Reduplication—when it is caused by pity—is found in Hosea: **Ephraim, like as I have seen Tyre, is planted in a pleasant place; but Ephraim shall bring forth his children to the slayer** [Hos. 9:13]. Also in Hosea: **How shall I give thee up, Ephraim, surrender thee, Israel: How shall I make thee as Admah, set thee as Zeboim? My heart is turned within Me**, etc. [11:8].[4] So, too, in Micah: **For her wound is incurable, for it is come even unto Judah**, etc. [Mic. 1:9]. Further, in Jeremiah: **Therefore my heart moaneth for Moab like pipes, and my heart moaneth like pipes for the men of Kir-heres** [Jer. 48:36]; **Therefore will it**[5] **wail for Moab, yea, I will cry out for all Moab** [48:31].

[4] Reduplication differs, of course, from all other varieties of repetition and from Adjunction mentioned above, for in this figure there is but one recurrence, and it springs either from anger or from pity, as plainly shown by the preceding examples. The same requirements do not hold for the other Figures of repetition mentioned. The power of Reduplication to arouse anger or pity is very great; it is as if a person should twice strike another on the same place which is already obviously sore and painful. The Figure can be used in all the Kinds of Cause, and its effect is called for in the Grand and Middle Styles.

CHAPTER 29

Interpretation[1]

[1] Interpretation[a] is the bringing back of a given thought in different words; the second thought, as it were, interprets and explains the first. For example: **I**

3. Hebrew: "according to" (כְּעַל), the same word as that which begins the verse.
4. Translation as in JV, but slightly adapted to exhibit the fact that there are only two occurrences of "how."
5. *Sic;* B: "I."

1. הַפִּתְרוֹן.

a. *R. ad H.* 4.28.38.

פרים, וכבשים, ועתודים לא חפצתי [יש׳ א׳ י״א]. וכן: רואיך אליך ישגיחו, אליך יתבוננו׃ ״הזה האיש מרגיז הארץ, מרעיש ממלכות?״ [שם י״ד ט״ז]. וכן: ואנו הדייגים, ואבלו כל משליכי ביאור חכה׃ ופורשי מכמרת על פני מים אמללו [שם י״ט ח׳]. וכן: הנה י״י בוקק הארץ ובולקה׃ ועוה פניה והפיץ יושביה [שם כ״ד
5 א׳]; שבת משוש תופים, חדל שאון עליזים׃ שבת משוש כנור [שם שם ח׳]. והנה מן ההכרח שהשומע יתעורר מהשבת הענין במלות שונות התעוררות מה.

[2] וכבר התפרסם למעלה מדברינו, שאפשר התחברות יפויים רבים במאמ׳ אחד מצדדים מתחלפים, מבלתי שיתחייב מזה בטל; והיו הדברים האלה על לבבך תמיד׃ יכונו יחדיו על שפתיך. ואפשר העשותו בכל סוגי הדבור, ויבקש
10 ענינו בנשא ובבנוני:

פרק ל׳

פ׳ הסבובי.

[1] הסבובי הוא מאמ׳ מורכב מהפכיים, באופן שהקודם במאמ׳ הראשון ישוב אחרון בשני, וכן להפך. והמשל: ולאהבה את שונאיך, ולשנא את אוהביך
15 [שמ״ב י״ט ז׳]; וכן ביחזקאל: כי אני י״י השפלתי עץ גבוה, הגבהתי עץ שפל [יח׳ י״ז כ״ד]; וכן: זאת לא זאת׃ השפלה הגבה, והגבוה השפיל [שם כ״א ל״א].

[2] וזה היפוי יתחלף מן החלוף מצד שתנאי החלוף שמאחד מהמאמרים יתחיב חברו, כמו שהתבאר׃ ואין הענין כן בזה המקום. ויבדל מן ההפוך, כי בזה היפוי תהפכנה התבות, כמו שהתפרסם, שהוא זולת מה שהתחייב בהפוך. וזה

3 [מים][ב] || 7 וכבר] וכזר[ב] || 9 ויבקש] יבוקש[ב] || 10 ובבנוני] ובבינוי[ד] || 11 פרק] פ׳[ב] || 12 פ׳] פרק[ד] ||
14 ולאהבה] לאהבה[ת] || 16 השפיל] השפילר[ב] || 17 היפוי] היפויי[ב] || 19 היפוי] היפויי[ב] ||

8–9 דב׳ ו׳ ו׳ | 9 מש׳ כ״ב י״ח ||

am full of the burnt-offerings of rams, and the fat of fed beasts; and I delight not in the blood of bullocks, or of lambs, or of he-goats [Isa. 1:11]. Similarly: **They that see thee do narrowly look upon thee, consider thee: "Is this the man that made the earth to tremble, that did shake kingdoms?"** [14:16].[2] Again: **The fishers also shall lament, and all they that cast angle into the Nile shall mourn, and they that spread nets upon the waters shall languish** [19:8]. And again: **Behold, the Lord maketh the earth empty and maketh it waste, and turneth it upside down and scattereth abroad the inhabitants thereof** [24:1]; **The mirth of tabrets ceaseth, the noise of them that rejoice endeth, the joy of the harp ceaseth** [24:8]. The hearer cannot but be rather stirred by the bringing back of the thought in different words.

[2] What we have said above has made it plain that the combination, in a single statement, of several different kinds of Figures is feasible, and need not result in absurdity; **and these words . . . shall be upon thy heart** [Deut. 6:6] constantly; **let them be established altogether upon thy lips** [Prov. 22:18].[3] This Figure can be used in all the Kinds of Cause, and its effect is called for in the Grand and Middle Styles.

CHAPTER 30

Reciprocal Change[1]

[1] Reciprocal Change[a] is diction compounded of a pair of discrepant thoughts, so ordered that what stands first in the first clause is last in the second, and vice versa. For example: . . . **in that thou lovest them that hate thee, and hatest them that love thee** [2 Sam. 19:7]. Similarly in Ezekiel: . . . **that I the Lord have brought low the high tree, have raised high the low tree** [Ezek. 17:24];[2] and: **This shall no more be the same: that which is low shall be made high, and that which is high made low** [21:31].

[2] Reciprocal Change differs from Reasoning by Contraries in that, as has been explained, in Reasoning by Contraries the indispensable condition is that one of the statements must necessarily follow from the other; but this is not the case here. Reciprocal Change is also differentiated from Antithesis, for, as was made clear, the terms are here reversed, whereas in Antithesis, reversal is not

2. KJV (adapted).
3. An "invented" example of the Figure.

1. Literally: "the rotative," "moving in circles": הַסִּבּוּבִי, i.e., chiasmus.
2. Modified from JV to exhibit JML's thought.

a. *R. ad H.* 4.28.39.

ההתחדשות יחייב ערבות אל השומעים, ובו מן הצחות מה שלא יעלם. ואפשר העשותו בכל סוגי הדבור, ויבוקש ענינו בבינוני יותר:

פרק ל״א

פ׳ ההתנדבות.

[1] ההתנדבות הוא מאמר כאשר יפרסם התנדבות דבר מה כלו בשלמות אל אשר חפצנו ביקרו, לעשות בו כחפצו. והמשל במגלת אסתר: ״הכסף נתון לך, והעם, לעשות בו כטוב בעיניך״ [אס׳ ג׳ י״א]. וכן: ״הנה ארצי לפניך· בטוב בעיניך שב״ [בר׳ כ׳ ט״ו]. וכן: ״לא אדוני, שמעני: השדה נתתי לך, והמערה אשר בו, לך נתתיה· לעיני בני עמי נתתיה לך· קבור מתיך״ [שם כ״ג י״א]. וכן בענין אביגיל: ותקם ותשתחו אפים ארצה· ותאמר: ״הנה אמתך לשפחה, לרחוץ רגלי עבדי אדני״ [שמ״א כ״ה מ״א]. וכן בענין ברזלי הגלעדי: ״הנה עבדך כמהם· יעבור עם אדני המלך, ועשה לו את אשר טוב בעיניך״ [שמ״ב י״ט ל״ח].

[2] ונכון העשותו בכל סוגי הדבור, ובבינוני ובשפל, ובפתיחה ובחתימה מחלקי המאמר:

פרק ל״ב

פ׳ המסופק.

[1] המסופק הוא מאמ׳ באשר ישאל מה טוב משני דברים, או יותר. והמשל במלכים: כשאמרו ישראל לרחבעם ״אביך הקשה את עלנו· אתה עתה הקל

3 פרק] פ׳[כ] || 4 פ׳] פרק[ר] || 5 התנדבות] ההתנדבו׳[ר] || 7 בטוב] כטוב[ר] || 8 שמעני‹אדוני›[כ] || 9 [נתתיה לך][כ] || 10 לרחוץ ‹את›[ר] || 11 הנה] והנה[ת] || 12 את אשר טוב] הטוב[כ] || 13 ובשפל] שפל[כ] || 15 פרק] פ׳[כ] || 16 פ׳] פרק[ר] || 17 משני] מב׳[ר] || 18 אתה] ואתה[ת] ||

required. Change of this kind affords delight to the hearers; it achieves a not inconsiderable elegance. The Figure can be used in all the kinds of Cause, and its effect is very often called for in the Middle Style.

CHAPTER 31

Surrender[1]

1. Surrender[a] is the dictional Figure whereby the offering of some thing, wholly and completely, to one whom we wish to honor, to do with as he likes, is communicated. For example, in the Scroll of Esther: **"The silver is given to thee, the people also, to do with them as it seemeth good to thee"** [Esth. 3:11]. Similarly: **"Behold, my land is before thee: dwell where it pleaseth thee"** [Gen. 20:15]. Again: **"Nay, my Lord, hear me: the field give I thee, and the cave that is therein, I give it thee; in the presence of the sons of my people give I it thee; bury thy dead"** [23:11]. And again, in the incident concerning Abigail: **And she arose, and bowed down with her face to the earth, and said: "Behold, thy handmaid is a servant to wash the feet of the servants of my Lord"** [1 Sam. 25:41]. And so too in the matter concerning Barzillai the Gileadite: **"But behold thy servant Chimham; let him go over with my lord the king; and do to him that which shall seem good unto thee"** [2 Sam. 19:38].

[2] Surrender can readily be used in all the Kinds of Cause, in the Middle Style and the Simple, and, of the Parts of the Discourse, in the Introduction and the Conclusion.

CHAPTER 32

Indecision[1]

[1] Indecision[a] is diction in which the question is asked, Which of two or more courses is the better, or best. An example is in Kings: When Israel had said to

1. Literally: ''volunteering,'' ''making of a free-will offering'': הַהִתְנַדְּבוּת.

a. *R. ad H.* 4.29.39.

1. Literally: ''the doubtful,'' ''dubious,'' ''problematic,'' ''questionable'': הַמְסוּפָּק.

a. *R. ad H.* 4.29.40.

מעבודת אביך הקשה ומעולו הכבד אשר נתן עלינו, ונעבדך״ [מל״א י״ב ד׳]· אמר א״כ: ויועץ המלך רחבעם את הזקנים אשר היו עומדים את פני שלמה אביו...לאמר: ״איך אתם נועצים להשיב את העם הזה דבר״ [שם ו׳]. ר״ל, ששאל להם מה היה יותר טוב משני דברים: להשיב הין על מה ששאלו· או להשיב את פניהם, ולא ישמע ולא יאבה. וכן בענין אבימלך, בשופטים: ״דברו נא באזני כל בעלי שכם, מה טוב לכם: המשול בכם שבעים איש, כל בני ירובעל, אם משול בכם איש אחד״? [שופ׳ ט׳ ב׳]. ויבוקש ענינו בשפל יותר:

פרק ל״ג

פ׳ ההמשכות.

[1] ההמשכות הוא מאמר יבואו בו מאמרים רבים על העשות הדבר, או בלתי עשותו· וישאר אחד מהם בהכרח משלילת כל מאמר מהבאים בספור זולתו. והמשל ממה שאמ׳ ירמיהו: כה אמר ה׳: אל יתהלל חכם בחכמתו· ואל יתהלל הגבור בגבורתו· ואל יתהלל עשיר בעשרו; כי אם בזאת יתהלל המתהולל, השכל וידוע אותי [יר׳ ט׳ כ״ב—כ״ג]. והוא מן המפרסם, שאם לא היה נופל במחשבת האדם שראוי להתהלל בענינים הנזכרים, בחכמה ובעושר ובגבורה, היתה האזהרה בזה מותר ולבטלה גמורה. ולזה התחייב בהכרח זה המאמ׳, שהדברים הנופלים ברשת הדמיון, שראוי להתהלל בהם, יעלו אל מספר ד׳: ר״ל, אם שיתהלל בחכמה· ואם בעושר· ואם בגבורה· ואם בהשכל וידוע; אבל אין ראוי שיתהלל לא החכם בחכמתו, ולא הגבור בגבורתו, ולא העשיר בעשרו· א״כ, ראוי שיתהלל בהשכל וידוע, וזהו הנשאר בהכרח משלילת האחרים.

1 ומעולו] מעלו[ד] | הכבד] הקשה[כ] || 5 [את][ד] || 8 פרק] פ׳[כ] || 9 פ׳] פרק[ד] || 11 וישאר] יישאר[כ] || 12 [כה אמר ה׳][ד] || 13 [ואל יתהלל עשיר בעשרו][ד] אל[ת] || 14 והוא <והוא>[כ] | נופל] שפל[כ] || 16 גמורה] גמור[כ] | ולזה] ולא[כ] || 19 העשיר] עשיר[ד] ||

Rehoboam, **"Thy father made our yoke grievous; now therefore make thou the grievous service of thy father, and his heavy yoke which he put upon us, lighter, and we will serve thee"** [1 Kings 12:4], we are subsequently told: **And king Rehoboam took counsel with the old men that had stood before Solomon his father . . . saying: "What counsel give ye me to return answer to this people?"** [12:6]. In other words, he asked them which of two courses would be better: to reply affirmatively to what the people asked, or, neither heeding nor consenting, to refuse them. So too in the incident concerning Abimelech, in Judges: **"Speak, I pray you, in the ears of all the men of Shechem: Which is better for you, that all the sons of Jerubbaal, who are threescore and ten persons, rule over you, or that one rule over you?"** [Judg. 9:2]. This Figure's effect is very often called for in the Simple Style.

CHAPTER 33

Elimination[1]

[1] Elimination[a] is diction in which several propositions about the performance or avoidance of some action are introduced, of which one alone necessarily remains after every other, of those coming into account, is negated. An example is afforded by Jeremiah's words: **Thus saith the Lord: Let not the wise man glory in his wisdom neither let the mighty man glory in his might, let not the rich man glory in his riches; but let him that glorieth glory in this, that he understandeth and knoweth Me** [Jer. 9:22–23]. Now manifestly, if it never came into anyone's mind that one might well glory in the advantages mentioned—wisdom, riches, and might—to warn against so doing would be superfluous and altogether vain. It therefore necessarily follows from this pronouncement that the things which do present themselves in the net of the imagination as those in which one may well glory are at least four in number: one may glory in wisdom, or riches, or might, or in understanding and knowing God. But it is improper for the wise man to glory in his wisdom, for the mighty man to glory in his might, and for the rich man in his riches. One may, therefore, properly glory only in understanding and knowing God,[2] this being the one good that perforce remains after the others have been negated.

1. Literally: ''duration,'' ''continuation''; ''development,'' ''conclusion'': הַהֶמְשֵׁכוּת.
2. The word ''God'' does not appear in our text at this point, but is to be understood from the Scriptural citation.

a. *R. ad H.* 4.29.40–41.

[2] וכן באמרו: אשרי האיש אשר לא הלך בעצת רשעים, ובדרך חטאים לא עמד, ובמושב ליצים לא ישב· כי אם בתורת י״י חפצו, ובתורת׳ יהגה יומם ולילה [תה׳ א׳ א׳ — ב׳]; הכונה בזה המאמ׳ להוכיח הדבר שראוי למענו שיאמ׳ לחושק בו ״אשריו״, ר״ל, שהוא מעותד להשיג ההצלחה התכליתית והתענוג האמתי הרוחני. וראוי שתדע שאין הרצון הנה ב״רשעים״ בעלי הפשעים והעברות, על דרך: ואתה חלל, רשע [יח׳ כ״א ל׳]· ישובו רשעים לשאולה [תה׳ ט׳ י״ח]. אמנם, זאת התיבה תשולח הנה על החרדים על הממון ומתמידים ההשתדלות בעניני העולם, כמו: לא ימלט רשע את בעליו [קה׳ ח׳ ח׳]· אל תרשע הרבה [שם ז׳ י״ז]· ובכל אשר יפנה ירשיע [שמ״א י״ד מ״ז]; ר״ל, בכל מקום שהיה פונה, היה מכוון עניינו בהשתדלות רב ועצום, עד שהיה מגיע מבוקשו.

[3] וכן גם כן, אין ענין ״חטאים״ הנה כמו: מחטאתו אשר חטא [וי׳ י״ט כ״ב]; אמנם, המכוון בו הדבר שאפשר שתשיגהו השגיאה, והיציאה מן האמת אל הכזב, והוא לא ידע ואשם, מלשון: אל השערה ולא יחטיא [שופ׳ כ׳ ט״ז]. ויהיה הרצון ב״חטאים״ בעלי החכמות העיוניות; כי אם יעמוד האדם בם לבד, אין ספק שיטעה בהרבה מן הדרושים, וביחוד האלקיים, באשר קצרה כח השכל להגיע עד תבונתם· עם שלא יתנו השלמות התכליתי אשר אנחנו, קהל י״י וסגלתו, נשיגהו באמצעות התורה הקדושה.

[4] גם ענין ״לצים״ ישולח לעולם על הדבור, כמו: להבין משל ומליצה [מש׳ א׳ ו׳]· מליצי רעי [איוב ט״ז כ׳]· יליץ משפט [מש׳ י״ט כ״ח], וזולתם; אלא שבסתם יאמר על המפליגים לדבר, ר״ל, יושבי קרנות המתלוצצים ותמיד לא יחשו מלספר מומי בני אדם בחנפי לעגי מעוג. והמכוון ב״לצים״ הנה, לפי מה שאחשוב, הם אשר שמו כל מעיינם בדבור — ר״ל, בחכמות הדבוריות, שהם דקדוק, הלצה, הגיון, וגם בפילוסופיא המדינית — שהם בעלי הדינים וההנהגות, המליצי׳ בעד האנשים ומדברים בענינם אם לטובה אם למות, ולשרשי, ולענש נכסים, ולאסרין. וקרא אלה ״לצים״, ואם באלה החכמות מן

1–2 בעצת...ישב] וכ׳[ד] || 2–3 ובתורת׳...ולילה] וכו׳[כ] || 3 בזה <להוכיח>[כ] || 4 שהוא מעותד] שמעותד[ד] || 7 אמנם] ואולם[כ] || 10 שהיה] שהוא[ד] | עניינו] ענייניו[כ] || 13 שתשיגהו] שתשיגיה[כ] || 14 ידע] ידע׳[ד] || 16 מן הדרושים] דרושי׳[ד] | האלקיים] באלקיים[ד] | באשר] כאשר[כ] || 17 [עד][כ] | תבונתם] תכונתם[ד] | עם] עד[כ] | התכליתי] התכלית[ד] || 19 [גם][ד] || 20 רעי] ריעיי[כ] || 23 בחכמות] בחכמת[ד] || 24 הדינים] המדינים[כ] || 26 ולענש] לענש[ד] | וקרא] ויקרא[ד] ||

14 וי׳ ה׳ י״ז || 17 במ׳ ט״ז ג׳ || 18 תה׳ קל״ה ד׳ || 21–22 יש׳ ס״ב ו׳ | 22 תה׳ ל״ה ט״ז || 25–26 עז׳ ז׳ כ״ו ||

[2] So too, when the Psalmist says, **Happy is the man that hath not walked in the counsel of the wicked, nor stood in the way of sinners, nor sat in the seat of the scornful; but his delight is in the law of the Lord, and in his law doth he meditate day and night** [Ps. 1:1–2], the statement is intended to demonstrate the one thing for love of which it is fitting to say of the lover, "Happy is he"—destined, in other words, to obtain the utmost good fortune and true spiritual bliss. You should know also that "wicked" here does not mean committers of trespass and transgression, as in **And thou, O wicked one, that art to be slain** [Ezek. 21:30], or in **The wicked shall return to the nether-world** [Ps. 9:18]. Rather, the word here connotes those who revere money and strive assiduously after the things of this world, as in **Neither shall wickedness deliver those that are given to it** [Eccl. 8:8]; **Be not overmuch wicked** [7:17];. . . **and whithersoever he turned himself he acted wickedly** [1 Sam. 14:47];[3]—wherever he might turn, he would attend to his schemes with such great energy that he would reach his goal.

[3] In precisely the same way, the "sin" of the "sinners" in this passage is not the same as in **for his sin which he hath sinned** [Lev. 19:22]; its intended meaning is rather some matter which it is possible for error, for departure from truth to falsehood, to overtake—some matter which, **though he know it not, yet he is guilty** [5:17]—the meaning expressed by "miss"[4] in **sling stones at a hair-breadth and not miss** [Judg. 20:16]. By "sinners," in our passage, is meant adherents of the speculative sciences; for if a man has understanding only of these, he will no doubt go astray in many inquiries, particularly in theology, wherein the faculty of reason falls short of arriving at comprehension of them; nor can the speculative sciences yield that utmost perfection which we, **the assembly of the Lord** [Num. 16:3] and **His own treasure** [Ps. 135:4], can obtain by way of the holy Torah.

[4] Furthermore, while the term "scornful" (*lēṣīm*) always implies speech, as in **to understand a proverb and a figure** (mᵉlīṣāh) [Prov. 1:6], **My friends scorn me** (mᵉlīṣay) [Job 16:20],[5] **mocketh** (yālīṣ) **at right** [Prov. 19:28], and in other examples, ordinarily the word denotes those who talk too much—those scoffers, that is, who sit idle in corners and **never hold their peace** [Isa. 62:6] from describing men's faults **with the profanest mockeries of backbiting** [Ps. 35:16]. In the present passage, however, I think "scornful" is intended to mean those who devote the whole of their study to speech—that is to say, to the verbal arts,[6] grammar, rhetoric, and logic, and also to political and ethical philosophy—the lawyers and statesmen who make speeches on behalf of men and speak in their cause, whether for good or for **death, . . . banishment, . . . confiscation of goods, or . . . imprisonment** [Ezra 7:26]. Although these arts do

3. Translated thus to exhibit JML's meaning.
4. "Miss" (יַחֲטִא) is formed on the same root as "sinners" (חַטָּאִים).
5. KJV.
6. The "*artes sermocinales*" (הַחָכְמוֹת הַדִּבּוּרִיּוֹת).

ההבנה אל העיוניות, והטוב המדותי, מה שלא יעלם· למה שאם כונו בהם
התכלית ויספיקו בהם מבלתי שיחרדו אל י״י ואל טובו — אל התורה אשר שם
משה להיות כל איש שורר בבית התהלה והתפארת, לחזות בנועם י״י — ישבו
במדרגת ״הלצים״ המפליגים תמיד לספר· ירבו, ידברו גבוהה גבוהה.

5 [5] והוא מבואר מאד, שאי אפשר שיעמוד מה שכונו קצת המפרשים בפרוש
אלה המלות. כי אם היה כדבריהם, מי הוא הסכל שיחשוב שבעל החטאות,
והרשע, והליצנות יאמ׳ בו ״אשריו״· עד שהוצרך המשורר לעקור זה הדעת
מעקרו, ולאמר, אשרי האיש אשר לא הלך, וכו׳? אבל מה שפי׳[1] אנחנו ניאות
מאד לענין, עם שהתבות תשארנה בבלתי זרות.

10 [6] ואחר התישב זה, נאמ׳ שהיה נופל במחשבה שהשלמות התכליתי הוא
באחד מארבעה, ר״ל; אם בקנינים, אשר ירמוז בהם בתבת ״רשעים״; ואם
בחכמות העיוניות, אשר יכוון אליהם במלת ״חטאים״; ואם בחכמות הדבריות
ובפילוסופיא המדינית, אשר רצה ב״לצים״; ואם בתורת י״י הקדושה. ואחר שזה
השלמות אינו באחד מאלה השלשה, ר״ל ״רשעים״ ו״חטאים״ ו״לצים״ —
15 דאדרבה, השלמות הוא במי שלא הרגיל עמהם הרגל רב — ישאר החלק
הרביעי, ר״ל, שמי שיאמ׳ לו ״אשריו״ הוא אשר בתורת י״י חפצו ויהגה בה יומם
ולילה. כאלו אמר שאין דבר שתהיה ההתמדה התדירה מותרת בו כי אם
התורה· ואם ביתר הדברים, ההרגל התדיר אסור, אלא שכבר ראוי לו להשתדל
בהשגתם השתדלות קצת, לתכלית הבנת הדעות התוריות אשר לא תלקחנה
20 על המשכל בלי ספק. והשכל והתורה לא יסתרו זה את זה, כאשר יחשבו
הפתאים ועתיקי משדים.

[7] והנה הלך בהדרגה. כי מאלה השלשה, החרדה על הממון, והקנין, ועניני
העולם הוא הרע הגדול, עד אי אפשר עמה שום שלמות· ולזה אמר ״הלך״
בערך אל ״הרשעים״, שאפי׳ ההליכה לא תותר בערכם. ואמר אחר זה
25 ״חטאים״, שאפשר היות בהם שלמות גדול, אלא שהשגותיו אינם מזוקקות

1 המדותי] המדותיי[ד] || 2 י״י] ה׳[כ] || 3 שורר] סורר[כ] | ‹לעולם הבא› לחזות[ד] | ישבו] שבו[ד] || 4 המפליגים] ומפליגים[כ] || 5–6 בפרוש אלה] בפ׳ אילו[כ] || 6 כדבריהם] בדבריהם[כ] || 8 מעקרו ‹וכו׳›[ד] | שפי׳[1] ‹בו›[כ] || 9 תשארנה ‹לעקור זה הדעת מעקרו›[כ] || 11 מארבעה] מד׳[ד] || 12 בחכמות] בחכמת[ד] | חטאים] רשעים[ד] || 14 השלשה] הג׳ | רשעים וחטאים] חטאים ורשעים[כ] || 15 דאדרבה] דאדררבה[כ] | הרגל] הרגיל[כ] || 16 בה] בו[כ] || 17 דבר] הדבר[ד] || 18 התורה] בתורה[ד] | ואם ביתר הדברים] אם וביתר [הדברים][ד] || 19 תלקחנה] תחלקנה[כ] || 20 והשכל] והסכל[כ] || 22 כי ‹מלאה הארץ›[כ] | [החרדה][כ] | ועניני] ונינני[ד] ||

2–3 דב׳ ד׳ מ״ד || 3 אס׳ א׳ כ״ב | יר׳ י״ג י״א | תה׳ כ״ז ד׳ || 4 שמ״א ב׳ ג׳ || 21 יש׳ כ״ח ט׳ ||

[1] J: שפירשנו.

contain considerable understanding of speculative philosophy and of ethical good, the Psalmist called such practitioners "the scornful" because, if they use these arts purposefully and persuade others by their means without reverence for the Lord and His good—**the law which Moses set** [Deut. 4:44] **that every man should bear rule in the house** [Esth. 1:22] of **praise and** of **glory** [Jer. 13:11], so as **to behold the graciousness of the Lord** [Ps. 27:4]—then they rank with "the scornful" who always exaggerage their tales: they **multiply . . . exceeding proud talk** [1 Sam. 2:3].

[5] It is quite obvious that what some commentators have fixed upon as the proper interpretation of these words cannot possibly stand. For if it were as they maintain, what fool is there who thinks that the words "Happy is the man" would be said of a person who indulges in sin, wickedness, and scorn, so that the Psalmist was constrained to eradicate this notion completely, and must say, **Happy is the man that hath** NOT **walked,** etc.? Our own interpretation,[7] on the other hand, is very well suited to the theme, and at the same time the words no longer seem strange.

[6] This established, we may say that it could occur to one to think that the utmost perfection is available by one of four means, to wit: by possessions, as suggested by the Psalmist in the word "wicked"; or by the speculative sciences, the intended meaning of his word "sinners"; or by the verbal arts and by political and ethical philosophy, which he meant by "the scornful"; or by the Lord's holy Torah. Since such perfection is available by means of none of these three, namely, "the wicked," "sinners," and "the scornful"—nay, perfection is rather available through one who is not very familiar with these—the fourth category alone is left; that is, the person of whom it may be said "Happy is he" is that one whose **delight is in the law of the Lord** and who **meditates** therein **day and night.** It is as though the Psalmist had declared that there is nothing in which constant diligence is licit except the Torah, and that as for the remaining categories, constant preoccupation with them is forbidden, although it is of course proper to make some effort to master them for the purpose of understanding those of the Torah's doctrines which cannot be taken to be indubitably rational. Reason and the Torah are not mutually contradictory, as think fools and those **that are drawn from the breasts** [Isa. 28:9].

[7] We see, then, that the Psalmist has used Climax.[8] For of these three categories, it is the reverence for money, property, and the things of this world that is the greatest evil, to the point that with this no perfection at all is possible; and that is why the Psalmist used the term "walk" with reference to "the wicked," since even "walking," so far as this category is concerned, is not permitted. He next used the term "sinners," through which perfection in greater degree is possible, although the achievements of this category are not refined and

7. I.e., JML's allegorical interpretation.
8. iv.20.

ונקיות מהטעות· ולזה התיר בהם ההליכה, ואמר "לא עמד". והביא "הלצים"
באחרונה, שהשגותיהם אמתיות, והם שומרות יותר מן הטעות ממה שיפילו בו
האנשים, עם הטוב הגדול הנמשך מהפילוסופיא המדינית· אלא שאין ראוי
לעמוד שם לעולם, ולא תותר בהם ההתמדה הגדולה, למען יתבונן[2] בבקר
5 בבקר בסודות התורה ובפינות שבטיה, וילמד לעשות את חקי האלקים ואת
תורותיו. ולכן, התיר בהם העמידה, ואמר "ישב", שהוא לשון נופל על עכבה
גדולה, כמו: ותשבו בקדש ימים רבים [דב׳ א׳ מ״ו]· ואתה י״י לעולם תשב [תה׳
ק״ב י״ג]. וכאלו רצה בזה, שבראשון מאלה אין ראוי לעמוד בו כלל· ובשני
אפשר בו שיעמוד קצת מן הזמן, אבל לא הרבה, כדי שיוכל לזקק דעותיו והסי׳
10 הטעיות, והמכשולים· אמנם, באחרון יוכל לעמוד בו יותר, להיותו נקי מן
הטעיות, אלא שאין ראוי להתאחר בו באופן יתבטל מן התורה, אשר תאות בה
ההתמדה אשר בתכלית. וזה המכוון ב"הלך", "עמד", ו"ישב", לא ענינם כאשר
הם, כי הוא מן הלשונות המפליגים. והתבונן העונש הכתו׳ בזה בסוף המזמור,
איך הלך בו גם כן בהדרגה, ומה מאד מורה על מה שאמרנוהו, ומסכים לו מכל
15 צד; וזה, שלא זכר האבדון בערך אל "החטאים", גם לא הזכיר "הלצים" בערך
כלל.

[8] והנה אם תפקחנה עיני השכל, זה המאמר הוא מסכים עם מה שאמ׳
ירמיהו: אל יתהלל חכם בחכמתו [יר׳ ט׳ כ״ב]· כי הוא כלל ב"חכם" כל
החכמות העיוניות, דבריות או בלתי דבריות; וב"גבור" כוון גם אל בעל ההנהגה
20 המדינית — שהוא גבור עומד כנגד יצרו· ו"אי זהו גבור? הכובש את יצרו" —
עם שהם גבורים, עושים דבריהם גזרות לשמור ולעשות, ולהם לבדם נתנה
הארץ. והוא מבואר שהשכל וידוע... ה׳ [שם שם כ״ג] היא התורה בעצמה, כי
לא ישוער זה זולתה.

[9] וזה היפוי מועיל מאד בראיות הלקוחות מן הסברה· ויבוקש ענינו בבינוני
25 יותר:

1 הלצים] ההלציי[ד] | 1 2 אמתיות] אמתות[כ] | שומרות] שמורות[כ] || 4 יתבונן[2] ‹יתבו› תתבונן[ד] ||
5 ובפינות] ופנות[ד] || 9 [אבל][ד] | והסי׳] יהסור[כ] || 10 באחרון] האחרון[כ] || 11 להתאחר] להתאחד[כ] |
יתבטל ‹בו›[ד] | תאות] תאוה[כ] | בה] בם[ד] || 12 וזה] וזהו[ד] | כאשר] באשר[ד] || 13 העונש] בענש[ד] |
[בזה][ד] || 15 בערך] בענש[ד] || 17 תפקחנה] תפקנ׳[ד] | השכל] שכלך[כ] || 18 [הוא][ד] || 19 [גם אל][ד] | בעל]
בעלי[ד] || 21 [ולהם][ד] || 22 לבדם] ולבדם[ד] | הארץ] לארץ[כ] ||

4–5 יש׳ נ׳ ד׳ || 5 יש׳ י״ט י״ג | 5–6 שמ׳ י״ח ט״ז || 17 יש׳ ל״ה ה׳ || 21 דב׳ כ״ח י״ג || 21–22 איוב
ט״ו י״ט ||

[2] *Litterae dilatabiles* in ד: יתבו.

wholly free from error; he therefore allowed "walking" in their case, but said "nor stood. . . ." Lastly he cited "the scornful," the category whose achievements are genuine, and which protect men against, rather than make them fall into, the error associated with the great good to be derived from political and ethical philosophy; but one must not "stand" therein forever, and great perseverance in it is not permitted, so that **morning by morning** [Isa. 50:4] one will study the secrets of the Torah and **the corner-stones of her tribes** [19:13] and learn to do **the statutes of God and His laws** [Exod. 18:16]. The Psalmist, therefore, did permit standing in the case of these, but used the word "sat," which is an idiomatic way of indicating long duration, as in **So ye abode**[9] **in Kadesh many days** [Deut. 1:46]; **But thou, O Lord, shalt endure**[10] **forever** [Ps. 102:13]. It is as though the Psalmist, in thus using Climax, had meant that, in the case of the first of these three categories, it is improper to abide by it at all; in the case of the second, that one may abide by it for a little time, though not long, in order to refine one's ideas and to remove errors and stumbling blocks; but that in the case of the last, one can abide by it longer because it is wholly free from error, except that it is not proper so to tarry in it that one will grow neglectful of the Torah, in which the greatest possible perseverance is appropriate. It is not the literal sense of "walked," "stood," and "sat" that is here intended, but that of the extended sense of the terms. Furthermore, consider the punishment recorded in the latter portion of the Psalm, how the Psalmist again used Climax, and how abundantly this bears out, and in every aspect accords with, what we have said. For he made no mention of perishing in regard to "the sinners," and no allusion at all to any punishment of "the scornful."

[8] Thus, if **the eyes of the** mind . . . **be opened** [Isa. 35:5], this statement by the Psalmist is seen to agree with Jeremiah's words: **Let not the wise man glory in his wisdom,** etc.[11] [Jer. 9:22]. For in using the term "wise man" the prophet implied all the theoretical sciences, whether verbal or other than verbal. By "mighty man" he meant both the holder of political leadership—"mighty" in the sense of one capable of withstanding his evil impulse: "Who is a mighty man? He that subdues his evil impulse"[12]—and those too who are mighty in the sense that they enact their words into decrees for others **to observe and to do** [Deut. 28:13], and **unto whom alone the land was given** [Job 15:19]. The words **that he understandeth and knoweth . . . the Lord** [Jer. 9:23] clearly refer to the Torah itself, for without the Torah such knowledge and understanding are inconceivable.

[9] This Figure is extremely useful in proofs drawn from conjecture, and its effect is very often called for in the Middle Style.

9. B: "sat" (וַתֵּשְׁבוּ).
10. KJV; B: "sit" (תֵּשֵׁב).
11. "Etc." not in text.
12. *Mishnah Ābhōth* 4:1.

פרק ל״ד

פ׳ הנבדל.

[1] הנבדל הוא כאשר יבאו מאמרים רבים נבדלים מבלי אות קושר. והמשל: כי עם מרי המה, בנים כחשים· בנים לא אבו שמוע תורת י״י [יש׳ ל׳ ט׳]. וכן: כי צו לצו צו לצו, קו לקו קו לקו· זער שם, זער שם [שם כ״ח י׳]. וכן: בהנחל עליון גוים, בהפרידו בני אדם· יצב גבולות עמים למספר בני ישראל [דב׳ ל״ב ח׳]. וכן: יזבחו לשדים לא אלוה, אלקים לא ידעום· חדשים מקרוב באו, לא שערום אבותיכם [שם שם י״ז].

[2] וזה מסכים עם המחולק בהעדר האות הקושר· ויתחלפו, שהעדר האות הקושר במחולק[1] הוא בין התיבות, ובזה היפוי בין המאמרים. וזה היפוי חזק ההערה אל הכעס או אל הרחמנות, עם שבו מן הקצור מה שלא יעלם; ויבוקש ענינו בדבור הנשא ובבינוני:

פרק ל״ה

פ׳ הנפסק.

[1] הנפסק הוא מאמ׳ אשר יותחל בו דבר מה ויפסק, כמו שאמר דוד מספר תכונות הרשע: אלה פיהו מלא ומרמות ותוך· תחת לשונו עמל ואון [תה׳ י׳ ז׳];

1 פרק] פ׳ᶜ || 2 פ׳] פרקᵈ || 4 המה] הואᵗ || 5 קו לקו [קו לקו]ᶜ | זער] זעירᵗ || 9 ויתחלפו] יתחלפוᶜ || 10 במחולק[1]] בנלחץᶜᵈ | המאמרים] המאמריᵈ || 12 ובבינוני] והבנוניᶜ || 13 פרק] פ׳ᶜ || 14 פ׳] פרקᵈ || 15 ויפסק] ויופסקᶜ || 16 [ותוך]ᶜ ||

[1] Corrected text.

CHAPTER 34

Asyndeton[1]

[1] The Figure is Asyndeton[a] when several separated statements are introduced without conjunctive particle. For example: **For they are[2] a rebellious people, lying children, children that refuse to hear the teaching of the Lord** [Isa. 30:9]. Similarly: **For it is precept by precept, precept by precept, line by line, line by line, here a little, there a little** [28:10]. Again: **When the Most High gave to the nations their inheritance, when He separated the children of men, He set the borders of the peoples according to the number of the children of Israel** [Deut. 32:8]. And again: **They sacrificed unto demons, no-gods, gods that they knew not, new gods that came up of late, which your fathers dreaded not** [v. 17].

[2] This figure agrees with Comma or Phrase[3] in that the conjunctive particle is lacking, but the two differ in that, in Comma, the particle is lacking between words, in Asyndeton, between statements. Asyndeton, though markedly concise, is powerfully evocative of anger or pity; its effect is called for in the Grand Style and the Middle.

CHAPTER 35

Aposiopesis[1]

[1] Aposiopesis[a] is diction in which some statement is begun, and then cut off, as David pointed out in describing the behavior characteristic of the wicked man: **His mouth is full of swearing[2] and deceit and secret guile; under his tongue is**

1. Literally: ''the separated,'' ''the set apart'': הַנִּבְדָּל.
2. *Sic;* B: ''. . . it is. . . .''
3. iv.13.

---

a. *R. ad H.* 4.30.41.

1. Literally: ''the cut off,'' ''the severed,'' ''the interrupted'': הַנִּפְסָק.
2. JV and KJV: ''cursing''; but that JML takes ''swearing'' to be the meaning can be seen from his subsequent interpretation. Other parts of the verse are also here translated to accord with JML's exposition.

---

a. *R. ad H.* 4.30.41.

וזה, שהרשע מפליג לחטוא בלב, בדבור, ובמעשה.

[2] וספר תחלה מה שבו מן העון והפשע בלב, ואמר שהוא אומר בלבו: ״בל אמוט· לדור ודור אשר לא ברע״ [שם שם ו׳]. כלומ׳: ״מה שבא בתורה מן הקללות והענשים הגדולים לעוברים על המצות לא יקום ולא יהיה בערכי, ולא תבואני צרה ותוכחה, שואה ומשואה״ — על דרך: והתברך בלבבו לאמר שלום יהיה לי [דב׳ כ״ט י״ח]. וזהו השרש המחטיאו, ואשר ישליכנו במצולות הפשעים והמרדים.

[3] וא״כ ספר מה שבו מן ״העון בלשון״, ואמר: אלה פיהו מלא [שם ז׳]; כלומ׳, שהוא מבטיח האנשים באלות ובשבועות, עד יגורם בחרמו, ויאספם למכמרתו. וזהו דרך אחד ממה שיחטא בלשון; עוד, יחטא באופן אחר, שהוא מרמה בלשונו בתכלית מה שאפשר· אמנם, יספר דרך תחבולה באופן לא ירגישו האנשים בו; וזה מה שרצה ב״מרמות ותוך״ [שם ז׳], והוא דרך שני.

[4] א״כ אמר: ותחת לשונו עמל ואון [שם]; ר״ל, שלפעמי׳ מתחיל לדבר ומכחיד הקצת ממנו תחת לשונו· אם שידו שם למו פיו ושותק, אם שאומר שאינו רוצה לסיים מה שהתחיל. וזהו יותר רע מכלם, מפני שמפליג החשד בלב השומעים, וישוער בו מן המרירות והרוע יותר ממה שהיה אם יאמרנו בפרסום.

[5] ובזה, מסכים זה היפוי עם ההעלמה; ויבדל ממנה, שההעלמה היא קודם הדבור או עמו, כמי שיאמר: ״איני רוצה לספר מה שבך מן המומי׳ והמעשים המגונים״, כמו שהמשלנו למעלה; והנפסק, הוא מתחיל לדבר, ואחר כך מפסיק, כמי שיאמ׳: ״אתה, אדם, כך וכך — איני רוצה לאמר יותר״.

[6] והמשל בזה עוד: אם תמתק בפיו רעה, יכחידנה תחת לשונו [איוב כ׳ י״ב]; ר״ל, שימתק לו הספור הרע והטלת המומים בבני אדם, וא״כ יכחידנה תחת לשונו, ואומ׳ שאינו רוצה לגמור ולסיים דבריו.

[7] ויבוקש עניינו בבינוני, ולפעמים בשפל:

1 שהרשע ‹הוא›ד || 2 בל] אלד || 4 יהיה] תהיהד | ולא] לא || 12 וזה] וזהוכ || 13 ותחת] תחתת || 14 ומכחיד] ומכחישד | שאומר] שיאמ׳כ || 18 הדבור או עמו]ד | המומי׳] המומיןכ || 20 כמי] במדרגה מי׳ | לאמר] לומרד || 21 [עוד]ד | תמתק] תמתיקת || 22 [לו]ד || 23 ואומ׳] ואמ׳ד || 24 עניינו] ענינינוד ||

5 יש׳ ל״ז ג׳ | צפ׳ א׳ ט״ו || 6 מי׳ ז׳ י״ט || 9 חב׳ א׳ ט״ו || 14 איוב מ׳ ד׳ ||

mischief and iniquity [Ps. 10:7]: the wicked man, namely, is exceedingly sinful in heart, speech, and action.

[2] David first described the iniquity and transgression in the heart of the wicked man, and said: **He saith in his heart: "I shall not be moved, I who to all generations shall not be in adversity"** [10:6]. In other words: "The curses and severe punishments laid down in the Torah for violators of the commandments will neither be fulfilled nor come to pass in my particular case, nor will there ever come to me **trouble and... rebuke** [Isa. 37:3], **wasteness and desolation**" [Zeph. 1:15]—an exemplification of **that he bless himself in his heart, saying, "I shall have peace"** [Deut. 29:18]. This is the root cause of his sinning, that which **casts** him **into the depths of** [Mic. 7:19] acts of transgression and rebellion against God.

[3] David next described the wicked man's "iniquity by tongue," saying: **His mouth is full of swearing;** in other words, the wicked person keeps making to other men promises bound by oaths and adjurations until he **catches them in his net and gathers them in his drag** [Hab. 1:15]. This is one way in which he sins by tongue. He sins in still another way by making the most deceitful possible use of his tongue, framing his tales with such cunning, indeed, that men will not see through them; this is the meaning of **deceit and secret guile,** and it is a second way.

[4] David then said: **Under his tongue is mischief and iniquity.** Sometimes, that is, the wicked man begins to speak, but withholds part of his speech "under his tongue," whether it be that he **lays** his **hand upon** his **mouth** [Job 40:4] and falls silent, or states that he is unwilling to finish what he had started to say. This is a more vicious expedient than any of the others because it creates much greater suspicion in the mind of the audience, and by means of it a greater amount of bitterness and vice will be imagined by the hearers than would be possible if he were to state it plainly in so many words.

[5] In respect of this withholding, the present Figure agrees with Paralipsis.[3] It differs, however, in that Paralipsis either precedes or accompanies the speech, as when one says, "I have no desire to tell the tale of your faults and your disgraceful deeds," like in the example we gave above; whereas in Aposiopesis, the speaker begins to speak and then breaks off, as when one says, "You, Sir, are thus—and thus, I have no desire to say more."

[6] Another example involving Aposiopesis: **Though wickedness be sweet in his mouth, he hides it under his tongue** [Job 20:13];[4] that is, though he would find it pleasant to describe evil and to lay men's faults at their door, he nevertheless **hides it under his tongue** and asserts that he has no wish to finish what he could say.

[7] The effect of Aposiopesis is one called for in the Middle Style, and occasionally in the Simple.

3. iv.24.
4. Here rendered in accordance with JML's interpretation.

פרק ל״ו

פ׳ הכלל.

[1] הכלל הוא העולה מן המאמ׳ והמתחייב ממנו. והמשל ממה שאמר הש׳ ית׳ ליהושע מן היעוד הטוב על כבוש הארץ, אם ישמור לעשות את חקי האלקים ואת תורותיו, ואמ׳: ״לא יתיצב איש לפניך, כו׳... רק חזק ואמץ מאד לשמור ולעשות, כו׳... לא ימוש ספר התורה״, כו׳ [יהו׳ א׳ ה׳ — ח׳]. ואמ׳ בתכלית הספור: ״הלא צויתיך חזק ואמץ· אל תערוץ ואל תחת...״[שם ט׳]. וזה הוא הכלל מכל זה הספור, כלומ׳: ״העולה מכל מה שנאמ׳, שאני צויתיך המצות; ואתה, חזק ואמץ לשמרם· וימשך לך מזה, על צד הגמול, שלא תערוץ ולא תחת, ואהיה עמך בכל אשר תלך.״

[2] והמשלים על זה הרבה· ויבוקש ענינו על הרוב בבינוני ובשפל:

פרק ל״ז

פ׳ ההצעה.

[1] ההצעה: ונאמ׳ אחר זה מעשרה יפויים שהם גם כן בתיבות, והם מסכימים עם הראשונים מזה הצד; ומתחלפים, למה שהנזכרים הם לפי הוראת התבות על דרך הפשט· אמנם אלה העשרה, התבות באו דרך משל, העברה, או דמיון. ונתחיל מן התמורה:

1 פרק] פ״[ג] || 2 פ׳] פרק[ר] || 3 [הוא][ג] |ממה] מה[ר] || השׁ׳] ה״[ג] || 4 [את][ג] || 5 לא] שלא[ר] || [מאד][ג] || 6 ולעשות] לעשות[ת] || 7 [הספור][ר] || 7–8 וזה הוא] וזהו[ר] || 8 [שנאמ׳][ר] || 11 על זה הרבה] הרבה על זה[ג] || 12 פרק] פ״[ג] || 13 פ׳] פרק[ר] || 14 [ההצעה][ר] |[זה][ר] || 16 הפשט] פשט[ר] |אלה] אלו[ר] |התבות] תיבות[ג] || 17 ונתחיל] ונחיל[ג] |התמורה ‹ונאמר›[ר] ||

4 יהו׳ א׳ ז׳ || 4–5 שמ׳ י״ח ט״ז ||

CHAPTER 36

Conclusion[1]

[1] Conclusion[a] is the sum of the statement made, and its necessary consequence. Our example is drawn from the goodly promise of the conquest of the land which the Lord, blessed be He, made to Joshua, if he would **observe to do** [Josh. 1:7] **the statutes of God and His laws** [Exod. 18:16]. The Lord said: **"There shall not any man be able to stand before thee. . . . Only be strong and very courageous, to observe to do. . . . This book of the law shall not depart . . ."** [Josh. 1:5–8]. At the end of the exposition, He said: **"Have I not commanded thee? Be strong and of good courage; be not affrighted, neither be thou dismayed, for the Lord thy God is with thee whithersoever thou goest"** [1:9]. These words are the Conclusion of this entire exposition. In other words: "The sum of all that was said is this: it is I who have enjoined the commandments upon you; do you be strong and of good courage in observing them, and this will have the rewarding consequence for you that you will neither be affrighted nor dismayed, and that I will be with you wherever you go."

[2] There are many other examples of Conclusion; its effect is called for mostly in the Middle Style, and in the Simple.

CHAPTER 37

An Advance Outline

[1] The proposal: In what now follows we shall treat ten Figures[a] which, as they too are word effects, agree in this respect with those first considered; yet they differ in that those treated above depend on the meaning of the words according to the literal sense,[1] whereas in the case of the ensuing ten embellishments, the words are used allegorically, tropically, or figuratively. We begin, then, with Onomatopoeia.

1. Literally: "General rule," "principle"; "total," "sum"; "inclusion," "generalization," "implication": הַכְּלָל.

a. *R. ad H.* 4.30.41.

1. But cf. the exegesis of Ps. 1 in iv.33.7, in which the words are interpreted not according to the literal, but in an "extended," sense.

a. Cf. *R. ad H.* 4.31.42 ff.

פרק ל״ח

פ׳ התמורה.

[1] התמורה היא מאמ׳ באו בו תיבה או תבות מושאלות או לקוחות דרך העברה. והמשל: שאגה לו כלביא... וינהום עליו כנהמת ים [יש׳ ה׳ כ״ט—ל׳]· יהמו ככלב ויסובבו עיר [תה׳ נ״ט ז׳]· וזולתם רבים. ויבקש ענינו בנשא ובבינוני: 5

פרק ל״ט

פ׳ הכנוי.

[1] הכוני הוא מאמ׳ יכונה בו אדם מה בזולת השם המיוחד לו, על צד האיבה או דבר מה זולת זה. והמשל: ״הראיתם...בן המרצח הזה״ [מל״ב ו׳ ל״ב]· ״בן נעות המרדות״ [שמ״א כ׳ ל׳]· קרבו הנה, בני עוננה, זרע מנאף ותזנה [יש׳ נ״ז ג׳]· 10 ״בן אדם, צופה נתתיך״ [יח׳ ג׳ י״ז]· והנוהג מנהגם. וזה היפוי נאות בכל סוגי הספורים, ובכל חלקי המאמר; ויבקש ענינו על הרוב בבינוני ובשפל:

1 פרק] פ׳[c] || 2 פ׳] פרק[r] || 3 בו] בה[c] || 4 עליו] עלי[r] || 6 פרק] פ׳[c] || 7 פ׳] פרק[r] || 9 המרצח] המרכח[c] ||

CHAPTER 38

Onomatopoeia[1]

[1] Onomatopoeia[a] is diction which contains one or more words that are used metaphorically, or that are to be taken in a tropical sense. For example: **Their roaring shall be like a lion. . . . And they shall roar against them like the roaring of the sea** [Isa. 5:29–30]; . . . **they howl like a dog, and go round about the city** [Ps. 59:7]; and there are many other examples. This Figure's effect is called for in the Grand and Middle Styles.

CHAPTER 39

Antonomasia or Pronomination[1]

[1] Antonomasia or Pronomination[a] is a Figure of Diction in which for some reason—hostile or otherwise—a certain person is called by another than his own, proper name. For example: **"See ye . . . this son of a murderer"** [2 Kings 6:32]; **"Thou son of perverse rebellion"** [1 Sam. 20:30]; **But draw near hither, ye sons of the sorceress, the seed of the adulterer and the harlot** [Isa. 57:3]; **"Son of man, I have appointed thee a watchman"** [Ezek. 3:17]; and there are others of like character. This Figure is appropriate in all kinds of Statement of Facts, and in all the Parts of a Discourse; its effect is, for the most part, called for in the Middle and Simple Styles.

1. Literally: "Exchange"; "substitution"; "permutation"; "change"; הַתְּמוּרָה.

---

a. *R. ad H.* 4.31.42.

1. Literally: "by-name," "surname"; "substituted expression"; "attribute," "epithet"; "pronoun," "pronominal suffix": הַכִּנּוּי.

---

a. *R. ad H.* 4.31.42.

פרק מ׳

פ׳ המכנה.

[1] המכנה היא מאמר יקרא בו שם לדבר לאי זה תואר, פנימי או חיצוני, קרה לענין ההוא. והיא על פנים רבים:

[2] — אם שנקרא דבר מה נמצא על שם מי שהמציאו בראשונה, והמשל: ויקרא לה נבח, בשמו [במ׳ ל״ב מ״ב]· ויקרא שם העיר כשם בנו, חנוך [בר׳ ד׳ י״ז].

[3] — אם שיקרא הממציא בשם הדבר אשר המציאו, כמו שנקרא שלמה המלך ״קהלת״, על שם הספר ההוא שהמציאו.

[4] — אם שיקרא בעל הכלי בשם הכלי, כמו: וקשתות נערים תרטשנה [יש׳ י״ג י״ח], ר״ל, בעלי הקשתות. וכן, לפי דעתי: ויבואו פתחי נדיבים [שם שם ב׳] ר״ל, בעלי החרבות· וקראם ״נדיבים״, שהיו אנשים חשובים, אשר מעולם אנשי השם; והוא כמו ״פתחי׳ נדיבים״, על דרך חלוני שקופים [מל״א ו׳ ד׳].

[5] — אם שיקרא העלול בשם העלה, כמו: והלילו שירות היכל [עמ׳ ח׳ ג׳], שהרצון בו פועלי השיר.

[6] — אם שתקרא העלה בשם העלו׳, כמו: ואור החמה יהיה שבעתים [יש׳ ל׳ כ״ו]; למה שהיא עלת החום, קורא אותה חמה.

[7] — אם שנקר׳ המקום בשם המקומם, והמשל: חטא חטאה ירושלם [איכה א׳ ח׳], ר״ל, היושבים בה; וכן: ויאמר מצרים, ״אנוסה מפני ישראל״, כו׳ [שמ׳ י״ד כ״ה].

1 פרק] פ׳[כ] || 2 פ׳] פרק[ר] || 3 לדבר] דבר[ר] | פנימי] פנמיי[כ] || 5 נמצא] שנמצא[כ] || 8 הדבר] תדבר[ר] | המציאו] המציאהו[כ] || 10 בשם] כשם[ר] || 16 העלו׳] העלולים[כ] || 17 קורא] קרא[ר] || 18 שנקר׳] שנקראם[כ] | חטא] חט[ר] || 19 מפני <בני>[ר] ||

12–13 בר׳ ו׳ ד׳ ||

CHAPTER 40

Metonymy[1]

[1] Metonymy[a] is a Figure of Diction in which something is called by the name of some chance qualification, internal or external, of that thing. Metonymy has many forms, as follows:

[2] (1) Something that now exists is called by the name given it by the person who first brought it into being. For example: **And Nobah went and took Kenath, and the villages thereof, and called it Nobah, after his own name** [Num. 32:42]; **. . . and he builded a city, and called the name of the city after the name of his son Enoch"** [Gen. 4:17].

[3] (2) The inventor is called by the name of his invention, as King Solomon was called *Koheleth* after the name of the book which he had produced.

[4] (3) The user is called by the name of the instrument: **And Bows[2] shall dash the young men in pieces** [Isa. 13:18], meaning the bowmen. So, too, I think: **Set ye up an ensign . . . that the noble Gates may come** [Isa. 13:2],[3] meaning the owners of those ruins; the prophet called them "noble" because they were men of importance, **that were of old the men of renown** [Gen. 6:4]. *Pithᵉ ḥē nᵉ dhībhīm* ["the gates of the nobles"] is here the equivalent of *pᵉ thāḥīm nᵉ dhībhīm* ["noble gates"], after the manner of *ḥallōnē shᵉ qūphīm* [1 Kings 6:4] ["the windows of broad-framed" = "broad-framed windows"].[4]

[5] (4) The effect is named instead of the cause; for example, **And the songs of the palace shall wail** [Amos 8:3],[5] where "the song-makers" are meant.

[6] (5) Or the cause is given the name of the effect; for example, **And the light of the sun shall be sevenfold** [Isa. 30:26]. Since the sun is the cause of heat, Isaiah calls it *ḥammāh* ["heat"].

[7] (6) The place is named instead of the occupant; for example, **Jerusalem hath grievously sinned** [Lam. 1:8], that is, its inhabitants have sinned; and so, too: **And Egypt said, "Let me flee from the face of Israel,"** etc. [Exod. 14:25].[6]

1. Literally: "that which gives a name, title"; "the surnamer, nicknamer"; "the name-substituter": הַמְּכַנֶּה.
2. JV and KJV: "their bows."
3. JV and KJV: ". . . that they may go into the gates of the nobles"; for "gate" in the sense of "leading citizens," cf. Ruth 3:11: ". . . the whole gate of my people. . . ."
4. JV: "windows broad within."
5. JV: "shall be wailings."
6. JV: ". . . so that the Egyptians said: 'Let us flee'," etc.

---

a. *R. ad H.* 4.31.43.

[8] — אם שיקרא המקומם בשם המקום, כמו: נעלה ביהודה ונקיצנה [יש׳ ז׳ ו׳].

[9] ושאר מה שנמצא בלשוננו מאופני זה ההתחלפות בארנו בלבנת הספיר, פרק ב׳ משער השמות. ויתחלף זה מהכנוי, למה שהוא על צד השבח והגנות, אשר אין הענין כן במכנה. ויבוקש ענינם בבינוני ובשפל:

פרק מ״א

פ׳ האריכות.

[1] האריכות הוא מאמר יבואו בו דברים רבים על צד הצחות אשר אין בהם הכרח להבנת הענין. והמשל: והנה נטיתי ידי עליך... ואתנך ביד שנאותיך, בנות פלשתים הנכלמות מדרכך זמה [יח׳ ט״ז כ״ז]; ולהבנת הענין היה מספיק שיאמר, ״ונתתיך ביד פלשתים.״ וכן: ואתה בן אדם, הנבא והך כף אל כף· ותכפל חרב שלישיתה, חרב חללים· היא חרב חלל הגדול החודרת להם [שם כ״א י״ט]; והיה מספיק שיאמ׳, ״ותכפל חרב שלישיתה... למען למוג לב והרבה המכשולים״ [שם שם כ׳].

[2] וכל ספרי הנבואה מלאים מזה היפוי· אשר יבואו בהם דברים רבים מתחלפים, על צד ההרחבה, להפליג הצחות והגדל המאמ׳. ויבוקש ענינו בנשא ובבינוני על הרוב:

3 בלשוננו] בלשונות[ב] || 4 פרק] פ׳[ב] || 6 פרק] פ׳[ב] || 7 פ׳] פרק[ד] || 9 ביד] בנפש[ת] || 10 ולהבנת] והלבנת[ב] || 16 ההרחבה] ההכרחה[ב] ||

[8] (7) Or the occupant is named instead of the place, as in **Let us go up against Judah, and vex it.**[7] [Isa. 7:6].

[9] The remaining kinds of such word substitution to be found in our language we have set forth in *Libh^e nath Hassappīr,*[8] Chapter II of the "Book of Nouns." The present figure differs from Antonomasia in that the latter functions in praise and blame, which is not characteristic of Metonymy. Both effects are called for in the Middle and Simple Styles.

CHAPTER 41

Periphrasis[1]

[1] Periphrasis[a] is diction in which several words not needed for the understanding of the theme may be introduced for the sake of elegance. For example: **Behold, therefore I have stretched out my hand over thee . . . and delivered thee into the hand of them that hate thee, the daughters of the Philistines, that are ashamed of thy lewd way** [Ezek. 16:27]. For understanding of the thought, it would have sufficed to say "**. . . and delivered thee into the hand**[2] **. . . of the Philistines.**" Similarly: **Thou therefore, son of man, prophesy, and smite thy hands together; and let the sword be doubled the third time, the sword of those to be slain; it is the sword of the great one that is to be slain, which compasseth them about** [21:19]. Here it would have been enough to say "**. . . and let the sword be doubled the third time . . . that their heart may melt and their stumblings be multiplied**" [2:19–20].

[2] All the prophetic books abound in examples of this Figure; numerous variations in wording are introduced by way of amplification to enhance elegance and give emphasis to what is being said. This Figure's effect is called for mostly in the Grand and Middle Styles.

7. The pronoun shows that the Judean territory is meant.

8. "The Pavement of Sapphire" (Ex. 24:10), JML's treatise on grammar (unpublished); cf. Int., §2 and n. 16, §3 and n. 151, and §5 (end).

1. Literally: "prolongation," "length": הָאֲרִיכוּת.

2. B: "unto the will" (בנפש).

a. *R. ad H.* 4.32.43.

פרק מ״ב

פ׳ הבלבול.

[1] הבלבול הוא מאמר יבואו בו דברים בבלבול, בחלוף הסדר הרגיל. וזה על שני פנים: אם בהפוך החלקים· אם בהתמצעות תיבות בין שני ענינים הראוים להיות יחד. משל הראשון: במותיך כחטאת [יר׳ י״ז ג׳] כמו ״כחטאת במותיך״. וכן: כאכל קש לשון אש [יש׳ ה׳ כ״ד] כמו ״כאכל לשון אש קש״. משל השני, בהושע: לי יזעקו ״אלקי ידענוך״ ישראל [הו׳ ח׳ ב׳], שהרצון בו ״לי יזעקו ישראל ׳אלקי ידענוך׳״ והתמצעו בין ״יזעקו״ ו״ישראל״ שתי תיבות, ר״ל, ״אלקי ידענוך״. וזה ההתמצעות ראוי שיעשה באופן ישאר המאמר מבואר, עם מה שבו מהצחות. ויבוקש ענינו על הרוב בבינוני ובשפל:

פרק מ״ג

פ׳ הגוזמא.

[1] הגוזמא הוא מאמר מגדיל הדבר יותר מן הראוי על צד ההפלגה. והמשל: ערים בצורות וגדולות בשמים [דב׳ ט׳ א׳]; חוצבי מרום קברו, חוקקי בסלע משכן לו [יש׳ כ״ב ט״ז]; בעדן גן אלקים היית· כל אבן יקרה מסכתך, אודם, פטדה, ויהלום, וכו׳ [יח׳ כ״ח י״ג]. ולפעמים בא עם הערכה ודמיון, והמשל: כל עץ בגן אלקי׳ לא דמה אליו ביפייו· ארזים לא עממוהו בגן אלקי׳... לא דמו אל סעפותיו... [יח׳ ל״א ח׳].

1 פרק] פ׳[כ] || פ׳] פרק[ד] || 4 [הראוים][כ] || 5 הראשון] הא׳[ד] | כחטאת] בחטאת[ת] || 6 השני] הב׳[ד] || 9 המאמר] מהמאמר[ד] || 10 ויבוקש] ויבוק[כ] | ובשפל] יותר[ד] || 11 פרק] פ׳[כ] || 12 פ׳] פרק[ד] || 14 בצורות וגדולות] גדלת ובצרת[ת] | חוצבי] חוכבי[כ] || 16 וכו׳] כו׳[כ] || 16–18 כל עץ...סעפותיו] ארזים לא... אלהים...לא דמו אל סעפותיו...כל עץ...ביפיו[ת] כל עץ בגן אלקים לא דמו אל סעפותיו[ד] ||

CHAPTER 42

Hyperbaton[1]

[1] Hyperbaton[a] is diction in which words are introduced in confusion, in other than the normal order. This Figure appears in two forms: either the several parts are reversed, or words are interposed between elements that rightly belong together. An example of the first, reversal: **thy high places, as the sin-offering"** [Jer. 17:3],[2] which is equivalent to "as the sin-offering for thy high places." Similarly, **as devoureth the stubble the tongue of fire** [Isa. 5:24][3] is equivalent to "as the tongue of fire devoureth the stubble." An example of the second form, interposition, in Hosea: **Unto Me shall cry "My God, we know Thee" Israel** [8:2];[3] here is meant "Israel shall cry unto Me, 'My God, we know Thee,'" but two words—"'My-God we-know-Thee'"—have been interposed between "shall cry" and "Israel." This kind of interposition should so be formed that the statement will remain clear while retaining its elegance. The effect of Hyperbaton is called for mostly in the Middle and Simple Styles.

CHAPTER 43

Hyperbole[1]

[1] Hyperbole[a] is diction which, by exaggeration, gives unusual emphasis to the thing spoken of. For example: **cities great and fortified up to heaven** [Deut. 9:1];[2] **that hewest thee out a sepulchre on high and gravest a habitation for thyself in the rock** [Isa. 22:16[; **Thou wast in Eden the garden of God; every precious stone was thy covering, the carnelian, the topaz, and the emerald,** etc. [Ezek. 28:13]. Hyperbole at times is introduced along with an appraisal and comparison; for example: **Nor was any tree in the garden of God like unto it in**

1. Literally: "confusion:" הַבְּלְבּוּל.
2. JML here wrongly cites B; JV ". . . thy high places, because of sin."
3. Translated in the order of the words in B, so as to exhibit JML's point.

---

a. *R. ad H.* 4.32.44.

1. Literally: "exaggeration," "overestimation": הַגּוּזְמָא.
2. *Sic*, B; JML: "fortified and great."

---

a. *R. ad H.* 4.33.44.

[2] וזה הרבה משיסופר· ויבוקש ענינו בנשא ובבינוני ובשפל:

פרק מ״ד

פ׳ ההמרה.

[1] ההמרה היא מאמר כאשר נבין הכל מן החלק, או להפך· או הרבים מן היחיד, או להפך. משל הראשון: פרשה ציון בידיה· אין מנחם לה [איכה א׳ י״ז]; ממה שאמר ב״ציון״, אבין שכן היה הענין בכל ערי יהודה. וכן: ותאמר ציון, עזבני י״י וי״י שכחני [יש׳ מ״ט י״ד]; לקח הנה החלק תמורת הכל.

[2] משל השני: וכל הארץ באו מצרים [בר׳ מ״א נ״ז]; אבין שזה המאמ׳ צודק בחלק מן הארץ לבד.

[3] משל השלישי: ואיש לא יעלה עמך· גם איש אל ירא בכל ההר [שמ׳ ל״ד ג׳]; הרצון בזה ״כל איש ואיש״. וכן: ויעבור יפתח אל בני עמון להלחם בם [שופ׳ י״א ל״ב]; יובן מזה כל העם אשר ברגלו.

[4] משל הרביעי: ויקבר בערי הגלעד [שופ׳ י״ב ז׳]· ר״ל, אחת מן הערים. וכן: ויונה ירד אל ירכתי הספינה, וישכב וירדם [יונה א׳ ה׳]· כלומ׳, אחד מן הירכתים.

[5] ויבוקש ענינו על הרוב בבינוני ובשפל:

2 פרק] פ׳[כ] || 3 פ׳] פרק[ד] || 4 היא] הוא[כ] | [או] הרבים[ד] || 6 [היה][כ] || 7 החלק] חלק[כ] || 8 מצרים] מצרימה[ת] || 9 [מן][כ] || 10 השלישי] הג׳[ד] | גם] וגם[ת] || 13 הרביעי] הד׳[ד] | אחת] אחד[כ] | מן הערים] מהערים[ד] ||

its beauty; the cedars in the garden of God could not hide it . . . were not like its boughs . . . [31:8].[3]

[2] Instances of this Figure are innumerable; its effect may be called for in the Grand, Middle, and Simple Styles.

CHAPTER 44

Synecdoche[1]

[1] Synecdoche[a] is our Figure of Speech when we understand the whole from the part or vice versa, or the plural from the singular or vice versa. An example of the first type, the whole understood from the part: **Zion spreadeth forth her hands; there is none to comfort her** [Lam. 1:17]; from what the text has said of "Zion" I understand that the same was true of all the cities of Judah. Similarly: **But Zion said: "The Lord hath forsaken me, and the Lord hath forgotten me"** [Isa. 49:14]; here the prophet has substituted the part for the whole.

[2] An example of the second type, the part understood from the whole: **And the whole earth came into Egypt** [Gen. 41:57];[2] I am to understand that this statement is accurate in respect of only a part of the earth.

[3] An example of the third type, the plural understood from the singular: **And a man shall not come up with thee, neither let a man be seen throughout all the mount** [Exod. 34:3];[3] here every individual man is meant. Similarly: **So Jephthah passed over unto the children of Ammon to fight against them** [Judg. 11:32]; from this is to be understood all the host who were being led by Jephthah.

[4] An example of the fourth type, the singular understood from the plural: **Then died Jephthah . . . and was buried[4] in the cities of Gilead[4]** [12:7], that is to say, in one of the cities of Gilead. And so too: **But Jonah was gone down into the sides of the ship; and he lay, and was fast asleep** [Jonah 1:5],[5] that is, had descended into one of the two sides of the ship.

[5] This Figure's effect is called for mostly in the Middle and Simple Styles.

3. *Sic,* M; C has garbled the citation. In B the two periods are in the reverse of the order given here.

1. Literally: "change," "exchange," "conversion": הַהֲמָרָה.
2. JV and KJV: "And all countries came": B has the subject (הָאָרֶץ) in the singular, the verb (בָּאוּ) in the plural.
3. Translated to exhibit JML's point.
4. *Sic,* literally, the Hebrew.
5. KJV.

a. *R. ad H.* 4.33.44–55.

פרק מ״ה

פ׳ הבלתי מורגל.

[1] הבלתי מורגל הוא מאמ׳ באשר תמצאנה תיבות בלתי מורגלות, קרובות לענין או דומות לו. והמשל: וכל העם רואים את הקולות [שמ׳ כ׳ י״ח]· ר״ל, שומעים. וכן: מרחוק יריח מלחמה [איוב ל״ט כ״ה]· ר״ל, מרגיש. וכן: ומתוק האור, וטוב לעינים...[קה׳ י״א ז׳]· הרצון ב״מתוק״ שהוא נאות.
[2] ויבוקש ענינו בבינוני ובשפל:

פרק מ״ו

פ׳ ההתיחסות.

[1] ההתיחסות הוא מאמ׳ ילקחו בו קצת דברים דרך משל ובהעברה, מצד הדמות מה נמצא ביניהם אשר למענו תעשה כהוגן. והמשל: ישושון מדבר וציה· ותגל ערבה, ותפרח כחבצלת [יש׳ ל״ה א׳]; המשוש הוא ענין מיוחס אל האדם, ונלקח הנה דרך דמיון· שהוצאת הפרחים מורה על טוב גדול במדבר וציה, כמו שהמשוש מורה על טוב האדם. וכן: כל הבשר חציר, וכל חסדו כציץ השדה [שם מ׳ ו׳]· הבשר הכלה במהרה המשילו לחציר ולציץ השדה, שהם נפסדים לשעתן.
[2] לפעמים יכונו בו הקצור, כמו: ואתם בערתם הכרם· גזלת העני בבתיכם

1 פרק] פ׳[כ] || 2 [פ׳][ד] || 3 באשר] כאשר[כ] || 4 [וכל העם][ד] || 5 מרחוק] ומרחוק[ת] || 8 פרק] פ׳[כ] || 9 פ׳] פרק[ד] || 11 ישושון] ישושום[ת] || 13 <על> דרך[ד] || 15 שהם] שהן[ד] || 16 נפסדים] נפסדי[ד] || 17 לפעמים] ולפעמים[ד] | [העני][כ] ||

CHAPTER 45

Catachresis[1]

[1] Catachresis[a] is a Figure of Diction in which are found unusual words that approximate, or resemble, the expression really intended. For example: **And all the people saw the thunderings** [Exod. 20:18],[2] that is, heard them. Similarly: . . . **he smelleth the battle afar off** [Job 39:25], that is, senses it. Again: **And the light is sweet, and a pleasant thing it is for the eyes** etc. [Eccl. 11:7]; by ''sweet'' is meant that the light is agreeable.

[2] This Figure's effect is called for in the Middle and Simple Styles.

CHAPTER 46

Metaphor[1]

[1] Metaphor[a] is diction in which certain words are taken as parable and in a transferred sense, because some resemblance obtains between the literal and transferred meanings which allows this appropriately to be done. For example: **The wilderness and the parched land shall be glad; and the desert shall rejoice, and blossom as the rose** [Isa. 35:1][2] Gladness is properly attributable only to man, but appears here through resemblance; for the bringing forth of the flowers is indicative of great good in the case of a desert and parched land, just as gladness is an indication of a man's good. Similarly: **All flesh is grass, and all the goodliness thereof is as the flower of the field** [40:6]; the prophet has likened the flesh, which quickly wastes away, to the grass and the flower of the field whose brief hour is soon done.

[2] The aim in using Metaphor is sometimes conciseness, as in: **For ye have**

1. Literally: ''the unusual, unaccustomed, unfamiliar, not habitually used'': הַבִּלְתִּי מוּרְגָּל.
2. KJV, JV (20:15): ''perceived.''

a. *R. ad H.* 4.33.45.

1. Literally: ''relation''; ''relationship''; ''tracing of pedigree''; ''the condition or state of being attributed or ascribed'': הַהִתְיַחֲסוּת.
2. The interpretation of R. David Qimḥi, here followed by JML, involves a tacit correction of יְשׂוּשׂוּן for יְשֻׂשׂוּם.

a. *R. ad H.* 4.34.45.

[שם ג׳ י״ד]; המכוון בבעור הכרם, שעשו אותו העני נקי מנכסיו, כמו שלא נשאר דבר בכרם אחר שבערו אותו; והנה בזה הלשון הוא מקצר. לפעמים יכוון בו נקיות הלשון, כמו: וידע אדם[1] את חוה אשתו [בר׳ ד׳ א׳]· תטחן לאחר אשתי [איוב ל״א י׳]; ספר ענין התשמיש בנקיות. לפעמים ירצו בו הגדלת הדבר, כמו: הוי מושכי העון בחבלי השוא· ובעבות העגלה חטאה [יש׳ ה׳ י״ח]. לפעמים המכוון בו המעטת הדבר, כמו: תהרו חשש, תלדו קש [שם ל״ג י״א]· אפרים רועה רוח ורודף קדים [הו׳ י״ב ב׳]. ולפעמים יכוונו בו הצחות לבד, כמו: שמים חשך לאור, ואור לחשך· שמים מר למתוק, ומתוק למר [יש׳ ה׳ כ׳].

[3] וראוי שיעשה זה היפוי בתבונה ודעת, באופן יראה בו ההדמות מזולת זרות. ואמר הפילוסוף בג׳ מההלצה שאין ראוי למליץ שישים מאמריו כלם במלות מסוג אחד, עד שיהיו כלם מושאלות, נכריות, או מפורסמות, אבל ראוי שיערב זה בזה; כי בזה יהיה המאמ׳ יותר חזק דמיון· לפי שכאשר יביאם מסוג אחד, ולא היה בהם דבר נכרי, לא יקנה בזה צחות ולא פליאה מניעה לנפש. ויבוקש ענין זה היפוי בנשא ובבינוני ובשפל:

פרק מ״ז

פ׳ ההשאלה

[1] ההשאלה, לפי המכוון בה הנה, היא מאמר אשר הכונה בו זולת מה שתורינה עליו התבות. ותתחלף מן ההתיחסות, שההתיחסות הוא בערך קצת

2 יכוון] <הוא> יכווין[כ] || 3 וידע אדם[1]] והאדם ידע[ת] || 4 ירצו] יריבו[כ] || 5 העון] עוון[כ] | ובעבות] ובעבותות[ר] וכעבות[ת] || 8 ואור] אור[ר] || 9 [בתבונה][כ] | ודעת] וכדעת[כ] | 12 [יותר][ר] || 13 לנפש] הנפש[ר] || 15 פרק] פ׳[כ] || 16 פ׳] פרק[ר] || 17 היא] הוא[ר] || 18 ותתחלף] והתחלף[ר] ||

[1] Reading taken from Gen. 4:25.

consumed the vineyard; the spoil of the poor is in your houses [Isa. 3:14].[3] The reference to the consumption of the vineyard was intended to mean that they had stripped the poor man in question of his possessions, just as nothing is left in a vineyard after it has been consumed by fire;[4] the use of such language thus enables the prophet to be brief. Sometimes the aim is decency of language, as in **And the man knew Eve his wife** [Gen. 4:1],[5] and in **then let my wife grind unto another** [Job 31:10]; each of these is a euphemistic description of the sexual act. Sometimes the intention is to magnify a matter, as in **Woe unto them that draw iniquity with cords of vanity, and sin as it were with a cart rope** [Isa. 5:18]. Sometimes it is meant to minify: **Ye conceive chaff, ye shall bring forth stubble** [33:11]; **Ephraim shepherdeth wind, and chaseth after the east wind** [Hos. 12:2].[6] And sometimes its sole purpose is elegance: **that put darkness for light, and light for darkness, that put bitter for sweet and sweet for bitter!"** [Isa. 5:20].[7]

[3] This Figure should be fashioned with understanding and awareness, in such a way that the resemblance will not seem bizarre. The Philosopher,[b] in Book III of the *Rhetoric,* says that a speaker should not couch all his statements in words of a single type, so that they are all metaphorical, strange, or ordinary, but should blend one sort with another. So doing, the speaker's discourse will be more strongly imaginative, for should he confine himself to words of a single type with nothing exotic about them, he would obtain neither elegance[8] nor any mentally stimulating surprise. The effect of this Figure is called for in the Grand, Middle, and Simple Styles.

CHAPTER 47

Allegory[1]

[1] As the word here implies, Allegory[a] is diction in which the meaning is something other than that literally indicated by the words. It differs from

3. Translated to exhibit JML's point.
4. The word ''consume'' also means ''burn'' (בִּעֵר).
5. In the wording here, JML combines Gen. 4:1 and 4:25; he is quoting from memory.
6. Translated to exhibit JML's point.
7. KJV.
8. T/A: ''foreignness, strangeness.''

---

b. T200/A281; cf. *Rhet.* 3.2 (1404b).

1. Literally: ''metaphorical use of a word,'' ''figurative meaning'': הַהַשְׁאָלָה.

---

a. *R. ad H.* 4.34.46.

התבות, וההשאלה היא בערך כל המאמ׳. ותבא אם על צד ההדמות· אם על צד ההגדלה או ההמעטה· אם על צד ההפך.

[2] משל הראשון: כרם היה לידידי בקרן בן שמן; ויעזקהו ויסקלהו ויטעהו שורק, כו׳ [יש׳ ה׳ א׳—ב׳]· שהוא מדמה ענין ישראל לזה הכרם, כמו שהתבאר בסוף המאמר. וכן: צופיו עורים כלם, לא ידעו... כלבים אלמים, לא יוכלו לנבוח· הוזים שוכבים, אוהבי לנום; והכלבים עזי נפש, לא ידעו שבעה [שם נ״ו י׳—י״א]; דמה ענין נביאי השקר לכלבים השומרים הצאן שהם ישנים, עד לא תשלם בהם השמירה המכוונת בם.

[3] והמשל על צד ההגדלה, מה שנא׳ ביחזקאל: ואחותך הגדולה שומרון, היא ובנותיה, היושבת על שמאלך· ואחותך הקטנה ממך, היושבת מימינך, סדום ובנותיה [יח׳ ט״ז מ״ו]; הנה, להגדיל עון יהודה וחטאתו, דמהו כאלו היתה אחותו שומרון וסדום.

[4] והמשל על צד ההפך: הנה חכם אתה מדניאל· כל סתום לא עממוך! [יח׳ כ״ח ג׳]; המכוון בזה חלוף מה שיראה ממנו, והוא שהיה סכל הרבה בערך אל דניאל.

[5] וכבר דברנו מהצחות הנופל בתבות דבר מספיק· וראוי לנו לדבר בצחיו׳ הנמצאים בספורים, כפי יכלתנו; ונתחיל מן המחלק, ונאמר:

פרק מ״ח

פ׳ המפקד.

[1] המפקד הוא מאמר כאשר התבאר חלוקת המשמרות והפקדיות הראויות לאיש ואיש, כפי מעלתו; והוא יעשה בדברים, ובערך אל פרטי המיוחד.

1 היא] הוא[ד] |המאמ׳] מאמ׳[ד] ||5 צופיו] צפו[ת] |<כלם> כלבים[ת] |יוכלו] יכלו[ר] ||10 שמאלך] שמאולך[ת] |ממך [היושבת][ר] ||11 דמהו] דמה[ד] |היתה] הידה[ד] ||14 [חלוף][ר] |שהיה] שיהיה[ד] || 16 בצחיו׳] בצחייות[ר] ||17 המחלק] החלק[ד] ||18 פרק] פ״[ר] ||19 פ׳] פרק[ד] ||21 המיוחד] מיוחד[ד] ||

Metaphor in that Metaphor involves some few of the words, while Allegory affects the entire statement. It comes in the form of a comparison, of a magnification or minification, or of a contrast.

[2] Our example of the first, the Figure in the form of a comparison: **My well-beloved had a vineyard in a very fruitful hill; and he digged it, and cleared it of stones, and planted it with the choicest vine,** etc. [Isa. 5:1 ff.]; the prophet is comparing the idea of Israel to this vineyard, as explained at the end of the passage [v. 7]. Similarly: **His watchmen are all blind, without knowledge, dumb dogs, they cannot bark; sleeping,[2] lying down, loving to slumber; yea, they are greedy dogs which can never have enough** [56:10–11]; Isaiah has likened the false prophets to dogs that sleep while on guard over the flock, so that the protection they are intended to afford is imperfect.

[3] Our example of the Figure in the form of a magnification is this statement in Ezekiel: **And thine elder sister is Samaria, that dwelleth at thy left hand, she and her daughters; and thy younger sister, that dwelleth at thy right hand, is Sodom and her daughters** [Ezek. 16:46]. Here, in order to magnify Judah's iniquity and sin, he has represented Judah as if Samaria and Sodom were each a sister of his.

[4] And the following is an example of Allegory in the form of a contrast: **Behold, thou art wiser than Daniel! There is no secret that they can hide from thee!** [28:3]. The actual meaning intended here—that the prince of Tyre was in fact a great fool by comparison with Daniel—is the contrary of what the verse appears to mean.

[5] Having said enough about the elegance procurable through words, we must now, as best we can, discuss the kinds of elegancies obtainable through whole descriptions. And we shall begin our treatment with the kind that achieves an apportionment.[3]

CHAPTER 48

Distribution[1]

[1] The Figure is Distribution[a] when explanation is made of the apportionment of functions and offices proper to each individual according to rank; the Figure is

2. So KJV, following the Jewish commentators and the Targum; JV: "raving."
3. Hebrew הַמְּחַלֵּק: "that which divides, apportions, distributes, assigns"; C has the reading החלק = "the part."

1. Literally: "the muster, appointment, appointed place": הַמִּפְקָד.

a. *R. ad H.* 4.35.47.

[2] והמשל ממה שאמר ישעיהו בפרשת הן לצדק ימלך מלך [יש׳ ל״ב א׳,
וכו׳]. וזה, כי בתחלה באר מה הראוי למלך: שהוא הגדול באמה ההיא שימלך
עליה, ולזה, צריך שיהיה גדול המעלה והחשיבות; אחר שהפחיתות והתכונות
הרעות בו מזיקות מאד, בהיות במדרגה מן היכלת לעשות בעם כטוב בעיניו.
5 לכן, יחס למלך הצדק, ואמר: לצדק ימלך מלך [שם א׳].

[3] וראוי שתדע, להבנת זה הענין, שהצדק הוא הפך הרשע. והצדק בסתם
היא תכונה תסדרנה ממנה כל הפעלות המדותיות, כפי מה שראוי במדה מדה·
כאלו תאמר, שיסודר ממנה הנדיבות, והגבורה, והפרישות, וזולתם, שהם
אמצעיות בין הקצוות; והרשע בסתם הפך זה. והמשפט הוא בערך אל הדברים
10 אשר יפול למענם הריב בין אדם לחברו· והוא רצון קיים ומתמיד בשופט לתת
לכל אחד מבעלי הריב כפי מה שיחייבהו הדין.

[4] והנה, מפני שהמלך הוא היותר מעולה, כמו שאמר, והשרים הם קרובים
אליו במדרגה, היושבים ראשונה במלכות, והיה הכרח החשיבות והמעלות כפי
מדרגת האנשים· חוייב בהכרח שהמלך ראוי שיהיה יותר שלם, ולזה יחס לו
15 הצדק שהוא השלמות אשר בתכלית, כמו שבארנו, ויחס לשרים מה שהוא
למטה ממנו, והוא המשפט, והוא המספיק. ואם תמצאנה להם מדות מה בלתי
אמצעיות, לא יזיקו כמו אם היה נמצא זה הדבר במלך· כי אם יבא הזק מה מן
השרים מצד פחיתות קצת מדותיהם, גבוה מעל גבוה שומר, ואפשר שיתוקן
המעוות על ידי המלך.

20 [5] ואפשר שתהיה למ״ד ״ולשרים״ [שם א׳] בלתי נוספת, כמו שחשבו קצת
המפרשים, ויהיה שיעור הפסוק כן: הן המלך, מן הראוי לו שימלך לצדק, ר״ל,
שיהיה צדיק בכל הדברים, וזה מה שראוי למלך; אמנם, מה שמספיק לשרים
הוא שישורו לעשות משפט לכל אחד מבעלי הריב.

[6] ואחר שבאר מן המשמרות מה הוא הראוי למלך ולשרים, ירד בהדרגה
25 אל האנשים החשובים, גדולי הארץ. וקרא אותם ״איש״ — כמו: ״איש אתה,
ואין כמוך בישראל״ [שמ״א כ״ו ט״ו]· כלם אנשים, ראשי אלפי ישראל המה [במ׳

5 לכן] לבל[כ] || 7 כל] בלי[כ] || 8 שיסודר] שסודר[כ] || 12 היותר] יותר[ד] || 18 השרים מצד פחיתות] השרים יותר פחיתות מצד[ד] || 20 למ״ד] למד׳[ד] לְמד[כ] | שחשבו] שיחשבו[ד] || 22 [אמנם][ד] || 25–26 איש אתה ואין] הלוא איש אתה ומי[ה] ||

---

13 אס׳ א׳ י״ד || 18 קה׳ ה׳ ז׳ ||

also applicable in respect of different kinds of things, or can be used in connection with particulars of some one category.

[2] Our example is taken from what Isaiah said in the passage beginning **Behold a king shall reign for righteousness** [Isa. 32:1 ff.].[2] He first explained the office proper to a king, that, as the greatest personage in the nation over which he reigns, he ought to be of the highest virtue and merit, since in him baseness and evil qualities can work great harm by virtue of the extent to which he can do with the people as he likes. The prophet therefore ordained righteousness for the king, saying **A king shall reign for righteousness.**

[3] For a proper understanding of this matter, you must know that righteousness is the opposite of wickedness. Absolute righteousness is the quality descending from which all ethical functions are ranked in the order proper to each one; as if you should say that liberality, courage, self-control, and the rest—which are means between the extremes—are ranked in an order descending from righteousness; and absolute wickedness is the opposite extreme.[3] Justice is concerned with the things over which contention arises between one man and another; it is a firm and persevering intention in a judge to grant to each of the contending parties according as the law requires.

[4] Now, because the king is the most distinguished personage, as the prophet said, and the princes are close to him in rank, **sitting first in the kingdom** [Esth. 1:14], and because the requirement of merit and virtue is according to men's rank, it is necessarily required of the king that he should be more perfect; the prophet therefore ordained righteousness for him, which, as we have explained, is the utmost degree of perfection, while for the princes he ordained, as sufficient, what is inferior to righteousness, namely, justice. Even should the princes chance to possess ethical values that are not at the mean, these are not likely to be as harmful as if this should be true of the king; for if some harm might come of the princes as a result of the baseness of certain of their ethical principles, **one higher than the high watcheth** [Eccl. 5:7], and what is crooked could be corrected by the king.

[5] It is possible that the *lāmedh* ["to," "for"] of *ūlᵉ sārīm* ["and to/for princes" (Isa. 32:1)] is not pleonastic, as some commentators have thought, but that the verse means virtually the following: It is indeed fitting for a king that he **reign for righteousness**—that is, that he be righteous in all things—and it is this that is appropriate to a king; for princes, however, it is sufficient that **they shall rule for** the doing of **justice** to each of the contending parties.

[6] Having explained what offices are proper to king and to princes, the prophet next descended a step in the social scale to the important men, the great of the land. He called them "**man**"—as in **"Thou art a man, and none is like to thee in Israel"** [1 Sam. 26:15],[4] and in **all of them men who were heads of**

2. Translated thus to accord with JML's interpretation.
3. Cf. ii.2.1–3.
4. *Sic,* JV: "Art not thou a valiant man? and who is like to thee in Israel?"

י״ג ג׳] — ואמר: והיה איש — ר״ל, כל אחד מנכבדי הארץ — כמחבא רוח [יש׳ ל״ב ב׳]. כלומר, שזה צד משלמות הנהגת המדינה, שיהיו בה גומלי חסדים ונדיבי עמים, עד יהיו העשירים למחסה ולמסתור לעניים האביונים, ולא יחוסו על צרורות כספיהם. ואם בהרבה מן הדברים יחטאו, הנה עליהם המלך
5 והשרים· יישרו ארחות עקלקלות, ויסקלו מסלת ההנהגות מאבן. אמנם, מן ההכרח לישוב העיר ולטוב הכולל, שתהיה להם תכונת הנדיבות והגמילות חסד, כי זה דבר בלתי נופל במצות המלך והשרי׳, להיות כל איש שורר בביתו ובקניניו בבית ובשדה. ולזה, אמר שיהיה זה ״האיש״ [יש׳ שם] מצד טבעו, בערך אל יושביה קצרי יד, כמקום[1] יוכל אדם להחבא בו מפני הרוח, וכסתר[1] [שם]
10 ינצל תחתיו מזרם [שם] מים רבים· ולהספיק להם מה שיצטרך, עד לא ירעבו ולא יצמאו, ויהיו כפלגי מים [שם] שישיבו נפש ההולכים בציות וארץ שואה ומשואה; ויהיה להם כצל סלע כבד בארץ עיפה [שם]; יומם השמש לא יכם. ושלש ורבע הענין בתבות מתחלפות, למען יחייבו הערה נפלאה בלבות האנשים· והוא מן הדרכים ההלציים.
15 [7] ואחר זה, ירד ג״כ בהדרגה אל דלת עם הארץ, ואמר: ולא תשעינה עיני רואים· ואזני שומעים תקשבנה [שם שם ג׳]. כלומר, שההכרח בערכם שיהיו להם עינים לראות — יראו ויקחו מוסר — ואזנים לשמוע לקול המלך והשרים ונכבדי הארץ; ויהיו כפופים תחתיהם, לשמור ולעשות ככל אשר יצוה אליהם — ובלעדם לא ירימו את ראשם ואת רגלם — למען לא יפלו ברשת הפשעים,
20 ויחוייבו להם מן העונש כפי הדבר אשר יחטאו עליו.
[8] ואחרי כן, ירד מדרגה אחרת אל ״הנמהרים״, אשר בחפזותם וסכלותם

1 כמחבא] במחבא[ד] ‖ 2 שיהיו] שהיו[ג] | בה] בהם[ד] ‖ 7 [שורר][ג] ‖ 9 כמקום[1]] במקום[כד] | וכסתר[1]] ובסתר[בד] ‖ 20 ויחוייבו] וחוייבו[ד] ‖ 21 ואחרי כן] אחר כך[ד] | בחפזותם] בפחזותם[ד] ‖

---

3 תה׳ מ״ז י׳ | יש׳ ד׳ ו׳ ‖ 4 בר׳ מ״ב ל״ה ‖ 5 שופ׳ ה׳ ו׳ | יש׳ ס״ב י׳ ‖ 7 דה״ב ל׳ י״ב | אס׳ א׳ כ״ב ‖ 8 בר׳ ל״ט ה׳ ‖ 10 יח׳ א׳ כ״ד ‖ 10–11 יש׳ מ״ט י׳ | 11 תה׳ ק״ה מ״א ‖ 11–12 איוב ל״ח כ״ז ‖ 12 תה׳ קכ״א ו׳ ‖ 15 מל״ב כ״ד י״ד ‖ 17 דב׳ כ״ט ג׳ | מש׳ כ״ד ל״ב | דב׳ כ״ט ג׳ ‖ 18 דב׳ כ״ח י״ג ‖ 19 בר׳ מ״א מ״ד ‖

---

[1] Corrected text.

the tribes of Israel [Num. 13:3][5]—and he said: **And a man shall be**—that is, every one of the important men of the land shall be—**as a hiding-place from the wind** [Isa. 32:2]. In other words, it is a feature of a perfectly governed State that it should include philanthropists and **princes of peoples** [Ps. 47:10], so that the rich may be **for a refuge and for a cover** [Isa. 4:6] to the poor and needy, not sparing of **their bundles of money** [Gen. 42:35]. Even if such men sin in many respects, still the king and the princes are above them: they straighten **tortuous ways** [Judg. 5:6][6] and **gather out the stones** from the **highway** [Isa. 62:10] of conduct. It is, of course, essential to the city's[7] tranquillity and to the public welfare that these men should themselves be naturally disposed to be liberal and beneficent, for this is not something subject to the **commandment of the king and of the princes** [2 Chr. 30:12], as **every man bears rule in his own house** [Esth. 1:22] and over his possessions **in the house and in the field** [Gen. 39:5]. The prophet therefore said that this **man** [Isa. 32:2], for those of the populace who are without means, would of his own nature be like a place in which a person might hide against the wind, and **a covert** beneath which to find safety from **the tempest** [Isa. 32:2] **of many waters** [Ezek. 1:24];[8] that he would supply the poor with what they need so that **they . . . not hunger nor thirst** [Isa. 49:10], but be **as by the watercourses** [32:2] which restore the soul of travelers **in the dry places** [Ps. 105:41] and a land **desolate and waste** [Job 38:27]; and that he would be to them **as the shadow of a great rock in a weary land** [Isa. 32:2]—**the sun** would **not smite** them **by day** [Ps. 121:6]. The prophet said the same thing thrice and four times in different words so that his words inevitably would have a marvellously stirring effect upon the hearts of men—a common rhetorical procedure.

[7] Isaiah next descended a further step in the social scale to **the poorest sort of the people of the land** [2 Kings 24:14], saying: **And the eyes of them that see shall not be closed, and the ears of them that hear shall attend** [Isa. 32:3]. In other words, the need in their regard was that they should have **eyes to see** [Deut. 29:3]—that they should **see and receive instruction** [Prov. 24:32]—**and ears to hear** [Deut. 29:3] the voice of the king, of the princes, and of the important men of the land. The poorer sort should subject themselves to these, **to observe and to do** [Deut. 28:13] according to all that might be commanded them—**without** them **should** they **not lift up** their **head or** their **foot** [Gen. 41:44][9]—in order not to fall into the net of transgression and become liable to the punishment for whatever crime they might commit.

[8] Lastly, the prophet descended still another step to "the rash," those who,

5. *Sic,* conflation of Num. 13:3 and 1:16? JV: "children" for "tribes."
6. *Sic,* B; JV and KJV: "byways."
7. JML's use of "State" and "city" interchangeably, as in this passage, reflects the political circumstances of the Italy of his day.
8. KJV.
9. Cf. Ps. 110:7 for "head."

חטאו חטאה גדולה או קטנה, ואמר שיתחייב בערכם שלבם יבינו לדעת [שם שם ד׳]· ושישובו מדרכם הרעה, ולא ילכו עוד אחרי שרירות לבם· יחזיקו במוסר, ולא ירפוהו, ויענדוהו עטרות להם· ויחדשו תכונה בלבם עד לא יתחייב ממנה ללכת בדרכי רשע. ואם היה החטא בדבור, ומצד מה שהלעיגו באנשים או דברו סרה, הגיע להם העונש הראוי, הוא מבואר שההכרח אליהם שיסכימו ל״מהר לדבר צחות״ [שם]· ר״ל, דברים יערבו לנפשות, ותהיינה אזניהם קשובות. ו״עלגים״ [שם] ו״לעגים״ מורים על ענין אחד, כמו ״כבש״/״כשב״, וזולתם.

[9] והנה ספר כל מדרגות אנשי המדינה, ר״ל, המלך, השרים, נכבדי הארץ, דלת עם הארץ, והחטאים — כי בכל דור ודור לא תנצל המדינה שלא יהיה בתוכה פשע וחטאת — ונתן לכל מדרגה חקה ומשמרתה; וזה משל מה שנעשה מזה היפוי בדברים.

[10] אמנם, משל מה שבערך אל פרטי מיוחד, ר״ל, היאך תהיינה משמרות האנשים בערכו, ובאי זו חזקה יחזיקוהו, הוא מה שאמ׳ אחר כן: לא יקרא עוד לנבל נדיב [שם שם ה׳]; ר״ל, שראוי להחזיק בכל אדם לפי מה שהוא, פן תחנף הארץ אם יעשה זולת זה.·

[11] וזה הרצון, לפי דעתנו, בזאת הפרשה: שהנביא יעורר על הדברים הראוים להנהגת כל מדינה — מדינה ומדינה ככתבה, ועם ועם כלשונו. אמנם, שהוא כוון בה בעבור ישראל· וסמך אותה לענין מלך אשור כי סבת ההצלה לישראל מידו היתה בעבור זה: למה שהמלך, והשרים והגדולים, ויתר העם היו במדרגה מן השלימות עד שנעשה בעבורם הנס הגדול ההוא ממפלת מלך אשור עם תעצומו ורומו, אשר כמוהו לא נהיה מימים רבים. והנרצה ב״כילי״ ו״נדיב״ ״נבל״ ו״שוע״, והמכון בפסוקים, כבר פרשתיהו למעלה.

[12] וזה היפוי הוא מעולה מאד בהדרכת הדברים המדיניים:

1 [או קטנה][ד] || 2 שרירות] ערירות[ד] || 5 להם] עלהם[ד] || 7 ועלגים] וע׳[כ] | [ולעגים][ד] || 9 השרים] והשרים[ד] || 10 והחטאים] והחוטאים[כ] | בכל] כל[כ] | ודור] ודוד[ד] || 13 שבערך] בערך[ד] || 14 אחר כן] א״כ[כ] || 18 [מדינה] ומדינה[ד] || 19 בה] בזה[ד] | ההצלה] ההצלת[כ] || 22 [ורומו][ד] || 23 בפסוקים] בפסויק[ד] ||

2 יר׳ כ״ו ג׳ | יר׳ ג׳ י״ז || 2–3 מש׳ ד׳ י״ג || 3 איוב ל״א ל״ו || 4 מש׳ ב׳ י״ג || 5 דב׳ י״ג ו׳ || 6 מש׳ י״ג י״ט || 6–7 תה׳ ק״ל ב׳ || 15–16 יר׳ ג׳ א׳ || 18 אס׳ א׳ כ״ב ||

in their haste[10] and folly, have committed sin, whether major or minor, and he said that what is required of them is that their **heart . . . shall understand knowledge** [Isa. 32:4]. They must **turn . . . from** their **evil way** [Jer. 26:3] **and not walk any more after the stubbornness of their . . . heart** [Jer. 3:17]; they should **take fast hold of instruction, let** it **not go** [Prov. 4:13], **bind it unto** them **as a crown** [Job 31:36], renovate the quality of their heart such that it would not require them inevitably **to walk in the ways of** wickedness [Prov. 2:13]. If their sin was one of speech, and if, because they mocked men or **spoke perversion** [Deut. 13:6], the proper punishment overtook them, then clearly they must agree to **be ready to speak plainly** [Isa. 32:4], that is, to speak words that are **sweet to the soul** [Prov. 13:19], so that men's **ears may be attentive** [Ps. 130:2]. *'illᵉghīm* [Isa. 32:4][11] and *lō'ᵃghīm* [''mockers''] have the same meaning, like *kebhes* and *kesebh* [''lamb''] and other similar doublets.

[9] The prophet has thus described every rank of the citizenry, that is, the king, the princes, the important men of the land, ''the poorest sort of the people of the land,'' and the criminal—for in no generation will a State escape the presence of transgression and crime within it—and he has assigned to each rank its duty and office. This, then, is an example of how to apply the Figure Distribution in the case of different things.

[10] An example of Distribution in connection with the particulars of some one category, that is to say, the kind of office which the several persons involved might have, and what qualification for it they might be held to have, is provided by the prophet's words in the next following passage: **The vile person shall be no more called liberal,** etc. [Isa. 32:5 ff.]. That is to say, every man must be held for what he is, lest otherwise **the land be . . . polluted** [Jer. 3:1].

[11] In our opinion, the purport of the present passage [32:1–4] is this: The prophet is calling attention to the several things proper to the governing of every State—**every province according to the writing thereof and . . . every people after its language** [Esth. 1:22]. The object of the prophet's concern here is, of course, Israel; he has, however, appended the passage to the material concerning the king of Assyria [Isa. 31:8 ff.] because Israel's deliverance out of his hand was so procured: because, that is, Israel's king, princes, notables, and the rest of the people were high enough in degree of perfection to warrant the accomplishment on their behalf of that great miracle, the downfall of the king of Assyria together with his might and pride, the like of which had not happened in many years. I have already commented above on the meaning of ''churl,'' ''liberal,'' ''vile person,'' and ''noble,'' and on the purport of these several verses [32:5–8].[12]

[12] This Figure is very useful in proffering guidance on affairs of State.

10. C: ''fecklessness''; but that ''haste'' (חפזות) and not ''fecklessness'' (פחזות) was the original reading seems to be proved by the fact that the *litterae dilatabiles* at the end of the line just preceding פחזות in C were חפ.

11. Usually: ''stammerers''—the word that appears in our verse.

12. iv.21.3–9 (Definition).

פרק מ״ט

פ׳ התוכחה.

[1] התוכחה היא מאמר יבואו בו תוכחות ראויות מצד האהבה, לא מצד
איבה או לעג. והיא נחלקת לשני חלקים, למה שממנה עצומה, ממנה קלה·
5 ואמר שהתוכיחה בזה המקום היא הנעשת מן האדם בערך אל מי שגדול הימנו.

[2] משל הראשון, התוכחה שעשה יואב אל דוד בענין אבשלום, שאמ׳:
״הובשת היום את פני כל עבדיך, הממלטים את נפשך היום, ואת נפש בניך
ובנותיך, ונפש נשיך, ונפש פלגשיך· לאהבה את שונאיך ולשנא את אוהביך; כי
הגדת היום כי אין לך שרים ועבדים· כי ידעתי היום כי לו[1] אבשלום חי, וכלנו
10 היום מתים, כי אז ישר בעיניך. ועתה, קום צא, ודבר על לב עבדיך; כי בי״י
נשבעתי, כי אינך יוצא, אם ילין איש אתך הלילה· ורעה לך זאת מכל הרעה
אשר באה עליך מנעוריך ועד עתה״ [שמ״ב י״ט ו׳—ח׳]. והנה, באו בזאת
התוכחה דברים המכעיסים אשר בתכלית· והכינו לזה המליצים בספריהם
תעלה ורפואה: לשכך חמתם בזכור מעלתם, חכמתם, ותבונתם, ושאר מה
15 שיצטרך להשיב חרב החרון אל תערה.

[3] משל השני, מענין שאול ברדפו אחריו ב׳ פעמים, ואמ׳ לו בראשונה:
״למה תשמע את דברי אדם לאמר: הנה דוד מבקש רעתך? הנה היום הזה ראו
עיניך, כו׳...ואבי ראה, גם ראה את כנף מעילך בידי, כו׳...ישפוט י״י ביני וביניך,
ונקמני י״י ממך· וידי לא תהיה בך. כאשר יאמר משל הקדמוני: מרשעים יצא
20 רשע· וידי לא תהיה בך. אחרי מי יצא מלך ישראל? אחרי מי אתה רודף? אחרי
כלב מת, אחרי פרעוש אחד. והיה י״י לדיין, ושפט ביני וביניך· וירא וירב את
ריבי, וישפטני מידך״ [שמ״א כ״ד י׳—ט״ז]. זאת תקרא תוכחה קלה· אמנם, מה
שאמ׳ לו בפעם השנית היה בה מן הקלות יותר [שם כ״ו י״ח]:

1 פרק] פ׳[כ] || 2 פ׳] פרק[ד] || 5 שהתוכיחה] שהתוכח׳[ד] | הימנו] הימינו[כ] || 6 הראשון] הא׳[ד] || 9 [כי] אין[ד] | לו[1]] לֹא[ת] || 11 ‹אם› אינך[כ] || 12 ועד] עד[ת] || 15 החרון] ההמון[ד] || 16 השני] הב׳[ד] || 17 ‹בני› אדם[כ] || 20 תהיה] יהיה[ד] || 21 [אחד][כ] | [את][כ] || 22 זאת] זו[ד] || 23 בה] בא[כ] ||

15 יח׳ כ״א ל״ה ||

[1] *Qᵉrē* for *kᵉthībh* לֹא.

CHAPTER 49

Frank Speech[1]

[1] Frank Speech[a] is diction containing deserved reproofs that are prompted by friendship, not by enmity or derision. The Figure is subdivided into two forms, a severer and a lighter; and Tully says that the rebuke meant here is that directed by the speaker against a superior.

[2] An example of the severer form is Joab's rebuke of David in the affair of Absalom when Joab said: **"Thou hast shamed this day the faces of all thy servants, who this day have saved thy life, and the lives of thy sons and of thy daughters, and the lives of thy wives, and the lives of thy concubines; in that thou lovest them that hate thee, and hatest them that love thee. For thou hast declared this day, that princes and servants are nought unto thee; for this day I perceive, that if Absalom had lived, and all we had died this day, then it had pleased thee well. Now therefore arise, go forth, and speak to the heart of thy servants; for I swear by the Lord, if thou go not forth, there will not tarry a man with thee this night; and that will be worse unto thee than all the evil that hath befallen thee from thy youth until now"** [2 Sam. 19:6–8]. As we see, this example of Frank Speech does indeed contain words likely to provoke extreme indignation; but the rhetoricians have in their books prepared a palliative and cure for this: to assuage the wrath of those thus rebuked by mentioning their virtue, wisdom, understanding and whatever else is needed to cause the sword of wrath[2] **to return into its sheath** [Ezek. 21:35].

[3] Our example of the lighter form is taken from the episode in which Saul twice pursued David. On the first occasion David said to him: **"Wherefore hearkenest thou to men's words, saying: Behold, David seeketh thy hurt? Behold, this day thine eyes have seen how that the Lord had delivered thee into my hand. . . . Moreover, my father, see, yea, see the skirt of thy robe in my hand. . . . The Lord judge between me and thee, and the Lord avenge me of thee; but my hand shall not be upon thee. As saith the proverb of the ancients: Out of the wicked cometh forth wickedness; but my hand shall not be upon thee. After whom is the king of Israel come out? after whom dost thou pursue? after a dead dog, after a flea. The Lord therefore be judge, and give sentence between me and thee, and see, and plead my cause, and deliver me out of thy hand."** [1 Sam. 24:10–16]. This may be called a light rebuke; to be sure the reproach addressed by David to Saul on the second occasion was even gentler.[3]

1. Literally: "rebuke," "reproof;" "chastisement," "correction": הַתּוֹכָחָה.
2. So M; C: ". . . the sword of the mob. . . ."
3. See 1 Sam. 26:18–20.

a. *R. ad H.* 4.36.48 ff.

פרק נ׳

פ׳ ההכנעה.

[1] ההכנעה הוא מאמר כאשר נפחית מן הטוב הנמצא בנו, או במשפחתנו, או בסרים אל משמעתנו, בין שיהיה טבעי או נקנה, לברוח מההתנשאות.
5 והמשל ממה שהשיב שאול אל שמואל; באמרו ״למי כל חמדת ישראל? הלא לך ולבית אביך?״ [שמ״א ט׳ כ׳], שהפחית משפחתו ושבטו, ואמר: ״הלא בן ימיני אנכי, מקטני שבטי ישראל, ומשפחתי הצעירה מכל משפחות שבטי בנימן? ולמה דברת אלי כדבר הזה?״ [שם שם כ״א].

[2] וכן, מה שהשיב דוד אל שאול, ברצותו ליתן לו בתו לאשה, ואמר: ״מי
10 אנכי, ומי חיי, משפחת אבי בישראל, כי אהיה חתן למלך?״ [שם י״ח י״ח]. וכן השיב א״כ לעבדי שאול: ״הנקלה בעיניכם התחתן במלך, ואנכי איש רש ונקלה?״ [שם שם כ״ג]. וכן, מה שאמר דוד לשאול: ״אחרי מי יצא מלך ישראל, אחרי מי אתה רודף? אחרי כלב מת, אחרי פרעוש אחד״ [שם כ״ד ט״ו]. וכן, מה שאמרה אביגיל לדוד: ״אל נא ישים אדני את[1] לבו אל איש הבליעל הזה, אל
15 נבל· כי כשמו כן הוא, נבל שמו, ונבלה עמו״ [שם כ״ה כ״ה]; ואמרה א״כ: ״יהיו כנבל אויביך, והמבקשים אל אדני רעה.״ [שם כ״ו].

[3] וזה היפוי רב התועלת להנצל מן הקנאה והאיבה: ״אוהב שלום ורודף שלום״. ויבוקש ענינו בשפל יותר:

1 פרק] פ׳ᶜ || 2 פ׳] פרקᵈ || 3 נפחית] נפחיתוᶜ | הנמצא] אשר נמצא || 5 למי] ולמיᵗ || 6 ולבית] ולכל ביתᵗ || 7 ומשפחתי] ומשפחתוᶜ | שבטי] שבטᶜ | בנימן] בנימיᵈ || 10 [אהיה]ᶜ | למלך] המלךᶜ || 14 ישים] ישיתᵈ | את[1]] אלᶜᵈ || 14–15 אל נבל] על נבלᵗ || 15 נבל שמו ונבלה עמו] וכוᵈ | יהיו] יהיᵈ ||

4 שמ״א כ״ב י״ד ||

[1] Corrected according to ת.

CHAPTER 50

Understatement[1]

[1] The Figure of Speech is Understatement[a] when, in order to avoid self-exaltation, we deliberately make little of the good that is in us, or in our family, or in those that **give heed unto** our **bidding** [1 Sam. 22:14], whether this good be natural or acquired. Our example is drawn from the reply made by Saul to Samuel. When Samuel said, "**And on whom is all the desire of Israel? Is it not on thee, and on all thy father's house?**" [1 Sam. 9:20], Saul deliberately depreciated the importance of his family and his tribe: "**Am not I a Benjamite, of the smallest of the tribes of Israel? and my family the least of all the families of the tribe of Benjamin? wherefore then speakest thou to me after this manner?**" [9:21].

[2] Of this sort, too, was the reply that David made to Saul, who had expressed willingness to give his daugher as wife to David: "**Who am I, and what is my life, or my father's family in Israel, that I should be son-in-law to the king?**" [1 Sam. 18:18]. And the reply that David subsequently made to Saul's servants was to like effect: "**Seemeth it to you a light thing to be the king's son-in-law, seeing that I am a poor man, and lightly esteemed**"? [18:23]. Again, David's word to Saul: "**After whom is the king of Israel come out? after whom dost thou pursue? after a dead dog, after a flea**" [24:15]. So, too, the words which Abigail addressed to David: "**Let not my lord, I pray thee, regard this base fellow, even Nabal; for as his name is, so is he: Nabal is his name, and vileness is with him**" [25:25]; and also her subsequent statement: "**let thine enemies, and them that seek evil to my lord, be as Nabal**" [25:26].[2]

[3] This Figure is very useful for sparing oneself envy and hostility; it is "one that loves peace and pursues peace."[3] The effect is in special demand in the Simple Style.

1. Literally: "humility," "humbleness," "submission": הַהַכְנָעָה.
2. Cf. i.7.25.
3. *Mishnah Ābhoth* 1:12.

---

a. *R. ad H.* 4.38.50.

פרק נ״א

פ׳ ההתבוננות.

[1] ההתבוננות הוא מאמר כולל, באופן צח וברור, מה שאפשר שימשך בעתיד מאשר עליו העצה.

5 [2] והמשל, ממה שאמר פרעה: ״הנה עם בני ישראל רב ועצום ממנו; הבה נתחכמה לו, פן ירבה· והיה, כי תקראנה מלחמה, ונוסף גם הוא על שנאינו, ונלחם בנו, ועלה מן הארץ״ [שמ׳ א׳ ט׳—י׳]. וכן אמרו שרי פלשתים אל אכיש, מענין דוד: ״השב את האיש, וישב אל מקומו אשר הפקדתו שם, ולא ירד עמנו למלחמה, ולא יהיה לנו לשטן במלחמה· ובמה יתרצה זה אל אדניו? הלא

10 בראשי האנשים ההם?״ [שמ״א כ״ט ד׳]. וכן, מה שאמר יהודה אל יוסף: ״ועתה, כבואי אל עבדך אבי, והנער איננו אתנו, ונפשו קשורה בנפשו· והיה, כראותו כי אין הנער, ומת· והורידו עבדיך את שיבת עבדך אבינו ביגון שאלה. כי עבדך ערב את הנער מעם אבי לאמר: ׳אם לא אביאנו אליך, וחטאתי לאבי כל הימים׳ ״ [בר׳ מ״ד ל׳ — ל״ב]. וכן, מה שאמר משה לה׳ בענין המרגלים: ״ושמעו

15 מצרים — כי העלית בכוחך את העם הזה מקרבו — ואמרו אל יושב הארץ הזאת״, כו׳... ״והמתה את העם הזה כאיש אחד, ואמרו הגוים אשר שמעו את שמעך, לאמר: מבלתי יכלת י״י להביא את העם הזה אל הארץ אשר נשבע להם, וישחטם במדבר. ועתה יגדל נא כח י״י״, וכו׳ [במ׳ י״ד י״ג — י״ז]. וכן, מה שכתבו רחום בעל טעם, ושמשי ספרא, לארתחששתא מלכא: ״כען ידיע להוא

20 למלכא, די הן קריתא דך תתבני, ושורייא ישתכללון, מנדה בלו והלך לא ינתנון, ואפתום מלכא תהנזיק״; ובסוף הענין: מהודעין אנחנה למלכא, די הן קריתא דך תתבני, ושורייא ישתכללון, לקבל דנא חלק בעבר נהרא לא איתי לך״ [עז׳ ד׳ י״ג — ט״ז].

1 פרק] פ׳[כ] || 2 פ׳] פרק[ד] || 8 מענין] מנינין[ד] | וישב] וישוב[כ] | <כל> אשר[כ] || 9 למלחמה] במלחמה[ת] | אדניו] אדונו[כ] || 11 כבואי] בבאי[ד] | איננו] אנינו[כ] || 12 [הנער][כ] || 14 וכן] כן[ד] || 15 יושב] יושבי[ד] || 17 נשבע] נשבעת[ד] || 18 וכו׳] כו׳[ד] || 19 טעם] שעם[כ] | ושמשי ספרא] וספרי[כ] | לארתחששתא] לארתחששת[כ] | להוא] ליהויא[ד] || 20 תתבני] תתבנא[ת] | ושורייא] ושורויא[כ] | לא] למו[כ] || 21 ואפתום] ואפתון[כ] | מלכא] מלכים[ת] | אנחנה] אנחנא[ד] | למלכא] למלכה[כ] || 22 תתבני] תתבנא[ת] | ושורייא] ושוריה[ת] ||

CHAPTER 51

Vivid Description[1]

[1] Vivid Description[a] is diction which clearly and lucidly sums up the possible future consequences of the course of action under deliberation.

[2] Our example is taken from Pharaoh's words: **"Behold, the people of the children of Israel are too many and too mighty for us; come, let us deal wisely with them, lest they multiply, and it come to pass, that, when there befalleth us any war, they also join themselves unto our enemies, and fight against us, and get them up out of the land"** [Exod. 1:9–10]. Similarly, the princes of the Philistines said to Achish concerning David: **"Make the man return, that he may go back to his place where thou hast appointed him, and let him not go down with us to battle, lest in the battle he become an adversary to us; for wherewith should this fellow reconcile himself unto his lord? should it not be with the heads of these men?"** [1 Sam. 29:4]. So too, Judah's words to Joseph: **"Now therefore when I come to thy servant my father, and the lad is not with us; seeing that his soul is bound up with the lad's soul; it will come to pass, when he seeth that the lad is not with us, that he will die; and thy servants will bring down the gray hairs of thy servant our father with sorrow to the grave. For thy servant became surety for the lad unto my father, saying: 'If I bring him not unto thee, then shall I bear the blame to my father forever'"** [Gen. 44:30–32]. Again, the words which Moses addressed to the Lord in the affair of the spies: **"When the Egyptians shall hear—for Thou broughtest up this people in Thy might from among them—they will tell it[2] to the inhabitants of this land. . . . Now if Thou shalt kill this people as one man, then the nations which have heard the fame of Thee will speak, saying: Because the Lord was not able to bring this people into the land which He swore unto them, therefore He hath slain them in the wilderness. And now, I pray Thee, let the power of the Lord be great,"** etc. [Num. 14:13–17]. And again, what Rehum, the commander, and Shimshai, the scribe, wrote to Artaxerxes the king: **"Be it known now unto the king, that, if this city be builded, and the walls finished, they will not pay tribute, import, or toll, and so thou wilt endamage the revenue of the king";[3]** and they ended as follows: **"We announce to the king that, if this city be builded, and the walls finished, by this means thou shalt have no portion beyond the River"** [Ezra 4:13–16].

1. Literally: "observation," "reflection," "meditation," "insight," "consideration," "study": הַהִתְבּוֹנְנוּת.
2. JV: "say."
3. *Sic*, JML; JV: "kings."

---

a. *R. ad H.* 4.39.51.

[3] וזה היפוי אפשר לו שיעורר כעס גדול, או רחמנות, בהגידו מה שאפשר שימשך, בקצור ובלשון ברור. ויבוקש ענינו בשפל יותר:

פרק נ״ב

פ׳ החלוק.

[1]החלוק הוא מאמר יחלק בו הדבר אל חלקים ידועים, עם באור כל אחד מהם. והמשל במלכים, משני המצורעים שהיו פתח השער, שאמרו: ״מה אנחנו יושבים פה עד מתנו? אם אמרנו נבא העיר, והרעב בעיר, ומתנו שם· ואם ישבנו פה, ומתנו. ועתה, לכו ונפלה אל מחנה ארם· אם יחיונו נחיה, ואם ימיתונו ומתנו״ [מל״ב ז׳ ג׳ — ד׳]. והנה בארו המיתה מצד הרעב: ואם היה זה בעיר, כל שכן אם ישבו פתח השער.

[2] וכן: לכו נא ונוכחה, יאמר י״י; אם יהיו חטאיכם כשנים, כשלג ילבינו· אם יאדימו כתולע, כצמר יהיו. אם תאבו ושמעתם, טוב הארץ תאכלו· ואם תמאנו ומריתם, חרב תאכלו; כי פי י״י דבר [יש׳ א׳ י״ח — כ׳]. והנה באר כל החלקים שהביא מצד שהש׳ ית׳ יעדם, אשר אין חליפות לו; ובזה יבדל מן החלוק שהוא אחד מחלקי המאמר.

ויבוקש ענינו בשפל יותר:

1 [גדול][ג] ‖ 2 בקצור] בין צור[ג] ‖ 3 פרק] פ׳[ג] ‖ 4 פ׳] פרק[ד] ‖ 6 שאמרו] שאמר[ד] ‖ 7 העיר] בעיר[ד] ‖ 8 ומתנו] ומתמנו[ג] ‖ 11 כשנים <כשנים>[ג] | אם] ואם[ד] ‖ 12 תאכלו] תאוכלו[ג] ‖

---

14 תה׳ נ״ה כ׳ ‖

[3] This Figure can arouse indignation or pity through its concise recital, in lucid language, of the possible consequences. The effect is most often called for in the Simple Style.

CHAPTER 52

Division[1]

[1] Division[a] is a Figure of Speech whereby the matter under discussion is divided into definite parts, with clarification of each. An example, in Kings, is afforded by the two lepers[2] **at the entrance of the gate,** who said: **"Why sit we here until we die? If we say: We will enter into the city, then the famine is in the city, and we shall die there; and if we sit still here, we die also. Now therefore come, and let us fall unto the host of the Arameans; if they save us alive, we shall live; and if they kill us, we shall but die"** [2 Kings 7:3–4]. The lepers thus clarified the subdivision of death by famine: if this could happen in the city, it must all the more be inevitable if they sat still at the gate.

[2] Similarly: **Come now, and let us reason together, saith the Lord; though your sins be as scarlet, they shall be white as snow; though they be red like crimson, they shall be as wool. If ye be willing and obedient, ye shall eat the good of the land; but if ye refuse and rebel, ye shall be devoured with the sword; for the mouth of the Lord hath spoken** [Isa. 1:18–20]. The prophet thus clarified all the parts which he had cited as the promises of the Name, blessed be he, Who **has no changes** [Ps. 55:20]. It is by such clarification that the Figure Division is distinguished from the division which is one of the Parts of the Discourse.[3]

The effect produced by the Figure Division is especially called for in the Simple Style.

1. הַחִלּוּק.
2. According to 2 Kings 7:3, there were four.
3. I.e., the Partition; cf. i.9.

a. *R. ad H.* 4.40.52.

פרק נ״ג

פ׳ המאסף.

[1] המאסף הוא מאמר כאשר הדברים המפוזרים והמפורדים בספור ארוך יהיו נכללים יחד· יתלכדו ולא יתפרדו. והמשל ממה שעשה ישעיהו, שכמעט כל מה שדבר מעונות ישראל, ומפשעיהם לכל חטאתם, כלל אותם בפסוק אחד, ואמר: הוי גוי חוטא, עם כבד עון, זרע מרעים, בנים משחיתים· עזבו את י״י, נאצו את קדש ישראל, נזורו אחור [יש׳ א׳ ד׳]. וכן, כל הנאמר מהשרים בארוכה, קבצם בפסוק אחד, ואמר: שריך סוררים, וחברי גנבים· כלו אוהב שוחד, ורודף שלמונים; יתום לא ישפוטו, וריב אלמנה לא יבא אליהם [שם שם כ״ג]. וכן, מה שאמ׳ מיכה: על הרע כפים להטיב· השר שואל, והשופט בשלום· והגדול דובר הוות נפשו הוא· ויעבתוה [מי׳ ז׳ ג׳].

[2] וזה היפוי גדול הסכנה לעורר השומעים אל הכעס והקצף הגדול· והוא טוב בכל סוגי הדבו׳, ובחלקי המאמ׳ — וביחוד בראיות הסברתיות; ויבוקש ענינו בנשא ובבינוני יותר:

פרק נ״ד

פ׳ הצחות.

[1] הצחות הוא מאמר כאשר ענין אחד יאמר באופנים מתחלפים· וזה נמצא ממנו בישעיה הרבה. והמשל: נדרשתי ללא שאלו, נמצאתי ללא בקשוני·

1 פרק] פ׳[כ] ‖ 2 פ׳] פרק[ד] ‖ 4 ישעיהו] ישעיה[כ] ‖ 6–7 זרע...אחור] כו׳[ד] | קדש] קדוש[ת] | נזורו] נזרו[ת] ‖ 8 בארוכה] בארכה[כ] | קבצם] קבצה[כ] ‖ 10 להטיב] להיטיב[ת] ‖ 11 [הוא][ד] ‖ 13 הדבו׳] הסבות[כ] ‖ 14 ובבינוני] בבינוני[ד] ‖ 15 פרק] פ׳[ד] ‖ 18 והמשל] המש׳[ד] | ללא] ללוא[ת] ‖

4 איוב מ״א ט׳ ‖ 5 וי׳ ט״ז ט״ז ‖

CHAPTER 53

Accumulation[1]

[1] Accumulation[a] is a Figure of Diction such that the points scattered and separated throughout a long recital are brought together into a united whole: **they stick together, that they cannot be sundered** [Job 41:9]. An example is provided by Isaiah's bringing together into a single verse virtually all the pronouncements he had made because of Israel's iniquities **and because of their transgressions, even all their sins** [Lev. 16:16], when he said: **Ah, sinful nation, a people laden with iniquity, a seed of evil-doers, children that deal corruptly; they have forsaken the Lord, they have contemned the Holy One of Israel, they are turned away backward** [Isa. 1:4]. Similarly, he collected into a single verse all that is stated at length about the princes, and said: **Thy princes are rebellious, and companions of thieves; every one loveth bribes, and followeth after rewards; they judge not the fatherless, neither doth the cause of the widow come unto them** [1:23]. A further example is Micah's statement: **Their hands are upon that which is evil to do it diligently; the prince asketh, and the judge is ready for a reward; and the great man, he uttereth the evil desire of his soul; thus they weave it together** [Mic. 7:3].

[2] This Figure is of great utility in arousing hearers to indignation and great wrath; it is valuable in all the Kinds of Cause, and in the several Parts of a Discourse—particularly in the proofs of conjectural issues; and its effect is called for in the Grand Style, but more frequently in the Middle.

CHAPTER 54

Refining[1]

[1] Refining[a] is a Figure of Speech such that a single theme is stated in several different ways; it is much in evidence in Isaiah. For example: **I gave access to**

1. Literally: "the collector," "the gatherer": הַמְּאַסֵּף.

a. *R. ad H.* 4.40.52 ff.

1. Literally: "clearness," "lucidity"; "elegance (of style)": הַצַּחוּת.

a. *R. ad H.* 4.42.54 ff.

אמרתי "הנני הנני" אל גוי לא קורא בשמי; פרשתי ידי כל היום אל עם סורר, כו' [יש' ס"ה א' — ב']. וכן: פחדו בציון חטאים, רעדה אחזה חנפים· "מי יגור לנו אש אוכלה? מי יגור לנו מוקדי עולם?" [שם ל"ג י"ד]. וכן, ביחזקאל: בת אמך את, גועלת אשה ובניה· ואחות אחותך את, אשר געלו אנשיהם ובניהם· אמכן חתית, ואביכן אמורי [יח' ט"ז מ"ה]. 5

[2] וזה היפוי בערך אל הפתרון הוא כיחס הכל אל החלק, למה שזה בערך אל המאמרי', והפתרון בערך אל התבות; ויען בזה היפוי מן הצחות אשר בתכלית, נקרא "צחות" סתם. ויבוקש ענינו בנשא ובבינוני יותר:

פרק נ"ה

פ' העכבה. 10

[1] העכבה הוא מאמר כאשר נתעכב על דבר אחד קיים זמן רב, אשר כל כח המאמ' סובב עליו, ונכפילהו ונשניהו פעמים רבות עד תשלום הספור. וטוליאו מתנצל לבלתי הביאו משל לצורך הספור, כי קשה להביאו מלשונם· ואני אביא לך בזה כמה משלים נכבדים ויקרים מדברי הנביאים הקדושים, שהם היו המליצים המפלגים. 15

[2] וראשונה, ממה שאמר י"י לירמיהו: וכי ישאלך העם הזה או הנביא או כהן, לאמר, "מה משא י"י?" ואמרת להם את־מה־משא: "ונטשתי אתכם," נאם

1 [עם] עב[כ] || 2 רעדה אחזה] אחזה רעה[ת] || 4 אשה] אישה[ת] | אנשיהם ובניהם] אנשיהן ובניהן[ת] || 6 כיחס] כי אם[כ] | החלק] החלוק[כ] || 9 פרק] פ'[כ] || 10 פ'] פרק[ד] || 11 הוא] היא[כ] || 13 לצורך הספור] לזה היפוי[ד] || 14 [כמה][כ] || 16 י"י] הש'[ד] || 17 משא י"י] משאיהם[כ] | להם] אליהם[ת] ||

them that asked not for Me, I was at hand to them that sought Me not; I said "Behold Me, behold Me" unto a nation that was not called by My name; I have spread out My hands all the day unto a rebellious people, etc. [Isa. 65:1–2]. Again: **The sinners in Zion are afraid, trembling hath seized the ungodly: "Who among us shall dwell with the devouring fire? Who among us shall dwell with everlasting burnings?"** [33:14]. Similarly, also, in Ezekiel: **Thou art thy mother's daughter, that loatheth her husband and her children; and thou art the sister of thy sisters, who loathed their husbands and their children; your mother was a Hittite, and your father an Amorite** [Ezek. 16:45].

[2] The present figure is related to Synonymy or Interpretation[2] as whole is to part: Refining relates to complete statements, Synonymy or Interpretation to words. It is because this Figure contains the utmost elegance that it is called Refining[3] without other qualification. Its effect is called for in the Grand Style, but more frequently in the Middle.

CHAPTER 55

Dwelling on the Point[1]

[1] Dwelling on the Point[a] is our Figure of Speech when we linger a long time over some one valid item upon which the whole force of what is being said turns, reiterate it, and repeat it a number of times before our recital is done. Tully apologizes for not introducing an example sufficient for the description,[2] for it is difficult to cite one from [speeches in] their language; but I shall here cite you several important and precious examples from the words of the holy prophets, who were the most preeminent of orators.

[2] First, then, an example from the word of the Lord to Jeremiah: **And when this people, or the prophet, or a priest shall ask thee, saying, "What is the burden of the Lord?" then shalt thou tell them what is burden: "And I will**

2. iv.29.
3. Literally, "elegance."

1. Literally: "lingering," "delay," "retention": הַעֲכָבָה.
2. M, literally: ". . . an example for the needs of the description (*or:* account)." C here reads, ". . . for not introducing an example of this Figure."

a. *R. ad H.* 4.45.58.

י״י [יר׳ כ״ג ל״ג]. והנה, כל זה המאמ׳ עד תשלומו סובב על ״משא י״י״, והוא
הנשנה פעמים רבות· ובאו בו גם כן דברים נכפלים, מקצתם בעצמם, ומקצתם
במלות שונות, כאשר יתבאר למתבונן בזה המאמר; ונמשך זה המאמר עד... יען
אמרכם הדבר הזה, ״משא י״י״, ואשלח אליכם לאמר, ״לא תאמרו ׳משא י״י׳ ״
5 [שם שם ל״ח].

[3] עוד, ביחזקאל: ואתה, בן אדם, שים פניך אל בנות עמך המתנבאות
מלבהן[1]· והנבא עליהן[1], וכו׳; ואח׳ כן: הוי, למתפרות כסתות על כל אצילי
ידים, ועושות המספחות על ראש כל קומה, לצודד נפשות! הנפשות תצודדנה
לעמי, ונפשות לכנה תחיינה? [יח׳ י״ג י״ז — י״ח]. והנה, כל זה המאמר בנוי על
10 ענין הנפשות, ובו העמידה הנה· וזה נשנה פעמים רבות עד... אשר אתם
מצודדות נפשים לפורחות [שם שם כ׳].

[4] עוד, ביחזקאל: בן אדם, ארץ כי תחטא לי למעול מעל, ונטיתי ידי עליה,
ושברתי לה מטה לחם, כו׳· וא״כ אמר: והיו שלשת האנשים האלה בתוכה, נח,
דניאל, ואיוב· המה בצדקתם ינצלו נפשם, נאם י״י אלקי׳ [שם י״ד י״ג — י״ד].
15 והנה, ענין זה המאמ׳ שתמנע להם ההצלה מן הענשים ההם, ואפי׳ יהיו בתוכם
הצדיקים הנזכ׳; ועל זה סובב כל המאמ׳, וזה מה שנשנה פעמים רבות עד סופו·
ונשנת הכרת הארץ ושוממותה בעונשים מתחלפים.

[5] עוד, ביחזקאל: ואחותך הגדולה שומרון היא ובנותיה, היושבת על
שמאלך· ואחותך הקטנה ממך, היושבת מימינך, סדום ובנותיה [שם ט״ז מ״ו].
20 והנה כל זה המאמר נבנה על שגדלה חטאתם מחטאת שומרון וסדום· והם
הנכפלים והנשנים עד סוף המאמר, ובהם העמידה תמיד; וקצת הדברים גם כן
נשנים במלות שונות, כאשר יתבאר למעיין בהם.

[6] וכאשר יכונן זה היפוי המליץ באופן נאות, יהיה בו מן הערת הלבבות
והמשכתם אל אשר יחפצהו שעור רב; ויבוקש ענינו בנשא בבינוני ושפל:

1 על] את[ר] |י״י] ה׳[כ] ||4 אמרכם] אמרתם[ר] |‹את› הדבר[ת] ||6–7 המתנבאות...וכו׳] כו׳[ר] ||7 ואח׳ כן ‹אמר›[ר] |אצילי ‹ארץ›[כ] ||8 ידים] ידי[ת] |על ראש] לראש[כ] ||9 בנוי] כנוי[ר] ||10 ובו העמידה] והעמידה[ר] ||12 [לי][כ] ||13 בתוכה] בתוכ׳[ר] ||14 י״י אלקי׳] אדני יהוה[ת] ||15 בתוכם] בתוכה[כ] ||16 הנזכ׳] הנז׳[כ] ||17 ושוממותה] ושוממותיה[כ] ||18 היושבת] יושבת[כ] ||19 שמאלך] שמאולך[ת] ||21 הדברים] דברים[ר] ||23 המליץ] במליץ[ר] ||

[1] Corrected according to ת.

cast you off, saith the Lord" [Jer. 23:33 ff.].[3] This whole discourse, from beginning to end, turns upon **the burden of the Lord,** the point that is frequently repeated; the discourse also contains a number of reiterations, some in the same words, some in different words, as will be obvious to anyone who studies it. And this discourse extends as far as the words **Because ye say this word, "The burden of the Lord," and I have sent unto you, saying, "Ye shall not say: the burden of the Lord"** [23:38].

[3] Again, in Ezekiel: **And thou, son of man, set thy face against the daughters of thy people, that prophesy out of their own heart; and prophesy thou against them,** etc. And immediately following: **Woe to the women that sew cushions upon all elbows and make pads for the head of persons of every stature to hunt souls! Will ye hunt the souls of my people, and save souls alive for yourselves?** [Ezek. 13:17–18]. Thus, the entire discourse is based upon the subject of souls, the point dwelt upon here; and this point is repeated many times, continuing through **even the souls that ye hunt as birds** [13:20].

[4] Another, in Ezekiel: **Son of man, when a land sinneth against Me by trespassing grievously, and I stretch out My hand upon it, and break the staff of the bread thereof,** etc; following this He said: **Though these three men, Noah, Daniel, and Job, were in it, they should deliver but their own souls by their righteousness, saith the Lord God** [14:13–14 ff.]. It is clearly the main theme of this discourse that the people cannot possibly be delivered from the punishments specified, not even if the aforementioned righteous men should be in their midst. Upon this point the entire discourse turns; it is therefore frequently repeated through to the end, with repetition, too, of the theme of the cutting off and desolation of the land by means of various punishments.

[5] Still another example in Ezekiel: **And thine elder sister is Samaria, that dwelleth at thy left hand, she and her daughters; and thy younger sister, that dwelleth at thy right hand, is Sodom and her daughters** [16:46]. This entire discourse is plainly based on the idea that the sinfulness of Judea is greater than that of Samaria and Sodom; words to this effect are reiterated and repeated through to the end and are constantly dwelt upon. Some points, moreover, are repeated in different words, as will be obvious to an observant student.

[6] This Figure, appropriately developed by the orator, has ample capacity to stir hearts and to impel them toward whatever he may wish. Its effect is called for in the Grand, Middle and Simple Styles.

3. JV: "... then shalt thou say unto them: 'What burden! I will cast you off.'"

פרק נ״ו

פ׳ ההגדה.

[1] ההגדה היא מאמר כאשר יביא המגיד א׳ או ב׳ או ג׳ מדברים, כל אחד לפי מה שיאות לו.

[2] והמשל משלמה המלך, בספר משלי, אשר יביא ״החכמה״ ו״התבונה״ מעוררות האנשים אל השגת הידיעות ההערה אשר בתכלית, ואמ׳: הלא חכמה תקרא· ותבונה תתן קולה? בראש מרומים עלי דרך· בית נתיבות נצבה [מש׳ ח׳ א׳—ב׳]. ואמר שהיא תרון, גם כן, ליד שערים... ומבא פתחים [שם שם ג׳]; והנה העיר בזה על תכונת הקול ההכרחי לפי מדרגת הספור· ולכן אמר ״תקרא״ ו״תתן קולה״ ו״תרון״, ר״ל, שהיתה נותנת הקול המיוחד לכמו זה הספור. והעיר גם כן על המקומות אשר ראוי לבחור למי שחפץ לעורר הלבבות אל הדרכים החשובים והטובים, למען עשות כיום הזה להחיות עם רב· ואמר שבמקומות הקבוצים הגדולים, שם יתנו צדקות י״י, במקהלות יברכו את י״י. והם מה שספר בכאן, ר״ל, ״ראש מרומים״ ״בית נתיבות״ ו״יד שערים״ ו״מבא פתחים״.

[3] והנה ״ראש מרומים״ ו״בית נתיבות״ הם מקומות האנשים בכלל· ו״יד שערים״ ו״מבא פתחים״ הם מקומות בעלי החכמה, על דרך... אל השערה אל הזקנים [דב׳ כ״ה ז׳]. וכאלו רצה בזה החכמה והבינה להעיר כל הלבבות· כעם ככהן, כנקלה כנכבד. וזה מה שאמר אחר כן גם כן: ״אליכם אישים אקרא״ — וזה המאמר שב אל נשיאי העדה... אנשי השם — ״וקולי אל בני אדם״ [מש׳ ח׳ ד׳]· המכוון בו יתר העם, מקצהו.

[4] והנה אמר ל״פתאים״ — שהם חסרי השכל וערומי המדע, גם משוללי ההנהגה — שיבינו ערמה [שם שם ה׳]. ושם ה״ערמה״ יאמר על קנין התחבולות המיוחדות בדבר דבר; וזה יהיה, אם בפילוסופיא המדינית, בחכמת ההלצה· ואם בפילוסופיא העיונית, בחכמת ההגיון. וזה, כי ״הפתאים״ הם

1 פרק] פ׳[ר] || 2 פ׳] פרק[ד] || 3 כאשר] באשר[ד] |א׳ או ב׳ או ג׳] אחד שנים או שלשה[ד] |כל] וכל[ד] || 4 לפי] כפי[ד] |לו <ההגדה>[ד] || 10 [ותרון][ר] || 12 עשות] עשותו[ד] עשה[ת] || 13 יברכו] ברכו[כת] || 14 נתיבות] נדיבות[ד] || 15 ראש] ראשי[ד] |נתיבות] נדיבות[ד] |[הם][ר] || 16 [אל] השערה[ת] || 17 רצה] רצו[ר] |הלבבות] הללבבות[ר] || 18 אחר כן גם כן] א״כ ג״כ[ר] || 19 השם] שם[ת] || 23 בפילוסופיא] בפילוסופיאה[ר] || 24 ההגיון] ההגון[ד] ||

12 בר׳ נ׳ כ׳ || 13 שופ׳ ה׳ י״א |תה׳ ס״ח כ״ז || 17—18 הו׳ ד׳ ט׳ || 19 במ׳ ט״ז ב׳ || 20 נחמ׳ ד׳ ח׳ | יש׳ נ״ו י״א ||

CHAPTER 56

Dialogue[1]

[1] The Figure of Speech is Dialogue[a] when the speaker quotes one, or two, or three persons, each speaking as is proper to him.

[2] Our illustration is furnished by King Solomon in the Book of Proverbs, who, introducing "Wisdom" and "Understanding" as urging men in the most stirring way to acquire knowledge, said: **Doth not Wisdom call, and Understanding put forth her voice? In the top of high places by the way, where the paths meet, she standeth** [Prov. 8:1-2]. **She crieth aloud** too, said Solomon, **beside the gates... at the coming in at the doors** [8:3]; here he has called attention to the quality of tone needed to conform with the dignity of the recital, and therefore used the words "call," "put forth her voice," "crieth aloud," meaning that Wisdom was "putting forth" the tone special to such a recital. He here also called attention to the backgrounds which one desirous of stirring hearts to ways worthy and fine should select, **in order to bring to pass, as it is this day, to save much people alive** [Gen. 50:20]; and he said that, in the places where large numbers of people foregather, **there shall they rehearse the righteous acts of the Lord** [Judg. 5:11], **bless... God in full assemblies** [Ps. 68:27]. Such are the backgrounds described here, namely, **the top of high places, where the paths meet, beside the gates,** and **at the coming in at the doors** [Prov. 8:2-3].

[3] Now "the tops of high places" and "where the paths meet" are places frequented by the generality of men; "beside the gates" and "at the coming in at the doors" are the places of those who possess wisdom, as shown by the usage in... **to the gate unto the elders** [Deut. 25:7]. It is as though Solomon here meant that wisdom and understanding were to arouse all hearts, **like people, like priest** [Hos. 4:9], the lightly esteemed as well as the person held in honor. This is what he said in the following verse too: **"Unto you, O men, I call"**—a reference to the **princes of the congregation... the men of renown** [Num. 16:2]—**and my voice is to the sons of men** [Prov. 8:4], meaning **the rest of the people** [Neh. 4:8] **one and all** [Isa. 56:11].

[4] At this juncture Solomon bade the **thoughtless**—those wanting in understanding, denuded of science, and even deficient in manners—to **understand prudence** [Prov. 8:5]. The term "prudence" denotes possession of the special skills of some one art; in ethical and political philosophy, the special skills are those of the art of rhetoric, in speculative philosophy those of the art of logic. He

1. Literally: "telling," "declaring"; "tale," "legend," "saga": הַהַגָּדָה.

a. *R. ad H.* 4.43.55.

הנעדרי הידיעה בכל ענין, ר״ל, אשר להם הסכלות העדרי· ואלה ראוי שיתחילו
באחד מן הנזכרים, לפי הדרך אשר יכוונו אליו. אמנם ״הכסילים״, אשר להם
הסכלות קניני, ר״ל, שידעים הדבר בחלוף מה שהוא, ראוי ש״יבינו לב״: ר״ל,
שיתנו בינה וחכמה בלבם, עד ידעו הדרך ישכון אור, ולא יגששו כעורים קיר.
[5] ואחר כך, אמר לבעלי הדיעה, היושבים לפני י״י: ״שמעו, כי נגידים אדבר·
ומפתח שפתי מישרים״ [שם שם ו׳]; ר״ל, שתדבר דבר נפלא הערך, מראשית
פרי ההשגות, ראוי לנגידים ולשופטי ארץ· ״ומפתח שפתיה מישרים״, ר״ל,
היושר אשר במדות ובדעות.
[6] והנה, זה הספור ארוך מאד, נמשך עד ״משחקת בתבל ארצו, ושעשועי
את בני אדם״ [שם שם ל״א]. ונמצאו בזה המאמר הרבה מן היפויים ההלציים:
אם הפתרון, הוא מה שאמ׳, ״ליד שערים״ ו״מבא פתחים״ [שם שם ג׳], שהם
דבר אחד· אם הצחות: ״כי טובה חכמה מפנינים, וכל חפצים לא ישוו בה״ [שם
י״א]· ״בטרם הרים הטבעו, לפני גבעות חוללתי״ [כ״ה]; — אם המשל מבלתי
נתינת הסבה: ״כלם נכוחים למבין, וישרים למוצאי דעת״ [ט׳]; — אם המשל עם
הסבה: ״קחו מוסרי ואל כסף, ודעת מחרוץ נבחר· כי טובה חכמה מפנינים״, כו׳
[י׳ — י״א]; — אם השוה: ״טוב פריי מחרוץ ומפז· ותבואתי מכסף נבחר״
[י״ט]; — אם החזרה: ״גאה וגאון, ודרך רע״, כו׳ [י״ג]; — אם המתדמה: ״כלם
נכוחים למבין, וישרים למוצאי דעת״ [ט׳]; — אם ההשבה: ״יראת י״י שנאת
רע· גאה וגאון, ודרך רע, ופי תהפוכות שנאתי״ [י״ג]; ואחרי׳ זולת אלה.
[7] והמשל, עוד, מזה היפוי: חכמות בחוץ תרונה, ברחובות תתן קולה·

1 ואלה] ואלו[ר] || 4 בלבם] ללבם[כ] || 5 ואחר כך] וא״כ[כ] | הדיעה] הדעת[ר] || 6 נפלא] כפלא[כ] || 7 ארץ] הארץ[ר] || 9 עד] עם[כ] || 11 מה] מאמ׳[ר] || 13 לפני] ולפני[ר] | מבלתי] מבלי[כ] || 14 נתינת] נתנת[כ] | נכוחים] נכונים[כ] | עם] על[כ] || 17 [רע][ר] | המתדמה] התמדה[כ] || 18 נכוחים] נכוכים[כ] ||

4 איוב ל״ח י״ט | יש׳ נ״ט י׳ || 5 יש׳ כ״ג י״ח || 6–7 דב׳ כ״ו ב׳ || 7 מש׳ ח׳ ט״ז ||

urges the "thoughtless" to "understand prudence," because they are without knowledge of any kind. Their ignorance, that is, arises from deficiency; and such as these ought to begin with one of the aforementioned arts, depending on which road they intend to take. The "fools," however, whose ignorance arises from acquisition—that is, whose acquired knowledge of something is the contrary of the fact—should **be... of an understanding heart** [Prov. 8:5b]: should put understanding and wisdom into their hearts, so that they may know **the way to the dwelling of light** [Job 38:19] and not **grope for the wall like the blind** [Isa. 59:10].

[5] Solomon next addressed those who possess intelligence, those **that dwell before the Lord** [Isa. 23:18]: **Hear, for I will speak excellent things, and the opening of my lips shall be right things** [Prov. 8:6]. Wisdom, that is, would speak a word of extraordinary value, **of the first of the fruit** [Deut. 26:2] of comprehension, one fit for leaders and **judges of the earth** [Prov. 8:16]; **and the opening of** her **lips** would **be right things** [8:6]—uprightness in morals and in ethical principles.

[6] Now this is a very long recital, continuing as far as the words . . . **playing in His habitable earth, and my delights are with the sons of men** [Prov. 8:31]. It abounds in Figures of Speech, as follows: (a) Synonymy or Interpretation:[2] Solomon's phrases **beside the gates** and **at the coming in at the doors** [8:3] come to the same thing. (b) Refining:[3] **For wisdom is better than rubies, and all things desirable are not to be compared unto her** [8:11]; **Before the mountains were settled, before the hills was I brought forth** [8:25]. (c) Maxim,[4] without an accompanying reason: **They are all plain to him that understandeth, and right to them that find knowledge** [8:9]. (d) Maxim,[5] with an accompanying reason: **Receive my instruction, and not silver, and knowledge rather than choice gold; for wisdom is better than rubies,** etc. [8:10–11]. (e) Isocolon:[6] **Better my fruit than gold, fine gold; and my produce than choice silver** [8:19]. (f) Transplacement:[7] . . . **to hate evil; pride and arrogancy, and the evil way,** etc. [8:13]. (g) Homoeoptoton,[8] **They are all plain** (nᵉkhōḥīm) **to him that understandeth, and right** (yᵉshārīm) **to them that find knowledge** [8:9]. (h) Adjunction:[9] **The fear of the Lord is to hate evil; pride and arrogancy, and the evil way, and the froward mouth do I hate** [8:13]. And there are other Figures besides.

[7] A further example of Dialogue: **Wisdom crieth aloud in the street, she uttereth her voice in the broad places; she calleth at the head of the noisy**

2. iv.29.
3. iv.54.
4. iv.10.
5. iv.10.
6. iv.15; the verse here is translated so as to exhibit the Figure.
7. iv.5.
8. iv.16.
9. iv.27.

בראש הומיות תקרא, בפתחי שערים, וכו׳, עד... ״ושומע לי ישכון בטח, ושאנן מפחד רעה״ [מש׳ א׳ כ׳—ל״ג].

[8] ויען אין הכונה ממני לפרש ספר משלי, עזבתי פי׳ כל הפסוקים למען לא אצא מכוונת הספר; והספקתי, במה שפרשתים, מצד מה שהם משל לזה היפוי.
5 ויבוקש ענינו בבינוני ובשפל יותר:

פרק נ״ז

פ׳ ההתנגדות.

[1] ההתנגדות הוא מאמר ימצא בו ההפוך מצד המאמרי, לא מצד התבות; והמשל: כי בם ידין עמים· יתן אכל למכביר [איוב ל״ו ל״א]. המכוון במאמ׳
10 הראשון הוא זולת המכוון במאמר השני, כי רצה במאמ׳ הראשון שה׳ ית׳ ידין עמים בגשמים, אם מצד העצרם, אם מצד היותם לפעמים גשמי קללה; והרצון בשני, שה׳ באמצעותם יתן אכל למכביר· וזה, בבואם בשעור הראוי לזרעים, בעתו יורה ומלקוש. אמנם, אין במאמרים האלה הפוך מצד התבות. ויבוקש ענינו בשפל ובבינוני:

1 עד] עוד^ר || 3 לפרש] עתה לבאר^ר || 4 שפרשתים] שפרשתי^ר || 6 פרק] פ׳^כ || 7 פ׳] פרק^ר || 10 הראשון הוא זולת] הא׳ אינו^ר | במאמר השני] בב׳^ר | הראשון שה׳] הא׳ שהש׳^ר || 12 שה׳] שהש׳^ר || 14 ובבינוני] ובינוני^ר ||

---

13 דב׳ י״א י״ד ||

streets, at the entrances of the gates, etc., continuing as far as **But whoso hearkeneth unto me shall dwell securely, and shall be quiet without fear of evil** [Prov. 1:20–33].[10]

[8] Since it is not my intention to expound[11] the Book of Proverbs I have refrained from interpreting all the verses in this passage, so as not to depart from the purpose of this book; and in the case of those verses which I have interpreted, I have considered it sufficient to do so only insofar as they exemplify the present Figure, Dialogue. The effect is one called for in the Middle Style, and more frequently in the Simple.

CHAPTER 57

Antithesis[1]

[1] Antithesis[a] is a Figure of Speech achieved through a contrast of clauses, not of words. For example: **For by these He judgeth the peoples; He giveth food in abundance** [Job 36:31]. The purport of the first clause is quite different from that of the second, for the first signifies that the Name, blessed be He, passes judgment on the peoples by means of the rains, whether through withholding them, or through the fact that they are sometimes rains of cursing;[2] and the second signifies that the Name, by means of the rains, gives food in abundance—that is, by the coming of the rains in the measure that seeds should have, . . . **in its season the former rain and the latter rain** [Deut. 11:14]. The contrast in these clauses is, of course, not verbal. The effect is in demand in the Simple and Middle Styles.

10. Note that JML never cites B by verse number, and only rarely by chapter, because such division of the Hebrew Bible had not yet come into general use among Jews in his day.

11. So M: the reading of C: ". . . now to make a commentary." As JML did write such a work, the changed reading may be the result of Conat's knowledge of such an intention on the part of JML, or that the latter had already begun it.

1. Literally: "opposition": הַהִתְנַגְּדוּת. "Word antithesis" (iv.6) is expressed by הִפּוּךְ ("contrary," "reverse").

2. Cf. "showers of blessing," Ezek. 34:26.

a. *R. ad H.* 4.45.58.

פרק נ״ח

פ׳ הערך.

[1] הערך הוא כאשר יתבאר הדמות שני דברים מתחלפים בענין מן הענינים. ותעשה לאחת מד׳ סבות: אם על צד הצחות· אם על צד הבאור· אם לפרסם יותר· אם לשום הענין לנגד עינינו. וכן יעשה באחד מד׳ פנים: אם מההפך· אם מהשלילה· אם מהקצור· אם מהיחס. וכל אחד מאלה הפנים יוחס אל אחת מהסבות הנזכרות.

[2] סבת הצחות תלקח מן ההפך; והמשל: הכמכת מכהו הכהו אם כהרג הרוגיו הורג? [יש׳ כ״ז ז׳]. ר״ל, שלא היה עונש ישראל מבלי מדה ושעור, כמו שהיה העונש המגיע לאויביו; אדרבה, היה הענין בהפך, שענשם היה במדה ובשיעור, כמה שנ׳: בסאסאה בשלחה תריבנה [שם שם ח׳]. והנה היה אפשר שיאמ׳, אם לא מפני הצחות, ״שה׳ ית׳ מגיע העונש לישראל במדה, מזולת שיעריך ענשם אל עונש האויבים״.

[3] וסבת הבאור תלקח מן השלילה; והמשל: כי לא אויב יחרפני, ואשא· לא משנאי עלי הגדיל, ואסתר ממנו [תה׳ נ״ה י״ג]. התבאר הדבר מצד שכאשר אין ראוי שנחוש אם משנאנו עלינו הגדיל, כן אין ראוי שנחוש אם יחרפנו, אלא שזה הדבר קשה לסבול מ״אנוש כערכנו״; וזה מה שאמ׳ אחר כן: ואתה, אנוש כערכי...[שם שם י״ד].

[4] סבת הפרסום יותר תלקח מן הקצור, כמו: כענבים במדבר מצאתי את ישראל, כבכורה בתאנה בראשיתה [הו׳ ט׳ י׳]· שהוא מאמר יותר קצר ממה שהיה אומר: ״אני מצאתי את ישראל במדבר, וחשקתי בהם חשק נפלא״, ולא היה כל כך מפורסם. אמנם, זה הדמיון מפרסמו פרסום רב, למה שהוא דבר נגלה להמון, הפלגת החשק כענבים במדבר וכבכורי התאנים.

[5] סבת תשומת הענין לנגד עינינו תלקח מההתיחסות; והמשל: ״הנה בטחת על משענת הקנה הרצוץ הזה, על מצרים· אשר יסמך איש עליו, ובא בכפו

1 פרק] פ׳[כ] || 2 פ׳ פרק[ר] || 4 לאחת] לאחד[ר] || 6 וכל] אם[ר] || 8–9 אם כהרג הרוגיו הורג] וכו׳[ר] || 11 ובשיעור] ושעור[ר] | כמה שנ׳] כמו שאמ׳[ר] || 12 שה׳] שהש׳[ר] || 14–15 [לא] משנאי׳[ר] || 16 אם] אב[כ] | 17 אחר כן] א״כ[כ] || מן] מ׳[ר] | [את][ת] || 21 [את][כ] || 23 החשק] החשך[כ] || 24 בטחת <לך>[ת] ||

CHAPTER 58

Comparison[1]

[1] Comparison[a] is such that it is made clear that two different things are alike in some one respect. This Figure is developed for one of four reasons: elegance, proof, greater clarity, or vividness. It is likewise developed in one of four forms: Contrast, Negation, Abridgment, or Connection. Each of these forms corresponds to one of the aforementioned reasons.

[2] The reason of elegance is served by Contrast. For example: **Hath He smitten him as He smote those that smote him? Or is he slain according to the slaughter of them that were slain by Him?** [Isa. 27:7]. Israel's punishment, that is to say, was not without measure and limit, as was that which overtook their enemies; the fact, rather, was the contrary, for their punishment was moderate in scope and limited, as stated in the text: **In full measure, when Thou sendest her away, Thou dost contend with her** [27:8]. If not for sake of elegance, it would have been possible to say: "The Name, blessed be He, brings punishment upon Israel in moderate measure, not permitting their punishment to be comparable to that of their enemies."

[3] The reason of proof is served by Negation. For example: **For it was not an enemy that taunted me, then I could have borne it; neither was it mine adversary that did magnify himself against me, then I would have hid myself from him** [Ps. 55:13]. The point is demonstrated on the score that as we ought not care if our enemy has magnified himself over us, so we ought not care if he taunts us, but on the part of a **man** who is our **equal** such conduct is hard to bear. Indeed, this is said by the Psalmist in the next verse: **But it was thou, a man mine equal, my companion, and my familiar friend!** [55:14].

[4] The reason of greater clarity is served by Abridgment, as follows: **As wilderness-grapes found I Israel, as the fig's first-ripe at first season** [Hos. 9:10].[2] The statement is briefer than if it had run: "I found Israel in the wilderness and conceived a marvellously great love for them," nor would this be as clear as the statement in the text. The comparison, in fact, confers great clarity, for it is a fact of which most people are aware that to be loved like grapes in the wilderness, and like first-ripened figs, is to be loved very deeply.

[5] The reason of vividness is served by Connection. For example: **"Thou hast trusted[3] upon the staff of this bruised reed, even upon Egypt; whereon if**

1. הָעֵרֶךְ.
2. Translated thus so as to illustrate JML's point. In B, Hosea's words are fewer in number than those in the paraphrase.
3. JV and KJV: "thou trustest."

a. *R. ad H.* 4.46.59 ff.

ונקבה׃ כן פרעה מלך מצרים לכל הבוטחים עליו״ [מל״ב י״ח כ״א]. וראוי שתדע, שתשומת נגד העין הוא כאשר נביא מה שהוא קודם הדבר, ומה שהוא במציאותו, ומה שהוא אחר הדבר. והנה, ימצא כלם בזה ההתיחסות, למה ש״הבטחון״ הוא הדבר הקודם ל״השען״׃ וה״השען״ הוא הענין בעצמו׃ ומה שימשך אחר זה הוא הצער הבא מן ה״נקוב״. וכן, היה רב שקה מעריך הבטחון אל פרעה כבטחון על המשענת, וההשען עליו כהשען על משענת הקנה הרצוץ׃ וכן, אמר שיתחייב אליהם מהנזק בזאת הסבה כאשר הענין בקנה; והנה ההזק הוא לפנינו. ולזה, יקרא זה ההדמות יחס או התיחסות, למה שיצטרך כאן יחס ג׳ דברים, כמו שבארנו.

[6] והנה, מה שצריך למליץ בערכים האלה שיסדרם באופן נפלא התקון, אם על צד הצחות׃ אם על צד הבאור׃ אם לפרסם יותר׃ אם לשום הענין מפורסם לעינינו׃ כאשר התבאר מהמשלים הנז׳. ויבוקש ענינו בנשא בבינוני ובשפל:

פרק נ״ט

פ׳ הדמיון.

[1] הדמיון הוא מאמר כאשר נביא מעשה או דבור על צד ההדמות עם שם האיש, בעל המעשה, או בעל הדבור ההוא׃ ובזה יבדל מהערך. כמו: ויעש אסא[1] הישר בעיני י״י, כדוד אביו [מל״א ט״ו י״א]; וכן: כאשר עשו לי בני עשו היושבי׳ בשעיר, וכו׳ [דב׳ ב׳ כ״ט]. ואפשר בערכו שבאותן הסבות בעצמן הכתובות בערך: יעשו עניין יותר צח, כאשר לא ילקח מפני דבר אחר, כי אם מפני הצחות׃ יותר מפורסם, כאשר ישיב היותר נעלם לברור׃ מבואר, כאשר ילקח הדמיון מהעניין שהוא יותר נגלה׃ וישים נגד העינים, כאשר יפרסם כל הדברים בדקות שהם קודם הענין, ועם מציאותו, ואחריו, כאשר התבאר במה שקדם.

ויבוקש ענינו בשפל יותר:

5 הצער] צער[ר] || 6 [וההשען עליו כהשען על משענת][ר] || 8 התיחסות] ההתיחסות[ר] || 11 לשום] לשים[כ] || 13 פרק] פ׳[כ] || 14 פ׳ הדמיון] מהדמיון[ר] || 17 [אסא[1]][כר] || 18 היושבי׳ בשעיר וכו׳] כו׳[ר] || 19 עניין] הענין[ר] || 22 שהם קודם] שקודם[ר] | במה] ממה[ר] ||

[1] Corrected according to ת.

a man lean, it will go into his hand, and pierce it; so is Pharaoh king of Egypt unto all that trust on him" [2 Kings 18:21].[4] We achieve vividness, you should know, when we introduce what obtained before the issue, what now is actually the case, and what the aftermath will be. All these phases, indeed, are present in this Connection, for the "trusting" is the condition precedent of the "leaning," the "leaning" is itself the matter of current concern, and the future consequence is the pain which will come from the "piercing." Rab-shakeh, then, was comparing confidence in Pharaoh to confidence in a staff, reliance upon Pharaoh to leaning upon the staff of a bruised reed; so too, he asserted that the injury caused by such confidence and reliance would as inevitably follow as in the case of the reed. The injury is thus vividly set before us. Such a comparison is called one of Connection or Relationship, because, as explained, a bringing of the three phases into relationship is required here.

[6] Thus, a speaker using these comparisons must arrange them with exceptionally fine exactness, either by way of elegance or of proof, either to achieve clarification or to confer vividness, as shown by the examples above. The effect produced by Comparison is called for in the Grand, Middle, and Simple Styles.

CHAPTER 59

Exemplification[1]

[1] The Figure is Exemplification[a] when, by way of comparison, we introduce some deed or utterance along with the name of its doer or author; by such naming Exemplification is distinguished from Comparison.[2] For example: **And Asa did that which was right in the eyes of the Lord, as did David his father** [1 Kings 15:11]. Again: **. . . as the children of Esau that dwell in Seir . . . did unto me** [Deut. 2:29]. Exemplification can be developed for the same reasons as those set forth for the Figure Comparison: they make a theme more elegant when the Figure is adopted for no other purpose than elegance; clearer, when it transforms into clarity what was very obscure; more plausible, when the example is taken from a matter that is almost self-evident; more vivid, when it makes plain in nice detail all the antecedent, currently actual, and subsequent circumstances, as has been explained in the chapter above.

This Figure's effect is quite frequently called for in the Simple Style.

4. Cf. iv.9.2–3.

1. Literally: "likeness," "resemblance"; "imagination"; "example"; הַדְּמְיוֹן.
2. iv.58.

a. *R. ad H.* 4.49.62.

פרק ס׳

פ׳ הצורה.

[1] הצורה הוא מאמ׳ כאשר נעריך תמונה לתמונה מצד התיחסות והדמות קרה לשניהם במראה או בעניין מה; וזה אפשר שיעשה אם על צד השבח, אם על צד הגנות. משל הראשון: ומראהו כמראה מלאך האלקי׳, נורא מאד [שופ׳ י״ג ו׳]; משל השני: דמיונו כאריה יכסוף לטרוף [תה׳ י״ז י״ב].

ויבוקש ענינו בבינוני ושפל יותר:

פרק ס״א

פ׳ הסימן.

[1] הסימן הוא מאמ׳ יתואר בו איש מהאנשים בסימני גופו, למען יודע באמצעותם. והמשל: אדמוני עם יפה עינים וטוב רואי [שמ״א ט״ז י״ב]; ויאמר ציבא אל המלך, ״עוד בן ליהונתן, נכה רגלים״ [שמ״ב ט׳ ג׳]; וכן: ותהי המלחמה בגת· ויהי איש מדון[1], ואצבעות ידיו ואצבעות רגליו שש ושש, עשרים וארבע במספר [שמ״ב כ״א כ׳]. וזה היפוי, אם יכוון בו ספור סימני הגוף בקצור, הנה בו מן היופי מה שלא יעלם.

ויבוקש ענינו בשפל יותר.

1 פרק] פ׳[כ] || 2 פ׳ הצורה] מהצורה[ר] || 4–5 אם על צד] או על[ד] || 5 הראשון] הא׳[ר] || 6 השני] הב׳[ר] || 8 פרק] פ׳[כ] || 9 פ׳ הסימן] מהסימן[ר] || 11 באמצעותם] באמצעו׳[ר] || 13 המלחמה] מלחמ׳[ר] עוד מלחמה[ת] || 14 ארבע] וארבעה[כ] וארבע[ת] | במספר][כ] מספר[ת] ||

[1] *Qᵉrē* for *kᵉthībh* מדין.

CHAPTER 60

Simile[1]

[1] Simile[a] is our Figure of Speech when we compare one form with another because of some relationship and resemblance that the two happen to bear in appearance or in function. It can be developed either in praise or in censure. For example, in praise: . . . **and his countenance was like the countenance of the angel of God, very terrible** [Judg. 13:6]; in censure: **He is like a lion that is eager to tear in pieces** [Ps. 17:12]. Simile's effect is called for most frequently in the Middle and Simple Styles.

CHAPTER 61

Portrayal[1]

[1] Portrayal[a] is diction in which some person is depicted in terms of the distinctive features of his body so that, through these, he is identifiable. For example: **Now he was ruddy, and withal of beautiful eyes, and goodly to look upon** [1 Sam. 16:12]; **And Ziba said unto the king: "Jonathan hath yet a son, who is lame on his feet"** [2 Sam. 9:3]; and too: **And there was . . . war at Gath, where was a champion, that had on every hand six fingers, and on every foot six toes, four and twenty in number** [2 Sam. 21:20]. This Figure, if the description of the distinctive physical marks is deliberately concise, has no little beauty. Its effect is very often called for in the Simple Style.

1. Literally: "form," "fashion," "figure," "shape"; "picture," "idol," "image": הַצּוּרָה.

a. *R. ad H.* 4.49.62.

1. Literally: "mark," "sign"; "omen," "symptom"; "mnemonic sign": הַסִּימָן.

a. *R. ad H.* 4.49.63.

פרק ס״ב

פ׳ התואר.

[1] התואר הוא מאמ׳ יתבאר בו איש מן האנשים מצד מדותיו, כמו: והאיש קשה, ורע מעללים, והוא כלבי[1] (שמ״א כ״ה ג׳].

5 [2] וכן: הורד שאול גאונך, המיית נבליך, כו׳... ואתה אמרת בלבבך: ״השמים אעלה, ממעל לכוכבי אל ארים כסאי· ואשב בהר מועד, בירכתי צפון; אעלה על במתי עב· אדמה לעליון״ [יש׳ י״ד י״א — י״ד]. תאר בזה המאמר נבוכדנצר בגאוה והתנשאות.

[3] וכן, ביחזקאל: יען גבה לבך, ותאמר: ״אל אני, מושב אלקים ישבתי״;

10 ואמ׳ אח׳ כך: גבה לבך ביפיך, שחת חכמתך על יפעתך [יח׳ כ״ח ב׳... י״ז]. מודיע חירם מלך צור בגאוה וגאון. וכן אמר בפרעה: התנין הגדול הרובץ בתוך יאוריו, אשר אמר: ״לי יאורי, ואני עשיתיני״ [יח׳ כ״ט ג׳]; ואמר אח׳ כך: אמור אל פרעה מלך מצרים, ואל המונו: אל מי דמית ביפיך? עוד, אמר: יען אשר גבהת בקומה· ויתן צמרתו אל בין עבותים, ורם לבבו בגבהו [שם ל״א ב׳... י׳].

15 [4] ואמר בתחלת עזרא: כה אמר כורש מלך פרס: ״כל ממלכות הארץ נתן לי י״י אלהי השמים״ [עז׳ א׳ ב׳]· תאר אותו בענוה ובמוסר; וכן: והאיש משה ענו מאד, מכל האדם אשר על פני האדמה [במ׳ י״ב ג׳].

ויבוקש ענינו בנשא בינוני ושפל:

1 פרק] פ׳ᶜ ||2 פ׳ התואר] מהתואר ᵀ ||3 [בו איש]ᵀ ||4 כלבי[1]] כליביᶜ ||7 במתי] במותיᶜ |נבוכדנצר] נבוכד נצרᵀ ||10 אח׳ כך] א״כᶜ ||11 חירם] חרםᵀ |התנין] התניםᵀ ||12 אח׳ כך] א״כᶜ ||13 ביפיך] בגדלךᵀ ||15 [כורש]ᵀ ||16 אלהי] אלקיᶜ ||

[1] *Qᵉrē* for *kᵉthībh* כלבו.

CHAPTER 62

Character Delineation[1]

[1] Character Delineation[a] is diction in which some person is clearly set forth in terms of his traits of character, as in the following: **but the man was churlish and evil in his doings; and he was of the house of Caleb** [1 Sam. 25:3].

[2] So too: **Thy pomp is brought down to the netherworld, and the noise of thy psalteries. . . . And thou saidst in thy heart: "I will ascend into heaven, above the stars of God will I exalt my throne; and I will sit upon the mount of meeting, in the uttermost parts of the north; I will ascend above the heights of the clouds; I will be like the Most High"** [Isa. 14:11–14]. In this speech, the prophet has characterized Nebuchadnezzar by the attributes of pride and self-exaltation.

[3] Likewise, in Ezekiel: **Because thy heart is lifted up, and thou hast said: I am a god, I sit in the seat of God** [Ezek. 28:2]; and following this, the prophet said: **Thy heart was lifted up because of thy beauty, thou hast corrupted thy wisdom by reason of thy brightness** [28:17]. Ezekiel here makes known to us Hiram, king of Tyre, in his pride and pomp. Similarly, of Pharaoh he said: **The great dragon that lieth in the midst of his rivers, that hath said: "My river is mine own, and I have made it for myself"** [29:3]; and following this: **Say unto Pharaoh king of Egypt, and to his multitude: Whom art thou like in thy beauty?**[2] [31:2]; and again: **Because thou art exalted in stature, and he hath set his top among the thick boughs, and his heart is lifted up in his height** [31:10].

[4] The statement at the beginning of Ezra—**Thus saith Cyrus king of Persia: "All the kingdoms of the earth hath the Lord, the God of heaven, given me"** [1:2]—attributed to Cyrus the qualities of humility and moral discipline. Thus too: **Now the man Moses was very meek, above all the men that were upon the face of the earth** [Num. 12:3].

The effect of this Figure is called for in the Grand, Middle, and Simple Styles.

1. Literally: "outline," "form," "figure," "shape"; "aspect," "visage," "attribute," "property"; "quality," etc.: הַתּוֹאַר.

2. *Sic,* B: "greatness."

---

a. *R. ad H.* 4.50.69 ff.

פרק ס״ג

פ׳ הספור.

[1] הספור הוא הגדת דברים מה קרו, עם הבאת עושי המעשה והמקבלים, מדברים כל אחד לפי מה שיאות לפי תכונתם; כמו הספור מהמלאכים עם אברהם [בר׳ י״ח ב׳–ט״ז] ועם לוט [שם י״ט א׳–כ״ג]· וספור יעקב עם עשו [שם ל״ב ד׳–ל״ג ט״ז] וספור ענין המרגלים [במ׳ י״ג א׳ — י״ד מ״ה] וענין פילגש בגבעה [שופ׳ י״ט א׳ — כ׳ מ״ח]· וזולתם רבים· אשר באו בהם שאלו׳ ותשובות, ותחנות, ומאמרים, כפי תכונת המדברים ההם. כאלו תאמר, שבני סדום היו מדברים בגאוה והתנשאות, כמו: ״האחד בא לגור וישפוט שפוט· עתה נרע לך מהם״, וכו׳ [בר׳ י״ט ט׳]; וזה היה נאות לפי טבעם מן הרוממות והגאון. ולוט היה מתחנן ומתנפל: ״אל נא, אחי, תרעו״, וכו׳ [שם שם ז׳]; וזה המאמר היה נאות לטבע לוט· גם כי היה מן הראוי לפי הענין, כי במקום האכזריות ועוות המשפט ראויה התחנה. וכן, בענין דבור יעקב והשלוחים ועשו: כי בערך יעקב והשלוחים, היתה ראויה התחנה והדבור המוסרי, כאשר הענין בעבדי המלך בערך אל המלך; אמנם עשו היה מדבר בגסות הרוח, כפי מה שהיה נאות לתכונותיו הרעות, אלא שהיה מראה אהבה וחבה בדבריו כדרך השרים אל אשר יאהבוהו.

[2] ובכלל, כל הספורים יבאו בהם מעשים ודברים מסכימים לטבע הענין ולתכונת האנשים אשר נקבו בשמות בספורים ההם. וזה הענין, ראוי שישמרהו אשר יבדה מלבו ספורים לא היו ולא נבראו; ויבוקש ענינו בשפל יותר:

1 פרק] פ׳[כ] ‖ 2 פ׳] פרק[ר] ‖ 4 [מה][ר] ‖ 7 בהם שאלו׳] בשאלו[רי] | ותחנות] ותואנות[כ] ‖ 8 [ההם][ר] ‖ 9 [עתה נרע לך מהם][ר] ‖ 10 [וזה...והגאון][ר] ‖ 11 [וכו׳][כ] ‖ 13 בענין] מעניין[כ] | 13–14 [ועשו... והשלוחים][ר] ‖ 16 השרים] הישרי[רי] ‖

---

19 דה״א י״ב ל״ב ‖ 20 מל״א י״ב ל״ג | שמ׳ ל״ד י׳ ‖

CHAPTER 63

Characteristic Statement[1]

[1] Characteristic Statement[a] consists of a telling of certain happenings, with introduction of those doing, or those affected by, the action as severally speaking in the manner appropriate to their characters. Examples are the narratives about the angels and Abraham [Gen. 18:2-16], the angels and Lot [Gen. 19:1-23], and Jacob and Esau [32:4-33:16]; those which recount the episodes of the spies [Num. 13:1-14:45] and of the concubine in Gibeah [Judg. 19:1-20:48]; and many others. These narratives contain questions and answers, entreaties, and declarations in keeping with the characters of the respective speakers. The inhabitants of Sodom, for instance, are made to speak with pride and arrogance: **"This one fellow came in to sojourn, and he will needs play the judge; now will we deal worse with thee, than with them,"** etc. [Gen. 19:9]; this was properly in accord with their proud and haughty nature. Lot, on the other hand, is made to entreat and grovel: **"I pray you, my brethren, do not so wickedly,"** etc. [19:7 f.]; this language was appropriate to Lot's nature and was, moreover, suited to the circumstances, for supplication is in point where cruelty and perversion of justice prevail. And so too in the account of the speaking done by Jacob, the emissaries, and Esau [Gen. 32:14-21; 33:3-15]: for on the part of Jacob and the emissaries, entreaties and polite speech such as a king's servants use in dealing with the king were appropriate. Esau, on the other hand, is made to speak in the coarse spirited way appropriate to his evil character, except that he is made to show in his words the warmth and affection which princes display toward one who enjoys their friendship.

[2] Generally, in all the narratives of Scripture, the actions and the speeches are consistent with the nature of the circumstances and the character of the persons involved—**who were mentioned by name** [1 Chr. 12:32]—in those narratives. The same rule should be observed by anyone who would **devise of his own heart** [1 Kings 12:33] tales of things that never were, and **such as have not been wrought** [Exod. 34:10]. The Figure's effect is very often called for in the Simple Style.

1. Literally: ''narrative,'' ''story''; ''narration,'' ''description,'' ''account'': הַסִּפּוּר. In *R. ad H.*, the corresponding term is *sermocinatio*.

a. *R. ad H.* 4.52.65.

פרק ס״ד

פ׳ ההעברה.

[1] ההעברה, בזה המקום, הוא מאמר תיוחס בו אחת הפעלות לאשר תמנע בערכם הפעלה ההיא. והמשל: גם ברושים שמחו לך, ארזי לבנון· ״מאז שכבת,
5 לא יעלה הכורת עלינו״; וכן: שאול מתחת רגזה לך לקראת בואך· עורר לך רפאים, כל עתודי ארץ· הקימו מכסאותם כל מלכי גוים· כולם ישנו ויאמרו אליך, כו׳ [יש׳ י״ד ח׳—י׳]. וכן: כי אבן מקיר תזעק· וכפיס מעץ יעננה [חב׳ ב׳ י״א]. וכן: הוי, חרב לי״י, עד אנה לא תשקוטי? הרגעי ודמי, הרגעי ודמי [יר׳ מ״ז ו׳]. וכן: ויקנאוהו כל עצי עדן אשר בגן אלקים [יח׳ ל״א ט׳]. וכן: ידברו לו
10 אילי גבורים מתוך שאול את עוזריו· ירדו, שכבו, הערלים, חללי חרב [שם ל״ב כ״א].

[2] וזה היפוי נפלא הערך כאשר תאות ההרחבה בלשון; ויבוקש ענינו בנשא ובבינוני:

פרק ס״ה

פ׳ הנותר.

15 [1] הנותר הוא כאשר ישאר במחשבה דבר לא הושם במאמר, וזה אם מפני התוספת· אם מפני הספק· אם מפני הנמשך· אם מפני ההפסקה· אם מפני הדמיון.

1 פרק] פ׳[ר] || 2 פ׳ ההעברה] <בזה המקום>[ר] מההעברה[ד] || 3 אחת] אחד || 6–7 [כולם ישנו ויאמרו אליך][ד] | ישנו] יענו[ת] || 7 יעננה] יענוה[ר] || 8 לא] לו[ד] | הרגעי ודמי [הרגעי ודמי][ת] | הרגעי...הרגעי] הרגיעי...הרגיעי[ד] || 9 אלקים] האלהים[ת] | [לו][ד] || 11 תאות] תשור[ר] || 12 ובבינוני] ובנוני[ר] || 13 פרק] פ׳[ר] || 14 פ׳] פרק[ד] || 15 [הוא][ר] ||

CHAPTER 64

Personification[1]

[1] Personification[a] in this Chapter means diction in which an emotion of some kind is ascribed to phenomena that are incapable of feeling it. For example: **Yea, the cypresses rejoice at thee, and the cedars of Lebanon: "Since thou art laid down, no feller is come up against us"** [Isa. 14:8]; and so too: **The nether-world from beneath is moved for thee to meet thee at thy coming; the shades are stirred up for thee, even all the chief ones of the earth; all the kings of the nations are raised up from their thrones; all they do repeat[2] and say unto thee,** etc. [14:9–10]. Similarly: **For the stone shall cry out from the wall, and the beam out of the timber shall answer it** [Hab. 2:11]. So too: **O thou sword of the Lord, how long will it be ere thou be quiet? . . . Rest, and be still, rest and be still** [Jer. 47:6].[3] Again: . . . **so that all the trees of Eden, that were in the garden of God, envied it** [Ezek. 31:9]. And again: **The strong among the mighty shall speak of him out of the midst of the nether-world with them that helped him; they are gone down, they lie still, even the uncircumcised, slain by the sword** [32:21].

[2] This figure is of surpassing value when Amplification is appropriate. Its effect is called for in the Grand and Middle Styles.

CHAPTER 65

Emphasis[1]

[1] The Figure is Emphasis[a] when some thought not expressly stated is nevertheless left in the mind of the audience—this whether through Hyperbole, Ambiguity, Logical Consequence, Aposiopesis, or Analogy.

1. Literally: "transfer," "removal"; "figurative sense," metaphor": הַהַעֲבָרָה.
2. B: "answer"; omitted in C.
3. B omits the last four words (dittography?).

a. *R. ad H.* 4.53.66.

1. Literally: "the remainder, remnant, residue": הַנּוֹתָר.

a. *R. ad H.* 4.54.67.

[2] מפני התוספת הוא, כשיאמ׳ יותר ממה שיסכים ממנו עם האמת; והמשל ממה שאמ׳ י״י להושע: ״קח לך אשת זנונים וילדי זנונים״ [הו׳ א׳ ב׳]׳ עוד, אמר: ״קח לך אשה אהובת ריע ומנאפת״ [שם ג׳ א׳]. נשאר במחשבה שזה אינו כמשמעו, ושהוא משל.

[3] משל השני, כאשר אפשר שיובנו מהעניין דברים מתחלפים, כמו: ״מה משא י״י?״ [יר׳ כ״ג ל״ג]׳ שאפשר שיהיה מלשון ״משא מדבר ים״ [יש׳ כ״א א׳], שהמכוון בו נבואה׳ ואפשר ג״כ שיהיה מענין ״כי תראה חמור שונאך רובץ תחת משאו״ [שמ׳ כ״ג ה׳]. והנה, נלקח בעבור אחד מאלה, ונשאר במחשבה זה הספק, ר״ל, מה המכוון מהם בו.

[4] משל השלישי — כאשר יאמרו הדברי׳ הנמשכים לדבר מה, הענין כלו ישאר במחשבה — כמו שבא בתורה, מעשיית קצת הענינים, אשר אינו נראה שקדם אליהם צווי; כאשר הענין כן בפרשת ״ויהי ביום השמיני״ [וי׳ ט׳ א׳], שנאמ׳: ויאמר אל אהרון: ״קח לך עגל בן בקר לחטאת״ [שם שם ב׳]. ולא נמצא שנצטוה משה על זה׳ ויען עשיית כמו אלה הדברים נמשכת אל הצווי שצוה בהם ה׳ יתב׳, ישאר הענין כלו במחשבה, ר״ל, הצווי והמעשה.

[5] משל הרביעי, ממה שאמ׳ למעלה בנפסק, שישאר דבר גדול במחשבה מהספקת המאמ׳.

[6] משל החמישי, כאשר ילקח הדמיון מבלתי הדבר אשר ידומה לו, כמו שנאמ׳ ביחזקאל, בנבואת צור: ואבדך, כרוב הסוכך, מתוך אבני אש [יח׳ כ״ח ט״ז]. וזהו הדמיון שנדמה בו חירם מלך צור׳ לכן, ישאר במחשבה הדבר כלו, הדמיון והדבר אשר נדמה; וכאלו אמר: ״ואבדך, חירם שנדמת לכרוב ממשח הסוכך [שם שם י״ד], מתוך אבני אש.״

[7] ויש בזה היפוי מן הערבות, ולפעמים מן הנאות, בהזדמן מי שיאות לו לדבר בזה האופן; ויבוקש ענינו בנשא בינוני ושפל:

2 וילדי זנונים ‹וכו׳›[ב] || 3 קח לך] אהב[ת] |ריע] רע[ת] || 5 השני] הב׳[ר] || 8 אחד] אחת[ב] || 9 מהם] מאלה[ר] || 10 משל] ומשל[ר] |השלישי] הג׳[ר] |הדברי׳] דברים[ב] || 12 בפרשת] בש״[ב] || 13 שנאמ׳] שנ׳[ב] || 14 משה על זה] על זה משה[ר] |כמו] כל[ר] || 15 ה׳] הש׳[ר] |יתב׳] יתע׳[ב] || 16 הרביעי] הד׳[ר] |בנפסק] בנספק[ב] || 18 [לו][ר] || 19 הסוכך] הסובך[ב] || 20 חירם] חרם[ר] || 21 שנדמת] שנדמה[ר] |לכרוב] לרוב[ב] || 23 ויש] וזה[ר] || 24 בינוני] ובינוני[ב] ||

[2] It is Emphasis through Hyperbole when obviously more is said than is consistent with truth. An example is afforded by what the Lord said to Hosea: "**Take unto thee a wife of harlotry and children of harlotry,** etc." [Hos. 1:2]; furthermore: **"Take unto thee[2] a woman beloved of her friend and an adulteress"** [3:1]. Left in our minds is the thought that this is not to be taken literally, but is a parable.

[3] An example of the second kind of Emphasis—through Ambiguity, when an expression can be understood in different ways—is **"What is the burden of the Lord?"** [Jer. 23:33]. It is possible that "burden" here has the same sense as in **The burden of the wilderness of the sea** [Isa. 21:1], where it means prophecy; and it is also possible that the meaning is that which it bears in **If thou see the ass of him that hateth thee lying under its burden** [Exod. 23:5]. The word was obviously chosen for the sake of one of these senses, and this ambiguity was left in the mind of the audience, namely, which sense was the one intended?

[4] Examples of the third form of Emphasis—when, as the Logical Consequences of some course have been expressed, the whole of the matter is left in the mind of the audience—are the Torah's citations of certain acts of compliance where no antecedent commandment can be discerned. Such is the case in the Torah portion *Sh^e mini,* (**And it came to pass on the eighth day** [Lev. 9:1]), where we read as follows: **And he[3] said unto Aaron: "Take thee a bull-calf for a sin-offering"** [9:2]. Now we do not find it stated that Moses had been thus commanded; but since the performance of such acts is the logical consequence of their having been commanded by the Name, blessed be He, the whole of the matter is left in our minds, that is, both the commandment and the fact that it was issued.

[5] The fourth form of Emphasis is exemplified above in what was said on Aposiopesis,[4] namely, that a point of greater persuasiveness than the actual utterance may be left in the mind of the audience.

[6] A typical example of the fifth form, when an analogue is adopted without mention of the thus depicted original, is provided by a statement in Ezekiel's prophecy against Tyre: **And I have destroyed thee, O covering cherub, from the midst of the stones of fire** [28:16]. Now this is the analogue through which Hiram, the king of Tyre is depicted; the entire matter, therefore—both the analogue and the original depicted by it—is left in our minds. It is as though Scripture had said: "And I have destroyed thee, O Hiram, thou who art depicted as **the far-covering cherub** [Ezek. 28:14], from the midst of the stones of fire."

[7] When the speaker happens to be one for whom it is appropriate to speak in this way, this Figure contains a measure of charm, and sometimes, even of beauty. Its effect may be called for in the Grand, Middle, and Simple Styles.

2. *Sic,* text; B: "Love."
3. Moses.
4. iv.35.

פרק ס״ו

פ׳ המספיק.

[1] המספיק הוא מאמ׳ אין בו יתר או פחות ממה שצריך, כמו: בני יפת: גומר, ומגוג, ומדי, ויון, ותובל, ומשך, ותירס [בר׳ י׳ ב׳]; וכן: ובני גומר: אשכנז, 5 וריפת, ותוגרמה [שם שם ג׳]; וזה הרבה. וראוי לעשות כשלא נצטרך להאריך, או שאין לנו פנאי, ואם היתה ההרחבה בלשון תועלת; ויבוקש עניננו בשפל:

פרק ס״ז

פ׳ נגד העין.

[1] נגד העין הוא מאמר משים הענין לנגד עינינו· וזה, בספרו מה שהיה קודם 10 הענין, ועם מציאותו, ואחריו באופן.

[2] והמשל משירת האזינו, שהיא מספרת בלשון צח ענין ישראל כלו· והתחיל מאז... מקדמי ארץ, והולך, מגדת ומספרת הדברים בכל דור ודור, עד סוף הגלות, ואמ׳: הרנינו, גוים, עמו· כי דם עבדיו יקום, כו׳ [דב׳ ל״ב מ״ג]. וכן, שירת דבורה תשית לנגד עינינו מלחמת סיסרא מתחלה ועד סוף — שנאמר: כן 15 יאבדו כל אויביך, י״י· ואוהביו כצאת השמש בגבורתו [שופ׳ ה׳ ל״א]. ועל זה הדרך הולכת פרשת ״הודע את ירושלם את תועבותיה״, הכתובה ביחזקאל [ט״ז ב׳, ואיל׳]· כי תספר ענין ישראל מהתחלת האמה, והולכת ומגדת דרכיהם ופשעיהם, לכל חטאתם, עד זמן יחזקאל· וכל זה בלשון מדברת גדולות ואמרות

1 פרק] פ׳[ג] ‖ 2 פ׳] פרק[ד] ‖ 3 יפת] יתר[ד] ‖ 4 ומדי] ומדיי[ג] ‖ 5 וריפת] ורפת[ג] ‖ 6 היתה] היה[ג] ‖ 7 פרק] פ׳[ג] ‖ 8 פ׳] פרק[ד] | העין] העַיין · העין[ג] ‖ 10 מציאותו] מציאות[ג] ‖ 15 [כל][ד] | אויביך] אויבך[ג] ‖ 16 [את ירושלם][ד] ‖ 17 ישראל] יש׳[ד] | [מהתחלת][ד] ‖

---

12 מש׳ ח׳ כ״ב–כ״ג ‖ 18 וי׳ ט״ז כ״א | תה׳ י״ב ד׳ | תה׳ י״ב ז׳ ‖

CHAPTER 66

Conciseness[1]

[1] Conciseness[a] is a Figure of Diction in which neither more nor less is said than is essential, as follows: **The sons of Japheth: Gomer, and Magog, and Madai, and Javan, and Tubal, and Meshech, and Tiras** [Gen. 10:2]; so too: **And the sons of Gomer: Ashkenaz, and Riphath, and Togarmah** [10:3]; instances are many. We should use this Figure when we have no need or time to speak at length, but when amplification might prove of advantage. Its effect may be called for in the Simple Style.

CHAPTER 67

Ocular Demonstration[1]

[1] Ocular Demonstration[a] is diction which sets the subject before our eyes by describing how matters stood before, during, and subsequent to its existence.

[2] Our example is the poem *Ha'ᵃzīnū* [Deut. 32:1–43], which in elegant language recounts all of Israel's history. Beginning with **of old . . . or ever the earth was** [Prov. 8:22–23], it continues with a narrative account of the history of each succeeding generation down to the very end of the Exile, whereupon it says: **Sing loud, O ye nations, the praises of His people; for He will avenge the blood of His servants,** etc. [Deut. 32:43].[2] So too, the Song of Deborah sets vividly before our eyes the war with Sisera, from beginning to end, where we read: **So perish all Thine enemies, O Lord; but they that love Him be as the sun when he goeth forth in his might** [Judg. 5:31]. The pericope, **Cause Jerusalem to know her abominations,** written in Ezekiel [16:2 ff.], proceeds in the same way; it narrates Israel's history from the nation's origins, and proceeds to tell of their ways and of their **transgressions, even all their sins** [Lev. 16:21]

1. Literally: "the sufficient, adequate": הַמַּסְפִּיק.

a. *R. ad H.* 4.54.68.

1. Literally: "before the eye": נֶגֶד הָעַיִן.
2. JV: "doth avenge." Messer Leon apparently regarded these words as a prophecy of the messianic age to come.

a. *R. ad H.* 4.55.68 ff.

מזוקקות.

[3] ויבוקש ענינו בנשא, בשפל, ובבינוני.

[4] ואל תתמה על קצת השמות אשר לפי הנראה הם ענין אחד, כמו "הדמות", "דמות", "דמיון", וזולתם· כי הוקשה מאד לקרא כל יפוי בשמו המיוחד לו; והנה טוליאו מחזיר השם בעצמו פעמיים, למה שבזה מן הקושי:

פרק ס"ח

פ׳ הצעה.

[1] ויען היו הנביאים בקיאי ההלצה, כמו שהתפרסם מענינם שאין ערוך אליהם במליצי האמות, התחייב שכל דבריהם יהיו אמרות טהורות, מזוקקות. והתחייב שאין בדבריהם זרות כלל; והדבר ההוא אשר יקרא זר אצל המדקדק הוא, אצל המליץ לענין, נאות לפי הענין ותמים ההספקה לשומעים. ולכן, כאשר התבוננתי בספרי הקדש, מצאתי בהם יפויים זולת הנזכרים, ואולי הם מיוחדים בלשוננו; והבאתי מהם קצת בזה המקום, אשר הכונה בו לדבר בענינם:

פרק ס"ט

פ׳ הנוסף.

[1] הנוסף הוא מאמ׳ יבא בו אות, תיבה, או מאמר נוסף, במקום לא יצטרך אל ההרחבה.

2 [בנשא][ד] || 4 דמות דמיון] דמיון דמות[כ] || 5 פעמיים] פעמים[כ] || 6 פרק] פ׳[כ] || 7 פ׳ הצעה] פרק ההצעה[ד] || 13 בזה <הלשון בזה>[כ] || 15 פרק] פ׳ || 16 פ׳] פרק[ד] || 17 יצטרך] נצטרך[כ] ||

---

9 תה׳ י"ב ז׳ ||

down to the time of Ezekiel—all this with a **tongue that speaketh great**[3] **things** [Ps. 12:4] and **words . . . refined** [12:7].

[3] The effect of Ocular Demonstration may be called for in the Grand, Simple, and Middle Styles.

[4] Let not the fact surprise you that a few of our terms, such as *hiddāmūth* [''resemblance,'' ''comparison,'' ''likeness''], *d^e mūth* [''likeness,'' ''image''; ''example''; ''shape''], *dimyōn* [''imagination''; ''likeness''; ''example,'' ''analogy''; ''appearance,'' ''form,'' ''figure,'' ''shape''], and others, seem apparently to have the same meaning. This is because it has proved very difficult to give each Figure a name special to it alone. Indeed, the difficulty involved is such that Tully himself uses the self-same term twice over.[4]

CHAPTER 68

An Advance Outline

[1] Now since the prophets were highly skilled in rhetoric—as by common consent they are held to be without peer among the orators of the Nations—it follows that all their utterances are **pure words . . . refined** [Ps. 12:7]. It also follows that there is no anomaly at all in their words; a construction that may be called anomalous by the grammarian may, to the orator developing a subject, prove appropriate to his theme and completely convincing to his hearers. Accordingly, therefore, as I have studied the Holy Books, I have found in them still other Figures than those thus far mentioned, Figures which perhaps are special to our language alone. And I have introduced some of them in this place, which is devoted to my treatment of the Figures.

CHAPTER 69

Pleonasm[1]

[1] Pleonasm is diction in which an extra (1) letter, (2) word, (or 3) phrase, is introduced at a point where such amplification is not essential.

3. JV: ''proud.''

4. E.g., *contentio* (antithesis) and *similitudo* (comparison) are each used in at least two senses in *R. ad H.;* see the index to Professor Caplan's edition, s.v.

1. הַנּוֹסָף.

[2] משל הראשון: אלה בני צבעון: ואיה וענה [בר׳ ל״ו כ״ד]; עוד בישעיה: לבזה נפש, למתעב גוי, לעבד מושלים· מלכים יראו וקמו, שרים וישתחוו [יש׳ מ״ט ז׳]; הוי״ו בהם לזולת ענין שמושי. וכן, בסוף התיבה: היושבי בשמים [תה׳ קכ״ג א׳]· חוצבי מרום קברו [יש׳ כ״ב ט״ז].

[3] משל השני: שם פחדו פחד [תה׳ י״ד ה׳]; וכן, ביחזקאל: כי עשק עושק· גזל גזל אח [יח׳ י״ח י״ח]; בשניהם, השם אחר הפעל נוסף יחשב.

[4] משל השלישי: יחי ראובן, ואל ימות [דב׳ ל״ג ו׳]; וכן, ביחזקאל: ויראה וישב[1] מכל פשעיו אשר עשה· חיה יחיה, לא ימות [יח׳ י״ח כ״ח]; מעט מזער, לא כביר [יש׳ ט״ז י״ד].

[5] ואמ׳ הפילוסוף שהאריכות, ואם הוא ממה שתקשה בו הבנת הענין, יקובל בו תועלת בהלצה אצל מה שיכוון ההלציי הרבות המאמר:

פרק ע׳

פ׳ החסר.

[1] החסר הוא מאמר יחסר בו אות, תיבה, או מאמר[1].

[2] משל הראשון; הנמצא בית י״י [מל״ב י״ח ט״ו]· כמו ״בבית י״י״; שני... שרי

1 אלה] ואלה[ת] || 5 [כי][כ] || 7 השלישי] הד׳[ר] || 8 וישב[1]] ויעש[כר] |חיה] חיו[ת] || 12 פרק] פ׳[כ] || 13 פ׳] פרק[ר] || 14 מאמר[1] ‹וקרא הפילוסוף בג׳ מההלצה זה המאמר בלתי נקשר ואמ׳ שהוא ב׳ מינים מין העדר אותיות הקשרים ומין העדר הממוצעים אשר בין חלקי המאמ׳› משל...[ר] || 15 שני] ושני[ת] ||

---

[1] Corrected according to ת *(qᵉrē)*.

[1] [Chapt. 70]. Here follows in ד sentence found in כ at par. 5 below.

[2] Examples of the first, Pleonasm by letter: **And these are the children of Zibeon: Aiah**[2] **and Anah** [Gen. 36:24]; further, in Isaiah: **To him who is despised of men, to him who is abhorred of nations, to a servant of rulers: kings shall see and arise, princes, and shall prostrate themselves**[3] [49:7]. The *wāw* [''and''] in these verses is without functional purpose. Likewise at the end of the word: the *yōdhs* at the end of *hayyōsh^e bhī* [''O Dweller''] in **O Thou that dwellest in the heavens** [Ps. 123:1],[4] and at the end of *ḥōṣ^e bhī* [''hewer''] in **thou that hewest thee out a sepulchre on high** [Isa. 22:16].

[3] Examples of the second, Pleonasm by word: **There do they fear a fear** [Ps. 14:5];[5] and similarly, in Ezekiel: **because he oppressed an oppressing, robbed a robbing of brother** [18:18].[6] In both, the noun following the verb may be considered pleonastic.

[4] Examples of the third, Pleonasm by phrase: **Let Reuben live, and not die** [Deut. 33:6]; and similarly, in Ezekiel: **Because he considereth, and turneth away from all his transgressions that he hath committed, he shall surely live, he shall not die** [Ezek. 18:28]; . . . **very small, not large** [Isa. 16:14].[7]

[5] The Philosopher[a] said that prolixity, though it may constitute an impediment to comprehension, is a means of rhetorical advantage when it is the orator's aim to expatiate.

CHAPTER 70

Ellipsis[1]

[1] Ellipsis is a Figure of Diction by which (1) a letter, (2) a word or (3) a phrase is omitted.[2]

[2] Examples of the first, an omitted letter: . . . *hannimṣāh bēth-'^{a}dhōnay* (**. . . that was found in the house of the Lord**) [2 Kings 18:15], where *bēth*

2. Literally: ''**and**-Aiah'' = וְאַיָּה.
3. The pleonasm: ''*and* shall prostrate,'' since ''shall prostrate'' would have sufficed; JV: ''princes, and they shall,'' etc.
4. KJV.
5. JV: ''There are they in great fear.''
6. JV: ''. . . because he cruelly oppressed, committed robbery on his brother.''
7. JV: ''. . . very small and without strength.''

a. T197/A277; cf. *Rhet*. 3.12.6 (1414a).

1. Literally: ''the needy, lacking, wanting, deficient''; ''defective (gram.)'': הֶחָסֵר.
2. Here, in C, appears the sentence of the next-to-last paragraph of this chapter, where, according to M, the sentence was originally placed.

גדודים היו בן שאול [שמ״ב ד׳ ב׳]· כמו ״לבן שאול״.

[3] משל השני: ויאמר ליוסף [בר׳ מ״ח א׳]· אם יחרוש בבקרים [עמ׳ ו׳ י״ב]; בא׳, תחסר התבה המורה על הפועל· ובשני, תחסר התבה המורה על הפועל, ועל הנפעל.

[4] משל השלשי: אל חכך שופר· כנשר על בית י״י [הו׳ ח׳ א׳]; המכוון בזה המאמ׳, שיתקע בשופר, כי האויב יבא מהר, כנשר, אל בית י״י· והנה יחסר כל זה ״כי האויב יבא מהר״. וכן, במיכה: איך ימוש לי· לשובב שדנו, יחלק [מי׳ ב׳ ד׳]; ר״ל, כאשר אנו חושבים שי״י ירצה לשובב שדינו, אז יחלק אותו בין האויבים· והנה חסר זה המאמ׳, ״כאשר אנו חושבים שי״י ירצה״, כו׳.

[5] וקרא הפילוסוף, בג׳ מההלצה, זה המאמ׳ בלתי נקשר, ואמר שהוא ב׳ מינים: מין העדר אותיות הקשׁרים, ומין העדר הממוצעים אשר בין חלקי המאמ׳.

[6] ויבוקש ענינו בבינוני ובשפל:

פרק ע״א

פ׳ המקיף.

[1] המקיף הוא מאמר בו תיבה כוללת ומקפת תיבות רבות, כמו: לא תלבש

3 בא׳] הראשון[כ] | התבה] תיבה || 5 השלשי] הג׳[ד] | [אל][ד] || 6 המאמ׳] המ[ד] || 7 ימוש] ימיש[ת] || 8 לשובב] למובב[כ] || 9 שי״י] שה׳[כ] || 10–12 [וקרא...המאמ׳][ד] (see note 1) || 13 ויבוקש] ויבקש[כ] | ענינו] עניני אלה[כ] | ובשפל] ושפל[כ] || 14 פרק] פ׳[כ] || 15 פ׳] פרק[ד] ||

[''house-of''] is the equivalent of *b^e bhēth* [''in the house of'']; *sh^e nē-sārē-gh^e dhūdhīm hāyū bhen-shā'ūl* **(Saul's son had two . . . captains of bands)** [2 Sam. 4:2], where *hāyū bhen-shā'ūl* [''were the son of Saul''] is the equivalent of *hāyū l^e bhen-shā'ūl* [''were to-the-son-of Saul''].

[3] Examples of the second, an omitted word: **And it came to pass after these things, that one[3] said to Joseph** [Gen. 48:1]; **Doth one[3] plow it[3] with oxen?** [Amos 6:12].[4] In the first of these passages, the word indicative of the subject of ''said'' is lacking, in the second, both that indicative of the subject and that indicative of the object of the verb.

[4] Example of the third, an omitted phrase: **The horn to thy mouth! As a vulture against the house of the Lord!** [Hos. 8:1];[5] this statement means that the horn should be blown because the enemy is coming speedily, like a vulture, to the house of the Lord; yet the entire phrase, ''because the enemy is coming speedily,'' is lacking. So too, in Micah: **How doth He remove it from me! Instead of restoring[6] our field, He divideth it** [Mic. 2:4); in other words: Just when we think that the Lord has graciously consented to restore our field, He divides it amongst the enemy; yet this clause, ''just when we think that the Lord has graciously consented,'' is lacking.

[5] In Book III of the *Rhetoric,* the Philosopher[a] called this figure Asyndeton, and said that it is of two kinds: one in which conjunctive particles are lacking, and the other in which no words are interposed between the several parts of the sentence.[7]

[6] This Figure's effect may be called for in the Middle and Simple Styles.

CHAPTER 71

The Inclusive Term[1]

[1] The Figure is the Inclusive Term when several words are included in, and brought together by, some one word; for example: **Thou shalt not wear** *sha'aṭ-*

3. Word absent in the Hebrew.
4. The text of this passage has long been held to contain an error of word division. It is now generally translated: ''Does one plow the sea with oxen?''
5. JV: ''Set the horn to thy mouth. As a vulture he cometh against the house of the Lord.''
6. Literally: ''to restore,'' or ''for the restoring of.''
7. Sentence transposed in C to the beginning of this chapter.

a. T197/A278; cf. *Rhet.* 3.11 (1413 b).

1. Literally: ''that which surrounds, encompasses, encloses; brings *or* knocks together'': הַמַּקִּיף.

שעטנו [דב׳ כ״ב י״א], ר״ל, ״שוע״, ״טווי״, ו״נוז״. וכן: לאסורים פקחקוח [יש׳ ס״א א׳]· המכוון בו פתיחת המאסר, כי הרצון ב״קוח״ ״מאסר״, למה שנלקחים שמה האנשים.

[2] ויבוקש ענינו בבינוני, ובשפל יותר:

פרק ע״ב

פ׳ המוקדם.

[1] המוקדם הוא מאמ׳ בו דבר היה אחר כמה שנים; כמו שנאמר במלכים: ״...הנה בן נולד לבית דוד, יושיהו שמו, וזבח עליך את כהני הבמות״, כו׳ [מל״א י״ג ב׳]. וכן: אל עין משפט, היא קדש, ויכו את כל שדה העמלקי [בר׳ י״ד ז׳]· ועדיין לא היה ״עמלק״. וכן: וירק את חניכיו, ילידי ביתו, שמנה עשר ושלש מאות, וירדוף עד דן [שם שם י״ד]· ו״דן״ לא נולד עדיין.

[2] ויבוקש ענינו בשפל:

1 ונוז] נוז[ד] |פקחקוח] פקח־קוח[ת] ||5 פרק] פ׳[כ] ||6 פ׳] פרק[ד] ||7 שנאמר במלכים] שנ׳ במלאׄכים[כ] ||
8 לבית] לבן[ד] |יושיהו] יאשיהו[ת] ||

nēz [''mingled stuff''] [Deut. 22:11]; included in this term are ''hackled'' (*shūʿa*), ''spun'' (*ṭāwūy*), and ''woven'' (*nūz*).[2] Similarly: **. . . and the opening of the prison to them that are bound** [Isa. 61:1];[3] *pᵉqaḥ-qōaḥ* included both ''the opening'' (*pᵉqaḥ*) and ''the prison'' (*qōaḥ*); the sense of *qōaḥ* [from *lāqaḥ* ''to take''] is ''prison,'' since it is thither that the men in bonds are taken (*nilqāḥīm*).

[2] This Figure's effect will be called for mainly in the Middle and Simple Styles.

CHAPTER 72

Anticipation[1]

[1] Anticipation is diction in which allusion is made to a phenomenon that was to come into being only some years later. An example is the statement in Kings: **"O altar, altar[2] . . . Behold, a son shall be born unto the house of David, Josiah by name; and upon thee shall he sacrifice the priests of the high places,"** [1 Kings 13:2]. Similarly: **And they turned back, and came to En-Mishpat—the same is Kadesh—and smote all the country of the Amalekites** [Gen. 14:7]; as yet, however, Amalek did not exist. Again: **And Abram . . . led forth his trained men, born in his house, three hundred and eighteen, and pursued as far as Dan** [14:14]; Dan, however, had not yet even been born.[3]

[2] This Figure's effect may be called for in the Simple Style.

2. JML's source for this haggadic interpretation of שַׁעַטְנֵז, as שׁוּעַ (hackled: the שׁ and ע of the word), טָווּי (spun; the ט of the word) and נוּז (woven: the נ and ז of the word), is *Mishnah Kilayim*, 9:8.
3. KJV.

1. Literally: ''that which is set before (in time), anticipated, made to be beforehand''; ''former, early'': הַמּוּקְדָּם.
2. The apostrophization is not cited by JML.
3. As Dan had not yet been born, mention of the territory later named after him is an anachronism tolerable only by virtue of this Figure.

פרק ע״ג

פ׳ המגזם.

[1] המגזם הוא מאמר נאמרו בו דברים אשר פשטיהם הם זולת מה שכוון בהם האומר; כמו: שמח, בחור, בילדותך [קה׳ י״א ט׳]· שהוא צווי דרך גזום, לא שהכונה מן האומר תהיה שהוא נכון לעשות כן, כמו שמעיד על זה סוף הפסוק, שאמ׳: ודע כי על כל אלה יביאך, כו׳ [שם שם]. וכן: עמדי נא בחבריך, וברוב כשפיך, כאשר יגעת מנעוריך, כו׳ [יש׳ מ״ז י״ב].

[2] ויבוקש ענינו בנשא, בינוני, ושפל:

פרק ע״ד

פ׳ המקביל.

[1] המקביל הוא מאמר בו תיבה תורה על הפך מה שהונחה להורות, כמו: כי אשה כושית לקח [במ׳ י״ב א׳]; תיבת ״כושית״ תורה על היופי, כמו שאומר התרגום. וכן: על דברי כוש בן ימיני [תה׳ ז׳ א׳] ״כוש,״ ר״ל ״יפה״, כי זה המזמור נאמ׳ על שאול, שהיה איש יפה: משכמו ומעלה גבוה מכל העם [שמ״א ט׳ ב׳]. וכן תיבת... חסד הוא [וי׳ כ׳ י״ז]· כי תיבת ״חסד״ תורה על היושר אשר בתכלית, ותורה הנה על דבר שהוא בתכלית מה שאפשר מהבלתי נאות.

[2] ויבוקש ענינו בשפל, ולפעמים בבינוני:

1 פרק] פ׳[כ] ‖ 2 פ׳] פרק[ד] ‖ 3 נאמרו] נאות[ד] | פשטיהם] בעניניהם[ד] ‖ 4 גזום] ג׳יים[כ] ‖ 6 [יביאך][ד] | [כו׳] וכו׳[כ] ‖ 7 כאשר] באשר[ת] | מנעוריך] מנעורך[כ] ‖ 9 פרק] פ׳[כ] ‖ 10 פ׳] פרק[ד] ‖ 11 שהונחה] שהוכחה[כ] ‖ 12 תיבת] תבה[ד] | היופי] היפוי[ד] ‖ 14 [איש][כ] ‖

CHAPTER 73

Irony[1]

[1] Irony is diction in which there are words whose ordinary sense is quite different from what the sayer really means; for example: **Rejoice, O young man, in thy youth** [Eccl. 11:9]. The imperative here is ironic; that the sayer's intention is not at all to urge that it is proper to act thus is attested by the end of the verse, where he says: **But know thou, that for all these things God will bring thee into judgment** [11:9]. Similarly: **Stand now with thine enchantments, and with the multitude of thy sorceries, even as[2] thou hast laboured from thy youth,** etc. [Isa. 47:12].

[2] This Figure's effect may be called for in the Grand, Middle, and Simple Styles.

CHAPTER 74

Inversion[1]

[1] Inversion is diction in which there is a word that connotes some contrary of what it is supposed to connote, as follows: . . . **for he had married a Cushite woman** [Num. 12:1]. Here, as the Targum says, the word ''Cushite'' connotes beauty. So also: . . . **concerning Cush, a Benjamite** [Ps. 7:1]; ''Cush'' here means ''handsome,'' for this Psalm treats of Saul, who was a handsome man: **from his shoulders and upward he was higher than any of the people** [1 Sam. 9:2]. Again, the word *ḥesedh* as used in . . . **it is a shameful thing** (ḥesedh) [Lev. 20:17]; for *ḥesedh,* which connotes the highest degree of uprightness, here signifies something at the lowest possible depth of unseemliness.

[2] This Figure's effect is called for in the Simple Style, and occasionally also in the Middle.

1. Literally: ''that which overstates, exaggerates'': הַמְגַזֵּם.
2. *Sic,* B: ''wherein.''

1. Literally: ''the opposite,'' ''parallel'': הַמַּקְבִּיל.

פרק ע״ה

פ׳ המסתיר

[1] המסתיר הוא מאמ׳ נאמר בו דבר רע בלשון נקיה· או שתאמ׳, תחת התיבה המגבלת, הבלתי מוגבלת, אפי׳ לא תהיה הכונה להסתיר הרע.

[2] כמו: ומן הבהמה אשר לא טהורה היא [בר׳ ז׳ ב׳]; ״אל בני, כי לא טובה השמועה״ [שמ״א ב׳ כ״ד]; יתיצבו בדרך לא טוב [תה׳ ל״ו ה׳]; ויאמר חותן משה אליו: ״לא טוב הדבר אשר אתה עושה לעם״ [שמ׳ י״ח י״ז].

[3] משל השני: וחרב לא אדם תאכלנו [יש׳ ל״א ח׳]; ולהכרית גוים לא מעט [שם י׳ ז׳]; הן קנאוני בלא אל [דב׳ ל״ב כ״א]; והנוהג מנהגם.

[4] ואמר הפילוסוף, בשלישי מההלצה, שהמלות המוסרות, והשמות בלתי נשלמים, והדבור בלתי שלם, ובכלל, השלילות כולן, והמלות המורות על ההעדר, הנה אמנם ראוי שיעשו ברוב אצל רמיזת ההכלמה, ואצל רצון העלמת הדבר והסתרתו; והם שיריים יותר מאשר הם הלציים.

[5] ויבוקש ענינו בבינוני:

פרק ע״ו

פ׳ הזרות.

[1] הזרות הוא מאמ׳ תבא בו תבה או תבות זרות לפי הדקדוק, לעורר על זרות הענין, להגדילו, ולרוממו, כמו שהתבאר מהפילוסוף בג׳ מההלצה.

1 פרק] פ׳[כ] || 2 פ׳] פרק[ר] || 5 לא] איננה[ר] || 6 יתיצבו בדרך] יתיצב על־דרך[ת] || 7 עושה לעם] כו׳[ר] [לעם][ת] || 8 השני] הב׳[ר] || 9 הן] הם[ת] || 10 בשלישי] בג׳[כ] || 11 שלם] נשלם[ט] | כולן] כלם[ר] || 12 ההכלמה] ההעלמה[ר] | ואצל <רמיזת>[כ] || 15 פרק] פ׳[כ] || 16 פ׳] פרק[ר] || 17 [תבה או][כ] || 18 [בג׳ מההלצה][ר] ||

CHAPTER 75

Euphemism[1]

[1] Euphemism is diction in which (1) an ugly term is expressed in chaste language, or in which (2) instead of the precise word, an indefinite expression will be used even though there is no intention to conceal the ugliness.

[2] Examples of (1): **and of the beasts that are not clean** [Gen. 7:2];[2] **"Nay, my sons, for it is no good report"** [1 Sam. 2:24];[3] **They set themselves in a way that is not good** [Ps. 36:5];[4] **And Moses' father-in-law said unto him: "The thing that thou doest to the people is not good"** [Exod. 18:17].[5]

[3] Examples of the second: **And the sword, not of men, shall devour him** [Isa. 31:8];[6] **and to cut off nations not a few** [Isa. 10:7]; **They have roused Me to jealousy with a no-god** [Deut. 32:21]; and similarly indefinite expressions.

[4] In Book III of the *Rhetoric,* the Philosopher[a] said that isolated expressions, parenthetical substantives, discontinued phrases, and, in general, all negative epithets and words indicative of privation, should for the most part be used only when we are hinting at the imputation of shame, and when we intimate that we would like to suppress thc matter and keep it secret. Such stylistic devices appertain more to poetry than to rhetoric.

[5] This Figure's effect may be called for in the Middle Style.

CHAPTER 76

Strange Usage[1]

[1] Strange Usage is diction in which one or more grammatically irregular words are introduced in order to call attention to, enhance, and heighten the

1. Literally: "that which hides, conceals, keeps secret": הַמַּסְתִּיר.
2. Chaste expression, because "that are not clean" is said rather than "that defile."
3. "No good," rather than "evil."
4. JV: "He setteth himself," etc.; cf. Prov. 16:29.
5. B omits ". . . to the people."
6. Identified by Qimḥi as the plague.

a. T197f./A278f.; cf. *Rhet.* 3.6 (1408a).

1. Literally: "anomaly," "irregular form or usage (gram.)," "strangeness," "abnormality," "exception (to a rule)": הַזָּרוּת.

[2] והמשל, ביחזקאל: ויהי בהכותם ונאשאר אני [יח׳ ט׳ ח׳]· והמה משתחויתם קדמה ׳לשמש [שם שם ח׳ ט״ז]; ויז נצחם על בגדי, וכל מלבושי אגאלתי [יש׳ ס״ג ג׳]. והנה, לקחנו אלה התבות הנה על סברת מי שיראה שאין בהם הרכבה, כאשר בארתי בלבנת הספיר.

[3] והנה התבאר, שענין שראה יחזקאל מההריגה העצומה עם הצלתו היה בתכלית הזרות, וכן ענין השתחואת האנשים ההם. אמנם ״אגאלתי״ בא לרומם הענין ולהגדילו· אשר לא היה נעשה אם ידבר בלשון המורגל. והנה הזרות יחקה הענינים הזרים, והרוממות הענינים הנשאים; ובכלל, כל ענין ועניין ראוי שיאמר בלשון תיוחס אליו.

[4] ויבוקש ענינו בנשא ובבינוני:

פרק ע״ז

פ׳ ההרכבה.

[1] ההרכבה היא מאמר תעמוד בו תיבה אחת במקום תבות; וזה נמצא בלשוננו הרבה, ואם הם בלתי נמצאות בלשון הערב כי אם על המעט; והם ממלות ההלציות, כאשר התבאר בהג׳ מההלצה.

[2] והמשל: ירדוף אויב נפשי [תה׳ ז׳ ו׳]· שהוא במקום ״ירדוף״, שהוא מן הקל, ו״ירדף״, שהוא מן פעל הדגוש; המכוון במאמ׳, ש״האויב״ מכוון בו היה רודפו ומרדפו לאחרים.

1 בהכותם] כהכותם[ת] |ונאשאר] ונשאר[כ] |אני] אש[כ] || 2 משתחויתם] משתחוים[כ] || 6 אגאלתי] אגלתי[ר] || 7 [בלשון][כ] |המורגל] המרגל[כ] || 8 [ועניין][ר] || 9 תיוחס] תיחס[כ] || 11 פרק] פ׳[כ] || 12 פ׳] פרק[ר] || 14 הם] הוא[ר] |נמצאות] נמצא[ר] || 15 בהג׳] מהג׳[ר] || 17 [מכוון בו][ר] || 18 רודפו <הוא בעצמו>[ר] ||

strangeness of the subject matter, as was explained by the Philosopher[a] in Book III of the *Rhetoric*.

[2] For example, in Ezekiel: **And it came to pass, while they were smiting, and** I WAS LEFT (wᵉnēshᵃ'ar)[2] [Ezek. 9:8]; **. . . and they** WORSHIPPED **the sun toward the east** (mishtaḥᵃwīthem)[2] [8:16]; and: **. . . and their lifeblood is dashed against My garments, and** I HAVE STAINED **all My raiment** ('egh'altī)[2] [Isa. 63:3]. We have here construed these words in accordance with the theory of those who hold that they do not contain a combination of regular forms, as I have explained in *Libhᵉnath Hassappīr*.[3]

[3] Now Ezekiel's vision of a tremendous massacre and of his own simultaneous deliverance was obviously extremely strange, and strange also was the matter of the sun-worship of those men [8:16]. As for the irregular *'egh'altī* [Isa. 63:3], it is introduced to elevate and enhance the theme of the verse—an effect that would not have been achieved if the prophet had spoken in ordinary and familiar language. The strangeness of Strange Usage, therefore, imitates strange subjects, the loftiness grand themes. In general, every subject should be expressed in language apposite to it.

[4] This Figure's effect may be called for in the Grand and Middle Styles.

CHAPTER 77

The Composite Word[1]

[1] The Composite Word is diction in which a single word stands in the place of several words. This Figure is frequently found in our language, although compounded words are only rarely found in Arabic; and words of this kind appertain to rhetoric, as explained in Book III of the *Rhetoric*.[a]

[2] For example: **Let the enemy pursue** (*yiraddōph*) **my soul** [Ps. 7:6]; *yiraddōph* here represents both the *qal*-form *yirdōph* ["pursue"] and the double middle radical *pi'el*-form *yᵉraddēph* ["cause to pursue"]; and the Figure's

2. "Grammatically anomalous" form.
3. JML's Hebrew grammar; see i.11.6 (n. 6).

a. T181; 185/A253; 256; cf. *Rhet*. 3.7 (1408b).

1. Literally: "the combining, compounding"; "composite," "compound," "composition": הַהַרְכָּבָה.

a. T190–1/A269; cf. *Rhet*. 3.2 and 3.3 (1404b and 1405a).

[3] וכן: מבליגיתי עלי יגון [יר׳ ח׳ י״ח] מרכב מ״מבליג״ ו״מבלגת״, כמו שבארנו בלבנת הספיר.

[4] וכן: ...כל היום שמי מנואץ [יש׳ נ״ב ה׳], מרכב מן פועל והתפעל· כלומר, שי״י היה מסבב שיהיה שמו נאוץ[1] בגוים בעד חטאות ישראל.

5 [5] ויבוקש ענינו בנשא ובבינוני.

פרק ע״ח

פ׳ הקודם.

[1] הקודם הוא מאמר אשר בו הכנוי טרם הידיעה, כמו: ותפתח ותראהו, את הילד [שמ׳ ב׳ ו׳]; אשר לא יעבדו אותו, את נבוכדנצר [יר׳ כ״ז ח׳]; וזולתם רבים.

10 [2] ויבוקש ענינו בשפל יותר:

פרק ע״ט

פ׳ ההגדלה.

[1] ההגדלה היא כאשר תבא בתיבה יחידה אות מורה על ההגדלה. והמשל:

3...כל היום] תמיד היום[ד] ותמיד כל היום[ת] || 4 שי״י] שה׳[כ] | נאוץ[1]] נואץ[כד] || 5 ובבינוני <נשלם הפרק>[ד] || 6 פרק] פ׳[כ] || 7 פ׳] פרק[ד] || 9 [אותו][ד] | נבוכדנצר] נבוכ׳ נצר[ד] נבוכדנאצר[ת] || 11 פרק] פ׳[כ] || 12 פ׳] פרק[ד] ||

[1] Corrected text.

purpose is that "the enemy" be understood to mean one who was both the pursuer of the speaker and the inducer of others to pursue him.

[3] Similarly: **Though man and woman would cheer me against sorrow** (mabhlīghīthī) [Jer. 8:18];[2] *mabhlīghīthī,* as we have explained in *Libh*ᵉ*nath Hassappīr,* is a composite of *mabhlīgh* ["one who cheers": *hiph'il* masculine participle] and *mabhlegheth* ["one who cheers": *hiph'il* feminine participle].

[4] Again: **And My name continually all the day is caused to be blasphemed** (minnō'āṣ) [Isa. 52:5]; *minnō'āṣ* is a composite of a *pu'al-* and of a *hithpa'el-*form; through Israel's sins, in other words, it was being brought about that the Lord's Name would be blasphemed among the nations.[3]

[5] This Figure's effect may be called for in the Grand and Middle Styles.[4]

CHAPTER 78

Prolepsis[1]

[1] Prolepsis is diction in which a pronoun anticipates the noun which identifies it, as follows: **And she opened . . . and saw it, even the child** [Exod. 2:6]; **. . . which will not serve him, namely Nebuchadnezzar** [Jer. 27:8];[2] and there are many other examples. The Figure's effect will be called for mainly in the Simple Style.

CHAPTER 79

Augmentation[1]

[1] The Figure is Augmentation when a letter indicating emphasis appears in a word otherwise complete in itself. Examples: **There is no** SALVATION **for him**

2. Translated to accord with what I think JML regards as the meaning of his "composite."
3. JV: "is blasphemed."
4. C here adds: "End of chapter."

1. Literally: "the preceding," "coming before": הַקּוֹדֵם; cf. iv.72.
2. KJV and JV: ". . . which will not serve the same Nebuchadnezzar"; cf. ii.13.27 (n. 13).

1. Literally: "enlargement," "enlarging," "magnification"; "exaggeration": הַהַגְדָּלָה. In the definition, I have translated it as "emphasis."

אין ישועתה לו באלקי׳ סלה [תה׳ ג׳ ג׳]; ולך לישועתה לנו [שם פ׳ ג׳]; אל י״י בצרתה לי [שם ק״כ א׳]; תבאתה לראש יוסף [דב׳ ל״ג ט״ז].

[2] ויבוקש ענינו בשפל, ולפעמי׳ בבינוני.

פרק פ׳

פ׳ הנשנה.

[1] הנשנה הוא מאמ׳ יבא בו הכפל הכנוי, או הכפל מלות הטעם, המורות על ענין אחד, כמו: ושתלתי אני [יח׳ י״ז כ״ב]; אמרתי אני[1] בלבי [קה׳ ב׳ א׳]; המבלי אין קברים [שמ׳ י״ד י״א]; הרק אך במשה [במ׳ י״ב ב׳]; והנוהג מנהגם.

[2] ויבוקש ענינו בנשא, ובשפל ובינוני:

פרק פ״א

פ׳ ההתעוררות.

[1] ההתעוררות הוא מאמר תבא בו אזהרה על העלם הדבר בדברים הנודעים לעורר העצבון, כמו: אל תגידו בגת, אל תבשרו בחצות אשקלון, פן תשמחנה בנות פלשתים [שמ״ב א׳ כ׳]; וכן, במיכה: בגת אל תגידו, בכה אל תבכו [מי׳ א׳ י׳].

[2] וזה היפוי הוא נפלא לעורר העצבון והקינה הנסמך בו; ויבוקש ענינו בנשא ובבינוני:

1 ולך] ולכה[ת] | י״י] ה׳[ל] || 2 תבאתה] תבואתה[ת] || 3 [בשפל ולפעמי׳][ר] || 4 פרק] פ׳[ל] || 5 פ׳] פרק[ר] || 7 [אמרתי אני בלבי][ר] [אני[1]][ל] || 8 והנוהג מנהגם] וזולתם[ר] || 10 פרק] פ׳[ל] || 11 פ׳ ההתעוררות] מהההתעוררות[ר] || 13 אל תבשרו] ואל תבשרו[ר] || 13–14 פן תשמחנה בנות פלשתים] כו׳[ר] || 14–15 בכה אל תבכו] כו׳[ר] בכה] בכו[ת] || 16 והקינה] והקצה[ל] | [הנסמך בו][ר] ||

[1] Corrected according to ת.

in God. Selah (yeshū'āh/yeshū'āthāh) [Ps. 3:3]; **. . . and come for our** SALVATION (yeshū'āh/yeshū'āthāh) [Ps. 80:3];[2] **In my** DISTRESS **I called unto the Lord** (ṣārāh/ṣārāthāh) [Ps. 120:1]; LET **the blessing** COME **upon the head of Joseph** (tābhō/tābhōthāh) [Deut. 33:16].

[2] The Figure's effects may be called for in the Simple Style, and occasionally in the Middle.

CHAPTER 80

Duplication[1]

[1] Duplication is diction containing two pronouns, or two particles, which have a single meaning, as follows: **I will take, I** [Ezek. 17:22];[2] **I, I said in my heart** [Eccl. 2:1];[3] **Because without—there were no—graves** [Exod. 14:11];[3] **Is it only but by Moses that the Lord hath spoken?** [Num. 12:2];[3] and the like.

[2] This effect may be called for in the Grand, Simple, and Middle Styles.

CHAPTER 81

Arousal[1]

[1] Arousal is diction containing an admonition to keep covert some known fact, so as to arouse sorrow, as follows: **Tell it not in Gath, publish it not in the streets of Ashkelon, lest the daughters of the Philistines rejoice** [2 Sam. 1:20]; similarly, in Micah: **Tell it not in Gath, weep not at all** [Mic. 1:10].

[2] This Figure is marvellously effective in stimulating grief and its attendant lamentation; the effect may be called for in the Grand and Middle Styles.

2. JV: ". . . and come to save us."

1. Literally: "the repeated, done again": הַנִּשְׁנֶה.
2. JV: "I will take, even I."
3. Translated thus in order to exhibit JML's meaning.

1. Literally: "the awakening," "waking," "stirring": הַהִתְעוֹרְרוּת.

פרק פ״ב

פ׳ הנסמך.

[1] הנסמך הוא מאמר כאשר[1] הסמוך והנסמך אליו מורים על ענין אחד, כמו: אדמת עפר [דנ׳ י״ב ב׳]; טיט היון [תה׳ מ׳ ג׳]; וזולתם רבים. ויבוקש ענינו בשפל 5 יותר.

[2] וימצאו בלשוננו יפויים זולת אלה שהבאנו· והספקתי על מה שאמרתי בזה, כי לא יקשה, עם מה שהעירותי הנה, לעמוד עליהם. ובכלל, כל הנמצא בכת׳ מדברי הנבואה והמדברים ברוח הקדש, אין בהם נפתל ועקש, לא גמגום כבדות או זרות על דרך האמת. כי איך ידבר אדון הלשון ותפארתו בתבות 10 ומאמרים כבדים, בלתי מזוקקים? זה לא יפול ברשת הדמיון, כל שכ׳ שהשכל ראוי שירחיק אותו.

[3] אמנם, הסבה הכללית בכל מה שאמרנו למעלה מאלה היפויים: למען יעברו הלשון המורגל מההמון. כי בזה הענין, יהיו תמימי ההספקה ויעוררו הלבבות; כי לא יתפעל האדם מהדבר שהוא רגיל בו. ואמ׳ הפילוסוף, בג׳ 15 מההלצה, כי כמו זה יקרה לבני העיר, שיפלאו מהנכרים הבאים עליהם ויכניעו להם נפשותיהם, וככה הענין במלות הנכריות אצל באם לשמע אוזן:

פרק פ״ג

הדברים שצריך להתרחק מהם או להתקרב אליהם.

[1] אמר אריסטו׳, בג׳ מההלצה, שראוי למליץ שיעשה מהשנוי׳ מה שהוא 20 מתיחס ומתדמה לעניין אשר בו ההספקה, לא פחות ולא יתר· וזה לפי מה

1 פרק] פ׳ᶜ || 2 פ׳] פרקᵈ || 3 כאשר[1]] אשרᶜᵈ || 4 טיט] מטיטⁿ || 6 אלה] אלוᵈ || 7 עם] עלᶜ | שהעירותי] שהערכתיᶜ || 8 בכת׳] ככתו׳ᶜ || 10 כל שכ׳] כ״שᶜ | שהשכל] שהכלᶜ || 12 אמנם הסכה] והסבתᵈ | [למעלה]ᵈ || 13 ויעוררו] ויתעוררוᶜ || 14 בג׳] בשלישיᶜ || 17 פרק] פ׳ᶜ || 19 אריסטו׳] אריסטוטולוᶜ ||

8 מש׳ ח׳ ח׳ || 16 איוב מ״ב ה׳ ||

[1] Corrected text.

CHAPTER 82

The Construct[1]

[1] The Figure is the Construct when both the governing and governed words of a construct expression signify the same thing, like **earth-of-dust** [Dan. 12:2],[2] **mud-of-mire** [Ps. 40:3],[3] and many others. This Figure's effect will be called for mainly in the Simple Style.

[2] Other Figures than those we have cited exist in our language, but I have contented myself with what I have said in this Book, for with the observations offered here the Figures are not difficult to understand. In general, whatever is found in Scripture of words of prophecy[4] and of those speaking by means of the Holy Spirit[5] **there is nothing perverse or crooked in them** [Prov. 8:8], no truly awkward stammering or real irregularity. For how should the Lord of language and its beauty speak in words and phrases that are awkward or unrefined? Such an incongruity is past imagining, and reason must all the more reject it.

[3] All the Figures we have treated above have the same general *raison d'être:* to transcend the familiar, everyday speech used by the mass of men. Accomplishing this, the Figures will prove wholly convincing and will stir hearts and minds; for nobody is moved by utterance with which he is completely familiar. In Book III of the *Rhetoric* the Philosopher[a] has said that just as it can happen that the inhabitants of a city will marvel at, and submit themselves to, foreigners who come to them, a like result can be obtained by foreign words when they come to **the hearing of the ear** [Job 42:5].

CHAPTER 83

Expressions Which Should Be Avoided or Sought

[1] Aristotle,[a] in Book III of the *Rhetoric,* said that the speaker should develop the kind of metaphor that is compatible with, and resembles, the means used to

1. Literally: "the supported"; "in the 'construct state' (gram.)": הַנִּסְמָךְ.
2. Literally: "And many of sleepers of earth-of-dust . . ."; KJV and JV: "And many of them that sleep in the dust of the earth. . . ."
3. KJV and JV: "miry clay."
4. Pentateuch, Joshua—II Kings, Isaiah, Jeremiah, Ezekiel, and the Twelve.
5. The Hagiographa.

a. T185/A260–1; cf. *Rhet.* 3.2.3 (1404b).

a. T188ff./A265 ff.; cf. *Rhet.* 3.2.7 (1405a).

שיכוון ההגדלה והבזוי בערך אל דבר אחד. שאם נרצה להגדיל עני׳ הגנבה בתכלית מה שאפשר, נאמר בגנב שהוא ״נלחם״· ואם נרצה לבזותו, נאמר שהוא ״לקח״, או ״הונה את עמיתו״. והנה כלם שבים אל לקיחת הממון מבלי רצון חברו, אלא שהמלחמה מגדלת עניינה, והאונאה מפחיתה.

5 [2] ועם כל זה, אין ראוי שיצא מסוג המאמר, אלא יגנה אותו או ייפהו בדברים שהם תחת הסוג ההוא. והמשל עוד, כי הבקשה והתחנה הם תחת סוג אח׳, והוא השאלה; והתחנה פחותה מהבקשה, וזה, שהתחנה תהיה ממי שהוא למטה, והבקשה מן השוה. וכאשר רצינו ליפות התחנה ולהגדילה, נקראה ״בקשה״· וכאשר רצינו לגנות הבקשה, נקראה ״תחנה״.

10 [3] והנה השנויים הנאים והמשלי׳ הם מהעניינים שהם אחדים במין· כמו שידומה האדם באדם המתיחס לו, ר״ל, שנדמה היפה ״כיוסף״. ואם לא יהיו אחדים במין, הנה יהיו אחדים בסוג הקרוב, כמו שנדמה האשה הנעימה אל הצביה; ואם אי אפשר, יהיו אחדים בסוג הרחוק, כמו אמרנו באשה התמימה שהיא ״ברה כחמה״. ואם לא יעלו אל סוג אחד, ואם היה רחוק, הנה הוא פחות.

15 [4] וראוי שיהיה הדבור הכתוב מה שתקל הבנת ענינו אצל קריאתו· והנאמר פנים בפנים מה שתקל פרישתו. והדבור הנקרא, אמנם תקל הבנת עניניו בעת קריאתו כשתהיינה בו אותיות מהדבקות וההפרדה; וצריך שישתדל בהנחת אותיות הקשרים במקומות אשר יחוייב שתהיינה בו.

[5] וראוי שישמר מהשמות הקרים, והם אשר מהם תקשה הבנת העניין.

20 ומהם, הדמות העניין אל מקרה רחוק או בלתי מפרסם, כמו שיקרא החלב ״הלבן״· כי ״הלבן״ הוא רב הכללות, ויקשה לשער רצונו בזה. ומהם, עשיית השמות הנכריים המפלגי הזרות הנמצאים בלשון האמה.

[6] והנה נשלם הנרצה ממנו בזה החלק:

1 אחד] אחר[ד] |עני׳] העניין[כ] ||2 בגנב] כגנב[כ] |נלחם] = حارب [א] ||3 שבים] שוים[כ] ||4 מגדלת עניינה] מגדלתה[ד] ||5 אין] אי׳[ד] |[אותו][כ] ||7 אח׳] אחר[כ] ||8 וכאשר רצינו] וכשרצינו[ד] |ולהגדילה] ולהגילה[ד] ||9 וכאשר רצינו] וכשרצינו[ד] ||10 והמשלי׳] ההמשלים[כ] |אחדים] אחרים[כ] ||11 כיוסף] ביוסף[ט] ||12 כמו] כגון[ד] ||16 הבנת] הבגת[כ] ||17 [אותיות][כ] אותות[ט] = علامات [א] ||19 העניין] הענ׳[ד] ||20 מפרסם] מפורס׳[ד] ||21 כי הלבן] שהלבן |רב] דם[כ] ||22 המפלגי] המופלגי[ט] ||

3 וי׳ כ״ה י״ז ||13 שה״ש ד׳ ה׳ ||14 שה״ש ו׳ י׳ ||

persuade, not the kind that is either short or in excess of these means—and this according as his purpose is to magnify or to depreciate a particular thing. If, for example, we wish to magnify a theft to the fullest possible extent, we shall say of the thief that he has "ravaged as in war,"[1] while if we wish to depreciate the deed, we shall say that "he took," or that "he wronged his fellow."[2] All these expressions, of course, refer to the taking of property from one's fellow without his consent, but "ravaging as in war" magnifies the theft, while "wronging" minifies it.

[2] At the same time, one should not depart from the class of statement one is making, but should disparage the theme, or adorn it, with words subsumed under that class. Again to illustrate, a request and a supplication are subsumed under one class—the question. But the supplication has less dignity than the request, because a supplication proceeds from an inferior, a request from an equal. When, therefore, we wish to adorn and enhance a supplication, we shall call it a "request," and when we wish to derogate a request, we shall call it a "supplication."

[3] Indeed, apt metaphors and similes derive from phenomena that are the same in kind, as when one man is likened to another of the same kind—I mean as when we say of a handsome fellow that he is "like Joseph." If the phenomena are not the same in kind, they should be as one in respect of a related class, as when we liken a graceful woman to a gazelle;[3] and if that is not possible, they should be as one in respect of a remoter class, as when we say of a woman of integrity that she is **pure as the sun** [Song of S. 6:10].[4] But if the phenomena involved may not be embraced by a single, albeit remote, class, then the metaphor or simile is of inferior quality.

[4] The contents of a written utterance should be easy to understand when read, and what is delivered face to face should be easy to explain. The sense of an utterance that is read is easy to understand during the reading only when it has conjunctive and disjunctive particles; and one must try to place the connective particles at the points where they are required.

[5] One should be on one's guard against frigid terms which will make the subject hard to understand. Among these is the figuring of the subject by some remote or obscure accident of it, like calling milk "the white"; for "white" is too general an accident, and it will be difficult to guess precisely what is meant by it. Also frigid is the use of the more bizarre of the foreign words to be found in the speaker's native language.

[6] We have now finished what we proposed to say in this section of our work.

1. T (hence JML): "did battle," "waged war," "fought" (נלחם); A: "despoiled," "plundered" (حارب).
2. A reminiscence of Lev. 25:17.
3. Cf. Song of S. 4:5.
4. JV: "clear as the sun."

קולופן: ד

[1] אמר אברהם, קטן המשפיעים ותלמיד הרופאים, הנסמך זעירא דמן חברייא, בכמ״ר שלמה כונת זלה״ה, הכותב בכמה קלמוסים בלא מעשה נסים:

[2] אל גנת אגוז השלמות ירדתי, וראיתי ספר מגיד אמרי שפר, מספר ספורים כספירים מפנינים יקרים. נחלק לד׳ שערי׳, כוללים כללים גדולים בשפה ברורה, לא יערכם זהב וזכוכית ואבן יקרה. 5

[3] וכמהו לא נמצא בינינו בחכמת ההלצה, אשר מישר למדבר דבורו, ויפק רצון האנשים במאמרו. ומי לא יחפוץ ביקרו, וגדלת התפארת הנותן בפשטי התורה והנבואה בכללה, ועטרת גדולה בדברי הקבלה? כאשר תראה בשער הראשון, פרק י״ג, פרק הזכירה, אחר אשר למד אותנו איכות הזכירה 10 המלאכותית, ומהותה, ועשיית המקומות והצורות; גם בשער הד׳, בפרק ל״ג, פרק ההמשכה, ובשאר המקומות — פשטים נפלאים, אין להם ערך בטובם.

[4] על כן אחזתיו, אף חבקתיו, והבאתיו אל חדרי משכיתי. ושלחתי ידי בקלמוסי, וכתבתיו לזכות בו את הרבים. והיה ביאת זה הספר בבית הקונה אותו לתוספת ברכה, והצלחה, וחיים, לו ולבניו אחריו, לתכלית הנמשך ממנו, 15 שיגדיל תורה ויאדיר:

[5] וישא משלו עליו ויאמר:

אחרי רואי ספר מכריז	נפת צופים אשביעך
אחזתי בו חבקתיו כי	בו אמרי יושר אורך
כשמו ריטוריקא כן הוא	ולך אל עולם אודך
כי המצאת זאת ליהודה	מיסר ליאון ואברכך.

20

4 שה״ש ו׳ י״א | בר׳ מ״ט כ״א || 5 מש׳ ג׳ ט״ו | צפ׳ ג׳ ט׳ || 6 איוב כ״ח י״ז | דנ׳ י״א ל״ח || 8 אס׳ ו׳ ו׳ || 13 יח׳ ח׳ י״ב || 16 יש׳ מ״ב כ״א || 17 במ׳ כ״ג ז׳ || 18 תה׳ י״ט י״א | תה׳ פ״א י״ז || 19 איוב ו׳ כ״ה ||

Abraham Conat's Colophon to the *Editio Princeps*

[1] Said Abraham, that least of the men of influence and disciple of the physicians, the ordained Rabbi who is the humblest of his colleagues, the s[on of our] h[onored] t[eacher], R[abbi] Solomon Conat [may he be] r[emembered] f[or life] e[verlasting]), who, without working miracles, writes with many pens:[1]

[2] **I went down into a nut-garden** [Song of S. 6:11] of perfection,[2] and saw a volume that tells of **goodly words** [Gen. 49:21], which, as gems of sapphire are **more precious than rubies** [Prov. 3:15], is more precious than a book of tales. It is divided into four books, containing, in **pure language** [Zeph. 3:9], principles of such great value that **gold and glass cannot equal** [Job 28:17] them, nor **precious stones** [Dan. 11:38].

[3] A like work on the art of rhetoric did not exist among us, one that directs a speaker's utterance aright so that he may win men's favor by his discourse. And who will not **delight in its splendour** [Esth. 6:6],[3] in the great glory which it gives to the literal meaning of the Torah and of the whole of Prophecy, and in the crown of greatness which it bestows upon the words of post-Mosaic Scripture? You can see such interpretation in Book I, Chapter 13, on Memory, following upon the instruction provided us on the nature and quality of artificial memory and the forming of backgrounds and images; it can also be seen in Book IV, Chapter 33, dealing with the Figure Elimination, and in the other Books, too—marvellous, inestimably valuable, interpretations of the literal meaning of Scripture.

[4] I therefore seized upon it, nay more, embraced it, brought it into my **chambers of imagery** [Ezek. 8:12],[4] set my hand to my pens, and wrote it out in order to bring many to benefit by it. May the coming of this volume into the house of him who acquires it constitute an accession of blessing, prosperity, and life for him and for his children after him, in consideration of the consequence it has in view, **to make Torah great and glorious** [Isa. 42:21].[5]

[5] **And he took up his parable** concerning it, **and said** [Num. 23:7]:

Having seen a book which proclaims:
"With **the honeycomb's flow** [Ps. 19:11] **would I satisfy thee**" [Ps. 81:17],
I seized upon it, embraced it, for
The **words of uprightness** [Job 6:25] in it I would teach thee.
'Tis even as its name, an Art of Rhetoric,
And I thank Thee, O God Eternal,
For having caused Judah Messer Leon
To create this work, and I bless Thee.

1. Abraham Conat here identifies himself (a) as an influential physician, (b) as an ordained Rabbi, and (c) as a scribe and printer; see the Int., §2, nn. 77–80, and §4 at n. 179.
2. JV: "garden of nuts;" the reference is doubtless to a collection of books on philosophy and theology (Int., §7, and n. 236).—What follows is written mainly in rhymed prose.
3. JV: "Whom . . . delighteth to honour."
4. I.e., his printing office.
5. JV: "to make the teaching great and glorious."

קולופון: כ

[1] לכל תְּכלה ראיתי קץ.
[2] וישא ר׳ אברהם קונטי משלו עליה ויאמ׳:

אחרי רואי ספר מכריז:	״נופת צופים אשביעך״
5 אחזתי בו, חבַקתיו, כי	בו אמרי יושר אורך.
כשמו, ריטוריקה, כן הוא·	ולך, אל עולם, אודך,
כי המצאת זאת ליהודה	מיסיר ליאון, ואברכך.

[3] והיתה השלמת זאת הריטוריקה ליל ד׳, בד׳ שעות בלילה, ר״ח מרחשוון, רל״ה לפרט האלף הששי, שהוא י״ב ימים לחדש אוטו׳. וכתבתיה אני, מנחם 10 יזיי״א, בכ״מ אליהו יצור״ו, מן האדומי׳, פה פירה העירה. והא׳, למען חסדיו שהגיעני להשלמתה ולכתבה, יגיעני לראות בשמחת בית הבחירה, עם כל ישראל חברים. אמן. לק״י.

2 תה׳ קי״ט צ״ו || 3 במ׳ כ״ג ז׳ || 4 תה׳ י״ט י״א | תה׳ פ״א י״ז || 5 איוב ו׳ כ״ה || 11–12 שופ׳ כ׳ י״א || 12 בר׳ מ״ט י״ח ||

Menahem de' Rossi's Colophon to the Ambrosian Library's Manuscript

[1] **I have seen an end to every** beginning[1] [Ps. 119:96].

[2] And Rabbi Abraham Conati[2] **took up his parable concerning it,**[3] **and said** [Num. 23:7]:

> "Having seen a book which proclaims:
> **'With the honeycomb's flow** [Ps. 19:11] **would I satisfy thee'** [Ps. 81:17],
> I seized upon it, embraced it, for
> The **words of uprightness** [Job 6:25] in it I would teach thee.
> 'Tis even as its name, an Art of Rhetoric,
> And I thank Thee, O God Eternal,
> For having caused Judah Messer Leon
> To create this work, and I bless Thee."

[3] This *Rhetorica* was completed on the night of Tuesday-to-Wednesday, at the 4th hour of the night, the first of the month Marheshvan, 235 of the specific enumeration of the Sixth Millennium [5235], which corresponds to the 12th day of the month Oct[ober, 1474]. I Menaḥem (m[ay he see] o[ffspring], h[ave length of] d[ays], a[men!]), s[on of our] h[onored] t[eacher], Elijah ([his] Roc[k] and [Redeemer protect him!]) de' Rossi transcribed it here in the City of Ferrara. And may God, Who, for His mercies' sake, has vouchsafed it me to reach the completing of its transcription, cause me to reach the beholding of the joy of the Chosen House, with **all Israel knit together** [Judg. 20:11]. Amen! **I w[ait] f[or] T[hy salvation], O L[ord]** [Gen. 49:18].

1. A play on words: *t^eḥillā* ("beginning") / *tikhlā* ("completeness, perfection").
2. *Sic:* with initial *qōph* and final *yōdh;* in C, Conat spells his name with initial *kāph,* and without the final *yōdh.*
3. The *Rhetorica* of Judah Messer Leon.

Index of Biblical Passages

The passages are located according to the pages of the English translation; the Hebrew original of any such passage will always be found on the immediately opposite even-numbered page. Roman type indicates passages cited by Judah Messer Leon in exemplification, illustration, or exegetical application of rhetorical rules and principles; italic type signifies passages that exemplify or illustrate figures of diction or of thought. Passages marked by an asterisk are those considered by Messer Leon to constitute divinely revealed repositories or sources of rhetorical doctrine; see p. liii, note 185, above. Not included in this index are the *loci* of the author's *m^e^līṣāh,* the scriptural phrases and verbal reminiscences imbedded in his parlance; see p. lxix for the manner in which these passages are identified in the Hebrew and English texts.

Index of Names and Subjects

Library of Congress Cataloging in Publication Data

Judah ben Jehiel, 15th cent.
ספר נפת צופים

English and Hebrew.
Title romanized: Sefer Nofet tsufim.
Added t.p.: Sēpher Nōpheth ṣūphim = The book of the honeycomb's flow.
Includes index.
1. Hebrew language—Rhetoric—Early works to 1800. 2. Bible. O.T.—Language, style. I. Rabinowitz, Isaac, 1909– . II. Title: Sefer Nofet tsufim. III. Title: Nofet tsufim. IV. Title: Sē Nōpheth sūphīm. V. Title: Nōpheth ṣūphīm. VI. Title: Book of the honeycomb's flow.
PJ4740.J813 1982 808′.04924 81-15273
AACR2